Canada College Library

3 9366 09574963 6

D0603792

Business Law

ASPEN COLLEGE SERIES

Business Law

Principles and Cases in the Legal Environment

Daniel V. Davidson

Professor of Business Law, Chair of Accounting, Finance & Business Law
Radford University

Lynn M. Forsythe

Professor of Business Law
Craig School of Business
California State University, Fresno

Brenda E. Knowles

Professor Emerita of Business Law
Indiana University, South Bend

Wolters Kluwer
Law & Business

AUSTIN   BOSTON   CHICAGO   NEW YORK   THE NETHERLANDS

© 2011 Aspen Publishers. All Rights Reserved.
http://paralegal.aspenpublishers.com

No part of this publication may be reproduced or transmitted in any form
or by any means, electronic or mechanical, including photocopy, recording,
or any information storage and retrieval system, without permission
in writing from the publisher. Requests for permission to make copies
of any part of this publication should be mailed to:

Aspen Publishers
Attn: Permissions Department
76 Ninth Avenue, 7th Floor
New York, NY   10011-5201

To contact Customer Care, e-mail customer.service@aspenpublishers.com,
call 1-800-234-1660, fax 1-800-901-9075, or mail correspondence to:

Aspen Publishers
Attn: Order Department
PO Box 990
Frederick, MD 21705

Printed in the United States of America.

1 2 3 4 5 6 7 8 9 0

ISBN 978-0-7355-9378-7

Library of Congress Cataloging-in-Publication Data

Davidson, Daniel V.
    Business law : principles and cases in the legal environment / Daniel V. Davidson, Lynn M. Forsythe, and Brenda
E. Knowles.
       p. cm.
    Includes index.
    ISBN 978-0-7355-9378-7
    1. Business law—United States. I. Forsythe, Lynn M. II. Knowles, Brenda E. III. Title.
    KF889.85.D38 2011
    346.7307—dc22

                                         2010044918

About Wolters Kluwer Law & Business

Wolters Kluwer Law & Business is a leading provider of research information and workflow solutions in key specialty areas. The strengths of the individual brands of Aspen Publishers, CCH, Kluwer Law International and Loislaw are aligned within Wolters Kluwer Law & Business to provide comprehensive, in-depth solutions and expert-authored content for the legal, professional and education markets.

CCH was founded in 1913 and has served more than four generations of business professionals and their clients. The CCH products in the Wolters Kluwer Law & Business group are highly regarded electronic and print resources for legal, securities, antitrust and trade regulation, government contracting, banking, pension, payroll, employment and labor, and healthcare reimbursement and compliance professionals.

Aspen Publishers is a leading information provider for attorneys, business professionals and law students. Written by preeminent authorities, Aspen products offer analytical and practical information in a range of specialty practice areas from securities law and intellectual property to mergers and acquisitions and pension/benefits. Aspen's trusted legal education resources provide professors and students with high-quality, up-to-date and effective resources for successful instruction and study in all areas of the law.

Kluwer Law International supplies the global business community with comprehensive English-language international legal information. Legal practitioners, corporate counsel and business executives around the world rely on the Kluwer Law International journals, loose-leafs, books and electronic products for authoritative information in many areas of international legal practice.

Loislaw is a premier provider of digitized legal content to small law firm practitioners of various specializations. Loislaw provides attorneys with the ability to quickly and efficiently find the necessary legal information they need, when and where they need it, by facilitating access to primary law as well as state-specific law, records, forms and treatises.

Wolters Kluwer Law & Business, a unit of Wolters Kluwer, is headquartered in New York and Riverwoods, Illinois. Wolters Kluwer is a leading multinational publisher and information services company.

With thanks (and love), as always, to my wife and best friend, Dee Davidson. And a special thanks to my co-author, Lynn Forsythe. It's been great working together once again.

—Dan Davidson

I want to thank my family for their love, support, and encouragement, especially Jim, Mike, and Mary Helen Poptanich and Aileen and Robert Zollweg. It was a pleasure to work with Dan Davidson again. His positive attitude makes the process more enjoyable and his suggestions greatly improve our book.

—Lynn M. Forsythe

Summary of Contents

Contents

Part I   Foundations of Law and the U.S. Legal System 1

Chapter 1: Introduction to Law 3

Chapter 2: Business Ethics   43

Chapter 3: The U.S. Legal System and Court Jurisdiction   77

Chapter 6: Torts 187

Chapter 7: Crimes and Business 221

Chapter 8: International Law 253

Part II	Contracts 289

Chapter 9: Introduction to Contract Law and Contract Theory 291

Chapter 10: Offer, Acceptance, and Consideration 317

Chapter 13: The Rights and Obligations of Third Persons 415

Part III   Sales and Leases 479

Chapter 15: Formation of the Sales Contract: Contracts for Leasing Goods 481

Chapter 16: Title and Risk of Loss 513

Chapter 17: Performance and Remedies 545

Chapter 18: Warranties and Product Liability 579

Part IV   **Negotiables   607**

Chapter 19: Introduction to Negotiables:
UCC Article 3 and Article 7 609

Chapter 20: Negotiability 635

Chapter 21: Negotiation and Holders in Due Course/Holders by Due Negotiation 661

Chapter 22: Negotiables: Liability and Discharge 693

Chapter 23: Bank-Customer Relations/ Electronic Fund Transfers 725

Part V

Debtor-Creditor Relations 753

Chapter 24: Secured Transactions: Attachment and Perfection 755

Chapter 25: Secured Transactions: Priorities and Enforcement 783

Chapter 26: Other Credit Transactions 813

Chapter 27: Bankruptcy 835

Part VI   Agency 875

Chapter 28: Agency: Creation and Termination 877

Chapter 29: Agency: Liability for Contracts   909

Chapter 30: Agency: Liability for Torts and Crimes 943

Part VII Business Organizations 971

Chapter 31: Formation of a Business 973

Chapter 32: Operation of a Business Organization 1015

Chapter 33: Business Terminations and Other Extraordinary Events 1061

Part VIII   Government Regulation of Business 1117

Chapter 36: Consumer Protection   1145

Chapter 37: Environmental Protection   1169

Chapter 38: Labor and Fair Employment Practices 1197

Part IX   Property Protection   1239

Chapter 39: Property and Joint Ownership   1241

Chapter 40: Intellectual Property, Computers, and the Law 1283

A BUSINESS-ORIENTED TEXT

Business Law: Principles and Cases in the Legal Environment provides students with a business-oriented introduction to the legal and ethical topics that affect business. This perspective may seem obvious. However, not all business law textbooks focus on the practice of business. Some fail to show students how the law will affect their future careers as business people. Our goal as business law and legal environment instructors is not to train lawyers, but to train future business people. The book is not organized along the lines of law school classes—for example, administrative law, agency, and remedies. Instead it is organized along the lines of how business people think about the law. For example, torts material may be in the agency chapters and remedies material may be in the contracts chapters.

Business people need to be able to anticipate and avoid legal problems. If legal problems occur, business people need to know how to recognize the nature of these problems and how to work with lawyers to achieve solutions. Legal problems, including lawsuits, are business problems that can and should be managed.

Our goals in this text are:

- To present in a student-friendly fashion a current and comprehensive introduction to the legal topics relevant to business;
- To demonstrate how these topics apply to business enterprises;
- To provide approaches for analyzing legal topics encountered in the practice of business; and
- To develop critical thinking skills and habits.

We also support the students and instructors using this text. Wolter Kluwer Law & Business offers a wide variety of supplementary materials for students and instructors.

eClass Business Cases

We have included an integrated, continuous business case or scenario. The eClass case is threaded throughout the text. The individual threads profile the experiences of a hypothetical business, eClass, owned and operated by a "local" group of student entrepreneurs. The entrepreneurs are introduced in Chapter 1. Each chapter begins with an Agenda that highlights some major legal issues from the chapter that are likely to be relevant to eClass. Within each chapter there are three eClass application boxes that address particular legal issues and call for students to offer guidance to the firm. Each application box is categorized by the relevant functional area of business—finance and accounting, international business, management, manufacturing, marketing, personal law, and sales. Application boxes pose questions including Business Considerations and Ethical Considerations. These questions ask students to go beyond the text and apply the concepts to a business entity. Many of the questions ask students to make business decisions informed by their knowledge of the law. The web materials that accompany the text also include International Considerations for the eClass thread cases for those seeking an international perspective.

Students in business schools often focus on one subject at a time. When they are in accounting class they think about accounting problems and when they are in business law they focus on business law. However, problems in a business generally overlap more than one functional area. A problem can be both a business law problem and a marketing problem. The problems are interdependent and not separate. In addition, business problems do not arise with labels attached. Business people need to be able to identify the subjects that are involved. Working with the eClass thread case helps students recognize the interdependent nature of business problems and business decision making. Students may not be able to provide a full answer to some of the questions posed. Some questions might require additional information or research to fully respond.

eClass thread cases are not intended to encourage business students to practice law without a license. It is illegal to practice law without a license and we are not advocating that students break the law in this regard. However, application is an important aspect of mastering material. Knowledge of the law is of little use if students do not know how or when to apply the knowledge. College students should ask themselves "how can I use this information?" The eClass case provides an opportunity for students to practice applying their knowledge of the law. Like our eClass entrepreneurs, business people do not call their attorneys to discuss every decision that may have legal ramifications. They often rely on their own knowledge and the information they gain from their friends and the Internet. (As we know, not all friends and Internet sites are well informed and provide reliable information.)

Exhibits

There are numerous exhibits in the text. These exhibits assist students in comprehending the material, but they are not intended to replace the text. They provide a visual aid to comprehension and learning. There are additional exhibits on the Web site.

TOPICAL COVERAGE

Our first goal is to present a current and comprehensive introduction to the legal topics relevant to business in a readable, accessible style. To achieve this goal, the book is divided into nine parts based on the typical topical coverage of undergraduate business law courses.

Part 1: Foundations of Law and the U.S. Legal System   Part 1 presents an overview of law and the legal system. Chapter 1, Introduction to Law, includes a discussion of ways to look at the law. It includes a discussion of theories of jurisprudence and how the law is viewed in different countries. Chapter 2, Business Ethics, focuses on how business people might apply ethical theories in making business decisions. Chapter 3 examines the U.S. court system and how courts obtain jurisdiction over cases. Chapter 4 examines a civil trial through a hypothetical accident involving our eClass entrepreneurs. It also discusses alternatives to the court system that business people can use. Chapter 5 discusses the constitutional bases for government regulation of business. Chapter 6 examines potential liability for torts. Chapter 7 addresses business crimes including computer crimes, espionage, and the Racketeer Influenced and Corrupt Organizations Act (RICO). Chapter 8 deals with international law.

Part 2: Contracts   Part 2 examines contract law and its importance in business transactions. The material includes an in depth discussion of the common law of contracts and information about how contract law is changing in response to the increase in e-commerce. Chapter 9 is an introduction to the law of contracts. Chapter 10 covers offer, acceptance, and consideration. Chapter 11 deals with capacity to contract, the reality of consent, and illegal contracts. Chapter 12 examines contract writings, including techniques courts use to interpret contracts. Chapter 13 discusses the rights and obligations of third parties. The section concludes with Chapter 14, Discharge, Breach, and Remedies.

Part 3: Sales and Leases   Part 3 addresses the law of sales and leases. Each of the first three chapters examines aspects of Article 2 of the Uniform Commercial Code (UCC), dealing with the Law of Sales. Each chapter includes coverage of Article 2A, the Law of Leases, and compares it to Article 2. Finally, each of these chapters compares the law of the international sale of goods, as embodied in the United Nations Convention on the International Sales of Goods (CISG), to the UCC. Warranties and Product Liability is the final chapter in this part. It highlights the potential impact that breach of warranty cases can have on a business. In contrast to a "mere" breach of contract, a breach of warranty case may result in substantial damages.

Part 4: Negotiables   Part 4 discusses Articles 3, 4, 4A, and 7 of the UCC. It includes a discussion of bank-customer relations, electronic funds transfers, and how the UCC revisions have changed the law of negotiable instruments.

Part 5: Debtor-Creditor Relations   Chapters 24 and 25 examine debtor-creditor relations by looking at secured transactions under revised Article 9 of the UCC with its significant revisions. Next is Chapter 26 dealing with Other Credit Transactions. This discussion includes payday loans, credit a business may extend to its customers, and credit a business may use to acquire assets or inventory. Chapter 27 examines the federal protections available for honest debtors under the Bankruptcy Abuse Prevention and Consumer Protection Act of 2005. The discussion compares Chapters 7, 11, and 13 of the Bankruptcy Act.

Part 6: Agency   Part 6 explains the agency relationship and its importance in conducting a business enterprise. It emphasizes the liability of the principal and agent for contracts entered into by the agent. It also focuses on the liability of masters and servants for torts and crimes committed by servants. Policies underlying the rules are also addressed. Protection of the business's confidential information and covenants not to compete are also discussed.

Part 7: Business Organizations   Part 7 treats the various types of business organizations in a unique manner. Rather than have separate chapters dealing with each business form, the text treats the types of organizations in a compare-and-contrast fashion within the chapters. The focus is on the advantages and disadvantages of the different structures for the operation of a business. The coverage includes the more traditional business forms, such as sole proprietorships, partnerships, and corporations. It also includes the newer business forms such as limited liability companies, limited partnerships, limited liability partnerships, and limited liability limited partnerships. This section also includes a discussion of securities regulation in Chapter 34.

Part 8: Government Regulation of Business   Part 8 addresses the regulatory issues regularly faced by businesses. Antitrust law is addressed in Chapter 35. Chapter 36, Consumer Protection, is devoted to consumer law and stresses concepts that relate back to Chapter 26, Other Credit Transactions. Chapter 37, Environmental Protection, addresses many of the major environmental statutes. Chapter 38, Labor and Fair Employment Practices, examines the rights and responsibilities of businesses and their employees.

Part 9 Property Protection   Chapter 39 addresses the types of property, property ownership, and the rights that owners have. It also discusses government regulation of real property. It includes a discussion of the forms of joint ownership and transfer on death ownership. It also addresses bailments of personal property. Chapter 40 addresses types of intellectual property, including copyrights, patents, trademarks, and trade secrets. It also includes a discussion of computers and the law.

APPLICATIONS

Our second goal is to demonstrate how the legal topics presented in the text apply to the practice of business. In addition to the thread case, *Business Law* includes the following features:

Court Cases

With the exception of Chapter 1, each chapter contains two court cases. After the chapter outline and eClass Agenda, each chapter begins with a Classic Case. This is an older court case, often a landmark legal decision. Each chapter then ends with a Contemporary Case, a more recent decision showing how courts today are applying concepts to recent legal disputes.

All the court cases show how the courts apply chapter concepts to actual disputes between litigants. Many of them are also illustrative as to how the parties could have avoided the dispute in the first place.

Court cases are organized into the following parts:

- Facts—the facts of the case
- Issue(s)—the question(s) that the court is deciding
- Holding(s)—the court's answer to the issue(s)
- Reasoning—the reasoning the court used in analyzing the question, reaching a decision, and explaining the decision to the public

The reasoning is excerpted from the language of the court. We have summarized the other three parts of the case.

There are Business Consideration questions and Ethical Consideration questions for the cases on the Web site for this book. These questions provide an opportunity for students to analyze business problems and utilize critical thinking skills further supporting our goals for this book. Business Consideration questions illustrate the effect of court cases on businesses and how business decisions may lead to litigation. Ethical Considerations specifically show how ethics constantly affects decision making. Ethics should be an integral part of business decision making.

You Be the Judge

After the Contemporary Case, each chapter has a You Be the Judge box. Many of the You Be the Judge boxes take their materials directly from current events. The boxes ask students to prepare an opinion that applies the law to the facts presented in the "box." By doing so, students will gain a greater appreciation for the difficulties involved in considering the alternatives and drafting an opinion.

Discussion Questions and Case Problems and Writing Assignments

Each chapter concludes with five Discussion Questions that ask students to test their knowledge of chapter material. The Discussion Questions are followed by three Case Problems and Writing Assignments. These questions ask students to apply ethical and legal concepts to actual situations. All the end-of-chapter materials can be used as study tools in reviewing the material, as class or small-group discussion material, or as writing assignments.

SUPPLEMENTAL RESOURCES

There is a Web site related to this text at www.aspenlegalcollege.com/davidson_business/. It has references to Web sites for students who want additional information. It also contains Internet Questions for students to improve their Internet search techniques and Key Terms for students to use in their study and review. For students who want more focus on International Law, it also contains International Considerations questions for the eClass thread case. It contains additional court cases with Business Consideration and Ethical Consideration questions. It includes additional Discussion Questions and Case Problems and Writing Assignments.

A new copy of this text comes packaged with four months of prepaid access to Loislaw's online legal research database, at http://www.loislawschool.com/.

Blackboard and eCollege course materials are available to supplement this text. This online courseware is designed to streamline the teaching of the course, providing valuable resources from the book in an accessible electronic format.

Instructor resources to accompany this text include a comprehensive Instructor's Manual, Test Bank, and PowerPoint slides. All of these materials are available on a CD-ROM or for download from our companion Web site.

AACSB CURRICULAR STANDARDS

The AACSB curricular standards relevant to business law and the legal environment of business state that the business curriculum should include ethical and global issues; the influence of political, social, legal and regulatory, environmental, and technology issues; and the impact of demographic diversity on organizations.

We believe *Business Law: Principles and Cases in the Legal Environment* uniquely satisfies these standards in a readable yet rigorous format.

Global issues are treated in several areas, beginning with Chapter 1 and its introduction to different legal systems. It continues with Chapter 8, International Law; the discussion of CISG in Chapters 15 through 18; and letters of credit in Chapters 8 and 26.

Chapter 2, Business Ethics, addresses the ethical theories and how they can be applied in business. Ethics questions follow the thread cases. In addition there are ethics questions for the court cases on the Web site.

We have created a text that we hope is intuitive, engaging, and oriented toward providing the legal skills students will need in the business world. Consequently, the contents of the book stretch beyond the mere presentation of "legal topics" to encompass the spectrum of "political, social, legal, regulatory, environmental, and technological issues." The pedagogical features are designed to support this approach.

The focus on applications, evidenced in the Agenda and the eClass business application thread case, uniquely contributes to showing how demographic diversity affects organizations. In the eClass case, the principals must understand the cultural and political challenges that a larger domestic and international market (and workforce) pose for them. These include issues ranging from employee privacy to labor law, and from employee use of eClass computers to sexual harassment. By following the case, students are immersed in these problems and are asked to offer advice as questions arise. This encourages sensitivity and an understanding of other points of view.

On another level, the principals and students learn that successful businesses today are often cross-functional. In this case, Ani, Meg, and Yousef need to recognize how the law applies to finance and accounting, international business, management, manufacturing, marketing, personal law, and sales. They also must be able to act on this knowledge. By assuming an advisory role with eClass, students have a unique glimpse at the cross-functional nature of many business activities today. *Business Law* supports the current trend toward integrating business disciplines.

ACKNOWLEDGMENTS

Writing a textbook is a rewarding endeavor. However, it is also a significant undertaking. It would not have been possible without the help and support of a number of people along the way. We have enjoyed working together on this project. We each prepared about half the chapters and commented on the drafts prepared by our co-author. We hope that our team effort has been successful and that you will enjoy using this book as much as we have enjoyed preparing it.

We want to thank Louis McGuire whose initial contact led us to Wolters Kluwer Law & Business. This book would not have been possible without the support of David Herzig who saw the need for a readable business law text with practical business applications. We are also indebted to our developmental editor, Betsy Kenny. Betsy's help and guidance improved the text as it evolved from the first draft to the final product. Troy Froebe and the rest of The Froebe Group carefully supervised the final stages of production. We have sincerely enjoyed working with all of them.

A special thanks to our families. They have tolerated the late nights and short deadlines. They provided helpful suggestions. Without their support and encouragement, we would not be able to accomplish our goal.

A sincere thank you to the following reviewers, whose suggestions, criticism, questions, and observations have helped us maintain our focus and write a text that contains the essential material and is user-friendly, readable, and enjoyable:

Ken Anderson, Mott Community College
Carol Brady, Milwaukee Area Technical College
Loretta Calvert, Volunteer State Community College
Elizabeth Dibble, Southwestern Illinois College
Norm Friedland, Nassau Community College
Paul Guymon, Harper College
Christie Highlander, Southwestern Illinois College
Christine Mooney, Queensborough Community College
Miriam Salholz, St. Francis College
John Thomas, Northhampton Community College
Ellen Tsagaris, Kaplan University
Deborah Walsh, Middlesex Community College

We also appreciate the encouragement and support of our students and colleagues.

Thank you, as well, to the contributing authors to this book. Corey Ciochetti, Associate Professor at the University of Denver, updated Chapter 5 on Constitutional Regulation of Business, and Patricia Elias, Adjunct Professor at the University of Denver, revised Chapter 34 on Securities Regulation.

Finally, we would like to acknowledge our co-author in previous editions, Brenda Knowles. Brenda did not actively participate in this edition, but many of her contributions remain as integral parts of the book.

Daniel V. Davidson
Lynn M. Forsythe

November 2010

Dan Davidson is an alumnus of the Indiana University—Bloomington College of Business and the Indiana University—Bloomington School of Law.

Professor Davidson has been teaching business law and legal environment classes since 1974, with stops at five different campuses over his career. He is currently teaching and serving (for the second time) as Chair of the Department of Accounting, Finance & Business Law at Radford University in Radford, Virginia.

Professor Davidson has previously served as a part of the author team on four other textbooks, and he has authored or co-authored numerous journal articles.

Professor Davidson has been the recipient of numerous teaching awards and several advising awards during his career.

Professor Davidson is married to Dee Davidson, a high school math teacher, and is the proud father of a son, Jaime, who is the marketing director for the Berkshire Theater Company, and a daughter, Tara, who is a high school English teacher.

Lynn M. Forsythe received her B.A. from The Pennsylvania State University and her J.D. from the University of Pittsburgh School of Law. She passed the bar examinations in the states of California and Pennsylvania. She is professor of business law at the Craig School of Business at California State University, Fresno.

Professor Forsythe has received numerous Craig School of Business awards, including the Research Award in 2008, and the Service Award in 2003 and again in 2006. She held the Verna Mae and Wayne A. Brooks Professorship of Business Law. She is a Coleman Fellow at the Lyles Center for Innovation and Entrepreneurship at California State University, Fresno. She is also a Craig Faculty Fellow in research for 2010-2012.

Professor Forsythe is the author or co-author of numerous articles on business law and business law pedagogy. She served as a part of the author team on three other textbooks. She has held the positions of editor-in-chief, staff editor, and reviewer for *The Journal of Legal Studies Education*. She is currently advisory editor. She received two recent best paper awards, the 2009 Western Academy of Legal Studies in Business Best Paper Award and the 2007 Allied Academies Conference Distinguished Research Paper Award.

Professor Forsythe is active in the Academy of Legal Studies in Business. She has served as the chair and vice-chair of the Business Ethics Section of the academy. She has served in the officer ranks of the Western Academy of Legal Studies in Business first from 1983-1987 and again from 2006-2009. She is currently the Proceedings Editor for the Western Academy of Legal Studies in Business.

Professor Forsythe is currently the Secretary of the Craig School of Business Chapter of Beta Gamma Sigma. She is also a Life Member of Alpha Kappa Psi.

Business Law

Part I

Foundations of Law and the U.S. Legal System

"I gnorance of the law is no excuse." The basic truth of this old adage seems simple and obvious. However, the simplicity of this basic truth tends to hide the complexity of the law. Each citizen—and resident—of this country has "constructive notice" of the law. This means that each person is expected to be aware of, and to abide by, all the laws of the land. The enormous scope of "the law" makes this expectation virtually impossible. No one person can realistically be expected to know *all* that the law entails, yet every person is expected to obey *every* aspect of the law—or to face possible sanctions for failing to do so.

Part I of this book will first help you to understand what law is, how it operates, and how it affects business. To successfully handle legal problems that arise in business, and to prevent many of these problems from arising, a businessperson needs to understand how the U.S. legal system operates. This part describes the powers and limitations of the federal government as set forth in the U.S. Constitution and the constitutional bases for government regulation of business. It describes the court system and how cases progress in the courts through the anatomy of a hypothetical civil suit involving eClass and its principals. It also discusses alternatives to the courts and why businesses may want to use these alternatives. It examines the differences between "private" wrongs, such as torts, and public wrongs called crimes.

Each part of this text will offer insights into various aspects of the law, especially the area of business law. A thorough knowledge of the law takes years of specialized study, but this text will begin to open doors of understanding for you, and to provide references to other sources for you to explore and study. We hope it will help to remove the "ignorance of the law [that] is no excuse."

Overview
eClass Needs Your Help!

What is eClass? Most people dream of owning their own business, of being their own boss, and of becoming successful entrepreneurs. Three friends in college have such a dream. Ani Yasuda, Yousef Alwazzan, and Meg Friesen are students at the local college. One day after their finance class they were discussing the online lectures, and they started brainstorming about how the online lectures could be more engaging. Ani and Yousef both enjoy role playing games (RPGs) and are knowledgeable in several programming languages. Meg has more background in marketing and production than in programming. The friends decided to start a new company called eClass. Its first product is going to be software for an academic platform for online lectures and courses, where the professor and students create and use avatars and move around a virtual classroom. They hope that their product will make the online component of classes more engaging and that students, even those at remote locations, will have a feeling that they are actually present in class. Of course, they are also hoping for financial success with eClass and its products. They intend to start with the platform for online lectures, but they may decide to expand into other electronic products, such as electronic books, online tutoring, and maybe even a competitor to Kindle, which could be used to read books electronically. They have developed a viable business plan, but they know that they will need help and advice as they work to implement their business plan.

While the eClass entrepreneurs will initially emphasize the online lectures platform, they hope to develop other platforms for class materials. Of course, eClass will need a lot of help and a lot of luck to be successful, and that is where you come in.

What is Your Role in eClass? Ani, Meg, and Yousef are just starting their business. While they will have an attorney to whom they can turn on various legal issues, they do not want to use their attorney every time a question arises. Instead, they would like to be able to ask *you* to be their consultant, since you are learning about business law. When a problem does arise that has business law implications, the friends would like to consult with you, asking you for advice and suggestions. Obviously, they do not want you to "practice law" (which would be illegal), but they would appreciate your help in determining whether an issue might have serious legal implications, how they might avoid legal problems, and when they should consult with their attorney.

eClass is, of course, a fictional company created and operated by fictional characters. But the use of this fictional business will illustrate how the legal concepts discussed in each chapter might apply in the business environment. Each chapter will begin with an "Agenda," which highlights some of the major issues relevant to a small business that are discussed in that chapter. Within each chapter there are three different scenarios, each of which addresses a particular issue that might arise in a business setting. For each of these scenarios you are asked to provide guidance and advice to the firm about the legal implications involved in that scenario. You are also asked to look at the business and ethical implications involved in the scenario. You will become a more enlightened consultant as you progress through the text. The problems you confront will involve many different functional areas of business besides law—management, marketing and sales, finance and accounting, international business—and even a few personal issues. This approach is intended to help you to recognize the interrelationships between the various business subjects. This recognition is important to a business's success. Business courses should be viewed not in isolation but as an integrated series of materials that, when properly combined, can help a business to maximize its chances for success.

The People Behind eClass Ani Yasuda is an accounting major with an emphasis in accounting information systems. She has written two role playing games as high school projects. She is currently a sophomore at the college.

Yousef Alwazzan is a junior majoring in entrepreneurship. He is concurrently working on a minor in computer science. He has some experience with computer programming.

Meg Friesen is currently a junior majoring in marketing. She recently completed an internship at a local public relations firm.

Samuel (Sam) Yasuda is Ani's brother and a good friend of Yousef and Meg. He is not a part of the eClass team, but he is interested in role playing games and he has offered to test the Beta versions of eClass software.

You are the consultant who will provide advice and guidance on potential legal issues—and other related topics—that the business encounters during its development. Without your considered input and suggestions the business is less likely to succeed, despite the dedication and expertise of the three entrepreneurs who are starting eClass.

1

Introduction to Law

Agenda

Ani, Meg, and Yousef need to understand what types of law will influence eClass. Will eClass be subject to federal regulation? To state regulation? To administrative regulation? How will these types of regulations affect eClass and its success? Most of the legal issues in business law involve civil law. Obviously, members of the firm need to concern themselves with numerous civil law topics. Should they also be concerned with criminal law? How does criminal law influence business?

What happens when a party to a lawsuit asks the court for a particular action as the remedy? Why are lawyers and courts so interested in prior court decisions?

These and other questions will arise as you read this chapter. Be prepared! You never know when the firm or one of its members will seek your advice.

[The cause of action is a criminal libel. In customs laws, a drawback is a reduction or refund of duties for goods.]

BARLOW v. UNITED STATES
32 U.S. 404, 1833 U.S. LEXIS 354 (1833)

FACTS Joseph Barlow allegedly made a false denomination of sugar, with an intent to defraud the revenue. Barlow admits that he made the entry to obtain a drawback on the export duties; but he denies that the entry was made by a false denomination. Barlow claims that the sugars are truly refined sugars, as they are listed in his entry. Under the statute, goods are subject to forfeiture to the federal government if a false entry is made in the office of the duty collector. Barlow argued that the federal statutes did not apply to his situation and that the sugar was refined sugar under the statute and was entitled to the refined sugar drawback.

ISSUE Is Barlow excused because he was ignorant of the law?

HOLDING No, ignorance of the law is no excuse. Barlow cannot avoid the forfeiture of the sugar.

REASONING Excerpts from the opinion of Justice Story:

. . . The next question is, whether the sugars were in this case entered by a false denomination. They were entered by the name of "refined sugars." They were, in fact, sugars known by the appellation of "bastar," or "bastard" sugards (sic), which are a species of sugars of a very inferior quality, of less value than the raw material; they are the residuum or refuse of clayed sugars, left in the process of refining, after taking away the loaf and lump sugar, which results from that process. The question is, whether this species of sugar is, in the sense of the acts of Congress, "refined sugar." These acts allow a drawback "on sugar refined within the United States."

It has been contended . . . that all sugars which have undergone the full process of refining, after they have arrived at the point of granulation, are properly to be deemed refined sugars, whether they have been clayed or not. In a certain sense, they may certainly be . . . deemed to be refined; that is, in the sense of being then clarified and freed from their feculence. But the question is, whether this is the sense in which the words are used in the acts of Congress.

The acts of Congress on this subject, are regulations of commerce and revenue; and there is no attempt in any of them to define the distinguishing qualities of any of the commodities which are mentioned therein. Congress must be presumed to use the words in their known and habitual commercial sense; not indeed in that of foreign countries, if it should differ from our own, but in that known in our own trade, foreign and domestic. . . . [S]till, if among buyers and sellers generally in the course of trade and business, the appellation "refined sugars," is exclusively limited to the products called lump and loaf sugar, and never includes bastard sugar, the acts of Congress ought to be construed in this restrictive sense. . . . [W]e think that there is a decisive and unequivocal preponderance of evidence to establish, that bastard sugar is not deemed, in a commercial sense, "refined sugar." The appellation is exclusively limited to . . . white refined loaf or lump sugars. This is established, not merely by the testimony of merchants and grocers, and persons in the custom house, but by the testimony of sugar refiners. A sale of refined sugars would be deemed by them not complied with by a delivery of bastard sugars. If this be so, it puts an end to the question, whether the sugars in controversy were entered by a false denomination. . . .

Were these sugars entered by a false denomination, happening by mistake or accident, and not from any intention to defraud the revenue? There was no accident in the case; there was no mistake in point of fact; for the party knew what the article was when he entered it. The only mistake, if there has been any, is a mistake of law. The party in the present case has acted, indeed, with his eyes open; against the known construction given to the acts by the government and the officers of the customs. He has not been misled; and his conduct . . . is not wholly free from the suspicion of an intention to overreach, and evade the vigilance of the custom house department. He has made every effort in his power to obtain the drawback, by passing off, as refined sugars, what he well knew were not admitted to be such by the higher government officers.

. . . [This case] presents the broader question, whether a mistake of law will excuse a forfeiture in cases of this description. We think it will not. . . . It is a common maxim, familiar to all minds, that ignorance of the law will not excuse any person, either civilly or criminally; and it results from the extreme difficulty of ascertaining what is . . . the interpretation of the party; and the extreme danger of allowing such excuses to be set up for

illegal acts to the detriment of the public. There is scarcely any law which does not admit of some ingenious doubt; and there would be perpetual temptations to violations of the laws, if men were not put upon extreme vigilance to avoid them. There is not the least reason to suppose that the legislature . . . had any intention to supersede the common principle. The safety of the revenue, so vital to the government, is essentially dependent upon upholding it. For mistakes of fact, the legislature might properly indulge a benignant policy, as they certainly ought, to accidents. The very association of mistake and accident, in this connexion [sic], furnishes a strong ground to presume that the legislature had the same classes of cases in view; accident, which no prudence could foresee or guard against, and mistakes of fact, consistent with entire innocence of intention. . . . Mistakes in the construction of the law, seem as little intended to be excepted by the proviso, as accidents in the construction of the law. . . . [I]t is the opinion of the court that the judgment of the circuit court ought to be affirmed. . . .

RELATIONSHIP AMONG LAW, ORDER, AND JUSTICE

Law

This book is about understanding the law of business. Before we begin our study, however, we must answer a basic question: What is *law*? Many definitions exist, ranging from the philosophical to the practical. Plato (427-347? B.C.), a Greek philosopher who studied and wrote in the area of philosophical idealism, said law was *social control*. Sir William Blackstone (1723-1780), an English judge and legal commentator, said law is rules specifying what is right and what is wrong. For our purposes, however, we shall define law as "rules that must be obeyed." People who disobey these rules are subject to sanctions that may result in their having to do something they would not voluntarily do, such as paying a fine or going to jail. Our society has many kinds of rules, but not all rules can be considered "law." A rule in baseball, for example, says that after three strikes the batter is out. This rule, however, is not law. All laws are rules, but all rules are not laws. What differentiates a law from a rule? Simply stated, *enforceability* separates laws from rules. People who do not follow the rules in baseball are not arrested or taken to court. They are simply ejected from the game. In contrast, people who break laws can be held accountable for their actions through court-imposed sanctions.

Many different types of legal rules exist. One legal rule defines a specific way to create a legal document, for example, a contract or a will. A second forbids certain kinds of conduct; criminal law is an excellent example of this kind of legal rule. (*Criminal law* is the body of law dealing with public wrongs called crimes.) A third type of legal rule was created to compensate persons who have been injured because someone else breached a duty. For example, when an automobile manufacturer negligently builds a car, and the manufacturer's negligence is the direct cause of an injury, the manufacturer may have to pay the injured person monetary damages. (*Negligence* is the failure to do something a reasonable person would do, or doing something a reasonable and prudent person would not do.) Rules that describe binding contracts, define crimes, and specify legal duties are generally rules about substantive law. (*Substantive law* is that part of law that creates and defines legal rights. It is distinct from the law that defines how laws should be enforced in court.) Exhibit 1.1 compares some of the major areas of law that are discussed in this book. Finally, rules exist that our legislative bodies and courts establish to take care of their everyday business. For example, all states have a rule concerning the

Exhibit 1.1

A Comparison of Tort Law, Criminal Law, and Contract Law

Type of Obligation	Tort Law	Criminal Law	Contract Law
How is the obligation created?	Civil law imposes duties on all people	Criminal law prohibits certain conduct or requires certain conduct of all people	Individuals agree on a contract thereby voluntarily assuming duties under the agreement
Who enforces the obligation?	Suit by injured plaintiff	Prosecution by a government entity	Suit by party to the contract
What is the burden of proof in court?	Preponderance of the evidence	Beyond a reasonable doubt	Preponderance of the evidence
What happens if the defendant loses?	Defendant can be required to pay for the injury caused	Defendant can be imprisoned, sentenced to probation, and/or fined	Defendant can be ordered to perform the contract or pay for the injury caused

Source: Courtesy of Lynn M. Forsythe, © Lynn M. Forsythe 2010

Exhibit 1.2

Duties in a Society

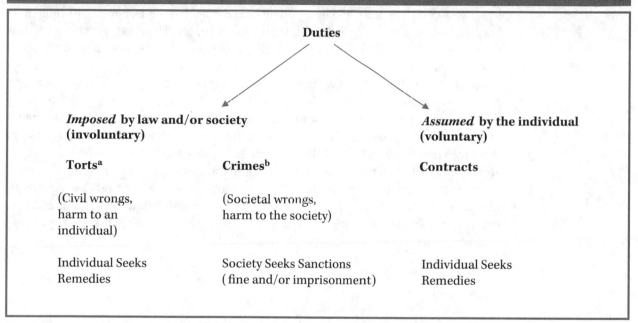

[a] Some torts may also be crimes. The victim of the crime can seek civil remedies while the state will seek criminal sanctions.
[b] Most crimes not only harm society, but also harm one or more individuals. The individuals who are harmed can seek civil remedies under tort law.

maximum number of days defendants will have to answer a civil lawsuit; this is an example of procedural law. (*Procedural law* is the law specifying the methods used to enforce legal rights or obtain compensation for the violation of these rights.) The distinction between substantive law and procedural law is important and will be revisited throughout our discussion of business law.

We will view the law as a body of rules that establish a certain level of social conduct, or of *duties*, that members of the society must honor. One way to view these duties is shown in Exhibit 1.2. The party or parties who are injured can seek enforcement of their rights in courts of law. Enforcement consists of one of three legal remedies: (1) paying money as damages or as a fine; (2) equitable relief, such as being subject to an *injunction*, a court order that directs a person to do or not do something; or (3) going to jail or prison.

Order

Order has different meanings in different contexts, and "an order" is significantly different from "order." The law usually considers *an order* as a legal command issued by a judge, while *order* is the absence of chaos. We are using *order* in this second context. *Chaos* is confusion and total disorganization, producing a disorderly society. If the laws of a society were always followed and never broken, perfect order would result. No crime would exist, and everyone would be safe. History, however, tells us that no society with perfect order has ever existed.

The words *law* and *order* are often linked together. It is natural to link them because, when the law is followed, there will be order. However, precisely because the law is not followed all the time by all the people, perfect order does not exist. Society is always *somewhat* chaotic and disorganized. One of the reasons people do not always obey the law is that they may not be aware of what the law is. However, our legal system *presumes* that everyone *is* aware of the law and what it requires. If the society did not presume that everyone knows the law, society would be more chaotic than it already is. In that case, individuals accused of breaking the law would have an excellent defense: They could argue that they did not know they were breaking the law, and the society would then have to prove the person's knowledge of the law before sanctions could be imposed. The presumption that everyone knows the law, and that "ignorance of the law is no excuse," removes this obstacle to enforcement of the law and also creates an incentive for citizens to study the law. Our educational system plays an important role in permitting us to learn the law.

Justice

Justice is a difficult term to define. Different theories of justice exist, and individuals have varying beliefs about justice. When we speak of *justice*, we normally mean "fairness." Although perfect justice *is* fair, there is more to the concept of justice than merely being fair. Justice, as used in the Anglo-American legal system, refers to both the *process* followed and the *results* obtained in the process. Courts try to *administer* justice in conformity with the laws of the territory. From a social perspective, justice may be affected as much—or even more—by appearances than by results. Thus, lawyers are required to avoid the *appearance* of impropriety in their dealings. If the public perceives that the system is not just, they will be less likely to accept the results the system provides. This, in turn, might lead to the destruction of the order developed in society through its laws and their enforcement.

The ultimate goal of any legal system should be attaining justice by continually searching for fairness and equity. Fairness is less abstract than justice, and thus it is easier to address on a practical level. Most people have a basic concept of "fairness" that can be applied to any given situation, even though those same people may not have a similar concept of "justice." For example, when you see a bully pick on a victim, you probably believe that this conduct is not fair. In this type of situation, the conduct is clearly unfair, and it also is clearly unjust. In most situations, however, it is difficult to determine what a fair-and-just result would be. For example, suppose that a wealthy individual is accused of committing a crime. That wealthy individual hires the best attorneys he or she can find, and—in a very public trial—is found not guilty by the jury. Many people might question whether this result is *fair*. While there may be doubts about the fairness of the result, the process followed in the legal system assures—at least to some extent—that the result of the trial is *just*.

The Nexus: Practicability

What we often refer to as "*the Law*" is really a system consisting of law, order, and justice. Combined, they make up the U.S. legal system. All the elements should balance in perfect equilibrium so that one element does not adversely affect any other. If we had total order, we would have very little justice; if we had total justice, we might have very little order. The *nexus* (link between elements) of the two concepts is the point of *practicability*. For example, to achieve perfect justice with respect to traffic violations, we need jury trials with counsel to ascertain precisely whether a driver did in fact violate the speed limit. However, the costs of such an approach are so prohibitive that no municipality or other local jurisdiction can afford to pay for it. As a result, most traffic courts tend to achieve "assembly line" justice rather than perfect justice.

LEGAL LANGUAGE

Many terms used in the law are also used in everyday speech, but often they have totally different meanings in the law. This text will define many of the terms for you in the chapter. There are also numerous law dictionaries available online. You might want to check—and bookmark—one or more of those online sources. The list of terms may seem endless: *offer, acceptance, consideration, guaranty, employee,* and so on. Because terms may have different connotations within the law, be on guard for subtle shifts in meaning. For example, the word "consideration" has a much different meaning in contract law than it does in "normal everyday" vocabulary. Remember to read in context and to be aware of legal meanings. If you are in doubt, read the passage again or check the definition.

In addition, it is impossible to discuss the law intelligently without reference to some words that are only defined in the law. Examples of this specialized vocabulary include *appellee, assignee, bailee, causa mortis, caveat venditor, estoppel,* and *quid pro quo*. Remember these three rules about our artificial language system to improve your mastery of this material:

1. Legal terms may appear to be synonyms with everyday words, but they often are not.
2. Legal terms may have more than one legal meaning.
3. Some legal terms have no relation to everyday language.

LAW OF BUSINESS

Origins of the Law of Business

In England, the law of business began as a private system administered outside regular law courts. (We will talk about the English law, because that is the source of most of U.S. law. However, business law had different origins in other countries, like the trading countries of the Mediterranean region and Asia.) In England, the law of business began as rules observed by business people in their dealings with one other. It was called the law merchant because it was administered in courts established in the various merchant guilds, commonly called Merchant Courts. Merchant Courts were not the official courts of England. (*Law merchant* is those rules of trade and commerce used by merchants in England beginning in the Middle Ages.) Eventually, it was integrated into the English common law court system. (In this context, *common law* is that unwritten law which is based on custom, usage, and court decisions. Court decisions themselves, however, are often written. Common law differs from statutory law, which consists of laws passed by legislatures.) Consequently, the law merchant is now recognized and enforced by the courts. We will generally consider the law merchant as part of the common law. Today, the law of business includes contracts, sales, negotiable instruments, secured transactions, agency, partnerships, and corporations, among other topics.

Why Study the Law of Business?

This textbook may be considered a primer in "prevention." The focus is on how to recognize legal problems, and then how to avoid these legal problems if possible, and then how to resolve them as quickly as possible if or when they do arise. The legislatures and the courts act in much the same manner, often attempting to prevent problems, but also providing remedies if the problems cannot be prevented or avoided. *Preventive law* is law designed to prevent harm or wrongdoing before it occurs. Many statutes are intended to prevent certain conduct by providing for sanctions against any persons who violate the statutory provisions. *Remedial law* is also an important aspect of the law. When a particular problem begins to arise, courts or legislatures may anticipate its future development and attempt to resolve the problem. The lawmakers, however, cannot predict or prevent every potential legal problem. Thus, the individual needs to know what he or she can do to prevent as many problems as possible.

You should understand the legal implications of what you are doing in your roles as a businessperson and a consumer. Otherwise, many actions may have unexpected legal consequences. If you understand the issues raised here and can apply your knowledge to particular business situations, you may save yourself great expense later. It is helpful to understand the legal environment in which a business operates. If business executives "scan" their environment, they can often identify trends. Sometimes a business or

eClass 1.1 Management

HEALTH INSURANCE FOR eCLASS EMPLOYEES

When Ani, Meg, and Yousef first began the firm, they gave virtually no consideration to providing health insurance benefits for eClass's employees. The young entrepreneurs purchased their health insurance through their college. The quotes for health insurance for eClass were very expensive. The firm has grown and expanded. Several of the employees have asked Yousef about a benefits package that would include health insurance coverage. They have also asked Yousef to see if any health insurance can be convertible into private coverage or portable to a new employer if any employee changes jobs. Yousef has asked you whether the firm should provide health insurance for the employees, and what the consequences of providing—or not providing—such coverage would be. What advice will you give him about providing health insurance?

BUSINESS CONSIDERATIONS   Should eClass provide health insurance as an employee benefit for its employees? What are the business implications—including taxation—if such coverage is provided? What are the business and legal implications if such coverage is not provided?

ETHICAL CONSIDERATIONS   Would it be ethical for eClass to provide coverage for Ani, Meg, and Yousef but not for other employees? What are the ethical implications of withholding insurance coverage from the firm's employees merely to increase its profits?

industry may impact the direction of the change, if they are alert to the changing environment. A business taking direct action is called proactive. (*Proactive* means to identify potential problem areas and actively participate in resolving them.) For example, industries may decide to self-regulate in order to persuade the legislature that government regulation is unnecessary. The video game industry created a rating system for games at least in part to avoid prospective legislative action. Not all businesses, however, are proactive. Some are *reactive*, waiting to see what develops and *then* reacting to those developments. They do not initiate change. They make change only when forced to do so. In general, business is a very practical subject. As you will see, the law of business is just as practical.

Another reason to study the law of business is that it will help you develop valuable decision-making skills. Legal style of analysis can be used in business decision making. This study will also sensitize you to particular situations in which you may need the assistance of a lawyer. Legal counsel can be helpful in the prevention of problems as well as in seeking remedies if a problem exists. For example, in the sale of commercial real estate you will discover that the buyer or seller needs the assistance of a lawyer *before,* rather than after, an earnest money contract is signed.

LEGAL SYSTEMS

When we speak of a "legal system" we are speaking of an entire range of people, rules, and processes. Every society and every culture is built around a system of some sort, and part of that system is likely to address the issues of rules, expectations, and enforcement. A legal system provides a structure for enforcing the rules in order to meet the expectations of the society. As previously mentioned, it will address law and order and will, hopefully, result in justice. In doing so, there are *needs* of the legal system that must be met in order to satisfy its *purpose*. These two areas are covered in the next sections.

The Needs of a Legal System

The Need to Be Reasonable   A legal system needs to be reasonable. It should rely on reasonable conclusions based on facts. Speeding laws are reasonable because one can prove that higher speeds on busy streets are related to an increase in the number of accidents.

In addition to being reasonable, laws need to be applied in a reasonable manner. A law stating that Juana, a consumer, will have property taken away from her if she does not pay for the property is certainly reasonable. It would be unreasonably applied if Juana stopped paying for the property and, without notice or warning, Ramiro, the seller, removed the property. Ramiro should inform Juana that the money is due and payable and then Juana should have an opportunity to explain why she does not owe the money. Then, if the money still is not paid, Ramiro could possibly repossess the property or seek other remedies through the legal process.

The Need to Be Definite   The law needs to be definite, not vague. For example, a law stating that all contracts "for a lot of money" must be in writing would be unclear about when a contract must be in writing, leading to confusion. The Statute of Frauds, however, states that all contracts for the sale of goods costing $500 or more must be in writing, which is very clear. If one has a contract for $499.99 worth of goods, it need not be in writing; but if the contract is for $500 or more of goods it must be in writing.[1] There is a definite point at which a writing is required.

Sometimes the law is unable to state precisely what one must do in all circumstances. In such cases, the law uses the word *reasonable* rather than set precise boundaries. If an automobile hits a pedestrian and causes injury, the pedestrian may sue the driver of the vehicle. In this situation, the law does not state that speed in excess of a particular amount is necessary in order to find the driver at fault. If the only information you had was that the speed limit was 55 miles per hour and the car was going 50 miles per hour, could you find the driver at fault? Under these conditions, the law would ask the question: Was the driver's conduct reasonable under the circumstances? If so, it will be written off as an accident without civil liability; if not, the driver will be liable for any injury to the pedestrian. In the final analysis, the law provides an answer. Thus, the law is definite.

The Need to Be Flexible   To say that the law needs to be both definite and flexible seems like a contradiction in terms. The law needs to be definite in order to establish a standard. In other respects, the law must be flexible so that it can be applied in many different *individual* situations. For example, if a drunk driver kills a family wage earner and the family files a wrongful death lawsuit, recovery would be based on the future earning capacity of the wage earner. (*Wrongful death* is unlawful death. It does not necessarily have to involve a crime.) It would not be based on a table of damages. If trees did not bend in the wind, they would break. Our legal system is like those trees: It must bend without breaking. However, because of this flexibility, our legal system loses some of its predictability.

The Need to Be Practical   Because people depend on the law to guide their actions, the law needs to be practical and oriented to action rather than to thought. However, there are thoughtful ideas supporting the legal system. The law must deal with real issues created by real people. For example, most courts will only decide real disputes between the parties. They will not decide hypothetical cases. Courts will also avoid cases where the issue is *moot* (abstract; not properly submitted to the court for a resolution; not capable of resolution) or where there is no real case or controversy. (A *case or controversy* is a case brought before the court where the plaintiff and defendant are really opposed to one another on significant issues.) When the plaintiff and defendant really agree with each other and are trying to get a court decision that they are correct, there is no real case or controversy.

The Need to Be Published   If we had the best set of laws imaginable but no one knew about them, they would be virtually useless and we would have chaos. Although ignorance of the law is no excuse, our system does try to provide notice of the rules and laws. In traffic law, for example, speed limits need to be posted so drivers know how fast they can legally drive. If no speed limits are posted, arbitrary enforcement would be the rule, and drivers would not know how fast they could legally drive. In general, people cannot voluntarily comply with secret laws and rules. Therefore, all laws need to be published. Once a law has been published, we can presume that all people know it. Consequently, ignorance of the law is no excuse. For example, even if you did not see the posted speed limit, the police will still enforce it.

Statutes are a good example of published laws. For example, the Patient Protection and Affordable Care Act of 2010[2] includes a tax credit on health care coverage expenses for small employers (with 25 or fewer employees).[3] It also prohibits insurance companies from excluding an individual's preexisting conditions.[4] Beginning in 2014, most citizens will be expected to have health care insurance, and those that do not will have to pay a penalty.[5]

The Need to Be Final   If a controversy exists and the parties use the legal system to resolve it, one thing is certain: At some point in time the matter will be resolved. It may not be resolved to the full satisfaction of the person who "won" the case, but it will be resolved. In this sense the law is like a political election. On election day, someone wins

Exhibit 1.3

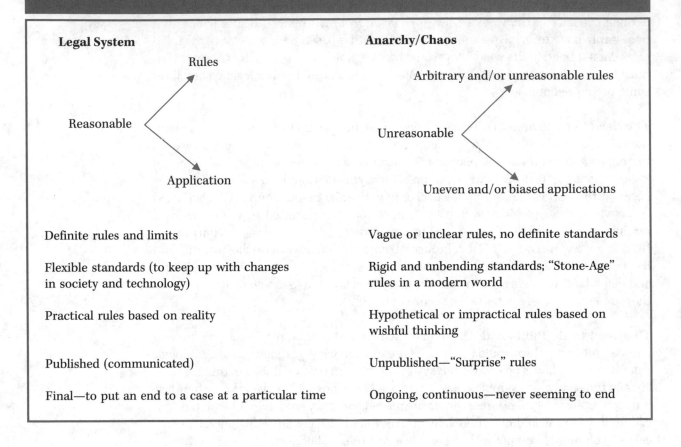

The Needs of a Legal System

Legal System	Anarchy/Chaos
Definite rules and limits	Vague or unclear rules, no definite standards
Flexible standards (to keep up with changes in society and technology)	Rigid and unbending standards; "Stone-Age" rules in a modern world
Practical rules based on reality	Hypothetical or impractical rules based on wishful thinking
Published (communicated)	Unpublished—"Surprise" rules
Final—to put an end to a case at a particular time	Ongoing, continuous—never seeming to end

and someone loses. The outcome may be delayed but eventually the results are final. In criminal law, if the defendant wins the case in trial court, the matter ends. In many situations, the prosecutor cannot appeal. A defendant who is convicted in trial court, however, can appeal to the highest court in the state system. If the defendant does not gain a reversal, the matter ends unless the U.S. Supreme Court chooses to review the case. Exhibit 1.3 outlines the needs of a legal system.

Compliance with the Law

A student of the law should note that people do not always comply with the law. When you observe people in your community repeatedly doing something, you might conclude that this behavior is lawful. This assumption may be unwise. For example, employers may repeatedly ask employees to violate the state labor code. During your study of business law, you should try to distinguish these three distinct questions:

1. What is the law about this topic?
2. How do people and businesses behave?
3. What should the law be on this topic?

Answers to these questions will vary based on the state or region under analysis. The most variance will occur about what the law should be. Individuals will disagree on the answer to this question, based on their views about jurisprudence and their ethical beliefs. Proactive businesspeople may suggest answers that will benefit their particular business enterprise or industry.

The Purposes of a Legal System

Achieving Justice   As previously discussed, justice is basically equated to fairness. Sometimes we achieve it and sometimes we do not. To some, the rule of *caveat emptor* (let the buyer beware) is a fair rule. The buyer cannot successfully seek redress in the courts if he or she did not thoroughly examine the goods.

Providing Police Power   Because justice is the ultimate purpose of a legal system, providing police power may be viewed as an intermediate purpose of a legal system. When most students see the term police power, they usually envision a uniformed police officer with a badge and gun. That, however, is just one part of what we call police power. Police power is inherent in all governments. This power allows for the creation and enforcement of laws designed to protect the public's health, safety, and general welfare.[6] Laws and ordinances concerning police, fire, sanitation, and social welfare departments in state and local governments stem from police power.

Maintaining Peace and the Status Quo   Ever since the days of ancient England, one of the clearest purposes of the law has been to "keep the King's peace." Most modern torts and crimes can trace their origin to a simple breaching of the King's peace. Today, laws that govern the relationships between private individuals, such as the laws governing assault, battery, trespass, and false imprisonment, are private forms of keeping the peace. Closely associated with keeping the peace is the concept of maintaining the status quo—that is, keeping things the way they are. It is natural for the law to maintain the status quo unless changing things will benefit society. It is possible to obtain a preliminary injunction from a court that will maintain the status quo until the lawsuit is finally resolved. The petitioner must allege and prove irreparable injury to obtain a preliminary injunction.

Providing Answers   On a philosophical level, the law should be just; but on a practical level, it should provide answers. Sometimes the answers the law provides are not satisfactory. If Melanie sues Troy, a neighbor, because Troy is allegedly creating

eClass 1.2 **Management**

SECURITY ISSUES

Yousef Alwazzan plans to visit Washington, D.C., next week for a conference on educational technology, including sessions at the Pentagon on possible uses of educational technology on some military bases. Ani and Meg recognize that this trip is important to eClass, but they are a little concerned because of the shooting at the Pentagon on March 4, 2010, and several other violent incidents at federal government facilities.[7] Yousef told them that there was little reason for concern since Pentagon security and the D.C. police have strengthened security around the Pentagon, including the application of some strict rules about people carrying weapons and/or acting in a suspicious manner. While Ani and Meg appreciate the extra security, they do not understand why different rules seem to apply to the Pentagon than exist in their hometown. They have asked you to explain how or why this is permitted. What will you tell them?

BUSINESS CONSIDERATIONS   Is it reasonable to have different legal rules about carrying weapons near the Pentagon than in other areas? Should the police apply the rules differently in this vicinity? Can a business impose different rules concerning the carrying of weapons on or around its workplace? What factors would cause a business to do so?

ETHICAL CONSIDERATIONS   Is it ethical for the government to have different rules near the Pentagon or the White House than it has in other places? What are the ethical implications of having special rules in certain specified areas or under certain conditions?

a nuisance on his property, and Troy wins the case in the trial court, then Melanie can appeal the decision to the next higher court. (*Nuisance* is the title we give to the unreasonable or unlawful use of a person's own property that interferes with another person's use and enjoyment of his or her property.) In most states this higher court is called an appellate court (court that has the power to review the decisions of lower courts). If an *appellate court* rules in favor of Troy, a further appeal may be taken to the state's highest court. In that court, Melanie may win and thereby receive a satisfactory answer. But whether she wins or loses, Melanie and Troy will be provided with an answer once the appellate process is completed.

Providing Protection   The law protects all kinds of interests. You have already seen that the law concerns itself with protecting individuals. The tort law of assault and battery is a classic example of protection of the individual. The law also protects persons less conspicuously when it protects their civil rights. Civil rights laws are extremely important in modern litigation and have their historical background in the first ten amendments to the U.S. Constitution, known as the Bill of Rights. (It is worthwhile for you to refresh your memory about the provisions in the Constitution.) Persons are protected in the free exercise of their speech, are free to choose or not to choose a religion, can peacefully assemble, and may petition their government for a redress of grievances. The U.S. Constitution contains the right to be protected from unreasonable searches and seizures, the right against compulsory self-incrimination of a crime, the right to a grand jury, the right against double jeopardy (a rule of criminal law that states that a person will not be tried in court more than once by the same government for the same criminal offense), the right to a jury trial, and the right to bail. Proponents argue that the Constitution provides a right to bear arms, but constitutional experts disagree on whether this is an individual right or a right to form a militia.

The government is also in the business of protecting *itself*. A government's self-protection is an ancient right that goes back to Roman law. It is based on the concept that if the *sovereign* (above or superior to all others; that from which all authority flows) is *truly* sovereign, it cannot be attacked legally. Because the sovereign is, by definition, supreme, it cannot be subject to attack nor can it be held liable to its inferiors. Thus, the rule of *sovereign immunity* was developed, shielding the sovereign from lawsuits against it, but permitting the sovereign to file lawsuits. This rule still stands, to some extent, although the federal government and many states have passed special statutes permitting individuals to sue them for *torts* (civil wrongs). See Chapter 6 for a discussion of torts.

Finally, the law is concerned with the protection of property. All property is characterized as either personal or real property. *Personal property* is all property with the exception of real property. In general, if property is movable or intangible, it is personal property. *Real property*, on the other hand, is land and whatever is affixed to land, such as a house. However, personal property can have dual meanings in law. In addition to the meaning above, it may also mean property that is owned by individuals, as opposed to public property that is owned by the government or the community. Our legal system has a variety of laws that protect both types of property.

Enforcing Intent   The law of contracts is based on freedom of contract. It is this rule that allows each of us to be our own "legislator" to a limited extent. We make our own "laws" of conduct, as long as the contracts into which we enter do not violate the general principles of contract law. For example, you may wish to enter into a contract with a supplier of goods. You may want to make the contract today so that it will immediately bind the other party. Perhaps you have found a good price and do not think you will find a better one. Your problem, however, is that you do not presently have the money to pay for the goods, but you know that you can easily resell them for an immediate cash profit within 10 days after delivery. You should, therefore, seek a provision in the contract stating that the buyer will pay the seller for the goods 11 or more days after receipt of the goods. Of course, if you cannot resell the goods within the 10 days as anticipated, you will have a financial problem. This is more a question of business judgment, however, than of law. If the goods or services in the contract were illegal, the contract would be void under contract law.

Providing Rehabilitation   Both criminal law and civil law are directed toward rehabilitation. Criminal law should, among other things, rehabilitate the criminal. Civil law is also involved in rehabilitation to some extent. Contract law provides rehabilitation for a party harmed by a breach of the contract. Tort law provides for a form of rehabilitation in the assessment of damages for the victim of the tort. The federal bankruptcy law is directed toward the rehabilitation of honest debtors.

Facilitating Commercial Transactions   One of the major characteristics of the U.S. legal system is that it facilitates commercial transactions. For example, very few automobiles would be sold in the U.S. if car dealers insisted on cash payment. Our national economy is still very reliant on the automobile industry. The prosperity of the steel, energy, and transportation industries are directly related to that of the automobile. Thus, reducing the number of automobiles sold could be harmful to the national economy. When U.S. automobile manufacturers suffered from the economic downturn in 2008-2009, the federal government offered bailout money to some of them. In addition, the extension of credit for the purchase of automobiles greatly facilitates trade. The use of checks and credit cards also accelerates commercial transactions. The taking of a security interest in goods expedites trade to persons who might otherwise not be in a financial position to make the purchase. (*Security interest* is a collateral interest taken in the property of another to secure payment of a debt or contract performance.) The U.S. legal system fosters free and open competition and facilitates trade. This characteristic of the legal system has done much to contribute to the business and financial power of the United States. Exhibit 1.4 outlines the purposes of a legal system.

Legal Systems in Other Countries

Sometimes we assume that all countries have the same or similar legal systems. This ethnocentric view can result in a rude shock when a U.S. citizen traveling in a foreign country continues to act the same as he or she would act at home. The U.S. citizen may find that behavior that is tolerated in the United States constitutes a crime in a foreign country, and that many of the protections he or she expects in the United States do not apply abroad. Other countries have different historical and sociological backgrounds. Citizens' values and government rules may differ from those in the United States. For example, life insurance isn't accepted under traditional Muslim law.[8]

With the exception of the United Kingdom, most of Europe, including France, Germany, and Sweden, follows civil law. In this context, *civil law* means that the legal system relies on statutory law. The statutes are grouped into codes, and the judges administer the codes. Judges, therefore, do not make law to the degree that they do in the United States. Under civil law, the judge relies primarily on the codes enacted by the legislative bodies.

Until recently, the former Union of Soviet Socialist Republics (USSR) followed a unique version of civil law. Owing to its socialist philosophy, private ownership of property was limited. The primary goal of this legal system was to preserve state

Exhibit 1.4

The Purposes of a Legal System

Purpose	Reason
Achieving justice	To provide "justice" so that the needs of the members of society are addressed.
Providing police power	To provide a social structure so that "wronged" individuals do not have to resort to self-help; to give society control of the system.
Maintaining peace and the status quo	To provide each member of society with a feeling of personal security and a structure on which each individual can rely.
Providing answers	To achieve practical justice; lets the members of society know what is expected of them and what they may reasonably expect from others.
Providing protection	To define and establish social guidelines and protect the entire society if any of these guidelines are not followed and obeyed.
Enforcing intent	To provide some method for permitting private agreements and for ensuring that these agreements are honored or enforced.
Providing rehabilitation	To allow a person who violates the guidelines of the society a second chance; recognizes that anyone can make a mistake.
Facilitating commercial transactions	To support freedom of contract and private ownership of property; each of these concepts encourages and promotes business transactions.

ownership of all means of production. Consequently, the USSR's law primarily consisted of public law such as criminal law. The law of property, contracts, and business organizations did not play a role. Many of the former Soviet republics are now beginning to engage in *privatization* (the process of going from government ownership of business and other property to private individual ownership). A body of private law is being developed as these countries move toward a more traditional civil law system. The new countries often rely on consultants, like attorneys from the United States, in developing their new system of commercial law.

In addition, the U.S. legal system is based on the law of precedents, with its strong dependence on previous court decisions. However, there are other countries, such as Mexico, where precedent is not important. In Mexico each judge does his or her best to fashion a fair result in the particular case before the court. In civil law systems, precedent is not significant. In the European Union (EU), the role of precedents is increasing. Decisions made by the EU Court of Justice become precedents in all the member countries. Although the EU is primarily a code system, it is moving toward the use of precedents and more of a common law approach.

There are a number of legal systems based on religious teachings. The Hindu legal system is one example. Their system is a personal and religious law system which states that Hindus should act in accordance with this law wherever they live. The Hindu system has been recorded in law books called *smitris*. Most Hindu law applies to family matters. Anglo-Hindu law evolved in most Hindu countries while they were British colonies, where judges were applying a combination of English and Hindu laws. When it gained its independence from the United Kingdom, India replaced Anglo-Hindu law with a civil code primarily based on Hindu law.

Muslims believe in Islamic law or *Shari'a*, which is based on the Koran and other religious writings. Saudi Arabia relies almost exclusively on Islamic law. Other countries apply Islamic law in some areas, such as family law, and supplement it with secular law. In 1998, the Pakistani Prime Minister, Nawaz Sharif, proposed a constitutional amendment to transform their legal system into an Islamic system. (The existing legal system was based on British common law.) Their constitution already permitted the courts to overturn any statute that is un-Islamic.[9]

A number of other religions also have legal systems, including Catholicism and Judaism. These religions generally provide their own tribunals for resolving disputes.

JURISPRUDENCE

In modern terms, *jurisprudence* can be defined as the "general or fundamental elements" of a legal system.[10] It is often thought of as the philosophy underlying the law. In Latin, jurisprudence means the "wisdom of the law." However, there are really many different "wisdoms" of the law reflected in a number of different philosophical views; these views vary based on the values inherent in the law, the development of the law, and its proper role in society. The law continues to change, and knowledge of the legal philosophies will improve your ability to understand the law and predict future trends. Here is a brief introduction to some of the philosophical approaches. Note that sometimes there is even disagreement among philosophers who subscribe to the same basic theory.

Natural Law Theory

The *natural law* theory holds that the law should be based on what is correct and moral. It is composed of these four concepts:

1. There are certain legal values or value judgments.
2. These values are unchanging because their source is absolute. Natural law theorists disagree about the sources. Theorists believe that they are Nature, God, or Reason.

3. These values can be determined by human reason.

4. Once they are determined, these values supersede any form of human law. Once the natural law is discovered, it nullifies any contradictory law created by humans.

This theory rests on some significant assumptions—the world is perceived as a rational order with values and purposes built into it; the laws of nature describe how things should be; and humans should use reason to grasp what should be done. Many early Greek philosophers were natural law theorists. In the history of Christian thought, the dominant theory of ethics has been the theory of natural law,[11] best exemplified by St. Thomas Aquinas.[12] Natural law theory is found in the words of the Declaration of Independence, "We hold these truths to be self-evident, that all Men are created equal, that they are endowed by their Creator with certain unalienable Rights. . .". The natural law theory focuses on fairness and justice, even though some disorder will result when individuals decide that the written law is not "natural law." Criticisms of natural law include whose values are to be included in the natural law and who determines whether a man-made law is unjust because it violates natural law.

Legal Positivism

Legal positivism is composed of three theoretical parts:

1. "[L]egal validity is ultimately a function of certain kinds of social facts."[13]

2. Social facts give rise to legal validity, which is authoritative due to some kind of social convention.

3. There is *no* overlap between notions of law and morality. This last part is in direct opposition to natural law theory.

Legal positivists disagree on the correct interpretation of these three theoretical parts. One alternate statement proposed by some positivists includes these primary beliefs: (1) law is the expression of the will of the legislator or sovereign, and must be followed; (2) morals are separate from law and should not be considered in making legal decisions, for example, judges should not consider factors outside the legal system such as contemporary community values; and (3) law is a closed system in which correct legal decisions are reached by reference to statutes and court precedents. (*Precedents* are decided cases that establish legal authority for later cases.) The *legal positivist* approach believes that the law is the result of lawmaking by a legitimate government. In the United States, this is primarily executive orders, legislation, court opinions, and administrative bodies. Under this theory, legality and morality are separated. The positive law approach promotes stability in the law and the supremacy of written laws. Criticisms of legal positivism include that it is too narrow and too literal-minded, and that its refusal to consider social, ethical, and other factors makes it static and unable to serve society well.

Sociological Theory

Under the *sociological* theory, the role of prior law in the form of precedents is minimized. The law's source should be contemporary opinion and customs. In creating statutes or court decisions, the legislator or judge should record community interests; familiarize himself or herself with the community standards and mores; and make a decision conforming to these standards. Criticisms of the sociological theory include that following the theory would make the law too unpredictable. Community standards change, and thus the law would be changing all the time. In a court decision relying on this theory, the judge may discuss sociological factors and current customs. For example, a court may consider "contemporary community standards" to determine whether a magazine is obscene.

Historical Theory

The *historical* theory holds that the law is primarily a system of customs and social traditions that have developed over time. It is very similar to the sociological school; however, its focus is more historical than contemporary. Each nation develops its own individual consensus about what the law should be. The law is an evolving system, and precedents have a significant role. Legitimacy is obtained from the historical will of a nation's people.

Law and Economics Theory

Law and economics theory applies classical economic theory and empirical methods to explain legal doctrines and to predict judicial decisions. It argues for using economic analysis as both a description about how courts and legislators behave and as a prescription about how courts and legislators *should* behave. The law and economics theory is closely allied with the University of Chicago, where it originated. It is sometimes called The Chicago School. This theory is commonly used in areas such as torts, contracts, and property law. Under the theory, the legal system should be viewed as a system to promote the efficient allocation of resources in society. For example, buyers and sellers in the market exchange goods or services of value. The exchange is maximizing value for both the buyer and seller. Richard Posner is currently a leader in law and economics theory. In his words,

> [M]any areas of law, especially the great common law fields of property, torts, crimes, and contracts, bear the stamp of economic reasoning. It is not a refutation [of this theory] that few judicial opinions contain explicit references to economic concepts. Often the true grounds of decision are concealed rather than illuminated by the characteristic rhetoric of judicial opinions. Indeed, legal education consists primarily of learning to dig

beneath the rhetorical surface to find these grounds, many of which may turn out to have an economic character.[14]

(*Rhetoric* is the art or science of using words effectively.)

The proper goal of statutory and common law is to promote wealth maximization, which can be accomplished by facilitating the mechanisms of the free market. Also, market transactions reflect autonomous judgments about the value of individual preferences. (*Autonomous* refers to the right of the individual to govern himself or herself according to his or her own reason.) Critics contend that this theory tends to be politically conservative and generally rests on only one type of economic philosophy to the exclusion of others. Another criticism is that the theory could be acceptable as a *descriptive theory* (theory that describes how things are and reports what is observed) to explain what the law is, but it is not helpful as a *prescriptive theory* (theory that states what people should do or what should occur).

Feminist Legal Theory

The *feminist legal* theory holds that the law does not treat women equally. The law is structured to promote the interests of white males and to exclude women. As with some of the other theories, there are a wide variety of views under this theory. Many feminist legal theorists are also concerned about persons of color. (There is also a critical race theory, which focuses on how people of color are excluded from the legal system.) Followers of feminist legal theory assert that the current legal system is dominated by men, and that women are often victimized and their perspectives ignored. They argue that the male perspective has shaped many areas of law including property, contract, criminal law, constitutional law, and civil rights law. They also contend that the law should consider the female perspective. For example, workplace behavior that may not seem harassing to men may seem harassing to women, and the law should address this accordingly. With the 1991 case of *Ellison v. Brady,*[15] federal courts began using the reasonable woman standard in cases where women were being sexually harassed

A 1998 Italian case attracted the attention of feminist legal theorists. The case was heard by Italy's highest criminal appeals court, which determined that an 18-year old girl was not raped, based in part, on the fact that she was wearing jeans. (For more details on the case, see Case Problems and Writing Assignments 1.) The ruling said that it is "common knowledge that it's nearly impossible to even partially remove jeans from a person without their co-operation, since this operation is already very difficult for the wearer."[16] It also said that "jeans cannot be removed easily and certainly it is impossible to pull them off if the victim is fighting against her attacker with all her force."[17] Eventually the alleged assailant was acquitted.[18] The decision sparked protests from Italy to California. "Denim Day," to commemorate victims of rape and assault, is an out-growth of these protests. On an historical note, rape has been considered a criminal felony in Italy only since 1996. Prior to that time, it was considered a "crime of honor" against the woman's family. A defendant could avoid punishment by agreeing to marry the woman or by proving that she had many sexual experiences.[19]

The feminist legal theory is criticized for being too narrow in focus and for failing to recognize changes taking place as more women enter the workforce, including the legal profession.

Critical Legal Studies Theory

The *critical legal studies* (CLS) movement holds that the content of the law in liberal democracies reflects "'ideological struggles among social factions in which competing conceptions of justice, goodness, and social and political life get compromised, truncated, vitiated, and adjusted.' The inevitable outcome of such struggles, [in] this view, is a profound inconsistency permeating the deepest layers of the law."[20] The law is not objective and neutral. The current law reflects a cluster of beliefs, which convinces people that they are living in a natural hierarchy, but that really this cluster of beliefs has been created by those in power. The elite uses these beliefs to rationalize their power. The elite maintains their power, wealth, and privilege using

Exhibit 1.5

Theories of Jurisprudence

Theory	Primary Characteristic
Natural Law	Source of law is nature, God, or reason.
Legal Positivism	Source of law is the legislature.
Sociological	Source of law is contemporary community standards and customs.
Historical	Law evolves over time based on custom and social traditions.
Law and Economics	Classical economic theory should be applied to all areas of the law.
Feminist Legal	Legal system is dominated by the perspective of white males; women's perspectives are ignored and women are victimized.
Critical Legal Studies	Law is a combination of legal and nonlegal beliefs; it must be critiqued to create social change and political growth.

law, economics, mass communication, and religion. In order to accomplish social and political change, the law must be examined and critiqued. The current law is a combination of legal and nonlegal beliefs that is used to maintain the status quo, especially in the political and economic spheres. This is accomplished by convincing others that those in power should remain in power. The legal system, including legal education, is a deceptive social mechanism for the preservation of power by those who currently have it. People can only free themselves of this perspective by critically examining these beliefs. Generally, people who subscribe to the CLS view wish to overturn the status quo. This theory is criticized as being basically a negative position; it does not have any concrete suggestions about how to change the social, political, and legal systems.

Exhibit 1.5 summarizes the foregoing philosophical approaches to jurisprudence.

SOURCES OF LAW

The U.S. legal system is based on the Constitution, treaties, statutes, ordinances, administrative regulations, common law, case law, and equity. Although each of the elements is separate, the elements are interdependent; together they constitute our system. These elements must be thought of as a system; a change in one element should not be considered in isolation. Such a change will affect one or more parts of the system. In a civil rights suit, a person may allege a violation of constitutional rights (Fourteenth Amendment), a statutory right (Civil Rights Act of 1964), an administrative regulation (Equal Employment Opportunity Commission guideline), past decisions of the court (*stare decisis* means to abide by, or adhere to, decided cases; it is the policy of courts to stand by decided cases and not to disturb a settled point of law), and equity (if all else fails, the person should win because it is fair). The important thing to remember is that all the parts of the legal system are interconnected and that the whole is more than the sum of the parts.

Constitutions

A *constitution* is the fundamental law of a nation. It may be written or unwritten. The British constitution is said to be unwritten. Clearly, the U.S. Constitution is written. It allocates the powers of government and also sets limits on those powers. Our founding fathers knew that all tyrants had two powers: the power of the purse and the power of the sword. The Constitution places the power of the purse exclusively with Congress and the power of the sword with the Executive branch. The Judiciary, our third branch of government, has neither the power of the purse nor the power of the sword. However, it has the power to interpret the meaning of the U.S. Constitution and to decide the constitutionality of the laws passed by Congress. In the case of *Marbury v. Madison*,[21] the U.S. Supreme Court for the first time applied the doctrine of *judicial review* (the power of the courts to say what the law is). That case held that the Supreme Court has the power to decide whether laws passed by Congress comply with the Constitution. If they do not, they are unconstitutional and thus of no force or effect. We discuss the unique nature of the Constitution further in Chapters 3 and 5.

Our states also have constitutions, and they are the fundamental laws of those states. The U.S. Constitution, however, is the supreme legal document in the United States and thus will take precedence over state constitutions in the event that there is a conflict between the documents, as provided for in the Supremacy Clause in Article VI of the Constitution.

Treaties

Treaties are formal agreements between two or more nations. Treaties are often categorized by the number of nations involved. *Bilateral treaties* involve two nations, and *multilateral treaties* involve more than two nations. Treaties that are recognized by almost all nations, such as the Geneva Convention, are labeled *universal treaties.* The United States enters into treaties for various purposes including providing protection, for example, through the North Atlantic Treaty Organization (NATO), and promoting trade, for example, through the North American Free Trade Agreement (NAFTA). Treaties are the only elements of our legal system that do not stem from the Constitution. Treaties are made, not with the authority of the Constitution, but under the authority of the United States. This difference is important because the power to make a treaty is a function of sovereignty and not one of a constitution. In most cases, treaties are negotiated by the President or his or her designee(s). The U.S. Constitution gives the Senate the power to approve treaties, and a two-thirds vote is required for approval.[22] The President sometimes involves senators in the negotiation process to help with the subsequent approval process.[23] The Senate has rejected relatively few of the treaties it has considered.[24] However, sometimes the President withdraws a treaty rather than have it defeated.[25] Other times the treaty dies in a Senate committee or is amended or changed by the Senate. In these situations, generally the other countries enter into further negotiations with the United States.[26] (The President can enter into executive agreements which are not subject to the approval process.[27]) The case of *Missouri v. Holland*[28] established that statutes passed in accordance with a valid treaty cannot be declared unconstitutional in the United States. While the Constitution is the supreme law of the land for domestic issues, once treaties are formed they become the supreme law of the land for international issues.

Statutes

Statutes are the acts of federal or state legislative bodies. They prohibit or command the doing of something. The word "statute" is preferred when one is referring to a legislative act to distinguish it from other types of laws, such as ordinances, regulations, common law, and case law.

One of the best examples of state statutory law is found in the Uniform Commercial Code (UCC). All 50 states, the District of Columbia, and the U.S. Virgin Islands have adopted at least portions of the UCC. Unfortunately for business people, some states adopted modified versions of the UCC, so you should check on the law in your state. The UCC is very important and, accordingly, is the subject of many of the chapters contained in this book. The UCC covers the following subjects: sales, leases, negotiable instruments, bank deposits and collections, fund transfers, letters of credit, bulk transfers, documents of title, investment securities, and secured transactions.

Ordinances

Ordinances are laws passed by municipal bodies. Cities, towns, and incorporated villages have the power to establish laws for the protection of the public's health, safety, and welfare. These entities are to be distinguished from counties, which generally do not have legislative power. Counties usually have the power to enforce state laws within their boundaries.

Administrative Regulations

Administrative regulations are rules promulgated by governmental agencies, most of which were created by the legislative branch of government. Examples of agencies include the Federal Trade Commission (FTC) on the federal level and an insurance commission on the state level. The rules and regulations of these entities have the full force and effect of law.

Common Law

Common law consists of the unwritten law of a country, based on custom, usage, *and* judicial decisions.[29] Common law is unique to the Anglo-American legal system, with its focus on precedents and following the opinions of prior cases. The development of the common law is depicted in Exhibit 1.6. All U.S. states, except for Louisiana, have a common law system.[30] Louisiana, like most European nations, has a code-based legal system. These code-based legal systems, commonly called civil law systems, rely on statutory authority in deciding cases rather than following precedent. If there is no statutory authority to decide a case, the court cannot issue a ruling in a civil law system. Courts in a civil law system lack the authority or power to "make law" through judicial rulings that establish precedent. By contrast, nations following the Anglo-American legal tradition do have the power to "make law" by establishing and following precedent and providing a "common law" for other courts to follow.

Exhibit 1.6

Common Law

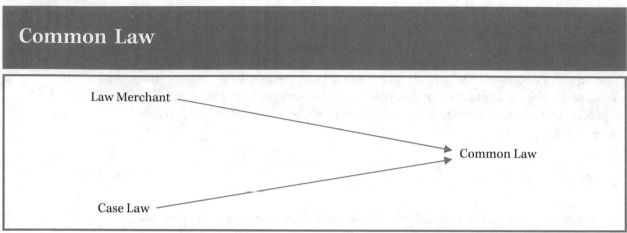

Case Law

Case law derives from the many reported court cases, and it is part of the common law previously discussed. Quite often, the judges must interpret statutes in order to apply them to actual cases and controversies. These interpretations place what lawyers call a "judicial gloss" on the statute. You will not fully understand a particular statute until you have read both the statute *and* the cases that have interpreted it. *Case law,* then, is the law as pronounced by judges.

The American Law Institute (ALI) is dedicated to promoting clarification of the law, improving the administration of justice, and drafting the Restatements of the Law. *Restatements* are not actually part of the law, rather they are treatises which summarize the law on a subject. When there are conflicting approaches, the *Restatement* "recommends" one of the alternatives. *Restatements* become part of the case law when a court relies on a particular section in reaching its opinion.

Stare decisis is an ancient doctrine that means the question has been decided. For example, if a particular legal point is well settled in a certain jurisdiction, a future case with substantially the same facts will be decided in accordance with the principle that has already been decided. This is one of the reasons that lawyers do a great deal of legal research. The doctrine of *stare decisis* is also called precedents. Even though a legal matter has been settled, it does not mean the legal system must remain static.

A precedent remains in effect until it is changed. (As previously mentioned, precedents do not play a major role in all legal systems.) It must be remembered that the legal system evolves. Lawyers and petitioners in court may try to persuade the court to modify precedents, and sometimes they are successful. Occasionally, the court will change or modify the precedents. When a court changes the precedents, it will generally support its decision with one of these three reasons:

1. The prior rule is out of date; it is not appropriate to present-day society.
2. The prior case is distinguishable because the facts are different in one or more significant details.
3. The judge or justice who made the prior ruling was incorrect or wrong.

Judges may be reluctant to state that the prior ruling was in error, especially if they participated in making the prior ruling. It is easier to state that someone else made an error. Judges *sometimes* do admit that the rule they fashioned earlier is not the preferred response to a particular legal problem.

When a court follows precedent it is striving to make the law *definite*, satisfying one of the needs of a legal system. However, as times and situations change, courts need to be able to change. The law would not be *flexible*, another need of a legal system, if precedents could never be changed. Courts have a difficult time balancing these two needs—definite and flexible—in applying the law within the area of precedents. *Brown v. Board of Education*[31] is an example of a court overturning precedents. In that case, the U.S. Supreme Court decided, contrary to prior decisions, that providing separate schools for black and white children was unconstitutional. This overturned the precedent, established in *Plessy v. Ferguson*,[32] that "separate but equal" schools were constitutional.

Dictum is language in a court opinion that is not necessary to the decision before the court. It is an observation or remark by a judge that is not necessarily involved in the case or essential to its resolution. These remarks or asides are not part of the precedents. Dictum can provide valuable clues about how that judge might decide future cases.

An opportunity to "make law," as it is called, occurs when jurisdictions are in conflict over a point of law. For example, many states are divided into various judicial districts, and courts in each of these districts may issue written legal opinions. If two or more districts have published conflicting opinions on a particular point, and the state's supreme court has *not* issued an opinion on the point, the time is ripe for the creation of a new rule, statewide, that will resolve the matter once and for all. Until the statewide rule is created, however, each court creates precedents for itself and for any courts directly under it. When there are no prior court decisions on a point of law, the court may state that the case is one of first impression. *First impression* occurs when an issue is presented to the court for an initial decision; the issue presents a novel question of law for the court's decision, and it is not governed by any existing precedent.

Equity

Equity is defined as a body of rules applied to legal controversies when no adequate remedy at law exists. These rules are based on the principles outlined by Justinian during his reign as the Byzantine emperor of Rome (A.D. 527-565): "to live honestly, to harm nobody, [and] to render to every man his due." These rules were developed outside the common law courts in England by an officer of the King called the chancellor. The primary reasons for development of equity were the unfair decisions made by the courts of law and the limited types of remedies available in them.

Today, the rules of law and equity are joined into one legal system.[33] The injunction is an equitable remedy, but before U.S. courts will issue an injunction, the person requesting it must show proof that the remedy at law would be inadequate. For example, if your neighbors are burning rubber tires on their property and the prevailing wind carries the obnoxious odor directly across your property, their action will destroy the peaceful use and enjoyment of your land. In general, no amount of monetary damages would be sufficient to allow them to continue to burn rubber tires. In that case, you would not have an adequate remedy at law, and you could request that the court issue an injunction to stop your neighbors from burning those tires. In a larger sense, however, equity may be viewed as a doctrine that results in the legal system's adhering to the principle of fairness. Exhibit 1.7 summarizes some of the differences between law and equity.

CLASSIFICATIONS OF LAW

Federal versus State Law

Our legal system is divided into two branches: federal and state. American lawyers must learn not only the law of their states but also federal law. In addition, lawyers should know the majority rule. The *majority rule* is simply the rule that most states have adopted. Quite often, a *minority rule*, which a smaller number of states follow, also exists. Rarely, if ever, do the various states agree on all aspects of a law. Exhibit 1.8 outlines the sources of the U.S. legal system. Note that there is some overlap between case law and common law.

Common versus Statutory Law

As discussed earlier, the legal system consists of both common and statutory laws. Judges in the United States and England generally have the power to "make law" by interpreting statutes or applying precedents, and those interpretations become "common" law. Judges also apply the statutory law. Statutory law refers to legislative enactments, the statutes passed by the legislative bodies of the state. Common law is "unwritten" law, law developed over time by judicial action. Common law fills the gaps where other sources of law do not cover a particular topic. Statutory enactments override common law, filling the gap with a statutory provision and eliminating the need for unwritten coverage.

Exhibit 1.7

Distinctions Between Actions in Law and in Equity[a]

Characteristic	In Law	In Equity[b]
Type of relief	Money to compensate plaintiff for his or her losses	Action, either in the form of ordering the defendant to do or not to do something, or in the form of a decree about the status of something[cd]
Nature of proceeding	More restricted by precedents	More flexible and less restricted by precedents, supposed to create equity (justice)
Time limit for filing lawsuit	Applicable period fixed by the statute of limitations[e]	A reasonable period of time as determined by the judge on a case-by-case basis[f]
Decider of fact	Jury trial, if requested by a party	No jury trial, judge decides the facts[g]
Enforcing a decision	Plaintiff may begin an execution of the judgment[h]	Plaintiff may begin contempt proceedings if the defendant does not perform as directed; defendant may be placed in jail and/or fined[i]

[a] Actions at law and those in equity are no longer as distinct as they once were. As a result, many states allow "combined" trials, with issues of law and issues of equity being tried together.

[b] Traditionally, a court of equity was called a court of chancery, and the judge was called a chancellor.

[c] Common equitable remedies include injunction, specific performance of a contract, rescission of a contract, and reformation (correcting or rewriting) of a contract.

[d] Courts would prefer to award monetary damages. Equitable relief is only granted when the plaintiff can convince the court that money would be inadequate.

[e] The statute of limitations period will depend on the state and the type of lawsuit. It will be a fixed period.

[f] If the plaintiff has waited too long to file suit under the circumstances, the judge will apply the doctrine of laches, and the suit will be dismissed.

[g] Some states permit the use of an advisory jury.

[h] In an execution, the clerk of the court issues a formal document and the sheriff seizes the defendant's money and/or other property. If property is seized, the sheriff will sell it and use the proceeds to pay the plaintiff.

[i] The court is authorized to place the defendant in jail until he or she complies (or agrees to comply) with the court decree.

Civil versus Criminal Law

The U.S. legal system also separates civil and criminal law. In this context, *civil law* is private law wherein one person sues another person. *Criminal law* is public law in which a government entity files charges against a person. For example, if a person

Exhibit 1.8

The Sources of Law in the U.S. Legal System

Authority	Source	Definition
F, S	Constitution	Supreme law of the land; fundamental basis of domestic law
F	Treaties	Not based on the Constitution; formal agreements between nations; fundamental basis of international law/relations
F, S	Statutes	Acts of the legislature; control of domestic conduct; subject to limits imposed by the Constitution
S	Ordinances	Laws passed by municipal bodies and designed to control purely local problems; subject to any limits imposed by statutes or by the Constitution
F, S	Administrative Regulations	Acts of administrative agencies; control of specific areas of conduct; subject to any limits imposed by statutes or by the Constitution
S	Common Law	Principles and rules that have developed over time and are based on custom and usage; provide rules when statutes and the Constitution do not
F, S	Case Law	Precedents, established interpretations of areas of law in which the courts define what the law is
F, S	Equity	Special rules and relief when "the law" does not provide a proper and/or adequate remedy

Legend: F = federal; S = state

becomes violently abusive and attacks another individual, inflicting bodily harm on the innocent individual, the district attorney, as the representative of a government entity, may prosecute the attacker for assault. If convicted, the attacker may go to jail or prison. In addition, the person who was injured may sue the attacker in court for money damages. The additional suit would not constitute double jeopardy or its civil law equivalent, *res judicata*, since two different theories of action exist: civil and criminal. (*Res judicata* is a rule of civil law that prevents a person from being sued more than once by the same party for the same civil wrong.)

There are a number of significant differences between civil and criminal law. One of the most significant differences is the burden of proof. In a civil case, the plaintiff must prove his or her case by a preponderance of the evidence. (A *preponderance of the*

eClass 1.3 Management

LOBBYING THE GOVERNMENT ON BEHALF OF eCLASS

Students and their families are understandably concerned about the price of textbooks and educational supplements. These citizens have lobbied members of the state legislature demanding a statutory price limit for the price of textbooks and supplementary materials, including eAccounting and similar products. Responding to the complaints, the state legislature is considering the enactment of a statute that sets the maximum price in the state for products like eAccounting. Ani, Meg, and Yousef would obviously like to stop the state legislature from enacting this proposed legislation because it might reduce eClass's profits from selling eAccounting in the state. Ani, Meg, and Yousef wonder what they can do, and turn to you for advice. What will you tell them?

BUSINESS CONSIDERATIONS   What options are available to eClass under these circumstances? What can—or should—a business do when it feels that proposed legislation will have a serious impact on the firm's profitability?

ETHICAL CONSIDERATIONS   Would it be ethical for a firm to attempt to influence potential legislation? What ethical considerations would arise should a firm decide to attempt to influence members of the legislature?

evidence means that the evidence on this side is stronger than the evidence on the other side. In other words, the greater weight of the evidence is on the plaintiff's side.) In a criminal case, the judge or jury must start with the presumption that the defendant is innocent, and the government must convince the judge or jury that the defendant is guilty *beyond* a reasonable doubt. (A *reasonable doubt* means a belief that there is a real possibility that the defendant is not guilty.)

Substantive versus Procedural Law

Substantive law deals with rights and duties given or imposed by the legal system. *Procedural law* is devoted to how those rights and duties are enforced. For example, the law of contracts is substantive law. The law of pleadings describes the steps used to enforce those rights or duties. (*Pleadings* are formal statements filed in court specifying the claims of the parties.) A controversy over the mental ability to form a valid contract is a substantive matter, but how one goes about getting the dispute into a court is a matter of procedure. Where one files the lawsuit, what must be alleged, how one notifies the defendant, and how long the defendant has to answer the allegations are all examples of procedural law. This book is devoted primarily to "substantive" law.

Public versus Private Law

Private law is the body of law that deals with the property and relationships of private persons. It includes the areas of *property law* (ownership and transfer of assets), *contract law* (rights and duties that arise from enforceable agreements), *tort law* (other private wrongs such as negligence, invasion of privacy, and defamation), and *business relationships* (agency, partnerships, corporations, and similar entities). *Public law* deals with the relations between private individuals and the government. It also deals with the structure and operation of the government itself. *Constitutional law* (law relating to the government and its activities), *criminal law* (law relating to offenses against the government), and *administrative law* (law relating to government agencies) are types of public law. Both private law and public law are very important to business decision making.

ROLE OF THE ATTORNEY

Legal issues are critical in all businesses, even though some businesses are subjected to more government regulation than others. Whether the business is faced with litigation or is practicing preventive law and attempting to avoid legal problems, attorneys can be important "partners" in a business. One of the primary purposes of this text is to assist you in speaking intelligently with your attorney and to enable you to more fully understand what he or she says to you. There may be situations when you are able to represent yourself in legal matters, such as negotiating a lease. When a person represents himself or herself in court, it is called appearing *pro persona*, or *pro per* for short. There are many situations when it is unwise to represent yourself and you should hire a competent attorney. You should evaluate how much is at stake, how much knowledge and skill you have, and whether you have adequate time to devote to the issue. The next section addresses how to select and hire an attorney.

Hiring an Attorney

Each state has a body of law dealing with the attorney-client relationship. Each state licenses attorneys to practice law within the state. State law generally addresses an attorney's obligation to his or her client and the extent of the obligation to keep client confidences.

Attorneys are generally paid a flat fee (a one-time fee), an hourly fee (based on an hourly rate), or a contingent fee (based on a percentage of the settlement or award.) Contingent fees are not permitted in criminal cases; in some states, they may be disallowed for other types of cases, too. The following should be helpful when you need to select an attorney:

1. Generate a list of potential lawyers by asking personal and business contacts. Try to find friends who have had a similar type of legal difficulty. Use *Martindale-Hubbell Law Directory*, West's Legal Directory (online), or directories maintained by your state bar association to discover additional information about the lawyers on your list. The Web site operated by Law.com has a law dictionary feature and a link to the *Martindale-Hubbell Law Directory* at http://www.law.com/. You can also locate a lawyer by using the West Legal Directory at the FindLaw Web site at http://directory.findlaw.com/.

2. Shop around and interview more than one attorney. Price, quality, and expertise are all important. An attorney with important expertise may cost less overall even though his or her hourly rate is higher.

3. When interviewing, ask lawyers about their experience in this particular area of the law. Also ask: What are the probable outcomes of your dispute? How long will the legal matter take?

4. Find out how the attorney is going to charge and what services you, as the client, will receive for the fee. For example, it is common in litigation for a fee to include a trial but no appellate work. Will a contingent fee be based on the award before or after expenses? If the attorney is going to charge an hourly rate, what is the smallest unit of time that is used for billing? In other words, will you be billed for 10 minutes or 15 minutes for a simple phone call to the lawyer? Try to avoid chitchat about extraneous topics if you are paying your lawyer by the hour. You don't want to pay your lawyer to discuss the basketball game or his or her new car with you.

5. What is a realistic estimate for the total bill and expenses? You should realize that it is more difficult to make a realistic estimate for some types of cases than others, particularly when the workload may depend on the decisions of the opponent. How often will the attorney send you a bill? Will the attorney put the estimate in writing? The estimate will help you decide whether it is worthwhile to go forward with the dispute. Will the attorney enter into a written contract with you?

6. Ask whether the fee will include private investigators, filing fees, expert witnesses, other attorneys, paralegals, photocopies, and so on. Generally, it does not. What other types of fees and expenses does the lawyer anticipate?

7. Ask for billings to be itemized. Itemized bills show the date and time of the work, the subject or type of work, and the hourly rate. It will also show when work is being done by paralegals.

8. Find out if you can take steps to reduce the legal fees. For example, you may be able to do some tasks yourself.

9. Ask if the attorney will need additional information from you.

10. Find out the attorney's procedure for handling billing disputes. Will the attorney charge for the additional hours spent on the billing dispute? Will the attorney agree to mandatory arbitration of the fee if the parties cannot resolve the dispute?

11. What are the alternatives to litigation? (See Chapter 4.) Does the attorney recommend any of them for this case? Does the attorney know any mediators or arbitrators who would be appropriate?

12. Try to discern whether client complaints have been filed against this attorney. Often, this information is made public and is available from the disciplinary agency for the state. This is generally the state bar association or the state supreme court.

13. Select the approach you plan to take with the case, and choose a lawyer whose style is similar to the approach you selected. Do you want someone who is extremely aggressive or more conciliatory?

14. Do *not* hire an attorney who is unable to communicate effectively with you or is unwilling to answer questions. Try to play an active role in your legal matters. If your lawyer does not listen or pay attention to you, you should consider hiring another lawyer.

Clients are sometimes dissatisfied with the services provided by their attorneys. Attorney-client relations do not always proceed smoothly. Some common "complaints" clients have include the manner in which the attorney (1) expedited the resolution of the matter; (2) kept them informed; (3) charged fees and expenses; (4) protected their rights and financial interests; (5) informed them about costs early in the process; and (6) did not act in a polite and considerate manner toward them.[34]

Resolving Problems with Legal Counsel

If a problem does arise from the attorney-client relationship, you should first try to resolve the problem with the attorney and/or the law firm. Begin with a clear letter expressing your concern and what you would like the attorney to do. If the problem is not resolved at this stage, you can fire the attorney and hire another. However, it may be costly for the replacement to become familiar with the dispute, and replacing an attorney may postpone the ultimate resolution of the legal matter.

If you believe the attorney breached one of the codes of ethics, you can report him or her to the disciplinary board. The American Bar Association (ABA) has a code of ethics for attorneys; however, most states also have their own codes of ethics. Copies are usually available from the library or the state Bar Association or disciplinary board. Bar Associations or disciplinary boards will not provide legal assistance to you but may investigate and take punitive action against the attorney, if appropriate. Most states have established a fund for clients who lose money because the attorney takes it from them and uses it inappropriately (for example, embezzles it). Practicing attorneys in the state are generally required to pay into the fund. As a last resort, you can sue the attorney for malpractice; however, then you will have to hire another attorney and begin a new litigation. In addition, it may be difficult for you to prove your damages, especially if you lost a lawsuit while the first attorney was representing you. Then the defendant will argue that even with another attorney, you still would have lost the suit.

You Be the Judge

In January 2010, the U.S. Supreme Court ruled that corporations and unions have a First Amendment right to buy political ads for or against specific candidates with their general funds. The court was divided in its 5-4 opinion in *Citizens United v. Federal Election Commission.*[35] The country's reception to the decision has also been divided. President Obama denounced the decision, and during his 2010 State of the Union Address, he said that the decision would lead to elections being "bankrolled by America's most powerful interests." Six of the nine justices attended the State of the Union Address. During Obama's comments, it appeared that Justice Samuel A. Alito Jr. was shaking his head and mouthing the words "not true." Justices normally sit quietly while the president speaks at the State of the Union. Although it is common for Presidents to criticize Supreme Court decisions and to ask Congress to pass legislation to override them, it is not common for Presidents to pointedly criticize the decisions at the State of the Union. Later, during questions at a law school speech, Chief Justice Roberts said, "First of all, anybody can criticize the Supreme Court without any qualm. Some people, I think, have an obligation to criticize what we do, given their office, if they think we've done something wrong. . . . On the other hand, there is the issue of the setting, the circumstances and the decorum. The image of having the members of one branch of government standing up, literally surrounding the Supreme Court, cheering and hollering while the court—according to the requirements of protocol—has to sit there expressionless, I think is very troubling." In a speech at another law school, Justice Clarence Thomas explained that he does not go to the State of the Union address and this controversy is an example of why. Chief Justice Roberts, who has attended every State of the Union since joining the court in 2005, has indicated that he may stop attending. Roberts said, "To the extent the State of the Union has degenerated into a political pep rally, I'm not sure why we're there." "Justice Antonin Scalia once said he no longer goes to the annual speech because the justices 'sit there like bumps on a log' in an otherwise highly partisan atmosphere." Should Supreme Court Justices be invited to attend the State of the Union speech? If the Justices are invited, should they attend? Would *you* make any changes to the manner that the State of the Union is handled? If so, what changes would *you* recommend? [See Robert Barnes & Anne E. Kornblut, "It's Obama vs. the Supreme Court, Round 2, Over Campaign Finance Ruling,"

Washington Post, March 11, 2010, p. A01, http://www.washingtonpost.com/
wp-dyn/content/article/2010/03/09/AR2010030903040.html (accessed 3/24/10);
Associated Press, "Supreme Court Chief Justice Roberts: State of the Union Has
'Degenerated into a Political Pep Rally,'" *NY Daily News*, March 10, 2010, http://
www.nydailynews.com/news/politics/2010/03/10/2010-03-10_supreme_court_chief_
justice_roberts_state_of_the_union_has_degenerated_into_a_po.html (accessed
3/24/10).]

Summary

Law consists of rules that must be obeyed because they are enforceable in courts of law. Order is the absence of chaos, and our legal system strives to create and to maintain order. Justice is fairness. Our legal system seeks constantly to balance law, order, and justice. Its ultimate goal is to achieve equilibrium.

The law is an artificial language system that includes everyday words with technical meanings. The law also uses words that are unique to the law. The law of business includes contracts, sales, negotiable instruments, secured transactions, agency relationships, partnerships, and corporations. By studying the law of business, you will learn how to avoid legal problems. If legal problems should develop, however, this knowledge will sensitize you to their ramifications. As a result, you will know when an attorney should be consulted.

A legal system needs to be reasonable, definite, practical, published, and final. A legal system should be focused on achieving justice. It does so by properly utilizing police power; by keeping the peace or maintaining the status quo when irreparable injury is threatened; by providing answers; by protecting people, property, and government; by enforcing intent; by rehabilitating people; and by facilitating commercial transactions. There are various philosophies about how the law works or how it should work.

Our legal system is like a three-dimensional chess game in which a move in one subsystem can affect other subsystems. The sources of law in the U.S. legal system are constitutions, treaties, statutes, ordinances, administrative regulations, common law, case law, and equity. The law is a multidimensional system, including common and statutory law, civil and criminal law, substantive and procedural law, and public and private law. The legal system is also composed of two branches—federal law and state law. A traveler or businessperson should not assume that the foreign law is similar to U.S. law.

Discussion Questions

1. Benjamin Franklin wrote, "Laws too gentle are seldom obeyed; too severe, seldom executed." Do you agree? Why or why not?[36]

2. What is the jurisprudential approach(es) of the following court opinion discussing whether an obligation to return an engagement ring should be based on fault?

   [T]he fault rule is sexist and archaic, a too-long enduring reminder of the times when even the law discriminated against women. . . . In ancient Rome the rule was fault. When the woman broke the engagement, however, she was required not only to return the ring, but also its value, as a penalty. No penalty attached when the breach was the man's. In England, women were oppressed by the rigidly stratified social order of the day. They worked as servants or, if not of the servant class, were dependent on their relatives. The fact that men were in short supply, marriage above one's station rare[,] and travel difficult abbreviated betrothal prospects for women. Marriages were arranged. Women's lifetime choices were limited to a marriage or a nunnery. . . . Men, because it was a man's world, were much more likely than women to break engagements. When one did, he left behind a woman of tainted reputation and ruined prospects. The law . . . gave her the engagement ring, as a consolation prize. When the man was jilted, a seldom thing, justice required the ring's return to him. Thus, the rule of life was the rule of law—both saw women as inferiors.[37]

3. John Rawls writes about justice and the elements that are necessary for a just society. He describes the "Bargaining Game," a theoretical community of men and women who get together to bargain for a completely new set of moral rules (laws) which they must all obey in the future. Once the rules are selected, the players must adhere to the rules, even if the rules are not in their self-interest in a particular situation. The players choosing the rules do not know their own position in society, talents, or abilities. Rawls calls this the veil of ignorance.[38] Rawls has been interpreted as saying, "In effect, the parties choose principles for the design of society as if their places in it were to be determined by their worst enemies."[39] What rules do you think the players would choose and why?

4. Jeremy Bentham (1748-1832), an English lawyer, is best known for his utilitarian philosophy that the object of law should be to achieve the "greatest happiness of the greatest number." Discuss the implications of the following statement based on your knowledge of common versus statutory law:

> Do you know how they make [common law]? Just as a man makes laws for his dog. When your dog does anything you want to break him of, you wait until he does it and then beat him. This is the way you make law for your dog, and this is the way judges make laws for you and me. They won't tell a man beforehand. . . . The French have had enough of this dog-law; they are turning it as fast as they can into statute law, that everybody may have a rule to go by. . . . [40]

5. In the United States, the general rule is that each party pays his or her own attorney's fees. There are a few exceptions provided under specific statutes. In Great Britain, the general rule is that the loser pays the winner's attorney's fees. Should the United States adopt the British rule? Why or why not?

Case Problems and Writing Assignments

1. In 1992, Rosa, an 18-year old woman in Southern Italy, went for a driving lesson. Rosa claims that the 45-year old instructor took her to a remote area and raped her. The instructor argued that the sex was consensual. The all-male panel of judges on the criminal appeals court concluded that Rosa

consented after considering that it is difficult to remove jeans without the cooperation of the wearer, Rosa waited several hours to tell her parents, and that Rosa returned to the driving school later that day for a driving theory lesson. The trial court convicted the instructor of gross indecency in public. The court of appeals held him liable for all of the offences. The Italian Supreme Court overturned the previous conviction from the court of appeals and remanded the case to the court of appeals. The Supreme Court said, "It is a fact of common experience that it is nearly impossible to slip off tight jeans even partly without the active collaboration of the person who is wearing them."[41] "[I]t is instinctive, especially for a young woman, to resist with all her strength one who is trying to rape her, and it is illogical to argue that a girl would supinely submit to a rape ... for fear of other hypothetical and certainly not more serious harm."[42] Do you agree with the Supreme Court's statements? Why or why not? Some information is lacking in the English language press. What additional information is important? [See "Judge Defends Rape-Jeans Ruling: 'We Have Complete Respect for Women,' Says Italian at Centre of Storm," *The Gazette* (Montreal), February 13, 1999, Art & Entertainment, p. D20; Benedetta Faedi, Rape, Blue Jeans, and Judicial Developments in Italy, 16 COLUM. J. EUR. L. ONLINE 13 (2009), http://www.cjel.net/online/16_1-faedi/ (accessed 3/29/10); Alessandra Stanley, "'Denim Defense': Court Ruling in Italy Rekindles Angry Debate About Rape, Justice//The Judges' Ruling—That a Woman Who Is Wearing Jeans Can't Be the Victim of Rape—Incensed the Nation and Prompted a Protest in Parliament," *Star Tribune* (Minneapolis, MN), February 17, 1999, p. 11A; and "The Denim Defense," *Sacramento Bee*, February 19, 1999, p. B6.]

2. Michael Fay, an American teenager, aged 18, was found guilty of spray-painting and throwing eggs at cars and possessing street signs in his room in Singapore. After Fay confessed, he was sentenced to four months in jail, fined $2,215, and subjected to six blows with a cane. This is a standard penalty for this type of behavior. Caning involves blows with a soaked rattan cane that is one-half inch thick. Prisoners often become unconscious during canings; however, a doctor revives them before the flogging continues. Caning causes severe pain and can cause serious bleeding and leave permanent scars. Prior to the caning, President Clinton and the parents (George Fay and Randy Chan) requested clemency from Singapore's president, Ong Teng Cheong. Is Fay's punishment under the Singapore criminal justice system appropriate? Why or why not? Is this a reasonable method to obtain law and order? Was it appropriate for the U.S. president to intervene? Why or why not? [See William Murphy, "Boy's Parents Losing Hope on Flogging," *Fresno Bee*, April 15, 1994, p. A13; Jim Steinberg, "Fresnans Split on Flogging Penalty," *Fresno Bee*, April 2, 1994, pp. B1 and B2.]

3. Under federal law, telemarketers must keep "do-not-call lists." If you get a call from a telemarketer and you don't want any more calls, be clear and direct. Ask them to put you on their "do-not-call list." Write down the name of the company and the date. If the company calls again, hang up and file a complaint with the Federal Trade Commission. The company faces fines of up to $10,000 per violation if they continue to call homes on the list. The Direct Marketing Association, an organization of mail-order companies and other direct marketers, also maintains a list of people who do not wish to be called. It is entitled Telephone Preference Service.[43] In a letter to the editor, Charlie Hollomon wrote, "If a telemarketer has a right to call, the citizen has a greater right to know who is calling. Instead of No-Call Lists, there should be OK to Call Lists, which citizens could use to indicate their willingness to receive solicitations. Telemarketers should then be required by law to be sure a citizen's phone is on such a list before calling."[44]

A number of states have passed or are considering statutes to protect consumers. For example, Louisiana and Pennsylvania enacted "Do-Not-Call List" statutes. A proposed statute to strengthen Nebraska's law was not successful. Telemarketing is a big industry in Nebraska. One of the opponents, State Senator Jon Bruning said, "Philosophically, it was a big government bill. People can simply not answer the phone or hang up the phone if they don't want to talk. I didn't think we needed government to step in and save us from the free market."[45]

Assume that your state has just enacted a tough statute providing for a "No-Call" list with penalties for violators. Three telemarketers responded by filing a class action suit. (A *class action suit* is a lawsuit involving a group of plaintiffs or defendants who are in substantially the same position as each other.) The case has been brought in *your* court. How will *you* rule? [See Asa Aarons, "Getting Your Name on Do-Not-Call List Can Pull the Plug on Telemarkerters," *Daily News* (New York), March 23, 1999, p. 18; Ed Anderson, "No-Call List May Quiet Phones; Bill Hangs Up on Telemarketers," *Times-Picayune*, May 20, 1999, p. A5; Federal Trade Commission's Press Release, National Do Not Call Registry Opens, June 27, 2003, http://www.ftc.gov/opa/2003/06/donotcall.shtm (accessed 7/25/10); Letter from Pennsylvania Attorney General Tom Corbett with links and enrollment information, http://www.lpsc.org/dncprogram.asp (accessed 7/25/10); Louisiana Public Service Commission Do Not Call Program Web site, with links and enrollment information, http://host.ntg.com/donotcall/; Realtor Mag, Official Magazine of the National Association of Realtors has a chart entitled "States with Established Do-Not-Call Laws" with information about the state lists, fines, and links to the state contact agency on its Web site at http://www.realtor.org/archives/donotcallapr02 (accessed 7/25/10) and links to its articles on Do-Not-Call Laws at http://www.realtor.org/library/library/fg707 (accessed 7/25/10).]

Notes

1. This section of the UCC was substantially revised in 2003. It will be $5,000 in the states that adopt the 2003 UCC revisions. Currently, no state has adopted the revisions. In 2010, the revisions were introduced in the Oklahoma legislature. "A Few Facts About the Amendments to UCC Articles 2 and 2A," National Conference of Commissioners of Uniform State Laws Web site, http://www.nccusl.org/Update/uniformact_factsheets/uniformacts-fs-ucc22A03.asp (accessed 6/7/10).
2. The Patient Protection and Affordable Care Act became Public Law No. 111-148. Thomas, http://thomas.loc.gov/cgi-bin/thomas (accessed 3/29/10).
3. Rob Wells & Shayndi Raice, "Summary of Patient Protection and Affordable Care Act," *Wall Street Journal*, March 21, 2010, http://online.wsj.com/article/BT-CO-20100321-704391.html (accessed 3/29/10).
4. Ibid.
5. Ibid.
6. Drysdale v. Prudden, 195 N.C. 722, 143 S.E. 530, 536 (1928).
7. Julian E. Barnes, "Gunman Open Fire Outside the Pentagon," *Los Angeles Times*, March 5, 2010, Part AA, p. 1; Peter Grier, "John Patrick Bedell: Did Right-Wing Extremism Lead to Shooting?; Authorities Have Identified John Patrick Bedell as the Gunman in the Pentagon Shooting. He Appears to Have Been a Right-Wing Extremist with Virulent Antigovernment Feelings," *Christian Science Monitor*, March 5, 2010.
8. "American Phoenix Will Provide Reinsurance to Oman Insurer," *Mealey's Litigation Report: Reinsurance*, February 11, 1999, vol. 9; no. 19.
9. "An Islamic Legal System?; Pakistan," *The National Law Journal*, September 14, 1998, p. A14; Beena Sarwar Lahore, "Rights—Pakistan: Nawaz Sharif's Use of Religion Fools No One," *IAC Newsletter Database*, Global Information Network, Inter Press Service, September 16, 1998.
10. Bryan A. Garner, *Black's Law Dictionary*, 7th ed. (St. Paul: West Publishing Co., 1999), p. 858.
11. James Rachels, *The Elements of Moral Philosophy*, 2d ed. (New York: McGraw-Hill, 1993), p. 50.
12. Ibid. More recently, John Finnis has written about natural law theory in *Natural Law and Natural Rights* (1980) and *Aquinas: Moral, Political, and Legal Theory* (1998). Richard W. Wright, "The Principles of Justice," 75 NOTRE DAME L. REV. 1859 (2000), n. 3 and 4.
13. Kenneth Einar Himma, *Natural Law*, The Internet Encyclopedia of Philosophy, last updated May 3, 2005, http://www.iep.utm.edu/natlaw (accessed 7/25/10).
14. Ibid., quoting Richard Posner, *Economic Analysis of Law*, 4th ed. (Boston: Little, Brown, and Company, 1992), p. 23. Posner

currently serves as the chief judge of the U.S. Court of Appeals for the Seventh Circuit.

15. 924 F.2d 872, 878 (9th Cir. 1991).

16. "Judge Defends Rape-Jeans Ruling: 'We Have Complete Respect for Women,' Says Italian at Centre of Storm," *The Gazette* (Montreal), February 13, 1999, Art & Entertainment, p. D20.

17. Alessandra Stanley, "'Denim Defense': Court Ruling in Italy Rekindles Angry Debate About Rape, Justice// The Judges' Ruling—That a Woman Who Is Wearing Jeans Can't Be the Victim of Rape—Incensed the Nation and Prompted a Protest in Parliament," *Star Tribune* (Minneapolis, MN), February 17, 1999, Source: *New York Times*, p. 11A.

18. Benedetta Faedi, "Rape, Blue Jeans, and Judicial Developments in Italy," 16 COLUM. J. EUR. L. ONLINE 13 (2009), http://www.cjel.net/online/16_1-faedi/ (accessed 3/29/10).

19. "The Denim Defense," *Sacramento Bee*, February 19, 1999, p. B6.

20. Kenneth Einar Himma, Philosophy of Law, *The Inernet Encyclopedia of Philosophy*, last updated April 19, 2009, http://www.iep.utm.edu/law-phil/#SH3b (accessed 7/25/10) quoting Andrew Altman, "Legal Realism, Critical Legal Studies, and Dworkin," *Philosophy and Public Affairs*, vol. 15, no. 2 (1986), p. 221.

21. 1 Cranch 137, 2 L. Ed. 60 (1803).

22. U.S. Constitution, Article II, Section 2.

23. Treaties, United States Senate Web page, http://www.senate.gov/artandhistory/history/common/briefing/Treaties.htm (accessed 3/24/10).

24. Ibid.

25. Ibid.

26. Ibid.

27. Ibid.

28. 252 U.S. 416 (1920).

29. One meaning of common law is the body of law derived by courts of law as opposed to courts of equity. *See* Garner, supra note 10, at p. 270.

30. Ibid.

31. 347 U.S. 483 (1954).

32. 163 U.S. 537 (1896).

33. Although it is one legal system, some states, like Delaware, still have separate courts of equity.

34. "When You Need a Lawyer," *Consumer Reports*, February 1996, pp. 34-39. The information in the report is based on a 1994 Consumer Union survey of members regarding their experiences with attorneys from 1991-1994. Consumer Union discovered that of the 30,000 respondents, clients involved in adversarial cases were more likely to be displeased with the legal services they received than those involved in non-adversarial matters. For example, 27 percent of the people who had hired an attorney for an adversarial matter were dissatisfied with the work performed by the lawyer.

35. 2010 U.S. LEXIS 766 (2010).

36. Benjamin Franklin, *Poor Richard Improved: Being an Almanack and Ephemeris . . . for the Year of our Lord 1756 by Richard Saunders*, printed and sold by B. Franklin & D. Hall, Philadelphia (1756), and at http://www.brainyquote. 3/21/10).

37. *Lindh v. Surman*, 702 A.2d 560, 1997 Pa. Super. LEXIS 3241 (Pa. Super. 1997), citing Aronow v. Silver, 538 A. 2d 851, 853 (N.J. Super. 1987). The Pennsylvania Supreme Court affirmed the decision of the lower courts to use a strict no-fault rule in *Lindh v. Surman*, 560 Pa. 1, 1999 Pa. LEXIS 3498 (1999).

38. John Rawls, *A Theory of Justice* (Cambridge, MA: Harvard University Press, Belknap Press, 1971).

39. Chandran Kukathas & Philip Pettit, *Rawls: A Theory of Justice and Its Critics*, (Palo Alto, CA: Stanford University Press, 1990), p. 39.

40. Jeremy Bentham, *The Works of Jeremy Bentham* (New York: Russell and Russell, 1962), p. 231.

41. Benedetta Faedi, supra note 18, quoting Cass., sez. III, 10 Feb. 1999.

42. Ibid.

43. Asa Aarons, "Getting Your Name on Do-Not-Call List Can Pull the Plug on Telemarkerters," *Daily News* (New York), March 23, 1999, p. 18.

44. Charlie Hollomon, "Letters: In My Opinion; Put Limits on Telemarketers," *Atlanta Journal and Constitution*, March 31, 1999, p. 17A.

45. Robynn Tysver, "'No Call' Phone List Hung Up: A Bill Targeting Unwanted Telemarketing Pitches Fails to Advance to the Next Round," *Omaha World-Herald*, April 8, 1999, p.11.

2

Business Ethics

Agenda

Ani, Meg, and Yousef need to understand and appreciate the ethical obligations and expectations under which they will operate eClass. A business today is expected to act ethically, even if it does not have any formulated ethical theory or formal statement of its ethical principles to provide guidance, and this expectation is likely to increase. The principals also need to realize that a business must satisfy the *social contract* it has with society, even if the business or its owners and managers don't realize that they have entered into such a "contract."

They must weigh their decisions, taking into account the potential impact—both beneficial and harmful—on each of the constituent groups of the firm. They may also want to decide how they should measure the ethical implications and impact of any business decisions. They will need to consider how a business manager knows what the social contract theory demands of the business. They will need to know who the constituents of the business are and how the conduct of the leadership of the business can affect each of these different constituent groups. These and other issues need to be addressed in covering the material in this chapter. Be prepared! You never know when the firm or one of its members will need your advice.

Classic Case

REGINA v. DUDLEY AND STEPHENS
14 Q.B.D. 273 (1884)

FACTS In July 1884, four British sailors were cast away in a storm 1,600 miles from the Cape of Good Hope in an open lifeboat. The only food the crew found aboard the lifeboat was two one-pound tins of turnips. They were able to catch a turtle on their fourth day at sea but had no other food beyond the turnips and the turtle through the 20th day. All four of the seamen were suffering from hunger and thirst by this time, and the youngest was delirious from drinking seawater. At that point in time, Dudley proposed that the other three should kill the youngest so that the other three would have food and liquid, and Stephens agreed. The next day, while Brooks was sleeping, Dudley killed the boy. While Brooks did not condone the act, he shared in the "bounty," and for the next four days the three men fed on the body and blood of the boy. They were rescued by a passing ship on the 29th day and taken to England, where they were arrested and charged with murder.

ISSUE Was the killing of the boy an act of murder or an act of self defense?

HOLDING It was an act of murder.

REASONING Excerpts from the opinion of Lord Coleridge, Chief Justice:

The court granted "that if the men had not fed upon the body of the boy they would probably not have survived to be so picked up and rescued, but would within the four days have died of famine." It also agreed "that the boy, being in a much weaker condition, was likely to have died before them . . . [t]hat under these circumstances there appeared to the prisoners every probability that unless they then fed or very soon fed upon the boy or one of themselves they would die of starvation. That there was no appreciable chance of saving life except by killing some one for the others to eat. . . ."

The court addressed the self-defense issue by examining the words of Lord Hale. In the chapter in which he deals with the exemption to murder created by compulsion or necessity, he stated: "If a man be desperately assaulted and in peril of death, and cannot otherwise escape unless, to satisfy his assailant's fury, he will kill an innocent person then present, the fear and actual force will not acquit him of the crime and punishment of murder, for he ought rather to die himself than kill an innocent; but if he cannot otherwise save his own life the law permits him in his own defence to kill the assailant."

The court recognized the stress the sailors faced, and acknowledged that the temptations they faced were powerful, but denied that these things created a "necessity" justifying homicide. "Nor is this to be regretted. Though law and morality are not the same, and many things may be immoral' which are not necessarily illegal, yet the absolute divorce of law from morality would be of fatal consequence; and such divorce would follow if the temptation to murder in this case were to be held by law an absolute defence of it. It is not so. To preserve one's life is generally speaking a duty, but it may be the plainest and the highest duty to sacrifice it. . . . It is not needful to point out the awful danger of admitting the principle which has been contended for. Who is to be the judge of this sort of necessity? By what measure is the comparative value of lives to be measured? Is it to be strength, or intellect, or what? It is plain that the principle leaves to him who is to profit by it to determine the necessity which will justify him in deliberately taking another's life to save his own . . . [I]t is quite plain that such a principle once admitted might be made the legal cloak for unbridled passion and atrocious crime. There is no safe path for judges to tread but to ascertain the law to the best of their ability and to declare it according to their judgment; and if in any case the law appears to be too severe for individuals, to leave it to the Sovereign to exercise that prerogative of mercy which the Constitution has intrusted to the hands fittest to dispense it. . . . It is therefore our duty to declare that the prisoners' act in this case was willful murder, that the facts as stated in the verdict are no legal justification of the homicide; and to say that in our unanimous opinion the prisoners are upon this special verdict guilty of murder."

[The court then proceeded to pass a sentence of death on the prisoners. Queen Victoria subsequently commuted the sentences, setting the punishment to be served by Dudley and Stephens at six months imprisonment.]

BUSINESS CONSIDERATIONS Assume that a business is facing serious economic problems. While there are several alternatives available, the easiest method of economic recovery for the business is to "cannibalize" (strip away the assets, leaving an empty shell) a subsidiary of the firm. What should the business do?

ETHICAL CONSIDERATIONS Is it possible to make a (superficially) persuasive ethical argument in support of the defendants on either an egoistic or a utilitarian basis, if one so desires? Can a persuasive argument be made under either the categorical imperative or the veil of ignorance?

INTRODUCTION

A number of people view "business ethics" as an oxymoron, a contradiction in terms. Some people make jokes about the topic, while others view any discussion of business ethics as an interesting academic exercise, but one without any *legitimate* use in the "real world." However, the events we have witnessed since 2002 have caused a change in attitude among even the most jaded of observers. The corporate scandals and the resulting loss of trust by the public has once again shown that ethics is important in business, and that even a *perceived* lack of ethics in a firm or in an industry can have devastating effects on the firm, the industry, or even the entire economy. Please keep the impact of these events, and the resulting economic harm, in mind while covering the material in this chapter.

ETHICS AND MORALITY

It is fairly standard for people to equate ethics with morality, and to use the words *ethics* and *morals* interchangeably. In so doing, they find it easier to discuss the topic of ethics. However, such usage is not altogether accurate. *Ethics* refers to a guiding philosophy—the principles of conduct governing an individual or a group.[1] By contrast, *morals* relate to principles of right and wrong behavior as sanctioned by or operative on one's conscience.[2] From the perspective of an individual, ethics and morals may, and frequently do, have the same meaning. However, from the perspective of a group—including a society—it is more appropriate to speak of ethics. Thus, when *we* speak of ethics, we will be talking about societal values, the accepted standard of conduct within a given society. In contrast, when *we* speak of morals, we will be talking about individual values, the accepted conduct *of* an individual *by* that individual. Exhibit 2.1 gives a few examples of how ethics and morals may be compared.

Exhibit 2.1

Ethics and Morals: A (Limited) Comparison

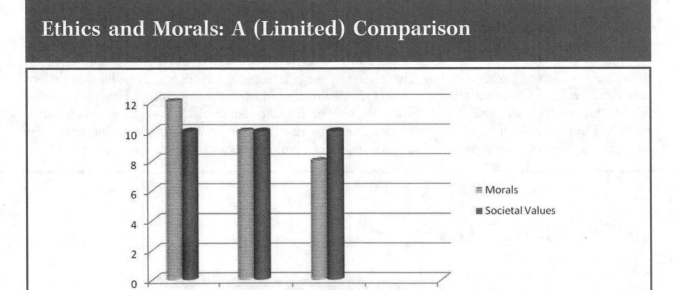

Source: Courtesy of Dan Davidson. Copyright August 2009

An individual with higher morals than society's values is one whose actions exceed those that are generally accepted. For example, while society may frown on jaywalking, it does not consider such conduct unethical. The person with higher morals might consider jaywalking to be wrong and immoral.

A person with lower morals than society's values is one whose actions, or at least whose accepted values, fall below those of society at large. Such a person may see nothing wrong with cheating or stealing.

Different societies may have different ethics, but the morals of any given individual should remain relatively constant no matter which society that person should happen to be in at any point in time. Ethical conduct is conduct that is deemed right—or at least accepted as not wrong—within a societal setting. Moral conduct is conduct that the individual considers right—or at least does not consider wrong—without regard to the attitude of the society.

To further complicate this already complex issue, societies also have standards that go beyond ethics. The ethical standards of a society reflect what is considered "right" and "wrong" within that society in a general manner. Some wrong behavior may be merely a matter of rude conduct, frowned on within the society, but not of sufficient seriousness or severity to merit more than a social dislike of the conduct. For example, conducting a loud cell phone conversation in a public place is likely to be considered rude, but it is not likely to be viewed as serious enough to merit an official sanction. Other "wrong" conduct may be considered much more serious, calling for more than a societal frown; this conduct may be so inappropriate for the society that the person who acts in this "wrongful" manner may be subjected to a fine or even to incarceration. To help ensure that people within a society act in a socially acceptable manner, the society enacts laws and regulations, usually with penalties attached for conduct in violation of the law or regulation in question. These laws enacted by society provide an ethical floor—a minimum standard of behavior that is expected from each member of that society.

Although it is a broad generalization, conduct that violates a law or a regulation of a society is generally deemed unethical by that society. This is not to say that all unethical conduct is also illegal; rather it says that all illegal conduct is generally viewed as unethical. Of course there are examples where some members of a society will act in a manner that violates a law or a regulation in order to force the society to reconsider its official position, with the aim of changing the law, and thereby changing the official social values the law affects. One such example involves Dr. Martin Luther King, Jr., and his encouragement of civil disobedience in the 1950s. His conduct was technically illegal—and thus could be viewed as unethical—at the time. However, the success of the Civil Rights movement ultimately changed the laws regarding equal rights and racial discrimination, thereby changing the social values reflected by the laws governing human rights in this country. Dr. King acted in a *moral* manner, effecting changes that, in turn, made his conduct ethical *in hindsight*.

If the personal morals of an individual call for conduct prohibited by society's ethics, however, there is a potential problem. For example, suppose a person feels that stealing is moral as long as the victim of the theft is wealthy. This person will encounter problems if he or she acts on the basis of this moral value by stealing from a wealthy victim. If this person decides to steal from the wealthy, he or she may be acting morally (adhering to his or her personal values), but will be deemed to have acted unethically by society (violating the society's values). Our society has deemed theft to be an illegal and an unethical act, and the person whose morals conflict with this value will find that society has deemed the conduct both illegal and unethical even though the conduct may have been acceptable, and thus moral, to the individual.

ETHICAL THEORIES

Before the topic of business ethics can be addressed, it is imperative to have at least an introductory exposure to some of the more widely cited ethical theories and principles. This section introduces several of these ethical theories and principles and compares them to one another. When we study these ethical theories, it is important to remember that there is no single "best" ethical theory everyone should follow. Each individual and each organization must choose the theory that best suits his, her, or its values and morals. The theory followed can be chosen in any fashion, even if that fashion seems entirely arbitrary to other people. The theory chosen can even be a combination of features from several different theories. For example, some people base their ethical beliefs on the Golden Rule (Do unto others as you would have others do unto you) while others select an "ends" approach (The outcome of the conduct determines its ethical nature). The important point is that a theory has been chosen and is being followed.

The study of ethics and of ethical principles is well known in philosophy, but it is relatively new to business. Studying ethical theories and principles is not nearly as "hard and fast" as most other business topics, and the problems and their solutions often are not obvious. Yet questions of ethics—particularly questions of business ethics—are among the most important questions the businessperson of the modern era will face in his or her career. The manager may face a "Hobson's choice" [3] among bad alternatives; or the decision may entail a trade-off between short-term gains and long-term gains; or the decision may involve short-term gains (or losses) compared to longer-term losses (or gains).

While ethics can be defined as the system, or code, of morals of a particular person, religion, group, or profession, [4] such a definition does not provide much help in the area of business ethics. Business does not fit neatly into any of the categories mentioned in this definition. Although a business may be recognized as a legal person, the business is not a "particular person," nor does any one individual sufficiently influence a business to provide moral or ethical modeling for the firm. Even though it is undoubtedly true that some businesspeople worship "the almighty dollar," business does not qualify as a religion in any realistic sense of the term. Likewise, the "group" to which business belongs is too diverse to have a single system or code of morals.

Similarly, "business" is not a single profession like medicine or law, susceptible to the adoption of a single code of professional conduct, or of ethics, if you will. Thus, for most people, the study of business ethics comes down to an analysis of the system or code of morals of a particular person, the specific businessperson whose conduct is being evaluated. Unfortunately, the ethical standard too often applied in this situation is the ethical standard of the observer and not that of the person being observed. To properly treat the ethical issues of a businessperson, some kind of analytic framework must be established and some basic understanding of the ethical parameters of business needs to be developed.

Consequential and Nonconsequential Principles

Before a framework for the analysis of business ethics can be developed, some decisions must be made as to what values and standards are being measured, and on what basis the measurement is being made. Two broad categories of ethical theories exist. Ethical theories may be based on either consequential (teleological) principles or on nonconsequential (deontological) principles.

Consequential principles judge the ethics of a particular action by the *consequences* of that action. Consequential ethics, therefore, determine the "rightness" or the "wrongness" of any action by determining the ratio of good to evil that a given action will produce. A person practicing consequential ethics needs to evaluate each of his or her possible alternative actions, measuring the good (and the evil) that seem likely to result from the alternatives. The "right" action is that action which is most likely to produce the greatest ratio of good to evil of any of the available alternatives. Among the major theories of ethical behavior under the consequential principles are egoism, utilitarianism, and feminism, also known as the "feminist philosophy." Each of these theories will be examined in more detail later in this section.

Nonconsequential principles tend to focus on the concept of *duty* rather than on any concepts of right and/or wrong: Nonconsequential ethical theories are rule-based. Under the nonconsequential approach, a person acts ethically if that person is faithful to his or her duty, regardless of the consequences that follow from being faithful to that duty.

In addition, society imposes duties to maximize the values society wants, and by meeting that duty the individual is furthering the interests of that society. The "categorical imperative" advanced by Immanuel Kant and the "veil of ignorance" advocated by John Rawls are two of the best-known theories in support of the nonconsequential principles of ethics. Both of these theories will be discussed in detail later in this chapter.

Consequential Ethics

Egoism The doctrine which assumes that self-interest is the proper goal of all human action is known as egoism.[5] (Do not confuse an *egoist*, a person who follows the ethical theory of egoism, with an *egotist*, a person who has an exaggerated sense of self-importance.) In the doctrine of egoism, each person is expected to act in a manner that will maximize his or her long-term interests. In so doing, society is expected to benefit because when each individual acts in a manner that produces the greatest ratio of good to evil, the sum of all of these individual "good-producing" actions within the society will produce the greatest total good for the society.

One common misconception about egoism is that all egoists are hedonistic seekers of pleasure who emphasize instant gratification. This misconception treats one's pleasure as being equal to one's best interests. In fact, an egoist may well decide to act in a "selfless" manner because doing so will further the long-term self-interest of that person to a greater degree than will any short-term pleasures he or she might be able to enjoy. An egoist may be willing to make a personal sacrifice today to receive some benefit in the future, and doing so is perfectly consistent with the doctrine of egoism. Similarly, an egoist may obtain self-gratification from performing acts that benefit others so that such actions further one's long-term interests by increasing one's satisfaction.

In the same manner that an individual may follow egoism, so may an organization. From an organizational perspective, egoism involves those actions that best promote the long-term interests of the organization. Thus, a corporation may establish a minority hiring program or a college scholarship program, and in so doing the corporation may well be acting in a purely egoistic manner. These programs may advance the long-term interests of the corporation by improving its public image, by reducing social tensions, or by avoiding legal problems that might otherwise have arisen. The short-term expenses incurred in such programs can be more than offset by future benefits so that the programs may appear to be generous and public-spirited when in reality they are undertaken for purely "selfish" reasons—as befits the ethical system of the particular firm.

Utilitarianism   The second major consequential approach to ethics is utilitarianism. To a utilitarian, the proper course of conduct to follow in any given setting is the course that will produce the greatest good (or the least harm) for the greatest number.[6] Rather than focusing on the interests of the individual (as an egoist would), the utilitarian focuses on the interests of the society. The ethical course of conduct is the one that best serves the interests of the social group as a whole, regardless of the impact on any individuals or any subgroups of the total social system. In theory, someone who is a utilitarian does not care if the "good" is felt immediately or if it is long-term in nature. The only concern is whether the "good" to be derived—whenever it is derived—produces the greatest quantity of "good" possible among the alternatives from which the choice was made.

There are two primary types of utilitarianism, *act utilitarianism* and *rule utilitarianism*. Act utilitarianism is concerned with individual actions and the effect of those actions on the social group as a whole more than it is concerned with obeying rules. An act utilitarian expects each person to act in a manner that will produce the greatest net benefit for the social group, even if such actions require the breaking of a social "rule." While it is felt that rules should generally be followed, exceptional situations may compel an act utilitarian to break the rules for the greater good of the society. Thus, to an act utilitarian, telling a "little white lie" may be the most ethical course of conduct in a given situation if telling the lie produces more total good than would be obtained by telling the truth, by avoiding the answer, or by any other alternative.

A rule utilitarian believes that strict adherence to the rules of the society will generally produce the greatest good for the greatest number. A rule utilitarian tends to follow all of the rules of the society without exception. This can lead to a problem in some situations. The rules that are followed can cause the rule utilitarian to become inflexible, especially when he or she faces a unique situation for which the rules were neither designed nor intended.

Feminism   Feminism, or the feminist philosophy (also called the ethics of caring), has gained in popularity recently. This ethical theory indicates that particular attention should be paid to the effect of decisions on individuals, especially those individuals in a close relationship with the decision maker.[7] This philosophy focuses on character traits such as sympathy, compassion, loyalty, and friendship. While decisions are still based on doing the greatest good, other factors must also be considered. Among these factors are social cooperation and the realization that in many situations the parties are not of equal power or ability. The structure of the society must be protected, and the rights and interests of the less capable people should be protected as well. This philosophy is still developing, but it bears watching in the future.

Nonconsequential Ethics

Kant and the Categorical Imperative   The nonconsequential principles of ethical theory are best exemplified by the categorical imperative developed by Immanuel Kant, an eighteenth-century German philosopher. Kant felt that certain universal moral standards existed without regard to the circumstances of the moment or the values of any particular society.[8] Under Kant's theory, when people follow these universal moral principles, they are acting morally and ethically. When people do not follow these universal principles, they are acting unethically. Individual variations and consequences are irrelevant. The universal moral principles impose a duty on each person, and the performance of that duty is what determines the "rightness" or the "wrongness" of any given action.

Kant also believed that there were perfect duties and imperfect duties. Perfect duties are those things a person must always do or refrain from doing, such as the duty of a merchant never to cheat a customer. Imperfect duties involve things a person should do, but not necessarily things a person must do. For example, a person should contribute to charities, but a person should not necessarily contribute to all charities, nor should a person have to contribute to any particular charity every time that charity solicits contributions.

Based on his theories, Kant developed his categorical imperative. The categorical imperative, simply stated, says that each person should act in such a manner that his or her actions could become the universal law. In a perfectly ethical and moral world, each person is expected to act as every person ought to act. The rules to be followed are unconditional, and adherence to these rules is imperative. If each person carries out his or her duty by following these "universal rules," society will be properly served by each individual.

Kant's approach to ethics is also applicable to organizations. An organization is judged in the same manner as an individual; the organization is expected to obey the categorical imperative, just as an individual is expected to obey it. The organization is to act according to its duty, with its actions being judged against the "universal law" standard—would such conduct be proper if all organizations were to act in the same manner? The organization is expected to act in a manner that discharges its duty to every aspect of society, which would include recognition of the rights of others and the duty owed to others.

Rawls and the Veil of Ignorance   John Rawls took the works of Locke, Rousseau, and Kant as a starting point to develop his own theory of justice.[9] Rawls viewed these earlier works as the foundation for a "contract theory" of justice, and he presented his conception of justice as a higher level of abstraction from the earlier theories. Rawls felt that a truly just society would be one where the rules governing the society were developed behind a veil of ignorance, behind which no person would know his or her personal characteristics. Since the people making the rules were making those rules while wholly ignorant of their unique combination of race, religion, color, gender, wealth, age, and/or education, they would enact rules they would be willing to live under regardless of which combination of factors they might, theoretically, possess; they would have to live under the rules they created once they stepped out from behind their veil of ignorance.

True justice can be obtained by the society with each member willing to live under the rules developed behind the veil. A proper constitution will be adopted; an appropriate method for legislation based on the constitution adopted will be created; a proper method for dispute resolution will be developed; and, finally, the application of rules to particular cases by judges and administrators, and the following of rules by citizens generally, will be implemented.[10]

These theories are summarized and analyzed as they apply in a business setting in Exhibit 2.2

Other Theories   There are other ethical theories that may also influence one's ethical outlook. Two of these are discussed very briefly.

Relativism. Ethical relativism states that two people or two societies may hold ethical views that are opposed to one another, and yet both may be correct. In other words, this theory takes the position that ethics and values are relative and may change from one location to another. While it is true that different societies have different values (i.e., the death penalty is a socially acceptable punishment in some societies, but not in others), the individual is more commonly governed by his or her *morals*, and personal morals do not change from one location to another. Relativism seems to be of more importance to sociologists and anthropologists than it is to ethicists.[16]

The Golden Rule. The Golden Rule theory of ethics advises each person to "do onto others as you would have others do onto you." This is a generally accepted principle in Judeo-Christian thought and an admirable rule for people to follow. However, as an ethical theory it is difficult to measure, and it is also difficult to define how to determine if one is following the principle in his or her conduct.

Exhibit 2.2

A Comparison of Ethical Theories

Ethical Theory	Positive Aspects in a Business Context	Negative Aspects in a Business Context
Egoism[11] (Consequential theory—An act is ethical when it promotes the best long-term interests of the firm.)	1. Provides a basis for formulating and testing policies. 2. Provides flexibility in ethical decision making for a business. 3. Allows a business to tailor codes of conduct to suit the complexity of its particular business dealings.	1. May ignore blatant wrongs. 2. Incompatible with the nature and role of business. 3. Cannot resolve conflicts of egoistic interests. 4. Introduces inconsistency into ethical decision making.
Utilitarianism[12] (Consequential theory— The most ethical decision is the one that produces the greatest good, or the least harm, for the greatest number of people.)	1. Provides a basis for formulating and testing policies. 2. Provides an objective manner for resolving conflicts of self-interest. 3. Recognizes the constituent groups of a business. 4. Provides the latitude in ethical decision making that business seems to need.	1. Utilitarians ignore conduct which appears to be wrong in and-of itself. 2. The principle of utility may be in conflict with the principle of justice. 3. It is very difficult to formulate satisfactory rules.
Feminism[13] (Consequential theory— The ethics of caring, it recognizes the importance of personal relationships in decision-making)	1. Provides a basis for formulating and testing policies. 2. Provides an objective manner for resolving conflicts of self-interest. 3. Recognizes the constituent groups of a business. 4. Provides flexibility in ethical decision making for business.	1. Places undue emphasis on those closest to the decision maker. 2. May be more concerned with the community than with the business. 3. It is very difficult to formulate satisfactory rules.
Kant and the Categorical Imperative[14] (Nonconsequential theory— Only when we act from a sense of duty do actions have ethical value.)	1. The categorical imperative takes the "guesswork" out of ethical decisions. 2. Introduces a needed humanistic dimension into business ethics decisions. 3. The concept of duty implies the ethical obligation to act from a respect for rights and the recognition of responsibilities.	1. Provides no clear way to resolve conflicts among duties. 2. There is no compelling reason that certain rules should be absolute.

Exhibit 2.2 Continued

Ethical Theory	Positive Aspects in a Business Context	Negative Aspects in a Business Context
Rawls and the Veil of Igno-rance[15] (Nonconsequential theory—Rational agents, unaware of their personal characteristics or places in society, choose the principles they wish to have govern the society.)	1. The veil of ignorance takes the "guesswork" out of ethical decisions.* 2. Introduces a needed humanistic dimension into business ethics decisions. 3. Implies the ethical obligation to act from a respect for rights and the recognition of responsibilities.	1. Uses the better-off members of society to assume the welfare of the worst-off. 2. There is no compelling reason for following universal principles that might be agreed to by members of the society

Source: Courtesy of Dan Davidson, copyright August 2009

* There is no "guesswork" because the rules that are to be followed have been established.

A SYNTHESIS FOR ETHICAL DECISION MAKING

Each of these ethical theories provides a possible framework for evaluating the ethics of a business and the ethics of the people who operate the business. Remember, there is no one universally accepted theory or approach to ethics in general, nor is there an accepted and universal approach to business ethics. Each firm in the business environment can select a theory of ethics to follow in developing its own ethical approach to conducting its business. Before choosing a theory, however, the businessperson should also take into account several other factors. These factors should include, but not be limited to, the short-term versus the long-term impact of any decisions, the constituent groups that will be affected by the decision being made (constituent groups are discussed later in the chapter), and the way in which the ethical decision fits within the laws and regulations affecting the business in this area.

One problem that many people face in making ethical decisions is recognizing that an ethical issue is present. Before you can use your ethical "tools" to make a decision, you need to realize that you are facing an ethical issue! When a business or economic issue is addressed, it is normally obvious that there are economic issues involved, and the decision that is made is then made on business and/or economic bases. However, the fact that an issue has business or economic implications does not mean that ethical issues are not also present. For example, while most people agree that slavery is wrong and that having slaves is unethical, slavery in the United States was allowed for decades, and often justified as being the natural order of things. In fact, slavery was economically beneficial for the slaveholders, and its existence was rationalized on moral grounds. In a similar manner, equal pay for women has been rationalized to justify the economic benefits to the employer rather than addressed as an ethical issue.

Once an ethical issue is identified within the problem being faced, it becomes easier to apply your ethical "tools" and to make a decision that includes consideration of the ethical issue and the proper resolution of the problem from an ethical, as well as a business/economic, perspective.

Perhaps a business would be best advised to seek a synthesis of these different theories, as tempered by the social contract theory, to develop an approach to ethical issues. After all, other people will judge the business, and they may view its decisions from a different ethical perspective. This approach would provide a structure for evaluating actions and options regardless of the ethical theory that most closely reflects the values of the business. One such synthesis is suggested by the work of Vincent Ruggerio.[17] Ruggerio suggests that there are three common concerns in ethical decision making: obligations, ideals, and effects. From this foundation we can develop a framework for ethical decision making without regard to whether the theory followed is a consequential or a nonconsequential theory. In making a decision, the following factors should be considered:

1. the obligations that arise from organizational relationships;
2. the ideals involved in any decisions that are made; and
3. the effects or consequences of alternative actions.

Any actions that honor obligations while simultaneously advancing ideals and have the effect of benefiting people can be presumed to be moral actions. Any actions that fall short in any respect become suspect.[18] This is not to say that these latter actions are necessarily unethical. However, since these actions have a negative impact on one or more of the areas of concern, the actions should be very carefully evaluated, and alternatives should be examined to see if a better alternative has been overlooked.

With this in mind, the firm should follow a two-step process in order to assure that it is making ethical decisions. The first step is to identify the important considerations involved (obligations, ideals, and effects). The second step is to decide where the emphasis should lie among these considerations. This approach allows the firm to apply its ethical principles to an ethical problem while also taking into account the social contract and the relative positions of each of the constituent groups of the business.

An individual, including a businessperson, may want to adopt a less formal approach to his or her ethical decision making. There are a number of informal approaches that can be used. Among the more popular—and effective—of these are the following:

1. The "Front Page" Test—Is this a decision or a course of action that the person would be comfortable seeing as the lead story on the front page of local and national newspapers?
2. The "Other Side of the Fence" Test—How would the decision maker feel if he or she was standing on the "other side of the fence" observing this decision being made by someone else?
3. The "What Would Your Mother Think" Test—Is this a decision that the decision maker's mother would be proud of when she learns about it?

While none of these possess the elegance of more formal models, each does provide an evaluation model that forces the decision maker to at least consider the impact of the decision from an outsider's perspective and may help in reaching a decision in which he or she can avoid embarrassment, if not take pride.

THE GAME THEORY OF BUSINESS

Business as an Amoral Institution

Historically, business was viewed by many as an amoral institution. Since any given business was inanimate, and since only animate objects could be expected to possess "morality," it stood to reason that a business was not expected to possess "morality." Because it could not be expected to be moral, it also could not be immoral. Morality and immorality were reserved for animate beings, and inanimate objects were *amoral*. This did not present much of a problem when most businesses were relatively small and local in nature. The owners and operators of businesses were known in the community, and even though the business was viewed as amoral, the owner or operator was held to community standards. Thus most businesses were operated in an ethical manner in order to keep the local customers satisfied. However, as businesses grew increasingly larger and more complex, this local flavor was lost. Businesses no longer operated in a restricted geographic market, and no longer had to adhere to community standards. Eventually, society began to demand some minimal ethical standards from businesses. Included among these standards were the expectations of fair play and honesty, and the expectation that a business would seek profits for its investors. If a business did not meet these demands voluntarily, society could seek intervention and help from the legislature, which would then, at least on occasion, enact statutes setting minimal standards for business behavior. If the business obeyed these laws, it met the duty of fair play; if the managers did not blatantly lie to the customers, the business met the duty of honesty; if the firm generated profits for its investors, it met this duty.

As an example, look at the court opinion in *Dodge v. Ford Motor Company*,[19] a 1919 opinion by the Supreme Court of Michigan. Ford Motor Company was an extremely successful enterprise at the time, and it was paying dividends reflecting that success. Between "ordinary dividends" of 5 percent *per month* and special dividends that had averaged more than *400 percent* per annum over the previous five years, the stockholders were receiving substantial returns on their investments. At that point in time, Henry Ford and the board of directors announced a change. While Ford would continue to pay regular dividends of 5 percent per month, there would be no more special dividends. Instead, the board announced its intention to reduce the price of new cars and to make substantial investments in socially beneficial programs for the employees and the community. Two of the stockholders, the Dodge brothers, filed suit to prevent this conduct proposed by Mr. Ford. The Michigan Supreme Court ruled that the board of directors of a corporation may *not* place the interests of the public ahead of the interests of the stockholders and may *not* divert corporate funds to non-corporate purposes. The board was instructed to continue to maximize profits and to leave any charitable or public benefit contributions for individuals who chose to make such contributions from their personal funds.

The *Dodge v. Ford Motor Company* case was viewed as a landmark opinion, providing guidance for boards of directors in closely held corporations. While this opinion deals directly with the conflict between the desire of the Ford board to provide for the workers and the challenge by shareholders who want dividends, the basic thrust of the opinion is that the board has a duty to the shareholders to maximize the return on their investments.

Notice what the court said a corporation is expected to do. Would such conduct by a corporation be considered ethical today? If not, what has changed? Investors still want a return on their investments, and they expect to receive dividends from the corporations in whom they invest. Businesses are still expected to earn a profit and to return at least a portion of that profit to the shareholders.

The "Game Theory"

As society and the courts began to recognize the existence of corporate duties, the concept of business as an amoral institution became untenable. If a business had duties, it also had some ethical responsibilities. These responsibilities, however, tended to be based on adherence to the "rules" and obeying those rules. If a business obeyed the rules and stayed within the law, it was deemed to be acting in an ethical manner. This approach to business ethics led to the development of the "game theory" as a means of judging the ethical stance of the business.[20] Basically, the game theory equates the operation of a business with playing a game, and the rules from the game were applicable to determine the ethics of the business. If a manager of a firm lied to his or her customers, the manager—and consequently, the business—had acted unethically. However, if the manager bluffed his or her customer, the manager—and the firm—may have acted in an ethical manner, presuming that bluffing is an acceptable part of the game being played. Bluffing is, after all, an accepted part of several games, including poker. Of course, one person's bluffing may well be another person's lying, but such conundra were left for others to solve.

There is a basic flaw in the game theory of business ethics. Game theories and game rules are fair and equitable only if all of the participants in the game are aware that a game is being played. If any of the participants do not realize a game is being played, they cannot be aware of the rules of that game, and thus will be at a disadvantage. To take advantage of people under such circumstances would not be ethical.

Under the game theory, a number of rules were developed and followed. For example, *caveat emptor* (let the buyer beware) was a "rule" of the business game for a substantial period in U.S. history. Similarly, *laissez faire* economic regulation was a rule of business in the United States. Business and its customers were aware of these rules and played the business game accordingly. Eventually, however, business began

eClass 2.1 **Sales/Manufacturing**

IS BUSINESS A GAME?

Meg was talking to Todd, one of her classmates. Todd seemed excited to learn that Meg was involved in starting a business. He pointed out that he, too, had formed a business, and that he was now doing quite well for himself. He then offered her some "free advice" for the business. He urged Meg to convince her fellow entrepreneurs to set their prices high for their consumer customers when they first enter the market, before there is much competition. He thinks that eClass's product is distinct enough, and will generate enough demand, that a significant portion of the public will pay dearly for the software. He also urged them to initially offer the most basic structure possible, allowing them to maximize their profits early, before any competitors enter the market. And he advised Meg to plan to roll out a "new and improved" version of the software with more features, features the principals planned to offer from the start, once any competition surfaces. As he pointed out, eClass can always increase its quality and lower its prices later, if or when competition arises. After all, business is "a game, just like *Monopoly,* only with real money." This advice bothered Meg, and she has asked your advice. To what extent is business "just a game"? If business is "just a game," what are the rules (if any) to the game?

BUSINESS CONSIDERATIONS What business problems might arise for eClass, or for any other firm, if it adopts the attitude Todd is recommending?

ETHICAL CONSIDERATIONS Can the ethical theory the firm follows help the principals in determining whether to listen to Todd's advice? Explain your reasoning.

to industrialize and to gain an increasing ability to produce for larger and larger markets. The game was no longer quite as fair as it had been before, and as the game became more one-sided in favor of business, the other "players" (the customers) began to seek new rules for the game. When business would not voluntarily change the rules, the customers asked the government to intervene. This led to government regulation of business and eventually an entirely new playing field on which the game of business was to be conducted. This new playing field is the one on which business must operate today.

THE SOCIAL CONTRACT THEORY

Many business executives today argue that U.S. business is too regulated by the government. These people see domestic business drowning in a sea of bureaucratic red tape while less-regulated foreign firms are assuming control of the economy. They want to be unfettered, set free from the "excessive" regulations imposed by the government and allowed to compete freely with foreign producers. Although this attitude can possibly be justified from a simplistic economic position, it fails to take into account two factors: the spillover costs society must pay when a business fails to act in a responsible and ethical manner, and the "social contract" between business and society. When businesses became too large for local control, the society sought legislative intervention to force compliance with social demands. This is the gist of the social contract theory. Business must comply with the demands of the society if it wants to continue to exist and to operate within that society. The social contract defines the permissible scope of business conduct and goes beyond the purely economic issues. If society wants more from business than profits, business must accept this mandate in order to survive in society. To do otherwise is to breach the social contract.

The social contract theory presupposes that a business can exist only because society allows it to exist, that a business must satisfy the demands of the society if it is to be allowed to continue. If business does not satisfy the demands of society, society will change the "rules of the game," and in so changing the rules, the permission that business now has may well be revoked. Today, society expects (and demands) more from business than mere profits. Environmental concerns, consumer safety and protection, and quality of life, among other things, must also be provided for in the production and distribution processes. If these added demands cause costs to rise, so be it. If business as we know it will not meet these demands voluntarily, these demands will be met by regulation—or by society's changing the form of business or the rules of doing business. Not only has the "game theory" of business been rejected by society, but the rules by which business is allowed to exist have also been changed by the social contract theory.

Some of the fraud allegations and reporting problems of 2002 show the potential impact of the social contract theory, and also show how rapidly the government can respond to change the "rules of the game" when a serious problem or crisis arises that causes a public uproar. The 1990s was a period of almost unparalleled growth and prosperity in the United States, and a significant number of people became rich—or richer, in some cases—during this extended period of positive financial growth. However, when the economy finally began to show signs of slowing, or even of entering into a downward cycle, many people were afraid that the goods times were coming to an end. While most businesses sought ways to minimize the harm of the downturn by seeking new markets and new strategies, downsizing, or making adjustments in their business policies and strategies, some businesses—and their executives—took a more "creative" approach to the problem. They elected to cheat! There were misstated financial records and reports, false earning reports, erroneous listings of expenses and income to make the "bottom line" look better on paper than it was in reality. Adelphia Communications, Enron, Global Crossing, and WorldCom, among others, were eventually exposed for their wrongdoing, and the fallout was tremendous. And the allegations of wrongdoing were not restricted to the corporate world. Arthur Anderson, one of the "Big Five" public accounting firms, was found guilty of security act violations. Martha Stewart was convicted of conspiracy to cover up a crime, lying (but not perjury), and obstructing justice in conjunction with insider trading charges in violation of the security laws.[21] The public was appalled, and the effect on the stock market was devastating.

The government acted promptly, and harshly, to address these problems. President George W. Bush condemned the corporate scandals, stating that "America is ushering in a new era of responsibility, and that ethic of responsibility must extend to America's boardrooms."[22] Congress responded quickly, passing the Sarbanes-Oxley Act of 2002, which requires, among other things, that chief executive officers and chief financial officers certify the accuracy of quarterly financial reports. Knowingly certifying an inaccurate report can result in fines of up to $1 million and incarceration for up to ten years.[23]

The private sector also became actively involved in addressing some of these issues. The Corporate Accountability and Listing Standards Committee of the New York Stock Exchange initiated a thorough review of its policies and procedures and released its report in June 2002. This report was designed to "enhance the accountability, integrity and transparency of [the NYSE's] 2,800 listed companies and to help restore investor trust and confidence."[24] By the second half of 2002 more than 100 companies had hired "ethics officers" to work with the management and the boards of directors and to conduct training courses dealing with various ethical issues.[25] Each of these responses involves the application of the social contract theory to a public outcry over perceived misconduct by business.

Beginning in mid-to-late 2008, and carrying over well into 2009, the world's economies suffered even more devastating blows than those felt by the United States in 2002. The virtual melt-down of the banking industry and the declines in the stock markets were as severe as had been seen since the Great Depression of 1929. Sub-prime loans, adjustable-rate mortgages (ARMs), bonuses paid to executives even when the firms they represented lost money, and other questionable actions by business once again created a call for governmental intervention. Governmental bailouts of troubled firms and industries (banks, automobile manufacturers) and new regulations were introduced. The long-term effects of these interventions have yet to be determined, but the need for action was evident under the social contract theory.

In dealing with the social contract theory and in evaluating the ethical stance of any given business, it is important to recognize that each business has a number of constituent groups and that each group of constituents will have different wants, needs, and desires. (How the constituent groups are viewed, and how they are counted, is a matter of interpretation. For simplicity's sake, we have listed the constituents as belonging to one of *four* distinct groups. More members or more groups could easily be used, if so desired.) The business manager must base decisions affecting the business, at least in part, on the impact these decisions will have on the various constituents. Some decisions will affect all of the constituent groups, although not equally. Others will only affect some of the groups. Some decisions will have a positive impact on some groups and a negative impact on others. Deciding how each group will be affected, and how much weight to give to each group, is essential in reaching ethical decisions. Exhibit 2.3 shows the constituent groups a corporation must consider.

Exhibit 2.3

Constituents of a Business

Owners and Creditors#

↑ ↓

Employees   →   ***The Business*** →   The Community
(including managers) ←   ←

↑ ↓

Customers

The arrows indicate that duties and obligations are owed in both directions, *from* the business to its constituents and *to* the business from its constituents. A business exists within a set of symbiotic relationships with its various constituents.

This group is sometimes referred to as "stakeholders"—A person or group that has an investment, share, or interest in something, as a business or industry. Dictionary.com. The term includes both owners and creditors of the business. There are numerous other definitions of "stakeholder," some of which are much broader and more inclusive than the definition used here. R. Edward Freeman, in his book *Strategic Management: A Stakeholder Approach* (Marshfield, Mass.: Pitman 1984), includes environmentalists, the media, government, and competitors, among others, as stakeholders. With a broad definition, as used here, there are few constituents. With a narrower definition, more constituents are involved, making the illustration more complex and making it more difficult to address constituent issues and concerns.

The social contract theory has influenced the development of Corporate Social Responsibility (CSR) as an obligation of management. CSR addresses, and potentially measures, the duties of a business as a good citizen or a good neighbor in its community. "While CSR does not have a universal definition, many see it as the private sector's way of integrating the economic, social, and environmental imperatives of their activities."[26]

Businesses owe duties to each of the constituent groups, and each of the constituent groups is likely to owe duties to the businesses. Thus, there is a reciprocal set of duties and expectations.

Consider the following example of how these duties can affect a business in its decision process. A firm has developed a new production method that will lower costs (which will lead to increased profits) while simultaneously making safer products. To adopt this new method will benefit two constituent groups, owners / creditors and customers. However, this new method will require relocating the plant, and it may produce a number of pollutants. Relocating the plant will cause harm to current employees who may be unable or unwilling to relocate and to the current community, which will suffer economic harm from reduced employment. The possible increase in pollutants will harm the community at the site of the new plant, although this harm will be offset to some extent by the increase in employment and the economic "ripple effect" a new plant will cause. Somehow a balancing of these competing interests must be undertaken in reaching a decision that reflects the best short-term and long-term interests of the firm.

The Changing Social Environment

Over the years, business has changed, and with it the attitudes of society toward business. The early days of commerce featured primarily local trade consisting of handcrafted goods produced and sold by local merchants and artisans. Under these circumstances, the rule of *caveat emptor* was followed, and the success of any business was, to a significant extent, dependent on the reputation of its owner/operator.

Eventually, business began to industrialize and to gain an increased capacity for productivity. As businesses began to produce more, they were able to expand their geographic markets from local to regional. This expansion caused some minor changes, although the buyer still had to beware. No longer could the buyer expect to be personally acquainted with the seller. Although the reputation of the seller remained important, much of the spread of that reputation was now by hearsay. The buyer and the seller were becoming separated by distance.

Industrialization continued to expand, and transportation and communication also grew and developed. The advent of the railroads allowed truly national business operations for the first time. With this opportunity to deal on a national scope, manufacturers became aware of "economies of scale." The age of "bigger is better" had arrived. Now *caveat emptor* took on more meaning. No longer could a buyer rely on his or her personal knowledge about a seller's reputation. Sellers were combining into trusts, and available substitutes for a seller's goods began to decline. Buyers were being thrust into a "take-it-or-leave-it" position.

For the first time, the public expectation of business made a drastic change. The public began to request government intervention to protect the consumer and the worker from "big business." The government responded with what business must have thought was a vengeance. The Interstate Commerce Commission, the antitrust statutes, the Securities and Exchange Commission, and a myriad of other agencies and acts were passed in relatively rapid succession.

Why did these changes occur? Fundamentally, because business was so busy meeting its own needs that it ignored the expectations and the demands of the public. Was business acting illegally? In most cases, no. Was business acting unethically? From our contemporary perspective, probably; from an historic point of view, probably not. The key point to remember is that, in most cases, business was being conducted in a manner that had been socially and legally acceptable up to that time. However, as society changed and as the demands of society changed, business failed to respond. Then, when business failed to respond, society sought legislative intervention. The end of the nineteenth century saw the birth of the social contract as an essential element of conducting business.

One example of the changing social environment is the area of "employment at will." An at-will employee is one who works for the employer only so long as both parties agree to the employment. There is no fixed term of employment, and either party may terminate the employment relationship at any time merely by giving notice to the other party. Historically, courts upheld the right of the employer to discharge an at-will employee "for good cause, for no cause, or even for cause morally wrong. . . ."[27] The employer's unlimited right to discharge an employee was too often abused by the

eClass 2.2 Marketing/Management

SHOULD ECLASS ADOPT A CODE OF ETHICS?

Ani and Yousef recently attended a business ethics seminar conducted by one of their professors. After attending this seminar and thinking about all of the corporate scandals that were recently discovered, Ani believes that eClass should adopt a formal "Code of Ethics" for the firm to follow. She asserts that such a code will help the company not only to respond to ethical dilemmas as they arise, but also to plan ahead in order to avoid ethical problems in the future. She also states that such a code, if properly publicized, can help the firm improve its profits. Yousef disagrees with Ani. He believes that since the business is run by people who are already ethical in their own lives, such a code in unnecessary. He also thinks that advertising any code of ethics is too much like "blowing your own horn," and is more likely to turn people off toward the firm than to attract them to do business with the firm. They have asked for your advice. What will you tell them?

BUSINESS CONSIDERATIONS   Why might it be a good idea to adopt a code for the business now, even if it is owned and operated by people who are already ethical? Why might such a code be a bad idea?

ETHICAL CONSIDERATIONS   If the firm is to adopt a code of ethics, what ethical theory do *you* believe should be selected as the foundation for the code? Explain your reasons.

employer, which led to a reevaluation of the traditional "at-will" doctrine. In *Pierce v. Ortho Pharmaceutical Corporation*,[28] the court ruled that, generally speaking, an employer in an employment-at-will state is free to terminate the employment relationship at any time, with or without cause. However, the court also stated that firing an employee for a reason that violates public policy could not be done in good faith and would result in liability for wrongful discharge.

Problems with Business Ethics

Any business that seeks to act in an "ethical" manner faces a basic problem. There are no fixed guidelines to follow, no formal code of ethics to set the standards under which the business should operate. Numerous professional organizations have their own codes of ethics or conduct. For example, the legal profession has the Code of Professional Responsibility; the medical profession has its Hippocratic Oath; the accounting profession has a code of ethics and also has generally accepted auditing standards (GAAS) and generally accepted accounting principles (GAAP); the real estate industry has a code of conduct; and various other groups or organizations have similar codes. However, "business" as a separate entity has no code, no "road map" of ethical conduct. The closest thing business has to an ethical guideline is the law. If a business is acting within the law, it is acting legally and is arguably meeting its minimum social requirements. However, this forces business into a reactive posture, always responding to legislative demands. It would seem that a proactive position in which business establishes its own path would be preferable.

Given this overriding problem, what can be done to provide a solution? At the present time, probably nothing can be done in the global, or even national, sense. But it may be possible for each industry to develop a code of ethics for that particular industry, in much the same manner that the real estate industry has developed a code for its members. If such an industry-wide approach does not prove feasible, each individual firm can develop its own personal code of ethics. Although such a micro-approach may not be ideal, it at least encourages business to embark on the journey toward formalizing its ethical posture.

The Human Factor   As was mentioned earlier, business was frequently viewed as an amoral institution in the past. Workers were expected to leave their personal values at the front gate when they reported to work, and then (presumably) to retrieve them at the close of the working day. At the same time, workers were expected to be loyal agents of the firm. Generally, this was interpreted to mean that if a course of conduct was beneficial to the employer, the employee was to follow that course. If a course of conduct was not beneficial to the employer, the employee was not to follow it. The attitudes and opinions of the employees were ignored.

The "loyal agent" attitude was described—and then rebutted—by Alex C. Micholos in his article "The Loyal Agent's Argument."[29] The loyal agent's argument presumes that the principal follows the ethical theory of egoism, and that the loyal agent must also act egoistically for the principal. The argument runs as follows:

1. As a loyal agent of the principal, I ought to serve his interests as he would serve them himself if he possessed my expertise.
2. The principal will serve his interests in a thoroughly egoistic manner.
3. Therefore, as a loyal agent of this principal, I must operate in a thoroughly egoistic manner on his behalf.

In order to operate in a thoroughly egoistic manner, a person acts in the way that best advances his or her interests, presuming that everyone else is doing the same thing.

The gist of the loyal agent's argument is that a truly loyal agent will put the principal first in any decisions where there are conflicting interests. Thus, the traditional argument supposes that a loyal agent is expected to act without regard to ethical considerations as long as the conduct puts the principal first. There is a major flaw in this traditional loyal agent's argument. Too many people feel that a loyal agent, if acting in a truly egoistic manner, has license—if not a duty—to act immorally and unethically if doing so will advance the interests of the principal. Micholos argued that the truly loyal agent must exercise due care and skill in the performance of the agency duties, and must act in a socially acceptable manner while furthering the interests of the principal. To do otherwise will have a long-term detrimental impact on the principal and will therefore be disloyal.

The Legal Aspect   The U.S. legal system contains numerous ethical components. For example, a person is presumed to be innocent until proven guilty in criminal law. Each person is entitled to due process of the law and to equal protection under the law. Protections exist against compulsory self-incrimination and cruel and unusual punishment. The Constitution provides for free speech, free exercise of religion, and the right to counsel, among other rights and guarantees.

Business law also attempts to reflect the ethical standards of the society and to promote ethical conduct in the realm of business. The law of sales imposes a duty on each party to a sales contract to act in good faith. Bankruptcy is designed to give an honest debtor a fresh start. Agency law imposes the duties of loyalty and good faith on the agent.

The laws that regulate business have developed, to a significant extent, under the social contract theory. Governmental regulations of business were enacted initially, in many cases, in response to a public demand for protection from the abuses and excesses of "big business." Antitrust laws were intended to control business and to protect the ideal of a free-and-competitive economy, while the Federal Trade Commission was established to stop unfair and deceptive trade practices.

Encouraged by the apparent success of the antitrust laws, the government began using statutes to force business to meet the demands of the public. The consumer movement of the 1960s led to a number of protective statutes by both the federal and state governments. The federal government was concerned with protecting consumer credit and consumer product safety. State governments tended to be more concerned with safety and with home solicitations. In either case, the government became involved only after a perceived problem was identified, public demands for protection were raised, and the business community failed or refused to adequately meet the demands of the public.

The 1960s and 1970s also saw an increased public awareness of and concern about pollution of the environment. Again, a number of protests and a great deal of public action were ignored by the business community in general, and once again governmental intervention was the tool used to address the problem. Governmental environmental protection statutes were intended to clean up the environment in order to protect the quality of life for present and future generations and for wildlife. Government involvement was triggered once more by the failure of the business community to address environmental issues the public had raised.

Similar steps were followed in other areas such as labor and fair employment. The public expressed a concern over how business was handling a perceived problem. Again, the steps business took toward solving the problem were less than the public demanded. Consequently, the legislature was asked to intervene on behalf of the public.

In virtually every circumstance, though, the statutory treatment of the problems adopted by the legislature is relatively rigid and potentially expensive for business. Similar protections could have—and should have—been developed within the business community, with a great deal less rigidity and a great deal less expense, had business been willing to meet the challenge directly. Instead, by waiting for the government response, business now has a much stricter regulatory environment in which to operate. More recently there have been adverse reaction in the legislature over bonuses paid to executives of companies that were bailed out and a new financial regulation bill was signed into law in response to the financial meltdown.[30]

In each of these areas, and in a number of others, the application of the social contract theory is apparent. Society perceived problems and demanded that corrective steps be taken to alleviate the problems. Business had an opportunity to take corrective steps in a manner devised by business but failed—or refused—to do so. At that point, the government stepped in to resolve the problem in a rigid, statutory manner when no satisfactory solutions were advanced by business. By failing to respond in a proactive manner, which would have permitted a custom-tailored, micro-focused solution by each affected business or industry, the business community was presented with a reactive, macro-oriented solution that must, by definition, extend across industry lines and that is intended to control all aspects of the business community with one broad regulation.

MULTINATIONAL ETHICS

There is an old adage that states: "When in Rome, do as the Romans do." This adage is very appropriate when considering business ethics in a multinational setting. If business ethics tended to be Kantian in nature, with firms throughout the world seeking—and then following—a categorical imperative, there would not be any problem. Since a categorical imperative is a perfect rule, one for which any and every exception has been developed, businesses would merely have to follow the resulting rules, and their actions would be ethical by definition. Unfortunately, there is no categorical imperative for business, nor are most businesses Kantian in their ethical perspectives. Thus, problems with business ethics exist, and these problems are compounded in an international environment.

A businessperson tends to follow his or her personal moral and ethical values and to apply these values in judging the ethics of others. While the "loyal agent's" argument stresses that a truly loyal agent will put the interests of the principal ahead of the interests of the agent, that same agent will normally only work for a principal whose interests and values can be reconciled with the interests and the values of the agent. If the demands and requirements of a job consistently conflict with the morals and the ethics of an employee, that employee will, or should, try to locate more acceptable employment before changing his or her ethical perspective. Be aware, however, that there are some who think that the employee becomes "desensitized" and begins to adopt the values of the employer. They start doing it the way the company has always done it. Similarly, the ethical stance of the firm is likely to be consistent with the ethical values of the society. If the firm does not conform to socially acceptable standards, the "social contract theory" is used to change the permissible scope of the firm's conduct.

Even if a business has a formal stated objective of acting in a socially responsible and ethical manner, problems may occur. What happens when that firm expands its operations into another country? What happens when a truly loyal and ethical agent of the firm is reassigned to a foreign post within the company? This expansion and/or reassignment may have serious ethical implications. The social contract between the new location and its businesses may well be different from the social contract between the firm and its domicile (home, legal residence) state, calling for a reappraisal of what is acceptable—or even desirable—behavior. For instance, a firm may open a new plant in a nation with very lax environmental protection statutes. This same firm, in its domicile state, has been an environmentally concerned business that has taken many pro-environment steps to reduce pollution in its production. If the firm tries to be as environmentally active in its new location, it will be at a short-term competitive disadvantage. If it seeks to be economically competitive, it will be acting in a manner contrary to its stated company policy of environmental concern and protection. What should the firm do?

Although there is no perfect solution, any firm that is considering expansion into another country needs to make every effort to learn about the cultural differences that exist between the two nations, and to take steps to reduce any culture shock or conflict prior to the expansion. The firm may consider hiring citizens of the other nation, or it may consider requiring an educational program to prepare its employees for the move. The employees should be taught as much as possible about the new country, and they should also be urged to "watch and learn." The firm and its employees should be aware that they are visitors, guests in another nation, and should act as they would were they personal guests at the home of a new friend. Above all else, the firm and its employees should avoid being judgmental. New countries and new cultures may seem strange and exotic, or they may merely seem different, but the new country will provide the social values that drive the social contract under which the firm will now be conducting business. Assimilation and acceptance are essential!

A RECOMMENDATION FOR BUSINESS

U.S. businesses need to develop a model or a framework of ethical behavior. It is more than likely that no single model can be developed that will apply equally to every industry within the U.S. economy, but it is possible to suggest a general outline for business. This general outline can then be tailored by each industry to the needs and the demands of that particular industry. For example, business should probably lean toward the consequential ethical theories rather than the nonconsequential theories. Consequential theories are more readily understood and more easily accepted by the public than the more esoteric nonconsequential approaches. Additionally, consequential theories are more flexible, and thus are more responsive to social and technological changes.

Regardless of the overriding theory, business should adopt a "synthesis" approach of resolving ethical issues. The firm should first identify the important considerations involved (obligations, ideals, effects) and should then decide where the emphasis should lie among these three considerations, especially with respect to its constituents (owners / creditors, employees, customers, community, etc.). This approach works well with any ethical principle adopted, takes into account the people to whom the firm

eClass 2.3 Marketing/Management

OPERATING eCLASS ETHICALLY

Ani, Meg, and Yousef have each seen numerous examples of what they consider unethical conduct, both in the workplace and in society at large. Yousef has several friends who are employed part-time in a sales capacity, and a number of them believe that it is perfectly legitimate to say virtually anything short of an outright lie in order to close a sale with a customer. They frequently "push the envelope" to the edge, grossly exaggerating qualities of the product being marketed, often to the detriment of the purchasers of that product. Meg knows a few information systems people who would not hesitate to claim credit for the work of others, and she also knows a few who would even assert privileges based on their seniority in order to gain credit for the work of others. (Of course, both know even more people who do not act in this manner, but these others do not disturb them.) Ani has seen people lie on their resumes or job applications, claiming accomplishments that were totally fictitious. She has also seen situations in which a person was hired who did not meet the criteria set out in the job description. This usually happened because the particular applicant knew someone who was able to influence the hiring decision, an example of "it's who you know, not what you know." All three of the principals believe that such conduct is generally harmful to a business and its reputation, especially with repeat customers. They also know they would like to operate this business ethically, but they don't know how to verbalize this goal. They have asked you for your advice. What will you tell them?

BUSINESS CONSIDERATIONS   Where might the principals look for examples of what they should or should not do? As one of the original entrants into this particular field, should eClass attempt to be proactive in establishing an ethics code, or should the firm wait for governmental guidance?

ETHICAL CONSIDERATIONS   Should the firm adopt a formal ethics code or policy as they begin the company, or should they be less formal until they see what sorts of ethical issues arise in the operation of the firm? What advantages are there for having a formal written code for a firm? What advantages are there to taking an informal and flexible approach to ethics?

must answer, and provides a framework for decision making that is comparable to other types of business decisions regularly made by managers.

Business should also consider its public relations image in deciding how to proceed within the consequential area. A utilitarian approach, one that is most concerned with the greatest good for the greatest number, is more acceptable to society than an egoistic approach. Society already tends to view business as egoistic—perhaps excessively so—without formally adopting such a theory as the driving force behind ethical considerations. Also, many people seem incapable of distinguishing between egoistic and egotistic. (Egoists measure their conduct on the basis of self-interest, choosing the course of conduct that will provide the greatest benefit to themselves. Egotists are self-centered, characterized by excessive references to themselves.)

Next, business should avoid rigid rules that force specific actions or reactions, especially with the rapid changes that occur with modern technology. This does not mean business should not have rules and standards, but, rather, that the rules and standards should be flexible enough to change as society and the business environment change. Business should also advocate the loyal agent's argument, while emphasizing that a truly loyal agent will act within the law while keeping the best interests of the principal in mind.

Whenever possible, businesses should learn to work with the government in establishing statutory regulations. By taking a proactive role in regulation, business can help to protect not only its own best interests, but also can show its concern for society and its various constituents.

The development of a comprehensive business ethic will not be easy, nor will it be greeted with open arms by all businesses or business leaders. The alternative, however, is excessive regulation, public distrust, and a general malaise in the business community. Proactive steps can be taken to benefit both business and society, which will ultimately benefit business.

Contemporary Case

HILL v. VERIZON MARYLAND, INC.

U.S. District Court, D. Maryland (2009)

FACTS Andy Hill filed suit against Verizon Maryland, Inc., alleging wrongful discrimination on the basis of an actual or perceived disability in violation of the Americans with Disabilities Act (ADA). Verizon Maryland argued that Hill did not qualify as a disabled person under the ADA and

cannot otherwise establish a prima facie case of disability discrimination.

Hill worked for Verizon for 27 years, beginning as a customer service representative. After 20 years, he was promoted to the position of service technician, a position he held until he retired in March 2006. According to Verizon's official job description, a service technician's duties include "climbing poles and ladders and working aloft."

Such employees were required to meet the medical standards set by Bell Atlantic and to satisfy the OSHA and company weight restrictions and guidelines. The weight restrictions applied by Verizon, in line with the standards established by OSHA and Verizon, limited workers to a maximum weight of 275 pounds, although "every attempt will be made to accommodate employees" who weighed between 275 and 325 pounds. Any employee whose weight exceeds 325 pounds is entirely precluded from performing aerial work. In March 2000, Hill's weight exceeded 325 pounds, and he was restricted to clerical work for the most part, although he retained his title and his salary. By January 2003, Hill's weight had fallen to below 325 pounds, and he resumed full-time duty as a service technician. However, by March 2004 his weight had increased to more than 400 pounds and remained above 400 pounds for the remainder of his time on the job. In March 2005, Hill was informed that he would be reclassified as a clerical assistant, with a pay decrease of $400 per week. Hill filed a grievance and was able to retain his pay grade and classification until April 2006. Hill voluntarily retired just before the reclassification took place. He then filed suit, claiming that the planned reclassification and pay reduction constituted constructive termination, making him unable to support his family, and was based on illegal discrimination against him because of his disability.

ISSUES Was Hill constructively discharged by Verizon? Was his separation from the company an illegal discrimination against a person with a disability?

HOLDING No, there was no evidence that Verizon acted in a manner sufficient to show constructive discharge. No, Mr. Hill did not establish that he had a recognized disability since, by his own testimony, he was able to perform most normal life activities and functions.

REASONING Excerpts from the opinion of Richard Bennett, Circuit Judge:

The Americans with Disabilities Act ("ADA") prohibits discrimination by a covered entity, including a private employer such as Verizon, "against a qualified individual" with a disability. . . . To establish a cause of action for disability discrimination, a plaintiff must show that (1) [he] has a disability, (2) [he] is otherwise qualified for the employment in question, and (3) [he] was excluded from the employment based on the disability. . . . [Hill] asserts that Verizon failed to provide him with reasonable accommodations. . . . To establish a *prima facie* failure to accommodate claim under the ADA, [Hill] must show "(1) that he was an individual who had a disability within the meaning of the statute; (2) that [Verizon] had notice of his disability; (3) that with reasonable accommodation he would perform the essential functions of the position . . . ; and (4) that [Verizon] refused to make such accommodations."

. . . "the case law and the regulations both point unrelentingly to the conclusion that a claim based on obesity is not likely to succeed under the ADA." . . . [Hill's] morbid obesity does not substantially limit a major life activity . . . The Court recognizes that Mr. Hill's obesity interferes with his quality of life . . . However, to be considered a disability under the ADA, an individual's impairment must be *substantially* limiting, which is a separate statutory requirement. . . .

"To prove constructive discharge, a plaintiff must at the outset show that his employer 'deliberately made [his] working conditions intolerable in an effort to induce [him] to quit.'" . . . "Plaintiff must therefore demonstrate: (1) that the employer's actions were deliberate, and (2) that working conditions were intolerable." . . . "However, mere dissatisfaction with work assignments, a feeling of being unfairly criticized or difficult or unpleasant working conditions are not so intolerable as to compel a reasonable person to resign." . . . the Court does not doubt that Verizon's actions were hard on Mr. Hill. They did not, however, constitute constructive discharge of his employment. The claim of "constructive discharge" is not meant to be an end-run around the ADA's main goal—to protect those truly disabled individuals who, because of stereotypes and prejudices concerning their general capabilities are denied employment opportunities.

Defendant's motion for summary judgment is granted.

BUSINESS CONSIDERATIONS Is it a good policy for a business to establish health and safety guidelines for its employees, or should the business just rely on the standards set by OSHA and the ADA? What benefits might a business derive by providing benefits related to the fitness and the lifestyles of its employees?

ETHICAL CONSIDERATIONS Is it ethical for a business to establish or require lifestyle guidelines or practices (weight standards, non-smoking requirements, etc.) for its employees? Would it be ethical to discharge an employee who failed to follow these standards or guidelines away from the workplace, although adhering to them at the workplace?

You Be the Judge

Delegate Phil Hamilton sponsored a bill that was to provide $500,000 to Old Dominion University (ODU) as start-up funds for a new teacher training center, the Center for Teacher Quality and Educational Leadership. Hamilton had also been in contact with the administration at ODU, seeking appointment as a faculty member to the center. In fact, he also designated the salary ($40,000) that he expected in this new position. When rumors began to circulate about a possible link between Hamilton's sponsoring of the bill to provide funding and his interest in acquiring a position in the new center, Hamilton denied that he had any contact with ODU prior to his introduction of the bill. However, a freedom of information request by the *Virginian-Pilot* newspaper resulted in the release of emails by ODU which made it clear that Hamilton expected to be hired by the center when he sponsored the center's startup funding.

Assume that the Virginia House of Delegates has initiated an action to remove Hamilton from the House, and that Hamilton has come before *your* court seeking an injunction to prevent his ouster. How will *you* rule in this situation? If the allegations are true, did Hamilton commit a crime in this situation? Even if there is no criminal liability, assuming that the allegations are true, do you believe that his conduct was unethical? Explain and justify your answer.

[See "PhilHamilton: Fired," *Blue Virginia* (August 20, 2009, http://www. bluevirginia.us/2009/08/phil-hamilton-fired.html; see also "A Shady Deal Brought to Light," *Roanoke Times* (August 27, 2009, http://blogs.roanoke.com/rtblogs/roundtable/2009/08/27/editorial-investigate-del-hamilton-openly/.)

Summary

It is important to distinguish ethics from morals. "Ethics" refers to either individual or group (including society) values, whereas "morals" refers to individuals' values and matters of conscience. Throughout this book we use ethics to refer to group or social values and morals to refer to individual values.

Over the history of this country, the social environment in which business operates has changed drastically. As the social environment has changed, the demands of society on business have also changed. Business, however, has been slow to recognize or to accept these changes.

For a substantial amount of time, business was judged by the "game theory." This theory does not take into account several factors, including the fact that the customers of a business may not be aware that a game is being played. Throughout most of the twentieth century and up to the present, business has been judged by the social contract theory. The social contract theory says that business must respond to the demands of the society, or the society will be permitted to change the "rules of the game" to ensure that business does comply with society's demands. If business does not act as society demands, society will request legislation to enforce compliance.

Even if businesses (and businesspeople) want to act ethically, it is difficult for them to do so. There are no clear-cut guidelines for most businesses to follow in adopting a code of ethics, and agreements among competing firms within an industry as to what should be done could be challenged as a conspiracy to restrain trade, a violation of antitrust laws. Still, some effort must be made. Business can make this effort by recognizing the human element—the fact that its employees are humans, with human wants, desires, and values. Business needs to recognize that unless it responds voluntarily, the legislature will often intervene. Business also needs to recognize that the courts are beginning to recognize ethical aspects to corporate conduct. Cases such as Madoff or the bonuses given to AIG executives will help to establish a new line of precedents concerning business ethics and the liability of the firms that fail to toe the ethical line.

The corporate scandals of 2002 have also led to a change in the social contract and to statutory and regulatory changes as well. Firms that engage in questionable activities, such as Adelphia Communications, Enron, Global Crossing, and WorldCom have an impact on firms and stakeholders well beyond the reach of the particular firm accused of wrongdoing. New laws and new rules will have a significant impact on executives for many years because of the unethical conduct of a relatively small group of executives for a relatively limited period of time.

Finally, business must make changes and develop ethical standards in a more global setting. Multinational trade carries with it multinational responsibilities, including meeting the ethical standards and expectations of other nations. The social contract business must follow will become more confusing and more restrictive as more and more businesses discover the profits of international trade.

Discussion Questions

1. What is the "social contract theory," and how does this theory affect the ethical conduct of business within the society in which that business operates? Does the United States follow the social contract theory?

2. What are the advantages and the disadvantages for a business that decides to be "proactive" in the area of ethics? What are the advantages and disadvantages for a business that decides to be "reactive" in this area? Based on your response, which option would better serve a business? Explain your reasoning.

3. Can the "game theory," which allows—and even encourages—bluffing, be reconciled with the basic social obligations and responsibilities a business is expected to perform? Should business follow the game theory in every situation, only in some situations, or in no situations? Explain and give examples where appropriate.

4. It has been established scientifically and medically that cigarette smoking is a health hazard, not only to the smoker, but also to those persons subjected to second-hand smoke. As a result, sales and profits for tobacco companies have declined substantially in the United States. Cigarette smoking is increasing in some parts of the world, especially in Asia, with a steadily increasing demand for American-made cigarettes. The sale of American cigarettes to this growing Asian market can generate literally billions of dollars in sales over the next few years. Many of the restrictions the tobacco companies face in the United States do not exist in these Asian nations, nor are there any restrictions on advertising. However, the health hazards posed by consumption of the product are the same as those faced in the United States. From an ethical perspective, what should American cigarette manufacturers do under these circumstances? Justify your answer and explain the theory under which you reached your conclusions.

5. John Rawls proposes that universal rules can be developed provided that these rules are developed behind a "veil of ignorance." How would such a veil of ignorance enhance or hinder the development of a business code of ethics for an industry?

Case Problems and Writing Assignments

1. Bernard Madoff orchestrated perhaps the largest Ponzi scheme in history, a $65 billion dollar fraud that affected thousands of investors, including a number of charities and universities, and contributed to the stock market decline in 2008. Madoff's firm was periodically under investigation for more than 16 years and was the subject of at least six "substantive complaints" between 1992 and 2008. One SEC official assigned to the investigation married Madoff's niece some time after he left the investigation, although he was seeing her during the investigation. A report released by the SEC in September 2009 acknowledged that investigators failed to scrutinize the firm's "consistently strong profits," that they did not follow up on inconsistencies in Madoff's testimony despite the fact that he was caught in "lies and inconsistencies" almost immediately. The SEC ended one phase of the investigation "abruptly" to focus on suspected mutual fund abuses.

   Assume that charges are filed in *your* court against various members of the SEC, including some of the investigators and the Chairman of the SEC, for dereliction of duty and criminal negligence.

rmation set out above, how would ...hical issues are raised in this sce-...enalties and/or sanctions, if any, ...osed on the SEC personnel? Explain and justify your answer. [See David Scheer & Joshua Gallu, "Madoff Scam Reaches Family of SEC Official Whose Unit got Tip," Bloomberg.com, http://www.bloomberg.com/apps/news?pid=20601087& sid=acsLM8lozhkY. See also Marcy Gordon, "Report Shows Investigators Botched Madoff Probes," Yahoo! News, http://abcnews.go.com/Business/wireStory? id=8497629/.]

2. Norris was hired as a mechanic by Hawaiian Airlines in 1987. The terms of Norris's employment were governed by a collective bargaining agreement between Hawaiian Airlines and the International Association of Machinists and Aerospace Workers. In 1987, during a routine preflight inspection of an airplane, Norris noticed that one of the tires on the plane was worn. After removing the wheel to replace the tire, Norris noticed that the axle sleeve was scarred and grooved (it should have been "mirror-smooth"), which could cause the landing gear to fail. He recommended that this axle sleeve be replaced, but his supervisor said that it should just be sanded smooth and returned to the plane. The sleeve was sanded and returned, and the plane flew as scheduled. At the end of the shift, Norris refused to sign the maintenance record indicating that the repairs had been performed satisfactorily and that the plane was fit to fly. When Norris refused to sign the maintenance record, he was suspended by his supervisor pending a termination hearing. Norris immediately went home and reported the problem with the sleeve to the Federal Aviation Administration (FAA). Norris then invoked the grievance procedure called for by the collective bargaining agreement. Following the grievance hearing, Norris was discharged for insubordination. Norris then sued the airline in Hawaii's circuit court for wrongful discharge, alleging that his discharge violated both the public policy of the Federal Aviation Act and the Hawaii Whistleblower Protection Act. The airline removed the case to the U.S. district court and asserted that Norris was not entitled to remedies due to the provisions of the Railway Labor Act (which has also covered airlines since 1936), which provides for mandatory arbitration proceedings to resolve such controversies. How should the court resolve this case? What ethical issues are raised by these facts? Would this case be resolved differently under ethical considerations than it would under legal considerations? [See *Hawaiian Airlines, Inc. v. Norris*, 114 S. Ct. 2239 (1994).]

3. Haworth was the blood bank supervisor at the Deborah Heart and Lung Center within the Deborah Hospital. Part of the responsibility of the blood bank was to collect blood samples from patients and to test those samples. The blood bank also ensured that there was an adequate supply of the proper blood type for the patient when the patient underwent surgery. Following an argument with his supervisor, Haworth destroyed an entire rack of patient blood samples. Following a leave of absence due to "stress," Haworth was offered a less stressful—but lower-level—job. Haworth refused to accept this reassignment, and the hospital discharged him at that time. Haworth claimed the discharge violated the Conscientious Employee Protection Act (CEPA). He alleged that the destruction of the blood samples was a communicative act designed to show his objection to an allegedly defective blood identification system and that the discharge was an illegal retaliatory act by the hospital. Was Haworth's conduct a communicative act, protected by the CEPA? How should a manager react when an employee takes actions that are contra to the firm's interests, but that may involve a legitimate protest by the employee? What if the manager believes the protest is not legitimate? [See *Haworth v. Deborah Heart and Lung Center*, 638 A.2d 1354 (N.J. Super. 1994)].

Notes

1. *Merriam Webster's Collegiate Dictionary*, 10th ed. (Springfield, MA: Merriam-Webster, 1993), p. 398.
2. Ibid., p. 756.
3. Hobson's choice, "The choice of taking either that which is offered or nothing; the absence of a real alternative," *Dictionary.com*.
4. William H. Shaw & Vincent Berry, *Moral Issues in Business*, 4th ed. (Belmont, CA: Wadsworth Publishing, 1989), p. 2.
5. Ibid., p. 51.
6. Ibid., p. 55.
7. Rogene A. Buchholz & Sandra B. Rosenthal, *Business Ethics, the Pragmatic Path Beyond Principles to Process*, (Upper Saddle River, NJ: Prentice-Hall, Inc., 1998), pp. 68-69.
8. Shaw & Berry, supra note 4, at p. 63.
9. John Rawls, *A Theory of Justice*, (Cambridge, MA: Belknap Press of Harvard University Press, 1971).
10. Ibid., pp. 195-201.
11. Shaw & Berry, supra note 4, at pp. 52-55.
12. Ibid., pp. 58-60.
13. Buchholz & Rosenthal, supra note 7, at pp. 68-69.
14. Shaw & Berry, supra note 4, at pp. 66-67.
15. Rawls, supra note 9, at pp. 195-210.
16. Hugh LaFollette, "The Truth in Ethical Relativism," Journal of Social Philosophy (1991), pp. 146-54.
17. Vincent Ryan Ruggerio, *The Moral Imperative* (Port Washington, NY: Alfred Knopf Publishers, 1973).
18. Shaw & Berry, supra note 4, at p. 77.
19. 170 N.W. 668 (Mich. 1919).
20. Albert Carr, "Is Business Bluffing Ethical?" Harv. Bus. Rev., (January-February, 1968).
21. Alan Reynolds, "Martha's Mistrial: The Insider Trading Accusation Came from a Cowardly Press Leak from a Congressional Committee," Cato Institute (March 9, 2004), http://www.cato.org/research/articles/reynolds-040309.html (accessed 7/30/2010).
22. "President Condemns Corporate Scandals," *The Roanoke Times*, June 30, 2001, p. A1.
23. "Reform has many CEOs rushing to comply," *The Roanoke Times*, August 9, 2002, p. A9.
24. "Where We Stand," *Your Market, Straight Talk for Investors*, The New York Stock Exchange (Time, Inc. Custom Publishing: New York Stock Exchange, July 2002), p. 3.
25. Jonathan D. Salant, "Ethics Officers to Teach the Lost Art of Fair Play," *The Roanoke Times*, November 1, 2002, p. 1.
26. "Corporate Social Responsibility," *Industry Canada*, ic.gc.ca., http://www.ic.gc.ca/eic/site/csr-rse.nsf/eng/Home/.
27. *Payne v. Western & Atl. R.R. Co.*, 81 Tenn. 507, 519-210 (1884).
28. 417 A.2d 505 (N.J. Super., 1980).
29. Tom L. Beauchamp & Norman E. Bowie, *Ethical Theories and Business*, 2nd ed. (Englewood Cliffs, N.J.: Prentice-Hall, Inc. 1983), p. 247.
30. See, e.g., "Troubled Asset Relief Program—TARP," Investopedia, http://www.investopedia.com/terms/t/troubled-asset-relief-program-tarp.asp; "Obama Says Big Bank Bonuses Prove That New Financial Regulation Law Was Needed," San Francisco Examiner, http://harrypottering.com/gossip/Obama-says-big-bank-bonuses-prove-that-new-financial-regulation-law-was-needed-3108023.html/.

3

The U.S. Legal System and Court Jurisdiction

Agenda

Ani, Meg, and Yousef never realized how important it is for owners and operators of a business to understand the complexities of the U.S. legal system until they began eClass. Now a number of questions have arisen. What, for example, do the eClass entrepreneurs need to know about state and federal court systems, or about the different types of jurisdiction? Might they be sued—or be forced to sue—in states other than their state of residence? How does a court obtain authority over business entitities? What types of cases might they encounter? For example, Ani, Meg, and Yousef obtained a U.S. copyright on eAccounting. However, they are not sure how well this copyright will protect eClass's software. Will the government protect eClass's copyright or does eClass have to bring suit itself? Can eClass test its copyright in court before a challenge arises, or will the firm have to wait until the software code is being used by someone else without authorization before they can sue? They have also discovered that they will have to use care to distinguish the rules applicable to the federal government and those applicable to the states.

These and other questions will arise as you read this chapter. Be prepared! You never know when the firm or one of its members will seek your advice.

Classic Case

INTERNATIONAL SHOE CO. v. STATE OF WASHINGTON

326 U.S. 310, 66 S. Ct. 154 (1945)

FACTS International Shoe was engaged in the manufacture and sale of shoes. It was a Delaware corporation with its principal place of business in St. Louis, Missouri. It maintained places of business in several states, but not in Washington. Its merchandise was distributed through several branches located outside the State of Washington. It had no office in Washington, made no contracts, and maintained no inventory there. During the years in question, International Shoe employed 11 to 13 salesmen under direct supervision and control of sales managers in St. Louis. These salesmen lived in Washington; their principal activities were confined to that state; and they were compensated by commissions based upon the amount of their sales. The commissions for each year totaled more than $31,000. The company supplied its salesmen with a line of samples which they displayed to prospective purchasers. On occasion they rented rooms to display samples. The cost of the rent was reimbursed by the company. The authority of the salesmen was limited to exhibiting their samples and soliciting orders at prices fixed by the company. The salesmen sent the orders to the company's principal office for acceptance or rejection. When the orders were accepted, the merchandise was shipped and invoiced from outside Washington. No salesman had authority to enter into contracts or to collect payment. Notice of the assessment was served on a salesman in the State of Washington, and a copy was mailed by registered mail to International Shoe at its address in St. Louis, Missouri.

ISSUES Without violating the Due Process Clause of the Fourteenth Amendment, can the State of Washington require International Shoe to appear in its courts? Also without violating due process, can Washington require International Shoe to pay the state unemployment compensation tax?

HOLDINGS Yes, to both questions. The State of Washington's suit and assessment of the unemployment contribution do not violate the Fourteenth Amendment.

REASONING Excerpts from the opinion of Chief Justice Stone:

. . . The statutes in question set up a comprehensive scheme of unemployment compensation, the costs of which are defrayed by contributions required to be made by employers to a state unemployment compensation fund. The contributions are a specified percentage of the wages payable annually by each employer for his employees' services in the state. . . .

53 Stat. 1391, 26 U. S. C. § 1606 (a) provides that "No person required under a State law to make payments to an unemployment fund shall be relieved from compliance therewith on the ground that he is engaged in interstate or foreign commerce, or that the State law does not distinguish between employees engaged in interstate or foreign commerce and those engaged in intrastate commerce." It is no longer debatable that Congress, in the exercise of the commerce power, may authorize the states, in specified ways, to regulate interstate commerce or impose burdens upon it. . . .

Since the corporate personality is a fiction, although a fiction intended to be acted upon as though it were a fact . . . it is clear that unlike an individual its "presence" without, as well as within, the state of its origin can be manifested only by activities carried on in its behalf by those who are authorized to act for it. . . . [T]he terms "present" or "presence" are used merely to symbolize those activities of the corporation's agent within the state which courts will deem to be sufficient to satisfy the demands of due process. . . . Those demands may be met by such contacts of the corporation with the state of the forum as make it reasonable . . . to require the corporation to defend the particular suit which is brought there. An "estimate of the inconveniences" which would result to the corporation from a trial away from its "home" or principal place of business is relevant in this connection. . . . "Presence" in the state in this sense has never been doubted when the activities of the corporation there have not only been continuous and systematic, but also give rise to the liabilities sued on, even though no consent to be sued or authorization to an agent to accept service of process has been given. . . . Conversely it has been generally recognized that the casual presence of the corporate agent or even his conduct of single or isolated items of activities in a state in the corporation's behalf are not enough to subject it to suit on causes of action unconnected with the activities there. . . . To require the corporation in such circumstances to

defend the suit away from its home or other jurisdiction where it carries on more substantial activities has been thought to lay too great and unreasonable a burden on the corporation to comport with due process. . . .

It is evident that the criteria by which we mark the boundary line between those activities which justify the subjection of a corporation to suit, and those which do not, cannot be simply mechanical or quantitative. . . . Whether due process is satisfied must depend . . . upon the quality and nature of the activity in relation to the fair and orderly administration of the laws which it was the purpose of the due process clause to insure. That clause does not contemplate that a state may make binding a judgment *in personam* against an individual or corporate defendant with which the state has no contacts, ties, or relations. . . .

But to the extent that a corporation exercises the privilege of conducting activities within a state, it enjoys the benefits and protection of the laws of that state. The exercise of that privilege may give rise to obligations, and, so far as those obligations arise out of or are connected with the activities within the state, a procedure which requires the corporation to respond to a suit brought to enforce them can, in most instances, hardly be said to be undue. . . .

Applying these standards, the activities carried on in behalf of appellant in the State of Washington were neither irregular nor casual. They were systematic and continuous throughout the years in question. They resulted in a large volume of interstate business, in the course of which appellant received the benefits and protection of the laws of the state, including the right to resort to the courts for the enforcement of its rights. The obligation which is . . . sued upon arose out of those very activities. It is evident that these operations establish sufficient contacts or ties with the state of the forum to make it reasonable and just, according to our traditional conception of fair play and substantial justice, to permit the state to enforce the obligations which appellant has incurred there. Hence we cannot say that the maintenance of the present suit in the State of Washington involves an unreasonable or undue procedure.

We are likewise unable to conclude that the service of the process within the state upon an agent whose activities establish appellant's "presence" there was not sufficient notice of the suit, or that the suit was so unrelated to those activities as to make the agent an inappropriate vehicle for communicating the notice. It is enough that appellant has established such contacts with the state that the particular form of substituted service adopted there gives reasonable assurance that the notice will be actual. . . . Nor can we say that the mailing of the notice of suit to appellant by registered mail at its home office was not reasonably calculated to apprise appellant of the suit. . . .

[Washington] . . . imposes a tax on the privilege of employing appellant's salesmen within the state measured by a percentage of the wages . . . The right to employ labor has been deemed an appropriate subject of taxation in this country and England . . . And such a tax imposed upon the employer for unemployment benefits is within the constitutional power of the states. . . .

THE FEDERAL CONSTITUTION

The Constitution of the United States is a unique document for two reasons: It is the oldest written national constitution, and it was the first to include a government based on the concept of a separation of powers. A copy of the Constitution is available on the Web site for this text. The U.S. Constitution was created in reaction to the tyranny of English rule; it was intended to prevent many of the problems the founding fathers felt were present under the English government. England has an unwritten constitution and a system of government that tends to merge the legislative, executive, and judicial functions. In contrast, our written constitution established a governmental structure that has three separate "divisions" and a series of checks and balances whereby the power of one branch is offset, at least to some extent, by that of the others.

History taught the persons who founded the United States that all tyrants had at least two powers—the power of the purse and the power of the sword. Consequently, they separated these powers by placing the power of the purse (fiscal and monetary control) in the legislative branch of government and the power of the sword (control over armed forces) in the executive branch. The third branch of government, the judicial branch, does not have the formal, written power that exists in the other branches of government. It does, however, possess what may be the most important power, at least from a constitutional perspective. The judicial branch has the power to decide where and how the other two branches may properly exercise their powers. This power was "created" by the court itself in the landmark case, *Marbury v. Madison*,[1] and is called the power of judicial review. We shall discuss judicial review in greater detail later in this chapter.

Allocation of Power

Legislative Power   Article I of the Constitution creates a Congress consisting of two houses: the Senate and the House of Representatives. Congress has the power to levy and collect taxes, pay debts, and pass all laws with respect to certain enumerated powers, such as providing for the common defense and general welfare, regulating commerce, borrowing and coining money, establishing post offices and building highways, promoting science and the arts, and creating courts inferior to the U.S. Supreme Court.

Executive Power   The U.S. Constitution, Article II, creates the executive branch of government by establishing the offices of President and Vice-President. The President is the commander-in-chief of the armed forces of the United States. In addition, the President has the power to make treaties and to nominate ambassadors, judges, and other officers of the United States. The Senate must confirm all presidential appointments, as well as ratify all treaties. Without Senate confirmation, the appointee cannot take office, nor will any treaty become effective for the nation. The Vice-President is the President of the Senate and also serves for the President when or if the President is unable to serve.

Administrative Agencies, an Additional Executive Power   Administrative agencies also wield power under the executive branch of government, even though they are not discussed in the U.S. Constitution. These agencies are sometimes called a fourth branch of government. They are generally created by Congress through the passage of a statute, often at the request of the executive branch. The statute that creates the agency is called the *enabling statute* and it specifies the power and authority of the agency. Most federal agencies have the power, within their authority, to make rules and regulations that are similar to statutes, and also to decide controversies involving these rules and regulations. (These controversies are resolved in administrative hearings; they are not cases in the literal sense of the word.) The exact authority and the organization of the agencies vary greatly. Administrative agencies exist on the federal, state, and local levels. See Chapter 5 for a more detailed discussion of administrative agencies.

Judicial Power   Article III of the Constitution vests federal judicial power in one Supreme Court and in such other inferior courts as Congress may create. The President nominates all U.S. federal judges; moreover, if they are confirmed by the Senate, they are permitted to serve in office for the rest of their lives, as long as their behavior is "good."

The actual wording of Article III limits rather than expands judicial power. Under Section 2 of Article III, generally the federal courts may only hear and decide cases or controversies (claims brought before the court in regular proceedings to protect or enforce rights or to prevent or punish wrongs). Legally, *cases or controversies* can be defined as matters that are appropriate for judicial determination. For a matter to be appropriate for judicial determination,

[t]he controversy must be definite and concrete, touching the legal relations of parties having adverse legal interests. It must be a real and substantial controversy admitting of specific relief through a decree of a conclusive character, as distinguished from an opinion advising what the law would be upon a hypothetical state of facts.[2]

Constitutional law has evolved through precedents so that, today, the following are not considered to be a case or a controversy:

- *Advisory opinions* (Opinions rendered by a court at the request of the government or of an interested party that indicate how the court would rule on a matter should such litigation develop.[3])
- *Moot cases* (Cases in which a determination is sought on a matter which, when decided, cannot have any practical effect on the controversy; a question is moot when it presents no actual controversy or where the issues have ceased to exist.[4])
- Lack of *standing* (Standing means that the party has a sufficient stake in an otherwise justiciable controversy to obtain judicial resolution;[5] a party who does not have such a sufficient stake lacks standing.)
- *Political questions* (Questions that the court refuses to decide, due to their purely political character or because their determination would encroach on executive or legislative powers.[6])

The doctrine of the separation of powers requires that *federal* courts deal only with judicial matters. An *advisory opinion* is one in which the executive branch or an interested party refers a question to the judicial branch for a nonbinding opinion. However, that is not the purpose of the federal judicial system. Accordingly, whenever a member of the executive branch requires an advisory opinion, the question is referred to the justice department within the executive branch for an opinion from the attorney general. Under the U.S. federal system of government, the attorney general is the appropriate person to issue an advisory opinion. Contrary to the federal rule, some state courts are empowered to give advisory opinions. The International Court of Justice and the courts of a number of other nations also will issue advisory opinions.

The federal courts will hear only cases that are appropriate for a judicial solution. *Moot cases* are those cases in which the matter has already been resolved or those cases in which any attempt at a resolution would have no practical effect. Sometimes the "resolution" occurs through the passage of time or a change in circumstances. In the case of *DeFunis v. Odegaard,*[7] the Supreme Court stated that the question of whether a student should be admitted to a law school was a moot case because by the time the Court could have issued its opinion, the student would have been on the brink of graduation. The law school informed the Supreme Court that regardless of the outcome of the suit, the law school would award DeFunis a degree if he passed his final quarter of coursework. Accordingly, as an example of judicial efficiency, the Court chose not to write an opinion on the merits of the suit.

Only persons who can demonstrate that they have actually been harmed or injured have *standing* to sue. Courts will generally define standing as having a direct and immediate personal injury. Courts use standing as part of the Article III limitation of federal judicial power to decide cases and controversies. In addition, statutes may grant standing to sue. For example, if you saw a person punch someone in the nose, you would not have standing to sue the aggressor for *assault* (a threat to touch someone in an undesired manner) or *battery* (the unauthorized touching of another person without either legal justification or that person's consent); only the person who was hit would have standing to sue because he or she was the one who was injured.

Even though many political questions in our society involve real controversies, the doctrine of our courts is that courts will not hear them. Why? While a political question may be considered a very real controversy, it is not considered to be a *judicial question* (a question that is proper for a court to decide). This rule is based on the concept of *judicial restraint*, a judicial policy of refusing to hear and decide certain types of cases. For example, if a citizen asserts that a state is not based on a democratic form of government, that claim will not be heard in a U.S. federal court because it is a political question. Similarly, if a citizen thinks that our nation's foreign policy is incorrect, our

eClass 3.1 Management

PRODUCT SAFETY LAWS

Yousef read an article in a business publication that predicted which states would pass the strictest product safety laws in the next 12 months. The author of the article thought that a number of the laws being proposed would be more consumer-oriented, and hence less "business-friendly," than the current statutes in those states. Ani, Meg, and Yousef believe that their products are not likely to be affected by such statutes at this point in time. However, Yousef is still concerned about the long-term effect on the company that could be caused by the passage of additional consumer-friendly state legislation. He asks what you would advise the company to do. What will you tell him?

BUSINESS CONSIDERATIONS   What practical steps can a business take to avoid the impact of a new product safety law proposed in a state? What legal steps can a business take to avoid a proposed product safety law? Can the firm avoid the jurisdiction of the state's courts? How?

ETHICAL CONSIDERATIONS   Is it ethical for a business to attempt to avoid product safety laws? Since product safety laws are enacted to protect consumers, would it be ethical for a firm to attempt to discourage state legislation that might harm the firm while helping consumers?

courts cannot be used to debate the point because foreign policy is a political question. What constitutes a political question, however, is not always clear. For instance, is *legislative apportionment*—the ratio of legislative representation to constituents—a political question? Historically, the courts have said no.

Now that the four limits that constrain judicial power have been discussed, we will consider the one concept that has expanded judicial power. When you read the Constitution, the specific power of judicial review is not mentioned. That is because it is a court-created power. In 1803, the Chief Justice of the U.S. Supreme Court, John Marshall, created this doctrine of the law in the landmark case of *Marbury v. Madison*.[8] This power is based on an interpretation of the Constitution, which states that our courts may examine the actions of the legislative and executive branches of government to ascertain whether those actions conform to the Constitution. If they do not, the courts have the power to declare those actions unconstitutional and, therefore, unenforceable. Thus under this doctrine, the Supreme Court can declare an act of Congress invalid if the congressional act does not conform to the Constitution. Similarly, the Court can declare conduct by the President, or any other member of the Executive branch, invalid if the conduct conflicts with the Constitution. This concept of judicial power does not exist in England, where the parliament is supreme. Therefore, the branch of government, which has neither the power of the purse nor the power of the sword, has significant power because it can determine what action by the other branches is legal. Since 1803, the power of U.S. courts to judicially review all actions of

eClass 3.2 Management

HOW TO PROTECT eCLASS'S COPYRIGHT

Meg is very concerned that another firm will "steal" the proprietary information behind eAccounting and produce and sell similar software at a lower price. Although eClass holds a copyright, Meg knows that copyrights are not always upheld in court. Consequently, she would like to file a suit with the court to determine if the copyright will be upheld *before* a competitor duplicates it. She asks you how she should proceed. What advice will you give her?

BUSINESS CONSIDERATIONS   What effect does uncertainty about the validity of a copyright cause for a business? What can a business do to reduce the risk? What technique or techniques would be most effective? Are businesses more or less concerned about protecting their patents?

ETHICAL CONSIDERATIONS   Analyze the ethical perspective of any business that would attempt to "steal" eClass's copyright or technology. Is commercial or industrial espionage an ethical method of doing business?

the legislative and executive branches of government has gone unchallenged. It has become the cornerstone of our doctrine of the separation of powers. Furthermore, this power of the Supreme Court to invalidate legislation also extends to all state legislation because of the Supremacy Clause in the federal Constitution.

The Watergate scandal, remembered by many as a low point in American history, may be viewed as a high point with respect to the doctrine of judicial review. In 1974, President Nixon was ordered to produce the now-famous Watergate tapes for use in a federal prosecution. Nixon claimed executive privilege and refused the order to turn over the tapes to the federal prosecutor. The Supreme Court, in a unanimous opinion, denied Nixon's claim and ordered him to release the tapes. President Nixon complied with the order of the Supreme Court, thus ending a constitutional crisis. Subsequently, Nixon became the first—and so far, only—U.S. President to resign from office.

Role of Judges   Despite the robes, the title, or the trappings of office, judges are people, too. As a result, the personalities of individual judges and justices may very well affect their rulings in any given case. The jurisprudential views of the judges impact the rulings in particular cases and the precedents being set for a jurisdiction. [For example, there are numerous articles about how Justice Ruth Bader Ginsburg's work experiences and views affect her decisions.[9] The same is true of other judges and justices. Justice Clarence Thomas made some pointed observations from the bench during a case involving cross burning that reportedly changed the tone of the proceedings.[10]] Judges who favor judicial restraint believe that the judge's role is to make sure that a law is legal and constitutional. These judges believe that if there is something wrong with the legal system, judges should not correct it. Corrections should be left to the legislature. For example, in addressing the asbestos litigation, Justice Souter writes, "[T]his litigation defies customary judicial administration and calls for national legislation."[11] Judges who are activists believe that their role is to encourage social change: these judges often believe it is not necessary to wait for the legislature to address the issue. The impact of the U.S. Supreme Court justices is particularly strong. The current justices on the Supreme Court are Chief Justice John G. Roberts, Jr., and Justices Samuel Anthony Alito, Jr., Stephen G. Breyer, Ruth Bader Ginsburg, Elena Kagan, Anthony M. Kennedy, Antonin Scalia, Sonia Sotomayor, and Clarence Thomas.[12]

Original Constitution

The original Constitution, signed on September 17, 1787, contained a number of rights pertaining to individuals. Among these is the right of *habeas corpus. Habeas corpus* is the name given to a variety of writs issued to bring a party before a court or judge. The original act is the English statute of 31 Car. II, c.2; it has been amended in England and adopted throughout the United States.[13] In Latin, habeas corpus means, "You have the body."[14] This right may be used by all persons who have been deprived of their liberty. There are special forms of the writ (a *writ* is a writing issued by a court in the form of a letter ordering some designated activity); however, when the words "writ of habeas corpus" are used alone, the writ is addressed to the person who detains an individual. The writ commands that person to produce the individual in a court and to comply with any order by the court issuing the writ. This is probably the most common form of the writ.

Another right established by the Constitution is that Congress may pass no bills of attainder. A *bill of attainder* is a "legislative trial" whereby a person is judged a felon or worse by act of the legislature and not by a court of law.

Congress also may not enact *ex post facto* laws. An *ex post facto* law is a law passed after an occurrence or act, which retrospectively changes the legal consequences of such act. For example, if a business entered into a perfectly legal transaction in January, then Congress cannot declare that transaction illegal in a statute passed after January. (Of course, Congress *can* declare similar transactions illegal in the future.) As used in the Constitution, the prohibition on *ex post facto* laws only applies to criminal law. This prohibition includes laws that make an act a crime; make a crime into a more serious crime; change the punishment for a crime; or alter the legal rules of evidence for proving a crime.[15]

These are some of the most notable constitutional rights. However, other individual rights, such as trial by jury in most criminal cases, were also written into the original Constitution.

Amendments to the Constitution

Four years after the U.S. Constitution was signed, the first ten amendments were passed. These amendments, known as the Bill of Rights, were designed to ensure that certain individual rights were protected. For example, the first amendment provides that "Congress shall make no law respecting an establishment of religion, or prohibiting the free exercise thereof. . . ." The first amendment provides the basis for the separation of church and state. In all, 27 amendments to the Constitution have been passed. The amendments to the Constitution reflect the citizens' concerns about particular topics and reflect changes in the society. The Constitution itself serves as the "supreme law of the land" for U.S. society.

THE COURTS AND JURISDICTION

Jurisdiction is the power of a court to affect legal relationships. We will examine four aspects of jurisdiction:

1. *Subject matter jurisdiction* (The power of a court to hear certain kinds of legal questions.)
2. Jurisdiction over the persons or property
3. Concurrent versus exclusive jurisdiction
4. Venue

Subject Matter Jurisdiction

In our discussion of the Constitution, we said that the Supreme Court was limited to deciding cases and controversies. In addition, Article III of the Constitution defines the Supreme Court's *subject matter jurisdiction* as including all cases in law and equity arising under the Constitution, the statutes of the United States, and all treaties. The subject matter jurisdiction granted to the Supreme Court is extensive. A state juvenile court, on the other hand, is limited solely to hearing matters concerning children, provided that the case or controversy also arose within that state and under its laws. If an adult were brought before a juvenile court, the court would lack subject matter jurisdiction. Because it may decide only matters concerning people under 18 years of age, a juvenile court is an inappropriate court for a case involving an adult. Likewise, a federal bankruptcy court may not decide a criminal matter because its jurisdiction is limited to bankruptcy matters. Subject matter jurisdiction determines which court is the "right" court to hear a particular type of case or controversy. However, *any* court that is allowed to hear cases of a particular type would have subject matter jurisdiction over any such case filed with the court.

Jurisdiction over the Persons or Property

In addition to the appropriate subject matter jurisdiction, a court must also have jurisdiction over the persons or property whose rights, duties, or obligations the court will decide. Basically, three techniques exist for obtaining jurisdiction over persons or property—*in personam, in rem,* and *quasi in rem.* First we will discuss *in personam jurisdiction,* the authority of the court over the specific person or corporation that can properly be brought within the control of the court.

***In Personam* Jurisdiction**   Jurisdictional questions do not arise over the person of the plaintiff, who filed the lawsuit. The plaintiff chooses to file the suit in a particular court and so implicitly consents to the court's jurisdiction. It is inconsistent to allow the plaintiff to file the suit and then complain that the same court lacks jurisdiction over him or her.

The *defendant* (the person who answers a lawsuit), however, does not choose the court. Often, if the defendant were given a choice, he or she would choose not to have any trial. If a trial *must* take place, he or she might well prefer to have it held elsewhere. The question, then, is how to get *in personam jurisdiction,* jurisdiction over the person, of the defendant. How or why can the court legally compel the defendant to attend, or properly enter a default judgment against the defendant who refuses to attend the trial? One technique is if the defendant consents to the court's jurisdiction. Consent can occur by merely responding to a lawsuit that has been filed. It can occur either by express consent or by failure to raise the issue of jurisdiction and, instead, responding to the legal questions. Consent can also be given prior to the lawsuit. This is commonly accomplished by a contract clause or by appointment of an agent to accept *service of process.* (The service of process is the delivery of a legal notice to inform the person served of the nature of the legal dispute.) A corporation is considered to have given consent when it registers with a state as a *foreign corporation* (a corporation that had its articles of incorporation approved in another state) and asks permission to conduct business in a state. Courts have concluded that a corporation that engages in business as a foreign corporation without the required registration has given implied consent.

A court will also have jurisdiction over a defendant who is physically present in the state when he or she is served with process. This would include a person who is on a trip to the state or even merely passing through the state on his or her way to another destination. Courts will generally decide that there is no jurisdiction over a defendant who is tricked into entering the state by the plaintiff. A corporation is physically present in a state in which it is *doing business.* (Doing business is also used as the basis of implied consent by some states.) For example, a corporation is doing business in a state in which it has stores, offices, warehouses, and regular employees. The courts have decided numerous cases about what constitutes doing business and have devised various tests for recognizing doing business. Two of these tests are: (1) whether the corporation's activities were single, isolated transactions or continuous and substantial activities; or (2) whether the corporation's agents were only soliciting offers in the state or were engaged in additional activities.

In the Classic Case of *International Shoe Co. v. State of Washington,*[16] the U.S. Supreme Court concluded that before a defendant is required to appear in a state court, the defendant must have certain *minimum contacts* with the state. Otherwise, the suit would offend traditional concepts of fair play and substantial justice. This case created a constitutional test for *in personam* jurisdiction. The defendant in this case was a corporation, but the ruling appears to apply to other business entities and individuals as well.

In personam jurisdiction also exists in the state of domicile. Domicile is a complicated legal doctrine (and most of its complexity is outside the scope of this text). Human beings have one and only one domicile. A person may choose his or her domicile or the law may assign it. *Domicile* is usually a person's home, the place where he or she is physically present and where he or she intends to remain for the time being. Domicile does *not* require that a person live in a state for a certain minimum period of time. Consequently, domicile contrasts with residency statutes that require, for example, a person to live in a state for a set period of time before voting in the state or being eligible for in-state tuition at its colleges and universities.

Suppose that both the plaintiff and the defendant are domiciliaries of Alaska; Alaska has jurisdiction over them. On the other hand, if the plaintiff is a domiciliary of Alaska but the defendant is a domiciliary of Oregon, Alaska *may* not have proper jurisdiction over the defendant. If the plaintiff wants to sue the defendant in a state court, the plaintiff might need to go to Oregon and sue the defendant there, since a *defendant's* state of domicile is almost always an appropriate forum. (*Forum* is the court that is or will be conducting the trial.) Potential jurisdiction in a federal court is discussed later in this chapter.

Corporations are domiciled in the state in which they are incorporated. They are also considered to be domiciled in the state where they have their corporate head-quarters, if this is a different state. A corporation may be sued where it is domiciled.

A corporation is *also* subject to *in personam* jurisdiction in all states in which the corporation does business because it is physically present there.

Most states have laws called *long-arm statutes*. The purpose of these statutes is to permit the state to exercise *in personam* jurisdiction when ordinarily this would not be possible. A common type of long-arm statute permits a state to exercise authority over a person who drives on its roads. This type of long-arm statute is also called a nonresident motorist statute. Suppose a resident of Nebraska drives a car on the roads of Kansas and injures a resident of Kansas. In that situation, the courts of Kansas would have *in personam* jurisdiction over the resident of Nebraska, because it would be unfair to require the resident of Kansas to go to Nebraska to sue. Other states have enacted much broader long-arm statutes. For example, Illinois enacted a statute that listed certain acts that would confer jurisdiction, if done in the state. California and Texas,[17] on the other hand, enacted long-arm statutes that provide for *in personam* jurisdiction whenever it complies with the U.S. Constitution. As with other matters under the control of the states, there is great variation among long-arm statutes.

The courts are facing a new problem in resolving whether *in personam* jurisdiction exists in cases involving the Internet. As Internet usage grows and as e-commerce expands, this area will attract a great deal of the attention of courts across the world. U.S. courts are relying on the precedent established by *International Shoe* and are applying the concepts from that case to Internet cases by analogy. One of the leading Internet cases is *Zippo Manufacturing Co. v. Zippo Dot Com, Inc.*,[18] which involved a dispute over the ownership of an Internet domain name. The District Court applied the criteria set out in *International Shoe* to determine if the defendant had "specific contacts" with Pennsylvania. It reformulated the criteria as follows:

> A three-pronged test has emerged for determining whether the exercise of specific personal jurisdiction over a non-resident defendant is appropriate: (1) the defendant must have sufficient "minimum contacts" with the forum state, (2) the claim asserted against the defendant must arise out of those contacts, and (3) the exercise of jurisdiction must be reasonable.[19]

From this the court decided that if a person enters into contracts with residents of another jurisdiction, and those contracts involve the knowing and repeated transmission of computer files over the Internet, personal jurisdiction over the person in that other jurisdiction would be proper. However, if a person simply posts information on an Internet Web site, there are not sufficient contacts with any "foreign" jurisdictions to permit the exercise of personal jurisdiction over the person posting the information. Such passive Web sites do no more than make information available. Between these two extremes lies the troublesome area. In this area a person might be involved with an interactive Web site that allows for the exchange of information between the person and the host computer. In these situations, personal jurisdiction will depend on the level of interaction and also on whether the exchange of information is commercial in nature.[20]

There are still a number of questions to be answered in this area. The ultimate resolution of some of these issues is likely to have a major impact on the future growth and development of e-commerce.

***In Rem* Jurisdiction**   If a state cannot obtain *in personam* jurisdiction on any of these grounds, another approach—called *in rem* jurisdiction—can be used. *In rem jurisdiction* is when the court has authority over property or status of the defendant that is located within the control of the court. *In rem* jurisdiction allows the state to exercise its authority over something such as land or a marital domicile within its

Exhibit 3.1

Methods to Obtain Jurisdiction over the Defendant

Type of Jurisdiction	Type of Judgment	Differences Between Individual and Corporate Defendants	
		Individual	*Corporation*
In personam			
Authority over a specific person or corporation within the control of the state. Authority may derive from consent, domicile, physical presence, or long-arm statutes.	Affects the person.	**Consent** Defendant consents to personal jurisdiction; consent can occur before or after a suit has begun. **Domicile** Defendant has a residence—usually a home—at which he or she is/has been physically present and intends to remain for the time being; individuals have only one domicile.[a] **Physical Presence** Defendant is served by hand while he or she is within the geographic boundaries of the state.[b]	**Consent** A corporation consents when it registers as a foreign corporation with the state.[c] **Domicile** A corporation is incorporated (has filed its articles of incorporation with the state) and/or has its corporate headquarters in the state. **Physical Presence** A corporation is recognized as "doing business" in the state.
In rem			
Authority over property or status within the control of the state. Settles ownership interests in property or status for all persons.	Affects the property or status.	The rules for individuals and corporations are basically the same.	

Exhibit 3.1 Continued

Type of Jurisdiction	Type of Judgment	Differences Between Individual and Corporate Defendants
Quasi in rem Authority obtained through property under the control of the state. Settles issues of ownership, possession, or use of property; or settles personal disputes unrelated to the property.	Affects the rights of specific people to property.[d]	The rules for individuals and corporations are basically the same.

[a] Some people are not capable of selecting domiciles for themselves; thus, they have domiciles determined for them by legal rules (for example, minors).

[b] Most states will decline to exercise jurisdiction if the defendant is brought into the state by force or enticed into the state by fraud.

[c] If the corporation fails to register, the court may imply consent from the act of doing business in the state. Generally, implied consent is limited to cases arising from the actual doing of business in the state.

[d] A successful plaintiff is limited to the value of the property.

boundaries. The court's judgment will affect everyone's rights in that "thing." It does not impose a personal obligation on the defendant. For example, if an individual or a corporation has real property in one state but resides in another, the state where the property is located can exercise *in rem* jurisdiction over the property in a *condemnation proceeding* (court proceeding to take property for public use or declare property forfeited).

***Quasi in Rem* Jurisdiction**   In this type of jurisdiction, the court determines the rights of particular persons to specific property. (It is distinct from *in rem* jurisdiction because a court with *in rem* jurisdiction will determine the rights of all persons in the thing. It differs from *in personam* jurisdiction because there is no authority over the person of the defendant.) *Quasi in rem* jurisdiction is authority obtained through property under the control of the court. The court obtains control of the property through one of two methods. In one, the property is within the jurisdiction of the court, and the plaintiff wishes to resolve issues of ownership, possession, or use of the property—for example, to foreclose a mortgage. In the second method, the dispute does not concern the property, but is personal to the plaintiff, such as a breach of contract or the commission of a tort. Jurisdiction will exist if the plaintiff can locate the defendant's property within the state and bring it before the court by *attachment* (seizure of the defendant's property) or *garnishment* (procedure to obtain possession of the defendant's property when it is in the custody of another person). Limitations exist on when attachment or garnishment is allowed. When the plaintiff's suit is successful, the recovery is limited to the value of the property. Exhibit 3.1 summarizes the techniques for obtaining jurisdiction over the defendant.

Service of Process   In cases of either *in personam, in rem*, or *quasi in rem* jurisdiction, there must be proper service of process on the defendant to inform him or her of the lawsuit. Proper service of process includes *actual notice*, in which one is personally served by an officer of the court or is mailed service by registered mail. If actual notice cannot be obtained after reasonable attempts to do so, notice may be served publicly by a posting on the property or in a newspaper. This is called *constructive service*. Proper notice may also include service at the office of the state's secretary of state. For example, when an out-of-state corporation registers in Delaware, the state may specify that process may be served on Delaware's secretary of state.

Concurrent versus Exclusive Jurisdiction

In certain cases, more than one court may exercise jurisdiction. If so, it is called *concurrent jurisdiction*. On the other hand, some subjects can be heard only by a particular court; this is called *exclusive jurisdiction*. Examples of exclusive jurisdiction in the federal courts are suits in which the United States is a party or suits that involve some areas of admiralty law, bankruptcy, copyright, federal crimes, and patent cases. Exhibit 3.2 illustrates the jurisdictional domains of federal and state courts.

Exhibit 3.2

A Comparison of Federal and State Court Jurisdiction

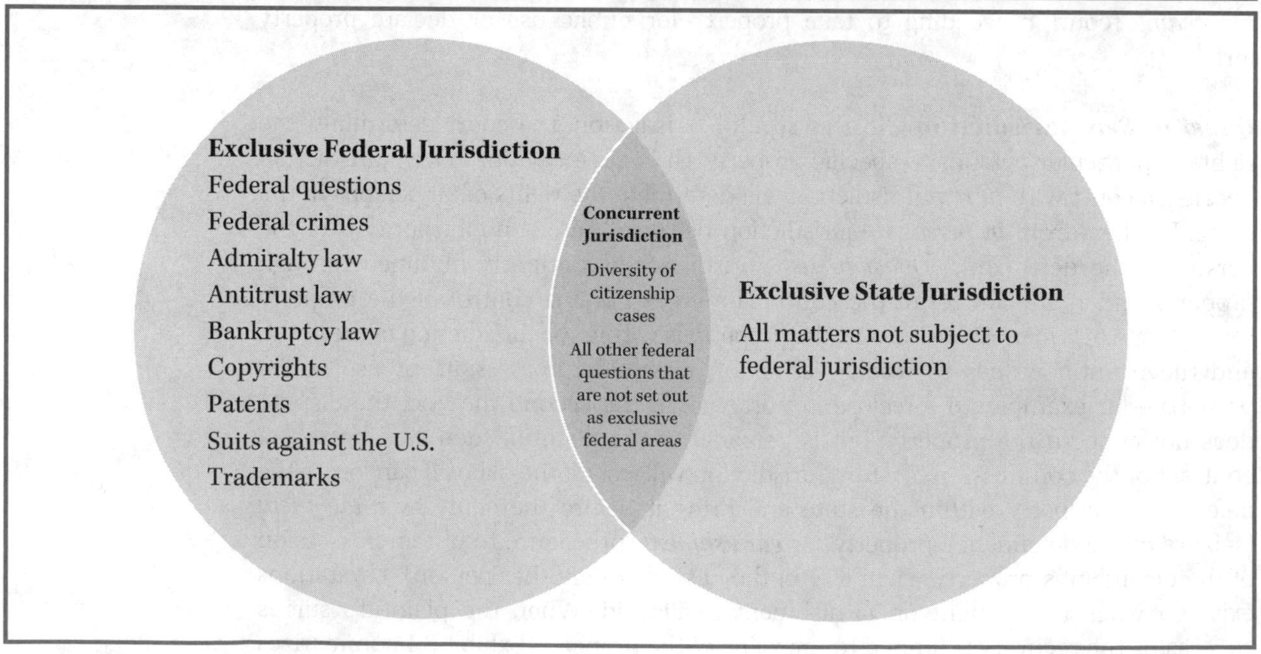

Exclusive Federal Jurisdiction
Federal questions
Federal crimes
Admiralty law
Antitrust law
Bankruptcy law
Copyrights
Patents
Suits against the U.S.
Trademarks

Concurrent Jurisdiction

Diversity of citizenship cases

All other federal questions that are not set out as exclusive federal areas

Exclusive State Jurisdiction

All matters not subject to federal jurisdiction

Venue

Once a court establishes that it has proper jurisdiction over the subject matter and the person, it must then ascertain whether proper venue exists. *Venue* literally means "neighborhood." In a legal sense, however, it means the proper geographical area or district where a suit can be brought. In state practice, it is usually a question of which county is appropriate. In federal practice, the question of venue is which federal judicial district is the appropriate one. In state practice, if both the plaintiff and the defendant are residents of the same state, *in personam* jurisdiction exists in that state's courts. But which of the state courts is best situated to hear the case? For example, venue could be proper in the area where an incident, such as an automobile accident, occurred. The residence of the defendant also may be considered in determining the proper venue. More than one court may have proper venue. The laws of each state spell out in great detail the appropriate courts that would have venue.

Choice of Laws

Choice of laws is the selection of which jurisdiction's laws should be applied to a particular incident; that is, what laws should govern the subject before the court. Although it is also called "conflict of laws," legal scholars argue that choice of laws is the more appropriate title. Another complication in this area is that the court will use choice of laws rules to determine the *substantive laws* (the law that creates, defines, and regulates rights) that should be applied to the dispute; however, the forum court will use its own procedural laws. (*Procedural law* is the method of enforcing rights or obtaining redress for the violation of rights). The following example is included to illustrate the complexity and importance of choice of laws issues. We will not attempt to resolve this example in this text because it is clearly too complex for an undergraduate course in the law of business, and the actual answer is likely to depend on where the case is filed. In other words the courts would probably disagree.

> *Julia, a domiciliary of Massachusetts, entered into a contract with Karen, a domiciliary of Vermont, while they both were in Connecticut. The contract concerned goods that were located in Maine and were to be shipped to New York. While the goods were in transit, they were stopped and taken by Dawn, a domiciliary of New Hampshire, who was a creditor of Julia. This situation raises many legal questions. What should Karen do to get the goods? In which state should the lawsuit be filed? And, specifically with reference to the choice of laws doctrine: What law should the court apply—the law of Massachusetts, Vermont, Connecticut, Maine, New York, or New Hampshire? It could be that Karen would win if the law of Massachusetts, Connecticut, or New York were applied but would lose if the law of Vermont, Maine, or New Hampshire were applied. Hence, choice of laws issues are quite important.*

Choice of laws issues are sometimes resolved by statutes that indicate which law should be applied. In business transactions, these issues may also be resolved by the parties' specifying which state (or national) law should apply. The courts generally will use the parties' selection as long as there is a reasonable relationship between the state selected and the transaction.

You need to be aware of the complexity of this matter and a good, simple solution to the problem—that is, stating in the written contract that if there should be any dispute concerning the contract, the laws of a particular state will apply. This is a form of *preventive law* and it is generally effective.

Federal Courts

In addition to the general grounds discussed previously with respect to jurisdiction, two specific grounds exist for federal jurisdiction: (1) federal question; and (2) diversity of citizenship *plus* amount in controversy.

Federal Question Jurisdiction   Federal question jurisdiction derives directly from Article III of the Constitution. *Federal questions* are questions that pertain to the federal Constitution, statutes of the United States, and treaties of the United States. Also included, today, are all regulations of federal administrative agencies. For example, if a person is denied a job because of race, that will raise a federal question because such discrimination raises concerns about violations of the Constitution, federal statutes, and federal regulations. If a publishing company brings an action asserting that another publishing company has infringed its copyright, it raises a federal question because copyright is both a constitutional and a statutory question. States do not have the right to issue copyrights, and state courts do not have the subject matter jurisdiction to decide copyright cases.

Diversity of Citizenship Jurisdiction   Federal question jurisdiction is not necessary when diversity of citizenship is present and vice versa. *Diversity of citizenship* exists when the plaintiff is a citizen of one state and the defendant is a citizen of another; it also exists when one party is a foreign country and the other is a citizen of a state. The primary reason underlying diversity jurisdiction is that if a citizen of Hawaii must file suit in Iowa in order to obtain jurisdiction over a citizen of Iowa, it is possible that the court of Iowa might favor its citizen over the citizen of Hawaii. In that case, the plaintiff can file suit in federal court if the plaintiff is worried about such potential favoritism.

When federal jurisdiction is based on diversity of citizenship, a further requirement exists: a *minimum amount* in question. Title 28, § 1332(a) of the United States Code requires that the amount in question must exceed $75,000 in diversity cases. In contrast, cases in which the federal courts have exclusive jurisdiction generally do not require a minimum amount in controversy. The purpose behind the amount is to prevent federal courts from dealing with trifles and to reduce the caseload in federal courts.

Exhibit 3.3

The Two Grounds for Federal Jurisdiction

For Federal Jurisdiction the Case Must Involve	
Either	*Or*
Federal Question The controlling law involves a federal statute, rule, or regulation; an issue of U.S. constitutional law; or a treaty. The case involves a consul or ambassador as a party. The case involves maritime or admiralty law. The United States is a party to the action. The case is between two or more states.	**Diversity of Citizenship** Parties on one side of the controversy are citizens of a different state than the parties on the other side. *and* **A Minimum Amount in Controversy (Excluding Costs and Interest)** The plaintiff must sue for more than $75,000.

Most federal cases are highly complex, and the precise amount is a matter that is often unknown when the lawsuit is filed. Accordingly, the courts look to the amount the plaintiff, acting in good faith, has determined to be in dispute. This is called the *plaintiff viewpoint rule.*

Another aspect of diversity jurisdiction is called complete diversity. *Complete diversity* requires that no plaintiff be a citizen of the same state as any of the defendants. This rule, however, poses complex problems when there are multiple plaintiffs and/or defendants. Complete diversity also prohibits having an alien plaintiff and an alien defendant in the same suit, even when the aliens are from different countries. (An *alien* is a person or corporation belonging to another country.)

Exhibit 3.3 depicts the two grounds for federal jurisdiction.

Specialized Courts

Congress has, from time to time, created courts of *limited* jurisdiction. At present, these courts include the claims court, the court of military appeals, the court of international trade, and the tax court. Congress has created *federal district courts* (trial courts in the federal court system) in every state. Each state has at least one; some states have many. Rhode Island, for example, has one district court, and Texas has four. The courts contained in each district constitute the general trial courts of the federal system.

All of the district courts are grouped into circuits. Currently there are 13 circuits. Each circuit has a court of appeals, which hears appeals from the trial courts. Courts of appeal do not retry the case; rather, they review the record to determine whether the

eClass 3.3 Management/Marketing

LAWSUIT AGAINST A SUPPLIER

Ani, Meg, and Yousef purchased a license for software from MicroSources, a California firm located in Silicon Valley. Assume that eClass is an Ohio corporation. eClass was unaware that the program was defective and used it in the eAccounting software. This caused the eAccounting software to malfunction. This software was sold to customers directly and through retail outlets. Customers have been calling eClass and complaining about the eAccounting program. This situation has also caused an increase in customer service calls. Ani, Meg, and Yousef are concerned about the short- and long-term effects on the company's finances and reputation. They ask you what the company should do. What will you tell them?

BUSINESS CONSIDERATIONS What can a business do to reduce the chance of purchasing defective supplies and software? Can eClass sue the software firm? In what court(s) could the suit be filed? What additional information will be necessary and why? Would filing the suit improve or harm eClass's reputation?

ETHICAL CONSIDERATIONS What should eClass do to protect its reputation? Are there any ethical restrictions on what eClass does to protect its reputation?

trial court made errors of law. Generally, a panel of three judges from the circuit hears appeals. Decisions of the court of appeals establish precedents for all district courts in the circuit. For the most part, the decisions of these *circuit courts of appeals* are final. In a very few cases, the parties can appeal to the U.S. Supreme Court.

The 13 federal judicial circuits and their seats are: First: Boston, Massachusetts; Second: New York, New York; Third: Philadelphia, Pennsylvania; Fourth: Richmond, Virginia; Fifth: New Orleans, Louisiana; Sixth: Cincinnati, Ohio; Seventh: Chicago, Illinois; Eighth: St. Louis, Missouri; Ninth: San Francisco, California; Tenth: Denver, Colorado; Eleventh: Atlanta, Georgia; Twelfth: District of Columbia, Washington, D.C.; Thirteenth: Federal Circuit, Washington, D.C. For details on the 13 federal judicial circuits, see Exhibit 3.4.

The *Supreme Court* sits at the apex of the U.S. judicial system. It is the only court created by the Constitution. The Constitution does not specify the number of judges, called justices, on the Supreme Court. The Supreme Court is led by the Chief Justice and it currently has 8 associate justices. [21] The justices are nominated by the President and confirmed by the Senate, and they serve for life. All federal judges—except those appointed to serve in the specialized courts—serve for life.

Exhibit 3.4

The Thirteen Federal Judicial Circuits

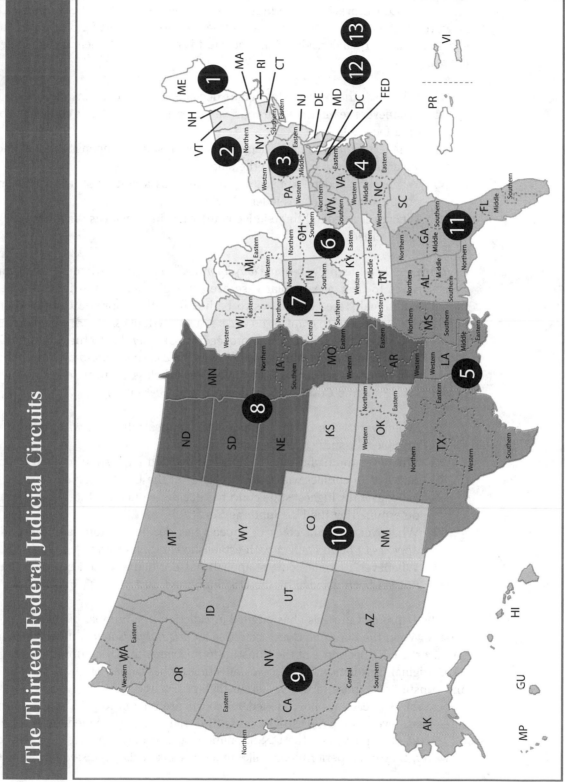

As mentioned previously, certain cases may be appealed to the Supreme Court. However, the court may affirm a case routinely without permitting oral arguments or giving the case formal consideration. The court is more likely to hear a case under the following conditions:

- Whenever the highest state court declares a federal law invalid;
- Whenever the highest state court validates a state law that is challenged based on a federal law;
- Whenever a federal court declares a federal statute unconstitutional and the government was a party to the suit;
- Whenever a federal appellate court declares a state statute invalid on the grounds that it violates federal law; and
- Whenever a federal three-judge court rules in a civil case involving an equitable remedy.

Certiorari   This means "*to be more fully informed*" and is used whenever the Supreme Court desires to hear a particular case even though there is no right of appeal. It permits additional state court cases to be heard by the Supreme Court. When the Supreme Court decides to grant *certiorari*, it issues a writ of *certiorari*, which orders the lower court to certify a record of the proceedings and send it to the Supreme Court. A minimum of four Justices must agree to hear the case on *certiorari*. Other than that requirement there are no hard-and-fast rules. Nevertheless, there are certain situations in which the Supreme Court is more likely to grant *certiorari:*

- Whenever two or more circuit courts of appeals disagree with respect to the same legal issue;
- Whenever the highest state court has decided a question in such a manner that it is in conflict with prior decisions of the U.S. Supreme Court;
- Whenever the highest state court has decided a question that has not yet been determined by the U.S. Supreme Court;
- Whenever a circuit court of appeals has decided a state law question that appears to be in conflict with established state law; and
- Whenever a circuit court of appeals has decided a federal question that has not yet been decided by the U.S. Supreme Court.

The Supreme Court also has original jurisdiction in a number of cases or controversies. When the Supreme Court exercises its *original jurisdiction* it serves as a trial court. Article III, Section 2 of the Constitution declares that the Supreme Court shall have original jurisdiction "In all cases affecting ambassadors, other public ministers and consuls, and those in which a state shall be a party."

Exhibit 3.5 describes how the federal courts are related to each other. There are three basic levels, the U.S. District Courts (the trial courts in the federal system), the U.S. Court of Appeals, and the U.S. Supreme Court. Federal agencies are not courts. However, they often perform court-like functions, also called *quasi-judicial* functions.

Exhibit 3.5

The Federal Judicial System

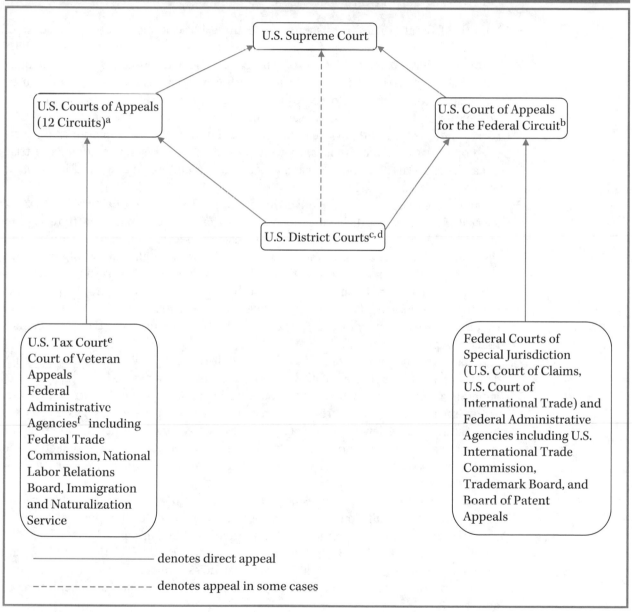

———————— denotes direct appeal

– – – – – – – – – – denotes appeal in some cases

[a] Includes D.C. Circuit.
[b] Takes appeals from some specialized courts.
[c] Bankruptcy courts exist as units of the district courts.
[d] Appeals from some federal agencies go to the U.S. District Courts.
[e] In some cases, there is Supreme Court review.
[f] Administrative agencies perform courtlike functions; however, they are not courts.

They are shown on the Exhibit to illustrate the appeal "path" from the agency to the court system.

State Courts

Like the federal system, most states have three basic levels: trial courts, court of appeals, and a supreme court. The names of the courts vary from state to state. States also have *inferior trial* courts. These may include municipal courts, juvenile courts, domestic relations courts, traffic courts, small claims courts, probate courts, and justice courts presided over by justices of the peace. (Historically, justices of the peace were not required to be lawyers. Many states have changed their rules and now require new justices of the peace to be lawyers.) For the most part, inferior trial courts are not *courts of record*—that is, there is no record or transcript made of the trial. In cases of appeals from their decisions, there is a *trial de novo,* "a new trial," in a regular trial court.

The more significant cases involving matters of state law originate in *courts of general jurisdiction* (courts having the judicial power to hear all matters with respect to state law). In some jurisdictions, two courts exist at this level. One court is charged with resolving all questions of law and the other with resolving all matters of equity. An example of a question of law is a suit seeking money damages. Most business law cases fall into this category. Equity suits, on the other hand, are those where the plaintiff is seeking a special remedy, such as an *injunction* (a writ issued by the court of equity ordering a person to do or not do a specified act), because monetary damages will not make the plaintiff "whole."

Each state has at least one *court of appeals.* It is usually called the supreme court. There are exceptions. In New York State, for example, the "Supreme Court" is a court of general trial jurisdiction, whereas the Court of Appeals is the highest court in the state. Sometimes intermediate courts of appeals also exist, as in the federal system. These appellate courts review the trial court record to determine whether the lower court made any errors of law. Appellate courts do not usually review decisions of facts made by the lower court. Some appellate courts hold trials *de novo*, which are exceptions to this general rule.

An example of a case history is *Bennis v. Michigan.*[22] It was originally decided by the Wayne County Circuit Court, then appealed (in this order) to the Michigan Court of Appeals, the Michigan Supreme Court, and then the U.S. Supreme Court.

Exhibit 3.6 describes a typical state system and its interrelationship with the federal system. State agencies, like federal agencies, are not courts; a person can appeal an unfavorable agency decision to the intermediate court of appeal in most states.

Exhibit 3.6

The Typical State Judicial System[a]

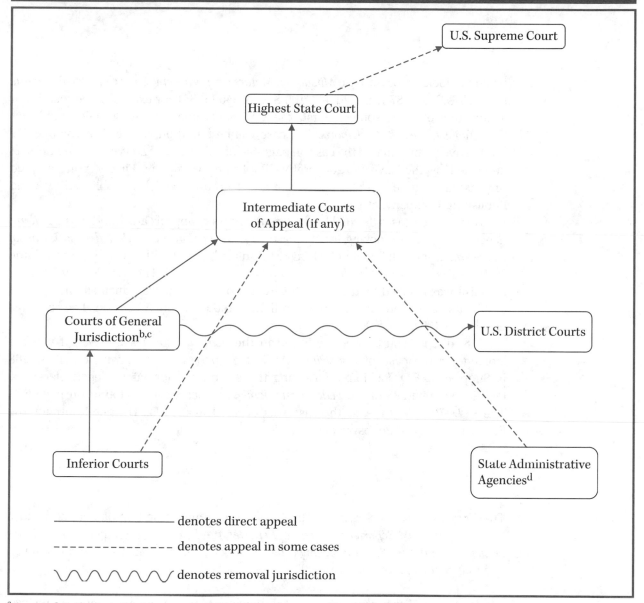

[a] As noted in the text, there is great variation among the states. The titles of the courts vary from state to state.
[b] The state trial courts may be divided into divisions, for example, the civil division, the criminal division, family court.
[c] Removal jurisdiction generally is exercised when the defendant asks that the case filed in one court be moved to the other court.
[d] Administrative agencies perform some courtlike functions; however, they are not courts.

HOW TO FIND THE LAW

We have already referred to some legal cases in this and previous chapters. Other cases will be cited in succeeding chapters. If you want to go to the library and read these or other cases in their entirety, you will need to know how to find the law.

Federal Court Cases

If you are looking for the case *Mitsubishi Motors Corporation v. Soler Chrysler-Plymouth, Inc.*, 473 U.S. 614, 87 L. Ed. 2d 444, 105 S. Ct. 3346 (1985), for example, you will find it in any one of three sources. First, the U.S. Government Printing Office publishes the official *United States Reports*. The case will be found on page 614 of volume 473. Alternatively, you can find the case on page 444 of volume 87 of *Lawyers Edition, Second*, published by the Lawyers Cooperative Publishing Company. Finally, you can find the case in volume 105 of the *Supreme Court Reporter*, which is published by West Publishing Company, at page 3346.

All reported cases decided by the circuit courts of appeals are found in the *Federal Reporter*. If you are looking for the case of *Johnson Controls v. United Association of Journeymen*, you will find it at 39 F.3d 821 (7th Cir. 1994). In other words, go to volume 39 of the *Federal Reporter, Third Series*, and turn to page 821. The *(7th Cir. 1994)* means the case was decided by the Seventh Circuit Court of Appeals, which sits in Chicago and hears cases from district courts in Illinois, Indiana, and Wisconsin. The case was decided in 1994.

U.S. district court cases are found in the *Federal Supplement Series*. If you are looking for the case of *Hoeflich v. William S. Merrell Co.*, you will find it at 288 F. Supp. 659 (E.D. Pa. 1968). Following the established format for legal references, look for volume 288 of the *Federal Supplement;* the case will be found on page 659. The *(E.D. Pa. 1968)* means the case was decided in the U.S. District Court for the Eastern District of Pennsylvania in 1968.

State Court Cases

The *National Reporter System* is published by West Publishing Company and includes the *Supreme Court Reporter*, the *Federal Reporter*, the *Federal Supplement, Federal Rules Decisions*, and the *Bankruptcy Reporter*. The reporter system also contains seven regional reporters for state cases. They are as follows:

1. *Atlantic Reporter*—Connecticut, Delaware, Maine, Maryland, New Hampshire, New Jersey, Pennsylvania, Rhode Island, Vermont, and the District of Columbia Municipal Court of Appeals

2. *Northeastern Reporter*—Illinois, Indiana, Massachusetts, New York, and Ohio
3. *Northwestern Reporter*—Iowa, Michigan, Minnesota, Nebraska, North Dakota, South Dakota, and Wisconsin
4. *Pacific Reporter*—Alaska, Arizona, California, Colorado, Hawaii, Idaho, Kansas, Montana, Nevada, New Mexico, Oklahoma, Oregon, Utah, Washington, and Wyoming
5. *Southeastern Reporter*—Georgia, North Carolina, South Carolina, Virginia, and West Virginia
6. *Southwestern Reporter*—Arkansas, Kentucky, Missouri, Tennessee, and Texas
7. *Southern Reporter*—Alabama, Florida, Louisiana, and Mississippi

These reporters contain most of the reported cases at the state supreme court and appellate court levels. Some significant trial court decisions are also included. Decisions of inferior courts are not included. The *National Reporter System* also includes the *Military Justice Reporter* and separate state reporters such as the *New York Supplement*, the *California Reporter*, and *Illinois Decisions*.

States generally also have their own system for publishing cases independent of the *National Reporter System*.

Computerized Legal Research

Legal research has entered the computer age. Two systems devoted to legal research are available—Lexis (part of Lexis/Nexis) and Westlaw. The techniques are similar, although the particular computer commands vary. Both systems allow you to indicate what material you wish to search and to enter key words for search terms. If your search terms are not appropriate or are too broad, you may not locate the desired material. Historical cases may not have been added to the data banks, but recent cases and articles generally are available. Manuals and handbooks specify which material can be retrieved from the system, including the years that are in the database.

There are also a number of sites on the World Wide Web that contain articles on statutory law, court cases, and government activity. Some of these sites are highlighted on the Web site for this text. Web sites can be established without much restriction, so care and patience are necessary. Some of the sites change addresses or stop operating. Consequently, the Web addresses may become dated. If you have a link that is outdated (no longer connects to the article or case indicated), return to the root Web site and begin your search from that point. Search engines like Yahoo can also be used to locate legal material. When conducting research on the Web, also remember that the information may not be reliable.

Contemporary Case

ELK GROVE UNIFIED SCHOOL DISTRICT v. NEWDOW

**542 U.S. 1, 124 S. Ct. 2301, 2004 U.S.
LEXIS 4178 (2004)**

The U.S. Supreme Court denied a rehearing in Elk Grove Unified School District v. Newdow, 542 U.S. 961, 125 S. Ct. 21, 2004 U.S. LEXIS 4886 (U.S., Aug. 23, 2004)

FACTS In the midst of World War II, Congress adopted the Pledge of Allegiance. Congress amended the Pledge 12 years later when it added the words "under God." Under California law, "every public elementary school" must begin each day with "appropriate patriotic exercises." Reciting the Pledge satisfies this requirement. The Elk Grove Unified School District satisfies the law by requiring each elementary school class to recite the Pledge. The School District permits students who object on religious grounds to abstain from the recitation.

Michael A. Newdow is an atheist whose daughter attended elementary school in the Elk Grove Unified School District. Each day the students say the Pledge. Because the Pledge contains the words "under God," Newdow objected on First Amendment grounds. Sandra Banning is the girl's mother. Although there are a number of custody orders, they give the mother the right to make decisions for her daughter if she and Newdow disagree. According to Banning, her daughter is a Christian who believes in God and has no objection either to reciting or hearing others recite the Pledge of Allegiance or to its reference to God.

ISSUE Did the noncustodial father have standing to raise the issue?

HOLDING No, the father did not have standing to raise the issue.

REASONING Excerpts from the opinion of Justice Stevens:

... "In essence the question of standing is whether the litigant is entitled to have the court decide the merits of the dispute". ... Even in cases concededly within our jurisdiction under Article III, we abide by "a series of rules under which [we have] avoided passing upon a large part of all the constitutional questions pressed upon [us] for decision." ... Always we must balance "the heavy obligation to exercise jurisdiction," ... against the "deeply rooted" commitment "not to pass on questions of constitutionality" unless adjudication of the constitutional issue is necessary. ... [O]ur standing jurisprudence contains two strands: Article III standing, which enforces the Constitution's case-or-controversy requirement ...; and prudential standing, which embodies "judicially self-imposed limits on the exercise of federal jurisdiction". ... The Article III limitations are familiar: The plaintiff must show that the conduct of which he complains has caused him to suffer an "injury in fact" that a favorable judgment will redress. ... [P]rudential standing encompasses "the general prohibition on a litigant's raising another person's legal rights, the rule barring adjudication of generalized grievances more appropriately addressed in the representative branches, and the requirement that a plaintiff's complaint fall within the zone of interests protected by the law invoked." ... "Without such limitations ... courts would be called upon to decide abstract questions of wide public significance even though other governmental institutions may be more competent to address the questions and even though judicial intervention may be unnecessary to protect individual rights." ...

One of the principal areas in which this Court has ... declined to intervene is the realm of domestic relations. ... "[T]he whole subject of the domestic relations of husband and wife, parent and child, belongs to the laws of the States and not to the laws of the United States.". . . [W]e have recognized a "domestic relations exception" that "divests the federal courts of power to issue divorce, alimony, and child custody decrees.". . . [A]lso . . . it might be appropriate for the federal courts to decline to hear a case involving "elements of the domestic relationship". . . .

Newdow's standing derives entirely from his relationship with his daughter. . . . [T]he interests of this parent and this child are not parallel and, indeed, are potentially in conflict. . . . Newdow's parental status is defined by California's domestic relations law. . . . [T]he Court of Appeals . . . concluded that state law vests in Newdow a cognizable right to influence his daughter's religious upbringing. . . . "[W]hile the custodial parent undoubtedly has the right to make ultimate decisions concerning the child's religious upbringing, a court will not enjoin the non-custodial parent from discussing religion with the child or involving the child in his or her religious activities in the absence of a showing that the child will be thereby harmed." . . .

Nothing that either Banning or the School Board has done . . . impairs Newdow's right to instruct his daughter in his religious views. . . . He wishes to forestall his daughter's exposure to religious ideas that her mother, who wields a form of veto power, endorses, and to use his parental status to challenge the influences to which his daughter may be exposed in school when he and Banning disagree. The California cases simply do not stand for the proposition that Newdow has a right to dictate to others what they may and may not say to his child respecting religion. . . . [I]t is improper for the federal courts to entertain a claim by a plaintiff whose standing to sue is founded on family law rights that are in dispute when prosecution of the lawsuit may have an adverse effect on the person who is the source of the plaintiff's claimed standing. When hard questions of domestic relations are sure to affect the outcome, the prudent course is for the federal court to stay its hand rather than reach out to resolve a weighty question of federal constitutional law. There is a vast difference between Newdow's right to communicate with his child—which both California law and the First Amendment recognize—and his claimed right to shield his daughter from influences to which she is exposed in school despite the terms of the custody order. . . . Newdow lacks prudential standing to bring this suit in federal court. . . .

You Be the Judge

Most states have both sales and use taxes. The state governments generally collect the sales taxes through the sellers in their states. When residents buy goods outside the state, including goods purchased on the Internet, generally the residents are supposed to report the purchase and pay the use tax. The use tax is intended to "back up" the sales tax. However, many residents do not report and pay the use tax. The California legislature, in its attempt to increase its tax revenue, is considering requiring Amazon.com and similar businesses to collect sales and use taxes.

The California legislature'sclaim to taxing Amazon.com is based on the existence of Web sites in California that are affiliates of Amazon.com. Affiliates "advertise Amazon products, provide links to the company's website and get a percentage of the resulting sales."[23] Both Amazon and Overstock have terminated their affiliate relationships with Web sites in states which enact these laws. Companies that act as affiliates stand to lose a substantial amount of revenue. A number of other states have enacted similar approaches, including New York, North Carolina, and Rhode Island. The New York law was challenged in court by Amazon and Overstock and has not been implemented.[24] (There is a federal effort to create a uniform system to tax online sales, but it is not likely to go into effect soon.)

Amazon is a Seattle corporation and claims that it has no store, warehouse, office buildings, or other physical presence in California.[25] However, Lab 126 is an Amazon.com company located in Cupertino, California. Lab 126 created the Kindle™ portable reader.[26]

Assume that California takes steps to force Amazon.com to collect use taxes on sales to California residents. Amazon.com files suit in your court claiming that California lacks jurisdiction. How would you rule and why? [See Evan Halper, "State Surfs the Web for Tax Revenue; Lawmakers Consider Forcing Amazon and Other Online Retailers to Collect on Sales," *Los Angeles Times*, February 20, 2010, Part AA, p. 1; Valerie Richardson, "Amazon Flexes Muscle in Online Sales-Tax Fight; States Target Internet Giant's 'Affiliates,'" *Washington Times*, March 23, 2010, Section A, p. 1.]

Summary

The federal Constitution is unique because it created the doctrine of separation of powers. As a result, our government is divided into three distinct branches: legislative, executive, and judicial. There is also an unofficial "fourth branch" of government, administrative agencies.

Judicial power has limits. For example, federal courts cannot issue advisory opinions or decide moot cases or political questions. In all cases, the plaintiff must have standing to sue. The doctrine of judicial review was created by Chief Justice John Marshall in the landmark case of *Marbury v. Madison*. The doctrine represents an expansion of judicial power, because it allows the Supreme Court to determine whether a statute passed by Congress is in compliance with the Constitution or whether the executive branch has acted in accordance with the Constitution.

Our court system is based on the concept of jurisdiction. Jurisdiction means the legal power to decide a case. It can be divided into subject matter jurisdiction, jurisdiction over the dollar amount (which is often considered an aspect of subject matter jurisdiction), and jurisdiction over the persons or property. There are basically three techniques for obtaining jurisdiction over the persons or property—*in personam, in rem*, and *quasi in rem*. The type of jurisdiction will affect the type of judgment the court can award.

Jurisdiction can be concurrent, in which more than one court can hear and decide a case, or it may be exclusive, in which case only one court can hear the matter. A federal district court's jurisdiction is based on either federal question or diversity of citizenship jurisdiction. In all diversity cases, the jurisdictional amount of over $75,000 must be met. Complete diversity is also required. The federal court system includes specialized courts, district courts, appellate courts, and the Supreme Court.

Discussion Questions

1. Where is the constitutional protection of habeas corpus found? What does the term mean?

2. Why is the identity of the individual Supreme Court justices important?

3. Describe long-arm statutes. Do they serve a legitimate state purpose? Do they make it easier to sue businesses? Do they make it easier for businesses to file suit?

4. What are the advantages and disadvantages of specialized courts, such as tax court or family court?

5. Go to the nearest law library, or Westlaw or Lexis terminal, and determine who were the attorneys for the parties in *Elk Grove Unified School District v. Newdow*, 542 U.S. 1, 124 S. Ct. 2301, 2004 U.S. LEXIS 4178 (2004).

Case Problems and Writing Assignments

1. Zachary Hood attended a first-grade class in a public school in Medford, New Jersey. As a reward, his teacher told students that they could select and read a story to the class. Zachary selected one of his favorites, the biblical tale of Jacob and Esau. His teacher decided that a Bible story would not be appropriate and would not allow Zachary to read his story out loud. The version that Zachary wanted to read does not mention God or the Bible. It is simply the story of two brothers who quarrel and then resolve their differences. The other students in the class were permitted to read the stories they chose. "[T]he case underscores the enduring tension between a teacher's right to supervise assignments and a student's right to express individual initiative." The teacher would have allowed Zachary to read the story to her privately. His parents wanted the story read aloud to the class. Eric Treene, an attorney with the Becket Fund for Religious Liberty, is representing the Hoods before the appellate court. He argues, "The government requires the school to be neutral to religion and this is being hostile to religion." How should the school respond? Why? [See Marjorie Coeyman, "First-grader Tests Ban on Religion in Class," *Christian Science Monitor*, June 15, 1999, p. 1.]

2. The Pasadena Crematorium and other funeral service companies allegedly sold human body parts and organs to a biological supply company. The body parts were allegedly removed without permission from the decedents being prepared for cremations or funerals. In the class action lawsuit, the plaintiffs sued for negligent infliction of emotional distress. The plaintiffs were relatives and friends of the deceased persons. Who has standing to sue in this situation? Would the alleged behavior of the crematorium and funeral homes be ethical? Why or why not? [See *Christensen v. Pasadena Crematorium of Altadena*, 2 Cal. Rptr. 2d 79 (1991).]

3. Bob Herbert, a columnist for the *New York Times*, wrote two tough articles accusing Nike Corporation of cruelly exploiting cheap Asian labor. Nike CEO Philip Knight replied in a letter to the editor that the *Times* published. According to Knight's letter,

"Nike has paid, on average, double the minimum wages as defined in countries where its products are produced under contract." He also stated that Nike contractors provide "free" meals and health care: Others report that they typically provide only subsidies. (Nike is headquartered in Beaverton, Oregon.) Marc Kasky, a community activist, sued, claiming that Knight's letter was false advertising and violated California law. He also alleged that Nike made numerous false statements about its hiring practices in Asia. This is based on a comparison between statements made by Nike representatives and statements by impartial parties. In May 2002, the California Supreme Court, in a four to three opinion, ruled that Knight's rebuttal was commercial speech, which enjoys less constitutional protection than regular speech and is more closely regulated by the government. Assume that you are on the U.S. Supreme Court and this case has been appealed to *you*. How would *you* rule and why? [See Roger Parloff, "Can We Talk?," *Fortune*, September 2, 2002, pp. 102-10.]

Notes

1. 1 Cranch 137, 2 L. Ed. 60 (1803).
2. Citations deleted. *Aetna Life Ins. Co. v. Haworth*, 300 U.S. 227, pp. 240-241 (1937).
3. *Black's Law Dictionary*, 6th ed. (St. Paul: West, 1990), p. 54.
4. Ibid., 1008.
5. Ibid., 1045.
6. Ibid., 1158.
7. 416 U.S. 312 (1974).
8. 1 Cranch 137, 2 L. Ed. 60 (1803).
9. Sheila M. Smith, "Comment: Justice Ruth Bader Ginsburg and Sexual Harassment Law: Will the Second Female Supreme Court Justice Become the Court's Women's Right Champion?" 63 U. Cin. L. Rev. 1893, Summer 1995.
10. Lawrence Hammack, "Supreme Court Takes Closer Look at Virginia Ban on Cross Burning," *Roanoke Times*, December 12, 2002, p. 4.
11. *Ortiz v. Fibreboard Corporation*, 1999 U.S. Lexis 4373 (1999).
12. Official Supreme Court Web site, "Biographies of Current Justices of the Supreme Court page," http://www.supremecourt.gov/about/biographies.aspx (accessed 4/2/10). In 2010, President Obama nominated Elena Kagan to replace Justice John Paul Stevens. Michael Scherer, "Court Nominee Elena Kagan: Let the Scrutiny Start," *Time Magazine*, May 10, 2010, http://www.time.com/time/politics/article/0,8599,1988179,00.html (accessed 7/26/10) and links to the confirmation hearings are available through the Washington Post, http://www.washingtonpost.com/wp-srv/package/supremecourt/2010candidates/elena-kagan.html?sid=ST2010070303036 (accessed 7/26/10).
13. *Black's Law Dictionary*, 7th ed. (St. Paul: West, 1999), pp. 715-16.
14. Ibid., 601.
15. Ibid., 601.
16. 326 U.S. 310 (1945).
17. Tex. Civ. Prac. & Rem. Code Ann. § 17.042 (1997).
18. 952 F. Supp. 1119 (W.D. Pa. 1997).
19. Ibid., 1122-23.
20. Ibid., 1124.
21. The number of associate justices is established in 28 U. S. C. § 1. Supreme Court of the United States, "A Brief Overview of the Supreme Court," http://www.supremecourt.gov/about/briefoverview.aspx (accessed 7/26/10).
22. 134 L. Ed. 2d 68 (1996).
23. Evan Halper, "State Surfs the Web for Tax Revenue; Lawmakers Consider Forcing Amazon and Other Online Retailers to Collect on Sales," *Los Angeles Times*, February 20, 2010, Part AA, p. 1.
24. Valerie Richardson, "Amazon Flexes Muscle in Online Sales-tax Fight; States Target Internet Giant's 'Affiliates,'" *Washington Times*, March 23, 2010, Section A, p. 1.
25. Ibid.
26. Lab 126 Web site, http://lab126.com/ (accessed 4/1/10).

4

Dispute Resolution

Agenda

While driving an eClass van, Yousef Alwazzan is involved in an accident with another vehicle, causing property damage to both vehicles and physical injuries to the parties inside the other car. The passengers in the other car are planning to file a lawsuit against Yousef and eClass. Ani, Meg, and Yousef want to know whether eClass is liable for Yousef's actions. They also want to know how eClass should defend itself in this situation. What steps should Ani, Meg, and Yousef take to minimize their involvement or the involvement of eClass in any future traffic accidents?

Ani, Meg, and Yousef do not *plan* to initiate any legal proceedings while conducting their business. They intend to be careful to minimize the risk of a lawsuit. They hope to select clients, customers, employees, and suppliers who will honor their contracts with eClass, so that eClass will not be forced to seek legal relief. They recognize, however, that inevitably they and/or the firm are likely to have a legal controversy. From discussions with you, and from their experience in the workplace, they realize that lawsuits can be time consuming and expensive. As a result, they would prefer to be able to settle any disputes or controversies in some alternative manner, if possible. Should they include mandatory arbitration provisions in their contracts with suppliers and retailers? Who should be specified as the arbitrator? Would it be better to include a provision for arbitration or a provision for mediation in their employment contracts? When might the firm want to "rent-a-judge" in settling a controversy? When is it better to negotiate than to litigate?

These and other questions will arise as you read this chapter. Be prepared! You never know when the firm or one of its members will seek your advice.

Classic Case

ALLIED-BRUCE TERMINIX COMPANIES, INC. v. DOBSON
513 U.S. 265 (1995)

FACTS In 1987, Steven Gwin, who owned a house in Birmingham, Alabama, bought a lifetime "Termite Protection Plan" (Plan) from the local office of Allied-Bruce Terminix Companies, a franchise of Terminix International Company. In the Plan, Allied-Bruce promised "to protect" Gwin's house "against the attack of subterranean termites," to reinspect periodically, to provide any "further treatment found necessary," and to repair damage caused by new termite infestations up to $100,000. The written contract provided that "any controversy or claim ... arising out of or relating to the interpretation, performance, or breach of any provision of this agreement shall be settled exclusively by arbitration."

In the Spring of 1991, Mr. and Mrs. Gwin wished to sell their house to Mr. and Mrs. Dobson. The Gwins had Allied-Bruce reinspect the house, and the Gwins were told that the house was free of termites. Soon after they sold the house and transferred the Termite Protection Plan to Mr. and Mrs. Dobson, the Dobsons found the house swarming with termites. Allied-Bruce attempted to treat and repair the house, but the Dobsons thought that Allied-Bruce's efforts were inadequate. They sued the Gwins, Allied-Bruce, and Terminix. Allied-Bruce and Terminix immediately asked the court for a stay so that arbitration could proceed. The court denied the request to stay due to a state statute that made written, predispute arbitration agreements invalid and "unenforceable."

ISSUE Was the arbitration clause enforceable against the Dobsons?

HOLDING Yes, the clause was enforceable against the Dobsons.

REASONING Excerpts from the opinion of Justice Breyer:

... Several state courts and federal district courts, like the Supreme Court of Alabama, have interpreted the [Federal Arbitration] Act's language as requiring the parties to a contract to have "contemplated" an interstate commerce connection.... Several federal appellate courts, however, have interpreted the same language differently, as reaching to the limits of Congress' Commerce Clause power.... We granted certiorari to resolve this conflict ...

[T]he basic purpose of the Federal Arbitration Act is to overcome courts' refusals to enforce agreements to arbitrate.... The origins of those refusals lie in "ancient times," when the English courts fought "for extension of jurisdiction—all of them being opposed to anything that would altogether deprive every one of them of jurisdiction." ... American courts initially followed English practice ... [W]hen Congress passed the Arbitration Act in 1925, it was "motivated, first and foremost, by a ... desire" to change this anti-arbitration rule.... It intended courts to "enforce [arbitration] agreements into which parties had entered," ... and to "place such agreements upon the same footing as other contracts." ...

Did Congress intend the Act also to apply in state courts? Did the Federal Arbitration Act pre-empt conflicting state anti-arbitration law, or could state courts apply their arbitration rules in cases before them, thereby reaching results different from those reached in similar federal diversity cases? ... The court concluded that the Federal Arbitration Act pre-empts state law; and it held that state courts cannot apply state statutes that invalidate arbitration agreements. ...

We must decide in this case whether that Act used language about interstate commerce that nonetheless limits the Act's application, thereby, carving out an important statutory niche in which a State remains free to apply its anti-arbitration law or policy. We conclude that it does not. ...

[Section] 2 [of the Federal Arbitration Act] gives States a method for protecting consumers against unfair pressure to agree to a contract with an unwanted arbitration provision. States may regulate contracts, including arbitration clauses, under general contract law principles and they may invalidate an arbitration clause "upon such grounds as exist at law or in equity for the revocation of any contract." ... What States may not do is decide that a contract is fair enough to enforce all of its basic terms (price, service, credit), but not fair enough to enforce its arbitration clause. The Act makes any such State policy unlawful, for that kind of policy would place arbitration clauses on an unequal "footing" directly contrary to the Act's language and Congress' intent.... For these reasons, we accept the "commerce in fact" interpretation, reading the Act's language as insisting that the "transaction" in fact "involve" interstate commerce, even if the parties did not contemplate an interstate commerce connection.... Consequently, the judgment of the Supreme Court of Alabama is reversed and the case is remanded for further proceedings consistent with this opinion.

LITIGATION

People in American society have a great many fears and concerns. Some of these fears may seem irrational to other individuals, for example, a fear of the dark or a fear of heights. Others are viewed as much more rational to most members of our society, for example, a fear of catching H1N1 flu or a fear of losing one's job. One area that causes fear and concern to the average person is involvement in the legal process. Someone might fear becoming involved in the legal process as a result of an automobile accident: That person may fear being sued and being required to pay damages or filing suit and seeking damages from another person.

This chapter explores the stages of a hypothetical case arising from such a situation. While this material may not alleviate the concern or the fear that you may have, it should help to shed some light on *what* is done, *why* it is done, and *how* it all ties together within the workings of our judicial system in a civil suit. Exhibit 4.1 sets out the six stages a *party* (plaintiff or defendant in the lawsuit) is likely to encounter in a civil *suit* (lawsuit, the formal legal proceeding used to resolve a legal dispute). Each of these stages is examined in more detail as we follow the progress of our hypothetical lawsuit through the legal system.

Costs of Litigation

Before an individual or business entity pursues litigation, he or she should consider the costs of the litigation. There are likely to be direct and obvious costs, and indirect, often hidden, costs. The kinds and amounts of fees will vary depending on the type of

Exhibit 4.1

The Six Steps Involved in Most Civil Lawsuits

Pleadings	The case begins by filing documents identifying the parties (the person suing and the person being sued), explaining what the claim is about, and asking the court to do something—usually to award monetary damages.
Service	The person being sued (the defendant) must be formally notified. Service is usually obtained by preparing a summons and then having the summons and a copy of the complaint personally delivered to the defendant.
Discovery	Both sides have to gather facts and information to prepare for trial. Discovery can involve examining documents, records, and other pieces of physical evidence as well as taking the statements of the parties and other witnesses.
Pretrial Motions	Parties request the court to make procedural decisions or other rulings by filing motions with the court. Motions are often in writing.
Trial	The court hears evidence offered by each side and decides issues of both fact and law.
Enforcing the Judgment	If a party wins a judgment at trial, he or she still has to collect the money awarded. A judgment can be enforced by putting a lien on property, garnishing wages, or obtaining a court order for the transfer of bank accounts or other property.

litigation. In order to make an informed decision about whether to sue or defend a suit, the parties should consider the probable outcomes of litigation. The parties should also consider the likelihood that alternative dispute resolution (ADR) will be effective and its costs. (*Alternative dispute resolution* consists of methods of resolving disputes other than traditional litigation.) Even though some forms of ADR are becoming more formal, time-consuming, and expensive, ADR may still reduce overall costs. The Association for Conflict Resolution (ACR) is concerned about conflict resolution, ranging from conflicts between nations to conflicts between family members.

There are a number of factors that a potential party should consider before deciding whether to initiate any lawsuit or agree to otherwise settle a dispute. Some of the more important factors include:

- The legal system is unpredictable, and a trial may be very time-consuming;
- It is difficult to determine the likelihood of winning the suit with any degree of certainty;
- The amount of money a party might win (or lose) may determine whether he or she wants to proceed with a trial or seek a settlement;
- The ability of the other party to pay any judgment might make suing a waste of time and money *or* may make suing seem like the best alternative available;
- The amount that the lawyer(s) would charge, and when the lawyers would bill;
- The amount of court costs, including filing fees;
- The additional fees that might be incurred, including the fees for expert witnesses (for example, accountants, economists, and doctors), fees for preparing exhibits, fees for medical tests and exams, fees for *depositions* (the formal process of asking a potential witness questions outside the courtroom, but under oath), and the cost for jury consultants;
- The availability of insurance to pay some of the costs of litigation. Some individuals purchase special legal insurance. Some other types of insurance pay the costs of litigation (for example, automobile policies generally pay the costs of defending the insured if there is an automobile accident);
- The amount of time that the parties, their families and friends, and company employees would spend in preparing for the litigation;
- The manner in which this lawsuit and/or additional publicity would affect the reputations of the parties;
- The effect on the continuing relationship between parties to the suit;
- The stress and emotional toll that the lawsuit will take on those involved;
- Personal time and effort, for example, employees may be preparing for the litigation in lieu of working on normally assigned employment tasks; and
- Distraction from personal and professional goals, for example, employees may be distracted from the goals of the enterprise.

This is a listing of some of the primary factors to be considered. In addition, there may be some hidden costs associated with the suit.

Litigation is also expensive for the court system. As a result, courts have rules to reduce the costs. For example, a court may permit a *class action lawsuit*, which is a lawsuit involving a group of plaintiffs or defendants who are in substantially the same situation. This is more efficient than facing the prospects of many individual lawsuits, each of which is likely to involve the same basic facts and issues of law. Of course, combining the plaintiffs or defendants into a class is not always appropriate.

Many courts have established additional procedures to make complex litigation run more efficiently and smoothly. For example, if there are 300 cases against four insurance companies, with each of the plaintiffs seeking recovery under the insurance policies for injuries allegedly suffered due to exposure to toxic mold, the court may designate an individual judge or panel of judges to handle the suits. In consultation with the legal counsel, the judge(s) may impose additional rules to aid in handling the cases. The judge may require things like electronic filing of complaints and motions. In civil practice, the *complaint* is the plaintiff's first pleading. It informs the defendant that he or she is being sued. Before filing the complaint, the plaintiff should consider whether the defendant is likely to be able to pay a judgment.

The Problem

Nic Grant, a college sophomore, saved some money earned from a part-time job to take his girlfriend, Nancy Griffin, to dinner at a very expensive and sophisticated restaurant on Mount Washington, overlooking the Point in downtown Pittsburgh. Nic called for Nancy at her apartment in Cranberry Township about 6:00 P.M. on June 6 and was driving through Butler County toward the restaurant when his car was struck by a white van with the eClass logo on it. The accident happened at the intersection of Route 19 (Perry Highway) and Rowan Road in Cranberry Township, Butler County.

Nic spent the next five days in the hospital. As a result, he did not show up for work and consequently lost his job. He was also unable to take his college final examinations or to complete his research projects for several of his classes. In fact, Nic was forced to withdraw from college for the semester. Nancy, who did not have a job, also suffered injuries from the impact and sought medical treatment. Nic's roommate, who is taking a course in business law, advised Nic that he and Nancy were likely to have a claim against the other driver and recommended that they consult a lawyer to learn what their potential rights might be.

Yousef Alwazzan, one of the principals and an officer of eClass, was in Pittsburgh to work at a trade show displaying electronic products. He worked at the booth in the Pittsburgh Convention Center from 8:30 A.M. until 5:30 P.M. on June 6, with a half-hour lunch break. Since none of the other principals of the firm could leave the eClass office for the trade show, Yousef had to work the booth by himself.

After a long and tiring day at the trade show, Yousef packed the sample products in the eClass van and left the Convention Center parking lot at 5:45 P.M. on the evening of June 6. Before heading home, he drove toward Butler, to a restaurant recommended by a friend, Trattoria Restaurant on Main Street. Yousef had directions from an Internet map site but was unfamiliar with the area. While he was trying to negotiate the streets, read the map he had printed out, and remember his friend's instructions, he was involved in an accident. The eClass van being driven by Yousef hit the car owned and operated by Nic Grant. (For purposes of this chapter, eClass is an Ohio corporation licensed as a foreign corporation doing business in Pennsylvania.)

Client's Interview with a Lawyer

Nic recognized that he needed legal assistance and consulted the local bar association. The local bar association referred Nic to an attorney, Lyn Carroll. (Chapter 1 contains additional information about hiring an attorney.) Nic called Ms. Carroll and scheduled an initial interview. At this initial interview, Nic recounted all the facts of that evening, to the best of his recollection. Nic then mentioned that he had not notified either the driver of the other vehicle or eClass. Ms. Carroll agreed to assist Nic in obtaining compensation and offered to help Nancy as well. Ms. Carroll recognized that it might be a conflict of interest for her to represent both Nic and Nancy, especially if Nic was also negligent in causing the accident. (In order for Lyn Carroll to comply with the ethics rules for attorneys, she would need to send each prospective client a letter disclosing the possible conflict of interest and seeking their consent to having her as the attorney for each despite this potential conflict.)

When meeting with Ms. Carroll, Nic asked a number of questions including what payment terms she would require in order to represent him, and whether there are any opportunities to negotiate or arbitrate a settlement rather than going to trial. Nic wanted to know if Ms. Carroll was willing to work towards a negotiated settlement and whether this would affect the amount of attorney's fees that would be owed. Following this initial meeting, Nic and Nancy agreed to meet with Ms. Carroll a few days later to discuss, read, and sign the client–attorney contract. As indicated in the contract, payment was to be based on a contingency fee. (A *contingency fee* is a fee to be paid to an attorney based on some contingency or event. The most common provisions are that the fee is due only if the case is settled or won.) Other bases for attorney's fees are not dependent on results: for example, flat rate and hourly rate fees. Whatever the fee arrangement, it is specified in the contract between the client and the attorney. The contract agreed to in this case appears as Exhibit 4.2.

Since eClass has insurance, an attorney hired by the insurance company is likely to be the "lead counsel" in this case. However, that attorney will focus on protecting the interests of the insurance company, not the interests of eClass. If eClass loses the case, the insurance company will pay for the damages covered by the insurance policy, and eClass will have to pay for any other damages. Consequently, in many situations the firm would hire its own attorney. The firm's attorney would normally work with the insurer's attorney, and the two of them would agree on the strategy to take. We will assume in this case that eClass has no liability over the policy limits and will not need its own attorney. We will refer to eClass and Yousef as the defendants. The insurance company is not really a defendant. It is providing insurance for eClass's liability. (In practice it is often difficult to decide whether to hire your own attorney in addition to the one hired by the insurer.)

In this case, the insurance company has selected Mr. Jones of the Pittsburgh law firm of Jones, Murphy, Sabbatino, and Schwartz, which specializes in defending against

Exhibit 4.2

Client-Attorney Contract

AGREEMENT

THIS CONTRACT entered into, by, and between NIC GRANT and NANCY GRIFFIN, hereinafter referred to as CLIENTS, and LYN CARROLL, hereinafter referred to as ATTORNEY, WITNESSETH:

1. Clients hereby retain and employ attorney to represent them in the prosecution of their claim and cause of action for damages sustained by them as a result of an automobile accident occurring June 6, 2011, on Route 19 and Rowan Road, Butler County, Pennsylvania, resulting in injuries and damages to clients.

2. Clients agree to pay attorney for her services rendered pursuant to this employment contract at the rate of twenty-five percent (25%) if the case is settled prior to trial and at the rate of thirty-three and one-third percent (33 1/3%) of the net amount recovered if the case goes to trial.

3. All necessary and reasonable costs, expenses, investigation, preparation for trial, and litigation expenses shall be initially paid for by attorney and then deducted from the amount of any settlement or recovery, and the division between the parties shall be made after deduction of said expenses. Furthermore, clients shall reimburse attorney for all such costs and expenses even if no recovery is made or, in the alternative, if the costs and expenses should exceed the amount of the recovery.

4. Attorney agrees to undertake the representation of clients in the prosecution of the above claims and causes of action, using her highest professional skill to further the interest of said clients in all matters in connection with their claims and causes of action, and to diligently pursue said claims and causes of action.

5. No settlement or other disposition of the matter shall be made by attorney without the written approval of clients.

IN WITNESS WHEREOF, the parties hereto have executed this instrument in triplicate originals this 17th day of June 2011.

CLIENT _____
NIC GRANT

CLIENT _____
NANCY GRIFFIN

ATTORNEY _____
LYN CARROLL

personal injury suits. The insurer has worked with Mr. Jones numerous times in past cases. Ani and Yousef scheduled an appointment to meet with Mr. Jones to discuss the case.

Even though the accident occurred in Butler County, the defendants can hire an attorney from Pittsburgh, located in Allegheny County. Attorneys are licensed at the state level and not the county level. Once licensed, the attorney can practice law anywhere within the state's jurisdiction. Rules of court and court procedures may vary somewhat from county to county, and the attorney will need to know or learn the rules in Butler County for this trial, as well as knowing the Pennsylvania Rules of Civil Procedure. Each state has its own rules of procedure for both civil and criminal trials, as does the federal court system. Civil trials conducted in federal court are controlled by the Federal Rules of Civil Procedure. The rules of procedure in many states are modeled after these rules.

Neither party is required to hire an attorney. Either the plaintiffs, the defendants, or both sides to the case could choose to represent themselves in court. This is called appearing *Pro se* (appearing in one's own behalf). This may be very unwise depending on the circumstances. A nonlawyer often mislabels concepts, misses key points, and is not familiar with the Rules of Civil Procedure.[1]

Investigation of the Facts

In the interviews with her clients and in subsequent telephone conversations, Ms. Carroll gathered information concerning the accident. On the basis of this preliminary information, she obtained medical releases from both clients in order to review the hospital and medical records of each of them. Nic also gave her copies of the hospital bills and the estimate for the car repair. Finally, Ms. Carroll obtained a copy of the police report filed by José Gonzalez, the officer who responded to the accident scene.

After reviewing the file, Ms. Carroll wrote to the university that Nic and Nancy had been attending for proof that they had withdrawn from classes after June 6, 2011. She also wrote to Nic's former employer for information about Nic's wages, normal work week, and proof that he was fired on June 10, 2011. Once all the material requested was in the file, her preliminary investigation was finished. She concluded that Nic was driving with Nancy in his car on Rowan Road, Cranberry Township, Butler County, when the car was struck by a van operated by Yousef Alwazzan. The van was owned by eClass and was decorated with permanent signs on both doors advertising eClass products. At this point, Ms. Carroll wrote a letter to Ani Yasuda, an officer of eClass. It appears as Exhibit 4.3. It is important that Ms. Carroll determine that there is basis for a suit, attorneys and clients who file frivolous lawsuits may be subject to penalties.

Negotiation of a Settlement

Upon receipt of the letter of notice, Ani Yasuda contacted eClass's insurance company to inform them of its contents. The insurance carrier immediately assigned an adjuster to the case. The adjuster contacted Ms. Carroll to ascertain the nature of the injuries. On the basis of this information, the adjuster attempted to negotiate a settlement by offering $17,027 to Mr. Grant and $5,680 to Ms. Griffin. Since the offers covered only

Exhibit 4.3

Letter of Notice

LYN CARROLL, J.D.
Attorney at Law
Suite 654
Butler Savings Building
Butler, Pennsylvania 15205

June 25, 2011

Ms. Ani Yasuda
President
eClass
9876 Appian Way
Maineville, OH 44444

Mr. Yousef Alwazzan
c/o eClass
9876 Appian Way
Maineville, OH 44444

RE: *Nic Grant and Nancy Griffin v. eClass and Yousef Alwazzan*

Dear Ms. Ani Yasuda and Mr. Yousef Alwazzan:

I have been retained by Mr. Nic Grant and Ms. Nancy Griffin to represent them in a cause of action arising from your van colliding with the car owned and operated by Mr. Grant on June 6, 2011. Ms. Griffin was a passenger in Mr. Grant's car at that time. My preliminary investigation indicates that the accident was caused by inattention and carelessness by your driver, Yousef Alwazzan, and by improper maintenance of your van.

Should you or your liability carrier wish to discuss this matter with me in order to achieve a just and equitable settlement, please contact me within twelve days from the date of this letter. If I do not hear from you or your representative within that period, I shall file suit against you without further notice.

Sincerely,

Lyn Carroll

LC:rj
cc: Mr. Grant
    Ms. Griffin

out-of-pocket expenses and did not include any allowance for lost wages or for pain and suffering, both Nic and Nancy rejected the offers. When no other offers were made by the insurer, Ms. Carroll filed suit on November 15, 2011. (Note that Nic Grant is claiming at least $16,000 and Nancy Griffin is claiming at least $8,000 in pain and suffering in addition to any other losses either of them will be able to prove.) In many situations, the negotiations would be more extensive. Ms. Carroll might have a conference with the insurance adjuster, eClass's attorney, or the insurance company's attorney in an effort to resolve the conflict and reach a settlement without resorting to a civil suit.

There is some advantage to waiting to initiate suit. Plaintiffs will want to know that their injuries are completely healed and no new injuries are discovered. In this case, waiting might also be an advantage to eClass, since Nic may obtain replacement employment. In general, a plaintiff must be sure to initiate his or her suit by filing the complaint before the statute of limitations expires. The suit should also commence before the memories of the parties and witnesses begin to fade. Before filing suit, the attorney should discuss alternatives to litigation with her clients.

Filing the Suit

The complaint should be definite, and it should contain sufficient information for the defendant to understand the nature of the litigation so that he or she can begin to prepare his or her defense. Exhibit 4.4 shows the plaintiffs' original complaint, which was filed in the *Court of Common Pleas* (title used in some states for trial courts of general jurisdiction). After it was filed, the prothonotary's office delivered a copy to the sheriff. (*Prothonotary* is the title used in some states to designate the chief clerk of courts.) In many states, the clerk of court's office performs the same functions as the prothonotary's office. The sheriff then serves copies of the complaint on all the defendants named in the complaint. Depending on the type of suit and the state, any responsible adult who is not a party to the suit may be able to serve the complaint. In some states, the complaint is accompanied by a *summons* (a writ commencing an action and notifying the person named that the person must appear in court to answer a complaint).

Since eClass is registered as a foreign corporation, its complaint was delivered by mail to Ani at the principal office of the corporation. Many states permit service of process on registered foreign corporations by delivery of the complaint to the state's own secretary of state. If either eClass or Yousef planned to claim that the court lacked jurisdiction over them or the lawsuit, they would have done it at this time instead of filing a general answer. (See Chapter 3 for a discussion of jurisdiction.)

Sometimes the defendant does not answer the complaint. In these cases, the court will generally enter a *default judgment*, a judgment in default of the defendant's

Exhibit 4.4

Plaintiffs' Original Complaint

Plaintiffs' Original Complaint
IN THE COURT OF COMMON PLEAS OF BUTLER COUNTY, PENNSYLVANIA
CIVIL ACTION

NIC GRANT	:	A.D. No. 23465
and	:	A jury trial is demanded.
NANCY GRIFFIN, Plaintiffs	:	
	:	
v.	:	
	:	
ECLASS[a]	:	
and	:	
YOUSEF ALWAZZAN,[b] Defendants	:	

NOW COME NIC GRANT and NANCY GRIFFIN, hereinafter called PLAINTIFFS, complaining of ECLASS, a foreign corporation doing business in the Commonwealth of Pennsylvania, and YOUSEF ALWAZZAN, hereinafter called DEFENDANTS, who may be served with citation by service, upon ECLASS's statutory agent and Mr. Alwazzan's place of employment, ANI YASUDA, 9876 Appian Way, Maineville, Ohio, and for cause of action would respectfully show unto the court that:

On or about June 6, 2011, plaintiffs were driving on Rowan Road, Butler County, Pennsylvania. As a result of defendants' negligence, plaintiffs have incurred, and will continue to incur, various medical expenses; they have suffered, and will continue to suffer, pain; Mr. Grant has been unable to work and has already lost wages in the sum of $10,000.00; Mr. Grant's ability to earn wages in the immediate future has been temporarily impaired; and plaintiffs have suffered a loss of tuition incurred in the course of furthering their education by having to leave school and by having to postpone their graduation date by one semester.

WHEREFORE, plaintiffs demand judgment against defendants, individually, jointly, and/or severally in an amount in excess of $50,000.00,[c] their costs, and all other proper relief.

LYN CARROLL, Attorney at Law
Suite 654
Butler Savings Building
Butler, PA 15205
(412) 555-0123

---

[a] If eClass was not a corporation, but was the name under which Ani, Yousef, and Meg did business, the complaint would name Ani Yasuda, Yousef Alwazzan, and Meg Friesen, d.b.a. eClass.

[b] Some states, including California, permit a plaintiff to include "John Doe(s)" as defendant(s) if the plaintiff does not know the true names of all the defendants. Then, the plaintiff can add the defendant(s) later, if it would be just to do so.

[c] Many courts require compulsory arbitration for smaller cases. For example, in Butler County, most cases under $35,000 will be referred to compulsory arbitration,[2] consisting of a panel of three attorneys who have agreed to serve as arbitrators.[3] A party not satisfied with this arbitrators' award may appeal to the Court of Common Pleas. Parties to any civil action may voluntarily agree to submit their dispute to the Butler County Mediation Program under Local Rules of Civil Procedure, Rule L212.1 (March 12, 2008).

appearance. In these cases, the court is only "listening" to the plaintiff's side, so the court generally awards the plaintiff what he or she is requesting. Default judgments are valid in civil cases if the court has proper jurisdiction, including jurisdiction over the defendant, and the defendant has been properly served in the case.

Exhibit 4.5 displays a copy of the defendants' answer. Most complaints and answers will be more detailed than these examples and must include individual numbered items specifying the elements that constitute the legal cause of action.

At this point in the proceedings, the plaintiffs have sued the defendants in a court of law and the defendants have filed an answer. Before trial, both attorneys may simplify the legal issues, amend their complaints and answers, and attempt to limit the number of expert witnesses, if any. The purpose is to reduce costs and the length of trial.

Pretrial Proceedings

At this point, the discovery process begins. *Discovery* is a general term that applies to a group of specific methods used to narrow the issues to be decided by the trial. Lawyers use the process to shorten the actual trial, if there is one, or to eliminate the need for a trial if the case can be settled. If one side sees that there is little hope they can win the suit, it is often in that party's best interests to settle the case. The scope of discovery is very broad. Generally, one can discover all information that is relevant even if it cannot be introduced as evidence during the trial. The standard used is whether the discovery request is reasonably calculated to lead to admissible evidence. Exhibit 4.6 depicts the five common discovery devices.

Depositions   Traditionally, a *deposition* is the reducing to writing of a witness's sworn testimony taken outside of court. The testimony begins with the witness swearing that the testimony will be truthful. If it is not, the witness can be held in contempt, as President Clinton was in Paula Jone's case.[4] Increasingly, attorneys also videotape the deposition. This is permitted in a number of jurisdictions, including federal courts (Federal Rules of Civil Procedure § 30[b][2]) and California courts (California Civil Procedure § 2025[p]). If the deposition is later used at trial, the jury will view the film of the deposition instead of having the deposition read to them. Generally, this is more interesting, and the jurors are more likely to pay close attention to the questions and answers. Depositions are used routinely today. They are used to preserve testimony from someone who, for good cause, may not be able to attend the trial. They are also used to impeach the witness when the witness appears at trial and gives evidence that conflicts with what he or she said at the time the deposition was taken. (To *impeach* means to question the truthfulness

Exhibit 4.5

Defendants' Original Answer

Defendants' Original Answer
IN THE COURT OF COMMON PLEAS OF BUTLER COUNTY, PENNSYLVANIA
CIVIL ACTION

NIC GRANT   :   A.D. No. 23465
and   :
NANCY GRIFFIN, Plaintiffs   :
                                             :
                                             :
                                             :
v.   :
                                             :
                                             :
ECLASS   :
and   :
YOUSEF ALWAZZAN, Defendants   :

NOW COME ECLASS and YOUSEF ALWAZZAN, defendants in the above styled and numbered cause, and for answer to Plaintiffs' Original Complaint would respectfully show unto the court:

Defendants deny each and every material allegation contained in Plaintiffs' Original Complaint. In addition, defendants allege that it was the negligent driving of Nic Grant that caused plaintiffs' injuries and the injuries of the defendants.

WHEREFORE, having fully answered, defendants pray that the complaint be dismissed, for their costs, and for all other proper relief, including damage to the eClass van.

JONES, MURPHY, SABBATINO,
   and SCHWARTZ
Suite 1010
First National Bank Building
Pittsburgh, PA 15205
(412) 355-0191

By_____

ATTORNEYS FOR DEFENDANTS

On December 12, 2011, the original of this answer was filed in the Prothonotary's office. A copy of this answer was mailed to Ms. Lyn Carroll, attorney for plaintiffs, Suite 654, Butler Savings Building, Butler, Pennsylvania 15205.

By_____

JEFFERSON JONES

eClass 4.1 **Management**

PREPARING TO MEET WITH THE ATTORNEY

Ani, Yousef, and Meg are preparing for their first meeting with Mr. Jones, and they are understandably nervous. They would like to know what information they should collect and take to the meeting. They would also like to know what they should expect at the meeting. They ask you to make a list of the information that would be legally relevant to this lawsuit. They also ask you what they should expect at this first meeting. What will you tell them?

BUSINESS CONSIDERATIONS   Frequently, a business will have certain items it wishes to treat in a confidential manner, but the business may need to reveal some or all of this information to its attorneys in preparation for a legal proceeding. What procedures should the business follow to maximize its protection while still being as open and honest as necessary with its counsel? What steps should the law firm take to protect the confidentiality of its clients?

ETHICAL CONSIDERATIONS   Suppose that the known facts make it relatively obvious that a business is liable for the wrongful conduct of one of its agents. Is it ethical for the business and its attorneys to use expensive and time-consuming delaying tactics in an effort to persuade the injured party to settle out of court? Would it be ethical to seek an alternative form of dispute resolution rather than going to trial?

of a witness using some evidence.) A deposition may be obtained from *any* party *or* witness.

Interrogatories   *Interrogatories* are written questions from one side to the other. Like depositions, interrogatories produce a written record of answers to questions. However, because both the questions and the answers are written, the answers are not as spontaneous as in a deposition. The answer is made under oath, but the respondent has the time to contemplate and carefully phrase the written answers to the questions posed. Often, a person's attorney will review a draft of his or her answers before they are returned. Interrogatories may be sent to any party to the lawsuit but *not* to other witnesses. That is, if a witness is neither a plaintiff nor a defendant, an interrogatory may not be obtained from that witness.

Exhibit 4.6

Discovery

Technique	Description	Purpose*
Deposition	Oral questions directed to a witness who is under oath	Used to preserve testimony or to impeach a witness
Interrogatories	Written questions directed to a party who responds under oath	Used to preserve testimony or to impeach a witness
Subpoena Duces Tecum	Order for the production of documents and things	Used to discover information and present it during the trial
Physical or Mental Examination	Request that a person submit to an exam by a doctor selected by the opposition	Used when physical or mental condition is an issue in the case
Request for Admissions	Request that opposing party admit that a statement is true	Used to reduce the number of items that must be proven at trial

*One purpose of all discovery techniques is to obtain information.

Production of Documents and Things   In many lawsuits, testimony alone is insufficient to win the case. In Nic and Nancy's case, Ms. Carroll also must introduce the records of the two doctors, the hospital, and the police report. Because of the circumstances, Ms. Carroll may also request that eClass produce records it possesses reflecting when and where the van was bought and any internal eClass communications used in tracking repair records and mechanical difficulties. The legal form used to obtain those documents is called a subpoena duces tecum. (A *subpoena duces tecum* is an order to appear with records or evidence at a trial.)

Physical or Mental Examination   Whenever the physical or mental condition of a party to the suit is in question, the court may order that party to submit to an examination by a physician. Here, both the present condition of the plaintiffs and their physical condition prior to the accident will potentially be in question, so a medical examination may be deemed necessary.

Request for Admission   One party can serve on the opponent a written request for an *admission*, which takes the form of a question asked by one party to which the answer is either yes or no. If the recipient fails to answer in a stated period of time (usually 30 days), the matter is deemed admitted. For example, Ms. Carroll may request an admission that Yousef Alwazzan was driving the van.

The Result of Discovery   As a result of the discovery process, the attorneys for the defendants, eClass and Yousef Alwazzan, informed their clients that it appears the accident was primarily caused by Yousef's negligence and his unfamiliarity with the streets. Mr. Jones recommended a settlement offer of $23,000 and Ani, Yousef, and Meg agreed. (A settlement offer is really an offer to negotiate.) Ms. Carroll informed her clients of the offer and recommended rejection. Nic and Nancy rejected the offer, and since the defendants made no additional offers, the case went to trial.

Pretrial Conferences   Many courts now use pretrial conferences to encourage the parties to settle the dispute themselves. However, not all judicial systems and judges favor these conferences. Often the pretrial conferences result in a settlement. Even if there is no settlement, the conference generally succeeds in further clarifying the legal and factual issues involved in the case. Depending on the situation, participation in settlement conferences may be mandatory or voluntary.

Businesspeople need to be aware that *many* courts require the parties to participate in pretrial conferences. Some jurisdictions base the requirement on the amount of damages. In Butler County, for example, during pretrial conferences, the attorneys meet with the judge. The parties are requested to be available either outside the courtroom or by telephone. Then, if a settlement offer is made, the attorney can quickly inform his or her client and obtain a prompt response. This procedure is common in many courts. Depending on the jurisdiction and the judge's preferences, the judge *may* take a very active role in attempting to fashion a compromise that would be acceptable to both parties. Some judges may be harsh with parties who do not accept reasonable settlement offers or who do not participate in pretrial conferences in good faith. In some jurisdictions, nonbinding arbitration may be required in addition to or instead of a settlement conference.

Demurrer   The purpose of a demurrer is to challenge the legal sufficiency of the other party's pleading as a pleading. For example, demurrers can be raised to the plaintiff's complaint, the defendant's answer, or the defendant's counterclaim. The grounds for a demurrer are usually limited by statute. Common grounds include failure to state facts sufficient to constitute a legal cause of action (general demurrer), lack of jurisdiction (special demurrer), lack of capacity to sue (special demurrer), and uncertainty or ambiguity (special demurrer).

A general demurrer only challenges defects that appear on the *face* of the pleading. At this point, the parties cannot produce additional evidence or sworn statements. Each jurisdiction has different requirements as to what constitutes a sufficient pleading and the amount of detail required. In deciding whether to grant a demurrer, the court must accept as true all the facts that were in the pleading. Assuming all the facts that are pleaded are true, the issue is whether they would entitle the plaintiff to any judicial relief. If the demurrer is denied, the party requesting the demurrer will be given time to answer. If the demurrer is granted, generally the losing party will be given permission to amend the pleading to make it sufficient.

Demurrers have been abolished before federal courts. In federal courts, a party would use a *motion* (request to a judge to take certain action. A motion is usually in writing.) to dismiss instead of a general demurrer. Motions to dismiss are discussed in the following section.

Motion to Dismiss   Depending on the jurisdiction, motions to dismiss can be raised on the same grounds as general or special demurrers. A motion to dismiss can be made after different pleadings. When a court considers a motion to dismiss, it *generally* accepts that the material facts alleged in the complaint are true. The pleading is construed in the light most favorable to the party who filed it. The pleading need only state a claim upon which relief can be granted. The purpose of a motion to dismiss is to avoid the expense of unnecessary trials.

If the motion to dismiss is granted, it may be with or without prejudice. If the motion is granted *without prejudice,* the plaintiff can amend and refile the complaint. The judge will often establish a deadline for amending the complaint. If the motion is granted *with prejudice,* the plaintiff cannot revise the complaint and the trial is terminated. In some jurisdictions, there is an absolute right to amend once. A motion to dismiss is a final decision in the case that can be appealed. Many of the cases in this text were decided on a demurrer or a motion to dismiss.

Motion for a Summary Judgment   A *motion for a summary judgment* is a request to the judge asking him or her to declare that side the "winner" because there are no material issues of fact. It is a technique for *going beyond the allegations stated in the pleadings* and attacking the basic merits of the opponent's case. Traditionally, it was difficult to obtain summary judgment, because most courts believed that its use violated the other party's right to a trial. Other courts indicated that there was no *right* to a trial when there was no genuine dispute about the facts. The modern view is that there is no right to a trial, and courts today are thus more willing to grant summary judgments.

This technique permits the examination of evidentiary material, such as admissions and depositions, without a full-scale trial. The purpose of a motion for a summary judgment is to avoid the expense of unnecessary trials. Consequently, it is usually decided before trial. Either party can file a motion for summary judgment. The party filing the motion must make an initial showing to justify the court's review. The opposing parties are entitled to have time to present their own materials. The length of time depends on the jurisdiction. The standard for granting a summary judgment is that *no genuine issue or no triable issue exists as to any material fact.* If this standard is satisfied, the moving party is entitled to a judgment as a matter of law. In some jurisdictions, the court will not consider the pleadings in making its decision. The court can grant a partial summary judgment on some issues or claims and not on others. In most courts, summary judgment is procedurally distinct from *judgment as a matter of law* even though they use essentially the same standard. It is also distinct from motions on the pleadings, which only permit the court to review the pleadings and do *not* permit review of evidence. Many of the court cases in this book were appeals of summary judgments by the party who lost.

On Nic and Nancy's behalf, Ms. Carroll introduced a motion for a summary judgment claiming that no material facts appear to be in dispute; rather, the case is merely a matter of applying the law.

The Trial

In Nic and Nancy's case, the judge denied the plaintiffs' pretrial motions and the legal process continued. The actual trial proceeding is governed by technical rules of trial practice. Generally, representation in court is best left to the attorneys. A good plaintiff or defendant, however, takes an active role in assisting the lawyer.

Jury Selection   A legal case can be resolved by a trial before a judge, without a jury. The judge then decides questions of fact *and* questions of law. Such a trial is often less expensive and less time-consuming. Nic Grant and Nancy Griffin agree with their attorney that a jury will generally favor the plaintiffs and their arguments, and they elect to have a jury trial. A request for a jury trial must be made in a timely manner. This was noted on the plaintiffs' original complaint (Exhibit 4.4).

Members of the jury are referred to as *petit jurors* (ordinary jurors on the panel for the trial of a civil or criminal action). Traditionally, civil juries consisted of 12 jurors. Some jurisdictions have reduced this number in civil trials. Generally, 6 to 12 jurors are used. In federal court, a civil jury also consists of 6 to 12 members.[5]

Alternate jurors may also be selected. Alternate jurors sit with the regular jurors and hear the evidence. If a regular juror becomes ill or has to leave the jury for some reason during the production of evidence, an alternate "joins" the jury and it continues to function. Without alternate jurors, the judge would have to select a new jury and begin the trial again. An alternate juror can substitute for a regular juror even during deliberations in some jurisdictions: The jury will then start its deliberations from the beginning.

Most states select potential jurors from the voter registration list or the list of licensed drivers or both. The prospective jurors may be required to complete a juror information form. The attorneys use this information to question potential jurors during the *voir dire* examination (examination of potential jurors to determine their competence to serve on the jury). Voir dire is an important part of the trial. Questions need to be asked in the proper manner to obtain helpful, accurate answers, without offending potential jurors. The information offered by the prospective jurors is used by the judge and counsel as the basis for challenging jurors as biased and, thus, ineligible to serve. The attorneys for both parties and/or the judge can ask questions. For example, an attorney may request that the judge ask any potentially embarrassing questions so that the attorney can try to maintain good rapport with the potential jurors. Generally, the procedure is that the attorneys submit written questions to the judge prior to voir dire. In some jurisdictions, the judge may control voir dire by asking all the questions of the potential jurors. At the opposite extreme—New York, for example—voir dire is conducted by the attorneys outside the courtroom; the judge is called in only if problems arise. The procedure depends on the rules of court and the judge's preferences in courtroom procedure. In civil disputes in Butler County, the judge usually conducts voir dire of all the prospective jurors at one time. In Nic and Nancy's case, for example, if a potential juror happened to work for eClass, Ms. Carroll would challenge that person and request that the judge excuse the person. On the other hand, if one of the prospective jurors was a member of Nic's fraternity, Mr. Jones would examine the student very carefully to see whether he or she would favor a fellow member.

Businesses are available that specialize in assisting parties in selecting sympathetic jurors. These jury consultants come from varying backgrounds including psychology, sociology, and marketing. They investigate the backgrounds of potential jurors and collect statistics about the reactions of some socioeconomic groups to trials generally and to issues that are expected to arise in the particular trial on which they are consulting.

Jury consultants sometimes arrange a *shadow jury* consisting of "jurors" with demographic backgrounds similar to the impaneled jurors. The shadow jury sits in the public area of the courtroom and members report their impressions of the evidence. This can be particularly helpful in highly technical cases, where there is a concern that the jurors may be confused by the details. Through this technique, attorneys can have continuous feedback on how their presentation is being perceived.

Another technique is the *mock jury*—the lawyers practice their case before a group of mock jurors with demographic backgrounds similar to those of the actual jurors.

Two methods exist for dismissing prospective jurors. First, a potential juror can be removed *for cause.* When a juror is removed for cause, generally an attorney first suggests to the judge that the juror will probably be biased. Challenges for cause occur if (1) the juror has a financial stake in the case or similar litigation; (2) if members of the juror's family have such an interest; or (3) there is reason to believe the juror will be partial. The judge then decides whether he or she agrees; if so, the potential juror is dismissed. The judge can also make this decision on his or her own initiative. (When a judge raises an issue on his or her own, we say that the judge does it *sua sponte*, which means voluntarily, without prompting or suggestion, of his or her own will or motion.) There is no limit on the number of potential jurors who can be removed for cause.

A second technique is to remove a prospective juror by the use of a *peremptory challenge.* Unlike removal for cause, each side is allotted a limited number of peremptory challenges. The judge decides the number of peremptory challenges prior to beginning the jury selection process. In federal court, for example, each side receives three peremptory challenges.[6] With peremptory challenges, the attorney does not need to discuss his or her reasons for wanting to remove the juror. The purpose of peremptory challenges is to allow each side to act on hints of bias that may not be provable or even rationally explainable. Some attorneys act on their intuition in deciding whom to eliminate from the jury. The attorney intuitively decides which potential jurors he or she trusts and which he or she does not trust. The attorney then uses peremptory challenges to eliminate those potential jurors in whom there is the greatest distrust. The use of these challenges is discretionary with the attorney. Historically, there have been no limits on the use of this discretion. Recent court decisions, however, have determined that one side may not use peremptory challenges to remove jurors of one gender,[7] religion, race, or color from the jury. (The precedents began with *Batson v. Kentucky*,[8] a criminal case. It is now used in criminal and civil cases.)

The decision about whether to exclude a person from the petit jury may be reached after that individual juror is questioned. In the alternative, it may be made after an entire set of jurors is sitting in the jury box. For example, the judge may then ask each

eClass 4.2 **Management**

SELECTING JURORS

Ms. Carroll and Mr. Jones are conducting the voir dire examination of a prospective juror, Andy Motz. Andy is a 23-year-old business student at the same university as Nic Grant and Nancy Griffin. His father, Ted Motz, is a senior claims supervisor at State-Wide Insurance Company. Ani, Yousef, and Meg believe that Mr. Jones should exclude this person from the jury. They ask you what additional questions Mr. Jones should ask Andy before making a decision whether to remove him from the jury. What additional information would be helpful in making a rational decision? If cause for removal cannot be established, should Mr. Jones use a peremptory challenge to remove this potential juror? What should Mr. Jones do if he disagrees with his clients on jury selection?

BUSINESS CONSIDERATIONS   Should the attorney for a business that sells high-tech, upscale products try to select jurors who have a relatively high-income level and a higher than average educational level? Would such a firm be better served by waiving their right to a jury trial and letting the judge serve as finder of fact?

ETHICAL CONSIDERATIONS   What ethical considerations enter into the jury selection process? Some wealthy parties to lawsuits are able to afford expensive jury consultants and profilers. Does this give them an unethical advantage over people who cannot afford such litigation support?

attorney in turn if the attorney has any objections to the jury sitting in the box. A judge may discuss eliminating jurors at both points. The techniques used for jury selection will depend on the rules of court and the judge's preferences.

Removal of Judges   California has a unique procedure that allows each party one peremptory challenge against the judge assigned to the case. This peremptory challenge must be filed before any proceedings begin in front of the judge being challenged.[9]

Most jurisdictions do not permit peremptory challenges to a judge; however, they have other procedures to disqualify a judge. A judge is not permitted to preside over any action in which he or she has any bias, has a financial interest, is related to any of the parties or attorneys, or there are any facts that would impair the judge's impartiality. For example, if the plaintiffs have appealed the judge's *gag order* (order by judge to be silent about a pending case) to the state supreme court, the judge may be biased. The judge may raise this issue *sua sponte* or it can be raised by one of the parties.[10]

Opening Statements   After the jury is chosen, each side has an opportunity to tell the jury what it intends to prove during the trial. This serves as an introduction to the party's case and helps the jury integrate the evidence that follows. The attorney for the plaintiff makes an opening statement, followed by the attorney for the defendant.

Direct Examination   After a witness has been sworn in, the attorneys question the witness. Witnesses who lie can be held in contempt. The plaintiffs' attorney questions his or her witnesses first. The rules of evidence include rules concerning what information an attorney may elicit from the witnesses as well as how an attorney may request the information. (A detailed discussion of these rules, however, is beyond the scope of this book.)

Trial attorneys are reluctant to ask questions when they do not know how a witness will respond. This is the reason for pretrial preparation of witnesses. Failure to adequately prepare can be disastrous.

Expert Witnesses   An *expert witness* is a witness possessing special knowledge who offers opinions based on facts that have been produced as evidence. For example, Nic Grant or eClass may call medical experts and accident-reconstruction engineers. Expert witnesses are permitted to testify concerning their opinions. They are allowed to state their own conclusions and to discuss hypothetical situations described by the attorneys. In this way, expert witnesses are distinguished from regular witnesses, who are not permitted to present opinions, conclusions, or respond to hypothetical questions. Courts may accommodate special witnesses, such as experts, by allowing them to testify when it is convenient for the witness's schedule.

Cross-examination   After Ms. Carroll questions each of her witnesses, Mr. Jones has an opportunity to question them. Skillful use of cross-examination by competent counsel is the best means to clarify matters brought up in direct examination. After the cross-examination, the party who called the witness (Ms. Carroll) *may* examine the witness again on redirect and the opposing party (Mr. Jones) *may* examine the witness on recross. The process of examination and cross-examination continues until Ms. Carroll has no other witnesses to call. Next, Mr. Jones directly examines his witnesses one at a time, and Ms. Carroll cross-examines each one until the defense has no further witnesses to call. At this point, both sides "rest" their cases.

Motion for a Directed Verdict   A motion for a directed verdict is addressed to the judge. It is usually requested at the close of the opponent's case. The standard used by the judge is whether the plaintiff has made a *prima facie* case (a case that is obvious on its face; it may be rebutted by evidence to the contrary) on which he or she is entitled to recover. If the plaintiff has *not* presented a *prima facie* case, the defendant is entitled to a directed verdict. In most jurisdictions, the judge cannot weigh the evidence—the judge must look solely at the evidence produced by the party against whom the motion is sought; accept any reasonable inference from that evidence; and disregard all challenges to the credibility of that evidence. (A minority of jurisdictions permit the weighing of evidence.) If the defendant's motion is granted, it means that the court has determined that the defendant must win as a matter of law.

If the motion is not granted, the trial will continue. After the presentation of the defendant's evidence, the plaintiff may request a directed verdict on the defendant's cross-complaint and/or the defendant can again request a directed verdict. Again, if either party's motion for a directed verdict is granted, it means that the court has determined that that party must win as a matter of law. In some states a motion for nonsuit is used in a similar manner.

Closing Arguments   After both sides rest, each has an opportunity to persuade the jury by reviewing the testimony, restating the significant facts, and then drawing conclusions from those facts that best support its position. Thus, each attorney takes the same body of evidence and attempts to reach a favorable conclusion by emphasizing the evidence favorable to his or her client and minimizing unfavorable evidence. This stage is called *closing arguments* or *summation*.

The Verdict   At the conclusion of closing arguments, the judge discusses the law with the jury and charges them to answer certain questions with respect to the evidence *adduced* (given as proof) at trial. As part of the charge, he or she instructs them in the applicable areas of law and defines any legal concepts. This is called the *charge to the jury* or *jury instructions*. Many states now have published standardized jury instructions so that the judge does not have to write new jury instructions each time.

The jury may be directed to reach a general verdict and/or a special verdict. In a *general verdict*, the jury is asked who should win the lawsuit and how much damage was suffered, if any. In a *special verdict*, the jury is asked specific questions about the relevant factual issues in the case.

After the jury withdraws from the courtroom, they *deliberate* on the evidence in private and attempt to reach a verdict. In many jurisdictions, the jury *may* request that parts of the evidence be "read back" to them during the deliberation process. In a civil case, many rules of court do not require a unanimous decision; some even authorize a decision by a majority vote of the jurors. In Pennsylvania, the verdict is valid if at least five sixths of the jurors agree to it.[11] In federal court, a unanimous jury must decide a civil case unless the parties agree to the contrary.[12] After the petit jurors reach a verdict, it is announced in open court. The *verdict* is the stated opinion of the jury. If the judge concurs in the verdict, he or she enters a judgment. This is the most common type of verdict.

In our case, the jury deliberated and held for the plaintiffs, Nic Grant and Nancy Griffin, for $21,026 and $5,498, respectively. The court then entered a judgment in those amounts for the two plaintiffs. The judgment is the court's official decision and appears as Exhibit 4.7.

Exhibit 4.7

Court's Judgment

Court's Judgment
IN THE COURT OF COMMON PLEAS OF BUTLER COUNTY, PENNSYLVANIA
CIVIL ACTION

NIC GRANT	:	A.D. No. 23465
and	:	
NANCY GRIFFIN, Plaintiffs	:	
	:	
	:	
v.	:	
	:	
	:	
ECLASS	:	
and	:	
YOUSEF ALWAZZAN, Defendants	:	

On the 9th day of November 2012, this cause came to be heard, plaintiffs appearing in person and by their attorney, LYN CARROLL, and defendants appearing in person and by their attorneys,[a] JONES, MURPHY, SABBATINO, and SCHWARTZ. All parties announcing ready for trial, a jury composed of Mae Brown and eleven others of the regular panel of the petit jurors of this court was selected and impaneled and sworn according to law to try the issues of fact arising in this cause. After the introduction of all the evidence, the instructions of the court, and the arguments of counsel, said jury retired to consider its verdict, and after deliberating thereon returned unto court the following verdict:

We, the jury, find in favor of the plaintiffs, Nic Grant and Nancy Griffin, and assess their damages at $21,026 and $5,498, respectively.

MAE BROWN, FOREPERSON

IT IS, THEREFORE, BY THE COURT, CONSIDERED, ORDERED, AND ADJUGED that the plaintiffs, NIC GRANT and NANCY GRIFFIN, are entitled to recover of and from the defendants, ECLASS and/or YOUSEF ALWAZZAN, the sums of $21,026 and $5,498, respectively, plus their court costs herein expended. Said judgment shall bear interest from this date until paid at the rate of SIX PERCENT PER ANNUM.[b]

Exhibit 4.7 Continued

ENTERED this 15th day of November 2012.[c]

_____
JUDGE

APPROVED AS TO FORM:

_____
Attorney for Plaintiffs

_____
Attorneys for Defendants

[a] This is plural because the defendants are represented by a law firm—Jones, Murphy, Sabbatino, and Schwartz.
[b] The rate of interest allowed depends on the jurisdiction. Butler County allows 6 percent.
[c] Notice that this is approximately one year after the lawsuit was initiated.

Judgment   In most cases, the judge will agree with the jury's verdict. The judge may disagree with the jury's verdict, however. In these situations, the judge may enter a _judgment notwithstanding the verdict._ Traditionally, this was called a judgment _non obstante veredicto,_ hence the abbreviation judgment n.o.v. When a judge declares a judgment n.o.v., he or she substitutes his or her own decision for that of the jury. Either a plaintiff or a defendant may be awarded a judgment n.o.v. A judgment n.o.v. is appropriate only if the jury's verdict is incorrect as a matter of law, that is, there is no substantial evidence to support the jury verdict. Most courts use the same standard as that used for a directed verdict. The court disregards all conflicts in the evidence, does not consider whether the witnesses are credible, and gives face value to the evidence in favor of the party who received the verdict. The party who won the original verdict will likely appeal the judgment n.o.v.

Post-Trial Proceedings

Execution and Attachment   Sometimes the defendant may "voluntarily" pay the judgment after losing the case. If that is not the case, the successful plaintiff will have to conduct the collection process himself or herself. This is usually accomplished by discovering the defendant's assets and obtaining permission (in a written legal document called a writ) from the court to attach them. The plaintiff then takes the writ to the court in the locality where the assets are located, completes a form requesting execution, pays a fee, and asks a sheriff, marshal, or constable to collect the described assets. State laws on execution and attachment vary.

Motion for a New Trial   Often, the losing party will request the court to either enter a judgment n.o.v. _or_ grant a new trial. A _motion for a new trial_ is filed with the same

Exhibit 4.8

Common Steps of a Trial

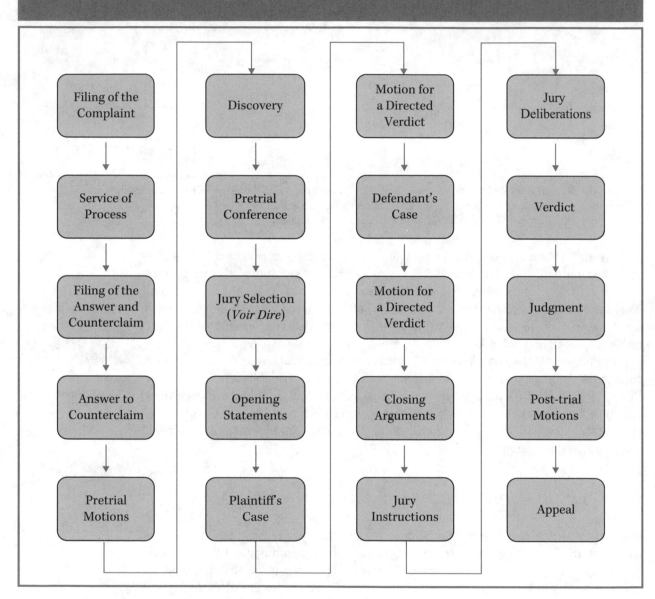

judge who originally heard the case, unless that judge is disabled or disqualified. The party making the motion is requesting the court to order a new trial. The party must justify the request and explain why a new trial is proper.

Common grounds for a motion for a new trial include: The judge committed a prejudicial error in conducting the trial; there were perceived irregularities in the jury's behavior; or the evidence was insufficient to support the verdict. In extremely rare cases, a new trial may be granted based on newly discovered evidence. To obtain a new trial on this basis, the moving party must show that the newly discovered evidence pertains to facts in existence at the time of trial, the evidence is material, and the moving party with reasonable diligence could not have obtained the information prior to trial. The latter requirement is to prevent a party from obtaining a new trial when the party was negligent in failing to obtain the evidence for the original trial. A new trial will *not* be granted because a party's attorney in the original trial was incompetent. A party who believes that the damage award is excessive *or* too small can also request a new trial. When the motion for a new trial is based on the amount of damages, a judge may, for example, grant a new trial unless a plaintiff agrees to accept a reduction in the amount of damages. This is called *remittitur*. Some states also permit granting a new trial unless a defendant agrees to accept an increase in the amount of the award. This is called *additur*. Obviously, conducting a new trial is expensive for the parties *and* the court system.

Appeal   After losing the decision, the attorneys for eClass might file a notice of appeal to hear the case before a higher court. The rules of court specify the time limit for filing a notice of appeal. Appeals, however, are limited to questions of law. In other words, the appellate court will generally not reverse a lower court unless the lower court made an error of law. In this case, the decision is in accordance with the law; consequently, eClass does not appeal. eClass now owes the plaintiffs $21,026 and $5,498, respectively.

If a case is appealed, the appellate court can *affirm* the decision, which indicates approval, or *reverse* the decision, which indicates an error of law. Appellate courts can affirm some parts of the decision and reverse others. Sometimes the appellate court reverses and *remands* the case because the lower court made a mistake of law, and the case is returned to it for correction. Exhibit 4.8 depicts the stages of a trial.

A Comment on Finality

One of the great virtues of the law is finality. When a cause of action has been litigated and reduced to a judgment and all appeals have been exhausted, the matter comes to an end. In this case, the doctrine of *res judicata* applies. *Res judicata* means that when a court issues a final judgment, the subject matter of that lawsuit is finally decided between the parties to the suit. This doctrine prevents further suits from being brought by the same parties on the same issues. In other words, the matter comes to rest. Remember, however, that *res judicata* does not prevent timely appeals nor does it prevent criminal proceedings based on the same behavior.

SMALL CLAIMS COURT

Another technique to reduce legal expenses is for a party to file the legal dispute in small claims court. Although this is still litigation, it significantly reduces the costs. This option permits a party to effectively represent himself or herself. Generally, the opponent can also appear without a lawyer. Small claims courts do not use legalese and standard rules of evidence. Quick resolution of disputes is usually available. The procedures in small claims courts vary from state to state. The jurisdictional amounts also vary—the upper limit may range from $1,000 (Mississippi and parts of Virginia) to $10,000 (parts of Tennessee).[13] In most states, Nic and Nancy's claims would exceed the jurisdictional limits of small claims court.

Some small claims courts publish booklets to assist parties in small claims actions. There may also be government employees who provide free or low-cost legal services to parties who are filing complaints in small claims courts. Participants do not need to be familiar with legal jargon; however, participants need to be organized and bring their witnesses and any physical evidence with them to the hearing. Participants should prepare a brief, coherent presentation of the case. It is also helpful to observe a couple of small claims cases in advance of the hearing date.

If the defendant does not show up on the trial date, the court hears only the plaintiff's side. Since only the plaintiff was heard, the court will rule for the plaintiff. This result is called a *default judgment*—the defendant defaults by failing to appear. If the plaintiff does not appear on the trial date, the case is dismissed.

ALTERNATIVE DISPUTE RESOLUTION (ADR)

The Need for Alternatives to a Civil Suit

Regular lawsuits are often expensive, and they are frequently time-consuming. A business that is plagued by frequent lawsuits will suffer financially, and the financial burden for businesses facing large class-action lawsuits may be even worse. As a result, many businesses may prefer to seek an alternative form of dispute resolution, such as arbitration. Even the federal government is participating in arbitration. For example, the United States arbitrated the value that was due to the amateur filmmaker Abraham Zapruder for seizing his film of the assassination of President John F. Kennedy.[14] There is normally a significant passage of time between the filing of a lawsuit and the resolution of the case by the court. Even if a plaintiff has what seems to be a good case, there is no guarantee that the plaintiff will prevail at trial. Product liability cases on average have a processing time of 530 days. Moreover, only 40 percent of the plaintiffs in these cases win.

For a business defendant, the time spent in preparing for the trial and then having officers attend the pretrial and trial proceedings represents a significant cost factor even if the business wins the case. Many businesses prefer to settle the case—the earlier the better—by paying the plaintiff and saving all the time and trouble that a trial requires. If an alternative means of resolving the dispute was available, those businesses would be likely to use it.

Alternatives to litigation do exist, and these *alternative* forms of *dispute resolution* are becoming increasingly popular. ADR provides a number of benefits:

- The burden on the court system is reduced.
- An injured party with a legitimate claim is likely to be compensated sooner. When one considers the time-value of money, this can be a significant factor.
- Businesses (and other defendants) are less likely to settle foundless claims merely for the sake of expediency and/or because the settlement is less expensive than the expenses of a trial.
- ADR is less adversarial, allowing the parties to reach a more amicable resolution. This, in turn, permits the parties to continue to do business together or to coexist in harmony in the future.

As a result of these—and other—benefits, the use of ADR is becoming more common, especially in the resolution of disputes involving a business. Increasingly, courts are *requiring* parties to attempt alternative methods of dispute resolution first, before allowing them to seek judicial remedies. Because these processes are usually less expensive and faster, they tend to create less tension in the relationship of the parties. This is particularly important in disputes between family members, such as child-custody cases, and in business situations where the parties may wish to continue to do business together. For example, difficulties arose when Whoopi Goldberg was filming *T. Rex*. The parties agreed to use arbitration whenever problems occurred so that they could continue to produce the film.[15] Continuity of relationship is not an issue in Nic Grant and Nancy Griffin's suit against eClass, since the parties do not have an on-going relationship. ADR can be used with more than two parties. However, for the sake of simplicity we will talk about two-party disputes.

ADR has its limits, and it is not appropriate for resolving every form of legal dispute. ADR cannot be used in criminal matters, for example, and it does not establish legal precedence. ADR may not result in a fair resolution if there is significant power imbalance. Power imbalance occurs when one of the parties to the dispute has a significant advantage over the other, such as workplace bullying where the employee's manager is the bully. Other types of advantages could be emotional strength, negotiating skills, or knowledge such as financial, legal, or technical knowledge. The impartial third party may be able to help "correct" some of the power imbalance depending on the intermediary's skill. In addition, some matters should be debated in a public forum, which is not provided by ADR. In both negotiation and mediation, a person can stipulate that he or she will not sign an agreement until it is approved by his or her lawyer or other advisor. When ADR is used within its limits, it usually provides quick and sure resolutions for a number of problems in a manner that is advantageous for all of the parties involved. Exhibit 4.9 summarizes the types of alternative dispute resolution which will be discussed below.

Exhibit 4.9

Types of Alternative Dispute Resolution

Type of Alternative Dispute Resolution	Definition	Example
Negotiation	The parties talk to each other and resolve their dispute.	Nicole and Pam are roommates. They each have annoying habits. They sit down and talk to each other and reach a compromise.
Mediation	The parties use an impartial third party (mediator) to help them communicate with each other and resolve their dispute.	Glenda and Robert are neighbors. They are not getting along very well. They agree to meet with a volunteer neighborhood mediator. The mediator helps them resolve their differences.
Arbitration	The parties present their evidence to an impartial third party (arbitrator) who makes a decision called an award. Before the arbitration begins, the parties decide if the arbitration will be binding or advisory on them.	Rosie works for an office supply store. When she started work, she agreed that she would submit any employment disputes to binding arbitration. The store also agreed to submit its disputes with Rosie to binding arbitration. Rosie feels that her boss is discriminating against her because she is a woman. Rosie and the store submit the dispute to binding arbitration.
Minitrial	The parties present their evidence to the arbitrator in a court-like setting. The arbitrator makes an advisory award. The parties then use the information to assist them in negotiating a solution.	Two competing car manufacturers have a dispute about the advertising practices of the other. They participate in a minitrial. After hearing the award, the manufacturers agree to change the content of their television commercials.
Rent-a-judge Trial	The parties present their evidence to a retired judge who serves as the arbitrator and makes an award.	A company and its primary supplier are having a dispute about the timing of shipments. They agree to submit their dispute to a rent-a-judge so that it can be resolved quickly and the shipments can continue.

Negotiation

Perhaps the earliest, and simplest, form of ADR is *negotiation*. Negotiation involves the discussion and resolution of a controversy by the parties involved. Negotiation is so common that most people do not even consider it as a form of ADR. Instead, they think of it as merely a method for settling disputes or controversies. That is the gist of ADR, however—settling a dispute or a controversy without resorting to the courts.

If the parties to the dispute recognize the wisdom in handling the dispute themselves and are willing and able to negotiate a solution acceptable to the parties, negotiation is an excellent method of dispute resolution. If the parties are able to resolve the matter themselves, with or without consulting their attorneys, they can probably save time and money. However, the parties may not *think* of negotiation as a possible solution, or they may not be *willing* to negotiate a settlement. Since negotiation is handled strictly by the parties, all interested parties must be willing to negotiate before it can serve as an effective method for resolving the dispute. For example, Nic and Nancy could try to negotiate a settlement with eClass's insurance company rather than take the case to trial. In so doing, they may wish to have Ms. Carroll assist them in the negotiation. The insurance adjuster or the attorney for the insurer may serve as the representative of the company.

Mediation

Mediation is similar to negotiation, although there is a significant difference. Mediation involves the use of an impartial third party, a *mediator*, who attempts to help the parties reach a mutually acceptable resolution to their dispute. Usually, just one mediator is used. The mediator does not act as a decision maker. Rather, he or she facilitates communication between the parties. The mediator listens to the parties and assists them in resolving their differences, or as many of the aspects of their dispute as possible. There are no formal procedures. The parties may choose to have a lawyer, a family member, or some other advisor present during the mediation. Generally, the mediator should not have any financial or personal interest in the result of the mediation without the written consent of all the parties. A prospective mediator should promptly disclose to the parties any circumstance likely to cause bias or the appearance of bias.

The advantages of mediation are that it is less expensive than litigation, it is quicker, and generally the results are perceived as more satisfactory. The American Arbitration Association (AAA) claims that its mediations are very effective with 85 percent of commercial matters and 95 percent of personal injury matters resulting in written settlement agreements.[16] Participants are generally more satisfied because they agreed to the result. Nic, Nancy, Ani, Meg, and Yousef could use mediation to attempt to resolve their dispute. The insurance company would also need to be represented if they are going to be asked for payment. The parties may use a commercial service to locate an appropriate unbiased mediator. The ABA Section of Dispute Resolution and the National Conference of Commissioners on Uniform State Laws (NCCUSL) has prepared the Uniform Mediation Act.[17]

Generally, the mediator does not impose a solution on the parties. Some mediators, however, take a more forceful role in attempting to fashion an agreement; others believe a more passive role is appropriate.

More than one mediation technique can be used in an attempt to resolve the disagreement. One mediation technique is *caucusing*. In this technique, the mediator meets with each party separately. Another mediation technique is *shuttle mediation*, where the mediator physically separates the parties during the mediation session and then runs messages between them.

Mediation sessions are private; usually only the parties, their representatives, and the mediator will be present. Other people generally may only attend with the permission of the parties and the mediator.

In most cases, mediation is successful; however, if it is not, the parties can use another ADR technique or submit their dispute for judicial resolution. Consequently, an important principle of mediation is confidentiality; otherwise, the parties will not discuss the issues freely. The parties must be confident that what they say or admit in mediation will not be used against them in court. The parties should agree to maintain the confidentiality of the mediation and not to rely on or introduce into evidence at any arbitration, judicial, or other proceeding (1) the views expressed by a party; (2) suggestions made by a party; (3) admissions made by a party; (4) proposals made by the mediator; (5) views expressed by the mediator; and/or (6) the fact that a party was or was not willing to accept a proposal. The mediator should not be required to testify or divulge records in any adversarial proceeding. No stenographic record is prepared of the mediation process. An American Arbitration Association (AAA) Mediation usually follows these steps:

1. Any party or parties to a dispute may initiate mediation by filing with the AAA a submission to mediation or a written request for mediation pursuant to these procedures. Where there is no submission to mediation or contract providing for mediation, a party may request the AAA to invite another party to join in a submission to mediation. Upon receipt of such a request, the AAA will contact the other parties involved in the dispute and attempt to obtain a submission to mediation.

2. Upon receipt of a request for mediation, the AAA will appoint a qualified mediator to serve. Normally, a single mediator will be appointed unless the parties agree otherwise or the AAA determines otherwise. If the agreement of the parties names a mediator or specifies a method of appointing a mediator, that designation or method shall be followed.

3. At least ten days prior to the first scheduled mediation session, each party shall provide the mediator with a brief memorandum setting forth its position with regard to the issues that need to be resolved. The mediator does not have the authority to impose a settlement on the parties but will attempt to help them reach a satisfactory resolution of their dispute. The mediator is authorized to conduct joint and separate meetings with the parties and to make oral and written recommendations for settlement.[18]

There is a disagreement about whether mediators should undergo some certification process and become "certified." The proponents of mediator certification believe that standards would encourage the confidence of the courts and the disputing parties. It would also ease the backlog in civil courts. The opponents to certification feel that it would limit the diversity of mediators at a time when this diversity is in demand. Lawyers, judges, psychotherapists, and ministers have entered the field of mediation. In addition, opponents argue that the profession is still developing and it is too early for certification; there are no adequate standards for certification. Certification at this time would be unfair and misleading to the public. In addition, there have been relatively few complaints against mediators.

A mediator should have good problem-solving skills and be fair. Roberta Kerr Parrott, a professional mediator, explains:

> The challenge is always, when there's conflict, to create a possibility for both sides, both parties, to win. To make sure that I'm quiet enough long enough to hear what the real issues are so that we're dealing with what people are feeling and thinking at the heart of the issue rather than dealing with the surface.[19]

Knowledge of the law, while important in some cases, is only one possible competency a good mediator needs. Other necessary skills for mediators include:

- patience, persistence, concentration, and focus toward the goal
- the ability to distinguish between stated positions of the disputants and their real interests
- the ability to remain positive and constructive, even with difficult parties
- the ability to maintain confidentiality
- the ability to remain unbiased in the search for the truth of the situation and the solutions that work best for all concerned under the circumstances
- the ability to secure a resolution that is truly satisfactory for the participants: substantively, procedurally, and psychologically[20]

Standards of Conduct   A model standards of conduct for mediators was drafted in 1994 and amended in 2005. The 2005 version has been endorsed by the American Arbitration Association, the American Bar Association, and the Association for Conflict Resolution. These standards do not have the force of law but may be viewed as the applicable standard for mediator behavior.[21] A summary appears as Exhibit 4.10.

The standards do not choose between the conflicting approaches to mediation; instead, they concentrate on the similarities between the approaches. One particularly difficult issue is how active a mediator should be. Some contend that a mediator should only *facilitate* the settlement of disputes. Others believe that mediators should *evaluate* the proposals and *comment* on the viability of an approach in court. A number of states, such as Florida, Indiana, and Texas, have adopted standards of conduct for mediators.[22]

Exhibit 4.10

Model Standards of Conduct for Mediators

A Mediator shall:

1. Recognize that mediation is based on the principles of self-determination by the parties.
2. Conduct the mediation in an impartial manner.
3. Disclose all actual and potential conflicts of interest reasonably known to the mediator.
4. Mediate only when the mediator has the necessary qualifications to satisfy the reasonable expectations of the parties.
5. Maintain the reasonable expectations of the parties with regard to confidentiality.
6. Conduct the mediation fairly and diligently, and in a manner consistent with the principle of self-determination by the parties.
7. Be truthful in advertising and solicitation for mediation.
8. Fully disclose and explain the basis of compensation, fees, and charges to the parties.
9. Have a duty to improve the practice of the profession.

Reprinted by permission of the American Arbitration Association, New York, NY.

Compensation   There is no hard-and-fast rule regarding the compensation of mediators. In fact, compensation among mediators can vary widely. For example, in the Boston area, mediators fees range from approximately $100 to $800 per hour.[23] Many mediators are volunteers who serve as mediators through various community organizations. Others are professional mediators who rely on mediation to provide much of their income. The parties should discuss the compensation issue and how the expenses will be shared before agreeing to submit their dispute to mediation.

Arbitration

Arbitration is the process of submitting a dispute to the judgment of a person or group of persons called arbitrators for resolution. The final decision of the arbitrator or panel of arbitrators is called an *award*. It is usually binding on the parties. *Advisory arbitration* is similar to traditional arbitration; however, it focuses on specific issues in the dispute, and the award is not binding on the parties. Television "judges" are arbitrators and not practicing judges, although some of them may have been judges in the past.

Arbitration begins with an agreement between the parties to arbitrate, usually in the initial agreement. The parties *can* agree to arbitrate after an actual dispute arises, if they are willing to do so. The terms in an arbitration agreement can vary widely. An agreement to arbitrate is basically a contract or a portion of a contract. Like all contracts, to be valid it must be based on *mutual assent*, meaning the parties must agree to be bound by exactly the same terms. If a party agrees to an arbitration clause

eClass 4.3 **Management**

SERVING AS A MEDIATOR

Meg has been asked to serve as a mediator in a dispute between two local firms that are each active in electronic research. Both firms agreed that their controversy should be resolved without taking the issue to court; and both agreed that Meg possessed the necessary qualifications to mediate their dispute. Meg is concerned about the request, and she has asked you whether she is qualified to serve as a mediator in this situation. What advice will you give her?

BUSINESS CONSIDERATIONS   Should a business adopt a policy concerning its officers serving as mediators in disputes? What are the possible drawbacks—or benefits—to having officers mediate disputes between other firms?

ETHICAL CONSIDERATIONS   Suppose a businessperson learned about certain new techniques or technical developments while serving as a mediator and this information would be of great use to the businessperson's firm. What ethical considerations would enter into any decision as to whether the information should be used? What legal considerations might enter into this situation?

because of *fraud* (when one party enters into a contract relying on a false statement of material fact) or *duress* (when one party enters into a contract due to a wrongful threat of force), the agreement will not be valid. (For a detailed discussion of what constitutes a valid contract, see Chapters 9-14.) Litigation may ensue if a party feels that the arbitration agreement was invalid. A judge would then determine the legality of the arbitration provision. AAA recommends a standard contract clause such as the one below. The language in brackets can be added when appropriate.

> Any controversy or claim arising out of or relating to this contract, or the breach thereof, shall be settled by arbitration administered by the American Arbitration Association in accordance with its Commercial [or other] Arbitration Rules [including the Optional Rules for Emergency Measures of Protection], and judgment on the award rendered by the arbitrator(s) may be entered in any court having jurisdiction thereof.[24]

Exhibit 4.11 illustrates the steps used in an AAA arbitration.

In arbitration, a hearing is held before an arbitrator or a panel of arbitrators. There are two types of arbitration—binding and nonbinding or advisory. In nonbinding arbitration, the parties can consider the decision but do not have to follow it. Generally, a

Exhibit 4.11

Steps in an AAA Arbitration

1. Arbitration is a creature of contract. In most cases, arbitration is initiated after a dispute has arisen between two parties who had included an arbitration clause in a business contract. The process is guided by time-tested AAA rules and procedures. The initiating party, or claimant, files a Demand for Arbitration with the appropriate AAA case management center. The respondent is given the opportunity to file a counterclaim. For existing disputes with no arbitration clause, parties may file a submission agreement with the AAA.
2. Based on the terms of the clause, an AAA case manager is designated and provides the parties with a list of qualified arbitrators relevant to the type of dispute and the parities' geographic locale.
3. Parties mutually select an arbitrator or arbitrators to hear and decide the case by striking and numbering names from the list until the arbitrator is selected. An acceptable hearing date and location is also selected.
4. The arbitrator(s) hears evidence from both parties, and yields a final and binding decision. The decision is rendered, in most cases, 30 days from the date of closing the hearing, or, if oral hearings have been waived, from the date of the AAA's transmittal of the final statements and proofs to the arbitrator.

American Arbitration Association, AAA Online Library, "Alternative Dispute Resolution Basics FAQs" (accessed 5/4/10). Reprinted with permission of the American Arbitration Association, New York, NY.

party *cannot* appeal the decision in binding arbitration. There are limited grounds for appeal, including problems of mutual assent in the agreement to arbitrate. Some courts will also consider an appeal if the arbitrator refused to admit evidence which would have been admissible in court.

Many states have statutes that provide for arbitration and the enforcement of the arbitrators' awards in the courts of the state. Statutes in Arizona,[25] California,[26] and Michigan[27] expressly authorize arbitration agreements, as does the Federal Arbitration Act.[28] At one time, the law did not favor arbitration because it was considered an improper means of avoiding the judicial system. This position is dwindling as arbitration—and other forms of ADR—are becoming more common and more widely accepted.

Various organizations offer panels of arbitrators. Parties may select their own arbitrator(s) or the arbitrator(s) may be selected by the organization. The AAA, for example, has a specific panel of arbitrators for commercial disputes. It also has panels for other types of disputes. The parties select their arbitrator from the panel members. Nic, Nancy, Ani, Meg, and Yousef could contact the AAA to obtain an arbitrator for their dispute.

Arbitrators charge about $400 to $700 a day.[29] Fees vary depending on the region and the type of case. Despite the expense, one finance company reported a 66 percent reduction in legal expenses by using arbitration.[30]

If both parties comply willingly with the arbitration award, no further action is required. If one side does not, court action to "confirm" the decision is necessary.

State Efforts to Restrict Arbitration　The states have developed their own individual approaches and laws to address arbitration issues. Some state statutes are more pro-arbitration than others. Some attempted to restrict the scope of arbitration. For example, some states (such as Alabama) did not permit arbitration clauses in consumer contracts, although they permitted the use of arbitration and arbitration clauses in other types of contracts.[31] The U.S. Supreme Court addressed this issue in *Allied-Bruce Terminix Companies, Inc. v. Dobson.*[32] The Alabama Supreme Court, relying on state law, had declared that a consumer did not have to go to arbitration as specified in the arbitration agreement. The U.S. Supreme Court heard the case on writ of certiorari to the Alabama Supreme Court and overturned that decision. It ruled that individual states could not regulate or prevent the use of arbitration by their statutes. The Federal Arbitration Act covers all transactions involving interstate commerce. For a more detailed discussion of what constitutes interstate commerce, see Chapter 5.

Statutory Coverage　Arbitration is subject to statutory coverage and provisions at the state, federal, and international levels. The statutory law is clarified by judicial interpretation at all levels. Parties seeking resolution of their disputes through arbitration should ascertain how arbitration is viewed and regulated at the level(s) in which they are involved.

At the state level, the Uniform Arbitration Act (1956) was adopted in 49 jurisdictions.[33] The NCCUSL has enacted the Uniform Arbitration Act (2000), which has been adopted by 13 states.[34]

At the federal level, the Federal Arbitration Act (FAA), originally enacted in 1925, provides some federal guidelines to be followed in arbitration. It also attempts to ensure that arbitration clauses be given the same protection and enforceability as any other contract clauses. Section 2 of the Federal Arbitration Act provides that a "Written provision in any maritime transaction or a contract evidencing a transaction involving commerce to settle by arbitration a controversy thereafter arising out of such contract or transaction . . . shall be valid, irrevocable, and enforceable, save upon such grounds as exist at law or in equity for the revocation of any contract."

At the international level, arbitration is most likely to be regulated by the 1958 UN Convention on Recognition and Enforcement of Arbitral Awards, an international treaty dealing with arbitration. This convention has been ratified by more than 110 nations.[35] In this hemisphere, the Inter-American Convention on International Commercial Arbitration also facilitates international arbitration.[36] The International Chamber of Commerce also supports and encourages arbitration; and many firms involved in international business seek to resolve their disputes through its arbitration provisions. The federal statute and the international treaties are designed to increase the acceptance and use of arbitration as an alternative method for resolving disputes.

Organizations　There are a number of organizations that actively support arbitration and provide both the forum in which an arbitration occurs and the arbitrator. Some of these organizations operate exclusively within the United States; others operate internationally. Within the United States, arbitration is supported by the

Judicial Arbitration and Mediation Services, Inc. (J.A.M.S.), which employs only former judges as arbitrators, the Federal Mediation and Conciliation Service, as well as the AAA. Internationally, the AAA (which operates both domestically and internationally), the International Chamber of Commerce, headquartered in Paris, and the London Court of Arbitration (which is *not* a court, despite the title of the organization) support arbitration.

The AAA administers approximately 150,000 cases per year.[37] Its services include arbitration, mediation, minitrial, *fact-finding* (a process where an arbitrator investigates a dispute and issues findings of fact and a nonbinding report), education, and training. When the AAA is involved in the arbitration process, it can refer a list of potential arbitrators, serve as an *intermediator* between the parties and the arbitrator in negotiating the arbitrator's compensation, and collect a deposit for arbitrator compensation. The AAA administrator handles the administrative details, so that the parties do not deal directly with the arbitrator. This helps ensure that the parties will not discuss the case privately with the arbitrator prior to the hearing. The AAA requires its arbitrators to issue awards within 30 days after the close of the hearings, unless the contract between the parties specifies another time limit.[38] Except in labor and international cases, the AAA does not encourage arbitrators to write lengthy opinions. Instead, it encourages them to write an itemized award.[39] It promulgates rules for specific types of arbitration, and it also has special procedures for large, complex commercial cases. The slogan of the AAA is "Speed, Economy, and Justice."

Minitrial

In ADR, the term *minitrial* describes a process in which the parties' attorneys present an abbreviated form of their case. The parties are permitted to use expert witnesses to support their case. A *neutral*, an unbiased person, chairs the case. Senior executives from the firms involved also attend the presentation. After the presentation, the senior executives meet in an attempt to resolve the dispute. Prior to the presentation, the parties usually specify what will happen if the senior executives are unable to settle the case. For example, if the senior executives *are* unable to settle the case, the neutral may be empowered to mediate or to provide a nonbinding advisory opinion informing the parties of the probable outcome of litigation. A minitrial would not be appropriate to resolve Nic and Nancy's claims.

Note that in court matters, judges use the term *minitrial* to refer to an abbreviated judicial proceeding on a few issues, for example, a minitrial on damages.

Rent-a-Judge Trial

A "rent-a-judge" trial is another alternative method of dispute resolution. When the parties elect to use this method, they pay a fee to a "judge" to settle the dispute. "Judges" in these cases are typically retired judges, people who are well trained in presiding over dispute resolution and who bring the reputation and prestige of their former positions to their current role. Rent-a-judge "cases" occasionally involve a "jury" of hired experts, particularly in technical cases.

The major advantage of the rent-a-judge option is that it is much faster than regular civil litigation. In addition, the proceedings are relatively private and do not become part of the public record. Many time-consuming trial procedures are eliminated in rent-a-judge trials, providing an additional savings of time and money.[40] These "trials" are significantly less formal and are generally conducted in conference rooms.

It is not uncommon for the parties in a civil case to wait four to five years before they can get their case to trial. These same parties can get their case to "trial" with a rent-a-judge in a matter of weeks. As a result, the use of rent-a-judge trials is growing more popular. Because all states accept some form of private resolution of cases, rent-a-judge resolutions are likely to become more common in the future. A number of companies now exist to assist clients in locating rent-a-judges. One company, Judicate, even has its own private courthouse in Los Angeles. In some jurisdictions, the clerk of court's office maintains a list of retired judges who are willing to serve as rent-a-judges. Depending on the jurisdiction, the decisions of rent-a-judges may be appealed to the public court of appeals.[41] Nic and Nancy might agree to using a retired judge from Butler County to serve as a rent-a-judge. If they are experiencing financial difficulty, the speed of using a rent-a-judge and the opportunity for a quick payment would be attractive.

Contemporary Case

CIRCUIT CITY STORES, INC. v. ADAMS

279 F.3d 889, 2002 U.S. App. LEXIS 1686 (9th Cir. 2002)

Writ of certiorari denied: Circuit City Stores, Inc. v. Adams, 2002 U.S. LEXIS 4060 (U.S. June 3, 2002).

On Remand from the United States Supreme Court

FACTS On October 23, 1995, Saint Clair Adams completed an application to work as a sales person at Circuit City. As part of the application, Adams signed the Circuit City Dispute Resolution Agreement (DRA). An employee cannot work at Circuit City without signing the DRA. If an applicant refuses to sign the DRA, Circuit City will not consider his application. The DRA says that an applicant agrees to settle "all previously unasserted claims, disputes or controversies arising out of or relating to my application or candidacy for employment, employment and/or cessation of employment with Circuit City, *exclusively* by final and binding *arbitration* before a neutral Arbitrator. By way of example only, such claims include claims under federal, state, and local statutory or common law, such as Age Discrimination in Employment Act, Title VII of the Civil Rights Act of 1964, as amended, including the amendments to the Civil Rights Act of 1991, the Americans with Disabilities Act, the law of contract and law of tort." Incorporated into the

DRA are rules that define the claims subject to arbitration, discovery rules, allocation of fees, and limit the amount of remedies. The employee is "required to split the costs of the arbitration, including the daily fees of the arbitrator, the cost of a reporter to transcribe the proceedings, and the expense of renting the room in which the arbitration is held, unless the employee prevails and the arbitrator decides to order Circuit City to pay the employee's share of the costs." The DRA does not require Circuit City to arbitrate its claims against the employee.

"Adams filed a state court lawsuit against Circuit City and three co-workers alleging sexual harassment, retaliation, constructive discharge, and intentional infliction of emotional distress under the California Fair Employment and Housing Act [FEHA] ... and discrimination based on sexual orientation under Cal. Labor Code § 1102.1." Circuit City filed a petition to stay the state court proceedings and compel arbitration pursuant to the DRA. The federal district court granted the petition. The court of appeals reversed on the ground that Section 1 of the Federal Arbitration Act (FAA) exempted Adams' employment contract from the FAA's coverage. The Supreme Court reversed and remanded the case to the court of appeals.

ISSUE Is Adams required to submit his employment-related disputes to arbitration?

HOLDING No, the Circuit City DRA is an unconscionable contract of adhesion and not binding on Adams.

REASONING Excerpts from the opinion of Circuit Judge Dorothy W. Nelson:

... The ... FAA was enacted to overcome courts' reluctance to enforce arbitration agreements. ... Section 2 of the FAA provides that arbitration agreements "shall be valid, irrevocable, and enforceable, *save upon such grounds that exist at law or in equity for the revocation of any contract.*" ... In determining the validity of an agreement to arbitrate, federal courts "should apply ordinary state-law principles that govern the formation of contracts." ... [G]eneral contract defenses such as fraud, duress, or unconscionability, grounded in state contract law, may operate to invalidate arbitration agreements. ...

Adams argues that the DRA is an unconscionable contract of adhesion. Because Adams was employed in California, we look to California contract law to determine whether the agreement is valid. ... Under California law, a contract is unenforceable if it is both procedurally and substantively unconscionable. ... When assessing procedural unconscionability, we consider the equilibrium of bargaining power between the parties and the extent to which the contract clearly discloses its terms. ... A determination of substantive unconscionability, on the other hand, involves whether the terms of the contract are unduly harsh or oppressive. ... The DRA is procedurally unconscionable because it is a contract of adhesion: a standard-form contract, drafted by the party with superior bargaining power, which relegates to the other party the option of either adhering to its terms without modification or rejecting the contract entirely. ... Circuit City, which possesses considerably more bargaining power than nearly all of its employees or applicants, drafted the contract and uses it as its standard arbitration agreement for all of its new employees. The agreement is a prerequisite to employment, and job applicants are not permitted to modify the agreement's terms—they must take the contract or leave it. ...

We find the arbitration agreement at issue here virtually indistinguishable from the agreement the California Supreme Court found unconscionable in ... [precedents]. [T]he DRA unilaterally forces employees to arbitrate claims against the employer. ... The provision does not require Circuit City to arbitrate its claims against employees. Circuit City has offered no justification for this asymmetry, nor is there any indication that "business realities" warrant the one-sided obligation. This unjustified one-sidedness deprives the DRA of the "modicum of bilaterality" that the California Supreme Court requires for contracts to be enforceable under California law.

... [T]he asymmetry is compounded by the fact that the agreement limits the relief available to employees.... Circuit City's arbitration agreement ... fails to provide for all of the types of relief that would otherwise be available in court, or to ensure that employees do not have to pay either unreasonable costs or any arbitrators' fees or expenses as a condition of access to the arbitration forum.... Because unconscionability is a defense to contracts generally and does not single out arbitration agreements for special scrutiny, it is also a valid reason not to enforce an arbitration agreement under the FAA. Indeed, the Supreme Court has specifically mentioned unconscionability as a "generally applicable contract defense[]" that may be raised consistent with § 2 of the FAA. ...

Under California law, courts have discretion to sever an unconscionable provision or refuse to enforce the contract in its entirety.... In this case, ... the objectionable provisions pervade the entire contract.... [T]he unilateral aspect of the DRA runs throughout the agreement and defines the scope of the matters that are covered. Removing these provisions would go beyond mere excision to rewriting the contract, which is not the proper role of this Court. ...

You Be the Judge

Jarek Molski had a motorcycle accident about 20 years ago, which left him confined to a wheelchair. Since that time, he has filed more than 400 lawsuits under the Americans with Disabilities Act (ADA). The ADA permits private individuals to file suit against public accommodations, such as restaurants and retail stores, if the public accommodation does not meet federal standards for access for the disabled. Successful plaintiffs earn money from their suits. Molski has asked that business owners who were not complying be fined $4,000 per day for every day they did not meet the standards. Fear of adverse decisions convinced many businesses to settle out of court. Molski reportedly earned hundreds of thousands of dollars in less than two years from his ADA litigation. In 2004, U.S. District Judge Edward Rafeedie called Molski a "hit-and-run plaintiff" and accused him of extortion of small businesses across California. In a very unusual action, the federal judge barred Molski from starting future litigation. The judge also barred Molski's attorney, Thomas E. Frankovich, from filing more suits without the judge's permission. If the judge's decision is appealed to *your* court, what would *you* decide? Is the decision fair to the plaintiff? Is it fair to his attorney? Remember that attorneys have an obligation to the court. [See Carol J. Williams, "Litigious Man Barred From More Lawsuits," *Fresno Bee*, November 18, 2008, p. B3.]

Summary

Lawsuits are based on factual circumstances. Therefore, it is the client's responsibility to reveal all the facts to his or her attorney. If all the facts are not known, the attorney might draw the wrong legal conclusion. If the facts warrant a lawsuit, one of the first things the attorney should do is to apprise the potential defendant of liability and seek to settle the case without filing a lawsuit.

Attorney's fees are an important consideration in deciding whether the client should sue. Nic Grant and Nancy Griffin had contingency fee arrangements, whereby if the plaintiffs had lost the case, their attorney would have received no fees. Other bases for attorney's fees also exist, including a flat rate or an hourly rate. In these cases, the attorney receives compensation whether or not the attorney wins the case. The fee arrangement is specified in the oral or written contract that creates the attorney—client relationship.

Before a lawsuit is filed, the attorney has a duty to investigate the facts to determine whether sufficient evidence exists to justify litigation. Before filing suit, an opportunity is usually provided for the parties to settle the matter, either through a settlement conference or arbitration.

After suit is filed, the discovery process takes place. Discovery is designed to narrow the legal issues, thus encouraging pretrial settlement or reducing the duration of the actual trial. During *voir dire*, the petit jury is selected for the trial. Potential jurors can be dismissed for cause or by use of a peremptory challenge. Consultants may be hired to assist the attorneys in selecting the jury and/or presenting an effective case before the jury.

The doctrine of *res judicata* means that when a court issues a final judgment, the subject matter of the case cannot be relitigated between the same parties. However, it does not prevent appeals from the final judgment.

Small claims courts provide relatively informal resolution for small civil claims. The rules and the jurisdictional limits of these specialized courts vary widely among the states.

The time, trouble, and expense associated with trials have led to an increasing emphasis on ADR methods. There are five major ADR methods. *Negotiation* is probably the oldest and most common form of ADR. The parties discuss their dispute and reach a mutually agreeable solution to the problem. Negotiation is only restricted by the willingness of the parties to compromise. *Mediation* is slightly more formal than negotiation. In mediation, the parties turn to a mediator, a third person who helps the parties to find a mutually acceptable solution. Mediators do not provide a solution; they provide a procedure for helping the parties reach a solution. The mediator facilitates communication rather than acting as a decision maker. *Arbitration* involves a third party, the arbitrator, who listens to the arguments of each party and then renders an award to resolve the controversy. The arbitrator is a decision maker. Arbitration is commonly *binding*, meaning that the parties agree to abide by the decision. *Minitrials* involve a neutral chairing a presentation of the evidence before the senior executives of the companies. After this presentation, the senior executives meet and attempt to settle the dispute. *Rent-a-judge trials* are a variation on arbitration, using a person in the role of "judge" rather than arbitrator to resolve a controversy. Rent-a-judges, often retired judges, preside over informal "trials" in private "courtrooms" to resolve disputes.

Discussion Questions

1. Is there any conflict of interest if Lyn Carroll represents both plaintiffs in this case? Why or why not? Is there any conflict of interest if Jefferson Jones represents both defendants in this case? Why or why not?

2. In the case of Nic Grant versus eClass and Yousef Alwazzan, suppose a jury is made up almost solely of people on public assistance. In your opinion, is this providing the parties with a fair trial? Why?

3. Some state and federal courts have significant waiting periods from the time of filing a lawsuit to a verdict. Court administrative offices generally compile and distribute that information. For example, in the 2007 fiscal year in federal district courts, the median length of time it takes for the District of Columbia—44 months, the Northern District of New York—40.5 months, the Eastern District of California—38 months, and the Middle District of Louisiana—38 months. Since these are median numbers, some cases continue much longer than that. Is it fair to expect litigants to wait so long? What factors contribute to these delays? What can be done to alleviate the delays?[42]

4. What are the advantages and disadvantages of including the following clause in an agreement to arbitrate: "The award shall include findings of fact [and conclusions of law]"?[43]

5. Parties who submit their claims to resolution with a rent-a-judge may be allowed to appeal the result of their "case" to the court of appeals. Will wealthy parties, who can afford to use rent-a-judge trials, lose interest in reforming the legal system if they can use private judging and still appeal to public appellate courts? Is that a concern? Why or why not?

Case Problems and Writing Assignments

1. On January 31, 1997, Judge Fujisaki instructed jurors in the civil trial of O.J. Simpson that they must "insulate themselves from all news media—watch no TV, listen to no radio and read no newspapers." He told them that he wanted to avoid sequestering the jury. A juror had just been removed from the trial for legal cause during deliberations; he was concerned that she might be giving interviews and did not want the jury tainted.

Jurors were also instructed to "have someone screen their phone calls, mail and faxes." The judge was concerned about reports that two jurors in the Simpson criminal trial were contacting members of the civil jury panel. They were allegedly trying to promote a deal for public appearances after the trial. Brenda Moran and Gina Marie Rosborough, two criminal jurors, announced a book deal shortly after the verdict in the criminal trial. Moran acknowledged writing a letter to the civil jurors recommending Bud Stewart as an agent. Both women stated that it was supposed to be delivered *after* the verdict, not while deliberations were going on. Faxes were sent to news producers offering to arrange interviews with three civil trial jurors in the case. The faxes were signed Bud Stewart, the agent mentioned in the letter from Moran.

Discuss the interrelationships between fair trials, the public's interest in obtaining information, and the media's business interests. It appears that Bud Stewart was attempting to get ahead of other agents. How could he have solicited business and clients without interfering with the legal process? [See Linda Deutsch & Michael Fleeman, "Simpson Juror Replaced; Talks Start Anew," *Fresno Bee*,

February 1, 1997, pp. A1 and A11; and "Juror Dismissed in Simpson Case," *Merced Sun-Star*, February 1, 1997, pp. A1 and A8.]

2. Justine Maldonado filed a sexual harassment lawsuit against the Ford Motor Company. Maldonado alleged that a supervisor, Daniel P. Bennett, sexually harassed her. Three other women have also sued Ford alleging sexual harassment by Bennett. Bennett was convicted in 1995 of the crime of exposing himself to three young women. This conviction was expunged from his record because he met the good-behavior requirements under Michigan law. There was no gag order in this case. Circuit Court Judge William J. Giovan dismissed Maldonado's suit because she and her lawyer, Miranda Massie, had discussed the case with reporters, including evidence that the court had said was inadmissible. Much of the information was a matter of public record. However, the judge said that it was an attempt to prejudice potential jurors and a violation of a Michigan law that forbids publicizing a conviction that has been expunged. According to the judge, "The behavior in question has been intentional, premeditated and intransigent. . . . It was designed to reach the farthest boundaries of the public consciousness." There has been other conflict between Massie and the judge. Massie had asked the judge to remove himself because a member of Ford's law firm handled a fund-raising event for his reelection. In addition, the judge said that Massie was disrespectful to him because she indicated to the media that it was difficult to get a fair trial against Ford in that town. Assume that the dismissal has been appealed to your court. How would you rule? Why? [See Danny Hakim, "Sex-Bias Suit Against Ford Is Dismissed on Trial Remarks," *New York Times*, August 27, 2002, C1.]

3. Annette Phillips worked as a bartender at a Hooters restaurant in Myrtle Beach, South Carolina. She alleged that a Hooters's official grabbed and slapped her buttocks. Phillips asked her manager for help and she was told to "let it

go." She quit her job. Phillips's attorney contacted Hooters, claiming that the attack and the restaurant's failure to deal with it violated Phillips's Title VII rights. Hooters responded that Phillips was required to submit her claims to arbitration.

In 1994, Hooters implemented an ADR program. Hooters conditioned eligibility for raises, transfers, and promotions upon an employee signing an agreement to arbitrate employment-related disputes. Phillips signed the agreement. The agreement said that Hooters and the employee agree to arbitrate all disputes arising out of employment, including "any claim of discrimination, sexual harassment, retaliation, or wrongful discharge, whether arising under federal or state law." It further stated "the employee and the company agree to resolve any claims pursuant to the company's rules and procedures for alternative resolution of employment-related disputes, as promulgated by the company from time to time. Company will make available or provide a copy of the rules upon written request of the employee." No employee was given a copy of Hooters's arbitration rules and procedures. Hooters sent a copy of the rules to Phillips's attorney.

Under these rules, the employee must provide the company with a notice of her claim at the outset, including the nature of the claim and the specific acts or omissions on which it is based. Hooters does not have to file a response or a list of its defenses. Simultaneously, the employee must provide the company with a list of all fact witnesses and a brief summary of the facts known by each one. The company does not have to reciprocate. Each party selects an arbitrator, and those two arbitrators select a third arbitrator. The third arbitrator must be selected from a list provided by Hooters. There is no input from the employee in the generation of the list. Hooters is free to make a list consisting solely of managers and people with family and/or financial relationships with Hooters. Nothing in the rules prevents Hooters from retaliating against arbitrators who rule against Hooters. Hooters may expand the scope of the arbitration to any matter, but the employee cannot raise any matter not included in the original notice. Hooters can move for summary dismissal of the employee's claims, but the employee cannot move for summary dismissal of Hooters's claims. Hooters may record the arbitration hearing by audiotaping, videotaping, or verbatim transcription. The employee cannot. Hooters can bring suit to cancel or modify an arbitral award, but the employee cannot. Hooters can cancel the agreement to arbitrate upon 30 days notice, but the employee cannot. Hooters reserves the right to modify the rules "in whole or in part," whenever it wishes and "without notice" to the employee. Hooters could even modify the rules in the middle of an arbitration. Hooters filed suit to compel arbitration. Phillips argues that she should not be required to arbitrate. Assume that you have been hired by Hooters to resolve the problem with Phillips. What would you do? You have also been assigned the responsibility to revise their arbitration program. What changes would you make? [See *Hooters of America, Inc. v. Phillips*, 173 F.3d 933, 1999 U.S. App. LEXIS 6329 (4th Cir. 1999).]

Notes

1. It is generally unwise for a lawyer to represent himself or herself even though he or she may know the rules, since the lawyer is emotionally involved in the case.
2. Butler County Local Rules of Civil Procedure, Rule L205.2 (b) Cover Sheet as amended September 15, 2009. Links for the Local Rules of Court are available at the Court Administration Office, Butler County, PA, http://www.co.butler.pa.us/butler/cwp/view.asp?a=1405&q=571308&butlerNav=|33535| (accessed 6/19/10).
3. Butler County Local Rules of Civil Procedure, Rules L1301 and 1302 (March 12, 2008).
4. David A. Lieb, "Clinton Ordered to Pay $90,000 in Penalty Fees in Jones Contempt Case," *Fresno Bee*, July 30, 1999, pp. A1, A22.
5. Federal Rules of Civil Procedure § 48.
6. See 28 U.S.C. § 1870.
7. See *J.E.B. v. T.B.*, 114 S. Ct. 1419 (1994).
8. 476 U.S. 79 (1986).
9. California Code of Civil Procedure § 170.6.
10. See 28 U.S.C. § 455 and California Code of Civil Procedure § 170.
11. See 42 Pa. C.S.A. § 5104.
12. Federal Rules of Civil Procedure § 48.
13. "Do-It-Yourself Justice—Small Claims Court," *Consumer Reports*, February 1996, p. 36.
14. Eric Lichtblau, "Zapruder Film Costs U.S. $16 Million," *Fresno Bee*, August 4, 1999, pp. A1, A5.
15. *Whoop, Inc. v. Dyno Productions, Inc.*, 75 Cal. Rptr. 2d 90 (Cal. App. 2d Dist. 1998).
16. American Arbitration Association, *A Guide to Mediation and Arbitration for Business People* (September, 2007), p. 2.
17. The primary concern of the Uniform Mediation Act (2001) is to keep mediation communications confidential. It was completed by the NCCUSL in 2001 and amended in 2003. It has been adopted by the District of Columbia, Idaho, Illinois, Iowa, Nebraska, New Jersey, Ohio, South Dakota, Utah, Vermont, and Washington. In 2010, it was introduced in Hawaii, Massachusetts, and New York. "A Few Facts about the Uniform Mediation Act (2001)(2003)," NCCUSL Web site, http://www.nccusl.org/nccusl/uniformact_factsheets/uniformacts-fs-uma2001.asp (accessed 4/4/10) and "Summary Uniform Mediation Act (2001)," NCCUSL Web site, http://www.nccusl.org/nccusl/uniformact_summaries/uniformacts-s-uma2001.asp (accessed 4/4/10).
18. American Arbitration Association, AAA Online Library, "Alternative Dispute Resolution Basics FAQs" (accessed 5/4/10). Reprinted by permission of AAA.
19. Quoted in Teresa V. Carey, "Credentialing for Mediators—To Be or Not To Be?," U.S.F. L. Rev. 30 (Spring 1996), p. 640.
20. Ibid., p. 641.
21. *Model Standards of Conduct for Mediators*, American Arbitration Association, American Bar Association, Association for Conflict Resolution, 2005, p. 3.
22. Richard C. Reuben, "Model Ethics Rules Limit Mediator Role: Despite Controversy, Standards Expected to Improve Respect for Profession," *ABA Journal*, January 1996, p. 25.
23. Boston Law Collaborative, LLC, "About Mediation and Other Methods of Dispute Resolution," http://bostonlawcollaborative.com/blc//faqs/about-mediation-and-other-methods-of-dispute-resolution.html (accessed 6/20/10).
24. American Arbitration Association, *Drafting Dispute Resolution Clauses—A Practical Guide* (September 1, 2007), p. 7. Reprinted by permission of AAA.
25. A.R.S. §§ 12-1501 to 1518.
26. 9 Cal. Civ. Proc. Code §§ 1280 *et seq.*, at § 1295.
27. Mich. Stat. Ann. §§ 27A.5040-27A.5065.
28. 9 U.S.C. §§ 1 *et. seq.*, at § 2.
29. "When You Need A Lawyer," *Consumer Reports*, February 1996, p. 39.

30. Curtis D. Brown, Esq., "New Law Lets Creditors Cut Court Costs," *Credit World,* July/August 1996, pp. 30-31.

31. Ibid.

32. 513 U.S. 265 (1995).

33. "A Few Facts about the Uniform Arbitration Act (2000)," NCCUSL Web site, http://www.nccusl.org/nccusl/uniformact_factsheets/uniformacts-fs-aa.asp (accessed 4/4/10).

34. It has been adopted by Alaska, Colorado, District of Columbia, Hawaii, Nevada, New Jersey, New Mexico, North Carolina, North Dakota, Oklahoma, Oregon, Utah, and Washington. In 2010, it was introduced in Alabama, Arizona, Massachusetts, Minnesota, and Pennsylvania. "A Few Facts about the Uniform Arbitration Act (2000)," NCCUSL Web site, http://www.nccusl.org/nccusl/uniformact_factsheets/uniformacts-fs-aa.asp (accessed 4/4/10).

35. American Arbitration Association, *Drafting,* supra note 24, at p. 16.

36. Ibid.

37. American Arbitration Association, "Statement of Ethical Principles for the American Arbitration Association, an ADR Provider Organization" (2007), http://www.adr.org/sp.asp?id=22036 (accessed 6/20/10).

38. American Arbitration Association, *Why Labor and Management Use the Services of the American Arbitration Association* (November 1993), p. 5.

39. American Arbitration Association, *Drafting,* supra note 24, at p. 30.

40. Deborah Shannon, "Rent-A-Judge," *American Way Magazine,* February 1991, pp. 33-36.

41. Ibid., p. 34.

42. Michael Doyle & John Ellis, "Cases Linger in Fresno District's Loaded Docket," *The Fresno Bee,* September 22, 2008, pp. A1 and A6.

43. American Arbitration Association, *Drafting,* supra note 24, at p. 36.

5

Constitutional Regulation of Business

Agenda

In its various activities, eClass probably will face fairly substantial regulation at both the state and the federal level. The firm will want to know *why* the government is able to regulate its efforts and *how* these regulations will affect them. Advertising of the products being offered will be subject to regulation. The principals may need to have the difference between personal speech and commercial speech explained, along with the reasons for different standards for the "freedom" of each type of speech. Several states are considering statutory restrictions or limitations on educational materials that could affect eClass. Should the firm consider challenging any such restrictions as violations of due process and/or equal protection? Most of this potential governmental oversight will subject the firm to administrative regulation as well. What protections are available to the firm when administrative regulations that affect the business are implemented?

These and other issues are likely to arise during your study of this chapter. Be prepared! You never know when the firm or one of its members will need your help or advice.

Classic Case

HEART OF ATLANTA MOTEL, INC. v. U.S.
379 U.S. 241 (1964)

FACTS The Heart of Atlanta Motel has 216 rooms available for its guests. It is located two blocks from downtown Peachtree Street and is readily accessible from two interstate highways. The motel solicits patronage from outside the state of Georgia through advertisements placed with various regional and national media, including nationally circulated magazines and more than 50 billboards alongside various highways in Georgia. The motel accepts conventions from outside the state, and approximately 75 percent of its patrons are residents of states other than Georgia. The motel refused to rent any of its rooms to African Americans. The government asserted that the motel could no longer discriminate on the basis of race under Title II of the Civil Rights Act of 1964 and ordered the motel to begin accepting African-American patrons.

ISSUE Is it constitutional for the government to apply Title II of the Civil Rights Act of 1964 to a private business that has interstate customers under the Commerce Clause?

HOLDING Yes. "The determinative test of the exercise of power by the Congress under the Commerce Clause is simply whether the activity sought to be regulated is 'commerce which concerns more States than one' and 'has a real and substantial relation to the national interest.'"

REASONING Excerpts from the opinion of Justice Clark:

... It is admitted that the operation of the motel brings it within the provisions of 201(a) of the Act and that [the motel] refused to provide lodging for transient Negroes because of their race or color and that it intends to continue that policy unless restrained. The sole question posed is, therefore, the constitutionality of the Civil Rights Act as applied to these facts. ... The Senate Commerce Committee made it quite clear that the fundamental objective of Title II was to vindicate "the deprivation of personal dignity that surely accompanies denials of equal access to public establishments." At the same time, however, it noted that such an objective has been and could be readily achieved "by congressional action based on the commerce power of the Constitution." Our study of the legislative record, made in light of prior cases, has brought us to the conclusion that Congress possessed ample power in this regard. ...

While the Act as adopted carried no congressional findings the record of its passage through each house is replete with evidence of the burden that discrimination by race or color places upon interstate commerce. ...

In framing Title II of this Act Congress was dealing with what it considered a moral problem. But that does not detract from the overwhelming evidence of the disruptive effect that racial discrimination has had on commercial intercourse. It was this burden which empowered Congress to enact appropriate legislation.... Congress was not restricted by the fact that the particular obstruction to interstate commerce with which it was dealing was also deemed a moral and social wrong. . . .

We, therefore, conclude that the action of the Congress in the adoption of the Act as applied here to a motel which concededly serves interstate travelers is within the power granted it by the Commerce Clause of the Constitution, as interpreted by the Court for 140 years. . . . How obstructions in commerce may be removed—what means are to be employed—is with the sound and exclusive discretion of the Congress. It is subject to only one caveat—that the means chosen by it must be reasonably adapted to the end permitted by the Constitution. We cannot say that its choice here was not so adapted. The Constitution requires no more.

AN HISTORICAL PERSPECTIVE

In the United States today, government heavily regulates business. This is especially true after the recent housing boom and bust and the corresponding mortgage crisis. Federal regulations address important issues such as environmental pollution, employee safety, wage and hour issues, and labor relations. The federal government also mandates that corporations accurately disclose material events, financial successes and failures, and, in some cases, how much top executives are paid. State regulations cover consumer protection, the selling of securities, loan rates, and highway weight limits. Local regulations cover issues such as zoning for commercial property and other building codes. And these represent only a few of the regulations that a business faces.

Pervasive governmental regulation of business, however, has not always been the case. As is often mentioned in American history texts, the United States was built on a *laissez faire* economy that reflected the belief that business operates best when uninhibited by the government. Business owners ran business and politicians ran government, and the two groups left each other alone. Buyers often were ignored, with *caveat emptor* ("let the buyer beware") being the rule of the land. Workers remained virtually unprotected. If they did not like their jobs, they could quit. If they did not go to work, they were fired. If they joined a union, they also were fired—and they quite often faced criminal conspiracy charges as well.

The nineteenth century was a great time to be an American entrepreneur, especially a wealthy one. These easy times came to an end, however. The general populace viewed too many "captains of industry" as "robber barons." Many people resented the abuse and mistreatment workers suffered. And, given the lack of land remaining for westward migration, people increasingly clamored for reform. Present-day governmental regulation emerged from these tumultuous times.

SHOULD GOVERNMENT REGULATE BUSINESS?

Yet, over the last few decades, people have been asking the question, "Should government regulate business?" The answer is either *yes* or *no*, depending on which type of business is at issue, what type of regulation is being discussed, and which level of government is involved. The answer also depends to some degree on whether the business involves international trade, domestic trade, or regional/local trade. Recently, the answer also involves whether the business is "too big to fail." In general, such a question involves a number of factors, and the answers may vary over time as the circumstances of the business change.

History shows that society needs some regulation—or intervention—by government. Governmental regulation typically takes two forms: social regulation (concern for such issues as workplace safety, equal opportunity, environmental protection, and consumer protection) and economic regulation (the behavior of firms, especially the firms' effects on prices, production, industry conditions for entry or exit, and so on). In 2010, over 2.7 million people work in federal agencies.[1] In fact, the federal government is the nation's largest employer. Obviously, had they not been working in the federal bureaucracy, presumably they could have worked at jobs producing other goods and services. Clearly, then, one must compare the costs—in terms of administration, compliance, and efficiency—of regulation with its perceived benefits.

Many people today believe this balance has tipped too far and has resulted in the overregulation of business. Indeed, the pervasiveness of the government's reach over business activities has led to cries for deregulation and a lessening of this glut of laws. Given the complexities of business at the advent of the twenty-first century, however, no one realistically believes that these laws magically will disappear.

Business's "social contract" requires that it pay heed to the various social and economic issues mentioned above. Somewhere between the extremes of overregulation and underregulation, a happy medium must exist so as to maximize the well-being of business, society, and government. Yet, as we learned in the preceding chapters, in the absence of the attainment of this balance, laws can become so burdensome on individuals that such persons can argue that the laws exceed the government's enumerated powers granted by the Constitution and often also the rights guaranteed to individuals by the Bill of Rights. Since the law in many instances views firms as legal, or *juristic*, persons, businesses also can assert various constitutional rights and thus curb what they view as excessive governmental regulation. Just as the Constitution stands as the guardian of individual rights, it also represents a significant weapon for businesses to use when they challenge the laws and regulations that affect them.

THE COMMERCE CLAUSE

Perhaps the single most important constitutional provision that affects business is the Commerce Clause. Article I, Section 8, Clause 3 of the Constitution states that Congress shall have the power "to regulate Commerce with foreign Nations, and among the several States, and with the Indian Tribes." The Commerce Clause grants Congress vast power to regulate the activities of businesses and also takes a large amount of power away from individual states to do the same. It also bans individual states from regulating to protect purely local economic interests at the expense of national economic interests. Also, Article I, Section 8, Clause 1 gives Congress the power to levy taxes. Finally, Article I, Section 8, Clause 18 allows the federal government to do whatever is "necessary and proper" in order to effectively implement its regulations of commerce. The interplay between these three powers forms the basis for much of the federal government's regulation of business.

The history of the Commerce Clause has been checkered. The founders understood that the basic failure of the Articles of Confederation was the federal government's inability to robustly regulate commerce. Therefore, they included the Commerce Clause to strike down unfair state laws affecting business, to open up channels of commerce, to facilitate the transportation of goods, and foster economic integration.

For better or for worse, the Commerce Clause itself does not define commerce. Therefore, the task fell to the Supreme Court and its power of judicial review. The Supreme Court initially had interpreted the clause, next expanded these interpretations, later contracted these interpretations, and then expanded them again. In 1824, the Supreme Court had its first occasion to interpret the Commerce Clause. Chief Justice Marshall's opinion in *Gibbons v. Ogden*[2] defined commerce as "the commercial intercourse between nations, in all its branches . . . regulated by prescribing rules for carrying on that intercourse." Marshall further noted that the federal government can regulate commerce that *affects* other states, even if that commerce is local in nature. Basically, the Supreme Court broadly claimed that commerce included all aspects of business operations—even if many of these operations transpired wholly within one state.

As a result of this interpretation, for nearly three quarters of a century, federal power to regulate business was broad. The Interstate Commerce Act of 1887 permitted the Interstate Commerce Commission (ICC) to regulate local railroad rates and local railroad safety because such issues directly affected interstate rates and safety.[3] The federal government also could regulate local grain and livestock exchanges because they, too, involved transactions that affected the rest of the nation.

Not all the court opinions of the period favored regulation by the federal government, however. In 1870, the Court upheld a state law that banned the sale of illuminating oils that could ignite at lower temperatures. The state passed the statute to protect its inhabitants from the danger posed by oil fires. The majority in *United States v. Dewitt* held that the ban was a valid use of a state's police power under the Tenth Amendment and that the Commerce Clause did not prohibit the use of this state power. In the 1873 Supreme Court decision *In re State Freight Tax*,[4] the Court stated that the Commerce Clause's phrase *among* meant *between*. As a result, this opinion held that the federal government could regulate only interstate (that is, between two or more states; between a point in one state and a point in another state) commerce. By limiting the definition of commerce to commerce between two or more states, the Court similarly contracted the federal power to regulate business. In its 1888 *Kidd v. Pearson*[5] decision, the Court ruled that commerce meant transportation. As a result of these opinions, federal regulation of business suddenly became restricted to actual interstate transportation and did not reach business deals that affected interstate business but that were conducted entirely in one state. Also, states were allowed some leeway to protect their citizens via their police power. Such transactions, defined as intrastate (that is, begun, carried on, and completed wholly within the boundaries of a single state), therefore remained beyond the scope of federal regulation.

This new, restricted definition of interstate commerce underlay the passage of the Sherman Act in 1890 (see Chapter 35 for a detailed treatment of this act). Indeed, this new definition of the federal authority to regulate business led the Court to narrower interpretations and, consequently, the Court's invalidation of many subsequent federal enactments. This period reflected back to the *laissez-faire* business philosophy of previous decades—at least until 1937.

A shift in the Court's restrictive view of the exercise of federal power did not occur until 1937. In *NLRB v. Jones & Laughlin Steel Corp.*,[6] which overturned 50 years of narrow interpretation, Chief Justice Hughes said:

> When industries organize themselves on a national scale, making their relation to interstate commerce the dominant factor in their activities, how can it be maintained that their industrial relations constitute a forbidden field into which Congress may not enter when it is necessary to protect interstate commerce from the paralyzing consequences of industrial war?

Thus, the Court had come full circle. As Justice Jackson noted in *United States v. Women's Sportswear Manufacturers Association*,[7] a 1949 case involving a Sherman Act challenge to a local price-fixing arrangement, "If it is interstate commerce that feels the pinch, it does not matter how local the operation which applies the squeeze." In upholding the right of the federal government to regulate the conduct in dispute, Justice Jackson provided us with both a picturesque definition of interstate commerce and the one most courts presently would accept as controlling.

This expansive definition of the reach of the federal government under the Commerce Clause also provided the federal government with a vehicle for ridding society of discrimination and bigotry, as the *Heart of Atlanta Motel, Inc. v. U.S.*[8] (our Classic Case) decision demonstrates. The Heart of Atlanta Motel had a policy of refusing service to blacks. The federal government challenged this policy as a violation of Title II of the Civil Rights Act of 1964, which prohibits racial, religious, or national origin discrimination by those who offer public accommodations. The government claimed that the motel was involved in interstate commerce and that federal intervention therefore was justifiable. The motel argued that it was a purely intrastate business and hence exempt from federal regulation under Title II. The Supreme Court held that because of its provision of services to interstate travelers, the motel was involved in interstate commerce. In reaching its decision, the Court focused on the following facts: (1) The motel was readily accessible from two interstate highways; (2) it also advertised in national magazines and placed billboards on federal highways; and (3) approximately 75 percent of its guests came from outside the state of Georgia. In the Court's view, allowing such discrimination would discourage travel by the black community. Furthermore, the motel was set up to serve interstate travelers; it drew much of its business from interstate travelers; and it was involved in interstate commerce. Hence, the Court concluded that Title II gave the government authority to prohibit Heart of Atlanta Motel, Inc.'s discriminatory practice of renting rooms only to white people.

The myriad of current state and federal laws has relegated this function of the Commerce Clause largely to a legal artifact. Nevertheless, you should remain mindful of the significance of the Commerce Clause largely in this historical context and its continuing importance as the jurisdictional basis for many federal regulatory schemes. In fact, the Commerce Clause has been a factor in recent civil and individual rights cases based on federal laws that prohibit convicted felons from owning guns and require convicted sex offenders to register within the state where they currently reside.

Exclusive Federal Power

Early on, court constructions viewed three areas as exclusive enclaves of federal regulation: commerce with foreign nations, commercial activities involving Indian tribes (that is, Native Americans), and commerce between the states (that is, interstate commerce). Courts generally have recognized that Congress enjoys plenary (that is, full; complete; absolute) power over foreign commerce or trade. For instance, the State of Washington does not have the authority to sign a treaty regulating tuna-fishing rights with Japan or Canada; only Congress has such power.[9]

Similarly, owing to the unique status that Native Americans have occupied in United States history, only Congress has the power to regulate such commerce. Congress's plenary power in this area stems from the quasi-sovereign status that historically has been accorded to Native American tribes. As such, Native American tribes have virtually complete control over their own reservations and land; the states have little say over reservation affairs. Federal law generally preempts even state or local regulation of off-reservation activities. This part of the Commerce Clause is referred to as the Indian Commerce Clause. Any federal law that is based upon the Indian Commerce Clause must deal with commerce that occurs on Indian reservations.

As we noted earlier, the phrase "among the several states" has spawned a great deal of litigation concerning when federal power over interstate commerce is plenary. Precedents over the years have established three such areas: (1) Congress's power to regulate the use of the channels of interstate commerce; (2) Congress's power to regulate the instrumentalities of interstate commerce (including persons and things); and (3) Congress's power to regulate activities that have a substantial relation to interstate commerce. Under the first two prongs, Congress can regulate interstate carriers, roads, television and radio stations, and so on. Congress also has the power to exclude from such interstate channels or facilities the goods, persons, or services designated by Congress as harmful to interstate commerce. Congress, then, under this federal police power, can stop the interstate shipment of stolen vehicles, diseased animals, spoiled meat, fungi-ridden fruit, or defective products. Businesses so affected can do little to challenge this exercise of federal power. Besides the channels or facilities of interstate commerce, Congress has plenary power to regulate all commerce or activity that affects more than one state. Note that even intrastate commerce may be subject to such federal control if the intrastate activity has a "substantial effect" on interstate commerce or if Congress rationally could conclude that the activity in question affects interstate commerce.

As the *Heart of Atlanta Motel* case indicates, it takes very little commercial activity to trigger the application of this federal power over commerce. To illustrate, in *Burbank v. Lockheed Air Terminal, Inc.*,[10] the Supreme Court struck down a local ordinance that prohibited jet airplane takeoffs during specified hours (11:00 P.M. to 7:00 A.M. local time). The Court invalidated this ordinance because of the need for national uniformity in airplane flight patterns (having this airport "off limits" for several hours could create clogs in air traffic) and because federal law, in the form of agencies concerned with aeronautical and environmental matters, preempted such local or state initiatives.

Clearly, though, this federal power is not boundless. For example, in *U.S. v. Lopez*,[11] the Supreme Court invalidated a federal law as exceeding congressional authority under the Commerce Clause. This was the first time the Court had struck down such a law in more than 50 years. Congress had made it a federal criminal offense for anyone to possess a firearm in a school zone. The Court held that the act exceeds Congress's authority under the Commerce Clause. Why? The possession of a gun in a local school zone in no sense constitutes an economic activity that might, through repetition elsewhere, have a substantial effect on interstate commerce. The advocates of the law argued that possession of firearms in a school zone could lead to violent crime, which, in turn, would hurt the national economy by (1) increasing the costs associated with violent crime; (2) reducing people's willingness to travel to areas they deem unsafe; and (3) threatening the learning environment, which would lead to poorly educated citizens. The Court, however, concluded that this argument demonstrated too tenuous a nexus to interstate commerce for the Court to sustain the law. Although not a business case, this decision may affect business in the future; the decision seems to cut back on 60 years of Supreme Court precedents that had shown broad deference to congressional authority to regulate activities that arguably affect interstate commerce. Five years later, the Court struck down part of another federal law—the Violence Against Women Act—on the same grounds in *United States v. Morrison*.[12] The court held that the effects of violence against women were primarily non-economic and that this subject had traditionally been regulated by the states. After *Lopez* and *Morrison*, Congress may not regulate non-economic activity that merely might, when considered cumulatively, have an effect on interstate commerce.

Concurrent State Power

In our interdependent domestic economy, virtually all businesses vie for market share with similar firms in other states. Consequently, Congress's sweeping power to regulate commerce seems practically absolute—even considering *Lopez* and *Morrison*.

Yet the states enjoy concurrent power with the federal government as to the regulation of commerce within the state. Just as the federal government wishes to promote the welfare of its citizens, so does each state. Hence, state regulation of economic matters is permissible as long as the regulation in question passes muster under a so-called "balancing" test that compares the burdens on interstate commerce caused by the regulation and the importance of the state interest that underlies the regulation. If a state regulation hampers interstate commerce in any way, the court is likely to strike it down under its Dormant Commerce Clause authority. The Dormant Commerce Clause—an implied power under the Commerce Clause—rears its head when Congress is silent on the issue but the state law at issue discriminates against out-of-state commercial interests.

Therefore, courts generally uphold valid state initiatives in furtherance of local health and safety measures that do not purport merely to protect local economic interests. For example, state regulation of milk products that involves testing or certification of the milk will survive a legal challenge based on the Commerce Clause unless the state's enactment discriminates in favor of in-state producers (that is, "local yokels") to the detriment of out-of-state producers and/or the costs of compliance, when compared with the putative benefits of the law, impose an unreasonable, or undue, burden on interstate commerce. In the absence of discrimination against out-of-state firms or the imposition of an undue burden, the states have concurrent power to regulate commerce.

The state's concurrent power to regulate commerce ceases, however, if the state regulation conflicts with federal law. As you may remember, the Supremacy Clause of Article VI of the Constitution invalidates such state legislation. If Congress expressly prohibits state regulation in a given area or if federal law impliedly preempts the regulatory area, federal law supersedes the state's power to regulate as well.

State powers of taxation can pose special problems under the Commerce Clause because the states' legitimate interest in increasing their revenues by taxing business entities may burden interstate commerce. As we will see later, such discriminatory taxes, in addition to violating the Commerce Clause, may pose due process and equal protection problems, too. Although Congress, pursuant to the Commerce Clause, can authorize or prohibit state taxation that affects interstate commerce, in the absence of such federal legislation, the states can tax corporations and other business entities.

State tax laws that single out—that is, discriminate against—interstate commerce usually violate the Commerce Clause. Nondiscriminatory taxation schemes—schemes that impose the same type of tax on local business or commerce as imposed on interstate entities—require courts to employ a "balancing" test in which they weigh the state's need for additional revenue against the burden imposed on interstate commerce by such taxes. Although entities of interstate commerce do not remain immune from paying state taxes, such businesses need only pay their fair share;

taxation that amounts to undue burdens, unfair discrimination, or multiple taxation generally does not survive challenges brought under the Commerce Clause (and perhaps not under the Due Process Clause, either).

For a state tax to be legal under the Commerce Clause, it must be applied to an activity that has a substantial *nexus* (or connection) with the taxing state; it must be fairly apportioned; it must not discriminate against interstate commerce; and it must be fairly related to the services provided by the state. Many courts then look at whether certain *minimum contacts* exist between the person, entity, or transaction taxed and the state levying the tax. If such state *jurisdiction* seems lacking, a violation of due process may have occurred.

Most of the precedents in this area involve state legislative schemes that tax goods shipped in interstate commerce; taxes imposed on firms doing business in a given state; and highway, airport, sales, and use taxes. As a businessperson, you should recognize the possible legal issues that may arise under such state tax laws.

Exclusive State Power

The state's plenary power to regulate commerce covers purely local activities that only very remotely affect other states. Given the interdependent nature of our economy and the Supreme Court precedents we have discussed, the instances in which a state has exclusive power over commerce remain comparatively rare.

Exhibit 5.1 provides a useful framework for understanding the analysis courts employ during their disposition of a challenge based on the Commerce Clause.

THE EQUAL PROTECTION CLAUSE

Another constitutional provision that acts as a curb on the government's power to regulate business is the Equal Protection Clause. The Fourteenth Amendment states: "[n]or shall any State . . . deny to any person within its jurisdiction the equal protection of the laws." Supreme Court precedents have determined that in most situations the Fifth Amendment's Due Process Clause provides that the *federal* government must guarantee equal protection to all persons as well. Basically, this guarantee means that when the government classifies people, it must treat similarly situated people similarly. It is interesting that the founders did not include such a provision within the seven articles of the Constitution itself. Many of the convention delegates reasoned that the federal government did not have the enumerated authority to treat similarly situated groups differently and that various state constitutional protections would be sufficient. History proved otherwise, and the Equal Protection Clause continues to help remedy the negative effects of slavery and other forms of invidious discrimination in America. In recent years, courts have used the Equal Protection Clause to protect a broad range of individual rights. Yet this provision also limits the types of regulations government can impose on businesses.

Exhibit 5.1

Commerce Clause Analysis

I. Areas of Exclusive Federal Regulation
   A. Commerce with foreign nations
   B. Commerce involving Indian tribes (i.e., Native Americans)
   C. Commerce involving the channels and facilities of interstate commerce
   D. Commerce that is interstate in nature or that originates in a single state but that has a "substantial effect" on interstate commerce
   E. Commerce where Congress has prohibited state regulation or where federal law impliedly preempts the regulatory area

II. Areas of Concurrent Federal and State Regulation
   A. "Balancing" test employed: the burdens on interstate commerce compared to the importance of the state interest underlying the state regulation are compared and evaluated
   B. State initiatives in furtherance of the state's "police power" (i.e., the promotion of the general welfare of the state's citizens) generally permissible unless:
      1. The state regulation imposes an undue or unreasonable burden on interstate commerce
      2. The state regulation discriminates in favor of in-state firms and against out-of-state firms
      3. The state regulation conflicts with federal law and thus is invalidated under the Supremacy Clause

III. Areas of Exclusive State Regulation
   A. Purely local activities with remote effects on other states' commerce

Whether applied to the protection of individuals' civil rights or businesses' rights, the Equal Protection Clause protects individuals and other entities only from invidious discrimination (that is, repugnant; discrimination stemming from bigotry or prejudice). What constitutes invidious discrimination? All governmental statutes and regulations classify (or discriminate) among groups. This kind of discrimination—mere differentiation—does not necessarily implicate the Equal Protection Clause, however. For example, when the government says professionals or businesses must secure licenses, the government is differentiating (discriminating) among people who need such licenses as a prerequisite for doing business and those who do not. But such differentiation *per se* does not constitute the discrimination banned by the Equal Protection Clause. Only when such differentiation stems from prejudice, bigotry, or stereotyping on racial, ethnic, gender, or similar bases does illegal discrimination result.

The Equal Protection Clause also prohibits only discrimination that derives from governmental (that is, so-called state) action; it does not reach actions taken by private individuals. Hence, under this clause, one can challenge only those actions taken by federal and state governments (or by any subdivisions or agencies thereof) pursuant to enacted laws or regulations.

Historically, few governmental actions were invalidated under the Equal Protection Clause—at least until the 1950s. Since then, the Supreme Court has developed various tests for determining the legality of economic regulations challenged under the Equal Protection Clause. As to each of these three possible tests, courts will review the legislative classification at issue with regard to the "fit" that exists between the means the legislative body has used to accomplish a desired end, or objective, and the impact the legislation has on the people affected by the regulation.

The Rational Basis Test

Under the traditional, or so-called rational basis, test, the government can distinguish among similarly situated persons if the statutory scheme—or classification—is rationally related to a legitimate state interest (or aim). Courts generally do not second-guess legislators' intent. Courts thus presume that the regulation is valid unless no conceivable justification exists for the law. Courts allow governmental entities wide latitude when, pursuant to their police power, these regulators enact social and economic regulations; courts only rarely invalidate such measures.

The rational basis test is the lowest level of scrutiny a court will place on governmental action. The only way a law will be struck down under this standard is if its provisions violate another constitutional provision or are irrational. An example of a law struck down under the rational basis test can be found in the case of *City of Cleburne v. Cleburne Living Center*.[13] In this case, a city ordinance required group homes for the mentally disabled to obtain permits because of resident concerns, potential harassment of residents by high school students, and zoning issues. The court held that the law violated the Equal Protection Clause because it was not rationally related to a legitimate aim of government. The law did not cover similar institutions such as hospitals or nursing homes, and the law played to prejudices in the community against the mentally disabled. These prejudices cannot be the foundation of a law when scrutinized under the Equal Protection Clause. This state law was too discriminatory—even under the deferential rational basis test.

Strict Scrutiny: The "Compelling State Interest" Test

If a regulatory measure involves invidious discrimination—that is, intentional discrimination against certain racial or ethnic groups—or limitations or restrictions of certain fundamental rights, courts will apply the strict scrutiny test. Under this test, courts presume that such regulations are *invalid*, only upholding those measures necessary to accomplish a compelling state interest. In these instances, the regulating body must show that the regulation is necessary in order to attain a compelling state interest, that no alternative, less burdensome ways exist to accomplish the state objective or goal, and that the regulation is tailored as narrowly as possible while still attaining the goal. Such arguments have rarely been successful.

Over the years, the Supreme Court has held that laws that impinge on so-called "suspect" classifications and thus burden the rights of African Americans, Hispanics, and Asian Americans must meet this compelling state interest standard. The Court has protected these groups from the application of such laws because these groups represent discrete, insular (that is, isolated from others) minorities whom other citizens view as unassimilable into American society and whom the government may easily identify because of the groups' immutable physical characteristics.

In order to justify the singling out of such disenfranchised groups (that is, groups restricted from enjoying certain constitutional or statutory rights owing to systemic prejudice or bigotry), the entity enacting the legislation must satisfy the compelling state interest test and the strict scrutiny approach that a court must apply to the law. For example, *Yick Wo v. Hopkins*[14] involved a denial of a permit to operate a laundry business. The city of San Francisco passed an ordinance requiring anyone operating a laundry business to obtain the consent of the board of supervisors in order to operate a laundry, and anyone without such consent was subject to arrest. Yick Wo was one of approximately 150 Chinese applicants who were denied such consent and arrested for

eClass 5.1 Management

CHALLENGING AN APPARENTLY UNCONSTITUTIONAL LAW

The firm has recently learned that the federal government has enacted a law requiring all new educational software vendors to provide auxiliary peripheral devices to users who are disabled. This new law does not apply to any educational software that was available on the market last year (the year before eClass was established), nor to any other type of software. In order to comply with the law, eClass will incur substantial costs that will either price its software out of the market or eliminate its profitability. The firm's members view this law as unconstitutional and wish to challenge it. If the firm's members ask you for your advice in this matter, what will you advise?

BUSINESS CONSIDERATIONS How should a business react to a proposed change in the law that will affect its current business practices? Should the business immediately begin the implementation of methods for complying with the new law, or should the business try to take steps to prevent or delay the effective date of the new law?

ETHICAL CONSIDERATIONS Is it ethical for the government to enact laws that apply to all customers so as to provide needed benefits or protections for a small number who require special accommodations in order to utilize the products covered? Would it be more ethical for the government to refrain from requiring such accommodations, thereby leaving some members of society unable to receive benefits otherwise generally available within society?

violating the ordinance. Since all of the approximately 80 non-Chinese consent seekers had been granted consent, the egregious denial of the license to Yick Wo violated the Fourteenth Amendment. Given the systemic prejudice against Chinese people at the time because of the widely held view that the Chinese were unworthy of citizenship, Yick Wo was a member of a discrete, insular minority who had suffered historical disenfranchisement. His immutable physical characteristics—the shape of his eyes and his skin color, for example—also made him more easily identified and singled out by the government. The city council could not show that its denial of Yick Wo's permit represented the only means of accomplishing the state interest (avoidance of fire hazards) allegedly involved here; hence, the city council had failed to show that its treatment of Yick Wo passed muster under the compelling state interest test.

Citing *Yick Wo v. Hopkins* and upholding its underlying predicates, the Supreme Court recently—in *Romer v. Evans*[15]—held that a referendum-based amendment to the Colorado state constitution that prohibited all legislative, executive, or judicial action at any level of state or local government designed to protect homosexual persons from discrimination was unconstitutional. The court found the amendment to be a status-based enactment that could not be justified or legitimately tied to a legitimate state interest. The Court—using only the rational basis test—concluded that the amendment instead "classifie[d] homosexuals not to further a proper legislative end but to make them unequal to everyone else. This Colorado cannot do. A state [under the Equal Protection Clause] cannot so deem a class of persons a stranger to its laws."[16]

Note that if the facts had been different in the *Yick Wo v. Hopkins* case and that if all the Chinese applicants had obtained their permits and all of the unsuccessful applicants had been white, the unsuccessful applicants presumably could sue under the Fourteenth Amendment for "reverse discrimination." The Supreme Court since 1989 has said that "benign" racial classifications used by the government for affirmative action purposes (for example, a city's deciding to award a certain percentage of city contracts to minority-owned businesses because of the city's desire to correct societal discrimination) will be judged under the strict scrutiny/compelling state interest test as well. *Adarand Constructors, Inc. v. Pena*,[17] which involved a challenge to a federal program that granted preferential treatment to minority subcontractors, reinforces this 1989 holding.

In *Adarand*, the Supreme Court held that reviewing courts must subject all racial classifications, imposed by whatever federal, state, or local governmental entity, to the strict scrutiny standard.[18] This case makes it clear that federal racial classifications, like those set up by a state, must serve a compelling governmental interest and must be narrowly tailored to further that interest. Under this standard, only affirmative action plans that respond to specific, provable past discrimination and that are narrowly tailored to eliminate such bias would be legal. Although the Court acknowledged that, practically speaking, it will be hard for the government to meet this test, the Court did not view its decision as dealing a fatal blow to the vast network of federal affirmative action programs that presently exist.

Recently, the court has ruled on a few major affirmative action cases in the arena of higher education—cases that might have a future impact on business. The challenged affirmative action programs do not cite historical discrimination as their impetus.

Instead, they are based on the idea that diversity is a valuable component of the educational experience. The court has upheld such programs if diversity is merely one aspect of the admissions decision (as opposed to part of an admissions quota) and only in the higher education context. On the other hand, public elementary schools are not allowed to justify admission preferences based on this "diversity for the sake of diversity" rationale. These education cases are important for business as companies begin to create affirmative action plans that seek to hire minorities solely for the sake of diversity. White male applicants are likely to sue, arguing reverse discrimination under the Equal Protection Clause. The court will likely use the precedents in the higher education arena combined with *Adarand* and its progeny to determine whether such corporate plans violate the Equal Protection Clause.

Just as the Equal Protection Clause prohibits virtually all legislation that burdens a suspect classification, it also subjects to the compelling state interest test any governmental action that penalizes or unduly burdens a *fundamental right* (that is, rights expressly or impliedly guaranteed in the Constitution). Accordingly, the Supreme Court has struck down laws that forbade a drugstore's selling birth control devices and a doctor's discussing birth control issues with his or her patients. The Court believed these laws implicate the right of privacy, interpreted by the Court as encompassing the marital relationship and procreation. Similarly, in our earlier example, had Yick Wo been a Presbyterian and the only unsuccessful applicants were Presbyterian while all successful applicants were members of other denominations, he could have argued that the city council's prior, publicly articulated, anti-Presbyterian sentiments had led to the penalizing of his First Amendment right of freedom of religion.

An Intermediate Level: The Substantially Important State Interest Test

In the 1970s, the Supreme Court flirted with the idea of placing gender-based laws under the strict scrutiny analysis, particularly if the challenged legislative enactment unduly burdened women. At that time, many commentators argued that, first, women represent a discrete, insular minority owing to their belated receipt of the right to vote, the existence of Married Women's Property Acts that denied women the capacity to contract, and so on. Second, women represent a group of individuals who manifest immutable physical characteristics; in other words, women's secondary sex characteristics ordinarily distinguish women from men and vice versa.

While the Court never accepted these arguments—apparently it believed the discrimination caused by gender-based laws failed to rise to the level of invidiousness found in most strict scrutiny cases—the Court carved out an intermediate tier of analysis for decision makers to use in evaluating challenges to gender-based laws. At this intermediate level, a "heightened scrutiny" test, regulations require more justification than a mere "rational basis," but less than a strict scrutiny is required. Any statutory schemes or regulations falling within this category must be "substantially related to an important state interest." If the enacting body cannot meet this test, courts will invalidate the legislation. Thus, older laws that prohibited women from entering certain occupations (say, becoming a barber) nowadays would be decided under this "heightened scrutiny" test. Similarly, if Yick Wo had been a woman and the city council's ordinance had said no woman can obtain a permit, the city council would need to show that its prohibition against women advanced a substantially important governmental objective. Otherwise, the ordinance would violate the Equal Protection Clause. Note that men are protected from burdensome laws as well. In *Craig v. Boren*,[19] the Supreme Court invalidated an Oklahoma law that allowed females to drink beer at age 18 but prohibited males from drinking beer until age 21.

Relying on these precedents, the Supreme Court has held that the exclusion of women by the Virginia Military Institute (VMI), a state college, violated the Equal Protection Clause. The Court characterized VMI's argument that the alterations to its "adversative" method of training that would be necessary to accommodate women would be so drastic as to destroy VMI's program and its mission to produce "citizen-soldiers" as falling well short of the showing necessary to justify the classification as "substantially related to an important state interest." The Court concluded that because neither VMI nor the State of Virginia had proffered an "exceedingly persuasive justification" for categorically excluding all women from VMI's programs, the school's policies were unconstitutional.[20]

THE DUE PROCESS CLAUSE

Besides guaranteeing equal protection, both the Fifth and Fourteenth Amendments protect against deprivations of "life, liberty, or property without due process of law." You probably associate the Due Process Clause with individual rights, and perhaps specifically with the protection of criminals, as mentioned in Chapter 7. For example, the government cannot deprive us of our lives (for example, by subjecting us to capital punishment) without according us due process. Similarly, the government cannot deprive us of liberty—interpreted by the Court to include one's freedom from physical restraints imposed without due process and in noncriminal contexts to include such issues as involuntary commitments to mental institutions. In the context of business, the term *liberty* also encompasses the right to contract and to engage in gainful employment.

Still, the life and liberty components of the Due Process Clause fade in importance compared to the property dimension of the provision. The Supreme Court has found few interpretive problems inherent in this third prong of the clause, perhaps because most of us more intuitively understand the concept property than we do the intangible concept *liberty*. Thus, the Court not surprisingly has construed the word *property* to include ownership of real estate, personal property, and money; but the Court also has extended the term *property* to entitlements to specific benefits set out under applicable state or federal law. If state action deprives us of property rights such as public employment, public education, continuing welfare benefits, or continuing public utility services, that deprivation cannot constitutionally occur in the absence of due process.

The due process required by notions of fundamental fairness involves two dimensions: procedural protections and substantive considerations.

Procedural Due Process

Before the government can deprive one of life, liberty, or property, one usually must be afforded some kind of hearing. Such hearings generally require notice to the aggrieved party, an opportunity for that person to present his or her side of the story, and an impartial decision maker. The government ordinarily can refrain from providing counsel, because counsel usually is not constitutionally required, although it is required in the case of indigent criminal defendants. The applicable rules and regulations, however, oftentimes allow counsel to be present. The timing of the hearing—whether it must occur before or after the deprivation of a protected interest—and the extent of the procedural safeguards afforded to the affected individual vary.

Courts generally balance the individual interests involved with the governmental interest in fiscal and administrative efficiency. Prior Supreme Court precedents have held that a hearing must precede, for example, the termination of welfare benefits, the government's seizure and forfeiture of real estate allegedly used in connection with the commission of crimes, termination of public employment, and prejudgment garnishment of wages. Evidentiary hearings prior to the termination of benefits need not occur in situations involving disability benefits, some terminations of parental rights, and some license suspensions (for example, failure to take a Breathalyzer test); but post-suspension hearings may be required in such circumstances.

For example, assume a state passes a law saying women can cut only women's hair and men can cut only men's hair. Patrick McCann, who runs a unisex barber shop, flouts the law and continues to cut women's hair. The state licensing board in response notifies him that it plans to revoke his license (state action has occurred), gives him a hearing in which he has an opportunity to present his side of the dispute, and convenes a panel (probably made up of other licensed barbers) that has no apparent biases against McCann. With these procedural steps taken against him, McCann ordinarily will not be able to use the Due Process Clause to challenge the subsequent revocation of his license; the hearing he has received apparently fulfills the requirements of procedural due process.

Substantive Due Process

The substantive aspects of due process, however, may hold more promise for McCann. The *substantive* dimension of due process focuses not on providing fundamentally fair procedures but on the content, or the subject matter, of the law. The theory is that individuals are protected by the Constitution when taking certain actions that the government would prefer that they do not take. One deprived of life, liberty, or property under arbitrary, irrational, and capricious social or economic laws may challenge such losses under the Due Process Clause. Under substantive due process principles, a regulation is invalid if it fails to advance a legitimate governmental interest or if it constitutes an unreasonable means of advancing a legitimate governmental interest.

Owing to its overuse in the first 30 years of the twentieth century, courts for many years viewed substantive due process as a discredited constitutional doctrine. In that earlier period, judges, by substituting their personal views for those of the legislatures that had enacted the laws, struck down a whole host of social and economic legislation. In the mid-1930s, however, the resurrection of the theory began. Today, courts generally defer to legislators' judgments regarding social and economic matters and thus presume such laws are valid unless the challenger can persuade the courts that the laws actually are demonstrably arbitrary and irrational. Judicial deference normally leads to the courts upholding such laws, as occurred in *Pacific Mutual Life Insurance Co. v. Haslip*,[21] where the Supreme Court upheld a jury award of punitive damages and the state's post-verdict procedures for reviewing such awards as reasonable.

Since the mid-1960s, the Supreme Court has used substantive due process primarily as a vehicle for protecting certain fundamental personal rights that are implied by constitutional wording and phraseology. Beginning in the mid-1960s, the Court has struck down on grounds of irrationality and arbitrariness state laws making the use of contraceptives by anyone, including married persons, illegal. Such laws impermissibly infringe on the so-called zone of marital privacy protected by the Court. In coming to this result, the Court viewed such legislation in a fashion virtually identical to strict scrutiny and applied something very akin to the compelling state interest test. The liberty component of the Due Process Clause also guarantees a competent person, who has clearly made his or her wishes known beforehand, the right to terminate unwanted medical treatment.[22] Laws holding otherwise can be challenged on substantive due process grounds.

As you studied this section, you probably noticed the complementary relationship between substantive due process and guarantees of equal protection under the law. Both constitutional guarantees mandate a rational fit between the objectives of the law and the group of people affected thereby. When all persons are subject to a law that deprives them of a life, liberty, or property interest, due process probably applies. When a law classifies certain people for certain purposes, the equal protection doctrine probably becomes the appropriate vehicle for challenging the law.

Under either theory, the Supreme Court since the mid-1930s has required judges to give great deference to legislative prerogatives when judges are called upon to review social legislation that does not involve personal fundamental rights. The same is true of economic legislation: Judges should uphold all such legislation unless the challenger can show the absence of any rational relationship to any legitimate governmental aim or interest. Proponents of the substantive due process theory claim that it is a natural extension of the protection of "liberty" in the Fifth and Fourteenth Amendments. They argue that no process is fair if it infringes upon a fundamental right. Opponents of the substantive due process theory claim that the Due Process Clause only requires fairness in the processes governments use to enforce regulations. They argue that the Supreme Court has gone too far in finding the substantive due process theory in the language of the Fifth and Fourteenth Amendments.

eClass 5.2 **Management**

CHALLENGING LOCAL LAWS

One city in which eClass has opened a retail outlet has announced that a new city ordinance will go into effect in three months. This new ordinance requires all firms selling interactive educational software to register with and be licensed by the city. eClass is the only firm that is currently selling such software in that city, and the firm believes that eClass has been singled out for discriminatory treatment by this ordinance. The firm members ask you what they can or should do under these circumstances. What will you tell them?

BUSINESS CONSIDERATIONS   Suppose that a city ordinance makes conducting business in a particular city too difficult or too expensive for a particular firm. Should the firm move its operation out of the city, or should it seek a variance or exemption from the city?

ETHICAL CONSIDERATIONS   Is it ethical for a business to pick and choose where it will operate based on local laws or regulations? What ethical considerations will such a decision raise?

THE TAKINGS CLAUSE

Besides guaranteeing procedural and substantive due process, the Fifth Amendment also provides that "private property [shall not] be taken for public use, without just compensation." This Fifth Amendment restraint on the power of the federal government applies to the states through the Fourteenth Amendment's Due Process Clause. Under this "takings" clause, the government can only take the property for a "public use" and must pay "just compensation" to the property owner whose property is taken.

In litigation, the disagreement between the parties often centers on whether a *taking* has occurred, in which case the Constitution obligates the government to pay just compensation, or whether the governmental action amounts only to *regulation* under the exercise of its police power, in which case no compensation is owed. While the Court has set out no clear formula for judging when a taking has occurred, any actual appropriation of property will suffice. For example, if the state through formal procedures condemns a business for the purpose of constructing a parking garage on a state college campus, a taking has occurred; and the state will have to pay just compensation to the owner of the property that was razed owing to the state's exercise of its power of eminent domain (a state or municipality's power to take private property for public use).

But less-than-complete appropriations of property may qualify as takings as well. For instance, the Court has held that federal dam construction resulting in the repeated flooding of private property and low, direct flights over private property located contiguous to federal or municipal airports constitute takings if the activities in question destroy the property's present use or unreasonably impair the value of the property and the owners' reasonable expectations regarding it.

As the *Lucas v. South Carolina Coastal Council*[23] case discussed in Chapter 39 demonstrates, a land use regulation that fails to substantially advance legitimate state interests or that denies an owner the economically viable use of his or her land is a taking subject to the Fifth Amendment. In the absence of such factors, zoning ordinances—the most common type of land use regulations—ordinarily pass muster under the Takings Clause even if the regulations restrict the use of the property and cause a reduction in its value, so long as the ordinances substantially advance legitimate state interests and do not extinguish fundamental attributes of ownership.

During the attempted taking, the government must afford the affected property owner procedural due process. However, the just compensation paid out by the governmental regulator need reflect only the fair market value of the property; the price paid need not compensate the owner for the sentimental value of the property, the owner's unique need for the property, or the gain the regulating body realizes by virtue of the taking.

The Supreme Court recently added to its property rights jurisprudence when it decided *Monterey, Calif. v. Del Monte Dunes at Monterey, Ltd.*[24] In this case, a firm sought to develop a condominium project on a parcel of environmentally sensitive land along the California coast. After the planning commission had rejected several plans and had imposed increasingly stringent demands on the developer over a period of five years, the firm filed a lawsuit under § 1983, which creates a duty to refrain from interfering with the federal rights of others and provides money damages and injunctive relief for violations of that duty that are effected under color of state law. In a 5-4 decision, the Court held that the developer was entitled to a jury trial on its regulatory taking claim. In doing so, the Court emphasized the narrowness of its ruling on the availability of jury trials in such cases. Indeed, the Court stressed that it was not setting out the precise demarcation of the respective provinces of judges and jury in determining whether a zoning decision substantially advances governmental interests. Nevertheless, the Court concluded that whether a challenged regulation has deprived a landowner of all the economically viable uses of his or her property is a jury question. The Court conceded that whether a land use decision substantially advances legitimate public interests involves a tougher call probably best understood as a mixed question of fact and law. In this case, however, the Court viewed the protracted sequence of the developer's applications and the city's rejections as sufficiently factbound to make the question of liability appropriate for a jury's consideration. The dissenters, in contrast, viewed such inverse condemnation (that is, an action brought by a property owner against a governmental entity that has the power of eminent domain; the property owner typically seeks just compensation for land taken for public use in situations in which the governmental entity does not intend to initiate eminent domain proceedings) cases as analogous to eminent domain proceedings in which no jury trial ordinarily is available because the measure of compensation required by the Fifth Amendment is the fair market value of the property on the date on which the property is appropriated.

The court has recently expanded the constitutional definition of taking property for "public use." In the case of *Kelo v. City of New London, Connecticut*[25] (our Contemporary Case), the majority opinion created a firestorm. The City of New London utilized its condemnation power to transfer property from private owners to private developers. Historically, condemnation proceedings transfer property from private owners to the government. The government then generally builds roads, bridges, railroads, government buildings, etc. New London argued that this private-to-private transfer was a public use even without a governmental building project because of the increase in tax dollars and jobs that would flow into the city when the developers created an urban center on the condemned land. The property owners argued that this private development was not a public use as required by the Constitution.

The court disagreed and ruled for the city. The majority opinion claimed that the city and not the developers was the primary beneficiary of the condemnation and that this was part of the "broader and more natural interpretation of public use." In response to *Kelo*, many states amended their takings laws to disallow condemnation and transfer for economic purposes. In 2006, President Bush issued an executive order that required the federal government to use its takings power only "for the purpose of benefiting the general public and not merely for the purpose of advancing the economic interest of private parties to be given ownership or use of the property taken."

Although we have emphasized only the Due Process and Takings Clauses of the Fifth Amendment, as you will learn from other chapters, this provision in the Constitution also prohibits *double jeopardy* (being tried twice for the same offense) and compulsory self-incrimination. Thus, the Fifth Amendment's many facets represent an effective curb on illegitimate governmental action taken against individuals or businesses.

THE FIRST AMENDMENT/ COMMERCIAL SPEECH

The First Amendment, as you remember, protects individual freedom of speech. Businesses, as legal (or *juristic*) persons, arguably enjoy protectable First Amendment rights as well. Indeed, commercial speech—speech that involves no more than commercial transactions, particularly the advertising of business products and services—does qualify for First Amendment protection. Although the Supreme Court has had difficulty in defining the term "commercial speech" with precision, one thing is clear: The parameters of this protection are not as broad as those given to individual speech.

Clearly, the government can—and does—regulate private expression. Freedom of speech—whether oral, expressive, or symbolic—is a *fundamental* right, but it is not an absolute right. In deciding whether to limit speech, the government engages in yet another balancing test in which it compares such factors as the importance of these rights in a democratic society, the nature of the restriction imposed by the law, the type and importance of the governmental interest the law purports to serve, and the narrowness of the means used to effectuate that interest. The commercial speech test set out in *Central Hudson Gas & Elec. Corp v. Public Serv. Comm'n of N.Y.*[26] laid out the test for commercial speech. Assuming the speech does no more than propose a commercial transaction (i.e., commercial as opposed to political, etc., speech), a four-part balancing test applies. First, the speech in question cannot be illegal or misleading. Second, the law regulating the speech must be based on a legitimate governmental interest—such as the health and safety of citizens. Third, the law must directly advance this interest. Fourth, the law must be narrowly tailored, using the least restrictive means available to effectively meet the governmental interest.

Courts ordinarily view laws that burden the content of individual speech ("content-based" regulations) by punishing some speech and favoring other speech as presumptively invalid. As a result, such laws must pass the "strict scrutiny/compelling state interest" (the "least restrictive alternative") test and be narrowly drawn measures designed to achieve such a compelling state interest. Courts can strike down substantially overbroad and vague laws (those that proscribe protected activity and thus "chill" others into refraining from the exercise of constitutionally protected expression). The government may outlaw defamation, advocacy of unlawful action, obscenity, and "fighting words." The government also can subject lawful speech to time, place, and manner regulation (it can require demonstrators to obtain permits, limit the demonstration to a certain venue, and so on).

Because the government can regulate and limit private expression, it comes as no surprise that the government can regulate commercial speech and even ban such speech that is false and misleading. Although the First Amendment protects commercial speech, the greater potential for deception and confusion posed by commercial speech allows the government to regulate even the content of commercial (as opposed to noncommercial) speech so long as the restriction serves and advances a substantial governmental interest and in a manner no more extensive than necessary ("sufficiently tailored") to achieve that governmental objective. For example, in 1994, the Supreme Court held in *Turner Broadcasting System, Inc. v. Federal Communications Commission (Turner I)*[27] that the provisions of the federal law that required cable television stations to devote a specified portion of their channels to the transmission of local programming (the "must carry" provisions) were not content-based laws. In 1997, after a remand for more fact finding, the Court—in *Turner II*—affirmed this holding.[28] The Court rejected the argument that these "must carry" provisions must be judged under the strict scrutiny/compelling state interest test and instead upheld the challenged provisions because they were sufficiently tailored to serve the important governmental interest relating to the preservation of local broadcasting. The recent challenges to Congress's attempt to regulate "indecent" content on the Internet (specifically, the Communications Decency Act of 1995, which outlawed the electronic transmission of lewd and indecent materials to anyone under age 18 and subjected to criminal penalties any commercial communication service that allows its system to be used for such transmissions) involve similar issues. The Supreme Court's invalidation of this law as illegal content-based blanket restrictions on speech[29] is a

eClass 5.3 Marketing/Law

ADVERTISING RESTRICTIONS

The firm recently decided that it needed to develop a catchy advertising campaign to increase the sale of its software. One of the ideas that Meg proposed was a commercial in which eAccounting is touted as "guaranteeing" a higher grade in the class and a better understanding of the material than is possible with any other course-support material on the market. Ani questions whether such an ad could be run without risk. She fears that the ad might be prohibited unless eClass has some evidence to support its "guarantee of success" claim. Meg and Yousef both believe that the firm has the constitutional right to run such an ad, citing the fact that freedom of speech applies to commercial speech as well as to individual speech, and that absent a showing of falsity, the government could not prohibit the use of this ad. However, the members have asked you for your opinion. What will you tell them?

BUSINESS CONSIDERATIONS   When a business, especially a relatively new business, begins to advertise, should it be conservative in asserting its quality until the business has established a public image, or should it be more assertive in its claims until or unless evidence shows that it overstated its quality?

ETHICAL CONSIDERATIONS   Is it ethical for a business to "puff" its products, asserting characteristics and quality for the product that fall within opinion rather than fact, and thus are not *literally* untrue, although the "puffing" is quite likely to cause customers to expect more from the product or service than it can provide?

harbinger of the types of issues that promise to provide a fertile field for continuing litigation.

In January 2010, the Court issued a landmark opinion concerning corporations' rights to political speech in *Citizens United v. Federal Election Commission*. In *Citizens United*, the Court dealt with the controversy surrounding business and political campaigns. Businesses have traditionally been allowed to speak in ways that do not propose merely a commercial transaction (i.e., political speech versus commercial speech). For example, businesses often donate money to political causes and committees. The Bipartisan Campaign Reform Act (BCRA) is a federal law that, among other things, banned direct campaign contributions from businesses to candidates for political office and more general contributions within a certain pre-election period.

In *Citizens United*, a non-profit group desired to run a documentary critical of Hillary Clinton, but refrained because of the BCRA. Instead, the organization sued, arguing that the campaign finance law infringed upon its freedom of political speech under the First Amendment. The court's majority opinion claimed that political speech

Exhibit 5.2

Summary of Constitutional Regulation Provisions

Constitutional Provision	Where Found	Application
Commerce Clause	Article I, Section 8, Clause 3 of the Constitution	Federal government has exclusive jurisdiction to regulate commerce with foreign nations, Indian nations, and among the several states (interstate commerce).
Equal Protection Clause	5th and 14th Amendments	Similarly situated people must be treated similarly. Any regulation that discriminates must meet the "rational basis" test; any regulation that discriminates on the basis of invidious discrimination or the infringement of fundamental rights must meet the "strict scrutiny" test and must be needed to meet a compelling state interest; and any regulation that discriminates on the basis of gender must meet the "intermediate" test, applying a "heightened scrutiny" to ensure that a substantial state interest is being met.
Due Process Clause (Procedural)	5th and 14th Amendments	Regulations must provide for procedural safeguards prior to removing "life, liberty, or property" from anyone affected by the regulation.
Due Process Clause (Substantive)	5th and 14th Amendments	Regulations must satisfy substantive guidelines prior to the removal of "life, liberty, or property" from anyone affected. The regulation cannot be overly broad and it must advance a legitimate state interest.
Takings Clause	5th and 14th Amendments	Property cannot be taken from a person by the government except when the taking is for a "public purpose" and the person is given "just compensation" for the property so taken. (Less-than-complete takings may also fall within this protection.)
Commercial Speech	1st Amendment	Commercial speech may be restricted, subject to a four-pronged test: the speech in question cannot be illegal or misleading; the regulation must be based on a legitimate governmental interest; it must directly advance this interest; and it must be narrowly tailored, using the least restrictive means available to effectively meet the governmental interest.

forms the heart of any democracy and that businesses are an important part of America's democracy. Therefore, many of the BCRA restrictions on corporate political speech were found to violate the First Amendment and were struck down. After *Citizens United*, corporations and labor unions possess the same political speech rights as individuals. Corporations are now allowed to conduct "electioneering campaigns" that support or denounce individual candidates prior to an election but are still banned from directly contributing to a politician's campaign.

ADMINISTRATIVE AGENCIES

Administrative agencies conduct much of the work of regulating business. Most of us are familiar with the three official branches of the federal government—the legislative, executive, and judicial—but we may tend to overlook the unofficial "fourth branch." This administrative "branch" of government has been especially active since the 1930s. The Great Depression and the presidency of Franklin Delano Roosevelt saw a tremendous growth in the use of administrative agencies as a major means of effecting regulation. Because a great deal of government intervention in the business sphere derives from the actions of administrative agencies, some familiarity with administrative law is essential to understanding governmental regulation of business.

Congress sets up administrative agencies; and since Congress "creates" them, Congress can terminate them. Hence, they are not an independent branch of government. They have only as much authority as the legislature delegates to them, and as a result, they must answer to Congress for their conduct. Congress establishes a basic policy or standard and then authorizes an agency to carry it out.

Once established, the agency will have certain quasi-legislative (partly legislative; empowered to enact rules and regulations but not statutes) and quasi-judicial (partly judicial; empowered to hold hearings but not trials) powers. The agency is allowed to pass rules and regulations within its area of authority and to hold hearings when it believes violations of its rules and regulations have occurred. In so doing, federal administrative agencies must follow the Administrative Procedures Act (APA), which mandates public participation and sets out the rules and procedures that such agencies must follow as they legislate, adjudicate, and enforce their regulations. The power of Congress to abolish any agency and the power of the courts to review any agency's conduct are considered sufficient control devices. It is believed that the agency will not exceed its authority or abuse its discretion as long as these two *official* branches of government keep a watchful eye on the agency's conduct.

Some of the constitutional provisions discussed earlier in the chapter limit the power of administrative agencies. Remember that an agency, in order to ensure procedural due process, must provide fairness in its proceedings. A person involved in a proceeding that affects his or her individual rights (those involving *adjudicative* facts) ordinarily is entitled to a hearing of some sort. Also remember that due process generally includes the right to present witnesses, the right to cross-examine witnesses, the right to an impartial decision maker, and possibly other rights as well. Agency proceedings involving only rule making or fact-finding concerning principles of general application (those involving *legislative* facts) usually require fewer procedural safeguards. Notice of the time, place, and purpose of the meeting might satisfy procedural due process in this context. The agency may only enact rules and regulations that bear a rational relationship to the agency's purpose or function. Under substantive due process doctrines, litigants may challenge unreasonable, arbitrary, and capricious administrative rules. Such rules also may deny the persons affected the equal protection of the law.

The respective agencies' enabling statutes ordinarily spell out the methods by which one can seek review of agency decisions. Those dissatisfied with treatment received at the hands of an administrative agency generally may ask a federal district or circuit court of appeals to review the administrative proceedings in question. Judicial review ordinarily focuses on four possible areas of agency error:

1. The agency violated procedural due process.
2. The agency violated substantive due process.
3. The agency otherwise violated the Constitution.
4. The agency exceeded its authority.

A court will review the proceedings only from the point of view of their legality. As to *questions of fact* (for example, what actually transpired), a court must follow the *substantial evidence rule*, which states that the agency's findings of fact *must* be upheld if such findings are based on substantial evidence. If instead the judicial review involves *questions of law* (for example, jurisdictional or procedural issues), courts remain free to substitute their judgment for the agencies'; courts need not give deference to the agencies' determinations regarding these issues.

Courts will review *discretionary* acts under the "abuse of discretion" rationale and will invalidate arbitrary, unreasonable, or capricious decisions.

Owing to the restricted nature of judicial review and the pervasive nature of administrative agencies in the business world, this area of regulation has become quite important today. A person who plans to advance very far in business is well advised to study administrative law in further detail.

Contemporary Case

KELO v. CITY OF NEW LONDON, CONNECTICUT
545 U.S. 469 (2005)

FACTS In 2000, the City of New London, Connecticut, approved a development plan that was projected to create more than 1,000 jobs in the community, to increase taxes and other revenues for the city, and to revitalize an economically distressed city, especially its downtown and riverfront areas. As part of this plan, the city reactivated the New London Development Corporation (NLDC), a private nonprofit entity, to assist in the planning and implementation of the plan. The NLDC was also designated as the city's development agent. In order to acquire the land to carry out this redevelopment, the NLDC purchased some land from willing sellers, but also found that some of the owners of targeted parcels of land were unwilling to sell. The development agent then proposed that the city use its power of eminent domain to acquire the balance of the property from the unwilling sellers for "just compensation." This proposal was accepted, and the city proceeded to exercise its power of eminent domain to acquire the property, which was then to be sold to private developers who would complete the development plan. Kelo and other "unwilling sellers" challenged the legality of the city's use of eminent domain in this manner.

ISSUE Does the city's proposed disposition of the property qualify as a "public use" with the meaning of the Takings Clause of the Fifth Amendment to the U.S. Constitution?

HOLDING Yes. This taking would be executed pursuant to a "carefully considered" development plan. There was no evidence of an illegitimate purpose. The plan was not adopted "to benefit a particular class of identifiable individuals," but rather to satisfy a legitimate public purpose.

REASONING Excerpts from the opinion of Justice Stevens.

... The trial judge and all the members of the Supreme Court of Connecticut agreed that there was no evidence of an illegitimate purpose in this case. Therefore ... the City's development plan was not adopted "to benefit a particular class of identifiable individuals."

On the other hand, this is not a case in which the City is planning to open the condemned land—at least not in its entirety—to use by the general public. Nor will the private lessees of the land in any sense be required to operate like common carriers, making their services available to all comers. But although such a projected use would be sufficient to satisfy the public use requirements, this "Court long ago rejected any literal requirement that condemned property be put into use for the general public." ... Not only was the "use by the public" test difficult to administer ..., but it proved to be impractical given the diverse and always evolving needs of society. Accordingly, when this Court began applying the Fifth Amendment to the States at the close of the 19th century, it embraced the broader and more natural interpretation of public use as "public purpose." ...

The disposition of this case therefore turns on the question whether the City's development plan serves a "public purpose." Without exception, our cases have defined the concept broadly, reflecting our longstanding policy of deference to legislative judgments in this field. ...

Those who govern the City were not confronted with the need to remove blight in the ... area, but their determination that the area was sufficiently distressed to justify a program of economic rejuvenation is entitled to our deference. The City has carefully formulated an economic development plan that it believes will provide appreciable benefits to the community, including—but by no means limited to—new jobs and increased tax revenue. ... To effectuate this plan, the city has invoked a state statute that specifically authorizes the use of eminent domain to promote economic development. Given the comprehensive character of the plan, the thorough deliberation that preceded its adoption, and the limited scope of our review, it is appropriate for us ... to resolve the challenges of the individual owners not on a piecemeal basis, but rather in light of the entire plan. Because that plan unquestionably serves a public purpose, the takings challenged here satisfy the public use requirement of the Fifth Amendment. ...

In affirming the City's authority to take [the] properties, we do not minimize the hardship that condemnation may entail, notwithstanding the payment of just compensation. We emphasize that nothing in our opinion precludes any State from placing further restrictions on its exercise of the takings power ... [T]he necessity and wisdom of using eminent domain to promote economic development are certainly matters of legitimate public debate. This Court's authority, however, extends only to determining whether the City's proposed condemnations are for a "public use" within the meaning of the Fifth Amendment to the Federal Constitution. Because over a century of our case law interpreting that provision dictates an affirmative answer to that question, we may not grant petitioners the relief that they seek. ...

You Be the Judge

The pharmaceutical firm, Eli Lilly and Co. (Lilly), has a Web site called www.prozac.com. From March 2000 through June 2001, Lilly offered a service called "Medi-Messenger," whereby the firm would provide individualized e-mail reminders concerning medication. Pursuant to its own privacy policy, Lilly assured all those who signed up for the Medi-Messenger service that "Eli Lilly and Company respects the privacy of visitors to its Web sites." The Lilly policy further specified that its sites "have security measures in place, including the use of industry standard secure socket layer encryption (SSL), to protect the confidentiality of any of Your Information that you volunteer." On June 27, 2001, Lilly sent all 669 subscribers to its Medi-Messenger service an e-mail that inadvertently included every subscriber's e-mail address in the "To" field. This disclosure was unintentional, and Lilly had never before made any inappropriate disclosures. Prompted by a complaint from the American Civil Liberties Union, the Federal Trade Commission (FTC) sought to hold Lilly legally accountable for this glitch based on Lilly's own privacy policy. Using as its jurisdictional basis the allegedly false or misleading representation that Lilly had made during the sign-up process for Medi-Messenger, the FTC claimed that Lilly had failed to implement internal measures and policies that protected the privacy and confidentiality of the personal information supplied by its customers. Among other things, the FTC suggested that Lilly should be held accountable not only for ensuring the sensitivity of the information supplied to it by its customers, but also for preventing cyber-attacks on such data.

Assume that Lilly and the FTC agree to settle this online privacy complaint. If you were representing the FTC, what specific provisions (or safeguards) would you require Lilly to include in its internal privacy policies so as to ensure that Lilly in the future would be able to maintain adequate controls on information security? [See 70 U.S.L.W. 2507-2508 (February 19, 2002).]

Summary

Governmental regulation of business is a fact of life in the modern business environment. Whether regulation takes the form of local zoning ordinances, state income taxation, or federal antitrust regulation, businesses today must address it. And the only way to deal with government regulation is to recognize and understand it. Federal regulation of business is based on the Commerce Clause of the U.S. Constitution, which authorizes Congress to "regulate commerce among the several states," along with Congress's taxing power and the Necessary and Proper Clause, also included in the Constitution.

Most regulation derives from the Commerce Clause. The Commerce Clause has been interpreted in such a way that federal regulation is permitted only if interstate commerce is involved. To qualify as interstate, the transaction must directly affect citizens of at least two different states or countries. If an interstate connection is present, federal regulation may be applied. The federal government exclusively regulates many aspects of business, but the states have concurrent power to regulate in certain areas. States can exercise exclusive regulatory power over commerce only rarely.

The Equal Protection Clause protects against invidious discrimination. Over the years, the Supreme Court has developed various tests for determining the legality of regulations challenged under this provision of the Constitution.

The Constitution's guarantee of due process has a distinct procedural dimension and a substantive dimension. These aspects guarantee fundamental fairness and freedom from the application of irrational, unreasonable, and arbitrary laws whenever the government deprives anyone of life, liberty, or property.

Under the Takings Clause of the Fifth Amendment, the government can take property for public use so long as the government pays just compensation to the affected property owner. Under a recent decision, public use can include condemnation and transfer of property to private developers to generate tax revenues for the government. In addition, the Fifth Amendment's prohibitions on double jeopardy and compulsory self-incrimination also serve as curbs on illegitimate governmental action.

The First Amendment protects commercial speech but to a lesser degree than it does individual speech. The government can ban misleading and illegal commercial speech and can even regulate other types of commercial speech as long as the restriction serves and directly advances a substantial governmental interest and does so in a manner no more extensive than necessary to achieve that governmental objective.

Much of the actual regulation of business is carried out by administrative agencies. Administrative agencies are created by Congress, and Congress then delegates to the agencies the authority to carry out certain duties. Agencies are involved in a large number of regulatory areas. In carrying out their responsibilities, these agencies are required to assure due process of law; and they are subject to judicial review to ensure that they conduct themselves properly.

Discussion Questions

1. How do you define the phrase interstate commerce? Do you accept or reject the Supreme Court's definition of this term? Why?

2. Discuss the factors courts must take into account in deciding whether a group is a "suspect classification" for purposes of equal protection analysis.

3. What does substantive due process mean? How does a court determine when a violation of this constitutional right has occurred?

4. How does procedural due process differ from substantive due process? What protections must the government provide to individuals and businesses under this aspect of the Fifth and Fourteenth Amendments?

5. What powers does the government enjoy under the Takings Clause? What rights does an individual or business have under this clause?

Case Problems and Writing Assignments

1. G & G Fire Sprinklers, Inc. (G & G) is a fire-protection company that installs fire sprinkler systems. G & G served as a subcontractor on several California public works projects. The California Labor Code (Code) requires that contractors and subcontractors on such projects pay their workers a prevailing wage that is determined by the state. At the time relevant here, if workers were not paid the prevailing wage, the contractor was required to pay each worker the difference between the prevailing wage and the wages paid, in addition to forfeiting a penalty to the state. The awarding body was required to include a clause to this effect in all contracts. The Code further authorizes the state to order the withholding of payments due a contractor on a public works project if a subcontractor on the project fails to comply with certain Code requirements. The Code permits the contractor, in turn, to withhold similar sums from the subcontractor. On the other hand, the Code permits the contractor, or its assignee, to recover the wages or penalties withheld by bringing suit against the awarding body. The awarding body retains the wages and penalties pending the outcome of the suit. In 1995, the state's Division of Labor Standards Enforcement (DLSE) determined that G & G, as a subcontractor on three public works projects, had violated the Code by failing to pay the prevailing wage and by failing to keep and/or furnish payroll records upon request. The DLSE issued notices to the awarding bodies on those projects, directing them to withhold from the contractors an amount equal to the wages and penalties forfeited owing to G & G's violations. The awarding bodies withheld payment from the contractors, who in turn withheld payment from G & G. The total withheld, according to G & G, exceeded $135,000. G & G then sued, claiming that the issuance of the withholding notices without a hearing constituted a deprivation of property without due process of law in violation of the Fourteenth Amendment. Should G & G win? [See *Lujan v. G & G Fire Sprinklers, Inc.*, 532 U.S. 189 (2001).]

2. In order to acquire the waterfront parcel of Rhode Island land at issue, Anthony Palazzolo and some associates formed Shore Gardens, Inc. (SGI) in 1959. Palazzolo eventually became the sole shareholder. Most of the property was then, and is now, salt marsh subject to tidal flooding. The wet ground and permeable soil thus would require considerable fill before significant structures could be built. Over the years, various governmental agencies rejected SGI's intermittent applications to develop the property. After 1966, no further applications were made for over a decade. Two intervening events, however, deserve mention. First, in 1971, the state created the Rhode Island Coastal Resources Management Council (Council) and charged it with protecting the state's coastal properties. The Council's regulations, known as the Rhode Island Coastal Resources Management Program (CRMP), designated salt marshes like those on SGI's property as protected "coastal wetlands" on which development is greatly limited. Second, in 1978, SGI's corporate charter was revoked, and title to the property passed to Palazzolo as the corporation's sole shareholder. In 1983, Palazzolo applied to the Council for permission to construct a wooden bulkhead and fill the entire marsh land area. The Council, in rejecting this application, concluded that it would conflict with the CRMP. In 1985, Palazzolo filed a new application, seeking permission to fill 11 of the property's 18 wetland acres in order to build a private beach club. The Council rejected this application as well, ruling that the proposal did not satisfy the standards for obtaining a "special exception," namely that the proposed activity serve a compelling public purpose. Subsequently, Palazzolo filed a lawsuit asserting that the state's wetlands regulations, as applied by the Council to his parcel, had taken the property without compensation in violation of the Fifth and Fourteenth Amendments. The suit further alleged that the Council's action had deprived him of "all economically beneficial use" of his property, resulting in a total taking that required compensation in the amount of $3,150,000, a figure derived from an appraiser's estimate as to the value of a 74-lot residential subdivision on the property. The lower courts ruled against Palazzolo on the grounds (among others) that (1) his takings claim was not ripe; (2) he lacked the right to challenge regulations predating 1978, the time when he had succeeded to the legal ownership of the property; (3) he would be unable to assert a takings claim based on the denial of all economic use of his property in light of the undisputed evidence that he had $200,000 in development value remaining on an upland parcel of the property; and 4) because the regulation at issue predated his acquisition of title, he could have had no reasonable investment-backed expectation that he could develop his property and, therefore, lacked any basis for recovery. Who had the stronger arguments—Palazzolo or the state? [See *Palazzolo v. Rhode Island*, 533 U.S. 606 (2001).]

3. In September 1992, the operators of the Women's Health Center (WHC), an abortion clinic in Melbourne, Florida, sought an injunction against certain anti-abortion protestors. At that time, a Florida state court permanently enjoined Madsen and the other protestors from blocking or interfering with public access to the clinic and from physically abusing persons entering or leaving the clinic. Six months later, WHC, complaining that access to the clinic was still impeded by the protestors' activities and that such activities also had discouraged some potential patients from entering the clinic and had had deleterious physical effects on others, sought to broaden the injunction. In issuing this broader injunction, the trial court found that, despite the initial injunction, protestors, by congregating on the paved portion of the street leading up to the clinic and by marching in front of the clinic's driveways, had continued to impede access to the clinic. The trial court found that as vehicles heading toward the clinic slowed to allow the protestors to move out of the way, "sidewalk counselors" would attempt to give the vehicles' occupants anti-abortion literature. The number of people congregating varied from a handful to 400, and the noise varied from singing and chanting to the use of loudspeakers and bullhorns. A clinic doctor testified that as a result of having to run such a gauntlet to enter the clinic, the patients, owing to heightened anxiety and hypertension, needed a higher level of sedation before they could undergo surgical procedures and thereby faced increased risks from such procedures. The noise caused stress not only for the patients undergoing surgery but also for those recuperating in the recovery rooms. Doctors and clinic workers, in turn, were not immune even in their homes. The protestors picketed in front of clinic employees' residences, rang the doorbells of neighbors, provided literature identifying the particular clinic employee as a "baby killer," and occasionally confronted the clinic employees' minor children, who were home alone. Given this and similar testimony, the state court viewed the original injunction as insufficient "to protect the health, safety and rights of women in Brevard and Seminole County, Florida, and surrounding counties seeking access to [medical and counseling] services." The state court, therefore, amended its prior order and enjoined a broader array of activities. Although the Florida supreme court had upheld the injunction, the Court of Appeals for the Eleventh Circuit had struck it down. At the U.S. Supreme Court, what constitutional arguments would the parties make? Who should win and why? If you were deciding this case on ethical grounds, with whom would you side—the protestors or the clinic and its personnel? Why? [See *Madsen v. Women's Health Center, Inc.*, 512 U.S. 753 (1994), modified at Schenck v. Pro-Choice Network of Western New York, 519 U.S. 357 (1997).]

Notes

1. *Statistical Abstract of the United States 2001*, 121st ed. (Washington, D.C.: U.S. Department of Commerce), p. 319.
2. 9 Wheat (22 U.S.) 1 (1824).
3. 24 Stat. 379 (1887).
4. 15 Wall. (82 U.S.) 232 (1873).
5. 128 U.S. 1 (1888).
6. 301 U.S. 1 (1937).
7. 336 U.S. 460, 464 (1949).
8. 379 U.S. 241 (1964).
9. The Supreme Court has held that the Commerce Clause grants Congress—and not the Executive Branch—exclusive power to regulate commerce with foreign nations (i.e., commerce between United States citizens and citizens of foreign nations).
10. 411 U.S. 624 (1973).
11. 514 U.S. 549 (1995).
12. 529 U.S. 598 (2000).
13. 432 U.S. 432 (1986).
14. 118 U.S. 356 (1886).
15. 517 U.S. 620 (1996).
16. Ibid., 635.
17. 515 U.S. 200 (1995).
18. Ibid., 202.
19. 429 U.S. 190 (1976).
20. *U.S. v. Virginia*, 518 U.S. 515, at 516 and 534 (1996).
21. 499 U.S. 1 (1991).
22. *Cruzan v. Director, Missouri Department of Health*, 497 U.S. 261 (1990).
23. *Lucas v. South Carolina Coastal Council*, 505 U.S. 1003 (1992).
24. 119 S. Ct. 1624 (1999).
25. 545 U.S. 469 (2005).
26. 447 U.S. 557 (1980).
27. 512 U.S. 622 (1994).
28. *Turner Broadcasting System, Inc. v. Federal Communication Comm'n*, 520 U.S. 180 (1997).
29. *Reno v. American Civil Liberties Union*, 521 U.S. 844 (1997).

6
Torts

Agenda

eClass recently has been victimized by some tortious activity. What steps can it legally pursue to protect its property interests? Gabino, a former eClass employee, is applying for new positions with several different firms; potential employers are calling Ani to inquire about Gabino's employment with eClass. What should Ani tell them when they call? A competitor has been advertising the merits of its software in comparison to another software program that looks like eAccounting. This "other software" is depicted as not performing very well. Although eClass is not specifically named in the advertisement, it seems obvious that the "other software" is eAccounting. Can the firm successfully sue this competitor for product disparagement in order to protect eClass's image and reputation? Also, a group of people have banded together to protest—or even prevent—the online use of software, and they have threatened to file invasion-of-privacy lawsuits based on the idea that the software can be used to collect personal information. Ani, Meg, and Yousef think that it is stretching the invasion of

187

privacy doctrine to claim that eClass's products invade peoples' privacy. Should they worry about these legal threats? What legal defenses might be available to them? What would occur if an employee were negligent in operating an eClass vehicle on "official" business? Who would be liable for any damages? eClass? The employee? Or both? What can our entrepreneurs do to avoid liability?

These and other questions will arise as you read this chapter. Be prepared! You never know when the firm or one of its members will seek your advice.

Classic Case

NEW YORK TIMES CO. v. SULLIVAN
376 U.S. 254, 1964 U.S. LEXIS 1655 (1964)

FACTS L. B. Sullivan was one of the three elected Commissioners of the City of Montgomery, Alabama. He sued four individual petitioners and the New York Times Company, claiming that he had been libeled by statements in a full-page advertisement about the civil rights movement that was printed in the *New York Times*. It is uncontroverted that some of the statements contained in the ad were not accurate descriptions of events that occurred in Montgomery. None of the statements in the ad named Sullivan, but he contended that the word "police" referred to him because he was the Montgomery Commissioner who supervised the Police Department. Sullivan contended that since arrests are ordinarily made by the police, the statement about arresting Dr. King would be read as referring to him.

The *Times* published the ad on an order from a New York advertising agency. The agency attached a letter from A. Philip Randolph, Chairman of the Committee, which certified that the persons who "signed" the advertisement had given their permission. The *Times*'s Advertising Acceptability Department knew Mr. Randolph and believed that he was a responsible person. It accepted the letter as sufficient proof of authorization following its established practice. These individuals testified that they had not authorized the use of their names and that they were unaware that their names were being used. "The manager of the Advertising Acceptability Department testified that he had approved the advertisement for publication because there was nothing to cause him to believe that it was false, and because it bore the endorsement of 'a number of people who are well known and whose reputation' he 'had no reason to question.'" No one at the *Times* tried to confirm the accuracy of the advertisement by checking it against *Times* news stories or by other confirmation.

ISSUE Does Alabama's libel law violate the freedom of speech and freedom of press?

HOLDING Yes, Alabama's libel law is unconstitutional.

REASONING Excerpts from the opinion of Justice Brennan:

...We hold that the rule of law applied by the Alabama courts is constitutionally deficient for failure to provide the safeguards for freedom of speech and of the press that are required by the First and Fourteenth Amendments in a libel action brought by a public official against critics of his official conduct. . . . [U]nder the proper safeguards the evidence presented in this case is constitutionally insufficient to support the judgment for respondent. . . . The publication here was not a "commercial" advertisement. . . . It communicated information, expressed opinion, recited grievances, protested claimed abuses, and sought financial support on behalf of a movement whose existence and objectives are matters of the highest public interest and concern. . . . That the Times was paid for publishing the advertisement is as immaterial . . . as is the fact that newspapers and books are sold. . . . Any other conclusion would discourage newspapers from carrying "editorial advertisements" of this type, and so might shut off an important outlet for the promulgation of information and ideas by persons who do not themselves have access to publishing facilities— who wish to exercise their freedom of speech even though they are not members of the press. . . .

The present advertisement . . . would seem clearly to qualify for the constitutional protection. . . . The constitutional protection does not turn upon "the truth, popularity, or social utility of the ideas and beliefs which are offered." . . . If neither factual error nor defamatory content suffices to remove the constitutional shield from criticism of official conduct, the combination of the two elements is no less inadequate. . . . It is true that the First Amendment was originally addressed only to action by the Federal Government. . . . But this distinction was eliminated with the adoption of the Fourteenth Amendment and the application to the States of the First Amendment's restrictions. . . . What a State may not constitutionally bring about by means of a criminal statute is likewise beyond the reach of its civil law of libel. . . . The fear of damage awards under a rule such as that invoked by the Alabama

courts . . . may be markedly more inhibiting than the fear of prosecution under a criminal statute. . . .

Allowance of the defense of truth, with the burden of proving it on the defendant, does not mean that only false speech will be deterred. . . . The constitutional guarantees require . . . a federal rule that prohibits a public official from recovering damages for a defamatory falsehood relating to his official conduct unless he proves that the statement was made with "actual malice"—that is, with knowledge that it was false or with reckless disregard of whether it was false or not. . . . [W]e consider that the proof presented to show actual malice [in this case] lacks the convincing clarity which the constitutional standard demands, and hence that it would not constitutionally sustain the judgment for respondent. . . . The case of the individual petitioners requires little discussion. Even assuming that they could constitutionally be found to have authorized the use of their names on the advertisement, there was no evidence whatever that they were aware of any erroneous statements or were in any way reckless in that regard. The judgment against them is thus without constitutional support. As to the Times, we similarly conclude that the facts do not support a finding of actual malice. . . . [T]here is evidence that the Times published the advertisement without checking its accuracy against the news stories in the Times' own files. The mere presence of the stories in the files does not . . . establish that the Times "knew" the advertisement was false. . . . [T]he record shows that they relied upon their knowledge of the good reputation of many of those whose names were listed as sponsors of the advertisement, and upon the letter from A. Philip Randolph. . . . [T]he persons handling the advertisement saw nothing in it that would render it unacceptable under the Times' policy. . . . We think the evidence against the Times supports at most a finding of negligence. . . .

We also think the evidence was constitutionally defective in another respect: it was incapable of supporting the jury's finding that the allegedly libelous statements were made "of and concerning" respondent. . . . There was no reference to respondent in the advertisement, either by name or official position. . . .

OBJECTIVES OF TORT LAW

Tort law is concerned with a body of "private" wrongs, whereas *criminal law*, which we shall study in Chapter 7, is concerned with "public" wrongs. Tort law has evolved over hundreds of years. It helps protect an individual's rights with respect to his or her property and person. It is a complicated body of law because of the long period of development and the various exceptions that have evolved in its application. In addition, tort law is based on common law; consequently, the rules can vary significantly from state to state. The discussion here, therefore, is fairly general.

Torts provide a mechanism for persons who have been wronged to seek remedies in our court system. In general, the remedy sought is money damages to compensate for the injury. People can avoid committing these wrongs by adhering to various "duties." For example, society recognizes a duty to refrain from physically injuring other persons or their property. Society also recognizes a duty to refrain from injuring the reputation of others.

Because tort law recognizes certain duties, it raises the policy question of exactly which rights society should protect through the imposition of duties. For example, should society recognize as a wrong only behavior intended to be a wrong? Should society also recognize as a wrong an unintended wrong due to someone's negligence? Should society also recognize as a wrong unintended behavior in which the person is not negligent? These are the questions discussed in this chapter.

Society has developed the body of tort law to resolve social and economic policy questions. The law has to take into consideration a number of factors including: the social usefulness of the conduct of a person; the interests asserted by the plaintiff; the justification (if any) for the defendant's conduct; the economic burden placed on the defendant if liability is imposed; and the question of spreading the cost of liability from one to many persons. The law also has the unique problem of respecting past decisions while maintaining the flexibility to provide solutions to modern problems. For instance, tort law has to adjust to technological advances such as defamation and invasion of privacy through the use of the computer.

THEORIES OF TORT LIABILITY

This chapter discusses intentional torts, negligence, and strict liability. Exhibit 6.1 depicts the three theories of tort liability. *Intentional torts* are those wrongs in which the persons being sued acted in a willful or intentional manner; they either wanted the act to occur or knew that the act would probably occur. Suppose that someone said something offensive to you, and you said, "If you don't apologize, I'll punch you in the nose." If that person did not apologize and you punched him in the nose, the law states that *you* are the party "in the wrong." When you punched the other person in the nose, you committed the tort of *battery* on the other person. Provocation is not an issue here, since generally the law does not recognize the privilege of striking someone for making offensive remarks. (In this context, a *privilege* is a defense where the defendant claims that his or her conduct was authorized or sanctioned by the law.)

The law of *negligence* is based on a concept of fault in which morality and law have been intermingled. How should society apportion the costs of accidents? Often, society has to make a moral statement when an injury occurs. Suppose a child darts out from behind a parked car an instant before an approaching driver reaches that point; the driver immediately brakes in an effort to avoid hitting the child but is unable to stop in time to avoid the accident. In all likelihood, this accident would be considered unavoidable—it occurred without any negligence on the part of the driver. The child, even though injured, would be denied any compensation from the driver for the accident.

Exhibit 6.1

The Three Theories of Tort Liability

TORT LIABILITY		
Intentional Torts	**Negligence**	**Strict Liability in Tort**
The accused acts in a willful or intentional manner.	The conduct of the accused is compared to the "reasonable and prudent" person.	The accused is generally involved in conduct that is deemed abnormally dangerous.
Involves a simple duty to avoid the act or conduct.	Involves a reasonable duty to avoid the act or conduct.	Involves a strict duty to be responsible for the harm caused.
There must be a showing of fault.	There must be a showing of fault.	There is no need to show fault.
The harm must be foreseeable.	The harm must be foreseeable.	The harm must be foreseeable.

On the other hand, if a child is walking across the street in a designated crosswalk and an automobile hits him or her because the driver is drunk or driving too fast, then society says that the driver breached a duty to drive the car in a reasonable manner. Accordingly, the driver will have to pay for damages suffered by the child. The amount of injury is not a factor in determining liability: what is relevant is how the injury occurred.

Since most negligence cases will not fall at the ends of the spectrum, as did the two examples above, the law has developed a test for determining whether negligence occurred in any given situation. The law applies the standards of the "reasonable and prudent person," comparing the conduct of this hypothetical individual to the conduct of the defendant. This topic is discussed in more detail later in this chapter.

Under *strict liability*, persons can be held liable to injured parties even if their conduct was neither intentional nor negligent. That is, they can be held liable even if the damage arising from their conduct was not their fault. Some activities are classified as either ultrahazardous or abnormally dangerous, and if injury results from activities fitting either of those categories, the actor will be held liable. For example, suppose you have a pet rattlesnake in a sealed glass cage and you place the cage in your backyard with signs on the fence that say: *Danger—Poisonous Snake, Beware*. If the snake somehow gets out and bites someone, you can be held liable for the resulting injuries despite your warnings or your best efforts to avoid injuring anyone. The law prevents you from trying to prove how careful you were. If your rattlesnake caused injury, you will simply have to pay. Increasingly, legislatures are creating strict liability for parents when their children intentionally cause injury to others.[1]

Duty

We live in a legal system in which we all have a duty to protect other persons from harm. The question the courts must examine is what degree of duty exists under any given set of specific circumstances. With respect to intentional torts, we all have a simple duty to avoid liability-causing behavior. However, with respect to negligence, we all have a "reasonable" duty to avoid this type of behavior. Generally, the law states that reasonable duty is a standard of ordinary skill and care, based on the facts of each individual case. In order to test for a duty in any particular situation, the law has constructed a person against whom the conduct of the defendant is to be compared. This purely hypothetical person is known as the *reasonable and prudent person*. Note that this hypothetical person is not perfect, he or she is merely reasonable and prudent.

Foreseeability

Both intentional torts and negligence are based on the concept of fault. Strict liability, to the contrary, is not. All theories of liability, however, require *foreseeability*, the knowledge or notice that a result is likely to occur if a certain act occurs.

Foreseeability addresses the likelihood that something will happen in the future. It is easy to see that if you point a loaded gun at someone and pull the trigger, you will cause that person harm. But suppose you get in your car and drive down a dark street, within the speed limit and with your lights on. A child darts out from behind a parked car, and you hit the child. Were you negligent, or was it merely an unavoidable accident? This is a more difficult question. Foreseeability is determined by what a "reasonable and prudent person" would expect. Thus, the foreseeability of a child darting into the street in front of your car would depend on such factors as the degree of darkness, the lateness of the hour, how densely populated the area was (for example, rural or urban, residential or business), other children observed in the area, signs regarding children at play, and so forth. Until these factors are considered, there can be no determination of the foreseeability of the child's action, and consequently of your negligence.

INTENTIONAL TORTS

Assault

Assault is wrongful, intentional conduct that would put a reasonable person or victim in immediate apprehension *or* fear of offensive, nonconsensual touching. Verbal threats alone are not an assault. Some movement toward the person must accompany the verbal threat. The threats of harm must be immediate: Threats of future harm are not sufficient to constitute an assault. The actor must have the actual or apparent ability to cause immediate harm to the victim. Pointing an unloaded pistol at a person, for example, is an assault if the victim has no way of knowing whether the pistol is loaded. The victim must feel apprehension: Actual fear is not required.

Battery

Some legal authorities have defined *battery* as a consummated assault. It is the wrongful, intentional, offensive, and nonconsensual touching of the victim. Touching an extension of the victim's body, such as a purse or backpack, also constitutes a battery. For example, removing a chair from underneath a person who briefly stood up and began to sit down again is a battery when the person who intended to be reseated instead hits the floor. The key element is that the actor intended the natural consequence of removing the chair: the victim falling to the ground. As far as the law is concerned, it is the same as pushing the person to the ground. On the other hand, if the removal of the chair was done innocently, and the ultimate result of having the person fall to the ground had been unintended, there is likely to be no tort of battery committed.

Conversion

Conversion occurs when a person intentionally exercises exclusive control over the personal property of another, usually the owner, without the permission of the owner. In such a case, the converter is liable for damages. If a person obtains possession of the property lawfully but is then told by the owner to return it and refuses to do so, that person is also a converter. If the owner seeks the return of the property in court, the lawsuit is one for *replevin* (an action to recover possession of goods taken unlawfully). Damages can also be obtained if the owner suffered harm during the conversion. Sometimes the owner does not desire the return of the property if, for example, it is now in damaged condition. In this case, the owner asks for reimbursement for his or her loss.

Defamation

Defamation occurs when an actor intentionally makes an untrue statement concerning a victim to a third person, and the statement injures the victim's reputation. As with other intentional torts, it is sufficient that the actor made the statement willfully. Notice that the defamatory remark must be *published*, which is defined as read or heard by others. Consequently, a negative remark made directly to the victim and which is not overheard by anyone else is not "published." The statement need not name the victim; however, the statement must be reasonably interpreted as referring to the victim. The statements must injure or reduce the victim's reputation among well-meaning individuals. If the actor curses at the victim, this will not injure the victim's reputation. It is interpreted more as an indication that the *actor* is extremely angry and may not be controlling his or her temper. Some courts apply the *libel-proof plaintiff doctrine* when the fact finder decides that the plaintiff's reputation for a trait is so poor that, with regard to that trait, it could not be further damaged by the statement.[2] A recent development in this area of law presents a potential problem for employers and supervisors. Disgruntled employees, especially those who have been discharged, have been suing their ex-employers for defamation. Some of these suits have been based on remarks made by the employer to some other workers. In addition, a number of former employees have sued for defamation due to comments made by the employer or supervisor to potential new employers, often as a result of the potential new employer contacting the former employer for a reference or "character check."

Two forms of defamation exist: *slander*, an oral statement that exposes a person to public ridicule or injures a person's reputation; and *libel*, a written or printed statement that exposes a person to public ridicule or injures a person's reputation. The reason for the two forms, each of which has different elements, is that each was developed in a different English court. *Slander*, which is spoken defamation, developed in the *English church courts* (the ecclesiastical courts that had jurisdiction over spiritual matters). *Libel* (written defamation) developed in the *Star Chamber* (an English common law court that had jurisdiction over cases in which the ordinary course of justice was so obstructed by one party that no inferior court could have its process obeyed). The tort of defamation is an important exception to the First Amendment's guarantee of free speech. Consequently, U.S. courts have modified some of the common law rules.

Slander is spoken communication that causes a person to suffer a loss of reputation. The common law rule distinguished between *slander per se* and *slander per quod*. *Slander per se* occurs when a person says that another person is seriously immoral, seriously criminal, has a social disease, or is unfit as a businessperson or professional. In those cases, there is no need to prove actual damages. *Slander per quod* is any other type of oral defamatory statement.

Libel is a written, printed, or other "permanent" communication that causes a person to suffer a loss of reputation. There are also two kinds of libel. *Libel per se* is libelous without having to consider the context in which the remark appeared. For example, if a newspaper printed a story that referred to a person as a "known assassin for hire," there is no need to show the context of the statement. On the other hand, *libel per quod* requires proof of the context. For example, suppose a television talk show host says that a particular woman just gave birth to a child. In order to prove that it was libel, the woman must prove that she is not married and that she has not made public information about her private life, including her unmarried cohabitation.

With the development of technology, the scope of libel has expanded from its historic basis. It is obvious that a book, a magazine, or a newspaper is written, so that defamatory remarks in any of these constitute a potential libel. Films and videos that contain defamatory remarks are also deemed libelous rather than slanderous. Since the medium containing the remark is relatively permanent, the remark can be "republished" any time the film or video is replayed. Thus, by analogy, these forms of communication are viewed as the equivalent of a writing rather than the equivalent of a spoken defamation. Electronic communications have created new areas for defamation, such as blogs, e-mails, social network sites, and Web sites.

The *New York Times Co. v. Sullivan*[3] case is a landmark in U.S. jurisprudence. The U.S. Supreme Court held that when a public official sues for libel, the public official must also prove that the false statement was made with actual malice in addition to the other elements of libel. The court defined actual malice as knowledge that the statement was false or with reckless disregard of whether it was false or not. Some courts actually call it *New York Times malice* instead of actual malice. Since 1964, the Court extended the definition of a *public official* to include candidates for public office as well as incumbents. The Court has also extended the holding to "public figures" as well as public officials. A *public figure* is a person who has a degree of prominence in society. Thus, a person who chooses to become active in society and who not only receives, but actually solicits, attention in the media will be classified as a public figure.

Disparagement

Disparagement occurs when a business product is defamed. Generally it requires that a person make a false statement about a business's products, services, reputation,

eClass 6.1 Marketing

UNFAIR ADVERTISING

Another firm in the educational software industry has been advertising that it has the best educational software on the market. The firm's ads do not name any competitors, but they do show what appears to be eAccounting next to their software. In the ads, "eAccounting" is not operating very well and generally seems to be an inferior product. Yousef wants to sue the other company for defamation, disparagement, or something similar. Meg is not sure that eClass has grounds to sue, but she is concerned about what these ads will do to eClass's image. Ani, Meg, and Yousef ask you what eClass's rights are in this situation, and what they would need to prove in court if they sue. What will you tell them?

BUSINESS CONSIDERATIONS   What practical steps can a business take to bolster its reputation? What could a business do to counteract negative publicity by a competitor?

ETHICAL CONSIDERATIONS   Is it ethical to use comparison advertising to create a false impression of a competitor's product? Is it ethical to intentionally create a negative impression of a competitor's product if you believe the impression is reasonably accurate? What moral obligations do you owe to competitors?

honesty, or integrity; the speaker publishes the remark to a third party; and the speaker knows the remark is false, *or* the speaker makes the statement maliciously and with intent to injure the victim. It is also called *trade libel*, if the statements are written, or *slander of title*, if the statements are oral. It is also sometimes called *product disparagement*. The Texas Beef Group's unsuccessful lawsuit against Oprah Winfrey for her statements about beef was based in part on product disparagement.[4]

False Imprisonment

False imprisonment is the unlawful detention of one person by another against the former's will, and without just cause, for an appreciable amount of time. This tort protects a person from the wrongful loss of liberty and freedom of movement. For example, if after the end of a college class your professor locks the door and says that no one can leave the room, that action is false imprisonment. Sometimes, standing in a doorway and refusing to let a person pass is also false imprisonment. As with other torts, there are defenses. For example, a privilege exists when a retail store's security officer has just cause to suspect a customer of shoplifting. If the security officer detains the customer, the security officer's acts will be privileged as long as the officer uses reasonable means in the detention.

Fraud

Fraud is an extremely complex tort. It concerns the misrepresentation of a material fact made with the intent to deceive. If an innocent person reasonably relies on the misrepresentation and is damaged as a result, the injured person may successfully sue for fraud. There are five elements of fraud:

1. A material fact was involved: An opinion usually will not constitute fraud (fact).
2. The fact was misrepresented (a falsehood).
3. The falsehood was made with the intent to deceive (*scienter*).
4. The falsehood was one on which another person justifiably relied (reasonable reliance).
5. That person was injured as a result (damage).

For example, if a jeweler sells a rhinestone as a diamond with the knowledge that it is a rhinestone, the action is fraud. If a bank customer knowingly obtains a loan on the basis of a false financial statement, it is fraud. If a corporation solicits persons to buy stock for the purpose of building a new plant when in reality the corporation wants the money to pay off existing liabilities, it is fraud. The list is virtually endless. Most states recognize both a tort cause of action and a contract cause of action for fraud, which is discussed in Chapter 11. The most significant difference between the two is that the injured plaintiff can request punitive damages for the tort of fraud.

Infliction of Emotional Distress

A growing body of law concerns situations that, for public policy reasons, are being recognized by courts and legislatures as torts. The law protects an individual from suffering *serious indignity* that causes emotional distress. This right, however, is balanced against the interest of the state in not opening the courts to frivolous and trivial claims. Many states require a physical injury in additional to emotional distress. In this context, an airline was liable when it unreasonably insulted a passenger on an aircraft. A mortician training school was held liable for mental distress to 23 people who took their loved ones to funeral homes and instructed that the bodies *not* be embalmed. In some of these cases, the deceased was going to be cremated. However, the training school "wrongfully" obtained the bodies and used them for instructional purposes in the embalming clinic.[5] A number of employees are suing their former employers for inflicting emotional distress. Most states recognize causes of action for both the intentional infliction and the negligent causing of emotional distress. The torts are often called the Intentional Infliction of Emotional Distress and the Negligent Infliction of Emotional Distress.

Intentional Interference with Contractual Relations

This tort occurs when a person (or business) intentionally interferes in a contract of another. It has various names depending on the state and may be called unlawful interference with contractual relations, interference with a contractual relationship, inducement of breach of contract, or procurement of breach of contract. It occurs when the defendant intentionally induces a party to breach his or her contract with the plaintiff, causing damage to the plaintiff. The defendant must be aware that a contract exists. In some jurisdictions, a defendant may have a privilege to interfere in the contractual relationship. However, the desire to compete *with* the plaintiff is not privileged. Many of the cases based on privilege involve defendants who have legal or fiduciary duties to the other party. *Interference with prospective advantage* is a closely related tort, which occurs when a person interferes with another person or business's potential business relationships.

Invasion of Privacy

Historically, no tort of invasion of privacy existed. However, our courts have begun to recognize that unwarranted or unreasonable invasions of privacy are *actionable*, ruling that these "invasions" furnish grounds for a legal action in some situations. *Privacy* refers to an individual's right to be left alone. Originally, this tort began with someone's peering into a home without permission. A person's privacy is invaded if that person becomes subject to unwarranted intrusions into his or her right to be left alone. These unwarranted intrusions have led to lawsuits and to the awarding of damages to the person whose privacy was invaded. Liability has been found for the public disclosure of private matters, such as playing a tape of a private citizen's telephone call without permission or a valid search warrant. In most states, simple invasion of privacy has been expanded to include: (1) appropriation of plaintiff's name, face, or likeness for commercial purposes; (2) presenting the plaintiff in a false light in the public eye; (3) intrusion on physical solitude; (4) public disclosure of private information; and (5) unauthorized use of the plaintiff's likeness or life story. For example, the use of a famous person's name, photograph, voice, song, or image in an advertisement without permission is an appropriation of the person's likeness. This version of invasion of privacy is often described as an invasion of the famous person's right of publicity, since he or she is deprived of the opportunity to sell his or her name or likeness to some other company. Publication is not required for most types of invasion of privacy. Unlike defamation, truth is not a defense. Under the First Amendment, the courts have created a privilege for the media when it is reporting on newsworthy events. Then, the media will be protected even when the news report is inaccurate, unless the error was made deliberately or recklessly. The types of invasion of privacy are illustrated in Exhibit 6.2.

Exhibit 6.2

The Tort of Invasion of Privacy

Type of Invasion of Privacy[a]	Definition	Example[b]
Appropriation of Name, Face, or Likeness	Defendant uses the plaintiff's name, face, or likeness for commercial benefit.	Company uses the picture of a sports figure in its advertising and claims that he prefers its energy drink.
False Light	Defendant publically attributes to plaintiff views or positions plaintiff does not hold.	Speaker falsely claims that an individual supported a particular candidate in an election.
Intrusion on Physical Solitude	Defendant interferes with the plaintiff's seclusion.	Individual takes a picture of a newscaster while she is alone in her hotel room and posts it on the Internet.
Public Disclosure of Private Information	Defendant reveals private information.	Manager informs co-workers that an employee is HIV positive.
Unauthorized Use of Likeness	Defendant publishes the plaintiff's likeness or life story.	Film company makes a movie about an athlete's life.

[a] Some states may not recognize all types of invasion of privacy. The categories listed may be combined in some states.
[b] These actions would not constitute invasion of privacy if the person gave consent.

Misappropriation of Trade Secrets

Misappropriation of trade secrets occurs when an actor unlawfully acquires and uses the trade secrets of another business enterprise. The victim must prove that a trade secret exists. A *trade secret* is some exclusive knowledge of commercial value that has been generated by the labors of a specific person or group of people. The owner must have implemented reasonable steps to protect the trade secret. The actor must have acquired it by some unlawful or improper means such as industrial espionage, theft, or bribery. Some states, like Texas, require that the actor acquire the secret as a result of a confidential relationship with the victim.[6] Texas also requires that the actor "use" the trade secret.[7] This tort is also called *theft of trade secrets*. Most states have adopted the Uniform Trade Secrets Act to codify their laws on trade secrets.[8]

eClass 6.2 **Management**

INVASION OF PRIVACY

Several people have complained that the various types of software, like eAccounting produced by eClass, should be banned. The basic argument put forward by these people is that once software is loaded on a computer, computer hackers might be able to use the software to discover personal information. One militant group of these people have formed an "action team" named "POPPN" (Protect Our Personal Privacy Now) that is threatening to file invasion-of-privacy lawsuits against every software manufacturer in the United States. eClass is not yet on solid financial ground, and Ani is concerned that such a lawsuit could bankrupt the firm before it has a chance to succeed. Meg seems less concerned, but she is still worried. She has asked you if Ani's fears are valid. What will you tell her? Why?

BUSINESS CONSIDERATIONS   Suppose that a business is facing the prospect of a number of lawsuits over its product. Should the business be proactive on the issue, or would it be better to wait and react to any suits that are filed? Why? If the firm chooses to be proactive, what should it do?

ETHICAL CONSIDERATIONS   Assume that a group is attempting to intimidate manufacturers in a given industry by threatening to file lawsuits unless the demands of the group are met. Is such behavior ethical? From an ethical perspective, how should the firms in the industry react to such threats?

RICO Violations

The Racketeer Influenced and Corrupt Organizations Act, commonly referred to by the acronym "RICO,"[9] is discussed in more detail in Chapter 7; however, it also deserves mention here. RICO is directed at a pattern of racketeering activity. A *pattern* means two or more racketeering acts within a ten-year period. Racketeering acts range from violent acts, such as murder, to less violent acts, such as mail fraud. The RICO statute includes a long list of racketeering acts. Individuals and businesses that are injured can sue those who are violating the statute. For example, on September 22, 1999, the U.S. Justice Department filed a civil RICO lawsuit against the tobacco industry.[10] Successful plaintiffs in a civil action may recover treble damages, attorney's fees, and reasonable court costs. (*Treble damages* are three times the amount of actual damages.) A criminal conviction is not a prerequisite to filing a RICO civil suit.

Trespass

In common law, trespass was one of the most common torts. Today, the general tort of "trespass" has evolved into some of the specific torts already discussed. The traditional tort of *trespass* continues to be used to protect property interests against nonconsensual infringements. There are two types of trespass—trespass to land and trespass to personal property. We will use the term owner in this section, but another person who has the right to possession of the land or personal property also can bring a lawsuit for trespass.

A person who goes onto the real property of another without permission is a trespasser. The trespasser must *intentionally* go onto the land. A person who accidentally goes on the land of another, for example, due to an automobile accident, may be negligent but is not trespassing. The trespasser does not need to realize that he or she is trespassing or that the land belongs to someone else. It is sufficient if the trespasser intends to go onto the land. For example, it would be trespass even if he or she reasonably believes he or she owns the land or has permission of the owner. Trespass can also occur by intentionally causing an object to go onto the land of someone else. The trespasser will be liable for any actual damages that he or she causes. The trespasser will be liable for nominal damages if there is no actual damage.

Trespass to personal property is also called *trespass to chattels*. It occurs if the trespasser's action is intentional. The intent required is that the trespasser intended to deal with the property in the manner in which he or she did. It is irrelevant if the trespasser thought he or she had the right to do so. The trespass may dispossess the owner or "intermeddle" with the owner's possession of the personal property. An example of intermeddling would be if the trespasser intentionally scratched the owner's car. The owner is not entitled to nominal damages for intermeddling; he or she can only collect actual damages. If the trespasser's actions dispossess the owner, the owner may have a choice of suing for trespass or conversion.

Exhibit 6.3 summarizes the intentional torts discussed in this chapter.

Defenses to Intentional Torts

As is true with the torts themselves, there is a great deal of variation from state to state in how the defenses are actually defined and what constitutes a defense. The following sections contain a brief description of some of the common defenses.

Consent   Even though a tort has been committed, the law may not compensate the injured party if, in fact, that person consented to the tort. Most cases involve issues of implied consent. (Courts find *implied consent* when the overall conduct of the parties raises a presumption that agreement was given.) The law will not infer consent unless it is reasonable under the circumstances. For example, football players obviously batter each other throughout the course of a game. Therefore, even though the tort of battery

Exhibit 6.3

Intentional Torts

Specific Tort	Definition	Defenses
Assault	Conduct that would put a reasonable person in apprehension of an immediate battery	Conditional privilege Consent Necessity/Justification Self-defense
Battery	Intentional offensive touching	Conditional privilege Consent Necessity/Justification Self-defense
Conversion	Intentional exercise of exclusive control over the personal property of another without permission	Necessity Consent
Defamation	Slander (spoken), libel (written) Statements that harm a person's reputation	Truth Absolute privilege (legal or congressional proceeding) Conditional privilege
Disparagement	Defamation of a business product, service, or reputation	Privilege
False Imprisonment	The detention of one person by another against his or her will and without just cause	Privilege Consent
Fraud	The misrepresentation of a material fact made with the intent to deceive	
Infliction of Emotional Distress	Causing a serious indignity or severe emotional distress	
Intentional Interference with Contractual Relations	Inducing a party to break his or her contract	Privilege
Invasion of Privacy	Unwarranted intrusions on the privacy of another	Privilege Consent

Exhibit 6.3 Continued

Specific Tort	Definition	Defenses
Misappropriation of Trade Secrets	Taking secret business data for unauthorized use	
Racketeer Influenced and Corrupt Organizations Act (RICO)	Violation of federal statute by engaging in a pattern of racketeering activity	
Trespass	Subjecting real or personal property to harm or infringement	Privilege Consent Necessity

may have been committed, it is not actionable because the law views each player as having consented to the touching. However, if a player intentionally exceeds the implied consent, he or she may be liable for the tort. For example, a professional boxer consents to being punched during the bout. However, most courts would hold that a boxer does not consent to being bitten in the ear during a match, or to being punched by the other fighter after the bout is over.

Privilege   Consent is given voluntarily, whether it is expressed or implied. The law also recognizes a defense that is not voluntary. Because the law seeks to protect certain social interests more than others, it developed the concept of privilege. Privilege may be recognized in a number of situations including:

- If someone moves to strike you, you have the ancient privilege of self-defense. Most states also recognize the privilege to defend family members.
- Retail businesspersons have a privilege to detain persons who they reasonably believe have committed theft.
- Persons whose property is stolen have the privilege of going onto another person's property in order to retrieve it.
- Judges and legislators have the privilege of saying things that might be defamation under other circumstances in order to stimulate debate and encourage independence of thought and action.

Necessity   Whenever a person enters another's land for self-protection, the law recognizes that as a necessity and disallows the nominal damages ordinarily awarded for trespass. For example, if you are in a boat on a lake and a storm suddenly develops, you may enter a private cove, tie up to a private dock, and find shelter on the land in order to protect yourself. Due to the necessity, no trespass exists. However, the law permits the landowner to collect actual losses if, for example, you use his or her

Exhibit 6.4

Effective Defenses Against Intentional Torts

Tort	Consent	Privilege	Necessity	Truth*
Assault	X	X		
Battery	X	X		
Conversion	X		X	
Defamation		X		X
Disparagement		X		Plaintiff must prove falsity
False Imprisonment	X	X		
Fraud				Plaintiff must prove falsity
Infliction of Emotional Distress				
Intentional Interference with Contractual Relations		X		
Invasion of Privacy	X	X		
Misappropriation of Trade Secrets				
Racketeer Influenced and Corrupt Organizations Act (RICO) Violations				
Trespass	X	X	X	

* In defamation, the defendant can use truth as a defense. In disparagement and fraud, the plaintiff must prove that the statement is false.

provisions while tied to his or her private dock. This example illustrates a *private necessity*, because the necessity applies only to you. There is also *public necessity*, where the act is for the public good. For example, if you destroy a person's orchard to prevent a fast moving fire from spreading to nearby homes.

eClass 6.3 Management

JOB REFERENCES FOR FORMER EMPLOYEES

Recently, eClass expanded by hiring three workers. Unfortunately, Ani, Meg, and Yousef have not had much experience in selecting employees. Two of the workers are excellent and fit in well with the business. The third, Gabino, was not a good fit and was fired after the first three weeks. Ani, Meg, and Yousef also suspect Gabino of falsifying company reports. Since his dismissal, Gabino has been applying for other jobs. Although he did not list eClass as a reference, Gabino did list eClass as his last place of employment. Consequently, potential employers have been calling eClass and leaving messages for Ani. They are understandably interested in why Gabino's employment lasted only three weeks. Ani knows she cannot avoid the messages from the four prospective employers much longer. She calls you to ask what she should do. What should she say and not say when she returns the calls? What will you tell her?

BUSINESS CONSIDERATIONS   Should a business adopt a policy regarding references for former employees? Is a business less likely to face liability if it only gives oral recommendations, or should it put everything in writing? Why?

ETHICAL CONSIDERATIONS   Is it ethical to give a good recommendation for a "bad" employee to help that employee obtain other employment? Is it ethical to give a bad recommendation for a good current employee to make it more difficult for him or her to leave the position?

Truth   Truth is one of the best defenses for the tort of defamation. A defendant will win if the defendant can prove that the statement was true. If an individual accuses a businessperson of being a crook and is sued for defamation, the actor will win if it can be proven that the businessperson is a "fence" for stolen property. Exhibit 6.4 (above) summarizes the defenses available against specific intentional torts.

NEGLIGENCE

Negligence exists when four conditions are met. First, the defendant must have owed the plaintiff a duty. Second, the defendant must have breached the duty by acting in a particular manner or failing to act as required. Third, the breach of that duty must be the actual, as well as the "legal," cause of the plaintiff's injury. Fourth, the breach must cause a harm or injury that the law recognizes and for which money damages may be awarded by a court.

Duty

The reasonable-and-prudent-person rule has been established in negligence law in order to determine the "degree" of duty. With respect to negligence, everyone has a "reasonable" duty to avoid the types of behavior that do not measure up to the standards of the reasonable and prudent person. This standard is more difficult to define, explain, and apply than is the standard of simple duty generally applied in cases involving intentional torts. Generally, the law states that *reasonable duty* is a standard of ordinary skill and care, based on the facts of each individual case.

If, while you are quietly fishing on the shore of a lake, you see a man 100 feet away fall out of his boat and begin to drown, does common law place on you a duty to help him? The answer is *no*! You do not have a duty to the man in this situation because you did not create the hazard in the first place. On the other hand, suppose you were in the boat with the man and you pushed him out of the boat as a joke, unaware that he could not swim. Now you will have a duty to help him. Since you have created the hazard, you have a duty to provide help to the man placed at risk by your conduct. Similarly, a person who owns a boatyard and rents boats to fishermen is not likely to have a duty to ensure the safety of every person who rents a boat merely because he or she is in the business of renting boats. However, if the person rents a boat to a fisherman and the boat springs a leak because it was defective or improperly maintained, thereby causing the fisherman to drown, the person renting the boats is likely to have breached his or her duty to rent safe boats and could face liability for negligence due to this breach of duty.

Foreseeability, in negligence, addresses the likelihood that something will happen in the future. It is determined by what a "reasonable and prudent person" would expect.

To test for a duty in any particular situation, the law has constructed a person against whom the conduct of the defendant is to be compared. This purely hypothetical person is known as the *reasonable and prudent person*. Again, it is important to remember that this "person" is not perfect, he or she is merely reasonable. Three areas help to define the reasonable and prudent person: knowledge, investigation, and judgment. There is also a statutory standard that is applied in certain situations.

Knowledge   As the amount of knowledge in the world increases, so does the amount of knowledge that the reasonable and prudent person is expected to possess. In this sense, the law presumes that everyone has complete knowledge of the law. If we have no knowledge of the law, how can we be expected to obey it?

Investigation   Investigation is closely related to knowledge. It is our obligation to find out. We assume that a reasonable person knows certain information. We also assume that the reasonable person will do research or tests to discover additional information. Before you drive a car, for example, the law presumes that you will have ascertained that the brakes are working properly. If you are a drug manufacturer, the law presumes that you will have discovered if your drug will cause any harmful side effects. If you have failed to do adequate testing, you will have violated the standard of care of a reasonable and prudent person. Note that a harmful side effect does not necessarily mean that the manufacturer is negligent. Some drugs do have harmful side effects for some or many patients; however, the drug is still beneficial for the majority to whom it is administered. In this case, distribution of the drug with proper warnings attached is permitted. The adequacy of the warning was an issue in a recent lawsuit against a manufacturer of the oral polio vaccine, when a father alleged that he contracted polio as a result of his daughter receiving the vaccine.[11]

Judgment   You have heard some people say that one person has "good" judgment or another has "bad" judgment. The law measures both persons against the same standard. In a tort case, the defendant must have acted reasonably or else he or she will be found to have breached the duty of reasonable care. We have no hard-and-fast rules here. The outcome always depends on the facts of each case. A missing fact, once supplied, can change the outcome. Before beginning any activity, the law expects people to consider questions such as: What is the likelihood that this particular activity will harm someone else? If harm might occur, what is the likely extent of the harm? What must I do to avoid risk to others?

Assume that you just purchased a new rifle and want to test it and adjust the sights (or scope) for maximum accuracy for the deer season. You find an isolated field in the country and set up a target at the base of a bald hill 300 yards away. No one else is present. After firing the first shot, however, you begin to attract a crowd. Assume that with each shot the crowd gets larger. At what point do you stop shooting to avoid injury to an innocent person? The decision to stop involves the exercise of reason. The exercise of reason is *judgment.*

Statutory Standard   In some cases, the law solves the problem of limits, like the ones just raised, by providing a standard contained in a statute. For example, most state traffic laws say that when it begins to get dark, all drivers are required to turn on their headlights. If, while traveling down a road at night without your lights on, you hit and injure a pedestrian, the law will conclude that you breached a standard of reasonableness no matter what your excuse. Most of these statutes provide a criminal penalty, but that penalty is irrelevant in a civil proceeding such as a tort case. In most states, breaching the statutory standard is *negligence per se* (inherent negligence; negligence without a need for further proof). However, the states are not in agreement as to whether this should be treated as a *conclusive presumption* where evidence to the contrary is not permitted. Some states, such as California,[12] instead treat *negligence per se* as a *rebuttable presumption*. The person is allowed to present evidence that, under the circumstances, violating the statutory standard was the most careful behavior.

Breach of Duty

In general, the plaintiff has to prove that the defendant caused injury by not adhering to the reasonable-and-prudent person standard. In some cases, that strict requirement of proof is relaxed because the law has developed the doctrine of *res ipsa loquitur*, which means, "the thing speaks for itself." To apply *res ipsa loquitur* in a case, the injury must meet the following three tests: (1) this occurrence would ordinarily not happen in the absence of someone's negligence; (2) the occurrence must be caused by a device within the exclusive control of the defendant(s); and (3) the plaintiff in no way contributed to his or her own injury. For example, if a patient agrees to an operation to remove infected tonsils and leaves the operating room with a surgical instrument embedded in her throat, there is no need to require direct testimony on the point. It speaks for itself; someone in the surgery room was negligent. In some states, *res ipsa loquitur* creates a presumption of negligence. Its effect is to shift the burden of proof from the plaintiff to the defendant(s). In this situation, the hospital personnel and the surgeons will each need to show that they were careful. In other states, the burden of proof remains with the plaintiff. *Res ipsa loquitur* creates an inference of negligence. Then the jury weighs the evidence, including the inference of negligence.

Causation

The heart of the law of negligence is causation. Causation has two components: actual cause and "legal" cause, which is also called proximate cause.

Actual Cause   The law determines whether X, an act by one party, is the actual cause of Y, a result affecting the other party. The courts examine whether "but for" the occurrence of act X, result Y would have happened. This is called the *but-for test*. For example, a defendant in an automobile accident case may have failed to signal a turn properly. But if the accident would have happened even if he had signaled properly, the failure to signal is not the actual cause of the accident. It fails the "but-for" test.

Proximate Cause   *After* actual cause has been established, the focus shifts to what the law calls *policy questions*. Such questions have nothing to do with whether the defendant actually did the act. What is decided here is whether the law should hold the defendant liable. At some point the law will say, "Enough." Beyond this point the defendant will not be held liable. To solve these policy questions, the law has developed a three-pronged test:

1. What is the likelihood that this particular conduct will injure other persons?
2. If injury should occur, what is the degree of seriousness of the injury?
3. What is the interest that the defendant must sacrifice to avoid the risk of causing the injury?

For example, if the defendant is negligent with respect to Emilio, and Carla tries to rescue Emilio and suffers some injury as a result, the defendant may be held liable for Carla's injuries as well as Emilio's because it is foreseeable that people will try to rescue someone in peril.

Harm

If the plaintiff is not injured, the defendant will not be held liable in damages. For example, Chad, speeding down a city street at 70 miles per hour, is clearly breaching the duty to drive in a safe and reasonable manner; but if no one is injured, no one can successfully sue for negligence. If harm is caused, it must be of a type for which the law allows damages to be awarded. For example, hurt feelings may be real, but the law does not generally award damages for hurt feelings.

Defenses to Negligence

Assumption of the Risk   Common law developed a doctrine in which the defendant will win if the defendant can prove that the plaintiff voluntarily assumed a known risk. For example, have you ever examined cigarette packages? They bear various warnings, some of which are "Surgeon General's Warning: Smoking by pregnant women may result in fetal injury, premature birth, and low birth weight," or "Quitting smoking now greatly reduces serious risks to your health," or "Cigarette smoke contains carbon monoxide." Historically, a longtime cigarette smoker who contracted lung cancer and sued the cigarette manufacturer has lost because the manufacturer defended on the basis of the plaintiff's voluntary assumption of the risk. (New scientific evidence is allowing the courts to reexamine tobacco company liability in this area.) Courts will generally apply assumption of the risk to a skier who breaks her leg while skiing on a mountain slope.

Contributory Negligence   Another defense at common law is *contributory negligence.* Suppose Justin wears a black raincoat at night and jaywalks across a busy street; he is hit by a car. If Justin sues and the defendant can prove Justin actually contributed to the injury, Justin will lose in a state that applies contributory negligence because contributory negligence would bar recovery. (In the legal sense, *bar* means to prevent or to stop.)

Comparative Negligence   In a growing number of jurisdictions, the doctrine of contributory negligence has been replaced by the doctrine of *comparative negligence,* through judicial precedents or legislative acts. Here, the fact finder (usually the jury) determines to what degree the plaintiff contributed to his or her own injury. Comparative negligence is generally perceived to be more fair; however, it may be difficult for the trier of fact to determine the relative faults. For example, if Jason is injured to the extent of $100,000 in damages but contributed 35 percent to his injury, he will be awarded $65,000 instead of losing completely, as he would under the doctrine of contributory negligence.

Jurisdictions may select from three variations of comparative negligence. *Pure* comparative negligence would allow the plaintiff to recover no matter how negligent he or she was. (For example, the California Supreme Court adopted pure comparative negligence in *Li v. Yellow Cab Co.*[13]) However, some jurisdictions feel it would be unfair to allow the plaintiff to recover if he or she was the primary cause of the injury, for example, if the plaintiff was 95 percent responsible for causing the accident. Consequently, two other variations prevent recovery to the party who was mostly to blame. One version only permits recovery if the plaintiff contributed less than 50 percent of the negligence to his or her injury. This is commonly called the "less than" type of comparative negligence. This is probably the most common variety of comparative negligence. Another version allows recovery if the plaintiff contributed 50 percent or less to his or her injury, which is commonly called the "equal to or less than" version. The differences may appear inconsequential, but they are significant to the parties of a lawsuit, who may be denied recovery because the jury concluded that they were each 50 percent at fault. The application of comparative negligence becomes difficult when there are more than two parties. States have different ways of handling multiple party situations. The effect of comparative negligence laws may be minimal in automobile accidents in "no fault" states. The National Conference of Commissioners on Uniform State Laws (NCCUSL) has adopted the Uniform Apportionment of Tort Responsibility Act (2002), which contains a modified comparative fault system.[14] Medical groups, insurance groups, and others advocate for change in the tort liability system, particularly as it applies to their businesses.

STRICT LIABILITY

Recall that with respect to intentional torts, everyone has a duty to avoid such behavior. With respect to negligence, we have a duty to use reasonable care. This section examines situations in which the law states that we have an absolute duty to make something safe, regardless of whether we are at fault or not. The law prescribes the situations in which there is strict liability.

Whenever a person undertakes an extremely hazardous activity and it is foreseeable that injury may result, that person can be held "strictly liable" if injury does result, whether or not the person was at fault. *Strict liability* is imposed without regard to fault. For example, if you use explosives on your property and by so doing cause windows to be blown out of an adjoining neighbor's house, you will be held liable no matter how careful you were in handling the explosives. Generally, the areas in which we have strict liability are set out in the applicable statutes and court precedents. *Rylands v. Fletcher*[15] is credited with creating this legal doctrine.

Through the development of the doctrine of strict liability, U.S. courts have shifted emphasis from ultrahazardous activity to dangerous activity, and the doctrine seems to be expanding in scope. Today, the following activities are considered strict liability activities in most states: the keeping of wild animals, the use of explosives, and dangerous activities. Some states have added strict liability for the owner of a motor vehicle if injury occurs when the driver has the owner's permission.[16] California imposes strict liability on parents for the willful misconduct of their minor children. There is a $10,000 limit on parental liability.[17] Strict liability does not automatically arise. It is created by court decisions or legislation. This is another area in which the legal system is making policy decisions about who should justly bear the loss.

NUISANCE

There are two types of nuisances—a private nuisance and a public nuisance. A private nuisance is the unreasonable interference with the interest of a person in the use or enjoyment of his or her land. An example would be a dairy farm that causes a stench on the neighbor's property. The neighbor could sue for a private nuisance. For the plaintiff to recover, it must be a situation where the interference would be offensive, inconvenient, or annoying to normal people in the community. The neighbor must not be either an overly sensitive person or a person who is using his or her land in an overly sensitive manner. In most states, the court will balance the utility of the defendant's conduct with the gravity of the harm the defendant is inflicting. In many situations the defendant's conduct is intentional, but that is not a requirement for the tort of nuisance. Nuisance can be based on intentional acts, negligent acts, or strict liability. For example, there may be strict liability for storing explosives in a residential neighborhood. Nuisance should be distinguished from the tort of trespass. Trespass interferes with the owner's *exclusive* possession of the land, but nuisance interferes with the owner's *use and enjoyment.*

A public nuisance causes an inconvenience or damage to the public at large (for example, if protestors block a highway). A private individual can only maintain an action for a public nuisance if he or she suffers a different type of injury than that suffered by the rest of the public. The private individual does not need to own land to sue for his or her private harm. For example, an individual who is operating a commercial fishery on a river that is polluted by the defendant's factory can sue for his or her private harm.

PRODUCT LIABILITY

Product liability is a growing concern of businesses. Manufacturers *and* distributors of products may be held liable based on these legal theories: (1) fraud in the marketing of the product; (2) express or implied warranties (warranties will not be discussed in this chapter, since they are based on contract theories); (3) negligence; and (4) strict liability. People who are injured by a product may claim and attempt to prove more than one theory of liability since these theories are not mutually exclusive.

Fraud in marketing will follow the general rules of fraud previously discussed in this chapter.

Negligence in product liability can include negligence in design, construction, labeling, instructions, packaging, and assembly. When an injured person uses the negligence theory for product liability, there must be a close causal connection between the negligence and the injury. The lawsuit will be subject to the usual defenses for negligence, including contributory negligence, comparative negligence, and assumption of the risk. To establish a negligent failure to warn claim, many states require the plaintiff to prove the following elements: (1) the defendant designed the product; (2) that the defendant knew or had reason to know that the product was likely to be unreasonably dangerous; (3) that the defendant had no reason to believe that the users would realize the risk; (4) that the defendant failed to use ordinary care in warning the user of the risk of harm; and (5) that the failure to warn directly caused the injury. In addition, the product must malfunction or fail.[18]

Strict liability for products is clarified by § 402A of the *Restatement (Second) of Torts*, and has been adopted by most states. *Restatement (Second) of Torts*, a publication of the American Law Institute (ALI), states the preferred version of the common law of torts. It is used by courts as an authoritative reference, but the *Restatement* is not binding on them. It becomes precedence in the court only after a judge has relied on a section and referred to it in his or her opinion.

Section 402A of the *Restatement (Second) of Torts* establishes the strict liability rule: A seller will be held liable for a product that contains a defect or is unreasonably dangerous to use. (*Unreasonably dangerous* seems vague to both laypersons and lawyers; there have been many court decisions attempting to define and clarify the term.) The defect must be in the product when it leaves the control of the defendant. As with other forms of strict liability, the plaintiff does not need to prove negligence or fraud in order to recover. Generally, the plaintiff must show that strict liability applies to this situation, that the product had a defect when it left the defendant's possession or was unreasonably dangerous, and that the plaintiff was harmed. Since this is a tort cause of action, the seller cannot avoid liability by disclaiming it. Contributory negligence by the plaintiff cannot be used as a defense. The manufacturer may prove the following defenses depending on the situation—*obviousness of hazard* (the risk in the product is evident, such as a sharp knife), product misuse by the plaintiff, and assumption of the risk. There is also a strict liability failure to warn theory. Missouri, for example, uses five elements for a strict liability failure to warn claim. They are: (1) the defendant sold the product in the course of its business; (2) the product was unreasonably dangerous at the time of sale when used as reasonably anticipated and without knowledge of its characteristics; (3) the defendant did not give an adequate warning of the danger; (4) the product was used in a reasonably anticipated manner; and (5) the plaintiff was damaged as a direct result of the product being sold without an adequate warning.[19] The courts often assume that if adequate warnings were given, the user would have heeded them. This is a rebuttable presumption in some states, including Missouri.[20] Another question is whether adequate information is available absent a warning from the manufacturer.

Section 402A of the *Restatement (Second) of Torts* has been considered the seminal document on product liability. However, ALI adopted significant revisions to § 402A and published them in *Restatement (Third) of Torts: Product Liability*.[21] ALI hopes this new document will shape product liability law in the future.

TORT LIABILITY OF BUSINESS ENTITIES

Before leaving this introduction to tort law, we should mention that businesses *can* be held liable for the torts of their employees. Initially, courts were reluctant to impose liability. Today, liability is more readily assessed. Liability is generally imposed through the doctrine of *respondeat superior*. *Respondeat superior* means that the superior should answer or pay for the torts of employees that occur in the course and scope of employment. *Respondeat superior* does not excuse the employee; the employee will be held liable in addition to his or her employer. *Respondeat superior* is discussed in detail in Chapter 30. The Federal Torts Claim Act permits some suits against the federal government for the torts of its workers.

Contemporary Case

ROE v. DOE
2009 U.S. Dist. LEXIS 59440 (N. Dist. CA 2009)

The parties in the dispute are listed as Richard Roe and John Doe. However, the real parties in interest are the plaintiff, Don A. Nelson, and the defendants, Mark Cuban and Dallas Basketball, Ltd.

FACTS Don Nelson is a former employee of the Dallas Mavericks basketball franchise. Nelson was employed by the Mavericks from December 1996 to August 2006. On or around July 1, 2003, Nelson and the Mavericks entered into a "Fifth Amendment to the Employment Agreement," which provided that Nelson would perform head coaching and general manager services for the Mavericks through June 30, 2006, and then perform five years of consulting services at $200,000 per year. The contract included a "non-competition" clause. In March 2005, Nelson and Cuban orally agreed that Nelson would step down as head coach but would continue to be paid the head coach salary. The written contract was not amended to reflect this change or to remove the consulting portion of the contract. Cuban was informed by his staff that Cuban was obligated to perform the consulting portion of the contract, but he stopped paying Nelson despite this advice. Then the Mavericks began negotiations with Nelson to amend the contract, but they were unable to come to an agreement. After the Mavericks missed a number of payments, Nelson accepted the head coaching position with the Golden State Warriors. When the Mavericks learned about the Warriors contract, they began withholding other compensation they owed to Nelson. During the dispute, Cuban appeared on the Murph & Mac radio show to promote his appearance on the television show "Dancing with the Stars." The radio show is broadcast throughout the San Francisco Bay Area. During Cuban's appearance on the show, he made several references to Nelson, including the statement that "I thought he tried to rip me off." Nelson sued Cuban for defamation.

ISSUE Is Nelson entitled to a trial on the issue of defamation?

HOLDING No, Nelson cannot produce sufficient evidence to prove defamation.

REASONING Excerpts from the opinion of United States District Judge Phyllis J. Hamilton:

[This case arose in the context of a motion to strike (or dismiss) the suit under the anti-SLAPP statute.[22] The essence of the suit is whether it is possible for Nelson to win on his defamation suit.]

... Nelson's burden is to make a prima facie showing of facts that would, if proved at trial, support a judgment in his favor. . . . "Defamation is an invasion of the interest in reputation. The tort involves the intentional publication of a statement of fact that is false, unprivileged, and has a natural tendency to injure or which causes special damage." . . . Defamation in its oral form is called slander, which is defined as a "false and unprivileged publication, orally uttered, and also communications by radio" . . . There can be no recovery for defamation without a falsehood. . . . Statements of opinion are not actionable. . . . ([A]pparent statements of fact may be deemed opinions "when made in public debate, heated labor dispute, or other circumstances in which an 'audience may anticipate efforts by the parties to persuade others to their positions by use of epithets, fiery rhetoric or hyperbole . . . '"). . . . [A] statement that implies a false assertion of fact, even if couched as an opinion, can be actionable. . . . An opinion loses its constitutional protection and becomes actionable when it is "based on implied, undisclosed facts" and "the speaker has no factual basis for the opinion." . . . [C]ourts must be cautious not to inhibit vigorous public debate about public issues, and should err on the side of allowing free-flowing discussion of current events. . . . [T]he test to be applied in determining whether an allegedly defamatory statement constitutes an actionable statement of fact requires that the court: (1) examine the statement in its totality in the context in which it was uttered or published; (2) consider all the words used, not merely a particular phrase or sentence; (3) give weight to cautionary terms used by the person publishing the statement; and

(4) consider all of the circumstances surrounding the statement, including the medium by which the statement is disseminated and the audience to which it is published. . . . [T]he court finds that the statements are non-actionable statements of opinion, rather than verifiable statements of fact. . . . The allegedly defamatory statements made by Cuban were phrased in terms of how he "felt" and what he "thought." . . . The statements were made on a sports talk show to an audience that would be expected to be familiar with Nelson, Cuban and the ongoing contract dispute. . . . [T]he audience was likely to understand that the statements made by Cuban were made for the purpose of persuading others to his position by the use of rhetorical hyperbole. . . . Accordingly, the court finds that Cuban's statements were not defamatory. . . .

Since public figures must prove by clear and convincing evidence that an allegedly defamatory statement was made with knowledge of falsity or reckless disregard for truth, a threshold determination in a defamation action is whether the plaintiff is a public figure. . . . There are two classes of public figures: (1) the "all purpose" public figure who has achieved such pervasive fame or notoriety that he becomes a public figure for all purposes and in all contexts; and (2) the "limited purpose" public figure, an individual who voluntarily injects himself or is drawn into a particular public controversy and thereby becomes a public figure for a limited range of issues. . . . The rationale for treating public figures differently from private citizens is that: (1) "'public figures usually enjoy significantly greater access to the channels of effective communication and hence have a more realistic opportunity to counteract false statements than private individuals normally enjoy'"; and (2) "public figures have invited the attention and comment they receive and must accept certain necessary consequences of their choice, including the risk false and injurious statements will be made about them." . . . The elements that must be present in order to characterize a plaintiff as a limited purpose public figure are: (1) there must be a public controversy . . . ; (2) the plaintiff must have undertaken some voluntary act through which he or she sought to influence resolution of the public issue; and (3) the alleged defamation must be germane to the plaintiff's participation in the controversy. . . . [T]he limited purpose public figure loses certain protection for his or her reputation only to the extent that the allegedly defamatory communication relates to his role in a public controversy. . . . [T]he court concludes that Nelson is a limited public figure for purposes of the statements made by Cuban on the Murph & Mac show. . . . Nelson must establish a probability that he can produce clear and convincing evidence that the allegedly defamatory statements were made with knowledge of their falsity or with reckless disregard of their truth or falsity. . . . "The reckless disregard test requires a high degree of awareness of the probable falsity of the defendant's statement. There must be sufficient evidence to permit the conclusion that the defendant in fact entertained serious doubts as to the truth of his publication." . . . This is a subjective test that focuses on the "defendant's attitude toward the veracity of the published material, as opposed to his or her attitude toward the plaintiff." . . . [Nelson's] allegations are insufficient to state a cause of action in a case where actual malice is required. . . .

You Be the Judge

In January 2010, the organization People for the Ethical Treatment of Animals (PETA) started an advertising campaign to discourage the wearing of fur in Washington, D.C. To promote the campaign, PETA created a photograph by mixing photos of Tyra Banks, Michelle Obama, Carrie Underwood, and Oprah Winfrey. The photograph made it appear that they were posing together at a special event. Some of the copy on the ad said, "FUR FREE and Fabulous!" and "Read all about it at peta.org." The ad was used as posters and on a PETA van.[23]

Mrs. Obama did not give consent for the use of her likeness nor has she publicly endorsed PETA. The picture of Mrs. Obama was taken from her official White House portrait. Her deputy press secretary has said, "Mrs. Obama does not wear fur." The White House asked PETA to remove the ad and they did. PETA refused to admit any wrong doing in producing and distributing the ad. Did PETA commit a tort? Assume that PETA refused to remove the posters and repaint the van and Mrs. Obama sued in *your* court. How would *you* rule and why? [See Lee B. Burgunder, "Fur-Free and Obamanable," *Western Academy of Legal Studies in Business 2010 Refereed Proceedings*.]

Summary

Tort law is designed to protect an individual's rights with respect to person and property. To do this, the law uses the concept of "duty." Tort law deals with "private" wrongs, whereas criminal law deals with "public" wrongs.

Three theories of tort liability exist: intentional torts, negligence, and strict liability. Intentional torts are those in which a person acted in a willful or intentional manner. Intentional torts to persons include assault, battery, defamation, disparagement, false imprisonment, emotional distress, and invasion of privacy. Invasion of privacy includes intrusion on physical solitude; unauthorized use of the plaintiff's likeness; presenting the plaintiff in a false light; and appropriation of the plaintiff's likeness for commercial purposes. Intentional torts to property include trespass, conversion, and misappropriation of trade secrets. Different torts have various defenses. Common defenses include consent, privilege, necessity, and truth.

Negligence is the unintentional causing of harm that could have been prevented if the defendant had acted as a reasonable and prudent person. Defenses to negligence suits include assumption of the risk, contributory negligence, and comparative negligence. Strict liability is a separate basis of tort liability because it is independent from intent or negligence. Our legal system, through the legislature and/or courts, has declared that if certain activities cause harm, the actor will be liable.

Central to a discussion of all three theories of liability are the concepts of duty and foreseeability. Duty imposes a certain kind of conduct and is action oriented. Intentional torts establish that one has a duty to avoid committing the tort. Negligence establishes that one has a "reasonable" duty to avoid it. Strict liability, on the other hand, establishes a strict duty so that no matter how reasonable the conduct, there is automatic liability if harm occurs. Foreseeability concerns the thought process. If the hypothetical reasonable and prudent person would have foreseen harm, liability exists.

Discussion Questions

1. Heather decides to go shopping at the XYZ Department Store. While she is in the sportswear department, the store detective suspects her of stealing a swimsuit. The detective approaches Heather and says, "Excuse me, but would you mind if I asked you a few questions?" She responds with, "Well, I'm really in quite a rush. I'm on my lunch hour and I have to get back to work." Nevertheless, she submits to the questioning, which lasts for 20 minutes. Has there been a false imprisonment? Would your answer be any different if the detective had said, "Excuse me, I suspect you of stealing a swimsuit. Would you mind if I asked you a few questions?"

2. A gorilla escapes from a traveling circus, enters a shopping center, and destroys $347,500 worth of property. The businesses whose property is destroyed decide to sue the circus to recover their damages. The circus can prove that it did not act negligently and that it was not at fault in the escape of the gorilla. Given this situation, will these lawsuits succeed against the circus?

3. E-Trade had a commercial created for the 2010 Super Bowl. It shows an E-Trade baby explaining to his cute baby girlfriend that he did not call because he was busy diversifying his portfolio

on E-Trade. She asks him, "And that milkaholic Lindsay wasn't over?" Lindsay Lohan has filed a $100 million lawsuit against E-Trade. Should she succeed? Why or why not?[24]

4. A manufacturer of chemical products markets suntan oil without sufficiently investigating the fact that under certain circumstances the vapors of the product become flammable. Suppose Amir uses the product, and as he rubs the oil on his arms, it ignites and burns him. Can Amir successfully sue the manufacturer for negligence? Why?

5. Professor Ortiz has established a listserver for her business law class. She posts procedural announcements on the listserver. She also uses the listserver to inform the class about interesting Web sites and to discuss journal articles and current events. Students can post information to the listserver. Professor Ortiz also communicates with students individually via e-mail. She will often inform them about their grades and comment on student work. One day, immediately after grading their second set of papers, she prepared an e-mail note to Nora Williamson. It said, "Nora, your last paper was extremely poorly written. It contained sentence fragments, incorrect usages of words, and numerous misspelled words. In addition, you seem to have misunderstood the assignment. Consequently, your grade on this assignment is a D–. Sincerely, Professor Ortiz." Professor Ortiz intended to send this message only to Nora; however, she accidentally hit the group reply function on her e-mail and sent the message to the entire class. There are two students named Nora in the class. Analyze the potential torts in this situation.

Case Problems and Writing Assignments

1. Douglas R. Tenbarge worked as a drywall installer. His primary duty was to apply drywall compound and tape along the seams of drywall panels with an Ames Auto Taper, known as a Bazooka. The Bazooka is a tube 56 inches in length and two and one-fourth inches in diameter used to apply joint compound and tape simultaneously to drywall seams in ceilings and walls. It weighs 7 pounds when empty and 20 pounds when filled to capacity with joint compound and a 500-foot roll of tape. The Bazooka is operated by holding it with both hands and applying pressure against the seam as the joint compound and tape are being fed out of the tube. The Bazooka requires repetitive wrist motions and the exertion of considerable pressure to apply the tape and compound. Lacking handholds, "the Bazooka is awkward to support and maneuver, particularly while doing overhead work." In 1991, after experiencing numbness in his hands and fingers, Tenbarge was diagnosed with carpal tunnel syndrome (CTS). In December 1992 and January 1993, Tenbarge underwent surgery on both wrists. He returned to work in April 1993, only to sustain an elbow injury. He underwent a third surgery late in 1993. Tenbarge filed suit against Ames, the manufacturer and renter of the Bazooka. Should the trial court have permitted the jury to consider whether Ames had a duty to warn Tenbarge? [See *Tenbarge v. Ames Taping Tool Systems, Inc.*, 1999 U.S. App. LEXIS 15028 (8th Cir. 1999).]

2. Rose Cipollone smoked cigarettes from 1942 until 1984, when she died. She smoked cigarette brands made by the defendant until 1968. She claimed that she started smoking because she wanted to imitate the "pretty girls and movie stars" in defendant's advertisements. Rose claims that she believed advertisements, which said, "Play Safe, Smoke [Liggett's] Chesterfield." and "Nose, Throat, and Accessory Organs not Adversely Affected by Smoking Chesterfield." In 1981, Rose was

diagnosed with lung cancer. Rose filed suit alleging that her cancer was caused by her use of the defendant's products for a 40-year period. Rose died before trial because of complications from the lung cancer. Thomas Cipollone, her son, continued the suit, individually and as a representative of her estate. The lawsuit requested compensation based on the following legal theories: strict liability, negligence, breach of warranty, intentional tort, and conspiracy. Did the cigarette manufacturers breach a duty to warn? Why or why not? What is the affect of the printed warnings imposed by federal statute on cigarette manufacturers beginning in 1969? [See *Cipollone v. Liggett Group, Inc.*, 505 U.S. 504 (1992). Aspects of the case were also considered by the Supreme Court at 502 U.S. 1055 (1992); 502 U.S. 923 (1991); and 499 U.S. 935 (1991). Lower courts considered the case at 893 F.2d 541 (3rd Cir. 1990); 789 F.2d 181 (3rd Cir. 1986); 649 F. Supp. 664 (NJ 1986); and 593 F. Supp. 1146 (NJ 1984).]

3. Caesar Barber, from the Bronx, NY, weighs 272 pounds. He filed a lawsuit against McDonald's,

Kentucky Fried Chicken, Wendy's, and Burger King for contributing to his weight. He has a number of health problems commonly associated with high weight—two heart attacks, diabetes, high blood pressure, and high cholesterol. He claims the fast-food chains deceived him with ads that said "100 percent beef" and that they created a de facto addiction. "The law of warnings is not designed for the best and brightest of us. . . . It is aimed at helping people who need to be told not to stand on the top step of a ladder or not to use a hair dryer in the bathtub." says John Banzhaf, a legal activism teacher at George Washington University Law School. All of the restaurants have nutritional information in their restaurants and online. Is there actual causation? Is there proximate causation? What other evidence would be helpful? [See Sheryl Y. Fred, "Super-Sized Plaintiff Attacks Fast-Food Chains," *Corporate Legal Times*, October 2002, The Insider, p. 75; Emily Heller, "Weighing Chances of Fast-Food Fat Suits," *Fulton County Daily Report*, December 13, 2002, Vol. 12, No. 13.]

Notes

1. See California Civil Code, § 1714.1.
2. *Church of Scientology Int'l. v. Time Warner, Inc.*, 932 F. Supp. 589 (S.D.N.Y. 1996), at pp. 593-94.
3. 376 U.S. 254, 1964 U.S. LEXIS 1655 (1964).
4. Barbara Wartelle Wall, "Following 'Oprah,' An Update on Food-Product Disparagement Laws," published at Gannett News Watch at http://www.gannett.com/go/newswatch/98/june/nw0619-8.htm (accessed 4/16/10) and Paul McMasters, "Section IV of Libel Law/Punitive Damages/Tort Actions of the First Amendment and the Media 1999 Online Outline" at http://www.mediainstitute.org/ONLINE/FAM99/LPT_A.html (accessed 8/15/10).
5. "Mortician Training Schools' Wrongful Acts Were Not Insured," *Death Care Business Advisor*, September 4, 1997, Vol. 2, No. 5.
6. *Texas Tanks, Inc. v. Owens-Corning Fiberglas Corp.*, 99 F.3d 734 (5th Cir. 1996).
7. Ibid.
8. The Uniform Trade Secrets Act, with the 1985 amendments, has been adopted in Alabama, Alaska, Arizona, Colorado, Delaware, District of Columbia, Florida, Georgia, Hawaii, Idaho, Illinois, Iowa, Kansas, Kentucky, Maine, Maryland, Michigan, Minnesota, Mississippi, Missouri, Montana, Nebraska, Nevada, New Hampshire, New Mexico, North Dakota, Ohio, Oklahoma, Oregon, Pennsylvania, South Carolina, South Dakota, Tennessee, U.S. Virgin Islands, Utah, Vermont, Virginia, West Virginia, Wisconsin, and Wyoming. (Although technically the U.S. Virgin Islands is not a state, the NCCUSL treats it as a state and for purposes of uniform laws we will also.) The following states have adopted the 1979 act, but not the 1985 amendments: Arkansas, California, Connecticut, Indiana, Louisiana, Rhode Island, and Washington. See the National Conference of Commissioners on Uniform State Laws (NCCUSL) Web site, "A Few Facts About the Uniform Trade Secrets Act," http://www.nccusl.org/Update/uniformact_factsheets/uniformacts-fs-utsa.asp (accessed 4/16/10).
9. See 18 U.S.C., §§ 1961 *et seq.*
10. Susan B. Garland, "Can a Tough-Guy Law Deck Big Tobacco?" *Business Week*, October 11, 1999, pp. 158, 160.

11. Michael Riccardi, "Drug Manufacturer Must Warn of Risks," *The Legal Intelligencer*, July 15, 1999, p. 4.

12. See Jury Instructions for Negligence Per Se, BAJI 3.45 (1992 Revision), *California Jury Instructions, Civil*, 7th ed. (St. Paul, MN: West Publishing Co., 1992). Drafted by the Committee of Standard Jury Instructions, Civil, of the Superior Court of Los Angeles County and used throughout the State of California.

13. 119 Cal. Rptr. 858, 532 P.2d 1226 (1975).

14. NCCUSL Web site, "Press Release: August 5, 2002, New Act on Tort Responsibility Completed," http://www.nccusl.org/nccusl/pressreleases/pr080502_TORT.asp (accessed 8/15/10).

15. L.R. 3 Ill. 330 (1868).

16. For example, California Vehicle Code, §17150.

17. California Civil Code, §1714.1.

18. *Tenbarge v. Ames Taping Tool Systems, Inc.*, 1999 U.S. App. LEXIS 15028 (8th Cir. 1999).

19. Ibid.

20. Ibid.

21. The *Restatement (Third) of Torts: Product Liability* was published in 1998. The American Law Institute (ALI) Web site, "Publications Catalog, Restatements of the Law—Torts: Product Liability," at http://www.ali.org/index.cfm?fuseaction=publications.ppage&node_id=54 (accessed 4/16/10).

22. A SLAPP lawsuit is a Strategic Lawsuit Against Public Participation. It is intended to discourage public participation on a public-interest issue. It is used to quiet those who want to object to a position on the issue. Anti-SLAPP statutes prevent some SLAPP lawsuits and encourage public discourse on the issue.

23. People for the Ethical Treatment of Animals (PETA) Web site Archives, "Help Make D.C. Fur-Free and Fabulous," shows a picture of the van at http://blog.peta.org/archives/2009/12/make_dc_fur_free.php (accessed 4/16/10).

24. *Monterey County Herald* (California), "Lohan Sues Over E-Trade Babies Spot," March 10, 2010; Anne Neville, "The Best and Worst Commercials from Super Bowl XLIV, from Betty White to Danica Patrick," *Buffalo News* (New York), February 7, 2010, Online Edition, Blogs, Pop Stand.

7

Crimes and Business

Agenda

eClass has recently been victimized by a series of minor crimes, including theft from its warehouse. This has led Ani, Meg, and Yousef to a general discussion of crimes, and especially of victim's rights when crimes are committed. Throughout this chapter, we consider what eClass and other businesses can do to deter criminal conduct and to reduce the likelihood of becoming victims of crimes.

The principals want to know whether, in general, eClass can be held liable for criminal activity committed by its employees on company time or on company property. For example, they want to know if eClass must pay any traffic tickets issued to employees who are driving company vehicles when they receive the tickets. They also want to know if the firm can be held liable if employees make unauthorized copies of computer software. They want to know who will be criminally responsible in these situations—the employee, eClass, or both. To answer these questions you will need to distinguish between criminal law and civil law throughout this chapter.

Suppose that Ani, Meg, or Yousef suspect an employee of storing drugs in his locker and selling the drugs at work. eClass has a zero tolerance policy on drug use and/or possession at work. Can the firm search the locker without permission? Can they ask the police to search the locker? Do they need probable cause in either circumstance? What are the legal restrictions on a private search?

These and other questions will arise as you read this chapter. Be prepared! You never know when the firm or one of its members will seek your advice.

Classic Case

NEW YORK v. BURGER
482 U.S. 691, 1987 U.S. LEXIS 2725 (1987)

FACTS Joseph Burger is the owner of a junkyard that dismantles automobiles and sells their parts. Five officers of the Auto Crimes Division of the New York City Police Department entered Burger's junkyard to conduct an inspection pursuant to New York Vehicle & Traffic Law § 415-a5.[1] The Division conducts 5 to 10 inspections each day. The officers asked to see Burger's license and his record of the automobiles and parts in his possession. Burger replied that he did not have a license or a record. The officers then announced their intention to conduct a § 415-a5 inspection. The officers checked the Vehicle Identification Numbers of several vehicles and determined that some were stolen. Burger was arrested and charged with possession of stolen property and operating as an unregistered vehicle dismantler.

ISSUES Is the warrantless search of an automobile junkyard unconstitutional, or does it fall within the exception for administrative inspections of highly regulated industries? Is an administrative inspection unconstitutional just because the ultimate purpose of the regulatory statute is the deterrence of criminal behavior and the inspection may disclose violations of the penal code?

HOLDINGS No, the search is constitutional because an automobile junkyard is a highly regulated industry. No, the fact that the statute was intended to deter criminal behavior and the inspection may disclose violations of penal statutes does not make it unconstitutional.

REASONING Excerpts from the opinion of Justice Blackmun:

... The Court long has recognized that the Fourth Amendment's prohibition on unreasonable searches and seizures is applicable to commercial premises. ... An expectation of privacy in commercial premises ... is ... less than a similar expectation in an individual's home. ... This expectation is particularly attenuated in commercial property employed in "closely regulated" industries. ...

Because the owner or operator of commercial premises in a "closely regulated" industry has a reduced expectation of privacy, the warrant and probable-cause requirements ... have lessened application ... This warrantless inspection[,] ... even in the context of a pervasively regulated business, will be deemed to be reasonable only so long as three criteria are met. First, there must be a "substantial" government interest that informs the regulatory scheme pursuant to which the inspection is made. . . . Second, the warrantless inspections must be "necessary to further [the] regulatory scheme." . . . Finally, . . . the regulatory statute must perform the two basic functions of a warrant: it must advise the owner of the commercial premises that the search is being made pursuant to the law and has a properly defined scope, and it must limit the discretion of the inspecting officers. . . . To perform this first function, the statute must be "sufficiently comprehensive and defined that the owner of commercial property cannot help but be aware that his property will be subject to periodic inspections undertaken for specific purposes." . . .

Searches made pursuant to § 415-a5 . . . clearly fall within this established exception to the warrant requirement for administrative inspections in "closely regulated" businesses. . . . First, the nature of the regulatory statute reveals that the operation of a junkyard, part of which is devoted to vehicle dismantling, is a "closely regulated" business in the State of New York. . . . The provisions regulating the activity of vehicle dismantling are extensive. An operator cannot engage in this industry without first obtaining a license, which means that he must meet the registration requirements and must pay a fee. . . . [T]he operator must maintain a police book recording the acquisition and disposition of motor vehicles and vehicle parts, and make such records and inventory available for inspection by the police or any agent of the Department of Motor Vehicles. The operator also must display his registration number prominently at his place of business, on business documentation, and on vehicles and parts that pass through his business. . . . [T]he person engaged in

this activity is subject to criminal penalties, as well as to loss of license or civil fines, for failure to comply with these provisions. . . . That other States besides New York have imposed similarly extensive regulations on automobile junkyards further supports the "closely regulated" status of this industry. . . .

This case . . . reveals that an administrative scheme may have the same ultimate purpose as penal laws, even if its regulatory goals are narrower. . . . New York, like many States, faces a serious social problem in automobile theft and has a substantial interest in regulating the vehicle-dismantling industry because of this problem. The New York penal laws address automobile theft by punishing it or the possession of stolen property, including possession by individuals in the business of buying and selling property. . . . [T]he State also has devised a regulatory manner of dealing with this problem. Section 415-a . . . serves the regulatory goals of seeking to ensure that vehicle dismantlers are legitimate businesspersons and that stolen vehicles and vehicle parts passing through automobile junkyards can be identified. . . .

. . . The discovery of evidence of crimes in the course of an otherwise proper administrative inspection does not render that search illegal or the administrative scheme suspect. . . . Finally, we fail to see any constitutional significance in the fact that police officers, rather than "administrative" agents, are permitted to conduct the § 415-a5 inspection. . . . [M]any States do not have the resources to assign the enforcement of a particular administrative scheme to a specialized agency. So long as a regulatory scheme is properly administrative, it is not rendered illegal by the fact that the inspecting officer has the power to arrest individuals for violations other than those created by the scheme itself. . . .

THE IMPORTANCE OF CRIMINAL LAW

Why should a business law textbook contain a chapter on criminal law? The reason is that businesses are constantly confronted with the *effects* of crimes such as computer crimes, embezzlement, and forgery, to name only a few of the crimes we discuss in this chapter. As can be seen in the Classic Case, a business can be subjected to police searches. In addition, there are a number of crimes with which a business can be charged. Therefore, to prevent a crime from happening, or to deal effectively with a crime once it has occurred, you need to know what constitutes a crime and its legal ramifications.

The criminal law developed through a long history of precedents. However, most states have codified their criminal laws. As you should expect, the exact rules vary from state to state. Begin by referring to Exhibit 7.1, which summarizes the primary distinctions between civil law and criminal law. Try to distinguish between the two areas throughout this chapter. Remember that one action or series of actions may constitute *both* a civil wrong and a criminal wrong. It will also be helpful to look at Exhibit 7.2, which examines the six steps in a typical criminal proceeding.

Exhibit 7.1

Distinctions Between Civil Law and Criminal Law

Question	Civil Law	Criminal Law
What type of action leads to the lawsuit or case?	Action against a private individual or business entity	Action against society
Who initiates the action?	Plaintiff	Government
Who is the attorney?	Private attorney	District Attorney (D.A.), State or Commonwealth's Attorney General, or the U.S. Attorney General
What is the burden of proof in the case?	Preponderance of the evidence	Beyond a reasonable doubt
Who generally has the burden of proof?	Plaintiff	Government

Exhibit 7.1 Continued

Question	Civil Law	Criminal Law
Is there a jury trial?	Yes, except in actions in equity	Yes, except in cases involving certain infractions and misdemeanors
What jury vote is necessary to win the case?	Jury vote depends on jurisdiction or agreement of the parties Often a simple majority or two-thirds jury vote is sufficient	Unanimous jury vote needed for the government to win a conviction
What type(s) of punishment is imposed?	Monetary damages or equitable remedies	Capital punishment, prison, fines, and/or probation

Exhibit 7.2

The Six Steps in a Typical Criminal Proceeding

1. Preliminary Hearing or a Grand Jury Hearing

A preliminary hearing is generally a public hearing where a magistrate considers the evidence against the accused and determines if there is probable cause to hold a criminal trial. The prosecutor need not present all the government's evidence at the preliminary hearing, just sufficient evidence to have the case go to trial. A grand jury, on the other hand, hears the evidence in secret: Generally, the witnesses appear before the grand jury one at a time. The district attorney appears before the grand jury and may lead the questioning of the witnesses. The grand jury determines if a crime has been committed and, if so, which individuals were likely to be involved in the commission of the crime. If a grand jury issues an indictment against an individual, there will be a trial.

2. Arraignment

The suspect appears before the court and is informed of the criminal charges and asked how he or she pleads. Generally, the amount of bail is set at this stage.

3. Discovery

Both sides have to gather facts and information to prepare for trial. Discovery can involve examining documents, records, and other pieces of physical evidence, as well as taking the depositions of witnesses or the parties themselves. Discovery is generally more limited in criminal cases than in civil cases. One of the concerns is that if the defendant knows who will testify for the government, the defendant, defendant's relatives, and friends may intimidate the witnesses. Some discovery actually occurs at the preliminary hearing and arraignment.

Exhibit 7.2 Continued

4. Pretial Motions

If the parties need the court to make procedural decisions or other rulings as the case moves toward trial, they do so by filing the appropriate motions with the court. In criminal cases, this may include a motion to suppress evidence that was illegally obtained by the police.

5. Trial

The court hears the evidence offered by both sides and decides issues of both fact and law during the process.

6. Sentencing

If the defendant is found guilty beyond a reasonable doubt, the defendant will be sentenced to jail, probation, parole, and/or to pay a fine.

OBJECTIVES OF CRIMINAL LAW

The objectives of criminal law are the protection of persons and property, the deterrence of criminal behavior, the punishment of criminal activity, and the rehabilitation of the criminal.

Protection of Persons and Property

Someone once said that a lock was designed to keep an honest person honest. It is for the same reason that the government declares certain conduct to be illegal. The government believes that all persons and their property should be protected from harm. In Chapter 6, you learned that tort law also protects persons and property. What is the difference? The primary difference between tort law and criminal law is that tort law may result in money damages being paid by the actor to the individual victims, whereas criminal law may result in loss of freedom by sending the actor to jail or prison. Private interests are served through the awarding of damages. The public interest, on the other hand, is served by punishing criminal activity. If all persons respected everyone else's person and property, there would be very little reason for criminal law. However, there is evidence that they do not. "There's an old saying . . . in fraud prevention circles called the 10-10-80 rule: 10 percent of people will never steal . . . , 10 percent of people will steal at any opportunity, and the other 80 percent of employees will go either way depending on how they rationalize a particular opportunity."[2]

Deterrence of Criminal Behavior

One method used to reduce criminal behavior is to present a sufficient *deterrent* (something that impedes or prevents) to antisocial behavior. The presumption inherent in criminal law is that if we make the punishment sufficiently harsh, people and businesses who contemplate criminal behavior will avoid it because they fear punishment. If people fear the punishment, they will not commit the criminal act. If sufficient people fear the punishment, there will be a reduction in that crime. The severity of the punishment is often an issue with corporate defendants. What constitutes a substantial penalty for an individual would be a minimal penalty for a corporation such as UBS Bank.[3]

Criminologists have noted that severity alone is not a sufficient deterrent. Individuals considering criminal behavior must also believe that they are likely to be identified and punished. If criminals believe that they will not be identified and tried or that they will not be found guilty in court, the deterrent effect will be reduced.

In our society, the Constitution states that there shall be no cruel and unusual punishment. If our laws allowed the death penalty for even minor offenses, there would probably be fewer minor offenses. But is that just? Most people would argue that the loss of one's life for stealing a loaf of bread seems too high a price to pay for fewer loaves of bread being stolen. Similarly, many feel that caning a teenager for vandalism or castrating a rapist is too extreme. The problem—at least in the United States—is to decide how much punishment will deter criminal behavior without being deemed excessive and, therefore, unconstitutional.

Punishment of Criminal Activity

Since we most likely cannot deter all criminal activity, our legal system accepts that a certain level of criminal activity will exist in society. Accordingly, we punish criminal activity for punishment's sake. There is no such thing as a free lunch: If a criminal takes something without paying for it, the criminal law makes that individual pay for it through deprivation of freedom for a period of time. Convicted criminals can be imprisoned, sentenced to probation, or fined. In addition, the use of criminal forfeiture as a punishment for certain crimes is growing. (*Criminal forfeiture* is when the government confiscates property as a punishment for criminal activity.)

Rehabilitation of the Criminal

Our criminal justice system does not *end* with imprisonment, probation, or a fine. Our government has designed various programs to educate and train criminals in legitimate occupations during the period of incarceration. Theoretically, then, criminals should have no reason to return to a life of crime. Sometimes a sentence is suspended; that is, it is not put into effect. In such cases, the court supervises the individuals' activities to ensure that they have learned from their mistakes.

eClass 7.1 **Management**

PROTECTING AGAINST CRIME

Ani, Meg, and Yousef have become somewhat concerned about crimes in their community, and how those crimes may affect eClass. They have read that the crime rate is rising in their community and across the country, and that crimes against small, closely held companies are particularly devastating. Ani, Meg, and Yousef wonder what they can do to protect their business and themselves without violating legal rules. They ask you for advice. What will you tell them?

BUSINESS CONSIDERATIONS   Suppose that a business decides to take aggressive steps to try to reduce crime in its community, especially crimes that affect the business itself. Would this be viewed favorably or unfavorably in the community? Why? From a business perspective, is public perception an important factor in making this decision? Why?

ETHICAL CONSIDERATIONS   If a business *did* decide to take aggressive steps to try to reduce crime in its community, its conduct would have to be practical as well as legal. Is this feasible? Would such a decision be ethical? What ethical considerations should constrain the firm's decision?

CRIMES VERSUS TORTS

It is important to remember that one act can be the legal basis for both a criminal lawsuit and a civil lawsuit. The two separate suits will not be barred by the doctrine of *res judicata*, nor by the rule against double jeopardy. In many situations, a *criminal act* (an act against the rules of society) will also involve an infringement on the social rights and expectations of an individual. If one act is both a crime and a tort, it may be prosecuted in the criminal system, and the harmed individual may be able to seek remedies in the civil system.

THE COMPONENTS OF CRIMINAL RESPONSIBILITIES

Generally, an individual is presumed innocent until proven guilty. The government has the burden of proving that the suspect is guilty *beyond a reasonable doubt*. (Beyond a reasonable doubt is the degree of proof required in a criminal trial. It is proof to a moral certainty; there is no other reasonable interpretation.) The government must prove all the parts of the crime.

There are two components, or elements, in every crime. In order for the defendant to be found guilty of an alleged criminal act, the state must prove that both elements are present to the degree specified in the state's criminal statute. The state must prove beyond a reasonable doubt that the defendant committed the prohibited criminal *act* and that the defendant possessed the necessary *mental state* at the time the act was committed. The wrongful act is called the *actus reus*, and the state of mind required for each crime is called the *mens rea*. If only one element is present, no crime exists. For example, if you decide to embezzle from your employer and then take no steps to implement your decision, you have not committed a crime. The intent was present, but no prohibited act occurred. Similarly, if you are smoking in a motel and your cigarette ignites the draperies in your room and causes the motel to burn down, you have not committed the crime of arson. A prohibited act occurred, but there was no criminal intent. In the latter case, you may be liable for negligence, but you have not committed arson. Even *if* an actor has committed a prohibited act and possessed the necessary criminal intent, no criminal conviction will occur unless the state can convince the jury of both elements beyond a reasonable doubt. (Note that the defendant is found not guilty, he or she is *not* found "innocent.")

The Act

The law generally imposes criminal liability only when an individual acts in a manner that is prohibited by law. Ordinarily, the prohibited act must be voluntarily committed by the person before criminal liability will attach. This means that a person who is forced to act illegally against his or her will does not act voluntarily and may not be legally responsible for the act. However, the court *may* still impose liability if it decides that the threat used to force the conduct was not sufficient to remove the free will of the actor. Also, some situations may *require* an individual to act or respond to the circumstances in a particular way. In these situations, a failure to act may be deemed a criminal "action" sufficient to justify prosecution by the government. This responsibility to act may be imposed by a statute or by judicial precedent.

Mental State

To be held criminally responsible for an illegal act, the actor must intend to do the act. Historically, various terms were used to describe this mental state: *consciously, intentionally, maliciously, unlawfully,* and *willfully*. Today, our approach to the problem is more systematic. This current approach involves the use of one of five terms, depending on the specific requirements of the statute. It defines more specifically the *degree* of intent than the prior terms. The terms commonly used are:

1. *Purpose*—An actor acts with purpose if it is his or her conscious objective to perform the prohibited act.

2. *Knowledge*—An actor acts with knowledge if he or she is aware of what he or she is doing.
3. *Recklessness*—An actor acts with recklessness if he or she disregards a substantial and unjustifiable risk that criminal harm or injury may result from his or her action.
4. *Negligence*—An actor acts in a criminally negligent manner if he or she should have known that a substantial and unreasonable risk of harm would result from his or her action.
5. *Strict liability*—An actor will be held strictly liable if he or she acts in a manner that our law declares criminal, even if none of the above four elements is present. This theory is used primarily for crimes that have a light punishment—for example, violating public health laws with respect to the sale of food. This theory is also used in statutory rape cases simply because our society has a vested interest in protecting our youth.

SERIOUSNESS OF THE OFFENSE

Criminal law classifies all offenses into three categories according to their level of seriousness. These categories are, from least to most serious, misdemeanors, felonies, and treason. Some states have an additional category called infractions or violations.

Infractions or Violations

Some states have a separate category for petty offenses called *infractions* or *violations*. They are generally punishable only by fines. Some examples include illegal gaming and disturbing the peace.

Misdemeanors

Misdemeanors are minor offenses that are punishable by confinement of up to one year in a city or county jail, a small fine, or both. Public intoxication, speeding, and vandalism are likely to be classified as misdemeanors.

Felonies

Felonies are major offenses punishable by confinement from one year to life in a state or federal prison, a large fine, or both. In some states, special capital felony statutes provide for the sentence of death. Murder, arson, rape, burglary, and grand theft are normally classified as felonies.

Treason

Treason is the only crime defined in the U.S. Constitution[4] and is the most serious offense against the government. It is currently defined as "Whoever, owing allegiance to the United States, levies war against them or adheres to their enemies, giving them aid and comfort within the United States or elsewhere, is guilty of treason and shall suffer death, or shall be imprisoned not less than five years and fined under this title but not less than $10,000; and shall be incapable of holding any office under the United States."[5] Treason is based on the concept that the person owed either a perpetual or temporary allegiance to the United States. Every citizen of the United States owes perpetual allegiance to it. Aliens who are domiciled in the United States owe temporary allegiance to it. If a citizen mutters words of discontent, the words by themselves will not constitute treason. The general view is that treason requires on overt act or a confession in court. The overt act does not have to be a crime by itself. The purpose of the overt act requirement is to show that the accused actually gave aid and comfort to the enemy. However, the overt act *can* be the oral or written communication of an idea, such as conveying military intelligence to the enemy or broadcasting radio shows of support and encouragement for the enemy.

Although some state constitutions and statutes make it a crime to commit treason against the state, there are few prosecutions under them. Treason is generally considered to be a crime against the nation.

Sedition

Sedition is an agreement, communication, or some other activity intended to incite treason or some lesser commotion against the public authority. It includes advocacy intended and likely to incite or produce imminent lawless behavior. Sedition may be committed by taking some preliminary steps, as compared to treason, which requires an overt act. If the plan is for some minor disturbance then, even if the plan is actually completed, it will be sedition instead of treason.

SELECTED CRIMES

We are unable to list all of the common crimes in this text. We will mention selected crimes that have applications for either detection or prevention in the marketplace. In many situations, it is the business that is the victim of the crime, not its perpetrator. It is possible for a business to be the perpetrator of a crime, and there are a number of criminal statutes aimed primarily at business activities. Some of the federal statutes directed at business activities are discussed in other chapters of the text. In this chapter, we discuss the federal Counterfeit Access Device and Computer Fraud and Abuse Act of 1984; Racketeer Influenced and Corrupt Organization Act (RICO); and the Currency and Foreign Transactions Reporting Act, among others.

The Currency and Foreign Transactions Reporting Act is a federal statute passed to prevent money-laundering and to require the filing of Currency Transaction Reports (CTRs). A *currency transaction report* is a report businesses must file if a customer brings $10,000 or more in cash to the business. The National Conference of Commissioners on Uniform State Laws (NCCUSL) has written the Uniform Money Services Act (2000) for adoption by state legislatures. It enhances enforcement of existing money laundering laws and provides a framework for dealing with nondepository providers of financial services. *Nondepository providers* are providers of services such as check cashing and currency exchange. While these businesses provide some financial services traditionally related to banking, these businesses do not hold client's deposits or provide other banking services.[6]

Murder/Manslaughter

Homicide is the killing of one human being by another. It is not necessarily a criminal act. It will *not* be a criminal act if the killing was lawful; for example, if there was a justification such as self-defense. *Murder*, however, is the willful, unlawful killing of a human being by another with *malice aforethought* (deliberate purpose or design). *Manslaughter* occurs when the killing is unlawful, but without malice. Manslaughter is usually divided into two categories—*voluntary* (upon a sudden heat of passion) or *involuntary* (in the commission of an unlawful act or in the commission of a lawful act without due caution). It is common for the state to charge a defendant with both murder and manslaughter and to let the decider of fact (the jury, if there is one; the judge, if there is no jury) determine which crime was actually committed.

Arson

Arson is the intentional or willful burning of property by fire or explosion. Originally, this crime was restricted to the burning of a house. Today, in most states, the crime has been expanded to include the burning of all types of *real property* (land and items of property permanently attached to land) and many types of *personal property* (property other than land).

Burglary

Burglary is the breaking and entering of a structure with the intent to commit a felony inside the structure. Originally, this crime was restricted to the breaking and entering of a house at night, but, like arson, it has been expanded to include other structures, such as stores and warehouses. The crime also is no longer limited to nighttime conduct, but can occur at any time of day or night.

Embezzlement

Embezzlement is the taking of money or other property by an employee who has been entrusted with the money or property by his or her employer. Businesses should establish practices and procedures to reduce the likelihood of being victimized by embezzlement.

Forgery

Forgery is the making or altering of a negotiable instrument or credit card invoice in order to create or to shift legal liability for the instrument. It generally consists of signing another person's name to a check, promissory note, or credit card invoice or altering an amount on any of those documents. To win any such case, the government must generally prove that the accused acted with the intent to defraud. A business entity should use care in maintaining checks and signature stamps. It should also reconcile bank statements to discover potential forgeries.

Credit Card and Check Legislation

Today, customers make extensive use of credit cards, *debit cards* (cards that transfer funds from customers's bank accounts to merchants's bank accounts), and checks. This creates a number of difficulties, particularly for mail order, e-commerce, and other businesses. For instance, criminals may steal an individual's credit card, debit card, or card number and use it to make substantial purchases. Card numbers may be obtained by accessing computer files where an owner has charged a purchase to his or her credit card. Duplicate copies of credit slips are also used to obtain numbers. There are also small machines that quickly swipe a card and retain the card information. Dishonest employees can obtain this information and then sell it to other criminals. Some states have enacted *separate* legislation making it a crime to misuse someone else's credit or debit card without permission. Other states treat this as a type of forgery. Criminals may steal the checks of an individual or business and forge the signature on the checks.

A different type of problem arises when the owner of a bank account writes checks when there are insufficient funds in the account. Most states have enacted statutes that make it a crime to write or transfer (make, draw, or deliver) a check when there are insufficient funds in the account. These are commonly called *bad check statutes*. Some states require the *mens rea* that the suspect intended to defraud the recipient of the check before any criminal liability can attach to the conduct.

Identity Theft

Identity theft occurs when a thief steals personal information, such as the name, address, Social Security number, and/or name of the employer, and then uses this

eClass 7.2 Marketing

E-COMMERCE SECURITY

Ani, Meg, and Yousef have been considering creating a Web site to sell eAccounting directly to customers. However, they are concerned about possible security breaches on their Web site, where hackers may "steal" customer information, such as credit card numbers, names, addresses, etc. How can eClass best protect itself and its customers from such dangers? Should it go forward with its plan? The principals have asked you for advice. What will you tell them? Why?

BUSINESS CONSIDERATIONS   How can a business provide security at its Web site? Is security important? Why?

ETHICAL CONSIDERATIONS   Is there a moral difference between theft of customer information by eClass employees and theft by others? Why?

information to access the victim's credit. The thief can obtain the personal information on the Internet, through public records, stealing mail from the victim's mailbox,[7] or going through the victim's trash. *Hackers* (outsiders who gain unauthorized access to computers or computer networks) may gain access to personal information through an individual's personal computer, an employer's computer systems, a business's records with whom the individual dealt, or a credit card company's records. In one case the hacker stole 80,000 credit card numbers.[8] In some cases, the thief may actually work for a credit card company or credit card department of a retailer. In some state or federal prisons, cheap inmate labor is utilized for various enterprises. In one case, the state was using inmates to process credit card applications, and some of the inmates were stealing personal information from the applications.

Once the thief has obtained the information, he or she may apply for credit using the victim's name or may access the victim's accounts, such as bank accounts, retirement accounts, or social security accounts.

Criminal Fraud

Fraud is a broad term that covers many specific situations. The tort of fraud was discussed in Chapter 6. The English courts were very reluctant to criminalize fraudulent behavior, preferring to allow tort law to resolve most situations. Over the years, legislation was passed in both England and the United States to overcome the historic view of "[we] are not to indict one for making a fool of another."[9] Today most states have statutes that cover variations of what is generally called *criminal fraud, false pretense*, or *theft by deception*. Most states require proof of the following elements to convict a person of criminal fraud:

- The speaker (or writer) made a false statement of fact;
- The statement was material, that is, the statement would affect the listener's decision;
- The listener relied on the statement; and
- The speaker intended to mislead the listener.

Note that the fraudulent party can be either the buyer or the seller. For example, suppose that a savings and loan creates the impression that certain real estate assets are worth $100,000 through the distribution of false appraisals in order to induce a person to invest in those assets. In fact, the assets are worth substantially less than the false appraisals show. The savings and loan and its officers could be found guilty of criminal fraud if an investor enters a partnership with the savings and loan involving the purchase, development, or other investment in those assets. The federal mail fraud statute[10] applies to fraud conducted, at least in part, through the mail. The federal wire fraud statute[11] applies to frauds conducted in part using telephone, radio, or television.

One type of fraud that has received a lot of notoriety recently is Ponzi schemes. Ponzi schemes are named after Charles Ponzi. However, he was not the first to operate such a scheme. In a Ponzi scheme, the money from later investors is used to repay early investors or to pay them dividends. The early investors generally receive "a high rate of return," attracting other investors to join the fund. Generally, there is no real revenue producing activity or investment. Eventually the scheme is uncovered when the "financier" cannot obtain sufficient new investment. Bernard (Bernie) Madoff was sentenced to 150 years in prison for the Ponzi scheme he ran. The government claimed that he operated the scheme for at least 20 years and caused $13 billion in net losses to investors.[12]

Larceny

Larceny is the wrongful taking and carrying away of the personal property of another without the owner's consent and with the intent to permanently deprive the owner of the property. The most common forms of larceny are shoplifting and pick pocketing. The use of force is not needed. Larceny is a serious problem for retail businesses. Merchandise is often lost through shoplifting. In addition, if customers feel unsafe due to pick pocketing, they will avoid certain stores and shopping centers.

At common law, the theft of a trade secret was not considered larceny. However, many modern statutes have changed that by recognizing the misappropriation of trade secrets as a theft. Some of these are federal statutes, including the National Stolen Property Act,[13] the Economic Espionage Act,[14] the mail fraud statute,[15] and the wire fraud statute.[16] There are also state statutes that specifically deal with the misappropriation of trade secrets. Espionage is discussed later in this section.

Robbery

Robbery is a form of aggravated theft. It is basically larceny *plus* the threat to use force or violence. To be classified as a robbery, the robber must use either violence or the threat of injury sufficient to place the victim in fear, and the robber then takes and carries away something either in the possession or the immediate presence of the victim. If the same property had been carried away without the use of violence or a threat of injury, the act would be a mere theft.

Espionage

The Economic Espionage Act of 1996 (EEA)[17] makes the theft of trade secrets a federal crime. It covers both domestic economic espionage, for example, by competitors,[18] and the theft of trade secrets to benefit foreign powers.[19] It was the first federal statute to provide criminal penalties for the misappropriation of trade secrets. Misappropriation of trade secrets is also called economic spying or *espionage*. When the EEA was being enacted, the FBI director, Louis Freeh, told a Senate panel that 23 countries are engaged in economic spying against U.S. businesses.[20] The Act makes espionage a federal crime punishable by 25 years in jail or a $25,000 fine for an individual offender. It also provides for fines of up to $10 million for companies found guilty of such conduct.[21] Under the EEA, almost anything can be a trade secret as long as the owner takes reasonable steps to keep it a secret and it has economic value because it is a secret.

Computer Crime

"The only secure computer is one that's turned off, locked in a safe, and buried 20 feet down in a secret location—and I'm not completely confident of that one either" (quote from Bruce Schneier, author of a book entitled *E-mail Security*).[22] Advances in computer technology have led to the development of new activities, some positive and some negative. Some of these negative behaviors are now recognized as crimes. Companies like the Gap, Hitachi America, PeopleSoft, Playboy Enterprises, and Twentieth Century Fox each attract from 1 to 30 hacker attempts per day.[23]

With our increased dependence on computers, computer criminals can create extensive damage. "The going estimates for financial losses from computer crime reach as high as $10 billion a year. But the truth is that nobody really knows. Almost all attacks go undetected—as many as 95% says the FBI."[24] In addition to civil liability for improper use, many states now recognize the following activities as computer crimes:

1. *Unauthorized use of computers or computer-related equipment.* This may include the use of business computers for personal projects, including homework and personal e-mail. It also includes transferring software purchased by a business to a personal computer.

2. *Destruction of a computer or its records.* Computer viruses destroy or alter records, data, and programs. Annually there are numerous virus alerts—some are fakes and some are legitimate. Businesses expend significant resources to protect themselves from viruses and to correct the damage they cause. This includes a virus that "infects" the computers in a college computer lab and subsequently infects students' travel drives and home computers.

3. *Alteration of legitimate records.* This would include altering a student's grade record in the registrar's office.

4. *Accessing computer records to transfer funds, stocks, or other property.* This would include entering a bank's computer system and transferring funds without authorization. For example, in 1994, Citibank discovered that Russian hackers made $10 million in illegal transfers. Initially the bank called in a private security firm. When Citibank finally spoke to the FBI and the media, it lost some of its top customers. Competitors lured customers away by promising them that the competitors' computer systems were more secure than those of Citibank.[25]

Congress enacted the federal Counterfeit Access Device and Computer Fraud and Abuse Act of 1984 to strengthen state attempts to deal with computer crime. The act criminalized the unauthorized, knowing use or access of computers in the following ways:

1. To obtain classified military or foreign policy information with the intent to injure the United States or to benefit a foreign country. This would include accessing classified Pentagon files. This constitutes a felony under the act.

2. To collect financial or credit information, which is protected under federal privacy law. This would include accessing credit card accounts to obtain credit card numbers and credit limits.

3. To use, modify, destroy, or disclose computer data and to prevent authorized individuals from using the data. This would include intentionally transferring a virus to a computer.

4. To alter or modify data in financial computers that causes a loss of $1,000 or more. (This would include the unlawful transfer of funds.)

5. To modify data that impairs an individual's medical treatment.

6. To transfer computer data, including passwords, which could assist individuals in gaining unauthorized access that either affects interstate commerce or allows access to a government computer. This would include the use of a "sniffer" program, which can hide in a computer network, record passwords, and then transfer this information to others.

The first category listed above constitutes a felony, and the remaining five categories constitute misdemeanors.

Computer users may engage in some of these new crimes. In addition, computer technology has enabled some individuals to commit more traditional crimes, but with a new, "high-tech" twist due to the use of a computer in the commission of the "traditional" crime. For example, Mark Johnson was investigated for a number of

eClass 7.3 Management

SHOULD eCLASS USE "OUT-OF-OFFICE" MESSAGES?

Meg read an article that people who post "out-of-office" messages on their email accounts experience an increase in computer hacking and theft. Meg is about to go to Detroit to represent eClass at a trade show for a week. She was planning to use an "out-of-office" greeting to let people know that her response would be delayed. Now she is not certain what she should do. She asks you for advice. What advice do you give her?

BUSINESS CONSIDERATIONS   Should eClass institute a general policy regarding the use of "out-of-office" messages? Why? Is there a concern about receiving flight itineraries via e-mail and sharing them with co-workers and family members? Why?

ETHICAL CONSIDERATIONS   What ethical issues should eClass consider in establishing a policy? What is the ethical perspective of computer hackers? Why?

computer-linked activities—computer fraud, computer "stalking" under the computer nickname "Vito," harassing and threatening computer users online, transporting a minor for sexual purposes, and sexual molestation.[26] Another example is *war-drivers* (drive-by hackers) who hack into vulnerable wireless computer networks from streets or parking lots to obtain information and/or plant sniffer programs. Often, the goal is to obtain credit card and debit card numbers to sell on the black market. A ring of hackers who hacked into the computers of Marshall's department stores and its subsidiary, TJ Maxx, stole up to 45 million credit and debit card numbers. The attack has already cost the parent company more than $130 million to settle with banks and customers.[27]

Corporate Liability for Crimes

Originally, courts held that a corporation was not answerable for crimes because the corporation was not authorized to commit crimes and, therefore, lacked the power to commit them. However, there is a growing trend in many states to hold corporations criminally responsible when their officers and agents commit criminal actions in the execution of their duties. Corporate directors, officers, and employees are also *personally* liable for crimes they commit while acting for the corporation. This trend is evidenced by court decisions, statutory law, and the Model Penal Code.[28] Another specific example is the California Corporate Criminal Liability Act, which enlarged the criminal liability of corporate managers.[29]

Corporate liability is more common when the corporation is accused of violating a statute that is *mala prohibita* (wrong because it is prohibited). In contrast, when the criminal act is one requiring a specific mental state, such as battery with intent to kill, the courts generally refuse to hold the corporation liable unless the corporation itself participated in the acts or a high-ranking official participated in the acts with the intent to benefit the corporation.

Corporate liability is sometimes limited to *white-collar crime.* Although this term does not have a precise meaning, it generally means crimes committed in a commercial context by professionals and managers. The officers and agents are generally tried separately and convicted for their behavior. When liability is imposed against the corporation, punishment is usually in the form of a fine.

RICO: Racketeer Influenced and Corrupt Organizations Act

The RICO statute[30] was included as part of the Organized Crime Control Act. According to the law's legislative history, it was the intent of Congress to remedy a serious problem: the infiltration of criminals into legitimate businesses as both a "cover" for their criminal activity and as a means of "laundering" profits derived from their crimes. RICO makes it a federal crime to obtain or maintain an interest in, use income from, or conduct or participate in the affairs of an enterprise through a pattern of racketeering activity.

Criminal prosecutors and plaintiffs' attorneys soon recognized the opportunity to use the statute against commercial enterprises. Plaintiffs' attorneys are involved because the statute permits individuals whose business or property is injured by a violation of RICO to file a civil action. Successful plaintiffs in a civil action may recover treble damages, attorney's fees, and reasonable court costs. For example, beneficiaries of group health insurance policies used RICO to sue the insurance company.[31] This is an example of the overlap between criminal and civil law systems. A prior conviction in a criminal suit is not required in order to file a civil RICO suit. Some observers contend that this is leading to unfounded lawsuits and out-of-court settlements by intimidated firms. The government can also file civil RICO actions. When the federal government proceeds with a civil suit, the burden of proof is lower. High civil penalties can provide a lucrative law enforcement technique.

Since its enactment in 1970, Congress has amended the law, which is incorporated in 18 U.S.C. §§ 1961-1968, and the courts have interpreted a number of its sections. The definitions of terms used in the statute are found in § 1961. Section 1962 lists the activities that are prohibited. Persons employed or associated with any enterprise are prohibited from engaging in a pattern of racketeering activity. A *pattern* constitutes committing at least two racketeering acts in a ten-year period. These racketeering acts are called *predicate acts* under RICO. Racketeering activity has been broadly defined and includes most criminal actions, such as bribery, antitrust violations, securities violations, fraud, acts of violence, and providing illegal goods or services.

Michael Milken was convicted under RICO of scheming to manipulate stock prices and of defrauding customers. Racketeering acts also include acts relating to the Currency and Foreign Transactions Reporting Act, which requires the filing of CTRs. RICO violations are added to other criminal charges when there is a pattern of corrupt behavior, such as bribery. Defendants may raise issues of double jeopardy when they are tried for both the predicate acts and the RICO violation. Courts generally determine that the prohibition against double jeopardy is not violated because the predicate acts and the RICO offenses are separate and distinct crimes.[32]

Criminal and civil penalties are described in U.S.C. § 1963, and §§ 1965-1968 cover procedural rules. Individuals convicted of criminal RICO violations can be fined up to $25,000 per violation, imprisoned for up to 20 years, or both. RICO also provides for the forfeiture of any property, including business interests, obtained through RICO violations. The property will be forfeited even if the property or business is itself legitimate. The defendant's assets can be temporarily seized before the trial begins to prevent further crimes. Some states have enacted their own RICO laws.

Since the federal RICO law is applied to legitimate business activities, it presents a potential concern for all business organizations, public and private. Recently, businesses have been lobbying for legislative amendments to limit the application of RICO.

SELECTED DEFENSES

The four classic defenses to criminal liability are duress, insanity, intoxication, and justification.

Duress

Duress exists when the accused is coerced into criminal conduct by threat or use of force that any person of reasonable firmness could not resist. Not all governments permit this defense. Those governments that recognize the defense vary with respect to the crimes to which it is applicable. Generally, the three essential elements of the defense are:

1. An immediate threat of death or serious bodily harm;
2. A well-grounded fear that the threat will be implemented; *and*
3. No reasonable opportunity to escape the threatened harm.

Insanity

Insanity exists when, as a result of a mental disease or defect, the accused either did not know that what he or she was doing was wrong or could not prevent himself or herself from doing what he or she knew to be wrong. The exact definition varies from state to state. This defense has been attacked for a variety of reasons, but the main complaint is that the definition is ambiguous. Although the defense is raised often, it is rejected in many of the cases in which it is raised.

Intoxication

Intoxication may be either voluntary or involuntary. Voluntary intoxication is not a defense unless it negates the specific intent required by a statute. For example, the crime of rape is said to require a general intent. Intoxication, therefore, would not be a valid defense. On the other hand, assault with the intent to commit rape is said to require specific intent. For that crime, intoxication may be a valid defense. Generally, involuntary intoxication is a good defense. *Involuntary intoxication*, for instance, can occur if one is forced to drink an alcoholic beverage against one's will or without one's knowledge. An example of the latter would be if a host offered a guest a soft drink; the host spiked the soft drink with drugs without the guest's knowledge.

The defense of intoxication is summarized in Exhibit 7.3.

Exhibit 7.3

Intoxication as a Defense

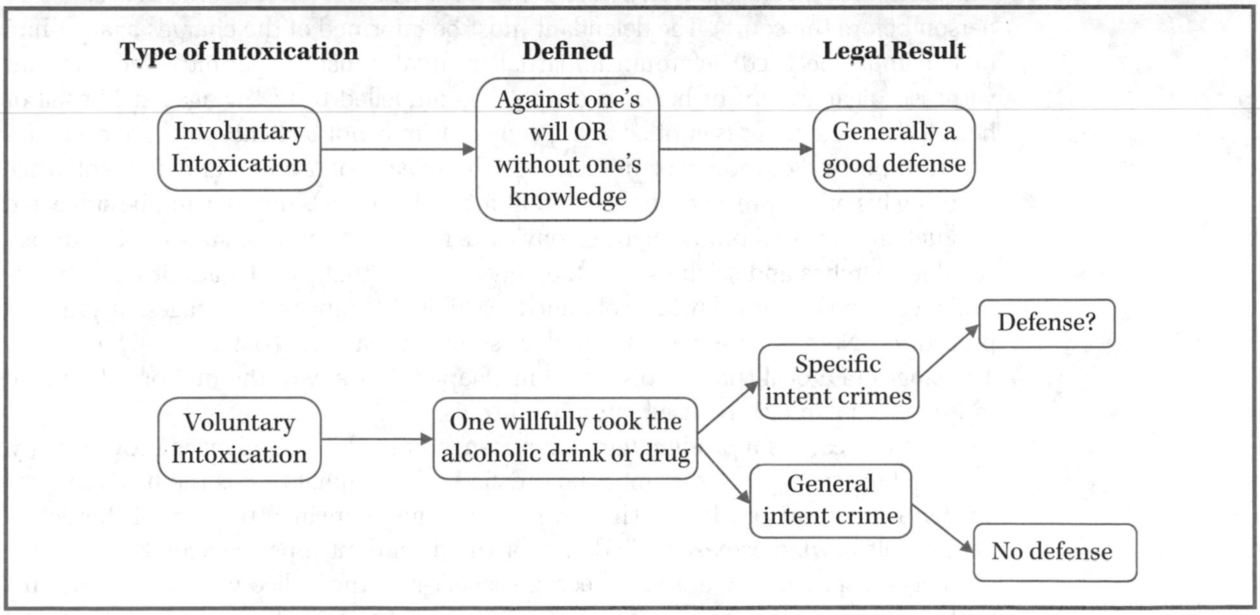

Type of Intoxication	Defined	Legal Result
Involuntary Intoxication	Against one's will OR without one's knowledge	Generally a good defense
Voluntary Intoxication	One willfully took the alcoholic drink or drug	Specific intent crimes → Defense? General intent crime → No defense

Justification

Justification exists when a person believes an act is necessary in order to avoid harm to himself or herself or to another person. The key to this defense is that whatever the person does to avoid harm must be lesser than the harm to be avoided. For example, sometimes property has to be destroyed to prevent the spread of fire or disease. A rancher's cows may be destroyed to prevent the spread of mad cow disease. A pharmacist may dispense a drug without a prescription if to do so would save a person's life.

THE LAW OF CRIMINAL PROCEDURE

Criminal procedure is the area of law that addresses the judicial process in a criminal case. It is concerned with ensuring criminal justice without unduly infringing on individual rights. The drafters of the U.S. Constitution were determined to avoid the excesses and abuses that had occurred under English rule. As a result, the area of criminal procedure was very important. There was a desire to protect the rights of the individual to the greatest extent possible without making law enforcement impossible.

The Constitution contains numerous criminal procedure provisions and protections, among them the guarantees of *due process* (the proper exercise of judicial authority as established by general concepts of law and morality) and *equal protection* (the assurance that any person before the court will be treated the same as every other person before the court). The defendant must be informed of the charges against him or her, must be tried before an impartial tribunal, must be permitted to confront witnesses against him or her, and cannot be compelled to testify against himself or herself. The defendant is entitled to a speedy trial, may not be held subject to excessive *bail* (the posting of money or property for the release of a criminal defendant while ensuring his or her presence in the court at future hearings), and may not be subjected to cruel and unusual punishment if convicted. No citizen may be subjected to unreasonable searches and seizures, and the only evidence that may be admitted at trial is evidence properly and lawfully obtained. Exhibit 7.4 depicts the stages of criminal procedure. Note that a criminal trial is similar to a civil trial in many respects. The stages of a civil trial are discussed in Chapter 4. Many of the motions discussed in Chapter 4 can also be used in criminal trials.

The law carries a *presumption* of innocence until the defendant is proven guilty, and the burden of proof that must be satisfied in a criminal trial is the heaviest such burden in U.S. jurisprudence. The government must convince the jury of the defendant's guilt beyond a reasonable doubt, or the defendant must be acquitted.

Legal disputes may arise between a suspect and the police who search the suspect's business, home, car, or person. Under the Fourth Amendment to the

Exhibit 7.4

The Common Stages of Criminal Procedure[a]

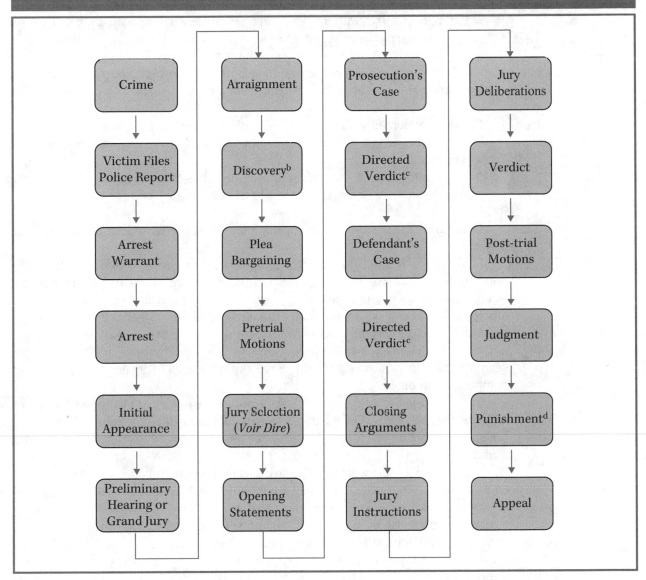

Crime	Arraignment	Prosecution's Case	Jury Deliberations
Victim Files Police Report	Discovery[b]	Directed Verdict[c]	Verdict
Arrest Warrant	Plea Bargaining	Defendant's Case	Post-trial Motions
Arrest	Pretrial Motions	Directed Verdict[c]	Judgment
Initial Appearance	Jury Selection (*Voir Dire*)	Closing Arguments	Punishment[d]
Preliminary Hearing or Grand Jury	Opening Statements	Jury Instructions	Appeal

[a] The exact order may vary.

[b] Discovery is more limited in criminal cases than in civil cases.

[c] Directed verdicts are not generally used *against* a criminal defendant.

[d] A criminal defendant may be imprisoned beginning at the time of the arrest, if the court determines that bail is not appropriate or if the defendant cannot raise the amount of bail.

Constitution, people are protected from unreasonable searches and seizures. When is a search and possible seizure legal? A search will be valid if any *one* of the following occurs:

- It is properly conducted under a legal search warrant based on probable cause.
- It is conducted without a warrant by officers acting with probable cause. In some situations, courts use a more reduced standard than probable cause. Most common examples of the reduced standards are when an officer "pats down" a suspect because the officer is concerned that the suspect has a concealed weapon or the evidence is in a motor vehicle that could be driven away.
- It is conducted with the permission of the owner of the property or a person with proper possession of the property, such as a tenant who rents an apartment.
- An emergency or exigent circumstance exists that requires police to enter onto the premises, such as a fire in the building.

Once police are legally on the property, they may observe and act on any criminal behavior they see.

Sometimes a business is subjected to a search. An example would be if the Occupational Safety and Health Administration (OSHA) wants to search a business for safety violations. On the other hand, sometimes the business wants to search an employee's locker, desk, or computer. The law in this area is very sophisticated and depends in part on: (1) who is actually doing the search; (2) the employee's expectation of privacy in the area; and (3) the basis for the employer's suspicion. The law about search and seizure is evolving rapidly, especially in the area of government searches of computers and offices.

In England, police who conduct illegal searches are punished by the police force for violating the rules. In the United States, we generally use a different approach. Evidence obtained through an illegal search may not be used in court; this is called *suppression of evidence.*

A police officer acting with probable cause may arrest and accuse an individual of committing a crime, or the arrest may occur under a warrant issued by a judge. A police officer who has probable cause to believe that a crime has been committed, or is being committed, may take the suspect into custody without obtaining a warrant. If an arrest warrant is used, it must be issued by a judge based on probable cause. The judge *may* find probable cause to believe that a crime has been committed solely on the basis of a sworn, written complaint that names the person to be arrested or adequately describes him or her.

Once arrested and charged with criminal conduct, the accused should be given a preliminary hearing. Preliminary hearings are not required in most jurisdictions if there has been a grand jury hearing. (A *grand jury* is a jury whose duty it is to receive complaints of criminal conduct and to return a bill of indictment if the grand jury is convinced a trial should be held.) At the preliminary hearing, a magistrate determines whether there is probable cause to proceed to a trial. The charges against the accused will be dropped if the magistrate decides that (1) there is no probable cause; (2) that there is not enough evidence to proceed to trial; or (3) that there is virtually no chance to obtain a conviction. Then the accused will be released from custody.

A grand jury may be involved in the pretrial stages of criminal proceedings. A *grand jury* is a panel charged with determining whether there is reason to believe that a person has committed a crime. After hearing the evidence presented by the prosecutor, the grand jury will issue an indictment if it believes that the accused has committed a crime. The government will then proceed to trial on the basis of this indictment, and a preliminary hearing is not required.

Once the grand jury has issued an indictment or the magistrate at a preliminary hearing has determined that probable cause exists, the accused is *arraigned* (called before a court to enter a plea on an indictment or criminal complaint). At the arraignment, the accused is informed of the charges against him or her, and if necessary, the court appoints an attorney to represent the defendant.

A common pretrial motion at this point is a motion for *change of venue*. In criminal cases, change of venue is requested if pretrial publicity was negative to the defendant. The defense counsel argues the location should be moved to ensure a fair trial for his or her client.

The defendant enters a plea to the charges. If the plea is guilty or *nolo contendere* (no contest; a plea in a criminal proceeding that has the same effect as a plea of guilty but that cannot be used as evidence of guilt), the court moves to the sentencing stage. If the defendant pleads not guilty, a trial date is set and, if appropriate, bail is set. If the court determines that the defendant is a flight risk, the court may refuse to set bail. For example, the district court judge determined that financier R. Allen Stanford, charged with operating a Ponzi scheme, was not eligible for release on bail.[33]

At the trial, the government has the burden of proving its case beyond a reasonable doubt, and it must satisfy this burden within the established rules of evidence. Any violation of the rules of evidence will result in the exclusion of the improper evidence, and often, the exclusion of the evidence will effectively undermine the government's case. When this happens, the defendant will be acquitted.

In criminal cases we still use 12 jurors plus alternates. An alternate replaces a regular juror who is not able to continue on the jury. A jury may be sequestered. When a jury is *sequestered*, jurors are not permitted to return home during the evenings and weekends. The jurors are kept separate from the rest of society so that others will not influence their views. Jurors are generally not sequestered in civil cases. For example, in the O.J. Simpson civil trial, Judge Fujisaki rejected the plaintiffs' request that the jury be sequestered stating that "there was no precedent for sequestering jurors at public expense in a civil trial . . .".[34]

If the jurors are deadlocked and are unable to reach a decision, it is called a *hung jury*. In 2010, Rod Blagojevich, former governor of Illinois, was tried for corruption. He allegedly attempted to get money or jobs in exchange for the Senate seat that became vacant when Barack Obama was elected President. The jury convicted him of 1 count, but was unable to reach a decision on the other 23 counts against Blagojevich and his brother. The prosecutors announced immediately that they will retry them. This retrial does not violate the prohibition against double jeopardy.[35]

If the defendant is found guilty, the court moves to the sentencing stage. Sentencing is governed by legislative guidelines to some extent, but the guidelines are normally very broad and somewhat vague. A great deal of judicial discretion is usually involved in sentencing especially for state crimes. Under current federal law, federal judges have much less discretion in sentencing for federal crimes than most state court judges. Federal judges rely heavily on the federal sentencing guidelines.

Contemporary Case

ARTHUR ANDERSEN, LLP v. UNITED STATES

544 U.S. 696, 2005 U.S. LEXIS 4348 (2005)

FACTS David Duncan headed Arthur Andersen's work for Enron, under the supervision of Michael Odom. On October 10, Michael Odom spoke at a general training meeting attended by 89 employees, including 10 from the Enron "engagement team." Odom urged everyone to comply with the firm's document retention policy. He added: " 'If it's destroyed in the course of [the] normal policy and litigation is filed the next day, that's great. . . . We've followed our own policy, and whatever there was that might have been of interest to somebody is gone and irretrievable.' " Arthur Andersen's policy stated that, "[i]n cases of threatened litigation, . . . no related information will be destroyed." It also provided that if Arthur Andersen is "advised of litigation or subpoenas regarding a particular engagement, the related information should not be destroyed."

On October 17, the SEC sent Enron a letter indicating that it had opened an investigation in August and was requesting certain information and documents. The letter was forwarded to Arthur Andersen on October 19. On October 20,

the Arthur Andersen Enron crisis-response team held a conference call, during which Nancy Temple, an in-house counsel, instructed everyone to "make sure to follow the [document] policy." On October 23, Duncan met with partners on the Enron engagement team and told them that they should ensure team members were complying with the document policy. Another meeting for all team members followed, during which Duncan distributed the policy and told everyone to comply. These, and other smaller meetings, were followed by substantial destruction of paper and electronic documents.

Throughout this time period, the document destruction continued, despite reservations by some of Arthur Andersen's managers. During an October 31 meeting with David Stulb, a forensics investigator for Arthur Andersen, Duncan picked up a document with the words "smoking gun" written on it and began to destroy it, adding "we don't need this." Stulb cautioned Duncan on the need to maintain documents and later informed Temple that Duncan needed advice on the document retention policy. On November 8, the SEC served Enron and Arthur Andersen with subpoenas for records. On November 9, Duncan's secretary sent an e-mail that stated: "Per Dave— No more shredding. . . . We have been officially served for our documents." Duncan was fired and later pleaded guilty to witness tampering. Arthur Andersen was indicted based on the document destruction between October 10 and November 9, 2001.

ISSUE Did the jury instructions properly convey the elements of corrupt persuasion?

HOLDING No, the jury instructions were in error.

REASONING Excerpts from the opinion of Chief Justice Rehnquist:

... [T]he United States Code provides criminal sanctions for those who obstruct justice. Sections 1512(b)(2)(A) and (B), part of the witness tampering provisions, provide in relevant part:

> "Whoever knowingly uses intimidation or physical force, threatens, or corruptly persuades another person, or attempts to do so, or engages in mis-leading conduct toward another person, with intent to ... cause or induce any person to ... with-hold testimony, or withhold a record, document, or other object, from an official proceeding [or] alter, destroy, mutilate, or conceal an object with intent to impair the object's integrity or availability for use in an official proceeding ... shall be [punished] ..."

... [O]ur attention is focused on what it means to "knowingly ... corruptly persuade" ... "We have traditionally exercised restraint in assessing the reach of a federal criminal statute, both out of deference to the prerogatives of Congress ... and out of concern that 'a fair warning should be given to the world ... of what the law intends to do if a certain line is passed' ... Such restraint is particularly appropriate here, where the act ... — "persuasion"—is by itself innocuous.... "[P]ersuading" a person "with intent to ... cause" that person to "withhold" testimony or documents from a Government proceeding or Government official is not inherently malign.... "Document retention policies," which are created in part to keep certain information from getting into the hands of others, including the Government, are common in business.... It is ... not wrongful for a manager to instruct his employees to comply with a valid document retention policy under ordinary circumstances. ...

Section 1512(b) punishes not just "corruptly persuading" another, but *knowingly ... corruptly persuading* another.... It provides the *mens rea*—"knowingly" ... "Knowledge" and "knowingly" are normally associated with awareness, understanding, or consciousness.... "Corrupt" and "corruptly" are normally associated with wrongful, immoral, depraved, or evil.... Only persons conscious of wrongdoing can be said to "knowingly ... corruptly persuade." ... [T]he jury instructions at issue simply failed to convey the requisite consciousness of wrongdoing.... [T]he jury was told that, "even if [petitioner] honestly and sincerely believed that its conduct was lawful, you may find [petitioner] guilty." ... The instructions also diluted the meaning of "corruptly" so that it covered innocent conduct.... The instructions also were infirm for another reason. They led the jury to believe that it did not have to find *any* nexus between the "persuasion" to destroy documents and any particular proceeding.... A "knowingly ... corrupt persuader" cannot be someone who persuades others to shred documents under a document retention policy when he does not have in contemplation any particular official proceeding in which those documents might be material. ...

You Be the Judge

About 2 P.M. on February 24, 2010, Dawn Brancheau, an animal trainer at Sea World in Orlando, Florida, was killed by Tilikum, a male orca. (Orcas are commonly called killer whales.) In front of the audience, Tilikum grabbed Brancheau and dragged her under the water. Brancheau was an experience trainer: She had worked at the park since 1994 and known Tilikum for 16 years. People for the Ethical Treatment of Animals (PETA), through its General Counsel Jeffrey Kerr, has asked the Florida State Attorney to file manslaughter charges against Sea World and its senior executives. PETA alleges that there has been a long list of previous attacks by orcas. A 1987 internal investigation by Sea World's parent company revealed 14 dangerous incidents within a four-month period. Tilikum killed a trainer at Sealand of the Pacific in British Columbia, and a park visitor was found dead and draped over Tilikum's back at Sea World. There have been at least six publicized attacks on trainers at Sea World parks since 2002. In 2006, an orca attacked a trainer at Sea World in San Diego. The California Division of Occupational Safety and Health investigated and concluded that it was "only a matter of time" before someone was killed. The agency withdrew its findings under pressure from Sea World. Assume that the Florida State Attorney files criminal charges in your court. How would *you* decide and why? [See Anika Myers Palm & Walter Pacheco, "The Nation; SeaWorld to Keep Killer Whale that Drowned Trainer," *Los Angeles Times*, February 26, 2010, Part A, p. 16; PETA Press Release, "Attorneys Allege Culpability: Record Shows SeaWorld Downplayed Risk of Injury and Death to Trainers Despite Long History and Government Warning," April 15, 2010, http://www.peta.org/MC/NewsItem.asp?id=14558 (accessed 4/16/10); Ed Pilkington, "Front: Whale Killing: They Played as Usual. Then He Drowned Her: Dawn Brancheau Had Known Tilikum the Whale for 16 Years. But SeaWorld Has Said the Orca Will Not be Destroyed." *The Guardian* (London), February 26, 2010, p. 2; and Daniel B. Wood, "Death of Sea World Trainer: Do 'Killer Whales' Belong in Theme Parks?; A Sea World Trainer Was Killed in Orlando, Fla., Wednesday by a 'Killer Whale.' Animal Rights Groups Say the Tragedy Shows Why the Giant Orcas Do Not Belong in Theme Parks," *Christian Science Monitor*, February 24, 2010.]

Summary

Criminal law is designed to protect persons and property from harm. In addition, it is designed to deter criminal behavior. Of course, the best protection is the absence of criminal activity; however, some criminal activity will always exist. Many believe that the law should punish criminals for their wrongful acts and/or try to rehabilitate them while they are incarcerated.

Criminal responsibility is based on two essential elements—a physical act and a mental state. The physical act must be overt. The mental state actually consists of one of the following: purpose, knowledge, recklessness, negligence, or strict liability. A similarity to civil law exists, but the interests protected are different: Civil law protects private interests, whereas criminal law protects public interests. Accordingly, one can be held liable twice for the same act, once in civil law and once in criminal law. This is not double jeopardy because there are two distinct bases of liability.

Most crimes are classified as misdemeanors, felonies, or treason. Misdemeanors constitute the least serious crimes; felonies are more serious. Treason, the most serious, involves acts to overthrow the government or provide aid, comfort, or information to another government.

The selected crimes discussed in the chapter include murder/manslaughter, arson, burglary, embezzlement, forgery, credit card and check crimes, fraud, larceny, robbery, espionage, computer crimes, and violations of the Currency and Foreign Transactions Reporting Act and the RICO statute. Courts may hold a corporation liable for crimes committed on its behalf. The criminal defenses mentioned are duress, insanity, intoxication, and justification.

The law of criminal procedure is very technical. An individual suspected of committing a crime can be arrested only upon probable cause. Probable cause is initially determined either by the arresting officer or by a judge issuing an arrest warrant. Once arrested, the accused is generally entitled to a preliminary hearing to determine if there is sufficient evidence to proceed to a trial. Grand jury hearings can also be used. The grand jury may issue an indictment if it believes the accused has committed a crime.

During a criminal trial, the government must prove its case beyond a reasonable doubt, and it must abide by numerous constitutional guarantees, such as due process, equal protection, and the rules of evidence. An accused person can be sentenced to a fine or imprisonment *only* after a conviction. A criminal defendant can be imprisoned pending trial because the magistrate determines that bail is not appropriate or the defendant is not able to post bail.

Discussion Questions

1. A man coated a carousel at Watkins Park in Indianapolis with skin-dissolving chemicals. Eleven children and one adult were sent to the hospital with irritated skins on their faces, hands, and legs.[36] Has the man committed any crimes? If so, which ones?

2. Meg went on her business trip to Detroit. Since she returned, she has noticed a couple of strange charges on her credit card. She suspected that she is a victim of identity theft. What should she do? What can you do to try to prevent identity theft?

3. Nazik's business was losing money. She decided to burn down her place of business, collect the proceeds of her insurance, and start over. The building burned down, but a homeless person sleeping in the building at the time was burned to death. What is Nazik's criminal

liability? Is she liable for arson, manslaughter, criminal fraud? Why?

4. Every day people die in police chases. Based on federal studies, about 40 percent of police chases end in crashes.[37] Oftentimes people are injured or killed. The suspect who is running from the police may be hurt or killed. The officer or bystanders may be harmed. How can the legal system balance the need to keep the peace and apprehend suspects with the need for public safety?

5. In an indictment that was unsealed on March 29, 2010, nine members of a militia group called Hutaree were charged with seditious conspiracy, attempted use of weapons of mass destruction, teaching the use of explosive materials, and

possessing a firearm during a crime of violence. According to the indictment, the Hutaree conspired to oppose by force the authority of the U.S. government. They viewed local, state, and federal law enforcement as the enemy and planned to engage them in armed conflict. The indictment alleged that they planned to kill a local law enforcement officer and then attack the other officers who gathered for the funeral using improvised explosive devices and explosively formed projectiles. The Hutaree leader obtained information about these devices from the Internet and e-mailed diagrams of the devices to others. They had begun gathering the materials for the devices. Assuming that the government can prove its case against these Hutaree members beyond a reasonable doubt, can it obtain a conviction for sedition? Why?[38]

Case Problems and Writing Assignments

1. Bernardo Garcia served time in prison for methamphetamine (meth) offenses. Shortly after Garcia's release from prison, two individuals told the police that Garcia was interested in manufacturing meth again. A store's security video system recorded pictures of Garcia buying the ingredients used in making meth. The police learned that Garcia was driving a borrowed Ford Tempo. They found the Ford Tempo parked on a public street near where Garcia was staying. Without obtaining a search warrant, the police placed a global positioning system (GPS) "memory tracking unit" underneath the rear bumper of the vehicle. Such a device receives and stores satellite signals that indicate the device's location. When the police later retrieved the GPS device, they were able to learn the car's travel history. Using the GPS information, the police learned that the car had been traveling to a large tract of land. The police obtained the consent of the tract's owner to search it. During the search they discovered equipment and materials used in the

manufacture of meth. While the police were conducting the search on the property, Garcia arrived there in his vehicle. The police found additional information by searching the vehicle. Did the police officers' use of the GPS system without a warrant violate the Fourth Amendment? Why? [See *United States v. Garcia*, 474 F.3d 994, 2007 U.S. App. Lexis 2272 (7th Cir. 2007).]

2. José Ignacio Lopez de Arriortua (Lopez) was a high-level General Motors (GM) executive when Volkswagen AG of Germany (VW) hired him as president after a "public and bitter" contest between GM and VW. (VW refers to VW of Germany only.) Much of the bidding war for Lopez's services was reported in newspapers like *The Wall Street Journal.* When Lopez eventually left GM for VW, he took other GM managers with him. Subsequently, GM documents were found in "possession" of these executives and in apartments frequented by them in Germany. GM contends that its proprietary information was taken, including designs for "Plant X," a new factory design that is supposed to improve flexibility.

GM has accused Lopez and VW of conspiring to steal company secrets when Lopez left GM in 1993. The VW board has been trying unsuccessfully to extricate itself from this conflict. German prosecutors filed criminal charges of industrial spying against Lopez in December 1996. In addition, U.S. federal judge Nancy Edmonds in Detroit has ruled that GM can proceed with a civil suit against Lopez and all of VW's top management.

Lopez resigned his position with VW on November 29, 1996. This occurred shortly after a federal judge decided that GM was permitted to file RICO charges against VW. If successful, GM would be eligible for treble damages.[39,40] Is it likely that VW violated RICO? Is it likely that Lopez and his colleagues who "relocated" to VW violated RICO? What critical evidence must be proven by GM? [*See* Daniel Howes, "Ex-GM Exec Faces Bribery Investigation: Automaker Isn't Included in Justice Department Probe, Source Says," *Detroit News*, February 19, 1997, p. A1; Daniel Howes and David Shepardson,

"U.S.: Lopez Probe 'Still Active:' Justice Department Vows to Keep Working on Espionage Case Against Ex-GM Official," *The Detroit News*, May 22, 1998, p. F1.]

3. Marjorie Knoller and her husband, Robert Noel, were keeping two huge presa canario dogs in their San Francisco apartment. When Knoller took the dogs out one day, the dogs savagely mauled and killed their neighbor, Diane Whipple, outside Whipple's apartment door as she returned home with groceries. After the death, Knoller and Noel were cavalier about the death and even blamed the victim. Knoller was convicted of second-degree murder, and she and her husband were convicted of involuntary manslaughter and having a mischievous dog that killed someone. Judge James Warren overturned Knoller's conviction of second-degree murder but let the other convictions stand. Assume that Warren's decision has been appealed to your court. What would you rule and why? [See Kim Curtis, "Judge Throws Out Murder Conviction of Dog-Attack Defendant," Associated Press Wire, June 17, 2002.]

Notes

1. The applicable portion of the statute is available on the Web site for this book.
2. Patricia Schaefer, "Employee Theft a Big Problem for Small Businesses," http://www.businessknowhow.com/manage/employee-theft.htm, © 2006 (accessed 6/17/10). Although government entities investigate and prosecute crimes, it is also important for businesses to be proactive in trying to deter crimes. Employee theft can be expensive and can damage a business's reputation.
3. In 2009, the Swiss bank UBS agreed to pay the U.S. government $780 million and admitted that it schemed to help Americans hide money from the I.R.S. David S. Hilzenrath and Tomoeh Murakami Tse, "Deal Marks End of Era for Swiss Banking, IRS to Be Given Names of Suspected Tax Cheats," *Washington Post*, August 20, 2009, at http://www.washingtonpost.com/wp-dyn/content/article/2009/08/19/AR2009081901395.html (accessed 8/17/10).
4. U.S. Constitution Article III, § 3.
5. 18 U.S.C.A. § 2381.
6. The Uniform Money Services Act (2000) has been adopted by Alaska, Arkansas, Iowa, U.S. Virgin Islands, Vermont, and Washington. (Although technically the U.S. Virgin Islands is not a state, the NCCUSL treats it as a state and for purposes of uniform laws we will also.) NCCUSL Web site, "A Few Facts about the Uniform Money Services Act (2000)" at http://www.nccusl.org/nccusl/uniformact_factsheets/uniformacts-fs-msa.asp (accessed 4/18/10) and "Summary Money Service Act (2000)" at http://www.nccusl.org/nccusl/uniformact_summaries/uniformacts-s-msa.asp (accessed 4/18/10).
7. Theft of mail is a felony in the United States.
8. "FBI: Hacker Stole 80,000 Credit Cards," *CNN.com*, December 9, 2002, at http://www.cnn.com/2002/TECH/internet/12/09/israel.hacker.ap/index.html (accessed 12/9/02).
9. See *Regina v. Jones*, 91 Eng. Rep. 330 (1703).
10. 18 U.S.C.A. §§ 1341-1347.

11. 18 U.S.C.A. § 1343.

12. Robert Frank and Amir Efrati, " 'Evil' Madoff Gets 150 Years in Epic Fraud," *The Wall Street Journal*, June 30, 2009, pp. A1 and A12; Review & Outlook Column on the Opinion page, "Madoff's Evil," *Wall Street Journal*, June 30, 2009, p. A14.

13. 18 U.S.C.A. § 2314.

14. 18 U.S.C.A. § 1832.

15. 18 U.S.C.A. § 1341.

16. 18 U.S.C.A. § 1343.

17. 18 U.S.C.A. §§ 1831-1839 (1996).

18. 18 U.S.C.A. § 1382.

19. 18 U.S.C.A. § 1381. One recent article focuses on the application of the EEA to the problem of Chinese espionage and encourages the government to revise the EEA to include stricter penalties for misappropriation to benefit a foreign government and to enact new comprehensive anti-hacking legislation. Jonathan Eric Lewis, "The Economic Espionage Act and the Threat of Chinese Espionage in the United States," 8 CHI.-KENT. J. INTELL. PROP. 189 (Spring 2009).

20. Richard Behar, "Who's Reading Your E-mail?" *Fortune*, February 3, 1997, pp. 57-70, p. 64.

21. "The Enemy Within: Christian Tyler Reports on How Cold War Spy Tactics Are Being Adapted to Big Business," *Financial Times* (London), April 12, 1997, p. 1.

22. Richard Behar, supra note 20, pp. 57-70.

23. Ibid., p. 70.

24. Ibid., p. 59.

25. Ibid., p. 64.

26. Jerry Bier, "Computer Stalker Trial Is Delayed," *Fresno Bee*, June 5, 1996, pp. B1 and B3.

27. The Secret Service did much of the investigation in this case. It is responsible for combating financial fraud in addition to its responsibility to protect public officials. Brad Stone, "A Global Trail That Revealed a Cyber-Ring," *New York Times*, August 12, 2008, p. A1.

28. See Model Penal Code (1985), § 2.07.

29. See California Penal Code, § 387.

30. See 18 U.S.C. §§ 1961 *et seq.*

31. See *Humana, Inc. v. Forsyth*, 119 S. Ct. 710, 1999 U.S. Lexis 744 (1999).

32. See *U.S. v. Bellomo*, 1997 U.S. Dist. Lexis 434 (S. Dist. N.Y. 1997).

33. Miguel Bustillo, "Stanford Declared a Flight Risk, Financier Denied Bail, to Remain in Jail Until Ponzi Trial; Lawyer to Appeal," *Wall Street Journal*, July 1, 2009, p. C3.

34. Linda Deutsch & Michael Fleeman, "Simpson Juror Replaced; Talks Start Anew," *Fresno Bee*, February 1, 1997, pp. A1 and A11.

35. Don Babwin & Michael Tarm, "Questions Hang Over Blagojevich Corruption Trial," *Washington Post*, August 13, 2010, at http://www.washingtonpost.com/wp-dyn/content/article/2009/08/19/AR2009081901395.html (accessed 8/17/10); Chris Bury, Michael S. James, Jessica Hopper & Christine Brozyna, "Rod Blagojevich's Narrow Escape: Ex-Illinois Gov. Guilty on 1 Count, but Jury Stymied on Other Charges; Case Grinds On; Could Get 5 Years in Prison; Prosecution to Try Again After Jury Hung on 23 Counts," ABC World News, August 17, 2010, at http://abcnews.go.com/WN/rod-blagojevich-trial-guilty-24-counts-jury-deadlocks/story?id=11411037 (accessed 8/17/10).

36. "Man Charged in Placing Chemical on Carousel," *Arizona Republic*, June 21, 1999, p. A8; "Police Say Chemical Coated on Carousel; National Briefs/Indiana," *Boston Globe*, June 21, 1999, p. A11.

37. Mike Madden, "It's Your Average Day in the U.S. and Someone Will Die in a Police Chase," *Fresno Bee*, July 11, 1999, p. A7.

38. Department of Justice Press Release, March 29, 2010, United States Attorney's Office Eastern District of Michigan, "Nine Members of a Militia Group Charged with Seditious Conspiracy and Related Offenses," at http://detroit.fbi.gov/dojpressrel/pressrel10/de032910.htm (accessed 4/1/10).

39. Daniel Howes, "Ex-GM Exec Faces Bribery Investigation: Automaker Isn't Included in Justice Department Probe, Source Says," *Detroit News*, February 19, 1997, p. A1; Daniel Howes & David Shepardson, "U.S.: Lopez Probe 'Still Active:' Justice Department Vows to Keep Working on Espionage Case Against Ex-GM Official," *Detroit News*, May 22, 1998, p. F1.

40. On January 9, 1997, GM and VW voluntarily settled their legal differences, thus avoiding costly and highly publicized litigation. Both sides officially apologized. The agreement specified that GM would get $100 million in cash, and VW promised to purchase $1 billion of GM parts over a seven-year period. German prosecutors have dropped the criminal charges. Brian Coleman, "Lopez Case Is Dropped in Germany," *Wall Street Journal*, July 28, 1998, p. A12.

8

International Law

Agenda

eClass needs to be aware of the importance of international business, even though the firm currently conducts its business in the United States. It is quite possible that the firm will be able to export its products to a number of other countries. It is also quite possible that similar firms in other countries will attempt to import their competing products into the U.S. market, thus competing directly with eClass and potentially reducing the firm's market share and/or profitability. Even if there is no international competition for the software, eClass may want to purchase equipment or supplies from a foreign vendor in some situations.

If eClass decides to export its product, what international markets should it look to initially? Does the North American Free Trade Agreement (NAFTA) make Canada and Mexico attractive markets? Does the European Union (EU) offer enough of an opportunity to make that a more attractive market? Are there any export or technical restrictions that might make it difficult for the firm to export its product? Are there any import restrictions that may hamper the ability of the firm to purchase equipment or supplies from other nations?

These and similar questions are likely to arise in the material in this chapter. Be prepared! You never know when the firm or one of its principals will need your help or advice.

Classic Case

FRIGALIMENT IMPORTING CO. v. B.N.S. INTERNATIONAL SALES CORP.
190 F. Supp. 116 (S.D.N.Y. 1960)

FACTS Frigaliment sued B.N.S., alleging that B.N.S. had breached its warranty in each of two contracts. In the first contract B.N.S. had agreed to sell Frigaliment 75,000 pounds of 2.5 to 3 pound chickens and 25,000 pounds of 1.5 to 2 pound chickens. The second contract called for 50,000 pounds of 2.5 to 3 pound chickens and 25,000 pounds of the 1.5 to 2 pound chickens, with the smaller chickens at a slighter higher price than in the first contract. Both contracts were signed on May 2, 1957. B.N.S. made two shipments to satisfy the first contract. The first delivery was a little short, but the shortage was made up in the second shipment. Following delivery, Frigaliment discovered that the larger chickens were not young chickens suitable for frying or broiling, but were older chickens, or fowl, considered to be stewing chickens. Frigaliment protested and B.N.S. stopped shipment of the chickens under the second contract. Frigaliment then sued, claiming that under the terms of the contract, all of the chickens shipped by B.N.S. were to be young chickens. B.N.S. asserted that its obligation was simply to ship chickens that met the description in the contract, and that it was not restricted to only young birds.

ISSUES How should the term chicken, as used in this contract, be defined? Does the party seeking a narrow interpretation of a term have the burden of proof in establishing the meaning? Can parol evidence be used to define an ambiguous term?

HOLDINGS The word chicken, standing alone, is ambiguous. The party asserting that a narrower definition has the burden of proving that this definition is appropriate, and parol evidence can be used to establish the meaning of the ambiguous terms.

REASONING Excerpts from the opinion of Circuit Judge Friendly:

The issue is, what is chicken? Plaintiff says "chicken" means a young chicken, suitable for broiling and frying. Defendant says "chicken" means any bird of that genus that meets contract specifications on weight and quality, including what it calls "stewing chicken" and plaintiff pejoratively terms "fowl." Dictionaries give both meanings, as well as some others not relevant here. To support its claim, plaintiff sends a number of volleys over the net; defendant essays to return them and adds a few serves of its own. Assuming that both parties were acting in good faith, the case nicely illustrates Holmes' remark "that the making of a contract depends not on the agreement of two minds in one intention, but on the agreement of two sets of external signs—not

254

on the parties' having meant the same thing but on their having said the same thing." ... I have concluded that plaintiff has not sustained its burden of persuasion that the contract used "chicken" in the narrower sense. ...

When the initial shipment arrived in Switzerland, plaintiff found ... that the 2½-3 lbs. birds were not young chicken suitable for broiling and frying but stewing chicken or "fowl"; indeed, many of the cartons and bags plainly so indicated. Protests ensued. Nevertheless, shipment under the second contract was made on May 29, the 2½-3 lbs. birds again being stewing chicken. Defendant stopped the transportation of these at Rotterdam.

This action followed. Plaintiff says that, notwithstanding that its acceptance was in Switzerland, New York law controls ... defendant does not dispute this, and relies on New York decisions. I shall follow the apparent agreement of the parties as to the applicable law.

Since the word "chicken" standing alone is ambiguous, I turn first to see whether the contract itself offers any aid to its interpretation. Plaintiff says the 1½-2 lbs. birds necessarily had to be young chicken since the older birds do not come in that size, hence the 2½-3 lbs. birds must likewise be young. This is unpersuasive—a contract for "apples" of two different sizes could be filled with different kinds of apples even though only one species came in both sizes. Defendant notes that the contract called not simply for chicken but for "US Fresh Frozen Chicken, Grade A, Government Inspected." It says the contract thereby incorporated by reference the Department of Agriculture's regulations, which favor its interpretation. ...

Defendant's witness [testified that] ... "[c]hicken is everything except a goose, a duck, and a turkey. Everything is a chicken, but then you have to say, you have to specify which category you want or that you are talking about." ... [I]n the trade "chicken" would encompass all the various classifications. ... [Another] testified that he would consider any bird coming within the classes of "chicken" in the Department of Agriculture's regulations to be a chicken. The specifications approved by the General Services Administration include fowl as well as broilers and fryers under the classification "chickens." ...

When all the evidence is reviewed, it is clear that defendant believed it could comply with the contracts by delivering stewing chicken in the 2½-3 lbs. size. Defendant's subjective intent would not be significant if this did not coincide with an objective meaning of "chicken." Here it did coincide with one of the dictionary meanings, with the definition in the Department of Agriculture Regulations to which the contract made at least oblique reference, with at least some usage in the trade, with the realities of the market, and with what plaintiff's spokesman had said. Plaintiff asserts it to be equally plain that plaintiff's own subjective intent was to obtain broilers and fryers; the only evidence against this is the material as to market prices and this may not have been sufficiently brought home. In any event it is unnecessary to determine that issue. For plaintiff has the burden of showing that "chicken" was used in the narrower rather than in the broader sense, and this it has not sustained.

This opinion constitutes the Court's findings of fact and conclusions of law. Judgment shall be entered dismissing the complaint with costs.

INTRODUCTION

Any business forecaster of the 1970s who had predicted the end of the Cold War, the political (and economic) collapse of the Soviet Union, the dismantling of apartheid in South Africa, or the possibility that the Czech Republic, Hungary, and Poland would become members of the North Atlantic Treaty Organization (NATO), might have been told to sell his or her story to the supermarket tabloid newspapers. Many people would also have been very dubious about the prospects for a strong, unified European community, a North American free trade zone, or a "war" on terrorism. Yet each of these events has taken place in just two generations, and these changes represent only some of the massive political and economic shifts that have occurred around the world in recent years. Hong Kong, the Asian economic powerhouse, has reverted to the control of the Chinese government.

More recently, most of the world's economies have suffered devastating downturns, affecting such things as employment, retirement, and real estate markets, as well as having a negative impact on world trade and international markets. The last quarter of the twentieth century was a time of unprecedented political and economic change, and the pace of change is continuing in this century. As a result, a businessperson must develop an international—even global—perspective in order to have the greatest chance for success.

Business in a Global Village

If U.S. businesses have learned one lesson in the past few years, it is, as Marshall McLuhan once said, that we all live in a "global village." Companies such as Coca-Cola and General Electric employ global advertising strategies. Other companies, including all of the major U.S. auto companies, have joint manufacturing and marketing agreements with their Japanese and/or European competitors. Numerous other firms and industries are also affected by the global market, some for the better and some for the worse. The textile firms of the American southeast find themselves competing with textiles imported from a number of other nations. Retail outlets across the country carry products manufactured in other nations. State governments are establishing departments to promote international trade by businesses located within the state. "Internationalization" is permeating society at virtually every level.

In 2000, the United States exported $1,070 billion in goods and services and imported $1,450 billion. By 2007, those figures had grown, with exports of $1,645 billion and imports of $2,346 billion.[1] When measured in goods and merchandise alone, U.S. exports have grown from $772 billion in 2000 to $1,148 billion in 2007. In that same time, U.S. imports of goods and merchandise have grown from $1,226 billion in 2000 to $1,968 billion in 2007.[2] In many cases, typically American companies such as McDonald's, General Motors, and Digital Equipment find most of their revenues or profits coming from overseas operations. Foreign investment in the United States doubled between 1985 and 1990. Marshall McLuhan was right: We are so economically interdependent on one another that we do live in a global village. To succeed in the business world of the twenty-first century, every businessperson must be familiar with the basic rules of international business.

Going "Global"

As communications and transportation have improved, buyers and sellers in different markets have been able to find one another more easily, which has made it easier for them to do business together. Technology has opened the global marketplace to businesses of all sizes, allowing them to sell their goods, services, and technology. Future advances in technology will make interactions between buyers and sellers in different markets even easier, increasing the potential for international trade and the likelihood—or even the need—for a business to "go global."

A business has many options once it decides to "go global." For example, as it develops its international customer base, the business may decide to change the way it organizes itself. The business may move from simple selling relationships toward direct investments in major foreign markets. Most businesses start their international operations simply by selling to foreign customers. They may exhibit their products at international trade fairs, or an international buyer may visit a potential seller on a buying trip or be referred to the seller by another satisfied international customer. Like any direct selling relationship, the parties govern their rights and obligations using a contract. Many of the concerns a seller or buyer would have in a local transaction will be the same in an international transaction. Others, however, are special to the international transaction.

Suppose that Acme Novelties, Inc., a company based in Arizona, decides to expand its business from national to international. Acme may be selling a variety of items to its traditional buyers in the United States, another variety of items to a Mexican business, and still other items to a buyer in Ireland. While business would appear to be good for Acme, not too long ago these sorts of contracts could pose serious problems for the firm. By entering into contracts with customers in three different countries, Acme would, at least theoretically, be facing potential legal problems under three entirely different sets of laws. While most of Acme's sales in the United States would be governed by the Uniform Commercial Code (UCC), the sale to the Mexican customer would possibly be influenced by Mexican law, which has a strong European influence and is based on the Napoleonic Code, and the sale to the Irish customer would possibly be influenced by Irish law, which has a strong English common law influence. In addition, the sale to the Irish customer could be affected to some extent by the European Union (EU), of which Ireland is a member, and its rules. The sale to the Mexican customer could be affected by the North American Free Trade Agreement (NAFTA), a treaty to which both Mexico and the United States are signatories.

What happens if the tendered goods are rejected by each of these buyers? Whose law will govern the rights and obligations of the parties? The UCC will govern the sales to the U.S. buyers but may not govern the international sales. The domestic laws of each buyer may be controlling. Mexican law is likely to be very different from either

Irish law or the UCC, which would normally be followed in Arizona. Similarly, Irish law is likely to be different from both Mexican law and the UCC. What is the seller to do?

Historically, experienced international traders would specify in their contracts which law would govern the transaction. Thus, the Arizona seller could have negotiated the contract so that the UCC was controlling in all three transactions from the example. Or the parties could have agreed to have any disputes settled by arbitration. International sales contracts would often call for any disputes to be arbitrated, rather than tried, so the parties could avoid using unfamiliar court systems and unfamiliar laws.

In 1988, the United Nations Convention on Contracts for the International Sale of Goods (CISG) went into effect. The CISG provides a law of sales contracts specifically for contracts between businesses in countries that have approved the convention. In the United States, the CISG replaces the Uniform Commercial Code in any sales transactions between a U.S. firm and a business from another CISG country. Fortunately, the CISG is much like Article 2 (the law of sales) of the Uniform Commercial Code, and provisions of the CISG are often similar to the UCC's provisions, so it should quickly become familiar to American managers. (Article 2 of the UCC, Sales, Article 2A of the UCC, Leases, and the CISG are discussed in detail in Chapters 16 to 19.)

As of May 18, 2009, 74 countries had ratified the CISG, including the United States and other important trading countries such as China, France, Germany, and several republics of the former Soviet Union. (The complete list of member nations is shown at the Web site for Chapter 15.) Over the next several years, the CISG is likely to become the law in even more countries. This should reduce the concerns faced by companies like Acme Novelties in the example above.

Doing Business in a Global Market

As a business grows, it may decide that it needs a more systematic effort to find customers in foreign markets. Often, it will turn to individuals or businesses in other major markets to act as go-betweens in attracting foreign buyers to the company's products. The business may seek an agent, or it may opt for a distributor. An agent is a person or company who finds buyers on behalf of the seller and usually is paid a commission for the resulting sales. The sales contract is still between the buyer and seller (although in a few cases the agent has the authority to accept orders on the seller's behalf). The buyer gets the goods directly from the seller and looks to the seller to solve any problems with the sale. A distributor, by contrast, buys goods from the seller and resells them directly to customers. The distributor bears the risk that the goods will not sell or that customers will fail to pay for the goods. Generally, customers look to the distributor for service after the sale. Businesses with intellectual property rights—such as patents, copyrights, and trademarks—sometimes find it best to sell to a foreign business the right to make, copy, or market the products covered by those rights. Generally, the buyer of the rights will pay a fee plus a royalty—that is, a percentage of the price or profit—on any products sold.

One very popular method for entering the international business environment is franchising. United States fast-food businesses have used franchising as the major

eClass 8.1 International Business

BENEFITS AND COSTS OF "GOING GLOBAL"

Yousef spends a considerable amount of time "surfing" the Internet, and he believes that eClass should use the Internet to take an international approach to its operations from the beginning. Meg doesn't think that the firm is ready to "go global" yet. She would prefer to approach this venture a bit more cautiously by beginning with a regional perspective. While she would like to see the firm grow to the point where it has a national—or even an international—market, she does not want to overextend now. Ani agrees with Meg. She doesn't think that eClass will be ready to "go global" in the near future, but she also doesn't think that it would hurt the firm if it at least "thinks globally" while it acts regionally. The members ask you for your opinion. What will you tell them?

BUSINESS CONSIDERATIONS   Should a newly created business operation be concerned with "going global," or should its emphasis be on survival for the short term in its natural regional location? When should a high-tech firm begin to think about global, or at least international, operations? Should a more traditional manufacturing firm approach this issue differently?

ETHICAL CONSIDERATIONS   Should the firm take international considerations into account in setting up its business practices and internal code of ethics, or should it leave such considerations for the future? How might such international considerations affect how the firm conducts its business or establishes its code of ethics?

method of entering foreign markets. In a franchise, a license is granted by the franchisor to allow the franchisee to conduct business under the name of the franchisor. This license covers primarily the trademarks, for example, brand names such as Big Mac®, Whopper®, or Century 21®. In return for a fee and royalty paid to the franchisor, the franchisee earns the benefit of the reputation of the trademarks, national and international advertising, and a wide customer base. Many U.S.-based franchisors have identified their largest growth opportunities as coming from international franchising.

Another method for entering the international marketplace is through a joint venture. *Black's Law Dictionary* defines a joint venture in the United States as "an association of two or more persons to carry out a single business enterprise for profit." In international business, joint ventures are viewed somewhat more broadly than that definition implies. The concept covers businesses such as General Motors and Toyota, who built a plant together in California to manufacture Chevrolets and Toyotas on the same production lines. It also covers groups of companies that cooperate in research and development activities and even those that jointly market products. The joint venture has proven itself a successful way for companies to enter new markets, because they get the benefit of local expertise from their joint venture partners.

In many instances, a growing international business will decide to incorporate an operation separately in another country. If the business controls the new corporation, then it is the parent, and the new corporation is the subsidiary. A subsidiary may be wholly owned by the parent company, or the parent company may have partial ownership. (In some countries, foreign businesses must involve local owners in the ownership and management of subsidiaries.)

Cross-Cultural Negotiations

The United States is geographically isolated from most of its trading partners. When the U.S. economy was the benchmark for the rest of the world, such isolation was not much of a problem. In those halcyon days, the U.S. international business was frequently able to employ a "take it or leave it" attitude, knowing that the other party had little choice but to "take it," unless the other party was willing to do without. Why? Not many alternative sources existed for many goods beyond the United States.

Such a situation no longer exists. International competition has become heated, and the emergence of alternative sources of goods and services has produced the need for international traders to become aware of cultural differences in dealing with their customers. If a customer can receive satisfactory goods or services from several sources, other factors besides quality or price may enter into the equation. The successful international businessperson needs to learn as much about his or her trading partners and their cultures as possible in order to present his or her goods and services in the best possible light.

While there are no universal characteristics of any given culture, there are certain guidelines that tend to hold true. Among these guidelines are the following: national negotiating styles; differences in decision-making techniques; proper protocol in the negotiations; the social aspects of negotiating; time, and how it is viewed by various cultures; the importance of developing personal relationships between the negotiators; and social mores and taboos.[3] For example, the American desire to get things done, and preferably to get them done quickly, is at odds with the Chinese approach to proceed more slowly, operating at a pace that is personally satisfying. Americans frequently make decisions based on a cost-benefit analysis, with little consideration given to face saving. By contrast, the Japanese consider saving face crucial in their social interactions. Many gestures are deemed to be acceptable in some cultures, but may be considered rude—or even obscene—in others. The ability of a businessperson to successfully navigate through the cultural differences of his or her trading partners is instrumental to success in the international arena.

Differences in language can also have an impact on cross-cultural negotiations and business dealings, as our Classic Case for this chapter demonstrates. When the parties to a contract speak different languages, the contract that each party *thinks* he or she entered may be significantly different from the contract that his or her trading partner *thinks* the parties entered.

EXTRATERRITORIALITY: U.S. LAWS, INTERNATIONAL APPLICATIONS

American businesses are used to operating under the laws of the U.S. However, as more and more businesses expand into foreign nations they will begin to face a dilemma. Obviously they will have to obey the laws of the nations in which they are operating. But will they also have to continue to obey the laws of the United States? Put another way, do the laws of the United States (or of any other sovereign nation) end at its borders, or do they reach across borders into other nations? This question is of major concern to international businesses. In addition, if domestic law does apply internationally, businesses need to know whether all domestic laws apply internationally, or if application is limited only to some laws.

Antitrust Law

The U.S. antitrust laws are intended to ensure that business in the United States is conducted on a level playing field by protecting competition. Various anticompetitive activities are prohibited by these statutes. For example, the Sherman Antitrust Act states in its first section that "every contract, combination . . . or conspiracy in restraint of trade or commerce among the several States, or with foreign nations, is declared to be illegal." Is this statute applicable internationally, or only domestically?

According to the precedent set in several cases, the United States does have antitrust laws with extraterritorial application. However, U.S. courts have not been in full agreement on the meaning of those statutes with respect to international commerce. Among U.S. courts, there has been no consensus on how far the jurisdiction should extend. Some courts use the "direct and substantial effect" test; they examine the effect on U.S. foreign commerce as a prerequisite for proper jurisdiction. Other courts have used a test that looks at whether a conspiracy exists that adversely affects American commerce.

In general, however, most courts prefer to evaluate and balance the relevant considerations in each case. The courts determine whether the contacts and interests of the United States are sufficient to support the exercise of extraterritorial jurisdiction. The U.S. Supreme Court even allowed an alleged violation of the Sherman Act to be decided by Japanese arbitration. In that case, *Mitsubishi Motors Corp. v. Soler Chrysler-Plymouth, Inc.,*[4] a firm in Puerto Rico entered into a contract with a Swiss firm and a Japanese firm. The contract specified that any disputes were to be resolved by submission of the case to the Japanese Arbitration Association. An antitrust issue arose in the case; and the Puerto Rican firm asserted that antitrust issues could not be resolved by arbitration, despite the contract's terms, but rather had to be settled by a U.S. federal court. The U.S. Supreme Court disagreed and compelled arbitration as provided for in the contract to settle the dispute.

In an effort to resolve the issue, Congress passed the Foreign Trade Antitrust Improvement Act[5] in 1982. This amendment to the Sherman Antitrust Act says that the courts need to examine the site of the injury in determining whether the antitrust laws apply. The Act is aimed at protecting the U.S. market from antitrust problems caused here, and attempts to exclude pure export activities from antitrust coverage.

The Foreign Corrupt Practices Act

Many businesses that are new to the international marketplace have some trouble understanding the different values of people from other cultures or the way business may be conducted in foreign nations. The differences may be relatively minor, or they may be substantial. One area that has been particularly troublesome involves payments to officials in other countries. If a business makes a payment to a foreign official, is the business giving that official a gift or is the official being bribed?

In an effort to address this problem and to provide guidelines for U.S. firms doing business in other nations, Congress passed the Foreign Corrupt Practices Act[6] (FCPA) in 1977. This act, an amendment to the Securities Exchange Act of 1934, covers foreign corrupt practices and provides accounting standards that firms must follow in reporting payments made to foreign officials. Significant amendments to the FCPA were made in 1988.

The FCPA only applies to firms that have their principal offices in the United States. The act prohibits giving money or anything else of value to foreign officials with the intent to corrupt. This is a very broad standard, but basically the act is intended to prevent the transfer of money or other items of value to any person who is in a position to exercise discretionary authority in order to have that person exercise his or her authority in a manner that gives an advantage to the donor of the "gift."

Interestingly, the act does not prohibit so-called grease payments to foreign officials, although these, too, may look like bribes. A grease payment is a payment to a person in order to have him or her perform a task or render a service that is part of the person's normal job. The "grease" is intended to get the person to do the job more quickly or more efficiently than he or she might have otherwise. By contrast, a payment that is made with the intent to corrupt is one that is designed to have the donee do something he or she might not have been obligated to do or to make a favorable choice among options.

Many businesspeople have claimed that the FCPA places American firms at a competitive disadvantage. These people argue that prohibiting American firms from making bribes means they are not able to compete with foreign firms, thus costing the American firms contracts, profits, and jobs. They argue that "everyone else is doing it, so why shouldn't we?" It is apparent that the U.S. Congress does not agree with them;

and the FCPA will continue to regulate payments made or gifts given to foreign officials by representatives of American companies for the foreseeable future.

Employment

As pointed out previously, U.S. antitrust law, at least in some cases, has extraterritorial application. Similar reasoning has led the courts to conclude that some U.S. employment laws also apply outside the domestic environment. Of particular concern are the nondiscrimination provisions of domestic employment law.

Congress has amended Title VII of the Civil Rights Act of 1964, extending protection against employment discrimination to Americans working for American companies, even when the employee is working in another nation. Thus, the protections of Title VII extend across national boundaries, at least for U.S. workers employed by U.S. firms, regardless of the location to which the worker is assigned.

FREE TRADE ZONES

At one time, it was necessary to know the laws of each of the countries involved in an international transaction. The complexity that entailed, as well as the increased number of countries in the world since the end of World War II, impeded international trade. In an effort to alleviate this problem, countries in common geographical areas have banded together to form economic unions to facilitate and expedite trade. The two most significant regional groupings are the European Union (EU), comprised of 27 European nations (as of January 2007), and the North American Free Trade Area, which includes the United States, Canada, and Mexico. Other groups in Asia, Africa, and Latin America are now looking to the examples set by these major regional groups to create a legal foundation for their own free trade areas.

The European Union

The European Union (EU) was created by the Treaty of Rome in 1957. Currently, the member states are Austria, Belgium, Bulgaria, Cyprus, Czech Republic, Denmark, Estonia, Finland, France, Germany, Greece, Hungary, Ireland, Italy, Latvia, Lithuania, Luxembourg, Malta, the Netherlands, Poland, Portugal, Romania, Slovakia, Slovenia Spain, Sweden, and the United Kingdom. In the Treaty of Nice, the EU proposed expansion of its membership, subject to approval by all of the current members. On October 21, 2002, Irish voters voted in favor of the proposal, completing the unanimous acceptance of the expansion.[7] Romania, Bulgaria, and Turkey have also applied for membership, but their applications have yet to be approved. In addition, Switzerland is preparing for a referendum on joining the EU. Obviously, the final composition of the EU will not be known for several more years.

eClass 8.2 International Business

INTERNATIONAL MARKETS AND FREE TRADE ZONES

Meg is excited about the marketing opportunities NAFTA provides for eClass. She believes that a strong potential market exists in Canada right now and that the Mexican market presents an even stronger potential market within the next few years. Yousef agrees with Meg, but he thinks that South America is the *real* opportunity for eClass. Yousef believes that NAFTA will expand soon and that any firm ready to capitalize on the opportunities in South America will be extremely successful. While Ani appreciates these sentiments, she believes that the firm's greatest chance for international sales lies with European customers, and she would like the firm to target the EU. They have asked you for your opinion. What will you tell them?

BUSINESS CONSIDERATIONS   Should the firm be concerned with an "either—or" position in considering international growth and expansion, or should it be more willing to consider planned expansion into both trade zones? Should the firm look only at these two trade zones (NAFTA and EU), or should it be concerned with expanding into any global markets that seem interested in the product?

ETHICAL CONSIDERATIONS   In considering expansion into new markets in other countries, what sorts of ethical issues might cause concern? Are there potential cultural issues the firm should consider? Might these potential cultural issues vary from one nation or free trade zone to another?

The purpose of the European Union is to establish a common customs tariff for outside nations importing goods into the community and to eliminate tariffs among EU members. In furtherance of this purpose, the EU has its own legislative, executive, and judicial branches. The treaty also covers the free movement of workers, goods, and capital within the community. It is aimed at accomplishing international cooperation. The EU is governed by the Council of Ministers, the European Commission, the European Parliament, and the Court of Justice. Exhibit 8.1 depicts the governing structure of the European Union.

Objectives Within the EU

The Treaty of Rome established four main objectives for the freedom of movement within the EU: the movement of goods, people, services, and capital. Since the treaty, the EU has developed a large body of law designed to achieve these four objectives.

Exhibit 8.1

The European Union

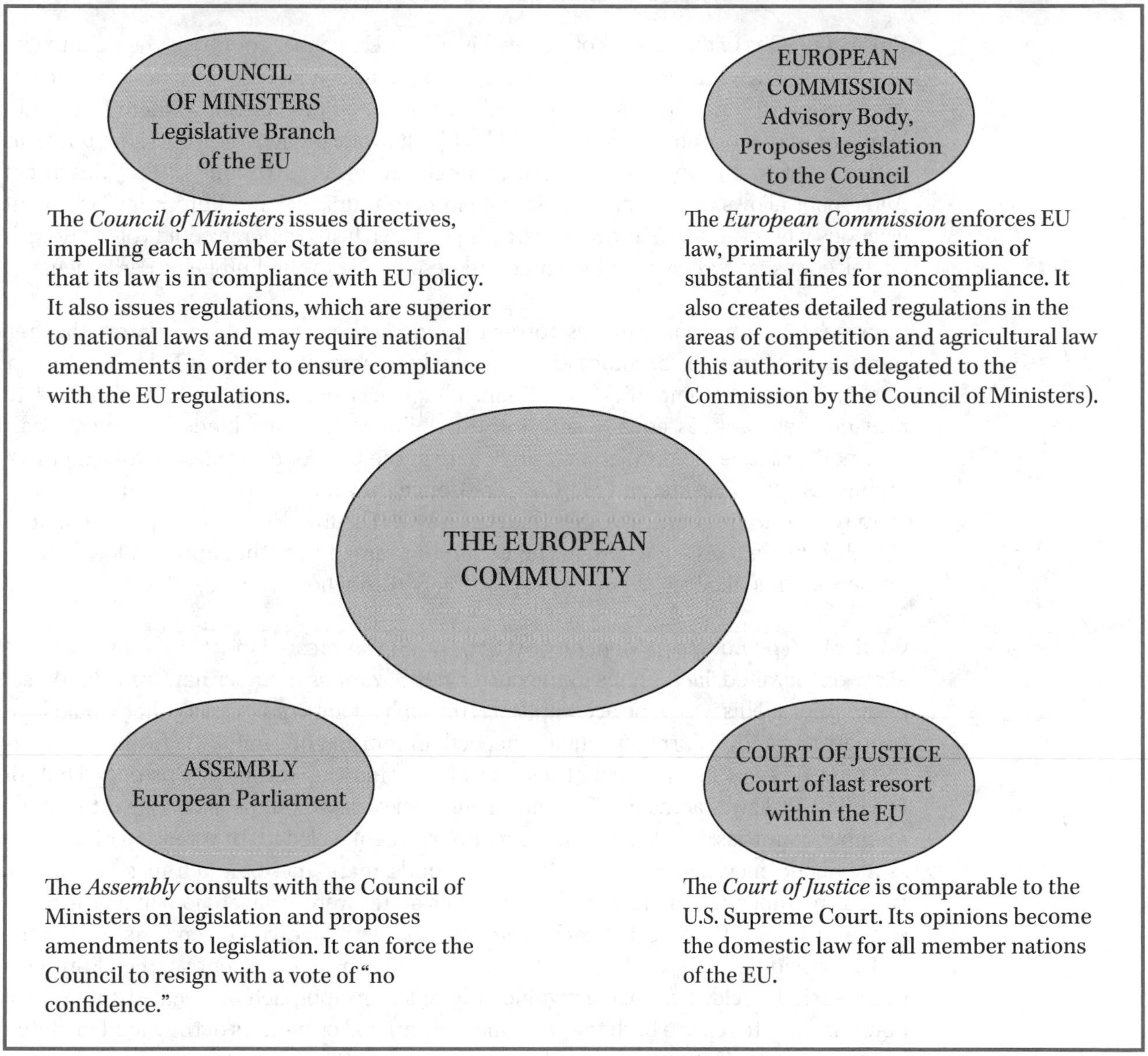

**COUNCIL
OF MINISTERS
Legislative Branch
of the EU**

The *Council of Ministers* issues directives, impelling each Member State to ensure that its law is in compliance with EU policy. It also issues regulations, which are superior to national laws and may require national amendments in order to ensure compliance with the EU regulations.

**EUROPEAN
COMMISSION
Advisory Body,
Proposes legislation
to the Council**

The *European Commission* enforces EU law, primarily by the imposition of substantial fines for noncompliance. It also creates detailed regulations in the areas of competition and agricultural law (this authority is delegated to the Commission by the Council of Ministers).

**THE EUROPEAN
COMMUNITY**

**ASSEMBLY
European Parliament**

The *Assembly* consults with the Council of Ministers on legislation and proposes amendments to legislation. It can force the Council to resign with a vote of "no confidence."

**COURT OF JUSTICE
Court of last resort
within the EU**

The *Court of Justice* is comparable to the U.S. Supreme Court. Its opinions become the domestic law for all member nations of the EU.

In 1986, the EU adopted the Single European Act, mandating the creation of a unified market by the end of 1992. In 1991, the heads of state of the EU member countries signed the Maastricht Treaty on European Political and Monetary Union, which strengthened the EU institutions and called for the establishment of a common currency, the European Currency Unit (ECU), by the close of the decade.

Goods   The EU has a customs union that is designed to eliminate customs duties among all member nations. In addition, the union has a common tariff with respect to trade between member nations and nonmember nations. As a result, no burdens are placed on trade between member nations, but a burden is placed on trade with countries outside the EU.

Persons   One of the benefits of citizenship in an EU member country is the right to free movement anywhere within the union. EU nationals and their families may reside anywhere in the EU. Students may enroll in vocational programs anywhere in the EU. Workers may work anywhere in the EU without work permits, on the same terms as nationals of that country. One of the more controversial provisions of the Maastricht Agreement allows any EU national to vote in both municipal and European Parliament elections wherever they may live. Thus, an Irish citizen living in Rome could vote in Rome's city elections, as well as vote for Rome's representative to the European Parliament.

Services   As the world moves toward a more service-oriented economy, the free movement of services becomes an increasingly important benefit of EU membership. Banks, insurance companies, and financial services businesses are now entitled to provide their services equally across the EU. Similarly, many kinds of professionals may now practice their professions anywhere in the EU. For example, doctors, dentists, architects, travel agents, and hairdressers—once they meet minimum requirements— all may practice in countries other than their own. The EU also gives people the right to establish businesses anywhere in the EU on the same terms that apply to local entrepreneurs, thus allowing them to operate freely throughout the EU.

Capital   The European Monetary System (EMS) was created in 1979. Its purpose is to allow only limited fluctuations in the currencies of various member nations from preset parity prices. This was to be accomplished through a joint credit facility that would lend support to an EMS currency when it needed an infusion of capital. To further stabilize the currencies of member countries, the EU created the European Currency Unit, or ECU. The ECU was actually a "basket" of currencies, based on the exchange rates of the member countries. In 1992, the Maastricht Agreement called for the creation of the ECU as a real currency, designed to replace the pounds, marks, pesos, and francs used in the various member nations. Not all of the member states were willing to join in on the move to the ECU, and the ECU left each member state with its own currency as well as the ECU, providing for some potential for confusion. Subsequently, the European Commission decided to take a significantly different approach. It decided to create a new currency to replace both the ECU and the national currencies of the member states.

This new EU currency, the "euro," was introduced effective January 1, 1999. The euro has been approved as the official currency of 15 of the 27 EU member states, and of 11other nations that are not part of the EU. The Euro is the single currency for more than 320 million people.[8] The euro replaced the ECU on January 1, 1999, at a conversion rate of 1:1. To help effectuate and smooth the transition, the European Commission enacted two Council Regulations. The first of these regulations provided for continuity of contracts, precision in conversion rates, and rounding rules to deal with this new currency.[9] The second regulation addressed the issues of substituting the euro for national currencies, the transition period for the changeover to the euro, the currency itself, and some other related issues or topics. Council Regulations were used because these regulations are applicable directly to the member states without the need for any national implementing legislation, debate, or other concerns.

Competition (Antitrust) Law in the EU

To create a truly common market, the EU needs extensive rules on competition. The Treaty of Rome set up the basic structure of EU competition law, and the Council of Ministers has issued a large body of directives and regulations. Further, the European Commission, as the law's main enforcer, has issued regulations and decisions implementing the law. The main concerns under competition law are covered in Article 85, Article 86, the area of negative clearances, and extraterritoriality.

Article 85   In a manner similar to U.S. antitrust law, Article 85 of the Treaty of Rome prohibits agreements, contracts, cartels, and joint activities that intend to restrict or distort competition within the EU. For example, price fixing, limiting or allocating markets, tying arrangements, and price discrimination are all prohibited under Article 85. However, Article 85 recognizes that some contracts benefit consumers by improving the production or distribution of goods or by promoting product improvements. The European Commission, therefore, can exempt activities from Article 85, either by issuing an individual exemption for a particular situation or by a block exemption for similarly situated businesses. An example of a block exemption would be the Commission guidelines for franchises; these tell potential franchise businesses which contract provisions are acceptable and which will bring Commission action.

Article 86   The second major EU competition law is Article 86 of the Treaty of Rome. It bars one or more companies from using a dominant market position to restrict or distort trade. Prohibited abuses of dominant positions include tying arrangements, price fixing, price discrimination, and other conduct similar to that prohibited under U.S. antitrust law. Either buyers or sellers can have dominant positions. The Commission and the Court of Justice of the European Union have defined dominance by a practical test: A firm or firms having the power to "act without taking into account their competitors, purchasers or suppliers" possesses a dominant position. (See *Europemballage Corp. v. Commission*, E.C.R. 215 (1973).) Thus, no specific market share is required; instead, the Commission looks at the firm's power to control suppliers and customers and its ability to prevent competition.

Negative Clearance   A business concerned about its actions violating either Article 85 or Article 86 can apply to the European Commission for permission to engage in activities that appear to violate EU competition laws. This permission is known as a negative clearance. If a negative clearance is granted, this means that the commission has reviewed the proposed conduct, and—if the business does what it has indicated—the commission will not prosecute it under either Article 85 or Article 86.

Extraterritoriality   The EU position on the reach of its power to regulate competition has expanded considerably over the last 20 years. It now appears that conduct anywhere can be subject to EU competition rules if it is intended to affect and does affect the EU market. The European Court of Justice has ruled that Article 85 has extraterritorial application if the conduct in question is intended to affect parties or businesses located within the European Union.[10] This should serve as a warning to companies that engage in activities lawful in their home country but that also affect the European market.

The North American Free Trade Agreement

One powerful alternative to the EU is the free trade partnership recently formed in North America under the North American Free Trade Agreement (NAFTA). The first piece of NAFTA went into effect in 1989, with the ratification of the Canada—U.S. Free Trade Agreement. As with its counterpart, the EU, one major purpose of the Canada—U.S. Free Trade Agreement was the elimination of tariffs on sales of goods between the two countries. The agreement called for the elimination of all tariffs between the nations by 1998. (As a practical matter, most such tariffs were already gone.) Goods qualify for tariff-free treatment if they are 50 percent North American in content. Also like the EU, the Canada—U.S. Free Trade Agreement made it easier for Canadian and U.S. citizens to work in each other's countries and for investments to flow across the border. Unlike the EU, however, the Free Trade Agreement did not set up a host of new institutions or require the two countries to give up much of their sovereignty. The only new institutions created by the agreement were binational panels of experts to be convened as needed to resolve trade disputes between the two countries. These expert panels replace the court systems for both countries in eligible cases.

In 1993, Mexico joined its Canadian and U.S. counterparts in the North American Free Trade Agreement. NAFTA creates a free trade area encompassing all of North America, a market large enough to compete successfully with Asian and European trade groups. There are still some concerns about NAFTA, but there is no concerted effort by any of the governments involved to rescind the agreement. Free trade with Mexico presents different concerns than it did with Canada. United States environmental and labor groups object to Mexico's reputation for having a lax legal environment, and Canadians worry about more jobs moving south.

There have been several proposals made over the past few years to increase and to strengthen NAFTA. In 1994, 34 nations from the Western Hemisphere agreed to negotiate a "Free Trade Area of the Americas" by 2005. Such a free trade zone would encompass virtually all of the Western Hemisphere, with 34 nations and more than 800 million citizens. This agreement was re-emphasized in April of 2001 when President Bush made his first speech to the Organization of American States. In this speech, the President reiterated the idea of a "Free Trade Area of the Americas" and pledged to lay the groundwork for such a zone.[11]

In July of 2002, the "Guayaquil Consensus"[12] was presented as the final document produced following a two-day summit meeting among leaders from ten

South American nations. The document proposes an increase in cooperation between the two major trading blocs in South America (Mersocur, made up of Brazil, Argentina, Uruguay, and Paraguay, with Chile and Bolivia as associate members; and the Andean Pact, made up of Venezuela, Colombia, Ecuador, Peru, and Bolivia), which will, in turn, lead to a better negotiating position with the United States. The ultimate goal is a hemisphere-wide free trade zone, a "Free Trade Area of the Americas," which is based on a combination of the members of NAFTA, Mersocur, and the Andean Pact into one large trade zone.

Other Free Trade Zones

There are a number of other free trades zones around the world, although none of the others possesses the economic might of either the European Union or NAFTA. For example, there are at least 4 free trade zones in Latin America. The Central American Common Market is comprised of Costa Rica, El Salvador, Guatemala, Honduras, Nicaragua, and Panama. The MERCOSUS Common Market is comprised of Argentina, Brazil, Paraguay, and Uruguay. The Andean Common Market is made up of Bolivia, Ecuador, Columbia, and Venezuela. And the Caribbean Community includes Barbados, Belize, Dominica, Jamaica, Trinidad-Tobago, Grenada, St. Kitts-Nevus-Anguilla, St. Lucia, and St. Vincent.

There are at least three African free trade zones as well. These include the Economic Community of West African States, the Economic and Customs Union of Central Africa, and the East African Community. There is also a treaty, the Treaty Establishing the African Economic Community, which has 51 signatories. This treaty is intended to create an African equivalent to the European Union.

Each of these free trade zones has the potential to influence international trade within its member states, and to help—or hinder—the economic growth and development of the member nations.

THE GENERAL AGREEMENT ON TARIFFS AND TRADE

Following World War II, the Western Allies envisioned an international economic organization that would provide leadership and coordination for international trade in the same manner as the United Nations was to provide in the political environment. A charter was drafted for an International Trade Organization (ITO) in 1948, but the charter was not adopted by enough nations, effectively shelving the ITO.

Prior to the proposed ITO charter, U.S. negotiators proposed a general agreement on tariffs and trades as a stepping-stone to prepare the way for ITO ratification. The Western Allies accepted this American proposal in 1947, creating the first General Agreement on Tariffs and Trade (GATT). When the ITO failed to generate sufficient support for ratification, GATT became the accepted framework for regulating international trade.

The GATT promoted free trade by seeking to reduce tariffs and quotas between nations. It promoted fair trade by defining such trade practices as unfair government subsidies of exports and dumping (selling goods below fair value on a foreign market). It also provided panels to resolve trade disputes. The GATT worked through "rounds" of discussions, during which countries agreed to reduce tariffs for all GATT members. The final round of GATT, known as the Uruguay Round, also raised non-goods-related issues, such as trade-related intellectual property rights, investment protection, services, and agricultural subsidies.

The Uruguay Round was frustrating for many of the participants, and a number of the objectives that were expected were not achieved. One major achievement, however, was the establishment of the World Trade Organization (WTO). The WTO is an international economic organization that is intended to provide leadership and coordination for international trade. Thus, 47 years after the ITO was defeated, a WTO has been created. The GATT did, indeed, provide an interim stepping-stone to the international organization, albeit for a much longer period than originally expected.

WORLD TRADE ORGANIZATION

The World trade Organization was created during the Uruguay Round of GATT discussions and officially established on January 1, 1995. However, the WTO is not merely an extension of GATT. The WTO has a completely different character than did GATT and a completely different mission. GATT was a multinational agreement, not an organization, and was intended to regulate trade in merchandise goods. There was no institutional foundation for GATT. By contrast, the WTO is an *organization* headquartered in Geneva, Switzerland, with a formal structure, a permanent staff, and a (sizable) operating budget. The WTO has expanded coverage to not only include merchandise goods, but to also cover some trade in services and to provide protection for intellectual property. As of July 2008, there were 153 member countries in the WTO, with several dozen more nations listed as "observers," most of which had applied for membership but which had not yet been admitted to the organization. (Among the nations that have applied for membership, but have not yet been admitted, are Russia and Vietnam.)[13]

The highest authority within the WTO is the Ministerial Conference, which is comprised of representatives from each member nation. The Ministerial Conference must meet at least once every two years and has the authority to make decisions on any matters under any of the multilateral trade agreements recognized by the WTO. While the Ministerial Conference is the highest authority, the day-to-day operations of the WTO are conducted by the General Council. The General Council serves as the Dispute Settlement Body of the WTO, and as the Trade Policy Review Body. It also reports to the Ministerial Conference. The General Council delegates a great deal of its responsibility to three other Councils—the Council for Trade in Goods, the Council for

Trade in Services, and the Council for Trade-Related Aspects of Intellectual Property Rights. Obviously, the WTO has a much wider responsibility than did GATT, covering areas other than international trade in goods.

Dispute resolution under the WTO is considerably quicker than was the case under GATT and promises to be much more effective. When controversies arise under the WTO, the dispute is submitted to a panel of trade experts. This panel will then have the authority to rule for one or the other of the complainants. When the panel rules for one of the nations, that nation will be given permission to retaliate against the other nation unless or until the losing nation changes the trade practice that was the subject of the dispute. In addition, the other member nations are expected to exert pressure on the losing nation to encourage a change in practice in order to ensure compliance. Since the member nations encompass a significant majority of world trade, such pressure and unofficial sanctions should prove to be very effective.

UNCITRAL

The United Nations Commission for International Trade Law (UNCITRAL) is perhaps the most important organization involved in addressing issues of private international trade. The U.N. General Assembly established UNCITRAL in 1966. This Commission attempts to provide harmonization of private international law in order to encourage and enhance international trade. UNCITRAL is actively involved in the development and enactment of U.N. Conventions dealing with international trade, such as the CISG and the Convention on the Recognition and Enforcement of Foreign Arbitral Awards. It is also actively involved in creating model laws and legal guides that are designed to serve as templates for the legislative bodies of any nations that are addressing international trade issues.

THE INTERNATIONAL ORGANIZATION FOR STANDARDIZATION (ISO)

The International Organization for Standardization (ISO) is an international body dedicated to developing uniform standards in a number of different areas, thus enhancing international trade. There are 163 nations and a myriad of standardizing bodies that belong to the ISO and help to establish the standards that will be followed by all of the member nations. According to the ISO:

"standards are documented agreements containing technical specifications or other precise criteria to be used consistently as rules, guidelines, or definitions of characteristics, to ensure that materials, products, processes and services are fit for their purposes."[14]

As an example, the ISO developed the standards used for credit cards, phone cards, and "smart" cards, specifying the optimal thickness for these cards, among other things. Such standards allow the cards to be used worldwide.

The ISO has developed the Agreement on Technical Barriers to Trade (TBT), also known as the "Standards Code," in an effort to reduce any impediments to trade due to differences between national regulations and standards. This Agreement "invites" the signatory nations to help ensure that the standardizing bodies within each nation accept and comply with a "Code of good practice for the preparation, adoption and application of standards" as embodied in the Agreement.[15] The ISO works closely with the World Trade Organization (WTO) in an effort to enhance the development of international trade. In fact, the TBT is also known as the WTO Code of Good Practice.

The ISO has also developed two sets of quality standards for businesses. The first, ISO 9000, deals with "quality management"; the second, ISO 14000, deals with environmental management. Firms may choose to seek ISO certification for their products under either of these plans. Such "certification" is voluntary for the firms seeking it, although the requirements can be quite rigorous. Neither ISO 9000 nor ISO 14000 is a *product* standard. Rather, both are *management system* standards. The *quality* standards of ISO 9000 address those features of a product or service that are required by customers of the firm and then address the production process that is followed by the firm as it seeks to ensure that these features are present. Similarly, ISO 14000 addresses what the firm does in its efforts to minimize any harmful effects on the environment caused by its activities.[16]

EXPORTS

In order to have truly international trade, some countries must import goods and other countries must export goods. Many students have a simplistic view of importing and exporting, not realizing that there are a significant number of problems to resolve in moving goods from one nation to another. These problems frequently begin with getting goods out of their nation of origin.

All exports leaving the United States must be licensed. For most goods and technology, the licensing process simply involves stamping a general license statement on the export documents. Some goods and technology, however, require validated licenses issued by the Department of Commerce, which maintains a commodity control list that gives the licensing status of thousands of export items. Businesses that export in violation of the export-licensing policy face criminal prosecution and loss of export privileges.

United States exports are regulated for three purposes. The first is to protect the nation in time of short supply. For example, Alaskan crude oil may be exported only if it does not adversely affect domestic supply. The second purpose is to protect national security. For example, exporting nuclear material to Iraq is not permitted currently. The third purpose is to further U.S. foreign policy interests. For example, all exports to Libya were banned in 1986 as a response to Libya's support of terrorism.

IMPORTS

Getting the goods out of their home country is only half the battle. Next, the goods must be moved into the nation of destination. All goods imported into a country must "pass" customs. Passing customs usually means paying a certain sum of money— known as a tariff or duty—at the port of entry, based on the type and value of the goods. For example, when Subaru imported the Brat motor vehicle into this country,

eClass 8.3 Manufacturing/Marketing

PRODUCTION AND LICENSE OF CALL-IMAGE INTERNATIONALLY

A European software manufacturer has expressed serious interest in selling the eClass program in Europe. However, while this firm would like to sell the software to colleges and universities in Europe, it does not want to import them. Instead, this firm has suggested that it be allowed to produce the software in a European-compatible version at its European locations and sell them within the EU. The manufacturer has suggested a licensing agreement that would designate it as the sole and exclusive distributor of any eClass software or other products for Europe. This manufacturer claims that by doing this both his firm and eClass will gain a significant share of the European market, and eClass will avoid any possible import duties, fees, or technical problems for its European sales. Ani is concerned that this could eventually be harmful to the firm, and she is also worried about possible repercussions involving the competition rules of the EU. She has asked for your advice on these matters. What will you tell her?

BUSINESS CONSIDERATIONS   What are the potential drawbacks for a domestic business if it allows a foreign firm to have an exclusive distributorship of its products and technology? Should the firm seek some other arrangement to better protect and position it for sales in other countries?

ETHICAL CONSIDERATIONS   Assume that the technology used by a business has substantial national security implications, but that the firm can acquire an export license. Without regard to profits, should the firm export its products despite the potential for compromising national security? What argument(s) support your response?

the U.S. Customs Service had to determine whether the Brat was a truck or a sports car. This was an important determination, since the duty to be paid differed depending on the category to which it rightfully belonged. If the Brat was a truck, it would require a larger duty than if it was a sports car. Subaru successfully argued that the Brat—despite the fact that it was a two-seat vehicle with a cargo bed—was a sports car. To further this argument, Subaru sold the Brat with two rear-facing plastic seats bolted into the bed of the cargo deck.

Once the type of import is determined, the analysis turns to its valuation. Is the proper valuation its wholesale value at the point of origin or destination, its retail value at the point of origin or destination, or a combination of those factors? In general, the transaction value of the goods is used. The transaction value is the price the importer paid for the goods, plus certain other necessary and related expenses.

The U.S. Customs Court has exclusive jurisdiction over civil actions challenging administrative decisions of the U.S. Customs Service.

One problem that is becoming increasingly serious involves the "dumping" of goods into foreign markets. "Dumping" involves the selling of goods in foreign markets at a price below that charged in the domestic market. Very commonly, a firm that is dumping goods in a foreign market has a protected market at home, so the firm is not concerned about retaliatory pricing in its home market. The firm can then sell its products in other countries at an unfair price, often to the detriment of the domestic firms in that other country. As a result, many nations have anti-dumping duties that are used to raise the cost of importing the goods, thus offsetting the cost advantage enjoyed by the dumped goods. The WTO has been involved in numerous cases involving allegations of dumping. For example, Mexico recently applied an anti-dumping duty to U.S. imports of high-fructose corn syrup, a sweetener used in soft drinks and food products. The U.S. challenged this duty, and the WTO determined that the duty violated the WTO trading rules. The WTO determined that Mexico had imposed the duty in order to protect its domestic sugar industry and not because U.S. firms were actually dumping the corn syrup in Mexico.[17]

LETTERS OF CREDIT

International traders also face special problems when paying for goods, services, and technology. In a domestic transaction, a seller can easily check the buyer's creditworthiness. If the buyer wrongfully rejects the goods, the seller is probably familiar enough with the market to know how to resell the goods or can have them returned fairly easily. In an international transaction, however, the seller will find it harder to check the buyer's financial status, harder to collect unpaid amounts from a foreign buyer, and more expensive or difficult to resell or reship rejected goods. To solve these problems posed by the international marketplace, buyers and sellers often use letters of credit to pay for goods, services, or technology.

When a letter of credit is used, the contract between buyer and seller will require the buyer to get a letter from its bank. The letter is the bank's promise that it will pay the contract price upon the seller's presentation of documents specified in the contract. To protect itself, the buyer will carefully specify which documents the seller must present to the bank to get payment. If the seller does not want to collect from a foreign bank, the contract can require the buyer to have a bank convenient to the seller that will confirm the letter of credit.

Suppose that Salesco, Inc., in California, contracts with Buyco, in Australia, for the sale of 5,000 electric motors at a total price of U.S. $5,000,000. The sales contract specifies that Buyco will pay by means of a letter of credit issued by First Australia Bank and confirmed by First San Diego Bank. The sales contract also specifies that payment will be made upon presentation of an invoice, packing list, export declaration, and negotiable on-board bill of lading (indicating the goods had been loaded on the ship). Buyco would go to its bank, First Australia, which would—for a fee—issue a letter stating the terms as specified in the contract. The bank would send that letter to First San Diego Bank, which would then write a letter to Salesco confirming the terms of the original letter of credit. Once Salesco obtained all the documents specified in the letter, it would go to its bank, First San Diego, which would compare the documents with the list in the letter of credit. If the documents were in order, First San Diego would pay Salesco and then forward the documents to First Australia, which would get payment from Buyco, then give Buyco the documents so it could take delivery of the motors. Exhibit 8.2 illustrates how the transaction would work.

Exhibit 8.2

Using a Letter of Credit in an International Sale of Goods

1. Buyco and Salesco enter into a sales contract, with Buyco agreeing to provide a letter of credit and Salesco agreeing to deliver 500 electric motors to Buyco.
2. Buyco goes to its bank, First Australia, to acquire a letter of credit to be paid to First San Diego Bank. The letter of credit specifies that payment is to be made on presentation to First San Diego Bank of an invoice, a packing list, an export declaration, and negotiable on-board bill of lading.
3. First Australia produces the letter of credit and sends it to First San Diego Bank.
4. First San Diego Bank receives the letter of credit and contacts Salesco confirming the terms of the letter of credit and the documents required in order for Salesco to receive payment.
5. Salesco arranges for the transportation of the goods, procures the necessary documents, and takes those documents to First San Diego Bank.
6. First San Diego Bank confirms that all required documents are present and in proper order and pays Salesco as per the letter of credit.
7. The paid letter of credit is returned to First Australia, which then pays First San Diego Bank for the letter of credit.
8. First Australia informs Buyco that the letter of credit has been paid and collects the amount of the letter, plus any fees, from Buyco.

As you can see, sellers are pleased to use letters of credit. They are paid for goods even before the buyer receives them, and they are paid even if the goods turn out to be defective. Buyers are less pleased to use letters of credit, but at least they know the goods are present, loaded, and ready for shipment before they pay for them. In order to further protect themselves, buyers can carefully specify which documents are required before the letter is to be paid. In some instances the buyer will also require a third party to inspect the goods as they are loaded for shipment. Buyers are also protected by the legal obligation that the documents the seller presents must strictly comply with the documents required in the letter of credit before the bank can pay the seller.

The importance of letters of credit is further emphasized by the fact that there is a United Nations Convention dealing with them, the *United Nations Convention on Independent Guarantees and Stand-by Letters of Credit,* drafted in New York in 1995. (This convention had only been signed by seven nations as of October 2002, although it went into effect January 1, 2000. The United States is the only major trading nation that had signed the convention. Other signatories include Belarus, Ecuador, El Salvador, Kuwait, Panama, and Tunisia.) In addition, International Standby Practices (ISP) 98 may now be incorporated into bank standby letters of credit, reflecting the importance of this area in international banking practices.[18] Letters of credit are dealt with in more detail in Chapter 15.

INFORMATION AND TECHNOLOGY

Historically, patent, copyright, and trademark protection extended only within the boundaries of each country. An inventor who wanted to protect an invention in any other countries would have to obtain a patent in each country. To complicate matters, some countries did not recognize exclusive patent rights in some kinds of products, such as pharmaceuticals. These countries felt it more important to deliver life-saving drugs to their people than to protect the profits of the pharmaceutical companies. Today, although no worldwide intellectual property rights exist, a real trend has grown toward international protection of copyrights, patents, and trademarks. In 1988, for example, the United States became the 80th member of the Berne Convention for the Protection of Literary and Artistic Works. A copyright holder who publishes a book in the United States will now receive the same protection in other member countries that local authors do.

The area of patent law is also moving toward international protection. The European Patent Convention allows only one filing and one patent examination to obtain protection in 18 countries. Similarly, the Patent Cooperation Treaty also allows only one patent application and examination to serve as a basis for patent filings in up to 47 countries, as of 1991.

Trademark law has also moved toward some international recognition, though not as quickly as the other areas of intellectual property protection. The Madrid Agreement—to which 42 countries (but not the United States) belonged as of

1996—allows one application to provide protection in all member countries. The EU has moved toward an EU-wide recognition of trademarks, but does not yet have uniformity. United States businesses have faced serious problems in recent years with counterfeit goods. Levi Strauss, Apple Computer, and other companies have reported large revenues lost due to imports that counterfeit company trademarks or patents. The United States has toughened its enforcement of the laws designed to oppose these counterfeiters. Section 337 of the Tariff Act of 1930 was amended in 1988 to allow any owner of a registered U.S. intellectual property right, who believes that an import infringes on that right, to apply to the U.S. International Trade Commission for an order banning the goods. This order can also fine the importer up to $100,000 per day or twice the domestic value of the goods. In addition, Congress amended the Trade Act of 1974 with a section called "Special 301," requiring the U.S. trade representative to identify countries that do not protect U.S. intellectual property rights. Once identified, the United States will negotiate improvements with those countries. If no improvements result, the United States must retaliate against those countries. Special 301 has been effective in getting many countries to improve their intellectual property laws.

NATIONALIZATION

Nationalization of privately owned business entities is a risk that exists primarily in developing countries. Nationalization is the act of converting privately owned businesses into governmentally owned businesses. In general, international trade can be carried on without fear of nationalization; the exporter merely ensures that payment is guaranteed before shipment of goods. However, international investment is not so simple a matter. To build and operate an aluminum plant or an oil refinery requires a large investment of capital. If, during the time the investment is paying for itself, it is nationalized, the result is usually a loss to the investor. It is for that reason, as well as for others, that international investment decisions usually require a shorter payback period than national investment decisions.

Is nationalization legal? It depends on your perspective. For the most part, from the viewpoint of the country that nationalizes a private property, some act of the legislature or head of state makes it legal within that country. From the viewpoint of international law, however, it may not be legal. If it does not comply with international law, it is termed a confiscation, not a nationalization. If it does comply with international law, it is called an expropriation. The key element is whether the state had a proper public purpose and, in addition, whether "just compensation" was paid for the property. No matter what it is called, there is little that can be done about it if it occurs. One means of insuring an investment against the risk of loss is by utilizing the facilities of the Overseas Private Investment Corporation (OPIC). OPIC furnishes low-cost insurance against nationalization, confiscation, lack of convertibility of foreign earnings, and general loss due to insurrection, revolution, or war. OPIC currently insures more than 400 projects in 50 countries.

ACT OF STATE DOCTRINE

One reason for the importance of seeking insurance protection for overseas investments is the act of state doctrine. The doctrine states that every sovereign state is bound to respect the independence of every other sovereign state and that the courts of one country will not sit in judgment on the acts of the government of another performed within its own borders. The concept of the act of state doctrine is embedded in the notion of sovereign immunity. Certainly each sovereign state recognizes all other states' sovereignty. But the act of state doctrine is not a specific rule of international law. International law does not require that nations follow this rule; and in the United States, the Constitution does not require it. Judicial decisions of the United States, however, have recognized the doctrine. The doctrine is based on the theory that a nation is not qualified to question the actions of other nations taken on their own soil. In fact, denouncing the public decisions of other nations can have a decidedly adverse effect on the conduct of a nation's foreign policy.

But what about a situation in which a U.S. bank held promissory notes issued by a group of Costa Rican banks payable in the United States in U.S. dollars? Would there be a lack of jurisdiction if the Costa Rican government, after the notes were signed, refused to allow the payments in U.S. dollars? Does the act of state doctrine apply? The Second Circuit said an emphatic no when it held that the situs (location) of the debt was in the United States and not Costa Rica and, therefore, the doctrine did not apply. [See *Allied Bank v. Banco Credito*, 757 F.2d 516 (2d Cir. 1985).]

SOVEREIGN IMMUNITY

In the traditions of international law, all nations are equal and sovereign. Thus, a nation is immune from suit for its actions, either by individuals or by other countries. To be sued, a nation must agree to give up its sovereign immunity. For example, the United States passed the Federal Tort Claims Act to allow individuals to sue the U.S. government for negligent or wrongful acts. On an international level, the doctrine of sovereign immunity causes businesses some trouble, especially because many governments operate businesses such as airlines, banks, auto companies, and even computer firms. The United States has taken actions to limit the effect of sovereign immunity in its courts. In 1976, Congress enacted the Foreign Sovereign Immunities Act, which declared that U.S. courts would not recognize sovereign immunity when the sovereign engaged in commercial, rather than political, activities. So, for example, a state-owned bank could be subject to suit over its failure to pay a letter of credit. The United States has also negotiated many bilateral investment treaties, containing provisions for other governments to waive the right to claim sovereign immunity.

The Foreign Sovereign Immunities Act was amended in 1996 with the passage of the Antiterrorism and Effective Death Penalty Act,[19] which permits American citizens to sue those foreign states officially classified as terrorist states for terrorist conduct that results in the death or injury of an American citizen. The Act also provides for punitive damages to be assessed against the terrorist state if it is found guilty of the prohibited conduct. (This provision is commonly referred to as the "Flatow Amendment.")

DISPUTE RESOLUTION

The best method of resolving an international business dispute is by providing a means for handling that contingency at the time the international transaction is created. Three principal options for settling a dispute are available: the International Court of Justice, national courts, and arbitration.

The International Court of Justice

The International Court of Justice (ICJ) has limited value in solving international business disputes. The ICJ is an agency of the United Nations, and its procedures were established in the United Nations Charter. A private person has no standing before the ICJ. Only nations may appear before the court. A private person who has a grievance against a state not his or her own must first secure the agreement of his or her own state to present the claim. If his or her state asserts the claim, the issue then becomes whether the other state will allow the matter to appear before the ICJ for resolution. Each state must agree to be bound by the court's decision; if they do not, there is no jurisdiction to hear the claim. Exhibit 8.3 lists the authorities the ICJ uses in reaching its decisions.

Exhibit 8.3

Authorities Used by the International Court of Justice

I   International Conventions
(treaties)

II   International Custom
(general practices accepted as law)

III General Legal Principles
(recognized by "civilized nations")

IV   Judicial Decisions and Teachings of Experts
(after it examines I, II, and III)

V   Ex Aequo at Bono
(that which is just and fair)

The International Court of Justice will use I, II, III, and IV as they apply. It will only use V if the parties agree.

National Courts

A private person can usually resort to settlement of a dispute with a foreign nation by seeking redress through the courts of that state. Private persons can sometimes obtain adequate relief in their native state's judicial system. For example, a favorable judgment from a U.S. court may be filed in another country and, under certain conditions, can execute on assets in the foreign country on the basis of the other country's judicial decision. U.S. courts are likely to enforce a judgment obtained in another country following a full and fair trial, before an impartial court, with an opportunity for the defendant to be heard. A biased or corrupt court or a case that did not give a defendant an adequate chance to defend against the claims of the plaintiff would probably lead a U.S. court to require a plaintiff to retry the entire claim in a U.S. court, rather than enforce the prior judgment.

The recognition of foreign judgments is not a matter of international law, but rather a matter of comity. As the U.S. Supreme Court stated in the landmark case of *Hilton v. Guyot*, 159 U.S. 113 (1895), comity is "the recognition which one nation allows within its territory to the . . . acts of another nation, having due regard both to international duty and convenience, and to the rights of its own citizens, or other persons. . . ." Comity is a matter of respect, goodwill, and courtesy that one nation gives to another, at least partly with the hope that the other nation will return the favor.

Arbitration

For variety of reasons, a particular international dispute may not be appropriate for resolution in the ICJ or national courts. In that case, international arbitration might be the best course of action. Many international commercial contracts include provisions for using arbitration. One hundred thirty-two countries, including the United States, have signed the 1958 United Nations Convention on the Recognition and Enforcement of Foreign Arbitral Awards (T.I.A.S. No. 6997) as of October 2002. The countries that have signed this convention have agreed to use their court systems to recognize and enforce arbitration decisions. The fact that so many nations have ratified this U.N. convention provides fairly persuasive evidence that arbitration is becoming the preferred method for resolving disputes in international business.

Online Dispute Resolution (ODR)

A new form of alternate dispute resolution (ADR) has recently developed. This new form takes advantage of technology to provide a method for resolving disputes online, without requiring either of the parties to travel or to be overly inconvenienced. Online Dispute Resolution (ODR) is now available in a number of circumstances. NAFTA has provisions for online dispute resolution, especially in a controversy between a consumer and a business, to encourage consumers to assert their rights even though the business from which they purchased the goods in dispute is in another nation. A significant number of e-commerce businesses, businesses that may well have customers in a number of countries, have provided for ODR as a part of the sales contract.

ODR is likely to involve mediation as the preferred method for resolving disputes. Each party submits its position to the online mediator, who then suggests settlement options to each party. However, the potential for growth is tremendous. All that is required to utilize this method is access to the Internet and a willingness to use the system. ODR can be synchronous or asynchronous; it can be extremely simple or relatively complex; and while it is now normally used only for mediation, it can also be used for arbitration. While this method of dispute resolution is relatively new, it is likely to become extremely common and widespread in a relatively short time.

Contemporary Case

TREIBACHER INDUSTRIE, A.G. v. ALLEGHENY TECHNOLOGIES, INC.

464 F.3d 1235, 2006 U.S. App. LEXIS 23252 (11th Cir. 2006)

FACTS Treibacher, an Austrian vendor of hard metal powders, agreed to sell specified quantities of tantalum carbide (TaC), a hard metal powder, to TDY Industries for delivery to "consignment." TDY originally intended to use the TaC in manufacturing operations in Alabama. However, after it received some of the TaC, TDY refused to take delivery of the balance of TaC. TDY also informed Treibacher that it (TDY) had no obligation to take delivery of or to pay for any TaC that it did not wish to use. Treibacher eventually sold the balance of the TaC, but at a lower price than called for in its contract with TDY. As a result, Treibacher filed suit against TDY for the balance of the amount that Treibacher would have received had TDY honored the original contract. At trial, the parties disputed the meaning of the term "consignment" as used in the original contract. TDY asserted that under common usage of trade, "consignment" meant that no sale occurred until

TDY actually accepted and used the product. Treibacher countered that, through course of dealings between these parties, "consignment" created a binding obligation to pay for all the goods ordered. Each party contends that its interpretation of "consignment" is consistent with the provisions of the CISG, the controlling statute in this case.

ISSUE Should usage of trade or course of dealings control in defining a word or a term under the CISG?

HOLDING Yes. The CISG specifically provides that usages they have agreed to and practices they have established are binding on the parties.

REASONING Excerpt from the opinion of Circuit Judge Tjoflat:

"We begin our analysis by discussing the CISG, which governs the formation of and rights and obligations under contracts for the international sale of goods ... Article 9 of the CISG provides the rules for interpreting the terms of contracts. Article 9(1) states that, "parties are bound by any usage to which they have agreed and by any practices which they have established between themselves." Article 9(2) then states that, "parties are considered, unless otherwise agreed, to have impliedly made applicable to their contract . . . a usage of which the parties knew or ought to have known and which in international trade is widely known to . . . parties to contracts of the type involved in the particular trade concerned." Article 8 of the CISG governs the interpretation of the parties' statements and conduct. A party's statements and conduct are interpreted according to that party's actual intent "where the other party knew . . . what that intent was," . . . but, if the other party was unaware of that party's actual intent, then "according to the understanding that a reasonable person . . . would have had in the same circumstances," . . . To determine a party's actual intent, or a reasonable interpretation thereof, "due consideration is to be given to all relevant circumstances of the case including the negotiations, any practices which the parties have established between themselves, usages and any subsequent conduct of the parties." . . .

The district court did not commit clear error in finding that, in their course of dealings, TDY and Treibacher defined the term "consignment" to require TDY to accept and pay for all of the TaC specified in each contract. The parties do not dispute that they executed, between 1993 and 2000, a series of contracts in which Treibacher agreed to sell certain hard metal powders, such as TaC, to TDY. In each instance, TDY discussed its needs with Treibacher, after which Treibacher and TDY executed a contract whereby Treibacher agreed to sell a fixed quantity of materials at a fixed price for delivery to "consignment." Treibacher then delivered to TDY the specified quantity of materials—sometimes in installments, depending upon TDY's needs. TDY kept the materials it received from Treibacher in a "consignment store," where the materials were labeled as being from Treibacher and segregated from other vendors' materials. As it withdrew the materials from the consignment store for use, TDY published "usage reports," which documented the

amounts of materials withdrawn. TDY sent the usage reports to Treibacher, and Treibacher, in turn, sent TDY invoices for the amounts of materials withdrawn at the price specified in the relevant contract. TDY then paid the invoices when they came due. In each instance, TDY ultimately withdrew and paid for the full quantity of materials specified in each contract.

A particularly telling interaction, the existence of which the parties do not dispute, occurred in February 2000, when a TDY employee . . . sent an e-mail to his counterpart at Treibacher . . . expressing TDY's desire to return unused portions of a hard metal powder, titanium carbonitride ("TiCN"), which Treibacher had delivered. [Treibacher's agent] . . . explained that TDY could not return the TiCN because TDY was contractually obligated to purchase the materials; Treibacher had delivered the TiCN as part of a quantity of TiCN that it was obligated to provide TDY under a contract executed in December 1999 . . . TDY subsequently used the TiCN and . . . paid. This interaction—evidencing TDY's acquiescence in Treibacher's interpretation of the contract—along with TDY's practice, between 1993 and 2000, of using and paying for all of the TaC specified in each contract amply support the district court's finding that the parties, in their course of dealings, construed their contracts to require TDY to use and pay for all of the TaC specified in each contract. . . .

In sum, the district court properly determined that, under the CISG, the meaning the parties ascribe to a contractual term in their course of dealings establishes the meaning of that term in the face of a conflicting customary usage of the term. The district court was not clearly erroneous in finding that Treibacher and TDY understood their contracts to require TDY to purchase all of the TaC specified in each contract and that Treibacher took reasonable measures to mitigate its losses after TDY breached. Accordingly, the judgment of the district court is AFFIRMED."

You Be the Judge

In 1981, Harry Carpenter, who was then chairman of the board and chief executive officer of petitioner W. S. Kirkpatrick & Co., Inc. (Kirkpatrick), learned that the Republic of Nigeria was interested in contracting for the construction and equipment of an aeromedical center at Kaduna Air Force Base in Nigeria. He made arrangements with Benson "Tunde" Akindele, a Nigerian citizen, whereby Akindele would endeavor to secure the contract for Kirkpatrick. It was agreed that, in the event the contract was awarded to Kirkpatrick, Kirkpatrick would pay to two Panamanian entities controlled by Akindele a "commission" equal to 20 percent of the contract price, which would in turn be given as a bribe to officials of the Nigerian Government. In accordance with this plan, the contract was awarded to petitioner W. S. Kirkpatrick & Co., International (Kirkpatrick International), a wholly owned subsidiary of Kirkpatrick; Kirkpatrick paid the promised "commission" to the appointed Panamanian entities; and those funds were disbursed as bribes. All parties agree that Nigerian law prohibits both the payment and the receipt of bribes in connection with the award of a government contract.

Environmental Tectonics Corporation, International, an unsuccessful bidder for the Kaduna contract, learned of the 20 percent "commission" and brought the matter to the attention of the Nigerian Air Force and the United States Embassy in Lagos. Following an investigation by the Federal Bureau of Investigation, the United States Attorney for the District of New Jersey brought charges against both Kirkpatrick and Carpenter for violations of the Foreign Corrupt Practices Act of 1977. Both parties entered guilty pleas.

Environmental Tectonics then brought a civil action in the United States District Court for the District of New Jersey against Carpenter, Akindele, petitioners, and others, seeking damages under the Racketeer Influenced and Corrupt Organizations Act, the Robinson-Patman Act, and the New Jersey Anti-Racketeering Act. The defendants moved to dismiss the complaint on the ground that the action was barred by the act of state doctrine. This case has been brought in *your* court. How will *you* rule on the motion to dismiss? What fact or factor is most influential to you in reaching your decision? [See *Kirkpatrick Co. v. Environmental Tectronics Corp.*, 493 U.S. 400 (1990).]

Summary

We live in an interdependent world. Consequently, businesspersons should be aware of the international implications of their business dealings. In addition to being familiar with the laws and customs of the countries where they do business, managers must be aware that competition and employment laws, among others, may reach beyond national borders.

Global trade agreements (such as GATT and the WTO) and regional free trade zones (such as the EU and NAFTA) are becoming much more important in the world economy. They provide businesses with frameworks for trade and, increasingly, with efficient access to large markets. These organizations have substantially changed the rules of the game in international business recently, and familiarity with them is essential if a businessperson desires success in the international arena. These organizations will serve as models for others all over the world in the years to come.

There is an increasing emphasis on private international trade law. Organizations such as UNCITRAL and UNIDROIT are attempting to draft model statutes that will help to increase international trade and to provide uniform coverage for businesses that operate across national borders. The International Organization for Standardization (ISO) encourages businesses to adhere to certain quality standards, and also encourage its member nations and organizations to look for methods of implementing such standards as broadly as possible. The WTO and the ISO are working together in a few areas to develop uniform standards and to establish codes of good conduct.

Changes in international trade, and in the emphasis placed on global development, have led to a number of "new" business concerns. Although imports and exports, labor, and information and technology have been recognized as important aspects of domestic trade for years, it is only recently that they have gained similar recognition in the international arena. Continuing development of regulation in these areas will shape the global market in the near future.

One risk to international business investment is nationalization. Nationalization is the taking of private property by a national government. If the nationalization complies with international law, it is called an expropriation. If it does not, it is called a confiscation. The act of state doctrine is used to justify the position that one country will not stand in judgment of the actions of other countries carried on within their own territories.

Sovereign immunity is a doctrine of law that a sovereign government cannot be sued unless it allows itself to be sued. International law provides three mechanisms for the resolution of international business disputes. The International Court of Justice (ICJ) is the appropriate forum when one nation sues another, provided that each nation agrees to the suit. Domestic courts are used for the resolution of disputes between citizens of different nations. Lastly, arbitration is used in international as well as domestic business disputes.

Dispute resolution is also changing as international business continues to grow and to develop. The International Court of Justice and the World Trade Organization have some provisions for dealing with transnational trade disputes. However, both of these are somewhat formal and require that a nation be involved before either will assert any jurisdiction. Of course, national courts can be used, as they have been used for resolving trade disputes within their respective nations for years. However, this is likely to be expensive, even by lawsuit standards, and at least one of the parties is likely to have a "home court advantage" that may be difficult to overcome. As a result, international trade is more likely to rely on non-judicial resolution. Arbitration has been a staple of international trade for generations, and it will continue to be used to resolve many disputes. And a new method, ODR, has recently been introduced and has tremendous potential as a method of resolving transnational disputes in a relatively quick and inexpensive manner.

Discussion Questions

1. Which recent agreements and enactments have increased the accuracy of the term "global village" in the area of international business? What, if anything, seems to be operating in a manner contrary to the concept of developing a global village?

2. What are the arguments in favor of restricting the application of a nation's laws to its territorial limits? What are the arguments in favor of expanding the application of a nation's laws beyond its territorial limits? Which set of arguments is more persuasive ethically?

3. What is the significance of the Treaty of Rome? How does the Treaty of Rome compare with the North American Free Trade Agreement (NAFTA)?

4. How do the United Nations Convention on Contracts for the International Sale of Goods (CISG), the General Agreement on Tariffs and Trade (GATT), and the World Trade Organization (WTO) affect international trade? To which types of international trade contracts does each of these (CISG, GATT, WTO) apply?

5. Three doctrines are often applied to international dealings: comity, act of state, and sovereign immunity. How does each of these doctrines affect international dealings and potential legal controversies?

Case Problems and Writing Assignments

1. In 1972, Ferdinand Marcos, President of the Philippines, incorporated Arelma, S.A. under Panamanian law. Arelma then opened a brokerage account with Merrill Lynch in New York, depositing $2 million. By 2000, the account had grown to nearly $35 million. During his presidency there were numerous allegations of criminal conduct and misfeasance, including human rights violations. A class action lawsuit (hereafter the Pimental class) by and on behalf of some 9,539 human rights victims was filed against Marcos in the U.S. District Court in Hawaii, resulting in a judgment against Marcos for nearly $2 billion. The Pimental class then claimed the right to attach the Arelma assets held by Merrill Lynch to satisfy a portion of its judgment.

When Marcos fled the Philippines in 1986, the Republic of the Philippines established a Commission that was charged with attempting to recover property wrongfully taken by Marcos during his reign as president. This Commission and the government of the Republic of the Philippines also claimed the right to attach the assets in the Merrill Lynch account.

Merrill Lynch filed an interpleader motion (a motion by a third person asking the court to determine which of two or more competing parties is entitled to property in the hands of the third person) to bring the government of the Republic of the Philippines and the Commission into the proceedings. The Republic of the Philippines and the Commission moved to dismiss the proceedings, asserting that sovereign immunity exempted them from the proceedings and that the proceedings could not be properly conducted without their participation.

The District Court refused the motion, dismissed the two parties from the proceedings, and awarded the Arelma assets to the Pimental class. The Republic and the Commission appealed. How should the court decide this appeal? How is sovereign immunity a factor in this case? [See *Republic of the Philippines v. Pimentel*, 128 S. Ct. 2180, 171 L. Ed. 2d 131, 2009 U.S. LEXIS 4889 (2008).]

286 Part I: Foundations of Law and the U.S. Legal System

2. PetroEcuador contracted with BP to purchase 140,000 barrels of unleaded gasoline. The contract specified that the gasoline have a gum content of less than 3 milligrams per 100 milliliters and an oxidation stability of 240 to be determined at the point of departure. BP purchased the gasoline from Shell Oil Company and time-chartered the M/T Tiber to transport the cargo from Texas to Ecuador. Following testing at the point of departure, the gasoline was loaded on board the M/T Tiber. When the cargo arrived in Ecuador, PetroEcuador rejected the shipment because the gasoline did not meet the contractual specifications for gum content or oxidation stability. BP later sold the gasoline to another purchaser at a loss of nearly $2 million.

BP sued the Tiber interests for breach of its duties and obligations under the charter party and bill of lading and for breach of bailment. BP also sued PetroEcuador for breach of contract and for wrongfully drawing against BP's letter of guarantee. BP and PetroEcuador settled their dispute, and BP continued with its cause of action against Tiber. BP's claim against Tiber hinged on the application of bailment law, which requires the bailor (BP) to make a prima facie case that the cargo was delivered to the bailee (Tiber) in good condition and was damaged while in the bailee's possession. The burden then shifts to the bailee to produce affirmative evidence that it exercised ordinary care. Tiber argued that its liability should be limited under the provisions of the Carriage of Goods by Sea Act. Application of this act would greatly reduce the potential liability of Tiber. However, Tiber did not challenge the application of the provisions of bailment law rather than the provisions of the COGSA at the district court level.

Should the Court of Appeals allow Tiber to raise the issue of the applicability of the COGSA at this stage when it was not raised at the trial? Explain and justify your answer. [See *BP Oil International, Ltd. v. Empresa Estatal Petroleos de Ecuador*, 2008 U.S. Appl LEXIS 914 (2008).]

3. Alberto-Culver, an American manufacturer based in Illinois, purchased from Scherk, a German citizen, three enterprises owned by Scherk and organized under the laws of Germany and Liechtenstein, together with all trademark rights of these enterprises. The sales contract, which was negotiated in the United States, England, and Germany, signed in Austria, and closed in Switzerland, contained express warranties by petitioner that the trademarks were unencumbered, and a clause provided that "any controversy or claim [that] shall arise out of this agreement or the breach thereof" would be referred to arbitration before the International Chamber of Commerce in Paris, France, and that Illinois laws would govern the agreement and its interpretation and performance. Subsequently, after allegedly discovering that the trademarks were subject to substantial encumbrances, Alberto-Culver offered to rescind the contract. Scherk refused, and Alberto-Culver filed suit for breach of contract and fraud. Scherk moved to dismiss the action, or, in the alternative, to stay the proceedings pending arbitration of the dispute before the ICC in Paris. The district court denied the motions by Scherk, ruling that the arbitration clause was unenforceable. The court of appeals affirmed, and Scherk appealed to the U.S. Supreme Court. How should the Supreme Court rule in this case? What reasons can you posit in support of the decision the Supreme Court should reach? If the contract was between two American businesses, would a different result be reached by the courts? [See *Scherk v. Alberto-Culver Co.*, 417 U.S. 506 (1974)].

Notes

1. U.S. International Trade in Goods and Services, 2000-2007, U.S. Census Bureau, released June 10, 2008, http://www.census.gov/compendia/statab/tables/09s1260.pdf.

2. Ibid.

3. Paul A. Herbig & Hugh E. Kramer, "Do's and Don't's of Cross-Cultural Negotiations," *Industrial Marketing Management*, 21 (1992) 287.

4. 473 U.S. 614 (1985).

5. 15 U.S.C. § 6a.

6. 15 U.S.C. § 78dd.

7. See "The Nice Treaty Ratification," The European Union Constitution, http://www.unizar.es/euroconstitucion/Treaties/Treaty_Nice_Rat.htm (accessed 7/30/2010); see also "EU enlargement after the Irish referendum," Socialism Today (Issue 70, November, 2002), http://www.socialismtoday.org/70/eu.html (accessed 7/30/2010).

8. "Euro—The Official Currency of the European Union," CoolPennyStocks.com (July 30, 2010), http://www.unizar.es/euroconstitucion/Treaties/Treaty_Nice_Rat.htm (accessed 7/30/2010).

9. Council Regulation (EC) No 2866/98 of 31 December 1998 on the conversion rates between the euro and the currencies of the Member States adopting the euro, EUR-Lex, http://eur-lex.europa.eu/LexUriServ/LexUriServ.do?uri=CELEX:31998R2866:EN:NOT/.

10. *Re Wood Pulp Cartel et al. v. Commission*, 4 C.M.L.R. 901 (1988).

11. Ian Christopher McCaleb, "Bush Envisions Western Hemisphere Free-Trade Zone," cnn.com, April 17, 2001, www.cnn.com/2001/ALLPOLITICS/04/17/bush.oas/.

12. "South American summit ends with free-trade agreement," *Roanoke Times*, Sunday, July 28, 2002, p. A16 (Associated Press).

13. "Understanding the WTO, Members and Observers," WTO Web site, at http://www.wto.org.

14. "What are standards," ISO Web site (7/17/2002), http://www.iso.ch/iso/en/aboutiso/introduction/index.html/. See also the ISO homepage at http://www.iso.org/iso/home.html for much more information.

15. "The Agreement on Technical Barriers to Trade (TBT)," ISO Web site (7/30/2010), http://www.wto.org/english/tratop_e/tbt_e/tbt_e.htm/.

16. "The Basics," ISO Web site, http://www.iso.ch/iso/en/iso9000-14000/tour/plain.html/.

17. "WTO Appellate Body rules in favor of U.S. in challenge to Mexico antidumping duties on high fructose corn syrup," World Trade Organization, Vol. 7, No. 11 (Transnational Law Associates, LLC, International Law Updates, Nov. 2001).

18. Robert J. Spjut, "Documentary and Standby Letters of Credit," EagleTraders.com, http://www.eagletraders.com/advice/doc_standby_letters_credit.htm/.

19. 28 U.S.C. §§ 1602-1011.

Part II

Contracts

The law of contracts forms the foundation of business law. Virtually every aspect of business involves contracts, as does much of a person's everyday life. When you rent an apartment, you sign—or orally agree to—a contract known as a lease. When you purchase food or arrange for utilities, you enter into a contract. When you take a job, you enter into a contract of employment. Any purchase of goods, services, or real estate involves some form of contract.

This part of the book examines the traditional elements of contract law—the common law of contracts. Later parts of the book consider various special types of contracts, among them sales, negotiable instruments, and secured transactions (that is, credit arrangements, covered by Article 9 of the UCC, in which the creditor retains a security interest in certain assets of the debtor). Increasingly, you will be contracting online, so an understanding of the "rules of engagement" for e-commerce contracts is vital as well. Keep in mind that all these specialized forms are merely variations on the basic form. To understand these specialized forms of contracts, you first need a thorough understanding of the common law of contracts presented in this part.

9

Introduction to Contract Law and Contract Theory

Agenda

eClass will enter into a large number of contracts as the business develops. eClass will have contracts with suppliers, customers, and employees. eClass is likely to have contracts with its insurer and its landlord, if it rents space. Ani, Meg, and Yousef will need to know how contract formation occurs, what types of contract to enter, and what rights and liabilities they undertake as a result of contract formation. It is quite likely they will turn to you for help and assistance at many stages along the way. Be prepared! You never know when the firm or one of its members will need your help or advice.

MILLER v. STEVENS

224 Mich. 626, 1923 Mich. LEXIS 972 (Sup. Ct. 1923)

FACTS Miller's business was selling coal. In the winter of 1920-21, Miller and George Stevens boarded at the same hotel in Grand Rapids where they became "hotel acquaintances." During their casual talks, Miller learned that Stevens owned a dyeing business known as the Parisian Dye House. Stevens was considering selling the business because he could not give it proper attention. The next summer, while Miller was trying to sell some coal to M. Deebs, he found out that Deebs was interested in starting a cleaning and dyeing plant. Recalling what Stevens had said about his dye house, Miller phoned Stevens to see if Stevens still wanted to sell his dye house and if Miller should send a man out to see him. Stevens indicated that he was willing to sell, and Miller brought the parties together. Negotiations resulted in the sale of the dye house to Deebs for $6,000. Prior to this time, Miller had never taken part as an agent or broker, in buying or selling or exchanging or offering for sale any business, business property, or good will of a business for others. Miller never advertised or held himself out as engaged in such business. At the circuit court, Miller recovered a judgment of $300 for his services in procuring Deebs to buy the business.

ISSUE Is Miller entitled to compensation based on an implied in fact contract?

HOLDING Yes, Miller is entitled to the compensation awarded by the lower court.

REASONING Excerpts from the opinion of Steere, J.:

... [The court also considered whether Miller violated a state statute making it unlawful for a person to engage in the business of "a business chance" broker without first obtaining a license. The statute coined and defined the title business chance broker.] The proofs are that plaintiff had never directly or indirectly offered or rendered services for others of the kind covered by the act prior to the occasion involved here. The question of his guilt turns on the one transaction. If his services on that occasion class him as a "business chance broker," ... he could not recover, under prevailing authorities. ... "Such statutes ... do not ordinarily apply to the case of a private individual not carrying on the business of a broker, and such an one may recover an agreed commission for a single sale though he had no license. ..." ... Plaintiff's regular business ... was selling coal on commission. ... [T]he courts have quite generally held that a single sale or act of a private citizen in relation to a vocation prohibited by statute without a license is not, standing alone, carrying on the forbidden business. Plaintiff's participation as an intermediary in negotiations for the deal involved here was not, under the circumstances shown, such an engaging in the business of a "business chance broker" as would, under the statutory definition, preclude his recovery for the services rendered.

Plaintiff's claim is based on an implied contract. He admits he made no claim for compensation until after the services were rendered. A contract is implied where the intention as to it is not manifested by direct or explicit words between the parties, but is to be gathered by implication or proper deduction from the conduct of the parties, language used or things done by them, or other pertinent circumstances attending the transaction. Where there is no express contract a contract may be implied in fact, where one engages or accepts beneficial services of another for which compensation is customarily made and naturally anticipated, and although there be no express stipulation between the parties for wages or price the law implies an understanding or intent to pay the value of the services rendered. Defendant contends . . . that the services were gratuitous and compensation an after-thought of plaintiff, because no mention of anticipated compensation was made by him when his services were offered, accepted and rendered and his first bill for pay thereafter was rendered . . . to "M. Deebs and George Stevens for sale of dye plant . . . , $6,000 cash, five per cent., $300.00". . . . Plaintiff testifies that he expected compensation for his services, which were rendered for defendant, accepted by him and continued during the negotiations at his request; that when the parties were closing the deal he heard Deebs say, "Miller will want $500 out of this" . . . ; that while he represented Stevens he did not at first know who was to pay . . . , and he learned that in those transactions the seller pays the commission.

While plaintiff's rendering a joint bill for his services to both Deebs and Stevens . . . was a proper matter for the jury to consider, . . . we cannot say as a matter of law it precluded the court from submitting the issue of fact of an implied contract to the jury. Plaintiff's testimony is positive that Stevens replied affirmatively to his inquiry as to whether he wanted to sell his dye house and accepted his offer to send Deebs to him, which opened the negotiations, and during their continuance he represented Stevens, did various things to help the deal along at his request, and at one time when the latter thought he had another prospective customer he told plaintiff that he was representing him and between the two they ought to land one of them, said he had an appointment with the other man at the Eagle hotel, had plaintiff take him over there in his car, saying . . . that plaintiff "should keep Deebs on the string". . . .

Plaintiff's testimony . . . raised an issue of fact for the jury. . . . The court correctly instructed the jury that absence of a broker's license did not bar recovery, submitting the issues of gratuitous service and implied contract under fair and proper instructions.

THE IMPORTANCE OF CONTRACT LAW

Of all the aspects of law examined in this text, none is as significant or pervasive in our lives as the law of contracts. Virtually every personal or business activity involves contract law: Charging a birthday gift on a credit card, buying and/or insuring a car, leasing an apartment, writing a check, paying for college, and purchasing textbooks and supplies all involve making contracts. An act as simple as filling a gasoline tank on your car or as complicated as purchasing a house involves contract law. Not only are we making a contract with the gasoline retailer, but the gasoline companies themselves receive much of their oil as a result of international contracts.

The Development of Contract Law

At early common law, contracts were not deemed to be of paramount importance. For example, Blackstone's *Commentaries on the Laws of England*, first published in 1756, devoted 380 pages to real property law but only 28 pages to contracts. Based on the organization of this treatise, the law of contracts apparently constituted a subdivision of the law of property rather than the independent branch of law as we know it today.[1] The concept of contracts did not merit much attention in that agrarian economy. Contract law increased in importance with the rise of a merchant class. Mercantile traditions grew out of the law merchant, which represented the accumulation of commercial customs from as early as Phoenician times. The merchant courts were separate from courts of law, and the merchants (or guilds) administered their own rules and customs. The evolution of commercial law remained outside the mainstream of legal development until the end of the seventeenth century. After the assimilation of the law merchant into the English common law, several acts of Parliament addressed commercial law subjects in the late 1800s.

Influenced by these English precursors, various legal bodies in the United States authored a wide variety of statutes covering U.S. commercial law, such as the Uniform Negotiable Instruments Law and the Uniform Sales Act. But the effectiveness of these acts was limited: Commercial remedies often differed from state to state, and the acts quickly became outmoded and not reflective of the current commercial practices. To effect an integration of inconsistent state statutes, the American Law Institute (ALI) and the National Conference of Commissioners on Uniform State Laws (NCCUSL) began working on what we call today the Uniform Commercial Code or UCC.[2]

By viewing commercial transactions as a single subject of the law, the UCC revolutionized prior approaches to commercial transactions. The drafters saw, for example, that a sale of *goods* (movable, identifiable, items of personal property) may constitute one facet of a commercial transaction. They also realized that a buyer may use a check for payment of the purchase price of the goods or that, alternatively, the seller may retain a *security interest* in the goods (a collateral claim against personal property or fixtures) to ensure payment of the balance of the debt. Consequently, the UCC included articles on sales, *negotiable instruments* (checks, drafts, notes, and certificates of deposit), bank deposits and collections, and *secured transactions* (Article 9 credit arrangements in which the vendor retains a security interest in certain assets of the debtor). The UCC fulfilled its original goals of (1) simplifying, clarifying, and modernizing the law governing commercial transactions; (2) permitting the continued expansion of commercial practices through custom, usage, and agreement of the parties; and (3) making uniform the law among the various jurisdictions [§ 1-102(2) and Comment 1]. Most states' commercial statutes, with minor variations, include the entire UCC. Louisiana is unique because it has adopted only some of the articles of the UCC. You can access the UCC, including the Official Comments, at http://www.law.cornell.edu/ucc/2/overview.html.

Contract law continues to evolve as more businesses and individuals create contracts online. Such contracts typically take three different forms: (1) business-to-business, or so-called B2B transactions; (2) business-to-consumer, or B2C transactions, such as AOL; and (3) consumer-to-consumer, or C2C, transactions, such as e-Bay. These changes pose issues that traditional contract law did not address. For centuries, the contracting parties either were face-to-face during their negotiations or communicated by sending signed documents by letter or telegraph. In contrast, the anonymity of online contracting, the virtual instantaneous transmissions of such dealings, and the paperless contracts that result raise concerns such as whether electronic communications suffice as offers and acceptances, the validity of electronic signatures, and the like. Despite these changes, most experts agree that traditional principles of contract law can adequately address most of the issues generated by online activities. Acquiring an understanding of the broad outlines of these new "rules of engagement" is an important dimension of business education in the twenty-first century.

The NCCUSL has proposed additional uniform statutes to deal with some of these issues. The 2002 Uniform Computer Information Transactions Act (UCITA) sets out a comprehensive set of rules for contracts related to computer information. Section 102 (10) of UCITA defines computer information as "information in electronic form which is obtained from or through the use of a computer or which is in a form capable of being processed by a computer." Thus, the act covers contracts involving the licensing or purchasing of software, computer games, online access to databases, online books, and the like. Certain exemptions apply. UCITA may govern only a part of a given transaction. UCITA has various parts that cover all aspects of such mass licensing arrangements from the formation of contracts through remedies for breaches of contracts. So far, only Maryland and Virginia have enacted UCITA.[3]

Another NCCUSL proposal is the Uniform Electronic Transactions Act (UETA).[4] Though both UCITA and UETA deal with e-commerce, they do so in divergent ways. For example, UETA supports all electronic transactions in business and governmental sectors (for example, electronic contracts, electronic signatures, and the use of electronic agents for electronic contracting) but does not impose rules on such transactions. UCITA, in contrast, limits its coverage to contracts involving computer information and imposes rules on such contracts. UETA will not apply to the parties' transactions unless they agree to use electronic commerce in these dealings. In contrast, UCITA applies to any agreement that falls within its scope.

The federal government enacted the Electronic Signatures in Global and National Commerce Act (known as the federal E-SIGN Act) in 2000. This federal law asserts that no contract, record, or signature may be denied legal effect solely because it is in electronic form. For contracting parties who have agreed to use electronic signatures, this statute makes electronic contracts and signatures as legally valid as hard copy, paper ones. The law exempts from its coverage certain transactions, such as court papers, wills, and health-insurance terminations; but experts predict that the E-SIGN Act will promote such Internet contracting activities as buying insurance or real estate online, obtaining mortgages online, and paying monthly bills electronically. These federal and state laws make commercial transactions more consistent from state to state. Such uniformity makes results more predictable without necessarily sacrificing the law's capacity to change when commercial practices dictate.

Uniformity and harmonization are also significant goals in the global marketplace. For example, the United Nations Convention on Contracts for the International Sale of Goods (CISG) provides coverage for international sales of goods that is similar to the coverage provided by Article 2 of the UCC for the sale of goods within the United States. (The CISG is discussed in some detail in the Sales material, Chapters 15-18.) CISG may apply to the sale of goods unless the parties agree to subject themselves to some other rule of law. Another example is European Union directives that cover some e-commerce transactions.

The law of contracts affects our most routine activities, and contract law still relies largely on settled common law rules. For this reason, this section emphasizes the broad categories of common law contracts and contractual situations. Many doctrines regarding modern-day contracts stem from "judge-made" law or precedents. Contract disputes decided on a daily basis in jurisdictions around the country significantly add to this body of precedents. Consequently, most of the discussion in Chapters 9-14 centers on common law contract principles—that is, principles derived from the judgments and decrees of courts. Exhibit 9.1 summarizes the sources of contract law.

Exhibit 9.1

The Evolution of Contract Law

Type of Law	Primary Coverage
Common law of contracts	Primary emphasis on real estate; historically geared to an agrarian society.
The Law Merchant	Initially, not really *law*, but rather the rules merchants used for self-regulation; eventually adopted by the British Parliament and made a part of the common law. Dealt with contracts between merchants and customers, especially consumers.
Uniform acts—various areas of coverage • Uniform Sales Act • Uniform Negotiable Instruments Act • Uniform Bills of Lading Act • Others	Covered specific areas of U.S. commercial law, without necessarily correlating with other related topics.
Uniform Commercial Code (UCC)	Successor to the various uniform acts in the U.S., this was the first compilation of the most significant areas of commercial law into a comprehensive code that also cross-referenced and correlated coverage of the different areas. Only applies within the U.S., but every state has adopted at least some parts of the UCC, if not the entire code.
United Nations Convention on Contracts for the International Sale of Goods (CISG)	An international treaty that addresses the sale of goods *between merchants* across national borders. CISG has many similarities to Article 2 of the UCC (the Law of Sales), but also has several significant differences. Businesses involved in international trade need to be aware of the coverage of this Convention.

Source: Courtesy of Daniel V. Davidson, © Daniel V. Davidson 2009

eClass 9.1 Sales/Management

WHAT TYPE OF LAW WILL GOVERN eCLASS'S CONTRACTS?

eClass will sell its software directly to a number of its initial customers, and the firm also will sell and install the software at some educational institutions. The sale to both types of customers involves the sale of *goods* (that is, movable, identifiable items of personal property) and thus is governed by the Uniform Commercial Code. However, the installation of the eClass software is a *service* and as such is governed by common law principles. Meg wants to know whether the contracts the firm enters will be governed in part by the UCC and in part by the common law of contracts or whether the court is more likely to determine that one aspect of the transaction "controls," so that the entire contract will be governed by the UCC or common law. What will you tell her?

BUSINESS CONSIDERATIONS   If a business provides both goods and services, should it price one higher than the other in order to imply which aspect of law—the UCC or common law—controls? Should the firm specify which aspect controls in the contract? Why?

ETHICAL CONSIDERATIONS   The sale of goods carries certain *warranties* if the seller is a merchant. Is it ethical to try to designate the contract as being primarily for services in order to avoid providing warranty protections to the customers?

DEFINITION OF A CONTRACT

Many definitions exist for the word "contract." In general, a contract is a legally binding and legally enforceable promise, or set of promises, between two or more competent parties. Put another way, a contract is "a promise or set of promises for the breach of which the law gives a remedy, or the performance of which the law in some way recognizes as a duty."[5] Most of us intuitively understand what a contract is. Still, situations exist that at first glance may appear to be contracts but are not.

Assume that you are a Jonas Brothers fan. The Jonas Brothers are in the United States for a concert tour. You are extremely eager to attend a concert by this group. A friend promises you a ticket to the show, and you of course are elated. Two days later, your friend calls to tell you he is taking an old flame instead of you. As you hang up, your anger and disappointment cause you to think about suing your friend. After all, you had an agreement, and he has broken a promise to you. You think you deserve to collect money damages for the harm you have suffered due to this "breach" of "contract" by your friend.

Does your agreement give rise to a legally enforceable contract? Will a court protect your expectations and award you damages? Probably not. Most courts will view this situation as a breached social obligation, not a breached contractual promise. You occasionally may read of people suing in small claims courts for the expenses incurred in making plans for dates that never occurred because they were "stood up." If the plaintiffs win these "contract" actions (and sometimes they do), higher courts generally overturn these decisions on appeal, determining that these situations are broken social obligations, not breached contracts. You need to be aware that a court will not consider all agreements to be "contracts."

Contrast the earlier situation involving the Jonas Brothers with this scenario:

You call a ticket outlet, order two tickets for the Jonas Brothers concert, and give your credit card number. When you arrive at the box office days before the concert to pick up your tickets, you learn the outlet has sold them to someone else.

Can you successfully sue this time? You probably can, because this situation involves more than a mere social obligation: It appears to have created binding obligations on both sides. If a court agrees, it will find that a contract existed and was breached, and it will award you damages. This illustrates the importance of that part of the definition of a contract that refers to a "legally enforceable" or "legally binding" agreement, because it means that not every promise, agreement, or expectation creates a contract.

ELEMENTS OF A CONTRACT

Given the law's emphasis on promises or mutual assent, it is not surprising that the first requirement for a valid contract is an agreement. An agreement consists of an offer and an acceptance of that offer. The law looks at the agreement from the viewpoint of a reasonable person and asks whether such a person would believe that an offer and an acceptance of that offer actually had occurred. Next, the parties must support their agreement with an exchange of consideration, the "bargain element" of a contract. Third, the parties must have capacity, the legal ability to contract. Fourth, the contract must reflect the genuine assent of each party. The concept of freedom of contract also implies that a contract must be entered into freely and voluntarily. If one party has entered a contract due to fraud or duress, for example, courts may be willing to set the contract aside owing to the lack of genuine assent by the disadvantaged party. Fifth, the subject matter of the contract must be legal. The legality of the bargain is questionable, for instance, if the parties have agreed to do something that violates a statute or public policy. Sixth, the element of form: In some cases, the law requires that a contract must be in writing in order to be enforceable. Oral contracts are generally valid and enforceable although they are risky due to the possible difficulty of proving the terms. However, some categories of contracts must be in writing to be legally enforceable by the court. (NOTE: If the parties enter into such a contract and each party performs, no one will question the lack of a writing. Such a contract is otherwise valid; it is just not enforceable by the courts.)

In summary, to be valid, a contract must be

- founded on an agreement (that is, an offer and an acceptance),
- supported by consideration,
- made by parties having the capacity to contract,
- based on the genuine assent of each party,
- grounded in a legal undertaking, and
- expressed in proper form, if applicable.

Each of these requirements is discussed in detail in Chapters 9-14. Exhibit 9.2 shows the elements of a contract.

CLASSIFICATIONS OF CONTRACTS

The law categorizes or distinguishes contracts in various ways. These categories are not always mutually exclusive, so several different terms may apply to the same contract. For example, suppose a restaurant orders produce from its supplier at set prices, and the supplier promises to deliver on a predetermined schedule. The understanding between these parties invokes several categories of contracts simultaneously: This agreement is an informal, bilateral, valid, *and* express contract.

Formal versus Informal Contracts

The distinction between formal and informal contracts derives from the method used in creating the contract. In early common law times, the contracting parties generally engaged in certain formalities (hence, the term formal). To be valid, for example, a contract had to be under seal; that is, the document had to be closed with wax and imprinted with one's seal, normally an insignia or distinctive mark. Very few contracts are under seal today because most jurisdictions have abolished that requirement for most contracts. Even the definition of "under seal" has changed: It has generally been replaced with an adhesive wafer or even a signature with a notation that says "under seal." This trend demonstrates that the need for ceremonies and formalities to ensure contractual validity has passed to a large extent. Perhaps the best known type of formal contract used in the United States today is a negotiable instrument, such as the check. Checks must meet certain formal elements in order to qualify for treatment as a check.

Informal (or simple) contracts are a more common category of contracts today. In these, the emphasis is not on the form or mode of expression but instead on giving effect to the promises of the parties. Informal contracts do not require a seal or any type of formality or specific format. Such contracts may be either oral or written and, in fact, may even be implied from the conduct of the parties.

Exhibit 9.2

The Elements of a Contract

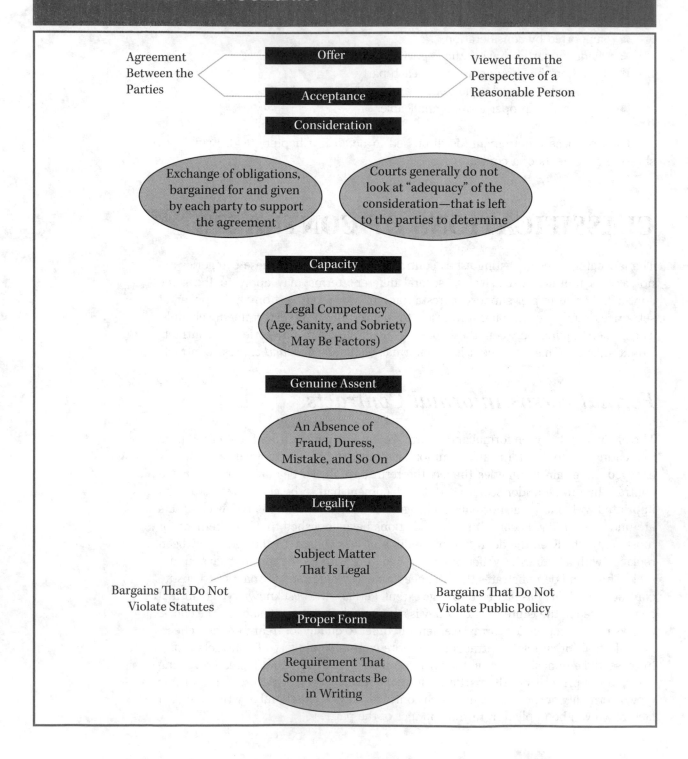

Agreement Between the Parties

Offer

Acceptance

Viewed from the Perspective of a Reasonable Person

Consideration

Exchange of obligations, bargained for and given by each party to support the agreement

Courts generally do not look at "adequacy" of the consideration—that is left to the parties to determine

Capacity

Legal Competency (Age, Sanity, and Sobriety May Be Factors)

Genuine Assent

An Absence of Fraud, Duress, Mistake, and So On

Legality

Subject Matter That Is Legal

Bargains That Do Not Violate Statutes

Bargains That Do Not Violate Public Policy

Proper Form

Requirement That Some Contracts Be in Writing

Unilateral versus Bilateral Contracts

Every contract has at least two contracting parties. The person who makes an offer (called the *offeror*) generally promises to do something or to pay a certain amount if the other person will comply with the offeror's request. The person who receives the offer is called the *offeree*. If the offeror requests a promise in return, the offer is for a *bilateral contract* (there will be promises on both sides.) However, if the offeror requests an action as acceptance, the offer is for a *unilateral contract* (there will be only a promise by the offeror, so there will be only a promise on one side.) If the offeror promises to pay the offeree $50 for raking the leaves in the offeror's yard, this contract is unilateral. Only one person, the offeror, has promised to do anything. The offeree accepts the offer by performing the requested act of raking the leaves. However, the offeree is not obligated to rake the leaves. Many contracts are unilateral because that is what the offeror intends. See Exhibit 9.3 for an illustration.

The case of *Kuhnhoffer v. Naperville Community School District 203*[6] illustrates the nature of unilateral contracts. From 1979 to 1988, Larry Kuhnhoffer worked for the Naperville Community School District #203 as a school bus driver. At the end of each school year, Kuhnhoffer received a letter from the school district thanking him for the previous year's work and inviting him to return as a driver in the fall. During the summer of 1988, the Naperville police department arrested Kuhnhoffer for driving under the influence of alcohol. This arrest resulted in the suspension of Kuhnhoffer's driving privileges for six months. When Dr. Michael Kiser, the school district's assistant superintendent, learned of this suspension, Kiser informed Kuhnhoffer that the district could not hire him as a school bus driver in the fall. Consequently, Kuhnhoffer sued for breach of contract. Because of the definition of unilateral contracts, Kuhnhoffer's suit was not successful. The judge ruled that the school district's offer constituted a unilateral contract offer. Because an offer of a unilateral contract is accepted by performance, no contract could result between Kuhnhoffer and the school district until he commenced performance. Without a valid license, Kuhnhoffer would be unable to fully perform his end of the bargain. Consequently, Kuhnhoffer could not accept and there could be no contract.

Exhibit 9.3

Bilateral Contracts and Unilateral Contracts

Bilateral Contracts	Unilateral Contracts
Promise	Promise
Offeror → Offeree	Offeror → Offeree
Promise	Action

In contrast, if the offeror makes a promise and requests that the offeree accept the offer by promising to do the requested act, a bilateral contract results because promises exist on both sides of the agreement. To use the earlier example, assume the offeror promises to pay the offeree $50 if the offeree will promise to rake the offeror's yard. When the offeree accepts by so promising, an exchange of promises has occurred, and a bilateral contract results from the parties' bargaining.

Valid, Voidable, Void, and Unenforceable Contracts

A *valid* contract is one that is legally binding and enforceable. There is an agreement and an exchange of consideration, and there are no issues regarding capacity, reality of consent, legality, or form. In contrast, a *voidable* contract is one that may be either affirmed or rejected at the option of one or more of the contracting parties, if that party can establish that he or she was "disadvantaged" in entering the contract. When a party lacks capacity or can show that he or she did not have real (voluntary) consent to the agreement, that party is disadvantaged and can elect to disaffirm (avoid) the contract. Remember that the agreement is valid until it is disaffirmed (avoided) by the disadvantaged party. For example, if a person buys a car in the belief that it was driven only 50,000 miles when in actuality it was driven 250,000 miles, that contract may be voidable on the basis of fraud or misrepresentation. (If the seller caused the buyer to believe that the car only had 50,000 miles, misrepresentation or fraud is likely to be found. But if the buyer makes a unilateral mistake in assuming the car had only been driven 50,000 miles, he or she may well have no recourse.) However, the contract remains valid and fully enforceable until the buyer disaffirms the agreement.

Void agreements, though they outwardly may appear to be contracts, can never have any legal effect. They never become contracts because they lack one of the essential elements of a contract (offer, acceptance, or consideration) or because the purpose of the alleged contract is illegal. An agreement to murder someone is void; a court will not enforce this agreement because it lacks the element of legality. (Not surprisingly, few lawsuits for breaches of these "contracts" are ever filed.)

On the other hand, it is possible to have a seemingly binding contract that will not be given effect in a court of law. Suppose, for example, that the contract involved is one that must be in writing (such as a contract for a sale of goods priced at $500 or more);[7] if this contract is oral, it will be *unenforceable*. Note that the contract otherwise appears to meet all the criteria of a valid contract, and the parties may well perform the contract to their mutual satisfaction. However, if one of the parties does not perform, the disappointed party cannot seek remedies or recourse in the courts due to the lack of the required writing.

Express versus Implied in Fact Contracts

There are two types of true contracts—express contracts and implied in fact contracts. An *express* contract is one in which the parties set forth their intentions specifically and definitely, either in writing or orally. Most contracts are of this type.

An *implied in fact contract*[8] is one that must be discerned or inferred from the actions or conduct of the parties. Even though the parties should have expressed their intentions more clearly, it still is possible to conclude that a true contract exists. The circumstances indicate that the parties intended to create an agreement by tacit understanding or by the assumption that an agreement exists. The elements of a contract implied in fact "are typically described as a request by the defendant for plaintiff's services ..., which are performed ... under circumstances in which the parties expect the plaintiff to be compensated ..." A common example occurs when a patient makes a doctor's appointment and comes to the doctor's office for medical services. The patient requested the services, and the parties should realize that the doctor expected payment.

Practically speaking, many agreements have express provisions and also include terms that must be discerned from the actions of the parties. Consequently, a given contract may not fall neatly into one or the other of these categories.

Executory versus Executed Contracts

An *executory contract* is one in which some performance or promise remains unfulfilled by one or more of the parties. For instance, if a person agrees to buy a king-sized mattress set from Honest John's, the contract is executory: The firm still must deliver the mattress set, and the buyer must pay for the set. If the buyer pays for the mattress set prior to delivery, the contract is still executory, even though the buyer has performed his or her part of the contract. As long as the contract is not fully performed by *both* parties it remains executory.

An *executed contract* is one in which all the parties have fully completed or performed all the obligations or promises set out in the agreement. In the last example, when Honest John's delivers the mattress set after payment, the contract will be executed. When a contract is executed, neither party has any further obligation. The term executed contract has another meaning: It can also mean a written contract that is signed. For example, the parties met in the attorney's office and executed the contract on June 5, 2011. The only way to determine the meaning is in context.

Quasi Contracts

Quasi contracts or contracts implied in law are not really contracts at all. It is unfortunate that we call them contracts because they are actually an equitable remedy[9] provided by a court to prevent the unjust enrichment of one party at the expense of the other. Under this theory, the court can "create" a contract (of sorts) for the parties, despite their wishes and intentions. Even though it may be clear that the parties did not actually contract with each other, the law may treat the parties as if they had. A quasi contract is a fiction engineered by a court to create justice between two parties. Some states recognize multiple theories under the category of quasi contract, for example, quantum meruit and unjust enrichment may be separate subcategories. An example is the Contemporary Case at the end of this chapter.

eClass 9.2 Personal Law

COLLECTING DAMAGES FROM A FRIEND

One of Yousef's friends, Eric, recently purchased a car stereo and a set of speakers for his new car. As a favor for Eric, Yousef installed the stereo and the speakers. In order to complete the installation, Yousef had to purchase some installation hardware and had to cut larger openings in the dash and the rear deck. By the time Yousef had obtained the installation hardware, cut the holes, and installed the stereo system, he had spent about four hours working on Eric's car. Once the installation was complete, Eric complained that, because Yousef had taken too long to complete the job, Eric missed an important appointment. Eric also complained about the holes Yousef had cut, alleging that they were not necessary and harmed the aesthetic look of the interior. Yousef was offended by this response to his "good deed" and decided that he should be compensated for his efforts. (He also would like an apology, but realizes that there *are* limits to his legal options.) He asks you whether he can recover for his time and expenses under either contract law or under quasi-contract. What will you tell him?

BUSINESS CONSIDERATIONS If a service business needs to modify or alter the customer's property in order to render the service, should the business obtain permission before making the modification or alteration, or should the business just complete the job? What legal issues might be raised by doing the alteration without prior permission?

ETHICAL CONSIDERATIONS Is it ethical for an employee to use his or her employer's tools and equipment to do favors for friends? What ethical issues arise when an employee does so?

To clarify the difference between a contract implied in fact and a quasi contract, consider this example:

> Kaila is sitting on her front porch at 111 Cedar Lane when a painting crew arrives. The painting crew has the wrong address (111 Cedar Lane instead of 1111 Cedar Lane, the address of the person who actually hired the painting crew). Kaila nevertheless allows the crew to paint her house and later tries to argue that since she did not request the services, she owes zero for them.

To prevent Kaila's unjust enrichment at the painters' expense, most courts will force Kaila to pay the painters under quasi contract. This payment can be based on either (1) making the painters whole, that is, putting them in the position the company would have enjoyed had a loss not occurred; or (2) making Kaila pay for the benefit she received (a newly painted house). The courts will not "gouge" Kaila by charging her an exorbitant price. A contract implied in fact does not exist here because of the lack of any facts suggesting that Kaila and the painting company had dealt with each other before the crew arrived at Kaila's house. Evidence of an intention to contract, however sloppy the execution of the contract, would have made this a true contract, or a contract implied in fact. Given the absence of any such evidence, the court instead creates a quasi contract to prevent Kaila's unjust enrichment.

Do not be misled into believing that every time one person receives a benefit, he or she will be liable in quasi contract. Remember that the policy underlying such recoveries is the avoidance of injustice. Kaila has to pay because she knowingly allowed the painters to proceed. If she was not present when the painting crew arrived and began to paint her house, the painters probably would not be able to hold Kaila liable for the services conferred on her. They were negligent and painted the wrong house. In these circumstances, it *is* fair to allow Kaila to retain the benefits bestowed on her. By the same token, a person who confers a gift (for example, assume Kaila's brother contracts with a painting company to redo Kaila's dilapidated house as a surprise for her) or one who volunteers a service (a neighbor who decides to paint Kaila's house while Kaila is away for the weekend) will not be able to recover later from Kaila in quasi contract. Similarly, a person who buys supplies in a mistaken belief that a contract exists, or who incurs foreseeable difficulties and later tries to make the recipient of the services pay for these extra costs or services, will probably not recover on a quasi-contractual basis. Still, remember that courts can, in a given circumstance, "make" a quasi-contract in order to avoid injustice.

Exhibit 9.4 shows the different classifications of contracts.

Exhibit 9.4

Classification of Contracts

Type of Contract	Definition	Example
Formal	A contract that is established through the use of certain rituals, ceremonies, or formalities.	Karma wants to pay for merchandise by a check. The check she writes is a formal contract.
Informal	A contract that is entered into by either oral or written statements or through the parties' conduct; requires no special rituals, forms, or format.	Trevor creates an oral contract to sell a used compact disc player to Kristen for $100.
Unilateral	A contract in which the offeror makes a promise in exchange for the performance of an act.	Leigh promises to pay $50 to the Salvation Army if Dexter completes a 10K walk-a-thon.
Bilateral	A contract in which a promise to perform is given in exchange for another promise to perform.	Stephanie promises to sell her dental practice and Frank promises to buy the practice.

Exhibit 9.4 Continued

Type of Contract	Definition	Example
Valid	One that manifests all the essential elements of a contract.	Teresa makes a contract to buy a new car from an automobile dealership.
Voidable	One that manifests all the essential elements of a contract and is legally binding unless disaffirmed by one or more of the contracting parties. Lack of capacity and lack of reality of consent allow disaffirmance (avoidance) of the contract.	Brian, who is aware of the extensive termite damage, enters into a contract to sell his termite-ridden house to Rosa, the buyer, who does not know about the damage. Rosa can disaffirm the contract due to Brian's fraud at the time of the contract's formation.
Void	One that lacks the essential elements of a contract. An agreement with an illegal purpose is void.	A contract in which Karen charges Denise a usurious rate of interest on a personal loan.
Unenforceable	One that manifests the essential elements of a contract but will not be enforced by a court of law.	Daniel borrows money from the bank. Sometime later, Jonathan makes an oral contract with the bank to guarantee the payment of Daniel's debt to the bank if Daniel fails to pay it.
Express	A contract in which the parties set out their intentions specifically and definitely.	Pete purchases a car from the General Motors dealership. The contract lists the price, the terms of the sale, the delivery date, and other details regarding the sale.
Implied in fact	A contract that exists despite the absence of explicit language showing that the parties intended to contract with each other.	Adam goes to the urgent care medical facility with a broken bone. He obtains medical care without discussing the cost. Adam implied that he wanted to enter into a contract for the medical care, and he will be obligated to pay for the treatment.
Quasi contract	An equitable remedy in which the court "creates" a "contract" in order to avoid injustice and/or the unjust enrichment of one party. This is not actually a contract, but the parties are treated as if a contract existed.	Chris goes to Country Hardware and purchases a welder to complete a project. Chris uses his credit card to pay. After he completes the project, he returns the welder to the store and obtains a credit on his card. The court might order Chris to pay the normal rental value of the welder in order to prevent unjust enrichment.

Exhibit 9.4 Continued

Type of Contract	Definition	Example
Executory	A contract in which some promise or obligation remains unfulfilled.	Lynda had a contract to sell a horse, saddle, and bridle to Greg. On the day of the delivery Lynda forgets to bring the saddle.
Executed	One in which all the parties have competed their promises or obligations under the terms of the agreement.	Andrew sells his truck to Kari for $8,000. On the date agreed, Andrew delivers the truck, keys, and vehicle registration and Kari delivers the cashier's check for $8,000.

eClass 9.3 Sales/Management

CONTRACTUAL CONSIDERATIONS

Ani, Meg, and Yousef realize that, in any potential contract, eClass must first ascertain whether common law or the Uniform Commercial Code will govern the transaction. However, Ani and Yousef still have trouble making this distinction. eClass will need to buy supplies to use in duplicating its software. It will need to contract with trucking firms to deliver its inventory to distributors across the country. If each of these contracts amount to $10,000 or more, are writings required? eClass is considering hiring a friend of Ani's to design the user interface for the eClass Web site. Would these agreements be governed by the UCC or common law? Ani and Yousef have asked for your advice on these matters. What advice will you give them?

BUSINESS CONSIDERATIONS   Why is it important for business practitioners to become well-versed in contract law? Should a business attempt to have its contracts governed by common law principles rather than by the UCC? Would it make a significant difference? Because eClass's products involve intellectual property, should the firm have its employees sign restrictive covenants to refrain, for a specified time and in a specified geographic area, from competing with eClass? What law will govern these contracts? Should these covenants also specify that employees may not divulge trade secrets and other proprietary, confidential information?

ETHICAL CONSIDERATION   What ethical issues might a software firm like eClass, which provides both goods and services, experience in its contracts that might not be faced by a firm that only provides services or only provides goods?

Exhibit 9.5

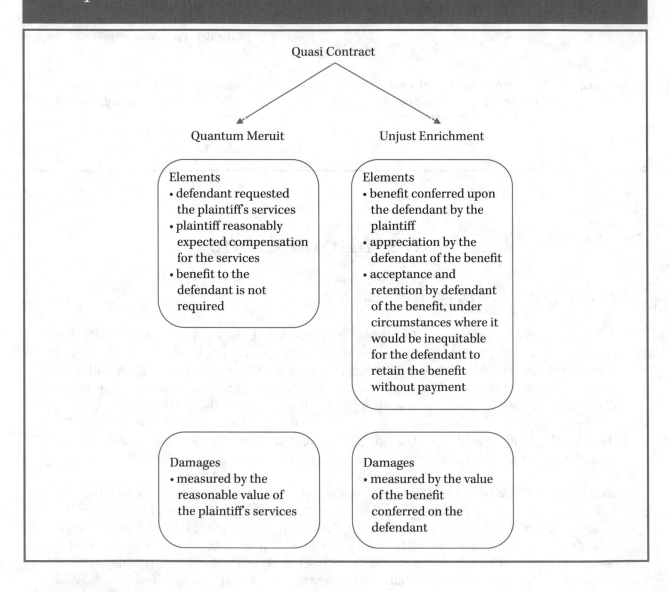

Quasi Contract Law in Wisconsin according to *Lindquist Ford, Inc. v. Middleton Motors, Inc.*

Quasi Contract

Quantum Meruit

Unjust Enrichment

Elements
- defendant requested the plaintiff's services
- plaintiff reasonably expected compensation for the services
- benefit to the defendant is not required

Elements
- benefit conferred upon the defendant by the plaintiff
- appreciation by the defendant of the benefit
- acceptance and retention by defendant of the benefit, under circumstances where it would be inequitable for the defendant to retain the benefit without payment

Damages
- measured by the reasonable value of the plaintiff's services

Damages
- measured by the value of the benefit conferred on the defendant

[The court labels the plaintiffs together as Lindquist except when that would be inaccurate or confusing.]

LINDQUIST FORD, INC. v. MIDDLETON MOTORS, INC.

557 F.3d 469, 2009 U.S. App. LEXIS 3747
(7th Cir. Wis. 2009)

FACTS Middleton Motors is a Ford dealership owned and operated by brothers Robert, Dave, and Dan Hudson. The brothers disagreed about how to best manage Middleton. For assistance Middleton looked to Lindquist Ford, another Ford dealership. Middleton sought a cash infusion from Lindquist and Craig Miller's services as a general manager in exchange for a profit-sharing agreement. Miller was the general manager at Lindquist. A general understanding was reached that Miller would take over as general manager of Middleton and Miller and Lindquist would be paid for these services, but the specifics of an agreement were not resolved. Nevertheless, the parties agreed that Miller would begin working at Middleton on April 21, 2003, and they would negotiate further terms and put the agreement in writing sometime later. Miller started working as general manager of Middleton while maintaining the same position with Lindquist. The parties continued to negotiate but never came to terms on the specifics of an agreement, and Lindquist never made a cash investment in Middleton. Middleton continued to sustain losses and fired Miller on March 24, 2004.

ISSUE Are the plaintiffs entitled to recovery under quantum meruit and/or unjust enrichment?

HOLDING Perhaps. The case should be remanded to the district court.

REASONING Excerpts from the opinion of Circuit Judge Sykes:

. . . [T]he heart of this appeal . . . requires a close analysis of quantum meruit, unjust enrichment, and the difference between implied-in-fact and implied-in-law contracts under Wisconsin law. . . . Wisconsin caselaw in this area can be confusing; the nomenclature and elements of proof are sometimes mixed up, leading to misconceptions about the nature and requirements of these discrete causes of action. . . . We think it helpful . . . to restate some . . . principles. Generally speaking, if the parties have made an enforceable contract and there is no ground for rescission, then breach-of-contract principles will govern the dispute. In the absence of an enforceable contract, . . . a plaintiff may turn to quasi-contractual theories of relief. . . . Unjust enrichment and quantum meruit are two such actions. . . . [E]ach of these claims has its own distinct elements of proof and measure of damages. . . .

In Wisconsin unjust enrichment is a legal cause of action governed by equitable principles. The action is "grounded on the moral principle that one who has received a benefit has a duty to make restitution where retaining such a benefit would be unjust." . . . To prevail on an unjust-enrichment claim, a plaintiff must prove three elements: "(1) a benefit conferred upon the defendant by the plaintiff, (2) appreciation by the defendant of the fact of such benefit, and (3) acceptance and retention by the defendant of the benefit, under circumstances such that it would be inequitable to retain the benefit without payment of the value thereof." . . . The measure of damages under unjust enrichment is limited to the value of the benefit conferred on the defendant; any costs the plaintiff may have incurred are generally irrelevant. . . . The value of the benefit may be calculated based on the prevailing price of plaintiff's services as long as those services benefited the defendant.

Unlike under unjust enrichment . . . a plaintiff can recover under quantum meruit even if he confers no benefit on the defendant. . . . Under quantum meruit, damages are "measured by the reasonable value of the plaintiff's services," . . . and calculated at "the customary rate of pay for such work in the community at the time the work was performed." . . . To take advantage of the more liberal recovery rule of quantum meruit, a plaintiff must prove . . . that "the defendant requested the [plaintiff's] services" and "the plaintiff expected reasonable compensation" for the services. . . . [In this quote, we] suspect what the . . . court meant was that the plaintiff must *reasonably* expect compensation, not that he must expect *reasonable* compensation. . . . [Q]uantum meruit is rooted in equity. If equity does not lie with the plaintiff, he will not recover under quantum meruit. . . . There are at least two ways to conceptualize the equity underpinnings of quantum meruit. One is to treat equity as another element of liability, as some states have. . . . Another is to treat equity as absorbed under . . . [the] requirement that a plaintiff must *reasonably* expect compensation; if equity does not lie on the plaintiff's side under the circumstances, his expectation of compensation is necessarily unreasonable. Under either approach, the result is the same. . . .

[Q]uantum meruit and unjust enrichment are quasi-contract actions (obligations imposed by law in the absence of a contract). . . . Wisconsin cases sometimes refer to quantum meruit as a contract "implied by law." . . . The Wisconsin Supreme Court distinguishes quantum meruit/ contracts implied by law from unjust enrichment, where there is no implied contract at all. . . . This distinction makes sense because there need not be any prior relationship between the plaintiff

and defendant for recovery under an unjust-enrichment claim. . . .

Wisconsin also recognizes contracts "implied in fact," but a "quasi-contract or contract implied-in-law differs markedly from a contract implied-in-fact." . . . Thus, Wisconsin recognizes two types of "implied contracts," but only implied-in-fact contracts rely on contract-formation and breach principles. . . . [W]e are convinced that the Wisconsin Supreme Court considers quantum-meruit actions to be conceptually separate from contracts implied in fact. . . .

[W]e conclude that the district court misconstrued the liability principles of quantum meruit under Wisconsin law and consequently mistried the claim. . . . [T]he district court correctly identified the three elements for liability under unjust enrichment. The question for us is whether the court correctly applied these elements. It was not clear error to find that Miller conferred a benefit to Middleton. Both sides presented evidence of what transpired at the dealership during Miller's tenure. The judge found Lindquist's evidence and argument on this point to be more credible and persuasive. On the second element of the claim, there is no question that Middleton accepted whatever benefit Miller conferred. Our concern lies with the third element of unjust enrichment—whether "it would be inequitable [for Middleton] to retain the benefit without payment." . . . The court oversimplified this aspect of the claim, essentially reducing it to this question: May an employer equitably withhold payment from an employee who worked for 11 months? The facts and context here make this claim more complicated. . . . [T]he district court excluded key areas of evidence relating to the parties' negotiations. . . . It also appears that the court excluded evidence that Middleton rolled back Miller's operational changes as soon as he left, perhaps to undercut Miller's claim that his efforts would eventually turn Middleton around. ... These evidentiary decisions flowed from ... the court's too-narrow view of the equitable element of unjust enrichment. Accordingly, this claim too must be retried.

If the court determines on remand that Lindquist expected to be paid only if Miller turned Middleton profitable and that Miller did not turn Middleton profitable after a fair attempt, then the court should enter judgment for Middleton under

both quantum meruit and unjust enrichment. If the facts are as Middleton describes them, then Lindquist gambled and lost on its bet. Equity requires that it internalize the consequences. ...

[Plaintiffs Lindquist and Miller recovered on remand. That opinion can be found at *Lindquist Ford, Inc. v. Middleton Motors, Inc.*, 665 F. Supp. 2d 1009, 2009 U.S. Dist. LEXIS 98748 (W.D. Wis. 2009).]

You Be the Judge

AmeriPro Search, Inc. was an employment referral firm that placed professional employees with interested employers. In May 1993, Elaine Brauninger, an agent of AmeriPro, contacted Fleming Steel Company (Fleming) and learned that Fleming was seeking an employee with an engineering background. Brauninger then contacted Seth Kohn, the president of Fleming, who was responsible for all decisions relating to employment and salaries. In their initial discussion, Brauninger advised Kohn that the fee for her services would equal 30 percent of the candidate's first year's salary. Kohn rejected this fee as too high. Kohn then told Brauninger that he and AmeriPro would determine the fee only after reaching an agreement to hire a candidate. Brauninger agreed and then sent Kohn résumés of potential candidates and a copy of AmeriPro's fee agreement. One of the candidates referred to Fleming was Dominic Barracchini. Kohn interviewed Barracchini on April 8, 1994, but did not hire Barracchini because Barracchini's salary request was too high. In February 1995, Barracchini called Brauninger because he had been laid off to inquire whether Fleming was still trying to fill the position for which he had previously interviewed. Brauninger never returned Barracchini's call. At Barracchini's initiative, Kohn interviewed and hired Barracchini as an engineer in June 1995. On September 6, 1995, AmeriPro sent Fleming a letter claiming entitlement to $14,400 for the placement of Barracchini with Fleming. When Fleming refused to pay the demanded fee, AmeriPro sued Fleming for the fee. How would you decide this dispute? Do you think AmeriPro and Fleming entered into a contract pursuant to which Fleming would pay AmeriPro a commission for placing Barracchini with Fleming? What, if anything, should AmeriPro have done to avoid this situation? [See *Ameripro Search, Inc. v. Fleming Steel Company*, 787 A.2d 988 (Pa. Super. 2001).]

Summary

The law of contracts affects us more often than any other area of law. Historically, contracts were of minor importance because a feudal society had little interest in protecting the parties' expectations. By the nineteenth century, contract law had outstripped property law in significance. The common law of contracts has been modified and in some areas superseded by the Uniform Commercial Code (UCC). The development of e-commerce has led to additional proposed statutes that states can enact into law, including the Uniform Computer Transactions Act and the Uniform Electronic Transactions Act. The federal Electronic Signatures in Global and National Commerce Act (the E-SIGN Act) promotes e-commerce by making electronic documents and signatures as legally valid as those involving paper and written signatures. The common law has also spawned numerous contract principles that affect the legal environment of business. Although the word "contract" has many definitions, it commonly means a legally binding and legally enforceable promise or set of promises between two or more competent parties.

Six requirements must be met for a contract to be valid: (1) an agreement (that is, an offer and an acceptance), (2) supported by consideration, (3) made by parties having the legal capacity to contract, (4) based on these parties' genuine assent, (5) grounded in a legal undertaking, and (6) expressed in proper form, if applicable. Contracts may be classified as formal or informal; unilateral or bilateral; valid, voidable, void, or unenforceable; express or implied; and executed or executory. These categories are not necessarily mutually exclusive.

A contract implied in fact consists of evidence of sufficient facts or conduct from which a court can conclude that the parties intended to enter into a binding agreement. A contract implied in fact is a true contract. A quasi contract is not a true contract. It occurs when a court "creates a contract" for the parties, despite their wishes and intentions, in order to create a just result. Not every situation in which a benefit has been conferred gives rise to a quasi contract.

Discussion Questions

1. Distinguish between a contractual obligation and a social obligation.

2. Name and define the six requirements for a valid contract.

3. Explain the following categories of contracts: (a) formal, (b) informal, (c) unilateral, (d) bilateral, (e) valid, (f) voidable, (g) void, (h) unenforceable, (i) express, (j) implied, (k) executory, and (l) executed.

4. What are the legal requirements for showing a quasi contract?

5. What is the Uniform Commercial Code, and why is it important?

Case Problems and Writing Assignments

1. Plaintiff Miguel Angel Gonzalez, a citizen of Mexico, was a highly ranked professional boxer. Defendant Don King was the chief executive officer and sole owner of DKP, a boxing promotional firm. This lawsuit involved two contracts. The first contract, dated February 15,

1996, was an exclusive promotional agreement between Gonzalez and DKP. The second contract, dated January 15, 1998, was a bout agreement for a boxing match with Julio Cesar Chavez held on March 7, 1998. The bout agreement incorporated some of the terms of the promotional agreement and also provided for a purse of $750,000 for the Chavez match. DKP paid this purse, a fact not disputed in this litigation. Paragraph 11 of the bout agreement, the focus of the dispute here, gave DKP the option to promote four of Gonzalez's matches following the Chavez match. The relevant portion of Paragraph 11 provided:

> In the event FIGHTER loses or draws the BOUT, or any option Bout, FIGHTER'S purse for each bout subsequent to such loss or draw shall be negotiated between PROMOTER and FIGHTER but shall not be less than AS PER PROMOTIONAL AGREEMENT unless a different sum is mutually agreed upon. The foregoing options as well as all other terms set forth in this Agreement are valid and enforceable regardless of the outcome of any bout provided for hereunder, i.e., win, lose or draw.

Pursuant to the terms of the promotional agreement, Gonzalez and DKP apparently agreed that if Gonzalez won the Chavez match, Gonzalez would receive at least $75,000 for the next fight, unless the parties agreed otherwise. Similarly, if Gonzalez lost the Chavez match, Gonzalez would receive at least $25,000 in subsequent matches, unless the parties agreed otherwise. Neither the promotional agreement nor the bout agreement explicitly stated the purse for subsequent matches in the event of a draw in the Chavez match. Since the Chavez match ended in a draw, the parties subsequently disputed whether the purse for subsequent matches could be determined with sufficient certainty to enforce the contract. Gonzalez contended that the omission of a purse for fights following a draw rendered the contract so indefinite as to constitute an unenforceable agreement to agree in the future. Should the

court accept Gonzalez's contention? Why or why not? [See *Gonzalez v. Don King Productions, Inc.*, 17 F. Supp. 2d. 313 (S.D.N.Y. 1998).]

2. In 1997, the Los Angeles County Metropolitan Transportation Authority (MTA) abolished its police force and entered into a contract with the County of Los Angeles to provide the MTA with law enforcement services through the County sheriff. Jack Herman was a former MTA police officer who did not pass the sheriff's review process. Neither the MTA nor the County offered him an alternative position. On the contrary, representatives of the MTA and the County met and mutually agreed not to place Herman in MTA or County employment. Section 2.1(A) of the contract states in relevant part:

> On the transfer date, all MTA [police officers] who elect to transfer to County and who have successfully passed the [sheriff department's] personnel review process shall transfer to County without any change in rank or loss in salary ... For sworn personnel who have not passed the [sheriff department's] personnel review process, the parties shall meet and reach mutual agreement on the placement of such personnel. ...

Herman contended that the latter provision of section 2.1(A) entitled him to employment with the MTA or a department of the County other than the sheriff's department in a job comparable in pay to his former position as an MTA police officer. The County argued that section 2.1(A) of the contract did not entitle Herman to employment with the County or the MTA for three reasons. First, the County asserted, the language providing "the parties shall meet and reach mutual agreement" on the placement of former MTA police officers leaves an essential element of the contract undetermined and therefore makes the contract void. Second, the County maintained, this language is also unenforceable because it purports to obligate the County "to employ another in personal service," employment otherwise prohibited by California's civil code. Finally, the County submitted, even if section 2.1(A) is enforceable, it does not require the MTA or the County to hire former MTA officers who do not meet the sheriff's standards in some other capacity—it only requires the parties to "agree on the placement of such personnel." According to the County, it had satisfied its obligations under the contract by meeting with the MTA and mutually agreeing on Herman's placement—the agreement being that he would not be placed with either agency. How should the court rule in this case? [See *Herman v. County of Los Angeles*, 119 Cal. Rptr. 2d 691 (Cal. App. 2 Dist. 2002).]

3. Morris Winograd had been John Keaton's insurance agent from the time Keaton was a young man. In 1993, Keaton left his job as a mechanic and opened a barbecue business on premises leased to him by George Williams. The lease ran from 1993 to 1999 with a monthly rental of $700. In 1995, Williams had financial difficulties and asked Keaton whether he would be interested in buying the premises. Keaton was not in a position to do so but suggested Winograd as a prospect for buying the property. Winograd eventually purchased the property to establish a new, more elaborate restaurant and bar to be known as Wynny's. Winograd consequently wanted to renovate the entire premises, including that portion occupied by Keaton's barbecue restaurant. According to Keaton, in or about September 1995, Winograd raised the question of buying out Keaton's business. Keaton said he responded with a price of $175,000, a figure Winograd agreed to pay. According to Keaton, pursuant to Winograd's requests, Keaton agreed to vacate the premises by December 1995, and to stay on to help Winograd run Wynny's. Around January 1996, Winograd began the renovations and also began paying a weekly salary for Keaton's services with respect to Winograd's new bar and restaurant. Keaton presented three independent witnesses (in addition to his daughter) to corroborate what he described as Winograd's promise to pay him a promissory note of $175,000 for his business. When Keaton sued for breach of contract, Winograd denied ever agreeing to pay Keaton anything for the barbecue business. Winograd also contended that the assets of Keaton's business had little, if any, value; that its earnings were negligible; and that whatever value it may have had did not approach $175,000. Winograd further claimed that Keaton had willingly terminated operation of his business so that Keaton could accept employment as manager of Wynny's, where he would be paid $800 per week—more than he ever could have earned from his barbecue restaurant. Had the parties entered into a contract concerning the sale of Keaton's business? If the court were to find the existence of an agreement, should the court nonetheless invalidate it for lack of specificity? [See *Satellite Entertainment Center, Inc. v. Keaton*, 789 A.2d 662 (N.J. Super. A.D. 2002).]

Notes

1. A.G. Guest, *Anson's Law of Contracts*, 26th ed. (Oxford: Clarendon Press, 1984), p. 1.
2. Bradford Stone, *Uniform Commercial Code in a Nutshell*, 2e (St. Paul, MN: West, 1995), pp. ix-x.
3. "A Few Facts About The Uniform Computer Information Transactions Act," NCCUSL Web site, at http://www.nccusl.org/Update/uniformact_factsheets/uniformacts-fs-ucita.asp (accessed 11/2/09).
4. UETA was completed by the NCCUSL in 1999 and has been adopted by Alabama, Alaska, Arizona, Arkansas, California, Colorado, Connecticut, Delaware, District of Columbia, Florida, Georgia, Hawaii, Idaho, Indiana, Iowa, Kansas, Kentucky, Louisiana, Maine, Maryland, Massachusetts, Michigan, Minnesota, Mississippi, Missouri, Montana, Nebraska, Nevada, New Hampshire, New Jersey, New Mexico, North Carolina, North Dakota, Ohio, Oklahoma, Oregon,

Pennsylvania, Rhode Island, South Carolina, South Dakota, Tennessee, Texas, U.S. Virgin Islands, Utah, Vermont, Virginia, West Virginia, Wisconsin, and Wyoming. (Although technically the U.S. Virgin Islands is not a state, the NCCUSL treats it as a state and for purposes of uniform laws we will also.) "A Few Facts About The Uniform Electronics Transactions Act," NCCUSL Web site, http://www.nccusl.org/Update/uniformact_factsheets/uniformacts-fs-ueta.asp (accessed 11/2/09).

5. *Restatement (Second) of Contracts*, § 1 (St. Paul, MN: American Law Institute Publishers, 1981).

6. 758 F. Supp. 468 (N.D. Ill. 1991).

7. The proposed revision to Article 2 of the UCC increases the amount to $5,000 or more. We will treat the topic here as if the 2003 revision to Article 2 has not been adopted.

8. It has been suggested that using the term implied in fact contract is unfortunate. Even though the contract is not expressed by words, it is still *expressed* through the parties' actions. John Edward Murray, Jr., *Grismore on Contracts*, Revised Edition, Student Edition, (Indianapolis, IN: The Bobbs-Merrill Company, Inc., 1965), p. 7.

9. In many states, quasi contract is considered an equitable remedy.

10

Offer, Acceptance, and Consideration

Agenda

As Ani, Meg, and Yousef work to launch eClass, they will enter into quite a few contracts. They also will buy goods and services from a number of businesses. Therefore, they need to know *how* to enter contracts, and they will need to know what legal effect different types of communications have on whether a contract exists. For example, will their advertising constitute an offer to form a contract?

eClass will enter into a number of contracts in order to produce and ship their software. The members of the firm want to be certain eClass is entering into legally binding contracts. One of their concerns centers on whether they are truly giving and/or receiving consideration in their contracts, and whether that consideration is adequate. They also want to avoid making or receiving any illusory promises in any of their agreements. They understand that bargaining, promises, and exchanges figure prominently in any determination of whether consideration exists. Yet they also have heard that in certain situations courts will enforce agreements despite a lack of consideration.

eClass presently confronts these and other contractual issues. Be prepared! You never know when the firm or one of its members will ask for your help or advice.

Classic Case

HOFFMAN v. RED OWL STORES, INC.

26 Wis. 2d 683, 1965 Wisc. LEXIS 1026 (Wisc. 1965)

FACTS Joseph Hoffman was interested in buying and operating a Red Owl grocery store. Hoffman had discussions with a number of Red Owl agents, including Edward Lukowitz. Hoffman mentioned that $18,000 was all the capital he had available to invest, and he was repeatedly assured that this would be sufficient to set him up in business as a Red Owl store. In1960, Hoffman thought it would be a good idea if he bought a small grocery store and operated it in order to gain experience in the grocery business. On the advice of Red Owl agents, Hoffman bought the inventory and fixtures of a small grocery store in Wautoma. After three months of operating this store, Lukowitz advised Hoffman to sell the store to Hoffman's manager and assured him that Red Owl would find a larger store for him elsewhere. Lukowitz told Hoffman and his wife that they would have to sell their bakery business and bakery building, and that retaining this property was the only "hitch" in the entire plan. On November 6, 1961, plaintiffs sold their bakery building for $10,000. Hoffman did not obtain a Red Owl store.

ISSUES Should the court recognize causes of action based on promissory estoppel? Do the facts in this case make out a cause of action for promissory estoppel?

HOLDINGS Yes, promissory estoppel should be used in Wisconsin. Yes, its use is justified in this case.

REASONING Excerpts from the opinion by C.J. Currie:

... Sec. 90 of Restatement, 1 Contracts, provides ... :

> "A promise which the promisor should reasonably expect to induce action or forbearance of a definite and substantial character on the part of the promisee and which does induce such action or forbearance is binding if injustice can be avoided only by enforcement of the promise."

... [Prior Wisconsin cases did not adopt the promissory-estoppel rule of the Restatement.] [N]o other possible theory has been presented to or discovered by this court which would permit plaintiffs to recover.... Many courts of other jurisdictions have seen fit ... to adopt the principle of promissory estoppel, and the tendency in that direction continues.... [T]he development of the law of promissory estoppel "is an attempt by the courts to keep remedies abreast of increased moral consciousness of honesty and fair representations in all business dealings." ... Because ... the doctrine of promissory estoppel ... is one which supplies a needed tool which courts may employ in a proper case to prevent injustice, we endorse and adopt it.

The record here discloses a number of promises and assurances given to Hoffman by Lukowitz . . . upon which plaintiffs relied and acted upon to their detriment. Foremost were the promises that for the sum of $18,000 Red Owl would establish Hoffman in a store. After Hoffman had sold his grocery store and paid . . . $1,000 on the . . . [building] lot, the $18,000 figure was changed to $24,100. Then in November, 1961, Hoffman was assured that if the $24,100 figure were increased by $2,000 the deal would go through. Hoffman was induced to sell his grocery store fixtures and inventory in June, 1961, on the promise that he would be in his new store by fall. In November, plaintiffs sold their bakery building on the urging of defendants and on the assurance that this was the last step necessary to have the deal with Red Owl go through. We determine that there was ample evidence to sustain the [jury's verdict] . . . with respect to the promissory representations made by Red Owl, Hoffman's reliance thereon in the exercise of ordinary care, and his fulfilment [sic] of the conditions required of him by . . . Red Owl. . . .

Originally the doctrine of promissory estoppel was invoked as a substitute for consideration rendering a gratuitous promise enforceable as a contract. . . . If promissory estoppel were to be limited to only those situations where the promise giving rise to the cause of action must be so definite with respect to all details that a contract would result were the promise supported by consideration, then the defendants' . . . promises to Hoffman would not meet this test. However, sec. 90 . . . does not impose the requirement that the promise . . . must be so comprehensive in scope as to meet the requirements of an offer. . . . Rather the conditions imposed are:

(1) Was the promise one which the promisor should reasonably expect to induce action or forbearance of a definite and substantial character on the part of the promisee?

(2) Did the promise induce such action or forbearance?

(3) Can injustice be avoided only by enforcement of the promise? . . .

We deem it would be a mistake to regard an action grounded on promissory estoppel as the equivalent of a breach-of-contract action. . . . [I]t is desirable that fluidity in the application of the concept be maintained. . . . While the first two of the . . . requirements of promissory estoppel present issues of fact which ordinarily will be resolved by a jury, the third requirement, that the remedy can only be invoked where necessary to avoid injustice, is one that involves a policy decision by the court. Such a policy decision necessarily embraces an element of discretion.

We conclude that injustice would result here if plaintiffs were not granted some relief because of the failure of defendants to keep their promises which induced plaintiffs to act to their detriment. . . .

THE FIRST STEP IN CONTRACT FORMATION

Agreement is the essence of a contract. An agreement is based on a valid offer by the offeror and a valid acceptance by the offeree. Because offer and acceptance are so important, courts closely examine the words and conduct of the parties to determine whether a *bona fide* (that is, a good faith) offer and acceptance are present. Although the offeror and the offeree can act through their agents as discussed in Chapters 28-30, for simplicity we will refer to just the offeror and the offeree.

Courts have developed numerous rules for checking the authenticity of the offer and the acceptance under common law principles. Under these rules, the threshold for contract formation remains high because courts require rather clear-cut statements that the parties are freely and voluntarily entering into a particular agreement. Conversely, under the more relaxed rules found in the Uniform Commercial Code (UCC) a court can *infer* a bona fide offer and acceptance from the conduct of the parties, even if the parties have omitted terms such as price, mode of payment, or mode of delivery. In this chapter, we discuss the reasons for these developments.

MUTUAL ASSENT

The initial phase of contract formation requires the assent of both parties to the agreement. The common law rules for contract formation required the parties to agree to exactly the same terms. Without this matching mutual assent, no agreement ever comes into existence and no contract is formed. However, it must be noted that contracts formed under and governed by the UCC do not require a "matching mutual assent." If the courts find that the parties acted like they had a contract, the court will treat them as if they have a contract. Contracts under Articles 2 and 2A of the UCC are discussed in more detail in Chapters 15 through 18.

THE OBJECTIVE THEORY OF CONTRACTS

The common law rules assume that there is a freedom of contract, and also that the parties have equality of bargaining power. This, in turn, assumes that the parties have freely and voluntarily consented to the formation of a contract. How do we judge whether the parties have mutually consented to the transaction? Common law rules tell us that the offeror has the right to set the terms of the offer (and to control the method by which the offeree accepts the offer). In so doing, the offeror must exhibit a clear and present intent to offer, and the offeree must exhibit a similar clear and present intent to accept.

To determine whether a valid offer exists, the law applies an *objective standard* (one that is capable of being observed and verified without being distorted by personal feelings and prejudices). Under common law, to decide whether an offer has been made, a court or a jury puts itself in the offeree's place to ascertain if a reasonable offeree would believe that the offeror was serious. Obviously, this result depends heavily on the facts. Courts *may* decide that you did not make an offer if you clearly are jesting, are excited, or are even visibly angry. Thus, a word to the wise: Beware of making "offers" you do not mean, since both common law and UCC principles may hold you to these statements.

OFFER

Let us look more closely at this first phase of reaching an agreement: the offer. An offer involves an indication (by a promise or another commitment) of one's willingness to do or refrain from doing something in the future. An offer implicitly invites another person to assent to the promise or commitment. The question then becomes what constitutes an offer in the eyes of the law. An offer has three parts: a clear intent to make a contract, a communication of the proposed terms to the offeree, and reasonably definite terms setting the parameters of the proposed contract.

Clear Intention to Contract and Definiteness of the Offer

Under the common law, an offer must show a clear intention to contract and be definite in all respects. An agreement to agree at some future time, for example, lacks these requirements for a common law offer. Similarly, statements of opinion, statements of intention, and preliminary negotiations do not result in bona fide offers because they lack definiteness. But reasonable people will differ as to what constitutes a clear, definite offer and what instead involves only preliminary negotiations or dickering.

   Since these are questions of fact that a judge or jury can later decide, be cautious. If you want to make an offer, be specific in all particulars. Haggling or dickering lacks definiteness regarding the details of the transaction and your intentions; consequently, such preliminary negotiations ordinarily are too vague to constitute a valid offer. Winning or losing a lawsuit can depend on how a court interprets the words expressed by the parties. For example, are the words "I can send you two trademark logos at $5,000 per logo" identical in intent to "I offer to sell you two trademark logos at $5,000 per logo"? Many people would view these statements as virtually identical, but a strict common law interpretation treats only the second statement as a bona fide offer. The law views the first statement as merely an indication of a willingness to negotiate or an invitation to negotiate.

Advertisements and Auctions

The law in general does not treat advertisements as valid offers because they normally lack sufficient specificity to be defined as such. Instead, the law views advertisements

eClass 10.1 Management

UNDERSTANDING CONTRACT FORMATION

One of the firm's salespersons, Chris, has been studying contract law in his Legal Environment of Business class. He explains to Meg that based on what he has been told in class, contracts are fairly technical and difficult to create. He believes that this principle gives eClass a great deal of latitude in discussing its product with potential customers because one can classify much of the conversation as mere "sales talk," and no offer will result. Meg is not sure that Chris has a thorough knowledge of contract law. Meg remembers that service contracts and employment contracts are often technical and that courts are likely to examine them very carefully. However, she also has heard that courts are much more likely to "find" contracts in the area of sales even if the courts conclude that the traditional common law requirements are lacking. Meg asks you for your advice. What will you tell her?

BUSINESS CONSIDERATION   What can a business do to protect itself from an overly exuberant sales force when the sales representatives are trying to make contracts with customers and earn more commission?

ETHICAL CONSIDERATIONS   Suppose a business, facing an agreement that will work to its disadvantage, identifies a possible loophole due to a technicality in contract law. Is it ethical for the firm to use this technicality to get out of the deal? Is it ethical to hold another party to a contract he or she does not realize is being formed?

as invitations to negotiate, asking persons to come into the store and make offers for goods at the prices indicated in the advertisements. Notice that this rule shows a pro-business perspective of the common law. A contrary perspective that advertisements constitute offers would presuppose that a merchant has an unlimited supply of merchandise. Consequently, the principle that advertisements ordinarily are not offers protects merchants from potential hardships. On rare occasions, however, an advertisement, catalog, circular, price list, or price quotation shows sufficient detail for a court to say that it is a valid offer.

Normally, courts require a showing that the merchant has placed some limitation on the advertised goods before courts will find that the advertisement constitutes an offer. For example, the merchant may have specified a time limit, such as "for one day only" in the advertisement. Or the merchant may have designated a quantity limit, such as "while they last" or "to the first 10 customers." In such a situation, the courts are somewhat more likely to find that the advertisement is an offer and not an invitation to deal or to negotiate. Again, courts refer to the objective standard of what a reasonable person would have thought.

Auctions are similar to advertisements in that the seller is not actually the offeror, although he or she may appear to be offering the goods for sale through the auctioneer. In reality, the law treats the *bidder* as the offeror. For a sale to occur, the seller must accept the bid. The seller can even refuse to sell to the highest bidder unless the auction is publicized as "without reserve." In an auction without reserve, the seller must let the goods go to the highest bidder; he or she cannot withdraw the goods if the price bid is too low. Once the auctioneer lets the hammer fall, the seller has accepted the bid. But until this point, the bidder can withdraw the offer and avoid the formation of a contract of sale. Section 2-328 of the UCC covers these points, which are discussed again in Chapter 16.

UCC and e-Commerce Variations to the Common Law Rules

Despite the common law requirement that an offer be definite in all its material (or essential) terms, you should be aware that the UCC relaxes this common law prerequisite in several significant ways. For instance, UCC § 2-204 states that a contract for sale of goods under the Code will not fail for indefiniteness as long as the parties have intended to form a contract and there is a reasonably certain basis for giving an appropriate remedy even though one or more of the terms of the agreement may have been left open. In addition, the UCC contains several so-called gap-filling provisions whereby the court can supply the terms—including price, place of delivery, and mode of payment—omitted by the parties.[1] The Code also validates *output contracts* (contracts that call for the buyer to purchase all the seller's production during the term of the contract) and *requirements contracts* (contracts in which the seller agrees to provide as much of a product or service as the buyer needs during the contract term), both of which would be too indefinite for common law courts to enforce.[2] Because the Code is predicated on the idea that commercial people (particularly merchants) want to deal with each other, it has eliminated some of the ticklish technicalities that impede contract formation under common law. You will learn more about these and other changes in common law brought about by the Uniform Commercial Code when you read Chapters 15 through 18. Like the UCC, the Uniform Computer Information Transactions Act (UCITA) endorses "gap fillers" if the contract is otherwise vague.[3] Both the UCC and UCITA impose a duty of good faith on the contracting parties; the parties need not refer specifically to this duty.

Still, online sellers should take great care in ensuring that any offer is clear and conspicuous. Among other matters, the sellers' Web sites should refer would-be buyers to a link that sets out the entire contract, including terms relating to remedies, payment, refunds and returns, privacy policies, dispute resolution mechanisms, and the like. Moreover, the offer should clearly indicate how to accept the offer. Ordinarily, the Web site includes a box stating "I agree" or "I accept the terms of the offer." The customer indicates acceptance of the offer by clicking on the box. Courts generally enforce such "click-on" agreements (also called "click-wrap agreements" or "click-on" licenses).

Communication of the Offer to the Offeree

Another requirement for a bona fide offer is that the offeror must communicate the offer to the offeree. At first glance this rule may seem nonsensical. How can a person accept an offer if he or she does not know it exists? Believe it or not, that sometimes happens. Suppose that Yessica is trying to sell some land, and several prospective buyers have looked at the property. Gurinder, one of these prospective buyers, writes a letter to Yessica in which he states, "I am willing to pay $80,000 for the property," signs and mails the letter. On that same day, Yessica writes a letter to Gurinder in which she states "I am willing to accept $80,000 for the property." Yessica signs her letter and mails it to Gurinder. It might appear that there is a contract in this situation. However, under common law rules there is no contract at this time. Each of the two parties is an offeror, communicating an intent to make a contract. However, though both parties are offerors on their letters (and offerees in the eyes of the other party), neither has accepted the offer put forward by the other party. While a contract may well result in this situation, technically there is no contract unless and until one of the parties communicates an acceptance of the offer to the other party.

This requirement of communicating the offer to the offeree sometimes arises in the context of "offers to all the world." Although most offers are made by one person to another, offers made to the general public or a similar class of large numbers of persons are perfectly legal. A reward, such as money for the arrest and conviction of the persons who vandalized an office building, represents the best example of such a general offer.

Exhibit 10.1

Offer: The First Phase of Reaching an Agreement

A *bona fide* offer by the offeror must:

- ■ Show a clear intention to enter into a contract.
- ■ Be *definite* in all respects.
- ■ Be *communicated* to the offeree.

Communications by the offeror that do *not* reflect a *bona fide* offer include:

- ■ Any *undisclosed* secret intentions.
- ■ Statements made in *jest* or in *strong excitement* as shown by objective evidence. (The "word" of the alleged offeror is not sufficient.)
- ■ Preliminary negotiations.
- ■ Price quotations, dickering, advertisements, and invitations to deal.

Even though there are court decisions to the contrary, most courts require that the party who performs the act contemplated by the reward (here, the identification of the vandals so as to lead to their prosecution and conviction) must have known of the reward and must have intended the act of identifying them as acceptance of that offer. Under this view, in order for a valid acceptance to occur, the offer must be communicated to the offeree. Under the rule followed in a majority of jurisdictions, then, a person who coincidentally identifies the vandals without knowledge of the reward is ineligible to receive the reward. Exhibit 10.1 summarizes the steps needed for reaching an agreement.

Termination of the Offer

Usually, offers satisfy these common law rules and will be legally effective. The next question that often arises concerns the duration of the offer; that is, how long will it remain open? Four methods for terminating an offer exist: (1) lapse; (2) revocation; (3) rejection; and (4) acceptance.

Lapse   Sometimes the offeror will specify in the offer when it will terminate. If so, the passage of time causes the termination (or *lapse*) of the offer. For instance, an offer may state, among other things, "This offer will remain open for 30 days." If the offeree has not accepted within this time, the offer automatically lapses after 30 days. The offeror is under no legal duty to communicate the fact that the offer has lapsed to the offeree. After 30 days, the offeror can make the same offer to anyone else.

In many cases, the offeror neglects to state any time period in the offer. In these situations, how long does the offeree have in which to respond? To avoid lapse, the offeree must accept within "a reasonable time." Determination of what constitutes a reasonable time becomes a question of fact that a judge or jury decides. The trier of fact will consider such things as industry conditions, customs, and usages of trade. In volatile commodities markets, an offer may lapse in a matter of seconds. On the other hand, a period of days or weeks may constitute a reasonable time if the offer involves the sale of real property in a slow market. To avoid such uncertainties, the offeror should state specifically when the offer lapses.

Lapse also may occur by operation of law. Regardless of the wishes of the parties, an offer automatically lapses upon the following occurrences: (1) the death or insanity of the offeror or offeree; (2) the supervening (an external or unexpected occurrence) illegality of the subject matter of the offer; or (3) the destruction of the subject matter involved in the offer. In other words, if Susan offers to sell some cattle to Joan, but Susan dies before Joan accepts, the offer automatically lapses. Assume Susan's cattle are in California and Joan's ranch is in Nebraska and, after the offer, Nebraska passes a statute prohibiting importing cattle from another state. The supervening illegality of the agreement will cause the contract to lapse. If lightning strikes the barn, starting a fire that kills the cattle, the offer also lapses. Communication to Joan is not necessary in any of these situations.

Revocation   Another method of terminating an offer is revocation. Under common law, the offeror possesses virtually unlimited rights to revoke an offer at any time before acceptance. The offeror need not use the word revoke, as long as an intention to terminate the offer is clear. In general, revocation does not become effective until it is communicated to (or received by) the offeree. Interestingly, such communication may be effective whether communicated directly or indirectly. Using our earlier example, Susan may state bluntly, "Joan, I revoke my offer to you." Alternatively, Joan may hear that Susan has sold the cattle to Leonard. In either case, an effective revocation has occurred.

Usually, Susan will be dealing only with Joan or, at most, with a few parties. This is not the case with a general offer to the public. If Denise lost her prize Dalmatian and has offered a reward for the return of or information about the dog, Denise need only revoke her offer in the same manner (or medium) in which she made the original offer. Because it is too burdensome to require Denise to communicate with every possible "taker" of her offer, public revocation suffices. It is even effective against a person who has not seen the revocation and who later comes forward with information about the dog.

Methods do exist for limiting this power of revocation by the Susans (and Denises) of the world. For example, by forcing Susan to promise to keep the offer open for a stated time, Joan can restrict Susan's power of revocation. The promise itself does not protect Joan from revocation. But if she takes an option on the cattle, Susan is legally bound to hold the offer open for the agreed-on period of time. (An *option* is a contract to keep an offer open for some agreed-on time period.) Joan will have to pay Susan for the option; but once she does so, Susan cannot sell the cattle to anyone else during the option period without breaching the option contract. Usually, Joan is under no obligation to exercise the option. If she does not, Susan can keep the money or other consideration paid to her for the option. If Joan does exercise the option, the money paid for the option may be subtracted from the purchase price. Whether Joan will have a "credit" for the amount paid will depend on the language of the agreement.

Finally, the equitable doctrine of promissory estoppel can prohibit offerors from revoking their offers. Promissory estoppel is a doctrine that prohibits a promisor from denying the making of a promise or from escaping the liability for that promise because of the justifiable reliance of the promisee. Under this doctrine, offerors can be prevented (estopped) from asserting a defense that would be available to them under common law. For Joan, the offeree in our earlier example, to successfully assert this doctrine, she must show that (1) Susan, the offeror, promised or represented to her that Susan would hold the offer open; (2) Joan relied on these promises or representations; (3) Joan consequently suffered a detriment (maybe Joan passed up the opportunity to purchase other cattle because she thought she would get Susan's); and (4) injustice can be avoided only by forcing Susan to keep the offer open. In several cases, plaintiffs have used this doctrine successfully to cut off the offeror's power of revocation. However, the rules for promissory estoppel are vague and it is difficult to predict whether a court will use it to rescue a plaintiff.

UCC and e-Commerce Variations to the Common Law Rules

Another exception to the rule that an offeror can revoke an offer at any time before acceptance is based on the "firm offer" provision of UCC § 2-205. An offer by a merchant to buy or sell goods which is in writing and signed by the merchant, and which by its terms gives assurance that it will be held open, is not revocable, for lack of consideration, during the time stated. If no time is stated, it will be held open for a reasonable time., In either situation the period will not exceed three months. The Code requires that merchants, as professionals, keep their word even if they received no consideration for their assurances.

Exhibit 10.2

Termination of an Offer

Type	Definition	Example
Acceptance by the offeree	Shows consent to the proposed terms; indicates an agreement which, if supported by consideration, creates a contract.	April made a written offer to Laurie. Laurie wrote "I accept" on the offer, she signed it, and returned it to April.
Rejection by the offeree	Shows an unwillingness to proceed on the terms proposed by the offeror. A counteroffer is deemed to be a rejection of the original offer.	Andrew made an offer to Jake. Jake told Andrew that his price was too high so Jake was not interested.
Revocation by the offeror	The offeror has the legal right to revoke his or her offer at any time prior to acceptance by the offeree. This right exists even if the offeror has promised to keep the offer open for a specified some time period. There are a few exceptions to this right.	Gilbert made an offer to Sarah. The next day Gilbert sent Sarah a text message revoking the offer. The offer is revoked when Sarah receives the text message (unless she has already accepted).
Lapse	Offers have limited lives, and if the offeree has not accepted the offer within that limited life span, the offer will expire due to the lapse of time.	Danielle made an offer to sell her business to Nathan. Danielle told Nathan he would have 30 days to consider her offer. At the end of the 30 days the offer would expire.

Source: Courtesy of Daniel V. Davidson, © Daniel V. Davidson 2010

Rejection   So far, we have discussed the offeror's power to terminate the offer. The offeree, of course, can refuse the offer and thereby terminate it. The law calls the offeree's power of termination rejection. Like revocations, rejections are not effective until communicated to (or received by) the offeror. For example, Joan can tell Susan that she no longer is interested in the cattle and thereby reject Susan's offer.

The usual rule holds that an offer cannot be accepted *after* lapse, revocation, or rejection, because the offer has already terminated. However, if the parties nonetheless still are willing to deal, there may be a valid agreement subsequent to one of these events. The parties generally are not obligated to continue the transaction unless they find it advantageous and agree to do so. Exhibit 10.2 summarizes the various methods for terminating an offer.

ACCEPTANCE

Acceptance is the usual mode of "terminating" an offer. This is a significant moment for the offeror and offeree because they have arrived at an agreement. Barring problems with consideration, capacity, genuineness of assent, legality, or proper form, a binding contract now exists.

Acceptance involves the offeree's assent to all the terms of the offer. Because this is so, the offeree's intention to be bound to the total offer must be clear. The offeree's mental reservations will not be binding on the offeror if they are not stated to the offeror. As with offers, courts apply the objective test to see whether the acceptance is valid. Generally, the method of acceptance (that is, oral, written, or implied through some act such as cashing a check) does not affect its validity. As we will see later in this chapter, there are some exceptions.

Mirror-Image Rule

Under common law rules, an acceptance must be clear and unconditional. This concept, called the *mirror-image* or *matching-ribbons* rule of common law, means that the acceptance must match, term by term, each of the provisions in the offer. Any deviation from these terms, whether by alteration, addition, or omission, makes the acceptance invalid and equivalent to a rejection of the offer originally made. This result follows from the offeror's power to set the terms of the offer and the acceptance under the common law.

Any deviation from the terms of the offer brings about a qualified acceptance, known as a *counteroffer*. Counteroffers terminate offers by replacing the prior offer with the new *counter*offer and reversing the status of the parties. There will not be an agreement unless the original offeror is willing to accept the (new) terms of the counteroffer. As you have seen in other contexts, the original offerors are not obligated to do so unless they still want to deal. Therefore, if you desire to enter into a contract with the offeror, you should pay close attention to the language of the acceptance.

Mere inquiries, requests, and terms implied by law, if part of the acceptance, do not invalidate it. Thus, if Mustafa offers to sell his car to Juanita for $2,000, and Juanita says, "I'll take the car at $2,000 as you offered, but I'd like you to throw in the snow tires," a valid acceptance probably exists. Juanita's added statement is a request, not a demand, and would not be treated as a counteroffer. Contrast this with Juanita's saying, "I accept if you throw in the snow tires." The latter statement sounds more like a requirement or a condition and may be viewed as a counteroffer, making the purported acceptance legally ineffective unless Mustafa is prepared to let Juanita have the snow tires as part of the deal.

UCC and e-Commerce Variations to the Common Law Rules

UCC § 2-207 continues its relaxation of common law rules by permitting a contract to arise between the parties, even if the offeree adds terms or includes different terms in the purported acceptance. This provision of the UCC reflects the drafters' knowledge of commercial practices, specifically the fact that buyers and sellers in commercial settings generally exchange their respective forms (that is, purchase order forms or order acknowledgment forms), which may contain contradictory terms. Rather than hamper commercial dealings by applying the common law rule, the UCC drafters permit a contract to arise between the parties unless the offeree expressly has indicated that his or her acceptance of the offer is conditioned on the offeror's assent to these additional or different terms.

Section 2-207 of the Code also sets out a scheme for determining the operative terms of the contract in these circumstances. For instance, between merchants, the additional terms automatically become part of the contract without the offeror's consent unless (1) the original offer expressly requires the offeree to accept the terms of the offer; (2) the additional terms materially alter the contract (that is, they would unfairly surprise or be unduly oppressive to the offeror); or (3) the offeror has notified the offeree that he or she will not accept the new terms. UCC § 2-207 states that conduct by both parties that recognizes the existence of a contract is sufficient to establish a contract for sale even though the writings of the parties otherwise do not establish a contract. You will learn more about these concepts in succeeding chapters, but for now, appreciate how the UCC alters the common law rules and the underlying rationales for these changes.

Manner and Time of Acceptance

To create a valid acceptance, the offeree must also avoid one other pitfall: The offeree must accept in exactly the mode specified, or *stipulated*, by the offeror in the offer. Thus, if the offeror says that acceptance must occur by telegram, a letter will not constitute an effective acceptance. Sending a letter in an attempt to accept legally would be viewed as a counteroffer. It is, in effect, a new offer. Similarly, if the offer says, "Acceptance required by return mail," an acceptance placed in the mail two days later is invalid. In addition, when the offer says, "Acceptance effective only when received at our home office," a contract will not arise until the offeror receives the acceptance.

Even though the offeror has the right to set the method of acceptance, the offeror may choose not to stipulate the mode necessary for a valid acceptance. In such cases, the offeree can use any *reasonable* medium of communication, as long as he or she acts within a reasonable time. Usually, the offeree will choose the same medium used by the offeror. By implication, this medium is a *reasonable* and therefore an *authorized* mode of communication. Hence, in the absence of a stipulated method of acceptance, if the offeror makes the offer via the mail, the offeree's mailing of an acceptance represents a reasonable (or authorized) mode of acceptance and thus a valid response. Another medium, such as the telephone, may be reasonable, and therefore authorized as well, if the parties have used this medium in their prior dealings or if local or industry custom sanctions it.

Use of an authorized mode of communication in either of these circumstances takes on particular significance because, in most states, these acceptances become legally effective *at the time of dispatch* (mailing, wiring, etc.) *if* the authorized means of communication is used. In order to be legally effective on dispatch, the communication must be properly addressed. If there is a charge to send the communication, the offeree must pay this fee. This is called the *mailbox rule*, or *implied-agency rule*, because the post office or telegraph office is *deemed* to be the agent of the offeror. (NOTE: The post office is not a true agent, but the use of the post office to send the offer implies that the post office is to be used for acceptance of the offer. By using the post office, the offeree is complying with the implied terms for accepting the offer.) To illustrate, assume that Charlotte did not stipulate the mode of acceptance for an offer that she mailed to Luis, the offeree, on September 28. Charlotte subsequently attempts to revoke the offer on October 1, only to learn that Luis mailed an acceptance to her on September 30. Since the offer was accepted on September 30, a contract existed as of that date; thus there is no longer a "mere offer" that Charlotte could revoke. (An *offer* can be revoked unilaterally by the offeror; an *agreement* cannot be revoked unless both parties agree to the revocation.) It is irrelevant that Charlotte did not receive the acceptance until after she attempted to revoke the offer. The law treats the post office as Charlotte's agent and thus concludes that the offeror "received" the acceptance on September 30, the date Luis deposited the letter with the post office. Because some letters never arrive, it is advisable, of course, for the offeree to obtain postal or telegraphic receipts in order to prove the date on which he or she actually dispatched the acceptance.

In contrast, where the offeree has used an unauthorized mode of communication but the exact mode was not specified, the strict rule states that the acceptance is ineffective until the offeror actually receives it; the mailbox rule is not applicable. Even so, some courts will enforce the agreement if the acceptance, even though communicated via an unauthorized mode, is timely, especially if the courts can construe the offeror's language about the proper mode as a mere suggestion rather than a stipulation or condition. UCC § 2-206(1)(a), by sanctioning acceptances "in any manner and by any medium reasonable in the circumstances," lends credence to such decisions.

As you can see, the time of contract formation is crucial. The mailbox rule allows acceptance, and hence a contract, to occur even before the offeror knows of the acceptance. Such an acceptance cuts off the offeror's right to revoke, because in order for an attempted revocation to be effective, it must occur prior to acceptance. Offerors can curtail the effect of the mailbox rule if they stipulate that acceptances will not be effective until received by them. Be aware that the mailbox rule applies *only* to acceptances: Revocations and rejections generally do not take effect until they are received by the recipient. Consequently, revocations and rejections do not become legally binding upon dispatch, as acceptances sometimes do. Receipt occurs when the communication is deposited or left for the recipient: The recipient cannot "prevent" receipt by refusing to open the communication.

Silence

As the previous discussion implies, some overt act necessarily accompanies acceptance. For this reason, acceptance requires a clear intent to accept. Thus, the settled weight of authority holds that mere silence by the offeree cannot constitute acceptance. However, in some isolated cases, the prior dealings of the parties may permit acceptance based on silence.

Bilateral versus Unilateral Contracts

The last major issue regarding acceptance concerns whether the contract, if formed, will be bilateral or unilateral. A bilateral contract is formed when the offeror promises to do something in exchange for a return promise to do something from the offeree. A unilateral contract is formed when only one party promises to do something in exchange for some action or performance by the offeree. By contrast, the weight of authority holds that an offer that contemplates the making of a *bilateral* contract may be accepted by either a direct communication of a promise to the offeror or a promise inferred from the offeree's conduct or other circumstances.

When the offer contemplates the formation of a *unilateral* contract, it usually is unnecessary for the offeree to communicate acceptance. The offeree accepts the offer merely by completing the act required in the offer. Subsequent notice to the offeror would be redundant because the offeror will learn of the acceptance when the offeree requests payment for the services rendered.

Disputes may arise between the parties as to how much time an offeree has to complete the performance mentioned in the purported unilateral contract. Assume the offeror says, "I'll pay you $50 to chop firewood for me," the offeree may think chopping wood at any time within the next two months will constitute a binding acceptance. On the other hand, the offeror may get nervous when the firewood is not in the wood rack within two weeks and, therefore, may make the same offer to someone else who completes the job more quickly. In such circumstances, the offeror

eClass 10.2 Sales

ACCEPTING OFFERS

Unbeknownst to Meg and Yousef, Ani has been negotiating for the purchase of two delivery vans for local deliveries. The auto dealership has the contracts ready and has asked that Ani stop by to sign the papers. Although she has indicated verbally that they probably will sign the agreements (she believes she can convince Meg and Yousef to do so), several weeks have passed without their having signed the papers. Ani is somewhat worried that the auto dealership will initiate a breach of contract suit against the firm. She seeks your advice as to whether her fears are unfounded or legitimate. How will you answer her queries?

BUSINESS CONSIDERATIONS   Why is it important for a firm to act diligently on all its obligations? What does a firm risk if it does not do so?

ETHICAL CONSIDERATIONS   Do you condone, on ethical grounds, Ani's action in this circumstance? Why or why not?

may not want to pay the first offeree for the wood delivered two months later; the offeror already has enough wood.

Because of such timing problems, courts remain somewhat hostile to unilateral contracts and, if possible, construe such alleged contracts as bilateral. More important, the contracting parties can avoid such timing problems by writing down all the pertinent details (delivery date, price, etc.) in advance, whether the offeror proposes a bilateral or a unilateral contract. Good planning, even in everyday affairs, helps avoid potential legal difficulties.

UCC and e-Commerce Variations to the Common Law Rules

UCC § 2-206(1)(b) specifies that unless the parties unambiguously indicate otherwise, "an order or other offer to buy goods for prompt or current shipment shall be construed as inviting acceptance either by a prompt promise to ship or by the prompt or current shipment of . . . [the goods] . . .": This section eliminates many of the distinctions made in the common law between bilateral and unilateral contracts. In the first instance, a bilateral contract is formed; in the second, a unilateral contract. Acceptance is effective in either case.

CONSIDERATION

Contract law addresses the importance of the parties' reaching an agreement. In addition, the law requires some evidence that the parties' agreement is mutual. One way for courts to find this "mutuality" is by determining that the parties have made an *exchange* of value. This exchange of value, the *quid pro quo* of contract formation, is called *consideration*. Familiarity with the doctrine's tenets is fundamental to an understanding of modern contract law.

Consideration indicates that some obligation or duty worthy of a court's protection genuinely exists. It also establishes that the parties are acting deliberately and intend to bind themselves to the terms of the agreement. One of the classic definitions of consideration states "A valuable consideration, in the sense of the law, may consist either in some right, interest, profit or benefit accruing to the one party, or some forbearance, detriment, loss or responsibility, given, suffered, or undertaken by the other."[4] Consideration consists of either a legal benefit to the promisor or a legal detriment to the promisee, bargained for and given in exchange for a promise. Both parties must give up or promise to give up consideration unless the contract is under seal. (In a number of states, contracts under seal do not require consideration.[5])

Consideration as an Act or a Forbearance to Act

Implicit in consideration is that the parties are promising to do something that they are not obligated to do or that they are promising to refrain from doing something that they are permitted to do. It is important to check the parties' language closely. Words that sound like promises actually may be *illusory* (that is, they derive from false appearances or are fallacious) because the parties really have not committed themselves in any manner. If one party never actually agrees to do anything (for example, if someone says, "I will sell you my farm for $80,000 if I feel like it"), the promise is illusory and unenforceable because consideration is absent.

Consideration is necessary for bilateral contracts and unilateral contracts. However, it may be more difficult to see in the latter situations. In unilateral contracts, consideration by one of the parties may be the actual act or a forbearance to act in lieu of a promise. In the latter situation, the consideration comes from refraining from engaging in a legal act. For example, suppose your parents promise to send you to Europe for the summer if you will earn straight A's in college this year. If you do, the agreement is supported by consideration and will be enforceable in a court of law, assuming you live in a state where family members can sue each other for breach of contract, and assuming that you are willing to risk your "domestic tranquility" by suing your parents.

Let us apply the definition of consideration to see why this agreement is enforceable. You waived your right to unlimited leisure time in exchange for your parents' promise. You and your parents bargained about the straight A's, so the trip is not a gift to you. You must do something (study more than you might like) or refrain from doing something (twittering, texting friends, or engaging in other leisure activities) to earn it. Furthermore, your parents, the promisors, promised a legal detriment (to pay for the cost of the trip) while you, the promisee, suffered a legal detriment (studying hard all year) as a result of this bargain. Your act of making perfect grades, therefore, has been given in exchange for your parents' promise to pay for your trip abroad.

Consideration as a Promise to Act or to Forbear

The earlier hypothetical bargain illustrates the formation of a unilateral contract. The analysis will be very similar, however, if your parents enter into a bilateral contract with you and you *promise* to earn straight A's in exchange for your parents' *promise* to send you to Europe. In this situation, the respective promises constitute the consideration to support the agreement, as long as the promises are genuine and not illusory. You can sue your parents if they do not pay to send you to Europe after you earn straight A's. On the other hand, your parents can probably sue you if you fail to earn straight A's as you promised.

Take this example one step further. For instance, if your parents breach this contract and you want to sue them, they may bargain with you to drop the lawsuit. If they promise to pay you $1,000 in exchange for your promise to forgo legal action and you accept this offer, you will have made another enforceable contract. Why? A promise to act or to forbear from a certain action, bargained for and given in exchange for another promise, constitutes consideration. Therefore, you should be able to convince a court to force your parents to pay, should they change their mind and refuse to do so: You surrendered your right to sue (and possibly prevail) in exchange for their promise to pay you if you did not pursue your potential legal remedies.

Adequacy of Consideration

Will your parents win in the earlier example if they argue that the $10,000 they will spend on your trip to Europe is too much, or that you really are doing nothing because becoming an honor student is insufficient to constitute a detriment to you? Usually your parents will lose, because courts generally are unreceptive to such arguments. The classic rule states courts will not inquire into the adequacy of the consideration. Courts instead will assume that the parties themselves remain the best judges of how much their bargain is worth and whether their performances are substantially equivalent. In other words, courts ordinarily will not second-guess the parties after the fact.

Exceptions to the general rule that courts will not inquire into the adequacy of the consideration do exist, however. If a court finds evidence of fraud, duress, undue influence, mistake, or other similar circumstances at the time of contract formation, adequacy of consideration becomes a more significant issue. Courts in these situations may permit one or more of the litigants to back out of the deal. In some circumstances the doctrine of unconscionability under either the common law or the UCC[6] also can form a basis for overturning bargains when the consideration appears to be grossly inadequate. But remember that courts do not routinely use this rationale to overturn bargaining between parties.

CONSIDERATION IN SPECIAL CONTEXTS

UCC and e-Commerce Variations to the Common Law Rules

The "firm offer" provision of UCC § 2-205 states that an offer to buy or sell goods by a merchant who gives assurance in writing that the offer will be held open may be irrevocable for a period of up to three months, even if no consideration has been paid to the offeror. Intended to encourage commercial activity that is free from haggling about "options," this provision dramatically changes the common law rules concerning consideration. Thus, even in the absence of consideration, courts will enforce a UCC firm offer. The same is true of contract modifications under the UCC: They, too, are enforceable without consideration under UCC § 2-209(1). In contrast, the common law would require consideration in both situations.

Courts ordinarily enforce output and requirements contracts as contracts supported by consideration. These courts reason that consideration is present in the form of the respective detriments suffered by the buyer and seller when they obligate themselves to deal exclusively with the other party. The promises underlying such contracts, then, are nonillusory and make the bargains enforceable.

Suretyship Contracts

Although the UCC has relaxed the requirement of consideration in some situations, the common law definitely requires consideration in suretyship contracts. Such contracts always involve three parties: a principal debtor, a creditor, and a *surety*. The surety agrees to be liable to the creditor in the event of the principal debtor's default. Such arrangements occur frequently in commercial transactions. For a more personal example, assume that Chan (the principal debtor) wishes to buy a new car. She may seek financing from a credit union (the creditor), which in turn may require that she bolster her credit (and decrease the credit union's risk) by having another person (such as her father or mother) sign the note as a surety. In so doing, the surety agrees to be primarily liable on the debt; the credit union can sue the surety if or when Chan defaults. The lender does not have to sue Chan first as a prerequisite to seeking payment from the surety.

If the principal debtor and surety simultaneously promise to pay the promissory note, a single consideration (the loan of money to Chan by the credit union) will support these promises. Given the presence of consideration, both promises will be enforceable. If, in contrast, the credit union lends the money for the car to Chan and later asks a surety to promise to pay in the event of her default, this second promise must be supported by new consideration before the surety's promise is legally binding. As will be discussed in the "Past Consideration" section of this chapter, Chan's preexisting obligation to the credit union (because the loan already has been made) does not constitute consideration for enforcing the surety's subsequent promise to pay the credit union.

Liquidated Debts

If one owes a debt to another person, partial payment of that debt is not consideration for full discharge of the obligation. For instance, assume Ravi has his dentist perform a root canal treatment on him. At the outset, the dentist tells Ravi the treatment will cost $1,090; and Ravi agrees that this is a fair price. If Ravi pays $550, he cannot successfully argue that this part payment is consideration for full discharge of the debt. The dentist will be able to argue that Ravi is under a preexisting duty to pay the entire $1,090. There is no consideration for accepting only $550 since both parties must give or promise to give a legal detriment. Consequently, Ravi is liable for the entire bill, or $1,090. It is crucial to note that the debt is *liquidated*; that is, the amount owed is not disputed. Ravi has agreed to pay $1,090, and he should not be allowed to escape this obligation. Allowing debtors to "escape" their obligation would throw commercial dealings into shambles!

Unliquidated Debts

Now let us assume that the debt is not liquidated. The amount of the debt may be in dispute because there has been no discussion of the price prior to performance, as in an implied in fact contract, or the parties agreed on a price but are unhappy with the product or service received. Suppose that Ravi in our prior example initially agreed to pay $1,090 for the root canal treatment. However, after the dentist treats him, Ravi continues to have soreness around the gums, and the treated tooth still is sensitive to changes in temperature. Although Ravi wants to live up to his obligation to pay his debt, he does not believe he should pay her the entire amount requested because he is dissatisfied with the results. At the point Ravi expresses these objections to the dentist, the debt is unliquidated; that is, the precise amount owed is in dispute. If Ravi sends the dentist a check for $550—particularly if he in some fashion indicates that this amount represents full payment for his entire indebtedness, such as writing "payment in full" on the memo line of the check—the dentist should understand that cashing Ravi's check permits Ravi to argue that he owes the dentist nothing more. The act of cashing the check shows that the dentist impliedly has agreed to accept $550 as full payment of the debt. Thus, the dentist is subject to the common law rule that payment toward an unliquidated debt that is intended and accepted as full payment is consideration for full discharge of the debt.

Instead, if the dentist wishes both to collect the entire $1,090 she alleges Ravi owes and to protect her rights fully, she should not cash Ravi's check for $550. Rather, she should return it to Ravi with a note stating that she is not agreeing to accept the tendered amount as full payment of the debt. If she is strapped for cash, she *may* be able to cash the check and try to preserve her rights against Ravi by endorsing it "with full reservation of all rights." Ideally, she should refrain from cashing the check to avoid the treatment of that partial payment as full payment of the debt.

Alternatively, Ravi and the dentist may negotiate and ultimately agree that $550 is the amount owed. In this case each suffers a legal detriment—Ravi, by giving up $550; the dentist, by giving up the right to hold out for more money—as a result of the bargained-for promise to pay. Both Ravi and the dentist also are giving up their rights to litigate the dispute. This notion of an exchange of rights is a hallmark of consideration.

One last note is appropriate. When Ravi and the dentist agree on the $550 sum, technically there is a compromise of the unliquidated debt. A *compromise* is the settlement of a disputed claim by the mutual agreement of the parties. Ravi and the dentist have negotiated the settlement of their dispute.

Composition of Creditors

Even though you will not study *bankruptcy* (the federal proceedings that are designed to give an "honest debtor" a fresh start) until Chapter 27, you probably are aware that the bankruptcy of the debtor poses serious financial risks for the creditor. In bankruptcy proceedings, a creditor ordinarily receives only a few cents on every dollar owed. Consequently, it often is in the creditor's best interest to give the debtor more time to pay (before the creditor forces the debtor into bankruptcy) or to agree with other creditors to accept smaller sums in full cancellation of larger claims through a composition agreement.

For an example of a composition agreement, suppose Doug (the debtor) owes Ann, Bill, and Cara (the creditors) $6,000, $4,000, and $2,000, respectively. The creditors each may agree to accept 50 percent of the respective debts as full satisfaction of their claims against Doug. Assume that Doug pays Ann $3,000, Bill $2,000, and Cara $1,000 under the agreement. Will the creditors be able to sue for the remainder of what is owed to them? If the courts were to apply the normal rules of consideration, the courts would conclude that Doug is not providing any legal detriment by paying a portion of his obligation. However, most states support composition agreements by:

(1) analogizing the result here to a settlement of an unliquidated debt situation;
(2) stating that the creditors who are entering into the agreement provide consideration for the other creditors who also agree; or
(3) making these agreements enforceable on public policy grounds.

These agreements help the debtor avoid the time and expense of bankruptcy, and the creditors generally receive more money than they would in a bankruptcy.

eClass 10.3 Finance/Management

ARRANGING CREDIT TERMS

eClass recently made a large sale to a private college. The college arranged credit terms with eClass and agreed to pay for the purchase over the next 24 months. Shortly after making this purchase, the college encountered some serious short-term financial difficulties. As a result, it has fallen behind in its payments to eClass and now faces the possibility of being forced into bankruptcy. The college is convinced that it can weather these problems and can become a profitable and viable entity again, *if* it can find a way to meet its short-term financial problems without resorting to bankruptcy. The college has asked eClass to agree to accept smaller monthly payments spread over the next 36 months. The college president states that his educational institution has proposed similar arrangements with several of its other creditors. The firm members ask you what they should do under these circumstances. What will you say? What is the legal significance of agreeing to the customer's proposal?

BUSINESS CONSIDERATIONS   Should a business that regularly sells on credit to its customers establish a policy for handling situations when its customers encounter financial problems, or should a firm handle each case individually as the situation arises? What are the benefits and the drawbacks to each approach?

ETHICAL CONSIDERATIONS   Is it ethical for a firm, after granting credit to its customers, to adopt a hard-line approach when any of the customers encounters difficulties? Is it ethical for a credit customer to threaten to resort to bankruptcy relief if the other party (that is, the creditor) balks at allowing the refinancing of the credit arrangement?

ABSENCE OF CONSIDERATION

There are circumstances where the courts will find a total absence of consideration and will not enforce the agreement that the parties have shaped. These circumstances are addressed in the following sections.

Illusory Promises

You will recall that promises that do not bind the promisor to a commitment are illusory promises. Such promises are made without any legal detriment to the promisor and hence are not supported by consideration. A promise "to order such goods as we may wish" or "as we may want from time to time" is not a genuine promise at all; it only appears to set up a binding commitment. Instead, it actually allows the promisor to order nothing. Such "will, wish, or want contracts," as they often are called, are void because they lack consideration. There is no real commitment by the promisor.

Contracts that purport to reserve an immediate right of arbitrary cancellation (any action that indicates a desire to terminate the obligations set out in the contract) fall into this category of contracts as well. Courts are hostile to attempted exercises of a right of arbitrary cancellation due to the potential unfairness of allowing one side, by merely giving notice of cancellation, to free itself from an agreement. Consequently, courts try to find some actual or implied limitations on the purported right of arbitrary cancellation so as to make it a nonillusory, or binding, promise. Since consideration will exist for such promises, the agreement will be enforceable.

Preexisting Duty

If one performs an act that one has a preexisting obligation to do, settled law holds that such a person has suffered no detriment. Likewise, a person suffers no detriment if he or she refrains from performing an act that he or she had a preexisting duty not to do. In both cases, no consideration is present to support the underlying promise or performance.

This principle often manifests itself in cases involving law enforcement officers. Assume you live next door to a policewoman, and she approaches you with this proposition: For $50 she will undertake extra patrols around your house when you are gone on a trip. Since this sounds like a good deal to you, you agree. But you have second thoughts later and do not pay her. When she sues you in small claims court, she probably will lose because she has a preexisting duty (imposed by law) to try to protect your home from burglars. In making those extra patrols, she has suffered no detriment; so consideration is lacking.

Besides obligations or duties imposed by law, preexisting duties may stem from contractual agreements. Numerous cases address these situations. For example, suppose G & H Painting Service has contracted with you to paint your basement for $900. Halfway through the job, the crew boss tells you that the crew will leave unless you agree to pay him $200 more. Because you are having a party in two days, you grudgingly say yes. On completion of the job, do you have to pay $900 or $1,100? Based on the doctrine of preexisting obligations, you generally will have to pay only $900, since the firm already owes you the duty of finishing the paint job. But if you subsequently want G & H to lay a concrete patio for you, your promise to pay another $500 in return for G & H's additional work on the patio is supported by new consideration—G & H did not obligate itself to construct the patio as part of the original agreement—and you must pay $500 more for this additional work.

To return to the earlier example, assume now that in the middle of winter a freakish humid spell causes a paint-resistant mold to grow in your basement. As a result, G & H has to paint the walls three times to cover the mold. If this blight arises after the firm begins the work, most courts will characterize it as an unforeseen or unforeseeable difficulty and will order you to pay the higher price. The same will hold true if you and the firm had canceled the original contract and had started anew with different promises and obligations. In both situations, consideration will support the new promises. Under the common law, strikes, inflation in the prices of raw materials, and lack of access to raw materials do not meet the test of "unforeseen or unforeseeable difficulties." Accordingly, new promises obtained on these bases ordinarily will lack consideration and thus will be unenforceable.

Moral Consideration

Remember that harsh outcomes sometimes result from the application of the doctrine of consideration. Promises made from a so-called moral obligation embody one such subcategory of consideration and ordinarily are not enforced. In general, courts adhere strictly to the requirement of consideration in these contexts.

For example, suppose your child has been saved from the jaws of a snarling Doberman Pinscher because of the efforts of a passerby. The woman who saved your child from the dog unfortunately suffers deep cuts that eventually require cosmetic surgery. Faced with such generosity, you offer to pay this Good Samaritan's lost wages while she is in the hospital. As time passes, though, you grow less willing to pay, and finally, you cease paying her altogether. If she sues you, you usually will win because a court will conclude that she has bestowed a gift on you—that is, saving your child. Consequently, no consideration was present. Note, too, that prior to the humanitarian gesture, there was no bargaining in exchange for your promise to pay. Another example of moral consideration is a promise to pay a relative based on the promisor's "love and affection" for the promisee. In most states, neither promise will be enforceable. However, in a few jurisdictions, courts will reject the settled rule and hold that the promisees are entitled to win. Remember, though, that this is the position taken by a minority of courts.

Past Consideration

Related to this doctrine of moral consideration is the doctrine of past consideration. This issue typically arises when a person retires and the company offers the former employee a small monthly stipend "in consideration of 25 years of faithful service." Since the old services are already executed (completed or finished), they are not consideration for a new promise. Neither bargaining nor an exchange of anything of value has occurred. The promise is not supported by consideration and will not be enforceable. As traditional legal authority holds, "Past consideration is no consideration."

EXCEPTIONS TO THE BARGAINING THEORY OF CONSIDERATION

As you should now realize, whether or not the parties have bargained with a resulting exchange of value appears crucially important under the common law rules surrounding consideration. Still, in the following four situations, courts will enforce agreements despite a lack of consideration: (1) promissory estoppel; (2) charitable subscriptions; (3) promises made after the statute of limitations has expired; and (4) promises to repay debts after a discharge in bankruptcy.

Promissory Estoppel

Earlier in this chapter, promissory estoppel was discussed in the context of preventing an offeror from revoking an offer. When warranted, courts apply this equitable doctrine in order to avoid injustice. Essentially, when promissory estoppel is a "substitute" for consideration, it operates the same way. In the words of § 90 of the *Restatement (Second) of Contracts*:

> A promise which the promisor should reasonably expect to induce action or forbearance on the part of the promisee or a third person and which does induce such action or forbearance is binding if injustice can be avoided only by enforcement of the promise.[7]

Accordingly, the law holds the promisor liable for failure to live up to his or her promise. In order to avoid injustice, the court prevents the promisor from denying his or her promise. Many states use the factors set out in § 90 of the *Restatement*. However, their application varies from state to state and case to case. Consequently, it is difficult to predict whether a litigant can successfully persuade the court to apply the doctrine.

For example, promissory estoppel *might* apply in the case of an employer who offered to pay Damian, a loyal employee, $1,000 a month when Damian retires. If the employer paid Damian $1,000 a month for 10 years, and Damian, expecting the stipends to continue, has given up opportunities for part-time employment, some courts will apply promissory estoppel and require the employer to continue the payments to Damian despite the absence of bargaining or of an exchange of anything of value.

Charitable Subscriptions

Suppose that a generous person wishes to donate an amount to a worthy charity and promises to do so. Later, this humanitarian zeal wanes, and the person no longer wishes to live up to the agreement. If you are the donor, what do you argue? In all likelihood, you will try to argue that you intended to bestow a gift. Since by definition a gift lacks consideration (there is neither bargaining nor an exchange of value), you will claim that you can avoid liability for this promise.

In some situations there is consideration in the form of a bargained for exchange and legal detriment. For example, if the hospital agrees to name the new wing after the donor (or a member of his or her family), that will constitute legal detriment on the part of the hospital in exchange for the promised funds. A business school might agree to name the school after a generous donor. Assume that there is no traditional consideration. If the donor puts the promise to the charity in writing and signs it, the donor has made a charitable subscription (subscription means "an act of the hand"), and the act of making a commitment by means of such a subscription is legally enforceable in some states. Even if there is no subscription, some courts believe that charitable institutions (like universities, hospitals, charitable agencies, or churches) serve noble purposes, and the court may use other theories to enforce the promise. The court might use promissory estoppel because the charitable institution relied on the amount pledged. The court may decide that all the donors are promising consideration, making the promises of the other donors binding, similar to the approach used by some states in the composition of creditors' situation. In the alternative, courts may simply enforce the promise on public policy grounds.

NOTE: a number of charities, such as a public television channel, offer something (a book bag, a CD, a DVD, or something comparable) in exchange for promised "donations" at various levels. In reality, the charity in this situation is offering to sell the item, that is, to give consideration, and the viewer who calls is buying the item, not making a donation.

Promises Made After the Expiration of the Statute of Limitations

State statutes of limitations set time limits on when creditors can bring suit against debtors for the sums owed to the creditors. Ordinarily, this period is from two to six years, after which the creditor cannot maintain suit against the debtor. Sometimes the debtor wants to repay the debt, even if this time limit has passed. In most of these situations, there will be no consideration; there is an absence of any bargaining, and the debtor's promise arguably represents moral consideration at best.

Yet under most state statutes and court decisions, the law will enforce the debtor's *new* promise to pay if it is in writing. Most states require that the writing acknowledge the debt and include a promise to pay it. The public policy of encouraging people to pay their debts generally forms the basis for this exception to the bargaining theory of consideration.

Promises to Pay Debts Covered by Bankruptcy Discharges

The same policy applies, and the result is similar, when a debtor promises to pay a debt covered by a discharge in bankruptcy. Again, generally no consideration underlies this

Exhibit 10.3

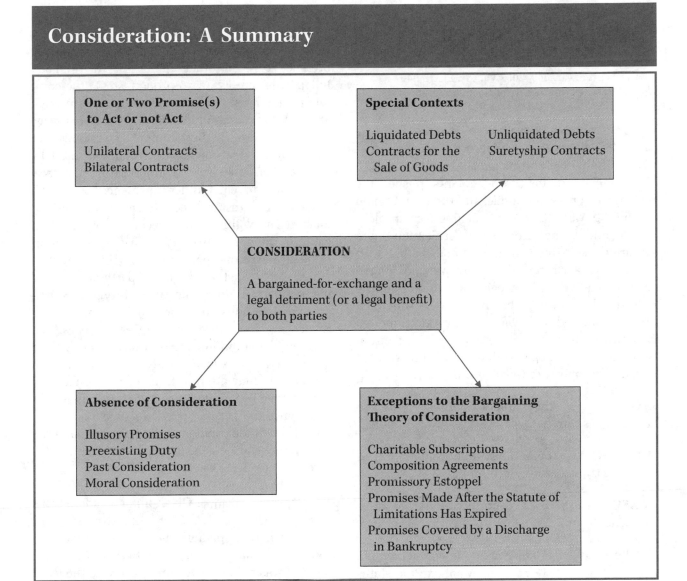

Consideration: A Summary

One or Two Promise(s) to Act or not Act

Unilateral Contracts
Bilateral Contracts

Special Contexts

Liquidated Debts   Unliquidated Debts
Contracts for the   Suretyship Contracts
 Sale of Goods

CONSIDERATION

A bargained-for-exchange and a legal detriment (or a legal benefit) to both parties

Absence of Consideration

Illusory Promises
Preexisting Duty
Past Consideration
Moral Consideration

Exceptions to the Bargaining Theory of Consideration

Charitable Subscriptions
Composition Agreements
Promissory Estoppel
Promises Made After the Statute of
 Limitations Has Expired
Promises Covered by a Discharge
 in Bankruptcy

new promise; but most states will allow the enforcement of the promise, provided that the debtor makes the promise to pay in full compliance with the reaffirmation provisions of the Bankruptcy Act and with a full understanding of the significance of this promise, as required by the Bankruptcy Code. Exhibit 10.3 offers a summary of how these principles are interrelated.

Contemporary Case

TRINITY HOMES, L.L.C. v. FANG

63 Va. Cir. 409, 2003 Va. Cir. LEXIS 349
(Cir. Ct. of the City of Norfolk, VA 2003)

FACTS Damon Stewart, an agent for the plaintiffs, alleges that he placed the acceptance in his facsimile machine, dialed the number for T.H. Nicholson, agent for the defendants, pushed the button to start the facsimile, and then went on an errand. Stewart's facsimile machine was an older version and did not provide any verification that a facsimile was being transmitted and/or that such facsimile was received. There are no phone records relative to the alleged transmission of the facsimile by Stewart. Shortly after the time that Stewart allegedly forwarded the facsimile to Nicholson, he received a phone call from Nicholson indicating that defendants did not wish to sell the property to the plaintiffs.

ISSUE Should the Mailbox Rule apply to acceptances sent by facsimile (fax) transmissions?

HOLDING Yes, the Mailbox Rule should apply to facsimile transmissions in Virginia.

REASONING Excerpts from the opinion of Judge Marc Jacobson:

... The Mailbox Rule was enunciated in [an English case in 1818]. ... The Mailbox Rule states that, once an offeree has dispatched his acceptance, it is too late for the offeror to revoke the offer. The Mailbox Rule has been accepted in most American jurisdictions and by the *Restatement of Contracts* [*Second*]. ... The Restatement addresses the issue of the application of the Mailbox Rule to electronic communication in § 64, which states: "Acceptance given by telephone or other medium of substantially instantaneous two-way communication is governed by the principles applicable to acceptances where the parties are in the presence of each other" [and not the Mailbox Rule]. ... [There is] a two-prong test: (1) the communication must be "substantially instantaneous"; and (2) the communication must be two-way. "The rationale of the Restatement's position is that when parties are conversing using 'substantially instantaneous two-way communication,' they are, in essence, in each other's presence." ... To be substantially instantaneous, the transmission must occur within a few seconds, or, at most, within a minute or two. ... For a communication to be two-way, one party must be able to "determine readily whether the other party is aware of the first party's communications, through immediate verbal response or, when the communication is face-to-face, through nonverbal cues." ... Further, if a communication is not two-way, "the offeror will not know exactly when the offeree accepts and may attempt to revoke the offer after the offeree has already sent his instantaneous acceptance to the offeror[]. ... In such a situation, the Mailbox Rule should continue to apply and the contract should be considered accepted upon dispatch of the offeree's acceptance." ...

The Supreme Court of Oklahoma considered this issue in *Osprey, L.L.C. v. Kelly-Moore Paint Co.,* ... [where applying] the Mailbox Rule, the court held that the faxed notice of the lease renewal was sufficient to timely exercise the lease renewal option because the notice was in writing and the delivery of the notice by fax transmission served the same purpose of the authorized methods of delivery. The court stated specifically: "the fax log and telephone records show that the notice was property transmitted to Osprey. Transmitting the fax *was like mailing an acceptance under the Mailbox Rule*, where an offer is accepted when it is deposited in the mail." ...

This Court concludes that the Mailbox Rule is applicable ... and thus the issue is one of fact, whether or not the facsimile transmission ... was actually forwarded or transmitted by Stewart to Nicholson. ... Stewart's fax machine was apparently one of early vintage and provided no verification of the transmission ... to Nicholson. Unlike the *Osprey* case, there was no fax log and/or telephone records to show that the fax was properly transmitted to Nicholson. Stewart cannot say with certainty if the fax actually went through other than to say that he placed the fax in the fax machine, turned it on, and then left before viewing and/or verifying its transmission. ... Stewart did not recall looking at the fax machine ... , when he returned later in the afternoon from his errand. The burden is on the Complainants to prove by preponderance of the evidence that the fax transmission ... was actually made and accomplished. The Court in considering the totality of the evidence and the totality of the circumstances, ... concludes that the burden has not been met ... and finds for the Defendants.

You Be the Judge

Gary Leavitt owned real property located in Scottsdale, Arizona. Leavitt financed his purchase of the property through a note and deed of trust, serviced by Wells Fargo bank. On July 22, 2008, Plaintiff sent a "partial payment" of $500 to Wells Fargo that contained a "restrictive endorsement" that said, "Upon endorsement of this payment, lender/payee agrees to the following new terms: suspended payment for 18 months, no late fees, no interest, no negative reporting to credit agencies. In the event of breach of new terms, lender agrees to forfeit balance and remove account from any and all credit reporting agencies." Wells Fargo cashed the check but has continued to charge late fees and interest and has reported the account as being late to the regional credit bureau. Wells Fargo then set a Trustee Sale of the property for January 13, 2009. Leavitt claims that he validly modified the terms of his mortgage loan through the restrictive endorsement placed on the $500 check and that Wells Fargo accepted those modifications by cashing the check without objecting to his proposed new terms. He claims that Wells Fargo breached the modified mortgage by assessing late fees and interest, by scheduling the Trustee Sale, and by reporting him to a credit agency. Was the original mortgage modified to include the new terms? [See *Leavitt v. Wells Fargo Bank, N.A.*, 2009 U.S. Dist. LEXIS 38258 (Dist. of Ariz. 2009).]

Summary

To have agreement, there must be an offer and an acceptance. Assent to a contract must be mutual, and the offeror can set the terms of both the offer and the acceptance under common law. An offer is an indication (by a promise or another commitment) of one's willingness to do or to refrain from doing something in the future. To be a genuine offer under the common law, the offer must manifest a clear and present intent to contract and be definite in all respects. The law usually construes advertisements as invitations for persons to come in and make offers for the goods at the prices indicated in the advertisements. An offer has no legal effect until the offeror communicates it to the offeree.

The four methods of terminating an offer include (1) lapse, (2) revocation, (3) rejection, and (4) acceptance. The offeror's power of revocation may be limited by option contracts, by the UCC "firm offer" provision, or by promissory estoppel. A bona fide offer and acceptance bring about an agreement. Acceptance involves the offeree's assent to all the terms of the offer. The acceptance must be clear and must be communicated to the offeror. Under the mirror-image rule of common law, an acceptance has to match, term by term, the provisions in the offer. A qualified acceptance—one that deviates from the original terms—is called a counteroffer. A counteroffer terminates the original offer and in effect brings about the rejection of the offer unless the original offeror is willing to deal on the new terms. If an offeree uses an authorized mode of communication, an acceptance may be effective on dispatch. If the offeror has not stipulated the mode necessary for a valid acceptance, use of any "authorized" mode of communication will make the acceptance effective on dispatch.

This is called the mailbox rule. If the offeree has used an unauthorized mode, acceptance actually must be received to be effective; the mailbox rule will be inapplicable. The mailbox rule does not apply to revocations or rejections.

Consideration is the bargain element of a contract. Consideration exists when there is an exchange between the parties as the result of a bargain, with each party either assuming a duty or surrendering a right as a result of the bargain. In unilateral contracts, consideration may take the form of an act or a forbearance to act. In bilateral contracts, the respective promises constitute the consideration. In the absence of fraud, duress, undue influence, or unconscionability, courts generally will not inquire into the adequacy of the consideration. Consideration is not required under the UCC provisions relating to firm offers and modifications of sales contracts.

The doctrine of preexisting obligations mandates that one pay a liquidated debt in full; part payment is not consideration for full discharge of the debt. In contrast, part payment of an unliquidated debt, if accepted as full payment, represents a compromise of the debt and is supported by consideration and cancels the debt.

Agreements based on illusory promises or promises grounded in preexisting legal duties lack consideration. The same is true of promises founded on moral obligations and on past consideration. The four exceptions to the bargaining theory of consideration are (1) promissory estoppel, (2) charitable subscriptions, (3) promises to repay made after the statute of limitations has expired, and (4) promises to repay debts covered by discharges in bankruptcy. In these situations, courts will give effect to agreements without consideration.

Discussion Questions

1. Is an advertisement a *bona fide* offer? Why or why not?

2. What are "counteroffers," and how do they arise?

3. Explain the term "mailbox rule" and its significance.

4. Why does the UCC dispense with requiring consideration in situations involving "firm offers" and contract modifications for the sale of goods?

5. Explain why part payment of a liquidated debt is not consideration for full discharge of the debt but part payment accepted as full payment for an unliquidated debt is.

Case Problems and Writing Assignments

1. The.TV Corporation International (dotTV) registers Internet domain names for a fee. In April 2000, dotTV auctioned off the domain name "Golf.tv." Je Ho Lim, a resident of South Korea, bid $1,010 for this domain name. On or about May 25, 2000, Lim received an e-mail entitled "E-MAIL INVOICE FOR DOMAIN REGISTRATION" in response to his bid. The e-mail said, "Congratulations! You have won the auction for the following domain name "—golf." Lim authorized a credit card payment to dotTV. Sometime later, however, dotTV notified Lim that "we have decided to release you from your bid." The company also told Lim to "disregard" the acceptance notification because it was an "e-mail error." Later, dotTV publicly offered the name "Golf.tv" at an opening bid of $1,000,000. Lim sued dotTV for breach of contract. Who should win this dispute and why? [See *Lim v. The.TV Corporation, International*, 121 Cal. Rptr. 333 (2002).]

2. Scott Specialty Gases (Scott) employed Diane Blair from January 1995 through March 1999 as the Plumstead Medical Products Division plant manager. After resigning on March 24, 1999, Blair filed a federal lawsuit alleging employment discrimination. Scott argued for dismissal of the lawsuit on the grounds that Blair had agreed to submit all employment-related claims to binding arbitration. Scott had placed a mandatory arbitration provision in an updated employee handbook that Scott had distributed to all employees in February 1998. Blair had been given the assignment of making sure that all the Medical Products' employees signed an "Acknowledgment of Receipt and Reading" of the revised handbook. Blair herself had signed such an acknowledgment on February 27, 1998. That acknowledgment stated that she had read the arbitration provision and agreed to submit any disputes arising out of her employment to a final and binding arbitration. The acknowledgment Blair had signed read:

> I understand that nothing in this Handbook can be modified or deleted, nor can anything be added in any way by oral statements or practice. Only the Executive Committee or Scott Specialty Gases can change this Handbook, and the change must be in writing. If Scott Specialty Gases makes any material changes, it will give me a copy of them, and by remaining employed by Scott Specialty Gases thereafter I will be deemed to have accepted these changes . . . .

In response to Scott's motion to dismiss based on the arbitration agreement, Blair claimed that the arbitration agreement lacked consideration and was not binding on her. Specifically, she claimed that Scott had not agreed to be bound to the arbitration and that Scott's unilateral ability to alter the agreement had rendered the agreement illusory. How should the court decide this case? [See *Blair v. Scott Specialty Gases*, 283 F.3d 595 (3d Cir. 2002).]

3. Gayle Moore and her husband bought a Suzuki four-wheel all-terrain vehicle (ATV) in May 1993 from Suzuki, Arctic Cat Motor Sports. At the time of the sale, the salesperson offered the Moores a $50 rebate to be issued on completion of an ATV rider safety class. On October 23, 1993, the Moores attended an ATV rider safety class held on the property of Hartley Motors, Inc. James Croak instructed the class using the curriculum of the ATV Safety Institute. Before starting the instruction, Croak requested that all participants sign a consent form and release. Moore did so. The driving portion of the class took place on a course marked with cones on unpaved ground. During the class, Moore drove her ATV through high grass beyond a cone marking the course. Her vehicle rolled up on a rock protruding from the ground. Moore suffered injuries as a result of being thrown from her vehicle. When Moore sued the instructor, the ATV Safety Institute, and Hartley Motors, Inc. for negligence, the defendants introduced the consent form and release that Moore had signed. Moore then argued that the release was invalid because she had received no consideration for signing it. She contended that the $50 rebate promised by the salesperson upon the completion of the course was to have been the consideration for her release of liability. Because she had not completed the course, she argued, the $50 rebate was unavailable. She submitted that because she had not received any consideration for the release, it was ineffective to protect the defendants from liability. Alternatively, Moore argued that the release was unconscionable and contrary to public policy. How would you decide this case? [See *Moore v. Hartley Motors, Inc.*, 36 P.3d 628 (Alaska 2001).]

Notes

1. UCC, §§ 2-305, 2-309, and 2-310.
2. Ibid., § 2-306.
3. UCITA, § 305.
4. Quoting from the Court of Exchequer's opinion in *Currie v. Misa*, L.R. 10 Ex. 153, 162 (1875), quoted in John Edward Murray, Jr., *Grismore on Contracts*, Revised Edition, Student Edition, (Indianapolis, IN: The Bobbs-Merrill Company, Inc., 1965), p. 80.
5. The doctrine of contracts under seal existed before the development of the doctrine of consideration. Contracts under seal do not require consideration unless there is a specific state law to the contrary. However, if the parties to a contract under seal promised consideration, they will be obligated to provide the promised consideration. Ibid., p. 137.
6. See UCC, § 2-302, which holds that a court may refuse to enforce a contract if it is shockingly unfair or oppressive.
7. *Restatement (Second) of Contracts* (St. Paul, MN: American Law Institute Publishers, 1981), § 90.

11

Capacity to Contract, Reality of Consent, and Legality

Agenda

Yousef has heard that some types of contracts are voidable. He is unclear about what this term means, but he definitely wants to avoid any contracts that are voidable at the option of the other party. Meg thinks that a large market for eClass software potentially exists among teenagers and young adults, and she thinks the firm should investigate this market. From both a professional and a legal perspective, Ani does not believe the firm should target this youth-oriented market. She prefers to have eClass focus on the parents and educational institutions.

The firm will have to decide how to advertise and market eClass's products. Should eClass use slick advertising that portrays the products as capable of doing more than they really do? Will adopting this strategy have any effect on the contracts they enter? Can the firm be held responsible for misleading ads that may constitute misrepresentation and fraud? The firm members also differ as to how "hard-line" eClass should be in securing a contractual agreement.

As eClass increasingly focuses on sales of its first product, eAccounting, the firm must make certain that its activities, as well as its contracts, involve legal undertakings. Otherwise, statutes and public policy may restrict the firm's ability to contract.

These and other questions are likely to surface in this chapter. Be prepared! You never know when the firm or one of its members will ask you for help or advice.

Classic Case

LEWIS AND QUEEN v. N.M. BALL SONS

48 Cal. 2d 141, 1957 Cal. LEXIS 173
(Cal. Supreme Ct. 1957)

FACTS George W. Lewis and Paul C. Queen operated a contracting business as a partnership called Lewis and Queen (plaintiff). Lewis had an individual contracting license, but Queen and the partnership of Lewis and Queen did not. Ball Sons (defendant) was awarded two contracts by California for the construction of separate sections of the Hollywood Parkway. Defendant entered into a contract with plaintiff to do much of the work. The defendant divided the work into four written contracts to hide the fact that the defendant was not doing fifty per cent or more of the work itself as required by the contract with the state. Some of these contracts were labeled rental agreements.

ISSUE Is the plaintiff partnership barred from recovering the rest of its fees because it does not have a contractor's license?

HOLDING Yes, the partnership itself needed a license. It was not sufficient that one of the partners had a license.

REASONING Excerpts from the opinion by Justice Traynor:

... Section 7028 of the Business and Professions Code makes it unlawful for "any person to engage in the business or act in the capacity of a contractor within this State without having a license ..." Section 7026 defines a contractor as "any person, who ... does himself or by or through others, construct, alter, repair, add to, subtract from, improve, move, wreck or demolish any building, highway, road ... or improvement...." "The term contractor includes subcontractor...." Section 7030 makes it a misdemeanor for any person to act in the capacity of a contractor without a license. Section 7031 provides that, "No person engaged in the business or acting in the capacity of a contractor, may bring or maintain any action ... for the collection of compensation for the performance of any act or contract for which a license is required ... without ... proving that he was a duly licensed contractor at all times during the performance of such act or contract." ... [S]ection 7025 states that the "person" required to have a license by section 7028 includes a partnership.

... [I]n spite of the form of the rental agreements plaintiff actually undertook to and did in fact "construct a highway"... and... acted as a contractor within the meaning of section 7026.... [W]hen the evidence shows that the plaintiff... seeks to enforce an illegal contract or recover compensation for an illegal act, the court has both the power and duty to ascertain the true facts in order that it may not unwittingly lend its assistance to the consummation or encouragement of what public policy forbids....

The "person" that did the contracting work, and was required... to have a license... was the partnership of Lewis and Queen, and it had no license. Nor did Queen individually.... [T]he board has never determined the qualifications of Queen.... Plaintiff claims that... Queen merely kept the books and sought out new business for the partnership. But the statutory provisions setting forth the qualifications for a license,... show that the Legislature was as much concerned to protect the public from dishonesty and incompetence in the administration of the contracting business as in the actual use of bricks, mortar, and earth-moving equipment.... Plaintiff's insistence that Queen knew nothing about actual construction... emphasizes the importance of the board's passing on his qualifications to engage in any aspect of the contracting business. The statute makes it clear... that if the contractor is a partnership, the experience, knowledge, and integrity of each partner is a vital consideration in determining whether to issue a license.... [I]t is not clear that Queen's activities were in fact confined to bookkeeping and the search for new business. He participated with Lewis in the negotiations that led to the execution of the contracts, and he "walked the job," apparently to determine what problems would be encountered if the work was undertaken. The conclusion is inescapable that plaintiff did not substantially comply with the licensing requirements....

[C]ourts generally will not enforce an illegal bargain or lend their assistance to a party who seeks compensation for an illegal act. The reason for this refusal is... deterring illegal conduct.... Section 7031 represents a legislative determination that the importance of deterring unlicensed persons from engaging in the contracting business outweighs any harshness between the parties, and that such deterrence can best be realized by denying violators the right to maintain any action for compensation in the courts of the state....

It is true that when the Legislature enacts a statute forbidding certain conduct for the purpose of protecting one class of persons from the activities of another, a member of the protected class may maintain an action notwithstanding the fact that he has shared in the illegal transaction.... The class protected by the statute includes those who deal with a person required by the statute to have a license.... However, when the person who was required to have a license but did not have one is himself a subcontractor,... he... is not to be protected from his own unlicensed activities. To allow him to recover would in fact destroy the protection of those who dealt with him, and they are in the class the Legislature intended to protect whether they are owners or general contractors.... [Plaintiff's] failure to obtain a license... made the transaction illegal.... General contractors as much as owners are entitled to raise the defense of lack of a license in the subcontractor. If they were not, section 7031 would be no deterrent to subcontractors, since they generally do look to the general contractor for compensation....

LEGAL CAPACITY

Capacity, the fourth requirement for a valid contract, requires that the parties to the contract have the legal ability to bind themselves to the agreement. Fortunately, the lack of such capacity (called incapacity) is the exception and not the rule. Hence, the burden of proof regarding incapacity falls on the party raising it as a defense to the enforcement of the contract or as a basis for rescission of the contract. Lack of capacity does not prevent the formation of a contract, rather it allows the incapacitated party a choice to ratify the contract or disaffirm it.

Indeed, the law often uses status as a basis for making distinctions that may protect or limit the legal rights of any persons falling within these classifications. For this reason, many jurisdictions determine that the contracts of minors, insane persons, intoxicated persons, aliens, and convicts are void or voidable. For most of these situations, the person being protected has the right to either enforce the contract or to disaffirm the contract. However, he or she has to decide whether to affirm or disaffirm the entire agreement; he or she cannot choose parts to affirm and parts to disaffirm. It is not required that the other party knows that the person lacks capacity. In earlier times, the common law also curtailed the contractual rights of married women. Most states have eliminated these restrictions, but some vestiges of these acts remain in a few states.[1] We now focus on the contracts of these individuals.

Minors

Most states, by statute, have decided that adult status occurs as early as age 18 for almost all purposes. (A common exception involves the purchase or consumption of alcoholic beverages.) A person under that age is a minor (or an infant). Some states allow for termination of infancy status upon marriage or *emancipation* (that is, the attainment of legal independence from one's parents).

Disaffirmance/Rescission   To protect minors in their dealings with adults (and businesses run by adults), the law allows minors to disaffirm (or avoid) their contracts with adults except in certain specialized cases, such as contracts involving *necessaries* (things that directly foster the minor's well-being). Recall that the minor can enforce the contract if it is to his or her benefit. When the minor decides not to perform the legal obligations contemplated in the agreement, he or she disaffirms the contract. Stated differently, the minor has the option either of performing the contract or avoiding it. The converse is not true: The adult who has contracted with a minor ordinarily will not be able to use the infancy of the minor to avoid the contract unless the minor releases the adult from the contract. As we will see, the minor's powers in a given instance may be quite broad. A business person can curtail a minor's powers of avoidance by insisting that a parent or other adult cosign the contract. In this fashion, the business can effectively limit the minor's power of rescission, or the ability to have the contract set aside. This is true because even if the minor disaffirms the contract, the adult cosigner still will remain liable on it.

Upon disaffirmance, the minor must return to the adult the property or other consideration that was the subject of the contract if this is possible. Strong policy reasons exist for this rule, called the *duty of restoration*. It clearly seems unfair to let the minor "have it both ways"—that is, rescind the contract and yet retain the consideration. The law, therefore, says that if the minor wants to avoid a contract, he or she must *totally* avoid it.

Sometimes the minor cannot return the property or other consideration because it has been damaged or destroyed. For example, Ace Used Cars will be very upset if, 10 months into the agreement, 17-year-old Marcie, who purchased a car from Ace, presents Ace with a demolished car and asks for all the money that she has paid. In most states, minors like Marcie will get exactly what they request because merely returning the car fulfills the minor's duty of restoration. In some states, however, Ace will be able to set off the costs of repairing the car from any payments that are being returned to Marcie. Courts in other jurisdictions will impose liability on minors like Marcie for the reasonable value of the benefit the minor received by having use of the car for the period prior to the rescission.[2]

Misrepresentation of Age   What if the minor intentionally misrepresents his or her age? For example, suppose our 17-year-old Marcie tells the salesperson at Ace Used Cars that she is 21 and uses a falsified driver's license as proof. If Marcie later tries to avoid the contract with Ace, can Ace argue that this intentional misrepresentation (fraud) prevents rescission? Some states hold that such a misrepresentation completely cuts off the minor's power of disaffirmance. Under the law of most jurisdictions, the minor still can disaffirm the contract in an age-misrepresentation case. However, Marci did commit the tort of deceit in this example, and Ace may be able to hold her liable for that tort. However, some states refuse to impose liability if it would indirectly cause enforcement of the contract that the minor has disaffirmed.

Changing the circumstances of the first example, assume now that Marcie had traded in another car when she purchased the now-demolished car from Ace. When she disaffirms the contract, Ace has to return the trade-in to the minor in order to fulfill the adult's corresponding duty of restoration. If Ace already has sold this car to a *bona fide purchaser* (a person who purchases in good faith, for value, and without notice of any defects or defenses affecting the sale or transaction) the minor cannot get the car back (as would be the usual result under the common law). However, Marcie can recover the price paid to Ace by the third party. This result occurs because UCC § 2-403 covers this transaction. Thus, the UCC has changed the common law.

The law does not require any special words or acts to disaffirm. Disaffirmances may be made orally or in writing, formally (by a lawsuit) or informally, directly or indirectly. The public policy considerations permitting a minor to disaffirm his or her contracts are very strong. In one case, the court allowed Kevin Green, a minor, to disaffirm his contract for the purchase of a Camaro even though the car had been wrecked and Kevin had received a settlement from his insurance company. Kevin had previously attempted to disaffirm, but the auto dealer refused to refund his purchase price unless Kevin first repaired the blown head gasket on the car. Under state law the dealer did not have the right to make this demand. Kevin then repaired the Camaro and was driving it when he was involved in an accident that totaled the car. The court allowed Kevin to disaffirm the contract and recover the purchase price he paid to the dealer.[3] The minor will not be held responsible for any property that was lost, stolen, or destroyed. While this ruling seems harsh, it emphasizes the point that adults should avoid contracting with minors.

The minor's power of disaffirmance, whether the contract is executory or executed, ordinarily extends through his or her minority and for a reasonable time after achieving majority. How long is "reasonable" becomes a question of fact for a judge or jury to decide in light of all the circumstances.

Ratification   Ratification means that the minor in some fashion has indicated (1) approval of the contract made while he or she is a minor and (2) an intention to be bound to the provisions of that contract. Ratification represents the opposite of disaffirmance and cuts off any right to disaffirm. Ratification cannot occur until the minor achieves majority status. Otherwise, the law's protection of minors would be meaningless.

Ratification takes two separate forms: express and implied. *Express ratifications* occur when the minor explicitly and definitely agrees to accept the obligations of the contract. The policy of protecting minors is so strong that many states require express ratifications to be in writing. The more common type of ratification occurs indirectly and is called implied ratification: It occurs through conduct that shows approval of the contract, even though the minor has said nothing specifically about agreeing to be bound to it. Failure to make a timely disaffirmance can constitute an implied ratification of an executed contract. Thus, a minor who is not diligent in disaffirming within a reasonable time after attaining majority will have impliedly ratified the contract. Such inaction does not ordinarily bring about the ratification of an executory contract, however. Some courts will hold that, by itself, partial payment of a debt usually is not equivalent to ratification, unless payment is accompanied by the minor's express intention to be bound to the contract.

Necessaries   Even in the absence of ratification, minors will be liable for transactions when the other party has furnished them with "necessaries." Necessaries are also called necessities or necessaries for life. Necessaries formerly encompassed only food, clothing, and shelter; but the law has broadened the doctrine to cover other things that directly foster the minor's well-being. The basis for the minor's liability is quasi contract, which you learned about in Chapter 9. (Remember that there can be no liability in contract law because of a lack of capacity.) If an adult has supplied necessaries to the minor, the law will imply liability for the reasonable value of those necessaries. Often the law will not impose liability on the minor for the cost of necessaries unless the minor's parents are unable or unwilling to discharge their obligation to support their child and pay for the essentials.

The definition of necessaries depends on the minor's circumstances or social and economic situation in life. In this sense, the rule is applied somewhat subjectively. Although food, clothing, and shelter are covered, is a fur coat a necessary for which the minor is liable? It may be, depending on the minor's social station. Similarly, loans for medical or dental services or education also may comprise necessaries in some situations. Numerous cases involve cars; and many courts hold that a car, especially if the minor uses it for commuting to and from work, is a necessary for which the minor remains liable.[4] The definition of what constitutes a necessary changes as community values and mores change.

Special Statutes   Legislatures in many states have passed special statutes making minors liable in a variety of circumstances. Under such laws, minors may be responsible for educational loans, medical or dental expenses, insurance policies, bank account contracts, transportation by common carrier (for example, airline tickets), and other expenses. These statutes protect the interests of those persons who deal with minors who exhibit the skills and maturity of adults.

Insane Persons

Like minors, insane persons (also called mental incompetents) may lack the capacity to make a binding contract. Under contract law, a person must be so mentally infirm or deranged as to be unable to understand what he or she is agreeing to or the consequences of the agreement. The mental or physical causes of such disability, such as Alzheimer's disease, mental retardation, stroke, senility, or alcohol or drug abuse—are irrelevant.

Effects of Transactions by Insane Persons   Some insane persons have been declared insane by the appropriate state court, for example, family court or probate court. Normally when a court declares that a person is mentally incompetent, the court follows that decision by appointing a guardian for him or her. (The *guardian* is the person legally responsible for taking care of another who lacks the legal capacity to take care of himself or herself.) After this appointment, future contracts of the incompetent person are void. Now, the only person who can contract for him or her is the guardian. The guardian's contracts on his or her behalf will be valid (assuming that there are no other problems with the contracts). In rare cases, the court declares the person mentally incompetent but does not appoint a guardian. This tends to occur when the court is having problems choosing the guardian. In this case, the future contracts by the insane person may be void or voidable depending on state law.

Given the relatively broad definition of "insanity" in contract law, it is quite possible to find a person who is considered insane even though that person has not been adjudged insane by a court. When there has been no adjudication, the contracts of the insane person are merely voidable, rather than void. To disaffirm a contract, the person using insanity as a defense must prove that he or she actually was insane at the time of contracting. If the person instead was lucid and understood the nature and consequences of the contract, that person is bound by the contract. This power of an insane person to avoid contracts also extends to the heirs or personal representative of a deceased insane person. The guardian of a living insane person possesses similar powers. Upon regaining sanity, a formerly insane person nonetheless may ratify a contract made during the period of insanity.

As with other voidable contracts, when the insane person (or his or her guardian or representative) seeks to disaffirm the contract, he or she should return any consideration that has been received. Sometimes the insane person no longer has the consideration. Often, this is due to some unwise behavior of the insane person, such as washing dishes wearing an expensive ring or not closing the gate behind a horse. In those cases, some courts make a distinction between whether the contract was fair to the insane person. These courts determine that if the contract is fair, the consideration received by the insane person must be returned or the insane person cannot disaffirm. On the other hand, if the contract was not fair and the insane person cannot locate the consideration, he or she can still disaffirm the contract. In effect, the court is deciding that there is overreaching by the other party in these cases. Even if the other party did not know that the person was insane, he or she should have known that there was something wrong.

Determining whether a transaction by an insane person is void, voidable, or enforceable depends heavily on the facts. Exhibit 11.1 summarizes the rules for insane persons. Notice that there are 2 basic categories if there has been a court adjudication, and 2 basic categories if there has not. If the insane person has a guardian, the guardian's contracts in his or her behalf will be valid.

Necessaries   Similar to the rules covering minors, the law also holds insane persons liable for necessaries in quasi contract. Generally, the same categories of goods and services are used. In the context of insanity, fewer controversies should arise regarding whether medical or legal services are necessaries—they probably constitute necessaries for which the insane person remains liable.

Exhibit 11.1

Contracts of Insane Persons

	Court Adjudication	No Court Adjudication	
Guardian Appointed	Void	Insane person must return the consideration in order to disaffirm.	**Contract Is Fair**
No Guardian Appointed	Void or voidable	Insane person need not return the consideration if he or she no longer has it; he or she can still disaffirm.	**Contract Is Unfair**

Intoxicated Persons

If a person is so thoroughly intoxicated that he or she does not understand the nature, purpose, and effect of the agreement, the person's mental disability approaches that of an insane person. A person who was in such a situation can try to disaffirm the agreement. Intoxication can be caused by alcohol, drugs, or a combination of them. Courts generally are hostile to avoiding contracts on the basis of intoxication except in unusual circumstances. Whether a court will permit disaffirmance depends on the degree of intoxication involved, which is a question of fact. Slight degrees of intoxication will not justify disaffirmance.

Whether the intoxication was involuntary or voluntary may bear on the result, too. If a plaintiff has plied the defendant with liquor, any resulting intoxication may factor into a court's finding of incapacity, fraud, or overreaching that may release the defendant from the agreement. This is especially true if defendant did not intend to ingest alcohol or drugs, but they were concealed in his or her beverage or food. Even voluntary intoxication sometimes can result in a voidable contract if the facts support this conclusion.

Upon regaining sobriety, the formerly intoxicated person either may avoid or ratify the contract. The rules about acting within a reasonable time apply here as well; if the person does not quickly disaffirm the contract, implied ratification will result.

Aliens

An *alien* is a citizen of a foreign country. Most of the disabilities formerly imposed on aliens have been removed, usually through treaties. Consequently, a *legal* alien ordinarily can enter into contracts and pursue gainful employment without legal disabilities, just as any U.S. citizen can. Some states limit an alien's right to own or inherit property, especially real property. *Enemy* aliens, or those who reside in countries with which we officially are at war, cannot enforce contracts during the period of hostility but sometimes can after the war ends. The contracts of illegal aliens are generally valid.

Convicts

In many states, conviction of a felony or treason carries with it certain contractual disabilities. For instance, laws may prohibit convicts from conveying property during their incarceration. Such disabilities, if applicable, exist only during imprisonment. Upon release from prison, these persons possess full contractual rights.

Married Women

Under early common law, married women's contracts were void. The law viewed women as their husbands' property and consequently lacking in capacity to make contracts and own real estate. This common law disability has been eliminated by

Exhibit 11.2

Contractual Capacity

Class of Person	Definition	Classification of Contract	Exceptions
Minors	Under the age of 18, unless emancipated	Voidable (upon return of consideration to seller)	1. Misrepresentation of age eliminates the power of rescission in some jurisdictions 2. Failure to rescind within a reasonable time after achieving majority (implied ratification) 3. Express ratification after achieving majority (necessity of a writing in some jurisdictions) 4. Necessaries (liability in quasi contract in some cases if parents are unable or unwilling to pay) 5. Special statutes making minors liable
Insane persons	Those adjudged insane and who have a guardian appointed	Void	1. Capacity of guardians to contract on the insane person's behalf
	Those insane but not adjudged so by a court	Voidable	1. Ratification possible during lucid periods 2. Special treatment if the insane person cannot find the consideration and the contract is unfair 3. Necessaries (liability in quasi contract in some circumstances)
Intoxicated persons	Slightly intoxicated persons	Valid	
	Seriously intoxicated persons	Possibly voidable, depending on other circumstances	1. Ratification possible upon regaining sobriety 2. Failure to rescind within a reasonable time after regaining sobriety in involuntary intoxication circumstances (implied ratification)

Exhibit 11.2 Continued

Class of Person	Definition	Classification of Contract	Exceptions
Aliens	Legal aliens	Valid	1. Some restrictions sometimes regarding ownership of real property
	Enemy aliens during hostilities	Void (sometimes deemed unenforceable) during hostilities	
	Enemy aliens after hostilities end	Valid	
	Illegal aliens	Valid	
Convicts	Convicts during incarceration	Void for certain types of contracts, valid for others	
	Convicts after release	Valid	
Married women	Women who are legally married	Valid	1. Some anachronistic restrictions remaining in a few states

statute or by judicial decision in almost all states. Exhibit 11.2 summarizes the contractual capacities of minors, insane persons, intoxicated persons, aliens, convicts, and married women.

GENUINENESS OF CONSENT

What seems to be a valid agreement in actuality may lack the parties' genuine assent. The law has to ascertain whether the consent given by each of the parties is real or whether the facts actually differ from those to which the parties have outwardly agreed. As a prerequisite for contract formation, the law requires reality (or genuineness) of consent. The existence of fraud, misrepresentation, mistake, duress, undue influence, or unconscionability may show a lack of genuine mutual assent.[5]

Fraud

Fraud is a word everyone uses fairly loosely. Basically, it consists of deception or hoodwinking; and it seems to involve a communication of some sort. But as one ancient case notes, "[a] nod or a wink, or a shake of the head or a smile" will do.[6] There are two types of fraud under contract law: fraud in the execution (also known as fraud in the inception or fraud in the factum) and fraud in the inducement. Fraud in the execution is relatively rare. In *fraud in the execution*, the victim is not aware that what he or she is signing is actually a contract. The victim thinks that he or she is signing something else, such as an ordinary letter or a contest entry form. When the court determines that there was fraud in the execution, the contract is void.

The more common type of fraud is fraud in the inducement. In *fraud in the inducement*, the victim is aware that the parties are entering into a contract, but he or she does not know the true nature of the agreement. If the court concludes that there is fraud in the inducement, the contract is voidable at the option of the victim of the fraud. The essence of fraud in the inducement is hard to pin down. One common definition states that fraud is a deliberate misrepresentation of a material fact with the intent to induce another person to enter into a contract that will be injurious to that person.[7] This definition can be broken down into six components or elements.

Elements of Fraud To constitute fraud, the misrepresentation or misstatement first must concern a fact. A *fact* is something reasonably subject to exact knowledge. For example, statements about the size of a car engine or the dimensions of a real estate parcel involve facts. To show this first element of fraud, the plaintiff will have to prove that the defendant misstated a fact. Predictions, statements of value, and expressions of opinions generally do not equate with misrepresentations of fact. Misstatements of law are not generally actionable as fraud either. In any given situation, it may be difficult to distinguish a fact from an opinion. Suppose a car salesperson says to you, "This little dandy will get you down the road at a pretty good clip. It has a great engine. It's a V-6, and those engines have been very serviceable." The first two remarks probably are opinions. They also may fall into the category of "seller's puff" (also called "dealer's talk" or "puffing"). Seller's puff is exaggerated opinions that sellers make in an attempt to sell goods or services. The statement about the type of engine probably constitutes a fact. You may be unhappy, for instance, if you find a V-8 engine in the car after you purchase it, or if you find out the V-6 engines have many problems and the salesperson knows this. You may want to argue that you have been a victim of intentional misrepresentation. Courts tend to discount statements of value because of genuine differences in the way people assess things. When Joe says, "That ring is worth a thousand dollars," most courts will refuse to call Joe's statement a fact. Such nonfactual statements of value ordinarily do not fulfill this first element of a showing of fraud. A common exception is if the person providing his or her opinion owed the victim a fiduciary duty to be truthful about his or her opinion. (*Fiduciary duties* are duties that arise from a relationship of trust or confidence that requires one who holds the special position of trust or confidence to act with the utmost good faith and loyalty.)

The second element of fraud a plaintiff must prove is that the fact that was allegedly misstated is a *material* or substantial factor. Depending on the jurisdiction, courts may use an *objective standard* (would it be material to a reasonable person) or they may use a *subjective standard* (whether it was material to this plaintiff). To use the earlier example, most people would probably care about the size of the engine, the mileage of the car, the number of previous owners, and whether the vehicle has been in a major accident. Misstatements about these facts may lead to liability for fraud.

The third element is one of the most difficult to prove: It is the defendant's knowledge of the falsity of his or her statements. This is called *scienter*, that is, guilty knowledge. In other words, at the time of making the statement, the defendant knew, or should have known, that he or she was misstating an important fact. Outright lies, of course, would meet this third requirement. Interestingly, the defendant also may be liable (1) for reckless use of—or disregard for—the truth, (2) for a statement made without verifying its accuracy when verification is possible, or (3) for making a statement when the defendant has no idea whether the statement is true or false. To illustrate the second situation, assume that a prospective buyer says to the homeowner, "I guess the property line extends to the fence, doesn't it?" The homeowner nods yes, even though the line actually does not extend that far. If the buyer purchases in reliance on this statement, a cause of action in fraud may result.

The fourth element is an *intent to deceive*. In other words, the purpose of the false statements is to induce the victim into entering the contract.

The plaintiff also must prove the fifth element that he or she *reasonably relied* on the deception. For example, if Tom inspects a lakefront cottage with a front porch that is on the verge of caving into the lake, a court will not allow him to cry "fraud" if the porch crumbles into the water one month after Tom buys the cottage. The same will be true even if the owner has said the cottage is structurally sound. Clearly, Tom should have been aware of such a *patent* (obvious) defect. However, if the damage instead derives from a *latent* (hidden/unobservable by the human eye) defect, such as carpenter ant infestation, Tom may win unless the court thinks Tom's failure to order a pest inspection is unreasonable.

The final element of a plaintiff's proof—*injury*, or *detriment*—normally is not difficult to show. In the last example, Tom can argue that his damages amount to the sum needed to rid the cottage of carpenter ants and to repair the dwelling. In many cases, the injury is that the plaintiff paid too high a price based on the fraud. In some cases, the plaintiff may ask for rescission of the contract. When a court grants rescission, both parties return any consideration that they have received. Courts generally do not require proof of injury if the plaintiff is requesting rescission. Fraudulent contracts are voidable at the option of the injured party. The facts of each case normally will dictate which remedy a plaintiff will pursue. The injured party, as plaintiff, faces a final pitfall: He or she must act as quickly as possible, or the court might decide that he or she waived the cause of action.

Silence   The common law held that "mere silence is not fraud." Silence denotes the total absence of any statement, so the rule arose that one cannot be liable for fraud unless one had said or done something. Remember that the first element requires a misstatement or misrepresentation of a fact.

In order to encourage disclosure and honesty in business transactions, many jurisdictions now reject this rule and require disclosure in certain instances. For example, in some states the seller must inform the buyer of any defects in a

eClass 11.1 Sales/Marketing

MARKETING AND SALES STRATEGIES

eClass needs to generate revenues very quickly at the launch of its business if it hopes to survive. As a result, Ani favors a very aggressive approach to the marketing of the firm's products. Yousef, in contrast, prefers a more cautious marketing strategy. Yousef believes that sales representatives who answer questions honestly and completely will build a loyal customer base and that a few lost sales initially are preferable to a number of lost customers in the future. Meg responds that, in the absence of robust sales early, the company's financial prospects remain so shaky that eClass will have few worries about customer concerns in the future because the enterprise will fail. All three have asked for your advice. What will you tell them?

BUSINESS CONSIDERATIONS   What sort of policy should a business adopt regarding the information a sales representative can or should communicate to customers? What factors will influence the firm's decision?

ETHICAL CONSIDERATIONS   Suppose a sales representative knows that a customer has an erroneous impression of the product, but the representative has no legal obligation to speak. Does the sales representative have an ethical obligation to speak? Why or why not? What should the sales representative do? Why?

house. Similarly, if the buyer asks a question, the seller must answer truthfully and correct any misconceptions that the buyer has. A seller's silence in such instances today may be the basis for legal liability. Still, the strict rule is that there generally is no duty to speak (that is, to disclose such facts).

Even the common law, however, deemed some situations so fraught with the possibility of injury or detriment that it placed a duty to speak on the party possessing the information. We have already examined situations involving latent defects. A duty to speak also arises in situations in which the parties owe each other fiduciary duties. For example, an investment advisor should inform all her clients of her part ownership in ABC Corporation before she suggests that her clients purchase ABC stock. Similarly, in applying for insurance coverage, one cannot be silent if the insurer asks questions about one's medical history. To avoid fraud, one must, for example, disclose the existence of a heart condition. In addition, if a statement made in preliminary negotiations is no longer true when the contract is to be signed, the statement must be corrected in order to escape a possible lawsuit based on fraud.

Misrepresentation

In general, everything previously discussed about the elements of fraud is true of a cause of action involving misrepresentation, with one notable exception: Misrepresentation lacks the elements of *scienter* and *intent to deceive*. Nevertheless, misrepresentation (often called innocent misrepresentation to differentiate it from fraud) can permit the victim to avoid the contract.

Suppose that Marcus received a watch from his uncle for his college graduation. The watch was allegedly a Rolex, and thus quite valuable. Marcus had no reason to doubt this allegation or to suspect that the watch was a "knock-off" (a fake Rolex.) Some time later Marcus was in need of money and decided that he should sell his watch to obtain the funds he needed. He sold the watch to Walter, a friend and co-worker, for several hundred dollars. After the purchase Walter took the watch to a jeweler to get it appraised so that he could add it to his homeowners insurance policy coverage. The jeweler told Walter that the watch was an imitation and only worth about $30. In this situation Walter could easily establish misrepresentation, disaffirm the contract, and recover the money he had paid after returning the watch to Marcus. It is quite likely that Walter could not prove *scienter* since Marcus did not know, and had no reason to know, that the watch was a fake. Since Walter cannot prove fraud, he probably cannot collect damages. *Misrepresentation*, or the innocent misstatement of a material fact that is relied on with resultant injury, makes the contract voidable at the option of the injured party. Rescission is a possible (and, in some jurisdictions, the exclusive) remedy. Again, the plaintiff must act in a timely manner so as not to waive the cause of action.

Practically speaking, most plaintiffs allege both fraud and misrepresentation in the same lawsuit. Fraud is harder to prove but more desirable from the plaintiff's point of view; successful proof of fraud brings with it the possibility of recovering damages under the tort of deceit. The elements of deceit are identical to those of fraud. Upon a showing of deceit, a court may award *punitive* damages (damages beyond the actual losses suffered) in addition to the actual (or compensatory) damages normally recoverable for fraud. But even if the plaintiff fails to prove fraud, recovery on grounds of misrepresentation is possible. At the very least, a showing of misrepresentation will form the basis for rescission.

Exhibit 11.3 describes the elements of misrepresentation and fraud; it shows the analysis a court may follow in determining the presence of either as a defense to a contract.

Mistake

Human nature is such that people often try to unravel transactions because they have made an error about some facet of the deal. Imagine the chaos if courts readily accepted these arguments. Such unpredictability would unduly hamper commercial transactions. On the other hand, the law stresses the importance of mutual assent in contract. Thus, the law, on policy grounds, wishes to set the contract aside if the error is so great that it has tainted the parties' consent to the agreement.

Exhibit 11.3

The Elements of Fraud and Misrepresentation

Has the defendant misrepresented a fact (as opposed to an opinion, a statement of value, or a prediction)?	YES	YES	NO
Is the misstated fact a material one?	YES	YES	NO
Does the defendant have knowledge of the falsity of the statement? (This is called *scienter*.)	NO	YES	
Does the defendant have an intent to deceive?	NO	YES	
Has the plaintiff reasonably relied on the defendant's misstatements (as opposed to unreasonable reliance)?	YES	YES	NO
Due to the defendant's misstatement, has the plaintiff suffered an injury or detriment?	YES	YES	NO
If the defendant has been silent, is silence justifiable in this situation?		NO	YES
Has the plaintiff also shown the tort of deceit?		YES	
Are punitive damages possible?		YES	
	Plaintiff has shown *misrepresentation.*		
		Plaintiff has shown *fraud.*	
			Plaintiff has shown neither *misrepresentation* nor *fraud.*

The legal doctrine of mistake tries to balance these competing interests. *Mistake* occurs when the parties are wrong about the existence or absence of a past or present fact that is material to their transaction. Note that the parties must be wrong about *material* facts. Legal mistake is not synonymous with ignorance, inability, or inaccurate judgments relating to value or quality. Courts will rescind contracts on the ground of mistake only if the error is so fundamental that it cannot be said that the parties were in agreement about the essential facts of the transaction. Mistakes as to law, in contrast, generally will not constitute grounds for rescission of the contract. Two kinds of mistakes exist: unilateral and bilateral (or mutual) mistakes.

Unilateral Mistake   As the term implies, in a unilateral mistake, only one party is mistaken about a material fact. The general rule, with some exceptions, holds that courts will *not* rescind such contracts. Unilateral mistakes frequently result from misplaced expectations of value. Let us suppose that Reza goes to an antique store to look for a Duncan Phyfe table. He finds a table he believes to be a Duncan Phyfe and, without mentioning his belief to the store owner, pays a hefty price for it. Later that evening, a friend informs him the table is not a Duncan Phyfe. If Reza tries to avoid the contract, he will not be successful because only he was mistaken about a material fact—that is, that the table was a Duncan Phyfe. He also was mistaken as to value. In such unilateral mistake situations, courts take a hands-off approach and leave the parties with the bargains they have made. Rescission of the contract ordinarily is not granted. However, the result here might differ if the store owner knew or should have known of Reza's error or if the owner acted fraudulently or unconscionably: then the court might allow rescission of the contract.

Similarly, courts use the concept of unilateral mistake in cases of mechanical errors in business computations. Such situations may arise if a contractor makes an addition error in computing a bid. The person soliciting the bid generally will choose the lowest bidder. Once the successful contractor/bidder recognizes its mistake, it will wish to rescind the contract. For example, assume Javier makes a bid to perform some work on Melvin's project. If Melvin accepted the bid and did not know or have reason to know of Javier's error, there will be a binding contract on the terms proposed by Javier in most states. However, there are court cases that indicate that Javier is able to rescind the contract if Javier notifies Melvin before Melvin has changed his position in reliance on the contract. Also, there are some court cases that indicate that even if Melvin has changed his position, Melvin's damages are limited to the damages incurred in his reliance on the bid. Courts take a different approach if Melvin knew or should have known of Javier's mistake in his computation. In these situations the mistake is said to be *palpable* (obvious or evident), and the court will decide that no contract was formed. In the prior example, assume that Javier's bid was 30 percent less than the next lowest bid. The court may decide that the difference is so significant that Melvin should have known that the bid contained a computation error. The rule about palpable errors only applies to computation errors or other errors that are very similar.

Bilateral Mistake   If both parties are in error about the essence of the agreement, bilateral (or mutual) mistake results. Courts will rescind such agreements on the rationale that, owing to a mistake about the existence, identity, or nature of the subject matter of the contract, a valid agreement has not occurred. If a mutual mistake of fact is present, generally either party may disaffirm this voidable contract. For example, assume an American company contracts with a foreign company (headquartered in New York) for hand-loomed rugs. The firms contract in April, but, unknown to both parties, a warehouse fire had destroyed the rugs in March. The destruction of the subject matter makes this contract voidable on the grounds of bilateral mistake: The parties have made an error regarding a significant fact—that the rugs existed at the time of contract formation.

Ambiguities, or uncertainties regarding the meanings of expressions used in contractual agreements, constitute another type of mutual mistake. If the American buyer believes that the term rugs means room-sized carpets, but, because of social or cultural differences, the international seller envisions rugs as smaller, that is, more comparable in size to wall hangings, this ambiguity may constitute mutual mistake. If so, rescission may be justifiable.

Reformation   If a court easily can remedy the mistake, a court may *reform* the contract, or rewrite it to reflect the parties' actual intentions. In the ambiguity example, assuming the rugs were obtainable, once the parties recognize the ambiguity, reformation would permit a court to make room-sized rugs the subject matter of the contract. (Reformation is an equitable remedy, and the court will only reform this contract if it is fair to do so.) If reformation is an appropriate remedy, the "rewritten" contract will be fully enforceable. Be aware, though, that large backlogs of court cases form a substantial impediment to reformation as a practical remedy. Therefore, it is important to use care to ascertain exactly what your agreement means to avoid a great many frustrations (and expenses).

The nature of electronic commerce and its reliance on *electronic agents* (computer programs and/or electronic or automated means) has given rise to concerns not only about when assent occurs (a topic covered in Chapter 10), but also about how to handle inadvertent errors. Virtually everyone has either pushed the wrong computer key or at least come close to doing so. To minimize the possibility of someone's unintentionally being bound to a contract, UETA § 10 allows one to avoid an automated transaction effected through an inadvertent error. Assuming a business-to-consumer (B2C) transaction where the business's (B's) electronic agent lacks any mechanisms for preventing or correcting an error, the consumer (C) may avoid the transaction and the legal consequences caused by the inadvertent error. In other words, if you meant to order two computer games but accidentally ordered 22 because you struck the "2" key twice or lingered on it too long, you could cancel this transaction if the online merchant has not put in place security procedures for detecting changes or errors. The consumer, upon learning that the Web site operator believes the consumer has entered into a transaction, must promptly inform the Web site operator (or Internet merchant) of the error and that he or she had not intended to be bound by the electronic record (the message about the 22 games). This provision of UETA seeks to encourage online firms and those who conduct business through Electronic Data Interchanges (EDIs) and other electronic agents to build into their systems security measures aimed at preventing such errors. This provision notes that when the special provisions do not apply, other law—including the common law rules of mistake—and the parties' contract (if any) will govern the transaction.

UCITA,[8] like UETA, protects consumers who have sent erroneous electronic messages that they did not intend to send by allowing such consumers to use the electronic error as a defense to contract formation. This provision defines an electronic error as one resulting from the online firm's use of an automated system that fails to provide a reasonable means for detecting and correcting any such errors. It penalizes firms that fail to provide such systems.

Duress

No genuine assent to the terms of an agreement results if a person assents while under duress. The person who assented under duress can ask for rescission of the contract and often he or she can sue for damages under tort law as well.

Duress involves the use of coercion to force a person to agree to a contract that he or she would not have entered absent the coercive threat. To constitute duress, the coercion must be so extreme that the victim has lost all ability to refuse the offer. The assent so acquired is not freely and voluntarily given, so the consent is not real. Courts look for evidence of physical threats or threats that, if carried out, will cause intense mental anguish. What constitutes duress depends on the jurisdiction and the facts, but duress commonly includes threats to harm the person, threats to harm a member of his or her family, threats to harm his or her property, threats to a person's livelihood (such as his or her business reputation), and threats to have the person unlawfully prosecuted for a crime. Courts, however, ordinarily do not view threats of civil suits as constituting duress.

Historically, duress required proving a threat of imminent bodily harm, and the threat had to be sufficient to "persuade" a reasonable person to agree in order to avoid the bodily harm. Recently, the doctrine of economic duress (also known as business compulsion) has arisen. *Economic duress* occurs when one party is forced to agree to a further, wrongful, and coercive demand (usually a price increase) in order to receive commodities or services to which he or she is entitled under the original contract. The party alleging economic duress ordinarily must show: (1) wrongful acts or threats by the defendant; (2) financial distress caused by the wrongful acts or threats; and (3) the absence of any reasonable alternative to the terms presented by the wrongdoer (that is, the injured party cannot obtain the goods or services elsewhere). Whether a court will grant recovery based on economic duress depends heavily on the particular facts of a given situation.

The earlier example of the hand-loomed rugs illustrates this concept. Assume that the foreign rug company has the only available hand-loomed rugs, and the American buyer has agreed to pay $2,500 per rug. Economic duress exists if the seller subsequently tells the American buyer that he can have the rugs only if he is willing to pay $4,000 apiece for them. Basing its decision on the concept of economic duress, a court may force the seller to sell the rugs at the original price of $2,500 or allow the American buyer after the fact to recover any difference in price.

As with most of the reality-of-consent situations, contracts made under duress ordinarily are voidable. The victim of the duress may choose to rescind the contract. If the victim has endured the coercive conduct for too long, his or her lack of action may amount to ratification of the agreement. Courts may find that the contract based on duress is void especially if the person being threatened is not aware that he or she is signing a contract.

Undue Influence

In contrast, undue influence involves taking advantage of a particularly close and trusting relationship with the victim. Some individuals who may have that close relationship include children, parents, spouses, accountants, doctors, housekeepers, and lawyers. *Undue influence* is the use of a relationship of trust and confidence to extract contractual advantages. The person in the fiduciary role may have the ability to unfairly sway the other party into agreeing to a contract by virtue of their relationship

eClass 11.2 Manufacturing/Management

SHOULD THE FIRM AGREE TO THE DEMANDS OF A SUPPLIER?

eClass has entered into a contract with Total Fabricator, Inc. (TFI), a manufacturing company, to duplicate, package, and label 2,000 units of eAccounting for $5 per unit. However, because of the likelihood that eClass will succeed, TFI also wants to produce the next 10,000 units at the same price per unit. To improve its leverage over eClass, TFI refuses to produce and ship the first 2,000 units of eAccounting for the agreed on price of $5 per unit unless eClass guarantees that TFI will have the contract for the next 10,000 units as well. Both Yousef and Meg know that, for a larger order, they can negotiate a better price per unit; however, they also know that, to ride the present wave of popularity relating to educational software, they must receive the first 2,000 units immediately and, therefore, must rely on TFI. The eClass firm members seek your advice. What legal risks are inherent in TFI's position? What legal remedy can eClass seek if it agrees to these terms now but wants to avoid this agreement later?

BUSINESS CONSIDERATIONS   How does a firm gauge when a "hard-line" position approaches illegality? Should a firm err on the side of caution and always disavow such an approach?

ETHICAL CONSIDERATIONS   Is the intersection of law and ethics represented by the Uniform Commercial Code's position on unconscionability advisable? Does the UCC section deviate too far from the principles of freedom of contract? Why or why not?

that would not have been agreed to with a non-fiduciary. Because of the domination by another, the contracting party actually has not exercised his or her free will in entering into the contract, but instead has given into the will or wishes of the other party. It can be difficult for courts to determine when the persuasiveness of the fiduciary has become so intense that the other party has lost their free will. But when they are convinced that this has occurred, they permit rescission of the challenged contract.

Unconscionability

Some courts have set contracts aside based on the doctrine of unconscionability or extreme unfairness. When considering unconscionability, the courts in many states examine whether there were procedural abuses when the contract was formed and/or whether the contract terms were unreasonably favorable to one side. The Uniform Commercial Code addresses unconscionability in § 2-302. Courts seem more likely to find unconscionability in consumer contracts and employment contracts than in other types of contracts. For example, in *Circuit City Stores, Inc. v. Adams*, the court found the employer's arbitration agreement unconscionable.[9] Unconscionability may signal a lack of meaningful assent to a contract and may justify a court's subsequent intervention on behalf of the injured party.

LEGALITY OF SUBJECT MATTER

U.S. contract law emphasizes bargaining and contract formation through the mutual agreement of the parties. Yet, the permissible boundaries of such conduct remain limited. Society at large may have a stake in the agreement the parties have forged. An agreement to bribe public officials or to murder someone, for instance, has definite repercussions for society that extend beyond the parties who agreed to the bargain. The law imposes a requirement that in order for the bargain to be recognized as a valid contract, the subject matter and purpose of the bargain must be legal. In this sense, the term *illegal contract* constitutes a misnomer; in general, a bargain cannot attain the status of a "contract" unless it is legal. Illegal "contracts" are void. Hence, any bargain, however innocent it seems, that involves a violation of a statute, common law, or public policy is void due to illegality.

Components of Illegality

A widely accepted definition of *illegality* states that a bargain is illegal if its performance is criminal, tortious, or otherwise opposed to public policy.[10] Both the subject matter of the bargain and the realization of its objectives must be permissible under state and federal statutes. Sometimes these statutes impose criminal penalties for their violation (for example, an agreement to engage in arson for money). Other statutes, however, may prohibit certain kinds of bargains (for example, a contract with an unlicensed contractor) without imposing criminal penalties on those who violate these statutes.

The desire to protect the public also underlies the prohibition of bargains involving tortious conduct (for example, an agreement between two parties for the purpose of defrauding a third person).

Even in the absence of an agreement that specifically violates a statute or requires the commission of a tort, courts may declare any bargain that will be detrimental to the public at large to be illegal on *public policy* grounds. Although the concept of public policy may fluctuate as different courts apply different standards, courts increasingly have used this rationale in a variety of contexts in which there appears to be no other technique for protecting the peace, health, or morals of the community. For instance, a bank may offer a rather one-sided night depository agreement in which it refuses to accept liability for a deposit placed in its after-hours slot, even if the loss stems from the negligence of its own employee and the depositor can prove that he or she actually deposited the amount in question with the bank. The concept of public policy—here the protection of depositors' expectations that the bank will take proper care of their deposits and the protection of consumers against one-sided agreements—will permit a court to invalidate such agreements on the grounds of illegality. A court may characterize such agreements as *exculpatory clauses* (portions of agreements in which one party agrees in advance not to hold the other party liable for certain losses for which the second party ordinarily would be liable) or *contracts of adhesion* (contracts in which the terms are not open to negotiation; so-called take-it-or-leave-it contracts). A court may construe the agreement as a contract of adhesion if, in these circumstances, depositors have no choice but to accept the bank's terms.

In general, an illegal bargain is void and unenforceable. This ordinarily is true whether the agreement is executory or fully executed. Usually a court merely leaves the parties where it finds them. Neither party, then, can sue the other. Exceptions to the general rule that courts will not give relief to parties who have created an illegal bargain do exist, however. We will address some of them later.

Mala in Se and *Mala Prohibita* Bargains

Early on, many courts became dissatisfied with the rule that illegal contracts are absolutely void. Some of these courts distinguished between bargains that violate statutes because they are evil *in themselves (mala in se)* and bargains that have been merely *forbidden by statute (mala prohibita)*. The first type (for example, an agreement to murder someone) fell within the general rule and was void. Some courts decided that bargains included within the second type were voidable rather than void, depending on the nature and effect of the act prohibited by the statute.

To illustrate, one case involved the sale of cattle in violation of a law stating that all cattle sold must be tested for brucellosis (a serious disease in cattle) within the 30-day period preceding the sale. The court clearly could have used this statutory violation as a basis for holding the agreement void. Yet the court concluded that this bargain was *mala prohibita*, rather than *mala in se*, because the contract was neither in bad faith nor contrary to public policy: The court enforced the contract.[11]

Courts almost universally recognize two types of agreements as *mala in se* bargains: agreements to commit a crime and agreements to commit a tort. The agreement mentioned earlier to commit arson could be called a *mala in se* bargain because the subject matter of the agreement itself, the commission of a crime, is morally unacceptable. The same would be true of an agreement to kill someone, a so-called murder "contract." Neither party can enforce such agreements; they are absolutely void. Likewise, an agreement that involves the commission of a tort is void. Such bargains may involve agreements to damage the good name of a competitor, to inflict mental distress on a third party, or to trespass against a person's real or personal property.

Determining whether a particular activity violates a statute (assuming the activity is not *mala in se*) is more difficult and requires that courts resort first to the words of the underlying statute. Courts then must assess the legislative intent and, finally, examine the social effects of giving or refusing a remedy in the particular situation.

Agreements That Violate Statutes

Courts ordinarily find certain categories of activities in violation of statutes. These undertakings include price-fixing agreements, performances of services without a license, contracts formed on Sunday, wagering, and usury contracts.

Price-Fixing Agreements   The purpose of price-fixing agreements generally is to restrain competition among competitors, allowing them to exploit the market without fearing "price wars" among themselves. The Sherman Antitrust Act declares such conduct to be a *per se* violation, finding the parties guilty upon a showing of price fixing. Price-fixing agreements also may violate state statutes; or, alternatively, courts may invalidate these arrangements on public policy grounds.

Performances of Services without a License   Agreements to perform services without a required license may constitute another type of statutory violation. To protect the public from unqualified persons, state statutes often require (or regulate) the licensing of professions such as law, medicine, and public accountancy and trades such as contracting, electrical work, and plumbing. Before the state grants a license, the would-be practitioner normally must meet the educational requirements and demonstrate competency by successfully passing an examination. The person who does not have the required license generally cannot enforce his or her bargains for performing such services. Some states distinguish regulatory licenses from revenue licenses which are discussed next. In these states, the absence of a regulatory license makes a contract void, but the absence of a revenue license does not.

The purpose of revenue licensing schemes is primarily to produce revenue rather than to protect the health and welfare of its citizens. For example, many cities require a business license. These licenses are generally a tax: The city does not test the applicant's knowledge of how to successfully operate a business. If the primary intent of the licensing requirement is to produce revenue, the lack of a license generally will not affect the contract between the parties, although the government entity may fine the person who failed to obtain the required license.

It pays to remember that courts have fairly wide discretion in these matters and may take into account such factors as the absence of harm resulting from failure to obtain the license, the extent of the knowledge of the persons involved, and the relative "guilt" of the respective parties. If, for example, a court deems the amount forfeited by the unlicensed professional sufficiently large to constitute a penalty, the professional ordinarily will be able to sue for the fee, despite the lack of a license. As mentioned earlier, even in statutes assigning criminal sanctions, courts will look closely at the legislative intent of the statute as they decide whether to give or to withhold remedies.

Sunday Closing Laws   Sunday closing laws (also called blue laws, Sabbath laws, and Lord's Day Acts) are so named because they prohibit the formation or performance of contracts on Sundays. These laws are troublesome because the existence and terms of such statutes vary widely from state to state. The statutes can be tricky because of the wide variation in what may be sold or done on Sunday. The most common type of statute prohibits the conducting of secular business, or one's "ordinary calling" (such as selling merchandise), on Sunday. You may be familiar with Sunday laws that forbid the sale of certain alcoholic beverages or forbid hunting. Exceptions usually involve works of charity or necessity, which one can undertake on Sunday without fear of sanctions.

In some jurisdictions, a violation of a Sunday statute voids the contract, unless the party seeking recovery can show, for instance, that he or she had no knowledge that the execution of the contract occurred on Sunday. He or she also can argue that the agreement, though initiated on Sunday, was not accepted until later in the week and thus actually ripened into a contract on another day.

Litigants in some jurisdictions have challenged the constitutionality of such statutes. These laws, by singling out Sunday as a "day of rest" from mercantile activity, may violate the First Amendment's prohibition against a governmentally established religion. State governments' enactments of such laws arguably put the interests of one religious group ahead of the interests of others. Courts have declared invalid the Sunday closing laws of some states.

Wagering Statutes   Wagering contracts and lotteries are illegal in certain states because of statutes prohibiting gambling, betting, and other games of chance. The underlying rationale for these laws focuses on protecting the public from the crime and familial discord often associated with gambling. To constitute illegal wagering, the activity must involve a person's paying consideration or value in the hope of receiving a prize or other property by chance. Wagering, in the legal sense, always consists of a scheme involving the artificial creation of risk; hence, insurance contracts or stock transactions, in which risk is an inherent feature, are not illegal wagering. On the other hand, courts may view raffles as unlawful wagering. For instance, because of the relatively soft demand in the housing market, some enterprising couples have attempted to raffle off their homes. The conduct of these people has violated the wagering statutes of some jurisdictions. Note that gambling casinos and government lotteries are legal in some states.

Online gambling represents a fast-growing sector of e-commerce, with an estimated 14.5 million participants annually. This activity has led to a number of recent legal developments. One issue involves whether the transactions of online bettors and online casinos—most of which are located in foreign countries—actually break the law. Some experts interpret a 1960s-era federal wire statute that prohibits placing bets on sports by telephone or wire as encompassing Internet transactions and thus banning online gambling. Several bills aimed at clarifying the statute have been introduced in Congress in recent years.

The gamblers themselves have also offered novel legal theories. Bolstered by the common law rule that gambling or wagering debts are void and uncollectable, some compulsive bettors have refused to pay the credit card charges used to finance their betting. In one California case, Cynthia Haines defaulted on more than $70,000 in off-shore gambling debts accumulated on numerous credit cards and gambling Web sites. When the card companies sued, she contended that she should win because Internet gambling is illegal in California and that gambling debts are not collectable in the state. The parties eventually settled out of court.[12] This and similar lawsuits has led several credit card companies either to refuse to accept Internet-related gambling charges or to formulate new rules governing this aspect of their business operations. Proposed legislation and concerns regarding gambling by minors have played a significant role in the development of such rules.

Usury Statutes   Usurious contracts occur when a lender loans money at a greater interest rate than state law permits. For usury to exist, there must be a loan of money (or an agreement to extend the maturity of a monetary debt) for which the debtor agrees to repay the principal at a rate that exceeds the legal rate of interest. In addition, the lender must intend to violate the usury laws. If these elements are present, the contract is illegal. In most states, a usurious lender will be unable to collect any interest and also may be subject to criminal or other statutory penalties. In some states, courts deny only the excess interest; the lender can recover the remaining interest and principal. In a few states, the agreement is void; the lender receives no interest or principal.

Because such wide variations exist among state usury laws, it is difficult to generalize one set of rules. States have various exemptions such as loans to corporations and short-term loans, especially where the lender will incur large risks. *Acceleration clauses* (contract clauses that advance the date for payment based on the occurrence of a condition or the breach of a duty) and *prepayment clauses* (contract clauses that allow the debtor to pay the debt before it is due without penalty) generally are not usurious. The same is true of service fees that reflect the incidental costs of making a loan—filing and recording fees, for example. Sales under *revolving charge accounts* (open-ended credit accounts) or *conditional sales contracts* (sales contracts in which the transfer of title is subject to a condition, most commonly the payment of the full purchase price by the buyer) ordinarily are not usurious even if the seller charges a higher-than-lawful rate. Two reasons have been forwarded to justify this position:

(1) A bona fide conditional sale on a deferred-payment basis is not a loan of money; and (2) the finance charge is merely a part of an increased purchase price reflective of the seller's risk in giving up possession of personal property (clothes, computers, MP3 players, and the like) that depreciates quickly in value.

Time-price differential sales contracts (contracts with a difference in price based on the date of payment, with one price for an immediate payment and another for a payment at a later date) may or may not be usurious, depending on the applicable state law and/or special consumer protection statutes. Time-price differential sales contracts involve an offer to sell at a designated price for cash (say, $6,000 for an entertainment center) or at a higher price on credit (say, $7,500). Even though the maximum legal rate of interest in this state may be 18 percent, the 25 percent actual rate represented by the credit price may not involve usury as long as the final price reflects the credit nature of the sale rather than an intent to evade the usury laws.

The trend today is to raise the maximum interest rate and to increase the exceptions to the usury laws. In addition, federally guaranteed loans allow interest rates that otherwise would violate state law. These factors have seriously eroded the original purpose of usury laws—the protection of debtors from excessive rates of interest. There is little uniformity in the various states' usury statutes; therefore, it is wise to consult these statutes if you have doubts about the legality of a particular transaction.

Agreements That Violate Public Policy

Judges more and more frequently resort to public policy as a basis for invalidating agreements. In holding that a contract is void on public policy grounds, a court is deciding the legality of the agreement in light of the public interests involved. Hence, public policy frequently becomes an alternative ground for finding illegality. To illustrate, a court may strike down a contract to fix prices because the agreement violates statutes (for example, the Sherman Act) or because the agreement will harm the public. However, because *public policy* is such a wide-ranging term, courts often have to balance competing interests in judging the legality of certain types of bargains. Keep this point in mind as you consider the following concepts.

Covenants Not to Compete   *Covenants not to compete* are express promises that a seller of a business or an employee who leaves a company will not engage in the same or similar business or occupation for a specific period of time in a certain geographic area. Such bargains may or may not be legal. If the buyer of a business or an employer has a legitimate interest in the "noncompete clause" and it is *reasonable* in *time* and in *geographic scope*, the clause will be legal in many states. (Agreements not to compete whose sole purpose is to curtail competition are illegal as restraints on trade—they violate the antitrust laws.) If a particular covenant not to compete is permissible but unreasonably restrictive in time or geographic scope, in some states the court has the power to rewrite the covenant so that it is reasonable, a process called blue-penciling. Blue-penciling is relatively rare, so people seeking covenants not to compete should not

eClass 11.3 Management

EMPLOYEE AGREEMENTS AND RELEASES

Ani, Meg, and Yousef want any employees (including family members) hired by eClass to sign a covenant not to compete with the firm anywhere in the United States for at least three years after leaving their employment with eClass. The firm members have asked you about the advisability of such a policy. What will you tell them?

BUSINESS CONSIDERATIONS What sort of policy regarding covenants not to compete should a business adopt? When would such a covenant be a good idea? When would such a covenant be impracticable? Explain.

ETHICAL CONSIDERATIONS Is it ethical for a firm to routinely require employees to sign covenants not to compete, even if the employee would not have access to any confidential business information? What ethical issues are raised by the use of such covenants?

expect courts to save them from illegal bargains. In fact, most courts reject this approach and will void the restrictive covenant and construe the agreement without any covenant not to compete.

As previously mentioned, competing policies complicate these situations. It clearly is unfair to unduly restrict the employment opportunities of the seller (or former employee) who must make a living. Similarly, to curtail this person's business activities or occupational activities in effect insulates the buyer (or former employer) from competition and thereby may result in higher prices. Consequently, when examining these covenants, many courts use public policy considerations. When California addressed the public policy considerations, it concluded that, in California, reasonable covenants not to compete will only be valid in contexts where an owner is selling or dissolving his or her business.[13] Eighteen other states also impose restrictions on employee covenants not to compete.[14]

Exculpatory Clauses Agreements to commit torts are illegal. Indeed, there is little justification to validate an agreement that stipulates an intentional breach of the duty of reasonable care to others. On the other hand, is anything illegal about a bargain in which one party tries in advance to limit his or her liability in a particular set of circumstances? Unfortunately, no clear-cut answer exists to this question. Courts judge the legality of such *exculpatory clauses*, or bargains in which one person agrees *in advance* to exonerate another person from liability, on a case-by-case basis.

For example, a dry cleaner may always write on its customers' tickets, "Not responsible for elastic and buttons." The dry cleaner can argue that by signing the tickets, customers agree to hold it harmless for any damages to elastic and buttons. Similarly, restaurants that have signs saying "Not responsible for belongings left in booths" attempt to achieve the same end. In general, these and other agreements in which one party promises not to hold the other liable for tortious or wrongful conduct are legal.

In some jurisdictions, statutes may control the issue of liability in particular situations. In the absence of statutes or clear precedents, however, courts look closely to see whether the party who agrees to assume the risk of the other's tortious conduct has done so voluntarily. In other words, the courts consider whether the party who has initiated the exculpatory clause has vastly superior bargaining power (or superior knowledge) over the other person. (Recall the bank depository example earlier in this chapter.) If so, courts may strike down the exculpatory clause as contrary to public policy.

If the court believes an *adhesion contract* exists—that is, a contract drafted by the stronger party in order to force unfavorable terms on the weaker party—the court probably will find the clause contrary to public policy and thus illegal. This finding is not an easy task, though. Courts necessarily will weigh a variety of factors, such as the age of the parties, their respective degrees of expertise, their mental condition at the time they signed the clause (for example, was the injured party drunk when he or she signed the exculpatory clause just before climbing onto the mechanical bull in Joe's Pub?), and whether the language of the clause was in fine print. After analyzing these and other facts and policies, the court assesses the legality of such clauses.

Exceptions: Upholding Illegal Agreements

The general rule, as mentioned earlier, holds that an illegal bargain is void, and courts will leave the parties to such agreements where they find themselves. Some situations do exist in which a party may bring a successful suit despite the fact that the alleged contract is based on an illegal agreement.

Parties Are Not *in Pari Delicto*   When one of the parties is less blameworthy than the other, the law states that the parties are not *in pari delicto* (they are not equally at fault or equally wrong). The court can allow the less-guilty person to recover for any losses suffered, if recovery serves the public interest in some way. It would not ordinarily serve the public interest if the contract is *malum in se*. In one common type of case, the less-guilty party belongs to the class of persons a statute was designed to protect. For example, the purpose of requiring roofers to obtain licenses is to protect members of the public, including Rhonda. Assume that Jared lacks the necessary license. If Rhonda hires Jared to install her new roof and Jared is negligent in the installation, some courts will allow Rhonda to sue Jared for damages because of his mistake. In the alternative, some courts will allow Rhonda to sue to enforce the contract if she decides that is in her best interests. On the other hand, if the roofing job is completed properly, Jared will not be able to sue Rhonda for payment under the illegal contract. Rhonda's position will be stronger if she is not aware that the contract is illegal, but many courts do not require this.

Exhibit 11.4

Legality as an Element of Contract Formation and Enforcement

Illegality ←——————————————→ **Legality**

Mala in Se Bargains
   (inherently and completely illegal)
a. "Agreements" to commit crimes
b. "Agreements" to commit torts

Mala Prohibita Bargains
   (illegal because forbidden by statute)
a. Price-fixing agreements
b. Performance of services without a
   license required under regulatory
   licensing schemes
c. Sunday closing laws
d. Wagering statutes
e. Usury statutes

Bargains Comprised of Subject Matters That Are Not Tortious, Criminal, or Otherwise Violate Public Policy

Bargains Involving Public Policy Considerations

a. Covenants not to compete

If unreasonable in time and/or geographic scope	If reasonable in time and geographic scope

b. Exculpatory clauses

If clauses are in fine print and drafter has vastly superior bargaining power	If clauses are conspicuous and parties have equal bargaining power

c. Agreements in which one party is
   not *in pari delicto*
d. Agreements in which one party
   repents before the illegal bargains
   are consummated
e. Agreements in which one party is
   justifiably ignorant or being
   protected by the statute
f. Agreements in which the legal
   portions can be severed
   from the illegal portions

Parties Are *in Pari Delicto* The law may allow recovery by the person who shows repentance by rescinding the illegal bargain *before* its performance. For example, assume that a partnership attempts to bribe a state senator to enact favorable legislation. This agreement would be illegal because it harms the public. If one of the partners attempts to rescind the transaction before delivery of the bribe, he or she can do so. The law calls this action repentance or repudiation. Recovery in these situations is generally based on quasi-contract. Courts justify the partner's recovery of the money he or she earlier directed to the senator because such a result furthers the public interest of deterring illegal schemes.

Partial Illegality Agreements may consist of several different promises supported by different considerations. While refusing to enforce those parts of the bargain that are illegal, courts can enforce the parts of the bargain that involve legal promises and legal considerations if the courts can sever (separate) these legal promises. However, if either the illegal promise or the illegal consideration (or both) wholly taints the agreement, courts declare the entire agreement void. For example, if a court finds a covenant not to compete unreasonable in scope, the judge may sever the illegal clause from the rest of the agreement. The court, however, ordinarily enforces the remainder of the contract (the sale of the business, for example), because the balance of the contract is perfectly legal; it is divisible from the illegal portion. In other words, after severing the illegal portions, courts will give effect to those provisions that constitute a legal contract.

Contemporary Case

COVINGTON v. GRIFFIN

19 So. 3d 805, 2009 Miss. App. LEXIS 692
(Miss. Ct. of Appeals 2009)

FACTS Ken Covington and Mitch Mosley, both savvy business men, each owned property adjoining Cremonia Griffin's land. Griffin was familiar with both men and had known their families as neighbors for many years. Griffin was a 67-year-old woman with mental health problems, who recently had been a patient at Alliance Mental Health Center, and was on medication for her mental condition at the time the option contract was signed. In the past, Covington and Mosley had approached Griffin multiple times about selling the property, but each time she refused, saying that she was not interested in selling it. Covington told Griffin that he was interested in the property if she ever decided to sell. On February 23, 2006, Griffin called Mosley and requested that he drive her from her apartment to her cousin's home. Griffin was not supposed to drive in her distressed condition. During the car trip, both parties agreed to stop at a Trustmark Bank. Mosley claimed that Griffin had agreed to sell the land during the car trip and that he took her to the bank that same day to sign and notarize an option contract that had already been prepared and brought to the bank by Mosley's wife. The option contract provided that Mosley would pay Griffin $1,000 in consideration for the option to purchase her land. The option contract also provided that Mosley would pay Griffin $1,000 dollars per acre for all of her land. Mosley gave her a check for $1,000 with "earnest money" written on it, but he said that she did not read the contract. Taking Griffin to the bank immediately denied her an opportunity to consult with family or an attorney and did not permit her time to study the contract. Griffin maintained that she never agreed to sell the land and was unaware that she was signing an option contract. She said that Mosley suggested that they go to the bank since she was about to go on a trip and might need some spending money. Mosley offered her $1,000 for spending money for her trip, and she believed that she was merely signing to show receipt of the check. Griffin testified that she never read the three-page option contract, and Mosley admitted that he never gave her a copy of it. Griffin attempted to return the check the next day after relatives explained to her that it was earnest money for the sale, but Mosley refused to accept it. Griffin never cashed the check, and she later instructed her brother to send it back to Mosley. Mosley and Covington recorded the option contract on the date it was signed. On May 11, 2006, Mosley and Covington filed a complaint to enforce the option contract against Griffin. In late August or early September 2006, Griffin returned from her trip to California.

ISSUE Was the option contract enforceable against Griffin?

HOLDING No. It was the result of unilateral mistake and unconscionability.

REASONING Excerpts from the opinion of Judge Ishee:

... [T]he two sides do not agree that there was even an intent to sell Griffin's property ... Griffin had been treated for mental illness throughout her life, and she had many persons assisting her with her daily transactions. ... Mosley and Covington

were vastly more sophisticated than Griffin and ... she did not have time to review the contract. ... "[E]quity will prevent an intolerable injustice such as where a party has gained an unconscionable advantage by mistake and the mistaken party is not grossly negligent." ... In order to rescind a contract on the basis of a unilateral mistake, it must be shown that: (1) "the mistake is of so fundamental a character that, the minds of the parties have never, in fact, met; or where an unconscionable advantage has been gained, by mere mistake or misapprehension"; (2) "there was no gross negligence ..."; (3) "no intervening rights have accrued"; and (4) "the parties may still be placed in status quo[.]" ... This Court finds no error in the chancellor's determination that Griffin was mistaken and that there had been no true meeting of the minds. ... [T]he acts of Covington and Mosley ... in getting the contract signed were questionable. They gained an unconscionable advantage by having an elderly lady with mental problems sign a contract that she did not know was a contract, which she did not review, and it was all settled almost on the spur of the moment, despite the fact that Griffin had repeatedly refused to sell the land. The error by Griffin was fundamental because she never even realized she was signing a contract; thus, there was no meeting of the minds. ... Griffin was not grossly negligent ... Covington and Mosley have failed to show that any intervening rights have accrued because of the contract, and Griffin attempted to return the check the next day. ... [T]he parties may still be placed in status quo. ...

Griffin ... had a history of mental illness and required assistance from others to handle her affairs. ... Griffin certainly suffered from a weakness of intellect. ...

[Griffin] was immediately taken to the bank after Mosley and Covington claim she changed her mind about selling the property. ... [S]he only had five to ten minutes to review the contract before signing it and . . . Mosley never explained what she was signing. . . . Griffin argues she misunderstood what she was signing and was unaware that it was an option contract. . . . Griffin argues that there was a great disparity in sophistication between the parties . . . Mosley owned a car dealership, was very familiar with sales contracts, and had personally bought and sold property on at least ten different occasions. . . . Covington attended two years of junior college, had experience in negotiating contracts as part of his business dealings, had purchased property in the past, and had an attorney's advice on those occasions. . . . Griffin claims that she had never sold property before, had worked in factory jobs, and required assistance to perform such tasks as purchasing airline tickets and signing rental agreements. . . .

There are five factors a court will consider when determining whether a contract is procedurally unconscionable: "1) lack of knowledge; 2) lack of voluntariness; 3) inconspicuous print; 4) complex legalistic language; 5) disparity in sophistication or bargaining power; [and] 6) lack of opportunity to study the contract and inquire about the contract terms." . . . [T]o enforce the option contract would be procedurally unconscionable. . . . Griffin was unaware she was signing a contract, which demonstrated both a lack of knowledge and lack of voluntariness; Griffin attempted to return the check as soon as she learned that it was for "earnest money"; there was a great and troubling disparity in sophistication between the parties; and . . . she was denied an opportunity to study the contract and gain advice from outside counsel before signing it. . . .

You Be the Judge

Jennifer Valdivia was 12 when she attended her first Major League baseball game. She attended the game with her 69-year-old grandfather, her 17-year-old brother, and one of his friends. She caught a baseball that was hit near where she was sitting. "The ball she caught was the ball from the 200th home run for Ryan Howard, an All-Star for the Philadelphia Phillies." Howard achieved this milestone in his 658th career game, earlier than any other Major League player.

The Marlins sent a team representative to get Jennifer and her brother, Gian Carlos, and escort them to the Phillies' clubhouse. "Their grandfather, a Cuban immigrant who doesn't speak English, stayed in his seat." Jennifer contends that a Phillies employee told her that if she gave them the ball, she could come back after the game, meet Howard, and have him sign the ball. She handed over the ball. They gave her some cotton candy and a soda. Jennifer and the rest of her group came to the clubhouse after the game, but Howard did not show up. A security guard gave Jennifer a ball autographed by Howard, but it was not the one she caught. It was clean and polished.

Jennifer's mother asked to have the ball returned. When the Phillies balked, the family hired Norm Kent, an attorney. Kent was unable to get the Phillies or Howard to return the ball, so he filed suit in Jennifer's behalf, seeking the return of the ball. The parties settled their suit shortly after this, and the ball was returned to Jennifer.

It has been said that "Letting fans keep the home-run balls they catch is a time-honored tradition. It's a way for ordinary fans to connect with the superstars—and to cash in on the catch if history has been made." Do you agree? Assume that the parties did not settle and this case is being heard in *your* court. If you were the judge, how would *you* decide this dispute? [See Wayne Drash, "Girl, 12, Slugged Back at Phillies Slugger," http://www.cnn.com/2009/US/10/09/florida.baseball.lawsuit/, October 9, 2009 (accessed 1/10/2010).]

Summary

Certain classes of people may lack capacity to contract. Generally, this means that people who lack capacity can choose to enforce or to disaffirm their contracts at their discretion. For example, the contracts of a minor often are voidable at the option of the minor, even when the minor has misrepresented his or her age. For minors, the power of disaffirmance ordinarily extends through the person's minority and for a reasonable time after attaining majority. After reaching majority, a minor may ratify, or approve, the contract. However, a minor may be liable for necessaries in quasi contract. The definition of necessaries depends on the minor's station in life and the parents' ability to provide for the minor.

The contracts of insane persons are generally voidable. To be insane, a person must be unable to understand the agreement or its consequences. Contracts entered into during periods of lucidity are enforceable. Insane persons are liable for necessaries, just as minors are.

Total intoxication may render a person incapable of entering into a binding contract, but slight intoxication will not. Courts generally are hostile to avoiding contracts on the basis of intoxication, except in unusual circumstances.

To have a valid contract, one also must prove that the assent of the parties is genuine. The existence of fraud, misrepresentation, mistake,

duress, undue influence, or unconscionability precludes reality of consent. Fraud is a deliberate misrepresentation of a material fact with the intent to induce another person to enter a contract. Predictions, statements of value, and opinions do not constitute fraud. Probably the most difficult element to prove is *scienter*, the defendant's knowledge of the falsity of the statement. The plaintiff's reliance on the deception must be reasonable, or the plaintiff will be precluded from recovering. Successful proof of fraud makes the contract voidable and justifies rescission. Innocent misrepresentation also may result in legal liability.

Mistake occurs when the parties are wrong about the existence or absence of a past or present fact that is material to their transaction. Two types of mistakes exist: unilateral where one person is in error and bilateral/mutual where both parties are in error. Courts generally will not rescind unilateral mistakes unless the other party knows, or should have known, of the mistaken party's error or uses it to take unconscionable advantage of the injured party. If a mutual or bilateral mistake of fact is present, either party can disaffirm the contract.

Duress exists when a person's will has been overridden as a result of another person's threats. Duress may be either personal or economic. Economic duress occurs when a seller, in order to extract a higher contract price, wrongfully or coercively withholds scarce commodities or services. Undue influence is the use of a relationship of trust and confidence to gain contractual advantages. The existence of unconscionability may signal a lack of meaningful assent to a contract and constitute grounds for a court's setting the contract aside.

In order to be a valid contract, the law imposes a requirement that the subject matter and purpose of a bargain must be legal. A bargain is illegal if its performance is criminal, tortious, or otherwise opposed to public policy. Some courts distinguish between bargains that violate statutes because they are evil in themselves (*mala in se*) and bargains that are merely forbidden by statute (*mala prohibita*). Many types of bargains violate statutes. Performances of services without a license may make the agreement void. Covenants not to compete and exculpatory clauses may be struck down on public policy grounds if they are too restrictive or one-sided. There are exceptions when courts may intervene in illegal contracts. These exceptions include agreements in which the parties are not *in pari delicto*, or of equal guilt; agreements in which one party repents before it performs the illegal bargain; and agreements in which courts can sever the legal portions from the illegal segments.

Discussion Questions

1. Why do savvy business people say, "Don't deal with minors"? Can minors disaffirm contracts if they have misrepresented their ages at the time of contracting?

2. Define *necessaries*. What happens if a minor or mentally incompetent person enters into a contract for necessaries?

3. How does silence relate to the legal theory of fraud? In what situations is there a legal duty to speak?

4. What are covenants not to compete? What standards do courts use to judge their legality?

5. Describe the four most important exceptions to the general rule that an illegal bargain is void.

Case Problems and Writing Assignments

1. John Hess was a passenger riding in a Ford pickup truck. At an intersection, a car driven by Charles Phillips struck the Ford truck, and the truck rolled over at least one and a half times. Hess suffered severe injuries and is now a paraplegic. Before filing a lawsuit, Hess made a claim against Phillips and his insurance company, Continental Insurance Company (Continental). Hess's attorney at the time negotiated with Brad Sommers, the claims adjuster for Continental, and settled Hess's claim against Phillips for $15,000, the policy limit. As part of the settlement, Hess signed a one-page boilerplate release form provided by Continental. This release stated that Hess "releases, acquits and forever discharges Charles Phillips, Continental Insurance and any and all agents and employees, UAC [the underwriters adjusting company] and any and [all] agents and employees and all other persons, firms, corporations, associations or partnerships of and from any and all claims, actions, causes of action, demands, rights, damages, costs, loss of service, expenses and compensation whatsoever" that Hess had or might have as a result of the accident. The release further stated that Hess "declare(s) and represent(s) that . . . this Release contains the entire agreement between the parties hereto. . . ."

Several months after signing the release, Hess hired a new attorney and filed suit against Ford Motor Company and others, alleging negligence, strict liability, and breach of warranty. In a separate lawsuit filed against Phillip and Continental, Hess asked for reformation of the release, specifically that the court strike the language discharging "all other persons, firms, corporations, associations or partnerships of and from any and all claims" on the ground of mutual mistake. The record showed that, at trial, Hess had testified that, before he had signed the release at his hospital bed, he had asked his first attorney about the contractual language at issue, and his attorney had told him the release was a standard form document. Hess then had testified that he had not intended to release Ford from liability. Hess's first attorney had testified that he had recommended settling with Phillips for the policy limit of $15,000, because an asset search had revealed that Phillips had no money. He further had testified that he had not intended to release Ford and that he had told Hess the release covered only Phillips, his insurance company, and the adjusting company. Finally, the attorney had stated that he had bought the Ford pickup truck involved in the accident for use as evidence in litigation against Ford after agreeing to settle with Phillips but before Hess had signed the release. Sommers, the former claims adjuster who had settled the case on behalf of Phillips and Continental, had testified that he and Hess's attorney had discussed Hess's intention to sue Ford and others and that Hess's attorney had told him (Sommers) he was settling with Phillips and Continental in order to defray future litigation costs. Sommers also had testified that Hess would not have settled and signed the release if it had discharged Ford. Finally, Sommers testified that he (1) had not intended to release Ford; (2) had not prepared the release or chosen the form used; and (3) had intended to protect Phillips and his insurance companies from "future exposure." Who had the stronger argument, Hess or Ford? Why? [See *Hess v. Ford Motor Company*, 117 Cal. Rptr. 2d 220 (2002).]

2. In 1995, 17-year-old David Cooper had been a member of the Aspen Valley Ski Club, Inc., for about nine years and was actively involved in competitive ski racing. At the beginning of the 1995-1996 ski season, David and his mother had signed a form entitled "Aspen Valley Ski Club, Inc. Acknowledgment and Assumption of Risk and Release." This form was an exculpatory clause that released the ski club from any liability from any claims that might arise from a member's participation in any ski club event. This release also included a "hold harmless" indemnification clause in which both David and his parents agreed to release the club from liability for future injuries and to assume all known and unknown risks. It provided that should a participant such as David incur personal injury (including death) or property damage during his participation in the ski clubs' programs and activities, he and his parents—not the club or its employees, even if the latter had caused his injuries—would bear the financial responsibility for any such injuries. The release would preclude a participant's suing the club and its employees for torts committed against the minor. On December 30, 1995, David was training for a competitive, high speed alpine race on a course set by David's coach, John McBride. During a training run, David fell and collided with a tree, sustaining severe injuries, including the loss of vision in both eyes. When David and his parents sued the ski club and McBride for negligence, the lower courts held that the release David's mother had signed was enforceable against David, despite his being a minor both at the time of signing the release and at the occurrence of the accident. The state supreme court granted review to determine whether public policy in Colorado permits a parent to release the claims of a minor child for future injuries and whether a parent may enter into an indemnification agreement that shifts the source of compensation for a minor's claim from a *tortfeasor* (the person or entity that commits a tort) to the parent. What particular public policy issues arise with parental releases of liability? If you were deciding this case, would these public policy aspects persuade you to uphold the parents' rights to sign such releases? Why or why not? [See *Cooper v. Aspen Skiing Company*, 48 P.3d 1229 (Colo. 2002).]

3. Jerie Pacurib was a willing, active participant in an illegal distributor pyramid scheme called Network. Using a promotional, chain-linked "gifting" program, Network led new members to believe that an unlimited pool of possible recruits was readily available to create new pyramid boards. In actuality, because Pacurib was a 20th-level investor, just to advance one level would have required an additional 8,388,608 new investors. Because pyramid schemes are doomed to fail, most states—including New York—viewed them as *malum prohibitum*. New York had specifically addressed the practices in the Martin Act, which was part of New York's General Business Law. Marlene Terez, one of the "founders" of the "gifting board" of which Pacurib would be a part, orally promised potential recruits (including Pacurib) that if they joined and then failed to get sufficient new recruits and/or the program did not work, she would return their money. At least one of the trial witnesses who corroborated this promise was a friend of Terez who had no stake in the outcome. Pacurib ultimately paid the $2,000 "gift" required for membership in Network. What could Pacurib argue as her basis for receiving a refund of the $2,000 she paid to Terez? Does illegality prevent Pacurib from recovering? [See *Pacurib v. Villacruz*, 705 N.Y.S.2d 819 (N.Y. City Civ. Ct. 1999).]

Notes

1. Depending on the jurisdiction, its Married Women's Property Act may expand or reduce the ability of married women to contract.
2. For a comparison of the law in the United States with the law in England, see Simon Goodfellow, "Note: Who Gets the Better Deal? A Comparison of the U.S. and English Infancy Doctrines," 29 Hastings Int'l & Comp. L. Rev. 135 (Fall 2005).
3. Kevin was allowed to retain the proceeds from his insurance coverage. According to the court, Kevin was entitled to the return of the purchase price he paid less the salvage value of the car. When a minor disaffirms a contract, he or she must return any consideration still in his or her possession which was the wrecked car. However, Kevin had transferred the wrecked vehicle to his insurance company under the terms of his policy. The wrecked car had a salvage value of $1,500. Star *Chevrolet Co. v. Green*, 473 So. 2d 157, 1985 Miss. LEXIS 2141 (Miss. S. Ct. 1985).
4. Whether a car is necessary may also depend on access to inexpensive and reliable public transportation.
5. Fraud, duress, and undue influence are also grounds to set aside gifts and wills.
6. See *Walters v. Morgan*, 3 Def., F. & J. 718, 724 (1861).
7. A.G. Guest, *Anson's Law of Contracts*, 26th ed. (Oxford: Clarendon Press, 1984), pp. 209-210.
8. Uniform Computer Information Transactions Act (UCITA), National Conference of Commissioners on Uniform State Laws, with 2000 and 2002 Amendments, © 2002.
9. 279 F.3d 889, 2002 U.S. App. LEXIS 1686 (9th Cir. 2002).
10. This definition is taken from the *Restatement (First) of Contracts* § 512, and augmented by the *Restatement (Second) of Contracts* § 178. *Restatement (Second) of Contracts* (St. Paul, MN: American Law Institute Publishers, 1981), § 178.
11. See *First National Bank of Shreveport v. Williams*, 346 So. 2d 257, 264 (La. App. 1977).
12. *Providian v. Haines*, No. CV980858 (Cal. Super. Ct. Marin Cty. Cross complaint filed July 23, 1998), as discussed in David I. Gold, "Note and Comment: Internet Gambling Debt Liability: Trouble Ahead? A Consideration of Providian v. Haines," 22 T. Jefferson L. Rev. 219 (Spring, 2000); and Pearson Liddell, Jr., Stevie Watson, William D. Eshee, Jr., Gloria J. Liddell & Robert Moore, "Internet Gambling on a Roll," 28 Seton Hall Legis. J. 315 (2004).
13. California Business & Professions Code §§ 16601, 16602, and 16602.5; and *Edwards v. Arthur Andersen*, LLP, 44 Cal. 4th 937, 2008 Cal. LEXIS 9618 (CA 2008).
14. Ala. Code § 8-1-1 (LexisNexis 2002); Colo. Rev. Stat. Ann. §§ 8-2-113(2)–(3) (West 2003); Fla. Stat. Ann. § 542.335

(West 2002 & Supp. 2007); Ga. Code Ann. §13.-8-2.1 (1982 & Supp. 2008); Haw. Rev. Stat. Ann. §480-4(c)(4) (LexisNexis 2009); La. Rev. Stat. Ann. §23.921 (1998 & Supp. 2009); Mich. Comp. Laws Ann. §445.772 (West 2002); Mont. Code Ann. §28-2-703 (2007); Nev. Rev. Stat. §613.200 (2007); N.C. Gen. Stat. §75-4 (2007); N.D. Cent. Code §9-08-06 (2006); Okla. Stat. Ann. tit. 15, §217 (West 1993 & Supp. 2009); Or. Rev. Stat. Ann. §653.295 (West 2003 & Supp. 2009); S.D. Codified Laws §53-9-11 (2004); Tenn. Code Ann. §47-25-101 (2001); Tex. Bus. & Com. Code §§15.50-52 (Vernon 2002); W. Va. Code Ann. §47-18-3(a) (LexisNexis 2006); Wis. Stat. Ann. §103.465 (West 2002). Some states have constitutional provisions, as well. *See* Ga. Const. art. III, §6, para. 5 (c).

12

Contract Writings and Interpretations

Agenda

Ani, Meg, and Yousef recognize that eClass will enter into a number of contracts in the near future. They plan to put many of their contracts in writing. They need to know which of their contracts *must* be in writing in order to be enforceable, and which contracts merely *should* be in writing, although they do not have to be. They also should understand how detailed their writings need to be and whether any of eClass's written agreements can be amended or altered orally. Ani, Meg, and Yousef would like to know how much technical language, or "trade talk," they can use in their written agreements, and how the courts will interpret this technical language.

They will look to you for help as they gain knowledge about these areas of the law. Be prepared! You never know when the firm or one of its members will seek your advice.

Classic Case

NELSON v. BOYNTON

44 Mass. 396, 1841 Mass. LEXIS 152
(Supreme Ct. of Mass., Essex, 1841)

FACTS In 1834, Stephen Nelson commenced a law suit against Ebenezer Boynton, William Boynton's father, on two of the father's promissory notes. Nelson attached the father's real estate as security. Before trial, William Boynton promised Nelson that if Nelson would discontinue the law suit, William Boynton would pay him the amount of the notes. The law suit was discontinued, but the notes were not paid. Nelson now brings a suit against William Boynton.

ISSUE Does the Statute of Frauds apply to William Boynton's promise?

HOLDING Yes, the Statute of Frauds applies and written evidence is required.

REASONING Excerpts from the opinion by Chief Justice Lemuel Shaw:

Questions depending upon this branch of the statute of frauds are often attended with some perplexity, on account of the difficulty in laying down a general rule, by which to distinguish a guaranty, or mere collateral promise for the debt of another, from an original agreement, upon a new and independent consideration, when the subject of the contract is the debt or default of another. . . . The statute . . . was this; "no action shall be brought whereby to charge the defendant upon any special promise to answer for the debt, default or misdoings of another person, unless the agreement, or some memorandum or note thereof shall be in writing, and signed by the party to be charged therewith . . .". The object of the statute . . . was, to secure the highest and most satisfactory . . . evidence, in a case, where a party, without apparent benefit to himself, . . . [promises to pay the debt of another,] and where there would be great temptation, on the part of a creditor, in danger of losing his debt by the insolvency of his debtor, to support a suit against the friends or relatives of a debtor, . . . by means of false evidence; by exaggerating words of recommendation, encouragement to forbearance, and requests for indulgence, into positive contracts. . . .

[T]o bind one person for the debt or default of another, there must not only be a promise or memorandum in writing, but such promise must be made on good consideration. The statute does not vary the . . . common law, as to what constitutes a valid and binding promise; to every such promise, whether oral or written, there must be a good consideration. A promise without consideration is bad by the common law . . . ; a promise on good consideration, without writing, if for the debt of another, is bad by the statute. . . . It is not enough . . . that a sufficient legal consideration for a promise is proved, if the object of the promise is the payment of the debt of another, for his account, and not with a view to any benefit to the promisor. . . .

The terms original and collateral promise, though not used in the [Massachusetts] statute, are convenient enough, to distinguish between the cases, where the direct and leading object of the promise is, to become the . . . guarantor of another's debt, and those where, although the effect of the promise is to pay the debt of another, yet the leading object of the undertaker is, to subserve or promote some interest or purpose of his own. The former, whether made before, or after, or at the same time with the promise of the principal, is not valid, unless manifested by evidence in writing; the latter, if made on good consideration, is unaffected by the statute, because, although the effect of it is to release or suspend the debt of another, yet that is not the leading object, on the part of the promisor . . .

[T]he statute does not apply, if the consideration, "spring[s] out of any new transaction, or move[s] to the party promising upon some fresh and substantive ground of a personal concern to himself." . . . [C]ases are not considered as coming within the statute, when the party promising has for his object a benefit which he did not before enjoy, accruing immediately to himself; but where the object of the promise is to obtain the release of the person or property of the debtor, or other forbearance or benefit to him, it is within the statute. . . . [In this case,] the court

are [sic] of opinion that the promise was within the statute of frauds; a promise to pay the debt of the father; . . . though made on good consideration, was not valid, without a promise or memorandum of the agreement in writing. . . . [T]he leading object and purpose were the relief and benefit of the father, and not of the son. It does not appear that the son had any interest in the estate released, or object or purpose of his own to subserve. It is the ordinary case of a son becoming . . . [liable] for the father's debt, in consideration of surceasing a suit, or other forbearance, and therefore, not being in writing, is within the statute. . . . [The trial court was in error and a new trial is granted.]

THE IMPORTANCE OF FORM

At this point, you should have a good grasp of the requirements of contract formation: agreement (offer and acceptance), consideration, capacity, reality of consent, and legality. In addition, according to the Statute of Frauds, certain categories of contracts must be in writing to be enforceable. These categories are discussed in the next section. The writing provides evidence that the parties actually entered into the contracts at issue, and it avoids the *perjuries* (false statements made under oath during court proceedings) traditionally and historically associated with these categories of contracts. In most other situations, the parties are free to contract orally, even though it may be unwise to do so.

In addition, once the parties reduce their agreement to writing, judges are wary of tampering with the contract. For this reason, the *parol evidence rule* states that oral testimony ordinarily is not admissible to add to, alter, or vary the terms of a written agreement. In certain situations, *parol* (oral or verbal) evidence will be admissible to clear up ambiguities. For example, even a relatively simple word like "ton" may be ambiguous when used in a contract: One of the parties may interpret "ton" as a "long" ton (2240 pounds) or as a metric ton (2204 pounds), while the other party interprets "ton" as a "short" ton (2000 pounds). If the parties take this controversy to court, the court may allow parol evidence of the customs and usages in each industry in order to define the term "ton." For this reason, an understanding of the Statute of Frauds and the parol evidence rule will be helpful in your understanding of contract law.

THE STATUTE OF FRAUDS

The ancestor of the present-day Statute of Frauds was called "An Act for the Prevention of Frauds and Perjuries," passed by the English Parliament in 1677. Parliament decreed that, to be enforceable, certain classes of contracts must be in writing. Parliament was concerned because there was little control over medieval juries, and perjury was widespread in lawsuits involving oral contracts.[1] Over time, the name was shortened, at least in common usage, to the Statute of Frauds. Be aware that this shortened name is somewhat misleading because these statutes deal with the requirement of a writing rather than with fraud. It helps to recall the original name of the statute in order to remember its purpose: An Act for the Prevention of Frauds and Perjuries, where the term *frauds* referred to the wholesale misrepresentations or perjured statements made to early English courts. Almost every state has a Statute of Frauds modeled on this original statute, although there are differences among the versions in the various states. One area of variance is the effect of non-compliance with the statute. The majority approach is to treat the contract as *unenforceable* against the party who has not signed the required writing. However, some states treat the contract as void.

Courts have been somewhat hostile to Statute of Frauds claims because of the injustice such statutes can cause. Consequently, some courts construe these statutes narrowly and find various rationales for removing the contract at issue from the coverage of the statute. This permits the court to give effect to oral contracts that otherwise would not be enforceable. By requiring all promises to be in writing, the wise businessperson or firm avoids such potential legal problems.

Types of Contracts Covered

Our discussion begins with the five categories of contracts historically covered by the Statute of Frauds in most states. Then we will discuss the categories added by the Uniform Commercial Code. The five historic categories are:

1. Contracts to answer for the debt of another if the person so defaults
2. Contracts of executors and administrators to pay estate debts
3. Contracts for interests in land
4. Contracts not capable of being performed within one year
5. Contracts made in consideration of marriage

Contracts to Answer for the Debt of Another If the Person So Defaults   Ordinarily, oral promises between two persons are perfectly valid and enforceable in court. When Linda orally promises to pay George $200 for a used fax machine and he orally promises to sell it to her, a contract exists between the two parties. We can call such promises original or primary promises because both parties have promised to be primarily liable on the transaction.

Sometimes people agree to be secondarily liable—that is, liable only in the event someone else (the debtor) defaults. Such agreements, called *collateral contracts*, are promises to answer for the debt or default of another. Collateral contracts are also called guarantee contracts or secondary contracts. Collateral contracts typically involve three persons: the debtor (the original promisor), the creditor (the promisee), and the third party, who generally is called a *guarantor* (one who makes a collateral promise to answer for the payment of a debt or the performance of an obligation if the person primarily liable fails to make payment or to perform). Notice that a collateral contract exhibits definite characteristics:

- There are three parties, the two parties to the contract and a third party who enters as a guarantor. [Not all three-party contracts are collateral contracts. For example, novations (discussed in Chapter 14) and third party beneficiary contracts (discussed in Chapter 13) are not collateral contracts.]
- There are two promises, one original (debtor to creditor) and the other secondary, or collateral (third party to creditor). It is not a collateral promise if the third party makes the promise to the debtor.
- The "second" promise is a promise to accept only secondary, or collateral, liability resulting from the default of the primary party. The guarantor's promise can occur before, after, or contemporaneous with the original promise.[2]

Exhibit 12.1 illustrates collateral agreements.

The *intent of the parties* determines whether a three-party transaction involves a collateral contract, which must be in writing to be enforceable, or an original contract, which may be enforceable even if oral. For example, Stan's grandson, Raymond, wants to purchase a car. Stan may sign the note Raymond has signed with a bank. This is a three-party situation (Stan, Raymond, and the bank), but it is not a collateral contract. Stan and Raymond are joint, original promisors to the bank. As such they each face joint and several liability on the loan. If Raymond defaults on the car payment, the bank can sue either Stan or Raymond. If, however, Stan wishes to be only secondarily liable

Exhibit 12.1

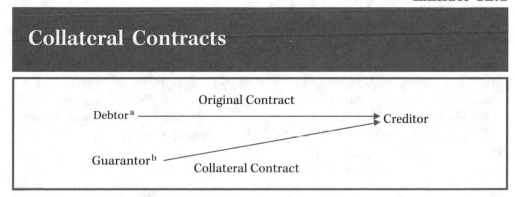

Collateral Contracts

[a]The debtor makes the original promise and has the primary obligation.
[b]The guarantor makes a promise, agreeing to be liable secondarily, upon the default of the debtor.

and the note is phrased accordingly, the contract is a collateral one. The bank must request payment from Raymond *without success before* it can attempt to hold Stan liable. Note that the intent and the wording of the parties are crucial in determining whether an original or collateral contract is involved. You should carefully examine the language being used to determine the type of liability Stan is "accepting."[3] By requiring any transaction that may be deemed a collateral contract to be in writing, the bank can protect itself from a defense based on the Statute of Frauds.

In the prior example, if Stan had been a surety (a concept discussed in Chapter 10), Stan would be accepting liability in all circumstances, and his liability would be primary and direct. Even though the promises of sureties are not generally considered collateral promises, a number of states include the promises of sureties under their Statute of Frauds.[4]

Because courts generally interpret the Statute of Frauds narrowly, they sometimes allow an exception to the rule that a collateral contract must be in writing to be enforceable. This is called the *leading-object* or *main-purpose* exception: When the third party agrees to be liable chiefly for the purpose of obtaining an economic benefit for himself or herself personally, the second promise, even if oral, will be recognized as an exception to the rule. The economic benefit can be either in the creation of the debt or its payment. Courts often wrestle with whether the situation involves a leading-object because it depends on the intention of the guarantor. Let us change our earlier example to one in which Stan orally tells the bank he will pay if Raymond defaults. When Raymond fails to pay and the bank sues Stan, Stan will use the Statute of Frauds as his defense: No writing exists, and the contract appears to be a collateral one. Suppose the bank can prove that before Stan entered into the agreement with the bank he had hired Raymond to make deliveries for him and had agreed to help Raymond get the car loan in order to make these deliveries. Then the bank may be able to show that Stan's "leading object" in making the promise primarily involved preventing economic loss to himself, and not providing a benefit to Raymond. Without the car, Raymond cannot make deliveries. Without having the deliveries made, Stan will lose business. Proving this, the bank can argue that the "main purpose" of Stan's conduct focused on protecting Stan's own economic position rather than Raymond's financial situation. If the court agrees, they may impose liability on Stan for his oral promise.

Contracts of Executors and Administrators to Pay Estate Debts   These promises arise when *executors* (persons appointed in a will by the testator to handle the estate) and *administrators* (persons appointed by an appropriate court to handle the estate) promise to pay claims against the estate out of their own personal funds. Ordinarily, these debts would be paid from estate assets, and if the estate was bankrupt or depleted, some creditors would not be paid. In order to protect the reputation of the deceased, the executor or administrator may feel obligated to personally assure that all the debts of the deceased are paid in full, and may even promise to pay them personally. While this may be a noble gesture, it is also unwise and unusual, and under the Statute of Frauds, the courts require a writing as evidence that such an agreement was made. Early court cases noted how closely this provision is related to the prior category,[5] and some states view these contracts as a subcategory of a promise to pay the debt of another.

Contracts for Interests in Land   Any agreement that involves buying, selling, or transferring interests in land must be in writing to be enforceable. *Mortgages* (conditional transfers of property as security for a debt), *leases* (contracts that grant the right to use and occupy realty), *easements* (limited rights to use and enjoy the land of another), and sales agreements transferring standing timber and buildings attached to the land should be in writing to satisfy the Statute of Frauds. Thus, if you orally offer to buy someone's house and the seller orally accepts your offer, this contract will be unenforceable because it does not comply with the Statute of Frauds.

Courts nevertheless will enforce oral contracts for the sale of land *if* the purchaser pays part of the purchase price *and*, with the seller's consent, the purchaser takes possession of the land and makes valuable improvements to it.[6] This equitable remedy is called the *doctrine of part performance*. For example, assume Greg moves onto Barry's land with Barry's oral permission, and tears down an old garage, repaints the entire house, and rebuilds a barn, all at Greg's expense. Before undertaking these actions, Greg also paid $5,000 to Barry toward the agreed purchase price. When Barry later tries to claim that there is no enforceable sales contract between the two due to the lack of any signed writing, a court can order specific performance of the contract despite noncompliance with the Statute of Frauds. Courts justify such an exception to the writing requirement on the ground that the *conduct* of both parties prior to litigation shows the existence of a contract. Courts in such cases conclude that the parties' actions can be explained only by the existence of such a contract. To avoid the unjust enrichment of the seller, equity also will give remedies in such situations.

Contracts Not Capable of Being Performed within One Year   This Statute of Frauds provision is also stated as contracts that are not to be performed within one year or a contract that cannot possibly be performed within one year from the date of making the agreement. To illustrate, an oral promise to haul milk for a dairy producer is invalid under the Statute of Frauds if the milk cannot be hauled in less than one year. For example, the parties enter into a contract on December 15, with the term of the contract to run from January 1 to December 31 of the following year. The starting period is the date of making the contract, or December 15 in our example. Therefore, to be enforceable under the Statute of Frauds this agreement must be in writing.

Courts interpret this requirement as whether *performance can possibly occur within one year's time*.[7] This interpretation has led to some rather strange results. A bilateral contract in which an employee promises to work for an employer "for the rest of the employer's life" in exchange for a salary sounds as if it cannot be performed within one year. However, the courts generally interpret such language to mean that since it is *possible* that the employer might die within a year, the oral contract is enforceable despite the Statute of Frauds. Courts do not examine whether it is likely that the employer will die within the year. In other words, the court does not consider evidence about the employer's age and health. Under this approach, if the contract in our earlier example obligated the hauler to transport the milk for "as long as the dairy farmer produces milk," such courts would reason that the dairy farmer possibly could cease operations within one year, thereby making the contract capable of being performed within one year from the date of formation.[8] Although a remote possibility, the fact that such a contingency could happen makes the oral contract enforceable and makes this section of the Statute of Frauds inapplicable. In most states the courts evaluate whether performance is possible as of the date that the parties enter into the agreement. They do not evaluate it in retrospect based on what actually occurs. So, the oral contract in the earlier example to work for the employer may actually last 30 years or more, yet still be valid under the Statute of Frauds.

A majority of the court cases make an exception and allow recovery for oral contracts that fall under this provision of the Statute of Frauds when one party to the contract has fully performed his or her promises within one year. In other words, the contract is fully executed on his or her side.[9] Courts also may apply promissory estoppel, which we discussed in Chapter 10, to allow recovery for contracts otherwise unenforceable under this provision.

Contracts Made in Consideration of Marriage Promises to pay money or to transfer property in consideration of a promise to marry must be in writing under the Statute of Frauds. For example, the statute would apply if the Benson family promises to transfer the ownership of their condominium in Florida to Pat Lloyd—if Pat promises to marry their daughter: The Statute of Frauds will require the Bensons' promise to be in writing. Under the Statute of Frauds, *premarital agreements* (also called antenuptial agreements or prenuptial agreements), which couples enter into before marriage and which spell out the disposition of the property when the marriage ends by death or divorce, ordinarily must be in writing to be enforceable. This provision of the statute does not apply to simple promises where two people become engaged and promise to marry one another. In some states, these simple promises to marry are expressly excluded by the language of the state statute.

Uniform Commercial Code Statute of Frauds The Uniform Commercial Code (UCC) also has several provisions dealing with the Statute of Frauds. They include:

- the sale of goods[10] priced at $500 or more (UCC § 2-201(1))[11]
- the lease of goods where the contract price is $1,000 or more (UCC § 2A-201)

[*NOTE: The proposed revision to Article 2 increases the amount for the sale of goods to $5,000 or more. We will treat the topic here as if the 2003 revision to Article 2 has not been adopted, but it would be a good idea to check your state statute to see which rule applies to your contracts—or, better yet, put all your contracts in writing to be on the safe side.*]

The Code defines goods as movable, personal property: It includes produce. Under § 2-201, however, there are some exceptions to the writing requirement. Courts will enforce oral contracts for the sale of goods, even for amounts of $500 or more, if (1) the goods are to be specially manufactured for the buyer and are not suitable for sale to others in the ordinary course of the seller's business; or (2) the buyer makes a partial payment or a partial acceptance, although the contract will be enforced only for the portion of goods paid for or accepted; or (3) the party being sued admits in court, or in court documents, that a contract was made for a certain quantity of goods. These same exceptions also apply to the lease of goods that otherwise would require a writing under the UCC.

UCC § 2-201 also contains a novel provision that may trap the unaware merchant. A merchant is defined by the UCC as a person who deals in goods of this kind, or otherwise, through his or her occupation, holds himself or herself out as having knowledge or skill peculiar to the practice or goods involved in the transaction. Section 2-201 states that a merchant who receives a *record* of a confirmation (for example, "This is to confirm our sale to you of 5,000 bushels of apples, #2 grade, at $1.25/bushel, delivery Tuesday /s/ Seller") from another merchant and does not use a record to object to the confirmation within 10 days is bound to the contract. (A "record" includes electronic communications such as an e-mail.) This provision is illustrated in Exhibit 12.2. The policy underlying this result is a familiar one: A valid oral contract must exist if the other merchant party does not object to the confirmation. The moral of this section of the UCC is: Merchants, answer your mail, e-mails, and faxes!

Section 2A-201 states that contracts for the lease of goods calling for total payments of $1,000 or more, excluding payments for options to renew or to buy, are not enforceable unless there is a sufficient writing. The writing must be signed by the party against whom enforcement is sought. For example, a contract for leasing a computer with lease payments of $1,000 or more must be in writing.

Interestingly, there is no comparable requirement in international sales of goods unless the parties themselves include such a requirement in their contract. The United Nations Convention on Contracts for the International Sale of Goods (CSIG), the most comprehensive statutory coverage of international sales contracts, has no provision comparable to the Statute of Frauds, nor does it require a writing for any types of contracts. In fact, the CSIG has no requirements as to form.

The Writing Requirement

The writing required to satisfy the Statute of Frauds is not unduly burdensome. In fact, there does not even need to be a written *contract*, per se. Courts are very liberal in what

Exhibit 12.2

Merchant's Rule Under UCC § 2-201

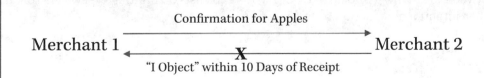

Failure to "object" in a timely manner will satisfy the need for a record, constituting proof of the agreement.

eClass 12.1 Management/Marketing

CONSULTANT CONTRACTS

Meg has a friend, Jessie, majoring in public relations. Jessie plans to have his own public relations firm after graduation. One day, Meg and Jessie were discussing eClass and its product line. Jessie shared some creative and interesting ideas for promoting eClass's products. Meg liked his ideas and suggested that eClass should hire Jessie and be his first client. Jessie agreed that this arrangement would be beneficial to eClass and his own public relations firm. Meg and Jessie orally agreed that Jessie would provide public relations and consulting services for eClass for a five year period. They also agreed that eClass would not hire any other public relations firm during that time. Neither Meg nor Jessie was familiar with the normal prices for these services, so they agreed to determine the fees later. Meg discussed this arrangement with you and asked for your advice. What will you tell her?

BUSINESS CONSIDERATIONS Should Ani, Meg, and Yousef have a policy on oral contracts? If so, what should it be? How can eClass ensure that its written contracts will cover most if not all the important terms? What sort of policy should eClass adopt regarding hiring consultants?

ETHICAL CONSIDERATIONS Once Meg and Jessie enter into this arrangement, what moral duties do they owe each other? Is it moral for Meg to hire Jessie without discussing it with Ani and Yousef? What moral duties does Meg owe to the other principals at eClass?

they accept as a writing. All that the Statute of Frauds requires is written evidence that the parties have reached an enforceable agreement. The writing may take the form of letters, telegrams, receipts, e-mails, or memoranda. However, the writing must, at a minimum, (1) identify the parties to the agreement, (2) identify the subject matter of the agreement, (3) set out all material terms and conditions of the agreement, and (4) be signed, at least by the party being sued. There may even be several writings that are "pieced together," such as the exchange of letters or e-mails, so long as these writings, when combined, all refer to the same transaction and show an agreement between the parties. (Under the UCC, a writing consists of "printing, typewriting, or any other intentional reduction to tangible form."[12])

The Signature Requirement

Similarly, anything intended by the parties as a signature will satisfy the Statute of Frauds. A signature is normally defined as "any mark, symbol, or device used with the present intent to authenticate a writing." This, of course, would include written signatures; but courts even have held stamped signatures or stationery letterheads to be sufficient. Both parties need not sign the memorandum, as long as the party against whom enforcement is sought signs it. A signature by his or her authorized agent will also be sufficient. Exhibit 12.3 explains the scope of the Statute of Frauds including the exceptions to the general rules.

Exhibit 12.3

The Common Law Statute of Frauds

Types of Contracts Covered (and Which Must Be in Writing)	Elements	Exceptions
Contracts to answer for the debt of another if the person defaults	1. There are three parties.	1.1. Not all three-party transactions are guaranty contracts.
	2. There are two promises, one original (debtor to creditor) and the other collateral (third-party guarantor to creditor).	
	3. The second promise is a promise to accept only secondary liability resulting from the default of another.	
	4. The intent of the parties determines whether a three-party transaction involves a collateral contract (which must be in writing) or an original contract (which can be oral and will still be enforceable).	4.1. The "leading object" or "main purpose" doctrine may apply.

Exhibit 12.3 Continued

Types of Contracts Covered (and Which Must Be in Writing)	Elements	Exceptions
Contracts by executors and administrators of estates	1. The executors or administrators have promised to pay estate claims out of their own personal funds.	
Contracts for an interest in land	1. The agreement involves buying, selling, or transferring interests in land. 2. Leases, easements, and sale agreements about standing timber and buildings attached to the land also are covered.	1.1. The doctrine of part performance may take the contract out of the statute.
Contracts not to be performed within one year of the date of their making	1. Contracts in which it is impossible to perform the contract completely within one year of the date of the creation of the contract are covered. 2. One party has completely performed within the one year. 3. Circumstances that justify the application of promissory estoppel may exist.	1.1. Courts narrowly interpret the provision by excluding contracts that can *possibly* be performed within one year, even if such performance is very unlikely.
Contracts made in consideration of marriage	1. One person has promised another person to pay a given amount or otherwise to perform a contractual duty in order to induce the person to enter a marriage.	1. Simple promises to marry each other are not covered.

The Statute of Frauds in e-Commerce

The e-commerce environment has spawned alternative approaches to the common law treatment of the Statute of Frauds. The thrust of UETA is that electronic records, electronic signatures, and the contracts that result from such transactions should be treated on a par with their paper-based counterparts. Accordingly, § 7 of UETA provides for the legal recognition of electronic records, electronic signatures, and electronic contracts. UETA § 2 (8) defines an "electronic signature" as an "electronic sound, symbol, or process attached to or logically associated with a record and executed or adopted by a person with the intent to sign the record." An electronic signature, then, includes (1) PIN numbers, (2) passwords, (3) clicking on a box labeled "I agree," and (4) encryption devices, to name a few. Yet, as discussed earlier, UETA does not override otherwise applicable substantive law. While § 8 makes it clear that "while the pen and ink provisions of such other law may be satisfied electronically, nothing in the Act vitiates the other requirement of such laws." Therefore, even though UETA § 9 (a) makes an electronic record or electronic signature attributable to a person as if it were the act of the person, this provision allows the determination of who signed the record to be established by any means (including effective security procedures). Section 9 (b) notes that the evidence used to determine the person to whom the electronic record or signature is attributable can be drawn from the context and surrounding circumstances, including the parties' agreement. Security procedures such as encryption help to verify the identity of the person who sent/signed the electronic record, a problem more prevalent in electronically based transactions because of the possibility of hacking. If the parties dispute the attribution of a signature or record, they may introduce any relevant evidence. An electronic signature that can be attributed to a given person would satisfy the signature requirement of the Statute of Frauds.

Unlike UETA, UCITA has a specific Statute of Frauds provision. But like UETA, UCITA's validation of both paper and electronic records encompasses electronic forms of authentication as signatures. UCITA'S Statute of Frauds provision (§ 201) requires an "authenticated record." As noted earlier, a "record" refers to information that is inscribed on a tangible medium (in writing) or that is stored in an electronic, retrievable format. A record becomes authenticated once it is signed or an electronic symbol linked with that record has been executed or adopted. Under UCITA § 201, a contract requiring a contract fee of $5,000 or more is not enforceable unless the party against which enforcement is sought has authenticated a record sufficient to indicate that a contract has been formed and which reasonably identifies the copy or subject matter to which the contract refers. The parties can, however, alter the requirements of this provision for future dealings. The exceptions set out in UCITA § 201 largely mirror the UCC's provisions as to merchants, admissions in court, and past performance; but the record must describe the subject matter (for example, the database that is being licensed) or the copies to which the agreement refers rather than goods, as would be the case under the UCC. UCITA dispenses with the need for a record if the agreement is a license for an agreed duration of one year or less or when the license may be terminated at will by the party against which the contract is asserted.

The federal E-SIGN statute, like UETA, validates but does not mandate the use of electronic signatures. In general, E-SIGN permits the use of electronic signatures in circumstances that otherwise would require manual signatures (also called wet signatures). Like UETA, E-SIGN does not alter substantive contract law.[13] Nevertheless, some critics argue that E-SIGN's fairly extensive consumer notification procedures may weaken the efficiencies otherwise realized by the statute's blanket endorsement of electronic signatures.

Contract Amendments

A number of legal questions arise when the parties to an agreement seek to amend their contract. Some of the issues dealing with consideration have already been addressed. The Statute of Frauds may apply to the contract amendment, requiring that the amendment be evidenced by a writing in order to be enforceable.

eClass 12.2 Sales/Manufacturing

CHECKING THE MAIL AND E-MAIL

Assume that eClass is producing its own inventory and that Ani and Yousef want to shut down the plant for two weeks and give all the employees a paid vacation. Ani and Yousef want all three principals during this time period to attend an international conference that will focus on many subjects of interest to them. Meg is concerned that, in this circumstance, communications sent to the firm will go unanswered. She suggests that they select an employee to check the daily mail and e-mails during their absence. Ani and Yousef do not like the idea of having an employee read eClass's letters and messages. They assert that because two weeks is a short time, all three can catch up with the mail and e-mails on their return. Meg insists that the firm cannot afford to ignore the communications sent to it for two weeks. They have asked for your advice. What will you tell them? Does the time involved affect your answer?

BUSINESS CONSIDERATIONS   Why is it important for businesspeople to read and respond to their mail and e-mails in a timely manner? What should a business do to protect itself when it regularly takes telephone orders for the sale of goods and those goods typically cost $500 or more?

ETHICAL CONSIDERATIONS   Is it ethical to hold a merchant responsible for communications received but unanswered (or even unread), when the same rules do not apply to a nonmerchant? Why does the distinction between merchants and nonmerchants matter?

Many written contracts specify that any subsequent modifications must be in writing. Assuming that the Statute of Frauds does not apply, most courts will still give effect to the oral modification. In the courts' view, the subsequent oral modification impliedly includes an agreement to abandon the requirement that modifications be in writing. The UCC provisions dealing with the sale of goods have a different rule; under UCC § 2-209(2), if the contract says that modifications must be in a signed writing, a signed writing will be required.

JUDICIAL INTERPRETATION

We have stressed the importance of a *meeting of the minds* of the parties to the contract. This phrase highlights one of the essential elements of a contract: The parties must have indicated, by their words or conduct, an intention to agree about some matter. Sometimes the parties do not express their intentions accurately and with complete detail. Because language is not always precise, it may later become apparent that the parties were not binding themselves to identical terms and courses of action. Disputes arise when this variance in expectations is discovered. If the parties cannot resolve these disputes amicably, courts must interpret what the contract "really says."

When the language of the agreement is confusing or ambiguous, *interpretation* is used to determine the meaning of the words and actions of the parties. When this occurs, it is likely to be difficult to ascertain the parties' real intent. Problems arise primarily because words are symbols of expression and can take on a multitude of meanings. Words do not exist in a vacuum. Determining how a certain party intended to use words or actions becomes a factual issue. A court must examine each party's understanding and conduct in the situation; it also must be conscious of how other reasonable persons would have understood these words and actions under similar circumstances. In deciding between the competing views, courts often consider the intentions of the parties through a frame of reference known as the "reasonable person." This perspective allows the court to choose the interpretation that would be most consistent with the expectations of a reasonable person in the same circumstances. Unreasonable expectations will not be protected.

Standards

Certain standards of interpretation have evolved over the years. Probably the most common is the standard of *general usage*, or the meaning that a reasonable person who was aware of all operative uses and who was acquainted with the circumstances would attach to the agreement. For example, Leighanne signs an agreement in which she pays $100,000 as a life membership fee for admission to a nursing home. The agreement states that for a trial period of two months, either Leighanne or the nursing home can suspend the agreement. If the agreement is "suspended," the $100,000 (minus $2,000 per month) will be returned. What if Leighanne dies after one month in the home? Can her estate recover the $98,000 by arguing that the agreement was "suspended" during the trial period due to Leighanne's death, or has the life membership fee been paid irrevocably? A court in a similar case applied general usage; it decided that a reasonable person in Leighanne's position would have understood the provision to mean that until life membership status were obtained, the nursing home should return the money (less the amounts specified) to her estate. The court also asserted that if the nursing home had intended to retain the money in the event of a probationary member's death, it should have expressly stated this fact in the contract. Under different facts, the court might have applied the standard of *limited usage* (the meaning given to language in a particular locale) instead of the standard of general usage.

Rules of Interpretation

To supplement the appropriate standard of interpretation (general usage or limited usage), courts also use *rules of interpretation* (also called *rules of construction.*) In most states, no one rule is conclusive. Authorities disagree as to the relative importance of these aids to interpretation. You should be aware of the following common rules. Courts should:

- Attempt to give effect to the manifested intentions of the parties.
- Take into account the circumstances surrounding the transaction.
- Examine the contract as a whole in order to ascertain the intentions of the parties.
- Give ordinary words their ordinary meanings and technical words their technical meanings, unless the circumstances indicate otherwise.
- Favor reasonable constructions over unreasonable alternatives.
- Give effect to the main purpose of the agreement and all its parts, if possible.
- Interpret the contract so that specific words or provisions control over general ones.
- Give effect to hand-written words over typed words and typed words over printed ones when there is a conflict. (*Printed words* are the words printed, or preprinted, on a form contract.) UCC § 3-114, dealing with negotiable instruments, says that typed words should be given effect over printed terms and that handwritten terms should prevail over both typed and printed words.
- Construe words most strictly against the party who drafted the agreement.
- Interpret contracts affecting the public interest in favor of the public.

These common rules of construction give the court a good "starting point" for interpreting written agreements and help to provide some sense of continuity and consistency in such interpretations.

Conduct and Usage of Trade

The *conduct* of the parties often aids in contract interpretation. If the court is in doubt, it will follow the interpretation placed on the agreement by the parties themselves. For example, when one party for years has accepted a grade of wool that is inferior to that called for by the contract specifications as satisfactory, evidence of this conduct will be admissible in determining how to interpret the other party's performance in relation to the contract specifications. UCC § 2-208 incorporates this rule of interpretation. Section 2-208 also addresses the roles that course of performance, course of dealing, and usage of trade have in contract construction. To characterize a situation involving judicial interpretation, one should answer the following questions:

1. Do the parties claim competing interpretations?
2. Can general usage resolve the conflict?
3. Can limited usage resolve the conflict?
4. Which rules of interpretation should the court employ?
5. How should the court resolve any conflicts among the rules of interpretation?
6. Is there any conduct of the parties or any "trade usage" that should be considered by the court in interpreting the contract?

THE PAROL EVIDENCE RULE

The *parol evidence rule* applies when the parties have a written contract.[14] Once there is a written contract, all previous oral agreements "merge" into the writing, and the written contract cannot be modified or changed by *parol evidence* (evidence given orally). Under the parol evidence rule, when the parties to a contract reduce their agreement to a writing with the intent that it embody the full and final expression of their bargain (a totally integrated contract), no other expressions—*written or oral*—made prior to or contemporaneous with the writing are admissible in court. By limiting the use of parol evidence, courts uphold the sanctity of totally integrated written contracts. The rule emphasizes the importance of the writings between the parties and provides the courts with a single source of proof as to the terms of contracts.

However, there are exceptions to the parol evidence rule. One of the important exceptions arises when the parties have a writing that is only a *partially integrated* contract. In a partially integrated contract, parol evidence can be used to (1) explain or define the terms used in the writing, or to (2) include consistent additional terms to the written terms in determining the complete contractual agreement.

Since the writing does not always provide conclusive proof as to whether the agreement is totally or partially integrated, the court must resolve this issue. Integration is discussed in the following sections. (In reading the following sections, note that "the parol evidence rule and the problems of interpretation must remain separate if they are to be understood."[15]) Exhibit 12.4 illustrates the parol evidence rule.

Exhibit 12.4

Application of the Parol Evidence Rule

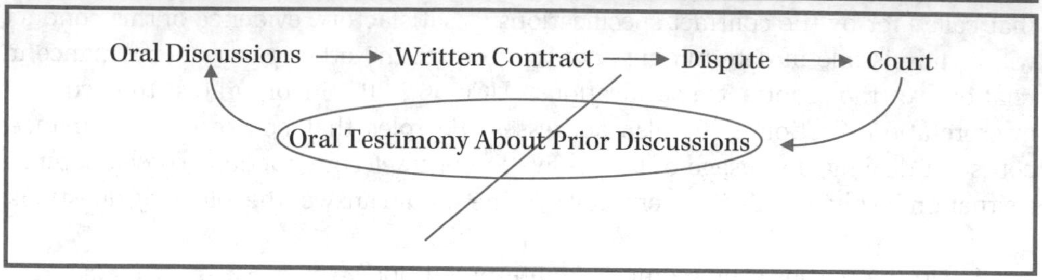

Oral Discussions → Written Contract → Dispute → Court

Oral Testimony About Prior Discussions

Rules of Integration

In general, the more formal and complete the instrument, the more likely a court will conclude that it is a *totally integrated* agreement. Courts use various tests to determine if the contract is totally integrated. One common test is the "face-of-instrument" test, where the court exams the "four corners of the writing" to determine if the parties intended the document to be totally integrated. Other jurisdictions use the "all-relevant-evidence" test, where the court reviews the document and extrinsic evidence to determine if the parties intended a total integration. Some contracts include clauses called *integration* or *merger* clauses. In these clauses, the parties declare that the writing is the full and final expression of all the terms in the agreement. Courts will then interpret the contract as totally integrated unless a party can show that the merger clause was induced by fraud or mistake.

Total Integration

A *totally integrated* contract is one that represents the parties' final and complete statement of their agreement. Such a contract can neither be contradicted nor added to by evidence of prior agreements or expressions. The law assumes that the writing supersedes the terms set out earlier in preliminary negotiations. Exhibit 12.5 illustrates some of the limitations on the use of parol evidence.

Partial Integration

If a writing is intended to be the final statement of the parties' agreement but is incomplete, it is a *partially integrated* contract. Such a writing cannot be contradicted by evidence of earlier agreements or expressions, but it can be supplemented by evidence of additional, consistent terms. Perhaps Leighanne and the nursing home orally agreed that her personal physician (rather than the nursing home's doctor) would provide needed medical care. If the parties leave out

Exhibit 12.5

Limitations Imposed on Parol Evidence

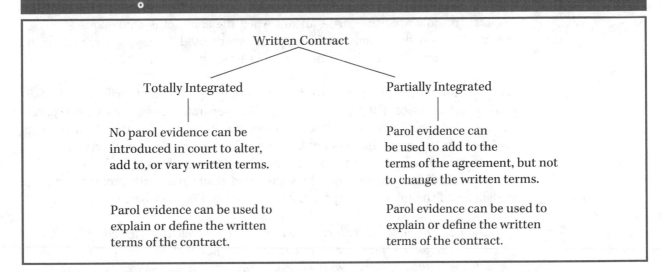

Written Contract

Totally Integrated | Partially Integrated

No parol evidence can be introduced in court to alter, add to, or vary written terms.

Parol evidence can be used to add to the terms of the agreement, but not to change the written terms.

Parol evidence can be used to explain or define the written terms of the contract.

Parol evidence can be used to explain or define the written terms of the contract.

this provision, the contract represents a partially integrated writing. Since this provision does not appear to contradict the original agreement, some courts may allow the parties to add it later.

Sometimes, the proponent of the parol evidence may acknowledge that there is one agreement but may argue that the parties intended to include only certain terms in the written contract. The proponent argues that it was their intent to leave the remaining terms "in parol." Courts may examine whether the subject matter of the parol evidence was mentioned at all in the contract. If it was, this strongly suggests that the writing was intended to cover that provision. The policy that underlies the parol evidence rule is not *as* compelling in situations in which the contract is partially integrated (that is, incomplete). In such cases, although the writing may not be contradicted by evidence of earlier terms, it may be supplemented by evidence of additional, consistent terms.

Exceptions to the Parol Evidence Rule

Courts will disregard the parol evidence rule and will admit parol evidence in certain circumstances, even when the contract is fully integrated. Although the exceptions and how they are applied may vary from state to state, parol evidence is generally admissible:

- To show sham, forgery, failure of consideration, or failure of a condition.
- To show fraud, duress, or mistake.

■ To show that the parties had a *condition precedent* to the agreement (a certain act or event that must occur before the other party has a duty to perform or before a contract exists). Courts may allow evidence about a condition precedent only if this evidence does not contradict the written terms of the contract.

■ To show what the parties meant when the contract is ambiguous.

■ To show the meanings of any special words used by the parties, such as the meanings that derive from custom or usage in an industry.

Although not strictly exceptions to the parol evidence rule, courts will also generally allow parol evidence if the parties entered into separate agreements with separate consideration and if only one of the agreements is in writing: Courts will allow parol evidence about the one that was not in writing. Courts also allow parol evidence about agreements made by the parties after the written contract was signed.

The following example shows how the court might deal with problems of parol evidence and the rules of interpretation in resolving a conflict between two parties.

Julian is trying to buy a "fully equipped" car. He enters into a written contract with the dealer for the purchase. The contract specifies that the car will be "fully equipped" upon delivery. When the car is delivered, Julian notices that there is no air conditioning in the car. He complains to the dealer, insisting that a fully equipped car includes air conditioning. The dealer disagrees, stating that fully equipped does not refer to air conditioning. If the parties cannot settle this dispute informally, a court may be asked to settle the case. If the judge believes the writing was a partial integration, he or she will need to scrutinize the entire transaction, including the car salesperson's representations and Julian's expectations. If, instead, the court decides the writing was a full integration of the agreement, neither the sales person's representations nor Julian's expectations will be considered. However, if the agreement is fully integrated, a judge may apply the standard of limited usage—the meaning of the term as understood locally and in the trade—to see whether a "fully equipped" car ordinarily includes air conditioning.

Parol Evidence Under the Uniform Commercial Code

Sections 2-202 and 2-208 of the UCC concern the parol evidence rule. Basically, the Code recognizes the rule but then weakens its impact by stating that the following types of evidence are admissible: (1) *a course of dealing* (previous conduct of the parties in their performance in *prior* contracts); (2) *usage of trade* (a regularly observed practice are in a trade); and (3) *course of performance* (previous conduct of the parties in their performance of *this* contract). Courts also can admit evidence of consistent, additional terms unless they find that the parties intended the writing as a complete and exclusive statement of the terms of the agreement. The Code also sets up priorities among these types of evidence: The express terms of the agreement control course of performance, course of dealing, and usage of trade. Evidence relating to course of performance, in turn, controls admissions about course of dealing and usage of trade. Sections 2A-202 and 2A-207 of the UCC provide parallel coverage and treatment of parol evidence in contracts for the leasing of goods.

As was the case with the Statute of Frauds provision, UCITA § 301 basically engrafts the common law parol evidence rule onto the parties' "confirmatory records" to protect the integrity of the terms the parties intended as the final expression of their agreement.

eClass 12.3 Manufacturing/Management

SUPPLIER'S CONTRACTS

Assume that eClass entered into a contract with Caine Software Company (CSC) to duplicate and package 2,000 units of eAccounting for the price of $10 per unit. Prior to entering into this agreement, Yousef met with Cody, the CSC representative. Yousef asked Cody if CSC would pay for shipping and insurance. Cody's response was yes, CSC would be responsible for insurance on the product up until the time the product left the CSC factory. Cody did not directly comment on the shipping costs. The written agreement was silent as to both shipping costs and insurance. When eClass received the shipment and the invoice for the software, it found that the cost of shipping the package was included as due and owing by eClass. Yousef called Cody to ask why this shipping expense was included when Cody had stated earlier that CSC would cover shipping and insurance. Cody replied that CSC had agreed to cover the insurance on the goods until they left the factory, which it did. He added that, under CSC's normal practices, the buyer was responsible for freight and insurance unless the contract specified otherwise. When he reviewed the written contract, Yousef did not see any mention of either shipping or insurance. Yousef asks you the following questions: If eClass sues CSC over these charges, how will the court decide which party is correct? Is the contract more likely to be fully integrated or partially integrated? What, if any, oral evidence might Yousef be able to introduce to support eClass's position in a lawsuit over these terms? What will you tell him?

BUSINESS CONSIDERATIONS   eClass wants to be more careful with future contracts. How should it change its business practices to avoid similar problems? What role do normal industry practices play in contract negotiations and interpretation?

ETHICAL CONSIDERATIONS   When one party to a negotiation asks for a concession, such as insurance, is it ethical to avoid the question or change the topic? Is it ethical to make oral promises and then intentionally not include the commitments in the written agreement and hope that the other party does not notice the omission?

Contemporary Case

BEATLEY v. KNISLEY

183 Ohio App. 3d 356, 2009 Ohio App. LEXIS 1878
(Ct. of Appeals, 10th Dist., Franklin County, 2009)

Discretionary appeal not allowed by *Beatley v. Knisley*, 123 Ohio St. 3d 1408, 2009 Ohio LEXIS 2692 (Ohio, 2009)

FACTS Defendants Katherine Knisley, Jaclyn Wanner, and Julianne L. Irene, all college students, began looking for rental housing in The Ohio State University campus area for the 2006-2007 school year. Lavon Baker, an agent for Jack K. Beatley, showed them various rental properties. Knisley and Wanner found a unit that they liked. Baker told Knisley and Wanner that they would have to satisfy three conditions before a lease on the unit would become binding. First, the girls needed to find someone willing to guarantee payments on their behalf and to sign a guarantor agreement. Second, the girls needed to submit a deposit of $1,460. And third, the girls needed to secure a fourth tenant to sign a lease. Baker informed Knisley and Wanner that they had only 24 hours to satisfy all three conditions. Knisley and Wanner completed rental applications and signed the lease that Baker gave them. None of the conditions appeared in the lease. Later that day, Irene visited Beatley's offices. Baker told Irene about the three conditions, and Irene signed the lease. Beatley approved defendants' rental applications, signed the lease, and withdrew the unit from the market. The defendants failed to satisfy any of the conditions. Defendants did not move into the unit at the beginning of the lease term, so Beatley sent them a letter stating that they owed him rent. Defendants expressed surprise because they never completed the three conditions.

ISSUE Should the defendants be permitted to testify in court about the alleged conditions?

HOLDING Yes, conditions precedent are exceptions to the parol evidence rule.

REASONING Excerpts from the opinion of Klatt, J.:

... The parol evidence rule is a substantive rule of law developed centuries ago to protect the integrity of written contracts. ... According to this rule, "'the parties' final written integration of their agreement may not be varied, contradicted or supplemented by evidence of prior or contemporaneous oral agreements, or prior written agreements.'" ... By prohibiting the introduction of extrinsic evidence to alter or supplement the parties' final, complete expression of their agreement, the parol evidence rule ensures the stability, predictability, and enforceability of written contracts and "'effectuates a presumption that a subsequent written contract is of a higher nature than earlier statements, negotiations, or oral agreements.'" ... Ohio courts have long recognized exceptions to the parol evidence rule. ... Among these exceptions is the allowance of extrinsic evidence to prove a condition precedent to a contract. ... Courts admit extrinsic evidence of a condition precedent because satisfaction of such a condition must occur before a contract comes into existence. ... [P]arol evidence establishing a condition precedent does not modify the terms of a written contract, but instead, determines whether the contract ever became effective. ... The parol evidence rule does not preclude evidence that contradicts the very existence or validity of an alleged contract.... [D]efendants ... testified that Baker told them that they had to perform three acts.... [T]he parol evidence rule would not prohibit this evidence....

The rule of contract integration is a corollary principle to the parol evidence rule, as the degree of integration determines whether the parol evidence rule applies to a contract.... Logically, ... where the parol evidence rule does not apply, neither does the rule of contract integration. Although the parol evidence rule does not preclude extrinsic evidence of a condition precedent, courts do not completely abandon the principles behind that rule when dealing with alleged oral conditions precedent. To preserve the integrity of the written contract, a party may not introduce extrinsic evidence of an oral condition precedent when the written contract addresses the subject matter of the condition precedent and the contractual terms are inconsistent with the condition precedent....

[This] lease addresses ... each of the alleged oral conditions precedent ... with varying degrees of specificity. With regard to the requirement that defendants' obtain a guarantor, the lease states that "[e]ach tenant may be required to have a Guarantor...." With regard to the requirement that defendants pay a $1,460 deposit, the lease provides that defendants "will be charged" one of the following: (1) a $1,460 "holding deposit" ..., (2) a liquidated damage fee ..., or (3) a $1,460 fee if Beatley re-rented the unit within 30 days ... With regard to the requirement that defendants find a fourth tenant ..., the lease only mandates that "[t]he premises shall be occupied by no more than 4 persons...." None of these provisions is inconsistent with the alleged oral conditions precedent. The requirement that defendants must obtain a guarantor is actually congruous to the relevant lease provision, as it resolves whether Beatley ... required defendants to secure a guarantor. Although the lease discusses the possibility that potential tenants may owe a "holding deposit" ..., that possibility does not conflict with a condition precedent that defendants must pay a deposit before the lease would become binding.... [T]he imposition of a maximum occupancy rate does not contradict the alleged oral condition precedent requiring a minimum occupancy rate. Because the lease terms and the alleged oral conditions precedent are not inconsistent, defendants may introduce extrinsic evidence of the three alleged oral conditions precedent.... [D]efendants have established a genuine issue of material fact that precludes summary judgment.... We ... reverse the [summary] judgment of the Franklin County Municipal Court, and we remand this matter to that court....

You Be the Judge

In 1969, the classic biker movie, "Easy Rider," was released with its anti-establishment and pro-drug use theme. This film is credited with making famous the song "Born to Be Wild," by Steppenwolf. The film is reported to have made $40 million, although it was produced for only $427,000. Dennis Hopper directed the film, co-wrote it with Peter Fonda, and co-starred in it with Fonda. Jack Nicholson and Phil Spector also acted in the film. Hopper alleges that he and Fonda originated the idea together. Fonda was the producer of the film. Allegedly, Fonda has taken one-half the net earnings, but Hopper has only received one-third. Hopper and Fonda did not write down their agreement about how they would share the profits and who would receive credit. Hopper filed suit against Fonda in February 1996, approximately 27 years after the film was released. Fonda claims "I am very articulate and I have an extraordinarily accurate memory." Eventually Hopper and Fonda settled their dispute. Assume that they have not, and the case was filed in *your* court. If you were the judge, how would *you* decide this dispute? [See Owen Bowcott, "From Easy Riders to Hard Cash, Increasingly, Big Showbiz Names Are Turning to the Law. Nowadays, It's Lights, Cameras, Legal Action," *The Guardian* (London), February 15, 1996, p. T7; Richard Conrad, "Get Hip to Hopper," *Herald Sun* (Australia), Wednesday, November 11, 2009, Amusements, p. 63; Shannon Kari, "Easy Rider Finds Gold in Person/Almost Three Decades Ago, Peter Fonda Created an Outlaw Archetype. Now He Is Drawing on His Father's Acting History to Escape It." *The Globe and Mail* (Canada), Thursday, June 12, 1997, p. C1; Sue Williams, "Dennis Hopper/Out of the Ashes," *The Weekend Australian*, Sunday, March 8, 1997, p. R05; and "Fonda Lashes Out at Studios," *Canberra Times* (Australia), Thursday, July 31, 1997, GT, p. 5.]

Summary

In accordance with the Statute of Frauds, certain types of contracts must be in writing to be enforceable. Under the common law, these include: (1) collateral contracts; (2) promises of executors and administrators to pay from their personal assets; (3) contracts for the sale or transfer of interests in land; (4) contracts not to be performed within one year from the date of their making; and (5) promises made in consideration of marriage. The Uniform Commercial Code (UCC) also has several Statute of Frauds provisions including the sale of goods priced at $500 or more and the lease of goods where the contract price is $1,000 or more. Under the common law and the UCC, very little in the way of a memorandum or signature is necessary to satisfy the Statute of Frauds. UETA, UCITA, and E-SIGN validate electronic forms of writings and signatures as satisfying the writing requirement of the Statute. The United Nations Convention on Contracts for the International Sale of Goods (CSIG) has no Statute of Frauds provision or any requirement for a writing for a contract, regardless of size or length of time.

Interpretation is the process of determining the meaning of words and other manifestations of intent that the parties used in forging their agreement. One common standard is the standard of general usage, or the meaning that a reasonable person who was aware of the alternative meanings and the circumstances would attach to the agreement. In the alternative, the court might apply the standard of limited usage or the meaning given to language in a particular locale.

A totally integrated contract represents the parties' final and complete statement of their agreement and cannot be contradicted. A partially integrated contract is intended to be the parties' final statement; but it is incomplete. It may be supplemented with consistent, additional terms. The parol evidence rule states that oral evidence is not admissible to alter, add to, or vary the terms of a totally integrated, written contract. If the contract is not totally integrated, parol evidence can be used more freely. However, it still cannot be used to alter or to vary the written terms in the contract. There are exceptions to the parol evidence rule. Parol evidence is generally admissible to show: (1) sham, forgery, failure of consideration, or failure of a condition; (2) fraud, duress, or mistake; (3) that the parties had a condition precedent to the agreement; (4) what the parties meant when the contract is ambiguous; and (5) the meanings of any special words used by the parties, such as the meanings that derive from custom or usage in an industry.

Discussion Questions

1. What are the most important characteristics of a collateral contract, or a contract to guarantee the debt of another if that person defaults? Also, explain the exception to the rule that collateral contracts must be in writing.

2. Describe the exceptions to the rules that (1) contracts for the sale of goods priced at $500 or more and (2) the lease of goods with payments of $1,000 or more must be in writing.

3. What is the process of contract interpretation?

4. eClass recently reviewed the standard form contracts the firm uses, and it decided to revise some of these contracts. As a part of this revision, Yousef suggested that the firm include a so-called "merger clause," stating that the written contract represented the parties' entire agreement and that the written terms superseded any previous oral communications. Is a "merger clause" a good idea for eClass? Why or why not?

5. What is the parol evidence rule? What are the exceptions to the rule?

Case Problems and Writing Assignments

1. In the early 1990s, PMC Corporation, a supplier of thermocouple wire and cable, began to sell its products to Houston Wire & Cable Company (Houston), a distributor of wire and cable products. In 1994, PMC and Houston began discussions about entering into a relationship in which PMC would provide training on thermocouple applications and other services to Houston and PMC would become Houston's primary vendor of thermocouple products. In late 1994, PMC's president, John Gehrisch, asked Houston to put in writing its commitment to purchase primarily from PMC. On January 4, 1996, Gehrisch wrote a letter to Tom Adelman, vice president of operations at Houston, in which Gehrisch requested a letter of intent from Houston confirming its recognition of PMC as its primary source for thermocouple products and confirming its intent to purchase thermocouple products amounting to a minimum of $800,000 per year and totaling $2,000,000 in 1995, $3,000,000 in 1996, and $4,000,000 in 1997. This amount represented Houston's total purchases of thermocouple products to cover both its corporate inventory and branch requirements. Although Houston could not guarantee that it would purchase a minimum of $800,000 per year, the parties noted PMC's need for a letter of intent from Houston so PMC could obtain leverage at its bank and would have something to give to the bank when it was negotiating for capital to

expand the factory. On January 13, 1995, PMC faxed Houston a draft of a revised agreement. The cover sheet characterized the draft as an intent to purchase that in no way locked Houston into purchases from PMC but merely indicated an intent. On January 17, 1995, Houston signed the revised version, which indicated Houston's acceptance in principle of the January 4 agreement and its addition of the following details:

> [Houston] expects to purchase in excess of $2,000,000 of thermocouple products in 1995.... While [Houston] cannot commit to exclusive purchase of this total from PMC, [Houston] recognizes PMC as a preferred supplier. As such ... PMC can expect to receive a major share of the total thermocouple business. It is not unrealistic to project total purchases by [Houston] from PMC to be in the $2,000,000 range in 1995, [$3,000,000 in 1996, and $4,000,000 in 1997]. It is also [Houston's] intent to purchase the major portion of this product from PMC.

After this correspondence, Houston's orders from PMC began to decrease. During a meeting on February 21, 1996, Houston informed PMC that it was planning to purchase the bulk of its thermocouple products from Belden, a competing manufacturer. In 1998, when PMC sued Houston for breach of contract, Houston argued that the writings in question were unenforceable under the Uniform Commercial Code's Statute of Frauds provision because they lacked the required element relating to quantity. Was Houston correct? [See *PMC Corporation v. Houston Wire & Cable Company*, 797 A.2d 125 (N.H. 2002).]

2. Ronald A. Yocca and others brought a class action against The Pittsburgh Steelers Sports, Inc., a National Football League franchise, and others. The Steelers had issued a brochure soliciting the purchase of stadium builder licenses (SBLs) for Heinz Field, a new football stadium then under construction. The brochure indicated that, for a one-time contribution to the cost of building the new stadium, the SBL purchasers would be assigned to a particular seating area (or section) in the stadium and would have the right to buy season tickets in that section for as many seasons as they wished. The actual seat assignments were to be made after the seats were physically installed in the stadium. The price of the SBLs ranged from $250 to $2,700 depending on where the purchaser wished to sit. The SBL Brochure contained colored diagrams of the planned stadium showing the various sections and showing the yard-lines of the playing field. The next to the last page of the SBL Brochure was headed "Before you sign" and contained, among other things, the following:

> You may apply for any Section you wish as your first preference. To ensure fairness, every application received by the November 30 deadline will be assigned a random computerized priority number and that priority number will be used to assign both sections and seats.... If you are ordering SBLs, you will be mailed a contract by the end of March 1999, notifying you of your [s]ection assignment. The contract must be signed and returned within 15 days. If the completed contract is not returned as required, your season ticket holder discount, seating priority and deposit will be forfeited.... Current season ticket holders who apply for [an] SBL [s]ection that corresponds with their current seat location in Three Rivers Stadium will be the first assigned to that [s]ection. If that is your choice, we will try to assign seats as close to your current seat location as the new stadium seating configuration will allow. All other seats in a given SBL [section] will be assigned using the random priority number. Assignment of your first preference is not guaranteed.

Interested parties were to fill out the application form and indicate their first, second, and third section choices. Yocca claimed that the defendants mailed two documents to the SBL applicants in October 1999, an "SBL Agreement" and "Additional Terms." The SBL Agreement incorporated by reference the Additional Terms, which, in turn, contained an integration clause stating that "This Agreement contains the entire agreement of the parties with respect to the matters provided for herein and shall supersede any representations or agreements previously made or entered into by the parties hereto." Yocca and the other plaintiffs alleged that they signed the SBL Agreement and paid the remaining installments for their SBLs. The plaintiffs claimed that when they took their seats in Heinz Field for the first time, they realized that the defendants had enlarged some of the SBL sections, causing their individual seats to be outside the SBL sections as depicted in the SBL Brochure, upon which they had relied when they filled out their applications. Yocca submitted that, based on the diagram in the SBL Brochure, he believed that Club I section seats would be somewhat between the 20-yard lines. However, Yocca's seats turned out to be at the 18-yard line. As a result, he submitted he would be forced to pay the higher Club I price for seats that, according to the SBL Brochure, should have been considered part of the less expensive Club II section and that he would have to do so for as long as he purchased season tickets. In rebuttal, the Steelers and the other defendants claimed that the integration clause in the "Additional Terms" portion of the October 1999 SBL Agreement barred the introduction of the parol evidence the plaintiffs had used to support their breach of contract claim. Evaluate the defendants' allegation that the October 1999 SBL Agreement superseded the parties' prior dealings, as well as the parol evidence rule's possible application to the plaintiffs' allegations. [See *Yocca v. The Pittsburgh Steelers Sports, Inc.*, 806 A.2d 936 (Pa. Comwlth. 2002).]

3. Monica Guzman's friend, Barbara Graves, rented a car from AAA Auto Rental in Bloomington, Indiana, and listed Guzman as an authorized driver. Guzman telephoned AAA to inform it that she would be driving the rental car to Chicago. At dusk about 25 miles from her destination, the battery light went on in the car. About 10 minutes later, the temperature light came on. Guzman continued to drive the car toward her destination; she passed a couple of exits from the interstate. The car eventually broke down on the interstate. Due to Guzman's failure to stop the car immediately after the warning lights had come on, the car's engine sustained damage from overheating. AAA had the car towed back to Bloomington where substantial repairs to the car's engine were made— including the resurfacing of the cylinder heads, a valve job, and the replacement of the fan relay switch. The towing and repair bills totaled nearly $1,000. Guzman testified that she had been afraid to pull off the highway. The trial court concluded that Guzman willfully had failed to stop because she was anxious to reach her destination, and it determined that Guzman had breached the car rental contract when she failed to return the car in good and safe mechanical condition. The trial court also found Guzman liable for the damages because she had "committed vandalism by the willful infliction of damage to this car by continuing to drive it after knowing it was not operating properly." The court relied on an Indiana statute governing motor vehicle rental companies and their contracts with customers, which permits rental companies to hold renters responsible for "physical damage to the rented vehicle . . . , resulting from vandalism unrelated to the theft of the rented vehicle." The trial court entered judgment in favor of AAA in the amount of $1,437, which represented the sum of the towing and repair bills and AAA's attorneys' fees. Guzman argued that the judgment was incorrect because the car had sustained mechanical, as opposed to physical, damages. She claimed the rental company could recover for mechanical/ engine damage only in the event of a collision. Is Guzman's interpretation logical or not? Why? [See *Guzman v. AAA Auto Rental*, 654 N.E.2d 838 (Ind. App. 1995).]

Notes

1. See John Edward Murray, Jr., *Grismore on Contracts*, rev., student edition (Indianapolis, IN: Bobbs-Merrill Company, 1965), § 265, p. 435. It is interesting to note that an earlier draft of the act required all contracts to be in writing. The act that was passed only listed six types of contracts. Ibid.

2. Usually, the guarantor enters the contract after the fact: However, he or she can enter prior to or at the same time as the primary agreement. For example, the guarantor may promise to guarantee the obligation *if* the creditor extends credit to the debtor.

3. Unfortunately, people use the term cosigner, and even surety, a number of different ways. The key is really the type of liability being undertaken by the parties. The label they use is not controlling.

4. The *Restatement (Second) of Contracts* actually labels this "The Suretyship Provision," in sections 112-123.

5. See *Harrington v. Rich*, 6 Vt. 666, cited in Murray, § 266, p. 438.

6. The type(s) of improvement that justify enforcement of the contract vary from state to state.

7. This apparently is an effort by the courts to construe this provision as narrowly as possible. Murray, § 270, p. 449.

8. If the contract provided for alternatives and one of them could be performed within one year, most courts would take the contract outside the Statute of Frauds.

9. It might be more logical for the courts to provide for quasi contractual recovery in these cases. However, most courts enforce the oral contract. Murray, § 270, p. 450.

10. The original Statute of Frauds included a provision dealing with the sale of goods. Under most circumstances it has been replaced by the UCC Statute of Frauds.

11. States have not yet adopted the revisions to Article 2 and 2A. In 2010, the National Conference of Commissioners of Uniform State Laws revisions were introduced in the Oklahoma legislature. "A Few Facts About the Amendments to UCC Articles 2 and 2A," http://www.nccusl.org/Update/uniformact_factsheets/uniformacts-fs-ucc22A03.asp. (accessed 6/7/10).

12. UCC § 1-202 (46).

13. E-SIGN specifies that it does not apply to a contract or record that is governed by the UCC. The new UCC § 1108 limits and supersedes E-SIGN. Uniform Commercial Code Task Force of the PBA Business Law Section, "Report on the Uniform Commercial Code Modernization Act of 2007," 78 PA BAR ASSN. QUARTERLY 83 (April, 2007).

14. Generally, the parol evidence rule is considered to be a rule of substantive law because it controls "what" the contract actually means. However, it also has impact on the evidence that can be introduced during a court case.

15. See Murray, § 97, p. 152.

13

The Rights and Obligations of Third Persons

Agenda

Ani, Meg, and Yousef know that some of the contracts they enter will involve third parties as well, and these third parties may also have contractual rights. For example, they believe that eClass's rights are involved each time an intermediary orders parts and supplies that are to be shipped directly to eClass. They also know that third party rights are involved when a shipment is lost or destroyed in the possession of a trucking company. Some of their clients may want or need to assign accounts receivables to eClass to pay for their purchases. The members would like to know what rights they would gain from the debtors who are obligated to pay these accounts and whether it would be wise to accept such an arrangement. They also want to know what risks eClass would assume. There will be times when eClass may need to hire other companies to install its software at distant locations. What rights and responsibilities would eClass have to the purchasers in these situations?

These and other questions will arise as you read this chapter. Be prepared! You never know when the firm or one of its members will seek your advice.

Classic Case

LAWRENCE v. FOX

20 N.Y. 268, 1859 N.Y. LEXIS 192
(Ct. of Appeals of New York, 1859)

[The Supreme Court is the trial court in the state of New York.]

FACTS[1] In November 1857, Holly loaned Fox $300 at Fox's request. Holly stated at the time that he owed that same amount to Lawrence for money he had borrowed from Lawrence that was due the next day. When Fox received the money, Fox promised to pay $300 to Lawrence the next day. This transaction was witnessed by a bystander. Fox's promise was made to Holly. It was not made to Lawrence or Lawrence's agent. Nor was it made in Lawrence's presence.

ISSUE Can Lawrence maintain a lawsuit against Fox?

HOLDING Yes, Lawrence is entitled to sue Fox on the debt.

REASONING Excerpts from the opinion of Judge H. Gray:

... [I]t is claimed that ... this promise ... was void for the want of consideration. It is now more than a quarter of a century since it was settled by the Supreme Court of this State [in precedents] ... that a promise in all material respects like the one under consideration was valid; and the judgment of that court was unanimously affirmed by the Court for the Correction of Errors. ... [Precedents] puts to rest the objection that the defendant's promise was void for want of consideration. ... In this case the promise was made to Holly and not expressly to the plaintiff; and this difference between the two cases presents the question ... as to the want of privity between the plaintiff and

defendant. As early as 1806 it was announced by the Supreme Court of this State, upon what was then regarded as the settled law of England, "That where one person makes a promise to another for the benefit of a third person, that third person may maintain an action upon it." ... This question was subsequently ... the subject of consideration by the Supreme Court, when it was held, that in declaring upon a promise, made to the debtor by a third party to pay the creditor of the debtor, founded upon a consideration advanced by the debtor, it was unnecessary to aver a promise to the creditor; for the reason that upon proof of a promise made to the debtor to pay the creditor, a promise to the creditor would be implied. ... The same principle is adjudged in several cases in Massachusetts. ... But it is urged that because the defendant was not in any sense a trustee of the property of Holly for the benefit of the plaintiff, the law will not imply a promise. I agree that many of the cases where a promise was implied were cases of trusts, created for the benefit of the promiser. ... The duty of the trustee to pay the *cestuis que trust*, according to the terms of the trust, implies his promise to the latter to do so. In this case the defendant, upon ample consideration received from Holly, promised Holly to pay his debt to the plaintiff; the consideration received and the promise to Holly made it as plainly his duty to pay the plaintiff as if the money had been remitted to him for that purpose, and as well implied a promise to do so as if he had been made a trustee of property to be converted into cash with which to pay. The fact that a breach of the duty imposed in the one case may be visited ... with more serious consequences than in the other, by no means disproves the payment to be a duty in both. ... "[T]hat a promise made to one for the benefit of another, he for whose benefit it is made may bring an action for its breach," has been applied to trust cases, not because it was exclusively applicable to those cases, but because it was a principle of law, and as such applicable to those cases.

... The cases cited ... establish the validity of a parol promise; it stands then upon the footing of a written one. Suppose the defendant had given his note in which, for value received of Holly, he had promised to pay the plaintiff and the plaintiff had accepted the promise. ... Very clearly Holly could not have discharged that promise. ... No one can doubt that he owes the sum of money demanded of him, or that in accordance with his promise it was his duty to have paid it to the plaintiff; ... the adjudications in this State ... have established the defendant's liability. ... The judgment should be affirmed.

ADDITION OF THIRD PARTIES TO THE CONTRACT

A contract affects the legal rights of the parties who directly enter into it. It may also influence the rights of other people. In some situations, these other people are so significant that they have legal rights under the contract and can file a lawsuit to enforce these contractual rights. In some of these situations, the third person is a significant party to the contract when the contract is initially formed; in others, the third person is added to the contract or affected by the contract at a later time. This chapter discusses what enforceable legal rights, if any, these third persons have under the contract.

THIRD-PARTY BENEFICIARY CONTRACTS

Persons and corporations who immediately receive rights in a contract to which they are not parties are called *beneficiaries*. It is really more appropriate to call this kind of beneficiary a *third person* because the additional person is not a party to the contract. However, we will use the common terminology and refer to this person as a *third party*. In some circumstances, the third person is *expected* to receive the benefits under the contract. These third persons are called "intended beneficiaries." They may be able to enforce the contract if the intended benefits are not conferred on them. In other circumstances, the third person is not necessarily expected to receive any benefits under the contract. Any benefits received by these third persons are incidental benefits. The benefits "spillover" to them, but that is not the intent of the parties making the contract. Such third persons do not have the right to enforce the contract if they never receive the "potential" benefits.

The two people who enter into the contract are commonly called the *promisor* and the *promisee*. A promisor may also be called an obligor, and a promisee may be called an obligee. Often, in third-party beneficiary contracts, the promise is to deliver goods to or perform a service directly for a third party. For example, Melanie is very busy; to save time in shopping for a Father's Day present and mailing it to her father in St. Cloud, Minnesota, she orders a basket of dried fruit and nuts from the Sierra Nut House Web site to be gift wrapped and delivered to her father. This arrangement is a third-party beneficiary contract; her father is the third-party beneficiary, and he is an intended beneficiary. A beneficiary does not need to know about the contract for the contract to be valid or to have any rights in the agreement.

Many businesses rely primarily on these contracts to achieve financial success. Examples include florist shops, singing telegram companies, mail-order companies that send fruit baskets, and life insurance companies.

Because these third parties are called beneficiaries, it is generally assumed that they receive something beneficial and good, but this is not always the case. In most states, the legal requirement for an *intended beneficiary* is that at least one of the contracting parties, usually the promisee, intended to have goods delivered to or services performed for the third party. The third party may not necessarily desire these goods or services. The beneficiary may, in fact, be displeased on receipt of the goods or services. An example is a singing telegram that embarrasses the recipient or is in poor taste.

An Incidental Beneficiary

The most important factor in determining the rights of a third party is whether the third party is an intended or an incidental beneficiary. When at least one of the original parties to the contract *meant* to affect a noncontracting person by establishing the contract, the noncontracting person is an *intended beneficiary*. Intended beneficiaries have legal rights in the contract. If the benefit or action to the noncontracting party was *accidental*, or *not intended*, this party is an *incidental beneficiary*.

For example, suppose Rosalia, an owner of a vacant city lot, decides to build a high-rise garage on it. Rosalia enters into a contract with a builder to construct the garage. Luke owns the neighboring lot with a high-rise office building on it. Luke is likely to benefit financially from the construction of the garage. However, if the builder does not complete the construction job and Rosalia decides not to sue for this breach of contract, Luke will not be able to sue to enforce the contract. In this situation, Luke is an incidental beneficiary because neither the builder nor Rosalia intended to benefit him. Consequently, he has no rights under the contract.

An Intended Beneficiary

An intended beneficiary does not have to be mentioned by name in the contract. It is sufficient for the parties to *clearly intend* to provide the beneficiary with rights under the agreement. In the absence of a clear expression of such an intent, the contracting parties are presumed to act solely for themselves. Sometimes the intended beneficiary may be one person from a group of people for whose benefit the contract was established. Automobile liability insurance, for example, is a contract between an insurance company and an automobile owner, but insurance is also partially for the benefit of drivers and pedestrians who share the road with the insured. (*Insureds* are persons or entities whose lives or property are covered under an insurance policy.)

When a faculty member is hired to teach, he or she signs a contract with the academic institution. Each of these two parties assumes certain duties toward the other, as specified in the contract. However, it is quite likely that the students at the institution are not mentioned in the contract. Do the students benefit from the employment contract? Of course they do. If there were no students there would be no need for any faculty. Are the students intended or incidental beneficiaries? Since they are one of the primary reasons for soliciting the faculty member's promise to teach, the students are intended beneficiaries; individual students do not need to be listed in the contract. Both the faculty member and the institution know that students are one of the primary reasons for the employment contract. Students would be viewed as intended beneficiaries of such faculty contracts in most states. The legal relationships in this example are diagrammed in Exhibit 13.1.

A Donee Beneficiary

The type of relationship between the promisee and the third party may affect the rights of an intended third-party beneficiary. If the promisee means to make a gift to the third party, the third party is a *donee beneficiary*. Life insurance policies are excellent examples of third-party beneficiary contracts. If a husband purchases a $100,000 life

Exhibit 13.1

Intended Beneficiary

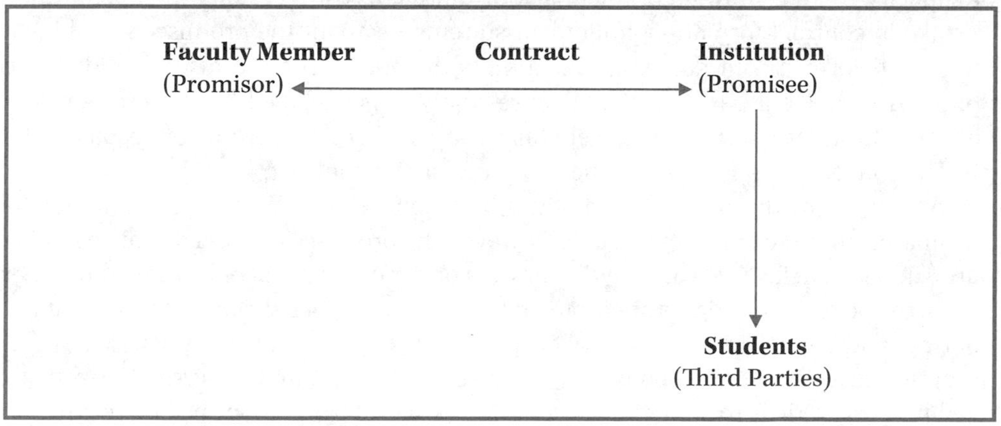

Faculty Member   Contract   Institution
(Promisor) ◄───────────────────────► (Promisee)
                                              │
                                              │
                                              ▼
                                          Students
                                          (Third Parties)

Exhibit 13.2

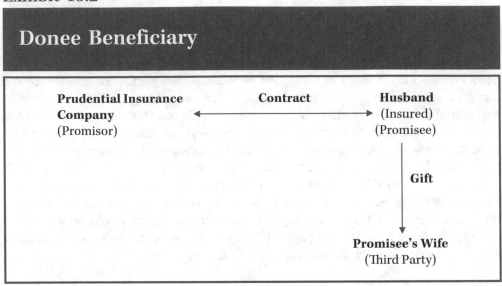

Donee Beneficiary

insurance policy from Prudential Insurance Company of America and names his wife as the beneficiary, she is a donee beneficiary. The husband has no legal obligation to purchase this insurance. (He might be under a legal obligation to purchase life insurance under some marital contracts or divorce decrees, but this is uncommon.) He is, in reality, planning a gift to his wife that will take effect at his death. She is a donee beneficiary. A donee beneficiary example is shown in Exhibit 13.2.

Prudential Insurance Company, the promisor, promises to deliver $100,000 to the promisee's wife if the promisee dies under situations covered by the policy. If Prudential refuses to pay, the wife may sue the company directly as an intended third party. Prudential (the promisor) can use the same legal defenses against the wife (the third party) as it can against the husband (the promisee). These defenses might include lack of capacity to enter into a contract, lack of mutual assent, illegality in the contract, mistake in contract formation, fraudulent statements about the promisee's health, an improperly formed contract, or cancellation of the policy. The promisor would not be obligated to make a payment if the cause of death is excluded by the terms of the contract. In addition, the courts generally will not force the promisor to pay if the promisee failed to perform his or her duty under the contract.[2]

According to the law in some states, the donee beneficiary's rights cannot be terminated after the contract is made. However, the promisee can still defeat the rights of the donee beneficiary by not performing his or her contractual obligations.[3] In other states, the beneficiary's rights are protected only when the beneficiary knows about the contract and has accepted it verbally or by reliance on its terms. If the beneficiary has accepted the contract, the beneficiary has a vested interest in it. (A *vested interest* is a fixed interest or right to something, even though actual possession may be postponed until later.) In these states, a beneficiary with a vested interest must consent before the promisor and promisee can mutually rescind the contract. This rule applies to both

Exhibit 13.3

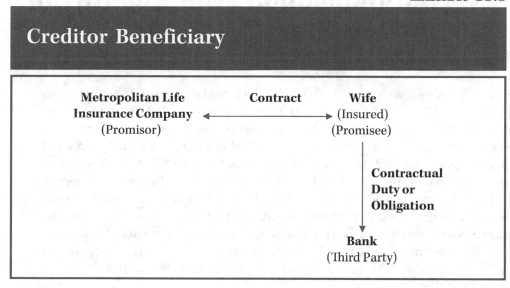

Contractual Duty or Obligation

donee and creditor beneficiaries. (A *creditor beneficiary* is a third party who is entitled to performance because the promisee owes him or her a contractual duty.) Even so, a donee beneficiary cannot prevent the promisee from taking some action that will defeat the rights of the donee beneficiary; for example, breaching the contract by refusing to pay for the goods or services.

A Creditor Beneficiary

The third party is a *creditor beneficiary* if the promisee owes a legal duty to the third party and that duty is being satisfied, in whole or in part, by the contract. In a contract between a college and a professor for teaching services, the third-party beneficiaries are students. The students are creditor beneficiaries because the college owes them a legal duty, to provide academic instruction, in exchange for the payment of tuition and fees. This is true even at state-supported colleges where tuition payments only constitute a portion of the cost of offering classes.

Another excellent example involves a life insurance policy. A working couple wishes to purchase a house with a $100,000 mortgage. The bank is willing to lend them $100,000 based on the value of the home and both of their salaries. Since the bank feels that the husband cannot afford the monthly payments without his wife's salary, the bank makes the loan contingent on the purchase of mortgage insurance on her life. (*Mortgage insurance* is insurance that will provide funds to pay the mortgage balance on a home if the insured dies.) The wife agrees to purchase a $100,000 mortgage insurance policy from Metropolitan Life Insurance Company, naming the bank as the beneficiary. The bank is a creditor beneficiary in this situation. This arrangement is diagrammed in Exhibit 13.3.

eClass 13.1 Management/Manufacturing

LIABILITY FOR DAMAGES IN SHIPPING

eClass placed an order for a specialized part for the equipment that duplicates the software on compact disks (CDs). The seller was Salma Systems, a manufacturer in Palo Alto, California. eClass was a bit concerned because this was the first time eClass had ordered from Salma Systems, and the part was very fragile. Salma Systems packed the part in a sturdy cardboard box, with foam pads to cushion it. Salma Systems then contracted with Vicente's Trucking to deliver the box to eClass. When the box was delivered two weeks later, there was substantial damage to the box and its contents. eClass believes that the part was in good condition when Salma Systems sent it, and that the damage occurred during the transportation. Assume that the contract between Salma and Vicente's Trucking said that Vicente's is liable for damage during shipment. Is Vicente's liable to eClass? Is eClass an intended third-party beneficiary of the Salma-Vicente's contract? Ani, Meg, and Yousef have asked you who is responsible to eClass. What will you tell them?

BUSINESS CONSIDERATIONS   What steps could Salma Systems have taken to further reduce the likelihood of loss? How might Vicente's Trucking and eClass have reduced the possibility of loss? How could/should eClass protect its interests in future situations like this one?

ETHICAL CONSIDERATIONS   Do Salma Systems and Vicente's Trucking owe eClass any ethical duties in addition to their legal obligations? Why or why not?

If the wife dies during the term of the mortgage, the bank is entitled to the proceeds from the insurance policy, and the bank can sue Metropolitan Life Insurance Company directly on the insurance contract if Metropolitan refuses to pay. Metropolitan can use any defenses that it had against the wife as defenses against the bank. It is important to remember that a third-party beneficiary cannot successfully claim any better rights than those provided to the promisee in the contract.

If the wife tries to cancel the policy, the bank can successfully sue the wife. Canceling the insurance policy and not replacing it is a breach of the loan contract. The bank, however, will probably allow the wife to substitute another policy from a different insurance company if the coverage is essentially the same. In practice, if the bank does not trust the wife to make the premium payments, the bank will require her to make the payments through the bank, which will then pay the premiums to the insurance company. This way the bank will be assured that the premium payments are made in a timely manner and that the insurance policy is still in effect.

The differences between donee and creditor beneficiaries are not significant. They both have basically the same rights against the promisor. A third party cannot successfully claim any better rights than those provided to the promisee in the contract. Although many states say that the rights of a creditor beneficiary are directly derived from the promisee, courts usually provide the same type of protection for the donee beneficiary as they do for the creditor beneficiary. The only real differences are their rights against the promisee, and even these differences are becoming less pronounced. The distinction between creditor and donee beneficiaries is excluded from the *Restatement (Second) of Contracts*,[4] which relies solely on the distinction between intended and incidental beneficiaries. The donee/creditor distinction is also beginning to disappear in some states, such as California.[5]

Analysis of Third-Party Beneficiary Contracts

In analyzing a situation involving a potential third party, the following questions should be addressed:

- Was the additional person involved from the beginning, or was that person added later?
- Did the promisee intend to benefit the third party, or was it an accident?
- Was the promisee making a gift to the third party, or was the promisee fulfilling a contract obligation to the third party?

DEFINING ASSIGNMENTS AND DELEGATIONS

If the third person becomes involved after the initial contract formation, that person is *not* a third-party beneficiary. Instead, the relationship may be an assignment or a delegation. To understand the distinction between assignments and delegations, remember the distinction between rights and duties. *Contractual rights* are the parts of the contract a person is entitled to *receive*. Examples include delivery of goods purchased, payment for goods sold, payment for work completed, and discounts for early payment. Payments owed to car dealers, mortgage companies, finance companies, and collection agencies are rights that are commonly assigned.

Contractual duties are the parts of the contract a person is obligated to *give*. Duties include working an eight-hour day, delivering goods that a customer orders, paying 15 percent interest on credit card charges, and providing repair services. Some duties may be performed by employees or delegated to others.

A general contractor will often use both assignments and delegations in carrying out his or her contractual obligations. The general contractor will subcontract (delegate) certain duties of a construction job, such as installing the roof. He or she may also assign certain rights, such as the right to receive payment for the work, to lenders who advanced the funds for the project. Remember that rights can be assigned, and duties can be delegated. In an assignment, the assignor transfers his or her rights to a third person, the assignee, usually through a contract. In a delegation, the delegator transfers his or her duties under a contract to a third person, the delegatee, usually through a contract. This may be confusing at times because many people, including judges and lawyers, are sometimes careless in their use of terminology, using the term "assignment" when a delegation is actually involved. Remember that duties *cannot* be assigned. A common example is a document that states "I assign all my rights and duties in the April 8 note with Gerald Weichmann." This would be an attempt to assign the rights and to delegate the duties, despite the language used in the document. The rules of law dealing with delegation will be applied to any attempts to "assign" contractual duties.

ASSIGNMENTS

An *assignment* occurs when a person transfers a contractual right to someone else. The transferor is called the *assignor*, and the recipient is called the *assignee*. The assignor "loses" the contractual right when the right is transferred to another party. The assignor's right has been extinguished, and now it belongs exclusively to the assignee. (*Extinguished* means destroyed or wiped out.) The other party to the original contract, the promisor, now has to deliver the promised goods or services to the assignee. The assignee is the only party entitled to them. For example, Mira (a tenant) rents a house from Jazmin (a landlord). Under the terms of the lease, Mira must pay $400 per month for rent. Jazmin is in default on a small business loan obtained from the bank and assigns the $400 per month rent payment to the bank. Therefore, Jazmin (the assignor) has relinquished the legal right to the money—that right now belongs exclusively to the assignee, the bank. This situation is diagrammed in Exhibit 13.4.

Formalities Required for Assignments

Generally, an assignment does not have to follow any particular format. Assignors must use words that indicate an intent to vest a present right in the contract in the assignee. This means that the assignor intends to transfer the right immediately, not at some time in the future. However, this does not mean that the word *assignment* must be used. A writing is not required unless the state Statute of Frauds applies. This includes the Statute of Frauds provisions in the UCC as adopted by the individual state. As with other contractual provisions, it is preferable to reduce the assignment to writing. The assignment must contain an adequate description of the rights being assigned.

Consideration, consisting of a bargained-for exchange and a legal detriment (or legal benefit) for both parties, is *not* required in order to have a valid assignment. (Consideration is discussed in detail in Chapter 10.) Although the assignee need not give up consideration in exchange for the contract right, consideration *is* generally present.

Exhibit 13.4

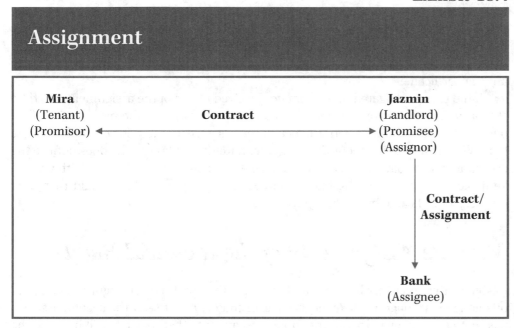

The existence of consideration affects the legal relationship between the assignor and the assignee—that relationship can be either a contract or a gift. However, the relationship is generally a contract, especially in business settings. In our earlier example, Jazmin (the landlord) assigns the payments to the bank so that the bank will not sue her or take other action to collect. People in business are not in the habit of making gifts to other businesspeople. A gift assignment occurs, for example, when Bradley, a sales representative for a pharmaceutical company, assigns the 10 percent Christmas bonus he earns to his eldest daughter, Brande, for her college education fund.

Notice of the Assignment

Because an assignment extinguishes the assignor's rights and creates rights only for the assignee, you would assume that the person obligated to perform must be informed about the assignment. Surprisingly, this is not a legal requirement. An assignment is perfectly valid even though the person obligated to perform is never told about it. An assignee may *want* to give notice to the promisor for a number of reasons, particularly if the assignor is potentially unethical or dishonest.

In many instances, the promisor is not told about the assignment, and the assignor receives the performance and then transfers it to the assignee. Suppose the promisor has not been given notice and delivers performance to the assignor and the assignor does not transfer it to the assignee, then the assignee will be limited to taking action against the assignor. This will be the result even if the assignor has absconded with the funds. Assume Keith owes Ileane $500 under their contract. Ileane assigns her payment to Wyanda. Neither one informs Keith about the assignment. Since Keith does not know about the assignment, he pays Ileane per their agreement. Ileane knows that she is not entitled to the payment, so most people in her position would transfer the funds to Wyanda. However, Ileane absconds with the funds. Since Keith was never informed of the assignment, Wyanda has no rights to assert against Keith. Wyanda's only rights are against Ileane.

If the person obligated to perform *has* received notice of the assignment and then still pays the assignor or delivers performance to the assignor, the person will still be obligated to pay or deliver performance to the assignee. In the prior example, assume that Wyanda tells Keith about the assignment. Keith decides that he does not like the assignment so he pays Ileane anyway. If Ileane absconds with the funds, Keith will still be liable to Wyanda, and he may be forced to pay Wyanda. Keith could then seek recovery from Ileane for the first payment.

Multiple Assignments of the Identical Right

In some cases, assignors have profited by selling the *same* contract right to more than one assignee through mistake, negligence, or fraud. Of course, if the second assignee has notice or knowledge of the prior assignment, that person will receive the assignment *subject* to the rights of the first assignee. In many cases, however, the second assignee lacks this notice. If the first assignment is revocable, the fact that a second assignment has occurred presents a relatively simple problem. Since the first assignment was revocable, the second assignment revokes the first assignment.

However, a second assignment presents a much more difficult problem in a few situations. If the second assignee (1) does not know about the first assignment, (2) did not take the assignment subject to the first assignment, and (3) the first assignment was not revocable, then a situation may exist in which two (or more) assignees each believe that he or she has the only assignment, and he or she expects to receive the complete performance from the promisor. In these situations, a dishonest assignor has deceived one or more assignees, usually for the assignor's monetary benefit.

Of course, dishonest assignors generally disappear with the funds and leave the innocent assignees to resolve their conflicting claims. What are these innocent assignees to do under these circumstances? Two broad theories are widely used by U.S. courts to resolve these problems.

The American Rule   The first of these theories is based on the belief that the first assignee to receive the assignment receives all the rights; after the first assignment has been made, the assignor has nothing left to assign to later assignees. This theory is usually called the *American Rule* or the *first-in-time approach*. The *New York Rule* is a variation of the first-in-time approach and is applied in some states.

For example, if Anita, the promisee, assigns her rights to Joel for value on January 1 and then assigns these same rights to Larry for value on January 15, Joel will receive the rights according to the American rule. The same results are likely to occur under the New York Rule variation. There are two primary exceptions where the first assignee will not "win" under the New York Rule: (1) if the first assignment is revocable, like an

Exhibit 13.5

Multiple Assignments of the Same Rights: The First-in-Time Approach (American Rule)

The first assignee takes the rights unless Assignment 1 is revocable.

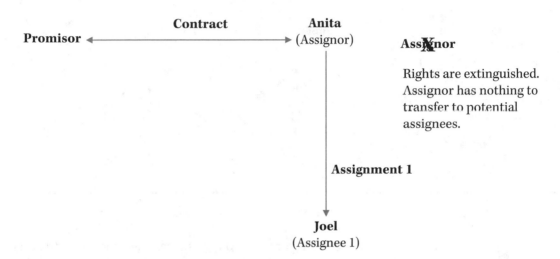

New York Rule

Additional exception: Assignee 1 fails to obtain documents evidencing Assignment 1.

Massachusetts Rule

Assignee 2 will have priority if Assignee 2 obtains the Assignment in good faith, for value, and does one of the following: obtains payment from Promisor, recovers a judgment against Promisor, obtains Promisor's promise to pay, OR receives tangible evidence of the claim.

undelivered gift; or (2) if the first assignee fails to obtain documents evidencing the assignment, thus enabling the assignor to "transfer" the rights to a second assignee.

Closely related to the New York Rule is the *Massachusetts Rule*, which is another slightly different first-in-time approach. Under this rule, the first assignee also has priority if the first assignment is not revocable. However, the second assignee will have the priority if the second assignee acquires the assignment in *good faith*, *for value*, and does any *one* of the following:

1. obtains payment from the promisor,
2. recovers a judgment against the promisor,

Exhibit 13.6

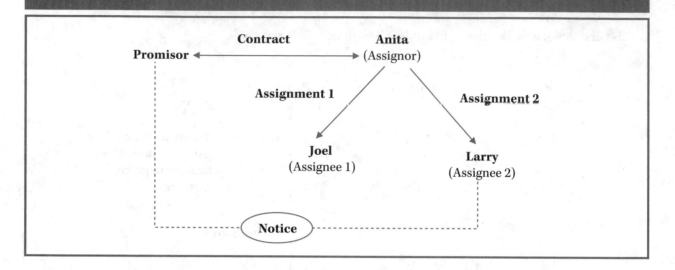

**Multiple Assignments of the Same Rights:
The First-to-Give Notice Approach (English Rule)**

3. obtains the promisor's promise to pay the assignee instead of the assignor, or
4. receives delivery of tangible evidence representing the claim.

See Exhibit 13.5 on the preceding page, which describes the first-in-time approach. The American rule and its variations are logical, but some states have not adopted the American rule or one of its variations. They use a different rule, which is discussed in the next section.

The English Rule   While many states do follow the American rule, some other states apply the rule that the first assignee to actually give *notice* to the promisor receives the right. This is called the *first-to-give-notice approach*, or the *English Rule*, which is followed in California, Florida, and a few other states. In the prior example, if Larry gives notice of the assignment to the promisor first, he will prevail under the English Rule, provided he takes for value without notice of the prior assignment to Joel. One of the policies underlying this rule is that a prudent assignee, who is about to pay value for the assignment, will check with the person obligated to perform. The promisor, who has notice of earlier assignments, will tell the prospective purchaser, and this information will prevent additional assignments. The advantage of giving notice should be obvious, especially under the English Rule. Exhibit 13.6 illustrates the first-to-give notice approach.

Assignor's Liability   Under each of these rules of law, the assignor who makes multiple assignments is likely to be held liable for fraud, and each of the injured parties can collect his or her damages from the assignor, *if* the assignor can be located, and *if* the assignor still has any assets. (Similar policy problems arise when multiple security interests are created in the same property or there are multiple transfers of the same property.) There is nothing inappropriate if a promisee (assignor) divides up the contract rights and assigns *different* contract rights to different assignees. For example, a landlord may assign the January and February rent payments to one assignee and the March and April rent payments to another.

Assignable Rights

Assignments have become an important aspect of our business and financial structure. They are important techniques for selling goods and improving cash flow. A common business practice among retail outlets is to sell expensive items on time. The retailer assigns the monthly payments to a credit corporation in exchange for cash and then uses the cash to buy more merchandise. A simple example of this practice occurs when a buyer purchases an automobile financed through a car dealership. Because of the importance of assignments in commercial transactions, courts are generally predisposed to allow assignments. This favorable perspective is obvious in the courts' treatment of contract assignments.

Assignments do not require the approval of the promisor. Even when the promisor objects to the assignment in court, the court will still generally allow it. To prevent an attempted assignment, the promisor must prove to the court that at least one of the following conditions will exist if the assignment is allowed:

- The assignment will materially change the duty of the promisor.
- The assignment will materially impair the chance of return performance or reduce its value.
- The assignment will materially increase the burden or risk imposed by the contract.

Basically, the promisor must convince the court that he or she will be in a substantially worse position if the assignment is allowed. These requirements are discussed in the *Restatement (Second) of Contracts* in § 317(2) and are also included in § 2-210(2) of the UCC. These provisions are applicable unless the language of the contract provides otherwise or the assignment is forbidden by statute or is against public policy.

When the promisor is asserting that the assignment materially changes the promisor's duty, the promisor is claiming that he or she will be required to perform a substantially different type or degree of work if the assignment is allowed. Many assignments involve assigning monthly payments. Because this simply requires that the promisor change the address on the payment envelopes, the promisor's duty is not substantially different following the assignment. As an example of a substantially different duty, suppose that Thad (a promisor) agrees to paint the exterior of any one house for $1,200, and he makes this promise to Lynda, who owns a 1,000-square-foot single-level house. Lynda enters into the contract with Thad and then

eClass 13.2 Finance

ACCEPTING ACCOUNTS RECEIVABLE AS PAYMENT OF DEBT

All Electronics, Inc. (AEI) is one of eClass's major retail distributors in Chicago. AEI has been suffering financial difficulties for over a year and currently owes eClass $65,000 for eClass software that it has already received. This $65,000 is 90 days past due, which causes Meg some anxiety. AEI has $40,000 in accounts receivable, most of which are current (not past due). AEI has suggested that it transfer its own accounts receivable to eClass. AEI would prefer to do this to discharge its entire obligation, but if this proposal is not acceptable to eClass, then AEI would, at least, like to transfer the accounts as partial payment of its obligation. Ani, Meg, and Yousef have never before accepted another firm's accounts receivable as payment, and they are unsure of the legal implications of doing so. They ask you for advice. What will you advise them?

BUSINESS CONSIDERATIONS   In order to decide if this is a sound business decision, what information should eClass obtain? What are the legal and business consequences of such an arrangement? What would be eClass's position if it accepted the transfer?

ETHICAL CONSIDERATION   Evaluate AEI's ethical perspective as it relates to AEI's proposal.

assigns the right to Joanne, who owns a 2,500-square-foot two-story house. Thad might convince the court that this assignment materially affects his duty. However, it is unwise for a promisor to enter into a contract that is ambiguous. Generally, a house painter like Thad will provide a bid to paint a specific house and will specify the address to avoid this type of problem.

If the assignment impairs the risk of return performance, it increases the chance that the promisor will not receive consideration from the promisee. For example, Chris wants to have her portrait painted; she locates a talented but struggling artist, Arturo, to paint the portrait for $200. Arturo explains that he needs the money to buy canvas and quality oil paint. Chris agrees to pay him the money on the first of the month, and Arturo is to start the portrait on the fifteenth. Later, however, Arturo wants to assign that payment to his landlord for unpaid rent. Consequently, Chris may convince the court that allowing this assignment will impair her chance of receiving the portrait since Arturo will still need supplies.

An assignment will not be allowed if it increases the risk or burden of the contract. If Arturo, the artist, tries to assign only $150 of the payment to his landlord, Chris might be able to convince the court that this assignment increases the burden or risk imposed by their contract, because Arturo might purchase inferior materials.

Not all types of assignments are favored. Some types of assignments are considered less desirable and are limited by state law. Common examples are prohibitions or limitations on the assignment of wages. Statutes in Alabama, California, Connecticut, the District of Columbia, Missouri, and Ohio generally prohibit the assignment of future wages. In addition, California, Connecticut, and many other states have special rules that apply to assignments of wages as security for small loans.[6] The legislature and the courts are also scrutinizing assignments of post-loss insurance payments. (*Post-loss* means after loss. These are obligations of insurance companies after a covered loss has actually occurred.)

Contract Clauses Restricting Assignments

Another example of court decisions that favor assignments is court interpretation of the language in the original promisor/promisee contract. Even if the contract states that "no assignment shall be made" or that "there shall be no assignment without the prior consent of the promisor," many courts will still allow the assignment. Courts *may* interpret these clauses as promises or covenants not to assign the rights. The assignor is then held legally responsible for making the assignment and must pay the promisor for any loss caused by the assignment. Often, the promisor cannot prove any loss in court, so this is a rather hollow right. These clauses can also be interpreted by courts as preventing the transfer of the contract *duties*. This latter approach is followed by § 2-210(3) of the UCC. If the contracting parties really want to prevent assignments, they must use clauses such as "all assignments shall be void" or "any attempt at assignment shall be null and void." Most courts will interpret this language as actually removing the power to make assignments.

Warranties Implied by the Assignor

An assignor who makes an assignment for value implies that certain things are true about the assigned rights. These implied warranties exist without any action by the assignor. The assignor's knowledge of the warranties is not required. The warranties include: (1) the right is a valid legal right and actually exists; (2) there are no valid defenses or limitations to the assigned right that are not specifically stated or apparent; and (3) the assignor will not do anything to defeat or impair the value of the assignment. These warranties need not be expressly stated but, instead, can be implied. If the assignor breaches the warranties, the assignee can sue successfully. The assignor and assignee may expressly agree to limit or exclude warranties.

Rights Created by the Assignment

An assignee obtains the same legal rights in the contract that the assignor had. If the assignee sues the promisor, the promisor generally may use the same defenses against the assignee as were available against the assignor. Examples of these defenses would include fraud, duress, undue influence, and breach of contract by the assignor. The promisor will not, however, be able to use every conceivable defense against an assignee.

Waiver of Defenses Clause

A waiver of defenses clause in a contract attempts to give the assignee better legal rights than the assignor had. Often, such a clause is part of a standard printed contract prepared by the assignee or assignor and signed by the promisor. Generally, the promisor (buyer) is not aware that the contract contains a waiver of defenses clause or does not understand what it means. In the clause, the promisor promises to give up legal defenses in any later lawsuit by the assignee. In other words, the promisor agrees not to exert defenses such as fraud in the inducement or breach of warranty against any subsequent assignees. Exhibit 13.7 shows the effect of a valid waiver of defenses clause on the promisor/assignee relationship.

If the waiver of defenses clause is effective, it reduces the promisor's bargaining power. For example, if a purchaser buys a product on time and the product is defective, a common reaction is to stop making payments. A waiver of defenses clause means that the buyer must continue to make the payments. Consequently, consumer groups and government agencies have often opposed waiver of defenses clauses because they reduce a consumer's bargaining power. Some states, including Alaska, Missouri, Ohio, Washington, and the District of Columbia, have statutes that forbid or limit the use of these clauses.[7] The Federal Trade Commission enacted a regulation barring these agreements in some consumer contracts.[8] Under UCC § 9-206(1) these clauses are generally enforceable against buyers or lessees of consumer goods unless the particular state has a different rule under its statutes or court decisions.

DELEGATIONS

Assignments and delegations may occur simultaneously. However, it is easier to understand delegations if they are analyzed as independent transfers. In fact, they are completely separate concepts that can and do occur independently. In a *delegation*, the promisor locates a new promisor to perform the duties under the contract. The original promisor is called the delegator, and the new promisor is called the delegatee. For example, suppose Cruz buys a new automobile from a Hyundai dealer. One of the terms of that contract is a promise by the dealer to provide certain warranty work on the car for three years. Later, Carmen, the mechanic employed by the Hyundai dealer, quits, and the dealer contracts with a local garage to do the warranty work. This particular delegation is illustrated in Exhibit 13.8. As with

Exhibit 13.7

Comparison of the Contract Rights of the Assignor and the Assignee

This exhibit assumes that the promisor has valid defenses that can be proven in court.

CONTRACT WITHOUT A WAIVER OF DEFENSES CLAUSE	CONTRACT WITH A VALID WAIVER OF DEFENSES CLAUSE
A. Lawsuit by Assignor	A. Lawsuit by Assignor
Defenses **Assignor** ——— **X** ———→ **Promisor**	Defenses **Assignor** ——— **X** ———→ **Promisor**
B. Lawsuit by Assignee	B. Lawsuit by Assignee
Defenses **Assignee** ——— **X** ———→ **Promisor**	Def**X**ses **Assignee** ——————————→ **Promisor**

Legend

Plaintiff ————————→ **Defendant**

———————— **X** ————→   The lawsuit will not be successful.

Def**X**ses   The defenses will not be successful.

assignments, there may be consideration for the delegation, but it is not necessary. If no consideration exists, the delegation is really a "gift" from the new promisor to the old promisor.

The purchaser of the car (Cruz) can sue the car dealer who made the promise to him if the warranty work is not performed. The purchaser can also generally sue the garage for failure to perform. In many states, the purchaser can sue both the dealer (delegator) and the garage (delegatee) at the same time, but the courts will only allow the purchaser to collect once.

The relationship between the delegator and the delegatee may be that of a contract or of a gift. If a contract relationship is present, the delegator has the right to sue the

Exhibit 13.8

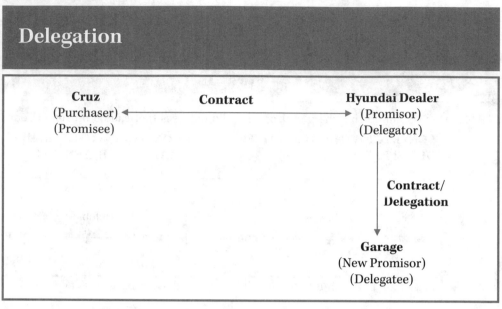

delegatee for nonperformance. If a gift relationship is present, the court would hold that the delegatee promised to make a gift in the future but failed to deliver it. Generally, promises to make gifts in the future are not enforceable without promissory estoppel. (*Promissory estoppel* is the doctrine used to enforce a gift promise based on the justifiable reliance of the promisee.)

Delegations do not occur unless the delegatee assumes the contract duties. This assumption can be either expressly stated or implied. The modern trend in court decisions is to imply the assumption of the duties, especially when there is an assignment *and* a delegation. Implied assumption of duties is also supported by the *Restatement (Second) of Contracts* and the UCC. An example of this occurs when the parties state that there is an "assignment of the contract" or an "assignment of all my rights under the contract." Unless there is a clear indication of a contrary intention such statements are generally interpreted as indicating (1) an assignment, (2) a delegation of the duties by the delegator, and (3) an acceptance of the duties by the delegatee. This position is followed by the UCC § 2-210(4) and the *Restatement (Second) of Contracts* § 328.

Delegations do not have the favored legal status that assignments do. Courts are more inclined to deny a delegation. If the contract between the promisor and the promisee states that "there shall be no delegations," the courts will prevent delegations. The same is true if the contract requires personal performance. Courts are also more likely to decide that a delegation is unfair to the promisee. Under UCC § 2-210(1), duties cannot be delegated if the agreement states that there will be no delegation or the promisor has a substantial interest in having the delegator perform the contract. The *Restatement (Second) of Contracts* § 318(2) states that delegations should not be

eClass 13.3 Marketing/Finance

ESTABLISHING A CUSTOMER SERVICE CENTER

eAccounting, one of eClass's products, is sold to consumers with 90 days of customer service. Consumers can extend the length of time for an additional fee. Currently, consumers must call eClass for customer service. Ani is considering establishing a call center for customer service. Ani feels this arrangement will improve the marketability of eAccounting and their other products. It will also improve the work flow at eClass. However, Ani, Meg, and Yousef are concerned about their relationship to the call center and their customers. They ask you about the legal and business effects of this decision. What do you tell them and why?

BUSINESS CONSIDERATIONS   What are the business advantages of such an arrangement? What are the disadvantages? What types of legal arrangements could eClass have with a call center? What will be eClass's obligations under these arrangements? If you were assisting eClass in drafting these contracts, what provisions would you include and why?

ETHICAL CONSIDERATIONS   Is it ethical to require a call center to also sell eClass products in addition to providing customer service? Why or why not?

allowed if the promisee has a substantial interest in having the delegator control or perform the acts promised. Consequently, personal service contracts generally cannot be delegated. UCC § 2-210(3) indicates that a contract clause that prohibits the assignment of "the contract" is to be construed as preventing *only* a delegation of the contract duties to the assignee.

Analysis of Assignments and Delegations

To characterize an assignment or a delegation situation, you should answer the following questions:

- Was the additional person involved from the beginning or added later?
- Did the additional person undertake to perform a contract duty or become entitled to a contract right? Or both?
- Did the language of the original contract prevent this transfer to an additional person?
- Did the type of rights or duties prevent this transfer to an additional person, because the transfer materially changes the rights or duties of a party?
- Is this transfer forbidden by state statute or public policy?

UNIFORM COMMERCIAL CODE PROVISIONS

When the UCC is applicable, businesspeople need to review the UCC assignment and delegation provisions. Certain types of assignments are excluded from the coverage of Article 9 by UCC §9-104—for example, claims for wages, interests under an insurance policy, claims arising from the commission of a tort, and deposits in banks. Under §9-201 and §9-203 of the UCC, provisions of Article 9 may be subordinated to state statutes regulating installment sales to consumers. Section 2-210 of the Code covers assignments and delegations under contracts for the sale of goods. However, some questions concerning assignments are not resolved in either Article 2 or Article 9 of the UCC. (This is only a brief overview of the code's provisions.)

Contemporary Case

PDG LOS ARCOS, LLC v. ADAMS (In re MORTG. LTD.)

2010 U.S. Dist. LEXIS 30926 (D. Ariz., 2010)

FACTS Mortgages Ltd. was in the business of lending money to commercial real estate developers. Mortgages Ltd. entered a $26 million construction loan agreement with PDG and a $10 million construction loan agreement with NRDP. The loans were documented with loan agreements, promissory notes, deeds of trust, guarantees, and other documents. Mortgages Ltd. sold "participations" in the loans to "Investors." The Investors received undivided fractional interests in the promissory notes and deeds of trust. The investors also received Assignments, which stated that "Assignor [Mortgages Ltd.] hereby assigns to Assignee the above-referenced interest in the following documents." NRDP and PDG's loans were not fully funded by the time of Mortgages Ltd.'s bankruptcy. NRDP and PDG asked the Investors for additional funding, which the Investors refused to provide. NRDP and PDG each filed suit against the Investors.

ISSUE Under Arizona law, does an assignment of a contract imply an assumption of duties?

HOLDING No, it does not, at least in the circumstance where the assignment is for financing.

REASONING Excerpts from the opinion of Judge Mary H. Murguia:

... In *Grant*, the Arizona Supreme Court considered whether the assignment of a contract carried with it an implied delegation of the duties owed by the assignor to the other original contracting party, the obligee. ... Finding that the defendant-assignee did not become indebted to the obligee, the court cited the "well-established rule" that assignment of a contract does not relieve the assignor of his duties to the obligee, nor "does it have the effect of creating a new liability on the part of the assignee to the other party to the contract . . . , because the assignment does not bring them together, and consequently there cannot be the meeting of the minds essential to the formation of a contract." . . . In *Norton*, the Arizona Supreme Court cited *Grant*'s "general principal[] that an assignment of a contract does not operate to cast on the assignee liabilities imposed by the contract on the assignor." . . . The *Norton* court noted that "a review of cases from other jurisdiction[s] discloses that many courts agree with this basic rule." . . . While suggesting . . . that because Arizona recognizes implied contracts, "it would be logical for us to recognize an implied assumption of duties by an assignee," the court concluded that the circumstances of the [*Norton*] case . . . did not require it to reach that question. . . . In the present case . . . , there was no express assumption of duties, therefore the Investors cannot be held liable for Mortgages Ltd.'s funding obligations . . . While the *Grant* court considered whether the assignment of a contract carried with it an implied delegation of the duties, it held to the contrary. . . .

The Bankruptcy Court found . . . that Appellants are not third-party beneficiaries of the assignments and therefore cannot enforce any obligations the Investors may have had to provide funds to Mortgages Ltd. Citing the "Arizona rule" that "for a person to recover as a third-party beneficiary of a contract, an intention to benefit that person must be indicated in the contract itself," the Bankruptcy Court concluded that nothing in the assignments between Mortgages Ltd. and its Investors indicated an intent to directly benefit the Appellants. . . .

[T]he Bankruptcy Court found that even if it were to conclude that Arizona would follow the *Restatement of Contracts* § 328, there were no facts alleged in the Complaints from which a delegation of duties could be implied. This Court agrees.

Under the presumptive approach, duties are not implicitly delegated to an assignee where "the circumstances indicate the contrary, as in an assignment for security. . . ." . . . The Bankruptcy Court noted that the purpose of the assignments to the Investors was to raise funds with which to fund the loans. While the Bankruptcy Court acknowledged that these assignments may not technically constitute securities because the Investors were intended to become the owners of the fractional interests in the notes . . . , it nevertheless held that the *Restatement*'s term "assignment for security" must be read broadly to include situations . . . where the assignment is "intended to make the assignee's investment a secure one." The Bankruptcy Court also found that the transaction documents demonstrated that "this was a financing transaction akin to the resale of collateralized debt obligations in the securities markets." Indeed, a review of these documents shows that the Investors had no control over the loans; at most, the Investors could have their interests diluted or liquidated. . . . [I]t was "not . . . a purchase of the business of Mortgages Ltd. where the buyer intended to take over the lending business and with it the obligation to fund the outstanding loan agreements." . . . [E]ven if the presumptive approach were adopted in Arizona, the assignments would not imply a delegation of duties. Important policy considerations support the Bankruptcy Court's conclusion. To extend the law by presuming a delegation of duties in the financing transaction at issue would negatively impact broader financial markets by making every investor potentially liable to the obligee. . . . "[B]y making the [assignee] a surety, not only will accounts receivable financing be discouraged, but transaction costs will undoubtedly increase for everyone . . . without any discernable benefit." . . .

[The Court agreed with the Bankruptcy Court's dismissal of NRDP and PDG's Complaints.]

You Be the Judge

PepsiCo, through its operating division of Pepsi-Cola Company, manufactured and sold soft drink concentrates for Pepsi-Cola soft drink products. PepsiCo entered exclusive bottling appointments (contracts) with individual bottlers throughout the United States. A bottling appointment authorized a bottler to manufacture and distribute Pepsi-Cola soft drink products within a defined, exclusive geographic territory. Bottlers could not directly or indirectly sell Pepsi-Cola soft drink products in another bottler's territory. Bottlers had a number of other duties including to vigorously promote and distribute the product line. Transshipment of any Pepsi-Cola soft drink product into the exclusive territory of another bottler undermined that bottler's rights under the bottling contract. Transshipments posed a threat to the distribution system. PepsiCo enacted a Transshipment Enforcement Program to investigate and fine bottlers who engaged in transshipment. When a bottler was fined, PepsiCo collected the fine and then paid the money to the offended bottler whose territory was violated. PepsiCo sent periodic memos to bottlers, reassuring them that it would enforce the exclusive territory agreements. Pittsburg Pepsi aggressively marketed Pepsi-Cola soft drink products in its territory, which included parts of Kansas and Missouri surrounding Pittsburg, Kansas. Bottling Group had the territory that surrounds the territory of Pittsburg Pepsi. Pittsburg Pepsi complained to PepsiCo that Bottling Group frequently transshipped into its territory. PepsiCo has largely ignored these complaints, so Pittsburg Pepsi sued Bottling Group. Could Pittsburg Pepsi be an intended third-party beneficiary of Bottling Group's contract with PepsiCo? If *you* were the judge, how would *you* decide this dispute? [See *Pepsi-Cola Bottling Co. of Pittsburg, Inc. v. PepsiCo, Inc.*, 175 F. Supp. 2d 1288, 2001 U.S. Dist. LEXIS 21429 (D. Kan. 2001).]

Summary

An additional person who is involved in a contract from the beginning may be a third-party beneficiary. An additional person who will receive benefits under a contract as an unintended consequence of the contract is an incidental beneficiary. Such a beneficiary has no rights under the contract and may not successfully sue either party to the contract if these unintended benefits never occur. If the promisor or promisee meant to affect the third person under the contract, that person will be an intended beneficiary and will have enforceable rights under the contract. Intended beneficiaries can file lawsuits to protect their own legal rights. If they sue the promisor, the promisor can use the same defenses that would be valid against the promisee. Creditor beneficiaries can sue a promisee who tries to cancel the contract. Donee beneficiaries generally will not be successful in a suit against the promisee because the donee beneficiary did not receive the promised gift.

An additional party who becomes involved after the contract is formed may be an assignee or a delegatee. An assignee receives a contract right from the transferor. An assignment extinguishes the contract right of the assignor and sets up this contract right exclusively in the assignee. The assignee is now entitled to performance under the contract. The assignee does not have to notify the promisor of the assignment. The assignee is better protected if he or she *does* give notice. This is especially important if the assignor makes multiple assignments of the same contract right.

In a delegation, a delegatee assumes the transferor's obligation to perform under the contract. The delegator will still be obligated to perform if the delegatee does not. Generally, courts will respect contract clauses that state that there shall be no delegations.

Discussion Questions

1. Legal Hit, Inc. makes contracts to deliver "benefits" to designated third-party beneficiaries. In the contract, Legal Hit agrees to have one of its employees throw a cream pie in the face of any target designated by the promisee. If you hired Legal Hit to deliver a cream pie "greeting" to your boss, what are the legal rights of Legal Hit, you, and your boss?

2. Should waiver of defenses clauses be enforced? What are the advantages and disadvantages of these clauses?

3. Andrew owes Clairise $100. Clairise assigns $25 of this amount to Diane. With knowledge of the assignment, Andrew pays the entire $100 to Clairise. Has Andrew discharged his duty to pay?[9]

4. What are the differences between assignees, delegatees, and third-party beneficiaries? In what ways are they similar?

5. What happens if the assignor assigns the identical contract right to three assignees? Who should recover from whom? Why?

Case Problems and Writing Assignments

1. On February 8, 1996, Church & Tower entered into a $25.4 million contract with Broward County to design and construct a 1,024-bed inmate facility, known as the North Broward Detention Center. The contract provided that the project was to be substantially completed within 548 days of the "project initiation" date. The anticipated completion date was October 4, 1997. A final certificate of occupancy was not issued until October 28, 1998. Sheriff Ken Jenne of Broward County filed a suit against the construction company, alleging that the delay caused him to incur over $13 million in labor and expenses because he had to transport inmates to other counties. Jenne was under a federal court decree to develop a plan for managing the jail population. Is Jenne an intended third-party beneficiary of the construction contract between the county and the construction company so that he can bring a lawsuit? [See *Jenne v. Church & Tower, Inc.*, 814 So. 2d 522, 2002 Fla. App. LEXIS 5226 (Fla. App. 4th Dist. 2002).]

2. Kurt L. VanVoorhies was a Senior Design Engineer for General Motors Corporation before he enrolled in graduate school at the University of West Virginia (WVU) to pursue a Ph.D. in engineering. He selected WVU specifically to work with one particular professor, Dr. James E. Smith. Smith and VanVoorhies investigated antennae for wireless power transmission. VanVoorhies's laboratory notebook indicated that he completed the first invention by June 3, 1991. In November 1991, VanVoorhies submitted an invention disclosure form to WVU describing that invention and listing Smith as a co-inventor. The WVU policy on inventions applies to "University personnel," who it defines as "all full-time and part-time members of the faculty and staff, and all other employees of the University including graduate and undergraduate students and fellows of the University." Under the

policy, "the University owns worldwide right, title and interest in any invention made at least in part by University personnel, or with substantial use of University resources, and unless otherwise agreed, this Policy applies to any invention conceived or first reduced to practice under terms of contracts, grants or other agreements." The inventor is required to cooperate with WVU in obtaining patents on the inventions. Inventors are compensated with 30 percent of the net royalty income received after subtracting the expenses incurred from the procuring and licensing of the patent. The assignment of the first invention to WVU states in part:

> The undersigned does (do) hereby sell, assign, transfer and set over unto said assignee, its successors and assigns, the entire right, title and interest in and to said invention or inventions, as described in the aforesaid application, in any form or embodiment thereof, and in and to the aforesaid application; ... also the entire right, title and interest in and to any and all patents or reissues or extensions thereof to be obtained in this or any foreign country upon said invention or inventions and any divisional, continuation, continuation-in-part or substitute applications which may be filed upon said invention or inventions in this or any foreign country; and the undersigned hereby authorize(s) and request(s) the issuing authority to issue any and all patents on said application or applications to said assignee or its successors and assigns.

VanVoorhies finished his dissertation and received his doctoral degree on December 29, 1993. On February 1, 1994, he began to work at WVU as a Post-Graduate Research Assistant Professor. VanVoorhies claims that he invented the second invention in the short interval between receiving his graduate degree and becoming an assistant professor. The second invention is based, at least in part, upon the technology in the first invention. Does VanVoorhies have an obligation to assign the second invention to WVU? Why or why not? [See *University of West Virginia Bd. of Trustees v. Van-Voorhies*, 278 F.3d 1288, 2002 U.S. App. LEXIS 1327 (Fed. Cir. 2002).]

3. Ray Larson and his sons, Michael and Robert Larson, contacted Glopak, Inc. They wanted to sell Glopak the intellectual property rights to an invention. The invention, a "bag and straw," allows single-serving beverages in a small pouch that can be drank using the enclosed straw. Glopak purchased the rights to the "bag and straw" and agreed to make royalty payments to the Larsons. The Larsons wanted to have their payments accelerated. Glopak did not consent. Glopak did allow the Larsons to sell their royalty payments to a third party. Dakota Partners purchased the right to receive the royalty payments in exchange for cash advances to the Larsons. Dakota Partners entered into two addendums with Glopak and the Larsons. Both agreements contained similar language. Addendum #2 provided, in part:

Glopak was requested by Larson on December 4, 1997, and Glopak has agreed, that payments which become due to Larson under Clauses 7c up to a maximum of Forty Thousand U.S. Dollars ($40,000.00 US) shall be paid to Dakota Partners . . .

Glopak agrees that it shall not offset any amount due under Clauses 7c and that said amount is absolutely due and owing.

Later, Glopak discovered that the Larsons were not the rightful owners of the rights to the "bag and straw." Glopak rescinded its agreements with the Larsons and refused to make payments to Dakota Partners. Dakota Partners filed suit against Glopak and the Larsons for breach of contract. The Larsons did not participate in the court suit. The trial court found that the Larsons made fraudulent representations to Glopak and that the contracts between Glopak and the Larsons were properly rescinded. Does the language quoted above contain a waiver of defenses clause? What affect does fraud have on the two addendums between Glopak, Larsons, and Dakota Partners? [See *Dakota Partners, L.L.P. v. Glopak, Inc.*, 2001 N.D. 168, 634 N.W.2d 520 (N.D. 2001).]

Notes

1. Facts were obtained from the court case, the reporter's notes, and Anthony Jon Waters, "The Property in The Promise: A Study of The Third Party Beneficiary Rule," 98 HARV. L. REV. 1109 (April, 1985).
2. Walter H. E. Jaeger, ed., *Williston on Contracts*, 3rd ed. (Mount Kisco, NY: Baker Voorhis, 1957), § 395, p. 1066.
3. Ibid., § 396, pp. 1067–70.
4. *Restatement (Second) of Contracts* § 302 and Introductory Note to Chapter 14, pp. 438-39.
5. *Allan v. Bekins Archival Service, Inc.*, 154 Cal. Rptr. 458 (Cal. App. Dist. 2 Div. 5 1979), n.8, p. 463.
6. *Restatement (Second) of Contracts*, Statutory Note to Chapter 15, pp. 7–9.
7. Ibid., p. 10.
8. 16 C.F.R. § 433.1-.3 (1975, as amended in 1977).
9. *Restatement (Second) of Contracts* § 326, Comment b, Ill. 1.

14

Discharge, Breach, and Remedies

Agenda

Ani, Meg, and Yousef realize that eClass may, from time to time, have customers who do not pay their bills as the bills become due. The firm members want to know what rights they will have in such situations. They also will be ordering equipment and components that must meet fairly exact standards. They wonder how they can word their contracts so that they will receive equipment and components of the desired specifications and what they can do if the suppliers do not meet these specifications. They are concerned—both as buyers and as sellers—with the time element in their contracts. How important is the time for performance? All three are unsure about the types of remedies they can seek if the other parties do not perform under the contracts.

These and other questions are likely to arise during this chapter. Be prepared! You never know when the firm or one of its members will seek your advice.

Classic Case

HADLEY v. BAXENDALE
9 Exch 341, 156 ER 145 (1854)

FACTS[1] The Hadleys carried on an extensive business as millers. Their mill was stopped by a breakage of the crank shaft. The broken shaft was sent to the engineers who made the machine to use as a pattern for making a new one. The Hadleys claim that their servant was informed that if the shaft was sent by 12 o'clock any day, it would be delivered to the engineers on the following day. After obtaining the information the shaft was taken to the defendants, before noon, to be shipped to the engineers. The shaft was not delivered for one week, because it was sent by canal rather than by rail. Consequently, the Hadleys' receipt of the new shaft was delayed for several days.

[There is some conflicting information, but this court concluded that at the time of the shipment, the Hadleys did not tell the defendants that this was their only mill shaft and that it was being sent to another company to make a replacement. The Hadleys also did not tell the defendants that the mill could not be operated until the Hadleys received a replacement.]

ISSUE Are the Hadleys entitled to lost profits due to the non-operation of their mill?

HOLDING No, the Hadleys are not entitled to lost profits when the defendant was not aware that the mill was not operational.

REASONING Excerpts from the opinion of Alderson B:

... Where two parties have made a contract which one of them has broken the damages which the other party ought to receive in respect of such breach of contract should be such as may fairly and reasonably be considered as either arising naturally, ie, [sic] according to the usual course of things, from such breach of contract itself, or such as may reasonably be supposed to have been in the contemplation of both parties at the time they made the contract as the probable result of the breach of it. If special circumstances under which the contract was actually made were communicated by the plaintiffs to the defendants, and thus known to both parties, the damages resulting from the breach of such a contract which they would reasonably contemplate would be the amount of injury which would ordinarily follow from a breach of contract under the special circumstances so known and communicated. But, on the other hand, if these special circumstances were wholly unknown to the party breaking the contract, he, at the most, could only be supposed to have had in his contemplation the amount of injury which would arise generally ... from such a breach of contract. For, had the special circumstances been known, the parties might have specially provided for the breach of contract by special terms as to the damages in that case; and of this advantage it would be very unjust to deprive them.

The above principles are those by which we think the jury ought to he [sic] guided in estimating the damages arising out of any breach of contract. It is said that other cases, such as breaches of contract in the non-payment of money, or in the not making a good title to land, are to he [sic] treated as exceptions from this ... But as, in such cases, both parties must be supposed to be cognisant [sic] of that well-known rule, these cases may ... be more properly classed under the rule above enunciated as to cases under known special circumstances, because there both parties may reasonably be presumed to con. template [sic] the estimation of the amount of damages ... In the present case, if we are to apply the principles above laid down, we find that the only circumstances here communicated by the plaintiffs to the defendants at the time the contract was made were that the article to be carried was the broken shaft of a mill and that the plaintiffs were the millers of that mill. But how do these circumstances show ... that the profits of the mill must be stopped by an unreasonable delay in the delivery of the broken shaft by the carrier to the third person? Suppose the plaintiffs had another shaft in their possession put up or putting up at the time, and that they only wished to send back the broken shaft to the engineer who made it; it is clear that this would be quite consistent with the above circumstances, and yet the unreasonable delay in the delivery would have no effect upon the intermediate profits of the mill. Or, again, suppose that, at the time of the delivery to the carrier, the machinery of the mill had been in other respects defective, then, also, the same results would follow. Here it is true that the shaft was actually sent back to serve as a model for a new one, that the want of a new one was the only cause of the stoppage of the mill, and that the loss of profit really arose from not sending down the new shaft in proper time, and that this arose from the delay in delivering the broken one to serve as a model. But it is obvious that, in the great multitude of cases of millers sending off broken shafts to third persons ... , such consequences would not, in all probability, have occurred, and these special circumstances were here never communicated by the plaintiffs to the defendants.

It follows ... that the loss of profits here cannot reasonably be considered such a consequence of the breach of contract as could have been fairly and reasonably contemplated by both the parties when they made this contract. For such loss would neither have flowed naturally from the breach of this contract in the great multitude of such cases occurring under ordinary circumstances, nor were the special circumstances, which, perhaps, would have made it a reasonable and natural consequence of such breach of contract, communicated to or known by the defendants. The judge ought ... to have told the jury that, upon the facts ... before them, they ought not to take the loss of profits into consideration at all in estimating the damages. There must, therefore, be a new trial in this case.

DISCHARGE OF THE CONTRACT

When parties contract with one another, each party naturally assumes that the other party will faithfully and satisfactorily perform the terms of their agreement. Consequently, whenever the parties do what the contract requires, the law says that they have discharged their duties under the contract. *Discharge* of a contract involves the legally valid termination of a contractual duty. Upon discharge, the parties have fulfilled their agreement; at this time, the parties' duties and obligations to one another end. The law groups the numerous methods for discharging contracts into four main categories: discharge by performance, discharge by agreement of the parties, discharge by operation of law, and discharge by nonperformance. Exhibit 14.1 explains the various methods for discharging a contract.

Exhibit 14.1

Methods of Discharging Contracts

Type of Discharge	General Rules
Discharge by performance	
1. Complete performance: the parties' exact fulfillment of the terms of the contract.	1.a. Complete performance based on completion of the contract by the tender of delivery and/or payment.
2. Substantial performance: less-than-perfect performance that complies with the essential portions of the contract.	2.a. The doctrine is only applicable to nonmaterial and nonwillful breaches. 2.b. The injured party can sue for damages resulting from the minor deviations: there has been substantial (as opposed to complete) performance.
Discharge by agreement of the parties	
1. Release: the surrender of a legal claim.	1.a. Release requires a writing, consideration, and an immediate relinquishment of rights or claims owed to another.
2. Rescission: the voluntary, mutual surrender and discharge of contractual rights and duties whereby the parties are returned to the original status quo.	2.a. Rescission may be either written or oral (subject to the Statute of Frauds), formal or informal, express or implied.
3. Accord and satisfaction: an agreement whereby the parties decide to accept performance different from that required by their original bargain and the parties' later compliance with the new agreement.	3.a. Actual agreement and subsequent performance is necessary.
4. Novation: a contract that effects an immediate discharge of a previously existing contractual duty, creates a new contractual duty or obligation, and includes as a party to this new agreement one who neither was	4.a. The assent of the promisee and the new promisor are required. 4.b. Novation differs from an accord and satisfaction in that it effects an immediate discharge of an obligation rather than a discharge

Exhibit 14.1 Continued

Type of Discharge	General Rules
owed a duty nor was obligated to perform in the original contract.	based on a subsequent performance.
	4.c. Novation also differs from an accord because it introduces a new party to the agreement.
Discharge by operation of law	
1. Bankruptcy: a court decree/ discharge of the debtor's contractual obligations.	1.a. The revival of the obligation is possible if done in compliance with applicable statutory provisions.
2. Statute of limitations: a definite statutory time period during which the plaintiff must commence a lawsuit or be barred forever.	2.a. The applicable time periods differ from state to state.
3. Material alteration of the contract: a serious change in the contract effected by a party to the contract.	3.a. The alteration must be done intentionally and without the consent of the other party.
Discharge by nonperformance	
1. Impossibility: an unforeseen event or condition that precludes the possibility of the party's performing as promised.	1.a. Discharge stemming from only objective (as opposed to subjective) impossibility.
	1.b. It includes such events as the destruction of the contract's subject matter without the fault of either party, supervening illegality, the death or disability of either party whose performance is essential to the performance of the contract, and conduct by one party that makes performance by the other party impossible.
2. Commercial frustration: the destruction of the essential purpose and value of the contract.	2.a. Destruction of the value of the contract brought about by a supervening event, not reasonably anticipated at the contract's formation.
	2.b. The term *commercially impracticable* is used in the UCC.

Exhibit 14.1 Continued

Type of Discharge	General Rules
3. Breach: the nonperformance of the obligations set up by the contract. a. Complete (or actual) breach.	3.a.1. A party's failure to perform a duty which is material and essential to the agreement; the other party is justified in treating the agreement as at an end.
b. Anticipatory breach: an unequivocal indication in advance by one of the contracting parties that he or she does not intend to abide by the terms of the contract.	3.b.1. Anticipatory breach is included in both the common law and the UCC.
4. Conditions: limitations or qualifications placed on a promise. a. Express conditions: those in which the parties explicitly or impliedly set out the limitations to which their promises will be subject.	4.a.1. Strict compliance with express conditions necessary to avoid a breach.

b. Constructive conditions: those read into the contract or implied in law in order to serve justice.
   c. Condition precedent: the occurrence of a particular event is required before the parties have an obligation to perform; failure of the event discharges the obligations of both parties.
   d. Condition subsequent: the occurrence of a particular event that cuts off all ongoing contractual duties and discharges the obligations of both parties.
	4.b.1. Substantial compliance with constructive conditions necessary to avoid a breach.

Despite the parties' original intentions, the possibility exists that one party will fail to live up to the contractual obligations. As you will learn, such nonperformance constitutes a breach of the contract and entitles the injured party to certain remedies. A *remedy* is a cause of action resulting from the breach of a contract. After the occurrence of a breach, remedies attempt to satisfy the parties' expectations when the contract was formed. Remedies fall into two main categories: those resulting from a court's exercise of its powers at law (*legal remedies*) and those arising from a court's use of its powers of equity (*equitable remedies*, or those arising from the branch of the legal system designed to provide fairness when there was no suitable remedy "at law").

Although you may have used the term *legal remedies* to encompass both types of relief, in this chapter you will learn to identify the sorts of situations in which it is appropriate for a court to order one kind of relief or the other. You also will learn that these types of remedies usually are mutually exclusive.

Discharge by Performance

Complete Performance   The simplest and most satisfactory method of discharge consists of *complete performance*, also known as *perfect tender*. (Yet, as we discuss later in this chapter, rendering complete performance may be easier said than done.) If Jonathan has agreed to deliver five carloads of wheat, and Vanessa has promised to pay $2,000 per carload, complete performance will occur when Jonathan makes the deliveries to Vanessa and Vanessa pays Jonathan. The parties' exact fulfillment of the terms of the contract satisfies the intent of their agreement and their reason for contracting. Complete performance also extinguishes all the legal duties and rights that the contract originally set up. Note, too, that performance will be complete if one of the parties tenders either the wheat or the payment: *Tender* is an unconditional offer to perform a contractual obligation by a party who has the ability to perform. That person will have completely performed the contract even if the other person does not accept the wheat or the payment.

As long as Jonathan is fulfilling Vanessa's reasonable expectations under the contract, discharge by complete performance will occur once the parties have met their respective obligations. Suppose that Jonathan does not live up to the letter of the agreement as to the quality of the wheat sent to Vanessa. Vanessa should give Jonathan prompt notice of these defects and should state formally that she expects complete performance. Vanessa's failure to take such actions may allow Jonathan to argue after the fact that Vanessa has waived her right to expect complete performance. Waiver is discussed later in this chapter.

Substantial Performance   In some circumstances, one party does not perform exactly as specified in the contract. In such cases, the recipient may question whether this degree of performance adequately fulfills the requirements of the contract. The issue raised by such a question involves the legal sufficiency of less-than-complete performance.

The law does not always require exact performance of a contract. Hence, minor deviations from the performance contemplated in the contract may still result in the discharge of the contract. This type of performance is called *substantial performance.*[2] Courts will only find that substantial performance has occurred if the performing party acted in good faith and provided performance that is "good enough" for a reasonable and prudent person. In other words, the essential purpose of the contract has been met. The party making the performance must have attempted to comply with the terms of the contract. In other words, the variances from the contract were unintentional. In addition, any variances that do exist must involve technical or minor details. Construction of a new house in which the contractor still needs to finish the woodwork or touch up the painting in certain rooms—assuming the contractor has completed everything else—probably constitutes *substantial performance*. A party who has substantially performed may receive the payment under the contract, less some amount in damages due to the less-than-perfect performance. Since the performance is not perfect, but rather is a notch below the parties' reasonable expectations, the other party can sue for the damages caused by the incomplete and/or imperfect performance.

Courts usually are more willing to apply the concept of substantial performance to construction contracts than to sales contracts. Why? In a sales contract, a disgruntled buyer has a duty to return or to reject defective goods, and it is relatively easy to do so. On the other hand, a dissatisfied landowner must keep the defective house or other structure. The possibility of the unjust enrichment of the landowner in construction situations makes the doctrine of substantial performance more attractive to courts in these circumstances.

Discharge by Agreement of the Parties

The parties themselves can specifically agree to discharge the contract. Provisions to that effect may be part of the original contract between the parties or part of a new contract drafted expressly to discharge the initial contract.

Release   Release represents a common method of discharging the legal rights one party has against another. To be valid, a *release* (1) should be in writing, (2) should be supported by consideration, and (3) should effect an immediate relinquishment of rights or claims owed to another. For example, a landowner may sign a release in which he or she agrees, usually in exchange for money, to discharge the builder from the original contractual obligations. Insurance companies commonly prepare releases that the injured parties must sign before the insurers will compensate the parties for their injuries.

Mutual Rescission   Sometimes the parties may find it advantageous to call off their deal. The law calls this process *mutual rescission* or *rescission*. Mutual rescission is a voluntary, mutual surrender and discharge of contractual rights and duties whereby the parties return to the original status quo. A valid rescission is legally binding. In general, rescission may be formal or informal, express or implied, and written or oral. Sometimes a rescission must be in writing under the Statute of Frauds, for example, UCC § 2-209 or the provisions dealing with real estate.

The simplest method of rescission involves the termination of executory bilateral contracts. If Jonathan and Vanessa in the earlier example *mutually agree to cancel* their transaction, *express rescission* has occurred. On the other hand, they may subsequently agree that Jonathan will deliver seven carloads of wheat instead of five. Substituting this later agreement for the original one brings about an *implied rescission* of the earlier agreement. Rescission is more difficult if the parties have entered a unilateral contract or one of the parties in a bilateral contract has already performed his or her duty, at least in part. The rescission may leave one party "enriched," perhaps unjustly, since that party has received at least partial performance, or it leaves one party "disadvantaged" since that party has often begun preparations to perform his or her duty. As a result, some courts will infer a promise to pay for the performance already rendered and/or expenses incurred before approving or allowing the rescission.

Accord and Satisfaction   Parties may agree to accept performance different from that required by their original bargain. The law calls such an agreement an *accord*. When the parties perform the action specified in the accord, *satisfaction* occurs, causing the discharge of the original claim by *accord and satisfaction*. The process of accord and satisfaction requires evidence of assent. An accord will not be legally binding unless and until the performance required by the accord is rendered. In most states if the performance does not occur, the other party can choose to sue on either the original promise or the accord.

Novation   A novation is a new contract that replaces a prior contract, and in which at least one of the parties to the original contract is replaced by a new party. By entering into a novation, the parties to the original contract agree to release one another from their obligations under that contract in exchange for the creation of a new contract in which at least one of the parties is replaced, although the benefits to be conferred are likely to be the same. Suppose, for example, that Andrea has a contract to "house sit" for Rob, agreeing to water his plants and care for his pets while Rob is on a cruise. Rob is going to pay Andrea for her services. Before the date of the cruise, Andrea learns of an opportunity to work on a project with her professor, but it will prevent her from house sitting for Rob. Fortunately, Andrea's roommate Carolyn is available to replace Andrea as the house sitter. Andrea notifies Rob and asks if this is acceptable to him. Rob knows and trusts Carolyn, and has no concerns about the change. All parties agree, and the original contract (Rob and Andrea's agreement) is discharged, replaced by the new contract (novation) between Rob and Carolyn. Such a novation is illustrated in Exhibit 14.2.

Exhibit 14.2

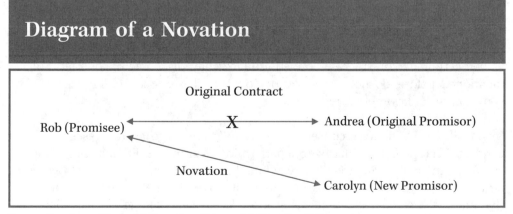

Diagram of a Novation

Original Contract

Rob (Promisee) ←——— X ———→ Andrea (Original Promisor)

Novation

Carolyn (New Promisor)

Source: Courtesy of Lynn M. Forsythe, © Lynn M. Forsythe 2009

Discharge by Operation of Law

The law itself can mandate the discharge of certain contracts. As you will learn in Chapter 27, bankruptcy decrees may grant honest debtors a discharge of contractual obligations by operation of law. Most of the time, a creditor will not receive the total owed, and yet, the discharge in bankruptcy prevents the creditor from later suing the debtor for nonperformance (usually nonpayment). However, most states allow the debtor to revive the obligation by a later promise to pay the creditor. This reaffirmation of the debt involves several stringent requirements under the Bankruptcy Act.

Statutes of limitations establish time periods within which litigants must initiate lawsuits. The length of the time period varies by jurisdiction and the nature of the claim. Noncompliance with these statutory time limits may discharge contractual claims by operation of law. For example, under the common law, one typically must bring claims for breach of contracts within six years of the date of the alleged breach. Filing a lawsuit after this time limit makes the claim unenforceable. When the transaction involves a sale of goods, UCC § 2-725 states that the injured party ordinarily must file suit within four years of the breach. The underlying claim is discharged by operation of law if the injured party fails to file a lawsuit within this period. Since these periods of limitations differ from jurisdiction to jurisdiction, the applicable state's statute should be checked. (The Statute of Limitations is an *affirmative defense*, which means that the defendant must raise the Statute of Limitations issue in order to avoid liability under the contract. The court will not ask the parties whether the claim is barred by the statute.)

The law also may grant a discharge of any contract that one of the parties to the agreement has materially altered. Before a court will apply this rule, it must be shown that the alteration was done intentionally and without the consent of the other party. Thus, if Jonathan, without Vanessa's permission, changes the price of each carload from $2,000 to $5,000 on the written contract, Vanessa can obtain a discharge of the contract through operation of law.

Discharge by Nonperformance

Under certain circumstances, nonperformance may discharge a contract. Still, as mentioned before, do not expect courts to apply these doctrines in order to save you from an unfavorable bargain.

Impossibility   The legal concept of *impossibility* refers to an unforeseen event or condition that precludes a party from performing as promised. For instance, using our earlier example of the contract between Jonathan and Vanessa, such events as (1) the destruction of the subject matter of the contract without the fault of either party (Jonathan's wheat burns before being loaded), (2) supervening illegality (after the contract's formation, the legislature passes a law making it illegal for trains to carry wheat into Vanessa's state), or (3) conduct by one party that makes performance by the other party impossible (in carrying out other deals, Vanessa contracts for every possible rail car so that Jonathan cannot procure the necessary cars to transport his wheat to complete their transaction) generally discharge contracts. These examples denote *objective impossibility* (*no one* could perform the contract in these circumstances; nonperformance of the contract is unavoidable).

Another instance of objective impossibility involves the death or disability of either party to a personal services contract. This contingency forms an exception to the general rule that a contract will be binding and not dischargeable despite the death or disability of either party, unless the parties have agreed otherwise. Objective impossibility would occur if Yessica hires Tong to paint her portrait, and Tong has a debilitating heart attack.

On the other hand, courts have held that circumstances involving subjective impossibility (as opposed to objective impossibility) will not discharge contractual obligations. *Subjective impossibility* consists of nonperformance owing to personal impossibility. The contract can be performed, but *this particular person* is unable to fulfill the contract obligations. For this reason, nonperformance owing to insolvency, shortages of materials, strikes, riots, droughts, and price increases ordinarily will *not* discharge contracts. However, some courts temporarily will suspend the duty to perform until the conditions causing the inability to perform have passed. More liberal courts may even discharge the contract if later performance will place an appreciably greater burden on the one obligated to perform. Given this division of opinion, the parties often will try to protect their rights by including express provisions covering the types of contingencies just described, such as a *force majeure*[3] clause. Still, it is up to the courts to evaluate the validity of any such clauses.

Commercial Frustration   Because of the harshness of the general rule that impossibility ordinarily will not discharge the performance called for in a contract, the doctrine of *commercial frustration* (or *frustration of purpose*) has recently emerged as a justification for nonperformance. Courts will not invoke this doctrine to excuse performance, however, unless the essential purpose and value of the contract have been frustrated. If the parties reasonably could (or should) have foreseen the "cause" of such frustration, courts will hold the nonperforming party to the terms of the bargain. Hence, courts will not utilize this doctrine to release parties from bad bargains. It is important to understand that in these cases performance is possible; but the value of the contract has been frustrated or destroyed by a supervening event that was not reasonably anticipated at the contract's formation. UCC § 2-615 uses the term *commercially impracticable* in like fashion to excuse nonperformance in cases of severe shortages of raw materials owing to war, embargo, local crop failure, and other similar reasons. Before courts will allow discharge, these factors must have caused a marked increase in price or must have totally precluded the seller from obtaining the supplies necessary for performance.

Actual Breach   *Breach of contract* occurs when one or more of the contracting parties fail to perform the obligations set up by the contract. Degrees of breach exist, which complicates the issue. A *complete* or *actual* breach of contract involves the nonperformance of a duty that is so material and essential to the agreement that the other party is justified in treating the agreement as at an end. UCC §§ 2-703 and 2-711 embrace this common law principle. Actual breach generally discharges the other party's obligation to perform under the terms of the contract. However, rather than cancel the contract upon breach, the injured (or nonbreaching) party may elect instead to hold the nonperforming party to the contract through various types of remedies, which we discuss later in this chapter.

Anticipatory Breach   Sometimes one of the contracting parties will indicate in advance, through words or conduct, that he or she does not intend to abide by the terms of the agreement. To illustrate, if Jonathan unequivocally tells Vanessa before the time performance is due that he will not send the wheat as scheduled, Jonathan will have wrongfully repudiated the contract. In legal terms, Jonathan's action is called *anticipatory breach* or *anticipatory repudiation*. In this situation, as with actual breaches, the injured party is not limited to discharging the contract but may seek any available remedies for the breach of contract.

The Uniform Commercial Code recognizes a kind of anticipatory repudiation in circumstances less definite than those allowable under the common law. UCC § 2-609

eClass 14.1 Management

DEFENSES TO CONTRACT ENFORCEMENT

Meg recalls that one of her professors mentioned that a number of subcontractors and service providers who encounter difficulties in meeting their contractual obligations try to use the defenses of impossibility, commercial impracticability, or commercial frustration when they fail to satisfy their contracts. eClass hires out much of its programming work, and Meg is concerned that these programmers may attempt to use these defenses if they are unable to meet their contractual obligations. She asks you what the firm should do to protect itself. What will you tell her?

BUSINESS CONSIDERATIONS   Should a business enter into contracts that it is not certain it can perform and then resort to commercial impracticability as an excuse *if* it cannot perform as promised? What legal risk is the business assuming if it uses such an approach to its obligations?

ETHICAL CONSIDERATIONS   Is it ethical for a business to avoid liability by asserting that its promised performance was made impossible or impracticable by some external factor? Is it ethical for a firm to try to collect damages when an external factor made the performance by the other firm impossible or impracticable?

states that when reasonable grounds for insecurity arise with respect to one party's performance, the other party may demand adequate assurances of due performance and suspend his or her own performance until such assurances are forthcoming. If 30 days pass without reply, the party who has demanded the assurances can deem the contract repudiated. For example, Vanessa's actual or apparent *insolvency* (the inability to pay one's debts as they become due) may cause Jonathan to invoke the provisions of § 2-609. If Vanessa does not respond by providing the requested "adequate assurances" of her ability to pay as called for in the contract within 30 days, Jonathan then may treat the contract as repudiated under UCC § 2-610.

Conditions   The presence of *conditions* in a contract may result in nonperformance that will justify discharge of a contract as well. A *promise* is a covenant where the promisor undertakes a duty to do something or to refrain from doing something. A *condition*, in contrast, is an act or event that limits or qualifies a promise. The condition must occur before the promisor has a duty to perform or to refrain from performing. Courts classify conditions in two ways. The first classification scheme emphasizes the *timing* of the qualifying occurrence (the condition) in relation to the promised performance. Three subsets of this classification include *conditions precedent, concurrent conditions*, and *conditions subsequent*. Exhibit 14.3 summarizes these conditions. The second classification scheme stems from the manner in which the conditions arise. Conditions created by the agreement of the parties themselves are called *express conditions*. In contrast, conditions created by law are deemed *constructive* (or *implied*) *conditions*.

Under the first classification scheme based on timing, an agreement may explicitly state that a certain act or event must occur *before* the other party has a duty to perform or before a contract results. If so, a *condition precedent* exists. For example, a person may promise (for consideration) to buy a car *if* the seller can deliver the car within ten days. A duty to buy the car does not arise unless and until the seller fulfills the condition. Thus, the timing of the condition and any later duty to perform go together. To be a condition precedent rather than a mere promise, the parties must indicate that the condition is an essential, vital aspect of the transaction. If the buyer in our example later wishes to sue for rescission of the contract or for damages on the ground that the seller did not deliver the car on time, the buyer will have to prove that delivery within ten days is essential to the transaction. A common condition precedent involves a buyer's signing a contract for the purchase of a new house subject to the sale of the buyer's current residence. The buyer views this provision as an important consideration regarding his or her willingness to enter into the contract.

Concurrent conditions obligate the parties *to perform at the same time*. Concurrent conditions where the parties agree to transfer the goods and the payment for them at the same time underlie most commercial sales.

A *condition subsequent* is any occurrence that the parties have agreed will cut off an existing legal duty. It also may be a contingency, the happening or performance of which will defeat a contract already in effect. When a sales contract involving grain states that the contract will be of no effect if fire destroys the grain, a condition subsequent exists. Genuine conditions subsequent are rare. What may sound like a

Exhibit 14.3

Conditions Based on Timing

Type	What Happens When the Condition Occurs (Timelines)
Condition precedent	Condition ——————————————— Contract The occurrence of the condition is required before the duty to perform is activated. "If (condition), then I will (perform)." For example: "If I am able to sell my current home by February 3rd, I will buy your house at the agreed-upon price." Failure or inability to sell the current home (the condition) negates the obligation to buy the house.
Condition concurrent	Tenders goods or performance Seller ⟵—————————————————⟶ Buyer Tenders payment The parties are expected to perform simultaneously, and the failure of one to perform excuses the obligation of the other to perform.
Condition subsequent	Contract ——————**X**————— Condition The occurrence of the condition will excuse a duty to perform that would otherwise be enforceable. "I will (perform) unless (condition)." For example: "I will sell you my textbook for business law at the end of the semester unless I fail the class and have to repeat it." The seller has a duty to sell the book at the end of the semester, but that duty will be negated if he or she does not pass the class and has to take the class again (the condition).

condition subsequent—for example, Acme Insurance will not pay for casualty losses if the premises are unoccupied—will be construed by many courts as a condition precedent. Courts that characterize such a provision as a condition subsequent will interpret the clause as stating that the occurrence of the condition (vacant premises) will cut off an existing legal duty (payment of the casualty loss). Other courts may say that it is a condition precedent (the premises must be kept occupied) that merely sounds like a condition subsequent because of the phrasing. This distinction can be procedurally significant. If it is a condition precedent, the insured has the burden of proof; if it is a condition subsequent, the insurer has the burden of proof. And when the evidence is conflicting, the party who has the burden of proof often loses.

Express conditions (for example, this sale can be consummated only by payment of cash) are those spelled out by the parties explicitly or impliedly in fact. A *constructive condition* is one not expressed by the parties, but rather read into the contract in order to serve justice (that is, the condition is implied in law). Differentiating between an express condition implied in fact and a constructive condition can be difficult. For example, a provision regarding place of delivery normally is an express condition precedent in a contract involving grain; but if such a condition is lacking, and there is no clear indication of the parties' intent, a court may imply that the place for delivery is the seller's place of business (see UCC § 2-308).

Nonperformance of an express condition precedent (such as posting a performance bond) causes a failure of the condition that nullifies the other party's duty to perform and discharges the contract. Similarly, the presence of an express condition subsequent (the occurrence of a particular event that cuts off all ongoing contractual duties) discharges the obligations of both parties.

It should be noted that a condition may require one party to perform "to the satisfaction" of the other party. In certain cases, such as those involving custom tailoring, some courts hold that in order to discharge the contract, the performing party must meet the personal, subjective expectations of the recipient. Other courts characterize the performance as substantial if the performance rendered will satisfy a reasonable person. Courts generally will apply this latter test when the parties base performance not on personal tastes or aesthetic preferences (as may be involved in our custom tailoring example) but rather on satisfaction as to merchantability or mechanical utility (as in the purchase of a car).

INTRODUCTION TO REMEDIES

When a person enters into a contract, he or she expects to receive the benefits of the bargain. When Rosalva makes a contract with Marquise, she expects Marquise to perform as he agreed. If Marquise does not so perform, and his nonperformance is not excused or discharged, Marquise is in breach. When this occurs, Rosalva does not receive the benefit she anticipated, for which she negotiated, and to which she was committed. As a result, Rosalva has the right to seek remedies from Marquise for his failure to perform. These remedies are most likely to be damages "at law," monetary

eClass 14.2 Manufacturing/Sales

ENSURING ACCEPTABLE PERFORMANCE

Meg has recently negotiated a preliminary agreement with a plastics manufacturer, PDG Plastiques (PDG), which calls for PDG to produce the plastic cases for the eClass software. Meg realizes that PDG will need to supply cases that meet eClass's specifications in order to work in its manufacturing and packaging process. She has asked for your advice on how to word the final written contract between eClass and PDG to ensure that eClass protects itself and so that the cases will meet eClass's specifications. What advice will you give her?

BUSINESS CONSIDERATION   Suppose a business is offered a very lucrative contract if it will produce a product to very specific standards. In deciding whether to accept the offer, what factors should the firm consider?

ETHICAL CONSIDERATIONS   Is it ethical for a person to enter a contract that requires his or her personal satisfaction with the other party's performance? What, if anything, would make this provision unethical?

damages that will give Rosalva the financial equivalent of the "benefit of her bargain." (In order to recover such damages, Rosalva has a duty to *mitigate*, or minimize, the damages she suffered). Sometimes money will not "make it right," and the payment of some amount will not give Rosalva the desired benefit. In these situations Rosalva may choose to seek remedies "in equity." These are non-monetary remedies that are designed to provide fairness to the non-breaching party by requiring the breaching party to do—or to refrain from doing—something ordered by the court. Each type of remedy will be examined in detail below. Exhibit 14.4 summarizes the various types of remedies.

DAMAGES

When one party breaches a contract, the other party is entitled to payment for lost expectations. The injured party can then bring an action for remedies, in this case damages. It is not necessary that the injured party have the ability to compute exactly what the damages are, as long as the losses represent the natural and proximate consequences of the breach. In computing damages, courts ask whether the breaching party should have foreseen that these injuries would result from a breach. If the nonperforming party should have foreseen the losses, courts will

Judicial Remedies for Breach of Contract

Type of Remedy	Definition	Example
Legal remedies	Damages resulting from a court's exercise of its power "at law" to award money for losses.	• Compensatory damages • Consequential damages • Punitive damages • Nominal damages (See below)
Compensatory damages	Damages awarded to a non-breaching party in order to compensate him or her for the actual, foreseeable harm or loss caused by the breach.	Court of law awarded Devonnel money because he had to purchase grapes from another vendor after Rosa breached their contract to provide grapes for his winery. The replacement grapes were more expensive so the court awarded Devonnel the difference between the two prices.
Consequential damages	Indirect or special damages springing from the effects or aftermath (i.e., the consequences) of the breach itself; not recoverable unless the breaching party knew, or should have known, at the time of contract formation, of the potential effect of a breach on the nonbreaching party.	Court of law awarded Lulu consequential damages. Lulu had a contract with Dolphin Pools to build a swimming pool for her. At the time of the contract, Lulu stressed that it was important that the pool be completed by June 1, because she was going to use the pool to teach swimming classes. Dolphin Pools promised that the pool would be completed by June 1, however, it did not complete the pool until June 15, and Lulu lost income from teaching swimming. Since Dolphin Pools knew of the reason for the June 1 deadline, it is responsible for the lost income from the two weeks delay.
Punitive damages	Monetary damages awarded to punish a party for willful, wanton, and malicious harm caused to a nonbreaching party. These damages are often relatively large in comparison to the actual damages suffered. Punitive damages are rare in contract disputes.	Court of law awarded Tracy treble damages under the statute.

Exhibit 14.4 Continued

Type of Remedy	Definition	Example
Nominal damages	Small sums that "recognize" that the plaintiff had a cause of action but the plaintiff suffered no measurable pecuniary loss.	Court of law awarded Pablo $25 because Edward breached their contract and failed to provide the motor he promised. However, Pablo located an equivalent motor that was less expensive.
Equitable remedies	Remedies arising from a court's use of its powers of equity. (The remedies can be granted by a court of equity or a court sitting in equity.)	• Rescission and restitution • Specific performance • Reformation • Injunction • Quasi contract (See below)
Rescission and restitution	A court order cancelling a contract and ordering the return of the previously rendered consideration or its value.	Court of equity ordered the rescission of a contract between Holly and Derek because Holly committed fraud in the inducement. Derek must return the watch he received from Holly and Holly must give Derek his money back.
Specific performance	A court order to render the performance promised in the contract.	Court of equity ordered Franco to deliver the Rembrandt painting to Kristin per the parties' agreement. Specific performance is normally only available for a unique item or object or an item or object that is currently not available elsewhere.
Reformation	A court order correcting an agreement to conform to the intentions of the parties.	Court of equity corrected the purchase price in a contract between Samantha and Neng for the sale of Neng's house. The written contract stated the price as $10,000, however, the parties agreed that the price would be $100,000.
Injunction	A court order requiring a person to perform an act or restraining a person from doing some act.	Court of equity ordered an opera singer not to perform a concert. The singer had contracted to sing a concert. When a more prestigious venue invited her to perform the same evening, she informed the first concert hall that she was going to breach. The court ordered her not to sing at the second venue.

Exhibit 14.4 Continued

Type of Remedy	Definition	Example
Quasi contract	A court order requiring that one who received a benefit pay for the benefit received so as to prevent the unjust enrichment of the other party. (Quasi contract may not be considered an equitable remedy depending on the state and the surrounding circumstances.)	Court of equity ordered Josh to pay Kasper for the unjust benefit that Josh received when he took Kasper's harvester without permission and used it on his own crops.

award damages to the injured party. The amount of damages awarded, of course, will depend heavily on the facts of the case.

Compensatory Damages

The most common type of damages is *compensatory damages*, or those sums of money that will place the injured party in the same economic position that would have been attained had the contract been performed. Such damages also are called *actual* damages. Injured parties may recover only the damages that the parties reasonably can foresee.

The 1854 English case *Hadley v. Baxendale*[4] enunciated this limitation on compensatory damages, which is still accepted by many courts today. Under the *Hadley v. Baxendale* rule, courts ordinarily will limit compensatory damage awards to those losses naturally arising from the breach, or those the parties may have reasonably contemplated or foreseen at the time of contract formation. Compensatory damages include all damages *directly* attributable to the loss of the bargain agreed on by the parties, including lost profits and any incidental expenses incurred as a result of the breach. If the breach involves a contract for the sale of goods, courts usually compute the difference between the contract price and the market price of the goods. Assume Miller Construction Company, a developer of real estate for its own particular purposes, orders three bulldozers from Precision Machinery Company and, unfortunately, none of the bulldozers functions properly. Miller should be able to recover the general or *direct damages* or losses caused by the defective equipment. Miller's costs of repairing the machines constitute one type of direct loss. Alternatively, if Miller has to buy new bulldozers at higher prices, Miller will be able to recover the costs associated with obtaining the replacement equipment. *Cover* is the purchase of replacement goods to substitute for those promised in the contract. Miller would use its right to cover if it purchased replacement bulldozers.[5]

Assume that Miller's bad luck continues. Antonio, a seller who contracted to sell land to Miller as an investment, fails to go through with this realty contract. Miller can sue Antonio, the reneging seller, for the difference between the price of this piece of land and the one Miller eventually purchases. Miller also can sue for such expenses as the additional brokers' fees or commissions involved in obtaining the second parcel of real estate, since these losses flow directly and foreseeably from Antonio's breach. However, in both cases Miller must deduct any expenses saved as a result of the breaches. (Miller would also have the right to seek specific performance, an equitable remedy, in the contract with Antonio, if it so desired. This is discussed in more detail below.)

Consequential Damages

Besides compensatory damages, it also is possible for plaintiffs like Miller to receive *consequential damages*. Consequential damages are those indirect or special damages—sometimes viewed as "spillover damages"—springing from the effects or aftermath (that is, the consequences) of the breach itself. Assume that Miller also loses a grading contract with the city because the bulldozers ordered from Precisions Machinery Company will not work. Miller also loses several rental contracts from retailers who wished to be part of a mall Miller was planning to develop on the real estate he had tried to purchase from Antonio. Can Miller sue Precision and Antonio for the losses accruing from these special circumstances and not just from the direct breaches? To determine whether there is liability, a court will apply the reasonable person test to see whether such lost contracts were a foreseeable result of the breaches by Precision and Antonio. A judge will not award purely speculative or conjectural damages; but if a court finds Precision and/or Antonio knew, or should have known, at the time of contract formation, of Miller's circumstances and the potential effect of their breaches on Miller, it may award incidental or consequential damages. The UCC in § 2-715 and § 2-710 also recognizes this doctrine.

Punitive Damages

In contrast to their willingness to make compensatory and consequential damages available to injured parties, courts generally will not allow the recovery of punitive damages in breach of contract situations. *Punitive*, or exemplary, damages are imposed not to compensate the injured party but to punish the wrongdoer so as to deter future conduct of this sort. The old common law rule was that punitive damages never were appropriate for breaches of contract. Though still rare, some statutes now permit the imposition of punitive damages in contractual situations (such as *treble damages*—a statutory remedy that allows the successful plaintiff to recover three times the damages suffered as a result of the injury). Furthermore, some courts have been willing to grant punitive damages in situations in which one party has acted willfully. An insurance company that unduly delays in paying legitimate claims may be subject to punitive damages in order to discourage this type of conduct. If the circumstances so warrant, consumer transactions also may form the basis for an award of punitive damages.

Since the 1990s, courts have wrestled with the issue of whether the Due Process Clause of the Fourteenth Amendment, which requires fundamental fairness, places some outer limits on a jury's otherwise unfettered discretion to award any amount of punitive damages, no matter how huge. The issue has risen because juries in many cases award large punitive damages in relation to the actual financial loss suffered by the party. In *Pacific Mutual Life Insurance Company v. Haslip,*[6] the U.S. Supreme Court acknowledged that it was possible for a punitive damage award to violate due process protections. However, the Court held that in this case the jury's punitive damages award based on the fraud of an insurance agent did not violate due process.[7] The Court based its conclusion on the fact that the procedural and substantive safeguards imposed by state law (including post-trial procedures that required trial courts to scrutinize all punitive damages awards) ensured the reasonableness of the amount of punitive damages and the rationality of the award in furthering the purposes of deterrence and punishment. In 1996, the Supreme Court voided a state court's award of punitive damages as being unconstitutional under the Fourteenth Amendment's Due Process Clause. In *BMW of North America, Inc. v. Gore,*[8] the Court held that a $2 million punitive damages award against BMW of North America, Inc. for BMW's fraudulent failure to disclose that it had repainted a new $40,000 car, thereby reducing the vehicle's value by $4,000, was "grossly excessive." The jury apparently had arrived at the $4 million punitive damages figure it had awarded by multiplying the $4,000 compensatory damages award by the 1,000 nationwide instances of BMW's similar nondisclosures of minor repairs. (The state supreme court used remittitur to reduce the punitive damages to $2 million.) The Supreme Court stressed that while Alabama had the right to protect its own citizens through the punishment of firms that engage in deceptive trade practices, such a state would not have the right, by the imposition of a punitive damages award or a legislatively authorized fine, to punish out-of-state activity that was lawful where it had occurred. While noting that the Court could not "draw a mathematically bright line" with regard to when the ratio between the compensatory and the punitive damages awards would become unconstitutional, the Court concluded that when, as here, the ratio was "a breathtaking 500:1," any such award must surely raise suspicion. In *Cooper Industries, Inc. v. Leatherman Tool Group, Inc.,*[9] the Court rejected the contention that a jury award of $4.5 million in punitive damages (the jury had awarded $50,000 in compensatory damages) was grossly excessive under *Gore.* The Court further held that when courts of appeals review district court determinations of the constitutionality of punitive damages awards, the courts of appeals should make a *de novo* review. In a *de novo* appeal or review, the court of appeals uses the trial courts' record but makes an independent review of the law and the facts. The Court continues to fill in the parameters of this important aspect of law, so you should watch for further developments in this area.

Duty to Mitigate

In determining whether to award damages and the amount of any damages, courts require the injured party to *mitigate* (or minimize) these damages, if possible. Courts impose this duty in the interest of fairness. The injured party must take affirmative steps to prevent the escalation of the losses brought about by the breaching party. Although the injured party has a duty to exercise due diligence to reduce the amount of losses, he or she is not required to incur undue risk, expense, or humiliation.

In our bulldozer example, courts will expect Miller to attempt to procure substitute bulldozers, assuming this is possible without undue risk or expense. If Miller does not undertake such reasonable steps, its failure to mitigate damages will limit the amount of damages it can recover. But if Miller can prove it was impossible to obtain substitute bulldozers at a reasonable price, most courts will excuse its failure to mitigate. The duty of mitigation does not require the injured party to go to superhuman lengths. If the risks or expenses would be unreasonably great, there is no duty to mitigate.

Liquidated Damages Clause

The parties may agree in advance that, upon breach of contract, a certain sum of money will be paid to the injured party. This agreement is called a *liquidated damages clause*. The amount to which the parties have agreed in advance fully satisfies any liability attendant upon the breach. Generally, courts will enforce such provisions if (1) the agreed-on amount is reasonable and not out of proportion to the injury likely to occur as a result of the breach and (2) calculation of the resulting damages in advance and with any accuracy will be difficult, if not impossible. Courts will determine that the clause is an unenforceable penalty if (1) the amount set grossly exceeds the probable damages if there is a breach, (2) the parties use the same amount for a variety of breaches including both major and minor breaches, and/or (3) a mere delay in making payment is included in the list of events triggering the payment of the specified amount. In the context of sales contracts, UCC § 2-718 takes a similar approach.

For an example, construction contracts typically have clauses assessing a per-day charge for delays in completing a building on time. Because it is difficult to ascertain the amount of damages that a breach of such a contract will cause, as long as the per-day charge is reasonable, courts generally uphold these clauses.

Courts will not enforce *penalties*, however. Penalties consist of amounts unrelated to the possible damages that may occur and usually are excessively large. Such an arbitrary lump sum, even if the parties have agreed to it in a liquidated damages clause, will be void.

Nominal Damages

You have learned that for most breaches of contract, an action for damages may be possible. However, in certain cases, especially those involving a minor or technical breach, the injured party sustains no actual losses or damages. A court may still decide to award a small amount of compensation (say $25) for the breach. This type of remedy

eClass 14.3 Management

LIQUIDATED DAMAGES CLAUSES

Ani recently suggested that eClass should begin to include liquidated damages clauses in its contracts with service providers. As she pointed out, damages are often difficult to calculate in these cases, and using a liquidated damages clause will eliminate that problem. Yousef pointed out that these clauses also could be used to set damages high enough to encourage service providers to make *every* effort to perform, since many of them will not be able to afford the effects of a breach. The firm members have asked for your advice. What will you tell them?

BUSINESS CONSIDERATIONS   Why would a business prefer to use a liquidated damages clause instead of trying to compute its actual damages in the event of a breach? What factors should be used in deciding what liquidated damages should be?

ETHICAL CONSIDERATIONS   Is it ethical to set liquidated damages so high that the other party cannot afford to breach its contract? What ethical issues does such a strategy implicate?

is called *nominal damages*. It is a token sum that a court will require the defendant to pay as an acknowledgment of the wrongful conduct in which he or she has engaged. Sometimes a court or jury awards nominal damages because the injured party has not been able to prove the amount of damages that he or she claims to have suffered. Upon proof of a breach, the injured party, therefore, is entitled only to nominal damages.

EQUITABLE REMEDIES

When the "at law" remedy of damages is unavailable, indeterminable, or inadequate, courts may award certain equitable remedies. The plaintiff's eligibility to receive such fairness-oriented relief will depend on the absence of bad faith on the plaintiff's part and similar factors. It is important to remember that a plaintiff will not necessarily receive equitable remedies just because he or she asks for them. Equitable remedies will only be granted under special or unusual circumstances. When they are available, the most significant types of equitable relief include rescission and restitution, specific performance, quasi contract, reformation, and injunction.

A court's power to award equitable remedies is discretionary; courts normally will *not* give equitable remedies if the injured party has "*unclean hands*" (that is, has shown bad faith or dishonesty in dealing with the other party); if the injured party has unduly delayed bringing the lawsuit (*laches*); if a *forfeiture of property* (the loss of property without compensation) will result from conferring an equitable decree; if the court itself necessarily will have to supervise the completion of the remedy granted; or if a remedy at law is available, determinable, and adequate.

Rescission and Restitution

As you saw earlier in this chapter, the parties may voluntarily agree to rescind, or set aside, their contract before rendering performance. This type of rescission discharges the contract. But rescission also may occur as a result of a material breach of the agreement. Rescission in this context refers to the cancellation or termination of the contract through restoring the parties to their pre-contract positions. Upon such rescission, the injured party may then ask for restitution.

Restitution is the legal term that describes the process by which the parties are returned to their original positions at the time of contract formation. It involves the return of the goods, money, or property involved in the contract or the recovery of the reasonable value of the services rendered. In essence, restitution relies on quasi-contractual principles rather than on the original agreement, because once rescission has occurred, the original contract no longer exists.

To avoid the unjust enrichment of the breaching party, the law permits restitution by allowing the plaintiff to sue in quasi contract in order to recover. In most jurisdictions, one cannot sue for both damages and restitution; damages and restitution constitute *mutually exclusive* remedies. The injured party must *elect* to pursue one remedy or the other. If Miller has paid Precision for the bulldozers, upon Precision's breach, Miller can treat the contract as at an end (that is, rescind it) and then recover the money (consideration) already paid to Precision in order to avoid the unjust enrichment of Precision. Alternatively, Miller can sue for damages. The *election of remedies* doctrine prevents Miller from recovering twice.

Specific Performance

Whenever the remedy represented by monetary damages is inadequate or unjust, the injured party may ask a court to order *specific performance*. In these cases, a court compels the breaching party to perform according to the exact terms of the agreement. Courts rely on uniqueness as one factor in deciding whether to grant specific performance. Specific performance generally can be awarded for contracts for the sale of an interest in land since land, by definition, is unique. For example, if you contract to buy a prairie-style home on the river, money damages for breach of that contract are unfulfilling: Money can buy a house similar to the one in the contract, but not that particular house at that particular location. The inherent uniqueness of real estate may convince a court to order the breaching party to convey the house to you—that is, give you specific performance—in order to create a just result. Specific performance also may be available if the goods called for in the contract are unique (artwork, antiques, and so forth) or, if not unique, the goods are in temporary short supply (a seasonal item that is not currently available on the market). If Franco breaches a contract to sell a Rembrandt painting, in the absence of fraud or illegality, a court can compel Franco to convey the painting to the buyer. But when the injured party easily can obtain the same or similar personal property from other sources, specific performance is not appropriate: Money damages will be adequate in these cases. Just as damages and restitution generally are mutually exclusive remedies, so too are damages and specific performance.

Money damages ordinarily will not satisfy the parties in situations involving personal services contracts. However, specific performance is normally viewed as an inappropriate remedy when a personal services contract is breached. The judge could order a person to work, but the judge would have difficulty ensuring that the person would work well. Judges will avoid ordering specific performance if it is not feasible or practical. Generally ordering a person to work against his or her will is not feasible.

Quasi Contract/Reformation/Injunction

Two concepts previously discussed, quasi contract and reformation, bear mentioning again, this time in the context of equitable remedies. *Quasi contract* involves circumstances in which a court creates a contract of sorts for the parties, despite their wishes and intentions, in order to prevent the unjust enrichment of one party. When the parties have not entered into a contract, but one party knowingly has received a benefit to which he or she is not entitled, an unjust enrichment has occurred. Given the absence of a valid contract, the injured party cannot seek contract-related remedies. In the interests of equity and fairness, however, the injured party may receive a restitution-based remedy, the reasonable value of the services rendered. *Reformation*, on the other hand, concerns a court's rewriting of a contract in order to remove a mistake and to make the agreement conform to the terms to which the parties originally agreed. (See the discussion of reformation in Chapter 12.)

An injunction is another type of equitable remedy. An *injunction* is a writ issued by a court of equity ordering a person to do or refrain from doing some specified act. This remedy does not arise often in contractual situations. However, an injunction would be an appropriate remedy for a personal services contract that is breached. While a judge will not order a person to work to fulfill a contract, the judge may be willing to prohibit that person from working in a similar field or for a competitor until such time as the person satisfies the original contract that he or she breached.

LIMITATIONS ON REMEDIES

The parties may attempt to limit the remedies available to the injured party in advance. Chapter 12 discussed such efforts in the context of exculpatory clauses. The UCC also permits the parties to limit remedies. However, if an exclusive remedy—as defined in the contract—fails in its essential purpose, UCC § 2-719 permits the injured party to seek any remedies available under the Code. Section 2-719 also forbids contractual limitations of consequential damages for *personal* injuries resulting from the use of consumer goods. The UCC labels limitations on these sorts of damages *prima facie* unconscionable, or damages that, on their face, are blatantly unfair and one-sided. On the other hand, the UCC does not characterize limitations of damages in purely *commercial* settings in this way.

WAIVER OF BREACH

Even though you have spent a great deal of this chapter studying the various remedies available to an injured party when the other party breaches the contract, recall that the injured party may be willing to accept less-than-complete performance. The law terms an injured party's giving up the right to receive the performance set out in the contract a *waiver of breach*. Once a waiver of breach occurs, the waiver in effect eliminates the breach; the performance required under the contract continues as if the breach never happened. In essence, waiver of breach precludes the termination or rescission of the contract; it serves as a method of keeping the contract operative between the parties. As usual, the nonbreaching party later can recover damages for anything that constitutes less-than-complete performance. Thus, if only one of the bulldozers delivered to Miller is slightly defective or if Precision is only slightly late in making what otherwise is a satisfactory delivery, Miller, in order to receive Precision's performance under the rest of the contract, may choose to waive such breaches.

A waiver of breach ordinarily applies only to the matter waived and not inevitably to the rest of the contract. The same is true of subsequent breaches of the contract: The first waiver normally will not cover additional, later breaches, especially when the later breaches bear no relation to the first one. However, the waiving party may want to stand on his or her rights after the first waiver and indicate unambiguously that he or she will not tolerate future breaches. This action will eliminate the possibility of the breaching party's arguing that the waivers were so numerous and systematic that the breaching party believed less-than-complete performance was acceptable for the duration of the contract. Still, waiver remains a common business response in those circumstances in which the continuation of the contract will further the interests of the injured party. Exhibit 14.5 describes some of the duties and rights of the parties.

Rights and Obligations of the Injured Party

Right or Obligation	Definition	Example
Liquidated damage clause (Right to damages specified in the contract)	A provision in a contract that a stated sum of money or property will be paid, or forfeited if previously deposited, if one of the parties fails to perform in accordance with the contract; clause is enforceable by a court unless it is unreasonable.	Melinda and Trevor enter into a contract for Trevor to design a marketing campaign for Melinda. The campaign is to be completed by May 1. The contract provides that Trevor will pay Melinda $50 a day for each day he is late in delivering the marketing campaign.
Mitigation of damages (Duty to minimize damages)	The nonbreaching party's duty to reduce the actual losses, if he or she is able to do so. If the nonbreaching party fails to minimize losses, he or she cannot recover in court the losses that could have been avoided.	Rachel enters into a contract to work for Anthony's accounting firm for one year at a specified salary. Anthony cancels the contract. Rachel does not seek a replacement position. The court will not award Rachel the lost salary if the court concludes that she could have obtained a replacement position of the same type.
Mutual rescission (Right to terminate a contract without liability)	An agreement by the parties to cancel a contract and return the consideration they have already received.	Marisol sold her boat to Rashad. Rashad decides that he is unhappy with the purchase. Marisol agrees to permit Rashad to return the boat and to refund the money to him.
Waiver of breach (Promisor abandons or relinquishes a legal right)	A party's relinquishment, repudiation, or surrender of a right that he or she has to seek a remedy for breach of contract.	David rents an office in a building owned by Luis. The lease says that rent is due on the first of the month. Despite the terms of the lease, David regularly pays on the fourth of each month, and Luis does not object to the late payments. Luis cannot later demand the rent on the first or treat the payment as late if it is received after the first but before the fourth of the month.

REMEDIES UNDER THE UNIFORM COMPUTER INFORMATION TRANSACTIONS ACT (UCITA)

UCITA's rules regarding contract discharge, breach of contract, and remedies resemble those provided by the UCC. For example, § 601 requires a party's performance to conform to the contract. If the performance fails to do so, in the absence of a waiver, the aggrieved party has a right to a remedy. In turn, the nature and extent of the remedy hinges on whether the failure to perform is minor or material. In this regard, UCITA follows the common law in making distinctions between material and nonmaterial breaches. UCITA § 701 notes that whether a party has breached the contract is determined by the agreement, or in the absence of an agreement, by UCITA's terms. According to § 701, among other things, a material breach is "a substantial failure to perform a term that is an essential element of the agreement" and the circumstances indicate that "the breach is likely to cause substantial harm to the aggrieved party." Nevertheless, § 701 explicitly states that an aggrieved party is entitled to remedies even for nonmaterial breaches. However, as § 701 makes clear, the aggrieved party can cancel the contract only if the breach is material. UCITA § 702 permits waivers of breach. Like the UCC, UCITA recognizes the doctrine of commercial frustration (§ 615) and anticipatory repudiation (§ 709).

Likewise UCITA mirrors the UCC by providing for cumulative remedies, including equitable remedies (§ 801). Specific performance is addressed in § 911.

UCITA also sets out general rules for calculating damages (§ 807); a liquidated damages provision (§ 804); a complicated statute of limitations provision (§ 805); and rules for discontinuing a licensee's access to the software, subscription service, or database that is the subject of the contract (§ 814). Pursuant to § 815, upon the cancellation of the license, the licensor can prevent the continued use of the contractual and informational rights in the licensed information that the licensee possesses. This so-called electronic self-help provision is probably the most controversial aspect of UCITA. With the exception of mass-market transactions, UCITA allows a licensor to disable the software or computer program from a remote location if the licensor believes the licensee has breached the contract. Moreover, a licensor that avails itself of this "electronic self-help" method is not liable for any losses caused unless the self-help is wrongful. The procedural safeguards set out in § 816 afford some protections to the licensee; for example, the requirement that the licensee must have separately manifested its assent to a contract term authorizing the self-help; that the licensor must give 15-days advance notice; that the licensor must specify the nature of the claimed breach; and that the licensor must provide the licensee with information that will allow the licensee to communicate with the licensor about the claimed breach. Still, the licensor's use of electronic self-help could, for example, abruptly shut down a licensee's human resources system and wreak havoc. Such concerns presumably underlie the reluctance of some states to enact UCITA.

Contemporary Case

SIMEONE v. FIRST BANK NATIONAL ASSOCIATION

73 F.3d 184, 1996 U.S. App. LEXIS 31 (8th Cir. 1996)

[Note that the court treats incidental damages as a separate category under Minnesota law.]

FACTS Frederick Simeone sued First Bank National Association (First Bank) for breach of contract. The contract called for First Bank to sell Simeone 1920-1930 era vintage Mercedes-Benz automobiles and parts which had been repossessed from a defaulting loan customer, Leland Gohlike. The contract listed four different vehicles and thousands of loose parts, including some which were no longer manufactured and were extraordinarily rare. First Bank agreed to sell the repossessed automobiles and parts to Simeone for $450,000, and Simeone paid 10 percent of the contract price as a down payment. Gohlike, the debtor, instituted a civil action against First Bank and its officers, claiming a violation of due process and seeking $13,000,000 in damages. Gohlike then obtained a temporary restraining order (TRO) to prevent the sale of the collateral. First Bank refused Simeone's tender of the balance of the purchase price and later returned his down payment with interest.

On or before November 4, 1985, First Bank entered into negotiations with Gohlike and his neighbor, James Torseth, to sell the automobiles and parts to Torseth in exchange for a purchase price slightly in excess of Simeone's and Gohlike's dismissal of his suit against the bank. Believing that it no longer had an obligation to sell the property to Simeone because of a condition in the agreement, First Bank subsequently sold the cars and parts to SMB, Inc., a corporation Torseth created for this purpose. SMB, Inc. later sold all of the cars and parts for $1,114,960. Two experts at trial testified that, because of their rarity, by late 1987 or early 1988 the vehicles and parts were worth over $3 million dollars.

In prior litigation and appeals it was determined that First Bank had breached the contract by failing to convey the property to Simeone, and the jury awarded him damages.

ISSUE Is the award of compensatory and consequential damages correct? Did Simeone fail to properly mitigate his damages? Is Simeone entitled to incidental damages?

HOLDING Yes, the compensatory and consequential damage awards are proper. No, Simeone had no obligation to purchase all the cars and parts from SMB to mitigate his damages. No, Simeone has been compensated for these same losses as compensatory and consequential damages.

REASONING Excerpts from the opinion of Circuit Judge Ross:

... [T]he evidence showed that the vehicles were rare, and in some cases unique, classic automobiles of historic significance. The disassembled parts ... were scarce commodities. ... Based on the evidence presented at trial, the jury concluded that, at the time of the breach, the value of the property owned by First Bank was $885,000 and the value of the property owned by the Quante Estate was $150,000, or a total market value of $1,035,000. [Both were included in the sales contract with First Bank.] The difference between this fair market value and the $450,000 contract price is $585,000, the amount of compensatory damages awarded. . . . The evidence clearly supports the jury's determination and the award of compensatory damages is affirmed. . . .

Under Minnesota law, recoverable consequential damages include:

> Any loss resulting from general or particular requirements and needs of which the seller at the time of contracting had reason to know and which could not reasonably be prevented by cover or otherwise. . . .

Under this section, consequential damages . . . are only proper if the seller had reason to foresee the particular requirements of the buyer, and even then only if such loss could not be prevented. The focus is on what the seller had reason to know. . . . The question of whether the buyer's consequential damages were foreseeable by the seller is one of fact to be determined by the trier of fact. . . . Simeone testified he told First Bank's broker that he intended to use the cars and parts for trading or possible resale to obtain additional cars. . . . Simeone contracted to purchase hundreds of automotive parts that the jury would reasonably presume would have to be either resold or assembled into something of increased value. The jury's determination that it was foreseeable that Simeone would seek to further his collection by engaging in sale or trade was not clearly erroneous. . . .

"The test of proper cover is whether at the time and place the buyer acted in good faith and in a reasonable manner, and it is immaterial that hindsight may later prove that the method of cover used was not the cheapest or most effective." . . . The burden of proof rests with the seller to establish that the buyer acted unreasonably in failing to prevent his own loss. . . . [T]he duty to cover "does not require an injured party to take measures which are unreasonable or impractical or which require

expenditures disproportionate to the loss sought to be avoided or which are beyond his financial means." . . . First Bank . . . contends that Simeone's consequential damages should be limited because he could have mitigated his damages by purchasing the vehicles and parts from SMB, Inc. at the increased price. The jury . . . rejected this argument. . . . [I]t is unreasonable to require that Simeone expend over $1,000,000, almost $700,000 more than the contract obligated him to pay, to purchase the cars and parts in order to effect cover and mitigate his loss. . . . First Bank made no showing . . . that Simeone even had such resources . . . or that it would be reasonable to require such cover. It is noteworthy that Simeone did, in fact, undertake efforts to effect cover when he ultimately purchased the 1929 SS Roadster from SMB, Inc. The purchase price of the Roadster exceeded that which Simeone had initially contracted to pay for all of the vehicles and parts. The suggestion that Simeone should have purchased the entire lot of automobiles and parts as a matter of law is not supported by the evidence. . . .

Under Minnesota law, "the controlling principle governing actions for damages is that damages which are speculative, remote, or conjectural are not recoverable." . . . However, a plaintiff's losses need not be proven with mathematical precision. "Once the fact of loss has been shown, the difficulty of proving its amount will not preclude recovery so long as there is proof of a reasonable basis upon which to approximate the amount." . . . Here, two experts in antique and classic cars testified as to the value . . . at the time of the breach as well as their appreciated value two years after the breach. This testimony was based on the expert's knowledge of the available market, the rate at which such unique cars appreciate in value because of their scarcity and desirability . . . , as well as the prices commanded by comparable vehicles. This testimony provides a reasonable basis upon which to support the jury's determination of consequential damages. . . .

Under Minnesota law, incidental damages resulting from a seller's breach are defined as:

> Expenses reasonably incurred in inspection, receipt, transportation and care and custody of goods rightfully rejected, any commercially reasonable charges, expenses or commissions in connection with effecting cover and any other reasonable expense incident to the delay or other breach.

.... The jury's award of incidental damages in this case represents a double recovery to the extent that it compensates Simeone for the difference between the contract price and the price he actually paid for the Roadster. Simeone was compensated for the difference between the contract price and the purchase price through both the compensatory and consequential damages awards. Since there is no other evidence of incidental damages, the award of incidental damages must be reversed. ...

You Be the Judge

Basketball superstar Michael Jordan filed a lawsuit claiming Karla Knafel had attempted to extort additional money from him in exchange for her silence about their relationship a decade earlier. Jordan argued that, due to Knafel's threats to publicly expose their relationship, he agreed and paid her $250,000. However, he asserted, he never agreed to pay Knafel any additional amount—let alone the $5,000,000 she claims he had promised.

In her countersuit, Knafel alleged that she and Jordan first met at an Indianapolis hotel where she was working as a vocalist. After an NBA referee had introduced her to Jordan, they had numerous long-distance telephone conversations before and after Jordan's marriage on September 2, 1989. When Knafel asked Jordan why he still wanted to see her, he allegedly responded that his marriage to Mrs. Jordan was a "business arrangement," that he considered his wife "hired help," and that he had married Juanita so as to maintain a favorable public image. Knafel and Jordan began a sexual relationship in December 1989. According to Knafel, they always engaged in unprotected sex, apparently out of Jordan's wishes, even thought Knafel had voiced her concerns about this matter to Jordan.

When Knafel learned she was pregnant in 1991, she believed the child was Jordan's, and she indicated to him that it was his child. (Legally, Knafel does not concede that Jordan is not the father. Two separate paternity tests have been conducted, and both indicate that Jordan is not the father.) She did not tell Jordan about the pregnancy because the Chicago Bulls were en route to winning Jordan's and the team's first NBA championship. Eventually, Knafel told Jordan that she was pregnant with his child, and he insisted that she have an abortion. Because of her personal beliefs, she refused. According to Knafel, Jordan wanted this relationship to remain out of the public eye because damage to his public image would result in the loss of endorsements. In 1991, Jordan allegedly offered to pay Knafel $5,000,000 when he retired from professional basketball in exchange for her agreement not to file a paternity suit against him and for her agreement to keep their romantic involvement private. Knafel accepted Jordan's offer and, as consideration for his promising payment of $5,000,000 when he retired from professional basketball, she agreed not to file a paternity action against him and to keep their romantic relationship confidential. When Knafel's child was born in July 1991, Jordan paid certain hospital bills and medical costs for the birth and sent roses to her at the hospital. Jordan also paid Knafel the sum of $250,000 for the mental pain and anguish that had arisen from their relationship.

In October 1993, Jordan announced that he was retiring from the Bulls. In March 1995, Jordan announced his immediate return to the Chicago Bulls. Knafel did not personally contact Jordan to demand his payment of the $5,000,000. She allegedly continued to rely on his assurance that he would pay her. In the summer of 1998, public speculation arose that Jordan soon would retire again. Knafel decided to see Jordan in Las Vegas, Nevada, where he was vacationing. During the course of their conversation, Knafel allegedly reminded Jordan of his obligation to pay her the money. He allegedly reaffirmed his 1991 agreement to pay her the $5,000,000 and said that he would have his Chicago lawyer contact her to arrange for payment. Jordan again retired from playing professional basketball.

When Jordan sued Knafel, she counterclaimed that Jordan's failure to pay her constituted a breach of their 1991 contract and his 1998 reaffirmation of it, causing her damages in the amount of $5,000,000 plus interest. Jordan claimed that any alleged agreement for $5,000,000 would be unenforceable because: (1) extortion agreements violate public policy; (2) there would be no consideration to support any such agreement due to Knafel's existing obligation to refrain from publicly exposing the relationship; (3) any such oral agreement would violate the Statute of Frauds; and (4) any such agreement would be barred by the applicable statute of limitations. Jordan also argues that any such agreement would be based on fraud because of Knafel's representations that he was the father and/or mutual mistake of fact about the paternity of the child. If *you* were the judge, how would *you* decide this dispute? [See *Jordan v. Knafel*, 378 Ill. App. 3d 219, 2007 Ill. App. LEXIS 1283 (Ill. App. Ct. 1st Dist. Div. 3, 2007), *Jordan v. Knafel*, 355 Ill. App. 3d 534, 2005 Ill. App. LEXIS 73 (Ill. App. Ct. 1st Dist. Div. 4, 2005), and Pleadings filed on October 14, 2002, and November 14, 2002, by Michael Jordan and Karla Knafel, respectively, in the Circuit Court of Cook County, Illinois; similar information is at http://www.thesmokinggum.com/archive/jordanextort1.html and http://www.thesmokinggum.com/archive/karlarespl.html (accessed 12/21/2002).]

Summary

Discharge of a contract refers to the legally valid termination of a contractual duty. Performance may be either complete or substantial. Both degrees of performance ordinarily discharge the contract. The parties themselves may agree to discharge the contract. Release, rescission, accord and satisfaction, and novation are examples of this method of discharging contracts. Bankruptcy decrees, the running of statutes of limitations, and intentional unauthorized material alterations of the contract will justify discharge of a contract by operation of law. Courts conclude that destruction of the subject matter, intervening illegality, or conduct by one party that makes performance by the other party objectively impossible excuse the resultant nonperformance. The doctrine of commercial frustration arose to mitigate the harshness of the common law's rejection of impossibility as a defense to nonperformance. Actual or anticipatory breach also may bring about discharge of the contract. Constructive conditions, the nonoccurrence of express conditions precedent, and the occurrence of express conditions subsequent also may discharge a contract.

Monetary damages are remedies "at law." Usually a party sues for compensatory damages, or the amount of money that will place the party in the same economic position that he or she would have enjoyed had the contract been performed. Courts may grant consequential, or special, damages if the facts warrant. The injured party has a duty to mitigate damages. Courts impose this duty in the interest of fairness. Courts impose punitive damages to punish the wrongdoer and to deter future malicious conduct. If the party sustains no actual damages, a court may award nominal damages. The parties may agree in advance on the sum of money to be paid for certain types of breaches. Such liquidated damages clauses are enforceable unless a court construes them as penalties.

When monetary damages are unavailable, indeterminable, or inadequate, courts may award equitable remedies. Rescission and restitution involve the termination of the contract through the restoration of the parties to the status quo. Monetary damages and restitution are mutually exclusive remedies. Specific performance is an equitable remedy that compels the breaching party to perform according to the terms of the agreement. Courts usually grant specific performance when the subject matter of the contract is unique: They are reluctant to grant specific performance in suits involving nonunique goods or personal services contracts. Quasi contract, reformation, and injunctions represent other types of equitable relief.

The injured party may choose to waive the breach in order to continue the contract. Waiver of breach, or the injured party's giving up the right to receive the performance set out in the contract, does not preclude the injured party's seeking recovery for damages resulting from the breach.

Discussion Questions

1. What is a complete, or material, breach of contract? What are the injured party's options when a complete breach occurs?

2. Explain the doctrine of impossibility and the doctrine of commercial frustration as they relate to contract discharge.

3. Define the duty of mitigation.

4. Under what circumstances is specific performance an appropriate remedy?

5. What are the legal consequences of waiving a breach of contract?

Case Problems and Writing Assignments

1. Katherine Lane enrolled her 18-month-old daughter in day care with Kindercare Learning Centers, Inc. On December 9, 1992, Lane dropped off her daughter at Kindercare's facility. Lane filled out an authorization form granting Kindercare's employees permission to administer prescription medication to her daughter that day. Just after 5:00 P.M., one of the employees placed the child, who had fallen asleep, in a crib in the infant room. At approximately 6:00 P.M., the employees, apparently unaware that Lane's daughter was still sleeping in the crib, locked the doors of the facility and went home for the evening. Shortly thereafter, Lane returned to the facility to get her daughter and found the facility locked and unlit. A police officer who responded to Lane's 911 call looked through a window of the facility and saw the child sleeping in the crib. Another officer broke a window and retrieved the child. The child was upset by the incident but was not physically harmed. When Lane went into the facility to retrieve her daughter's belongings, she apparently found the medication authorization form and observed that it had not been initialed to indicate that an employee had given the medication to the child. As a result of the incident, Lane alleged that she had suffered emotional distress. Michigan law allowed the recovery of emotional damages for breach of contracts of a personal nature but not for breaches involving commercial contracts. Should Lane prevail on her claim in this case? [See *Lane v. Kindercare Learning Centers, Inc.*, 588 N.W. 2d 715 (Mich. App. 1998).]

2. Franconia Associates and other property owners participated in a federal program that promoted the development of affordable rental housing in areas conventional lenders traditionally did not serve. Pursuant to this program, the owners, in exchange for low-interest mortgage loans issued by the Farmers Home Administration (FmHA), agreed to devote the owners' properties to low- and middle-income housing and to abide by related restrictions during the life of the loans. The owners' promissory notes included provisions concerning prepayment of the program loans. However, the Emergency Low Income Housing Preservation Act of 1987 (ELIHPA), as amended, placed permanent restrictions on the prepayment of such loans. Franconia and the other owners, filing suit under the Tucker Act, claimed that ELIHPA abridged the absolute prepayment right set forth in their promissory notes and thereby effected a repudiation of their contracts. In dismissing these contract claims as untimely under § 2501 of the Tucker Act—which provides that a claim "shall be barred unless the petition thereon is filed within six years after such claim first accrues"—the Court of Federal Claims concluded that the claims first accrued on the ELIHPA regulations' effective date. The Federal Circuit ruled that, if the government's continuing duty to allow the owners to prepay their loans was breached, the breach occurred immediately on ELIHPA's enactment date, over nine years before the owners had filed their suit. In holding that the statute of limitations would bar the owners' claims, the court also rejected the owners' argument that ELIHPA's passage qualified as a repudiation, so that their suit would be timely if filed within six years of either the date performance fell due (the date they rendered prepayment) or the date on which they elected to treat the repudiation as a present breach. Should the Supreme Court affirm the Federal Circuit's decision? [See *Franconia Associates v. United States*, 536 U.S. 129 (2002).]

3. Warren Kobatake and other nursery owners whose plants were allegedly damaged by Benlate 50DF, a fungicide manufactured by E.I. Dupont de Nemours and Company, settled a product liability case with Dupont. Pursuant to the terms of the settlement agreements, the plaintiffs executed general releases in which they released and discharged Dupont from any and all liabilities relating to the fungicide. The parties also promised that the releases represented the parties' complete agreement. Some time afterward, the plaintiffs discovered information that led them to believe that Dupont had acted improperly and fraudulently during its defense of the previous litigation by, among other things, scheming to destroy harmful evidence and presenting perjured testimony. Two years after unearthing these facts, the plaintiffs sought to rescind the settlement agreements on the basis of fraud in the inducement. How should the court rule in this case? What factors would the court consider? Why would a large, well-known firm like DuPont put its reputation on the line and engage in the questionable behavior alleged here? Would a code of ethics have helped to prevent these improprieties? [See *Kobatake v. E.I. DuPont de Nemours and Company*, 162 F.3d 619 (11th Cir. 1998).]

Notes

1. The Court Reporter wrote the facts as was typical for English Appellate cases during this time period.
2. The substantial performance doctrine is also called the substantial-compliance rule.
3. A *force majeure* clause is a contract clause that excuses performance and discharges the contract upon the occurrence of certain external events beyond the control of the parties. These clauses are normally restricted to natural occurrences such as flood or earthquake, but may include other specified events that were not expected to occur, but are designated by the parties as excusing performance if they do occur.
4. 156 Eng. Rep. 145 (Ex. 1854).
5. Leasees and licensees of software can also obtain cover.
6. 499 U.S. 1 (1991).
7. There was conflicting evidence before the Court, but it appeared that punitive damages of $840,000 were awarded by the jury. The conflict is due to the wording of the award.
8. 517 U.S. 559 (1996).
9. 532 U.S. 424 (2001).

Part III

Sales and Leases

The early common law of contracts was inappropriate—if not inadequate—for a commercial society. The common law was developed in an agrarian society, and it reflected the relative importance of land and a corresponding lack of importance for commercial transactions, especially the sale of goods. Over time, however, commercial transactions became increasingly important, and the law became less relevant to the realities of the society. As a result, during the late Middle Ages, merchants developed their own set of rules and regulations, the law merchant, as a means for regulating commercial transactions. Eventually, in the sixteenth century, the law merchant was absorbed into the common law, providing "official" recognition of the growing importance of commercial transactions to the society. The sociological and technological advances of the twentieth century made the law merchant as outmoded for this era as the original common law had been for the Industrial Revolution. Once again, new rules were developed and codified, first in such statutes as the Uniform Sales Act (USA) and the Uniform Negotiable Instruments Law (NIL), and then later in the Uniform Commercial Code (UCC). The UCC covers multiple areas of commercial law, including provisions dealing with the sale of goods (Article 2) and the leasing of goods (Article 2A).

The UCC provides coverage for sales and leases within the United States, but it does not provide coverage for international transactions. Firms involved in international trade also need to be aware of their rights and obligations, but contracts between firms in different nations make such awareness difficult. One potential solution to this problem can be found in the United Nations Convention on Contracts for the International Sale of Goods, the CISG.

The next four chapters discuss how contracts involving the sale or lease of goods are formed; the rules that govern performance, title, and risk of loss; how warranties and liabilities operate in these transactions; what remedies are available for a breach in a sales contract; and how international laws may affect the sales of goods outside the borders of the United States.

[NOTE: The NCCUSL was at one point working on Article 2B, which was intended to apply to the sale and licensing of computer software, but that project failed when the ALI withdrew its support. Subsequently, the Uniform Computer Information Transaction Act (UCITA) was prepared and disseminated to the states as a complement to the UCC. As proposed, UCITA will govern all contracts for the development, sale, licensing, support and maintenance of computer software and for many other contracts involving information.[1] To date, only two states have adopted UCITA. The importance of the coverage of information technology, including software, cannot be overstated, and this is a topic that needs to be closely monitored by all businesses and business people. It also, not coincidentally, applies to our thread case involving Ani, Meg, Yousef, and eClass.]

15

Formation of the Sales Contract: Contracts for Leasing Goods

Agenda

eClass will be considered a merchant in the sale of its software in the United States. What does it mean to be considered a "merchant" in the sale of goods? Does merchant status carry any special benefits or burdens that non-merchants do not possess? Why should it matter if eClass is considered a merchant?

The firm expects to be selling its products to a significant number of purchasers. Some of these purchasers will also be merchants, and some will be consumers. Should the firm negotiate each contract separately, entered into the traditional "give and take" of the marketplace, or would the business be better served by using a standard form contract, basically treating each sale as being virtually the same as every other sale? Does the status of the purchaser have any impact on this decision?

If things go as hoped, eClass will also be making sales to some foreign customers and may have to order some of its diskettes from foreign suppliers. Will Article 2 of the UCC still govern these transactions, or will some other law control these international contracts?

These and other questions need to be addressed in covering the material in this chapter. Be prepared! You never know when the firm or one of its members will seek your advice.

Classic Case

MILLER v. NEWSWEEK, INC.
660 F. Supp. 852, 1987 U.S. Dist. LEXIS 4338 (Del. 1987)

FACTS In August 1982, Daniel Miller, a commercial photographer, was asked by the *New York Times* to photograph Irving Shapiro, former chairman of the board of DuPont, as he embarked on a new career as a corporate attorney. Miller accepted the *Times* assignment and shot 72 photos of Shapiro in his new office. The *Times* used one of the photos in its story on Shapiro, but all 72 photos remained the property of Miller. Some time later, *Newsweek* decided to do a story on Shapiro and wanted some pictures to accompany its article. F. Joseph Dwyer, *Newsweek*'s photo researcher, contacted Miller and asked Miller to send all of his Shapiro photos to *Newsweek* so its photo editors could have the "luxury of editing" the pictures themselves. The parties reached an agreement that *Newsweek* would pay Miller the "space rate" for any pictures used in connection with the article, and *Newsweek* sent a courier to pick the negatives up at Miller's home.

Miller claims that he included a document known as a Delivery Memo along with the negatives and that this Delivery Memo provided the terms for the contract between Miller and *Newsweek*. However, there is no evidence that anyone at *Newsweek* ever read, signed, or agreed to the terms included in the memo.

Newsweek never ran the Shapiro article, so it did not use any of the photographs Miller had taken. Unfortunately, the 72 negatives were never returned to Miller. *Newsweek* admits that it cannot find the negatives, and they are presumed to be lost. As a result, Miller sued *Newsweek*, seeking $108,000 in damages for the loss of the 72 photographic negatives he had sent to *Newsweek*. He is arguing that *Newsweek* breached its contract, embodied in the Delivery Memo, by not returning the negatives, and that *Newsweek* breached its duty as a bailee by losing the negatives. *Newsweek* denies that it has any liability under either claim.

ISSUES Did *Newsweek* breach the contract as set out in the Delivery Memo? Did *Newsweek* breach its duty as a bailee?

HOLDINGS No, as to the alleged breach of contract. Yes, to the bailee question.

REASONING Excerpts from the opinion of Latchum, Senior Judge:

"A preliminary dispute between the parties centers on the applicability of Article II of the Uniform Commercial Code ("UCC") to the transaction herein. Newsweek contends that if a contract does exist between the parties, it is a bailment contract, not a sales contract, and thus not within the scope of Article II ... Miller responds that Article II applies to "all transactions in goods," not just sale transactions, and is thus applicable to bailment contracts . . .

Miller offers the following interpretation of the parties' dealings in support of his position that the Delivery Memo constitutes a valid contract. Miller maintains that the first contact between the parties, the Dwyer telephone call, was an invitation by Newsweek for Miller to submit an offer. Miller's conduct in sending the Shapiro negatives, accompanied by the Delivery Memo, then constituted an offer to enter into a contract with the terms expressed in the Delivery Memo . . . Newsweek's conduct in accepting the negatives, without objecting to the terms of the Delivery Memo, . . . then . . . constituted an acceptance of the contract and its terms under Section 2-204 of the UCC. . . .

The Court has a totally different view of the legal significance of the parties' contacts. The uncontroverted evidence demonstrates that a valid and enforceable contract was formed during the initial telephone conversation between Miller and Dwyer. . . . The Court finds that this conversation manifested a clear and unambiguous intention on the part of both parties to enter into a binding agreement. Nothing more is required for a valid and enforceable contract to exist under Article II. . . .

A valid and enforceable contract having been formed on the telephone, the Delivery Memo constituted a written confirmation of an existing contract under section 2-207 of the UCC. Section 2-207 applies in situations . . . where an oral agreement has been reached and one or both of the parties send written confirmation of that agreement including additional terms not previously discussed. . . . The fact that the confirmation contains additional terms has no affect on the validity of the original acceptance. . . . As between merchants, the additional terms become part of the contract unless they materially alter it or the opposing party has previously objected to them or does so within a reasonable time. . . .

The Delivery Memo contains numerous terms not contained in the original oral contract. . . . However, Miller's contract claim is based on the liquidated damages and late penalty clauses of the Delivery Memo only. Thus the Court will limit its discussion of section 2-207 to those clauses.

Neither the text of section 2-207 nor its comments expressly define the phrase "materially alter." Even so, some courts have inferred one possible test from the comments. A term materially alters a contract if incorporation of that term would result in surprise or undue hardship to the party opposing the incorporation. . . .

Both the liquidated damages and late penalty clauses would result in surprise and undue hardship to Newsweek if incorporated into the oral contract. In forming the original agreement the parties never discussed any liquidated damages or late penalty provisions. . . . The parties never focused on the possibility that the film might be returned late or not at all. . . . To include these terms in the contract simply because they appeared in a unilateral proposal offered by Miller would surely result in a surprise to Newsweek, especially considering that Newsweek's employees never read the Delivery Memo . . . as was the common practice in the industry. . . .

In sum, the court finds that incorporation of the liquidated damages and late penalty clauses into the contract would materially alter the contract, and they must therefore be disregarded. . . .

Based on the above, the court concludes that the terms of the Delivery Memo are not enforceable against Newsweek and Miller's claim for liquidated damages and late penalties under those terms must fail. . . . [The issue dealing with breach by the bailee was resolved in favor of Miller, who ultimately recovered $16,250, plus interest, for the lost negatives.]

INTRODUCTION

The common law coverage of contracts provides a good framework for studying agreements between people. As society has progressed and developed in England and in the United States, however, some elements of the common law have become outdated. When this occurs, the law-making bodies often step in to try to resolve the problems presented by a changing society. One early result of this legislative intervention is the Statute of Frauds (the original statute was enacted by the English Parliament in 1677), which requires that certain types of contracts be in writing in order to be enforceable. Another—and more contemporary—example of legislative intervention to help the law keep pace with society is the Uniform Commercial Code (the first UCC was adopted in the United States in 1954). The UCC was developed by the National Conference of Commissioners on Uniform State Laws. It is designed to update and modernize the law of commerce in code form and to reflect modern commercial reality.

Under the early common law, contract law developed primarily to reflect the importance of land in the economy of England. The common law treatment of contracts involving the sale of land was quite extensive, whereas the treatment of contracts for the sale of goods was sparse. As a merchant class began to develop in England, the merchants realized that the common law did not adequately treat their contracts or their contractual concerns. As a result, the merchants developed their own law, the law merchant (lex mercatoria). Eventually, the law merchant was adopted by parliament as an official part of English law, giving official status to the merchants and their transactions under the law.

This same legal tradition was followed in the United States after its formation. Since the United States had been a part of England, and since the courts in existence were based on English law, it was natural for the United States to follow English laws initially. By the early twentieth century, the law merchant was still in effect, but it was substantially out of date. As a result, the Uniform Sales Act (USA) was enacted to update and modernize the law merchant in the United States. While the USA was significantly more modern than the law merchant, it, too, was quickly out of date.

The Uniform Commercial Code (UCC) was adopted in 1954 to reflect contemporary commercial practices. The UCC replaced the USA and the NIL (the Uniform Negotiable Instrument Law), among other areas. The Uniform Commercial Code is organized into sections, with each section covering a different aspect of commercial law. For example, the UCC replaced the USA with Article 2, which governs the sale of goods. Other sections of the Code include Article 2A, which deals with the leasing of goods (many modern transactions involve leasing goods rather than buying them); Article 3, which deals with negotiable instruments (checks, a form of negotiable instrument, are often used to pay for goods); Article 4, which deals with banks and customers; Article 4A, which deals with fund transfers; Article 5, which deals with letters of credit (a standard method of payment, especially when the parties are separated geographically); Article 7, which deals with documents of title (often used in sales of goods between merchants); and Article 9, which deals with secured transactions (goods are often used as collateral when goods are sold on credit).

The UCC has been adopted, in whole or in part, in all 50 states. (Louisiana, with its French heritage and its tradition of following the Napoleonic Code, has not adopted all

eClass 15.1 Management

WHAT TYPE OF LAW WILL MOST AFFECT eCLASS?

The firm's members have been discussing the various types of law that are likely to affect their business and trying to decide what type of law will be most important in governing their business. Meg is convinced that federal regulatory provisions and statutes will be most important, especially copyright law, Federal Communication Commission rules and regulations, and laws affecting computers and computing technology. Ani agrees that federal laws will have a large impact, but she believes that traditional common law principles, especially in the area of contract law, will be most important since the firm will generate its revenues from contracts with its customers. Yousef is of the opinion that, since eClass will be selling goods, the most important area of law will be Article 2 of the UCC, at least until the firm begins to make international sales. They have asked you for your opinion. What will you tell them?

BUSINESS CONSIDERATIONS   A new business, especially one in a high-tech industry, is likely to be subjected to numerous types of legal and administrative regulations. Is any one type of regulation more important than the others? Should a business try to deduce which areas of law or administrative regulation will most affect it before it begins doing business, or should the firm just seek compliance with *all* areas of the law which affect it?

ETHICAL CONSIDERATIONS   Should a business be more concerned with evading regulations, avoiding regulations, or complying with regulations? Explain your reasoning. What ethical issues are raised by efforts to evade regulation? By efforts to avoid regulation?

sections of the Code. In particular, Louisiana has not adopted Article 2 or Article 2A. South Carolina has not adopted Article 2A. All the other states have adopted both articles.) Thus, the coverage and the principles of the Code are applicable virtually nation-wide, even though the Code itself is state law. This uniformity allows widespread understanding of the rules and the reasonable expectations that the rules followed in one state are likely to be followed in other states as well.

The NCCUSL proposed a revision to Articles 2 and 2A in 2003. Despite the efforts of the commission, as of January 1, 2009, neither of these revised Articles has been adopted by any state.[2] Some of the proposed changes seem to be long overdue, and the recommendations for addressing electronic transactions, consumer contracts, and "battle of the forms" issues, among others, appear to be an improvement over the current coverage. This is an area that needs to be watched very closely, since any changes will have an immediate and widespread impact.

While the UCC has basically been adopted throughout the United States, it is not applicable internationally unless the parties to an international contract specify that the UCC will control, or unless the contract is entered into in the United States, with the parties agreeing to be governed by U.S. law while also "opting out" of the provisions of the United Nations Convention on Contracts for the International Sale of Goods (CISG). As international trade increases, the need for a uniform set of legal rules and guidelines will increase. The closest thing to a uniform set of international laws governing such trade that we have at present is the CISG. The CISG is similar in many respects to Article 2 of the UCC.

THE SCOPE OF ARTICLE 2

Article 2 of the UCC (Sales) deals with the *sale* of *goods*. This is a somewhat limited topic when compared to all the types of contracts that a party might enter. However, most of us will enter into more contracts for the sale of goods than any other types of contracts.

To understand the scope of Article 2, we need to know what is covered. Thus, we must begin by defining a "sale" and then by defining "goods." According to § 2-106(1) of the UCC, a *sale* is defined as the passing of title from the seller to the buyer for a price. This is the only definition of a sale in Article 2, but there are several related and similar terms that also need to be examined. For example, the words *contract* and *agreement*, when used in Article 2, refer to either the present or the future sale of goods. *Contract for sale* covers both a present sale and a contract to sell goods in the future. A *present sale* is a sale made at the time the contract is made. *Goods* are defined in § 2-105(1) of the Code. According to that section, goods mean "all things that are movable at the time they are identified to the contract." The Code lists several things that are specifically *included* as goods, such as specially manufactured items, the unborn young of animals, growing crops, and things attached to land, if they are to be separated from the land for their sale. The Code also specifically *excludes* some things, declaring them *not* to be goods. Examples are money when used as a payment for sale, investment securities, and things in action, such as rights under a contract yet to be performed. (Things in action are also sometimes referred to as choses in action.)

Sometimes, states will exempt certain transactions from sales law coverage because they want to protect a practice that the states see as good for society. For example, hospitals that provide blood, blood products, and human tissues provide a service that is deemed essential to society. By classifying such procedures as "services" rather than "sales," even though recipients pay for the blood or tissue provided, the legislatures of a significant number of states have opted to protect the hospitals. This means that the protections afforded by Article 2 do not apply to these transactions. Public policy considerations seemingly favor protecting the hospitals, thus furthering the general welfare of the community, over applying sales laws and protections, including warranty protections, to individuals who may suffer grievous loss due to receiving tainted or diseased blood or tissue.

Transactions under Article 2 must involve two persons. One is the buyer—the person who purchases, or agrees to purchase, the goods. The other person is the seller—the person who provides, or agrees to provide, the goods covered by the contract.

The law of sales is very broad. It covers every sale of goods, whether made by a seller who is a merchant or by one who is a non-merchant, and whether made to a buyer who is a merchant or to one who is a non-merchant. Regardless of the status of the parties, Article 2 controls the sale. However, the status of the parties will affect the duties and obligations of the parties involved in the sale; the key factor here is the status of the parties as merchants or non-merchants.

Merchants are held to a higher standard than non-merchants. A merchant is defined as a person who deals in the type of goods involved in the sale, *or* a person who claims to be (or is recognized as) an expert in the type of goods involved in the sale, *or* a person who employs an expert in the type of goods involved in the sale (§ 2-104). A person who is represented by an agent or a broker or any other intermediary who, by his occupation, holds himself out as an expert is deemed to be a merchant. Any other person is viewed as a non-merchant.

A merchant is required by the terms of the Code to act in good faith, to cooperate with the other party in the performance of the contract, and to act in a commercially reasonable manner in the performance of the contract. For a merchant, acting in good faith means "honesty in fact and the observance of reasonable commercial standards of fair dealings in trade."[3] A merchant is also required to act in a commercially reasonable manner, which means not only that the conduct must comply with the normal fair dealings and practices of the trade (good faith), but also that it rests on normal business practices which should be typical of and familiar to any person in business. A non-merchant is required to act in good faith and to cooperate with the other party in the performance of the contract. (The good faith of a non-merchant only requires "honesty in fact in the conduct or transaction involved."[4]) However, a non-merchant is not required to act in a commercially reasonable manner. Thus, as previously stated, a merchant is held to a higher standard of conduct than is expected of a non-merchant. Further, merchants are presumed to give an implied warranty of merchantability in their contracts, whereas a non-merchant does not give such an implied warranty. Obviously, the status of a party as a merchant or as a non-merchant is an important consideration in determining rights and duties under the sales contract.

FORMING THE SALES CONTRACT

A contract for the sale of goods under Article 2 is formed in basically the same manner as a contract that is formed under the rules of common law. However, a sales contract can be formed with much less formality or rigidity than is required by common law. For example:

- The common law requires an exact agreement, a "mirror image" between the offer and the acceptance; the Code recognizes that a contract can be made in any manner sufficient to show agreement. Under Article 2, a contract exists whenever the parties *act* as if they have an agreement.

- The common law requires that the acceptance has to comply exactly with all the terms of the offer. Any variation is treated as a counteroffer (an attempt to vary the terms of the original offer) rather than as an acceptance; the Code allows acceptance in any manner and by any medium that is reasonable under the circumstances.

- The common law seemingly imposed barriers and rigid rules for forming a contract in order to make contract cases difficult to establish. In an effort to reflect commercial reality, the Code will sometimes recognize a contract that would not be considered binding under the common law. For example:
  - In § 2-204(2), the Code recognizes that a contract exists even though the time of the agreement is uncertain.
  - In § 2-204(3), the Code permits a contract to stand even though some other terms (such as price or quantity) are omitted from the agreement. Under the common law, the omission of any of these terms would negate the existence of a contract. The courts would rule that the attempt to form a contract failed due to the "indefiniteness of the terms."
  - Under the UCC, if the parties intend to have a contract and if remedies can be found in case there is a breach, the mere lack of some terms is often deemed unimportant. A contract will be found to exist, and the missing terms will be supplied under other provisions of the Code.

As in the common law, a contract for the sale of goods needs both an offer and an acceptance. These technical requirements are covered by UCC § 2-206, which states that, unless an offer obviously requires otherwise, it can be accepted in any manner reasonable under the circumstances. Suppose the seller received an offer that included the following clause: "Acceptance must be made by sending a white pigeon carrying your note of acceptance tied to its left leg." Under the common law, a seller could accept this offer only by tying a note to the left leg of a white pigeon. If the message was tied to the right leg or if the pigeon was gray, the seller would be deemed to have made a counteroffer. Under the Code, the seller can accept by complying exactly with the terms of the offer (tying a message to the left leg of a white pigeon), by nearly complying (tying a message to either leg of a pigeon, or using a gray pigeon rather than a white one), or by using any other method of accepting that is reasonable under the circumstances. Under some circumstances, the Code even permits the acceptance of an offer by performing rather than by communicating or by communicating rather than performing, depending upon the terms of the offer and the conduct of the offeree.

For example, an offer to buy goods may call for the offeree to show acceptance of the offer by prompt shipment of the goods. Under the common law, the seller could accept this offer *only* by making a prompt shipment of the goods. However, under the UCC, the seller can accept this offer, thus creating a contract, in any of the following ways:

1. The seller can promptly ship conforming goods to the buyer.
2. The seller can promptly ship nonconforming goods to the buyer.
3. The seller can notify the buyer that the goods will be shipped promptly.

Thus, the UCC permits acceptance in at least three different ways, while the common law only permitted acceptance in one exact manner. Notice that in the second method of acceptance under the UCC, the seller would not only have accepted the offer but would also (possibly) have breached the contract that was entered into by shipment-as-acceptance. The seller shipped the goods, thus accepting; and the seller shipped nonconforming goods, thus breaching the contract. However, according to § 2-206(1)(b), a seller who receives an order or other offer, with the offer calling for acceptance by prompt shipment, may ship nonconforming goods as an *accommodation* to the buyer, and the shipment will not be treated as an acceptance of the offer. In order to qualify as an accommodation shipment, however, the seller must seasonably notify the buyer that nonconforming goods have been shipped and that the buyer has the option of accepting these (counteroffered) goods or rejecting them and returning them to the seller at the seller's expense. If the seller fails to give the required seasonable notification, the buyer may treat the goods shipped as an acceptance of the offer—and as a breach of the contract.

The seller who accepts an offer by means of a prompt or current shipment must be careful for another reason. Assume the seller accepts by promptly shipping the goods but does not notify the buyer that the goods have been shipped. If the buyer neither receives the goods nor hears from the seller within a reasonable time, the buyer may treat the offer as lapsed before acceptance. When this happens, the buyer has no duty to pay for the goods when they finally arrive (if they finally arrive). This could leave the seller with unsold goods at some distant point, no ready buyer for the goods, and no contract remedies available since there was no contract due to lapse, and thus no breach by the buyer.

Exhibit 15.1 illustrates some of the differences between the common law of contracts and the provisions of Article 2 of the UCC.

Standard Form Contracts

Very often, both parties to the contract are merchants, and they are transacting business over a substantial distance. When this situation occurs, it is common to have the offer made on a standard form prepared by the offeror and the acceptance made on another standard form, this one prepared by the offeree who is trying to accept the offer. (A standard form is a preprinted contract form, often with blanks left in certain key places for later completion as the final contract terms are agreed to by the parties.) Under common law principles, using two different forms with two different sets of terms would mean that there was no "meeting of the minds," no true agreement, and thus no contract was formed. However, the Code recognizes that businesses often use standard forms and that these standard forms frequently differ. To reflect "commercial reality," the Code makes allowance for these differences, recognizing the existence of a contract when such forms are exchanged. Under § 2-207(1), an acceptance that is made within a reasonable time is effective, even if it includes terms that add to or differ from the terms of the original offer. The only exception is when the acceptance is expressly made subject to an agreement with the new or different terms.

Exhibit 15.1

Comparing the common law of contracts with Article 2 of the UCC

Common Law	Article 2
Requires offer + acceptance + consideration to have a contract.	Requires offer + acceptance + consideration to have a contract.
Requires a "mirror image" agreement. The offer and the acceptance must "mirror" one another in every aspect.	Does not require a "mirror image." Article 2 allows acceptance in "any reasonable manner."
Any variation in an attempted acceptance is viewed as a counteroffer, terminating the original offer and reversing the roles of the parties (offeror and offeree).	A variation from the terms of the offer in the attempted acceptance is not treated as a counteroffer unless the variation materially alters the terms of the attempted contract. Again, acceptance in "any reasonable manner" creates an agreement.
All material terms must be agreed upon to create a contract.	Some terms may be omitted—left open—without affecting the formation of the contract. For example, the time of delivery, the place of delivery, the method of payment, even the quantity of goods covered by the contract can be left open for later completion.
Does not allow output contracts or requirement contracts, since each is viewed as too vague to form a binding contract.	Both output contracts and requirement contracts are permitted.
Generally requires "perfect tender" in order to show performance of the contract. The seller must deliver exactly what was ordered in exactly the manner called for in order to show performance.	Allows variations in performance and does not require "perfect tender." The seller may even deliver nonconforming goods *as an accommodation* without being in breach.

Even if the purported acceptance includes new or different terms, the Code provides a solution. The new terms are treated as proposed additions to the contract. If the contract is between merchants, the new terms become a part of the contract unless one of the following conditions exists:

1. The offer explicitly limits acceptance to the terms of the offer.
2. The new terms materially alter the contract.
3. The offeror objects to the new terms within a reasonable time.

Exhibit 15.2

A "Conflict of Form" Resolution

If the *offer* includes a Term or Clause	If the *acceptance* includes an *Additional* Term or Clause
And the acceptance includes the same proposed term or clause, the term or clause will become part of the contract.	*And* the offeror does not object to the additional term with a seasonable time, the proposed additional term or clause will become part of the contract, *unless* the proposed additional term materially alters the rights or duties of the parties in performing the contract.
And the acceptance is silent as to the the term or clause, the term or clause will become part of the contract.	
And the acceptance includes the opposite of the term or clause, the two conflicting terms cancel one another and the term or clause is not mentioned—positively or negatively—in the contract.	*But* the offeror *does* seasonably object to the inclusion of the term or clause, the proposed clause will *not* become part of the contract.

If the contract is not between merchants, the courts will not normally uphold the new terms unless it can be shown that both parties accepted them. If the offeree proposes different terms, § 2-207(3) controls. This section states that when the parties act as if they have a contract, they have a contract. And if they have writings, the writings will be construed consistently, so that an agreement exists. The written contract will consist of the terms on which the parties agree, as well as the terms included by one party without any objection by the other party. But it will not include any terms that contradict other terms, or that have been objected to by one of the parties, or that materially alter the basic agreement. Exhibit 15.2 shows how a "conflict of forms" problem would be resolved.

[NOTE: The proposed 2003 revisions for Article 2 greatly simplify the language for addressing "battle of the forms" issues. Under this proposal, terms that the records[5] of the parties agree on and which are intended as the final expression of their agreement are included and may not be contradicted by evidence of any prior agreement or contemporaneous oral agreement, but may be supplemented by consistent additional terms. (§ 2-202) According to the proposed revisions to § 2-207, if conduct by both

eClass 15.2 Sales

STANDARD FORM SALES CONTRACTS

eClass will be making most of its sales of its software to consumers rather than to merchants. Ani thinks they should use a standard order form for all of the sales to consumers, and that they should word the form in a manner that provides contract protection to eClass. She also suggests that the firm may want to draft a more complex standard form contract for sale of the software when the buyer is a merchant. Yousef agrees that a standard order form for consumer purchases is a good idea, especially if it is included in the "shrink-wrap" of the package to ensure that consumer buyers always have to read and agree to the terms in order to access the diskette to install the program. However, he would prefer to have the firm negotiate its contracts individually in sales to merchants, thus allowing the firm to bargain based on the relative size of the order and the importance of the individual customer. They have asked you for your opinion. What will you tell them?

BUSINESS CONSIDERATIONS   Is the standard order form eClass is considering a "standard form contract"? Why might a business want to use a standard form for sales to individuals who are not merchants, but not to merchant buyers? What are the advantages to using a standard form contract?

ETHICAL CONSIDERATIONS   If a business uses a standard form contract, should that standard form include "fine print" clauses that are advantageous to the firm, or should it avoid using such language? Why? What ethical issues are raised by including contract terms on the shrink-wrap of a product such as software?

parties recognizes the existence of a contract although their records do not otherwise recognize a contract, the terms of the contract will be:

    a. Terms that appear in the records of both parties;
    b. Terms, whether in a record or not, to which both parties agree; and
    c. Terms supplied or incorporated under any provisions of this Act (Article 2).]

Firm Offers

Another area that gets special treatment for merchants under the Code is that of firm offers. Under common law, an offer could be freely revoked by the offeror at any time before its acceptance. This right to revoke existed even though the offeror might have "promised" to keep the offer open for some specified time period. (If the offeree wanted a guarantee that the offer would remain open, the offeree had to enter into an option contract, giving consideration to the offeror for the benefit of having a guaranteed time period to decide.) Such a situation makes it very difficult for the offeree to make detailed plans based on the offer.

The Code recognizes that the offeree may have to make plans and explore options before accepting an offer, but may still need to be able to rely on the offer being available if and when the decision to accept is reached. The offeree may be harmed if an offer that is supposed to be "open" is revoked. To eliminate this potential problem, the Code guarantees that *firm offers* cannot be freely revoked before acceptance. Firm offers are only given by merchants. If a merchant promises in writing to keep an offer open and unmodified for some specified time and signs the writing, a firm offer exists. The offer cannot be revoked by the offeror during the time the offeror agreed to keep the offer open. And if no time was specified, the offer cannot be revoked for a "reasonable time." To place some limit on this, the "reasonable time" cannot exceed three months.

Statute of Frauds

So far, the discussion has focused on the intent to have a contract and the Code's recognition that a contract exists in such a situation. However, some technical rules still exist that will override intent. One of these involves the Statute of Frauds, which requires that a contract for the sale of goods for $500 or more must be evidenced by a writing in order for it to be enforceable. According to § 2-201of the Code,[6]

> "a contract for the sale of goods for the price of $500 or more is not enforceable by way of action or defense unless there is some writing sufficient to indicate that a contract for sale has been made between the parties and signed by the party against whom enforcement is sought or by his authorized agent or broker. A writing is not insufficient because it omits or incorrectly states a term agreed upon but the contract is not enforceable under this paragraph beyond the quantity of goods shown in such writing."

[NOTE: The proposed revision to Article 2 increases the amount to $5,000 or more. We will treat the topic here as if the 2003 revision to Article 2 has not been adopted, but it would be a good idea to check your state statute to see which rule applies to your contracts—or, better yet, put all your contracts in writing to be on the safe side.]

The Official Comments state that there are only three definite and invariable requirements for the writing:

1. The writing must evidence a contract for the sale of goods;
2. The writing must be "signed," which includes any authentication; and,
3. It must specify a quantity of goods covered by the contract.

An oral agreement that falls within the coverage of the Statute of Frauds is normally unenforceable. However, the Code attempts to recognize modern commercial

eClass 15.3 MANAGEMENT

HOW SHOULD eCLASS COMMUNICATE WITH ITS CUSTOMERS?

A local retail teaching supply store sent a letter to eClass requesting a discounted price for the firm's software since the store sells mainly to teachers. This retailer wanted an idea of how much of a discount he might be able to get, especially if he guaranteed a specified number of copies of the product sold every year. Meg thinks eClass should reply by e-mail, citing its ease and its speed. She believes that if the firm can accustom its clientele to using e-mail, the firm can save a significant amount of money in postage, increase the speed of communications, and be more efficient. Yousef would prefer to reply to the customers in the manner the customers use to initiate contact. He thinks that this will allow the firm to operate in the "comfort zone" of the customer, with long-term benefits since the customers will communicate in the manner to which they are accustomed. Ani agrees with Meg, but she is concerned that e-mail communications, while much quicker, may have negative legal implications. They have asked you to provide some guidance in this area. What will you tell them?

BUSINESS CONSIDERATIONS   Communications with customers or potential customers may well have legal implications. Should a business have a policy concerning communications? Should the policy, if one exists, be for all communications, or should it depend on the status of the other party?

ETHICAL CONSIDERATIONS   Is it ethical for a business to communicate with a customer in a manner that is not normal for that customer, thus potentially putting the customer at a disadvantage? Should a business impose its standards on a customer just because the business is more comfortable using those standards, whether in communications or in some other area?

practices in this area as well. If the parties have any writing (a note, a memorandum, or "other writing") signed by the party being sued, that writing is sufficient to satisfy the statute. (This is the common law rule.) Terms that are omitted or incorrectly stated in the writing will not defeat the proof of the contract's existence. When both parties are merchants, however, a slightly different rule applies. Suppose one merchant sends a written confirmation that would be binding on the sender. Under common law rules, the sender would be bound by the writing, but the other party would not be since he or she did not sign it. Under the UCC, the other merchant will also be bound by this written confirmation unless he or she objects to its contents in writing within ten days after receiving it. This rule forces merchants to read their forms and to cooperate with other merchants.

An interesting evolution to the Statute of Frauds requirements has taken place recently. New statutory coverage recognizes the possibility that electronic communications can satisfy the writing requirement, and thus can satisfy the Statute of Frauds. Under the Electronic Signatures in Global and National Commerce Act (E-SIGN),[7] an "authenticated" electronic communication will suffice as a writing if the transaction affects interstate or foreign commerce. Further, the Uniform Electronic Transactions Act (UETA)[8] recognizes "authenticated" electronic communications for intrastate transactions. Thus, electronic communications such as e-mails or faxes will meet the requirement of a "writing" for Statute of Fraud purposes under Article 2 in most intrastate transactions and in all interstate transactions, with the expectation that the UETA will eventually be adopted by virtually all of the states.

Finally, § 2-201(3) of the Code lists three exceptions to the general provisions of the Statute of Frauds:

1. No writing is needed when the goods are to be specially manufactured for the buyer and are of such a nature that they cannot be resold by the seller in the ordinary course of his or her business, and when the seller has made a substantial start in performing the contract.
2. No writing is needed if the party being sued admits in court or in the legal proceedings that the contract existed.
3. No writing is needed for any portion of the goods already delivered and accepted or already paid for.

When the parties have a written agreement, the parol evidence rule applies; that is, the writing is meant to be the final agreement, and the writing cannot be *contradicted* by any oral agreements made at the same time as, or before, the written document. If the writing is intended as a *total integration* of the agreement, the writing is viewed as the entire contract. No additional terms can be introduced. However, even with a total integration the writing can be *explained* or *supplemented* by additional evidence, including parol (oral) evidence. For example, either party may show that course of dealings, usage of trade, or course of performance gives special meaning to certain terms contained in the writing. If the writing is only deemed to be a partial integration of the contract, evidence can be introduced to show additional terms that are also a part of the contract, even if those terms are not included in the writing. Either party may introduce evidence of additional consistent terms to fill out any apparent gaps in the written agreement.

Course of dealings refers to any prior conduct or contracts between the parties. Prior conduct between the parties sets up a pattern that either party may reasonably expect will be followed in the present setting. *Course of performance* involves repeated performances between the parties in their present contract. If neither party objects to the performance, it is considered appropriate to continue such performance. *Usage of trade* refers to a widely recognized and accepted industry practice. When usage of trade is proven, it is expected to be followed by the parties.

In interpreting a contract, the court will first look to the express language used by the parties. Whenever possible, the court will read the express language of the agreement and then consider the course of performance, any course of dealings, and any usages of trade in a consistent manner. If a consistent interpretation is not possible,

Exhibit 15.3

Bill of Sale

BILL OF SALE

Vehicle License No. or
Vessel CF No.

_____

Vehicle or Hull Identification No.	Make	Body Type	Model	Year

_____

For Motorcycle Only:
Engine No.

_____

For the sum of _____Dollars

($_____) and/or other valuable consideration in the amount of $_____,

the receipt of which is hereby acknowledged, I/We did sell, transfer and deliver to

_____
(BUYER)

_____
(ADDRESS)

On the _____ day of _____ 20_____ my/our right, title and

Interest in and to the above described vehicle or vessel.

I/WE certify under penalty of perjury that: (1) I/WE are the lawful owner(s) of the Vehicle/vessel and (2) I/WE have the right to sell it, and (3) I/WE guarantee and will Defend the title of said vehicle/vessel against the claims and demands of any and all Persons arising prior to this date and (4) the vehicle/vessel is free of all liens and Encumbrances.

Signature of Seller _____ Date _____

Address of Seller _____

_____

however, express terms control any other interpretation. Course of performance controls either course of dealings or usage of trade, and course of dealings controls usage of trade.

Course of dealings and course of performance are normally based on current or prior conduct of the parties with one another. As such, both standards are, or have been, practiced by the parties, and they are readily apparent to both parties and are difficult for either party to deny. Some trade usage patterns are less obvious, especially since the usage of trade may be applicable to situations in which one (or even both) of the parties are not merchants. For example, in California it is a standard usage of trade to use a formal bill of sale to transfer an automobile, truck, or boat by contract (see Exhibit 15.3). It is generally the obligation of the parties to acquaint themselves with the usages of trade that apply and to comply with them if necessary.

[NOTE: The proposed revision to Article 2 found in § 2-201(1) would increase the threshold for application of the Statute of Frauds to $5,000, a tenfold increase over the current law.]

SPECIAL RULES UNDER ARTICLE 2

The basic assumption under Article 2 is that both parties will be acting in good faith, with the seller selling and the buyer buying. And, of course, all is done according to the terms of the contract. If that was all that Article 2 said, the rules of contracts from common law would be more than adequate to cover sales. The true value of the Code's coverage of sales is what it provides if, or when, the contract is defective, incomplete, or unclear in some area.

For example, § 2-302 makes provisions for unconscionable contracts or contract clauses. Unconscionability means so unfair or one-sided as to shock the conscience. Unlike the common law, which presumed that equal bargaining power existed, the Code realized that some parties can "force a bargain" on the other party, and such forced bargains may be unconscionable to the party who was forced into the bargain. If the court feels that a contract is unconscionable, it may refuse to enforce the contract. If the court feels that only a clause of the contract is unconscionable, it normally will enforce all of the contract's terms except the challenged clause.

Open Terms

The Code also recognizes that the parties may intend to have a contract even though the contract may omit some elements. In an effort to give the parties the "benefit of their bargain," the Code allows the omitted terms to be filled in by the court. (Remember from Chapter 12, the court may complete a contract for the parties, but it will not write or make a contract for the parties.)

What happens when, for example, the parties intend to create a contract but fail to set a price? In such a case, § 2-305 controls. Under this section, the price can be set by either of the parties or by some external factor. If nothing is said about price, the price is a reasonable price at the time of delivery of the goods. If the price is to be set by one of the parties, that party must set the price in good faith. A bad faith price may be treated by the other party as a cancellation of the contract, or the other party may set a reasonable price and perform the contract.

Sometimes the parties set a price and otherwise agree to contract terms, but fail to provide for delivery. Again, the Code provides a method to save the contract and to resolve the problem. Three different delivery sections may be utilized.

First, under § 2-307, the seller can make a complete delivery in one shipment unless the contract allows for several shipments. However, if the seller tenders a partial delivery and the buyer does not object, the seller can continue to make partial shipments until the buyer objects.

Second, § 2-308 covers the place for delivery. If the contract is silent as to the place of delivery, delivery is at the seller's place of business. (Law students often miss this point. At first glance, it seems illogical. In reality, it is very logical. When a person buys a toaster or a can of beans, that person takes delivery at the store—the seller's place of business.) If the seller has no place of business, delivery is at the seller's residence. If the goods are known by both parties to be at some other place, that place is the proper place for the delivery.

Third, § 2-309 covers the time for delivery. If the contract is silent about when delivery is to occur, delivery is to be within a reasonable time. Reasonable time here means reasonable in both clock time and in calendar time. The seller is to make delivery during normal business hours (clock time), and the seller is not allowed to delay unduly the number of days before delivery (calendar time).

In addition to these rules, the Code resolves several other potential problems. Under § 2-306, the Code specifically allows requirement contracts and output contracts. In a requirement contract, the seller provides all of a certain good that the buyer needs. In an output contract, the buyer purchases all of a certain good that the seller produces. Both types of contracts were often declared unenforceable at common law since they were too indefinite in terms. Exhibit 15.4 summarizes the treatment of open terms in a sales contract.

Options

The Code also deals with options. If a contract calls for an unspecified product mix, the assortment of goods is at the buyer's option. If the contract is silent as to how the goods are to be shipped, the shipping arrangements are at the seller's option. However, if a party having an option delays unduly, the other party may act. A party may elect to wait until he or she hears what is being done by the other party or may proceed on his or her own. Thus, if the buyer does not notify the seller as to the product mix desired, the seller may delay shipping any goods, and the delay is excused. Or, the seller may select his or her own assortment and ship it, providing the act is in good faith. Or, the seller may treat the delay as a breach of contract by the buyer and seek remedies for the breach.

Exhibit 15.4

Open Terms in Sales Contracts		
Open Term	**Treatment**	**Code Section**
Price	The buyer or the seller sets the price in *good faith*, if the contract so provides; or	§ 2-305(2)
	The price is a reasonable price at the time and place of delivery.	§ 2-305(1)
Delivery	If no place for delivery is mentioned, delivery is at the seller's place of business or the seller's home if the seller has no place of business.	§ 2-308(a)
	If the goods to the contract are identified, and if both parties know the goods are at a place other than the seller's location, delivery is presumed to occur at the location of the goods.	§ 2-308(b)
	If the time for delivery is not mentioned, delivery is to occur within a reasonable time considering the nature of the goods [calendar time] and the nature of the buyer's business [clock time].	§ 2-309
Payment	Payment is expected at the time and place of delivery unless some other payment terms are specified; payment is to be made in any commercially reasonable manner.	§§ 2-310, 2-511(1)
	If the seller insists on payment in cash, but did not specify cash payment in the contract, the buyer must be given a reasonable time to procure cash for the payment.	§ 2-511(2)

Cooperation

As a final and overriding obligation, the parties are required to cooperate with one another in the performance of their duties. Any failure to cooperate or any interference with the performance of the other party can be treated as a breach of contract or as an excuse for a delayed performance.

THE SCOPE OF ARTICLE 2A

Article 2A covers leases, specifically the leasing of *goods*. [Note that this article does not address apartment leases, which are governed under other provisions of the state's laws.] When the National Conference of Commissioners on Uniform State Laws decided to codify the coverage of leases, the drafting committee looked for comparable areas for guidance. Eventually they decided that Article 2 of the UCC was most analogous to leases, and they used this article for guidance in their efforts. The coverage of leases was originally embodied in the Uniform Personal Property Leasing Act, which was approved by the National Conference of Commissioners on Uniform State Laws in 1985. It was decided, however, that this coverage would be better suited for inclusion in the UCC, and the Uniform Personal Property Leasing Act was reworked into its present form as Article 2A. In August 1986, the conference approved Article 2A for promulgation as an amendment to the UCC. The Council of the American Law Institute approved and recommended the article in December 1986; and the Permanent Editorial Board of the Uniform Commercial Code approved the article in March 1987. All of the states except Louisiana and South Carolina had adopted Article 2A.

Article 2A applies to "any transaction, regardless of form, that creates a lease."[9] This broad statement provides coverage for a "consumer lease," a "finance leases," or an "installment lease" contract. As used in this article, "lease" means "a transfer of the right to possession and use of goods for a term in return for consideration, but a sale, including a sale on approval or a sale or return, or retention or creation of a security interest is not a lease. Unless the context clearly indicates otherwise, the term includes a sublease."[10]

Article 2A is intended to provide the same sort of broad coverage to leases, regardless of form, that Article 2 provides for sales. With the increasing use of leases by both merchants and non-merchants, such coverage gives a welcome—and necessary—uniformity to this area of the law.

CONTRACTS FOR LEASING GOODS

Much of the coverage from Article 2 was carried into Article 2A, with appropriate changes made to reflect the inherent differences between a sale and a lease. Amendments were also made to Articles 1 and 9 to make these areas consistent with the new coverage of leases as provided in Article 2A. The article is designed to help protect the basic tenets of freedom of contract by permitting the parties to vary certain terms of their lease agreements. At the same time, the parties cannot vary such staples of the UCC as the requirements that the parties act in good faith and in a reasonable manner and that they exercise due diligence and due care.

Article 2A has five parts, as opposed to the seven parts in Article 2. Part 1 contains general provisions. Part 2 covers the formation and construction of lease contracts. Part 3 covers the effect of lease contracts, including enforceability. Part 4 deals with the performance of lease contracts. Part 5 concerns defaults and remedies.

The scope of Article 2A is restricted to leases of goods. It does not include "security leases," which are already provided for in Article 9. Similarly, there is no need for a lessor to file any financing statement or other document in order to protect his or her interest in the leased property. Lessees are entitled to warranty protections similar in scope and coverage to those protections given to buyers of goods under Article 2. Thus, there are both express and implied warranties given to lessees.

Parties to a lease, the same as parties to a sale, are classified as merchants or non-merchants. Protections are provided for a lessee in the ordinary course of business, a person who leases goods in the ordinary course of business and in good faith and without knowledge that the lease is a violation of the rights of a third person.

Article 2A recognizes two basic types of leases, consumer leases and finance leases. It also recognizes an "installment lease" contract, with some special provisions for this type of agreement. A consumer lease is defined as a lease made by a lessor who regularly engages in the business of making leases and which is made to a lessee (excluding an organization) for personal, family, or household usage. In order to qualify as a consumer lease, the total payments called for, excluding renewals or options to buy, may not exceed $25,000. A finance lease is a lease in which the lessor (1) does not select, manufacture, or supply the leased goods, (2) the lessor acquires the goods in connection with the lease, and (3) the lessee either receives a copy of the contract under which the lessor acquired rights to the goods before the lease is signed or the lessee's approval of the contract under which the lessor acquires rights to the goods is a condition to the effectiveness of the lease contract. An "installment lease" contract is one that authorizes or requires the delivery of goods in separate lots to be separately accepted, even if the contract contains a clause stating that each delivery is to be viewed and treated as a separate lease.

A lease contract may be made in any manner sufficient to show agreement between the parties, including the conduct of the parties. Similarly, a lease contract can be entered even though some of the terms of the contract are omitted, provided that the parties intended to make a lease and there is a reasonably certain basis for giving appropriate remedies in the event of a breach.

Leases may also be subject to the rules providing for firm offers. A merchant who makes a written offer to lease goods to or from another party in a signed writing is deemed to have made an irrevocable offer when that writing gives assurance that the offer will be held open. The offer may not be revoked for the time stated in the writing. If no time period is stated, the offer is irrevocable for a reasonable time. In no event may the period during which the offer is irrevocable exceed three months. Further, if the offeree is the party who makes the firm offer on a form prepared by the offeree, the offeror must sign the form before the offer is considered "firm," and therefore irrevocable.

The Statute of Frauds for leases requires a writing for any lease that calls for total payments, excluding options for renewals or options to buy, of $1,000 or more. If the total payments are less than $1,000, an oral contract is valid and enforceable. Article 2A also recognizes the same three exceptions to the Statute of Frauds as are recognized under Article 2 if there is no writing and the lease has total payments of $1,000 or more (specially manufactured goods, admission in a legal proceeding by the party against whom enforcement is sought, or to the extent the goods have been received and accepted).

CONTRACTS FOR THE SALE OF GOODS IN AN INTERNATIONAL SETTING

Business is rapidly "going global," with international trade increasing each year. A significant portion of international trade involves the sale of goods, with the balance comprised of services. Whether goods or services are involved, the trade entails contracts between the parties. Most of these contracts will be performed with little or no problems—at least legally. However, some of these contracts will not be performed or will not be performed satisfactorily, and legal issues will arise due to the inadequate performance. These legal issues may well present legal problems beyond the "mere" problem of the alleged breach of contract.

There are more than 200 separate nations today, each with its own (somewhat) unique legal system. A business that is involved in international sales of goods may do business with firms in any—or even all—of these separate nations. Familiarity with each of these legal systems would be impractical at best. Yet a person who does business with a person in another nation may be subject to the laws of that other nation in a contract action. Obviously this presents a logistical problem for the international trader.

In addition, there are many different languages used in the world. Communication between people who speak different languages can make international trade more difficult than national trade between people who share a common language and a culture. Recall the *Frigaliment Importing Co.* case from Chapter 8. The simple word "chicken" caused serious legal problems in that case. As technological advances are made and as international trade increases, translation problems and misunderstandings are also likely to increase. As the *Frigaliment* case indicates, the potential for confusion or misunderstanding as to what meaning is in effect in a given contract is present with any international sales contract.

Determining which laws are in effect and need to be followed also provides for potential confusion or misunderstanding to a much greater extent in international trade than in domestic trade. This potential for confusion, in turn, has had a negative impact on the growth and development of international trade. Something new was needed to reflect the increasingly international nature of business as the twentieth century progressed. This "something new" became the United Nations Convention on Contracts for the International Sale of Goods, the CISG.

The United Nations Convention on Contracts for the International Sale of Goods

The CISG was drafted at the behest of the United Nations to provide for international sales what Article 2 of the Uniform Commercial Code (UCC) provides in the United States for domestic sales, a uniform set of rules governing sales contracts. There had been earlier attempts to provide regulations for international sales, most notably the efforts arising from the international diplomatic conference in The Hague in 1964.

The United Nations instituted the Conference on International Trade (UNCITRAL) in 1968, charging this conference with the task of unifying the international law governing sales. To help ensure broader acceptance of its actions, the conference was composed of representatives from numerous countries, with broad diversity in the legal traditions and the economic status of the represented states.

Meeting once a year, UNCITRAL took nine years to prepare draft conventions dealing with the international sale of goods and with the formation of international sales contracts. These two drafts were combined into one draft convention in 1978, and that combined convention was submitted to an official diplomatic convention convened in Vienna in 1980 by the United Nations General Assembly.

The final language of the CISG was approved at the Vienna Conference in 1980. Sixty-two nations participated in the Vienna conference, and these nations helped in the drafting of the Convention. By having such broad participation (one commentator characterized the participants as 22 Western nations, 11 socialist nations, and 29 third-world nations[11]), the Convention provides compromise standards that should eventually prove acceptable to most of the world. There were 20 signatory nations, including the United States. (The U.S. Senate unanimously ratified the CISG in 1986.) The CISG became effective January 1, 1988, for all of the ratifying nations.

As of May 18, 2009, the UN Treaty Section reports that 74 nations have signed and/or ratified the Convention. These nations are listed in an exhibit on the Web site for this chapter.

Domestically, there are numerous legal traditions that various nations follow, and there are various levels of economic development among the member nations of the United Nations. Both of these differences present problems in deriving a uniform set of laws to govern the international sale of goods. Common law nations, such as England, the United States, and the numerous nations that are—or have been—heavily influenced by England, traditionally follow a less rigid system in forming and performing sales contracts. Civil law nations, including most of Europe except for England, follow a more rigid system in which statutes provide the entire framework of the sales contract. Nations that follow Islamic law, including most of the Middle East, have different expectations regarding contract law. Socialist nations prefer much more controlled terms and allow much less flexibility in forming contracts, establishing prices, and dealing with remedies. Industrialized nations have different expectations than developing—or "third-world"—nations. All of these differences have made the creation and ratification of the CISG very difficult.

Despite these differences, and despite the difficulties, a Convention was agreed on and ratified by 44 (as stated, now up to 74) nations. This Convention holds out the hope for a truly uniform international law governing the sale of goods. In the interim, the CISG may provide the controlling law for international sale-of-goods contracts under two different sets of circumstances:

1. The contract for the sale of goods is made between firms from different countries, if both countries have ratified the Convention.

2. The contract for the sale of goods designates that the law of a particular country will be the applicable law governing the contract, provided that the country whose laws will be applicable has ratified the Convention.

[NOTE: A list of the nations that have adopted the CISG is available on the Web site for this chapter.]

SCOPE OF THE CISG

The CISG provides the framework for the international sale of goods in much the same way that Article 2 of the UCC provides the framework for the domestic sale of goods in the United States. However, students should avoid drawing too strict a comparison between the UCC and the CISG. Not all the subjects covered by the UCC are also covered by the CISG, nor does the CISG extend to as many sales as does Article 2. For example, the CISG does not apply to the sale of goods intended for personal or household use unless the seller neither knew nor should have known that the goods were being purchased for personal or household use.[12] By contrast, Article 2 does apply to such purchases by a consumer, even providing warranty protection to the consumer in many such situations. See Exhibit 15.5.

The CISG applies to contracts for the sale of goods between parties whose places of business are in different *states* (when used in this sense, states means nations), provided that those different states are signatory states to the CISG, *or* provided that the parties have agreed to follow the laws of one of the two nations and that nation is a signatory state. In addition, the International Chamber of Commerce has recognized the CISG as part of the Lex Mercatoria and regularly applies the terms of the CISG to controversies involving the international sale of goods that are submitted to the International Chamber of Commerce for arbitration.

There are some other significant differences between the UCC and the CISG, and some of these differences may prove troublesome for U.S. businesses (as well as businesses from other common law nations) new to the international marketplace. For example, under common law, in order to have a contract there must be (1) an offer, (2) an acceptance, and (3) consideration. The CISG does not mention "consideration"—a basic element of contract formation in common law countries. Instead, the CISG view is that since consideration is part of the formation of the contract, it relates to the "validity" of the contract. Validity-of-the-contract issues are to be determined by applicable national law, not by the CISG.

Another formation-of-the-contract issue involves acceptance. Unlike consideration, which is a matter to be resolved under applicable national law, the CISG does address the issue of acceptance. Under common law, an acceptance is effective when sent by the offeree (the "mailbox rule"), placing the risk of misdelivery or nondelivery on the offeror. Under civil law, an acceptance is not effective until it is received by the offeror, placing the risk of misdelivery or nondelivery on the offeree. These two positions are diametrically opposed. This means that in a civil law nation, an offer can

Exhibit 15.5

A Comparison of UCC Article 2 and the CISG

Article 2	CISG
Contract formation requires an offer, an acceptance, and consideration.	Contract formation requires an offer and an acceptance, but there is no requirement of consideration.
Acceptance is generally valid when sent (the "mailbox rule"), even if never received by the offeror.	Acceptance is not valid until received by offeror.
An offer can generally be revoked at any time prior to acceptance.	An offer can be revoked at any time prior to the time when an acceptance is *sent*, even though the acceptance is not valid until received.
A "firm offer" is irrevocable for the time stated, and if no time is stated, is irrevocable for a reasonable time.	An offer that the offeror promises to hold open *or* that the offeree reasonably believes will be held open is irrevocable for the time stated or for a reasonable time.
Contracts for the sale of goods in an amount of $500 or more must be in writing in order to be enforceable.	There is no writing requirement under the CISG, although the parties may, in their agreement, require a writing before a contract exists.

be revoked by the offeror at any time prior to his or her receipt of an acceptance. In a common law nation, the offer cannot be revoked once an acceptance has been sent by the offeree.

In Article 18(2), the CISG states that an acceptance is effective when it reaches the offeror—the civil law rule. However, it also states, in Article 16(1), that an offer may not be revoked after an acceptance has been *sent* (even though it may not yet have been received)—a variation on the common law rule. Finally, Article 18(3) says that an acceptance is effective as soon as the offeree shows acceptance by beginning to perform—another concession to common law traditions.

Another difference involves the need for a written agreement for some contracts. Many U.S. firms are used to the applicability of the Statute of Frauds, requiring that a contract for the sale of goods (subject to numerous exceptions) must be in writing if the contract is for $500 or more. These parties may be shocked to learn that the CISG specifically states that oral contracts for the sale of goods are enforceable.[13] Since there is no need for any writing, U.S. firms may believe that they are still in the negotiations (prewriting) stage while their non-U.S. counterparts (especially if those counterparts are from civil law nations) will believe that an oral agreement has been reached and will be expecting performance. If the CISG is the statute governing the sale, a contract may very well exist, and the U.S. firm will have to perform despite the lack of a writing.

Common law nations treat offers as freely revocable at any time prior to acceptance, unless the offeree has an option or unless the parties are governed by the UCC and a merchant has made a firm offer. Civil law countries generally treat an offer that states a time limit as irrevocable. Thus, there is a basic difference between common law and civil law in this area. The CISG generally adopts the common law approach, making the offer freely revocable at any time prior to acceptance. However, there are two important exceptions to this general approach, both based on civil law:

1. The offer is irrevocable where the offer states that an acceptance must be made within a stated time; and
2. The offer is irrevocable if it was reasonable for the offeree to rely on the offer remaining open, and the offeree did, in fact, rely on the offer remaining open.[14]

Thus, an offer that says the offeree has 20 days to accept is deemed to be irrevocable for the 20-day period even though the offer does not take the form of a firm offer as provided for in the UCC. In addition, the CISG provides a promissory estoppel-like exception when the facts of the case make it appear that the offeree relied on the fact that the offer would remain open and will be harmed if the offer is not held open for the time indicated in the offer. (Note that the CISG does not require the offeror to reasonably expect the offeree to rely to his or her detriment, as the common law would.)

Contemporary Case

GREAT WHITE BEAR, LLC v. MERVYNS, LLC

2007 U.S. Dist. LEXIS 31224
(S.D.N.Y. 2007)

FACTS Great White Bear alleged that it entered into a contract with Mervyns on or about March or April of 2005, with the contract calling for Mervyns to place orders for clothing for $13 million at cost, allowing for a 10 percent deviation down (meaning as little as $11.7 million) over an 18-month period. Great White Bear also alleged that over the course of the contract the relationship deteriorated, so that "representatives of Mervyns ... handled the Great White Bear account in a deliberately counterproductive way, lacking entirely in good faith and in breach of the agreement by frustrating performance thereunder, so that Great White Bear was set up to fail." In January 2006, Mervyns informed Great White Bear that the contract was finished and that Mervyns would be placing no additional orders. At that time, Mervyns had only ordered $2.3 million, substantially short of the minimum amount of $11.7 million called for in the contract.

When Great White Bear sued, Mervyns raised as its defense the absence of a writing, in violation of the Statute of Frauds. Great White Bear countered that there was, in fact, a writing sufficient to satisfy the Statute of Frauds and that the contract was fully enforceable.

ISSUE Was there a writing sufficient to satisfy the Statute of Frauds requirement under New York state law?

HOLDING Yes, the email produced by Great White Bear was a sufficient writing to satisfy the requirements of the Statute of Frauds.

REASONING Excepts from the opinion of Richard M. Berman, U.S.D.J.:

Defendant argues that Great White Bear "has not and cannot plead a writing sufficient to satisfy the Statute of Frauds." . . . Plaintiff counters that a March 31, 2005 e-mail from Great White Bear to Mervyns is a "writing in confirmation" and "takes the case out of the Statute of Frauds". . . .

"Under the New York statute of frauds, a contract for the sale of goods for the price of $500 or more is not enforceable 'unless there is some writing sufficient to indicate that a contract for the sale was made between the parties and signed by the party against whom enforcement is sought or by his authorized agent or broker.' . . . Where there is 'no writing signed by the party against whom enforcement is sought,' the alleged oral agreement may fall within the so-called 'merchants' exception" to the Statute of Frauds . . . allowing "merchants A and B [to] orally agree to a sale of goods for $500 or more, and [if] merchant A within a reasonable time sends merchant B a written

confirmation of the contract, merchant B would [then] lose the Statute of Frauds defense unless merchant B gives a written objection within ten days after receiving the confirmation." . . . "[I]n deciding whether writings are confirmatory documents . . . neither explicit words of confirmation nor express references to the prior agreement are required, and the writings are sufficient so long as they afford a basis for believing that they reflect a real transaction between the parties". . . .

The . . . Complaint includes an allegation that "Great White Bear's Danny Fodiman . . . sent an e-mailed writing to Mervyn's Scott Jeffries confirming the agreement . . . The e-mail, dated March 31, 2005, states that 'collections [i.e., knits, wovens, jackets, and pants] would be $9,000,000 at cost and active [wear] would be $4,200,000 at cost over an 18 month period." . . . The March 31 E-mail also states that $3.2 million "could be aggressive" and "may be 10% high"—a reference to Plaintiff's allegation that the alleged contract allowed for a 10 percent downward deviation in the total contract price.

The March 31 e-mail "afford[s] a basis for believing that [it] reflects a real transaction between the parties" at this stage in the case. . . .

The parties are directed to appear at a status/settlement conference with the Court on May 30, 2010. . . . The Court directs the parties to engage in good faith settlement negotiations prior to the conference with the Court.

[Note that while the court did not decide the case, it did determine that an e-mail confirmation is a sufficient writing to satisfy the requirements of the Statute of Frauds.]

You Be the Judge

Fleetwood Homes manufactures mobile homes, and CMH Homes, Inc. is an authorized Fleetwood Homes dealer. David and Loria Doyle purchased a new Fleetwood mobile home from CMH in April of 2006. CMH provided the Doyles with various express warranties at the time of the sale, including a warranty that all repairs and replacements necessary due to defects in materials or workmanship would be provided free of charge during the warranty period. Additional warranties were set forth in a warranty booklet and owner's manual provided by Fleetwood Homes. Another portion of the agreement called for CMH to install the mobile home at the location designated by the Doyles.

Following the installation, the Doyles alleged that CMH had installed the mobile home at the wrong location, that the installation was not done in the manner agreed upon by the parties, and that CMH had caused damage to the mobile home by failing to follow installation instructions provided by Fleetwood Homes. The Doyles further alleged that after moving in to their new home, they discovered numerous nonconformities caused by "substandard, defective, and/or negligent manufacture, delivery, and installation" that "substantially impaired the use, value and/or safety of the home." CMH and Fleetwood were contacted and asked to make repairs, as per the warranties given in the contract, but the Doyles asserted that Fleetwood and CMH "failed and/or refused to repair the home in a timely manner so as to bring it into conformity with the warranties set forth" in the contract. At that point, the Doyles informed both Fleetwood and CMH that they intended to reject and/or revoke their acceptance of the mobile home.

The Doyles then filed suit against both Fleetwood and CMH, asserting that both parties had breached their duty of good faith. The defendants answered that the complaint filed by the Doyles failed "to state a claim upon which relief can be granted" and asked the court to dismiss the lawsuit. According to the defendants, the UCC does not allow an independent cause of action for "failure to perform in good faith," but rather that the doctrine of good faith is merely a means of measuring other aspects of performance.

This case has been brought in *your* court. How will *you* decide whether a party can be held liable for a breach of its duty to act in "good faith"? What is the most important fact or factor influencing your decision? [See *Doyle v. Fleetwood Homes of Virginia, Inc.*, (S.D. W. Va., 2009).]

Summary

This chapter introduces the law of sales, Article 2 of the Uniform Commercial Code, the law of leases, Article 2A of the Uniform Commercial Code, and the CISG, the United Nations Convention on Contracts for the International Sale of Goods. It is important to distinguish sales contracts from other types of contracts. Article 2 attempts to deal with "commercial reality" in the sale of goods, whereas common law developed strict and rigid rules for the treatment of contracts. Article 2 also recognizes the difference between a merchant—a person who "specializes" in dealing with a particular type of goods—and a non-merchant—a "casual dealer" in the goods. The Code provides built-in flexibility in the formation of sales contracts. Intent, rather than form, is the key element in sales. Offers and acceptances are likely to be found if the parties act as if they have an agreement. The Code even provides methods to supply missing terms, if it seems appropriate to do so in order to carry out the wishes and intentions of the parties. The Statute of Frauds remains operative under Article 2, but its provisions are less restrictive than they are under common law. Three exceptions to the Statute of Frauds are built into the Code, and the past dealings of the parties may also be taken into consideration in deciding what the parties have agreed to do. Some general obligations are imposed on the parties to prevent or minimize abuses of the less rigid rules of Article 2. The parties are required to act in good faith, they may not act unconscionably, and they must cooperate with one another. Performance options are available to either party if the other party fails to cooperate fully or properly.

Article 2A was enacted because of the growing importance of personal property leases in our society. Many people today lease goods rather than purchase them. Historically, leases were governed by common law, whereas sales of goods have been governed by the UCC since 1954. Despite the similarity between a sale of goods and a lease of goods, there was likely to be a different outcome in a lawsuit. For quite some time courts have drawn analogies between leases and sales and then applied Article 2 provisions to leases. This will no longer be necessary with the enactment of Article 2A.

Work on an international law of sales began in 1930, prior to World War II, when the International Institute for the Unification of Private Law tried to develop uniform coverage in this area. The initial work was submitted to an international conference at The Hague following World War II and resulted in the creation of two conventions, one dealing with the formation of sales contracts and one dealing with the performance of sales contracts. Unfortunately, neither convention has been widely adopted. The United Nations created an International Conference on International Trade and charged it with creating an international law governing sales. This led to the United Nations Convention on the International Sale of Goods (CISG), which was approved at the Vienna Conference in 1980 and became effective January 1, 1988, for all ratifying nations.

The CISG was created by compromises among the various factions that make up the United Nations. There were disagreements among common law, civil law, and Islamic law nations; between developed and developing nations; and between capitalist and socialist nations. Despite these differences, a Convention was created and has been ratified or adopted by 74 nations as of May 2009. The CISG covers formation-of-contracts issues; seller obligations and rights; buyer obligations and rights; and remedies for both sellers and buyers. Ratifying nations have the option of not ratifying all sections of the CISG, but most have opted to follow the entire Convention.

Discussion Questions

1. What does Article 2 of the UCC govern? What does Article 2A of the UCC govern? How is it different from Article 2? What does the CISG govern? How does the coverage in each of these areas differ from the common law of contracts as followed in the United States?

2. The status of "merchant" carries with it certain duties and expectations under the UCC. What are the three separate tests that the UCC uses to determine whether a person in a sales or a leasing contract is a merchant? How are merchants treated differently from non-merchants under the UCC? Why do you think this difference in treatment exists?

3. What is a *firm offer* under either Article 2 or Article 2A, and how is a firm offer treated differently from a similar offer at common law? Does the CISG have anything analogous to the *firm offer* provisions of the UCC?

4. Generally speaking, how can an offer be accepted under the law of sales? How is this different from the *mirror image* requirement for acceptance at common law? Why does the UCC provide for a different method of acceptance than the common law provides? Are the rules concerning acceptance different under the provisions of the CISG?

5. Assume that a buyer sends the seller a *purchase order*, a form offering to buy a certain quantity of goods. The seller subsequently returns an acknowledgement form accepting the offer. When these two forms are compared, it is discovered that they do not agree on every point. Do the parties have a contract under Article 2? If so, what are its terms? If not, why? Would the same result occur under the provisions of the common law?

Case Problems and Writing Assignments

1. Citipostal, Inc. acquired certain mobile communications equipment as lessee under a self-described "finance lease." The lease, assigned to Unistar Leasing shortly after its inception, provides for a term of 12 months and for a "down payment" of $2,084.62 and 11 additional monthly payments of $525.21 plus tax. The lease further provides that Citipostal has the option to purchase the equipment for $1 upon fulfillment of its lease obligation, and that it may exercise the purchase option by furnishing written notice no later than 90 days prior to expiration of the lease term. The lease further provides in relevant part: "If upon expiration or termination, you do not exercise the Purchase Option, at our option (a) we may remove the equipment and you agree to pay us an amount equal to a minimum of two monthly payments, or (b) the equipment will continue to be held and leased by you for successive one-year periods at the same monthly rental in the original lease subject to the rights of either party to terminate the lease upon twelve (12) months written notice (at the end of the 12 months you will deliver the equipment to us under the terms of this paragraph)."

Citipostal took possession of the equipment and made all of the monthly payments required by the lease. It did not, however, furnish notice that it would exercise its option to purchase the equipment for $1. After expiration of the lease term, Unistar continued to render monthly invoices, which Citipostal duly paid, for a period of 18 months. Upon realizing that it had paid some $10,233.72 more than the total amount required to be paid over the lease term, Citipostal commenced this action to recover all lease payments made after expiration of the lease term based upon causes of action for breach of contract, fraud, and conversion. In addition, Citipostal sought to recover all lease payments made based upon a cause of action for usury.

Citipostal contends that the parties' transaction is a security agreement under UCC § 9-105, thus creating a security interest, and is not a lease. Unistar contends that the transaction is a finance lease, as provided for in UCC § 2A-103(1)(g), and not a security agreement, noting that the lease specifically provides that it is "a 'finance lease' as that term is defined in UCC Article 2A." If the agreement is a security agreement, Citipostal will prevail, but if it is a finance lease Unistar will prevail.

How should the court decide this case? Does the fact that the parties themselves refer to the transaction as a "finance lease" strengthen Unistar's position? What is the most important fact or factor in making your decision? [See *Citipostal, Inc., v. Unistar Leasing*, 283 A.D.2d 916; 724 N.Y.S.2d 555; 2001 N.Y. App. Div. LEXIS 4526; 44 U.C.C. Rep. Serv. 2d (Callaghan) 691 (2001).]

2. PetroEcuador sent BP an invitation to bid for supplying 140,000 barrels of unleaded gasoline deliverable "CFR" to Ecuador. "CFR," which stands for "Cost and Freight," is one of 13 International Commercial Terms (Incoterms) designed to "provide a set of international rules for the interpretation of the most commonly used trade terms in foreign trade." Incoterms are recognized through their incorporation into the Convention on Contracts for the International Sale of Goods (CISG). BP responded favorably to the invitation, and PetroEcuador confirmed the sale on its contract form. The final agreement required that the oil be sent "CFR La Libertad-Ecuador." A separate provision, paragraph 10, states, "Jurisdiction: Laws of the Republic of Ecuador." The contract further specifies that the gasoline have a gum content of less than 3 milligrams per 100 milliliters, to be determined at the port of departure. PetroEcuador appointed

Saybolt, a company specializing in quality control services, to ensure this requirement was met.

To fulfill the contract, BP purchased gasoline from Shell Oil Company and, following testing by Saybolt, loaded it on board the M/T TIBER.

The TIBER sailed to La Libertad, Ecuador, where the gasoline was again tested for gum content. On learning that the gum content now exceeded the contractual limit, PetroEcuador refused to accept delivery. Eventually, BP resold the gasoline to Shell at a loss of approximately $2 million.

BP sued PetroEcuador in Texas for breach of contract, and PetroEcuador filed a notice of intent to apply foreign law. The district court applied the Texas choice of law rules and determined that Ecuadorian law governed, as per the contract. Under Ecuadorian law, a seller is required to deliver conforming goods at the destination. Since the gasoline was determined not to be conforming at the destination, BP would be in breach. However, BP argued that the applicable Ecuadorian law should be the CISG since both Ecuador and the U.S. are signatories of the Convention, and that under the CISG, use of the term "CFR" demonstrated the parties' intent to pass the risk of loss to PetroEcuador once the goods were delivered on board the TIBER.

How should the court decide this case? Is the CISG part of "Ecuadorian law" for purposes of international trade, or did the parties truly mean to follow the *domestic* law of Ecuador in this contract, or the Ecuadorian laws governing international sales? [See *BP Oil International, Ltd. v. Empresa Estatal Petroleos de Ecuador*, 332 F.3d 333; 2003 U.S. App. LEXIS 12013; 200 A.L.R. Fed. 771 (5th Cir. 2003).]

3. Kane, a professional photographer, shipped 45 photographic transparencies to Avanti Press via Federal Express. Federal Express lost the transparencies sometime during the shipment. Admitting that it had lost the package, Federal Express paid Kane $100 as per the shipping contract the two parties had entered when Kane shipped the package of transparencies (apparently he decided not to insure the package for its alleged value). Kane then filed suit against Avanti for $67,000, the alleged value of the transparencies. Avanti denied liability. According to Kane, Avanti had requested that he submit the transparencies so that Avanti could consider the pictures for possible inclusion in its greeting card collection, and had even sent Kane a shipping number to use with Federal Express, so that Avanti was paying the shipping fees. Because of these allegations, Kane asserts that Avanti had risk of loss. Avanti argues that this controversy does not involve the sale of goods, so that Article 2 does not apply because this was not the sale of goods, but of an intangible, the images contained on the transparencies. According to Avanti, since this was not a sale of goods, the risk of loss provisions of Article 2 do not apply, and any claim Kane might have is against Federal Express. Further, under the Federal Express contract, Kane has been paid for his loss. Was this a sale of goods, governed by Article 2 of the UCC, or the sale of an intangible, governed by the common law? Should Article 2 apply by analogy even if this is *not* a sale of goods? [See *Kane v. Federal Express Corp. et al.*, 2001 Conn. Super. LEXIS 2536, 45 U.C.C. Rep. Serv. 2d (Callaghan) 730, (Conn. 2001)].

Notes

1. Uniform Consumer Information Technology Act (UCITA), *Bad Software: A Consumer Protection Guide*, found at http://www.badsoftware.com/uccindex.htm.
2. Keith A. Rowley, "UCC Legislative Update," found at http://www.abanet.org/buslaw/committees/CL190000pub/newsletter/200901/subcommittees/developments.pdf
3. U.C.C. § 2-103(1)(b).
4. U.C.C. § 1-201(19).
5. "Records" is a broadened definition of "writings" to include electronic communications such as an email, as defined in UETA and E-SIGN.
6. The proposed revisions to Article 2 make a substantial change to this provision. According to § 2-201 (1) of the revised Code, "A contract for the sale of goods for the price of $5,000 or more is not enforceable by way of action or defense unless there is some record sufficient to indicate that a contract for sale has been made between the parties and signed by the party against which enforcement is sought or by the party's authorized agent or broker. A record is not insufficient because it omits or incorrectly states a term agreed upon but the contract is not enforceable under this subsection beyond the quantity of goods shown in the record."
7. 15 U.S.C.A. § 7001 *et seq.*
8. Promulgated by the NCCUSL, the UETA is currently enacted in 39 states, with another 4 states having similar statutes.
9. Section 2A-102.
10. Section 2A-103(j).
11. Alejandro M. Garro, "Reconciliation of Legal Traditions in the U.N. Convention on Contracts for the International Sale of Goods," *The International Lawyer* 23 (Summer 1989), p. 433 at 444.
12. United Nations, Convention on Contracts for the International Sales of Goods, Article 2.
13. Ibid., Article 11.
14. CISG, Article 16(2)(b).

16

Title and Risk of Loss

Agenda

As the business continues to grow, eClass will be expanding its operation, hiring more employees, and leasing or purchasing more items.
The principals are concerned that some of the items they purchase or lease may be damaged during shipment and would like to know how to minimize their risk if this occurs.

There has also been an increased interest from several retailers who would like to offer the software to the public. While eClass is delighted at the prospect of more sales, the principals are concerned about the added burden and risk of shipping their product to these retail outlets. They need to decide how to deliver the goods to these buyers. Among their considerations are deciding which delivery terms they are most comfortable using and whether the firm might be responsible for any loss or damage to the goods while they are being delivered.

Sales to individual consumers also present some problems. Some individuals want to receive a diskette containing the program, while others prefer to just download the software from the eClass Web site. Does this mean that some of their contracts are for the sale of goods (the diskettes) while others (the download sales) fall outside the coverage of Article 2, or does the law consider all of these sales to be the sale of goods? Be prepared! You never know when the firm or one of its members will seek your advice.

Classic Case

EBERHARD MANUFACTURING COMPANY v. BROWN

61 Mich. App. 268, 232 N.W.2d 378, 1975 Mich. App. LEXIS 1527 (Mich. App. 1975)

FACTS Eberhard Manufacturing entered into a sales contract with Stanley M. Brown under a distributorship agreement. Eberhard shipped the goods to Brown, but the goods were lost in transit. Since he never received the goods, Brown never paid for them. Eberhard sued to recover the price of the goods sold, and Brown counterclaimed for damages, alleging that Eberhard was the party in breach.

Eberhard contended that the goods were sold "F.O.B., seller's factory," making the contract a shipment contract and placing the risk of loss on Brown. Brown, on the other hand, contended that the parties had entered into a destination contract, with the risk of loss remaining on Eberhard until the goods were delivered at the buyer's location.

ISSUE Which party had the risk of loss?

HOLDING Brown. The court determined that this was a shipment contract.

REASONING Excerpts from the opinion of J.H. Gillis, Judge:

... On appeal both parties point to ... [§ 2-509(1)] as controlling. Plaintiff, however, cites subsection (a)

and defendant subsection (b). Subsection (a) states the rule where the contract is a "shipment" contract, in which case risk of loss passes to the buyer where the goods are duly delivered to the carrier; subsection (b) states the rule where a contract is a "destination" contract, in which case risk of loss passes to the buyer when the goods are duly tendered at the destination.

An agreement of the parties would control as to who has the risk of loss. ... The parties here did not expressly agree on who was to bear the risk of loss. The contract contained no F.O.B. term. ... There was testimony by plaintiff that its goods are sold F.O.B. place of shipment, plaintiff's factory. That testimony might be evidence of a usage of trade. ... It was not proof that the parties had agreed, expressly or in fact, as to who had the risk of loss.

Under Article 2 of the Uniform Commercial Code, the "shipment" contract is regarded as the normal one and the "destination" contract as the variant type. The seller is not obligated to deliver at a named destination and bear the concurrent risk of loss until arrival, unless he has specifically agreed so to deliver or the commercial understanding of the terms used by the parties contemplates such delivery ... Thus a contract which contains neither an F.O.B. term nor any other term explicitly allocating loss is a shipment contract.

Defendant argues that since the goods were to be shipped to defendant's place of business in Birmingham, the contract required plaintiff to deliver the goods "at a particular destination". . . . Defendant's position is that "ship to" substitutes for and is equivalent to an F.O.B. term, namely F.O.B. place of destination. But that argument is persuasively refuted by the response that a "ship to" address must be supplied in any case in which carriage is contemplated. Thus a "ship to" term has no significance in determining whether a contract is a shipment or destination contract for risk of loss purposes.

Other buyers have occasionally argued that the "ship to" term made the contract into a destination contract. Courts have properly rejected this argument. . . .

[F]indings of fact by the trial court are not to be set aside unless clearly erroneous. The findings of fact here . . . were clearly supported by testimony. . . .

INTRODUCTION

What is *title* and why is it important? What is *risk of loss* and why is it important? Are these two topics related, interrelated, or independent? The answer to these questions is the focus of this chapter.

Title is defined as "the union of all elements (as ownership, possession, and custody) constituting the legal right to control and dispose of property."[1] When a buyer enters into a sales contract, he or she expects to *own* the goods once the contract has been performed; that is, he or she expects to acquire *title* to the goods being purchased. The UCC reflects this concern with its definition of a sale. According to § 2-106(1), a *sale* "consists of the passing of title from the seller to the buyer for a price." The section then refers to § 2-401 for an explanation of the "passing of title." We discuss passing of title in more detail later in this chapter. By contrast, when parties enter into a contract to lease goods, title is not an issue. A lease is defined in § 2A-103(j) as "a transfer of the right to possession and use of the goods for a term in return for consideration." This section goes on to state that a sale, including a sale on approval or a sale or return (both discussed later in this chapter) or the retention or creation of a security interest, is *not* a lease.

TITLE TO GOODS UNDER ARTICLE 2 OF THE UCC

Historic Importance

Under common law and under the Uniform Sales Act, title was of paramount importance. The Uniform Sales Act was concerned with when title passed from the seller to the buyer because it tied many other aspects of the sales contract to the issue of title. For example, the party who had title also had risk of loss. Thus, if the goods were damaged or destroyed after the contract was entered but before the buyer had possession of the goods, the risk of loss for the damaged or destroyed goods was on the party who had title. The Uniform Sales Act determined that title passed when the parties intended for title to pass. If the parties did not specify when they intended title to pass, the Act provided certain guidelines. If the goods to the contract had been identified, title passed at the time of the formation of the contract. If the goods had not yet been identified to the contract when the contract was made, title passed when the goods were subsequently identified to the contract by the seller and delivered to a carrier for delivery (shipment contract), unless the seller was required to pay for the transportation. In that case, title passed when the goods arrived at the destination (destination contract). Finally, if the goods were sold to the buyer "on approval," title passed to the buyer when the buyer approved the goods. And if the sale specified that the buyer had the right to return the goods (sale or return), title passed to the buyer upon delivery but would revest in the seller upon their return by the buyer.[2]

While this approach worked, and had worked for literally centuries, it did not really address the practical issue of how to allocate the various risks and responsibilities of modern commercial practice. One source refers to the Uniform Sales Act approach as the "lump concept" approach in which the location of title determined virtually every other aspect or issue in the contract.[3] A more contemporary approach, one that reflected modern commercial concerns and practices, was needed than this "lump concept," which blindly located title and then rigidly applied the rules. That more contemporary approach can be found in Article 2 of the UCC.

Risk of loss refers to financial responsibility for goods that are lost, damaged, or destroyed during the performance of a contract. The parties are allowed to expressly agree in the sales contract for how risk of loss will be allocated. If they do not so agree, § 2-509 and § 2-510 provide the guidelines for when risk of loss moves from the seller to the buyer. Section 2-509 provides for risk of loss when there is no breach of contract by either party. Section 2-510 discusses the effect that a breach of contract by one of the parties has on how risk of loss may be modified or altered due to the breach. These issues are addressed in detail later in the chapter.

The Modern Rule Under the UCC

Section 2-401 of the UCC addresses the "passing of title" issue. This section states that title cannot pass under a contract for sale prior to the identification of the goods to the contract, and that once the goods are identified, the buyer acquires a "special property" in the goods without regard to the location of title. The section provides that, unless the parties otherwise explicitly agree, title passes from the seller to the buyer at the time and place where the seller completes his or her performance with reference to delivery of the goods. If the goods are not to be moved, title passes to the buyer with any documents of title delivered by the seller, and if no documents of title are involved, title passes at the time and place the contract is made. Finally, if the buyer rejects or refuses the goods or revokes his or her acceptance of the goods, title revests in the seller. Since these rules sound strikingly similar to the rules under the Uniform Sales Act, you *might* (should) be asking yourself, "What's the big deal?" The "big deal" is found in the first paragraph to § 2-401.

The first paragraph of § 2-401 specifically states that all the rights, duties, and remedies of any party apply without regard to title, unless title is specifically referred to in the provisions of the particular section. Thus the UCC has separated the concepts of title and risk of loss in favor of a "narrow approach."[4] This means that the UCC makes provision for the passage of title from the seller to the buyer for a price (the definition of a sale) and also provides a method of ascertaining the location of title for those instances where it is important, but frees up the concept of risk of loss to allow the parties to address that issue in the context of contract performance and the reasonable expectations of each party. This is a significant improvement from the rigid, title-is-determinative approach of the pre-Code rules.

When *does* the location of title matter in a sales contract? Title might matter for inheritance purposes. For example, if one of the parties to the sales contract dies, the heirs of that party might be able to assert a claim to the goods as part of the estate of the decedent, *if* the decedent had title to the goods. Title might matter for taxation purposes. Suppose that a state imposes a sales tax for any sales of goods within the state. A buyer from that state and a seller from a different state enter into a sales contract. If title passes at the *seller's* location, it can be argued that the sale occurred in the seller's state, so that no sales tax is owed in the buyer's state.[5] And of course, the location of title is still important in the area of creditor rights. A creditor of one of the parties may be able to assert a claim against any goods that belong to that party. Thus, creditors are very anxious to know where title lies. This also helps to explain the UCC's treatment of consignments. The Code is very careful in spelling out the rights of each party when creditors are involved. Section 2-402 deals with the rights of creditors of the seller when goods are sold. The rights of an unsecured creditor of the seller are limited by the rights of the buyer to recover the goods once the goods are identified to the contract. In a legal tug-of-war between the buyer and a creditor of the seller, the buyer normally will win if the goods have been identified as the goods covered by the sales contract.

When the seller is a merchant, and he or she sells the goods in the ordinary course of business, the buyer purchases the goods "free and clear" of any claims of the seller's creditors. Should the seller subsequently default on his or her credit obligations, the creditors will *not* have the right to go to the buyer in an effort to repossess the goods. The buyer obtained title from the seller in the contract, and any rights the seller's creditors may have possessed in the goods have been cut off. (More treatment of this topic is found in Chapters 24 and 25 in the coverage of secured transactions, Article 9 of the UCC.) If the seller is a merchant and he or she sells the goods to the buyer *not* in the ordinary course of business, the sale is likely to be treated as a Bulk Sale, which is governed by Article 6 of the UCC (in those states still following Article 6) or by the state's bulk sales provisions. Bulk sales provisions are designed to protect creditors of the bulk seller. In this situation, if the creditors of the seller had a perfected security interest in the goods, those creditors can proceed against the goods in the hands of the buyer. Since the sale was made *not* in the ordinary course of business, the creditors retain their rights. While the buyer acquired title to the goods, he or she acquired that title *subject to* the perfected rights of the seller's creditors.

Exhibit 16.1 shows how title passes under Article 2 of the UCC. These same rules apply whether the seller has valid title or voidable title, a topic discussed below.

What happens when, as sometimes happens, the seller "sells" goods but retains possession? The seller's creditors would normally think that so long as their debtor has possession of the goods, he or she still owns those goods, and the creditors may be able to acquire and sell the goods to pay the debt if the debtor defaults on his or her credit. But suppose that the debtor defaults on the debt, the creditors show up asserting one or more claims against various goods in the possession of the debtor, and the debtor asserts that he or she sold the goods to another person. Assuming that the purported buyer shows up and presents an apparently valid bill of sale or other receipt, what happens to the creditors of the "seller"? In such a case, the

Exhibit 16.1

The Passing of Title

Method of Delivery by Seller	When Title Passes to Buyer Under § 2-401
Delivery by Carrier	
• With a shipment contract	When the seller surrenders the goods to the carrier and makes arrangements for shipment.
• With a destination contract	When the carrier tenders delivery to the buyer at the destination.
Delivery via Warehouseman	
• With a document of title	When the document is delivered to the buyer (the negotiability of the document is irrelevant).
• Without a document of title	At the time and place of the contract.
Personal Delivery by the Seller	
• The seller is a merchant	At the time and place of the contract.
• The seller is not a merchant	At the time and place of the contract.

Note: If the buyer rejects the goods, whether rightfully or wrongfully, title *revests* in the seller; if the buyer rightfully revokes his or her acceptance, title *revests* in the seller.

seller's creditors can treat the sale as void if the retention by the seller is fraudulent under state law. Historically, the seller's only defense was to show that he or she was a merchant who retained the goods in good faith in the ordinary course of business, and then only if the goods were retained only for a commercially reasonable time. Thus, a seller who holds identified goods in "layaway" would have a valid defense to a fraudulent retention charge. But a seller who holds the goods without a valid reason could be in trouble.

Different states treat the issue of fraudulent retention differently. Three possible rules exist for a state to follow. In some states, a fraudulent retention by the seller is treated as a conclusive presumption of fraud; if a seller sells goods and then retains possession of those goods for any reason other than a commercial reason, the seller is deemed guilty of fraud. Other states view retention of the goods by the seller after the sale as *prima facie* proof of fraud; the seller is presumed to be guilty of fraud unless the seller is able to show good cause for the retention. In other states, the retention of the goods by the seller is viewed merely as one bit of evidence, to be viewed together with all the other evidence, in determining whether a fraud has occurred.

The enactment of Article 2A, Leases, has further complicated this issue. Article 2A specifically recognizes the validity of a sale and leaseback arrangement, provided that the buyer in the sale portion of the deals acts in good faith and gives value for the goods purchased. Sale and leaseback arrangements have become very popular in a number of industries, especially construction, and the increase has presented numerous problems with the former attitude toward sellers who retained possession of the goods following the sale. The specific authorization of this sort of dealing under Article 2A should reduce the problems and help to clarify this area of law.

Sellers with Voidable Title

As a general rule, any person who sells goods can transfer to the buyer only those rights that are equal to or less than the rights the seller possesses in those goods. Thus, the person who has *valid* title (that is, the owner of the goods) can sell the goods and pass valid title to the buyer. A person who has *void* title (that is, a thief) has *no* true title to the goods and passes void title to the buyer. The true owner of the goods may legally reclaim the goods from the person who bought the goods from the thief, if and when the true owner discovers the location of the goods.

However, a special exception to this general rule exists under Article 2. A person who has *voidable* title may legally transfer rights that are better than he or she possesses in the goods. A person with voidable title may legally pass full and valid title to a buyer if that buyer is a good-faith purchaser for value. For example, a person who acquires goods through fraud or misrepresentation has voidable title to those goods. The person who was defrauded or who was the victim of the misrepresentation may avoid the transaction and recover title to the goods if the avoidance occurs while the defrauding or misrepresenting party still has possession of the goods. However, if the defrauding or misrepresenting party sells the goods to a bona fide purchaser for value before the victim of the wrongdoing makes any attempt to avoid the transaction, the buyer may have full and valid title to the goods.

Voidable title does not exist only in cases such as fraud or misrepresentation. Voidable title also exists in situations involving *entrustment.* An entrustment occurs when there is:

> any delivery and acquiescence in retention of possession regardless of any conditions expressed between the parties to the delivery or acquiescence and regardless of whether the procurement of the entrusting or the possessor's disposition of the goods has been such as to be larcenous under the criminal law.[6]

Commonly, an entrustment involves a situation in which possession of the goods is given to a merchant who regularly deals in goods of that kind (often for repairs). The entruster, the person who delivers possession of the goods to the merchant, gives the merchant voidable title, which gives the merchant the legal power to transfer all of the entruster's rights to a buyer who purchases the entrusted goods from the merchant *in the ordinary course of business.* An owner who takes his or her goods to a merchant for repairs entrusts those goods to the merchant. If the merchant happens to sell the entrusted goods to a customer in the ordinary course of business, and if the customer acted in good faith, the customer takes valid title to the goods.

Of course, the entruster does have rights and remedies against the merchant to whom the goods were entrusted. If the entrustment involves a party who obtains the goods but who is not a merchant in goods of that kind, the entrusted party can transfer good title to any good faith purchaser for value. [*Alamo Rent-a-Car, Inc. v. Mendenhall,* case 16.1 on this text's Web site, is an excellent case for discussing this issue.] The following two examples show the difference between an entrustment to a merchant and an entrustment to a non-merchant.

> *Betty took her watch to Roger's Jewelry to have it repaired. Roger's sells new and used watches in its normal business dealings. If a customer comes into the store and "purchases" Betty's watch, that customer will own the watch. Betty's only recourse will be to sue Roger's for her loss. By entrusting the watch to Roger's, she gave Roger's the legal power to transfer good title to any buyer in the ordinary course of business who purchases the watch from Roger's.*

> *Roger took his watch to Betty's Radio Shop to have it repaired. Although Betty's does not deal in watches, Betty sometimes repairs watches for her friends, and she agrees to do this for Roger. If a customer comes into Betty's and purchases Roger's watch, Roger may be able to recover the watch from the customer. Since Betty does not deal in watches, the transaction with Roger was not an entrustment to a merchant. However, if the person who bought the watch bought it as a good faith purchaser for value, the buyer would still acquire good title due to the entrustment of the watch to Betty by Roger.*

INSURABLE INTEREST

"An insurable interest, in its broadest sense, is a relation between the insured and the event insured against such that the occurrence of the event will cause substantial loss or injury of some kind to the insured."[7] When dealing with sales or leases, the term *insurable interest* refers to the right to purchase insurance on goods to protect one's property rights and interests in the goods. Section 2-501 provides the general guidelines for determining whether an insurable interest exists in the sale of goods, and § 2A-218 provides the guidelines for determining whether an insurable interest exists in the leasing of goods. The buyer gains an insurable interest when existing goods are identified to the contract, even if the goods are nonconforming. If the goods are not identified, the buyer gains an insurable interest once identification occurs. Likewise, if the goods are not yet in existence, the buyer gains an insurable interest as soon as the goods come into existence.

The seller has an insurable interest in the goods for as long as the seller retains title to or any security interest in the goods; and either party has an insurable interest if that

eClass 16.1 Finance/Management

WHO HAS AN INSURABLE INTEREST?

eClass recently began negotiations for the purchase of several new laptops from an online merchant (an e-tailer), with delivery to be made via Federal Parcel Service. While the firm was able to negotiate a good price on the laptops, this is still a relatively large expenditure, and the principals are concerned about the probability that the computers will arrive in good condition. Yousef thinks the firm should purchase insurance on the computers, with coverage during the shipment. Ani would prefer not to spend any funds unless absolutely necessary and believes the firm should negotiate a contract in which the seller has risk of loss. Meg agrees, to some extent, with each of the others. However, she doubts that the firm can get insurance coverage before the firm acquires possession of the computers, so she would prefer to have the seller assume the risk of loss during shipment. Ani has asked you what options are available to eClass in this situation and which option would be best under the circumstances. What will you tell her?

BUSINESS CONSIDERATIONS   When does a buyer acquire an insurable interest in goods being purchased? When does a seller lose its insurable interest in goods being sold?

ETHICAL CONSIDERATIONS   Does the allocation of an insurable interest raise any ethical questions or concerns? Would it be ethical for a seller to choose a less expensive and possibly riskier method of shipment when a buyer purchases insurance to cover the shipment since the seller may no longer be at risk of loss?

party also has a risk of loss. Notice that title is not necessary for an insurable interest to exist. Insurance provides an important protection when a party has any risk of loss for the affected goods, so knowing when an insurable interest arises can be extremely important.

RISK OF LOSS UNDER ARTICLE 2 OF THE UCC

The term risk of loss refers to the financial responsibility between the parties if the goods are lost, damaged, or destroyed before the buyer has accepted them. Notice that risk of loss refers to the relationship between the buyer and the seller. It does not refer to the possibility that an independent carrier of the goods or a warehouseman or bailee hired to store the goods may be liable. Nor does it refer to the possible liability of any insurer of the goods or of their delivery. The allocation of risk of loss normally depends on the method of performance called for in the contract, passing from the seller to the buyer once the seller completes his or her delivery obligations under the terms of the contract.

A buyer who has risk of loss must pay the seller for the goods if the goods were properly shipped. This situation arises most commonly in a shipment contract: If the seller shipped conforming goods, but during the journey the goods were damaged, destroyed, or lost, the buyer is liable and must perform the contract as agreed. Of course, the buyer may have recourse against the carrier, the warehouseman, or against an insurer for the loss, but such recourse involves a separate contract or relationship and does not affect the buyer's liability to the seller.

If the contract involved is a destination contract, the seller bears the risk of loss. In this situation, any lost, damaged, or destroyed goods are the responsibility of the seller. The seller will be required to ship more goods or to make up the loss to the buyer in some other manner. And the seller will then have to proceed against the carrier, the warehouseman, or the insurer for any remedies that may be available under the carriage or storage contract or the insurance coverage.

In contracts that do not involve the use of an independent carrier, the risk of loss will frequently depend on the status of the parties, the terms of the contract, and how adequately the parties have performed. Several possibilities are explored next.

Breach of Contract

If the seller breaches the contract by sending nonconforming goods, risk of loss remains with the seller until either the seller cures the defect or the buyer accepts the goods despite the nonconformity. In order for this provision to apply, the goods must be so nonconforming that the buyer may properly reject the tender of delivery. Sometimes the buyer accepts the goods that the seller sends but later finds them to be nonconforming. When this occurs, the buyer often has the right to revoke acceptance. When accepting the goods, the buyer assumes risk of loss. When the nonconformity is discovered and the acceptance is revoked, what happens? The buyer retains risk of loss, but only to the extent of the buyer's insurance coverage. Any loss in excess of the buyer's insurance rests on the seller because the seller breached the contact. It would not be fair to have the buyer assume risk of loss when the seller is the party at fault in the underlying agreement, nor would it be fair to allow the buyer to recover the complete loss from the seller and to also recover from the insurance company for its payment under the insurance policy.

Sometimes the buyer breaches a contract, usually by repudiation, after the goods are identified but before they are delivered. In such a case, risk of loss has not yet shifted from the seller to the buyer. As a result, the risk still rests on the seller. However, since the buyer is in breach, any loss in excess of the seller's insurance coverage rests on the buyer, applying the same reasoning as set out above. Of course, the buyer will face this possible loss only for a commercially reasonable time, at which point the buyer is relieved of the burden of risk of loss. He or she also still faces the burden of being in breach of contract and may well face liability for that breach.

No Breach of Contract

If the contract is not breached, risk of loss is much more technical. It is difficult to determine where risk of loss resides until the entire contract is reviewed. The UCC recognizes four distinct contract possibilities to allocate risk of loss when the contract has not been breached. In addition, the parties can agree by contract to allocate the risk.

The first situation arises in a contract whereby the seller sends the goods by means of a carrier. If the goods are sent by means of a shipment contract, risk of loss passes to the buyer when the goods are delivered to the carrier. This is true even if the seller reserves rights in the goods pending payment. In contrast, the seller may enter into a destination contract with the carrier. Risk of loss, then, does not pass to the buyer until the goods are properly tendered at the point of destination. Once the goods are made available to the buyer, the buyer has risk of loss.

The second situation arises when the goods are in the hands of a bailee, and they are not to be physically delivered. When the bailee is holding the goods, the contract must be very carefully analyzed. The contract may call for the seller to deliver a negotiable document of title to the buyer. If so, risk of loss passes when the buyer receives the document from the seller. If the seller is not to use a negotiable document of title but does use a nonnegotiable document, risk of loss passes only after the buyer has a reasonable opportunity to present the document to the bailee. And sometimes no document at all is used. In such cases, risk of loss passes to the buyer only after the bailee acknowledges the rights of the buyer in the goods.

The third situation arises when the goods are in the possession of the seller and a carrier is not to be used. Under these circumstances, the status of the seller is the key. If the seller is a merchant, risk of loss does not pass to the buyer until the buyer takes

Exhibit 16.2

Allocation of Risk of Loss

Risk of Loss With No Breach of Contract—§ 2-509

Method of Delivery by Seller	When Risk of Loss Passes to Buyer
Delivery by Carrier	
• With a shipment contract	When the seller surrenders the goods to the carrier and makes arrangements for shipment.
• With a destination contract	When the carrier tenders delivery to the buyer at the destination.
Delivery via Warehouseman	
• With a negotiable document of title	When the document is delivered to the buyer.
• With a non-negotiable document of title	After the buyer receives the document *and* has a reasonable time to notify the warehouseman of his or her rights in the goods.
• Without a document of title	Upon the warehouseman's acknowledgement of the buyer's rights in the goods once the warehouseman has been notified of the sale.
Personal Delivery by the Seller	
• The seller is a merchant	Upon *actual* delivery of the goods to the buyer.
• The seller is not a merchant	Upon *tender* of delivery of the goods to the buyer.

Risk of Loss With a Breach of Contract—§ 2-510

When Breach is Discovered	Allocation of Risk of Loss
• Tender of delivery fails to conform, buyer rightfully rejects	Risk remains with seller until the seller cures or the buyer accepts the goods despite the nonconformity.
• Buyer rightfully revokes an Acceptance	Risk is with the buyer to the extent of the buyer's insurance, if any; any loss beyond the buyer's insurance is treated as remaining with the seller from the beginning.
• Buyer repudiates or otherwise breaches before risk has passed	Risk is with the seller to the extent of the seller's insurance, if any; any loss beyond the seller's insurance lies with the buyer for a commercially reasonable time.

eClass 16.2 Sales

METHODS OF SELLING

Meg contacted a local college bookstore to ask if it might be interested in carrying the eClass software along with its other computer-related items. The bookstore seemed interested but did not want to make a commitment to purchase the software outright. Instead, the store manager asked Meg if eClass might be interested in entering into a "sale-or-return" arrangement so that if the software did not sell, the bookstore would be able to return any unsold diskettes. According to the bookstore manager, this is a normal practice with textbook publishers and a number of other suppliers that deal with the bookstore. Meg would like to get the eClass product into college bookstores, but she is unsure about the potential problems that a sale-or-return arrangement might present for the firm. Before discussing the matter with Ani and Yousef, she decided to ask what *you* think of the idea and what risks and benefits might be involved in a sale or return. What will you tell her?

BUSINESS CONSIDERATIONS   A firm trying to break into an established industry might have to decide whether it is better to try to gain a market share through price competition or through the use of a nonstandard marketing method, such as a sale-or-return arrangement. What are the benefits to using sale or return rather than reduced price to gain market recognition and share? What are the potential drawbacks to this approach?

ETHICAL CONSIDERATIONS   The rights of the creditors of a retail merchant are different in regard to the merchant's inventory if the merchant has goods through a consignment than they are if the merchant has the goods through a sale-or-return contract. If the merchant carries inventory under both bases, what are the ethical obligations of that merchant to provide its creditors with adequate information regarding the inventory? What concerns might the seller or the consignor have about the potential claims of the buyer's creditors?

possession of the goods. If the seller is not a merchant, risk of loss passes on tender of delivery to the buyer. The following two examples show how risk of loss varies with the status of the seller.

Joan is a used-car dealer. She enters a contract with Bob to sell him a car. She tells Bob that the keys are in the car and to go pick it up at any time. Before Bob gets there, the car is destroyed by a fire. Since Joan is a merchant, she still has risk of loss. She will have to provide Bob with another car or refund his money.

Jack is not a car dealer and is not considered a merchant in the sale of cars. He enters a contract to sell his car to Marie. He tells her the keys are in the car and she can pick it up at any time. This is a tender of delivery. Before Marie gets the car, it is destroyed by a fire. She must bear the loss since Jack was a non-merchant and he had tendered delivery.

The fourth set of circumstances applies to a sale on approval. Here, risk of loss remains with the seller until the buyer accepts the goods by approval of the sale. Of course, the various ways the buyer can accept should be kept in mind.

Finally, the parties can agree to allocate risk of loss in any way they wish. Risk of loss can be divided in any manner the parties feel is proper. Such an agreement must be very explicit or the Code provisions just discussed will be applied.

Exhibit 16.2 illustrates the allocation of Risk of Loss under Article 2 of the UCC. It might be helpful to compare how title passes (Exhibit 16.1) with how risk of loss passes. This is a substantial change from the treatment at common law or under the Uniform Sales Act, where title was paramount and risk of loss was simply assigned to the party with title.

SPECIAL PROBLEMS

The commercial world is crowded with businesses trying to get, or trying to keep, "a foot in the door"; or just looking for a new gimmick that will provide an edge. As a result, some special forms of business dealings have arisen. The UCC has attempted to deal with two of these special areas: "sale on approval" and "sale or return." Both of these forms of business dealings resemble yet another form: consignments. The Code deals with these special areas in §§ 2-326 and 2-327.

Sale on Approval

A sale on approval exists if the buyer "purchases" goods primarily for personal use with the understanding that the goods can be returned, even if they conform to the contract. The buyer is given a reasonable time to examine, inspect, and try the goods at the seller's risk. Neither title nor risk of loss passes to the buyer until and unless the buyer "approves" (accepts the goods). The seller retains both title and risk of loss during the buyer's "approval" period, even though the buyer has possession of the goods. The buyer is deemed to have accepted the goods if one of the following occurs:

1. The buyer signifies acceptance.
2. The buyer does not return the goods.
3. The buyer subjects the goods to unreasonable usage.

The following example involves a contract for sale on approval.

Sam "purchases" a new lawn mower with a 30-day "free home trial." He uses the mower six times in three weeks, cutting his lawn and in no way abusing the product.

After the third week, Sam returns the mower and refuses to pay the purchase price. Since this was a sale on approval and Sam never approved, he is not responsible for payment.

Sale or Return

A sale or return exists if the buyer "purchases" goods primarily for resale with the understanding that the unsold goods may be returned to the seller, normally at some specified future date, even if they conform to the contract. In this situation, both title and risk of loss lie with possession of the goods. Goods stolen from the buyer cannot be returned, so they are "sold" to the buyer. The seller must be paid for them. The following example indicates how the purpose of a sale or return differs from the purpose of a sale on approval.

Sam "purchases" some automobile stereo systems from Smooth Sounds, Inc., on a sale-or-return contract. Sam displays one of the stereos in his service station. If a customer wants an auto stereo system, Sam will sell it and install it. Sam can return any unsold units to Smooth Sounds for a refund or for credit on future goods. However, a thief breaks into Sam's station and steals the stereos. Sam must pay Smooth Sounds for the stereos since he cannot return them.

It should be noted that there is a strong presumption *against* any delivery of goods to a merchant for resale of those goods being treated as a sale on approval, or of any delivery of goods to a consumer being a sale or return of those goods.[8] When goods are delivered to a merchant buyer, it is assumed that the transaction is either a normal sale or a sale or return. Similarly, when goods are delivered to a consumer, it is assumed that the transaction is either a normal sale or a sale on approval.

Consignment

In a consignment, the owner of the goods allows a consignee to display and sell the goods for the owner/consignor. The UCC treats such an arrangement as a sale or return unless one of the following occurs:

1. The consignor ensures that signs are posted specifying that the goods on display are consigned goods.
2. The consignor proves that the creditors of the consignee were generally aware of the consignments.
3. The consignor complies with the rules for secured transactions under Article 9 of the UCC.

Obviously, the Code has severely limited, although not entirely eliminated, consignments in the modern business world. Most such arrangements today are treated merely as sale-or-return contracts.

Auctions

Auctions receive special mention in § 2-328. In an auction, the auctioneer, on behalf of the seller, sells the goods to the highest bidder. The auctioneer does not normally give the same warranties to a buyer that other sellers of goods give. A sale at auction is not complete until the auctioneer accepts a bid. Even then, if a bid is made while the auctioneer is in the process of "knocking down," the auctioneer may elect to reopen bidding. The goods at an auction are presumed to be put up "with reserve." An auction will be deemed "without reserve" only if, by its terms, it is specifically and expressly stated to be "without reserve." With reserve means that the auctioneer may declare all the bids to be too low and may refuse to accept any bids or to make any sale. In contrast, if the auction is without reserve, the highest bid made must be accepted and a sale made.

What if the seller enters a bid, directly or indirectly, in an effort to drive up the bidding? The winning bidder in such a case may choose to renounce his or her bidding and to avoid the sale or may elect to take the goods at the last good-faith bid before the seller entered the bidding.

LEASES UNDER ARTICLE 2A OF THE UCC

In much the same manner as under Article 2, Article 2A is not overly concerned with the concept of title. Article 2A specifically separates title and possession. It states that the provisions governing leases apply whether the lessor or a third party has title to the leased goods, and whether the lessor, the lessee, or a third party has possession of the leased goods.

Risk of loss with respect to the leased goods varies depending upon the type of lease involved. In a finance lease, risk of loss passes to the lessee under the provisions of § 2A-219. If the lease is other than a finance lease, risk of loss is retained by the lessor. If the leased goods are in the hands of a bailee and risk of loss is to pass to the lessee, rules similar to those under Article 2 are followed in allocating risk of loss:

- If the goods are in the possession of a bailee and delivery is to occur without movement of the goods, risk of loss passes to the lessee upon the bailee's acknowledgment of the lessee's right to possession of the goods. (Since there is not a sale, there will not be a document of title involved in such a situation.)
- If the goods are to be delivered to the lessee by a carrier, the carriage contract is presumed to be a shipment contract, passing risk of loss to the lessee when the goods are duly delivered to the carrier. If a destination contract is specified, risk of loss passes to the lessee when the goods are duly tendered at the destination.
- If the goods are to be delivered to the lessee by the lessor, passage of risk of loss depends upon the status of the lessor. If the lessor (or the supplier, in the case

of a finance lease) is a merchant, risk of loss passes to the lessee when the goods are actually delivered to the lessee. If the lessor is not a merchant, risk of loss passes to the lessee upon tender of delivery.

TITLE TO GOODS UNDER THE CISG

Article 1 of the CISG states that:

> This Convention governs only the formation of the contract of sale and the rights and obligations of the seller and the buyer arising from such a contract. In particular, except as otherwise expressly provided in this Convention, it is not concerned with:
>
> (a) the validity of the contract or of any of its provisions or of any usage;
> (b) the effect which the contract may have on the property in the goods sold.

Thus, the CISG is not concerned with title—or with a number of other issues that seem important to American businesspersons. The CISG "applies to contracts for the sale of goods between parties whose places of business are in different States and either both of those States are contracting States or the rules of private international law lead to the law of a Contracting State."[9] It would seem the Convention treats title as a "validity question," and "validity questions" are resolved by the applicable laws of the forum state rather than under the provisions of the CISG.

Despite the lack of specific treatment of the title issue, however, the CISG does *imply* how title should be treated under the provisions of the Convention. Article 41 obligates the seller to deliver goods which are free from any right or claim of a third party, unless the buyer agreed to take the goods subject to that right or claim, unless the right or claim is based on industrial property or other intellectual property of the third party. (These claims by a third party based on industrial or other intellectual property of the third party are very similar to the UCC's implied warranty against infringements, which is discussed in Chapter 18.) Thus, while the CISG does not expressly discuss title, there appear to be warranty provisions that assure the buyer will receive title to the goods upon performance by the seller.

RISK OF LOSS UNDER THE CISG

The CISG treats risk of loss in a manner that is very similar to the way in which Article 2 treats risk of loss. Like Article 2, the CISG allocates risk of loss based on how the seller is to deliver the goods to the buyer.

If a common carrier is to be used to transport the goods from the seller to the buyer, the type of carriage contract arranged by the seller determines when risk of loss passes to the buyer. If the sales contract does not designate a destination at which the seller is to deliver the goods, risk of loss passes to the buyer when the goods are handed over to the first carrier.[10] If the seller is obligated to turn the goods over to the carrier at a particular location, risk of loss will pass to the buyer when the goods are handed over to the carrier at that location.[11] The risk of loss will pass to the buyer in either of these circumstances, even if the seller is permitted to retain documents that control the disposition of the goods by the carrier.

If the contract for sale is made while the goods are in transit, risk of loss passes to the buyer upon the conclusion of the contract.[12] Thus, if goods are in a ship at sea and the buyer and seller enter into a contract for the sale of those goods, the buyer assumes risk of loss as soon as the contract is entered, and the seller will be able to enforce the contract and collect the contract price, even if the goods are lost, damaged, or destroyed while at sea.

If the goods are not to be transported by carrier and are not in transit, the risk of loss passes from the seller to the buyer when the buyer either takes possession of the goods *or* fails to take possession of them within a reasonable time after the goods have been placed at his or her disposal, *if* such failure to take possession is a breach of the contract.[13]

STANDARD SHIPPING TERMS

If both parties to a sales contract are merchants, it is a fairly common practice for the parties to the contract to agree that the seller will have the goods delivered to the buyer by a third person, a "common carrier." This is such a common occurrence that the parties have developed standardized terms that are used in the contract to describe the carriage by the third party. These standardized terms are a sort of commercial "shorthand" that merchants use. While the terms do describe the carriage, they also carry other important meanings, including an allocation of risk of loss. And once again, the terms used internationally are different—at least in meaning, even if not always in "letters"—from the terms used under the UCC.

Standard Terms Under the UCC

Every shipping contract must take one of two positions: It is either a *shipment* contract or it is a *destination* contract. In a shipment contract, once the seller makes a proper contract for the carriage of the goods and surrenders them to the care of the carrier, the goods belong to the buyer. The buyer has title and risk of loss. The seller has performed his or her part of the contract. In contrast, in a destination contract, the seller retains title and all risk of loss until the carrier gets the goods to the buyer or wherever the goods are supposed to go under the contract. The seller has not performed until the goods reach their destination.

Under § 2-303, the parties can agree to allocate or share the risk of loss during transit. This sort of arrangement seems to be the exception rather than the rule, however. Most parties seem to ignore the problem of loss during shipment until a loss occurs. And, at that point, it is too late to begin negotiating about what to do if one occurs. Because of this normal oversight, and because so many shipments use standard terms, the UCC allocates risk of loss when the parties to a contract use any of these standard shipping terms. If the parties do not designate how loss is to be allocated, and if the contract does not specify whether it is a shipment contract or a destination contract, the law presumes that the contract is a shipment contract. Thus, once the seller properly transfers the goods to the carrier and makes arrangements for the transportation of the goods, the title and the risk of loss pass to the buyer.

FOB

FOB means "free on board." A seller frequently quotes a price for the goods to the buyer "FOB." This quoted price represents the total cost to the buyer for the goods (including any transportation or loading expenses incurred) at the place named as the FOB point. The buyer is responsible for any costs incurred beyond the FOB point named in the contract. Free on board may be either a shipment contract term or a destination contract term, depending on the place named. If the contract terms are FOB and the named place is the place of shipment (the seller's location), the contract is a shipment contract. Once the seller has the goods loaded by the carrier, the seller has performed fully. If the contract terms are FOB and the named place is the destination (the buyer's location), the contract is a destination contract. The seller has not performed until the goods arrive at the final point, and thus the seller faces the risk of damages during transit.

FAS

FAS means "free along side" and is a standard shipping term for seagoing transportation. This term is normally followed by the name of a vessel and the name of a port. When a seller quotes the price to the buyer "FAS," the seller is telling the buyer that this is the total cost of the goods, including any expenses incurred, to get the goods to the named location. Again, the buyer is responsible for any costs incurred (loading, transportation, insurance, and so on) beyond the FAS point named in the contract. The seller is required only to get the goods to the named vessel and port. Having done so, the seller has performed. The buyer then has all the risks of loading, transporting, and unloading the goods. The buyer is responsible from the dock of shipment to the buyer's location. There is a recent trend to treat FAS as a seagoing FOB term, with the term being either a shipment contract or a destination contract, depending on the named port. This current usage is gradually replacing the more traditional and more correct treatment of FAS as a shipment contract term, with ex-ship being the more traditional and more correct term for a destination contract.

Ex-Ship

The term ex-ship always involves a destination contract. The seller quotes the buyer an "ex-ship" price, which means the price the buyer is to pay to receive tender of the goods from the named ship at the named dock. Like FAS, ex-ship indicates that the transportation is by sea. However, now the seller is responsible for getting the goods both to the named vessel and port and unloaded from the vessel. Here the seller shoulders the risks of loading, transportation, and unloading the goods. Until the goods reach the destination dock, they are the seller's responsibility.

CIF and C & F

CIF means cost, insurance, freight. C & F means cost and freight. When either of these terms is used, the seller quotes a lump-sum price to the buyer. That single price will include the cost of the goods, the freight to get the goods to the buyer, and possibly the cost of the insurance to cover the goods during the carriage. Both terms are deemed to be shipment contracts, with the buyer assuming all the risks associated with the transportation. Under both terms, the seller pays the carrier for the transportation and then includes these freight charges as part of the price quoted to the buyer. The buyer repays the seller for the expenses of the carriage.

No Arrival, No Sale

Under a no arrival, no sale contract, the seller faces the risk of loss if the goods are damaged or destroyed during transit. However, even if the goods are damaged or destroyed, the seller may not be responsible to the buyer to perform the contract. If it can be shown that the seller shipped conforming goods, and if it is not shown that the seller caused the loss or damage, the seller is released from the duty to perform. If the goods shipped were not conforming or if the seller caused the loss, however, the seller is still obligated to ship conforming goods.

COD

COD means collect on delivery. COD is a destination contract with a special feature: The buyer is required to pay for the goods on tender by the carrier but is not permitted to inspect the goods until payment has been made. If the buyer is unable or unwilling to pay on tender, the goods are returned to the seller, and the buyer is likely to be sued and found liable for breach of contract.

eClass 16.3 Management/International Business

COMMUNICATION

Yousef was recently contacted by Carlos, one of his friends who handles sales for NRW. NRW sells a product called InvenTrakR, a Radio Frequency Identification (RFID) chip. A European company told Carlos that it is interested in purchasing thousands of InvenTrakR units, provided that the price is reasonable and that delivery can be made relatively promptly. Carlos sent an e-mail to the European headquarters of the business and suggested that the units should be sent FOB the seller's warehouse. The buyer replied that it would like to receive the goods much more promptly than that. Carlos was confused by this reply and has asked Yousef what the European company meant by that comment. Since Yousef was also unsure, he asks you what the comment meant. What will you tell him?

BUSINESS CONSIDERATIONS   International sales carry a number of benefits for both parties, but there are also a number of risks, including misunderstandings due to language differences and law differences. How can a business ensure that the terms it uses, especially delivery terms, have the same meaning to both parties?

ETHICAL CONSIDERATIONS   Is it ethical for a business to insist that the primary language of its managers be used in all of the international contracts to reduce the chance of misunderstanding the terms of the agreement? What should a business do when a potential contracting party speaks a different language in order to provide protection for both parties?

Standard Shipping Terms in International Trade (IncoTerms)

International sales of goods under the CISG are *expected* to be between merchants, and it is *expected* that the goods will be moved from one nation to another—often after passing by, through, or over several other nations while en route. Very often these goods will be transported by third parties serving as common carriers. And once again, there are standard terms that have been developed and which serve as a sort of commercial "shorthand" between the parties to the contract. However, these provisions are not found in the CISG.

In 1936, the International Chamber of Commerce first developed the "International Rules for the Interpretation of Trade Terms," which provides for one uniform meaning for *in*ternational *c*ommercial *terms*, or IncoTerms. These Inco-Terms became widely known and followed and are encouraged by trade councils, courts, and international experts. The International Chamber of Commerce has amended the general provisions of these IncoTerms a number of times, most recently in 1990. These "IncoTerms 1990" have no automatic legal standing and are only applied if the parties agree to accept them and so state in their contract. Because there are terms (i.e., FOB) that are used as IncoTerms and are also used in the UCC, the parties should also ensure that their contract designates the applicable source of the term. For example, the contract should say FOB (IncoTerms 1990) if the parties want the IncoTerms interpretation of FOB to control in the contract. It is also important for businesses that do not customarily use IncoTerms to be very careful in using them. Many American firms use FOB as a matter of course. If these firms are using IncoTerms, they probably mean to use the term "FCA" in order to provide the same responsibility as "FOB" provides under the UCC.

There are four broad categories of IncoTerms, with each category placing different burdens and responsibilities on the buyer and the seller. These categories are designated by letters—"E" terms, "F" terms, "C" terms, and "D" terms.

"E" Terms

There is only one "E" term, EXW, which stands for "ex-works." Under this term, the seller fulfills its obligation when the goods are made available to the buyer at the seller's premises. The seller is not responsible for loading the goods or for clearing the goods for export. The buyer bears all risks and responsibilities. The "E" term represents the minimum obligation the seller can face.

"F" Terms

"F" terms require the seller to hand over the designated goods to a nominated carrier free of any risk or expense to the buyer. There are three basic "F" terms.

The first is FCA, which means free carrier. To satisfy this term, the seller must hand over goods to a named carrier, cleared for export, at the named location. The name of the location will follow the term, as in "FCA London."

The second is FAS, which means free along side. The seller must place goods alongside a named vessel at a named port with all fees and risks covered to that point. The buyer assumes responsibility and risk once the goods reach the docks alongside the named vessel.

The final "F" term is FOB, which means free on board. As an IncoTerm, FOB transfers risk and responsibility to the buyer as soon as the goods "pass over the ship's rail" at the named destination port. The seller must clear the goods for export under this term, which is only used for sea or inland waterway transportation internationally.

"C" Terms

"C" terms imply that the seller must bear certain costs under the contract. There are four "C" terms.

The first "C" term is CFR, which stands for cost and freight, and is normally followed by a named location, such as Lisbon. The seller must clear the goods for export and bears all risks until the goods pass over the ship's rail at the port of shipment. CFR is only used for sea or inland waterway transportation.

The second "C" term is CIF, which is the same as CFR, except that the seller must also insure the goods during the carriage. The insurance to be carried need only be a minimum (contract price plus 10 percent), unless the agreement sets a different rate.

The third "C" term is CPT, which means carriage paid to (named location). The seller makes arrangements for shipping the goods to a named location, pays the freight or carriage charges, and delivers the goods to the carrier. At that point, the risk transfers to the buyer.

The final "C" term is CIP, which means cost and insurance paid to (named location). The seller has the same obligations as under CPT, plus the obligation to procure insurance (again at minimum coverage) to protect the buyer's potential risk of loss.

"D" Terms

The final type of IncoTerm is the "D" term, which refers to a named destination; the duty of the seller depends on the particular "D" term used.

The first "D" term is DAF, which means delivered at frontier. The seller must make the goods available and clear the goods for export at a named place, but prior to the clearing of customs at the next country. This term is most common with overland transportation of the goods, normally by rail or by truck.

The second term is DES, which means delivered ex-ship at some named port. The seller must make the goods available to the buyer on board the ship, prior to clearing the goods for import, at the named port. This is a seagoing transportation term.

A similar term, again used with seagoing transportation, is DEQ, which means delivery ex-quay. The seller in a DEQ contract is to place the goods on the quay (dock) cleared for importation before the risk passes to the buyer.

DDU, which stands for delivered duty unpaid, may be used for any type of transportation. The seller is to get the goods to a named destination with all fees paid except for import fees and costs, which are to be borne by the buyer.

A similar term, again valid with any type of transport, is DDP, which means delivered duty paid. With this term, the seller is to get the goods to the named destination with all costs paid, including import duties and taxes, and cleared for importation.

Exhibit 16.3 compares the standard shipping terms used under Article 2 of the UCC and the IncoTerms developed by the International Chamber of Commerce. Note that in several cases the *terms* are the same, but the *meaning* of the terms is different. Businesspersons need to exercise care in their international contracts to be certain that the delivery term used carries the meaning the businessperson intended.

Exhibit 16.3

A Comparison of Standard Shipping: UCC and InCoTerms

UCC Terms	Meaning	InCo Terms	Meaning
C&F	Cost and Freight—seller quotes buyer a price for the goods plus freight. Buyer has risk of loss.	CFR	Cost and freight—seller clears goods for export and bears all risks until the goods pass over the ship's rails—used for water transport.
CIF	Cost, Insurance, Freight—same as C&F, plus seller procures insurance in the buyer's name.	CIF	Cost, Insurance, Freight—same as CFR, plus seller insures the goods during transport.
		CPT	Carriage Paid—seller makes arrangements to ship the goods to a named destination, pays the freight, and delivers the goods to the carrier. Buyer takes risk when carrier acquires goods.
		CIP	Cost and Insurance Paid—same as CPT, plus the seller procures insurance to cover the buyer's risk.
		DAF	Delivered at Frontier—seller makes goods available and cleared for export at a named location, but prior to clearance of customs. Normally used for overland transport.
Ex-ship	Ex-ship—seller makes goods available on the dock beside a ship at a named port. Used with water transport. Seller has all risk until the goods reach the dock.	DES	Delivered ex-ship—seller makes goods available on board a ship, prior to clearance for import. Used with water transport.
		DEQ	Delivered ex-quay—seller places goods on the quay (dock) cleared for import before risk shifts to the buyer. Used with water transport.
		DDU	Delivered Duty Unpaid—seller gets goods to a named destination with all fees paid except for import duties. Used with any transport.

Exhibit 16.3 Continued

UCC Terms	Meaning	InCo Terms	Meaning
		DDP	Delivered Duty Paid—same as DDU, except the seller has also paid import duties, taxes, and fees.
		EXW	Ex-works—seller makes goods available to the buyer at the seller's premises. Buyer is responsible for all risks upon tender of delivery.
		FCA	Free Carrier—seller transfers goods to a named carrier, cleared for export.
FAS	Free Along Side—seller gets the goods to a named vessel at a named port, with all fees paid to that point. Buyer has risk during loading. Only used with water transport.	FAS	Free Along Side—seller gets the goods to a named vessel at a named port, with all fees paid to that point. Buyer has risk during loading. Only used with water transport.
FOB	Free On Board—seller quotes a price for goods, with all fees paid, to the location named. Buyer has risk from that point. Used with all forms of transport.	FOB	Free On Board—seller is responsible for getting the goods "over the rail" of a named vessel at a named port, and cleared for export. Only used with water transport.
COD	Collect on Delivery—buyer is to pay for the goods upon tender at the buyer's location. Can be used with any form of transport.		
No Arrival-No Sale	Seller has risk during transport, but is excused from additional obligations if the goods are lost or destroyed during carriage.		

Contemporary Case

LINDHOLM v. BRANT
925 A.2d. 1048, 2007 Conn. LEXIS 264 (Conn. 2007)

FACTS Anders Malmberg, a Swedish art dealer, served as an art advisor to Kirsten Lindholm and her husband for more than 30 years. He handled all of the art purchases and sales by the Lindholms, including the 1987 purchase by Ms. Lindholm of "Red Elvis," a painting by Andy Warhol, for $300,000. The only evidence of this transaction was an invoice she received from Malmberg and written on Malmberg's stationary. This painting was subsequently loaned to various museums as part of a Warhol exhibition.

In 1996, the Guggenheim Museum sponsored an exhibition of Warhol paintings that would travel to various European venues before concluding in New York City. Peter M. Brant, a member of the Guggenheim board of trustees, owned several Warhol paintings, and he agreed to lend some of these to the exhibition. He also agreed to help arrange for the museum to borrow Warhol paintings from some other owners, including the "Red Elvis" painting. The "Red Elvis" did become part of the exhibit, bearing an identification plaque reading: *"Private Collection, Courtesy Anders Malmberg, Malmo, Sweden."*

In 1998, Mr. Lindholm initiated divorce proceedings against his wife. Ms. Lindholm then enlisted the aid of Malmberg in selling some works of art. They entered into an agreement that designated Malmberg as her agent for the purpose of selling "certain works," although which works were to be sold was not stated. However, Ms. Lindholm did not discuss selling "Red Elvis," nor did she ever agree to do so.

In 1999, Mr. Brant was attempting to purchase additional Warhol painting, including "Red Elvis." He was told that Malmberg had purchased the "Red Elvis" and was willing to sell it. In February 2000, Brant agreed to pay Malmberg $2.9 million for the "Red Elvis" painting, and following negotiations to work out the details of payment and delivery, Brant took possession of the painting on April 12, 2000.

In January 2001, Ms. Lindholm agreed to sell "Red Elvis" to a Japanese buyer for $4.6 million and instructed Malmberg to have the painting delivered to the buyer. At that time, she was unaware that Malmberg had already sold the painting to Brant. In June 2001, Ms. Lindholm read a magazine article reporting that Brant had purchased "Red Elvis." Ms. Lindholm contacted Brant, informing him that she had not authorized the sale of the painting and demanding its return. When he refused, she filed suit to recover the painting. Brant's defense was that he was a buyer in the ordinary course of business and had acquired all of Ms. Lindholm's rights in the painting.

ISSUES Was the painting entrusted to Malmberg, thus giving him voidable title? Was Brant a buyer in the ordinary course of business?

HOLDINGS Yes, to both issues.

REASONING Excerpts from the opinion of Sullivan, J.:

We are required ... to determine whether the defendant followed the usual or customary practices and observed reasonable commercial standards of fair dealing in the art industry in his dealings with Malmberg. ... [T]he defendant presented expert testimony that the vast majority of art transactions ... are "completed on a handshake and an exchange of invoice." It is customary to rely upon representations made by respected dealers regarding their authority to sell works of art. A dealer customarily in not required to present an invoice establishing when and for whom he bought the artwork or the conditions of the purchase. . . .

We agree . . . that a merchant buyer has a heightened duty to inquiry when a reasonable merchant would have doubts or questions regarding the seller's authority to sell. We further conclude that the steps that a merchant must take to conform to reasonable commercial standards before consummating a deal depend on all the facts and circumstances surrounding the sale. . . . [T]he defendant took the extraordinary step of hiring counsel to conduct an investigation and to negotiate a formal contract of sale on his behalf . . . In addition, during the course of the investigation, the defendant's counsel conducted both a lien search and an Art Loss Register search that revealed no competing claims to Red Elvis. . . . [Brant] had little reason to doubt Malmberg's claim that he was the owner of Red Elvis, and any doubts he did have reasonably were allayed by relying on . . . assurances that Malmberg had bought the painting from [Lindholm] because she needed money due to her divorce. . . . [Brant's] concerns were further allayed when Malmberg delivered Red Elvis to a bonded warehouse in Denmark, the delivery location . . . agreed to in the contract of sale. . . . At the time of the sale, the painting was on loan to the Guggenheim, whose policy it was to release a painting only to the true owner, or to someone the true owner had authorized to take possession. . . . Knowing that the Guggenheim would release the painting to an authorized party only, it was reasonable for the defendant to believe that Malmberg was the true owner of the painting. We conclude that these steps were sufficient to conform to reasonable commercial standards for the sale of artwork under the circumstances and, therefore, that the defendant had status as a buyer in the ordinary course of business.

You Be the Judge

Step-Saver was a computing firm that helped customers find and deploy the optimal computer system for each customer. In response to the needs of doctors and lawyers to have a multi-user system readily accessed from anyone in the office, Step-Saver looked at a number of available software packages. The Software Link provided a multi-user software package called Multilink Advanced that seemingly met all of the requirements Step-Saver wanted, and the two firms began negotiations for a contract. After several telephone calls in which Step-Saver asked questions and detailed its technical needs, and received appropriate responses from The Software Link, Step-Saver placed an order for the software. Following these negotiations, each party sent confirming documentation to the other, capturing the terms of their agreement.

Step-Saver ultimately purchased 142 copies of The Software Link and combined this software with other software and hardware in a package for its medical and legal office customers. Unfortunately, problems quickly developed, apparently due to the fact that Multilink Advanced did not work compatibly with the rest of the package. When Step-Saver sued, The Software Link asserted that it was not liable. The Software Link alleged that the "box top license" found on the software's packaging became a part of the contract. This box top license asserted that the customer had not purchased the software, but rather had acquired a license to use it. It also purported to disclaim any warranties and to limit liability for any problems encountered. Step-Saver denied that this language was part of the contract, pointing out that it had never been discussed in the telephone negotiations nor included in the final documentation.

This case has been brought in *your* court. How will *you* decide this controversy? What is the most important fact or factor affecting your decision? [See *Step-Saver Data Systems, Inc. v. Wyse Technology*, 939 F.2d 91 (3d Cir. 1991).]

Summary

In this chapter, we examined the concept and importance of title to goods. Under the UCC, title passes at any time the parties agree. If the parties do not agree, title passes when the seller completes his or her performance. Title can revest in the seller if the buyer refuses to accept the goods, rejects them, or revokes the acceptance. The primary area in which title is important today is that of creditor rights.

The concept of risk of loss is much more important under the Code than it is under common law. Risk of loss refers to the party—buyer or seller—who must bear the burden of lost, damaged, or destroyed goods when the loss occurs during the performance stage of the contract. Risk of loss is allocated in a similar manner in both a sale of goods and in the leasing of goods under a finance lease. In a nonfinance lease, risk of loss remains with the lessor throughout the lease.

Some special problems have developed from modern business practices. Before the adoption of the UCC, consignments were frequently used to sell goods. Today, consignments have virtually been replaced by sale-on-approval and sale-or-return contracts. Each of these areas is specifically treated under Article 2. Special treatment is also provided for consignments and for auctions under Article 2.

Article 2A separates title and possession, and allocates risk of loss to the parties based on the type of lease contract involved. In a finance lease, risk of loss passes to the lessee in the same manner as risk of loss passes to the buyer in a sales contract. For example, if a carrier is involved, the passage of risk of loss is determined by whether the delivery is a shipment contract or a destination contract. If the lease is other than a finance lease, risk of loss remains with the lessor and does not pass to the lessee.

The CISG was created by compromises among the various factions that make up the United Nations. There were disagreements among common law, civil law, and Islamic law nations; between developed and developing nations; and between capitalist and socialist nations. Despite these differences, a Convention was created and has been ratified or adopted by 74 nations as of May 2009. The CISG views title as a validity of the contract issue to be addressed under the law of the forum hearing the case. It treats risk of loss similarly to the treatment afforded under the UCC, with an emphasis on the seller's delivery duties in determining how risk of loss will be allocated. The parties to a sale often use standard shipping terms. The meaning of these "standard terms" will depend on the context in which they are used. If the contract is governed by the UCC, one interpretation applies. However, if the contract involves an international sale of goods, a different interpretation is likely to apply. The UCC classifies any carriage contract as forming either a shipment contract or a destination contract and imposes the burdens and responsibilities on each party accordingly. In a shipment contract, the buyer bears the risks of loss or damage during transportation. In a destination contract, the seller bears the risks of loss or damage during transportation.

The International Chamber of Commerce developed the "International Rules for the Interpretation of Trade Terms," which provides uniform meanings for these IncoTerms. IncoTerms are broken down into four broad categories, with each category imposing different burdens and responsibilities on the parties to contracts when they use standard shipping terms. The categories are "E" terms, "F" terms, "C" terms, and "D" terms.

Discussion Questions

1. Under Article 2 of the UCC, when does title pass from the seller to the buyer in a sale of goods contract? Under the CISG, when does title pass from the seller to the buyer in a sale of goods contract?

2. Two parties enter into a sales contract under Article 2 of the UCC. The contract calls for the seller to send the goods to the buyer via a common carrier. The seller would like to use a *shipment* contract, while the buyer would prefer a *destination* contract. What is the legal effect of a *shipment* contract as compared with that of a *destination* contract? How can a party tell if the delivery terms involve a shipment contract or a destination contract?

3. Under Article 2 of the UCC, when does risk of loss pass from the seller to the buyer? Under Article 2A of the UCC, when does risk of loss pass from the lessor or supplier to the lessee? When does risk of loss pass from the seller to the buyer under the CISG?

4. Suppose that goods are to be *consigned* to a merchant for sale. What would the owner/consignor need to show in order to establish that the goods in the hands of the merchant were consigned goods rather than goods that had been sold under a sale-or-return (or other sales) contract? Why might the owner/consignor want or need to establish that a consignment exists?

5. A buyer and a seller enter into a contract for the sale of goods, and the parties agree that the goods will be shipped to the buyer "FOB" the buyer's place of business. What does this mean if the contract is governed by the UCC? What does this mean if the contract is an international sale of goods, with the standard terms interpreted as an ICC IncoTerm? If the buyer would prefer one interpretation to the other, what can he or she do to ensure that such an interpretation will be used?

Case Problems and Writing Assignments

1. In June 2001, a group called ArtColl Trust purchased "Mystery of the Beach" ("the painting") from a European seller. On May 26, 2004, ArtColl Trust assigned the painting to Deca Trust, and on the same day, Deca Trust and MIN entered into a consignment agreement. MIN's obligations under the agreement were to take possession of the painting for the purpose of making and receiving offers on its sale.

The consignment agreement stated that MIN had to obtain Deca Trust's written consent before removing the painting from MIN's New York premises. The agreement also stated that MIN did not have authority to sell the painting without Deca Trust's approval. The agreement limited MIN to selling the painting for a gross price of not less than $7 million. MIN was permitted to sell the painting for less, provided that Deca Trust received at least $6 million in net sales proceeds after MIN took its commission. Deca Trust and MIN added an amendment to their consignment agreement on December 20, 2006, to allow the painting to be loaned to the Museum of Modern Art ("MoMA") for a Munch exhibition from January 30, 2006, through May 26, 2006.

The Wurth Entities are based in Germany and Switzerland. Wurth KG owns a museum called Museum Wurth, and the Wurth Entities acquire more than 1,000 paintings a year and earn income from the public display of their painting collections. In early 2006, an art consultant and dealer named Christoph Graf Douglas contacted Sylvia Weber, the curator for Museum Wurth, to tell her that "Mystery of the Beach" was for sale. Douglas is allegedly also a co-owner of a separate art-consulting business in New York with Nash, MIN's director. The Complaint alleges that the Wurth Entities and MIN had worked together on art sales and purchases on previous occasions.

In response to Douglas's call about "Mystery of the Beach," Weber allegedly told Douglas to contact MIN and have MIN contact her. A MIN employee named Lucy Dew then contacted Weber in February 2006 and sent a photo of the painting to Weber. The Complaint states that the Defendants "instructed one of their agents to view the Painting in New York" in connection with their interest in purchasing the painting.

On April 7, 2006, a Wurth Museum representative e-mailed Dew and asked whether the painting was still available. At some point between April 7 and May 18, Weber allegedly phoned MIN and asked MIN to ship the painting to Germany. The painting returned to MIN from the MoMA exhibit on May 12, 2006, and MIN shipped it to Germany on May 18. Before the painting was shipped, MIN and the Defendants allegedly agreed on a purchase price

of $6.5 million. Despite the clear language of the consignment agreement, MIN never notified Deca Trust of its dealings with the Wurth Entities or that it had shipped the painting to Germany.

Sometime between May 24 and May 31, Weber telephoned MIN and said that the Wurth Entities would purchase the painting. Over the next several weeks, Defendants and MIN discussed how the painting would be invoiced, and on June 14, 2006, Wurth International wired $6.5 million to MIN's account at First Republic Bank in New York City.

Once the sale was complete, MIN finally advised Deca Trust of the Defendants' interest in and subsequent purchase of the painting. MIN director Nash allegedly contacted Tara Coram, Senior Curator for Deca Trust, on June 21, 2006, and said that he had a prospective buyer for the painting for $6.5 million. Nash asked that he be able to retain a commission that would leave Deca Trust with only $5.85 in net proceeds. On July 6, 2006, after Deca Trust rejected Nash's proposal, Nash told Coram that he had already sold the painting for $6.5 million, and Nash informed Coram that he was no longer in possession of the painting. At Deca Trust's request, Nash sent a letter to Defendants requesting return of the painting and cancellation of the sale, but Defendants refused.

Deca Trust has sued to recover the painting from Wurth, arguing that Wurth never acquired title. How should the court resolve this dispute? What is the most important fact or factor influencing your decision? Should this case be resolved under the UCC, the CISG, or the common law of contracts? Why? [See *Brown v. Mitchell-Innes & Nash, Inc.*, 2009 U.S. Dist. LEXIS 35081; 68 U.C.C. Rep. Serv. 2d (Callaghan) 599 (S.D. N.Y. 2009).]

2. Chicago Prime, a Colorado corporation, and Northam, a partnership formed under the laws of Ontario, Canada, are both wholesalers of meat products. On March 30, 2001, Chicago Prime contracted to sell Northam 1,350 boxes (40,500 pounds) of pork back ribs. Northam agreed to pay $178,200.00 for the ribs, with payment due within seven days of receipt of the shipment.

The contract also set forth a description of the ribs, the price, and the date and location for pick-up.

Chicago Prime purchased the ribs specified in the contract from meat processor Brookfield Farms. When a pork loin is processed at Brookfield, it is broken into various segments, one of which is the back rib. After processing, Brookfield packages back ribs "flat" (horizontally), layer by layer, in 30-pound boxes. The ribs are placed first in a blast freezer and then transferred to an outside freezer, where they remain until shipped.

In addition to its own freezers, Brookfield stored the ribs at issue in this case in as many as two independent cold storage facilities: B&B Pullman Cold Storage and Fulton Market Cold Storage. According to Brookfield's temperature logs and quality control records for its own facilities, the ribs were maintained at acceptable temperatures and were processed and maintained in accordance with Brookfield's procedures. Records presented at trial also indicate that the ribs were stored at or below acceptable temperatures during the entire time they were in B&B's possession. The parties offered no evidence regarding storage of the ribs at Fulton.

On April 24, 2001, Brown Brother's Trucking Company, acting on behalf of Northam, picked up 40,500 pounds of ribs from B&B. Chicago Prime, the seller, never possessed the ribs. When Brown accepted the shipment, it signed a bill of lading, thereby acknowledging that the goods were "in apparent good order." The bill of lading also indicated, however, that the "contents and condition of contents of packages [were] unknown." The next day, Brown delivered the shipment to Northam's customer, Beacon Premium Meats. Like Chicago Prime, Northam, the buyer, never possessed the ribs. Upon delivery, Beacon signed a second bill of lading acknowledging that it had received the shipment "in apparent good order," except for some problems not at issue in this case.

Under the terms of the contract, Northam was obligated to pay Chicago Prime by May 1, 2001. Sandra Burdon, who negotiated the contract on behalf of Northam, testified that on that date, Northam had

no basis for withholding payment. In fact, she thought that a check had been sent to Chicago Prime prior to May 1, 2001, but subsequently discovered that the check had not been mailed. On May 2, 2001, Chicago Prime, not having heard from Northam, demanded payment.

On May 4, 2001, Beacon began "processing" a shipment of ribs and noticed that the product appeared to be in an "off condition." Beacon asked Inspector Ken Ward of the United States Department of Agriculture to examine the product. Ward inspected the ribs at the Beacon facility, found that the meat "did not look good," and ordered Beacon to stop processing it. Ward then placed a "U.S. Retained" tag on the shipment, noting "yellow, green, temperature, abused, spoiled," and had the ribs placed in Beacon's freezer. The same day, Northam and Chicago Prime learned of a potential problem with the ribs.

Inspector Ward returned to Beacon on May 7 and 8, 2001, and examined both frozen and thawed samples of the product. On May 23, 2001, Dr. John Maltby, Ward's supervisor, also conducted an on-site inspection of the ribs. Dr. Maltby reviewed Beacon's shipping records and temperature logs from the relevant time period and found no "anomalies" or "gaps." In addition, he examined approximately 20 cases of ribs and prepared a written report. According to this report, Beacon gave Dr. Maltby two pallets of frozen ribs untouched by Beacon, as well as some of the product that Beacon had reworked. Looking inside the intact pallets, Dr. Maltby found ribs stacked both horizontally and vertically, with some frozen individually and others frozen together in larger units. The individually frozen ribs were "putrid," while the ribs frozen in larger units were "good."

Examining samples of the thawed, reworked product, Dr. Maltby found putrid, green, slimy ribs, but no sign of temperature abuse. He concluded in his report that the inspected product was rotten, that it arrived at Beacon in a rotten condition, and that it appeared to have been "assembled from various sources." Dr. Maltby also concluded that there was no opportunity for salvage and that all of the product should be condemned. The same day, the USDA issued a Notice of Receipt of Adulterated or Misbranded Product, and the entire shipment of 1,350 boxes of ribs was condemned. After Northam informed it of the results of Dr. Malby's inspection, Chicago Prime continued to demand payment and eventually filed suit.

Chicago Prime has sued for the contract price, alleging that title and risk of loss had passed to Northam and that, as a result, Chicago Prime was entitled to payment. Northam denied any liability, asserting that Chicago Prime had breached the contract so that risk of loss never passed to the buyer. How should the court decide this case? What fact or factor most influenced your decision? [See *Chicago Prime Packers, Inc. v. Northam Food Trading Co.*, 408 F.3d 894; 2005 U.S. App. LEXIS 9355 (7th Cir. 2005).]

3. Shared Imaging, Inc., an American corporation, purchased a mobile magnetic resonance imaging system from Neuromed Medical Systems & Support, GmbH, a German corporation, and agreed to accept the system "CIF (cost, insurance, freight) New York Seaport." The contract also provided that German law would govern resolutions of disputes, that Neuromed would retain title until final payment, and that acceptance by Shared Imaging was "subject to inspection." The system was delivered in good working order at a port for transport but was damaged and needed extensive repair when it arrived in Illinois. Two companies that insured the system during transport paid a claim filed by the buyer, and they filed a subrogation claim against Neuromed.

Neuromed asserted that under the provisions of the CISG and the meaning of CIF as applied by the CISG, it was not liable. The insurance companies alleged that since the buyer was a U.S. corporation, and since the contract was for the sale of goods, the UCC applied, including the interpretation of CIF under the UCC.

How should the court resolve this case? What fact or factor most influenced your decision? [See *St. Paul Guardian Insurance Company v. Neuromed Medical Systems & Support, GmbH*, 2002 U.S. Dist. LEXIS 5096 (S.D. N.Y., 2002).]

Notes

1. *A Handbook of Basic Law Terms*, Bryan A. Garner, ed., p. 217 (St. Paul: West Group, 1999).
2. Uniform Sales Act, § 19, Rules 1-5.
3. Bradford Stone, *Uniform Commercial Code in a Nutshell*, pp. 39-43 (St. Paul: West Group, 2002).
4. Ibid., pp. 43-46.
5. Ibid., p.47.
6. UCC § 2-403(3)
7. Edwin W. Patterson, *Essentials of Insurance Law*, § 22 (2d ed., 1957).
8. UCC § 2-306, Official Comments.
9. Explanatory Note by the UNCITRAL Secretariat on the United Nations Convention on Contracts for the International Sale of Goods, Part One, A. 7.
10. CISG, Article 67.
11. Ibid.
12. CISG, Article 68.
13. CISG, Article 69(1).

17

Performance and Remedies

Agenda

eClass purchases diskettes for its software from several different suppliers and outsources most of its packaging. As a result, the firm has little direct control over the quality of its final product when it is shipped to the customers. The customers who purchase the downloadable version of the software have few problems or complaints about the software unless a technical issue such as compatibility with the customer's computer and operating system becomes a concern. The principals realize that some of the diskettes may be defective, resulting in customer complaints that some of the sales involve defective products. There is a very real possibility that the firm will be sued or will have to file suit in some of these situations. The principals are concerned about what they can expect from their suppliers and what duties they owe to their customers. They are also concerned about the types of remedies that may be available to them or that may be asserted against them. They are likely to have a number of questions for you in these areas. Be prepared! You never know when the firm will be asking you for advice.

Classic Case

MAPLE FARMS, INC. v. CITY SCHOOL DISTRICT

76 Misc. 2d 1080, 352 N.Y.S.2d 784, 1974 N.Y. Misc. LEXIS 1070 (S. Ct. N.Y. 1974)

FACTS Maple Farms had a contract with the City School District of Elmira to supply milk for the District's schools. The contract called for Maple Farms to supply milk at a set price of $0.0759 per half pint for the 1973–74 school year. The School District based its budget on this price. Maple Farms asserts that this price was based, at least in part, on the cost of raw milk at the time of the contract. (The price of raw milk is controlled by the U.S. Department of Agriculture through the New York–New Jersey Milk Administrator.) By November 1973, the price of raw milk increased 23 percent from the price at the time of the contract, at which point Maple Farms asked the School District to release Maple Farms from the contract and to put the contract out for rebidding. The School District refused, and Maple Farms filed suit seeking a termination of the contract due to legal "impossibility" or "impracticability" due to events not contemplated by the parties at the time of contract formation.

ISSUE Does the substantial increase in cost constitute a legal impossibility or impracticability sufficient to excuse Maple Farms from its performance obligations under the contract?

HOLDING No. Where economic hardship alone is involved, performance will not be excused.

REASONING Excerpts from the opinion of Judge Charles B. Swartwood:

. . . The plaintiff spells out in detail its costs based on the June and December prices of raw milk and shows that it will sustain a loss of $7,350.55 if it is required to continue its performance on the same volume with raw milk at the December price. Its contracts with other school districts where it is faced with the same problem will triple its total contemplated loss. . . .

The plaintiff goes to great lengths to spell out the cause of the substantial increase in the price of raw milk, which the plaintiff argues could not have been foreseen by the parties because it came about in large measure from the agreement of the United States to sell huge amounts of grain to Russia and to a lesser extent to unanticipated crop failures.

The legal basis of the plaintiff's request for being relieved of the obligation under the contract . . . is the doctrine known variously as "impossibility of performance" and "frustration of performance" at common law and as "excuse by failure of presupposed conditions" under section 2-615 of the Uniform Commercial Code.

The common law rule is stated in Restatement of Law, Contracts (vol. 2, § 454) as follows: . . . "impossibility means not only strict impossibility but impracticability because of an extreme and unreasonable difficulty, expense, injury or loss involved." . . .

Section 2-615 of the Uniform Commercial Code states in part: "Except so far as a seller may have assumed a greater obligation and subject to the preceding section on substituted performance:

> (a) Delay in delivery or non-delivery in whole or in part by a seller . . . is not in breach of his duty under a contract for sale if performance as agreed has been made impracticable by the occurrence of a contingency the non-occurrence of which was a basic assumption on which the contract was made or by compliance in

good faith with any applicable foreign or domestic governmental regulation or order whether or not it later proves to be valid."

The Official Comment, No. 3 to that section points out that the test or impracticability is to be judged by commercial standards. Official Comment No. 4 states: "increased cost alone does not excuse performance unless the rise in cost is due to some unforeseen contingency which alters the essential nature of the performance . . . for that is exactly the type of business risk for which business contracts made at fixed prices are intended to cover."

Applying these rules to the facts here, we find that the contingency causing the increase in the price of raw milk was not totally unexpected. The price from the low point in the year 1972 to the price on the date . . . of the contract in June 1973 had risen nearly 10% and any business man should have been aware of the general inflation in this country during the previous years and of the chance of crop failures. . . .

There is no precise point . . . at which an increase in price of raw goods above the norm would be so disproportionate to the risk assumed as to amount to "impracticality" in a commercial sense. However, we cannot say on these acts that increase here has reached the point of "impracticality: in performance of the contact in light of the risks that we find were assumed by the plaintiff. . . .

The plaintiff's motion is denied and the defendant is granted summary judgment dismissing the complaint.

PERFORMANCE OF A SALES CONTRACT

General Obligations

The performance of a sales contract seems very simple and straightforward. The seller delivers the goods to the buyer, who accepts the goods and pays for them. In practice, this is very often what occurs. However, the exceptions to this simple and straightforward process provide a myriad of possibilities which need to be explored and explained if a businessperson is to be able to protect his or her interests in this area. The performance obligations must be examined, as must the intervening rights of the parties. We have already discussed the topics of *title* (who owns the goods at any particular point in time) and *risk of loss* (who is financially and legally responsible for any loss, damage, or destruction of the goods during performance), as well as "standard shipping terms" and "special problems" in Chapter 16. Those issues may affect the performance obligations of the parties and the availability of remedies, so keep them in mind as you study the materials in this chapter.

To further complicate this seemingly simple and straightforward area, there may well be an issue as to what law governs the transaction, depending upon the domicile of the parties. If both parties are U.S. citizens and the contract is formed within the United States, the applicable law is likely to be Article 2 of the UCC. However, if either—or both—parties are non-residents of the United States, there is a good chance that some other law will control. If so, the controlling law is increasingly likely to be the CISG, more formally known as the United Nations Convention on Contracts for the International Sale of Goods. While both the UCC and the CISG expect the seller to deliver the goods to the buyer and then the buyer to inspect the goods and to pay for them, they differ in a number of ways in deciding how the parties can meet these expectations, and also in treating what happens if one or the other of the parties does not perform as is expected. A number of these differences will be addressed in this chapter.

SALES UNDER ARTICLE 2 OF THE UCC

The parties to a sales contract are required by the Uniform Commercial Code to act in good faith. In addition, any merchant who is a party to a sales contract is obligated to act in a commercially reasonable manner. These two standards are broad enough that they could adequately regulate the basic sales contract. The drafters of the Code decided, however, that more specific provisions were needed to supplement these rules and standards.

The most basic and obvious obligation is spelled out in § 2-301. Under that section, the seller is to transfer and deliver conforming goods to the buyer. The buyer is then to accept and pay for the goods so delivered. Both parties are to perform in accordance with the terms of the contract.

Conforming goods are goods that are within the description of the goods as set out in the contract. Payment by the buyer will normally be made at the time and place of delivery and will be made in money. However, the Code permits payment in money, goods, realty, or "other."[1] The manner of payment, whatever the form, will normally be spelled out in the contract.

The Code presumes that both parties will be acting in good faith, with the seller selling and the buyer buying.[2] In addition, if one of the parties to the contract is a *merchant*, the merchant is expected to observe the reasonable commercial standards of fair dealings in the trade.[3] And, of course, everything is being done according to the terms of the contract. If that was all that Article 2 said, the rules of contracts from common law would be more than adequate to cover sales. The true value of the Code's coverage of sales is what it provides if, or when, the contract is defective, incomplete, or unclear in some area.

Cooperation

As a final and overriding obligation, the parties are required to cooperate with one another in the performance of their respective duties. Any failure to cooperate or any interference with the performance of the other party can be treated as a breach of contract or as an excuse for a delayed performance.

Seller's Duties

The seller in a contract for the sale of goods has a very simple basic duty: The seller is to *tender delivery* of conforming goods according to the terms of the contract. The parties can agree to make delivery in any manner they desire. If they do not agree, or if they simply fail to consider how delivery is to occur, the Uniform Commercial Code covers the topic for them. Section 2-503 explains tender of delivery. The seller has properly tendered delivery by putting and holding conforming goods at the buyer's disposition and then notifying the buyer that the goods are available. Normally, the contract will tell the seller when and where to make the goods "available." When it does not, the seller must make his or her tender at a reasonable time and place, and the buyer must provide facilities suitable for receiving the goods. This all sounds technical and confusing, but in practice delivery is fairly simple. There are five possible ways delivery can occur:

1. The *buyer* personally takes the goods *from* the seller.
2. The *seller* personally takes the goods *to* the buyer.
3. The *seller ships* the goods to the buyer by means of a common carrier.
4. The goods are in the hands of a *third person* (bailee), and *no documents of title* are involved.
5. The goods are in the hands of a *third person* (bailee), and the seller is to deliver some *document of title* to the buyer.

If the seller properly tenders delivery under any of these situations and the goods are conforming, the seller has performed his or her duty under the contract.

Tender entitles the seller to have the buyer accept the goods and entitles the seller to receive payment for the goods. If the buyer and seller make the delivery personally and directly (possibilities 1 and 2), proper tender is obvious. The seller will provide properly packaged goods to the buyer. The buyer will accept the goods and pay for them. Very neat and very simple. If the goods are in the hands of a third person, referred to as a bailee, delivery becomes somewhat more complicated. The seller in these cases must either provide the buyer with a negotiable document of title covering the goods (possibility 5) or get some acknowledgment from the bailee that the goods now belong to the buyer (possibility 4). If the buyer objects to anything less than a negotiable document of title, the seller must provide a negotiable document in order to prove that a proper tender of delivery was made.

The UCC treats the topic of documents of title in Article 7. This article, entitled "Warehouse Receipts, Bills of Lading, and Other Documents of Title," specifies the rights and duties of all relevant parties in the handling of documents of title, whether those documents are negotiable or nonnegotiable. In addition to the coverage of a document of title by Parts 1 and 2 (for a warehouse receipt) or Parts 1 and 3 (for a bill of lading), both Parts 4 and 5 of this article deal with warehouse receipts and bills of lading if the document of title is negotiable. In order to reduce the amount of statutory coverage involved, and to avoid the problems of determining whether there has been "due negotiation" of the document making the holder a "holder by due negotiation" (a favored position under the law), most commercial warehousemen and common carriers simply issue nonnegotiable documents of title to protect themselves. These two areas limit and control how a seller of stored goods may tender delivery to a buyer.

None of the methods of delivery that have been described is very troublesome. The problems in understanding delivery normally arise when a common carrier enters the picture (possibility 3). Now the seller must give the goods to the carrier, the carrier must transport the goods to the buyer, and the buyer must accept the transported goods and make payment for them. As one might expect, the more parties involved in a transaction, the more likely that problems and confusion will enter the picture.

The seller must provide for reasonable carriage of the goods, taking into account the nature of the goods, the need for speed, and any other factors that will affect delivery. The seller must then obtain and deliver to the buyer any necessary documents concerning the carriage, and the seller must promptly notify the buyer of the shipment. Again, all these steps seem obvious, and none should cause any undue problems or hardships. The problems arise when the parties use technical and/or legal terms without understanding their meaning. This area generally involves the use of standard shipping terms, a topic discussed in Chapter 16. We also compared and contrasted the standard shipping terms used in the United States under the UCC with the standard shipping terms used in international sales of goods, *IncoTerms*, in Chapter 16.

Intervening Rights

Once the seller's single duty has been performed, the focus of the sales contract shifts. Even though the seller has performed, it is not yet time for the buyer to perform. First, the buyer has an intervening right, the right to inspect the goods. If this inspection results in a discovery of some nonconformity, the seller may have a right to cure the defective performance to avoid a breach. Only after these intervening rights have been exercised or waived does the duty of the buyer to perform arise.

Inspection   The right of the buyer to inspect the goods is covered in § 2-513. This section empowers the buyer to inspect the goods in any reasonable manner and at any reasonable time and place. This includes inspection after the goods arrive at their destination, if the seller ships the goods. The buyer bears the expense of inspection. This serves two functions: (1) It encourages the buyer to use a more reasonable method of inspection (since the buyer must pay for it); and (2) it eliminates "phantom" inspections, with the expenses billed to the other person. If the inspection reveals that the goods do not conform to the contract, the buyer is entitled to recover the expenses of the inspection from the seller, along with any other damages the buyer may be entitled to recover.

There are two circumstances in which the buyer is required to pay for the goods before being allowed to inspect them. If the contract calls for payment against documents or if it is COD, inspection before payment is not allowed. However, such a pre-inspection payment is not treated as an acceptance under the Code.

In contrast, if the right to inspect the goods before payment exists, a pre-inspection payment is treated as an acceptance. If the buyer fails to inspect, or refuses to inspect, or inspects poorly, the buyer may waive some rights. Any defects that should be noticed or discovered by a reasonable inspection may not be raised, argued, or relied on after an unreasonable inspection. The one exception is when the seller promises to correct, or cure, the problem and then fails to do so. In other words, unless the defect is hidden (so that a reasonable inspection would not reveal it), the buyer must "speak now or forever hold his peace."

Cure   Often the buyer will discover on inspection that the goods do not conform exactly to the description in the contract. When this happens, the buyer must make a decision. Either (1) the nonconformity is minor, or of little or no consequence, in which case the buyer will normally accept the goods despite the nonconformity; or (2) the goods are too different from those described in the contract to be acceptable. When this happens, the buyer must promptly notify the seller, specifying in detail the problems with the goods that result in nonconformity. If the time for performance has not yet expired, the Code gives the seller a chance to avoid being held in breach. The seller may cure the defect in the goods, putting the goods into conformity with the contract. However, the cure must be completed within the time period in which the original contract was to be performed. No extension of time is permitted without the buyer's permission.

Occasionally, a seller ships nonconforming goods and reasonably expects the buyer to accept them despite the nonconformity. Such an expectation may be realistically based on typical past dealings between the parties, prior performances between the parties, or industry standards. In such a case, if the buyer decides to stand by the literal terms of the contract and refuses to accept the nonconforming goods and so informs the seller, the UCC gives the seller a right to cure even if the time for performance is past. If the seller informs the buyer of an intention to cure the defect, the seller is given a reasonable time to cure by substituting conforming goods so that the seller's performance is in compliance with the contract. The following example addresses this issue.

A merchant seller and a merchant buyer have done business together over several previous contracts, each of which involved the sale of a particular component part the buyer uses in its manufacturing process. Each of these previous contracts called for the seller to deliver the component part Brand A. On at least one prior occasion, the seller did not have an adequate supply of Brand A to satisfy the contract, so the seller substituted Brand B (a competing brand with similar characteristics and price), and the buyer accepted the substituted component without objection. In the current contract, the seller once again had an inadequate supply of Brand A and decided to fill the contract by shipping Brand B instead. When the delivery was tendered, the buyer rejected the goods because the component was not Brand A, as called for in the contract. Since the seller reasonably believed that the substitution would be acceptable (based on their prior dealings), the seller will have a reasonable time to ship conforming goods in order to satisfy the contract. If this had been the first time the seller had shipped substitute parts, there would not be a reasonable belief that they would be accepted (unless such a belief was based on industry standards), and there would not be an extension of time to allow the seller to perform.

While a seller who reasonably believes that the substitute goods will be accepted is given an extension of time to satisfy the contract, the seller will not be given unlimited time or opportunity to cure the defect. This has often been a problem in automobile cases.

Buyer's Duties

The buyer's duties with respect to the sales contract arise after the seller's duties have been completed and the intervening rights of the parties have been exercised, if these intervening rights in fact exist in the contract. Since the buyer is not required to inspect the goods, a failure to inspect operates as a waiver, and the buyer's duty to perform arises. If the buyer inspects and discovers a defect, the seller may have a right to cure. If the seller does in fact cure, the duty of the buyer arises. The buyer has a duty to accept the goods and to pay for the goods.

Acceptance   When delivery of the goods is tendered, the buyer has three options:

1. He or she can accept the entire shipment, without regard to the conformity of the goods.
2. He or she can reject the entire shipment, without regard to the conformity of the goods.
3. He or she can accept some of the goods and reject the rest of the shipment.

The buyer's options are illustrated in Exhibit 17.1.

If the buyer accepts the entire shipment, the seller may view the contract as properly performed and is entitled to payment for the goods as called for in the contract. If the buyer rejects the entire shipment, either the seller is in breach for tendering delivery of nonconforming goods or the buyer is in breach for rejecting a proper tender of delivery. One of the parties will be entitled to damages due to the breach of the contract by the other party. If the buyer decides to accept some of the goods and to reject the rest, there is a limitation imposed by the Code. The buyer must accept *all* conforming goods and may then *also accept* as many nonconforming goods as he or she desires. This means that the seller breached the contract, at least in part, and that the buyer will be entitled to some remedies.

Obviously, the decision of the buyer to accept—or to reject—the goods is of paramount importance. The UCC states that the buyer accepts the goods and thus

Exhibit 17.1

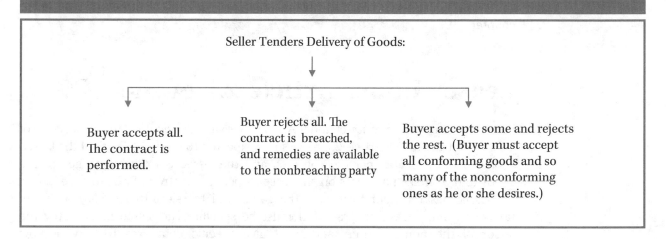

Buyer's Options Upon Tender of Delivery

Seller Tenders Delivery of Goods:

Buyer accepts all. The contract is performed.

Buyer rejects all. The contract is breached, and remedies are available to the nonbreaching party

Buyer accepts some and rejects the rest. (Buyer must accept all conforming goods and so many of the nonconforming ones as he or she desires.)

is obligated to pay for them, in a number of ways. After having had a reasonable time to inspect the goods, the buyer is deemed to have accepted them in any one of the following ways:

1. By signifying that the goods conform to the contract.
2. By signifying that the goods do not conform, but that they will be retained and accepted despite the nonconformity.
3. By failing to make a proper rejection of the goods if they are nonconforming.
4. By doing anything that is not consistent with the seller's ownership of the goods. (Since the buyer is attempting to reject the goods, he or she must treat the goods as if they still belong to the seller. Any conduct by the buyer that is not consistent with this hypothetical ownership of the seller is taken as proof that the buyer owned the goods, and had therefore accepted them!)

As mentioned earlier, acceptance obligates the buyer to pay for the goods at the contract price. It also prevents rejection of the accepted goods unless the defect was hidden or the seller promised to cure the defect and then failed to do so. Also, the acceptance of any part of a commercial unit is treated as an acceptance of the entire commercial unit.

Payment   Once the seller tenders delivery and the buyer accepts (or fails to reject properly), the buyer has a duty to tender payment. Likewise, in the case of a COD contract or a payment against documents, the buyer has a duty to tender payment. The buyer is allowed to tender payment in any manner that is normal in the ordinary course of business, typically by check or draft. A seller who is not satisfied with this can demand cash. But in so doing, the seller must allow the buyer a reasonable extension of time to obtain cash. This would normally be viewed as at least one banking day. Once the buyer tenders payment, the normal contract for the sale of goods is fully performed. Each of the parties received what it wanted, and nothing further is required. However, some contracts present special problems, some of which will be discussed later in the chapter.

Leases Under Article 2A of the UCC

Performance of a lease contract under Article 2A is virtually identical to performance of a sales contract under Article 2. The lessor is expected to tender delivery of the leased goods to the lessee as per the contract, and the lessee is expected to accept the goods and to make payments on the lease as per the contract. Prior to acceptance, the lessee has the right to inspect the goods and to reject the goods if they are nonconforming. Again, the rejection must be specific. The lessee must notify the lessor of the nonconformity and must give specific details as to why or how the goods do not conform. The lessor may then have the opportunity to cure the defect, putting the goods in conformity with the contract.

Article 2A specifies that the lessor is expected to make a *perfect tender.*[4] If the goods or the tender fail in any way to conform to the lease contract, the lessee may reject the goods. Of course, the lessee may also choose to accept the goods despite the nonconformity, and he or she may choose to accept some of the goods while rejecting the rest, provided that all conforming goods are accepted.

Obviously, Article 2A is modeled to a significant extent on Article 2. The manner in which the lessor can tender delivery is virtually the same as the manner in which a seller can tender delivery. The intervening rights of the parties between tender of delivery and acceptance and payment are the same. The need for specificity in rejecting an improper tender is the same. And the options of the lessee are virtually the same as the options of a buyer.

Sales Under The CISG

The CISG provides the framework for an increasing number of international sales of goods contracts. The CISG also expects the seller to tender delivery of the goods to the buyer as per the contract, and it expects the buyer to accept the goods and to pay for them, presuming, of course, that the goods conform to the contract. The CISG also imposes a duty of good faith on the parties.[5] The CISG provides the buyer with the opportunity to inspect the goods prior to acceptance and obligates the buyer to notify the seller of any nonconformity in the goods within a reasonable time. The seller may well have an opportunity to cure any nonconformity in order to avoid a breach. The similarities are obvious, but in practice there are some important differences that a businessperson must keep in mind when dealing in the international environment.

One major difference involves the buyer's right to inspect the goods. U.S. sellers operating under the provisions of the UCC expect their buyers to inspect the goods tendered for delivery and to give specific reasons for any rejection. A failure to properly reject is treated as an acceptance of the goods as tendered, making the buyer liable for the purchase price. Under the CISG, a buyer may not rely on any lack of conformity as a reason to reject the goods unless notice of the nonconformity is given to the seller within a reasonable time. This sounds like the UCC rule, but there is an important difference. The CISG states that there is a time limit of *two years* for the giving of notice, unless the contract includes an agreement setting a different time.[6] To further confuse U.S. firms, even if the buyer fails to give the required notice of nonconformity, Article 44 of the CISG allows the buyer to "reduce the price . . . or claim damages, except for the loss of profit, if he has a reasonable excuse for his failure to give the required notice."

Obligations of the Seller

Chapter II of the CISG covers the obligations of the seller of goods under the Convention, and Chapter III covers the obligations of the buyer. These chapters include remedies for breach of the contract among the obligations, which reflects the basic implication of the Convention that a contract for the sale of goods is expected to be performed by both parties to the contract.

The obligations of the seller under the CISG can be found in Articles 30 through 44 of the Convention; these articles are broken down into three sections. The first section is general, calling for the seller to deliver goods, turn over any relevant documents, and surrender any property in the goods as provided in the contract. The second section deals with the conformity of the goods and with any claims by third parties. The third section deals with remedies that are available upon breach by the seller (see the Remedies Under the CISG section below).

Section I   Articles 31 through 34 describe the obligations of the seller in a contract under the CISG. Under the provisions of Article 31, if the seller is not specifically obligated to deliver the goods at a particular place, then he or she is expected to follow these guidelines:

1. If the contract involves carriage of the goods, the seller is to hand the goods over to the first carrier for transmission to the buyer.
2. If the goods are not to be carried, the seller is to place the goods at the buyer's disposition, either where the goods are known by both parties to be located or at the seller's place of business.

Article 32 deals with contracts involving carriage of the goods by an independent carrier. It specifies that the seller must notify the buyer of the consignment of the goods to the carrier, must make the reasonable and necessary contracts for carriage of the goods, and must either procure insurance on the goods or give the buyer sufficient information regarding the goods and the carriage to permit the buyer to procure insurance.

Articles 33 and 34 deal with the proper time for delivery and with the handing over of any necessary documents relating to the goods as a part of the performance duty.

Section II   Made up of Articles 35 through 44, Section II deals with conformity of the goods and possible claims by third parties. This section specifies that the goods must be fit for their normal and intended purpose, fit for any particular purpose of which the seller was aware at the time of the contract, and are properly packaged in order to be deemed conforming. Conformity is measured at the time when the risk of loss passes to the buyer, although the seller may cure any nonconformity if the goods are delivered prior to the delivery date as set out in the contract. The buyer is expected to examine the goods as promptly as practical and to notify the seller of any nonconformity in a timely manner, or the buyer loses his or her right to object to any nonconformity in the goods delivered. This section was hotly debated at the conference, and a compromise was reached on this topic. The buyer is given special rights here in that the buyer has up to two years to assert that the goods contain a hidden defect. In addition, a buyer who fails to give timely notice of a defect can still deduct the "value" of the defect from the contract price, provided that the buyer has a "reasonable excuse" for a failure to give timely notice.[7]

The seller is also expected to deliver goods to the buyer that are free of any rights or claims of any third parties, and the seller can be held liable to the buyer and to the third party for any violations of this obligation.

Obligations of the Buyer

Chapter III of the CISG covers the obligations of the buyer under the contract, which consists of the duty to accept the goods and to pay for them. This chapter is also broken down into three sections. Section I, comprised of Articles 54 through 59, discusses the duty of the buyer with respect to payment of the contract price for the goods. Section II, which consists solely of Article 60, explains taking delivery. Section III, made up of Articles 61 through 65, discusses remedies upon a breach by the buyer (see the remedies under the CISG section below).

Section I   This section specifies the payment obligation of the buyer under a number of different sets of circumstances. If the contract is silent as to payment, the buyer is to pay the price generally charged for such goods at the time and place of the conclusion of the contract. If the price is to be based on weight and the method for determining weight is not specified, it is presumed to be net weight. If no place for payment is specified, the buyer is to pay the seller at the seller's place of business or at the place where any documents are handed over, if payment is to be "against documents." In addition, unless the contract specifies a different time, the buyer is to pay for the goods when the goods or the documents are made available by the seller.

Section II   Article 60 is the only article included in this section. This article specifies that the buyer is to take delivery by doing all the acts that are necessary and could reasonably be expected in order to allow the seller to deliver the goods, and in actually taking delivery of the goods.

REMEDIES

The overwhelming majority of sales contracts are performed by the parties as expected. The seller tenders conforming goods to the buyer at the time and place of delivery. The buyer then inspects the goods, accepts them, and pays the seller the price agreed to in the contract. Of course, not every tender is letter-perfect; but when the tender of delivery is flawed, the seller normally cures the defect. Again, the parties are left with their bargain as agreed.

In some cases, however, the tender is never made, or it is made in so insubstantial a manner that it is treated as a breach of contract. Furthermore, some sellers refuse to cure a defective performance or lack the time to do so, and some buyers refuse to pay the agreed price or are unable to do so. Under these circumstances, the other party must look to remedies to minimize the effect of the breach.

This section examines remedies first from the seller's viewpoint and then from the buyer's. In either case, certain remedies will be available at some times, and other remedies will be available at other times. The last part of the section explores some technical rules that affect how and when remedies may be sought or established.

Seller's Remedies

If the buyer wrongfully rejects goods, refuses to pay for the goods, or otherwise breaches the contract, the seller is entitled to remedies. The remedies available to the seller depend on when the buyer breaches. The seller has six possible remedies if the breach occurs before acceptance. If the breach happens after acceptance, the seller has two possible remedies. Exhibit 17.2 summarizes the types of preacceptance and postacceptance remedies available to the seller. Each of these is discussed in turn.

Preacceptance Remedies of the Seller   If the buyer breaches the contract before accepting the goods, the seller may seek up to six different remedies. The seller does not have to choose just one possible remedy: As many of the six can be used as are needed in the particular case.

The first possible remedy is to withhold delivery of the goods. The seller does not have to deliver or to continue delivering goods to a buyer who is not willing to perform the contract properly. In addition, if the seller discovers that the buyer is insolvent, the seller may withhold delivery unless the buyer pays in cash all prior charges and the cost of the current shipment.

Exhibit 17.2

Seller's Remedies Under Article 2

Preacceptance Remedies

1. Withhold delivery of goods identified to the contract but still in the seller's possession.
2. Stoppage in transit.
3. Resell the goods, including raw materials purchased to produce the goods, and any goods listed as work in process, resold as scrap, salvage, or other.
4. Sue for the *contract*. This includes the right to identify goods to the contract and the right to complete work in progress.
5. Sue for *damages* suffered due to the breach, whether based on a resale of the goods, lost profits, or some other measure.
6. Cancel any future performance obligations under the contract.

Postacceptance Remedies

1. Sue for the amount still due under the contract.
2. Reclaim/Recover the goods (provided that the buyer is insolvent *and* that the seller asserts this right within 10 days of delivery, *or* that the buyer made a written misrepresentation of solvency, which waives the 10-day limit).

The second possible seller's remedy is a little more complicated. It is known as stoppage of delivery in transit. To use this remedy, the goods must be in the possession of a third person—a carrier or a bailee. If the seller discovers that the buyer is insolvent, the seller may stop delivery of any goods in the possession of a third person. If the buyer breaches the contract, the seller may also be able to stop the delivery; however, before the seller can stop delivery because of a breach, the delivery must be of a planeload, carload, truckload, or larger shipment. The seller also must make provisions to protect the carrier or the bailee before a stoppage is permitted. The seller must notify the carrier or bailee in enough time to reasonably allow a stoppage and must indemnify that carrier or bailee for any charges or damages suffered because of the stoppage.

The third remedy allows the seller to sue for the contract. This remedy does provide a potential burden to the seller, however. If or when the buyer pays the contract price, the seller must tender delivery of the goods. Thus, a seller who sues for the contract must be prepared to perform the contract upon the buyer's performance.

The fourth seller's remedy gives the seller the right to resell those goods that are still in the seller's possession. A seller who does resell the goods, and who does so in good faith in a commercially reasonable manner, may also be able to collect damages from the buyer. The seller may elect to resell in a public sale or in a private sale and may resell the entire lot of goods as a unit or make the resale by individual units. All the seller has to do is establish that the resale was conducted in a commercially reasonable fashion. This means that the method, time, place, and terms all must be shown to be reasonable. And the seller must give the breaching buyer notice of the sale, if possible. Normally, the issue of reasonableness will be raised in a private sale, but if he or she is given notice, the buyer has little opportunity to defeat the resale. In a public resale, reasonableness is well defined. Except for recognized futures, the resale can be made only on identified goods. It must occur at a normal place for a public sale unless the goods are perishable. The breaching buyer must be given notice of the time and place of the resale. Notice must be given as to where the goods are located so prospective bidders can inspect them. If the seller fails to meet any of these criteria, the resale is not commercially reasonable, and therefore, the seller cannot recover any damages. If the seller resells the goods for more than the contract price, an interesting situation arises. If the buyer breached, the seller may keep the excess. If the buyer rightfully rejected the goods, the seller may still keep the excess, but now the excess is defined as anything above the buyer's security interest.

The fifth option available to the seller is to sue the buyer, either for damages or for lost profits. If the seller has not yet completed the goods or has not yet identified the goods to the contract, the seller normally will be content to sue for damages. In such a situation, damages are determined by taking the difference between the contract price and the market price at the time and place of breach, adding any incidental damages incurred, and then subtracting any expenses avoided. The seller may discover that the damages computed in this manner do not put him or her in as good a position as performance of the contract would have. If so, the seller may instead elect to sue for lost profits. The seller will show the profits that full performance would have netted and sue for this amount plus the recovery of any expenses reasonably incurred due to the breach. The seller may decide to resell the goods and then to sue for any losses or damages not recovered in the resale. If so, the damages are figured by deducting the resale price from the original contract price, adding consequential damages incurred due to the buyer's breach, and then subtracting any expenses saved by not having to deliver the goods to the original buyer.

Remedies 3, 4, and 5 allow the seller to exercise some discretion in the treatment of unidentified goods. If the buyer breaches the contract, the seller may identify goods to the contract that were unidentified before the breach, thus helping to establish damages. Also, the seller may decide either to complete goods that were incomplete or to stop production and resell the goods for scrap. Either of these options may be used, provided that the seller is exercising reasonable business judgment.

The seller's final preacceptance remedy is the right to cancel. On giving notice to the buyer, the seller can cancel all future performance due to the buyer under the contract. Cancellation does not discharge the buyer or hinder the seller in collecting or enforcing any other rights or remedies resulting from the breach; it merely terminates the duties of the seller under the contract due to the breach by the buyer.

eClass 17.1 Sales/Finance

SHOULD eCLASS USE CREDIT SALES TO INCREASE MARKET SHARE?

Ani would like to offer the software to a number of retailers on credit terms. She is convinced that if the firm can get these merchants to carry the product, the company's name will become more widely known quickly, accelerating the firm's growth. Yousef is concerned about cash flow, especially during the initial stages of development of the firm. He would prefer to have the firm require payment on delivery, or very shortly thereafter. Ani has argued that extending credit is not such a great risk since the firm can just repossess their product if any buyer defaults. However, Yousef is not sure that the firm will be allowed to "just go in and repossess" any units if the buyer defaults. The firm asks you for advice. What will you tell them?

BUSINESS CONSIDERATIONS   A new company in an industry may have trouble getting its product into stores unless it is willing to take some chances, including making credit sales. What should a company do to maximize its protection if it decides to sell goods on credit? Are the Article 2 postacceptance remedies adequate for the firm's protection? Do any other articles, used in conjunction with Article 2, increase the seller's protection?

ETHICAL CONSIDERATIONS   Suppose that a credit customer is having a temporary cash flow problem, but will probably be able to meet its debt obligation to your company in the near future. Should your company play "hardball" and demand payment when due, be "caring creditors" who allow the debtor a bit of leeway, or take a position somewhere between these extremes? How can the position you choose be justified ethically?

Postacceptance Remedies of the Seller   Once the goods have been accepted by the buyer and the buyer has breached the contract, the seller may seek either or both of two remedies.

The first of these remedies is by far the more common. The seller may sue the buyer for the price of the goods. Since the buyer has accepted, the buyer's duty to pay is established. Thus, winning the case is almost a certainty. Many buyers who do not pay, however, are unable to pay. They are insolvent. In such a situation, winning the case is a Pyrrhic victory—the winner suffers nearly as much as the loser.

If the buyer has accepted goods and the buyer is insolvent, the seller will possibly seek the second available postacceptance remedy: The seller will attempt to reclaim the goods. To do so, the seller must prove that the following two conditions have been satisfied:

1. The buyer received the goods on credit while insolvent.
2. The seller demanded the return of the goods within 10 days of delivery to the buyer.

This second remedy is obviously of limited value, since many businesses operate on credit terms providing for payment after 30 days (or longer), and the seller has only 10 days in which to act. But there is one exception. If the buyer misrepresented his or her solvency in writing to the seller within three months before delivery, the 10-day limit does not apply. In practice, many sellers extend credit in conjunction with a security interest (as provided for in Article 9 of the UCC) to protect themselves from the drawbacks presented by the "reclaim the goods" postacceptance remedy. Otherwise, if the seller discovers that the buyer is unable to pay after the goods have been accepted, the seller may find himself or herself with little hope of ever collecting the full contract price.

It is possible, at least in theory, for a seller to use all eight potential remedies in a single contract upon a breach by the buyer. In order to use all eight possible remedies, the circumstances would have to be unusual (to say the least), and the conduct of the buyer would have to fit within certain guidelines. Although such a confluence of circumstances is highly unlikely, it could happen, as is shown in the following example.

Tariq entered into a contract with Jamal that called for Jamal to produce and deliver 1,000 video games to Tariq each month for the next 12 months. Tariq was to make payments for each shipment within 30 days of receipt. Jamal did not ordinarily allow deferred or delayed payment, but Tariq had provided a written financial statement that presented a picture of a very profitable business. (As it turned out, the financial statement was fraudulent; Tariq was, in fact, insolvent at the time of the contract.) Jamal purchased sufficient raw materials to produce 8 months' worth of goods and began the manufacturing process. The performance of the contract can be summarized as follows:

1. *The first two monthly shipments were sent to Tariq.*
2. *The third monthly shipment had been turned over to a common carrier for delivery.*
3. *The fourth monthly shipment was ready for pickup by the common carrier when Jamal learned that Tariq was insolvent.*
4. *The goods for monthly shipments 5 through 8 were, at that time, in various stages of "work in process."*
5. *The balance of the raw materials to complete the contract had been ordered by Jamal.*

Jamal decided to seek any and all remedies that might be available under Article 2. Jamal first looked at the preacceptance remedies. He decided to withhold delivery of the fourth shipment to the carrier and to notify the carrier to stop the goods that were already in transit (the third shipment). The goods in shipments 3 and 4 had been identified to the contract, as was the work in process. Jamal decided to stop the work in process and to sell the partially completed goods for scrap. He also decided to resell the completed goods that were stopped in transit and the goods withheld from delivery. Jamal also called Tariq and canceled all future performance on the contract due to Tariq's insolvency. Jamal sued for damages on shipments 3 through 8 and for lost profits on shipments 9 through 12. Jamal then decided to exercise the postacceptance remedies. He reclaimed all the unsold goods still in Tariq's possession from shipments 1 and 2 and sued for the amount due under the contract for all goods that Tariq had disposed of before Jamal was able to assert his right to reclaim the goods from Tariq.

Buyer's Remedies

The buyer also has a range of possible remedies. Like the seller, the buyer's remedy options depend on the timing of the breach. The buyer has six preacceptance and three postacceptance remedies available. These remedies are summarized in Exhibit 17.3. We then discuss each of them in turn.

Preacceptance Remedies of the Buyer   Before the buyer accepts, the seller may breach by nondelivery or by delivery of nonconforming goods. Under either circumstance, the buyer may elect any or all of the following remedies.

The buyer's first remedy is to sue for damages. The buyer is allowed to recover the excess of market price over contract price at the time of breach and at the place of delivery. Any additional damages are added to this amount. The amount is then reduced by any expenses the buyer saved because of the breach.

The second remedy available to the buyer is that of cover. The buyer covers by buying substitute goods from another source within a reasonable time of the breach. If

Exhibit 17.3

Buyer's Remedies Under Article 2

Preacceptance Remedies

1. Sue for damages for breach of contract.
2. Cover (buy substitute goods elsewhere) and sue for damages for any losses due to the efforts and expenses of covering.
3. Seek *specific performance* (for unique goods) or *replevin* (for common goods that are temporarily not available through cover).
4. Claim any identified goods still in possession of the seller, *provided that* the goods have already been paid for *and* the seller has become insolvent *and* it is within 10 days of the payment for the goods.
5. Resell any nonconforming goods tendered by the seller and in the possession of the buyer. (NOTE: the buyer has possession but has not accepted the nonconforming goods.)
6. Cancel any further obligations under the contract.

Postacceptance Remedies

1. Revoke the acceptance (requires either a hidden defect that substantially impairs the value of the contract or a failure by the seller to cure after promising to do so in order to get the buyer to accept nonconforming goods).
2. Sue for damages for breach of contract.
3. Use *recoupment* by deducting the alleged damages from the contract price still owed to the seller (the buyer must notify the seller of an intent to recoup before using this remedy).

the goods obtained through cover cost more than the contract price, the buyer can collect the excess costs from the breaching seller, plus other expenses incurred in effecting cover.

The third remedy is available if the goods cannot be obtained by cover. The buyer may seek specific performance or replevin. If the goods are unique, the court may order specific performance; and the seller will have to deliver the goods in accordance with the contract. If the goods are not unique but are unavailable from other sources at the time, replevin is available. Once the buyer shows an inability to cover, the court may order replevin.

The fourth remedy is probably rare in actual practice. If the seller has identified the goods to the contract, and if the buyer has paid some or all of the contract price, and if the seller becomes insolvent within 10 days of receipt of the payment, the buyer can claim the identified goods. The likelihood of this chain of events occurring is not very high. But if it does occur, the buyer is protected.

The fifth remedy available to the buyer frequently baffles and amazes students: Under appropriate circumstances, the buyer may resell the goods. (Students frequently ask, "How can someone resell goods that were never accepted and thus never sold in the first place?") This remedy becomes available when the seller ships nonconforming goods to the buyer. On receipt of the nonconforming goods, the buyer must notify the seller of the nonconformity. Furthermore, if the buyer is a merchant, the buyer must request instructions from the seller as to disposal of the goods. If no instructions are given (or if the seller asks the buyer to resell the goods on the seller's behalf), the buyer must attempt to resell the goods for the seller. The resale must be reasonable under the circumstances. A buyer who does resell the goods will be allowed to deduct an appropriate amount from the sale amount for expenses and commissions, and may then apply the balance of the sale proceeds to the damages resulting from the breach. Any excess must be returned to the seller.

The final preacceptance remedy available to the buyer is the right to cancel. On discovery of a breach by the seller, the buyer may notify the seller that all future obligations of the buyer are canceled. Cancellation will not affect any other rights or remedies of the buyer under the contract.

Postacceptance Remedies of the Buyer   Once the buyer has accepted the goods, the focus shifts. A buyer who accepts cannot reject the goods, since accepting and rejecting are mutually exclusive. However, the buyer may be able to revoke the acceptance. Revocation is permitted only if the following criteria are met:

1. The defect must have been hidden; or the seller must have promised to cure the defect, but no cure occurred.
2. The defect must substantially impair the value of the contract.

While a hidden defect is not necessarily rare, a hidden defect that also substantially impairs the value of the contract may well be rare. If something is so wrong with the goods that the buyer's rights are substantially harmed, that problem would seem to be one that a reasonable inspection should reveal. A substantially impairing defect that is not cured when cure is promised is probably more common.

eClass 17.2 Manufacturing/Management

ADDRESSING DELIVERY PROBLEMS WITH A SUPPLIER

The firm that supplies the diskettes for the eClass software has recently been troubled by labor problems. Its employees were out on strike for several weeks, and the company has virtually exhausted its inventory of the diskettes. When the strike ended last week, the president of the company called Meg to let her know that the strike was over and that the company expected to be back in regular production in a matter of days. He also explained that the strike has depleted the company's inventory and that the next scheduled shipment of diskettes to eClass would be several days late. Meg thinks the firm should be patient with the supplier and let that company get back up to normal production. She points out that eClass can handle the temporary diskette shortage with virtually no trouble, and the supplier has been cooperative with the firm in the past. Ani believes that the strike was just a harbinger of problems to come in dealing with the supplier. She would like the firm to cancel its contract due to the delay in delivery, sue for damages, and seek a new supplier. Yousef is concerned that there could be more delays beyond those the supplier anticipates, but he does not want to just drop the contract with the supplier. The members have asked you for your advice as to the best alternative for the firm. What will you tell them?

BUSINESS CONSIDERATIONS   Does the fact that one or more remedies are available mean that a business should *use* those remedies? Should a business base its decisions on the fact that remedies are available, or should it view remedies as a last resort after all else has failed?

ETHICAL CONSIDERATIONS   Is it a better business practice to work problems out in an equitable manner or to hold the other person to the literal terms of the bargain? Should loyalty to a supplier be a factor in deciding whether to sue or to be patient?

If the buyer properly revokes acceptance, the buyer is treated as if he or she rejected the initial delivery, and the buyer is then permitted to assert any or all of the available preacceptance remedies that apply to the case.

The buyer is more likely to accept the goods and later discover a defect or other breach that is not sufficient to permit a revocation. When this happens, the buyer will select the second possible remedy, suing the seller for damages. Damages are likely to be measured by comparing the value of the goods as delivered with the value that the buyer would have received if the goods that were delivered had conformed to the contract. Damages can also be established as the expense the buyer incurs in having the defects in the goods repaired by a third person.

The third remedy available to the buyer allows the buyer to deduct damages from the price due to the nonconformity, but keep the goods (recoupment). Normally, this third remedy will be used together with the second. The buyer must notify the seller that the buyer intends to deduct damages caused by the seller's breach from the contract price still owed to the seller for the contract. If the seller agrees, the matter is concluded. If the seller disagrees, he or she will either need to negotiate with the buyer to reach an agreement, or the seller will have to sue the buyer for any alleged underpayment of the balance due on the contract.

MODIFICATIONS

The parties to the contract are allowed to tailor their remedies to fit their particular contract and their particular circumstances. For example, the parties may, by expressly including it in the contract, provide for remedies in addition to the remedies provided by the Uniform Commercial Code. Or, they may provide for remedies in lieu of those provided by the Code. Or, they may place a limit on the remedies that may be used. If the parties so desire, they can select one remedy that is to be used as the exclusive remedy for their particular contract. (When an exclusive remedy is selected, it must be followed unless circumstances change so that the remedy no longer adequately covers the damages.)

Consequential damages may be excluded or limited by the parties in the contract. Such an agreement will be enforced unless the court finds it to be unconscionable. The parties may also provide for liquidated damages if the provision is reasonable, the difficulty of setting the loss is substantial, and establishing actual loss would be inconvenient, if not impossible. Of course, if the amount designated as liquidated damages is found unreasonable or unconscionable or is deemed to be a penalty, the clause is void.

Sometimes the seller justifiably withholds delivery from the buyer when the buyer has paid part of the contract price. In such a case, the buyer, even though in breach, can recover any payments made in excess of any liquidated damages called for in the contract, or, if there is no liquidated damages amount, the lesser of 20 percent of the total contract value or $500.

SPECIAL PROBLEMS

In determining when remedies may be obtained and what remedies to seek, several special problems may arise. The court may be asked to determine whether a breach has occurred or whether the contractual performance was excused. If there has been a breach, the courts may need to determine when it occurred. There may be a problem with the expectations of the parties or a question as to whether a party is capable of performing as scheduled. And sometimes there is just a special circumstance involved that requires special treatment.

(Anticipatory) Repudiation

Occasionally, one of the parties to a contract will repudiate his or her obligations before performance is due. If such a repudiation will substantially reduce the value expected to be received by the other party, the other party may choose one of three courses of conduct:

1. He or she may await performance for a commercially reasonable time despite the repudiation.
2. The nonrepudiating party may treat the repudiation as an immediate breach and seek any available remedies.
3. The nonrepudiating party may suspend his or her own performance under the contract until there is a resolution of the problem.

A repudiating party is allowed to retract the repudiation at any time up to and including the date performance is due, *if* the other party permits a retraction. No retraction is allowed if the nonrepudiating party has canceled the contract or has materially changed his or her position in reliance on the repudiation. A retraction re-establishes the contract rights and duties of each party.

Excused Performance

Sometimes, a seller may be forced into a delay in making delivery, may not be able to make delivery, or may have to make only a partial delivery. Normally, this would be treated as a breach. Some of these situations fall into the area of excused performance, however, and hence are not treated as a breach. Performance is excused, in whole or in part, if performance has become impracticable because of the occurrence of some event whose nonoccurrence was a basic assumption of the contract. Also, performance is excused if the seller's delay or lack of performance is based on compliance with a governmental order or regulation.

If the seller has an excuse for less than full performance, the seller must notify the buyer seasonally. If performance will be reduced but not eliminated, the seller is allowed to allocate deliveries among customers in a reasonable manner. On receiving notice of a planned allocation due to some excuse, the buyer must then elect whether to terminate the contract or to modify it. Modifying it means accepting the partial delivery as a substitute performance. A failure to modify within 30 days will be treated as a termination.

Adequate Assurances

When the parties enter a contract for the sale of goods, each expects to receive the benefit of the bargain made. If, before performance is due, either party feels insecure in expecting performance, the insecure party may demand assurances of performance.

The insecure party must make a written demand for assurance that performance will be tendered when due. Until the assurances are given, the requesting party may suspend performance. If no assurance is given within 30 days of the request, it is treated as repudiation of the contract.

Duty to Particularize

When the buyer rightfully rejects goods, the buyer must do so properly. If the goods are rejected owing to a curable defect, the buyer may reject only by stating exactly what the defect is. A failure to do so will preclude the use of that defect to prove breach in court. And if the buyer cannot prove breach, the seller will be deemed to have performed properly. Thus, a failure to particularize can result in the buyer being required to pay for nonconforming goods or in other liability to the seller.

STATUTE OF LIMITATIONS

Any lawsuit for breach of a sales contract must be started within four years of the breach, unless the contract itself sets a shorter time period. (The time period cannot be less than one year.) The fact that a breach is not discovered when it occurs is not material. The time limitation begins at breach, not at discovery. This reemphasizes the need for a buyer to inspect goods carefully and completely in order to protect his or her interests.

REMEDIES IN LEASING CONTRACTS UNDER ARTICLE 2A

Article 2A provides for remedies in the event a lease contract is breached. As under Article 2, the remedies available depend to a significant extent on when the breach occurs. A brief synopsis of the remedies is set out below.

Lessor's Remedies

If a lessee wrongfully rejects goods tendered under the lease, wrongfully revokes acceptance, fails to make payments when due, or repudiates the lease, the lessor may:

1. Cancel the lease contract.
2. Proceed respecting goods not identified to the lease contract.
3. Withhold delivery of the goods and take possession of goods previously delivered.

   4. Stop delivery of the goods by any bailee.
   5. Dispose of the goods and recover damages, or retain the goods and recover damages, or, in a property case, recover rent.

If a lessee is otherwise in default, the lessor may exercise the rights and remedies provided in the lease, as well as those listed in Article 2A.

Lessee's Remedies

If a lessor fails to deliver goods in conformity with the lease contract or repudiates the lease contract, or the lessee rightfully rejects the goods or justifiably revokes acceptance of the goods, then the lessee may:

   1. Cancel the lease contract.
   2. Recover as much of the rent and security as has been paid; but in the case of an installment lease contract, the recovery is that which is just under the circumstances.
   3. Cover and recover damages as to all goods affected, whether or not they have been identified to the lease contract, or recover damages for nondelivery,

If the lessor fails to deliver the goods or repudiates the contract, the lessee may also:

   1. Recover any goods that have been identified to the contract.
   2. Obtain specific performance or replevin.

If the lessor is otherwise in default under a lease contract, the lessee may exercise the rights and remedies provided in the lease contract and/or those included in Article 2A.

REMEDIES UNDER THE CISG

Remedies for Breach by the Seller

Section III of Chapter II specifies remedies that are available to the buyer upon a breach of the sales contract by the seller. In addition, Articles 74 through 77 provide damages that may be available to either the buyer or the seller upon a breach by the other party. The CISG also specifically states that a party is not deprived of any rights to claim damages if that party seeks other remedies under the Convention as well. If the seller fails to deliver conforming goods or fails to meet any other aspect of the agreement, the buyer may seek any or all of the appropriate remedies from the alternatives shown in Exhibit 17.4.

Exhibit 17.4

Buyer's Remedies Under the CISG

1. The buyer may require the seller to perform, unless the buyer has chose another remedy that is inconsistent with performance by the seller.
2. The buyer may require the seller to deliver conforming substitute goods or to cure any nonconformity, if the seller delivered nonconforming goods.
3. The buyer can set an additional time for performance, provided that the seller is notified of this extension. (The buyer may not seek any other remedies during this extended time.)
4. The buyer can declare the contract avoided if the seller does not deliver the goods within the time permitted under the contract (or before the time extension expires).
5. If the seller delivered nonconforming goods, the buyer can reduce the price paid to the seller to reflect the value of the goods delivered.
6. If the seller tenders delivery prior to the agreed delivery date, the buyer can accept or refuse to accept the goods; if the seller tenders delivery of a larger shipment than called for in the contract, the buyer may accept any or all of the excess amount, paying for any accepted goods at the contract rate.

Remedies for Breach by the Buyer

Section III of Chapter III specifies the remedies that are available to the seller upon a breach of the sales contract by the buyer. Again, Articles 74 through 77 provide damages that may be available as well. Recall also that the CISG specifically states

Exhibit 17.5

Seller's Remedies Under the CISG

1. The seller may require the buyer to pay the contract price, to take delivery of the goods, or to perform any other obligations under the contract, unless the seller has chosen another remedy that is inconsistent with this remedy.
2. The seller can set an additional reasonable time during which the buyer can perform, provided that the buyer is notified of this extension. (The seller may not seek any other remedies during this extended time.)
3. The seller can declare the contract avoided as to any unperformed parts of the contract.
4. If the contract calls for the buyer to specify any form, measurement, or other feature of the goods and he or she fails to do so, the seller may supply such specifications if he or she does so within a reasonable time.

that a party is not deprived of any rights to claim damages if that party seeks other remedies under the Convention as well. If the buyer fails to accept delivery of the goods or fails to pay for the goods as agreed, the seller may seek any or all of the appropriate remedies from the alternatives shown in Exhibit 17.5.

Damages

Section II of Chapter IV specifies damages that may be available to either party under the Convention following a breach of the contract by the other party. These damages may be available even if other remedies are also sought by the nonbreaching party.

The basic measure of damages under the CISG is "a sum equal to the loss, including loss of profit, suffered by the other party as a consequence of the breach. Such

eClass 17.3 Finance

WHAT DAMAGES WOULD BE APPROPRIATE?

Meg's father manages an automobile repair shop that works on both foreign and domestic cars. One of his customers drives an older model Peugeot, and this customer expends a great deal of attention on the car—a gift from her grandfather when she graduated college. She recently asked Meg's father to order some parts for the car, and he contacted the Peugeot Company in France to place the order. Unfortunately, when the parts were tendered for delivery at the garage, Meg's father was not in, and the assistant manager refused the delivery. The carrier made a second unsuccessful effort to deliver the goods, then notified Meg's father of the refused tender and asked what it should do with the goods. Meg's father, in turn, asked Meg for her opinion. Meg believes that this contract is governed by the CISG, and she is not as familiar with the terms of the CISG as she would like. She is also unsure as to who should be held liable for any extra expenses due to the failed tenders of delivery that have already occurred. She has asked you for advice in this situation. What will you tell them?

BUSINESS CONSIDERATIONS   The CISG provides the possibility of specific performance as a remedy, regardless of the nature of the goods. It also requires each party to mitigate damages. Does seeking specific performance following a breach help to mitigate damages, or are these two policies contradictory?

ETHICAL CONSIDERATIONS   Is it ethical to provide for a remedy that requires a business to do what it promised to do, but then failed to do (specific performance)? Would seeking another remedy be more ethical?

damages cannot exceed the loss which the party in breach foresaw or ought to have foreseen at the time of the conclusion of the contract."

If the contract is avoided and the buyer then purchases replacement goods, the buyer is entitled to the difference between the price of the replacement goods and the original contract price, plus any other damages computed under the prior damage provisions. If the contract is avoided and the seller then resells the goods, the seller is entitled to the difference between the resale price and the original contract price, plus any other damages computed under the prior damage provisions.

If the contract is avoided and there is a current price for the goods covered by the contract, the nonbreaching party can recover the difference between the current price and the contract price, plus any other damages allowed under Article 74, without the need to purchase (by the buyer) or resell (by the seller). In any case, the party seeking damages must take any and all reasonable steps to mitigate damages, or the other party can use the failure to mitigate as grounds for reducing the damages assessed to the level that would have been attained with mitigation.

The international sale and movement of goods should continue to expand over the foreseeable future. This means the CISG will become increasingly important to the U.S. domestic business environment in the future, although it will not replace the UCC in its importance. Business will need to be aware of the differences between the CISG in international agreements and the UCC domestically, because conduct that is merely a preliminary negotiation under the UCC may well be a binding contract under the Convention.

Contemporary Case

DAVIDSON COTTON MEXICO v. TEKMATEX, INC.

2006 U.S. Dist. LEXIS 71226 (W.D. N.C. 2006)

FACTS On October 23, 2000, Davidson Cotton entered into a sales contract with Tekmatex, Inc., in which Davidson agreed to purchase 48 textile looms and ancillary equipment and services for a total price of $4,562,538. Davidson made a down payment to Tekmatex in the amount of $1,280,153.25. In July 2001, Davidson wrote a letter to Tekmatex indicating that it was canceling the sales contract because it had been unable to secure sufficient financing to proceed with its facility in Mexico. Davidson acknowledged that Tekmatex had delivered two training looms, invoiced at a value of $190,525.00, and requested a refund of the balance of the down payment in the amount of $1,090,878.25. Davidson also requested details of any applicable design-specific expenses allocable to the delivered looms so that those expenses could be deducted from the amount of the refund requested. Tekmatex responded by asserting unequivocally that, under the terms of the contract, the down payment was non-refundable. Tekmatex urged Davidson to retract what it characterized as a repudiation of the contract and urged Davidson to perform its contractual obligations. Instead, Davidson responded by again requesting a refund of the balance of the down payment, and requested documentation supporting costs and expenses incurred by Tekmatex relating to the contract. Davidson also indicated that once an agreement had been reached on the amount of those charges for which it was requesting documentation, those charges could be deducted from the amount of the refund requested. On November 7, 2001, Tekmatex responded by stating Davidson was in breach of the contract, and it maintained that the damages it incurred due to Davidson's breach exceeded the amount of the down payment. Tekmatex refused to return any portion of the down payment. Davidson subsequently filed suit, contending that Tekmatex breached the parties' contract for sale of textile looms and other equipment. Tekmatex filed a motion to dismiss for failure to state a cause of action.

ISSUES Did Davidson repudiate the contract? Was Davidson, the buyer, entitled to the recovery of any portion of the down payment?

HOLDING Yes, Davidson's attempt to cancel was, in effect, a repudiation of its obligations under the contract. Perhaps. That is an issue to be decided by the court on remand.

REASONING Excerpts from the opinion of Robert J. Conrad, Jr., Chief District Judge:

"In deciding a motion to dismiss for failure to state a claim, the Court must construe the complaint liberally in favor of the plaintiff, taking as true all well-pleaded factual allegations and all reasonable inferences which may be drawn therefrom . . . Neither party disputes that the Sales Contract is a valid contract, or that the defendant has not refunded the down payment . . . Because the Sales Contract is a contract for the sale of goods, its interpretation is governed by the Uniform Commercial Code as adopted by North Carolina ("UCC"). . . .

The plaintiff-buyer asserts it has paid a down payment under a contract for sale of goods—some 48 machines—and has filed a Complaint to get at least part of the down payment back. Prior to filing suit, the plaintiff stated, in its "cancellation" of the contract letter, its clear determination not to perform the balance of its obligations under the contract. . . . The defendant had partially performed by delivering two of the machines, which the plaintiff accepted. In simplest terms, the plaintiff alleges it paid one fourth of the contract price for goods, but received only two of the promised forty-eight machines in return.

A motion to dismiss for failure to state a claim, which considers the facts only in the light most favorable to the plaintiff, tests only the sufficiency of those facts to support a claim against the defendant. The offset language of the cancellation provision of the contract suggests that there may be unresolved obligations of the defendant toward the plaintiff with respect to the down payment. . . . An action may be maintained by the plaintiff to enforce those obligations. . . . Moreover, to determine if a claim for breach has been stated, one notes at the outset that the UCC recognizes cancellation as a remedy not for a buyer who does an anticipatory repudiation of a contract, but for one who does a rightful rejection of goods or a justifiable revocation of acceptance. . . . Such a wronged buyer certainly would have a claim to pursue on the contract. Under the facts alleged in the complaint, the plaintiff-buyer cannot claim to have been wronged in either sense. Under the terms of the contract in this case, however, the parties have elevated the buyer to claimant status in circumstances where cancellation occurs "for any reason," not just the ones recognized by the statute. The "cancellation provision" specifies that should the buyer cancel the contract for any reason, the buyer, will pay "at least the following stipulated damages . . ." including . . . certain costs incurred by the seller. The items of damage mentioned are explicitly non-exclusive, thus opening the door for assessment of other items of damage, and defeating the plaintiff's contention that the defendant's obligation to return the down payment is absolute. This provision further contemplates the possibility of cancellation by the buyer before complete performance by the seller ... To that extent, the clause modifies the definition of "cancellation" found in [§ 2-106(4)]. A claim to enforce the rights of a cancelling party under these circumstances is therefore implicitly acknowledged by the contract itself. Such a claim has been stated. The cancellation provision further may be said to recognize that cancellation amounts to a breach by the buyer, by specifying minimum stipulated damages to which the seller would be entitled. Cancellation in this context is equivalent to anticipatory repudiation by the buyer. In this case, the plaintiff buyer is admitting a controversy arguably entailing its own breach, invoking the contract's terms to limit the damages to which seller is entitled, and seeking the Court's aid to enforce a return of that portion of its down payment to which it may be entitled. ... For the foregoing reasons, the plaintiff has stated a claim in respect to breach of contract upon which relief may be granted, and the defendant's motion to dismiss the claim for breach of contract will be denied. ...

You Be the Judge

Zapata, a Mexican corporation, had a contract with Lenell, a U.S. wholesale baker of cookies, which called for Zapata to supply cookie tins to Lenell, to be used in packaging the cookies for resale. Zapata alleged that Lenell had breached the contract by failing to pay for a number of shipments of the tins. (There were a total of 110 invoices involved in this lawsuit, with total payments of nearly $900,000 at issue.) As a result, Zapata sued for the amount owed plus prejudgment interest and attorneys' fees in the amount of $550,000. Zapata prevailed at trial, receiving a judgment of about $1.75 million, $850,000 in damages, $350,000 in interest, and $550,000 in attorney's fees. Lenell appealed the judgment.

The court determined, and both parties agreed, that the case was governed by the CISG since both Mexico and the United States are signatories and the parties had not "opted out" of the CISG's coverage. The only issue of contention was the award by the trial court of the $550,000 in attorneys' fees to Zapata. Lenell argued that attorneys' fees should not be awarded in this case, pointing out that the CISG does not make provision for such an award. Zapata countered by asserting that the CISG also did not prohibit the imposition of attorneys' fees, instead providing for all "damages for breach of contract by one party consist(ing) of a sum equal to the loss, including loss of profit, suffered by the other party as a consequence of the breach," providing that the consequences were foreseeable by the breaching party. Zapata then asserted that when a party breaches a contract, it should expect to get sued, and it is foreseeable that the lawsuit will result in attorneys' fees.

In contract law, there are two competing rules for the imposition of attorneys' fees. One rule, the "American rule," requires the prevailing party in a lawsuit to pay its own attorneys' fees unless there is a statute-specific provision for the imposition of attorneys' fees and other litigation expenses, such as is found in antitrust, pension, or copyright cases. The other rule, the "English rule," calls for the losing party to pay the attorneys' fees and other litigation expenses of the winning party. The English rule is followed in most countries, while the American rule is limited primarily to application in the United States.

This case has been brought in your court. How will you decide this case? What is the most important fact or factor affecting your decision?

Does the lack of any provision in the CISG make the application of the American rule more appropriate, or does it make the application of the more widely followed English rule more appropriate? [See *Zapata Hermanos Sucesores, S.A. v. Hearthside Baking Company, Inc.*, 313 F.3d 385, 2002 U.S. App. LEXIS 23675 (7th Cir. 2002).]

Summary

Although most sales contracts are fully performed and the performance is normally satisfactory, sometimes a nonperformance occurs. When nonperformance is found, the innocent party usually seeks remedies for breach of contract.

When the buyer fails to perform, the seller will seek remedies. The available remedies depend on when the buyer breached. If the buyer breached before acceptance, the seller will seek one or more of six preacceptance remedies. If the buyer accepts the goods and then breaches, the seller will seek one or both of two postacceptance remedies. By the same token, if the seller breaches, the buyer will seek remedies. Again, the buyer's available remedies will depend on when the seller breached. If the seller breached before the buyer accepted the goods, the buyer may seek one or more of six preacceptance remedies. If the seller breaches after the buyer accepts, the buyer has up to three available postacceptance remedies.

Occasionally, a nonperformance turns out not to be a breach. It may involve a special problem that excuses performance or affects the rights of the innocent party. Great care must be exercised by both parties in these special problem areas.

Leases are also normally performed properly by both parties. Again, however, sometimes breaches occur. When they do, the breaching party is held liable for those damages that the nonbreaching party suffers. Article 2A lists specific remedies that are available, and also specifically states that the parties are entitled to those damages called for in the lease contract as well as any of the remedies listed in the article. These Code remedies are very similar in nature and application to the remedies provided by Article 2.

The CISG also provides remedies when the sales contract is breached. The remedies are not very similar to those found in Article 2, nor do they distinguish between pre- and postacceptance remedies. Basically, the nonbreaching party can require the other party to perform the contract unless the nonbreaching party has resorted to other remedies. The nonbreaching party can also extend the time for performance, thus encouraging the other party to perform, or can declare the contract avoided. Of course, numerous other remedies may be available under the other applicable laws of the nature in which the suit is filed.

Discussion Questions

1. What constitutes a proper *tender of delivery* under either Article 2 or Article 2A of the UCC? What constitutes a proper *tender of delivery* under the terms of the CISG? Does the manner of delivery called for in the contract determine what is required in order to have a proper tender of delivery?

2. What is the right of inspection, and how does it affect the performance obligation of the parties in a sale or lease of goods under the UCC? What is meant by "cure," and how does it affect the performance obligation of the parties in a sale or lease of goods under the UCC?

3. How long does a buyer of goods have to inspect the goods and to inform the seller of any nonconformities under the UCC? How does this compare to the time for inspection and notification under the CISG? Why is there such a significant difference in the time allowed?

4. What is an anticipatory repudiation, and how does it affect contracts formed under the law of sales? Does a repudiation have the same meaning and impact under the law of leases?

5. What is an "adequate assurance," and when does a party to a sales contract have the right to request such an assurance? What is required in order to maker a proper request for an adequate assurance?

Case Problems and Writing Assignments

1. Zhong Ya Chemicals (USA) entered into two contracts with Industrial Chemical Trading for the sale of vitamin E powder. ICT ordered 5,000 kg of vitamin E powder from Zhong Ya on July 2, 1998. Delivery was tendered, together with an invoice for $77,329.05, and ICT accepted the powder. One year later, ICT attempted to revoke the acceptance. In February 1999, ICT ordered and took delivery of another 2,000 kg of vitamin E powder. When delivery was tendered, ICT refused to pay the $28,000 purchase price, alleging that the goods were nonconforming. (ICT offered no proof of nonconformity at trial.) ICT made no payments on either of the two shipments, and Zhong Ya sued for damages for breach of both contracts, seeking $105,329.05 plus interest.

ICT denied liability, arguing that it had revoked its acceptance of the first shipment and rejected the second shipment. It further argued that Zhong Ya had failed to mitigate damages, as is required under Article 2 of the UCC. Zhong Ya asserted that it was entitled to the full amount called for on the invoices due to ICT's failure to pay for either shipment.

The court had to decide (1) whether ICT properly revoked the first shipment, (2) whether ICT properly rejected the second shipment, (3) whether Zhong Ya failed to mitigate damages, and (4) whether Zhong Ya was entitled to preacceptance remedies, postacceptance remedies, or no remedies on each of the shipments. How should the court decide these four issues? Explain and justify your reasoning. [See *Zhong Ya (USA) Ltd. v. Industrial Chemical Trading*, Inc. 2001 U.S. Dist. LEXIS 19184 (S.D.N.Y. 2001).]

2. Plexus Publishing, a British publishing company, was engaged in preparing a book titled "Rock 'n' Roll Babylon" that portrayed the lives of rock and roll celebrities. W. H. Smith Publishers, a Delaware corporation, was interested in purchasing 25,000 copies of an American edition of the book when it was finished. After lengthy negotiations, the parties entered into a contract, and W.H. Smith made a down payment of $25,875 toward the ultimate price of the books. This contract included a clause that gave W. H. Smith the right to review the finished text and illustrations, and, if in the opinion of its counsel the book was libelous or that it might infringe on any copyrights, to require Plexus to "make or cause to be made such changes or deletions as may be necessary, in the opinion of such counsel, to make the work fit and acceptable for publication, or else the publisher (Smith) shall have the absolute right to terminate the agreement and recover" from Plexus any amounts paid.

W. H. Smith received a copy of the completed manuscript soon after the contract was signed. Shortly thereafter, W. H. Smith notified Plexus that the manuscript was unacceptable, since it contained libelous materials, and that W. H. Smith was exercising its right to terminate the contract, demanding the return of the down payment. Plexus disputed W.H. Smith's right to terminate the contract without first allowing Plexus the opportunity to correct the allegedly objectionable material (to cure the defect). W. H. Smith then sued.

W. H. Smith alleged that the contract was the sale of goods, which means it was covered by Article 2 of the UCC, and that § 2-718 gave it the right to seek restitution—the recovery of the down payment less $500. Plexus asserted that the contract was not for the sale of goods, but rather was for work, labor, and services, and that under contract law, it is entitled to retain the down payment and to recover losses it sustained as a result of the breach.

How should the court resolve this dispute? Was this a contract for the sale of goods or a contract for work, labor, and services? Explain and justify your reasoning. [See *W.H. Smith, Inc. v. Plexus Publishing, Limited*, 557 F. Supp. 546, 1983 U.S. Dist. LEXIS 18987 (S.D.N.Y. 1983).]

3. Purina Mills, Inc. (subsequently Purina Mills, LLC) entered into a contract with Less for the sale of feeder pigs and weanling pigs. The contract called for Less to purchase approximately 15,000 weanling pigs each year from November 25, 1997, through December 31, 2007, with the pigs to be delivered in approximately 28 deliveries each year, and with Less agreeing to feed the pigs Purina nutritional products. It further specified that Purina had the right to terminate the agreement if Less failed to make timely payments, with Purina giving written notice of the intent to terminate and the reason for the termination, and Less having 15 days to cure the breach. If Less did not cure within the 15 days, Purina could then provide a second written notice terminating the agreement.

On August 14, 2002, Less made a prepayment of $15,000 on his account and accepted a shipment of pigs priced at $9,888. On August 16, 2002, Less accepted another shipment of pigs priced at $6,544. After deducting the prepayment, Less still owed $1,432, an amount that remained unpaid. On August 21, 2002, Less did not accept a scheduled delivery of pigs due to alleged financial difficulties, and has not purchased any more pigs from Purina since the August 16 delivery. Purina gave written notice of an intent to terminate the contract unless Less cured the defect. When Less did not reply or cure the defect, Purina exercised its right to terminate the contract 15 days later. Purina then sued for the amount owed plus damages for breach for the remaining 5+ years of the contract, alleging that Less had repudiated his obligations by his conduct in August of 2002. Less argued that Purina Mills, LLC was not a proper party to the controversy since he had entered a contract with Purina Mills, Inc., a business entity that no longer existed. He also asserted that Purina Mills had not mitigated its damages and had used an improper market price for weanling pigs in calculating the damages being sought. According to Less, if the contract had been performed, Purina Mills would have realized a profit of $3 per pig, or $45,000 per year, giving total damages of approximately $500,000, substantially less than the $13 million Purina Mills was seeking. Purina Mills, LLC responded that it had changed its business organization form legally under Delaware law, that Purina Mills, Inc. had then properly assigned its rights under the contract to its successor, Purina Mills, LLC, and that under the provisions of the UCC, an aggrieved seller is allowed to select any appropriate remedies when there is a breach of contract.

How should the court resolve this controversy? What is the most important fact or factor affecting your decision? Does a duty to mitigate damages include a duty to select the least favorable remedy, the one providing the smallest amount of damages, when filing suit? [See *Purina Mills, LLC v. Less*, 295 F. Supp. 2d 1017, 2003 U.S. Dist. LEXIS 23247 (N.D. IA, 2003).]

Notes

1. UCC § 2-304.
2. UCC, § 1-203.
3. Official Comments to UCC § 1-203.
4. § 2A-509(1).

5. CISG, Articles 7 (1), 60 (a).
6. CISG, Article 39.
7. CISG, Article 44.

18

Warranties and Product Liability

Agenda

While most customers will be pleased with the eClass products, some customers will encounter problems. Since the cost of the software is so low, it is unlikely that an individual consumer will complain too much if he or she has a problem with the product, but complaints or lawsuits are still a possibility. Thus, while being sued is not likely, any such lawsuits filed due to problems with the software could have serious legal and financial implications. As a result, the firm wants to establish a warranty strategy for the firm that will provide appropriate protection for the firm while also providing reasonable protection for the customers. Should the firm attempt to exclude any warranties? Should the firm attempt to impose a liability cap in its contracts? How should warranty information be disseminated to customers? Should different methods be used for consumers than are used for merchants? These, and other questions, may arise in this chapter. Be prepared! You never know when the firm or one of its members will call on you for advice.

Classic Case

WEBSTER v. BLUE SHIP TEA ROOM
198 N.E.2d 309, 347 Mass. 421 (1964)

[This case has one of the most delicious opinions ever written (pun intended), combining a pinch of history with a dollop of common sense in resolving the case.]

FACTS Webster, a native of New England, ordered a cup of fish chowder in the Blue Ship Tea Room, a "quaint" Boston restaurant. While eating, she choked on a fish bone in the soup, requiring her to undergo two esophagoscopies at the Massachusetts General Hospital. Webster sued the restaurant, alleging breach of the implied warranty of merchantability.

ISSUE "[W]hether a fish bone lurking in fish chowder, about the ingredients of which there in no other complaint, constitutes a breach of the implied warranty of merchantability under applicable provisions of the Uniform Commercial Code."

HOLDING No. "No chef is forced to reduce pieces of fish in chowder to miniscule size in an effort to ascertain if they contain any pieces of bone . . . [and this] does not constitute a breach of implied warranty under the Uniform Commercial Code."

REASONING Excerpts from the opinion of Justice Reardon:

This is a case which by its nature evokes earnest study not only of the law but also of the culinary traditions of the Commonwealth which bear so heavily upon its outcome. It is an action to recover damages for personal injuries sustained by reason of a breach of implied warranty of food served by the defendant in its restaurant. . . .

The plaintiff, who had been born and brought up in New England (a fact of some consequence), ordered a cup of fish chowder. Presently, there was set before her "a small bowl of fish chowder." . . . "She started to eat it, alternating between the chowder and crackers which were on the table with . . . [some] rolls. . . . After 3 or 4 spoonfuls she was aware that something had lodged in her throat because she couldn't swallow and couldn't clear her throat by gulping and she could feel it." This misadventure led to two esophagoscopies at the Massachusetts General Hospital, in the second of which . . . a fish bone was found and removed. The sequence of events produced injury to the plaintiff which was not insubstantial. . . .

As the judge put it in his charge [to the jury], "Was the fish chowder fit to be eaten and wholesome? . . . [N]obody is claiming that the fish itself wasn't wholesome. . . . But the bone of contention here—I don't mean that for a pun—but was this fish bone a foreign substance that made the fish chowder unwholesome or not fit to be eaten?" . . .

The plaintiff has vigorously reminded us of the high standards imposed by this court where the sale of food is involved . . . serving to bolster her contention of breach of warranty.

The defendant asserts that here was a native New Englander eating fish chowder in a "quaint" Boston dining place where she had been before; that "[f]ish chowder, as it is served and enjoyed by New Englanders, is a hearty dish, originally designed to satisfy the appetites of our seamen and fishermen"; that "[t]his court knows well that we are not talking of some insipid broth as is customarily served to convalescents." . . . Notwithstanding these passionate entreaties we are bound to examine with detachment the nature of fish chowder and what might happen to it under varying interpretations of the Uniform Commercial

Code. Chowder is an ancient dish preexisting even "the appetites of our seamen and fishermen." . . .

Our literature over the years abounds in references not only to the delights of chowder but also to its manufacture. A namesake of the plaintiff, Daniel Webster, had a recipe for fish chowder which has survived into a number of modern cookbooks and in which the removal of fish bones is not mentioned at all. One old time recipe recited in the New English Dictionary study defines chowder as "A dish made of fresh fish (esp. cod) or clams, stewed with slices of pork or bacon, onions, and biscuit. 'Cider and champagne are sometimes added.'" Hawthorne, in The House of the Seven Gables . . . speaks of "[a] codfish of sixty pounds, caught in the bay, [which] had been dissolved into the rich liquid of a chowder." . . .

The recitation of these ancient formulae suffices to indicate that in the construction of chowders in these parts . . ., worries about fish bones played no role whatsoever. This broad outlook on chowders has persisted in more modern cookbooks. "The chowder of today is much the same as the old chowder. . . ."

Thus, we consider a dish which for many long years, if well made, has been made generally as outlined above. It is not too much to say that a person sitting down in New England to consume a good New England fish chowder embarks on a gustatory adventure which may entail the removal of some fish bones from his bowl as he proceeds. We are not inclined to tamper with age old recipes by any amendment reflecting the plaintiff's view of the effect of the Uniform Commercial Code upon them. . . .

[W]e consider that the joys of life in New England include the ready availability of fresh fish chowder. We should be prepared to cope with the hazards of fish bones, the occasional presence of which in chowders is, it seems to us, to be anticipated, and which, in the light of a hallowed tradition, do not impair their fitness or merchantability. . . .

Thus, while we sympathize with the plaintiff who has suffered a peculiarly New England injury, the order must be

Exceptions sustained. Judgment for the defendant.

INTRODUCTION

It is increasingly important for businesses to be aware of the scope of warranties and of the potential impact of product liability. A substantial number of very large judgments have been handed down against merchant sellers and/or manufacturers due to a breach of warranty or on the basis of product liability. Many of these judgments have been awarded to consumers of the goods, non-merchant buyers who have suffered harm when a product did not measure up to the reasonable—or guaranteed—expectations of the consumer purchaser. While it is true that warranty protections also extend to merchant buyers, and that some merchant buyers may have a claim against his or her seller based on product liability, this areas seems to be more important to non-merchant buyers who suffer harm due to the product in question, and this chapter emphasizes the rights of the consumers and the corresponding obligations of the merchant sellers against whom the claims are

eClass 18.1 Marketing/Sales

ADVERTISING THE PRODUCT

Ani wants to advertise the firm's software extensively in computing magazines, with ads extolling the benefits to be derived from using the software and testimonials from satisfied customers that will "grab" the readers and, hopefully, spur sales. Meg and Yousef agree with Ani in principle, but they suggest that the ads should be more low-key. They prefer a "soft sell" approach that does not create any inflated expectations in the minds of purchasers. Ani thinks this approach is too conservative, especially given the cost of such ads. She also wonders what possible harm could come from the fact that some people who read the ads and purchase the software end up disappointed with its performance. The principals have asked for your advice. What will you tell them? What other suggestions regarding advertising—and any potential related liability—might you want to provide?

BUSINESS CONSIDERATIONS   Visual ads can be very effective, especially with the technological devices available today. Computer enhancements can place famous people from the past in contemporary settings, and "morphing" can allow the advertiser to transform products from, or to, something else. While such ads can be effective, they can also be misleading. How much care should an advertiser take to ensure that an ad does not create express warranties that the advertiser will then have to honor?

ETHICAL CONSIDERATIONS   From an ethical perspective, should commercials include some disclaiming language informing the viewers that the depictions in the commercial were performed under controlled conditions, possibly with special effects and computer enhancement, in order to prevent viewers from getting the wrong idea about the capability of the advertised products?

filed. Remember that a warranty claim involves an alleged breach of contract, and as such, this area falls within the broad category of "remedies" (covered in Chapter 17), but it is treated separately due to the fact that the claims often involve personal injuries suffered by the buyer, not just a loss in value of the goods due to the alleged defect in the goods.

A warranty is defined as "a promise that a proposition of fact is true."[1] Since a warranty involves a promise, it becomes a part of the contract. This is especially important in the sale of goods. Warranty protection is very often the best protection that a buyer can have in a sale. There are two types of warranties in sales: express and implied. (There are also statutory warranty provisions, but these tend to be informational rather than coverage-based.) The fact that one type of warranty is present does not mean that the other type is absent. In fact, both types will frequently be present in one contract.

At common law, the courts presume that the parties to a contract have equal bargaining power. The courts also strongly believe in "freedom of contract." Thus, they were reluctant to interfere in the contractual relationship. Historically, the rule of *caveat emptor*—let the buyer beware—was regularly followed. As the commercial world matured, the relative positions of the parties to a sales contract began to change. Businesses grew larger, and the location of the business became more likely to be geographically removed from the location of the individual buyer. It became less likely that the parties would truly have equal bargaining power. It also became less likely that the seller of the goods had also manufactured them. The courts and legislatures began to seek means of protecting consumers. Implied warranties (and statutory warranty provisions) and product liability provided those means. The consumer has thus now become so protected that many people feel the modern rule of commerce is *caveat venditor*—let the seller beware!

EXPRESS WARRANTIES

An express warranty can only be *given* by the seller; it is not present until such time as the seller gives it. However, once given, such a warranty is said by the UCC to be a part of "the basis of the bargain." Section 2-313 mentions three different ways in which the seller creates an express warranty.

1. Any affirmation of a fact or a promise that relates to the goods creates an express warranty that the goods will match the fact or the promise.
2. Any description of the goods creates an express warranty that the goods will match the description.
3. Any sample or model of the goods creates an express warranty that the goods will conform to the sample or the model.[2]

Any of these three methods creates an express warranty if it is a part of "the basis of the bargain." It is not necessary for the seller to use words such as "warrant" or "guarantee." It is not even necessary for the seller to *intend* to create an express warranty. All that is necessary is that the seller employs one of these methods in a manner that causes the buyer to reasonably believe that a warranty covering the goods has been given.[3]

The Uniform Sales Act, which preceded the UCC, required the buyer to show reliance before an express warranty was found. The UCC seems to have removed the requirement of proving reliance. Instead, reliance appears to be presumed. The rule under the Code is that the seller must disprove the existence of an express warranty. In other words, if the buyer can prove the seller affirmed a fact, described

Exhibit 18.1

Finding an Express Warranty

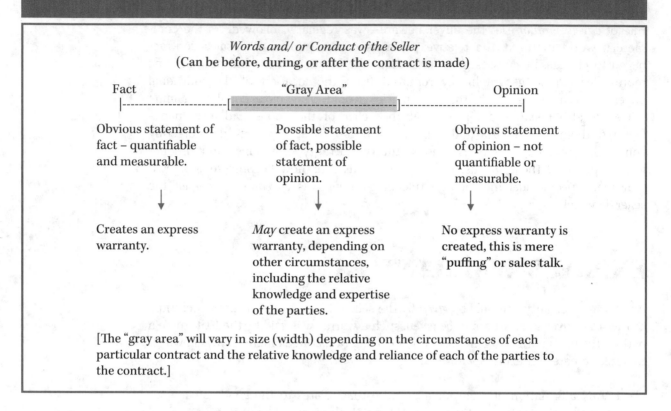

Words and/ or Conduct of the Seller
(Can be before, during, or after the contract is made)

Fact	"Gray Area"	Opinion
Obvious statement of fact – quantifiable and measurable.	Possible statement of fact, possible statement of opinion.	Obvious statement of opinion – not quantifiable or measurable.
Creates an express warranty.	*May* create an express warranty, depending on other circumstances, including the relative knowledge and expertise of the parties.	No express warranty is created, this is mere "puffing" or sales talk.

[The "gray area" will vary in size (width) depending on the circumstances of each particular contract and the relative knowledge and reliance of each of the parties to the contract.]

the goods, or used a model or a sample, an express warranty is presumed. To disprove the existence of the warranty, the seller must show proof that the conduct described by the buyer was not the basis of the bargain. If such proof cannot be shown, the express warranty is present, and it will be included in the contract.

Express warranties focus on *facts*. Mere opinions of the seller are not taken to be warranties. The seller is also allowed a certain amount of "puffing," also known as "sales talk." However, there is often a fine line between opinion and fact, and the seller should be extremely careful. If a statement is quantifiable, it is likely to be treated as a fact. If the statement is relative, it normally will be treated as opinion. Thus, the statement "this car gets 30 miles per gallon" likely would be treated as a warranty. But the statement "this is a good car" likely would not be a warranty. The problem lies with comments that fall between these two extremes.

Exhibit 18.1 illustrates the difficulty faced by the court in deciding whether something is a matter of fact or a matter of opinion. There is a great deal of gray area between things that are obvious facts and those that are obviously opinion, and the court has the task of deciding whether something within this gray area is a fact or an opinion.

If a statement that falls between an obvious fact and an obvious opinion was made by the seller, the court must decide how to interpret this statement in terms of warranty protections. To do so, the court must weigh the relative knowledge of the parties, the reliance (if any) the buyer placed on the seller, the likelihood that the seller was aware of any reliance, and any other pertinent facts that influence the balancing of interests of the two parties. Thus, if the seller conveyed an impression that seemed to be based on facts to the buyer, the court may decide that there was an assertion of facts and, therefore, may find an express warranty exists, despite the intent of the seller.

The seller also needs to be careful in advertising. Advertisements that claim certain characteristics for a product may also be treated by the courts as affirmations of fact and thus as express warranties. The following example shows how an advertisement may be viewed by the court in an express warranty case.

A television advertisement for the Pick Pen Company, manufacturers of disposable ballpoint pens, shows a couple on a picnic. The couple removes a can of fruit juice from the picnic hamper, only to discover that they forgot to bring a can opener. One of them reaches into a pocket, removes a Pick Pen, and uses the uncapped pen to punch a hole in the top of the can. The couple smiles, the camera pulls back, and a voice solemnly intones, "Pick Pens! For 99¢, it's not just a great writing instrument."

A customer who has seen this commercial decides to use his or her Pick Pen to open a can. Unfortunately for the customer—and for the Pick Pen Company—the pen shatters, and plastic shards enter the customer's wrist and hand, causing serious injury to the customer. An argument could be made that the commercial had created a belief in the mind of the customer that this use was expressly warranted, that the pen was suitable for use as a can opener in addition to its normal use as a writing utensil. If, however, the Pick Pen Company used a disclaimer in the commercial—normally by scrolling script across the bottom of the screen— asserting that the pen should not be used for this purpose, or not to attempt this sort of action "at home," the courts might be less likely to find that the commercial created an express warranty for this use.

Finally, the Code considers the *timing* of the statement or conduct from the buyer's perspective. Under § 2-209(1), a modification of a sales contract is valid without consideration. This means that the seller can create an express warranty before the contract is formed (through sales talk, negotiations, or even commercials); while forming the contract (in the language used in the agreement or in oral commitments made while forming the writing); or even after the contract is formed (through continued reassurances to the buyer that he or she has made a "good deal"). As a result, sellers should remember two things:

1. If they know a fact, they should state it honestly.
2. If they do not know a fact, they should not speculate! It is too easy to give an express warranty without realizing it.

Wat Henry Pontiac Co. v. Bradley[4] is one of the landmark cases in express warranty law. In 1944, Mrs. Bradley went to the Wat Henry Pontiac Company to purchase a used car. Mrs. Bradley asked many questions, and the seller assured her that the car in question was in good condition. When Mrs. Bradley stated that she had to drive to Camp Shelby, Mississippi, with her seven-month-old child to see her husband, the salesman allegedly said: "This is a car I can recommend" and "It is in A-1 shape." However, Mrs. Bradley was not allowed to take a "test drive" in the car, allegedly because of wartime gas rationing. Eventually, Mrs. Bradley bought the car and drove it home. Several days later, after she set out for Camp Shelby, the car broke down and required extensive repairs. Mrs. Bradley sued for breach of express warranties concerning the car. The sales manager testified that he gave no warranties in the sale and that he had explained to Mrs. Bradley at the time of the sale that there were no warranties covering the car. The court disagreed! The court pointed out that Mrs. Bradley was not generally knowledgeable concerning automobiles, and she was ignorant of all of the facts concerning this car in this case. The defects in the car were hidden, and the buyer was denied the opportunity to take a test drive during which the defects might have been discovered. The seller was an expert in automobiles. He repeatedly reassured her as to the quality of the car (albeit in general and non-quantifiable terms) throughout the sale process, from negotiations through the closing of the deal, and possibly even thereafter. His statements concerning the condition of the car, when viewed with her inability to personally examine the car prior to the sale, created express warranties and not mere opinion. Many of the principles of express warranty law now included in the Code seem to be based, at least indirectly, on the court's language from this case.

IMPLIED WARRANTIES

As pointed out in the preceding section, express warranties are a part of the contract. They are not present until given by the seller. The court will not find an express warranty unless it is created by the seller as a part of the "basis of the bargain." Thus, a careful seller will not give many—if any—express warranties until—and unless—so desired.

In contrast, implied warranties are *imposed* by operation of law, subject to certain limitations involving the status of the seller. If the circumstances are correct for the imposition of implied warranties, these warranties will automatically be present in the contract unless they are voluntarily "surrendered" by the buyer, generally because the warranties were excluded by the seller. If the language of the contract includes specific language excluding one or more of the implied warranties and the buyer agrees to that language, the buyer has "surrendered" the protections afforded by the excluded warranties.

The UCC recognizes four types of implied warranties: the warranty of title, the warranty against infringement, the warranty of merchantability, and the warranty of fitness for a particular purpose. Some, all, or none of these warranties may be present in any given sales contract, depending on the circumstances surrounding the transaction and on the status of the seller of the goods.

Warranty of Title

Every contract for the sale of goods carries a warranty of title by the seller unless such a warranty is excluded by specific language warning the buyer that title is not guaranteed or unless the sale is made under circumstances that put the buyer on notice that title is not guaranteed. Absent one of these two conditions, a warranty of title exists to protect the buyer. A warranty of title ensures the buyer of the following:

1. The transfer of the goods by the seller is proper.
2. The buyer is receiving good title.
3. The goods are free of hidden security interests, encumbrances, or liens.

In other words, the buyer is assured that no one may assert a hidden lien or claim to the goods that is superior to the claim of the buyer. (Note that this warranty does not assure the buyer that there are no liens or claims on the goods that may be superior, but only that there are no *hidden* liens or claims.)

Section 2-312 of the UCC specifies that every seller of goods gives an implied warranty of title unless the contract contains specific language that the warranty is being excluded or the circumstances of the sale are such that the buyer should realize that the seller does not warrant title. Thus, a merchant who is entrusted with goods gives a warranty of title if the merchant sells the entrusted goods to a good-faith purchaser. If the merchant has voidable title to the entrusted goods, the buyer receives good title, and there is no breach of the warranty. However, if the goods entrusted to the merchant have been stolen, the person who purchases the goods from the merchant would receive void title, and the merchant would be liable for breach of the implied warranty of title.

Warranty Against Infringement

The implied warranty against infringement is unique in that it can be given by either the buyer or the seller, although it is normally given by the seller. (None of the other implied warranties can be given by the buyer.) The infringement protected against is the rightful claim of any third person concerning the goods.

Patent infringement is probably the most common type of problem dealt with under this warranty, but another area that is becoming increasingly important is copyright infringement. Videotapes, audiotapes, and computer software normally are copyrighted, and all are easy to copy without a great deal of equipment, expertise, or expense. Experts estimate that pirated copies of copyright-protected materials cost each of these industries a tremendous amount of money, possibly even billions of dollars per year. As a result, more attention is being paid to the protection and

eClass 18.2 Management

WARRANTIES AND INFRINGEMENTS

One of the firm's customers wrote a letter complimenting the firm for the quality of the eClass software. In the letter, the customer commented that the software was very "SIMS^{TM}-like," which made its use especially appealing to students who were involved in cyber role-playing games and activities. This comment caused Meg to think that the firm may have inadvertently infringed on a trademarked software program, opening it up to possible liability not only to the holder of the SIMS^{TM} rights for trademark infringement, but also to any customers who have purchased eClass for breach of the warranty against infringement. She has asked you for your opinion on this matter. What will you tell her?

BUSINESS CONSIDERATIONS   What sort of policy should a firm have for dealing with items that are likely to be protected by a patent, copyright, or trademark? How can a firm be certain that it is not infringing rights when it produces or uses a product?

ETHICAL CONSIDERATIONS   Patent litigation can be extremely expensive, and it is not unusual for a court to declare the patent invalid, ruling that the product was not "new, useful, or non-obvious." Is it ethical for a business to infringe a patent, hoping to prevail in court by having the patent declared invalid?

enforcement of copyrights. As this trend continues, an increase in the number of cases involving the warranty against infringement will likely occur.

In order for a seller to give this warranty, the seller must be a merchant who regularly deals in the type of goods involved. A buyer who gives the warranty against infringement need not be a merchant. Any buyer who furnishes specifications to the seller in order to have the seller specially manufacture the goods described warrants against infringement if the seller complies with the specifications.

Warranty of Merchantability

Probably the most commonly breached, and the most commonly asserted, implied warranty is the warranty of merchantability. A warranty of merchantability is given whenever a merchant of goods, including a merchant of food or drink, makes a sale. It is a very broad warranty, designed to assure buyers that the goods they purchase from a merchant will be suitable for the normal and intended use of goods of that kind. Failure to satisfy any of the following six criteria means that the goods are not merchantable and that the warranty has been breached.

1. The goods must be able to pass without objection in the trade, under the description in the contract.
2. If the goods are fungible, they must be of fair average quality within the description.
3. The goods must be suitable for their ordinary purpose and use.
4. The goods must be of even kind, quality, and quantity.
5. The goods must be adequately contained, packaged, and labeled as required under the agreement.
6. The goods must conform to the promises and facts contained on the label, if any.

Merchant sellers have been found liable for breaching this warranty because of such things as bobby pins in soft-drink containers, worms in canned peas, a decomposing mouse in a soda bottle, and a hair dye that caused the buyer's hair to fall out.

Because many merchantability cases involve disputes over food and drink, the courts have developed special tests to determine merchantability in these cases. Early cases involving food were decided under the "foreign–natural" test. Under the foreign–natural test, "foreign" objects found in the food constitute a breach of warranty, whereas "natural" objects found in the food do not constitute a breach. Thus, a chicken bone found in a chicken salad sandwich does not involve a breach since chicken bones are "natural" to chicken. But a cherry pit found in a chicken salad sandwich is "foreign" and thus establishes a breach. While the results under the foreign-natural test were easy to predict, they often seemed unfair. Eventually a somewhat fairer test was developed, the "reasonable expectations" test. The reasonable expectations test has supplanted the earlier foreign-natural test in most, if not all, jurisdictions. Under the reasonable expectations test, the court attempts to establish what a reasonable person expects to find in the food. A reasonable person does not expect to find a "foreign" object in the food, so any foreign object found constitutes a breach. However, a reasonable person may not expect to find a "natural" object in the food either, so finding such a natural object can also constitute a breach. Thus, a chicken bone in a chicken salad sandwich might show a breach if it is unreasonable to expect to find a bone in such a sandwich. The reasonable expectations in any given case are a question of fact.

One such case, *Webster v. Blue Ship Tea Room*,[5] our Classic Case from earlier in this chapter, is considered a classic in the law. The case involved a woman (Webster) who ingested a fish bone while eating a bowl of fish chowder in a Boston restaurant. The bone became lodged in her throat, and she required surgery to remove the bone. The court recognized that Webster was a native New Englander and that she had ordered a seafood dish in a waterfront restaurant in Boston. The court's opinion then treated her presumed knowledge of the preparation of fish chowder, along with a relatively detailed history of fish chowder as a New England dietary staple. The court concluded that a reasonable person eating fish chowder in a New England restaurant would reasonably expect to find fish bones in the chowder, so that the chowder was, in fact, merchantable. This opinion illustrates one approach a court might take in deciding a merchantability-of-food case.

Merchants whose contracts primarily provide services do not give the implied warranty of merchantability for those services. A number of cases involving tainted blood have been decided, with the courts tending to view the provision of blood by a hospital as a "service" rather than a "sale," thus negating any claim that the tainted blood provided to the patient constituted a breach of the warranty of merchantability. Other states have specifically excluded warranty protections in the provision of blood, blood products, and other human tissue.

Warranty of Fitness for a Particular Purpose

Any seller, whether a merchant or a non-merchant, may give the implied warranty of fitness for a *particular* purpose (remember that the warranty of merchantability refers to fitness for a *normally intended or expected* purpose). In order for this warranty to come into existence, all of the following conditions must be present:

1. The seller must know that the buyer is contemplating a particular use for the goods.
2. The seller must know that the buyer is relying on the seller's skill, judgment, or knowledge in selecting the proper goods for the purpose.
3. The buyer must not restrict the seller's range of choices to a particular brand or price range or otherwise limit the scope of the seller's expert judgment.

The following examples show how this warranty may be found in a contract.

Bethany is in an appliance store looking at washing machines. She tells the sales clerk that she has a rather large family and needs a washer that can handle loads of 15 pounds. The sales clerk shows her a particular model and states that "this machine can easily handle loads of 15 pounds." Bethany buys the washer, only to discover that it will not handle such large loads. The store has breached the implied warranty of fitness for a particular purpose. Even though the washer may work very well on loads of up to 12 pound, it will not handle the size of load that the customer had specifically mentioned and which the sales clerk assured her that it would handle.[6]

Charles, who likes to travel, stops by a used car lot while shopping for a truck. While talking with the salesman, Charles mentions that he needs a truck that can haul his camper on his vacation over the summer. He also specifies that he only wants a vehicle that costs less than $10,000. The salesman shows him the available trucks on the lot that fall within the price range Charles has designated, and after a few test drives, Charles agrees to buy one of them. Unfortunately for Charles, the truck does not have adequate power to haul the camper, and the hauling causes transmission problems in the truck. Since Charles limited the salesman's options by specifying a price range, there is no warranty of fitness for a particular purpose, and Charles will not be able to recover from the dealership under this theory.

WARRANTY EXCLUSIONS

The seller can modify or exclude warranties. The simplest way to exclude an express warranty is not to give one. If the seller is careful, no express warranties will exist. Sometimes, a seller will create an express warranty orally but will attempt to exclude any express warranties in writing. In this case, the court will turn to UCC §2-316(1). The court will read the warranty and the exclusion as being consistent with one another, if possible; otherwise, the warranty will override the exclusion. Excluding or modifying implied warranties is not so easy. To exclude or modify a warranty of merchantability, either orally or in writing, the word *merchantability* must be used. If the exclusion is written, the exclusion must be conspicuous. To exclude or modify a warranty of fitness for a particular purpose, the exclusion must be written, and it must be conspicuous; no oral exclusions of fitness are allowed. Under §2-316(3), it is possible to exclude all implied warranties of quality (which normally do not exclude title or infringement protections) under three sets of circumstances:

1. Language such as "as is" or "with all faults" must be used properly so that the buyer is duly informed that no implied warranties are given.
2. If the buyer has thoroughly examined the goods or has refused to examine them before the sale, no implied warranty is given for defects that the examination should have revealed.
3. Under course of dealings, course of performance, or usage of trade, implied warranties are not given as a matter of common practice.

SCOPE OF WARRANTY PROTECTION

If warranties do exist, the next question to be answered is: Who do the warranties protect? At common law, the answer is simple but unsatisfactory. Since the warranty is a part of the contract, it extends only to a party in privity of contract. Any party not in privity of contract would not be covered by the warranty, regardless of whether that party was a foreseeable user or consumer of the warranted goods. Thus, the buyer is covered, but no one else is protected. The UCC has changed this. Section 2-318 contains the following three alternative provisions, and each state has selected one of the alternatives:

1. Warranties extend to any member of the buyer's family or household or any guest in the buyer's home if it is reasonable to expect that person to use or consume the goods.
2. Warranties extend to any natural person (human being) who could reasonably be expected to use or consume the goods.
3. Warranties extend to any person (remember, a corporation is a legal person) who could reasonably be expected to use or consume the goods.

Exhibit 18.2

Implied Warranties

Warranty	Covers	Given by	Exclusion
Title	Title to the goods. Warrants that there are no hidden security interests, liens, or other claims against the goods and that the seller had good title or the right to sell the goods.	All sellers, unless excluded by the seller *or* the circumstances of the sale are such that the buyer had no reason to expect the warranty	Specific language in the contract excluding the warranty. Note that a general exclusion clause—"there are no warranties, express or implied"—does not exclude the warranty of title. It only excludes merchantability and infringement warranties.
Against infringements	Infringements of the rights of third persons, especially for infringements of intellectual property rights of the third person (patents, copyrights, trademarks, etc.).	A merchant seller who regularly deals in goods of the kind involved in the sale. Can also be given by a buyer who provides specifications to the seller, if the specifications result in an infringement by the seller in meeting the specifications.	Exclusions must be in writing, must be specific, and must be conspicuous.
Merchant-ability	Goods must be fit for their normal and intended use.	Merchant sellers.	Exclusions can be oral or written, although proving an oral exclusion is likely to be difficult. Can be excluded generally (language such as "with all faults" or "as is" or "there are no warranties, express or implied") or specifically. If the exclusion is specific, it must be conspicuous, and it must contain the word merchantability.
Fitness for a particular purpose	A particular—as opposed to a "normal and intended"—use for the goods the buyer is purchasing, *if* the buyer makes the seller aware of the particular use *and* relies on the seller's expertise in making the purchase.	Any seller who, at the time of the sale, has reason to know of the buyer's particular purpose of the goods and knows that the buyer is relying on the seller's skill and judgment in selecting the goods.	Must be in writing. As with merchantability, the writing may be general or specific, and it must be conspicuous.

eClass 18.3 Sales

WARRANTIES

Yousef recently attended a seminar discussing common problems faced by new businesses, and one of the problems discussed was with warranties and the potential liability a firm faces if it breaches its warranties. Yousef became concerned that the principals had not given enough thought to the potential liability that eClass could be facing and decided to make some recommendations to the others about limiting or excluding their warranties in an effort to avoid liability if something should be wrong. Among the options he considered was the use of a warranty exclusion on the "shrink wrap" packaging on the software and a general exclusion of all warranties on the jewel case holding the diskette. He has asked for your advice. What will you tell him?

BUSINESS CONSIDERATIONS   A firm like eClass produces one product that it sells primarily to consumers, although it also has some sales to merchant buyers who will re-sell the product to consumers. Should such a business develop a strategy for its treatment of warranties based on the status of the customer, or should it just follow one warranty strategy for all of its products?

ETHICAL CONSIDERATIONS   Is it ethical for a business to advertise in a manner that suggests that the customers are getting a *full* warranty when in fact the customers are getting a *limited* warranty? Is it ethical to attempt to exclude all warranty protections in selling a product to consumers?

The seller may not exclude or modify the extension of the warranties to those third-party beneficiaries.

Exhibit 18.2 compares the implied warranties.

STATUTORY WARRANTY PROVISIONS

Before 1975, consumers faced certain problems in the area of warranty law: Many manufacturers disclaimed warranty protection, leaving the consumer with little or no protection; and most manufacturers put the warranty terms inside a sealed package, so the consumer did not even know what warranty provisions were being offered until after the sale was completed. The warranty terms inside the package frequently were in the form of a warranty card. The instructions told the buyer to complete the card and return it to the manufacturer in order to obtain his or her warranties. In fact, these cards often specified that the buyer was agreeing to accept the express warranties the manufacturer was offering as the exclusive warranties in the contract. By completing and returning the card, the buyer was surrendering any implied warranties he or she possessed in exchange for a very restricted (frequently a 60- or 90-day) express warranty coverage proposed by the merchant.

As a result of these problems, the Magnuson-Moss Warranty Act was passed and took effect in 1975. This law covers any consumer good manufactured after January 3, 1975. The manufacturer must provide the consumer with presale *warranty information.* The manufacturer also should set up informal settlement procedures to benefit the consumer. The manufacturer does not have to give any express warranties under the statute. However, according to the law, a manufacturer who does give an express warranty must designate it as either full or limited. To qualify as a full warranty, the warranty must meet at least four requirements:

1. It must warrant that defects in the goods will be remedied within a reasonable time.
2. It must conspicuously display any exclusions or limitations of consequential damages.
3. Any implied warranty must not be limited in time.
4. It must warrant that if the seller's attempts to remedy defects in the goods fail, the consumer will be allowed to select either a refund or a replacement.

Any warranty that is not full is limited. In a limited warranty, implied warranties may be limited to a reasonable time, frequently the same time as the express warranties given in the contract by the seller. There may also be limits on when the buyer can select a refund or a replacement.

Note that Magnuson-Moss does not provide warranty protection. All that this law requires is for the manufacturer or seller who deals in consumer goods to inform the consumer of his or her warranty protections. The Magnuson-Moss Warranty Act is a disclosure law, designed to ensure that consumers are made aware of the warranty protections available with different products so that the consumer can make an informed and intelligent choice between products based on all of the available information, including warranty coverage.

PRODUCT LIABILITY

While a great deal of energy and emphasis is placed on warranty law and warranty protections, this is not the only area in which buyers and consumers are protected from injuries caused by goods they have purchased and/or are using. Because they are a part of the contract, warranty protections are obvious to the buyer and the seller. Less obvious to the buyer, and to many sellers, are the other sources of remedies to which the buyer may be entitled. These other remedies may well be broader, they often last longer, and they frequently lead to larger judgments for injured parties. Sellers, in particular, need to be aware of the potential liability they face for injuries caused by the goods they sell beyond the liabilities imposed under warranty law.

Assume that a person is injured while using goods he or she has purchased, and he or she decides to seek remedies for the injury suffered. The first alternative many people consider is a breach of warranty claim. However, in many cases the warranty protections do not extend to the injury suffered, or the warranty protections have expired. When such a situation occurs, the injured party is not necessarily left without remedies. He or she may discover that, although warranty protections are lacking, potential remedies are still available under tort law. The injured party may be able to assert negligence against the manufacturer, or may even be able to establish strict tort liability against the manufacturer or the seller of the goods.

Negligence

At common law, negligence can be used in only two circumstances: The buyer can argue breach of duties established by the privity of contract between the parties; or the buyer can argue that the goods are innately dangerous, so that privity of contract is not necessary in order to establish the liability of the seller or the manufacturer.

An injured party trying to establish that the tort of negligence occurred has to show the requisite elements of negligence: duty, breach of duty, harm, and proximate cause. Duty, the first element, is often the most difficult to establish. The injured party has to show that he or she is in privity of contract with the negligent party in order to establish that the seller owes a duty to the buyer. If there is privity, the contractual relationship establishes a duty by the seller to provide reasonably safe goods. The buyer next has to establish that this duty has been breached. This is normally done by showing that the goods provided are not reasonably safe for their intended use. The injured party then has to show that he or she was injured while using the goods and that the injury was *proximately caused* by the seller's breach of duty. This presents a relatively difficult task for the buyer. Even if the buyer can establish that the goods are not reasonably safe, that an injury did occur, and that there is a proximate causative link between the defect and the injury, establishing a duty owed by the manufacturer to the buyer is hard to show. In most instances, the injured party is in contact only with an innocent intermediate party and not with the negligent manufacturer. The manufacturer would argue that it only owes a duty to its buyer, the intermediate party. The intermediate party would assert that it has not breached any duty owed to the injured party. The lack of privity thus negates the duty element, effectively removing the possibility of suing the manufacturer for negligence.

Historically, an injured user who was able to argue that the goods were innately dangerous had an easier time establishing his or her case, if the innate danger of the goods could be shown. If the goods were found to be imminently or inherently dangerous, privity was not required. However, establishing the imminent or inherent danger of the product is more difficult. A product is deemed to be imminently dangerous if it is reasonably certain to threaten death or severe bodily harm as produced and/or sold. An item is considered to be inherently dangerous if it is dangerous by its nature. Imminent danger is most commonly found in negligent production; inherent danger is most commonly found in negligent use.

The difficulty of establishing either of these bases for proving that the manufacturer is liable for injuries serves as an effective shield from product liability at common law. However, times change, and so did the law's approach to product liability. In 1916, U.S. courts effectively laid the privity defense to rest in product liability cases. In the landmark case of *MacPherson v. Buick Motor Co.*, the owner of a Buick automobile was injured when the wooden spoke wheel of his automobile broke while he was driving the car. MacPherson sued Buick for his injuries. Buick denied liability for two reasons. It had not produced the wheel, but rather it had purchased the wheel from a supplier; so, if liability attached to the defect in the wheel, the supplier should be the liable party. Buick also claimed lack of privity in that MacPherson had purchased his car from a dealer, not from the Buick Motor Company. The court rejected both arguments made by Buick, allowing the injured plaintiff to recover damages from Buick despite a lack of privity. Other courts quickly adopted the *MacPherson* rule, and, as a result, privity of contract is seldom asserted as a negligence defense today.

Strict Liability in Tort

The other basis for recovery frequently asserted by an injured party is strict liability in tort (also referred to frequently as strict liability or strict tort liability). Strict liability in tort appears to be a public policy area. It is possible for a manufacturer to disclaim warranty provisions, leaving a purchaser without the protections envisioned by warranty law. Similarly, an injured consumer may not be able to establish the necessary elements for a successful negligence suit. Nonetheless, there seems to be a general feeling that an injured consumer should be able to recover from *someone*, and the manufacturer is seen as the best available source for recovery. Not only is the manufacturer normally better able to absorb the loss than the injured consumer, but the manufacturer is also in a position to pass the cost on to society in the form of higher prices for the goods.

The basis for this theory of recovery is found in *Restatement (Second) of Torts*, § 402A. Section 402A is widely followed by the courts of the United States. The section states:

> **(1)** One who sells any product in a defective condition unreasonably dangerous to the user or consumer or to his property is subject to liability for physical harm thereby caused to the ultimate user or consumer, or to his property, if
>
> **(a)** the seller is engaged in the business of selling such a product, and
> **(b)** it is expected to and does reach the user or consumer without substantial change in the condition in which it is sold.

(2) The rule stated in subsection (1) applies although

(a) the seller has exercised all possible care in the preparation and sale of his product, and

(b) the user or consumer has not bought the product from or entered into any contractual relation with the seller.

Note that this provision applies only to a merchant, that the merchant must sell a "defective" product that is "unreasonably" dangerous to the consumer, and that the product must reach the consumer without any substantial change in its condition. If these three criteria are satisfied, and if the consumer is injured using the product, the manufacturer can be held liable even though it used all possible care in the production of the product and even though there is no allegation of negligence.

This basis for liability imposes a substantial potential burden on the manufacturer. The "defective condition unreasonably dangerous to the user or consumer" referred to in part 1 is often measured at the time the injury occurs and not at the time the product was produced. Thus, a manufacturer who produces a product with a long useful life may face liability in the future, due to technological advances in the industry after production of the product but before the product is removed from service. The manufacturer can be found liable under this section for defects in design, defects in construction, or for failing to warn the consumer of a known danger commonly faced when using the product. This is one of the reasons for the warning on the blade platform on power lawn mowers ("Keep hands and feet from under mower while in operation."), the warning label on the power cords of electric hair driers ("Keep away from water—Danger"), and other labels or tags on consumer goods. This could also be an argument for planned obsolescence of products. A product whose useful life is supposed to end before too many technological advances can be made is less likely to lead to liability for the manufacturer.

LEASES

Article 2A provides many of the same types of protections to lessees that Article 2 provides to buyers. Thus, when goods are leased, the lessee receives certain warranties, and these warranties are either the same as, or at least analogous to, the warranties given to the buyer in a sale of goods. There are some differences in a few of the warranties, but these differences are due to the difference in the reason the contract is entered. As you can see, these differences are more in style or terminology than in the types of coverage provided. The lessee receives express warranties on the same basis as a buyer of goods does. Express warranties are created when the lessor makes any affirmation of fact or promise that relates to the character, quality, or nature of the goods. These express warranties become part of the basis of the bargain. The lessor also provides express warranties based on descriptions of the goods or by providing any sample or model of the goods being leased. Article 2A of the UCC specifically excludes any statements as to the value of the goods, as well as any statement purporting to be merely the lessor's opinion or commendation of the goods, from attaining the status of an express warranty.

Lessees also receive four implied warranties in their lease contracts. These implied warranties are: the warranty against interference, the warranty against infringement, the warranty of merchantability, and the warranty of fitness for a particular purpose. The warranty against interference is similar to the warranty of title under Article 2. It warrants that, during the term of the lease, no person holds a claim to or interest in the goods that will interfere with the lessee's use and enjoyment of the goods. The other three implied warranties are the same for lessees as they are for buyers. Warranties under Article 2A can be excluded in the same manner as they are excludable under Article 2.

Product liability claims are also available against the lessor or the manufacturer in a lease agreement. The same sorts of claims would be asserted, and the same defenses would be available.

THE CISG

The CISG does not expressly provide for warranties as the UCC does. Instead, the warranties protections provided under the CISG are implied from the language of some of the articles of the Convention. Nonetheless, if warranties are found to exist and those warranties are breached, the buyer will be entitled to remedies. Also remember that the CISG is not meant to apply to the sale of goods to consumers under most circumstances, so any breach of warranty claims under the CISG are most likely to involve merchant buyers and merchant sellers. Thus, the remedies sought are quite likely to be "normal" sales remedies rather than remedies given to an injured consumer. As such, the assessment of damages is likely to be much smaller, relating to the value of the contract rather than to personal injury, harm, or loss.

Article 8 of the CISG says that any statements or conduct of either party are to be interpreted according to the intent of the party making the statement or carrying out the conduct. If the intent of the party cannot be determined from the circumstances, statements and conduct are to be interpreted as a reasonable person would interpret them under the circumstances. If the statements or the conduct were intended to create a warranty, *or* if the intent cannot be determined, but a reasonable person would interpret the statements or conduct as creating a warranty, then a warranty has been created. Since this warranty exists because of the intentional conduct of the parties, the warranty would be viewed as an express warranty.

Article 9 provides that the parties are bound by any practices they have established between themselves, and to have impliedly made any common trade usages part of their contract. Thus, if it is normal trade usage to provide warranties in these types of contracts, those warranties will become part of the particular contract unless the agreement specifically excludes such trade usage. These trade usages may well include some implied warranty provisions, especially if one of the parties to the international sale of goods is a U.S. firm, which commonly has implied warranties as a part of its trade usage, and the other party knew or should have known of that trade usage.

Article 35 requires the seller to deliver goods that are of the quantity, quality, and description required by the contract and that are contained or packaged in the manner required by the contract. This article goes on to state that, unless otherwise agreed, the goods are nonconforming unless they are fit for their ordinary use and purpose[7] and, also, unless they are fit for any particular purpose made known to the seller at the time of the contract.[8] These provisions sound strikingly similar to the UCC's provisions for the implied warranties of merchantability (fit for normal use) and fitness for a particular purpose. The CISG even has a similar limitation on the provisions regarding particular purpose: This finding of nonconformity does not apply in the "particular purpose" area where the circumstances show that the buyer did not rely, or that it was unreasonable for him to rely, on the seller's skill and judgment. Article 35 also states that the goods must be properly contained and packaged, and that the goods must possess the qualities of goods that the seller has held the goods out as possessing, based upon the use of any model or sample. Thus, while the CISG does not use the word "warranty," it contains provisions that require the same sorts of protections as the implied warranty provisions of Articles 2 and 2A of the UCC.

The CISG does not make any provisions for product liability. It appears that international sales of goods treat the issue of product liability or negligence under the applicable national laws of the forum court. Of course, the UCC does not provide for product liability or negligence either. These areas are both areas of state law developed through the common law traditional and applied by the forum court when appropriate.

ISO 9000

The CISG is not the only major international agreement involving business and the sale of goods. Numerous free trade zones have been established in the recent past, greatly affecting trade both within and outside of these zones. (See Chapter 8 for a brief discussion of free trade zones.) A number of other initiatives that will have an impact on international trade have also been adopted or proposed. It appears that international business will be a focal point for uniform law for the foreseeable future.

Product quality and quality control are topics that have attracted a substantial amount of attention in the global marketplace. The concerns with these topics led to the promulgation and eventual adoption of an international quality-control standard, ISO 9000.

The International Standards Organization (ISO) is an international agency head-quartered in Geneva, Switzerland. The ISO was established to develop uniform international standards in certain specified areas. The ISO is comprised of representatives from the national standards organizations of a number of countries; they have joined their efforts in an attempt to create certain uniform international standards. The first major success was in the area of quality control—ISO 9000.

ISO 9000 is not a standard. Rather, it is a mechanism providing a comprehensive review process and overall guidelines. By following this review process and the guidelines, companies can ensure that their products comply with the quality standards established for their industry. ISO 9000 is a set of five international standards concerning quality management and quality assurance in the production process. Firms that decide to participate in the program register with the national standards body and acquire an ISO number. As the number of registered firms increases, the importance of participation also increases. Many firms that are active in international trade require ISO 9000 participation as a condition to entering a contract. Quality standards may have a significant impact on international sales over the next few years.

It is quite possible that ISO 9000 compliance will become even more important in the future. Not only might ISO certification become mandatory for the importation of goods into some free trade zones, but the presence or absence of ISO 9000 certification might become an aspect of product liability litigation. Firms that possess such certification might, arguably, be deemed to satisfy minimum quality standards for their products unless the injured party can prove some form of negligence or some other basis for recovery. Firms that do not possess the certification might be presumed to lack the necessary minimum quality standards, placing the burden on the firm to establish its lack of liability. Such presumptions are merely speculative now, but as ISO 9000 certification expands, this could change.

Contemporary Case

ACUSHNET CORPORATION v. G.I. JOE's, INC.
2006 U.S. Dist. LEXIS 73254 (Ore. 2006)

FACTS In March 2005, G.I. Joe's placed an order with Cam Golf, a supplier of golfing equipment, for a total of 396 dozen Titleist Pro V-1 golf balls. Acushnet is the manufacturer of Titleist golf balls, and although G.I. Joe's had a direct account with Acushnet for some golf items, it did not have a direct account with Acushnet for Titleist golf balls. Consequently, G.I. Joe's obtained what appeared to be Titleist golf balls from Cam Golf. G.I. Joe's had

been buying golf balls from Cam Golf for several years. During 2005, all Titleist golf balls sold by G.I. Joe's were purchased from Cam Golf. G.I. Joe's sold the Titleist golf balls to its customers.

On April 19, 2005, one of G.I. Joe's customers complained to the manager of the Eugene, Oregon, store that the Titleist golf balls he had purchased were "seconds," or counterfeits, because the laminate on the golf balls came off after one round of golf. G.I. Joe's pulled all of its remaining stock of Titleist golf balls from its shelves, about 138 dozen, and contacted Cam Golf's president, Don Bach, about the customer's complaint. Mr. Bach told

G.I. Joe's that it could return the golf balls for full credit, which G.I. Joe's did.

Meanwhile, a G.I. Joe's customer had complained to Acushnet that there was something wrong with the golf balls he had purchased from the G.I. Joe's, and Acushnet determined that the customer had purchased counterfeit golf balls. Acushnet then sent an investigator to purchase golf balls from the G.I. Joe's store in Puyallup, Washington, and determined that these golf balls were also counterfeit.

On May 27, 2005, Acushnet commenced this action against G.I. Joe's. G.I. Joe's answered and filed a third-party complaint against Cam Golf, alleging that Cam Golf breached its warranty of non-infringement. Acushnet and G.I. Joe's settled, with G.I. Joe's paying Acushnet $25,000 and incurring $19,350 in attorneys' fees.

ISSUES Did Cam Golf breach its warranty against infringements by selling counterfeit or "second" Titleist golf balls to G.I.Joe's? Is G.I. Joe's entitled to claim the amount of the settlement as consequential damages?

HOLDINGS Yes. The golf balls Cam Golf sold to G.I. Joe's infringed Acushnet's trademark, resulting in the infringement lawsuit. Yes. Since Cam Golf did not intercede to defend it must pay the settlement amount to G.I. Joe's.

REASONING Excerpts from the Opinion of Judge Dennis James Hubel:

G.I. Joe's has proffered evidence that the Titleist golf balls sold by G.I. Joe's in March 2005 were infringing, and that the only Titleist golf balls G.I. Joe's sold during that period were originally obtained from Cam Golf. Cam Golf neither admits nor denies that the golf balls it sold to G.I. Joe's were infringing, despite claiming that it has investigated the matter. Cam Golf admits that

G.I. Joe's ordered 396 dozen Titleist golf balls from Cam Golf on March 1 and March 28, 2005, and that Cam Golf filled those orders. Cam Golf neither admits nor denies that it sold the accused Titleist golf balls to G.I. Joe's. . . . The U.C.C. provides that the warranty of non-infringement is imposed on a seller who is a merchant regularly dealing in goods of the kind. Cam Golf is such a merchant. G.I. Joe's has produced evidence that Cam Golf breached the warranty of non-infringement, and Cam Golf has not countered that evidence. In the absence of any genuine issue of material fact, G.I. Joe's is entitled to summary judgment on the issue of Cam Golf's breach of the warranty of non-infringement.

Cam Golf argues that the amount G.I. Joe's paid to Acushnet may not be recovered as consequential damages because the payment was by settlement rather than pursuant to a judgment.

I find this argument unpersuasive. First, the Oregon U.C.C. "vouching in" provision . . . is not mandatory. The statute provides:

(5) Where the buyer is sued for breach of a warranty or other obligation for which the seller is answerable over:

(a) The buyer may give the seller written notice of the litigation. If the notice states that the seller may come in and defend and that if the seller does not do so the seller will be bound in any action against the seller by the buyer by any determination of fact common to the two litigations, then unless the seller after seasonable receipt of the notice does come in and defend the seller is so bound.

(b) If the claim is one for infringement or the like . . . the original seller may demand in writing that the buyer turn over to the seller control of the litigation including settlement or else be barred from any remedy over and if the seller also agrees to bear all expense and to satisfy any adverse judgment, then unless the buyer after seasonable receipt of the demand does turn over control the buyer is so barred.

(6) The provisions of subsection[s] ... (5) appl[ies] to any obligation of a buyer to hold the seller harmless against infringement or the like. ...

You Be the Judge

Alex Hardy was driving his Chevrolet S-10 Blazer when he was involved in a one-vehicle accident. Hardy was thrown from the vehicle, allegedly because the door latch failed, and he suffered serious and permanent injuries as a result of the accident. Hardy was paralyzed from the waist down. During the trial, Hardy admitted that he had been drinking beer immediately before he began his fateful drive. He also admitted that he was not wearing a seat belt at the time of the accident. Finally, he admitted that he had fallen asleep at the wheel of his vehicle while driving and was asleep at the time of the accident. However, Hardy also asserted that none of these factors were involved in the crash or the subsequent injuries. According to Hardy's theory, the axle of the truck broke, causing the crash. As a result of the crash, the vehicle rolled over, the door latch failed, and Hardy was thrown from the truck. Thus, according to Hardy, the vehicle did not conform to his expectations, the defects were hidden so that a reasonable inspection would not reveal them, and General Motors was in breach of its contract. A jury awarded Hardy $50 million in compensatory damages and an additional $100 million in punitive damages. General Motors has appealed this case to *your* court. How will *you* rule on this appeal?

This case was decided in Alabama, a state that has had numerous very large jury verdicts of late. Should a business that operates in multiple states consider *not* doing business in Alabama—or any other "pro-plaintiff" state—due to the fear of potentially crippling jury awards of damages? Is it ethical for a plaintiff who admittedly had been drinking and who admittedly fell asleep at the wheel while driving to sue the manufacturer of the vehicle for injuries suffered in a subsequent accident? Is it ethical for a jury to award a huge verdict to a plaintiff simply because the defendant has "deep pockets" and can afford to pay the award?

[See "Tort Reform Advocates Condemn GM Jury Award," *Detroit News* (June 5, 1996) http://detnews.com/menu/stories/50879.]

Summary

Warranty law and product liability are two major areas of consumer protection—a subject that has been receiving an increasing amount of attention for some years. Warranty protection comes in two broad forms: express warranties, which are given by the seller; and implied warranties, which are imposed by law. There are also statutory warranty provisions, which are primarily concerned with disclosures to consumer-purchasers. Warranties are considered a part of the contract covering the sale of goods. Warranties may be excluded by the seller or surrendered by the buyer. The method of exclusion depends on the type of warranty involved.

Generally speaking, warranties extend to parties other than the buyer of the product, provided that the other parties are foreseeable users or consumers of the product. Each state has adopted one of three alternatives for the extension of warranty protections beyond the buyer of the goods.

The Magnuson-Moss—Consumer Product Warranty Act provides statutory coverage in the warranty area. Magnuson-Moss provides for disclosure of the warranty protections extended to purchasers of consumer goods. It does not provide substantive protections for the purchasers, but it does provide a method for making consumer purchasers aware of what sorts of warranty protections are provided in the contract.

Under product liability, the manufacturer or the seller may be held liable because of negligence in making, designing, or packaging the product. The manufacturer may also be held strictly liable, despite any lack of due care. This is true if the product, in its normal use, is imminently or inherently dangerous.

Leases also carry protections for the lessee in the area of warranty law. Lessees can receive express warranties when the lessor creates a belief in the mind of the lessee as to the character, quality, or nature of the goods being leased. Lessees also enjoy the protection of four implied warranties. These warranties are analogous to the implied warranties of Article 2.

The CISG contains language that seems to provide for warranty coverage, although the word "warranty" is not used. It provides that statements or conduct of the parties is to be interpreted as the parties intend, and if such intent cannot be ascertained, the statements or conduct is to be interpreted as a reasonable person would interpret them. This can be interpreted as allowing the parties to create express warranties if they so desire, or if a reasonable person would believe they had done so. The CISG also provides that the goods must be fit for their normal use and properly packaged, and must conform to any samples or models provided by the seller in order to be deemed as conforming to the contract. This is similar to the UCC's merchantability provisions. The CISG also states that goods must be suitable for a particular use of which the seller was aware at the time of the contract, unless the buyer can be shown not to have relied on the seller's expertise. This is similar to the UCC's fitness for a particular purpose provisions.

Discussion Questions

1. According to Article 2 of the UCC, what is necessary before a seller is deemed to give a buyer express warranties in a sales contract? What is necessary to give a lessee express warranties in a lease contract under Article 2A? Does the CISG make any provisions for the granting of express warranties in an international sale of goods?

2. What does a seller warrant to the buyer in the implied warranty of title? What does the lessor warrant to the lessee in the implied warranty against infringement? Does the CISG have any comparable protections in its coverage?

3. When does a buyer of goods receive an implied warranty of merchantability under Article 2 of the UCC? When does the lessee of goods receive an implied warranty of merchantability under Article 2A of the UCC? What assurances does the buyer or lessee receive with this warranty?

Does the CISG provide a warranty of merchantability under its coverage?

4. What is the purpose of the Magnuson-Moss Warranty Act? What is the difference between a full warranty and a limited warranty under the Magnuson-Moss Act?

5. What are the requirements that must be satisfied before a seller will be found liable for strict tort liability under § 402A of the *Restatement (Second) of Torts*?

Case Problems and Writing Assignments

1. Cooper and a friend, Turner, were sitting under Cooper's carport in June 2007. They had a lit citronella candle on the floor between them. The candle consisted of a citronella scented paraffin and wax contained within a metal bucket-shaped container. Cooper had purchased the candle between two and four years earlier and had stored it, uncovered, on a shelf in the carport. Cooper did not remember where she purchased the candle, but she did not purchase it from the Old Williamsburg Candle Company. There was a label attached to the bottom of the container warning against attempting to extinguish the candle with water, but Cooper claimed never to have read, or even noticed, the warning. She did claim to have used the candle several times previously to "ward off bugs" without problems or difficulties.

On the night of the incident, Cooper and Turner had been sitting on lawn chairs under the carport for several hour, and had been burning the candle for a portion of that time. When they decided to end their evening visit, Cooper attempted to blow out the candle. However, the wick failed to extinguish. Turner then went into the house and drew water from the tap into a Pyrex cup. He then poured the water over the candle in an attempt to extinguish the flame. The candle began "snapping and popping" but still did not extinguish. Rather, it began to burn

more "aggressively," so Turner decided to attempt to smother the flame. While Turner was looking for a suitable cover to smother the flame, the candle exploded, spewing flames and hot wax and paraffin over Cooper's lower body. She suffered severe burns over 11 percent of her body. As a result, she was unable to work, and she incurred substantial medical and hospital bills. She filed suit against Old Williamsburg Candle to recover for her injuries and expenses, alleging product liability, breach of the implied warranty of merchantability, and negligence. Old Williamsburg has denied liability, asserting that Cooper's failure to properly use the candle, and her failure to obey the warning contained on the bottom of the container should relieve Old Williamsburg of any liability.

How should the court rule in this case? What was the most important fact or factor influencing your decision? [See *Cooper v. Old Williamsburg Candle Corp.* (M.D. Fla. 2009).]

2. Spooner Farms of Puyallup, Washington, sells certified root stock for raspberry plants. Barbara Berry is a commercial berry grower in Michoacan, Mexico. Berry purchased 3,150 pounds of raspberry root stock from Spooner in December 2003, and the root stock was shipped to Mexico in February and March of 2004. Berry intended to use this root stock to plant 74 acres of raspberries, but since there wasn't enough root stock to plant this many acres, she propagated the root stock through a method known as "etiolation," which is allegedly a common practice in Mexico. She then planted the propagated root stock to complete planting of the 74 acres, but she claims that the plants propagated from the Spooner root stock produced fruit that was "malformed and crumbly." She then sued Spooner Farms, claiming breach of the implied warranty of merchantability, citing the inferior fruit produced by the plants as evidence that the root stock was not fit for its normal and intended purpose.

Spooner Farms denies liability, asserting that it did not sell the root stock that produced the "malformed and crumbly" fruit, but rather that Berry had produced that root stock. According to Spooner Farms, it could not be held liable for breach of warranty for a product that it did not provide or sell.

How should the court decide this case? Should the implied warranty of merchantability, which admittedly attached to the original order of root stock, also extent to additional root stock propagated from the original product? Explain your reasoning. [See *Berry v. Spooner Farms, Inc.* (W.D. Wash. 2009).]

3. HCT purchased a number of plastic non-slip shims from Korolath and used those shims in 18 different construction projects. After it had completed the projects, HCT allegedly had to replace all of the shims, which were defective in that they failed to bear the loads placed on them, at great expense in time and money. HCT is suing for breach of contract, breach of warranty, and product liability.

The shims were made from high impact polystyrene (HIPS), made from recycled styrene, with rubber added to provide greater flexibility. The HIPS used to produce the shims were an economy version that had no specifications indicating compression strength. This product, sold "off catalog," is variable in nature and inconsistent in quality. Spartech, which produced the shims, claimed that Korolath knew this about the product and purchased it despite its nature. Korolath denied this, claiming that it had been ordering a custom blend from Spartech under a 1986 contract, but that Spartech breached that contract by sending this particular batch. According to Korolath, if it is liable to HCT, then Spartech is liable to it.

Assuming that the shims provided by Korolath to HCT were, in fact, defective, what should be the outcome of this case? Is Korolath liable to HCT for any or all of the grounds asserted by HCT? Is Spartech liable to Korolath under any or all of those same grounds? Explain and justify your reasoning. [See *High Concrete Technology v. Korolath of New England* (S.D. Ohio 2009).]

Notes

1. *Black's Law Dictionary*, rev. 6th ed. (St. Paul: West Group, 1990), p. 1586.
2. UCC § 2-313(1).
3. UCC § 2-313(2).
4. 210 P.2d 348 (Supp. Ct. Okla. 1949)
5. 198 N.E.2d 309 (1964).
6. This example was derived from "Understanding Warranties," Free Advice, found at http://law.freeadvice.com/resources/gov_material/ftc_business_guide_to_fed_warranty_law_understanding_5_87.htm
7. CISG Article 35 (2)(a).
8. CISG, Article 35 (2)(b).

Part IV

Negotiables

egotiables" can take many forms. Negotiable *instruments* consist of checks, notes, drafts, and certificates of deposit. All of these forms are governed by [Revised] Article 3 of the Uniform Commercial Code (UCC), "Negotiable Instruments." Checks are also governed to a significant extent by Article 4 of the UCC, "Bank Deposits and Collections." "Negotiables" can also take the form of negotiable documents of title. Documents of title are governed by Article 7 of the UCC, "Warehouse Receipts, Bills of Lading and Other Documents of Title." Article 8, "Investment Securities," also deals with an area historically included with "negotiables." Our emphasis in this section is on negotiable instruments, although we also address negotiable documents to a limited extent.

In general, negotiable instruments are short-term instruments that arise out of commercial transactions. Millions of such instruments are signed each day, not only because they are a safe and convenient means of doing business, but also because they are acceptable in the commercial world as credit instruments and/or as substitutes for money. Documents of title are not as widely used, but they also have an important place in our commercial law.

This part of the text explains how and why negotiables are widely used and accepted in the modern commercial world. In addition, the topics of funds transfers (Article 4A of the UCC), electronic funds transfers, and bank—customer relations will be discussed.

19

Introduction to Negotiables: UCC Article 3 and Article 7

Agenda

eClass will need an initial source of funds in order to get established. Ani, Meg, and Youisef may need to obtain loans for the business. What will they need to do, and what legal implications may arise if they sign promissory notes on behalf of the firm?

The business will have bills and obligations that it needs to meet periodically. Should eClass try to pay all of its bills in cash, or should the firm have some sort of checking account? If a checking account is opened, what legal rights and duties will be involved for the firm? What rights and duties will be involved for the principals?

Many customers of eClass will wish to pay their bills by checks. Accepting these checks will create a risk, albeit small, for the firm. Should the principals adopt a policy against accepting checks in order to avoid this risk? What might such a policy mean for the firm and its chances of success?

eClass will also be selling its software to customers online, with payment to be made via computer. What area of law covers such payments?

Is there a difference between credit card payments and electronic fund transfers? If so, which is safer for the firm?

If eClass orders any goods or equipment from a remote supplier, how are these shipments likely to be handled? Should the firm insist on the use of negotiable documents of title, or should it insist that all documents of title be nonnegotiable? What legal significance is attached to the negotiability of these documents of title?

These and other questions will arise during our discussion of law of negotiables. Be prepared! You never know when the firm or one of its members will seek your advice.

Classic Case

STATE OF MONTANA v. CROSS
1992 Mont. Dist. LEXIS 106 (1st Dist., 1992)

[This is an interesting case. The rules of interpretation for a negotiable instrument provided a valid defense in a criminal case.]

FACTS Pauline Cross entered into an agreement on January 9, 1991, with Miracle Ear Center of Kalispell to purchase two Miracle-Ear hearing aids. The cost of each hearing aid was $ 950, for a total purchase price of $ 1,900. On or about February 11, 1991, Cross issued a check, to be drawn on her account at The State Bank of Townsend, to a representative of Miracle Ear in exchange for the two hearing aids. Shortly thereafter, the check was dishonored and returned by The State Bank of Townsend, stamped "NOT PAID" and "N.S.F.," allegedly for lack of funds in Cross's account to cover the draft.

Criminal charges were filed against Cross, accusing her of issuing a bad check. Montana law states that a person commits the offense of issuing a bad check when she issues or delivers a check or other order upon a real or fictitious depository for the payment of money knowing that it will not be paid by the drawee bank.

ISSUE Did Cross issue a check for an amount that she knew would not be paid by her bank?

HOLDING No. She had no reason to know that the bank would not pay the check as issued.

REASONING Excerpts from the opinion of Judge Sherlock:

Defendant contends that the check she issued is ambiguous as to the amount and, as such, the civil rules regarding negotiable instruments will apply. The Court agrees.

The criminal statutes of this state do not define a "check," Therefore, we must turn to the provisions of the Uniform Commercial Code for guidance. Under [§ 3-104] . . . a "check" is defined as an instrument which contains an unconditional promise or order to pay a sum certain in money, payable on demand or at a definite time, and payable to order or to bearer. . . .

The amount of Defendant's check stated in words was "Nineteen ———— no/100 Dollars." The amount of the check stated in figures was "$1,900.00." Because the words and the figures on the check in question differ as to their amount, the Court must again look to the civil code and that section that controls negotiable instruments. When an ambiguity exists in a draft or check [§ 3-118] . . . provides rules of construction that are to be applied in determining the amount for which the check was drawn. Subsection (c), of the statute provides: "Words control figures except that if the words are ambiguous figures control."

Under the applicable commercial law in force at the time of the alleged offense, it can be determined from the face of the check that the words in question are not ambiguous and as such will control as to the amount for which the check was drawn. Therefore, Defendant's check is determined to be written and payable for $19.00.

The record in this case contains no evidence that this amount, $19.00, would not have been paid by Defendant's depository, The State Bank of Townsend, because of insufficient funds. Therefore, the felony charge of issuing a bad check pending against Defendant should be dismissed.

The Court should note that it is possible in most cases to apply either the bad checks provisions . . . or the general section on theft . . . to bad check activities. However, the laws defining criminal offenses are not rubberbands to be stretched to cover any social purpose, however worthy. The prosecution of this matter should have properly occurred under the statute defining the offense of theft. The State is therefore granted leave to file an amended information.

Therefore, the Court HEREBY ORDERS, ADJUDGES, AND DECREES that Defendant's motion to dismiss is GRANTED. . . .

HISTORIC OVERVIEW

An industrial or a commercial society needs to use some forms of documents or instruments in order to function efficiently. Documents and instruments provide evidence of the transactions and also provide convenience for their users. When goods are transported or stored, some document is needed to reflect their transportation or their storage. When goods are sold and paid for, unless the sale is a cash transaction, some instrument or documentation is needed to reflect the payment while providing some safety for the parties involved. This is especially true if the transaction is not a "face-to-face" transaction, since sending cash payments by means of the mail or via commercial carrier is, at best, somewhat risky.

Negotiable instruments of various types have been present in nearly every society that has developed a substantial commercial system. Instruments very similar to the contemporary promissory note date back to about 2100 B.C. The merchants of Europe were using negotiable documents and instruments on a broad scale by the thirteenth century. In fact, the use of drafts was so widespread that a substantial portion of the *Law Merchant* was devoted to the proper treatment of these instruments.

Negotiable instruments had become so pervasive by the late nineteenth century that the English Parliament enacted the English Bills of Exchange Act in 1882 to govern the use of such instruments in England. Following the example of the English Parliament, the National Conference of Commissioners on Uniform State Laws drafted the Uniform Negotiable Instruments Law (NIL) for the United States in 1896. Each of these statutes merely attempted to codify and formalize the common law rules that had been developed over the years in their respective nations. In the United States, the NIL was designed to unify and codify the rules and laws of each jurisdiction regarding all negotiable commercial documents. However, since negotiable commercial documents included checks, drafts, notes, certificates of deposit, bills of lading, warehouse receipts, and investment securities, the breadth of the topical coverage made the NIL unwieldy and difficult to apply to the commercial world of the twentieth century.

One of the objectives of the UCC is to comply more readily with the demands of the modern business world. By the mid-twentieth century, it was obvious that the coverage of the NIL was too broad. In an effort to reflect "commercial reality," the topical coverage contained in the NIL was updated and divided into different articles, and these articles were then included in the UCC. The original Article 3, "Commercial Paper," dealt only with negotiable *instruments* in their various forms. Other articles dealt with other aspects of what had been covered for the previous 50-plus years by the NIL.

The Code has been adopted by every state in the union except Louisiana, and Louisiana has adopted some portions, including original Articles 3 and 4, which deal with commercial paper and with bank—customer relations. However, changes in banking laws and banking practices, and the increased use of instruments that were not covered by the original Article 3 (i.e., "share drafts" issued by credit unions), led the National Conference of Commissioners on Uniform State Laws (NCCUSL) to develop and propose the 1990 revision of Article 3 and the related amendments to Article 4.

Articles 3 and 4 are based on a paper payment system, and that system has changed dramatically. In the early 1950s, about 7 billion checks were processed annually.[1] However, the American Banking Association anticipated a major increase in checking activities and developed the MICR[2] line technology, a more efficient method for processing checks. By 1988, the Federal Reserve estimated that there were approximately 48 billion checks written annually,[3] and nearly 50 billion checks, worth about $47.4 *trillion*, were written in 2000.[4] The number of checks written in the United States has been declining, however, down to 42 billion in 2001, 37 billion in 2003, and 30 billion in 2006.[5] There were also some changes in federal banking law, especially in the Expedited Funds Availability Act,[6] and with the Federal Reserve, which enacted Regulation CC.[7] The revision to Article 3 involved a change of name, from "Commercial Paper" to "Negotiable Instruments," and a change in scope, to encompass more types of instruments. The amendments to Article 4, Bank Deposits and Collections, not only take into account the changes to Article 3, but also more accurately reflect modern banking practices and contemporary usage of instruments. As of May 2004, the Revised Articles 3 and 4 have been adopted in 48 states and the District of Columbia (New York and South Carolina have not yet adopted the revised version). As a result, our coverage here will only discuss Revised Article 3, which will henceforth be referred to simply as Article 3.

In revising Articles 3 and 4, the UCC's treatment of negotiable instruments has been modified to reflect modern commercial reality. The articles now provide statutory treatment that is in line with the advances provided by growth and technology, and with the changes in federal laws and banking practices. The UCC has also standardized and clarified the rules governing documents of title. Both warehouse receipts and bills of lading are covered in Article 7 of the Code. Article 7 retains many of the traditional rules and views of documents of title, while also codifying the contemporary use of these documents in the U.S. legal system. Each of these articles is discussed in some detail in the remainder of this chapter.

THE SCOPE OF ARTICLE 3

Article 3 of the Uniform Commercial Code covers *negotiable instruments*. A negotiable instrument is a written promise or order to pay money to the order of a named person or to bearer. Although Article 3 provides most of the coverage of negotiable instruments, there are also provisions in other articles of the UCC that affect negotiable instruments. For example, a number of definitions from Article 1 apply in Article 3. Article 4, Bank Deposits and Collections, and Article 9, Secured Transactions, also affect the coverage of negotiable instruments. In fact, Article 3 specifies that its (Article 3's) provisions are "subject to" the coverage in Articles 4 and 9.[8] The scope of Article 3 is somewhat narrow, being restricted solely to negotiable instruments, as defined in § 3-104. Further, Section 3-102(a) states that Article 3 does *not* apply to money, to payment orders governed by Article 4A, or to securities governed by Article 8. Thus, one finds that Article 3 covers negotiable instruments but not other types of commercial or negotiable documents, and that two other articles of the Code may supplement, complement, or override the provisions of Article 3. To fall within the coverage of Article 3, an instrument must qualify as a "negotiable instrument." If an instrument does not qualify, it is likely to be governed by common law provisions, primarily in the area of contract law.

The revision to Article 3 provides for substantially different coverage of negotiable instruments and also significantly expands the definition of what constitutes a negotiation instrument. This new treatment is found in § 3-104. This section is important enough, and complex enough, that we have reproduced it virtually in its entirety, with the first portion set out here and the balance set out in "Functions and Forms," below.

§ 3-104 Negotiable Instrument.

(a) Except as provided in subsections (c) and (d), "negotiable instrument" means an unconditional promise or order to pay a fixed amount of money, with or without interest or other charges described in the promise or order, if it:

1) is payable to bearer or to order at the time it is issued or first comes into possession of a holder;

2) is payable on demand or at a definite time; and

3) does not state any other undertaking or instruction by the person promising or ordering payment to do any act in addition to the

payment of money, but the promise or order may contain (i) an undertaking or power to give, maintain, or protect collateral to secure payment, (ii) an authorization or power to the holder to confess judgment or realize on or dispose of collateral, or (iii) a waiver of the benefit of any law intended for the advantage or protection of an obligor.

(b) "Instrument" means a negotiable instrument.

(c) An order that meets all of the requirements of subsection (a) except paragraph (1), and otherwise fills within the definition of "check" in subsection (f) is a negotiable instrument and a check.

(d) A promise or order other than a check is not an instrument if, at the time it is issued or first comes into possession of a holder, it contains a conspicuous statement, however expressed, to the effect that the promise or order is not negotiable or in not an instrument governed by this article.

Thus, the first part of § 3-104 gives us the broad general outline of what constitutes a negotiable instrument. It is an unconditional promise or order to pay a fixed amount of money, and it contains no other "undertaking" or "instruction" by the person who promised or ordered the payment. Notice, also, that a negotiable instrument must be payable "to bearer" or "to order" at the time it is issued or first comes into the possession of a holder *unless* the instrument qualifies as a check. A check will be considered negotiable even if it lacks this wording, the "words of negotiability" that is discussed in Chapter 20. It should also be noted that any writing that looks like an instrument *except a check* will *not* be negotiable (and hence, not an instrument) if it contains a conspicuous statement that it is not negotiable.

This means that a person who issues a *check* must abide by the provisions of Article 3, even if the check does not contain "words of negotiability," but a person who issues any other type of writing that *appears* to be an instrument may "opt out" of coverage under Article 3 by placing a *conspicuous* term on the face of the instrument excluding it from treatment as a negotiable instrument.

USES OF NEGOTIABLE INSTRUMENTS

Negotiable instruments are widely used in our economy. They are used as a substitute for money. They are used for convenience. They are used as credit instruments. They are used to pay bills, to buy things, and to borrow. Some of the most important uses of each type are set out in the following sections.

Checks

The most commonly used type of negotiable instrument is a check. Many people use checks rather than cash for daily purchases. Checks are regularly written to the supermarket for groceries, to the utility companies to pay bills, to the landlord to pay the rent, and to the bank to make loan payments. In addition, many working people receive their salaries or wages in periodic paychecks from their employers. (Of course, many people also now have automatic deposits of their pay made electronically. This is a type of electronic fund transfer, one of the topics discussed in Chapter 23.)

Checks are widely used because they are easily written, easily carried, and widely accepted. Carrying and using checks is safer than carrying and using cash. If a person loses a blank, unsigned check, no harm is likely to occur. All that was lost was a piece of paper. However, if a person loses cash, the money is gone. The bank will not take an unsigned check, but it will take lost money. Great care should be taken with checks, particularly signed ones. A signed check, otherwise blank, is nearly as good as cash. Anyone finding such a check can complete the blanks and possibly receive cash for it as completed, to the detriment of the depositor/"drawer."

The revision to Article 3 recognizes a number of specialized drafts as "checks" within the coverage of § 3-104. Each of these specialized checks has the primary use of serving as a substitute for money. However, they also have some aspect that distinguishes them from traditional or "regular" checks. For example, a cashier's check is a check drawn by a bank against that same bank and then issued to the person who purchased it. Cashier's checks and teller's checks are commonly used by a purchaser who wants to guarantee payment to the payee. Both cashier's checks and teller's checks are treated as "cash equivalents" by the payee, based on the assumption that the bank will honor the check upon presentment.[9] The bank issuing the cashier's or teller's check is referred to as the "obligated bank," and it must honor the check unless the bank itself has a reason for non-payment. Any alleged defenses by the remitter cannot be used by the bank to avoid liability.[10] Payees are willing to accept either of these checks because the payee knows that there are sufficient funds available, and because the issuing bank is not likely to have any reason not to pay the check upon proper presentment.

A traveler's check is a special type of check used by people who are away from home and want the security of having checks that will be accepted. A traveler's check is signed once by the drawer upon purchase, but it requires a second signing by that same drawer (a countersigning) before it can be negotiated. The payee knows that a bank is holding the funds used to purchase the traveler's check, so there is no danger of insufficient funds; and the payee can compare the countersignature to the "authenticating" original signature, minimizing the risk of a forgery. A credit union check (formerly called a "share draft") is simply a check drawn against a credit union. As banks become more and more specialized, many individuals are turning to credit unions to handle their personal banking needs, simply because the credit union specializes in individual accounts, and the fees imposed are normally substantially less.

Drafts

Businesses often use drafts to pay for merchandise ordered, especially when the buyer and the seller are in different states. Drafts may be payable "at sight" (i.e., on demand,

eClass 19.1 Finance

CO-MAKERS FOR COMPANY LOANS

When eClass was first formed, the firm needed to borrow some money. The bank's lending officer seemed very willing to make the loan, but not if the borrower was to only be eClass. She insisted that the principals had to be co-makers of the note, with each of them signing the note as both an individual and as a principal of eClass. While they were not entirely comfortable with this arrangement, the three principals agreed to the terms because they needed the funds the loan would provide. After, Ani felt that the bank had treated them unfairly, and she suggested that they seek a new bank for future activities. Meg and Yousef were not sure that they had been treated unfairly. However, in deference to Ani's opinion, they have asked you for your advice. What will you tell them?

BUSINESS CONSIDERATIONS   It is common in business classes to discuss the advantages and disadvantages of various forms of business. One advantage that is frequently cited for the corporate form is the limited liability of the investors. However, when a corporation is newly formed, it has no "track record" upon which a bank or other lender can rely. Should a bank refuse to lend money to a newly formed corporation without requiring any cosigners until the business has established itself? Should it insist that the principals act as cosigners on any loans?

ETHICAL CONSIDERATIONS   Is it ethical for the principals in a business to attempt to avoid any potential liability by forming a corporation, an LLC, or an LLP?

the first time the drawer has "sight" of the draft after its issue), or they may be time drafts (i.e., they will be payable at a future time, either a specific date or a specific time after "sight"). Often, the seller of goods will send a draft to the buyer for acceptance. If the buyer accepts, he or she has agreed to pay any holder who makes proper presentment. Such a draft is called a trade acceptance.

With the recent liberalization of federal and state banking laws and regulations, a number of changes have occurred in the area of negotiable instruments. One of these changes has been in the area of drafts. Today, some financial institutions other than banks offer accounts similar to the checking accounts offered by banks. These drafting accounts offer the same privileges for these depositors as are available to depositors of banks. Technically, however, these are not checking accounts. There are some minor differences, especially with respect to Article 4 of the UCC and in the requirements regarding account statements.

Promissory Notes

Promissory notes are most often used as instruments of credit. They are also used as evidence to show a pre-existing debt. When a person borrows money from a bank, finance company, or other type of commercial lender, the borrower will normally be required to sign a promissory note; this signed note proves the existence of the debt, the amount owed, the manner of repayment, and any other terms important to the loan agreement. Notes are so widely used that special types of notes have been developed. Real estate loans normally involve a mortgage note. Automobile loans usually involve an installment note. Many banks also use a device called a commercial loan note or a signature note for short-term unsecured loans (loans made without collateral).

Certificates of Deposit

A certificate of deposit (CD) is an instrument issued by a bank evidencing a debt owed to a depositor. These instruments commonly call for the bank to pay to a proper presenter the amount deposited plus interest at a stated future date. Although regularly thought of as a type of special savings account, CDs are really credit instruments. They are *promissory notes* of the bank that recognize money "borrowed" by the bank from the "depositor," the person who loaned the money to the bank. Most banks today issue non-negotiable certificates of deposit which are not covered by the provisions of Article 3.

FUNCTIONS AND FORMS

Negotiable instruments have two major functions: They are designed to serve as a substitute for money, and they are designed to serve as credit instruments. In satisfying either use, they carry certain contract rights, certain property rights, and some special rights due exclusively to their nature as negotiable instruments. Every negotiable instrument is presumed to be a contract, but not every contract is a negotiable instrument. The difference between a contract and a negotiable instrument is one of form. To be negotiable, an instrument must be (1) current in trade and (2) payable in money. These criteria are obviously too broad and too vague to be of much practical significance. Accordingly, Article 3 has more fully defined the requirements an instrument must meet in order to be negotiable. These elements are discussed in detail in Chapter 21.

As mentioned earlier, UCC § 3-104 defines the various types of negotiable instruments. These definitions include the following, as described in the remaining subsections of 3-104:

(e) An instrument is a "note" if it is a promise and it is a "draft" if it is an order. If an instrument falls within the definition of both "note" and "draft," a person entitled to enforce the instrument may treat it as either.

(f) "Check" means (i) a draft, other than a documentary draft, payable on demand and drawn on a bank or (ii) a cashier's check or teller's check. An instrument may be a check even though it is described on its face by another term, such as "money order."

(g) "Cashier's check" means a draft with respect to which a drawer and drawee are the same bank or branches of the same bank.

(h) "Teller's check" means a draft drawn by a bank (i) on another bank, or (ii) payable at or through a bank.

(i) "Traveler's check" means an instrument that (i) is payable on demand, (ii) is drawn on or payable at or through a bank, (iii) is designated by the term "traveler's check" or by a substantially similar term, and (iv) requires, as a condition to payment, a countersignature by a person whose specimen signature appears on the instrument.

eClass 19.2 Finance/Management

WHERE SHOULD eCLASS HAVE ITS CHECKING ACCOUNT?

Yousef has his personal checking account with a credit union, and he is very pleased with the service he receives. He is strongly urging the firm to place the eClass checking account with the credit union to take advantage of the lower fees and what he perceives as more personal service. Ani has dealt with a local bank for several years, and she is also generally pleased with the service and treatment she receives with her bank. Meg has recently opened an account with a large regional bank, and she likes the services available through such a bank. She thinks that this is the sort of bank the firm should utilize for its checking account. While each of the principles can see advantages to having the firm's account with the same bank as at least one of them has a personal account, they have also heard that a commercial bank has certain benefits for a business. They have asked you for your advice. What will you tell them? (Before answering, you might want to contact a local bank and a local credit union for information, suggestions, and guidance.)

BUSINESS CONSIDERATIONS   What services would a business want and/or reasonably expect from a bank? How are these services different from those that an individual would want and/or reasonably expect on his or her account?

ETHICAL CONSIDERATIONS   Many banks today are beginning to charge customers fees and service charges for using an automated teller machine (ATM). Some banks are also imposing fees when a customer enters the bank and uses a human teller when the transaction could have been handled by an ATM. Is the imposition of a fee or a service charge for normal and expected banking services ethical? How does such an arrangement affect a business account, as compared to a personal account?

(j) "Certificate of deposit" means an instrument containing an acknowledgment by a bank that a sum of money has been received by the bank and a promise by the bank to repay the sum of money. A certificate of deposit is a note of the bank.

Every instrument must contain either an order or a promise to pay a fixed amount of money. If the instrument contains an order, it is a draft. If the instrument contains a promise, it is a note. The category of drafts includes checks, which are simply specialized forms of drafts. The category of notes includes certificates of deposit, which are simply specialized forms of notes. Drafts, also known as "order paper," are most commonly used as a substitute for money. Notes, also known as "promise paper," are most commonly used as credit instruments, providing proof that credit has been extended and showing evidence of the terms of payment for that credit.

PAPER CONTAINING AN ORDER ("THREE-PARTY" PAPER)

The distinctive features of paper containing an order (order paper), or three-party paper, are that each instrument contains an order to pay money and that at least three legal roles are involved on each instrument. The order element is pointed out in the following sections, while the rules governing this class of negotiable instrument are explained later. The three roles involved on order paper are: the drawer, the drawee, and the payee. As noted, this class consists of drafts, including checks in the various forms checks can take.

Drafts

A draft is an instrument in which one party, the drawer, issues an instrument to a second party, the payee. The draft is accepted by the payee as a substitute for money. The payee expects to receive money at some time from the third party, the drawee. The reason the payee expects to receive money from the drawee is contained in the basic form of the instrument. As will be pointed out, the drawer issues an *order* to the drawee to pay a sum of money. This order, coupled with the three roles involved, distinguishes drafts from promise paper. The components of a draft are shown in Exhibit 19.1.

Checks

The most common type of order paper is a check. A check is a special type of draft. Like a draft, a check necessitates the involvement of three parties, but there are two differences. A check is, by definition, a demand instrument; in contrast, a draft may be a demand

Exhibit 19.1

A Draft

41618

(1)
WORLDWIDE EXPORTS, INC.
1313 Mockingbird Lane
Metropolis, USA

Date_____**(2)**_____

To _____**(3)**_____

(4)   **(5)**
Pay to the Order of _____**(6)**_____ $___**(7)**___

_____**(8)**_____ Dollars

For _____**(10)**_____   _____**(9)**_____
                                        Authorized Signature

Legend: (1) The drawer. (2) The date of issue. (3) The drawee (can be any third party, including a bank). (4) The order. (5) The words of negotiability. (6) The payee. (7) The amount, in numbers. (8) The amount, in words. (9) Authorized signature of drawer. (10) Reason for issuance.

instrument or a time instrument. Furthermore, a check must be drawn on a bank or payable at or through a bank; in contrast, anyone may be the drawee on a draft. Article 3 now specifically includes cashier's checks, teller's checks, traveler's checks, and checks drawn against credit unions within the definition of "checks" to better reflect contemporary usage of that term. Exhibit 19.2 shows the various elements of a check.

In the case of both a check and a draft, the drawee is obligated to the drawer. This obligation is normally a debt or contractual obligation owed to the drawer by the drawee. When the drawer orders the drawee to pay, the drawer is directing the drawee as to how the debt or contractual obligation should be discharged or partially discharged. The order to the drawee to pay, coupled with the obligation to pay, assures the payee or a subsequent holder that payment will (normally) be made by the drawee at the appropriate time.

Exhibit 19.2

A Check

1492

Isabelle Issuer
104 Palace Drive
Anytown, USA

(6) ____ 20____

(1)   (2)
Pay to the Order of _____**(3)**_____ $ __**(4)**___

_____**(5)**_____ Dollars

Last National Bank, N.A. **(8)**
Metropolis, USA

Memo _____   _____**(7)**_____
101010101 :   123456789   1492

Legend: (1) The order. (2) Words of negotiability (*preferred*, but no longer *required*, on a check). (3) The payee. (4) The amount, in numbers. (5) The amount, in words. (6) The date of issue. (7) The drawer's signature. (8) The drawee (must be a bank).

The Order   All drafts (including checks) contain an order. The drawer orders the drawee to pay the instrument. The language used is not a request. The drawer does not "ask," or "hope," or even "expect" the drawee to pay. The drawer demands that payment be made. If you look at Exhibit 19.1 or Exhibit 19.2, you will see that the drawer tells the drawee to "Pay to the order of (Payee)." It should also be noted that the *order* is the word **pay**; the phrase "to the order of" is not the order. This phrase is a term of negotiability; its meaning will be explained later, when negotiability is discussed.

The Drawer   The person who draws an order instrument, who gives the order to the drawee, and who issues the instrument to the payee is known as the drawer. This person originates the check or the draft. The drawer does not pay the payee directly. The drawee is expected to pay the payee or the holder, upon proper presentment. That is why the drawer gives the drawee the order. The drawer expects the order to be obeyed because of a prior agreement or relationship between the drawer and the drawee. If the order is obeyed, the drawee pays the payee or holder, and both the drawer and the drawee have performed.

Exhibit 19.3

The Parties on Order Paper

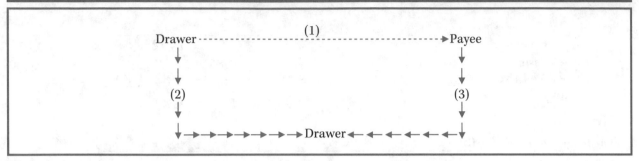

Legend: (1) The drawer issues the order instrument to the payee. The instrument contains an order directed to the drawee. (2) The payee (or an indorser or holder) presents the order instrument to the drawee in order to collect. The drawee is expected to obey the order given to it by the drawer by accepting and paying the instrument. (3) Assuming that the drawee obeyed the order, the drawer or the drawer's account is charged for the amount of the instrument.

The Drawee   The party to whom the order on the draft is directed is the drawee. The drawee is told by the drawer to "*Pay* to the order of" the payee. It is the drawee who is expected to make payment to the presenting party. However, the drawee has no duty to the payee or to the holder to pay, despite the order. The only duty the drawee has is a duty owed to the drawer. The duty of the drawee is to accept the instrument. Before acceptance, there is only the prospect that the drawee will pay when the time for payment arrives. Once the drawee accepts, the drawee has a contractual obligation to pay the presenter. This relationship is shown in Exhibit 19.3.

The Payee   The payee is the person to whom the instrument is originally issued. The payee may be specifically designated, as in "Pay to the order of Jane Doe"; the payee may be an office or title, as in "Pay to the order of Treasurer of Truro County"; or the particular payee may be unspecified, as in "Pay to the order of bearer." The payee may decide to seek payment personally, or the payee may decide to further negotiate the instrument. The words "to the order of" allow the payee to order the drawee to make payment to some other party. ("To the order of" means to whomever the payee orders, literally allowing the negotiation of the instrument.)

PAPER CONTAINING A PROMISE ("TWO-PARTY" PAPER)

The distinctive features of paper containing a promise (promise paper), or two-party paper, are that each such instrument contains a *promise*, and that only *two* parties are necessary to fulfill the legal roles involved on the instrument. This class of negotiable instruments involves notes, including certificates of deposit. These two parties are known as the maker and the payee.

The term "two-party" is confusing to many people. Many stores have signs prominently posted stating that they do not accept "two-party checks." These so-called two-party checks are, in reality, checks that have been negotiated by the payee to a later holder. The store does not want to accept a check unless it receives it directly from the drawer. But there is no such legal creature as a check that is "two-party paper."

The promise element of promise paper is pointed out in the following sections, and the rules governing this class of negotiable instrument are explained later.

(Promissory) Notes

The promissory note is the oldest known form of negotiable instrument. It is normally used as a credit instrument, executed either at the time credit is extended or as evidence of a pre-existing debt not yet repaid.

In a note, one party (the maker) promises to pay the other party (the payee) a sum of money at some future time. The promise may call for a lump-sum payment, or it may call for installment payments over time. The note may specify the payment of interest in addition to the principal; it may have the interest included in the principal; or it may be interest free. The note may recite details about collateral. Despite any or all of these possibilities, the basic form is constant. Such an instrument is shown in Exhibit 19.4.

Certificates of Deposit

A certificate of deposit (or a CD, as it is frequently called) is a special type of note issued by a bank as an acknowledgment of money received, with a promise to repay the money at some future date. Many people think of a CD as a "time savings account," in contrast to a passbook savings account. In reality, though, a CD is not a savings account at all. It is most commonly a time deposit of money with a bank.

Most banks today do not offer *negotiable* certificates of deposit, instead offering a nonnegotiable alternative that, technically, is not governed by Article 3. *Investopedia* refers to negotiable certificates as NCDs, and defines them as "A certificate of deposit with a minimum face value of $100,000."[11]

In today's world, a certificate of deposit is a short-term, large denomination CD primarily issued to institutional investors. It appears that for most individuals, the negotiable CD has become extinct.

Exhibit 19.4

A Promissory Note

---

(1)

Friendly Finance LLC
221B Baker Street
Our City, USA

Loan No. _____

Borrower(s)   **(2)**
Name(s) _____ and _____
       (first)   (last)   (first)   (last)

Address _____

_____
    (3)   **(4)**   **(5)**   **(6)**

I/We promise to pay to the order of **Friendly Finance LLC** the sum of $_____

_____**(7)**_____ Dollars, plus
interest at a rate of twelve percent (12%) per annum. Payment is to be made in one payment no later than two
(2) years from the above date at the address of the payee, 221B Baker Street, Our City, USA.

_____**(8)**_____   _____**(9)**_____

_____**(8)**_____   _____**(9)**_____
(Borrower's Signature)   (Date)

Legend: (1) The lender/payee. (2) The borrowers/makers. (3) The promise. (4) The words of negotiability. (5) The payee.
(6) The amount, in numbers. (7) The amount, in words. (8) The signature of the makers. (9) The date.

The Promise   Promise paper is so-called because it contains a promise. The maker of the instrument *promises* to pay an amount of money to the payee or to a holder. The instrument does not say that the maker "might' pay, or will "probably" pay, or will "agree" to pay. The instrument says that the maker *promises* to pay the payee or a holder.

Exhibit 19.5

The Parties on Promise Paper

Maker   (1) ⟶ Payee

Maker ⟵ (2)   Payee or Holder

Legend: (1) The maker issues the promissory note to the payee, promising to pay the payee (or a subsequent holder) upon proper presentment. (2) The payee (or a subsequent holder) presents the promise paper to the maker, expecting to receive payment as per the promise.

The Maker   The duties performed by the drawer and the drawee on order paper are effectively combined in promise paper: Both duties fall to the maker. The maker makes the promise—"I promise to pay to the order of (the payee)"; the maker issues the instrument to the payee; and the maker pays the instrument upon proper presentment. However, there is one important difference from order paper. While the drawee is not obligated to any holder until acceptance, the maker is liable to a holder from the date of issue of the instrument. This obligation is shown in Exhibit 19.5.

The Payee   As in order paper, the payee is the party to whom the instrument is originally issued. Again, the payee may be specifically designated by name, or designated by title or office, or unspecified (Pay to the order of bearer). The payee on promise paper is the person to whom the promise is made by the maker. By contract, the payee on order paper is the person to whom the drawee is directed or ordered to make payment.

THE SCOPE OF ARTICLE 7

The UCC treats the topic of documents of title in Article 7. This article, entitled "Warehouse Receipts, Bills of Lading, and Other Documents of Title," specifies the rights and the duties of all relevant parties in the handling of documents of title, whether those documents are negotiable or nonnegotiable. Part 2 of Article 7 deals with warehouse receipts; Part 3 deals with bills of lading; Part 5 deals with the negotiation and transfer of a document of title. Note that these provisions apply to the documents of title without regard to their negotiability. While Article 3 only deals with negotiable instruments, Article 7 deals with all relevant documents of title.

USES AND FORMS OF DOCUMENTS OF TITLE

The essential use of a document of title is to reflect the rights of the owner when the goods are turned over to the custody and care of a bailee, whether for storage or for carriage. A secondary use of a document of title, especially if the document is negotiable, is to enable the owner to transfer title to the goods without having to reclaim possession of the goods from the bailee in order to make a sale. The owner can negotiate the document of title, and in so doing, the owner also transfers title to the goods to the person receiving the document by means of the negotiation.

Warehouse Receipts

A warehouse receipt is a document issued by a person who takes goods for storage. There is no particular form that a warehouse receipt needs to take, but most will contain at least the following provisions:

1. The location of the warehouse;
2. The date the receipt for the goods is issued;
3. The number of receipts (receipts are numbered consecutively);
4. A statement as to whether the stored goods will be delivered to the bailor (a nonnegotiable receipt) or either to the bearer, or to a named person, or that person's order (a negotiable receipt);
5. The fees and expenses for the storage (unless the goods are stored in a field warehousing arrangement);
6. A description of the goods or the packages stored; and
7. The signature of the warehouseman or his or her agent.

The warehouseman assumes a duty to exercise due care in the handling of the goods and a duty to deliver the goods as agreed in the receipt at the close of the storage period.

The warehouseman assumes liability for any damages to the goods stored with him or her if the damages are caused by a failure to exercise reasonable care.

eClass 19.3 Financing/Sales

BILLS OF LADING

The principals of eClass recently decided to purchase some new computer hardware from a retailer in another state. This new hardware is quite expensive, but the firm needs to remain as "cutting edge" as possible in its hardware, in part to ensure that new versions of eClass will operate properly with new hardware and software as it hits the market. Ani has been handling all of the negotiations with the retailer. After their initial discussions, Ani reported to Meg and Yousef that she liked the price she was quoted, but she was concerned that the retailer would only be willing to make a contract if the goods were shipped via negotiable bill of lading, with payment terms of "2/10, net 30." Ani told the retailer that she would let her know if this was agreeable to the others and that she would get back in touch the following day. Ani thinks they should agree to these terms, but she would like a bit more information before deciding. Yousef thinks the firm should require the use of *either* a negotiable bill of lading *or* the credit terms, but not both. Meg is unsure of what she would recommend without more information. The three of them have asked for your advice. What will you tell them?

BUSINESS CONSIDERATIONS   Should a business have a policy concerning the use of either credit terms or negotiable bills of lading? Does the frequency with which the firm does business with a particular customer affect how you answer this question?

ETHICAL CONSIDERATIONS   Should a request from a first-time customer that a negotiable document of title be used raise any concerns or worries? Are there ethical implications to the use of a negotiable document of title that might be avoided if the document was not negotiable?

The warehouseman also acquires a warehouseman's lien on the goods for the storage and transportation charges, insurance, and expenses reasonably necessary to preserve the goods.

Bills of Lading

A bill of lading is issued by a carrier who is taking possession and custody of the goods for the purpose of transporting the goods, normally from a seller to a buyer. The person

628 Part IV: Negotiables

who arranges the transportation is the consignor; the person to whom the goods are to be delivered is the consignee; the carrier is the issuer of the bill of lading. The bill must adequately describe the goods covered by the bill and must designate whether the goods were consigned to a particular consignee (nonnegotiable), or to a named consignee or order, or to the consignee or bearer (negotiable). The carrier is liable for any misdescription or irregularity unless the document is properly qualified by words such as "contents of package unknown," "shipper's weight and count," or comparable language.

Contemporary Case

WHITAKER v. LIMECO CORP.
2010 Miss. LEXIS 182 (S. Ct. Miss., 2010)

FACTS R.W. Whitaker and Monty Fletcher loaned William Kidd $750,000 in connection with what later became a failed effort to purchase a hockey team in Tupelo. At the time, Kidd was the managing director of Limeco, and he allegedly promised Whitaker and Fletcher that, to the extent Kidd could not pay back the loans, Limeco had sufficient assets to repay the loans in full. Whitaker and Fletcher assert that Kidd concealed the fact that Limeco had no assets. Kidd shared with the Plaintiffs certain financial records and books that showed the corporation to be a solvent corporation possessing sufficient assets to repay the loans.

On July 1, 2002, the parties entered into what they referred to as promissory notes (referred to as the "Fletcher note" and the "Whitaker note") to memorialize the terms of the loan agreements they had made in early 2002. Both Fletcher and Whitaker were granted a continuing lien on Limeco's monies, securities, and/or other property for the entire amount of the promissory notes (each in the amount of $375,000).

On December 11, 2003, Whitaker and Fletcher filed suit against Kidd and Limeco, but the suit was dismissed due to faulty service of process. Finally, on September 18, 2007, they sued again, claiming that Kidd and Limeco had breached the promissory notes. [There were other claims as well, but they were also dismissed.] The trial court ultimately found the suit to be time-barred due to the trial court's determination that the notes did not meet the statutory requirements to be considered negotiable instruments and were, therefore, subject to a three-year breach-of-contract statute of limitations, as opposed to the six-year statute of limitations for a breach-of-promissory-note cause of action.

ISSUE Were the notes Whitaker and Fletcher received promissory notes, and thus negotiable instruments?

HOLDING No. The two notes lacked "words of negotiability" and, therefore, were not negotiable instruments.

REASONING Excerpts from the opinion of Carlson, Presiding Justice:

The Plaintiffs argue that the notes entered into by Kidd, each in the amount of $375,000, met all of the statutory requirements for negotiable instruments pursuant to [§ 3-104]; thus, the complaint was timely filed within the six-year statute of limitations. . . .

The trial court dismissed the Plaintiffs' complaint on the basis that neither of the promissory notes . . . was a negotiable instrument under [§ 3-104] because neither of the notes contained the required "words of negotiability." As a result, the trial court found that the notes were not subject to the six-year statute of limitations applicable to negotiable instruments. . . . Instead, according to the trial court, the notes were subject to the three-year statute of limitations for breach-of-contract claims. . . .

[§ 3-104] defines a negotiable instrument as follows:

Except as provided in subsections (c) and (d), "negotiable instrument" means an unconditional promise or order to pay a fixed amount of money, with or without interest or other charges described in the promise or order, if it:

(1) Is payable to bearer or to order at the time it is issued or first comes into possession of a holder. . . .

The statutory definition of "payable to order" is found in [§ 3-109(b)], which states:

A promise or order that is not payable to bearer is payable to order if it is payable (i) to the order of an identified person or (ii) to an identified person or order. A promise or order that is payable to order is payable to the identified person. . . .

What the Plaintiffs identify as the "Whitaker note" reads as follows: "On demand, for value received, I promise to pay to R.W. Whitaker . . . the sum of Three Hundred, Seventy-five Thousand Dollars ($ 375,000)." The written agreement identified as the "Fletcher note" contains identical language. The Plaintiffs argue that this meets the statutory definition of "payable to order" and urge this Court to interpret [§ 3-109(b)] as defining "payable to order" as follows: payable "to the order of an identified payee," payable to an identified payee, or payable "to order." In support of their argument, the Plaintiffs cite the canon of statutory construction that statutes written in the disjunctive set forth separate and distinct alternatives. . . .

However, interpreting [§ 3-109(b)] as defining "payable to order" as payable to an identified payee or payable to order is contrary to how the majority of jurisdictions interpret the Uniform Commercial Code's statutory requirements for negotiable instruments. In order to meet the requirements of a negotiable instrument:

[A] paper or instrument generally must be payable to order or to bearer at the time it is issued or comes into the possession of a holder. This means that notes payable simply to a specific payee, and not to the order of the payee or to the payee or order, are not negotiable. . . .

Thus, the words "payable to the order of" or payable "to [identified payee] or order" must appear within the instrument in order to qualify it as a negotiable instrument, and since the promissory notes in today's case do not contain this language, they cannot be deemed to be negotiable instruments. . . .

You Be the Judge

In March 1976, J. Monte Williamson, the owner of a 16.65 percent interest in Lake Manor Associates, a partnership, agreed to sell his partnership interest, 50 percent to H. Louis Salomonsky and 50 percent to Tiffany H. Armstrong. In return, Salomonsky and Armstrong each agreed to give Williamson 400 shares of a certain stock valued at $15.00 a share, with a total worth of $6,000, and a noninterest bearing note in the amount of $4,000 for the balance. The notes were executed on March 15, 1976. On that same date, the parties executed an agreement which was incorporated in the notes by reference and which itself referred to the notes.

The agreement set forth various conditions which had to be satisfied before the debt evidenced by the notes became due and payable. The evidence established that these conditions were met in October 1981.

In early 1982, Williamson made an oral demand for payment upon Salomonsky. Later, by letter dated May 18, 1982, Williamson demanded payment from both Salomonsky and Armstrong. On June 7, 1982, when no payments were forthcoming, Williamson filed two separate suits on the separate notes and related agreement.

In the trial court, Salomonsky and Armstrong defended on the grounds that the March 15, 1976, notes were negotiable instruments under the UCC; that the notes were demand instruments; that a five-year statute of limitations applied to the notes; that the statute of limitations began to run on March 15, 1976; and that the suits filed on June 7, 1982, were therefore untimely.

Williamson denied that his claims were barred by the statute of limitations. Instead, he alleged that the two writings were nonnegotiable and that the statute of limitations did not begin to run until all of the conditions and contingencies in the original writing were satisfied, which occurred in October of 1981. To support his allegations, Williamson pointed out that both "notes" contained the following language:

FOR VALUE RECEIVED, the undersigned promises to pay to the order of J. MONTE WILLIAMSON, ... the principal sum of Four Thousand Dollars ($4,000.00), *payable as set forth in that certain agreement dated March 15, 1976*, an executed copy of which is attached hereto and made a part hereof by this reference.

The issue to be resolved is whether the writings in question are negotiable instruments, meaning that Article 3 of the UCC controls, or nonnegotiable instruments, and therefore, that the case must be decided under principles of contract law.

This case has been brought in *your* court. How will *you* decide? What is the most important fact or factor in support of your decision?

[See *Salomonsky v. Kelly*, 349 S.E.2d 358, 232 Va. 261 (Va. S. Ct. 1986).]

Summary

"Negotiables" are an important part of the modern commercial world. Negotiable *documents* cover goods that are placed in the hands of a bailee, either for storage or for transportation. Negotiable *instruments* are used as a substitute for money or as a credit instrument. Both are governed by the UCC.

Article 3 of the UCC involves negotiable instruments. These negotiable instruments are "current in trade" and are payable in money. There are two major classes of negotiable instruments, and each major class contains two types of instruments. The first class, paper containing an order ("order paper"), is comprised of checks and drafts. Checks and drafts are used primarily as a substitute for money. There are three legal roles involved on "order" paper: the drawer, who "draws" (drafts) the instrument and issues the order; the payee, to whom the instrument is issued; and the drawee, the party who is ordered to pay the instrument upon proper presentment.

The second class of negotiable instruments, paper containing a promise ("promise paper"), is comprised of promissory notes and certificates of deposit. Promise paper is used principally as a credit instrument. There are two legal roles involved on promise paper: the maker, who makes the promise to pay and who issues the instrument; and the payee, to whom the instrument is issued.

The recent revision to Article 3 has greatly expanded the concept of "checks," making the article more closely reflect contemporary business practices. The revision also removed some of the older, more technical aspects of negotiable instrument law.

Documents of title, including negotiable documents, are governed by Article 7 of the UCC. The two primary types of documents of title are warehouse receipts, issued by a bailee who accepts goods for storage, and bills of lading, issued by a carrier who accepts possession of goods for transportation. However, Article 7 is much more flexible than Article 3. Any other document which, in the regular course of business or financing, is treated as a document of title is recognized as falling within the coverage of Article 7.

Discussion Questions

1. Who is expected to make payment on negotiable instruments that are designated as "order paper"? Who is expected to make payment on negotiable instruments that are designated as "promise paper"? Why are different parties expected to pay on these different instruments?

2. Article 3 of the UCC was revised in 1990. Why was Article 3 revised, and what effect did these revisions have on the law governing negotiable instruments?

3. How does Article 3 define a "check"? Why is this definition important in negotiable instrument law? Given the increased use of debit cards and credit cards, why is it necessary for the UCC to pay so much attention to checks and their regulation?

4. What is a document of title under the provisions of Article 7? How is a negotiable document of title different from a nonnegotiable document of title?

5. What sort of limitation or qualification can a carrier use on a bill of lading to protect itself from liability if the goods delivered are mislabeled or improperly identified? Is it ethical for a carrier to use such language, effectively shielding itself from liability for damages to the goods carried?

Case Problems and Writing Assignments

1. On October 16, 1989, Harris Trust and Savings Bank sold to Siena Publishers the book inventory and accounts receivables of Bookthrift Marketing following a foreclosure on Bookthrift by the bank. Siena agreed to pay $2,250,000 for the assets on an "as is, where is" basis. The sale was financed by the bank, as evidenced by a demand note signed by the president of Siena dated October 19, 1989. In this demand note, Siena promised to pay to the bank on demand the sum of $2,250,000, representing the purchase price of the Bookthrift assets. Siena also agreed to grant the bank a purchase money security interest in all of Siena's accounts receivable, general intangibles, inventory, and equipment. The bank properly perfected its security interest, filing its UCC-1 with the appropriate offices during November 1989. At some time prior to August 31, 1989, Metro Services, Inc. had provided fulfillment and warehousing services for Bookthrift. (Fulfillment services include the receipt and unloading of books from delivering carriers, storage of the books, picking, counting, packing, loading, and shipping the books, and so forth.) Metro was also indebted to Harris Trust and Savings Bank, and Metro also defaulted on its loans. The bank arranged for NCI to purchase Metro's assets. This sale was consummated on August 31, 1989, with the bank receiving full payment for Metro's debt, and NCI purchasing all of Metro's assets except accounts receivables. (This means that NCI did not receive the fulfillment services contract claims against Bookthrift and thus against Siena.) On August 29, 1990, NCI and Siena entered into a fulfillment services agreement. On March 18, 1992, Siena filed for relief under the Bankruptcy Act. At that time, Siena was in default on its fulfillment services agreement with NCI and was unable to pay the note from Harris Bank. Both Harris Bank and NCI claimed priority on the assets of Siena. The bank argued that it had a valid perfected security interest. NCI argued that it had a valid possessory warehouseman's lien, and that this lien had priority over the bank's security interest. Did the fulfillment services agreement give NCI a warehouse receipt on the assets of Siena? Explain. Which party, the bank or NCI, should have priority in this case? Why? Should NCI have adopted a policy to help protect its interests when it entered into a fulfillment services agreement? [See *In Re Siena Publishers Associates*, 149 B.R. 359 (1993).]

2. Lassen is an experienced construction lender. It is his practice before entering into a loan agreement to conduct an independent analysis of the financial condition of the borrower. He conducted such an analysis before making the loans in this case. Lassen had a continuing business relationship with Kopfmann Homes, Inc., a builder in the Minneapolis area. Between 1985 and 1990, Lassen made a number of loans to Kopfmann through an account Lassen had with First Bank. In 1986, on the basis of Lassen's recommendation, Kopfmann opened its own account with First Bank. In early 1990, Lassen entered into two loan agreements with Kopfmann. The contracts called for Kopfmann to construct two homes. Each loan was secured by a mortgage. Later that year, Lassen purchased five cashier's checks (totaling nearly $170,000) from First Bank and delivered these checks to Kopfmann. Each of the checks was jointly payable to Kopfmann and Chicago Title Insurance Company. Kopfmann presented each of these checks to First Bank without the indorsement of the title company. First Bank accepted each of the checks, depositing the proceeds into Kopfmann's account. Subsequently, Kopfmann defaulted on the two loans from Lassen. Kopfmann also failed to pay the subcontractors on the two construction jobs. Lassen then sued First Bank, alleging breach of contract, conversion, and fraud. Lassen argued that the bank had a duty to ensure that all required indorsements were present on the checks before accepting them. The bank denied liability to Lassen, asserting that he was not a party to the contracts since the checks in question were cashier's checks, with the bank as both drawer and drawee. Did the bank breach its contracts with Lassen, who purchased the cashier's checks, by not obtaining the indorsements of both joint payees on the checks prior to accepting them? Was it ethical for the bank to deny any obligation to Lassen, the purchaser of the cashier's checks, for its failure to require the indorsements of both joint payees? What more could Lassen have done to protect his interests? [See *Lassen v. First Bank Eden Prairie*, 514 N.W.2d 831 (Minn. App. 1994).]

3. Universal Premium Acceptance Corporation provides financing to policyholders to pay their insurance premiums. In the fall of 1991, Walter Talbot of the W. Talbot Insurance Agency in Lancaster, Pennsylvania, requested Universal to provide financing for his customers who needed funds to pay premiums on policies issued by the Great American Insurance Company. Universal accepted Talbot's proposal and sent him the necessary documents, including blank drafts. The face of each instrument contained Universal's name and address in the top left corner and a large UPAC logo in the top center. Below UPAC's address was printed "PAY AND DEPOSIT ONLY TO THE CREDIT OF: _____ INSURANCE CO." with a space for the amount. On the lower right side of the instrument were blanks for the policyholder's name, the insurance agency name, and a line for 'SIGNATURE OF PRODUCER OF RECORD/ BROKER/AGENT." In the lower right hand corner beneath the signature line appeared the name and address of the Landmark Bank. The back of each instrument contained pre-printed language: "Acceptance of this draft acknowledges Universal Premium Acceptance Corporation's interest in the unearned or return premium(s) and that we have issued a policy(ies) to the named applicant (insured) in the amount of the premium indicated." Between September 1991 and July 1992, Talbot signed drafts

for more than $1 million in favor of Great American but did not deliver them to the insurance company. Instead, he arranged for his confederate to forge the indorsement of Great American and deposit the drafts in an account they opened at defendant York Bank under the name of "Small Businessman's Service Corporation." York deposited the drafts without securing the indorsement of Small Businessman's Service Corporation and transmitted them to Landmark, Universal's bank in St. Louis. As part of the scheme, Talbot and his associate set up a dummy "Great American Insurance Company" office in Lancaster and furnished its address and telephone number to Universal. To verify that Great American had issued a policy, Universal would contact that office. After assurances from Talbot's cohorts there that the transaction was in order, Universal would then authorize Landmark to pay the draft. After the fraud was discovered, Talbot was convicted and imprisoned. Universal recovered part of its loss from Talbot and then filed suit in its own behalf and as assignee of Landmark against York. The complaints asserted claims under Articles 3 and 4 of the Uniform Commercial Code as enacted in Pennsylvania, as well as for negligence and conversion. The district court granted summary judgment for York, and Universal appealed, contending that the limiting language as to the payee of the drafts did not permit York to deposit them in the Small Businessman's account, that the fictitious payee provision did not apply, and that the negligence claim should not have been resolved in York's favor. Were the drafts negotiable instruments under Article 3? Did the blank indorsements convert the drafts to negotiable bearer instruments? Is York protected from liability by the fictitious payee rule? What sort of policies or procedures should Universal have established to help prevent this sort of situation from arising? [See *Universal Premium Assurance Corporation v. York Bank and Trust Company*, 69 F.3d 695 (3d Cir. 1995).

Notes

1. Prefatory Note to Article 3, *Uniform Commercial Code, 2001 edition* (St. Paul: West Group, 2001), p. 287.
2. Magnetic Ink Character Recognition, the required encoding on all checks issued in the United States.
3. Ibid.
4. "Cars Keep Getting Grounded, but Cash and Checks Are Still King," *Bankrate.com*, March 6, 2002, http://www.bankrate.com/msn/news/cc/200220212a.asp.
5. "Federal Reserve Banks Announce Reduced Number of Check Processing Sites and Accelerated Restructuring Schedule," Financial Services Policy Committee (November 6, 2008).
6. 12 USCS §§ 401 *et seq.*
7. 12 CFR § 229.
8. UCC § 3-102(b).
9. UCC § 3-411, Official Comment.
10. UCC § 3-411.
11. "What Does Negotiable Certificate of Deposit (NCD) Mean?" Investopedia, A Forbes Digital Company, http://www.investopedia.com/terms/n/ncd.asp.

20

Negotiability

Agenda

eClass will be receiving payments from its customers in various ways. While some will pay by cash, others will use debit cards or credit cards. However, many of the customers will pay by issuing a check or a draft. While the principals of eClass do not anticipate any problems, they will need to know if these checks or drafts are negotiable under Article 3, or nonnegotiable and, therefore, governed by other areas of the law. eClass will also be issuing its own instruments to purchase supplies and materials, to pay bills, and to operate the business. Will the instruments issued by the firm be negotiable? Will it matter if the instruments issued by eClass are *not* negotiable?

The firm will be relying on common carriers a great deal, both for receiving shipments of materials and for shipping finished goods to their commercial customers. These shipments via common carrier will use bills of lading. Being relatively new to the operation of a business, Ani, Meg, and Yousef are not very familiar with bills of lading, and they are unsure whether they should use negotiable bills or nonnegotiable bills.

These and other questions will arise during our discussion of negotiability. Be prepared! You never know when the firm or one of its members will seek your advice.

Classic Case

RESERVE PLAN, INC. v. SCHLEIDER

208 Misc. 805, 145 N.Y.S.2d 122, 1955 N.Y. Misc. LEXIS 3291 (Mun. Ct., N.Y. 1955)

[This case was decided under the provisions of the Negotiable Instruments Law (NIL), but the same result should occur under Article 3, § 3-104(a) today.]

FACTS Schleider executed the document in question on May 5, 1954, as an obligation to pay for certain dental work that was to be performed by his dentist, who was listed as the payee on the document. The document called for the payment of $480, with payment to be made in 24 monthly installments of $20 each, beginning June 5, 1954. On May 7, 1954, the dentist transferred the document to Reserve Plan. (Reserve Plan asserts that this transfer was a negotiation of a promissory note.)

Schleider alleges (1) that the payee dentist did not perform the dental work as agreed, and as a result, Schleider is still in serious need of dental care; (2) that the dentist neglected and refused to furnish this care; and (3) that Schleider was not informed that the document he signed was a negotiable instrument, but rather that he was told it was only a contract with a provision for installment payments.

Reserve Plan argues that the document in question is a promissory note, a type of negotiable

instrument; and that Reserve Plan took the note as a holder in due course and was entitled to the unpaid balance of this note.

ISSUE Is this document a negotiable instrument?

HOLDING No. The document does not contain an unconditional promise to pay a sum certain and thus is not a negotiable instrument.

REASONING Excerpts from the opinion of Bennett, Judge:

The question arises as to whether the agreement is in fact a negotiable instrument. If it is then the defenses asserted would not be available against this plaintiff. However, if the instrument does not conform to the requirements of the Negotiable Instruments Law of the State of New York, such defenses may be asserted against the present holder.

Section 20 of the said Negotiable Instruments Law provides in subdivision 2 thereof as follows: "Must contain an unconditional promise or order to pay a sum certain in money", in setting forth the elements of a promissory note.

Examination of the instrument in suit discloses that the same contains this proviso, "In case of death of maker all payments not due at date of death are cancelled". Can it then be said that the form of the instrument sets forth an unconditional promise to pay a sum certain? It appears to this court that such essential element is definitely lacking. ... [W]hen such instruments contain special stipulations and their payment is subject to contingencies not within the control of their holders, they are, by established rules, deprived of the character of negotiable instruments, and become exposed to any defense existing thereto, as between the original parties to the instrument. It is essential by such rules that such paper should provide for the unconditional payment to a person, or order, or bearer, of a certain sum of money at a time capable of exact ascertainment." ...

[In a prior case the] Court of Appeals defined a promissory note in the following terms: "A promissory note is defined to be a written engagement by one person to pay absolutely and unconditionally to another person therein named, or to the bearer, a certain sum of money at a specified time or on demand. ... It must contain the positive engagement of the maker to pay at a

certain definite time and the agreement to pay must not depend on any contingency, but [must] be absolute and at all events."

It is obvious from the foregoing that the document herein does not meet the required standards above mentioned for although the sum specified as payable is stated to be $480, such payment would be contingent on the maker continuing to live during the twenty-four months during which the installments were payable. By the terms of the said agreement, the contingency was always present during the said twenty-four months that a lesser amount would be payable in the event of death of the maker.

For the foregoing reasons the court finds that the instrument does not constitute a negotiable promissory note and that the defendant is entitled to assert his defenses which raise issues of fact that can only be determined by a trial. Accordingly the motion [for summary judgment] is denied.

INTRODUCTION

Negotiable instruments have a special place in business law. Perhaps the most important aspect of negotiable instruments is that they provide *liquidity*. They can readily be exchanged for cash, often at face value. Checks are almost always traded at face value unless the check has been dishonored. Notes and drafts, especially time drafts, may be discounted by the "purchaser" due to the fact that they will not be paid until later. (The time value of money factors into the discounting of the instrument.) Negotiable instruments are "current in trade," which means that they are widely used and widely accepted. A person who accepts a negotiable instrument, whether as the payee or as an indorsee, knows that the instrument can easily be negotiated to another person for goods, services, payment on an account, or for cash. This combination, the ease of transferability (negotiability) combined with the liquidity of the instrument, ensure that such instruments will continue to occupy this special place, especially in business.

Every negotiable instrument is a contract and carries with it, at a minimum, the rights that a person would enjoy under contract law. As you remember from contract law, a person possessing rights under a contract can *assign* those rights to another person. The person who assigns his or her rights—the assignor—is expected, although not required, to give notice to the party who will be conferring the benefits—the obligor—that an assignment has been made, and the assignor will identify the person to whom the rights were transferred—the assignee. You should also remember that the assignee takes the rights assigned under the contract subject to *any* and *every* defense the obligor could assert against the assignor. These two things, taking the benefits subject to any defenses and the need for the assignor to give notice, make assignments a less-than-popular method for transferring benefits under a contract.

While a negotiable instrument is also a contract, it is a contract given special treatment under the law. Since a negotiable instrument is a contract, the benefits called for in the instrument can be assigned, the same as the benefits under other types of contracts can be assigned. But, as we just discussed, assignments are not a very good method for ensuring that the assignee will receive the benefits the assignor is trying to transfer. Unless there is more protection given to the holder of a negotiable instrument than the protection given to the assignee of a contract's benefits, negotiable instruments would just be a specialized type of contract. The protection given to holders, and to holders in due course, provides particular benefits when a negotiable instrument is involved that go beyond those available in other contracts.

A person in possession of a negotiable instrument by means of a negotiation is called a *holder* (think of the holder as roughly analogous to an assignee for now).

Exhibit 20.1

Comparison of an Assignment and a Negotiation

Assignment:	A is obligated to B under the terms of a contract.
	B (the assignor) assigns his rights to C (the assignee).
	C takes the same rights under the contract as B. C will be subject to any and all defenses that A could assert against B, *and* C will not be able to assert any rights against A unless and until A is notified of the assignment.
Negotiation:	A is obligated to B, and A (the drawer or maker) issued a negotiable instrument to cover the obligation payable to the order of B (the payee).
	B (the payee) negotiates the instrument to C (a holder *or* a holder in due course).
	C takes the same rights as B, *plus* C has no need to notify A of the negotiation since possession of the instrument is adequate notice. C also takes the rights of a *holder* and may be able to assert the rights of a *holder in due course.* Thus, C may have greater rights than B and may be able to enforce the instrument against A even if A would be able to avoid honoring the obligation if B was attempting to enforce it.

The holder of a negotiable instrument has all of the rights of an assignee under contract law, *plus* any rights conferred by Article 3. While an assignee can only assert rights equivalent to those of the assignor, the holder of a negotiable instrument may be able to assert greater rights than those possessed by the person from whom the holder acquired the instrument. In addition, a holder may be able to attain the status of *holder in due course*, in which case this holder in due course of a negotiable instrument will be permitted to collect the money (receive the benefits under the contract), despite virtually any defenses the maker or drawer can assert. (There are some defenses that not even a holder in due course can overcome. The various defenses will be discussed in Chapter 21.) This is the primary reason that negotiable instrument law is so important! The holder of a negotiable instrument has all of the rights of an assignee under contract law, plus any additional rights conferred on him or her by Article 3 of the Uniform Commercial Code (UCC). Not only that, but the instrument, if correctly made or drawn, will move easily through the commercial world as a substitute for money and/or as a credit instrument. Exhibit 20.1 compares the assignment of contract rights with the negotiation of a negotiable instrument.

FORMAL REQUIREMENTS FOR NEGOTIABILITY: ARTICLE 3

In order to qualify for the special treatment accorded to negotiable instruments, the document in question must qualify as a *negotiable instrument* under the guidelines set out in Article 3. There are six requirements set out in Article 3 that must be met before an instrument is deemed negotiable, and the instrument in question must meet each and every one of these requirements in order to fall within the coverage of Article 3. Any missing element removes the instrument from Article 3 and places it under the coverage of the common law. The basic requirements for negotiability are set out in § 3-104 (a) of the UCC, which provides that:

Section 3-104. Negotiable Instrument

(a) Except as provided in subsections (c) and (d), "negotiable instrument" means an unconditional promise or order to pay a fixed amount of money, with or without interest or other charges described in the promise or order, if it:
(1) is payable to bearer or to order at the time it is issued or first comes into possession of a holder;
(2) is payable on demand or at a definite time; and,
(3) does not state any other undertaking or instruction by the person promising or ordering payment to do any act in addition to the payment of money, but the promise or order may contain (i) an undertaking or power to give, maintain, or protect collateral to secure payment; (ii) an authorization or power to the holder

to confess judgment or realize on or dispose of collateral; or (iii) a waiver of the benefit of any law intended for the advantage or protection of an obligor.

Two other important definitions must also be reviewed before the discussion of negotiability can commence. Both of these definitions are found in § 3-103, and each defines one of the words used in § 3-104(a). As defined in the article:

Section 3-103. Definitions

(a) In this Article:

(6) "Order" means a *written* instruction to pay money signed by the person giving the instruction. The instruction may be addressed to any person, including the person giving the instruction, or to one or more persons jointly or in the alternative but not in succession. An authorization to pay is not an order unless the person authorized to pay is also instructed to pay. [Emphasis added]

(9) "Promise" means a *written* undertaking to pay money signed by the person undertaking to pay. An acknowledgment of an obligation by the obligor is not a promise unless the obligor also undertakes to pay the obligation. [Emphasis added]

These two sections, when read together, give the requirements for a negotiable instrument. Thus, to qualify as a negotiable instrument, the instrument in question must:

1. contain a written promise [§ 3-103 (a)(9)] or a written order [§ 3-103 (a)(6)]; and
2. be signed by the maker [§ 3-103 (a)(9)] (promise paper) or by the drawer (order paper) [§ 3-103(a)(6)]; and
3. contain an unconditional promise or order to pay a fixed amount of money, with or without interest or other charges described in the promise or order [§ 3-104(a)];
4. be payable *to bearer* or *to order* at the time it is issued or first comes into possession of a holder [§ 3-104(a)(1)];
5. be payable *on demand* or *at a definite time* [§ 3-104(a)(2)]; and
6. *not* state any other undertaking or instruction by the person promising or ordering payment to do any act in addition to the payment of money [§ 31-4(a)(c)].

These elements are shown in Exhibit 20.2. Remember that every one of the elements must be present in order for the writing to be deemed negotiable, with *one* exception—checks do not have to have the "words of negotiability" in order to be negotiable. (There is another area in which checks receive special treatment, the statutory provisions of "Check 21," which is discussed later in this chapter.) Other than this one exception, the absence of any element negates negotiability. If a writing is not negotiable the paper can still be valuable even though it does not meet the requirements of negotiability, it just does not have the protections provided by the UCC. The person holding the paper would only have his or her (potential) contract

Exhibit 20.2

The Elements of Negotiability

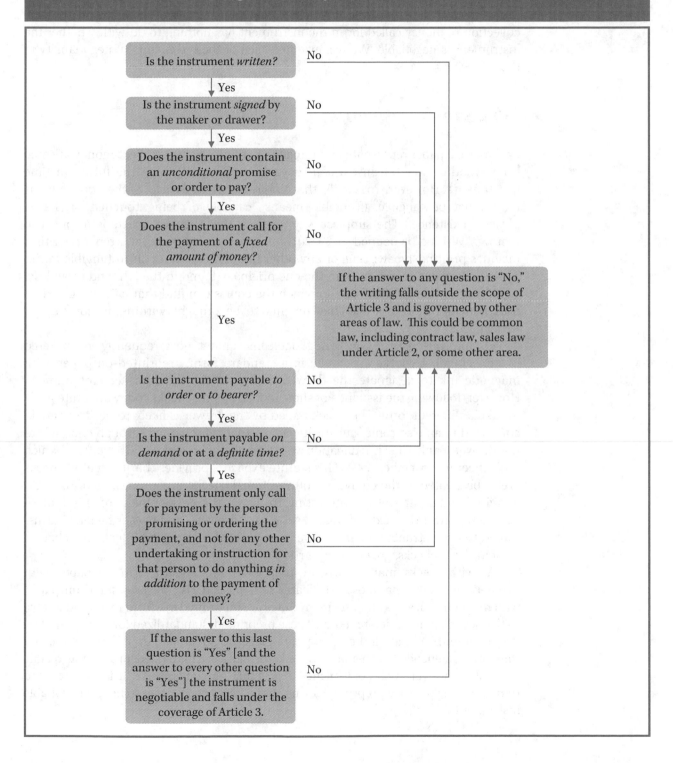

Is the instrument *written?*

No

Yes

Is the instrument *signed* by the maker or drawer?

No

Yes

Does the instrument contain an *unconditional* promise or order to pay?

No

Yes

Does the instrument call for the payment of a *fixed amount of money?*

No

Yes

If the answer to any question is "No," the writing falls outside the scope of Article 3 and is governed by other areas of law. This could be common law, including contract law, sales law under Article 2, or some other area.

Is the instrument payable *to order* or *to bearer?*

No

Yes

Is the instrument payable *on demand* or at a *definite time?*

No

Yes

Does the instrument only call for payment by the person promising or ordering the payment, and not for any other undertaking or instruction for that person to do anything *in addition* to the payment of money?

No

Yes

If the answer to this last question is "Yes" [and the answer to every other question is "Yes"] the instrument is negotiable and falls under the coverage of Article 3.

No

rights under the common law. As you will see in our subsequent discussion, this can be an important consideration for the person in possession of the paper.

It should be emphasized that negotiability has nothing to do with *validity* or *enforceability*. If an instrument is negotiable, this merely means that the instrument is governed by the provisions of Article 3. The enforceability of the instrument or the collection of money called for in the instrument has nothing to do with whether the instrument is negotiable. We will examine each of these elements of negotiability in the following sections.

Writing Requirement

Commercial paper represents an intangible right, the right to collect money at some time, whether now (an instrument payable on demand) or in the future (a time instrument). However, to satisfy the requirements of Article 3, the proof of this right must be tangible. (Tangible means "capable of being touched," it has a physical existence.) The simplest way to prove that the right exists is to put it in writing. "Writing" is defined in § 1-201(46), which states that: " 'written' or 'writing' includes printing, typewriting, or any other intentional reduction to tangible form." This is a broader definition than the one originally found in the NIL and provides a significant amount of flexibility in which the courts can find that a "writing" exists, thus allowing more types of instruments to be brought within the coverage of Article 3.

For many people, the type of negotiable instrument most frequently encountered is a check. Most checks are issued in a standard form, preprinted on paper, with magnetic ink to designate the drawee bank and the drawer's account number. However, following the issuance of such an instrument, checks today are quite likely to take a different form. The check issued by the drawer is likely to be "truncated," converted to an electronic "substitute check" that is forwarded through channels to the drawee bank. Check truncation was formally approved by "Check 21,"[1] which took effect in November 2004. This statute explicitly provides that truncated checks are to be treated as the equivalent of traditional checks, any provisions of the UCC notwithstanding. It will be interesting to watch the development of this type of transaction over the next few years as drawers, drawees, and payees become accustomed to check truncation and as we move toward recognizing "electronic checks" as being true checks, governed by Article 3.

As with checks, many drafts are preprinted, in standard form, on paper, with magnetic ink encoding; most certificates of deposit (CDs) are preprinted on paper, with magnetic ink encoding; and many notes are preprinted in a form readily adaptable to the needs of the lender/preparer. These preprinted, standardized forms are familiar, they contain blanks at all the appropriate places to streamline their completion, and they are pre-encoded with magnetic ink to make computerized processing readily available. However, such convenience is just that—a convenience. It is important to remember that use of a preprinted form is not a necessity in order to have a negotiable instrument.

A negotiable instrument is equally valid when prepared by handwriting on a scratch pad, or on a blank sheet of paper, or on virtually any other relatively permanent thing. For example, several years ago, on a television series entitled *Love American Style*, a couple was marooned on a desert island. The only thing they had for entertainment was a deck of cards. According to the plot, they spent their time playing gin. When they were rescued, the young woman had won $1 million from her fellow castaway. As evidence, she had a check . . . written on her stomach! Despite the comedic implications, such a check would (theoretically) be valid.

In another (possibly apocryphal) example, a disgruntled taxpayer completed his tax return on April 15. When he mailed his return, he included a check for the taxes due and a note. The note said: "You've been trying to get it for years, and you've finally succeeded. Here's the shirt off my back." The note was pinned to his check, which was written on his undershirt. However, the joke was on him. The IRS cashed it! (A friend at an IRS Service Center insists that whenever a check written on a shirt, underwear, etc. is received the staff has a good laugh!)

eClass 20.1 Finance/Management

SIGNING BUSINESS CHECKS

eClass will be issuing a significant number of checks initially, and the number is likely to increase as the business grows. Ani, Meg, and Yousef have agreed that the firm's checks should be signed by two of them, and all three of their signatures are on file with the bank. However, Meg has pointed out that it will take up a lot of time every month just signing checks, and that there should be a better way for the firm to "sign" its checks, to improve efficiency and time management. She would like to have the firm invest in a software package that will prepare checks, keep a check register, and even sign the checks automatically. They have asked you for your advice. What will you tell them?

BUSINESS CONSIDERATIONS   Many businesses have lost money due to inadequate internal auditing practices and/or poor controls, especially in the handling of checking accounts. What sorts of practices and controls should a business have in place to minimize the risk of suffering such losses?

ETHICAL CONSIDERATIONS   Is it ethical for a business to try to "play the float" by writing checks before deposits are available, in the hope—or the expectation—that the funds will be available when the checks are presented to the bank? (Consider the likely impact of Check 21 in preparing your answer to this question.)

Signature Requirement

On a check or a draft, an order is given by the *drawer.* On a note or a CD, a promise is given by the *maker.* Given the widespread use of preprinted forms as negotiable instruments, some protection is needed from fraud or trickery. The UCC tries to minimize the potential for fakery by requiring a *signature* by the maker or the drawer. A signature is deemed to be an "authentication" of the document or writing to which the signature is attached. As such, it has great legal significance. Most people think of a signature as a manual subscription, an autograph. Although a manual subscription is, obviously, a signature, it is not the only possible type of signature.

A corporation, being an inanimate object, cannot sign its own name. Yet corporations need to "sign" negotiable instruments, particularly checks. The instruments can, of course, be signed by agents of the corporation. But even this is impractical. Some corporations issue thousands of checks each month. An "authorized signer" could spend an entire career "autographing" checks for the corporation, laboriously attaching his or her manual subscription to checks, drafts, and notes every working day. If "autographs" were the only method of signing, someone would have to occupy such a boring position in virtually every company.

Fortunately, the UCC solved this problem. The solution is found in § 1-201(39), which states that: "'signed' includes any symbol executed or adopted by a party with present intention to authenticate a writing." Thus, the party who is signing an instrument can use *any* symbol he or she desires, so long as the symbol is used with the "present intent" to authenticate the writing. This means that, for example, a corporation can use a stamp or imprinter of some sort to sign checks. Likewise, a negotiable instrument can be signed by affixing an X, or a thumbprint, or any other intentionally affixed symbol. (Note that while a number of banks are now requiring a thumbprint along with the indorsement of the presenter before accepting checks drawn against the bank when the presenter does not have an account with the bank, this is not a "signing" as defined by the Code, merely a protective device for the bank. Remember that a *signature* is a mark or symbol that authenticates an instrument. An *indorsement* is used to transfer rights by a holder of a negotiable instrument and is not considered a signature as used in the UCC.)

While the Code permits the maker or drawer to use any symbol he or she desires to authenticate a writing, care and common sense should be exercised in this area. There are practical problems with adopting any unusual types of signatures. These problems deal more with the acceptability of the instrument than with the negotiability of it. An unusual signature may be so strange that people will be hesitant to accept it or the instrument containing it. The unusual signature also must be proved by the person trying to claim the instrument.

It makes no difference where the instrument is signed. Although it is normal to sign in the lower right-hand corner of the face of the instrument, the signature can be anywhere. For example, in a note beginning "I, Mary Smith, promise to pay," Mary Smith's signature can be placed following the word "I," or Mary Smith can sign in the lower right-hand corner, or the lower left-hand corner, or in any other location on the face of the instrument, and her signature would be sufficient if it appeared to a reasonable person that the signature was placed by Mary Smith in an attempt to authenticate the underlying writing.

Unconditional Promise or Order Requirement

Negotiable instruments are designed to move easily through the commercial world. To serve effectively as a substitute for money, a negotiable instrument must be freely transferable. It also needs to be "current in trade," which means that it must be in a form that people are willing to accept. These needs are met by the requirement that the promise made, or the order given, be unconditional. A person taking possession of a negotiable instrument wants to know that payment can reasonably be expected under *every* circumstance. A prospective holder would not be eager to accept an instrument that says payment *might* be made or will be made *only if* something happens. The holder wants an unconditional commitment that the money will be paid.

Because of its importance, the Code has gone to great lengths to define "unconditional." Section 3-106 lists the requirements that must be met to make the promise or order conditional. These requirements will be set out here, with a brief explanation inserted between each of the four subsections of the Code section. According to this Code section:

> **(a)** Except as provided in this section [3-106], for the purposes of [negotiable instruments], a promise or order is unconditional unless it states (i) an express condition to payment, (ii) that the promise or order is subject to or governed by another writing, or (iii) that rights or obligations with respect to the promise or order are stated in another writing. A reference to another writing does not of itself make the promise or order conditional.

There appears to be a presumption that every promise or order is unconditional unless a condition is obvious from reading the instrument. For example, if an instrument says "payment to be made only if [statement of condition] that instrument would contain an express condition and would not be negotiable." Similarly, if an instrument contained a clause stating that the payment of the instrument is governed by a separate document or writing, the instrument would be conditional and, therefore, nonnegotiable. However, if the instrument merely refers to another writing, there is no condition attached to payment, and negotiability would not be affected by the reference. Thus, a notation that the instrument is issued as "Payment for Invoice #67542" would not be conditional, and such a notation would not affect negotiability.

> **(b)** A promise or order is not made conditional (i) by a reference to another writing for a statement of rights with respect to collateral, prepayment, or acceleration, or (ii) because payment is limited to resort to a particular source of funds.

This subsection makes a significant change in the law of negotiable instruments, again emphasizing the effort to remove conditions from written promises or orders unless they are very explicit. Before the revision to Article 3, the "particular fund" doctrine made an instrument conditional, hence negating negotiability, any time the instrument required payment from a particular fund, unless the drawer or maker was a governmental entity. Many students have wondered why a check drawn by a person against his or her personal account was not drawn against a "particular fund." The (technically accurate) explanation was that the check was not drawn against that person's deposited funds, but rather against any or all of the funds in the bank, with the person's account being merely a bookkeeping notation telling the bank where to "post" the check, which seemed to be an evasive answer at best, and begged the question at worst. This particular rule was confusing at best, and its demise was long overdue.

(c) If a promise or order requires, as a condition to payment, a countersignature by a person whose specimen signature appears on the promise or order, the condition does not make the promise or order conditional. If the person whose specimen signature appears on an instrument fails to countersign the instrument, the failure to countersign is a defense to the obligation of the issuer, but the failure does not prevent a transferee of the instrument from becoming a holder of the instrument.

This subsection appears to be intended specifically to permit the inclusion of traveler's checks within the coverage of Article 3. Notice that the absence of a required countersignature does not remove the instrument from the coverage of Article 3; it merely provides a defense for the issuer. The instrument is still negotiable, and the person in possession of the instrument is not prevented from being classified as a holder of the instrument.

(d) If a promise or order at the time it is issued or first comes into possession of a holder contains a statement, required by applicable statutory or administrative law, to the effect that the rights of a holder or transferee are subject to claims or defenses that the issuer could assert against the original payee, the promise or order is not thereby made conditional for the purposes of Section 3-104(a); but if the promise or order is an instrument, there cannot be a holder in due course on the instrument.

This subsection reflects the Code's recognition of the "Federal Trade Commission Holder in Due Course Rule" as it affects consumer credit transactions (explained in the next chapter), while also recognizing that other statutory or regulatory enactments may also occur in the future. By addressing this issue in general terms, the Code greatly simplifies the task facing courts that would otherwise have to interpret the effect of these enactments on (1) whether they created a condition and (2) whether it would be possible to attain holder in due course (HDC) status under the enactment if it was determined that the provision did not create a condition and that the instrument was therefore negotiable.

eClass 20.2 Finance

PROMISSORY NOTES AND INTEREST RATES

Ani recently contacted the firm's bank, inquiring about current rates on loans. The bank's lending officer informed Ani that the firm had recently been reclassified by the bank and was now eligible for a "prime plus" rate on its loans. When Ani shared this information with the others, Meg was pleased, but Yousef was skeptical. He wanted to know exactly what a prime plus rate meant, and he also wanted to know if a "note" that called for interest at "prime plus" was negotiable. The principles have asked for your advice. What will you tell them?

BUSINESS CONSIDERATIONS   The revisions to Article 3 greatly expanded the permissible terms that can be used in an instrument without affecting negotiability, especially in determining interest on an instrument. Are these changes better or worse for a borrower? To whom is the negotiability of an instrument most important; the maker, the payee, or a holder?

ETHICAL CONSIDERATIONS   Is it ethical to use a phrase for describing the interest on an instrument that may be misinterpreted by third persons? Is it ethical to use any unclear or inexact language in an instrument?

Fixed Amount of Money Requirement

In order to serve as a substitute for money, and in order to be current in trade, a negotiable instrument must provide for payment at some point in time, and it must call for that payment in "money." A holder of a negotiable instrument reasonably expects to know how much money is to be received when the instrument is ultimately paid. The amount is commonly specified exactly, which makes the determination simple, but this is not necessary to satisfy the "fixed amount of money" requirement. Article 3 does not address this requirement specifically. Instead, several sections of the Code need to be read in combination to determine what a "fixed amount of money" means. First, we will look at how money is defined in the Code, then we will look at how to arrive at a "fixed amount." Money is defined in § 1-201(24), and the treatment of an instrument that calls for payment in foreign money is explained in § 3-107. According to these sections:

1-201(24) "Money" means a medium of exchange authorized or adopted by a domestic or foreign government and includes a monetary unit of account established by an intergovernmental organization or by agreement between two or more nations.

3-107. Instrument Payable in Foreign Money

Unless the instrument otherwise provides, an instrument that states that it is payable in foreign money may be paid in the foreign money or in an equivalent amount in dollars calculated by using the current bank-offered spot rate (the foreign exchange price at which a currency will be delivered) at the place of payment for the purchase of dollars on the day on which the instrument is paid.

Thus, money is a medium of exchange that has been authorized or adopted by a government. (The earlier requirement that money was defined as "legal tender" has been rejected in favor of this broader definition.[2]) While an instrument may be worded in terms of "foreign" money, Article 3 permits the payment of that instrument in *either* the foreign currency *or* in the equivalent of the foreign currency in U.S. dollars at the time and place of payment of the instrument, *unless* the instrument itself specifies the form of payment. Now that the definition of "money" has been established, we must turn to the meaning of "fixed amount."

Historically, in order to meet the requirement that the instrument called for the payment of a fixed amount of money, the total amount to be paid had to be calculable from the face of the instrument. This requirement raised the "four-corners" rule. All the necessary information for the calculation of the amount to be paid had to be on the face of the instrument, within the "four corners" of the instrument, even if the calculation has not yet been done. This requirement no longer applies under the new standards, at least with regard to interest.

When an instrument calls for the payment of a definite amount, as a check does, the "fixed amount" is obvious. A check for $100 orders the payment of $100 regardless of when the check is presented for payment. Any non-interest bearing instrument provides an easily determined fixed amount of money to be paid. The problem with determining the fixed amount arises when interest is to be paid on the instrument. Given the current practice of variable rate notes, and of tying interest to the "prime rate," the provisions for determining a fixed amount of money needed to be revised, and the old "four corners" rule needed to be retired. The provisions for interest are set out in § 3-112. An instrument is presumed to be issued without interest unless interest is specifically called for in the instrument.[3] However, if interest is called for in the instrument, the interest will run from the date of the instrument. The significant change in the treatment of interest is found in § 3-112(b), which states:

> Interest may be stated in an instrument as a fixed or variable rate or rates. The amount or rate of interest may be stated or described in the instrument in any manner and may require reference to information not contained in the instrument. If an instrument provides for interest, but the amount cannot be ascertained from the description, interest is payable at the judgment rate in effect at the place of payment of the instrument and at the time interest first accrues.

This means that an instrument can call for the payment of interest at a variable rate, for example, "the prime rate," and it still satisfies the fixed amount of money requirement.

eClass 20.3 Finance/Management

HOW SHOULD THE FIRM HANDLE A MONEY ORDER?

eClass recently received a writing from one of its customers intended as a payment on the customer's account. The writing had a heading stating that it was a "Money Order," and below this heading it stated "Pay to eClass_____ $100.00." When this payment was received, the principles discussed what it meant and how it should be treated. Meg said that money orders are valid methods of payment and that the firm should just deposit it as it would any other payments. Yousef said that he thought the money order was actually a check and that the firm should treat it as a check. Ani was of the opinion that both Meg and Yousef were correct and that it really didn't matter unless the money order was dishonored. They have asked for your advice. What will you tell them?

BUSINESS CONSIDERATIONS   Why might a firm be hesitant to accept a "money order" as payment from a customer? Should a firm be more or less confident in collecting on a "money order" than on a check?

ETHICAL CONSIDERATIONS   Is it ethical to refuse payments from customers unless the payments are submitted either in cash or by means of a traditional check? Is it ethical for a customer to submit payment in an unusual manner?

Words of Negotiability Requirement: "Pay to the Order of" or "Pay to Bearer"

To be negotiable, even if every other element is present, an instrument generally must contain "words of negotiability." (There is one exception to this rule, which is discussed blow.) The words of negotiability are "Pay to the order of (name of payee)" or some variation of this phrase, or "Pay to bearer" or some variation. The reason these words are so important is that the law reads them as authorizing the free transfer of the instrument. Failing to use one of these terms can be viewed as a denial of the intention to permit free transferability of the instrument, and, therefore, as a denial of negotiability.

When Article 3 was revised, a special exception was added to this rule as it relates to the treatment of checks. An instrument that meets all of the requirements to be negotiable *except* for being payable "to order" or "to bearer" at the time of its issue, *and* which otherwise falls within the definition of a "check" as set out in § 3-104(f) is a negotiable instrument *and* a check.[4] This is true even if the instrument is described on its face as being some other type of instrument, such as a "money order." Thus, if an instrument is payable on demand and drawn on a bank, and it meets every requirement for negotiability *except* that it does not contain either of the "words of negotiability" phrases, it is still considered a check, and as such, it is still negotiable. (At the time of the revision of Article 3, many credit unions were using instruments that stated "Pay to (name of payee)," rather than the more widely accepted "Pay to the order of (name of payee).") Since credit union instruments were now to be recognized as checks, and since so many of the instruments using this form were available, the revised Article 3 simply decided to recognize these forms and to carve out a special rule for checks. In addition, this exception prevents a person from simply deleting or striking out the words "the order of" on a preprinted check, and thereby removing the paper from the coverage of Article 3.[5]

However, if an instrument other than a check that is otherwise negotiable calls for payment by stating "Pay to Pete Jones" (rather than "Pay to the order of Pete Jones"), it is *not* negotiable. By the terms of the instrument, only Pete Jones is authorized to receive payment; he cannot transfer payment by negotiation (although he may be able to *assign* his right to receive payment under contract law). And since the instrument is not a check, the special exception does not apply. However, an *indorsement* that says "Pay to Pete Jones" would not affect negotiability. Indorsements cannot negate negotiability once it exists, nor can an indorsement "create" negotiability where it did not previously exist. (Negotiability is based on the information on the front (or face) of the instrument, and an indorsement is normally on the back of the instrument.)

To be payable "to order," the terms of the instrument must state that it is payable to the order or assigns of a specified individual, or to a specified individual, or to the individual's order. The designated individual may be a person, as in "Pay to Paula Lopez or order"; an office, as in "Pay to the order of the Treasurer of Washington County"; an estate or trust, as in "Pay to the order of the Johnson Estate"; or an unincorporated association, as in "Pay to the XYZ Partnership or order." An instrument payable to order requires an endorsement to be further negotiated.

If no particular individual is designated, the instrument must be payable to bearer to be negotiable. An instrument is payable to bearer when, by its terms, it is payable to bearer or to the order of bearer; or to "cash" or the order of "cash"; or to a named person or bearer, as in "Pay to Joe Jakes or bearer" or "Pay to the order of Joe Jakes or bearer" (§ 3-109). An instrument is also considered payable to bearer if no payee is stated. No indorsement is legally needed to negotiate an instrument payable to bearer, although most holders will request (or demand) an indorsement for added protection. (The meaning and the importance of indorsements is discussed in Chapter 21.)

Determinable Time Requirement: Payable on Demand or at a Fixed Time

A holder wants to know not only how much money will be paid (fixed amount in money), but also *when* payment can be expected. The question of when will depend on the terms of the instrument, but in order to be negotiable, the instrument must be payable either on demand or at a definite time. This element of negotiability is discussed in § 3-108 of Article 3, which provides that:

(a) A promise or order is "payable on demand" if it (i) states that it is payable on demand or at sight, or otherwise indicates that it is payable at the will of the holder; or (ii) does not state any time for payment.

(b) A promise or order is "payable at a definite time" if it is payable on elapse of a definite period of time after sight or acceptance or at a fixed date or dates or at a time or times readily ascertainable at the time the promise or order is issued, subject to rights of (i) prepayment, (ii) acceleration, (iii) extension at the option of the holder, or (iv) extension to a further definite time at the option of the maker or acceptor or automatically upon or after a specified act or event.

(c) If an instrument, payable at a fixed date, is also payable upon demand made before the fixed date, the instrument is payable on demand until the fixed date and, if demand for payment is not made before that date, becomes payable at a definite time on the fixed date.

The payee or holder must be able to tell when the instrument is payable by looking at the face of the instrument. Unless the instrument specifies that it is to be paid at some future date (payable at a definite time) it is payable on demand. An instrument is payable on demand when payment is to be made on sight, or at presentment, or when no time for payment is stated. Any form of instrument may be payable on demand, but promise paper (notes and CDs) normally is payable at a definite (future) time and is not payable on demand. A check must be payable on demand, by definition. A draft other than a check may be payable on demand, or it may be payable at a definite time.

An instrument is payable at a definite time if, by its terms, it is payable at a time that can be determined from its face. This definite time frequently will be some stated future date, such as "September 24, 20XX," or it may be at some time after a stated date, such as "90 days after March 3, 20XX." Either of these dates would be definite even if some provision were made for accelerating the payment date. They also would be definite with a provision for extending the time if the holder, maker, or acceptor has the option of extending the time. However, the extension must be a predetermined definite period, not to exceed the original term if the maker or acceptor has the option.

The UCC also stipulates that payment is at a definite time if payment is a stated period after sight (i.e., after presentment). Thus, an instrument calling for payment "60 days after sight" is payable at a definite time even though that definite time cannot be ascertained until after "sight" is established. Although the holder must act (present the instrument to the drawee to establish the date of sight), once the act is done, the date for payment is definite.

However, one must be careful in this area. Payment is not at a definite time if it is to occur only upon an act or occurrence that is of uncertain date. For example, an instrument payable "30 days after Uncle Charlie dies" is probably not negotiable, since the holder would have to go outside the instrument to determine the time of occurrence before the time to pay the instrument could be set. (The language of the revised Article 3 that a definite time exists if the time or times are "readily ascertainable at the time the promise or order is issued" may change this area. We will have to wait for judicial interpretations to see how broadly or how narrowly this provision will now be construed.)

The "Exclusive Obligation" Requirement

The final requirement for determining negotiability is that the promise or the order contained in the instrument is the only *undertaking* or *instruction* of the person making the promise or giving the order. The person promising or ordering payment must not have any other "undertaking or instruction" to do any other act in addition to payment of the money. The Code uses the terms "undertaking" and "instruction" rather than "promise" or "order" because both promise and orders are specifically defined in Article 3 as only involving written promises or order to pay money.[6] Thus, undertaking and instruction are meant to be broader and to include oral commitments or other written commitments beyond the coverage of Article 3. The promises and orders governed by this Article are *exclusively* those written promises and orders that call for the payment of money, and have no other commitments or obligations tied to the writing.

CONSTRUCTION AND INTERPRETATION: ARTICLE 3

Article 3 takes a very short-and-simple approach to construction and interpretation. Basically, § 3-114, which covers contradictory terms, provides the coverage in this area. According to this section:

> If an instrument contains contradictory terms, typewritten terms prevail over printed terms, handwritten terms prevail over both, and words prevail over numbers.

This coverage is very brief and seems to be very specific. However, despite its brevity, this is an area that is likely to require some litigation to provide additional guidelines as to how courts plan to interpret ambiguities that do not fall exactly within the language of the section. Ultimately, judicial decisions will provide the parameters for this area.

CHECK TRUNCATION AND CHECK 21

To truncate literally means "to shorten by or as if by cutting off,"[7] or "to make something shorter or briefer, especially by removing the end of it."[8] When we speak of check truncation, we are not speaking of cutting the end off of a check, but we are speaking of cutting the processing method. According to the definition of "truncate" in the statute itself:

> The term "truncate" means to remove an original paper check from the check collection process and send to a recipient, in lieu of such original paper check, a substitute check (including data taken from the MICR line of the original check or an electronic image of the original check), whether with or without subsequent delivery of the original paper check.[9]

The desire to implement check truncation is not new to Congress. In fact, Congress has been interested in encouraging check truncation since at least 1987, if not earlier. In 1987, Congress passed the Expedited Funds Availability Act,[10] a statute that provided mandatory guidelines for when funds deposited by a bank customer must be made available to the customer. In that act, Congress directed the Board of Governors of the Federal Reserve System to consider establishing regulations for Federal Reserve banks and other depository institutions to provide for check truncation as a means of improving the check processing system.[11] In fact, the Expedited Funds Availability Act provided the Board of Governors with the authority to regulate all aspects of the check payment system and "directed that the exercise of such authority by the Board superceded any State law, including the Uniform Commercial Code, as in effect in any State."[12]

In October of 2003, Congress passed Public Law 108-100, the *Check Clearing for the 21st Century Act*, which President Bush signed into law on October 28, 2003. The law became effective as of October 28, 2004.[13] Despite the title attached to this statute, the primary thrust of the law is to implement check truncation. However, the implementation of check truncation is expected to speed the check-clearing process, thus making funds available sooner for the payee on a truncated check, as well as for the bank or banks that handle the check before its final acceptance and payment by the drawee bank. Of course, this benefit to the payee and to the banks involved in the process has a counterpoint: the potential detriment to the issuer of the check due to the fact that his or her account will be debited more quickly due to the increased speed of the check-clearing process. This means that the issuer of the check (the drawer) will find that he or she has much less "float," possibly increasing the likelihood of having the check refused (dishonored) by the drawee bank due to non-sufficient funds in the account.

Check 21 has three stated objectives, or purposes: (1) to facilitate check truncation by authorizing substitute checks; (2) to foster innovation in the check collection system without mandating receipt of checks in electronic form; and (3) to improve the overall efficiency of the nation's payments system.[14] Thus, the law is designed to *facilitate* check truncation by encouraging the use of substitute checks, but it is to do so without *mandating* that any party must use a substitute check, most likely in electronic form.

While the law does not mandate that a substitute check must be used, it does provide that "a person may deposit, present, or send for collection or return a substitute check *without an agreement* with the recipient . . ."[15] (emphasis added). This means that a party wishing to truncate a check may do so without seeking approval or permission from the drawer of the check or from any prior holder of the check. Further, the law provides that any such substitute check is the legal equivalent of the original check for all purposes, under any provisions of any federal or state laws, and this applies to every person affected by the check or its substitute, provided that:

a. The substitute check accurately represents all of the information on the original check, both front and back, as of the time of truncation, and,

b. That the substitute check bears the legend: "This is a legal copy of your check. You can use it the same way as you would use the original check."[16]

One protection the law provides is that any bank that transfers, presents, or returns a substitute check, whether in electronic or paper form, for consideration gives warranties to the transferee. The bank warrants that the substitute check meets all the legal requirements to be deemed as the legal equivalent of the original check, and it also warrants that no party will receive presentment or return of the substitute check, any other substitute check, or the original check in such a manner that the party will be asked to make any payments based on a check or substitute that has already been paid.[17]

It will be interesting to follow the courts as they issue opinions dealing with this new area of law and try to fit their opinions into the precedents established under the UCC over its 50-plus years, along with earlier opinions under the Uniform Negotiable Instruments Law.

REQUIREMENTS FOR NEGOTIABILITY: ARTICLE 7

Article 7 of the UCC provides the coverage of documents of title. Where Article 3 is very strict in determining whether the Article applies to a particular writing, Article 7 is much more relaxed in determining what it covers. One reason for this difference is that Article 3 *only* applies to negotiable instruments. If a writing is not negotiable, it does not fall within the coverage of Article 3 and is governed by other areas of law. However, Article 7 applies to "Warehouse Receipts, Bills of Lading, and Other Documents of Title." In order for Article 7 to apply, all that needs to be shown is that the document in question is a document of title. The negotiability of the document is not relevant to the document's coverage by Article 7. Nonetheless, the negotiability of a document of title may be important, and the Article does have provisions for determining whether a document of title is negotiable. Section 7-104 states that a document of title is negotiable if:

1. by its terms the goods are to be delivered to bearer or to the order of a named person; or

2. where recognized in international trade, if it runs to a named person or assigns.

Every other document of title is deemed to be nonnegotiable. In fact, a bill of lading that is consigned to a named person is not made negotiable by a provision that specifies that the goods are only to be delivered against an order signed by a named person. Obviously, Article 7 is more concerned with the rights of the parties to the goods than it is concerned with the rights of the parties in the documents covering the goods.

Whether the document of title is negotiable or nonnegotiable, the bailee has a duty of care. If the bailee fails to exercise due care and the goods are damaged or destroyed, the bailee is liable.

Even though Article 7 is more concerned with rights in the goods, there are certain rights to be gained if the document of title is negotiable, especially if the party qualifies as a holder by due negotiation. In addition, a holder by due negotiation can exist only if the document of title is negotiable. (This topic is covered in more detail in Chapter 21.)

Contemporary Case

GERBER & GERBER v. REGIONS BANK

266 Ga. App. 8, 596 S.E.2d 174, 2004 Ga. App. LEXIS 206 (Ga. App. 2004)

FACTS Stafford worked as a real estate closing secretary at G&G for over two years. During this time, she stole 29 cashier's checks received by G&G during real estate closings, which checks the payees had endorsed in blank during the closings. She then endorsed these checks herself and deposited them into her personal account at Regions Bank. She also stole ten checks made payable to G&G, which she endorsed in blank on behalf of G&G (forging Sanford Gerber's signature). She then endorsed the forged checks in her own name and deposited them into her personal account at Regions Bank. Throughout this time, G&G had its escrow and other accounts at Regions Bank and deposited thousands of checks amounting to $150 million to $200 million into those accounts every year. G&G would

endorse each deposited check with a rubber stamp for deposit into the G&G account.

The thefts were made possible because G&G did not restrictively stamp the checks immediately at closing but waited until sometime after the closing, during which interim period the checks were kept in an open file left in an area accessible to all G&G employees. Also, at times Stafford was allowed to be the person to stamp and account for the checks. The amount stolen approximated $180,000. Stafford confessed to the thefts and later she plead guilty to criminal charges and received a 30-year sentence (five years to serve). She claimed to have spent the money.

G&G sued Regions Bank to recover the stolen $180,000, alleging counts of conversion and negligence in that the bank improperly accepted the forged checks as well as the true-endorsed cashier's checks into Stafford's personal account. Regions Bank moved for summary judgment, arguing that as a matter of law it had acted appropriately under the Uniform Commercial Code in accepting the checks.

ISSUES Did the bank act improperly in accepting the cashier's check endorsed by Stafford? Did the bank act improperly in accepting the checks with G&G's endorsements forged by Stafford?

HOLDINGS No. The cashier's checks were bearer paper, which the bank handled properly. Possibly. While G&G was negligent in allowing the forgeries, the bank has not established that it acted in good faith in its handling of these checks. This issue must be resolved by a jury.

REASONING Excerpts from the opinion of Miller, Judge:

With regard to the blank-endorsed cashier's checks, the court correctly granted summary judgment in favor of the bank. Under ... [UCC § 3-420(a)] a bank converts an instrument if the bank "makes or obtains payment with respect to the instrument for a person not entitled to enforce the instrument or receive payment." The holder of an instrument is a person entitled to enforce the instrument, even though the person is in wrongful possession of the instrument ... A person is a holder of a negotiable instrument if that person possesses the instrument and the instrument is payable to bearer. ... An instrument is deemed payable to bearer if it is endorsed in blank (i.e., not specially endorsed). ... "When indorsed in blank, an instrument becomes payable to bearer and may be negotiated by transfer of possession alone until specially indorsed." ...

Accordingly, when here the payees of the cashier's checks endorsed the checks in blank, the checks then became bearer paper and could—similar to cash—be transferred by possession alone ... Sanford Gerber even admitted to this well-known fact in his deposition. Thus, Regions Bank quite properly accepted the endorsed-in-blank cashier's checks from the person in possession of them and

deposited the checks into that person's account. The court did not err in granting Regions Bank summary judgment on G&G's causes of action arising out of these checks.

More problematic, however, are the forged checks. Although these were also endorsed in blank, the payee's signatures were forgeries and were therefore ineffective as endorsements by the payee. ... Accordingly, Stafford was not entitled to enforce the instruments or to receive payment thereunder, and Regions Bank converted the instruments when it made or obtained payment on them by allowing them to be deposited into Stafford's personal account. ...

Regions Bank argues that G&G failed to exercise ordinary care, which substantially contributed to the making of the forged signatures. Regions Bank contends that accordingly G&G was precluded ... from asserting the forgery against the bank. Indeed, where some evidence shows that the corporate payee acted negligently in failing to prevent the forgery of its endorsement, a jury should decide whether that negligence substantially contributed to the making of the forgery—but only if the defendant bank in good faith paid the instrument or took it for value or for collection. ... In 1996 the General Assembly amended the applicable definition of "good faith" to mean "honesty in fact and the observance of reasonable commercial standards of fair dealing." ... Thus, even assuming the evidence established as a matter of law that G&G's actions substantially contributed to the making of the forgeries at issue, the question here is whether there is a disputed issue of fact as to Regions Bank's good faith (its honesty in fact and its observance of reasonable commercial standards of fair dealing) in regard to its accepting the forged checks as deposits in Stafford's account.

Regions Bank has presented evidence that it knew nothing of the possible forgery at the time it accepted the checks. The first Regions Bank learned of the forgery was from G&G after the fact. G&G has presented no evidence to contradict this, and thus the undisputed evidence shows Regions Bank's honesty in fact. . . .

However, disputed evidence does exist on the question of whether Regions Bank's actions were in observance of reasonable commercial standards of fair dealing. Significantly, reasonable commercial standards of fair dealing are different from reasonable commercial standards of due care. "Although fair dealing is a broad term that must be defined in context, it is clear that it is concerned with the fairness of conduct rather than the care with which an act is performed. Failure to exercise ordinary care in conducting a transaction is an entirely different concept than failure to deal fairly in conducting the transaction." . . .

You Be the Judge

Thomas J. Stafford was a farmer in Chesterfield County. He had two children, a daughter, June S. Zink, and a son, Thomas L. Stafford. He also developed a residential subdivision on a parcel of land that he owned. He built four houses in the subdivision, each on a separate subdivided lot, and sold each of the four houses. In each instance, Stafford took back a purchase money note from the purchaser, with the note secured by a deed of trust. Each of the four notes was payable to the order of Thomas Stafford, and each of the notes was indorsed by Stafford as follows: "Pay to the order of Thomas J. Stafford or June S. Zink, or the survivor." Proceeds from the notes were deposited into a "collection account" with a local bank. The account was maintained in the name of "Thomas J. Stafford and June S. Zink, as joint tenants with right of survivorship." Thomas J. Stafford died, and his son insisted that the four purchase money notes and the balance in the "collection account" properly belonged in the estate, to be distributed according to the will of the deceased. June Zink argued that the notes and the balance of the "collection account" properly belonged to her, as survivor, in accord with the indorsements on the notes and the provision that the account named her as one of the "joint tenants with right of survivorship." The daughter also asserts that the notes were negotiated to her, as evidenced by the indorsements on each, giving her rights. The son argues that the notes were not negotiated—or even transferred—to June Zink, and that the various writings were merely a failed attempt to create a gift.

This case has been brought before *your* court. How will *you* decide? In rendering your opinion, be certain that you consider the following issues: What should a person who operates an unincorporated business do to ensure that the assets of the business—or even the business entity—are preserved in the event of his or her death? And how could the notes in this case have been written to ensure that the daughter had rights in the notes *ab initio*? [See *Zink v. Stafford*, Lawyers Weekly, www.lawyersweekly.com/va/opin/supreme/1980283 (January 18, 1999).]

Summary

This chapter examines the technical requirements for negotiability of an instrument under Article 3. The first requirement is that the instrument be written or reduced to tangible form. Next, the instrument must be signed by the maker or the drawer. The promise (for notes or CDs) or the order (for checks or drafts) must be unconditional. The instrument must call for the payment of a fixed amount of money—a medium of exchange authorized or adopted by a domestic or foreign government. In addition, the time of payment must be at a definite time, or it must be payable on demand. Finally, the instrument must contain "words of negotiability." This means it must be payable "to order" or "to bearer," although a special exception for this rule exists if the instrument is a check in all other respects. Checks do not need to include the "words of negotiability" in order to be treated as negotiable instruments.

In case the instrument contains ambiguities, the Code provides a method of interpretation. Handwriting takes precedence over typing and over printing. Typing takes precedence over printing, and words take precedence over numbers.

Check truncation and "Check 21" may signal the beginning of electronic "negotiable instruments." This statute provides that truncated checks— checks converted to electronic images—are to be treated as equivalent to "traditional" checks, any contrary terms of the UCC notwithstanding. The advances in technology, the various statutes that authorize and recognize electronic signatures, and the benefits in terms of speed and accuracy with electronic communications may ultimately result in the treatment of many different types of electronic communications as negotiable instruments, although for now only "truncated checks" will enjoy such treatment.

Article 7 of the UCC governs documents of title. Documents of title may be negotiable or nonnegotiable. The requirements for negotiable documents under Article 7 are much less stringent than the requirements for negotiability under Article 3. Article 7 is more concerned with the goods than it is with the documents covering the goods, but it does provide some special protections if the document is negotiable and the holder qualifies as a holder by due negotiation.

Discussion Questions

1. How does the UCC define a "signature"? Why is the signature requirement so important in determining whether an instrument is negotiable?

2. In order to qualify as a negotiable instrument, the promise or the order must be "written." How does the UCC define "written," and how is that definition modified for negotiable instruments? How does Check 21 affect this requirement for negotiability in dealing with truncated checks?

3. In order to be a negotiable instrument, the writing must call for payment *either* on demand *or* at a definite time. Why is an instrument that is payable "30 days after sight" considered to be payable at a definite time, while an instrument payable "30 days after my birthday" is not considered to be payable at a definite time?

4. The courts have consistently held that an "IOU is not a negotiable instrument." Below is a typical IOU. Why would such an instrument be deemed nonnegotiable? Be specific.

	March 17, 20XX
Betty,	
IOU $350	
Jane Doe	

---

5. What is required by Article 7 in order for a document of title to be deemed negotiable? Is this more or less rigorous than the requirements for negotiability under Article 3? Why is there a difference in the requirements of negotiability under the two articles?

Case Problems and Writing Assignments

1. This case arises from a dispute between a brother and a sister over the interpretation of their mother's last will and testament, and especially the treatment of a check written by the decedent just prior to her death. James H. Creekmore, Jr. and Judith Carolyn Creekmore are the only children of the decedent, Ruby Lamm Creekmore. During her final illness, Ruby executed a last will and testament. This will disposed of her assets, including real property, personal effects and shares of a closely held corporation denominated in the will as "Lamm Development Corporation," also known as Lamm Development Co. of Wilson, Inc." ("LDC"). LDC was a corporation organized by the Lamm and Creekmore families to hold certain real property in Wilson, North Carolina. Until her death, Ruby was an officer and stockholder of the corporation. Under the terms of the will, Judith Creekmore was to receive 50 percent of her mother's stock in a life estate, and then Judith and James were each to divide the balance of their mother's estate equally. On February 6, 1994, prior to her death, Ruby gave a $10,000 check to Judith. According to Judith's affidavit, Ruby asked her not to deposit the check until after March 1, 1994, because she did not want the check to appear in her February bank statements, to which James had access. On November 15, 1994, James filed a complaint seeking a declaratory judgment to construe Ruby's will. In its final declaration, the court ruled that the estate had an obligation for payment to Judith Creekmore of the $10,000 check dated February 7, 1994. James appealed this judgment, arguing that the check did not constitute a completed gift since it had not been cashed prior to the death of the drawer. James believed that the $10,000 should be a part of the estate, to be divided equally between him and his sister. Was the delivery to Judith Creekmore by her mother of a $10,000 check a completed *inter vivos* gift, and thus properly excluded from the estate? Is it ethical for a relative to challenge the alleged wishes of a decedent in hopes of gaining a larger inheritance? [See *Creekmore v. Creekmore*, 485 S.E.2d 68 (N.C. App. 1997).]

2. Kindy agreed to purchase four diesel engines from Hicks, with Hicks agreeing to deliver the engines to Kindy. The purchase price was $13,000. Kindy agreed to wire transfer $6,500 and to pay the remainder by check. The check was not to be cashed until the engines had been delivered. Kindy wrote and mailed a post-dated check to Hicks in June of 1989. This check had two different amounts on its face: $6,500 in numbers on the number line, and $5,500 imprinted with a check imprinting machine on the line where words normally appear. Kindy stated that he had intentionally put two amounts on the check, reasoning that the bank would call him to find out which amount was to be paid, allowing him to tell the bank whether to honor the check (if the engines had been delivered) or to dishonor the check (if the engines had not been delivered). Hicks presented the check to the Galatia Bank on June 10, 1989, and the bank honored the check for $5,500. A bank employee altered the amount in the normal "number" location, changing the "6" in $6,500 to a "5" so that the amounts in each area were in agreement. The check was subsequently presented to the drawee bank, which refused it. Galatia sued Kindy for the amount of the check. Kindy denied liability, asserting that he had a defense (nondelivery) and that the bank was a mere holder. Was Galatia Bank a holder in due course and thus entitled to recover from Kindy on the check? Do imprinted numbers, located where the words are normally located, take precedence over numbers placed where the numbers are *normally* placed on a check? Does the answer to this question have any implications for businesses that use imprinting machines to "emboss" the amount on checks issued by the company? [See *Galatia Community State Bank v. Kindy*, 821 S.W.2d 765 (Ark. 1991).]

3. O'Mara, a West Virginia corporation with its principal place of business in Steubenville, Ohio, operated 15 Bonanza restaurants. O'Mara hired GSD, an accounting firm, to manage its accounting and other financial matters. Included in GSD's services were the computation of O'Mara's weekly federal withholding taxes, preparation of checks for deposit of these taxes, and reconciliation of bank statements. Smith was the sole owner of GSD, and also owned 20 percent of O'Mara. Thompson was the comptroller for both O'Mara and GSD. Smith encountered financial

difficulties beginning in 1979, and Smith and Thompson devised a plan whereby Smith would embezzle O'Mara's withholding taxes. This scheme involved indorsing the withholding checks, which were payable to the order of the Heritage Bank, as follows:

> Pay to the order of The First National Bank & Trust Company in Steubenville, Ohio FOR DEPOSIT ONLY GAIL SMITH DEVELOPMENT #009-215, W. Gail Smith.

Heritage Bank accepted each of these checks with this indorsement without question. When O'Mara discovered what had happened, it sued Heritage Bank (along with two other banks similarly involved) to recover the funds. The banks denied liability, asserting that the checks as issued were "bearer" instruments, not "order" instruments. Were these checks "bearer paper" so that Heritage Bank acted properly in accepting them? [See *O'Mara Enterprises, Inc. v. People's Bank of Weirton*, 420 S.E.2d 727 (W.Va. 1992).

Notes

1. 12 U.S.C. 5002.
2. Official Comments to UCC § 1-201(24), Comment 24.
3. UCC § 3-112(a).
4. UCC § 3-104(c).
5. Official Comments to UCC § 3-104, Comment 2.
6. Official Comments to UCC § 3-104, Comment 1.
7. *Merriam-Webster Online Dictionary*, http://www.m-w.com/.
8. *Cambridge Dictionaries*, http://dictionary.cambridge.org/.
9. 12 U.S.C. 5002 § 3 (18).
10. 12 U.S.C.A §§ 4000 *et seq.*
11. 12 U.S.C. 5001 § 2(a)(1).
12. Ibid., § (a)(2)(A) and (B).
13. "Check Truncation ('Check 21')," Association for Financial Professionals, http://www.afponline.org/pub/gr/i_checktrunc.html.
14. Ibid., § (b)(1)(2) and (3).
15. 12 U.S.C. 5003 § 4(a).
16. Ibid., § 4(b)(1) and (2).
17. 12 U.S.C. 5004 § 5.

21

Negotiation and Holders in Due Course/Holders by Due Negotiation

Agenda

eClass will be receiving a number of checks from its customers. How should the checks be handled? How should they be indorsed? Does the method of indorsement make any difference legally?

Occasionally the firm will receive a check that was originally issued to one of the firm's customers as payee, and that customer will then turn the check over to eClass as payment on his or her account. Does it matter if the customer transfers such a check to the firm without indorsing the check? If the firm wants an indorsement, what type of indorsement will the firm be entitled to receive from the transferring customer? What type of indorsement would the firm prefer?

eClass will also be using checks to make payments on the firm's various accounts. If a problem subsequently arises between the payee and eClass, can the firm avoid paying any checks already issued due to this problem, or might it be forced to pay the check despite the problem?

If the checks are deposited, when will the funds be available for the firm to use? Suppose that some of the checks they deposit are dishonored by the bank. What rights can the firm assert? Against whom will they be able to assert these rights?

These and other questions may arise during our discussion of the topics in this chapter. Be prepared! You never know when the firm or one of its members will seek your advice.

Classic Case

BANK OF NORTH CAROLINA, N.A. v. THE ROCK ISLAND BANK

471 F. Supp. 1301, 1979 U.S. Dist. LEXIS 11957 (C.D. Ill. 1979)

FACTS On June 5, 1969, William J. Kearney, the president of Rock Island Bank (RI), delivered to Lorraine Realty Corporation a letter of irrevocable and unconditional commitment to purchase a $400,000 Promissory Note from its holder in due course. Some time thereafter Sumner Financial Corporation (SFC) endorsed the note to the Bank of North Carolina (NC), receiving the discounted amount of $354,000. Lorraine Realty ultimately received $300,000 through SFC.

Mr. Kearney did not have authority to issue the commitment. Neither the Loan Committee nor the Board of Directors of RI were consulted or advised about the transaction. The commitment was not reflected on RI's books until in 1970, when RI authorities were contacted by examiners for the Federal Reserve System.

NC gave notice to RI of its intention to tender the note to RI for payment at its maturity on June 5, 1971. The note was duly tendered for payment through the Federal Reserve System and received by RI upon that transmittal on June 8, 1971.

RI refused to pay the note and NC filed suit. RI contends that NC failed to prove that it was a holder in due course of the note, thus failing to establish its right to recover on the commitment signed by Kearney. NC asserted that it must be presumed to be a holder in due course unless it appears that there is a defense against the note.

ISSUE Which party has the burden of proof regarding holder in due course status?

HOLDING The party asserting holder in due course status has the burden of proving its status.

REASONING Excerpts from the opinion of Morgan, Judge:

Allocation of the burden of proof upon the question of holder in due course is a critical issue which must be resolved at the outset. RI takes the position that this is a suit upon the contract created by the letter of credit, and that the obligation to purchase the note is limited to purchase from a person who is a holder in due course. It argues that NC had the burden . . . of proving its "holder-in-due-course" status to prove a *prima facie* right to recover. . . . Conversely, NC relies upon the Commercial Code, and contends that it is presumptively a holder in due course until and unless it appears that there is a defense against the note. . . .

Historically, the concept of a holder in due course derives from common law decisions in the area of what was termed the law merchant. The concept was devised to accord credibility to commercial paper. Basically, ... any defense not patent upon the face of a particular negotiable instrument could not be asserted against a bona fide purchaser of the instrument for value in good faith and without notice of such defense or infirmity.

As subsequently codified by legislative enactment, extending through the current Uniform Commercial Code, that same concept was embodied as the holder in due course principle. A holder in due course is a party who takes an instrument for value in good faith and without notice of any defense against the instrument. ...

Concomitantly, with that substantive concept designed to protect the free negotiability of instruments, there was developed a procedural concept that a holder of negotiable paper need only produce and substantiate the paper and adduce proof that payment was in default, to prove a *prima facie* right to recover. A duty upon his part to prove his status as a bona fide purchaser, for value and without notice, could arise only upon the assertion of a defense to the negotiable instrument involved. That procedural concept is now codified in the Commercial Code, § 3-307(2), (3). ... Section 3-307 applies only to a suit upon the instrument itself. It is codified in Part 3 of the Code, which defines and establishes the rights of holders of negotiable instrument. ...

In a suit upon a negotiable instrument itself, the Section presumes a right to recovery, upon proof of the instrument, until and unless it is shown that a defense does exist. Section 3-307(2), (3).

Plaintiff's argument thus misconstrues its own complaint. Its argument would be valid if RI were the maker of the note and if the suit were grounded upon the note itself [which it is not]. ... What NC does contend is that the refusal of RI to pay the note upon presentment was a breach of the contract of RI to purchase the note if the same remained unpaid at maturity. It was thus incumbent upon NC to prove, *prima facie*, its own compliance with the conditions stated in the RI letter, one of which was that RI would purchase from a "holder in due course," upon compliance by such holder with the notice and tender requirements stated in the letter.

The Commercial Code has a relevant bearing upon this issue to the extent that it does provide the legal definition of a holder in due course, to-wit, a holder who takes an instrument for value, in good faith, and without notice of any defense against the instrument. ... NC's proof was limited to the identification of a cancelled NC cashier's check, dated July 31, 1969, payable to SFC.

Clearly, NC did not adduce the proof necessary to show that it was a holder in due course and thus entitled to recover upon the RI letter of credit. Defendant's motion for judgment at the close of plaintiff's case ... was therefore meritorious and is entitled to be allowed.

TRANSFER

Negotiable instruments are intended to "flow" through the commercial world. In order to "flow," the instrument needs to be freely transferable from person to person. The form these transfers take determines the rights that can be asserted by each person obtaining possession of the instrument.

The Uniform Commercial Code (UCC) defines a *transfer* as a delivery by any person other than the issuer for the purpose of giving the person receiving the instrument the right to enforce the instrument.[1] A transfer, whether by negotiation or not, confers on the transferee the rights possessed by the transferor, including the rights of a holder in due course (HDC) if the transferor has those rights.[2] Thus, as was discussed in the previous chapter, a transfer of a negotiable instrument is treated like an assignment of a contract right. The transferee receives any and all rights of the transferor. While this is, in effect, the same as an assignment of the rights under a contract, this is not an ideal position, and if negotiable instruments could only be transferred—treated the same as an assignment—they would not be as readily accepted as they are in the modern commercial world.

NEGOTIATION

Obviously, something more is needed to protect the possessor of the negotiable instrument and to facilitate the free flow of negotiable instruments through commercial channels. The UCC provides this "something more" by making provision for *negotiations* of the instruments, and by providing for the possibility of special protections for some of the recipients of these negotiations, providing they qualify as *holders in due course.*

The Code defines a negotiation in § 3-201(a) as: "a transfer of possession, whether voluntary or involuntary, of an instrument by a person other than the issuer to a person who thereby becomes its holder." The Code then explains what is required to negotiate an instrument in § 3-201(b): "Except for negotiation by a remitter, if an instrument is payable to an identified person, negotiation requires transfer of possession of the instrument and its indorsement by the holder. If an instrument is payable to bearer, it may be negotiated by transfer of possession alone."

For example, a check that says "Pay to the order of Ollie Oliver" must be indorsed by Ollie Oliver along with a transfer of its possession before it can be negotiated. If Ollie simply transfers possession of the check to another person without indorsing it, the transfer would be an assignment. The terms imposed by the drawer—pay to the order of Ollie Oliver—require that Ollie prove he is transferring his rights. His indorsement provides that proof.

In contrast, a check that says "Pay to the order of bearer" does not need to be indorsed to be negotiated. Transfer of possession alone is enough to show negotiation. The terms imposed by the drawer at the time of issue—pay to the order of bearer—tell the drawee that anyone in possession, that is anyone *bearing* the instrument—is entitled to payment. However, the recipient of the instrument may well insist on having an indorsement even though none is required, for reasons explained in the next section.

The Code even makes allowance for negotiations that may be subject to rescission by the negotiating party. Section 3-202 addresses this issue, providing that:

(a) Negotiation is effective even if obtained (i) from an infant, a corporation exceeding its powers, or a person without capacity, (ii) by fraud, duress, or mistake, or (iii) in breach of duty or as part of an illegal transaction.

(b) To the extent permitted by other law, negotiation may be rescinded or may be subject to other remedies, but these remedies may not be asserted against a subsequent holder in due course or a person paying the instrument in good faith and without knowledge of facts that are the basis for rescission or other remedy.

Such protection for the subsequent parties would not be available in a "mere" assignment, but it is available under the provisions of Article 3, providing protection for holders in due course and for parties who pay the instrument in good faith, protections beyond those they would enjoy under traditional contract law.

eClass 21.1 Finance

SHOULD THE FIRM INSIST ON HAVING AN INDORSEMENT?

eClass recently received a complaint from one of its customers. The customer wanted to give the sales person a check as payment for a software package. The check was originally written by another person and was payable to the order of "bearer." The customer, who was not the drawer, wanted to merely deliver the check to the sales person as payment for the product, but the sales person insisted that the customer needed to indorse the check prior to delivering it or it would not be taken as payment. The customer refused to indorse the check, left the store without paying for the product, and called the firm to complain. Yousef believes that the sales person should have avoided this scene by accepting the check. After all, as he pointed out, the check was payable to bearer and did not require any indorsements. Meg disagreed, pointing out that the sales person was protecting the firm by insisting on an indorsement on the check. They have asked for your opinion. What will you tell them?

BUSINESS CONSIDERATIONS   Should a business have a policy regarding accepting checks drawn by someone other than the person trying to negotiate the check to the business (so-called "two-party checks")? If a business is going to accept checks from a payee or other holder, should the business insist on getting an indorsement? Why?

ETHICAL CONSIDERATIONS   Is it ethical for a person who wants to negotiate a check drawn by another person to refuse to indorse the check before transferring it, even if an indorsement is not legally necessary?

INDORSEMENTS

Section 3-204 defines an indorsement. According to this section of the Code:

> "Indorsement" means a signature, other than that of a signer as maker, drawer, or acceptor, that alone or accompanied by other words is made on an instrument for the purpose of (i) negotiating the instrument, (ii) restricting payment of the instrument, or (iii) incurring indorser's liability on the instrument, but regardless of the intent of the signer, a signature and its accompanying words is an indorsement unless the accompanying words, terms of the instrument, or other circumstances unambiguously indicate that the signature was made for a purpose other than an indorsement...

This means that a signature on a negotiable instrument is *presumed* to be an indorsement unless some other purpose is *unambiguously* shown as the purpose for the signature's placement on the instrument. There are two reasons that this is important. First, any instrument payable "to order" requires an indorsement before it can be further negotiated. Second, and perhaps more important, each and every indorsement is a separate contract *added to* the contract that the instrument itself represents, and to any other indorsement contracts already present on the instrument. Indorsers are assuming contractual liability to the person to whom they transfer the instrument and to every subsequent holder or transferee of that instrument. For this reason, many people will not accept the negotiation of a bearer instrument unless the holder indorses it. Even though bearer paper may legally be negotiated by delivery alone, the transferee usually demands the added security of an indorsement, thereby adding the indorsement contract and its rights to the rights represented by the instrument itself.

There are two reasons for indorsing an instrument. One reason is to affect negotiation. The other is to affect liability. The indorsements that affect negotiation will tell the holder:

(1) that another indorsement is needed to negotiate the instrument further (a special indorsement);

(2) that no further indorsements are needed in order to negotiate the instrument further (a blank indorsement); or

(3) that the instrument has been restricted to some special channel of commerce such as banking (a restrictive indorsement).

The indorsements that affect liability either:

(1) admit and/or agree to honor the contract of indorsement (an unqualified indorsement). or

(2) expressly deny any liability on the indorsement contract (a qualified indorsement).

Every indorsement must affect negotiation as well as liability. Thus, each indorsement must fit one of the boxes in the matrix shown in Exhibit 21.1.

Exhibit 21.1

The Indorsement Matrix

	Unqualified	*Qualified*
Special	(1) Designates the next holder so an additional indorsement is required; does not deny liability for the indorsement contract.	(2) Designates the next holder so an additional indorsement is required; denies contract liability for the indorsement.
Blank	(3) Does not designate the next holder, making the instrument "bearer paper"; does not deny liability for the indorsement contract.	(4) Does not designate the next holder, making the instrument "bearer paper"; denies contract liability for the indorsement.
Restrictive	(5) Attempts to restrict or limit future negotiation of the instrument, as in "for deposit only"; does not deny liability for the indorsement contract.	(6) Attempts to restrict or limit future negotiation of the instrument, as in "for deposit only"; denies contract liability for the indorsement.

Notice that each box in the matrix is numbered. We will use these numbers to refer back to the matrix as we discuss some examples of the various types of indorsements. Throughout the examples, we will be using the check shown in Exhibit 21.2.

Exhibit 21.2

The Check as Issued

Isabelle Issuer
104 Palace Drive
Anytown, USA

1492

August 10   20 __ XX __

Pay to the Order of __ Pauline Payee __ $ __ 200.00 __

Two Hundred and XX/100 _____ dollars

Last National Bank, N.A.
Metropolis, USA

Memo _____   *Isabelle Issuer*

101010101:   123456789   1492

Exhibit 21.3

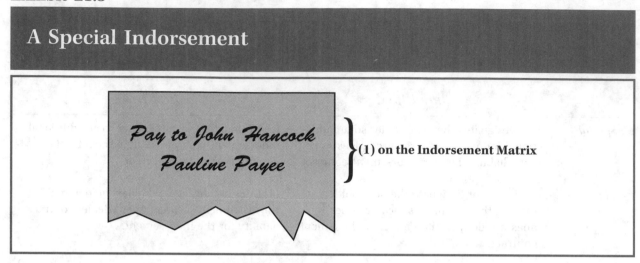

A Special Indorsement

Pay to John Hancock
Pauline Payee

}(1) on the Indorsement Matrix

Special Indorsements

A special indorsement specifies the party to whom the instrument is to be paid or to whose order it is to be paid. This means that a special indorsement makes (or leaves) the instrument payable "to order." Even if the instrument was issued as bearer paper, a special indorsement will make it payable "to order." The party specified will have to indorse it before it can be negotiated further. Exhibit 21.3 is an example of a special indorsement.

Blank Indorsements

A blank indorsement does not specify the party to whom the instrument is to be paid. The normal form of a blank indorsement is a mere signature by the holder. Such an indorsement makes the instrument bearer paper. As such, it is negotiable by transfer of possession alone, without any need for further indorsements. In Exhibit 21.4, a blank indorsement has been added to the previous special indorsement. Note that at this point the check has every indorsement that is necessary for negotiation. Should the check now be lost or stolen, the finder or the thief could effectively negotiate it. To protect against such an occurrence, § 3-205(c) empowers the holder to *convert* a blank indorsement into a special indorsement by writing, above the signature of the indorser, words identifying the person to whom the instrument is now made payable. This is shown in Exhibit 21.5. Here a holder added the words "Pay to M. Spillback, or

Exhibit 21.4

A Blank Indorsement

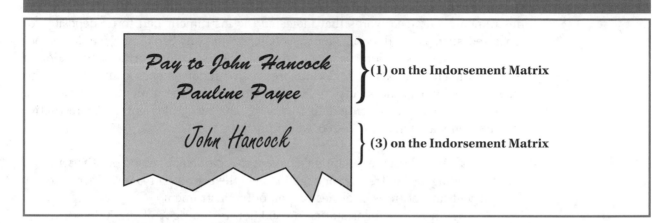

Exhibit 21.5

Conversion of a Blank Indorsement to a Special Indorsement

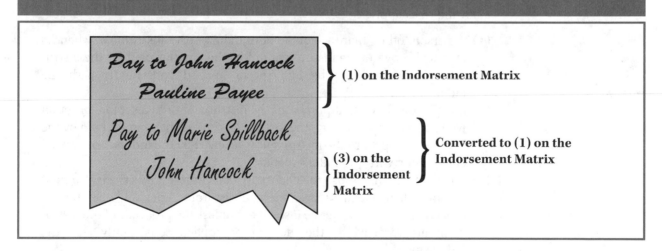

order" above John Hancock's indorsement. This phrase could have been added by John Hancock when he negotiated the check to Marie Spillback. More likely, Marie Spillback added the phrase after she received the check from John Hancock. By adding the phrase, he or she has protected Marie Spillback against losing her right in the event that she should lose the check or have it stolen.

Restrictive Indorsements

A restrictive indorsement purports to restrict or prohibit any further negotiation of the instrument. Prior to the revision of Article 3 it was not uncommon for a person to use an indorsement that contained a condition restricting any further negotiation of the instrument, contained words that indicated the instrument had to be deposited or collected, such as "for deposit," "for collection," or "pay any bank," or the indorsement had some other restriction specifying a permissible use before further negotiation of the instrument was allowed. Because restrictive indorsements could be used to effectively eliminate the ability to *negotiate* a negotiable instrument, the revision to Article 3 paid special attention to this area. The new rules governing restrictive indorsements are found in § 3-206, which provides:

> **(a)** An indorsement limiting payment to a particular person or otherwise prohibiting further transfer or negotiation of the instrument is not effective to prevent further transfer or negotiation of the instrument.
>
> **(b)** An indorsement stating a condition to the right of the indorsee to receive payment does not affect the right of the indorsee to enforce the instrument. A person paying the instrument or taking it for value or collection may disregard the condition, and the rights and liabilities of that person are not affected by whether the condition has been fulfilled.
>
> **(c)** If an instrument bears an indorsement . . . using the words "for deposit," "for collection," or other words indicating a purpose of having the instrument collected by a bank for the indorser or for a particular amount, the following rules apply:
>
> (1) A person, other than a bank, who purchases the instrument when so indorsed converts the instrument unless the amount paid for the instrument is received by the indorser or applied consistently with the indorsement.
>
> (2) A depository bank that purchases the instrument or takes it for collection when so indorsed converts the instrument unless the amount paid by the bank with respect to the instrument is received by the indorser or applied consistently with the indorsement.
>
> (3) A payor bank that is also the depositary bank or that takes the instrument for immediate payment over the counter from a person other than a collecting bank converts the instrument unless the proceeds of the instrument are received by the indorser or applied consistently with the indorsement.

Thus, under the new rules, a restrictive indorsement that purports to restrict payment or negotiation may be disregarded by the indorsee, with no affect on the rights or liabilities of the indorsee, unless the restrictive indorsement restricts further negotiation of the instrument to banking channels. When a restrictive indorsement restricts the instrument to banking channels ("for deposit" or "for collection"), it is a valid restriction, and any person who subsequently deals with that instrument without ensuring that the funds are applied consistently with the indorsement is deemed guilty of conversion. Thus, the revision to Article 3 establishes that only those restrictive indorsements that restrict the instrument to banking have any meaning or effect, but that the ones that do so restrict the instrument have a very serious and substantial effect.

One possible reason for this change in the treatment of restrictive indorsements is the importance placed on the negotiability of the instrument governed by Article 3. Remember that negotiability is determined by the information contained on the *face* of the instrument, and that indorsements are normally placed on the *back* of the instrument. Once an instrument as issued satisfies all the tests of negotiability, the instrument is deemed to be negotiable and no indorsement can be allowed to remove its negotiable status.

In Exhibit 21.6, item (5) shows a restrictive indorsement.

eClass 21.2 Finance

DEPOSITING COMPANY CHECKS

One of the new employees has been given the responsibility of preparing the deposits made by eClass. This employee takes the checks that have been received, stamps the back of the check with a rubber stamp reading "eClass" and the company's address, and then puts the checks in an envelope until they are taken to the bank for deposit. Meg is concerned that the employee is not being careful enough with the checks, and that this treatment poses a potential financial risk to the firm. Yousef thinks that Meg is overreacting. He thinks that since the checks have been indorsed, the firm is safe. However, he wants to be certain, so he has asked for your advice on this matter. What will you tell him?

BUSINESS CONSIDERATIONS   How should a business handle checks to reduce its risk of loss through embezzlement, theft of the checks, or other similar problems? Does the method of indorsement used on the checks make any difference?

ETHICAL CONSIDERATIONS   Assume that a firm permits its employees to indorse checks in blank, and then suffers a financial loss when some of these checks are stolen and negotiated further. Is it ethical for the firm to blame the employees for mishandling the checks? Should the firm share in the blame for permitting this method of indorsing?

Exhibit 21.6

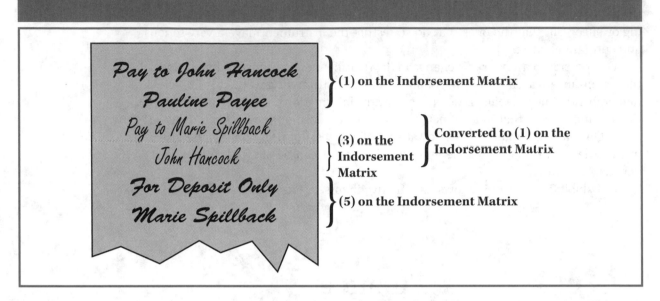

It should be noted that each of these sample indorsements refers to the unqualified indorsement column of the matrix set out in Exhibit 21.1. The reason for this is contained in UCC § 3-415, Obligation of Indorser, which provides:

> **(a)** ... If an instrument is dishonored, an indorser is obliged to pay the amount due on the instrument

> (i) according to the terms of the instrument at the time it was indorsed; or (ii) if the indorser indorsed an incomplete instrument, according to its terms when completed [presuming that the completion was authorized]. The obligation of the indorser is owed to a person entitled to enforce the instrument or to a subsequent indorser who paid the instrument under this section.

> **(b)** If an indorsement states that it is made "without recourse" or otherwise disclaims liability of the indorser, the indorser is not liable under subsection (a) to pay the instrument.

Under this section, an indorsement is presumed to be *unqualified*. To be qualified, the indorsement must contain specific words of qualification. An unqualified indorsement carries with it a contractual commitment to pay the amount due on the instrument if there is a dishonor. The indorser is committed to the indorsee (the person to whom the instrument is transferred by indorsement) or to any later holder if the instrument is dishonored and proper notice of the dishonor is given. The normal order of payment among the indorsers is the reverse of the order in which they indorsed the instrument. Thus, on a dishonored check, which had four indorsers, indorser four would collect from indorser three, who in turn would collect from indorser two, who in turn would collect from indorser one. (For example, Spillback would proceed against Hancock, who would proceed against Payee, who would proceed against Issuer. This is known as the secondary chain of liability, and will be discussed in detail in the next chapter.)

A qualified indorsement is one that denies contract liability. The indorser includes words such as "without recourse" in the indorsement. These words have the legal effect of telling later holders that the qualifying indorser will not repay them if the instrument is dishonored. By accepting a qualified indorsement in a negotiation, the later holders also agree to the contract terms of the qualified indorsement. In Exhibit 21.7, each of the earlier indorsements is shown as unqualified; in Exhibit 21.8, the same indorsements are shown as qualified. Note the specific language necessary to change an indorsement from the presumed unqualified indorsement to a qualified indorsement.

HOLDER

At the beginning of this chapter, we examined the transfer of negotiable instruments. It was pointed out that a *transfer* leaves the transferee in the role of an *assignee*. It also was stated that a *negotiation* leaves the transferee in the role of a *holder*. The role of a holder is important in negotiable instruments. A holder takes an instrument by

Exhibit 21.7

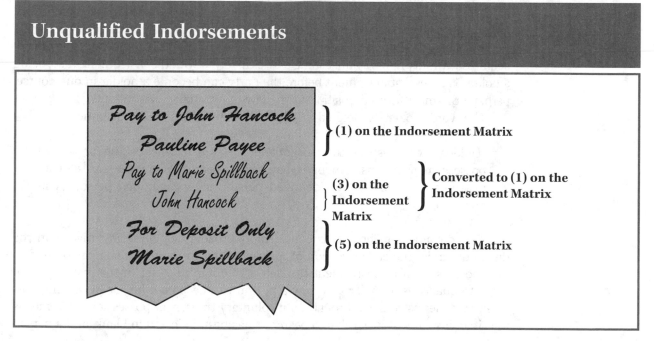

Unqualified Indorsements

Pay to John Hancock
Pauline Payee
} **(1) on the Indorsement Matrix**

Pay to Marie Spillback
John Hancock
} **(3) on the Indorsement Matrix** } **Converted to (1) on the Indorsement Matrix**

For Deposit Only
Marie Spillback
} **(5) on the Indorsement Matrix**

Exhibit 21.8

Qualified Indorsements

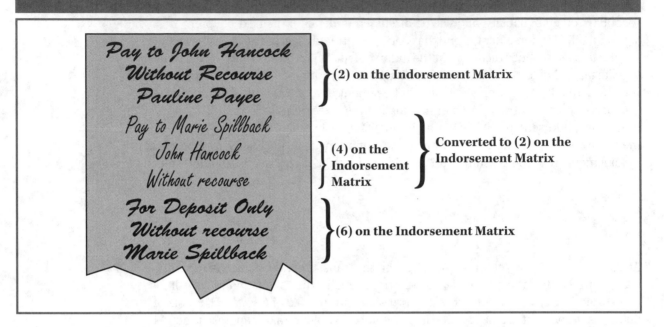

transfer, giving the holder all of the rights that his or her transferor possessed. However, a holder also acquires personal rights that may well be above and beyond those rights conferred by the transfer. Thus a holder can have better rights than the person from whom the holder received the negotiation. A holder normally acquires contractual rights against several parties involved with the instrument. A holder also normally acquires warranty rights against some parties involved with the instrument. Also, being a holder is an essential element before the party can become a holder in due course, perhaps the most favored position in the law of negotiable instruments.

The word "holder" is defined in § 1-201(20). According to the definition:

"Holder," with respect to a negotiable instrument, means the person in possession if the instrument is payable to bearer, or, in the cases of an instrument payable to an identified person, if the identified person is in possession.

This definition of "holder" is considerably broader and more inclusive than the definition under the earlier version of Article 3. Prior to the revision, a person had to take possession of an instrument through a voluntary transfer of the instrument in order to qualify as a holder. But now a person can become a holder by gaining possession of the instrument through an involuntary transfer of possession. This means that if an instrument is payable to bearer or has been indorsed in blank, and a person *steals* the instrument, the *thief* becomes a holder![3] A holder has the right to transfer, negotiate, discharge, or enforce the instrument in the holder's own name. However, a holder is subject to any defenses on the instrument that a maker or drawer can assert.

HOLDER IN DUE COURSE

To overcome even one of the defenses on the instrument that may be available to the maker or drawer, the holder needs to acquire *holder in due course* (HDC) status. Great care needs to be exercised here. The burden of proof for establishing HDC status lies with the person claiming the status. A holder must prove he or she is a holder in due course; such status is not presumed. A holder or an assignee is subject to any defense the drawer or maker can assert. A holder in due course is subject only to *some* defenses of the maker or drawer. The holder in due course prevails over *most* available defenses.

When the NIL was initially enacted, and for quite some time thereafter, instruments commonly remained in circulation for quite a while after they were issued. Under these circumstances, the instruments were regularly treated as substitutes for money, and the protection of the holders of the instrument was a very significant concern. The rules regarding holders in due course were developed to protect holders of negotiable instruments in these situations. Modern commercial practice and changes in banking laws, rules, and regulations has reduced the likelihood that an instrument will remain in circulation for very long today, reducing somewhat the practical importance of the holder in due course rules. Nonetheless, the Code still devotes a considerable amount of attention to HDC status, beginning with the definition of a holder in due course as set out in Section 3-302:

> Subject to subsection (c) [precluding HDC status for parties who acquire an instrument through extraordinary purchases, acquisitions outside the ordinary course of business, and the like] and Section 3-106(d) [statutory language that removes the availability of HDC status contained on the face of certain instruments], "holder in due course" means the holder of an instrument if:
>
> **(1)** the instrument when issued or negotiated to the holder does not bear such apparent evidence of forgery or alteration or is not otherwise so irregular or incomplete as to call into question its authenticity; and
> **(2)** the holder took the instrument (i) for value, (ii) in good faith, (iii) without notice that the instrument is overdue or has been dishonored or that there is an uncured default with respect to payment of another instrument as part of the same series, (iv) without notice that the instrument contains an unauthorized signature or has been altered, (v) without notice of any claim to the instrument described in Section 3-306, and (vi) without notice that any party has a defense or claim in recoupment described in Section 3-305(a).

Thus, in order to qualify as an HDC, the holder must take an instrument that *appears* to be regular, complete, and authentic when he or she acquires the instrument, *and* the instrument must be taken (1) for *value*, (2) in *good faith*, and (3) *without notice* of defects or defenses affecting the instrument.

The appearance of the instrument at the time the holder takes possession of it should not be too difficult to establish. Similarly, the issues of value and good faith are relatively simple to establish. However, sometimes the various notice issues can be difficult to prove. Each of these three elements of holder in due course status is discussed in the following sections.

For Value

In order to qualify as an HDC, a holder must give *value* for the instrument. Under Article 3, value is more than consideration. Holders in due course merit special protection because they have already *performed* their obligation or they are irrevocably committed to perform. Thus, if they are not protected, they lose more than "opportunity costs." Since they have already performed, they are "out" the value of the performance. If they were not protected on the instrument, they might also wind up being "out" on the instrument, thus causing them to lose twice, the actual loss of their uncompensated performance and the opportunity cost of the unpaid or dishonored instrument.

Section 3-303 sets out five methods of giving value for an instrument. Notice that each method involves actual performance by the holder, not just a commitment to perform in the future. The first method involves an instrument issued or transferred for a promise of performance, to the extent the promise has been performed. The second method arises when the transferee acquires a security interest or other lien in the instrument, other than a lien obtained in a judicial proceeding. Third, the instrument is issued or transferred as payment of, or as security for, an antecedent claim against any person, whether or not the claim is due. Fourth, the instrument is issued or transferred in exchange for another negotiable instrument. Fifth, the instrument is issued or transferred in exchange for an irrevocable obligation to a third person by the person taking the instrument. Once the holder can prove that value was given, the holder goes on to the next test.

In Good Faith

The next requirement is that the holder must take the instrument in *good faith*. Historically, good faith was defined as "honesty in fact." This provided a relatively simplistic standard, and one that was very hard to measure. It seemed that good faith was assumed, and the person challenging HDC status for a holder had to establish a *lack* of good faith in order to negate this element of the HDC requirements. This requirement was actually being measured by a negative test. The holder acted with good faith if bad faith was not shown. Traditionally, in order to show a lack of good faith, it had to be proved that the holder either had actual knowledge of a defect in the instrument or ignored facts that would have shown the defect. Usually, all the holder needed to do was to allege that he or she had acted with/in good faith. (This test was referred to by one court as the "white heart, empty head" test because of the presumption that the parties acted with good faith absent some showing of knowledge or gross negligence.) Very few cases involved bad faith.

The revision to Article 3 has changed the requirement of good faith and its measurement significantly. Article 3 now provides in § 3-103(a)(4) that "'Good faith' means honesty in fact and the observance of reasonable commercial standards of fair dealing." With this new definition of "good faith" the courts require the holder to show that he or she has "observed reasonable commercial standards" in order to establish that he or she has acted with good faith in the transaction. The requirement that a holder must have "observed reasonable commercial standards of fair dealing" provides a relatively broad test that is not specifically defined. Thus, the courts will have to decide whether the holder meets this standard by looking at the context of the transaction. It seems that this section is now more concerned with the fairness of the conduct of the parties than it is with the care with which the parties have acted.[4] This new standard is likely to make "good faith" a much more meaningful test in cases in which HDC status is alleged, and it will be interesting to watch how the courts apply this newer, stricter standard.

eClass 21.3 Finance/Management

WHAT CONSTITUTES NOTICE?

eClass received a "writing" from one of its customers as payment in full of the customer's account. The "writing" looked like a typical draft except for a statement typed in bold-faced type across the top of the paper. The statement said "**This is NOT a negotiable instrument.**" Everything else on the paper had the look and the form of a draft, including the statement to "Pay to the order of eClass." When the paper was presented to the person to whom the order was directed, that person refused to honor the writing, and returned the paper unpaid. The principals want to know if this is a draft and also what they can or should do. They have asked for your advice. What will you tell them?

BUSINESS CONSIDERATIONS.   Should a business develop a policy for what types of writing it will accept as payment and what types of writing it will refuse, if offered as payment? Why might such a policy be a good idea?

ETHICAL CONSIDERATIONS.   Is it ethical for a person to issue what *looks* like a negotiable instrument, but to include a disclaimer of negotiability, thus "opting out" of the coverage of Article 3? What ethical issues are raised by such conduct?

Without Notice of Defenses or Defects

The final requirement to establish holder-in-due-course status is that the holder takes the instrument without notice of any defenses or defects on the instrument. *Notice* is present if a reasonable person would know that there was a defense or a defect, or if a reasonable person would be suspicious and would make further inquiry before accepting the instrument.

The Code provides a broad statement concerning notice in § 3-302(2), but it does not list many specific facts that constitute notice or specific facts that do not constitute notice, leaving this area for judicial interpretation to a much greater extent. According to this section, in order to satisfy the "without notice" requirement, the holder must take the instrument:

> **(iii)** without notice that the instrument is overdue or has been dishonored or that there is an uncured default with respect to payment of another instrument issued as part of the same series,
>
> **(iv)** without notice that the instrument contains an unauthorized signature or has been altered,
>
> **(v)** without notice of any claim to the instrument described in Section 3-306 (claims of a previous holder to recover the instrument or to rescind the negotiation), and
>
> **(vi)** without notice that any party has a defense or claim in recoupment described in Section 3-305.

Thus, to qualify as an HDC, the holder cannot have notice that the instrument is overdue or has been dishonored. He or she also cannot have notice that there is an unauthorized signature or an alteration of the instrument, that another party has asserted a claim to recover the instrument by legal means or to rescind a previous negotiation. And finally, he or she cannot have notice of any *other* defense or claim against the instrument. Of these elements, the fact that in instrument is overdue *will* be apparent on the face of the instrument most of the time. The fact that an instrument has been dishonored *might* be apparent on the face of the instrument (the instrument may have been stamped "NSF" or "Payment Stopped" upon prior presentment to the drawee bank, for example). An alteration also *might* be apparent on the face of the instrument, especially if someone has stricken through something on the instrument and replaced it with something else. But it is quite likely that any defenses or claims against the instrument, and any claims to recover the instrument or to rescind a prior negotiation will not show on the face of the instrument and will not be apparent to a holder exercising ordinary care in accepting the instrument through a negotiation.

In § 3-304, overdue instruments are defined. According to this section:

> **(a)** an instrument payable on demand becomes overdue at the *earliest* of the following times:
>
> **(1)** on the day after the day demand for payment is duly made;
>
> **(2)** if the instrument is a check, 90 days after its date; or

(3) if the instrument is not a check, when the instrument has been outstanding for a period of time after its date which is unreasonably long under the circumstances of the particular case in light of the nature of the instrument and usage of the trade.

(b) With respect to an instrument payable at a definite time the following rules apply:

(1) if the principal is payable in installments and a due date has not been accelerated, the instrument becomes overdue upon default under the instrument for nonpayment of an installment, and the instrument remains overdue until the default is cured;

(2) if the principal is not payable in installments and the due date has not been accelerated, the instrument becomes overdue on the day after the due date;

(3) if a due date with respect to principal has been accelerated, the instrument becomes overdue on the date after the accelerated due date.

(c) Unless the due date of principal has been accelerated, an instrument does not become overdue if there is default in payment of interest but no default in payment of principal.

Other Facts That Are Considered Notice   Some of the things that have traditionally served as notice of a defect or a defense affecting an instrument are set out here. A purchaser of a negotiable instrument has notice of a defect if the instrument is incomplete in some material respect. Thus, a missing signature or a missing amount would be notice. So would a missing date on a time instrument. But a missing date on a demand instrument, such as a check, is not notice since it is not material. It is not material because a demand instrument is payable at issue, and even if it is not dated, it has been issued. The simple fact of its existence proves that it has been issued. Notice of a defect also exists if the instrument is visibly altered or bears visible evidence of a forgery. Notice exists if the instrument is irregular on its face. This means that an erasure or a "striking out" of an obligation of a party or of an amount is notice of a defect. A holder who takes an instrument stamped "NSF" (not sufficient funds), or "Payment Stopped," or "Paid" would have notice of a defense or defect on the instrument. It has been presented, and it has been dishonored or paid. The holder knows this by looking at the face of the instrument.

Facts That Are Not Considered Notice   Traditional interpretations of Article 3 have shown that the following facts, standing alone, are not notice of a defense or defect on the instrument, even if the holder has knowledge of the fact:

1. The instrument was antedated or post-dated.
2. The instrument was issued or negotiated for an executory promise, unless the holder has notice of defenses to the promise.
3. Any party has signed as an accommodation party.[5]

4. A formerly incomplete instrument was completed.

5. Any person negotiating the instrument is or was a fiduciary.

In addition, it is not treated as notice if any party has filed or recorded a document, if the holder would otherwise qualify as an HDC. In addition, before notice is effective, it must be received in a time and a manner that give a reasonable opportunity to act on the information. Notice must be received before the holder receives the instrument. Once the holder has received the instrument, later notice is irrelevant.

EFFECT OF HOLDER IN DUE COURSE STATUS

The status of holder in due course is a preferred legal position. The HDC takes an instrument free of personal defenses that the drawer or maker may be able to assert in order to avoid paying the instrument. Although the holder in due course is subject to real defenses, he or she will be able to enforce the instrument against any other defense or defect. This position is far superior to that of a mere holder or an assignee. A holder or an assignee is subject to any and every defense or defect in the instrument, real or personal. A mere holder, an assignee, or a transferee takes possession of a negotiable instrument subject to every available defense. In contrast, an HDC takes the instrument subject only to real defenses. The HDC is not subject to personal (sometimes referred to as limited) defenses.

A personal defense is one that affects the agreement for which the instrument was issued. It does not affect or challenge the validity of the instrument. The underlying agreement, the reason the instrument was issued, is the point of contention. A real defense, on the other hand, questions the legal validity of the instrument.

Personal Defenses

The most common types of personal defenses are those available on a simple contract. The most common of these contract defenses are failure of consideration, fraud, duress, and breach of warranty. In addition, the holder frequently may be faced with the personal defenses of nondelivery, theft, payment, or any other cancellation.

Most of the simple contract defenses were covered in Part 3, "Contracts," and need no further review here. However, fraud does need some added coverage because negotiable instrument law recognizes two types of fraud. One type, fraud in the inducement, is a personal defense. The other type, fraud in the execution, is a real defense.

Fraud in the inducement is a personal defense because the fraud committed is a fraud related to the agreement. The maker or drawer intentionally and knowingly issues a negotiable instrument to the payee. However, this issue is made to support an underlying agreement, and the agreement is based on fraudulent representations. The underlying contract is voidable because of the fraud, but the instrument is valid, subject only to a personal defense. (Fraud in the execution is discussed in the following section.)

Of the other personal defenses not based on simple contract defenses, only one will be covered here. Nondelivery of the instrument needs special treatment. To issue an instrument, the maker or drawer must deliver the instrument to the payee or to an authorized representative of the payee. If the payee gains possession of the instrument without the knowledge or consent of the maker or drawer, the defense of nondelivery is available against a mere holder. Another type of nondelivery occurs when the maker or drawer gives the payee possession, but with a condition attached before delivery is effective. The condition may be that the payee must perform some act before he or she can treat the instrument as "delivered," and the act is then not performed. Technically, delivery never occurred because the condition was never satisfied, and the defense of nondelivery can be raised as a personal defense.

Recoupment

On occasion the person who issues a negotiable instrument may be able to assert a claim, not against the instrument, but against payment of the full amount of the instrument. When this happens, the issuer is said to have a claim in recoupment. For example, suppose that a buyer purchases some equipment from a seller, paying for the equipment by issuing a check payable to the order of the seller. The buyer accepts the equipment when it is delivered, but discovers a defect in the equipment. The buyer then decides to pay for repairs to the equipment rather than revoking his acceptance of the goods. While the buyer has accepted the goods, it is quite likely that the seller has breached one or more warranties in the sale. In this case, while the buyer is obligated to pay for the goods (the goods were accepted upon tender of delivery), the buyer also has a claim against the seller for the damages discovered after the acceptance, and may well be allowed to reduce the amount that is owed to the seller for the goods by the amount of the damages ("recouping" his losses). If recoupment is allowed, the issuer pays the amount of the instrument minus the amount of any damages incurred. The instrument is still being paid, but it is not being paid in full!

Under the former version of Article 3, this sort of situation was classified as a general "failure of consideration," and was treated as a personal defense of the issuer. However, this treatment was deemed too vague, and was open to too many possible interpretations. As a result, the revision to Article 3 does not mention "failure of consideration," instead preferring to treat specific types of failures more directly. In § 3-305 (a)(3), claims in recoupment are specifically covered. According to this section, the right to enforce the obligation of a party to pay an instrument is subject to the following:

(3) A claim in recoupment of the obligor against the original payee of the instrument if the claim arose from the transaction that gave rise to the instrument; but the claim of the obligor may be asserted against a transferee of the instrument only to reduce the amount owing on the instrument at the time the action is brought.[6]

Section 3-305(b) goes on to state that the right of a holder in due course to enforce the instrument is not subject to any claim of recoupment against a person other than the holder.

This change in emphasis removes a personal defense that existed under the previous coverage of Article 3, failure of consideration. But it allows the issuer of the instrument to "net out" the amount owed on the instrument if the issuer has a claim in recoupment against the original payee, unless the party seeking payment is a holder in due course. This still provides adequate protection for an HDC, it protects other holders who do not possess HDC status to some extent, and it leaves the issuer in the position he or she would occupy under Article 2 while allowing the issuer to use a negotiable instrument to make payment for the goods.

Real Defenses

A real defense, sometimes referred to as a universal defense, challenges the validity of the instrument itself. If a real defense can be established, the negotiable instrument is voided by operation of law, and *no one* can enforce the instrument. Thus, even an HDC will lose to a real defense. It should be kept in mind that if a maker or drawer alleges a real defense, the maker or drawer must establish the defense as real. A failure to do so will normally still leave a valid personal defense, but such a defense will not prevail against a holder in due course. Section 3-305(a)(1) of the UCC lists the four defenses that are valid against an HDC. There are two additional potential real defenses, found in § 3-403 and § 3-407, which are also discussed here.

Infancy   The first real defense is infancy (or minority), but only "to the extent that it is a defense to a simple contract." Infancy refers to the period before a person attains majority status and gains complete contractual capacity. Thus, anyone who is not yet 18 years of age is still, legally, an infant, or a minor. To determine whether infancy is a real defense, state law must be examined. If the statutes or cases in the state where the instrument is issued allow infancy to be asserted as a defense to the underlying contract, the infancy may also be raised as a real defense on the instrument. Even if state law does not give such a broad defense, it is still useful as a personal defense; however, a holder in due course can override that defense.

Duress, Lack of Legal Capacity, or Illegality   The second real defense is "duress, lack of legal capacity, or illegality of the transactions which, under other law, nullifies the obligation." Again, the relevant state law will be controlling. If the state statutes or prior cases void the transaction, the instrument also is voided. If not, the defense is merely personal in nature. An example would be the issuance of a check to pay a gambling debt. If gambling agreements are illegal in the state, a defense exists on the instrument, but it is probably only a personal defense. However, if the check contains a notation that it is meant as payment for a gambling debt, the defense becomes real. The instrument itself now reflects the illegality.

Other types of illegality that might affect a negotiable instrument, and hence operate as a real defense on the instrument, include usury, agreements that violate public policy, and attempts to do business in a state when not licensed to do so.

Fraud   The third real defense is "fraud that induced the obligor to sign the instrument with neither knowledge nor reasonable opportunity to learn of its character or its essential terms." In this defense, the maker or drawer must prove two things: (1) lack of knowledge of the instrument signed and (2) no reasonable opportunity to discover the nature or terms of the instrument. To establish this defense, the maker or drawer must prove that discovering the nature of the signed instrument was not reasonable at the time of signing. Such proof will be virtually impossible unless the signing person is either illiterate or is involved in a strange set of circumstances. The following hypothetical case illustrates such a setting.

Freddy Hornet, a famous rock musician, was signing autographs outside a theater after a performance. Sonya Smith, among others, shoved a paper in front of Freddy for him to sign. However, the paper she shoved was a promissory note, payable to her order, for $50,000. Freddy signed it without reading it, and Sonya left the theater area. Sonya later sued Freddy to collect the money called for in the note. If Freddy can prove these facts, he may have a real defense and will not have to pay the note.

[NOTE: Check fraud is becoming a significant problem, especially with the growing use of telechecks and pre-authorized payments. Several web sites are devoted to this topic, some of which are available at the web site accompanying this text. While the check frauds referred to at these sites may not qualify as a real defense in every case, it is worth examining these sites for some helpful hints.]

Discharge in Insolvency   The fourth real defense is a "discharge of the obligor in insolvency proceedings." This area basically refers to a discharge in bankruptcy proceedings. Bankruptcy is a federally guaranteed privilege, and federal law prevails over conflicting state law. The federal bankruptcy law discharges the enforceability of the instrument, creating a statutory real defense on the instrument.

Forgery   Section 3-403 of the Code treats a forgery—or any unauthorized signature—as ineffective against anyone except the person who signed. Thus, a forgery of the signature of the drawer or of a draft or the maker of a note is ineffective against the person whose signature was forged. However, if the drawer or maker ratifies the signature, the signature becomes authorized, and thus effective against that person. In addition, if the drawer or maker contributed to the forgery, the defense is "reduced" to a personal defense, it is no longer valid against a holder in due course.

Material Alteration   Section 3-407 provides that an unauthorized material alteration is a real defense to the extent of the alteration. An HDC can still enforce the instrument as issued, but would have to seek recovery for the altered terms from the person who altered the instrument without authorization. Again, if the drawer or maker contributed to the alteration, the defense becomes merely personal, and is not effective against a holder in due course.

Section 3-406 provides the standards for determining whether an unauthorized signature or an unauthorized alteration becomes merely a personal defense. According to this section, "a person whose failure to exercise reasonable care substantially contributes to an alteration of an instrument or to the making of a forged signature on an instrument is precluding from asserting the alteration or the forgery against a person who, in good faith, pays the instrument or takes it for value or for collection." It is important to note that if a person who contributes to a forgery or a material alteration is liable to some parties who do not have HDC status. A person who acts in good faith in paying for an instrument or taking the instrument for value or collection is protected, along with an HDC.

THE SHELTER PROVISION

Remember that we stated earlier in this chapter that a transfer of an instrument is treated like the assignment of rights under contract law. You should also remember that an assignee takes the same rights as were held by his or her assignor. This same rule holds true with the transfer of a negotiable instrument. This provision is spelled out in § 3-203(b), which states:

> Transfer of an instrument, whether or not the transfer is a negotiation, vests in the transferee any right of the transferor to enforce the instrument, including any right as a holder in due course, but the transferee cannot acquire rights of a holder in due course by transfer, directly or indirectly, from a holder in due course if the transferee engaged in fraud or illegality affecting the instrument.

This provision, generally known as the "shelter provision," simply states that once an HDC is involved with an instrument, every subsequent holder can assert the rights of an HDC without having to prove his or her status, with one exception. No one who engaged in any act of fraud or other illegality affecting the instrument can then "launder" his or her involvement by having the instrument negotiated to an HDC and then acquiring or reacquiring the instrument and asserting the shelter provision.

It must also be noted that a transferee who takes an instrument by a means other than by negotiation may have to establish his or her rights to the instrument, and may also have to establish the rights of his or her transferor *as an HDC* in order to make use of the protection of the shelter provision.[7]

STATUTORY LIMITATIONS

The protected status given to holders in due course makes abuses possible. If a payee obtains an instrument by wrongful means and then negotiates it to an HDC, the maker or drawer will nearly always be obliged to pay the instrument. As will be seen in the next chapter, the maker or drawer can sue the payee to recover the money paid. However, the payee must be found to be sued; and the finding may not be easy. If the payee and the HDC are working together, the maker or drawer is easily taken, usually with no chance of recovering.

Because of this potential, the Federal Trade Commission (FTC) passed a regulation in 1976 designed to protect consumers. This regulation modifies the holder in due course rules in some circumstances. If a consumer credit transaction is involved, the instrument used must contain the following notice, printed prominently:

ANY HOLDER OF THIS CONSUMER CREDIT CONTRACT IS SUBJECT TO ALL CLAIMS AND DEFENSES WHICH THE DEBTOR COULD ASSERT AGAINST THE SELLER OF GOODS OR SERVICES OBTAINED HERETO OR WITH THE PROCEEDS HEREOF. RECOVERY HEREUNDER BY THE DEBTOR SHALL NOT EXCEED AMOUNTS PAID BY THE DEBTOR HEREUNDER.

The effect of the rule is to make even an HDC subject to any defenses available against the payee, which is a tremendous protection for the consumer. This rule may have a great impact on the use of consumer credit contracts in the future.

If the notice is present in a consumer credit transaction, any holder of the instrument has agreed by the terms of the instrument to remain subject to any defenses of the maker or drawer. This means that a consumer could avoid payment to any HDC in possession of the instrument if the consumer could avoid payment to the payee. This is true even if the notice is included in a credit contract with a nonconsumer, as is pointed out in *Jefferson Bank & Trust Co. v. Stamatiou.*[8] In that case, Stamatiou purchased a truck from Key Dodge, signing a note that was subsequently assigned to Jefferson Bank & Trust. Although Stamatiou was purchasing the truck for a commercial purpose, the note Stamatiou signed included the FTC HDC limitation (Apparently, the sales manager at the dealership used the consumer loan form by mistake). When the truck broke down, Stamatiou rescinded the contract and ceased making payments on the loan. The bank sued, alleging that it was entitled to recover on the note due to its status as an HDC. Stamatiou raised the FTC restriction on the protections afforded to an HDC and denied liability, and the court agreed with his argument. While the protection was *intended* for consumer credit transactions, it *could* be used in a commercial loan, and would be given full force and effect when it was. Since the clause was in the note, Stamatiou was allowed to assert his personal defense against the bank despite its HDC status, and was therefore not obligated to pay the note.

This case is still viewed by many people as the definitive case in this area. The new restriction on HDC status included in the revision to Article 3 is based, at least in part, on this opinion. Section 3-302(g) states that the protections given to a holder in due course are subject to any law limiting the status as a holder in due course in particular classes of transactions. This section is intended to recognize the impact of the FTC HDC rule, as well as any comparable rules or statutes passed by any state, and to remove any uncertainty as to whether HDC protections exist in such a situation.

HOLDER BY DUE NEGOTIATION

When a negotiable warehouse receipt is issued calling for delivery of the goods to the order of a named individual, or to bearer, the document of title is negotiable. As such, it can be negotiated by indorsement and delivery (if the goods are to be delivered "to order") or by delivery alone (if the goods are to be delivered "to bearer"). When a document is negotiated to a person who purchases the instrument in good faith and the purchaser takes the document without notice of any defense against or claim to the goods or the document, the instrument has been "duly negotiated." This makes the recipient of the document a *holder by due negotiation* (HDN), a somewhat preferred and protected status in the area of documents of title, although neither as preferred nor as protected as an HDC in the area of negotiable instruments.

A holder by due negotiation is assured of the following rights:

1. Title to the document
2. Title to the goods the document represents
3. All rights accruing under the laws of agency or estoppel, including the right to goods delivered to the bailee after the document was issued
4. The direct obligation of the issuer of the document to hold or to deliver the goods according to the terms of the document and free of any claims or defenses of the issuer except those specified in the document or specified in Article 7

In contrast, if the document is not negotiable or was not negotiated despite its negotiability, or if the purchaser either did not act in good faith or had notice of a defense or claim against the document, he or she cannot be an HDN. In this situation the recipient only acquires the rights and the title the transferor possesses or has the authority to convey. Further, if the document is nonnegotiable, the rights of the recipient may be defeated by any claims or defenses that arise after the transfer but before the bailee receives notice of the transfer.

Contemporary Case

TRIFFIN v. TRAVELERS EXPRESS COMPANY, INC.

370 N.J. Super. 399, 851 A.2d 667, 2004 N.J. Super.
LEXIS 231, (N.J. Sup. Ct. App. Div. 2004)

FACTS Seventeen Travelers Express money orders were stolen from a pharmacy in Brooklyn. Each of the stolen money orders was then signed and cashed by either Checks Cashed Etc., LLC or G & R Check Cashing Corp. However, the signatures placed on the money orders were unauthorized. When Travelers Express learned of the theft it placed stop payment orders on the money orders, which were subsequently dishonored by the drawee bank.

Checks Cashed Etc., LLC and G & R Check Cashing Corp. then assigned their rights in the money orders to Robert J. Triffin, who commenced suit against twelve individuals whose signatures appear on the money orders, but made no attempt to serve them with process. Triffin also sought relief against Travelers Express Company, Inc., which defended the claim by asserting that the money orders were stolen and the signatures appearing on the money orders were unauthorized.

ISSUE Was Triffin a holder in due course? Was Triffin entitled to recover the amount of the money orders from Travelers Express?

HOLDING No, Triffin was not a holder in due. No, Triffin was not entitled to recover from Travelers Express.

REASONING Excerpts from the opinion of Fisher, Appellate Division Judge

Travelers asserted . . . without contradiction, that the seventeen money orders were stolen from a Brooklyn pharmacy. Once alerted to the theft, Travelers stopped payment, but the money orders were presented to and cashed by Triffin's assignors. . . .

When a lost or stolen money order, unsigned by the purchaser, is later presented by the thief or finder, the majority view is that the issuing bank is not liable. . . . This approach was followed in *Trump Plaza Assocs. v. Haas* . . . where we rejected the contention that personal money orders are "the equivalent of cash or have the credit of the issuing bank behind them." Instead, we re-enforced an earlier holding that "a personal money order is a check and that a bank should not be deemed to have accepted a money order merely because its name and logo are printed on the face of the instrument." . . .

The money orders in question contain . . . [a] description of Travelers' role in the transaction— "Issuer/Drawer: Travelers Express Company, Inc."—which logically persuades that, in a normal transaction, Travelers is ultimately intended to be the drawer of the money orders. . . . And, while it is true that the nature of a transaction between Travelers and a purchaser . . . required that the purchaser deposit the amount of the money order with Travelers and pay the required fee for the service . . . the purchaser, by taking those steps, becomes authorized to execute the money order as the agent or representative of the drawer, Travelers. When these events lawfully occur, the terms of the instrument require Travelers to pay the money order. Triffin, thus, correctly argues that Travelers is the drawer in . . . [the] transaction. However, Triffin incorrectly disregards the significance of the particular transactions between the thieves or finders of these stolen money orders and his assignors, as well as the undisputed fact that none of these money orders contains an authorized signature.

687

It is true that a document may be signed in a great variety of ways, including by embossing a name on an instrument. But an effective signature requires that an instrument be "executed or adopted by a party with present intention to authenticate." . . . While Travelers' name is embossed on the money orders and alongside the words "Issuer/Drawer," the remainder of the document clearly indicates that an additional signature—that of the purchaser—is required to authenticate the writing. . . . To be authenticated and effective, the instruments required authorized signatures in the "purchaser, signer for drawer" space. Since there was no dispute that the money orders in question were stolen and the signatures were not made by purchasers—because the money orders were not purchased—we must conclude that the money orders do not contain authorized signatures.

While the signatures in the "purchaser, signer for drawer" spaces on these money orders were made by persons who were not purchasers, these signatures may still have significance because the Uniform Commercial Code does not conclude that such signatures are nullities. Instead, the Code describes such signatures as "unauthorized." . . . An unauthorized signature, however, is "ineffective except as the signature of the unauthorized signer in favor of a person who in good faith pays the instrument or takes it for value." . . . Accordingly, Triffin could not obtain relief on these money orders against anyone other than the persons who actually signed on the lines marked "purchaser, signer for drawer." . . .

We . . . note that any . . . negligence on the part of the owner of an instrument could only preclude it "from asserting the alteration or the forgery against a person who, in good faith, pays the instrument or takes it for value or for collection," i.e., a holder in due course. . . . Here, Triffin could not claim that his assignors were holders in due course. The good faith requirements of holder in due course status were not present here, as demonstrated by the absence of any evidence that Triffin's assignors heeded any of the warnings on, or sought any information about, the money orders. . . .

Each money order contained a warning on the reverse side:

> This Money Order will not be paid if it has been forged, altered, or stolen and recourse is only against the presenter. This means that persons receiving this money order should accept it only from those known to them and against whom they have effective recourse.

Each money order contained a statement . . . advising that information concerning the money order could be obtained from Travelers, whose address and toll free telephone number were also provided. Thus, a simple, toll free telephone call would undoubtedly have revealed that the instruments were stolen. Triffin's assignors, especially because they are in the business of making a profit by cashing such instruments, cannot claim holder in due course status by blithely and blindly cashing such instruments. The very appearance of these money orders . . . , should have caused Triffin's assignors, to be suspicious about their legitimacy, and should have prompted them to seek information from Travelers. By failing to do so, Triffin's assignors could not be deemed holders in due course. . . .

You Be the Judge

Under a sales agreement, exporter Mega Power, Inc. (Mega Power), agreed to ship electronic goods from Korea to importer Audiobahn in America. Mega Power sold its right to receive Audiobahn's payment for the shipment to Kookmin Bank by issuing bills of exchange (the term "bill of exchange" is a synonym for "draft"), in the amounts of $256,414.98 and $63,254.40, respectively. The bills of exchange specified Kookmin Bank as payee, payable within a specified period of time upon acceptance by Audiobahn. Mega Power also provided Kookmin Bank with bills of lading for the shipped goods, so that Audiobahn would receive title to the shipped goods only after it had accepted the bills of exchange. Audiobahn accepted the bills of exchange, thus obligating itself to pay for the shipped goods.

Audiobahn failed to satisfy the bills of exchange, first because of cash flow problems, and later because of offsets arising from previous disputes it had with Mega Power and related companies. Because Audiobahn failed to pay the bills of exchange, Korea Export Insurance Corporation (KEIC), as underwriter, paid the amount owed to Kookmin Bank (Korea Export Insurance Corporation (KEIC) underwrites bills of exchange purchased by Korean banks from Korean exporters to finance the shipments of goods to other countries, including the United States). KEIC also obtained from Mega Power letters of assignment giving KEIC Mega Power's rights under its sales agreement with Audiobahn.

Asserting its subrogation and assignment rights, KEIC sued Audiobahn for the two unpaid letters of exchange. Following a bench trial, the court determined that Kookmin Bank was a holder in due course of the letters of exchange, and that KEIC stood in Kookmin's shoes. The court, however, determined that KEIC was required to provide Audiobahn notice of KEIC's rights to receive payment "at its earliest opportunity." The court held that prompt notice to Audiobahn was a condition subsequent to KEIC maintaining its holder in due course status. Finding neither Mega Power nor KEIC provided prompt notice of KEIC's interest, the trial court entered judgment in Autobahn's favor.

KEIC has appealed this decision to your court. How will you resolve this case? Kookmin Bank was a holder in due course, but KEIC never took the trade acceptances by negotiation, so how can KEIC assert the rights of a holder in due course? What was the most important fact or factor influencing *your* decision? [See *Korea Export Ins. Corp. v. Audiobahn*, California Court of Appeal, 4th App. District, 2008).]

[NOTE: In ruling in Audiobahn's favor, the trial court also expressed concern for the financial harm Audiobahn would suffer by losing its offsets against Mega Power, which had declared bankruptcy. The appellate court ruled that this concern does not support the abrogation of KEIC's statutory rights.]

Summary

A negotiable instrument can be transferred in a number of ways. The original transfer from the maker or the drawer is an issue. Once issued, it can be further transferred by assignment or by negotiation. An assignment gives the assignee no special rights or protections. In contrast, a negotiation may confer some individual rights on the recipient. When a negotiation occurs, the transferee becomes a holder.

Most negotiations involve the use of an indorsement. Indorsements may affect further negotiation, and they may affect the possible liability of the parties. Special, blank, and restrictive indorsements affect negotiations. Qualified and unqualified indorsements affect liability.

Once a negotiation occurs, the holder has the opportunity to achieve the most favored status in commercial paper: He or she may become a holder in due course. An HDC is a holder who takes an instrument in good faith, for value, and without notice of any defenses or defects on the instrument.

A holder in due course can defeat a personal defense. A real defense will defeat a holder in due course. In addition, a person who takes an instrument *after* a holder in due course is normally allowed to assert the rights of an HDC due to the shelter provision. Thus, once an HDC has possessed the instrument, subsequent parties can assert the rights of an HDC regardless of their status, with a few minor exceptions.

The Federal Trade Commission enacted a special rule in 1976 to protect consumers. The rule denies any protection against any defenses, even for an HDC, on a consumer credit instrument.

Article 7 provides for special protections in handling negotiable documents of title. A person who acquires a negotiable document of title and who purchases the document in good faith without notice of any defenses or defects qualifies as a holder by due negotiation. This status confers benefits beyond the benefits acquired in the document itself.

Discussion Questions

1. Is the distinction between a mere transfer and a negotiation important in determining the rights of a party in possession of a negotiable instrument? Why might this distinction matter to the party in possession of the instrument?

2. How can a holder indorse an instrument to minimize his or her potential secondary liability on the instrument in the event of a dishonor upon presentment? What, if anything, will such an indorsement tell the indorsee?

3. Amita issued Carol a check payable to the order of Carol. Carol sold the check to Lynn, but neglected to indorse it at the time of the sale.

At that point, what legal status would Lynn possess? What duty, if any, would Carol owe to Lynn? Would Carol have any different duties or obligations if she had given the check to Lynn as a gift, again without any indorsement?

4. Terry issued a check to Phil. Phil indorsed the check and delivered it to Irene. The name on the payee line of the check had originally read "Ben," but Terry had crossed out Ben's name and replaced it with Phil's name. To show what he had done, Terry initialed the change on the payee line. Under these circumstances, can Irene qualify as a holder in due course on the check? Explain your reasoning.

5. Charles had a note issued by David. Charles discovered that David was about to go through a bankruptcy, so he negotiated the note to Richard. Richard qualified as a holder in due course. David filed for bankruptcy, and Richard sued David to collect on the note. What are Richard's rights against David? Why?

Case Problems and Writing Assignments

1. Harry H. Wagner is the president of Harry H. Wagner & Son, Inc., a residential and commercial construction company located in Lima, Ohio. Wagner has worked for the company, which was founded by his father, for thirty-one years. In the past 20 years, Wagner & Son has built approximately 156 duplex units, which it owns and leases as residential rental property. The properties had been financed through various local banks at interest rates of 8.0 percent, adjustable in small increments every three to five years. Wagner had no difficulty paying these loans. Wagner eventually sought to refinance these rental properties for estate planning purposes, and approached American Heritage Mortgage Company of Ohio for assistance in arranging and securing this refinancing. Wagner hoped to secure a fixed interest rate of seven to eight percent to increase the properties' long-term profitability. Wagner eventually agreed to borrow the money from AMC Bank at a fixed rate of 10.9 percent. Wagner agreed to these terms, at least in part, because he thought that AMC had orally agreed to refinance the loans at a fixed rate between seven and eight percent after the loans had "seasoned" for about twelve months. On February 10, 1997, Wagner closed on the loans with AMC by executing approximately 60 notes totaling $11 million at an annual interest rate of 10.9 percent per annum. Thereafter, AMC sold the mortgage notes on the secondary market to various banks. The properties failed to generate the income necessary to support the note payments at the new, higher rates, and Wagner eventually defaulted on the payments. The various banks that had purchased the notes then declared the debts due and initiated foreclosure proceedings. Wagner objected to the foreclosure proceedings, claiming, among other things, that he had defenses on the notes including fraud, misrepresentation, promissory estoppel and breach of contract. According to Wagner's assertions, the oral promises from AMC Bank provided him with defenses on the notes and those defenses were good against the various banks that had purchased the notes. Each of the banks claimed to be a holder in due course on any notes held by that bank, and they denied that Wagner's alleged defenses were valid against them. How should this case be resolved? Did the various banks act in good faith in their dealings with AMC? Were the various banks holders in due course of the notes they held? Were the alleged personal defenses raised by Wagner valid against these banks? What ethical issues are raised by the facts in this case? [See *Bankers Trust Company v. Harry H. Wagner & Son, Inc., et al.*, 2001 Ohio App. LEXIS 5947 (Ohio App. 3d App. Dist. 2001).]

2. On October 30, 2006, Southern Plumbing issued a check for $288.00 to Robert Olivarez as an advance for work to be performed. Several hours later, Olivarez informed Southern Plumbing that he could not perform the work and he would destroy the check. Robert Zamora, on behalf of Southern Plumbing, told Olivarez he would place a stop-payment order on the check. However, Olivarez endorsed and cashed the check at The Money Box. When The Money Box presented the check to the bank for payment, the check was returned with the notation, "payment stopped." According to The Money Box, it notified Southern Plumbing by certified mail that the check had been returned, and that The Money Box expected payment of the check and a $20.00 returned check fee. The envelope, however, reflects the letter was "returned to sender, not deliverable as addressed, unable to forward."

When the check and returned check fee were not paid, The Money Box sued Southern Plumbing for the amount owed on the check plus interest, the returned check fee, and reasonable attorneys' fees.

The Money Box alleged it was entitled to judgment as a matter of law because it is the holder of Southern Plumbing's check, it took the check in good faith, without knowledge of any claims or defenses to the instrument, and it paid value for the check.

Southern Plumbing argued that it should not be held liable in this case. According to southern Pluming, Olivarez "did not present, endorse in the presence of, nor deliver the check to [The Money Box]" because he was in custody at the Bexar County Jail after being arrested. It also argued that The Money Box must have "cashed the check without acquiring proper identification or verification by any form of photo identification" since Olivarez was in jail at the time the check was cashed. Finally, Southern Plumbing asserted that it could not be held liable because it was never given notice prior to the filing of the lawsuit that The Money Box was a possible holder in due course.

How should this case be decided? Was The Money Box required to notify Southern Plumbing that it was claiming holder in due course status prior to filing its suit? [*See* Zamora v. The Money Box, County Court at Law No. 7, Bexar County, Texas (2009).]

3. On August 6, 2001, defendant Frederick Jones signed a lease with Mullinax for a new 2001 Ford Taurus. Under the lease, Jones agreed to make 36 monthly payments of $523.70. Jones's sister, Moore, cosigned the lease. Mullinax then assigned the lease to Ford Motor Credit.

Jones repeatedly failed to make his payments on time and in December 2003, stopped making payments entirely. Ford Credit repossessed the Ford Taurus on November 16, 2004, and then sold the car at auction for $5,700, leaving a deficiency balance of $7,997.52.

Ford Credit sued Jones and Moore for the deficiency balance. Jones did not appear, and the court entered a default judgment against him. However, Moore denied liability and filed a crossclaim against both Mullinax and Ford Motor Credit Company. [Moore's crossclaim against Mullinax was based on alleged violations of Ohio's Retail Installment Sales Act (RISA) and its Consumer Sales Practices Act (CSPA). She made the same claim against Ford Motor Credit. These issues are not addressed in this case problem.] Moore alleged that Ford Motor Credit was "derivatively liable" because Mullinax had "knowingly taken advantage of her inability to understand the terms of the lease," and then assigned the note and lease to Ford Motor Credit. Ford Motor Credit denied liability, asserting that it was a holder in due course on the note, and Moore's alleged defense was only a personal defense. [The note signed by Jones and Moore did not contain the required anti-holder-in-due-course language required by the FTC on a consumer credit instrument.]

Should the court find that Ford Motor Credit Company was "derivatively liable" on the note, or does Ford Motor Credit's HDC status shield it from such liability? What effect does the absence of the anti-holder-in-due-course language in the note have on the claim of FMCC? [See *Ford Motor Credit Co. v. Jones*, Court of Appeals of Ohio, 8th District (2009).]

Notes

1. UCC § 3-203(a).
2. UCC § 3-203(b).
3. UCC § 3-201, and Official Comment 1.
4. UCC § 3-103(4), and Official Comment 4.
5. An accommodation party is one who signs a negotiable instrument in any capacity for the purpose of lending his name and credit to another party to the instrument; an accommodation is a surety.
6. UCC § 3-305(a)(3).
7. UCC § 3-203, Official Comment 2.
8. 384 So.2d 388 (La. 1980).

22

Negotiables: Liability and Discharge

Agenda

eClass is likely to receive a few "bad" checks in the course of its business, and the firm will need to know what its rights are in those situations. Since the firm is involved in a technology-intensive industry, Ani, Meg, andYousef would like to accept "telechecks" as payment for their goods, but they are unsure what their rights and/or liabilities might be with a telecheck. They are especially concerned with what happens if a telecheck is dishonored.

The firm has borrowed money from its bank in order to make some needed improvements. However, the bank recently informed the firm that it had "sold" the firm's note to another financial institution. The principles would likc to know what this will do to their potential liability and to the liability of the firm. They would also like to know what impact this will have on their possible future dealings with their bank.

These and other questions will arise during our discussion of these topics. Be prepared! You never know when the firm or one of its members will seek your advice.

VAN METER DRILLING CO. v. J.R. KUBELKA

544 So. 2d 547, 1989 La. App. LEXIS 964
(5th Cir. La. App., 1989)

FACTS Kubelka worked under the supervision of Cliff Van Meter for Sea Drilling Corporation. In 1981 the two men joined with Richard Hoskin, A. T. Webber, Jr. and W. A. Hines to form Van Meter Drilling Company as a sub-S corporation.

At the initial incorporation of the company, each principal made a cash contribution to capital. Defendant's check for $7,000.00 written on January 30, 1981 represented his share. Subsequently, each man executed a promissory note secured by a letter of credit to the Company. This claim is based on Kubelka's note for $25,500.

The business purpose of the Company was to act as general managing partner in Van Meter Limited Partnership I (Partnership). The Partnership was formed to own and operate land drilling rigs. Two such rigs were purchased by the Partnership with permanent financing from Manufacturers Hanover Leasing Corporation, (Manufacturers). The Company guaranteed the loan using the promissory notes and letters of credit as collateral.

In 1983 the price of oil decreased; the Partnership fell on hard times and defaulted on its loan. Manufacturers repossessed the oil rigs and called in the letters of credit given by Van Meter, Webber and Hines. The letters of credit issued on the accounts of Hoskin and Kubelka had expired. The balance of the Company's debt was forgiven by Manufacturers.

Offers were made by the Company to both Hoskin and Kubelka to fulfill their obligations on the promissory notes by paying half of the face amount. Hoskin accepted and Kubelka refused the offer. Consequently, the Company filed this action on Kubelka's promissory note.

Kubelka asserts that no consideration for the note existed. He further contends that the assertion of the affirmative defense of lack and/or failure of consideration shifted the burden of proof to the Company to show that consideration existed at the time the note was executed and did not wholly or partially cease to exist subsequent to execution of the note.

ISSUE Must the holder of a note prove that consideration was given at the time the note was issued before it can enforce the note against the maker?

HOLDING No. Consideration is assumed when a negotiable instrument is issued. The maker or drawer would need to prove an absence of consideration.

REASONING Excerpts from the opinion of Sol Gothard, Judge:

Kubelka asserts that no consideration for the note existed. He further contends that the assertion of the affirmative defense of lack and/or failure of consideration shifted the burden of proof to the Company to show that consideration existed at the time the note was executed and did not wholly or partially cease to exist subsequent to execution of the note. A burden which, Kubelka asserts, was not met by the Company.

That conclusion depends on a version of the facts presented in defendant's brief which are not consistent with the facts presented at trial. Kubelka contends that the promissory note in question was executed merely as a method to secure financing for the purchase of drilling rigs to be owned and operated by the Partnership. Thus, there was never any consideration for the note which was used solely as a security device. . . .

At trial, Cliff Van Meter testified that the Company was to be capitalized by a combination of cash and promissory notes from each of the share holders. The note executed on September 4, 1981 by Kubelka represented partial payment for his stock. . . .

The defendant testified in his own behalf. He stated that he was unsure of the exact purpose of the promissory note but understood it to be necessary to secure financing. However, he admitted on cross-examination that he did not expect to receive his 5.6% of the shares of the Company for only $7,000 cash and knew that the note of $25,500 was "to make up the thirty-two, five that would buy the 5.6 percent eventually." . . .

Under the circumstances we find that the promissory note was given in partial payment for stock received. We find further neither the absence of, or failure of consideration which would preclude recovery by the Company on the note executed by Kubelka.

The note meets the statutory requirements for negotiability. It is signed by the maker, contains an unconditional promise to pay a sum certain in money on demand and is payable to order. . . . Being in possession of an instrument issued to its order, the Company is the holder of the note . . . and has a right to enforce payment. . . .

When Manufacturers forgave the balance of the debt on the principal obligation owed by the Partnership, the Company was released from its obligation as surety. The extinction of the principal obligation extinguishes the suretyship. . . . That transaction in no way affected Kubelka's obligation on the promissory note. . . .

BASIC CONCEPTS

Negotiable instruments are used as a substitute for money. However, at some point, the holder of the instrument is going to want the money for which the instrument has been substituted. Normally, this desire will lead to a presentment to the maker or drawee. In most cases, the maker or drawee then will pay the money as called for by the instrument, the instrument will be canceled, and its commercial life will terminate. Unfortunately, such a series of events does not happen every time. Some makers or drawees refuse to pay the presented instrument—they dishonor it. When this occurs, the issue of secondary liability arises. Some holders inadvertently fail to make a proper presentment. When this occurs, the issue of discharge arises. These possibilities are shown in Exhibit 22.1. You may want to refer back to this exhibit as you move through this chapter, keeping the roles and responsibilities of the various parties in mind.

Exhibit 22.1

The Movement of a Negotiable Instrument

Issue → *Negotiation(s)* → *Presentment* → *Acceptance and Payment*
(Primary Liability Accepted)

Or

→ *Dishonor (Primary Liability Denied,*
Secondary Liability Claims Arise)

Issue	The initial negotiation of an instrument by delivery. Normally delivery is to the payee, although it may also be delivered to a remitter.
Negotiation	The transfer of an instrument by indorsement and delivery (payable to order) or by delivery alone (payable to bearer), in which the transferee becomes a holder.
Presentment	Demand made to the primary party (drawee on order paper/maker on promise paper) for the acceptance and/or payment of the instrument.
Acceptance	Commitment by the primary party to accept and/or pay the instrument as presented. Releases secondary parties from potential secondary liability.
Dishonor	Refusal by the primary party to accept the instrument as presented; activates secondary liability of the prior parties on the instrument.

THE CHAINS OF LIABILITY

The term liability, when used with negotiable instruments, refers to an obligation to pay the negotiable instrument involved. There are several possible types of liability in commercial paper. The obligation to pay may be based either on primary liability or on secondary liability. The liability also may be based on contract principles, warranty principles, or the admissions of one of the parties.

Primary Liability

Every negotiable instrument has a primary party, and every negotiable instrument has secondary parties. The primary party is the party who is expected to pay the instrument upon proper presentment. The secondary parties are the parties who face conditional liability if or when the primary party refuses to pay the instrument upon proper presentment.

The maker of a note is the primary party on that note. It is the maker to whom the holder will look for payment, and it is the maker who is normally expected to pay the note on its due date. Similarly, the drawee is the primary party on a check or a draft. It is the drawee to whom the holder will first look for payment of the order instrument, and it is the drawee who is normally expected to pay the order instrument, either on demand or on its due date.

A substantial difference exists between the position of the primary party on a note and that of a primary party on a check or a draft. On a note, the maker is primarily liable as soon as the note is issued. This is because the primary party, the maker, is also the person who gives the promise to pay. The maker is in a contractual relationship with the payee from the time he or she issues the instrument. By contrast, the drawee is normally *not* primarily liable on a check or a draft at the time the check or draft is issued. Primary liability will not arise until a holder presents the instrument and the drawee accepts the instrument as presented. (This is not true if the instrument is a cashier's check, certified check, or teller's check.)

The reason the drawee is not normally liable on an order instrument upon issue is that there are usually two contractual relationships involved in order paper: the first contract is the contract between the drawer and the payee, the reason for the issuance of the instrument; the second contract is between the drawer and the drawee, the reason the drawee is expected to obey the drawer's order upon proper presentment. No contractual relationship exists between the drawee and the payee on the negotiable instrument issued by the drawer unless or until the drawee accepts the instrument, thereby agreeing to honor the order given by the drawer. Thus, a note has a commitment of primary liability from the time of its issue (the maker is legally obligated to the payee or any subsequent holders), but a check or a draft has a mere *expectation* that primary liability will exist at a future time. (The drawee has not yet made a commitment to the payee or any subsequent holders; its commitment is to the drawer.)

On most negotiable instruments the primary party does, in fact, pay the instrument, honoring the primary liability of the instrument. Occasionally, however, the primary party does not honor his or her primary liability. When this happens, the holder of the dishonored instrument may seek recovery from one of the secondary parties on that instrument.

Secondary Liability

The drawer of a check or a draft is obligated to pay that draft or check if the instrument is dishonored.[1] This means that the drawer of the instrument is a secondary party on the instrument. In addition, the payee and any indorsers of any negotiable instrument—a check, a draft, a note, or a certificate of deposit—are each secondary parties on that instrument. Secondary parties face potential secondary liability on the instrument. A secondary party agrees, by acting either as the drawer, the payee, or as an indorser, to pay the instrument if certain conditions are met. Remember, though, that secondary liability is conditional liability. The secondary parties can only be held liable if the conditions are satisfied or if the secondary party waives the need for the conditions to be met. To hold a secondary party liable on his or her contract (represented by the indorsement or signing of the instrument), a person holding the instrument must prove all three of the following actions:

1. Presentment of the instrument was properly made or presentment was excused.
2. The primary party dishonored the instrument upon proper presentment.
3. Notice of the dishonor was properly given to the secondary party or notice has been waived or excused.

It should also be recalled that there are two types of potential secondary liability: contractual liability and warranty liability. Any indorsement that is unqualified (indorsements are presumed to be unqualified) gives a contract to the indorsee and to every subsequent holder that, upon proper presentment and dishonor, the indorser will "buy" the instrument back. However, indorsers who use a qualified indorsement deny this contractual liability. Nonetheless, they, too, face potential secondary liability based on the warranties they give upon transfer and/or presentment. (This warranty liability will be discussed later in the chapter.)

Obligation of the Drawer

The drawer of a draft faces potential secondary liability for any drafts issued if the draft is dishonored upon presentment. Section 3-414 spells out the obligations of the drawer, stating that:

> If an unaccepted draft is dishonored, the drawer is obligated to pay the draft (i) according to its terms at the time it was issued or, if not issued, at the time it first came into possession of a holder, or (ii) if the drawer signed an incomplete instrument, according to its terms when completed. . . . The obligation is owed to a person entitled to enforce the draft or to an indorser who paid the draft under Section 3-415.[2]

If the draft is accepted upon proper presentment, and the acceptance is by a bank, the drawer is discharged.[3] However, if the draft is accepted by a drawee and the drawee is not a bank, the drawer is not automatically discharged. Instead, if the drawee accepts the draft and later dishonors the instrument, the drawer faces the same liability as would be faced by an indorser under the provisions of § 3-415.[4] If the drawer wishes to avoid liability, he or she can issue a draft—but not a *check*— "without recourse." The drawer of a check cannot deny secondary liability in this manner. By using this qualifying language, the drawer is denying his or her potential secondary liability on the draft from the date of issue, thus negating the liability provisions of § 3-414 (b). And since the qualifying language is on the face of the instrument, the payee is aware of the denial of secondary liability from the time the draft is issued.

Obligation of the Indorser

In a similar manner, the indorsers of a negotiable instrument have certain obligations. The indorsers of any negotiable instrument face potential secondary liability for any instruments indorsed that are dishonored upon presentment. Section 3-415 spells out the obligations of the indorsers, stating that:

> (a) Subject to subsections (b), (c), (d), (e), and to Section 3-419(d), if an instrument is dishonored, an indorser is obliged to pay the amount due on the instrument (i) according to the terms of the instrument at the time it was indorsed, or (ii) if the indorser indorsed an incomplete instrument, according to its terms when completed . . . The obligation of the indorser is owed to a person entitled to enforce the instrument or to a subsequent indorser who paid the instrument under this section.

There are a few exceptions to this basic rule as set out in subsection (a). If the indorser used a qualified indorsement to indorse the instrument, he or she is not liable under subsection (a) to pay the instrument.[5] The indorser is also not liable:

1. if notice of any dishonor is required in order to hold the indorser liable, and such notice is not given;[6]
2. if the instrument is accepted by a bank after the indorsement was made;[7] or
3. if the indorsed instrument is a check and the check is not presented to the drawee bank or deposited within thirty days of the day the indorsement was made.[8]

These chains of liability are shown in Exhibit 22.2.

Exhibit 22.2

The Chains of Liability on Negotiable Instruments

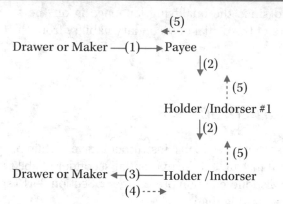

The potential primary liability moves in a clockwise manner, following the *solid* lines: (1) is the issue, (2) is/are negotiations, (3) is presentment. If the drawee (order paper) or the maker (promise paper) accepts the instrument it is accepted and paid, discharging all further liabilities.

If the drawee or maker dishonors the instrument on presentment (4), secondary liability (5) is activated. Secondary liability moves counterclockwise, following the *dashed* lines. Note that the number of holders/indorsers may be larger or smaller than the number shown in this exhibit.

ESTABLISHING LIABILITY

As we showed in Exhibit 22.1, negotiable instruments have a normal movement pattern. The instrument is issued, and it may then be negotiated to one or more holders. At some point in time a holder is expected to make *presentment* of the instrument to the primary party. When presentment is made, one of two things will occur. Either the primary party will *accept* the instrument (and pay it, either at the time of acceptance or at a later time), or the primary party will *dishonor* the instrument, refusing to pay it. If the instrument is accepted, primary liability is accepted and the instrument will be paid and removed from circulation. If the instrument is dishonored, primary liability is refused and secondary liability is activated. These stages are examined in detail in the following sections.

Presentment

Presentment is a demand for acceptance or for payment of a negotiable instrument. The demand is made to the maker of a promise instrument, or to the drawee of an order instrument, or to the acceptor of a previously accepted instrument. The party making presentment is called the presenter. The rules governing presentment have been changed somewhat in the current version of Article 3 to more accurately reflect the treatment of negotiable instruments today. The current rule regarding presentment is found in Section 3-501. This section is set out below, with a brief explanation of each subsection immediately following that subsection.

Section 3-501. Presentment

(a) "Presentment" means a demand made by or on behalf of a person entitled to enforce an instrument (i) to pay the instrument made to the drawee or a party obliged to pay the instrument or, in the case of a note or accepted draft payable at a bank, to the bank, or (ii) to accept a draft made to the drawee.

(The holder *demands* payment and/or acceptance from the drawee of order paper or the maker of promise paper. If the instrument is a note payable at a bank or is an accepted draft, the holder demands payment from the bank.)

(b) The following rules are subject to Article 4, agreement of the parties, and clearing-house rules and the like:

(1) Presentment may be made at the place of payment of the instrument and must be made at the place of payment if the instrument is payable at a bank in the United States; may be made by any commercially reasonable means, including an oral, written, or electronic communication; is effective when received by the person to whom presentment is made; and is effective if made to any two or more makers, acceptors, drawees, or other payees.

(The holder is to make presentment at the proper place. This means at the place of payment of the instrument. If the place of payment is a U.S. bank, presentment *must* be made at that bank. Presentment may be made in any reasonable manner, and is deemed effective when the presentment is received by the primary party.)

(2) Upon demand of the person to whom presentment is made, the person making presentment must (i) exhibit the instrument; (ii) give reasonable identification and, if presentment is made on behalf of another person, reasonable evidence of authority to do so, and . . . sign a receipt on the instrument for any payment made or surrender the instrument if full payment is made.

(The presenting party must satisfy the reasonable demands or requests of the primary party in order to establish the rights of the presenting party. This includes showing the instrument, showing proof of identity, and signing a receipt for any payments made on the instrument.)

(3) Without dishonoring the instrument, the party to whom presentment is made may (i) return the instrument for lack of a necessary indorsement, or (ii) refuse payment or acceptance for failure of the presentment to comply with the terms of the instrument, an agreement of the parties, or other applicable rules of law.

(If the instrument lacks a necessary indorsement at the time of presentment, the primary party can refuse to accept the instrument, and this refusal is *not* treated as a dishonor. It is also deemed *not* to be a dishonor if the primary party refuses the accept or pay the instrument due to an improper presentment for other reasons, including the terms of the instrument itself, an agreement of the parties, or any applicable rules of law regarding presentment.)

(4) The party to whom presentment is made may treat presentment as occurring on the next business day after the day of presentment if the party to whom presentment is made has established a cut-off hour not earlier than 2 p.m. for the receipt and processing of instruments presented for payment or acceptance and presentment is made after the cut-off hour.

(This allows primary parties, especially banks and other financial institutions, to establish an "end of business day" time, and to treat any activities after that time as occurring on the next business day. Thus, a presentment made at 3:00 P.M. on a Tuesday is treated as being made on Wednesday. Since the primary party has a deadline for taking action after a proper presentment, it is important to know the day on which presentment was made.)

The previous version of Article 3 required that presentment be made by mail, or through a clearinghouse, or at a place specified in the instrument. The presentment "at a place specified in the instrument" implied, at least, that the presentment had to be made by the holder by having the holder be physically present *with the instrument* at that place. Thus, presentment required the production of the instrument itself if the presentment was to be proper. This has changed dramatically in the revision to Article 3. Presentment can now be made in the "traditional" manner by using the mail, or a clearinghouse, or by physically appearing at the place specified in the instrument. But presentment can also be made *orally* or *electronically*. Obviously, the instrument itself will not be physically present in either an oral or an electronic presentment. Thus, if the parties have agreed to an oral or an electronic presentment, the requirement that the instrument be exhibited by the presenter at the request of the primary party [§ 3-501(b)(2)(i)] does not apply. This would allow an acceptance of the instrument—or a dishonor—by the primary party without that person actually seeing the instrument.

If the presentment is made through the mail, presentment occurs when the mail is received. (This places the danger of postal delay on the presenting party.) If the presentment is to be made at a specified place and if the person who is to receive it is not there at the proper time, presentment is excused. This makes the drawee or the maker responsible for being at the proper place at the proper time. It also removes a possible worry from the presenting party—that the drawee or the maker will be absent when presentment is due, and will then deny that a presentment was ever made to that drawee or maker. If a note is payable at a bank in the United States or a draft is to be accepted at such a bank, the note or draft must be presented at that bank.

The rules of presentment are very important because presentment must be properly made before a dishonor can be shown. Dishonor also must be shown before any secondary party (except the drawer) can be held on his or her liability. The only exception to this rule is if presentment is excused.

The rules that govern presentment are fairly straightforward. The holder must make presentment within a reasonable time, or the presentment is improper. The reasonable time concept has two components: The time must be reasonable in both a clock sense (time of day) and a calendar sense (day of the week). In every case, presentment must be made at a reasonable time of day—that is, during normal working hours. An alleged presentment made at a bank or business address at 3 A.M. would be improper and would not be effective to prove a dishonor. Article 3 as revised has no time requirements for presentment, leaving the determination of whether presentment was made in a timely manner for interpretation based on the terms of the instrument and on other provisions of the Code.

Instruments that are payable at a definite time must be presented on or before the due date in order to establish that proper presentment was made. Demand instruments are treated differently. The holder of a check must present the check to the drawee bank within 90 days of its date or its issue, whichever is later, to hold the drawer liable on that check. A delay beyond this 90-day period will not excuse the drawer from liability on the underlying obligation, but it will excuse the drawer (and any secondary parties) from liability on that particular check. The drawer may be forced to redeem the check by paying cash or by issuing a new negotiable instrument to replace the original check.

Indorsers also have an interest in proper presentment. An indorser of a check is released from the contract liability of the indorsement if the check is not presented within thirty days of the date of indorsement. In order to hold the indorsers liable for the indorsement contract on other demand instruments, presentment must be made within a reasonable time from the date of the indorsement. If the instrument is payable at a definite time, the presentment must be made by that time in order to hold the indorser to the indorsement contract.

Once presentment is made, the focus shifts to the maker, drawee, or acceptor. If the presentment is made for acceptance alone (as when a presenter asks a bank to certify a check), the drawee (the bank in this example) has until the close of business the next business day to accept the instrument. (If the holder agrees—in good faith—another business day may be granted to the drawee to decide whether to accept the instrument.) If the presentment is made for acceptance and payment (or for payment alone, if acceptance occurred previously), payment must be made before the close of the business day on which the presentment was made. (Some short delay in paying the instrument is permitted if the drawee, acceptor, or maker needs to investigate whether payment would be proper.) Any delay beyond these time limits is treated as a dishonor of the instrument presented.[9]

Persons receiving a presentment do have some protection. They can require some proof from the presenter of the presenter's right to have the check; requesting this proof is not treated as a dishonor. They can require the presenter to show them the instrument. They can demand reasonable identification of the presenter. They can require a showing of authority to make the presentment. They can demand the surrender of the instrument upon payment in full. If the presenter fails or refuses to comply with any of these requests, the presentment is considered improper. However, the presenter is allowed a reasonable time to comply with any of the requests.

Acceptance

When the drawee decides to accept an instrument, the drawee must sign the instrument. By signing the draft or check, the drawee agrees to honor the instrument as presented. This act of acceptance fixes the primary liability of the drawee. (Remember: An order instrument has no primary liability until it has been accepted by the drawee.)

The acceptance can be made even if the instrument is incomplete, but it must be made for the instrument as presented. Suppose the drawee tries to change the terms of the draft in the acceptance. The presenter can treat this as a dishonor or can agree to the changed terms. However, if this draft-varying acceptance is agreed to by the presenter, the drawer and every prior indorser are discharged from secondary liability on the draft.

If a draft is accepted by a bank, the drawer and any indorsers who indorsed the draft prior to its acceptance are all discharged from secondary liability.

Dishonor

An instrument is dishonored when proper presentment is made and acceptance or payment is refused. A dishonor also occurs when presentment is excused and the instrument is not accepted or paid. [Under UCC § 3-501(b)(3)(i), the return of an instrument for lack of a proper indorsement is not a dishonor.] The failure of the primary party to accept the instrument within the proper time is also a dishonor. A check returned because of insufficient funds or because of a stop-payment order is dishonored. A refusal by the primary party to accept the instrument is a dishonor, subject to the limitations in § 3-501(b)(3). Dishonor is a denial of primary liability, and it activates the secondary liability of indorsers and of the drawer (refer back to Exhibit 23.2, The Chains of Liability on Negotiable Instruments). Remember that before dishonor, the secondary parties faced only potential secondary liability. The act of dishonor may, and usually will, move this liability from potential to actual.

eClass 22.1 Finance/Law

DISHONORED CHECKS

One of the checks received as a payment on an account from a customer was returned by the bank for insufficient funds. As is the firm's usual practice, Ani has redeposited the check twice, and both times it was returned dishonored. This is the first time the firm has received a check that the bank did not honor on either the first of the second time it was deposited, and Ani is not sure what the firm needs to do. Yousef remembers hearing something about the need to give notice of a dishonor within three days of the dishonor in order to preserve your rights on a dishonored instrument against prior parties. Meg agrees that notice must be given, but she is not sure that there is a three day time limit. However, both Meg and Yousef are concerned that by redepositing the check the firm has waived its right to collect from the drawer, and that the amount of the check has been lost. They have asked you for advice. What will you tell him?

BUSINESS CONSIDERATIONS.   A number of businesses will hold a dishonored check for a short time and then "re-run" the check through the bank in the hope that the drawer has made a deposit and that the check will be honored the second time through banking channels. Is this a good practice or a bad practice? Why? Should the business give the customer who wrote the check notice that the check has been dishonored, but that the firm plans to "re-run" the check soon?

ETHICAL CONSIDERATIONS.   Most banks impose a service charge on their customers for every check presented against the customer's account and dishonored. Is it ethical to present a check more than once, thus potentially increasing the service charges imposed on the customer by the bank, and to have the business also impose a service charge as the payee for a check that is dishonored? When does submission of a check stop being good business and start being an attempt to punish the drawer for writing a bad check?

Notice

The holder of a dishonored instrument has an obligation to give notice to prior parties in order to establish their secondary liability. The notice may be given to any or all persons who may be secondarily liable on the instrument, and it may be given by any person who has received notice. Thus, if the presenter/holder gives notice of dishonor to Indorser 2, Indorser 2 may then give notice to Indorser 1, and so on. The notice may be given in any commercially reasonable manner, including an oral, a written, or an electronic communication. It may be given in any terms or in any form, as long as it reasonably identifies the instrument and states that it has been dishonored or has not been paid or accepted.

Article 3 is concerned with protecting the rights of the holder of a dishonored instrument. Allowance is made for an error in the description of the instrument in the notice. A misdescription will not affect the validity of the notice unless it misleads the person being notified. The notice must be given in a timely manner. Again, there has been a significant change in the time limit for notice under the revised Article 3. This new provision is found in Section 3-503, which provides that:

> **(c)** Subject to Section 3-504(c), with respect to an instrument taken for collection by a collecting bank, notice of dishonor must be given (i) by the bank before midnight of the next banking day following the banking day on which the bank receives notice of dishonor of the instrument, or (ii) by any other person within 30 days following the day on which the person receives notice of dishonor. With respect to any other instrument, notice of dishonor must be given with 30 days following the date on which dishonor occurs.

Section 3-504(c) excuses giving notice of the dishonor within these time limits, if the delay is caused by circumstances beyond the control of the person giving notice, and if that person acts with reasonable diligence once the reason for the delay is removed. [Prior to the revision, the time limit for a bank was the same—its midnight deadline on the next banking day. However, other parties only had three days after they learned of the dishonor to give notice, or they lost their secondary liability contract claim. The new rules are obviously much more favorable for secondary parties.]

It is normal for each party to give notice to the party who transferred the instrument to him or her. However, sometimes this transferor cannot be found or, when found, cannot pay. For that reason, a holder should give notice to every prior party who can be located. This increases the chances that the holder eventually will recover on the dishonored instrument.

A failure to give proper or timely notice will operate as a release from the conditional secondary liability for all the secondary parties except the drawer, unless the need to give notice is either excused or the need to receive notice is waived. Failure to give notice, or giving improper notice, may release other secondary parties, but it does not release the drawer or maker.

Frequently, the duty to make presentment or to give notice is waived or excused. When these situations arise, § 3-504 of the Code governs the situation. Under subsection (a), a delay in making presentment is excused if any of the following are true:

1. The person entitled to make presentment cannot with reasonable diligence make presentment.

2. The maker or acceptor has repudiated an obligation to pay the instrument, or has died, or is involved in an insolvency proceeding.

3. The terms of the instrument state that presentment is not necessary in order to enforce the obligation of the indorsers or the drawer.

4. The drawer or indorser whose obligation is being enforced has waived present-ment or otherwise has no reason to expect or right to require that the instru-ment be paid or accepted.

5. The drawer instructed the drawee not to pay or accept the instrument or accept the draft or the drawee was not obligated to the drawer to pay the draft.

Under subsection (b), notice of dishonor is excused if any of the following are true:

1. By the terms of the instrument, notice is not necessary to enforce the obligation of a party to pay the instrument.

2. The party whose obligation is being enforced waived notice of dishonor.

3. Presentment was waived, which also constitutes a waiver of notice.

TYPES OF LIABILITY

A negotiable instrument is a contract with special treatment under the law. One recognition of contract law principles is found in UCC § 3-401. This section states that "a person is not liable on an instrument unless (i) the person signed the instrument, or (ii) the person is represented by an agent or representative who signed the instrument and the signature is binding on the represented person . . .". However, once such a signature is found, the signing—or represented—party faces potential liability. The type of liability depends on the capacity in which it was signed. Again, the Code helps. As was pointed out earlier, § 3-204 states that every signature is presumed to be an indorsement unless the instrument clearly indicates that the signature was made in some other capacity by the signing party.

It is important to remember that there are two types of contracts involved with negotiable instruments. The first type of contract is represented by the instrument itself. The maker of promise paper and the acceptor of order paper give a contract. Each agrees to pay the instrument according to the terms of the instrument at the time of his or her engagement, or as completed if it was incomplete. The drawer of order paper promises to pay any holder or any indorser the amount of the instrument if it is dishonored. The second type of contract is the contract encompassed in the indorsement.

eClass 22.2 Finance

SEEKING RECOVERY FOR A BAD CHECK

One of the checks the firm deposited into its account has been returned by the bank. The check has an "Account Closed" stamp on its face. The check was originally issued by James Smitts, payable to the order of Harriet Rudzinski. Ms. Rudzinski, a customer of the firm, had indorsed the check "Pay to eClass, Harriet Rudzinski" and forwarded it to the firm as payment for a software purchase she had ordered. Meg has asked you what the firm can do to recover the amount of this check, and from whom the firm should seek recovery. She also wants to know if the firm should refuse to accept indorsed checks payable to the order of someone other than eClass in the future. What advice will you give her?

BUSINESS CONSIDERATIONS.   Many businesses have a policy of not accepting what they call "two-party checks," checks that were drawn to the order of a payee who now wants to indorse the check over to the business. What reasons might a business have for this policy? Do the protections afforded by Article 3 make such a policy unnecessary?

ETHICAL CONSIDERATIONS.   Is there an ethical issue raised when a person indorses a check over to a new holder rather than depositing the check into his or her own account and then writing a check to that person? Is it ethical for a business to refuse to accept a check indorsed by the payee when there are legal protections for the business if the check is dishonored?

Indorsement Liability

The indorsers of commercial paper also give a contract by the act of indorsing, unless the indorsement is qualified. By the act of indorsing, the indorser promises that upon dishonor, and proper notice, he or she will pay the instrument as indorsed to any subsequent holder. The indorsers are presumed to be liable to one another on a dishonored instrument in the order indorsed, moving from bottom to top.

Two other parties may be involved in contractual liability on commercial paper: the accommodation party and the guarantor. Each of these parties has special potential contract liability. An accommodation party is a person who signs an instrument to "lend his name," or his credit, to another party. He signs as a favor, usually without getting anything out of the transaction. The accommodation party is liable to subsequent parties in the capacity in which he signed. If required to pay because of his secondary liability, he is entitled to recover from the party for whom he signed as an accommodator. A person signing an instrument is presumed to be an accommodation party and there is notice to all subsequent holders that the instrument was signed for accommodation if the signature is an anomalous indorsement (any indorsement made by a person who is not a holder of the instrument is considered anomalous), or if the signature is accompanied by words indicating that the indorser is acting as a surety or as a guarantor with respect to the obligations of another party to the instrument.

If the signature of a party to an instrument is accompanied by words indicating unambiguously that he or she is guaranteeing collection, rather than guaranteeing the payment of the obligation of another party to the instrument, that party is endorsing as a guarantor. Article 3 has reduced the obligation of a guarantor somewhat. A guarantor is obliged to pay the amount due on the instrument to any person entitled to enforce the instrument, but only if:

1. An execution of judgment against the party whose obligation was guaranteed has been returned unsatisfied, or
2. The party whose obligation was guaranteed is insolvent or involved in an insolvency proceeding, or
3. The party whose obligation was guaranteed cannot be served with process, or
4. It is otherwise apparent payment cannot be obtained from the party whose obligation was guaranteed.[10]

[NOTE: The Federal Trade Commission has enacted its Federal Trade Commission Credit Practices Rule, which went into effect in 1985, in an effort to provide some protection to accommodation parties, especially co-signers on notes. This rule requires lenders to provide disclosure to co-signers and other accommodation parties as to the serious nature of signing as an accommodation.]

Warranty Liability

In addition to the basic contract liabilities just discussed, persons who present or transfer negotiable instruments make certain warranties. These warranties also carry with them the possibility of liabilities, and warranty liabilities cannot be disclaimed as easily as contract liabilities. An indorser may deny contract liability by the use of a qualified indorsement, but warranty liability is still present even if the indorsement is qualified, unless the qualified indorsement also specifically excludes warranties. An indorser could qualify the indorsement so that warranties are also excluded, even though endorsing with such a qualification to later holders makes the indorsement highly unusual. The indorser who would use such an indorsement would be well protected, but the instrument would be very difficult to transfer since few subsequent holders would be willing to accept such a negotiation.

The warranties involved in negotiable instruments are set out in § 3-416 and § 3-417 of the UCC. Section 3-416 provides for transfer warranties, while § 3-417 provides for presentment warranties. Any person who transfers an instrument for consideration gives transfer warranties to his or her transferee. In addition, if the transfer is by indorsement the transferee gives the transfer warranties to every subsequent transferee. Notice that the instrument does not need to be negotiated, and the transferee does not have to give value in order to have transfer warranties arise.

The transfer warranties provide protection to the transferee(s) in the following five areas:

1. The warrantor (transferor) is a person entitled to enforce the instrument.
2. All signatures on the instrument are authentic and authorized.
3. The instrument has not been materially altered.
4. The instrument is not subject to a defense or claim in recoupment of any party which can be asserted against the warrantor.
5. The warrantor has no knowledge of any insolvency proceedings commenced with respect to the maker or acceptor or, in the case of an unaccepted draft, the drawer.

Transfer warranties cannot be disclaimed on checks. Notice of any breach of the transfer warranties must be given to the warrantor within 30 days after the claimant has reason to know of the breach of warranty in order to have maximum protection. After 30 days the liability of the warrantor is reduced by any amount the warrantor can show was lost due to the delay.

If an unaccepted draft is presented to the drawee for payment or acceptance and the drawee pays or accepts the draft, the person making presentment and any previous transferees of the draft give presentment warranties to the drawee. The presentment warranties provide the following three protections to the drawee:

1. The warrantor is, or was, at the time the warrantor transferred the draft, a person entitled to enforce the draft or authorized to obtain payment or acceptance of the draft on behalf of a person entitled to enforce the draft.
2. The draft has not been altered.
3. The warrantor has no knowledge that the signature of the drawer is unauthorized.

Again, these warranties cannot be disclaimed on a check, and again notice of a claim for breach of the warranty must be given within 30 days of the time the drawee has reason to know of the breach. Any losses suffered by the warrantor as a result of a delay beyond the 30 days reduce the liability of the warrantor.

The new provisions of Article 3 have removed presentment warranty protections from promise paper, have removed the added protections that were formerly available with a qualified indorsement, and have added a time limit within which the person claiming damages based on a breach of warranty must give notice in order to have maximum protection.

Exhibit 22.3 summarizes the order of liability on a negotiable instrument.

Exhibit 22.3

Liability on a Negotiable Instrument

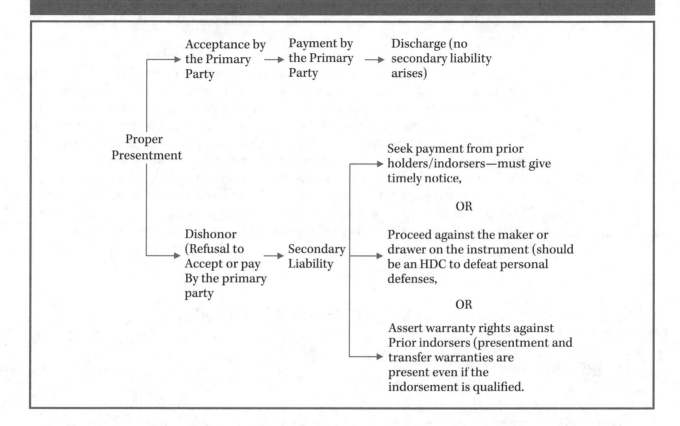

SPECIAL PROBLEMS

As was pointed out earlier, a person's signature or the signature of a person authorized to represent him or her, must appear on an instrument before that person can be held liable on the instrument. Thus, a forgery or an unauthorized signature is normally of no legal effect. However, an unauthorized signature can be ratified by the named person, and it then becomes fully effective. The rules governing unauthorized signatures can be found in § 3-403. These rules are relatively simple and straightforward:

(a) Unless otherwise provided in this Article or Article 4, an unauthorized signature is ineffective except as the signature of the unauthorized signer in favor of a person who in good faith pays the instrument or takes it for value. An unauthorized signature may be ratified for all purposes of this Article.

(a) If the signature of more than one person is required to constitute the authorized signature of an organization, the signature of the organization is unauthorized if one of the required signatures is lacking.

(b) The civil or criminal liability of a person who makes an unauthorized signature is not affected by any provisions of this Article which make the unauthorized signature effective for the purposes of this Article.[11]

Any unauthorized signatures are ineffective against the person whose name is signed, unless that person chooses to ratify the signature after the fact. The unauthorized signature is effective against the person who did, in fact, sign, and will expose that person to liability for the signature or it will transfer any rights that the signer might possess in the instrument, provided that the person who takes the instrument takes it for value or who pays the instrument in good faith. Unauthorized signings include both forgeries and signatures made without actual, implied, or apparent authority.[12]

Even with such a straightforward set of rules, there are some special circumstances that arise often enough to require special rules and special treatment. In particular, situations involving *imposters* and situations involving *fictitious payees* demand special rules and special treatment beyond the provisions for unauthorized signatures.

eClass 22.3 Management/Law

FORGERIES

eClass received a check from a customer recently as payment for a purchase. Yousef was concerned when the check was received because there seemed to be something unusual about the signature. However, he decided not to do anything about it and the check was included in the firm's deposit. Unfortunately, the check was eventually returned by the bank with a notation that the drawer's signature was a forgery. Yousef is concerned that he may have done something wrong or that the firm may now face liability on the check because he failed to act on his suspicions initially. He asks you if he has done anything wrong and if the firm is now at risk. He also would like to know what the firm's rights are on the check. What will you tell him?

BUSINESS CONSIDERATIONS   Should a business have a policy of requiring identification and a specimen signature from any of its customers who want to pay by check? How could such a policy be implemented if the business receives payments by mail?

ETHICAL CONSIDERATIONS   Is it ethical for a business to refuse to accept a check if the business doesn't like the way an indorsement looks? Should businesses select customers on the basis of the legibility of the customer's signature?

An "imposter" is a person who pretends to be the person to whom an instrument is payable. The imposter pretends to be the actual payee in order to induce the issuer of the instrument to deliver the instrument to the imposter, believing that the instrument is being delivered to the intended payee. Situations involving imposters arise when there is a legitimate reason for issuing the instrument and the person named as payee has a legitimate claim to the instrument, but the issuer is tricked into issuing the instrument to a person claiming to be the payee. A "fictitious payee" is a person who obtains an instrument that either (a) is made payable to the order of a legitimate person, but one who has no legitimate claim to the particular instrument, or (b) is made payable to a nonexistent person, a "fictitious" payee.

Section 3-404 provides the coverage for both imposters and for fictitious payees. According to § 3-404:

> **(a)** If an imposter, by use of the mails or otherwise, induces the issuer of an instrument to issue the instrument to the imposter, or to a person acting in concert with the imposter, by impersonating the payee of the instrument or a person authorized to act for the payee, an indorsement of the instrument by any person in the name of the payee is effective as the indorsement of the payee in favor of a person who, in good faith, pays the instrument or takes it for value or for collection.
>
> **(b)** If (i) a person whose intent determines to whom an instrument is payable ... does not intend the person identified as payee to have any interest in the instrument, or (ii) the person identified as payee of an instrument is a fictitious person, the following rules apply until the instrument is negotiated by special indorsement:
>
> **(1)** Any person in possession of the instrument is its holder.
> **(2)** An indorsement by any person in the name of the payee stated in the instrument is effective as the indorsement of the payee in favor of the person who, in good faith, pays the instrument or takes it for value or for collection.

These two subsections seem to place the risk of loss on the issuer of the instrument when an imposter or a fictitious payee is involved. While this is generally true, the provisions of each of these subsections are limited to some extent. If the person who pays the instrument or who takes it for value or for collection does not exercise ordinary care in acquiring the instrument, and if the failure to exercise ordinary care substantially contributes to the loss resulting from paying the instrument, the person suffering that loss can recover the portion of the loss suffered because ordinary care was not exercised.

The following hypothetical cases illustrate these two special problem areas.

Fred stole a radio from Herb. Fred then approached Thelma, told her that he was Herb, and offered to sell the radio to her. Thelma wrote a check payable to the order of Herb to pay for the radio. Under the impostor rule, Fred may effectively indorse the check by writing Herb's name, UCC § 3-403 on unauthorized signatures notwithstanding. Thelma intended to write a check to Herb, Fred pretended to be Herb, so Fred is an imposter and his indorsement of the check in Herb's name is effective against Thelma.

Steve works for Acme. Part of his job is preparing checks to be sent to various suppliers and creditors of the firm and then taking those checks to Mr. Burton to be signed for the company. Steve slipped a check payable to Hall and Associates in among the other checks for Mr. Burton to sign. In fact, no money was owed to Hall and Associates. If Steve later removes the phony check and indorses it "Hall and Associates," the indorsement is valid under the fictitious-payee rule, UCC § 3-403 notwithstanding. Steve intended to have a check drawn payable to the order of Hall and Associates, while he also intended for Hall and Associates to have no interest in the check. Thus, the check is payable to a fictitious payee, and Steve's indorsement of the check in the name "Hall and Associates" is effective against Acme.

A related problem area is the area of fraudulently indorsed instruments, especially by dishonest employees. Again, the problems in this area are common enough and significant enough to require special attention and treatment under the Code. Section 3-405 addresses the employer's responsibility for fraudulent indorsements by employees. The section uses a broad definition of employees, including independent contractors and employees of independent contractors who are retained by the employer. "Fraudulent indorsement" is defined as:

> **(i)** in the case of an instrument payable to the employer, a forged indorsement purporting to be that of the employer, or
>
> **(ii)** in the case of an instrument with respect to which the employer is the issuer, a forged indorsement purporting to be that of the person identified as the payee.

Section 3-405 imposes responsibility on the employer for these fraudulent indorsements if a subsequent party took the instrument containing the fraudulent indorsement in good faith, and either pays the instrument or takes it for value or for collection. The fraudulent indorsement is effective against the employer, who will then need to seek recovery from the employee who appended the fraudulent indorsement to the instrument.

One other "special problem" needs to be addressed. On some occasions a instrument is lost, stolen, or destroyed prior to its presentment, and the person who was in possession of the instrument prior to its loss, theft, or destruction would like to collect the amount owed despite the absence of the instrument itself. The situation arises frequently enough that the Code has two sections addressing the problem.

Section 3-309 deals with the enforcement of lost, destroyed, or stolen instrument. Section 3-312 is more specific, dealing with lost, destroyed, or stolen cashier's checks, teller's checks, and certified checks. Under the provisions of § 3-309, a person who is *not* in possession of an instrument will still be allowed to enforce the instrument, if:

(i) the person was in possession of the instrument and entitled to enforce it when the loss of possession occurred,

(ii) the loss of possession was not the result of a transfer by the person or a lawful seizure, and

(iii) the person cannot reasonably obtain possession of the instrument because the instrument was destroyed, its whereabouts cannot be determined, or it is in the wrongful possession of an unknown person or a person that cannot be found and is not amenable to service of process.[13]

Of course, the person seeking to enforce the missing instrument must prove the terms of the instrument and also must prove his or her right to enforce the instrument. And the person seeking to enforce the instrument will not be able to procure a judgment unless the court is assured that the person who will have to pay is adequately protected against loss in the event that another person should surface with a valid claim seeking to enforce the instrument.[14]

Section 3-312 is similar, but more complicated. The drawer or the payee of a certified check, or the remitter or the payee of either a teller's check or a cashier's check must make a written "declaration of loss" regarding the missing check. This declaration is made under penalty of perjury and states that the party making the declaration lost possession of the check and that the loss was not the result of a transfer or a lawful seizure, and that possession of the check cannot reasonably be obtained. If the bank pays the claimant the amount of the check and the check itself is subsequently presented to the bank by a person possessing the rights of a holder in due course, the claimant must refund the proceeds to the bank or to the HDC.[15]

DISCHARGE

The term discharge means to remove liability or potential liability on a negotiable instrument. A discharge can take place in a number of ways. Some methods discharge all the parties, and others discharge only a few. The most important and most common types of discharge are explained in the following sections.

Payment

The most common type of discharge is the payment or other satisfaction of the instrument. In the vast majority of cases, the primary party pays the instrument on presentment and cancels it (or otherwise marks it as paid). If this were not so, negotiable instruments would not be so readily accepted in the commercial world. There are only two exceptions to payment operating as a discharge. A payment will not operate as a discharge when it is made in bad faith to a thief or to a person holding through (receiving the instrument from) or after (receiving the instrument from a party who received it from) a thief. Also, it will not operate as a discharge if the paying party makes a payment that violates a restrictive indorsement. (Note: An intermediary bank or a nondepository bank may be discharged even though it ignores the restrictive indorsement, provided it acts in good faith.) In these examples, the bad faith of the payer does not remove liability. The proper party, the person who should have received payment, is still entitled to payment, and the liability of the wrongfully paying party remains.

Tender of Payment

If a party tenders payment in full to a holder when an instrument is due, or later, and the holder refuses the payment, a discharge occurs. The party tendering payment is discharged to a limited extent. No additional interest can be added to the instrument after the date of the tender, nor can any other costs or attorney's fees be added to the instrument. Any other parties on the instrument (indorsers, drawers, and the like) are totally discharged if, to collect on the instrument, they could theoretically have sued the party who refused the tender of payment if the instrument was dishonored.

Cancellation and Renunciation

A holder may discharge a party by canceling that party's signature on the instrument or by canceling the instrument itself. Cancellation may be shown either by striking out a portion, such as one signature, or by striking out the entire instrument. It can also be shown by destroying or mutilating a signature or the entire instrument. To be effective, the cancellation must be done intentionally.

Renunciation operates as a discharge whenever the holder delivers a written and signed statement to the discharged party that renounces (gives up) any rights against that person. Such a discharge is good against the renouncing party but not against any later holders, unless they were aware of the renunciation.

Impairment

Under the UCC section on impairment, a holder may elect to release some party from liability on the instrument. Or a holder may decide to release some collateral that is being used to secure payment of the instrument. However, in so doing, the holder also will discharge some or even all of the secondary parties on the instrument. When the holder releases a particular prior party, the holder also releases any other prior party who might have had recourse against the originally released party. In addition, when a holder releases collateral, the holder releases every prior party, since each prior party might have had recourse against the collateral. The following are the only two exceptions to these rules:

1. If a prior party agrees to the release of another party or to a release of the collateral, this prior party is not discharged by the release.

2. If the holder expressly reserves rights against a party, that party is not released or discharged. However, the releases by the holder are also not effective as far as the nondischarged party is concerned. In other words, the party who was expressly not discharged does not have any change in his or her position.

Other Discharges

If a party is a former holder of an instrument and later reacquires it, a partial discharge occurs. Any person who held the note between the two holdings of the reacquiring party is discharged from liability to the reacquiring party. Also, if the reacquiring party strikes out the indorsements of the intervening persons, they are totally discharged on the instrument. For example, if George holds a note, indorses it to Betty, and then buys it back from Betty, Betty is discharged from liability to George.

A fraudulent material alteration also acts as a discharge. If the alteration is fraudulent and material, any party who does not consent to the alteration is totally discharged from liability under most circumstances. A holder in due course may still enforce the instrument as it was originally issued, even though it has been materially altered.

Finally, an undue delay in making presentment operates as a discharge for all prior indorsers. An undue delay in giving notice of a dishonor will also operate as a discharge of all prior indorsers, and may even discharge a drawer or maker.

Contemporary Case

J. WALTER THOMPSON, U.S.A., INC. v. FIRST BANKAMERICANO

518 F.3d 128, 2008 U.S. App. LEXIS 4540 (2d Cir. 2008)

FACTS On October 31, 2001, J. Walter Thompson, U.S.A (JWT), an advertising agency, issued a check in the amount of $ 382,210.15 payable to one of its vendors, Outdoor Life Network. The Check was issued from JWT's checking account at Bank of America (BoA). At an unknown date, an unknown person altered the payee on the Check to "Diversified Business Enterpises [sic], Inc" and deposited the Check into an account maintained by Diversified Business Enterprises at First BankAmericano (FBA). FBA then presented the Check to the Federal Reserve Bank of New York, which, in turn, presented it to the Federal Reserve Bank of Atlanta. The Atlanta Fed then presented it to Bank of America via BoA's check processing facility in Georgia. BoA debited $ 382,210.15 from the Account of JWT and transmitted the payment through the bank collection system to FBA, which, presumably, deposited the funds into the account held by Diversified Business Enterprises. Later, JWT discovered that the payee of the Check had been altered, notified BoA the same day of the alteration and the fact that BoA had made a payment on the altered Check, and sought to have its Account credited for the amount of the Check. BoA did not credit the Account but, instead, demanded that FBA remit the proceeds of the Check to BoA. FBA refused to do so.

At the time of the events at issue, BoA had a program in place to identify potentially fraudulent checks (the "Positive Pay Program" or "Positive Pay"), and JWT subscribed to this service during the relevant time period. Positive Pay permitted BoA to match check numbers, dates, and amounts on the checks that were presented to BoA with a list provided by JWT prior to payment of a check. If the Positive Pay Program identified a discrepancy in any of this information, BoA would not make payment on the check. At the time of the instant fraud, Positive Pay did not have the capability of matching payee names, a capability that arguably would have detected the fraud here.

When BoA refused to credit JWT's account for the amount of the Check JWT sued, alleging that BoA was negligent and had violated its duties under the UCC. BoA, in turn, filed a third-party complaint against FBA and the Atlanta Fed for violations of the transfer warranty and presentment warranty provisions of Articles 3 and 4 of the UCC.

FBA and the Atlanta Fed argued that JWT and BofA each had been negligent in not taking additional steps to prevent check frauds such as this, and that such negligence should shield them from liability.

ISSUE Did JWT's failure to take certain preventive measures constitute negligence which "substantially contributed," to the alteration of the check?

HOLDING No. There was no showing that JWT failed to exercise ordinary care or that it had been negligent in handling its account with BofA.

REASONING Excerpts from the opinion of Jose A. Cabranes, Circuit Judge:

FBA and Atlanta Fed contend that, upon learning of the prior instances of fraud, JWT should have (1) closed the Account and (2) instituted a payee matching system to detect future fraud. They argue that JWT's failure to take these steps constituted negligence that substantially contributed to the alteration of the check and JWT should . . . be estopped from asserting the alteration against BoA.

The Fourth Circuit addressed the issue of drawer negligence in . . . a case arising from the theft and alteration of a check drawn on an account from which six checks had been stolen previously. . . . The defendant in that action contended that the drawer's failure to implement certain precautionary measures to prevent check theft— specifically, sending checks via an electronic funds transfer system or Federal Express rather than through the mail—constituted a failure to exercise ordinary care that "substantially contributed to the alteration." The Fourth Circuit rejected this argument. Because the prior thefts "constituted a very small percentage" of the checks issued by the drawer, were relatively remote in time, and were committed by individuals then believed to be in custody, the drawer's decision to continue using regular mail to send its checks hardly amounted to "a failure to exercise ordinary care, much less a failure to exercise ordinary care that substantially contributed to the alteration." . . .

Here, FBA and the Atlanta Fed contend that, in light of the prior instances of fraud, JWT should have (1) closed the Account and (2) instituted a payee matching system to detect future fraud. Based on the facts before us, however, we conclude that ordinary care did not compel JWT to adopt either of these measures. [A few] previous incidents of altered checks resulted in *de minimis* losses compared to the significant costs which JWT would have incurred by closing the Account. In addition, FBA came forward with no evidence showing that had JWT closed the Account and drawn checks on a different account, the new account would have been less susceptible to check theft, thereby averting the theft giving rise to this litigation. Under these circumstances, closing the Account would not have been a reasonable, much less a necessary, exercise of ordinary care. . . . JWT reasonably relied on BoA's Positive Pay fraud detection service with the technological limitations that existed at the time. . . .

We further hold that a defense based on a drawer's alleged post-alteration negligence is foreclosed by the plain language of U.C.C. § 3-406. When a drawer's own negligence "substantially contributes" to the alteration of a check, the drawer is "precluded from asserting the alteration" against a collecting or presenting bank, such as FBA, that processes the check in good faith. . . . The lack of payee matching cannot, as a matter of logic, have "substantially contributed" to the alteration at issue in this litigation. A payee matching mechanism identifies check fraud when an altered check is presented to the drawee/payor bank for payment, in other words, after the alteration has already occurred. Because this technology detects alterations after the fact, but does not prevent them in the first instance, JWT's alleged failure to adopt payee matching cannot have "contributed" or "set the stage" for the alteration. We therefore conclude that JWT's alleged failures to take certain preventive measures suggested by FBA here did not constitute negligence which substantially contributed to the alteration of the Check.

You Be the Judge

Clean World is an environmental engineering company specializing in providing pollution control services. Clean World was looking for a new accountant for the firm. Nicholas Fredich placed an ad for a fictitious bookkeeping position, and used the information obtained from one of the applications to steal the identity of an accountant, Robert Landrum. Using this stolen identity, Fredich applied for and obtained a job with Clean World as its new accountant. (Clean World has run a credit check on Robert Landrum, and had also contacted a person who was allegedly a former employer of Robert Landrum, but who was, in fact, a co-conspirator with Fredich. Since the credit check and the reference both provided positive information, Clean World hired the applicant.) After several weeks on the job, "Landrum" informed his supervisor that his mother-in-law had died suddenly, and he ("Landrum") would need a few days off. In fact, Fredich had obtained a number of checks from the firm's checking account with MidAmerica Bank, had accessed the software for preparing checks on the firm's account, had forged the signature of the officer authorized to sign company checks, and had deposited checks totaling $137,445.02 and drawn against the company account into his account with TCF Bank.

WhenClean World learned of the forgeries, it sought recovery of its money from MidAmerica Bank, alleging that the bank had wrongfully paid the checks over a forged signature. MidAmerica, in turn, sought to recover the funds it had paid out from TCF Bank, alleging that TCF had breached its presentment warranties since it presented checks that contained forged signatures.

MidAmerica Bank denied that it was liable because Clean World's conduct in allowing virtually unlimited access to the blank checks and the software caused, or substantially contributed to, the forgeries. Clean World denied that its negligence, if there was any, was a contributing factor to the forgeries.

TCF denied that it was liable to MidAmerica since MidAmerica failed to assert, and also failed to prove, that TCF had knowledge of the forgeries, thus negating the presentment warranty protections.

This case has been brought in *your* court. How will *you* decide the case? What fact or factor most influenced your decision in each of the controversies?

[See *Clean World Engineering, Ltd. V. MidAmerican Bank*, FSB, 341 Ill. App. 3d 992, 793 N.E.2d, 110 (2003)]

Summary

As formal contracts, negotiable instruments carry certain contract responsibilities and liabilities. The maker of promise paper has primary liability on the instrument from its issue date. The drawee of order paper faces potential primary liability. However, once the drawee accepts the instrument, the drawee has primary liability. If the primary liability is denied or refused, every prior holder is secondarily liable. In addition, the drawer of order paper is secondarily liable on a dishonored instrument.

For the holder to enforce the primary liability of the instrument, proper presentment must be made to the maker or drawee. Proper presentment can now be made electronically, as well as through one of the traditional methods. Proper presentment also may include demands made on the presenter for him or her to establish identity. This can include requiring a "thumbprint signature" as part of the identification. At that point, the primary party will either accept the instrument or dishonor it. If dishonor occurs, the holder will give notice to prior parties to establish their secondary liability.

If an instrument is lost, stolen, or destroyed, the party who is entitled to enforce the instrument may still be allowed to seek collection from the primary party. In order to do so, that person will need to establish the loss of possession was not due to a transfer or a lawful seizure, and that he or she cannot reasonably obtain possession of the missing instrument. The person will also need to prove the terms of the instrument *and* his or her right to enforcement. Similar rules apply if the missing instrument is a cashier's check, teller's check, or certified check.

Negotiable instruments carry both contract liability and warranty liability. The warranty liability may be transfer warranty liability or presentment warranty liability. Transfer warranties exist on all negotiable instruments that are transferred for consideration. Presentment warranties only apply to order paper that is presented to the drawee for acceptance or payment.

The final stage for most instruments is discharge. Discharge can be, and normally is, based on payment or satisfaction. Some discharges are partial, discharging either a portion of the liability or a few of the parties. Tender of payment is a partial discharge. Cancellation, renunciation, and impairment are all discharges of some of the secondary parties.

Discussion Questions

1. What is meant by "primary liability" under Article 3, and when does it exist on a negotiable instrument? What is meant by "secondary liability" under Article 3, and when does it exist on a negotiable instrument? Is it possible for a party to be both primarily and secondarily liable on the same instrument at the same time?

2. In order to show proper presentment, what must the presenting party establish? What are the rights of the primary party when a presentment is made? How have these rights changed in light of the increase in check fraud?

3. Who or what is an "imposter" under Article 3? Who or what is a "fictitious payee" under Article 3? How is an indorsement by an imposter or by a fictitious payee treated? What reasons exist for this special treatment of the indorsements of imposters and fictitious payees?

4. Presume that a holder makes proper presentment of a negotiable instrument and that the instrument is dishonored upon presentment. The holder now has three options. What are the three options available to the holder of an instrument that has been dishonored after proper presentment? Under what circumstances should the holder pursue each—or all—of the options available? Explain your reasoning.

5. When a person indorses a check, that person gives an additional contract to the indorsee, the contract of indorsement. How long is that indorsement contract valid? What must the indorsee (or a subsequent transferee) do in order to hold the indorser of the check to the indorsement contract?

Case Problems and Writing Assignments

1. Pauline Pagani was an employee of Maryland Industrial Finishing Company, Inc. (MIFCO) from 13 April 1989 through 23 February 1990. In June of 1989, Pagani began embezzling funds by depositing some of MIFCO's checks into her own account at Citizens Bank of Maryland, rather than depositing the checks into MIFCO's account at Citizens. She continued this practice until February of 1990, when Brenda Alexander discovered the embezzlement. MIFCO later sued Citizens to recover the funds that were deposited into Pagani's personal account. MIFCO alleged, among other things, that Citizens converted the checks under the UCC, and that Citizens was negligent. At trial, Brenda Alexander testified that MIFCO is a small company with seven employees and that it has had an account with Citizens since 1976. Alexander also testified that she instructed Pagani that when MIFCO received a check from a customer, she should retrieve the invoice from the file, mark it paid, and write on it the check information, and to then place the invoice in the "paid" file. Pagani was also instructed to indorse the check by stamping the back with two stamps—one with the name and address of MIFCO and the other containing the words, "For deposit only." Pagani was then directed to deposit the indorsed checks into MIFCO's account at Citizens Bank and to file a copy of the deposit slip in MIFCO's files. MIFCO contends that the indorsements by Pagani were "unauthorized" since she did not make the

indorsements restrictive, as she had been instructed to do, and thus the bank should be liable for accepting checks with unauthorized indorsements. The bank argues that the indorsements were authorized, and that is should not be held liable for the disloyalty and/or dishonesty of an employee of the MIFCO.

How should the court decide this case? In reaching your decision you should address the following issues:

> Was the bank liable under conversion, negligence, or breach of warranty theories? What ethical issues are raised by the facts in this case? How might the parties have acted differently if they were more concerned with ethics than with law?

[See *Citizens Bank of Maryland v. Maryland Industrial Finishing Co.*, Inc., 659 A.2d 313 (Md. 1995).]

2. Texas Stadium Corporation ("TSC") is the lessee of Texas Stadium in Irving, Texas. Candace Pratt worked as an accounts payable clerk for TSC from late 1988 until August 1993. As part of her job, Pratt prepared TSC checks, which were later signed by authorized officers of TSC. While employed at TSC, Pratt embezzled money from TSC. As part of her embezzlement scheme, Pratt established a d/b/a account at Savings of America (SOA) in the name of Candace A. Pratt d/b/a AAA Lawn Maintenance Service and Repair ("AAA"). To effect her embezzlement scheme, Pratt would prepare a check for an actual vendor, and after having the check signed by an authorized officer of TSC, Pratt would alter the check by either changing the payee name to a version of the AAA name or by adding the AAA name above the original payee name. Pratt also used other methods to embezzle money from TSC. One such method was to prepare a TSC check in a version of the AAA name and then deposit it into her account once it was signed. Once Pratt obtained the appropriate signatures and deposited the checks in her d/b/a account, SOA then forwarded the checks to TSC's bank, and the checks were paid in due course. In all,

Pratt deposited 206 checks in her account, totaling $1,060,052.10. After discovering Pratt's scheme, TSC filed suit against Pratt and SOA to recover the money Pratt embezzled. TSC alleged causes of action against Pratt and SOA for negligence, conversion, money had and received, and breach of warranty. In July 1994, SOA moved for summary judgment on all of TSC's claims. After hearing the evidence and arguments of counsel, the trial judge granted summary judgment in favor of SOA without specifying the basis for his ruling. TSC and Pratt then entered into an agreed judgment. TSC appeals the summary judgment granted in favor of SOA. Was Savings of America liable to TSC on the checks under any of the theories advanced by TSC in its complaint? Should the "fictitious payee" rule protect SOA in this case? What should Texas Stadium Corporation have done differently in order to prevent this sort of loss? [See *Texas Stadium Corporation v. Savings of America*, 933 S.W.2d 616 (Tex. App.-Dallas 1996).]

3. Woods Code 3, d/b/a Americom, gave its former bookkeeper, Terrie Johnson, signature authority to transact business on Americom's bank account with Woodforest National Bank, N.A. From 2000 to 2005, Johnson wrote hundreds of Woodforest account checks that she then deposited into her personal checking account with Chase. Some of the checks were made payable to Johnson and indorsed by her signature, but many of them were signed in blank or made payable to fictitious accounts or payees before being indorsed and deposited into Johnson's personal account. Chase accepted each of these checks for deposit into Johnson's account, and Woodforest, in turn, honored each of the checks, paying Chase the amount called for.

When this scheme was discovered, Americom sued Chase (now operating as JP Morgan Chase Bank, N.A.), seeking recover of the funds deposited into Johnson's account. Americom alleged that Chase was guilty of "aiding and abetting breach of fiduciary duty" under the applicable Texas state statute. In support of its assertion, Americom pointed out that tellers at Chase accepted checks for deposit into Johnson's account that were not made payable to Johnsons' order; Americom also asserted that some of the checks were not indorsed, since Johnson had only put her account number on the back of these checks, never signing her name or otherwise adding an indorsement. Chase responded that none of the tellers had any evidence that the checks Johnson was depositing were not authorized;

Chase also argued that the placement of only the account number on the back of the check was a sufficient indorsement for checks that were only being deposited into the designated account.

How should the court decide this case? What are the most important facts or factors that should influence the court's decision? [See *Woods Code 3 v. JPMorgan Chase Bank*, Tex. App., 9th District (2009).]

Notes

1. UCC § 3-414(b).
2. Ibid.
3. UCC § 3-414(c).
4. UCC § 3-414(d).
5. UCC § 3-415(b).
6. UCC § 3-415(c).
7. UCC § 3-415(d).
8. UCC § 3-415(e).
9. UCC § 3-502(a).
10. UCC § 3-419(d).
11. UCC § 3-403.
12. UCC § 1-201(43).
13. UCC § 3-309(a).
14. UCC § 3-309(b).
15. UCC § 3-312.

23

Bank-Customer Relations/ Electronic Fund Transfers

Agenda

eClass will need to open at least one account, and more than likely it will need several different accounts, with its bank. What sorts of accounts might the firm need? There are several different types of financial institutions in the community, including credit unions, savings and loans, and commercial banks. What sort of financial institution should eClass deal with? Each of the principals in the firm has an ATM card and at least two different types of credit cards. Should the firm also have an ATM card or a credit card?

What are the rights and responsibilities of the firm in its dealings with a bank? Are the rights and responsibilities of a business different than the rights and responsibilities of an individual customer?

How can the firm transfer funds quickly and safely without using checks or other types of negotiable instruments? The firm will receive a number of payments each month by check. How soon after depositing these checks into the firm's account will the funds be available? How can the firm minimize the risk that any checks it accepts may be dishonored by the drawee bank upon presentment?

These or similar questions may arise during our discussion. Be prepared! You never know when the firm or one of its members will seek your advice.

Classic Case

CALIFORNIA BANK v. DIAMOND

144 Cal. App. 2d 387, 301 P.2d 60, 1956 Cal. App. LEXIS 1730 (Cal. App. 2d Dist. 1955)

FACTS H. Grabell and Sons issued a check dated September 15, 1952 and payable to the order of Herbert Diamond some time prior to September 4, 1952. On September 4, 1952 Grabell placed a stop payment order on the check with California Bank, the drawee. Some time later Diamond negotiated the check to E. B. Corbin, who presented it to the drawee bank for payment on February 5, 1954. The check as presented contained the endorsements of Diamond and Corbin. The bank accepted and paid the check as presented.

At some time prior to Diamond's negotiation of the check to Corbin the date on the check was changed from September 15, 1952 to September 15, 1953. Also at that time, Diamond informed Corbin that he had not yet earned the money represented by the check.

On March 3, 1954, Grabell demanded that the bank return the sum of $67,275 (the amount of the check) that had been paid to Corbin. The bank, in turn, demanded that Corbin return the sum, and also demanded that Diamond return the sum to either Grinell or the bank. Neither party returned the sum or any part of it. (The bank recognized

that if Corbin was a holder in due course it was not entitled to recover the amount of the check from him.)

The bank then sued Corbin to recover the amount of the check. The trial court rendered judgment against Corbin, who appealed.

ISSUE Was Corbin a holder in due course?

HOLDING No, Corbin had actual knowledge of Diamond's lack of title to the check, and therefore he was not a holder in due course.

REASONING Excerpts from the opinion of Paul Nourse, Judge:

By the finding in question, the Court found that at the time Corbin took the check from Diamond, Corbin had notice of an infirmity in the instrument and a defect in the title of Diamond. From the facts the court had already found that there was an infirmity in Diamond's title in that he received a check subject to an agreement on his part that he would not negotiate it until certain machinery had been delivered to Grabell, and that this machinery was not delivered. Corbin testified that at the time he purchased the check from Diamond, Diamond told him of the conditions upon which he held the check and told him that he was not then entitled to cash it. Corbin thus had actual notice of an infirmity in Diamond's

726

title and did not become a holder in due course. . . . The court made further findings that Corbin did not act in good faith in purchasing the check and in failing to make inquiry of Grabell concerning the check; but these findings are of no importance inasmuch as the evidence clearly shows actual knowledge on Corbin's part on the infirmity of Diamond's title. . . .

The judgment is affirmed.

BASIC CONCEPTS

In the United States today, nearly every business organization has a checking account. In addition, many, if not most, of the adults in this country have checking accounts. Many workers still receive their pay by check. Checking account information is normally required on credit and loan applications, and increasingly, is asked for on job applications. Millions of checks move through the economic system each day. Yet few people actually understand the basic rules and regulations of the checking system they are using. The advent and widespread use of debit cards and electronic banking has made having and using an account easier than ever. However, it has made understanding the rules and regulations relating to these accounts more complex because now the customer is dealing with traditional checking accounts and with electronic fund transfers (EFTs).

A new customer walking into a bank follows the signs that lead to the "New Accounts" desk. Upon sitting down at this desk, the novice depositor is inundated with seemingly trivial information and details. Several different types of accounts—interest plus checking, free checking, ready-reserve checking, and so on—are briefly mentioned in passing; multiple colors and styles of checks are displayed; a "signature card" is handed to the customer with instructions to "sign at the X"; a deposit ticket is prepared; and a deposit is made in the customer's name in a new account. Before really knowing what has happened, the new customer is back on the street, the proud possessor of a personal checking account. More likely than not, the customer has no idea of what all this means legally.

By signing a signature card, the customer has entered a multirole legal relationship with the bank. The signature card represents a contract with the bank that the customer accepts on signing the card, even though he or she probably is unaware of any of its terms or conditions. In addition, the customer is now governed by Article 4 of the Uniform Commercial Code (UCC), which covers Bank Deposits and Collections. Article 4 was revised, together with Article 3, in 1990. As of May 1999, forty-seven states and the District of Columbia have adopted the revised versions of both Articles (New York, Rhode Island, and South Carolina still follow the earlier versions of both Articles). The customer has entered into an agency relationship and has agreed to a debtor–creditor relationship, as well. In addition, if the customer requested and accepted a check card/debit card/ATM card, he or she is also agreeing to abide by the terms of the Electronic Fund Transfers Act, a federal law, as well as the bank's rules and regulations involving the use of such cards. This includes an agreement regarding the imposition of fees for using the card.

The contract that the customer entered into is relatively simple. It covers things like service charges that can be imposed by the bank for various services, minimum balance requirements for the customer's account, and technical terms and conditions. Likewise, the coverage afforded by Article 4 of the Code is fairly simple; basically, it spells out the mandatory rights and duties of each of the parties. These will be dealt with later in this chapter.

The agency portion of the agreement is a complete surprise to most depositors. To put it simply, the bank is the agent and the depositor is the principal. An agent is required to obey any lawful orders of the principal that deal with the agency. This explains, in part, the language used on a check. The depositor (principal) is ordering the bank (agent) to "*Pay* to the order of" someone. The check does not say, "Please pay" or "I would appreciate it if you would pay." It says, "**PAY!**" This language is an order, and the order is usually lawful. Therefore, the bank must obey that order or face possible liability to the depositor for the disobedience, providing that the order issued by the principal is lawful.

The final relationship varies based on the situation. Normally, the customer will have a positive balance in the checking account. As a result, the customer is a creditor of the bank, and the bank is a debtor of the customer. Occasionally, the bank will pay an overdraft on the customer's account. When this happens, the customer has a negative balance in the account, and the roles reverse. Now the bank is a creditor of the customer, and the customer is a debtor to the bank.

THE CUSTOMER: RIGHTS AND DUTIES

The duties of a bank customer are relatively few and straightforward. The first and main duty of a customer is to act with due care and diligence. Whether writing a check, inspecting a monthly statement, or indorsing a check, or whether making a deposit or cashing a check, the customer is required to act in a careful and reasonable manner. If customers remember that it is their money being handled, and that carelessness could cause them to lose that money, they are more likely to be careful. In addition, the customer is expected to prepare and issue checks in a non-negligent manner, and is to exercise reasonable care and promptness in examining statements and items delivered to the customer by the bank.

Customers have several rights they may exercise. They may stop payment on a previously issued check, and they may collect damages from the bank if the bank errs in the handling of the account to the customer's financial detriment. But before they can exercise these rights, customers must show that they have acted properly and/or that the bank has acted improperly. For example, suppose that Louis issues a check to pay for some merchandise. The merchant presents the check to the bank for payment, and the bank dishonors the check. Louis is now likely to have some problems with the merchant. He may have to pay the merchant a "handling fee" or a "service charge" for the returned check. He may face a lawsuit filed by the merchant to collect the amount of the check plus costs and interest. In many states a person may face a criminal charge for passing "hot" (bad) checks. But what if the dishonor was due to an error by the bank, not to any carelessness or wrongdoing on Louis's part? Louis will still have to settle his own problems with the merchant, but the criminal action will be dropped. And, Louis will be able to proceed against the bank for recovery of the damages he might have suffered in this ordeal.

Wrongful Dishonor

According to UCC § 4-402, the bank is liable to its customer for any damages proximately caused by a wrongful dishonor of the customer's check. Note that this section also limits damages *under this Article* to *actual* damages proved by the customer. Those damages may include damages for an arrest or prosecution, or any other consequential damages. While this section restricts damages the customer can recover to actual damages, "other" damages, including punitive damages, might be available under "other rules of law" if the court deems such damages appropriate.[1] (There was some controversy concerning available damages when a check was wrongfully dishonored for a reason other than mistake under the previous version of Article 4. The language of § 4-402 was changed to eliminate this controversy by deleting the reference to "dishonor due to mistake" and limiting damages for wrongful dishonor to actual damages.)

From the language used in the revision to § 4-402 it sounds as if the customer will end up in a reasonably good position if the bank wrongfully dishonors a check drawn by the customer: The customer will recover the "handling fees," the interest, and any other costs paid to the merchant; the customer will recover any damages related to the arrest; and the bank will end up taking all the losses on this case. In seeking damages from the bank, however, the customer must prove that the bank's conduct was the proximate cause of the losses suffered by the customer. If the bank can show that the customer contributed to the loss, the bank may be able to avoid liability for the dishonor of the customer's check. The following hypothetical case represents the type of problem that might prevent the customer's recovery.

> *Roberto owed Mustafa $600. Roberto wrote Mustafa a check for the $600 to pay off the debt, but he post-dated the check so that he would have time to make a deposit in order to ensure that his account had sufficient funds to cover the check. Unfortunately, Mustafa presented the check to the bank prior to the date on the check (remember, the check was post-dated) and before Roberto had an opportunity to make a deposit. The bank dishonored the check and imposed its service charge for returning a check against Roberto's account. Even though the check was presented prior to its date and the bank ignored the date on the check, this would not be a wrongful dishonor. A bank is not obligated to honor a post-dating unless the customer has notified the bank in advance[2] and provided an adequate description of the*

eClass 23.1 Finance

ISSUING A STOP PAYMENT ORDER

eClass recently issued a check to pay for some office supplies, including labels for the firm's software and for the jewel cases in which the software is packaged. When the supplies were delivered Meg noticed that the labels for the diskettes and for insertion into the jewel cases were not properly centered. In addition, the design was blurred and had a very "amateurish" appearance. While the labels *could* be used, the principals all believe that it would reflect poorly on the firm to use these labels on their product. They have complained to the supplier and demanded that replacement labels be prepared that show the information clearly and distinctly. However, since they have already issued a check in payment, they are concerned about a lack of leverage with the supplier. Ani suggests that they issue a stop payment order on the check, but Yousef is not sure that this is the right thing to do, fearing that this might cause future problems with the supplier, and also worrying that the bank may pay the check despite the stop payment order. They have asked you for your opinion. What will you tell them?

BUSINESS CONSIDERATIONS   Should a business issue a stop payment order on a check before trying to resolve a controversy over performance with the payee of the check? What drawbacks might there be for trying to resolve the matter first?

ETHICAL CONSIDERATIONS   Is it ethical to issue a stop payment order on a check when only a portion of the goods or services for which the check was issued is defective? How might the use of a stop payment order be abused?

post-dated check to allow the bank to act on it. In addition, the bank has no duty to pay an overdraft unless it has a prior agreement with the customer concerning overdrafts on the account. If Roberto has any complaint in this situation it should be made to Mustafa, the party who did not honor the post-dating of the check as he (apparently) had agreed to do when he accepted delivery of a post-dated check.

Stop Payment Orders

A customer has a right to order the bank to pay by issuing a check. The customer also has a right to order the bank *not* to pay by issuing a stop-payment order to the bank. If this stop payment order is issued properly, the bank must obey the order to stop payment on the check. The bank may be held liable for any damages proximately caused by its failure to obey a properly issued order to stop payment. Of course, the burden of proving damages is on the customer who issued the stop payment order.

The stop payment order must be given to the bank in a time and manner that gives the bank a reasonable opportunity to act on the order. In other words, the bank must receive a complete description of the check (number, payee, amount, date, reason) with enough "lead time" to allow the bank to react to the order. A minimum of a few hours is normally required, but it may take as long as a full banking day to get the word out to the bank's various branch offices.

The customer can give either an oral or a written stop-payment order. A stop-payment order is good for six months, but it lapses after 14 days if the original order was oral and it was not confirmed in writing within that 14-day period. A written order can be renewed for additional six-month periods. Of course, every renewal will entail another service charge.

If the customer properly gives the bank a stop-payment order, and the bank pays the check despite the order, the customer may be able to collect damages from the bank. To do so, the customer will have to prove that he or she suffered damages because the check was paid. To prove this, he or she will have to show that the presenter could not have collected from him or her (the customer) if payment had

eClass 23.2 Finance/Management

UNAUTHORIZED PAYMENTS BY THE BANK

While reconciling eClass's latest bank statement, Ani found a listing for an item that was not reflected in the check register. When she asked, neither Meg nor Yousef could remember issuing a check for the amount of the listed item. Ani wants to call the bank to complain and to demand that the money be re-credited to the firm's account, but Yousef thinks that they should wait for the next statement to see if perhaps the bank made a mistake in posting the item to the account, and has subsequently discovered and corrected the error. Meg is concerned that if the firm delays it may be waiving some of its rights. They have asked you for your opinion. What will you tell them?

BUSINESS CONSIDERATIONS   Should a business have a policy for reconciliation of its bank statement? If so, what should that policy include? What sort of policy or practice should an individual follow in reconciling his or her bank statement?

ETHICAL CONSIDERATIONS   Is it ethical for a bank that has made an unauthorized payment on a customer's account to *not* re-credit the account simply because the customer delayed in reporting the transaction? Is it ethical for a customer who delayed reporting an unauthorized payment to still seek recovery from the bank even though the customer's delay may have affected the bank's rights?

been stopped by the bank as the customer ordered. If the presenter could enforce the check against the customer (drawer), then the customer will not be able to collect any damages from the bank for paying the check despite the stop-payment order. If payment is stopped by the bank, the drawer may be sued by the holder in an effort to recover his or her money.

The Duty to Inspect Bank Statements

Section 4-406 addresses the customer's duty to inspect his or her bank statements. The bank will periodically send statements to the customer showing the activities on the account for the statement period, typically one month. The statement must include *either* the cancelled items (paid checks) *or* it must provide adequate information for the customer to reasonably be able to identify the items listed on the statement. Section 4-406(a) states that the bank's statement provides sufficient information to the customer "if the item is described by number, amount, and date of payment." If the bank returns the paid items, the customer should retain them for a period of seven years. If the bank does not return the paid items, § 4-406(b) provides that "the person retaining the items [the bank] shall either retain the items or, if the items are destroyed, maintain the capacity to furnish legible copies of the items until the expiration of seven years after receipt of the items." This section adds the requirement that if the customer requests an item from the bank, the bank must provide the requested item or a legible copy of that item within a reasonable time. This is an important provision since the paid item is proof of payment and may be needed as evidence in a legal proceeding involving the customer.

The customer has certain duties once he or she receives the periodic statement of account. The customer is expected to examine the statement, to reconcile his or her account with the statement provided by the bank, and to discover and to report any unauthorized signatures or alterations on any items included in the statement. Section 4-406(c) provides that the customer must "exercise reasonable promptness" in examining the statement to determine whether any of the items paid by the bank were not authorized due to an alteration of the instrument or due to the presence of a signature of the drawer that was not authorized. If any such items are discovered, the customer must *promptly* give the bank notice of this fact. If the customer fails to exercise "reasonable promptness" in meeting these duties, he or she may be unable to recover from the bank for any unauthorized payments.

According to § 4-406(d), if the bank can prove that a customer failed to exercise reasonable promptness in examining the statement and reporting any problems, the customer will be precluded from asserting against the bank:

(1) the customer's unauthorized signature or any alteration on the item, if the bank also proves that it suffered a loss by reason of the failure; and

(2) the customer's unauthorized signature or alteration by the same wrongdoer on any other item paid in good faith by the bank if the payment was made before the bank received notice from the customer of the unauthorized signature or alteration and after the customer had been afforded a reasonable period of time, not exceeding 30 days, in which to examine the item or statement and notify the bank.

These rules make it sound as if the customer *must* (1) examine his or her statement, (2) discover any unauthorized payments made by the bank due to the fact that the item either contains a signature that was not authorized by the customer or the item was altered without the customer's authorization, and (3) notify the bank of the problem in a reasonably prompt manner not to exceed thirty days, or the customer will lose his or her rights against the bank. However, that is *not* what the rules mean.

The bank can only avoid liability to the customer for paying an unauthorized item if the customer does not give the bank prompt notice *and* the bank can prove that it suffered a loss due to the delay. If the bank cannot prove that it suffered a loss due to the delay, the bank will still be liable to the customer. The real protection for the bank here arises when the *same* wrongdoer has signed more than one item without authority or has altered more than one item without authority, and the bank has paid these subsequent items in good faith. If the customer failed to notify the bank of the problem with reasonable promptness when the first such item was included in a statement, and the bank paid subsequent items in good faith before it was notified, the customer cannot recover for the subsequent items paid by the bank. Since the customer failed to notify the bank with reasonable promptness, the bank can treat these subsequent signatures or alterations by the same wrongdoers as *authorized* by the customer.

The Code seems to limit the customer's right to recover to those situations in which the customer gives reasonably prompt notice, which is not to exceed 30 days. In fact, a customer has one year after the statement or the item is made available to discover and report the unauthorized signature or alteration before he or she is absolutely precluded from asserting the improper payment of any item by the bank.[3]

Finally, even if the customer would otherwise be precluded from recovering from the bank under § 4-406(d), the customer may still have recourse. If the customer can prove that the bank did not exercise ordinary care in paying the item, and that this lack of ordinary care substantially contributed to the customer's loss, the loss will be allocated between the bank and the customer based on the degree of fault that can be allocated to each party.[4] And if the customer can prove that the bank did not pay the item in good faith, the customer can recover for all of his or her loss, and none of the preclusions under § 4-406(d) apply.

The rules regarding examination of the statement require a customer to discover that his or her "signature" was not authorized, or that the item has been altered. These rules do not address the issue of an unauthorized indorsement. Obviously, a drawer should recognize his or her own signature or should be aware that he or she had not authorized a particular item to be signed. Similarly, the customer should be aware of the amount of any items issued and should recognize when such an item has been altered. But the customer cannot be expected to know the indorsement of the payee or of any subsequent holders, so the "reasonable promptness" standard would impose an unreasonable burden on the customer. Accordingly, the Code gives the customer three years from the statement date to discover that an indorsement was not authorized and to notify the bank of this fact.[5]

THE BANK: RIGHTS AND DUTIES

The overriding duty of the bank is the duty to exercise ordinary care. Section 4-103(a) allows the parties a certain amount of flexibility, but only within limits. According to this section, the parties can vary the effects of the provisions of Article 4, but the bank cannot disclaim its responsibility for a lack of good faith or for a failure to exercise ordinary care, nor can the bank limit the measure of damages for any lack of good faith or any failure to exercise ordinary care. The "ordinary care" standard is intended to allow banks to change their practices over time as the ordinary standards and practices of the banking industry change, while helping to insure that any particular bank will be held to the current standards of the industry. To further reflect this intent, § 4-103(b) specifies that "Federal Reserve regulations and operating circulars, clearinghouse rules, and the like have the affect of agreements under subsection (a), whether or not specifically assented to by all parties interested in items handled." Obviously, "all parties interested" would include the bank and the customer, but it may also include indorsers or other parties having an interest in the account.

Banks face other duties beyond those imposed by § 4-103. Since the bank is the agent of the customer, it has the duties of an agent. This means, among other things, that it must obey any lawful orders of the customer. This duty to obey gives the bank a very important right: It can charge to the customer's account any item that is properly payable from the customer's account. The bank can pay the check even if the payment creates an overdraft. The bank can also pay a check that was incomplete when issued and then completed by some later holder. The bank may even know that a holder, and not the drawer, completed the check and still pay it as completed. The only exception is when the bank has notice that the completion was improper or was done in bad faith.

Stale Checks

In accordance with the rules that govern timely presentment, the bank may refuse to honor any "stale" checks.[6] A "stale" check is one that is more than six months old and has not been certified. If the bank dishonors a stale check, it is not liable to the customer for any damages, nor can the dishonor be treated as a wrongful dishonor. Alternatively, the bank may, at its option, honor a stale check. Again, the bank will not be liable for any damages suffered by the customer if it honors the check in good faith. It should be remembered that a written stop payment is good for six months, the period after which a check becomes stale. Suppose a customer issues a written stop-payment order. Six months elapse without the check ever being presented, and the customer does not renew the stop-payment order. The payee now presents the check to the bank. The check is stale. A stop payment order had been in effect on that check.

Suppose the bank honors the check despite these two apparent problems. If the bank can prove it acted in good faith, it will face no liability for its payment of the stale check the customer once tried to stop.

Death or Incompetence of a Customer

Under traditional agency rules, if the principal dies or becomes incompetent, the agency terminates by operation of law. After this termination, if the agent continues to perform its agency duties, the agent becomes personally liable, and the principal has no liability. (This is the traditional rule for agencies. Many states have modified this rule so that the death of the principal does not automatically terminate the agency if doing so would cause an undue hardship. See Chapter 29 for a detailed discussion of this topic.) This rule would be impractical with negotiable instruments, so the UCC expressly changed it. As applied to the bank–customer relationship, agencies do not automatically end at the instant of the principal's death or incompetence. Under § 4-405(a), the bank is fully authorized to perform its banking functions on the account of a customer who has died or has become incompetent until the bank knows of the occurrence and has had adequate time to react to the news. Even if the bank knows of the customer's death, its power to act is not terminated. Section 4-405(b) permits the bank to continue to honor checks drawn on the account for 10 days after the date of a death unless a stop payment is placed on the account by an interested party.

The Bank's Right of Subrogation

Sometimes banks make mistakes. A bank may honor an instrument that had a stop-payment order covering it, or it may do something else that allows the customer to recover damages from the bank. When this happens, the bank has some protection: It is entitled to subrogation. Subrogation means the bank is given the rights that some other parties could have raised if the bank had not made improper payment. UCC § 4-407 gives the bank three different sets of rights to assert through subrogation:

1. The rights of a holder in due course on the item against the maker or drawer;
2. The rights of the payee or any other holder of the item against the maker or drawer either on the item or under the transaction out of which the item arose; and
3. The rights of the drawer or maker against the payee or any other holders of the item with respect to the transaction out of which the item arose.

Thus, the bank may assert the rights of the drawer, the payee, the holder, or of any other interested party in the transaction. From this buffet of rights, the bank can select the set of rights that gives it the greatest likelihood of winning the case.

The Bank's Rights with Legal Notice

A bank may acquire knowledge or receive legal notice affecting a particular item or affecting a customer's account. What must the bank do in this situation? What rights can the bank assert? This area is addressed in § 4-303, which says:

> **(a)** Any knowledge, notice, or stop-payment order received by, legal process served upon, or setoff exercised by a payor bank comes too late to terminate, suspend, or modify the bank's right or duty to pay an item or to charge its customer's account for the item if the knowledge, notice, stop-payment order, or legal process is received or served and a reasonable time for the bank to act thereon expires or the setoff is exercised after the earliest of the following:
>
> > **(1)** the bank accepts or certifies the item;
> > **(2)** the bank pays the item in cash;
> > **(3)** the bank settles for the item without having a right to revoke the settlement under statute, clearing-house rule, or agreement;
> > **(4)** the bank becomes accountable for the amount of the item under Section 4-302 dealing with the payor bank's responsibility for late return of items; or
> > **(5)** with respect to checks, a cutoff hour no earlier than one hour after the opening of the next banking day after the banking day on which the bank received the check and no later than the close of that next banking day or, if no cutoff hour is fixed, the close of the next banking day after the banking day on which the bank received the check.
>
> **(b)** Subject to subsection (a), items may be accepted, paid, certified, or charged to the indicated account of its customer in any order.

This section specifies the rights of the bank any time a customer of the bank is involved in a bankruptcy proceeding, a garnishment, or some other legal process in which one or more parties is seeking to assert a claim against the customer's account. The bank is allowed to pay the item or otherwise settle on the item without liability to the legal claims of third person, so long as the bank exercises "ordinary care" in handling the item and follows its normal practices and procedures. So long as the bank follows these rules it will not be held liable by a third person asserting a legal claim against the customer for making a "wrongful payment" in contravention of any legal proceedings or other claims asserted by the third person.

The Account Contract

The bank has the right to enforce the terms of its contract with the customer. Among other things, this right allows the bank to impose certain service charges and fees against many of its customers each month. The bank may be able to collect a specific amount every month, it may be able to collect a specific amount in any month the customer's account balance falls below a certain amount, or it may be able to charge a specific amount for every check written by the customer. The bank will impose a service charge for handling a stop-payment order. Likewise, it may charge a customer when it pays an overdraft or when it dishonors a check, if honoring it would have created an overdraft. These service charges are specified in the contract formed when the customer signed the signature card.

SPECIAL PROBLEMS

Two areas deserve further mention: certified checks and unauthorized signatures.

Certified Checks

A certified check is one that has already been accepted by the drawee bank. In other words, the bank has assumed primary liability and agreed to pay the check on a later presentment. Certification can be done at the request of the drawer or of any holder. A refusal by the bank to certify the check is not a dishonor.[7] How does certification occur? Either the drawer or a holder presents the check to the bank and requests certification. If the bank agrees to certify, it follows certain steps. First, it charges the account of the customer and credits its own "Certified Check Account." Thus, the money is held by the bank in the bank's own account, and the customer has already "paid" the amount of the check. Second, the bank punches a hole in the encoded account number of the check, or otherwise "disables" the account number, to ensure that the check will not be paid a second time on a later presentment. Third, a stamp is made on the face of the check, and the terms of the certification are written into the stamped form.

If the drawer seeks and receives the certification, the drawer remains secondarily liable until final payment. However, if a holder seeks and receives the certification, the drawer and all prior indorsers are discharged from liability.

Unauthorized Signatures

Under UCC § 1-201(43), an unauthorized signature is one made without any authority, express or implied, and it includes a forgery. An unauthorized signature is wholly inoperative against the person whose name was signed unless that person later ratifies the signing. It cannot be used to impose liability on the purported signer. However, in some circumstances, an unauthorized and unratified signature is still binding on the purported signer. According to § 3-406, if a person contributes to the unauthorized signing through negligence, he or she will be held liable to any good faith holder of the instrument.

Many businesses "sign" checks by means of a stamp. The business may leave the stamp and its checks in a place where they are easily reached by a nonauthorized person (most likely a thief). Such conduct on the part of the business is negligent, and the negligence may lead to the unauthorized "signing." In such circumstances, the business may not later assert the defense that the signing was unauthorized if the holder is a holder in good faith. Notice that the holder does not have to be a holder in due course; the fact that the holder is in good faith is sufficient. The negligence of the wronged party is the key: The wronged party must be negligent, and the negligence must cause the loss. Otherwise, the unauthorized signature cannot be used against the person whose name was signed.

FUNDS TRANSFERS: ARTICLE 4A

Changes in banking laws, the growth of international business, and technology have affected the banking industry to a significant extent, beginning in the last quarter of the twentieth century. The savings and loan industry crisis of the 1980s led to numerous changes in banking regulations. International trade frequently requires that large amounts of money be transferred from one nation to another quickly. Technology has reduced the need for personnel, and made automated banking much simpler. Each of these changes has moved banking ahead, while many of the banking regulations have lagged behind. However, the distance between banking practice and banking regulation is narrowing.

Bank customers have long had a need for a particular type of funds transfer, the wire transfer. However, this type of funds transfer has not been uniformly regulated until very recently. Now the UCC has developed Article 4A to provide uniform coverage in the area of funds transfers within the United States. As of July 1998, Article 4A had been adopted by all 50 states and the District of Columbia.

Fund transfers are commonly used to provide a rapid movement of funds from one account to another without the use of a traditional negotiable instrument. A "funds transfer" is defined in § 4A-104 as:

> the series of transactions, beginning with the originator's payment order, made for the purpose of making payment to the beneficiary of the order. The term includes any payment order issued by the originator's bank or an intermediary bank intended to carry out the originator's payment order. A funds transfer is completed by acceptance by the beneficiary's bank of a payment order for the benefit of the beneficiary of the originator's payment order.

Note that the funds transfer is defined as a *series* of transactions. The person who is transferring the funds—the "originator"—places the funds transfer order with his or her bank. This bank—the "originator bank"—then transfers the funds to the next bank—an "intermediary bank"—in line. This intermediary bank, in turn, will transfer the funds to the next bank, until, ultimately, the funds reach the "beneficiary bank." Once the funds reach the beneficiary bank, they are credited to the account of the beneficiary, completing the funds transfer. Each transaction is deemed to be only

eClass 23.3 Finance/Management

FUNDS TRANSFERS

The firm is nearing an agreement with an e-tailer (an on-line retailer) that could result in a significant increase in sales of the software. The e-tailer's proposal includes quarterly payments to the firm of the revenues generated from the sale of eClass software, but the method of payment is still being negotiated. Yousef is willing to let the retailer pay for the order by check. Ani would prefer that the customer sends either a cashier's check or a certified check. Meg has pointed out that, given the "time value" of money, the sooner the firm receives the funds the better they will be. She thinks that the firm should insist on a wire transfer of the funds as soon as the e-tailer prepares the quarterly statement. They all agree that the time value of money is important, and they like Meg's idea, but they want more information before they make a final decision. They have asked you your opinion. What will you tell them?

BUSINESS CONSIDERATIONS   What benefits accrue to a seller who receives payment by funds (wire) transfer? What disadvantages does the buyer who pays by funds (wire) transfer experience? When should a business insist that it be paid by wire transfer rather than by negotiable instrument?

ETHICAL CONSIDERATIONS   Is it ethical to ask a buyer to pay for goods by funds (wire) transfer upon receipt? Should the buyer be given some sort of discount since the seller will be receiving his or her funds so quickly, as compared to when the funds would be available if the buyer sent a negotiable instrument?

between the two parties directly involved. Thus, the transfer between the originating bank and intermediary bank one is a transaction between them, and the originator has no rights against the intermediary bank if something goes awry.

Section 4A-302 provides guidance for receiving banks in carrying out the funds transfer. If the sender of the funds transfer order specifies how the funds transfer is to be carried out, the receiving bank must follow these specifications. If no specifications are provided, the receiving bank is allowed to use any means that are reasonable under the circumstances, including first class mail, if such a method is appropriate under the circumstances.

Finally, § 4A-108 specifically excludes coverage by Article 4A in any area already governed by the Electronic Funds Transfer Act, as that Act may be amended from time to time. Thus, the UCC will provide state coverage for funds transfers, but will defer to federal regulation of Electronic Fund Transfers (EFTs), which are discussed in the next section.

FUNDS TRANSFERS: ELECTRONIC FUNDS TRANSFERS

Recent technological advances have provided banking with a new method of doing business and with a new type of service. This new method of doing business is the electronic funds transfer (EFT), which allows for computerization of checking accounts and for faster (theoretically), more accurate banking transactions.

Electronic fund transfers are regulated by the Electronic Funds Transfer Act (15 U.S.C. 1693), which became effective in 1980. This statute provides the basic legal framework for EFTs, granting extensive authority to the Board of Governors of the Federal Reserve System. In addition, various agencies are granted enforcement power,[8] with special enforcement power given to the Federal Trade Commission for any areas not specifically reserved to the specialized authority of other named agencies. This method of financial dealing eventually may make the current checking or drafting account obsolete, or nearly so, due to the delays and expenses of handling checks or drafts when compared to electronic banking.

The purpose of the Electronic Fund Transfer Act is "to provide a basic framework establishing rights, liabilities, and responsibilities of participants in electronic fund transfer systems."[9] The primary objective of the statute is the provision of individual consumer rights in electronic fund transfers.

The Act defines an electronic fund transfer as "any transfer of funds, other than a transaction originated by check, draft, or similar paper instrument, which is initiated through an electronic terminal, telephonic instrument, or computer or magnetic tape so as to order, instruct, or authorize a financial institution to debit or credit an account."[10] It also requires any financial institution providing EFTs to its customers to provide those customers with periodic statements for each account that the customer may access through the use of an EFT. These periodic statements must be provided at least monthly for each monthly cycle in which an EFT occurred, or every three months, whichever is more frequent.[11]

There are five methods for electronically transferring funds recognized by the Act: POS transactions; ATM transactions; telephonic transactions; preauthorized transactions, whether deposits or withdrawals, and on-line (electronic) banking.

Point of Sale (POS) Transactions

The first method is the point-of-sale (POS) transaction, involving the use of a POS terminal and a "debit" card. In a POS transaction, the customer presents the merchant with a debit card, the merchant imprints the card and has the customer sign, and the funds are transferred from the customer's account to the merchant's account. The transaction is similar in format to the use of a credit card, but there should be no delay in receiving the money from the sale for the merchant. Unfortunately, the use of a POS transaction is often no faster or safer for the merchant than the use of a check. In most parts of the country, the POS transaction must be processed through a clearinghouse in the same manner as a check, making the transfer of funds to the merchant no faster than it would be with a check. In addition, the cost is slightly higher for a POS transaction than for a check when a clearinghouse is involved.

Debit/ATM Cards

A second, and more familiar, method is the use of automated teller machine (ATM) transfers. The bank customer inserts his or her card in the machine, enters his or her personal identification number (PIN), and selects a transaction. The customer can make a deposit, a withdrawal, a transfer from one account to another, a payment, or a number of other banking transactions.

Telephonic Transactions

If the bank is a participant in a network, the customer may be able to authorize payments to predetermined accounts by phone. Here, the customer calls the bank and, using the buttons on a touch-tone phone, can designate preselected "payees" who will be paid an amount determined by punching in the amount of the "electronic check" so that the funds are automatically transferred.

Preauthorized Transactions

Finally, there are preauthorized automatic payments and preauthorized direct deposits. In both cases, regular amounts are deducted from, or added to, the customer's account balance on designated dates to ensure that payment (or credit) is received without any worries about forgetting to send in the check or drive to the bank to make the deposit.

Online (Electronic) Banking

Online banking provides most of the traditional banking services to customers, but offers these services through an internet connection rather than through the use of the mail or a visit to a bank by the customer. These services are offered "24/7/365," meaning that the customer can, theoretically, access the Web site and make transactions any time of day or night any day of the year. Basically the only restriction is internet access. If the customer's internet connection is down or the server is off-line, the online bank is "closed." Otherwise, the bank is always "open" and ready to serve its customers. Many customers use online banking to pay bills, to find out whether—and when—a given check or charge cleared, and to keep closer tabs on their account balance or balances. The convenience of the service, combined with a growing comfort level with internet transactions in general, make online banking an increasingly popular option. Customers should keep in mind, however, that they still have the same duties to the bank that Article 4 imposes for traditional "paper" banking. The ease and speed of on-line banking do not eliminate the need to exercise reasonable care.

Rights and Duties with EFTs

In general, a consumer who uses EFTs has the same types of rights and duties as a consumer who has a checking or drafting account with a financial institution. For example, a customer can place a stop-payment order on a preauthorized payment by notifying the bank orally or in writing at least three days prior to the date for preauthorized payment. A consumer can recover damages from a financial institution for failure to make EFT payments as instructed, provided the consumer has sufficient funds on deposit.

Numerous protections also exist for the consumer who is using EFTs. For example, consumer liability is limited in case of unauthorized use of an account, provided the consumer gives proper and timely notice to the bank. A consumer is expected to give the bank "proper and timely" notice of the loss or theft of his or her card or other means of access to his or her account in order to minimize liability. If the consumer gives such "proper and timely" notice, the consumer's liability is limited to the lesser of the amount of money or value accessed wrongfully or $50. "Proper and timely" notice is generally defined as notice given within two business days after the consumer learns of the loss or theft. If the consumer gives notice, but the notice is not "proper and timely," his or her liability is still somewhat limited under the statute. In this case liability is the lesser of $500 or the amount of unauthorized electronic fund transfers that occur between the time when the consumer should have given notice (two business days after discovery) and the date on which notice was actually given. The bank has the burden of proof to establish either that the use was in fact authorized or that the customer did not give proper and/or timely notice.

As the public becomes more familiar and more comfortable with EFTs, the use of this form of money management will grow and develop. As that happens, the use of checks will begin to decline. The decline will be gradual at first, but over the next few decades we may do virtually all our banking electronically.

THE EXPEDITED FUNDS AVAILABILITY ACT

For years bank customers complained about the delays they experienced in gaining access to funds they deposited. It was fairly common for a bank to impose a "waiting period" of up to ten days after a check was deposited before the customer was allowed to use the funds. It was also not uncommon for a customer to issue checks that were dishonored by the bank even though the funds were, at least theoretically, available, simply because the check was presented to the bank during the "waiting period" before the customer could use the funds. In an effort to address this problem, Congress passed the Expedited Funds Availability Act[12] (EFAA) in 1988. This Act provides federally mandated guidelines for when funds must be made available to the customer.

Under the provisions of the EFAA and Regulation CC,[13] its implementing regulations, there are specified time limits for when a customer can write a check against funds deposited with the bank and for when the customer can withdraw cash from funds deposited with the bank. The Act also takes into account *what* the customer deposited, *where* the deposit was made, and the location of the drawee bank, if the deposit was of a check acquired by the customer. There are also some exceptions written into the law for the treatment of new accounts and for those situations in which a customer has a history of issuing bad checks.

If the customer makes a deposit of cash, a cashier's check, a certified check, a government check, a check drawn against the customer's bank, or by means of a wire transfer, and the deposit is made with a teller, the customer can write checks against the amount deposited the next business day. If the deposit is made at one of the bank's ATMs the customer can write checks against the funds on the second business day after the deposit.

If the customer makes a deposit of a *local* check, but not a check drawn against the customer's bank, the customer can write checks for the first $100 the next business day. The customer can then write checks for the balance of the check, up to $5000, on the second business day. If the check is for more than $5000, the customer cannot write checks on the balance over $5000 until the *ninth* business day.

If the customer makes a deposit of a *non-local* check, once again the customer can write checks for the first $100 the next business day. However, since the check in not local, the customer must wait until the *fifth* business day to write checks for the balance of the check, up to $5000. And, once again, if the check is for more than $5000, the customer cannot write checks on the balance over $5000 until the *ninth* business day.

If the customer would like to withdraw cash, rather than write a check, from the deposited funds the rules are slightly different. The customer can withdraw up to $100 cash the next business day after the deposit. He or she can then withdraw up to $400 more on the same day as those funds would be available for covering checks, and the balance can be withdrawn in cash the day *after* the funds would be available for covering checks.

CHECK TRUNCATION

Check truncation, the changing of a check into an electronic or digital image of the check, has become a reality with the enactment of the Check Clearing for the 21st Century act (also known as Check 21).[14] This Act went into effect October 28, 2004.

The reason behind this move is to speed up the flow of instruments through the system and to allow banks to handle more checks and with greater efficiency, although it should also provide significant savings for banks since it will reduce the expenses associated with storage of cancelled items.

Under the provisions of Check 21 a bank has the option of changing a check it receives into a digital copy of the check, and the digital copy is then processed through the banking system. The bank that truncates the check (changes it into a digital copy) has no duty to retain the original or to forward it to the drawee bank. This digital copy is deemed a "substitute check," and it carries the same rights for the drawer as the original check. According to the FDIC, Check 21 affects check writers and depositors in the following ways:

- If you are used to getting your canceled checks back to you when you get your account statement, you may now be getting a "substitute" check. A substitute check is a high-quality paper reproduction of both sides of the original check. A substitute check is a legal equivalent of the original check.
- It is more important than ever to avoid bouncing checks. A check deposited in a bank generally travels by airplane and truck until it reaches the paying bank, typically about one or two days later. As a result of Check 21, more checks will be processed electronically . . . and faster!
- Check 21 does not require your bank to return your original check to you. However, Check 21 ensures that you have the same legal protections when you receive a substitute check from your bank as you do when you receive an original check.
- If you notice a problem with a substitute check, you should contact your bank as soon as possible. Check 21 provides a special process that allows you to claim a refund when you receive a substitute check from a bank and you think there is an error because of the substitute check. In general, you should contact your bank no later than 40 days from the date your bank provided the substitute check or from the date of the statement that shows the problem.[15]

The substitute check (known in the industry as an Image Replacement Document) must contain all of the information on both the front and back sides of the original check, including all indorsements and the MICR line. It must also state that it is a legal copy of the original check.[16]

The National Automated Clearing House Association (NACHA), the Herndon, Virginia-based electronic payment association, adopted its final rules on check truncation in October of 2001. Among the reasons cited for making this change were that billers would get their money more quickly and more reliably, that automated clearing house transactions eliminate "float," and that most banks process automated clearing house debits before they process checks, making electronic items more likely to be honored.

TRANSFERABLE RECORDS

Check 21 is the first step in moving negotiable instruments into the electronic realm. Telechecks (discussed in Chapter 22), truncated checks, and the recently created "transferable records" point to the likelihood that more and more negotiable instruments will be transformed from their current tangible form to an electronic form or to a digital form.

The term "transferable record" was first used in the Uniform Electronic Transactions Act (UETA), and was then picked up in the Electronic Signatures in Global and National Commerce Act (E-SIGN). Simply stated, a transferable record is the electronic equivalent of a promissory note.[17]

A transferable record cannot be used unless the obligor (the "maker" if it were truly a promissory note) expressly agrees to execute a "negotiable instrument" in electronic form. A further restriction applies in that E-SIGN only permits the use of a transferable record if the obligation is secured by real property. The UETA, by contrast, refers to negotiable instruments and documents without imposing any limitations.

Given the recent growth of electronic transactions, the enactment of such statutes as UETA and E-SIGN, and the passage of Check 21, it is quite possible that the first steps in another "revolution" in negotiable instrument law have been taken. This is an area of law that is worth watching.

Contemporary Case

SPACEMAKERS OF AMERICA v. SUNTRUST BANK

271 Ga. App. 335, 609 S.E.2d 683, 2005 Ga. App. LEXIS 43 (Ga. App. 2005)

FACTS Jenny Triplett applied to Spacemakers for a bookkeeping position in November 1999. Her employment application listed no prior employment, and the application did not ask about her criminal history. Spacemakers neither asked her about her criminal history nor conducted a bankground check. Had it done so, it would have learned that Triplett was on probation from a 1997 conviction for thirteen counts of forgery in the first degree, theft by taking and theft by deception. All of these convictions were the result of Triplett forging the checks of previous employers.

Spacemakers hired Triplett and delegated to her the sole responsibility of maintaining the company's checkbook, reconciling the bank statements, and preparing financial reports. Dennis Rose, the president of Spacemakers, signed the checks that Triplett prepared, and no other employees or officers checked on her work or the financial records.

On January 2, 2000, Triplett forged Rose's signature on a check for $3000 and payable to the order of her husband's company, Triple M Entertainment Group, which was not a vendor for Spacemakers. By the end of her first full month on the job she had forged five more checks payable to Triple M, and over the following nine months she forged an additional fifty-nine checks payable to Triple M. The total amount of these sixty-five forged checks was in excess of $500,000.

On October 13, 2000, a SunTrust loss prevention employee visually inspected the largest of these forged checks ($30,670), became suspicious of the signature, and immediately contacted Dennis Rose. A copy of the check was faxed to Rose, who knew that Triple M was not a Spacemaker vendor and also that he had not signed or authorized the check. A Spacemaker employee informed Rose that Triple M was owned by Triplett's husband. The police were called and Triplett was arrested.

On November 9, 2000, Spacemakers sent a letter to SunTrust demanding that the bank credit the Spacemaker account for $523,106.03 as reimbursement for the forged checks. SunTrust refused, contending thatSpacemakers' failure to give timely notice of the forgeries barred its claim. Spacemakers then filed suit against SunTrust for negligence, conversion, and unauthorized payments of forged checks.

ISSUE Is Spacemakers entitled to recover from SunTrust for the payment of these sixty-five forged checks?

HOLDING No. Spacemakers failed to give timely notice or to satisfy its obligations with regard to reconciling its bank statements and is thus barred from recovery.

REASONING Excerpts from the opinion of Ellington, Judge:

In granting summary judgment to the bank, the trial court found that Spacemakers could not recover for the first forged check from January 2000 because it failed to notify the bank of the forgery within 30 days of receiving its bank statement, as required by [§ 4-406] The trial court also found that, under the same provision, Spacemakers could not recover for the 64 subsequently forged checks because they were all forged by the same person who forged the first

check. Further, the court found that there was no evidence that the bank failed to exercise ordinary care in the payment of the checks. . . .

[§ 4-406] imposes upon a bank customer the duty to promptly examine its monthly statements and to notify the bank of any unauthorized transaction. If the customer fails to report the first forged item within 30 days, it is precluded from recovering for that transaction *and for any additional items forged by the same wrongdoer.* . . . The underlying justification for this provision is simple: one of the most serious consequences of the failure of a customer to timely examine its statements is that it gives the wrongdoer the opportunity to repeat his misdeeds. . . . Clearly, the customer "is in the best position to discover and report small forgeries before the [same] wrongdoer is emboldened and attempts a larger misdeed." . . .

In this case, the undisputed evidence showed that Spacemakers hired as a bookkeeper a twice-convicted embezzler who was on probation, then delegated the entire responsibility of reviewing and reconciling its bank statements to her while failing to provide any oversight on these essential tasks. The bookkeeper began forging checks within weeks of taking control of the company's checkbook . . . [and] made all the checks payable to her husband's company, which had never been a Spacemaker vendor. There is every reason to believe that, if Spacemaker had simply reviewed the bank statement of January 2000, it would have discovered the forgeries. More importantly, it would have been able to timely notify the bank of its discovery and avoided its subsequent losses of almost $475,000. Clearly, Spacemakers' extensive and unnecessary loss due to forgery is precisely the scenario that the duties created by [§ 4-406] were designed to prevent. Accordingly, we find that Spacemakers is precluded as a matter of law from asserting claims based upon the forgeries in this case. . . .

You Be the Judge

In 2002, Mary Christelle, the mother of David Hernandez (president of Essential Technologies of Illinois, or ETI), purchased a $50,000 cashier's check from her Charter One account. ETI deposited this check in its account with MidAmerica Bank. Four days later, Christelle asked Charter One to stop payment on the cashier's check, and Charter One placed a stop payment order on the cashier's check. When MidAmerica presented the check for payment, Charter One refused to honor the check, instead returning it to MidAmerica with a "Payment Stopped" stamp on the face of the check. MidAmerica then sent the check back to ETI after removing the $50,000 previously credited to the ETI account from that account. Within two weeks of the return of the dishonored cashier's check to ETI, its account had fallen to a negative balance of more than $50,000.

In 2006 MidAmerica filed suit against Charter One to recover the value of the dishonored cashier's check. MidAmerica alleged that Bank One had improperly stopped payment on the cashier's check in violation of § 3-411 if the UCC. Charter One admitted that it had stopped payment on the cashier's check, but argued that the check had been issued in furtherance of a fraudulent scheme or due to mistake, and thus that Charter One should not be held liable. (Charter One also filed a third-party complaint against Christelle, Hernandez, and ETI, but that does not affect the issues in this case.)

MidAmerica asserts that a bank cannot stop payment on a cashier's check. Charter One counters that a bank is permitted to stop payment on a cashier's check when the check was procured by fraud. To support its position, Charter One pointed out that § 4-403(a) provided that "A customer . . . may stop payment on any item drawn on the customer's account or close the account by an order to the bank describing the item or account with reasonable certainty." MidAmerica rebutted this argument by alleging that a cashier's check is not drawn on a customer's account, but rather is drawn against the issuing bank, so that § 4-403(a) does not apply.

This case has been brought in your court. How will *you* decide the case? What is the most important fact or factor affecting *your* decision? After deciding, consider whether it is ethical for a bank to stop payment on a cashier's check, teller check, or comparable instrument. [See *MidAmerica Bank v. Charter One Bank*, 232 Ill.2d 560 (Ill. S. Ct. 2009)]

Summary

The most frequently used negotiable instrument is the check. As a result, special attention must be paid to the bank–customer relationship. When a customer opens a checking account, a multirole relationship is created. The bank and the customer have a contract, they are involved in an agency relationship, they have a debtor-creditor relationship, and they are controlled by Article 4 of the UCC and a number of regulations promulgated by the Federal Reserve Board. In addition, a number of statutory enactments also affect the relationship.

Obviously, the customer is obligated to obey the terms of the contract with the bank. The customer is also expected to exercise reasonable care. They are required to inspect their statements carefully and promptly for any irregularities, alterations, or unauthorized signings, and to notify the bank of any problems encountered with "reasonable promptness." They may also issue stop-payment orders to the bank. Since the bank is the agent of its customers, it is obligated to obey such orders.

Banks are required to operate with ordinary care, and to abide by the terms of the contract with the customer. The bank must pay properly drawn checks if the customer has sufficient funds, must obey the lawful orders of the customer to "pay" or to "stop payment," and must act in good faith.

Certified checks and unauthorized signatures can present special problems. A certified check is one that has been accepted by the bank and then circulated through the normal channels of commerce. Unauthorized signings are sometimes caused by the negligence of the customer; in such a case, the bank is not liable for honoring the unauthorized signing.

Funds transfers are the "wave of the future" for banking and for businesses. There are two major areas of funds transfers: electronic funds transfers, governed by the Electronic Funds Transfer Act; and funds (wire) transfers, governed by Article 4A of the UCC. By using the capacity and the speed of computers and by eliminating the paper required for traditional checking accounts, funds can be moved more quickly, more accurately, and more efficiently than is possible with checking accounts. This developmental area will continue to grow and to spread over the next several years.

The Expedited Funds Availability Act regulates when banks must make funds available to customers. This law has reduced the time that a bank can "hold" funds before the customer can access the monies deposited. The check Truncation Act, passed in 2004, greatly increases the speed and the ease of handling of checks. Check truncation involves scanning a check and then replacing it with an electronic or a digital "duplicate" that is treated as the equivalent of the check. Transferable records, which are, for lack of a better term, electronic "promissory notes" have also been introduced. The use of transferable records and the potential for truncating checks should, in the near future, bring Articles 3 and 4 and the EFTs into much closer harmony.

Discussion Questions

1. What is a "stop-payment" order? Why must a bank obey a customer's order to "stop payment" on a check? What should a stop-payment order include? Can a bank customer issue a "stop payment" order on a preauthorized payment—an EFT—periodically charged to the customer's account? What is required for a customer to place a stop payment order on a preauthorized charge, a type of electronic fund transfer? What liability does the bank face if it fails to honor this stop payment order? How does this compare to the liability of a bank that fails to honor a stop payment order on a check?

2. What is the bank's liability to a customer when the bank wrongfully dishonors one of the customer's instruments? What limitations are imposed on this liability?

3. What is an electronic funds transfer? What current methods can a customer use to transfer funds electronically? What advantages, if any, are provided by EFTs over payment by negotiable instrument?

4. What is the Expedited Funds Availability Act and how does it affect the bank-customer relationship? If a customer deposits a $10,000 check drawn on a bank within the same region, when can the customer access the funds deposited? Would this access be different if the check was drawn against a bank from outside the same region as the depository bank?

5. What is "check truncation"? How does the Check Truncation Act affect the bank-customer relationship? What effect, if any, does this act have on a customer's checking account and the related duties of the customer with regard to his or her checking account?

Case Problems and Writing Assignments

1. MRF Resources, Ltd. maintained a checking account with Merchant's Bank, as did Galit Diamond, Inc. On May 20, 1993, the bank certified a check drawn by MRF, payable to Galit Diamond in the amount of $58,958. Upon receipt of the check, Galit presented it to Merchants for payment, and the bank posted the funds to Galit's account on that same day. Shortly thereafter, MRF's president informed Merchants that the certified check was forged. As a result, the bank placed a hold on Galit's account. Meanwhile, on June 1, Galit presented Merchants with a funds transfer application accompanied by a check drawn on its Merchants account in the amount of $30,030. The check was intended to cover a funds transfer for $30,000 and the bank's fee for that service. The application directed a credit to the Israeli bank account of Ilan Gertler, the supplier of approximately 60 percent of Galit's diamond inventory. Without rejecting the application or informing Galit that a hold had been placed on its account, Merchants held onto the funds transfer application and check. Gertler eventually received the funds, but a week later than expected. Because the late transfer tainted Galit's creditworthiness, Gertler severed its business relationship with Galit, greatly damaging Galit's ability to conduct its business profitably. Galit alleged that Merchants Bank was liable in damages for wrongfully freezing its account and claimed that Merchants' handling of the certified check violated various provisions of Article 3 of the Uniform Commercial Code, giving rise to liability under Article 4. Merchant's Bank denies any liability. According to Merchant's Bank, the transaction is governed completely by Article 4A, and Article 4A does not make allowance for consequential damages. Galit denies that Article 4A provides exclusive coverage, pointing out that the problem arose from the handling of a cashier's check, and thus must be decided under all three articles—3, 4, and 4A. How should this case be decided? What do you think is the key factor in deciding this case? [See "Diamond Dealer Denied Consequential Damages Allegedly Sustained When Bank Delayed Execution of Funds Transfer," *New York Law Publishing Company, New York Law Journal*, www.lexis-nexis.com (October 20, 1997).]

2. In July 2003, Phil Giannino, an authorized agent of Phil & Kathy's, Inc., arranged for Phil & Kathy's bank to wire $1,500,000 from the firm's account to Safra National Bank, where the funds were to be placed in a designated beneficiary account. The payment order requested by Giannino identified the beneficiary as "Banco de Brasil SA/Proteknika Do Brasil." Harris Trust and Savings Bank, the originating bank, processed the request for the payment order that same day. Unfortunately, the beneficiary account was misidentified, making completion of the wire transfer impossible. Phil & Kathy's was so informed the next day. The firm then contacted the Brazilian bank, which advised the firm to change the name of the beneficiary to "Blue Vale." Giannino then returned to Harris Trust and made a second $1,500,000 payment order, this time to Blue Vale. After Giannino left the bank, an officer of Harris Trust sent the first of three urgent wires to Safra National Bank asking it to amend the original payment order so that the proper beneficiary, Blue Vale, would receive the funds.

Safra Bank received the second payment order, processed it, and on the following business day the funds were successfully credited to the Blue Vale account. Five business days after the original order was placed, Safra Bank successfully credited Blue Vale with another $1,500,000, the amount specified in the original order. When Phil & Kathy's learned that Blue Vale had received the amount called for twice, it filed suit against Safra Bank to recover the second payment, plus interest and costs. According to Phil & Kathy's, since no true beneficiary was identified in the original order, the order was cancelled by operation of law and thus the second payment (payment of the first order) was improper and Safra should be liable for the firm's loss. Safra rebutted this argument by asserting that the UCC gives banks a five business day "window" in which to allow amendments to payment orders, and that the payment order only becomes void by operation of law if no payment is made at the end of the fifth business day.

How should the court rule in this case? What is the most important fact or factor affecting your decision? From an ethical perspective, should the bank have contacted Phil & Kathy's when it realized that it was processing two payments to the same beneficiary within such a short time period before sending the funds on to the Brazilian bank? [See *Phil & Kathy's, Inc. v. Safra National Bank of N.Y.* (S.D.N.Y. 2009)]

3. Robert J. Triffin is in the business of purchasing dishonored checks at a discount, and then collecting the amount owed on these checks. Triffin entered into five separate contracts with Richmond Financial Services, Inc., a check cashing company, to purchase Richmond's rights in five dishonored checks drawn against Third Federal Savings Bank, and issued by VFW Post 22. Each of the five checks had been cashed by Richmond, which then deposited the checks into its account with Wachovia Bank. Wachovia, in turn, credited Richmond's account and sent the checks to the Federal Reserve Bank in Philadelphia. The Federal Reserve Bank then presented electronic copies of the checks to Third Federal Savings Bank for payment. Third Federal paid the Federal Reserve Bank and changed the VFW account for the amount of each of the checks. However, VFW Post 22 informed Third Federal that the checks were forgeries, presenting affidavits in support of its claim. As a result, Third Federal printed electronic copies of each of the checks, stamping on the face of each "RETURNED UNPAID— OTHER FORGERY." On the back of each check was stamped:

> This is a photographic facsimile of the original check, which was endorsed by the undersigned and reported lost, stolen, or destroyed, while in the regular course of bank collection. All prior endorsements and any missing endorsements and the validity of this facsimile are hereby guaranteed, and upon payment hereof in lieu of the original check, the undersigned will hold each collecting bank harmless from any loss suffered, provided the

original check is unpaid and payment is stopped thereon. Third Federal Savings Bank.

Triffin sued Third Federal seeking payment on the five checks, alleging that Third Federal had breached its contract and its warranties because the facsimiles returned to Richmond did not include the legend: "THIS IS A LEGAL COPY OF YOUR CHECKS YOU CAN USE IT THE SAME WAY YOU WOULD USE THE ORIGINAL CHECKS." According to Triffin, absent this legend he was unable to sue the forger to recover on the checks, and therefore the bank should be held liable for breaching its warranties. Third Federal, on the other hand, asserted that it did not have an obligation to issue substitute checks because the original instruments were dishonored due to forgery, and that the notice it provided satisfied it warranty obligations.

How should the court rule in this case? What is the most important fact or factor affecting your decision? From an ethical perspective, should the bank have included the legend on the returned checks, or was the notice of dishonor due to a forgery sufficient? [See *Triffin v. Third Federal Savings Bank* (N.J. Super. 2008).]

Notes

1. UCC § 1-106.
2. UCC § 4-401(c).
3. UCC § 4-406(f).
4. UCC § 4-406(e).
5. UCC § 4-111.
6. UCC § 4-404.
7. UCC § 3-409(d).
8. Section 1693o(a).
9. Section 1693(b).
10. Section 1693(a)(6).
11. Section 1693(d)(c).
12. 12 USCA §§ 4000 *et seq.*
13. 12 CFR Part 229.
14. Pub. L. 108-100.
15. Check Clearing for the 21st Century Act, Federal Deposit Insurance Corporation Web site http://www.fdic.gov/consumers/consumer/alerts/check21.html.
16. Check 21 Requirements, http://www.accram.com/check21_research.html.
17. Jane K. Winn, "What Is a 'Transferable Record,' and Who Cares?," *BNA Electronic Commerce & Law Report*, 1060 (October 25, 2000).

Part V

Debtor-Creditor Relations

The use of credit is integral to the U.S. economy. People purchase homes on credit; they purchase automobiles on credit; they purchase major appliances on credit; and they purchase a number of other, less expensive or less valuable items on credit. In addition, businesses often use credit to obtain equipment, raw materials, and inventory. Such widespread use of credit will, on occasion, cause problems for the creditor, as well as presenting a number of concerns to the debtor who may not be able to pay for the credit as originally scheduled or intended.

Secured transactions are used to protect some creditors by providing a hedge against losses if or when the debtor defaults on the contract. Secured transactions give the creditor rights to the collateral used as security so as to minimize the potential losses that arise when the debtor fails to repay the credit in a timely manner. The law of secured transactions establishes the requirements for creating the security interest (attachment) and for perfection the security interest. The law also provides for establishing priorities among competing security interests and competing creditors.

Many different types of credit are used in the United States, especially by consumers. Collateralized loans of various types are used, as are signature loans and credit card transactions. There are a number of laws designed to provide consumer protections in credit transactions and guidance for the creditors who deal in these areas.

Bankruptcy law is intended to give an "honest debtor" a "fresh start" by allowing the honest debtor to eliminate or restructure his or her debts. The bankruptcy law is designed to protect debtors who encounter financial difficulties beyond their control, while also protecting the interests of the creditors to a significant extent. There are also provisions allowing a business debtor to reorganize in order to save the business while protecting the interests of the business's creditors.

24

Secured Transactions: Attachment and Perfection

Agenda

eClass entered the market at a very opportune time, and it has enjoyed moderate success. However, in order to expand the business and to take advantage of the firm's potential for growth, the business may need to borrow money from time to time. Ani, Meg, and Yousef would like to know how they can borrow money on the most favorable terms available and what sorts of collateral they can use to obtain those terms. They also want to know what it means to them and to other creditors if the firm is asked to grant a security interest in assets to secure a loan. The firm also expects to be asked to extend credit to some of its customers as the business grows and enters into larger contracts. What should eClass expect from its customers to whom it extends credit? How can the firm best protect its interests if it agrees to extend credit? What rights might eClass gain if it retains a security interest in any credit sales, and what should it require as collateral in such loans?

These and similar questions will arise as you study this chapter. Be prepared! You never know when the firm or one of its members will seek your advice.

Classic Case

IN RE COUNTY GREEN LIMITED PARTNERSHIP
438 F. Supp. 693, 1977 U.S. Dist. LEXIS 14662
(W.D. Va. 1977)

FACTS County Green Limited Partnership (CGLP) was organized for the purpose of acquiring a parcel of land located in Campbell County and constructing an apartment complex on the land. The project was financed through a $2,250,000.00 loan by the First and Merchants National Bank. CGLP gave First and Merchants a deed of trust and a security agreement as collateral for the loan. On June 12, 1974, First and Merchants recorded the deed of trust in the Clerk's Office of the Circuit Court of Campbell County, Virginia; filed a financing statement covering the property described in the security agreement in that office, and filed the financing statement in the Office of the State Corporation Commission.

CGLP contracted with the County Green Development Corporation, a construction company organized to serve as general contractor for the project, including furnishing the necessary appliances. The Development Corporation entered into an agreement with Goldberg, Inc., under which Goldberg would furnish these appliances. Goldberg retained a security interest in the appliances and filed financing statements in the Office of the State Corporation Commission of Virginia on May 21, 1975, and in the Office of the Clerk of the Circuit Court of the City of Lynchburg on May 24, 1975.

From May 25, 1975, through September 15, 1975, Goldberg delivered $90,867.40 worth of appliances. However, monthly title examinations conducted by First and Merchants in the Clerk's Office of the Campbell County Circuit Court failed to reveal any financing statements filed by Goldberg. First and Merchants did at one point receive a letter relative to equipment shipped by Goldberg together with a nearly unreadable photostatic copy of a portion of the front side of the security agreement constituting a part of the agreement between the Development Corporation and Goldberg, Inc. At no time prior to November 12, 1975, the date on which the partnership filed its bankruptcy petition, did First and Merchants have any knowledge of any financing statements filed by Goldberg with respect to the appliances at issue, and it was not until November 12, 1975, that Goldberg filed a financing statement in the Circuit Court of Campbell County, Virginia, covering the appliances sold to the Development Corporation.

ISSUE Which secured creditor, Goldberg, Inc. or First and Merchants, has the priority security interest in the appliances?

HOLDING First and Merchants had priority, based on the first to file or perfect provisions of Article 9 of the UCC.

REASONING Excerpts from the opinion of Chief Judge Turk:

The Bankruptcy Court determined that Goldberg failed to file a financing statement in Campbell

County, but, nevertheless, determined that as of July 10, 1975, had a superior secured interest under . . . § 9-401(2) . . . which provides that a financing statement filed in an improper place may nevertheless be effective against "any person who has knowledge of the contents of such financing statement." The Bankruptcy Court reasoned that First and Merchants obtained knowledge of the contents of the Goldberg security agreement by virtue of its receipt of the partial copy of Goldberg's security agreement on the 10th of July, 1975. . . . As both Goldberg, Inc. and First and Merchants have competing security interests the question becomes which interest is entitled to priority. With certain inapplicable exceptions . . . § 9-301(1)(a) . . . provides that "an unperfected security interest is subordinate to the rights of persons entitled to priority under § 9-312." . . . § 9-312(5)(a) . . . in the pertinent part, provides that in all cases not governed by the other rules of . . . [§ 9-312], priority between conflicting security interests in the same collateral is determined according to the time of filing or perfection whichever is earlier with the first party to file or perfect having priority. As the other provisions of . . . [§ 9-312] are inapplicable priority in the present case is governed by the first to file or perfect rule. Pursuant to the relevant provisions of . . . [§ 9-401] the proper places for Goldberg to have filed were in the Office of the State Corporation Commission and the Office of the Clerk of the Circuit Court for Campbell County, Virginia. . . . Therefore, Goldberg neither filed nor perfected prior to the date on which County Green Limited Partnership filed its petition in bankruptcy. . . . Consequently, as First and Merchants both filed and perfected prior to the time that Goldberg either properly filed or perfected there can be no question but that First and Merchants has priority. . . .

Irrespective of what it has conceded to be an improper filing, Goldberg, Inc. has argued that it is entitled to priority under . . . § 9-401(2). That section makes certain improper filings effective against any person who has knowledge of the contents of the erroneously filed financing statements. . . . The Bankruptcy Court determined that by virtue of First and Merchants' receipt of the partial copy of Goldberg's security agreement with the accompanying Goldberg letter, it obtained "knowledge of the contents of the Goldberg security agreement, within the meaning of the statute, to make a good faith filing by Goldberg effective against the security interest of the bank," as of July 10, 1975. . . . This . . . conclusion . . . is incorrect for at least two reasons. First, knowledge of the contents of the security agreement is not the test established by . . . [§ 9-401(2)]. That section requires knowledge of the contents of the improperly filed financing statement. Second, if the . . . opinion is read to mean that it has determined that First and Merchants had knowledge of the contents of the misfiled financing statement then it is clearly erroneous . . . "[a] person 'knows' or has 'knowledge' of a fact when he has actual knowledge of it." The parties stipulated that prior to November 12, 1975, First and Merchants had no "knowledge of any financing statements filed by Goldberg with respect to the appliances. . . ." Given this fact, it is difficult to perceive of how a party can know the contents of something which he does not know exists. . . .

The Uniform Commercial Code is a carefully planned and systematic compilation of logic and experience. Words are painstakingly defined and used in accordance with their intended impact on the everyday commercial transaction. A security agreement is not the same thing as a financing statement. Had the legislature intended for knowledge of a security agreement to be the same as knowledge of the contents of a financing statement it could have said so. Furthermore, such an expanded reading . . . tends to circumvent the pure race aspect of [§ 9-312(5)]. . . . First and Merchants . . . is entitled to a first priority security interest to the full extent of its loan.

THE NEED FOR SECURITY

According to an old song, "love makes the world go 'round." While this may be true, love does not provide much help in the business environment. Indeed, from a business perspective, *credit* may be what makes the *business* world go 'round. Businesses extend credit with the expectation that they will be repaid, with interest. Generally, the interest rate charged will, to some extent, reflect the risk the creditor believes he or she is assuming. The greater the risk assumed by the creditor, the higher the cost of the credit to be paid by the debtor. Debtors realize that they will be expected to pay for the use of credit, but they would prefer to receive as much credit as they need while paying as little for that credit as possible.

Security interests in general, and secured transactions in particular, can be used to help both parties in credit situations. The creditor is given "security" in the form of a claim against assets of the debtor, thus reducing the risk faced by the creditor. With this lowered risk, the creditor is willing to extend credit to the debtor at a lower cost. The debtor, in turn, is given credit at a lower cost without much, if any, additional risk. Admittedly, the debtor has granted the creditor rights against one or more assets of the debtor in the event that the debtor defaults, but the creditor would have rights against the debtor in the event of a default with or without any security interest.

There are numerous types of security interests that can be used. Many home-owners acquire a mortgage loan to purchase their homes, granting the lender a security interest against the home and the property as security. In many automobile loans the lender takes a lien against the title of the automobile. Some lenders want to take physical possession of the securing asset until such time as the loan is repaid, a method referred to at common law as a *pledge*. In this chapter we will address secured transactions as they are defined—and restricted—by Article 9 of the UCC. This article has been amended several times, most recently with revised Article 9. Revised Article 9 went in effect January 1, 2001 in most states, and by January 1, 2002 it was in effect in all of the states.

CREDIT FINANCING AND ARTICLE 9

The UCC, including the original Article 9, was originally proposed in 1951. This original version was basically a compilation of many of the laws and interpretations of secured transactions that were then in existence. Since then Article 9 has been amended several times. The 1962 revision made substantial changes to the law in this area, and the 1972 Official Text of Article 9 differed substantially from the 1962 official text. While most of the states had adopted the 1972 version of Article 9, some states were still following the 1962 version. Then in 1999 the NCCUSL completed its far-reaching revision of Article 9 and presented it to the states for consideration and adoption. The reaction was surprising. The states quickly adopted this latest revision, and by January 1, 2002, the newly revised Article 9 was in effect in every state.

These latest revisions to Article 9 were significant, and while they are meant to simplify the treatment of secured transactions, they required a period of adjustment for businesspeople and their attorneys. Among other things, this newest version of Article 9, now simply called "Secured Transactions," expands the scope of property available for secured transactions. For example, the revision permits creditors to create original security interests in deposit accounts and in software that is embedded in goods. In addition, revised Article 9 has eliminated the need for the multiple filings required by prior versions of the Code. Instead, under the revision, creditors will need to file only in the state where the debtor is domiciled. Other than fixture filings, the creditor need only file centrally, not locally. This change replaces the earlier mixed system of centralized and local filings. This new provision also clarifies the place for filing if the debtor is an international entity or individual. Again, the drafters' intent focuses on facilitating such credit arrangements. Revised Article 9 also permits electronic filings, making the filing process potentially faster and easier for the creditor. The revision also revised many of the prior rules on priorities when competing creditors assert claims as to certain classes of collateral.

The use of secured transactions is very common in business, so an understanding of the material is important to most businesspeople. It is not unusual to have a manufacturer who is a secured creditor in a number of transactions, while simultaneously occupying the role of debtor for one or more credit transactions in which he or she purchased equipment or raw materials. This manufacturer is in the position of having one or more security interests in his or her role as creditor, while also being subject to one or more security interests in his or her role as debtor.

To illustrate how a secured transaction may be used, assume that Bart Brown has opened a new restaurant and he needs to purchase a freezer and a cash register for his new business. He has enough cash on hand to make a substantial down payment toward both of these assets, but he cannot afford to pay the full price for either of them at this time. In this situation, he may be able to enter into a secured transaction with each of the sellers. For example, he may pay part of the sale price in cash, financing the balance of the price with the sellers. Bart will then receive possession of the items in exchange for giving each of the sellers a security interest in the equipment being sold. (Such a transaction is called a *purchase money security interest* or *PMSI*. PMSI's will be discussed in detail later in the chapter.) Using such a security interest "secures" payment by the buyer so that if Bart does not pay one of the sellers, that seller will have a priority claim against the goods and can repossess those goods in partial satisfaction of the debt owed by Bart. The creditors in this example could also have taken a security interest in assets other than the equipment they were selling to Bart, or they could have taken a security interest in other assets along with a claim against the equipment. (Taking an interest in other assets would *not* involve a PMSI.) Such decisions are left to the creditor and the debtor.

Thus, a secured transaction frequently allows buyers to receive goods more quickly than if they were forced to pay cash, while permitting the creditors (often the sellers, but other creditors may be involved) to protect themselves by retaining the right of repossession of the collateral in the event of a buyer's nonpayment. However, to ensure that they will have a priority claim against the equipment (or other collateral), these creditors must comply with the Article 9 rules relating to attachment and perfection; they should also be aware of the rules that establish priorities among multiple creditors, each asserting rights. These concepts are developed further in this chapter and in Chapter 25.

The terminology used in Article 9 is fairly specific, and it is important to use these terms correctly in any discussion of secured transactions. Applying this terminology to our example, the two seller/creditors are characterized as the *secured parties* ("a lender, seller, or other person in whose favor there is a security interest, including a person to whom accounts or chattel paper have been sold").[1] Bart, of course, is the *debtor* ("the person who owes payment or other performance of the obligation secured, whether or not he owns or has rights in the collateral, and includes the seller of accounts or chattel paper").[2] Bart and the seller presumably have entered into a *security agreement* ("the agreement which creates or provides for a security interest").[3] The freezer and cash register constitute *collateral* ("the property subject to a security interest").[4] Article 9's application is very broad: It may cover relatively simple business transactions like the one we have described, or it may extend to more complex forms of business financing, such as accounts receivable financing.

SCOPE OF ARTICLE 9

The revision of Article 9 changed and expanded the scope of the Article's coverage, providing Article 9 protections to a wider range of collateral. The newly defined scope can be found in § 9-109. This section provides the following definition.

> **§ 9-109. Scope.**
> **(a)** [**General scope of article**.] Except as otherwise provided in subsections (c) and (d), this article applies to:
>
> **(1)** a transaction, regardless of its form, that creates a security interest in personal property or fixtures by contract;
> **(2)** an agricultural lien;
> **(3)** a sale of accounts, chattel paper, payment intangibles, or promissory notes;
> **(4)** a consignment;
> **(5)** a security interest arising under Section 2-401, 2-505, 2-711(3), or 2A-508(5), as provided in Section 9-110; and
> **(6)** a security interest arising under Section 4-210 or 5-118.

The provisions set out in (a)(5) refer to security interests involved in a sale or lease of goods, and allow the creditor to retain a security interest in the goods until such time as the debtor acquires possession of the goods without requiring the creditor to file or otherwise act to perfect his or her interest. The provisions set out in (a)(6) refer to security interests by a bank (§ 4-210) or the issuer of a letter of credit (§ 5-118), to the extent that the bank or the issuer has given value for the instrument or for the letter of credit, without regard to the "normal" rules for creating a security interest otherwise set out in Article 9. These are special rules more fully defining the scope of the article.

The definition of a *security interest*, the key component of the scope of Article 9, is found in UCC § 1-201 (37). According to this definition, a *security interest* means "an interest in personal property or fixtures which secures payment or performance of an obligation. The term also includes any interest of a consignor and a buyer of accounts, chattel paper, a payment intangible, or a promissory note in a transaction that is subject to Article 9." This definition goes on to define several things that are *not* security interests:

- the special property interests of a buyer of goods upon identification of the goods to the contract; or
- the rights of a seller or lessor of goods under Articles 2 or 2A to retain or acquire possession of the goods.

This section also states that the retention or reservation of title by a seller of goods notwithstanding shipment or delivery to the buyer is limited in effect to the reservation of a security interest in those goods.

The personal property or collateral that will be subject to a security interest takes many forms. The Code categorizes collateral according to either (1) the *nature* of the collateral or (2) its *use*. Thus, *documents* (warehouse receipts, bills of lading, and other documents of title); *instruments* (drafts, certificates of deposit, stocks, and bonds); *proceeds* (whatever is received upon the sale, exchange, collection, or other disposition of collateral or proceeds); and the three kinds of collateral mentioned earlier—*accounts, chattel paper*, and *general intangibles*—represent the types of collateral the Code classifies primarily on the basis of their *nature*.

Goods, the most common type of collateral, are categorized on the basis of their *use* by the *debtor*. According to the Code, *goods* include all things that are movable at the time the security interest attaches or that are fixtures.[5] If goods are purchased for personal or household use they are treated as *consumer goods*.[6] Thus, a debtor may give a security interest in his or her household furniture or personal computer to a secured party. Goods purchased primarily for business use are classified as *equipment*.[7] Bart's freezer and cash register, in our example, are equipment collateral, as are such goods as corporate-owned office furniture and computers for the business. *Farm products* are a special category of equipment. The Code defines *farm products* as crops, livestock, or supplies used or produced in farming operations.[8] This means that a farmer may give a security interest in wheat, corn, cows, or even milk, since the Code covers the products of crops or livestock in their unmanufactured states as well. Goods that a business intends to sell or lease, as well as the raw materials that the business will use or consumer are viewed as *inventory*.[9] The items on a merchant's shelves or the food in a restaurant's refrigerator would be inventory. The last type of goods that the Code delineates is *fixtures*. Fixtures are goods that have become so related to particular parcel of real property that an interest in them arises under real property law.[10] Furnaces and central air-conditioning units, once installed in a building, are fixtures.

Exhibit 24.1 Shows the different classes of collateral and how each is treated.

When goods are used as collateral, the goods must be classified as one—and only one—type of goods. The classifications are mutually exclusive, and the classification is determined by the use made of the goods by the debtor. In borderline cases the principal use to which the debtor has put the property determines the type of collateral involved. Because the Code's rules regarding perfection, priorities, and default often turn on the type of collateral involved, as we shall see in Chapter 25, it is important to know which category of collateral is present in a given transaction.

A secured transaction is a *consensual* arrangement between the debtor and the creditor in which the debtor consents to the use of certain of his or her assets as

Exhibit 24.1

Classes of Collateral

Classes/Types of Collateral	Definition
Documents	Warehouse receipts, bills of lading, and other documents of title
Instruments	Checks, drafts, certificates of deposit, stocks, and bonds
Proceeds	Anything received upon the sale, exchange, collection, or other disposition of collateral or proceeds. The "replacement" for collateral due to its disposition by the debtor.
Accounts	A right to payment of a monetary obligation, whether or not earned by performance.
Chattel Paper	A record or records providing evidence of both a monetary obligation and a security interest in specific goods; specific goods and the software used in the goods; specific goods and licenses of software used in the goods.
General Intangibles	Any personal property, including things in action, other than accounts, chattel paper, commercial tort claims, deposit accounts, documents, goods, instruments, investment property, letter-of-credit rights, letters of credit, money, and oil, gas, or other minerals before extraction. The term includes payment intangibles and software.
Goods	Tangible personal property; all things that are moveable at the time the security interest attaches. Goods are classified by their use by the debtor as either consumer goods, equipment, farm goods inventory, or fixtures.

collateral, and the creditor then consents to the granting of credit, subject to the creditor's claim against that collateral. In our earlier example, we can say that Bart and the sellers of both the freezer and the cash register have each consented to this commercial transaction. Since personal property is involved (the freezer and register are goods), Bart has agreed to let the sellers retain an interest in the goods until Bart pays for them (a method of ensuring the performance of Bart's obligations); and the sellers, in turn, have agreed to give the goods to Bart now (even though the sellers have not received the total purchase price for them) in exchange for the right to repossess the items if Bart fails to pay. This transaction therefore fulfills all the requirements of an enforceable security interest.

Article 9 only applies to consensual security interests in *personal property*. Article 9 applies to the sale of motor vehicles, although the security interest is shown as a lien on the certificate of title issued by the state. The normal rules of Article 9 apply to vehicles held as inventory by a dealer. In some cases, a transaction, although covered by Article 9, also may be subject to other state statutes governing usury, retail installment sales, and the like (for example, the Uniform Consumer Credit Code). In the event of a conflict, the provisions of any such statute, and not Article 9, are controlling.

On the other hand, Article 9 does *not* apply to a security interest that arises by operation of law rather than through the agreement of the parties. Examples of such situations include a mechanic's lien or a judgment lien asserted against any of the assets of a debtor. For example, assume that Bart, our erstwhile restaurateur, hires a building contractor to renovate the restaurant. When the remodeling work is completed, Bart finds that he is unable to pay for the work. The contractor would be able to assert a *mechanic's lien* against Bart. The lien represents the money Bart owes for the labor and materials involved in the remodeling of the restaurant. Since Bart and the contractor did not agree in advance that the contractor would have an interest in Bart's restaurant, this is a nonconsensual arrangement that arises as a consequence of the parties' *status* (the contractor is a creditor who now is using the restaurant as security for the debt Bart owes) rather than as a result of *mutual consent*. Since it is not a consensual arrangement, it is not an Article 9 security interest.

Similarly, if Bart loses a lawsuit but does not pay the judgment, the plaintiff in that lawsuit can assert a *judgment lien* against property belonging to Bart, giving the victim the right to levy (as used in this situation, to levy means to seize) on that property in an effort to satisfy the judgment previously won. Again, there is no agreement between Bart and the judgment creditor that the property will be used as security for the debt, so this is a nonconsensual arrangement and it will not be governed by Article 9.

Article 9 also does not apply to transactions involving the use of real property or real estate as collateral, with the exception of some treatment of fixtures. This means that Article 9 has no application to real estate mortgages or on landlords' liens.

One test a person can use in deciding whether Article 9 applies is to ask whether the transaction is *intended* by the parties to have effect as a security interest. If the answer is *yes*, Article 9 probably covers the transaction.

eClass 24.1 Management/Finance

SOURCES OF FINANCING

The firm needs a quick infusion of capital, and Ani and Meg would like to have the firm borrow some money for business operations. However, they expect that the bank will want some sort of collateral before making any loans to eClass. Neither Ani nor Meg wants to use her personal assets as security for any credit they receive, but they are not sure whether eClass has any assets that can be used to secure the loan. They ask you what assets eClass might have that would be useful as collateral for any loans they seek. What will you tell them?

BUSINESS CONSIDERATIONS   How can businesspeople who are starting a closely held business acquire financing without using their personal assets as collateral? Is it a good idea for the owner/managers of small businesses to have their personal and their professional assets so closely entwined in the business venture?

ETHICAL CONSIDERATIONS   Is it ethical for a lender to insist that the owners of a start-up business use their personal assets as security for loans extended to the business? What ethical principles does this situation involve?

ATTACHMENT: THE CREATION OF A SECURITY INTEREST

As was previously mentioned, a secured transaction is a consensual relationship between the debtor and the creditor. If the debtor repays the creditor as agreed to by the parties, there is no controversy and no problems will arise. But if the debtor does not repay the creditor, the creditor will probably want to enforce the security interest agreed to by the parties. In order to do so, the creditor needs some proof that such an arrangement exists. This proof is established by *attachment*. Attachment establishes the rights of the creditor versus the debtor, vis-à-vis the collateral covered by the agreement. However, attachment alone does *not* provide the creditor with any advantage over other, potentially competing, creditors who may seek to enforce their claims in that same collateral.

Attachment creates the security interest in the collateral, and it establishes the rights of the creditor in the collateral.[11] Following attachment the creditor can assert rights superior to those of the debtor in the collateral if or when the debtor defaults on the agreement, usually due to non-payment of the debt. In addition, attachment is necessary before the creditor can *perfect* his or her interest. (Perfection establishes the rights of the creditor to the collateral against everyone *except* the debtor.)

According to the UCC, there are three requirements that must be met before attachment occurs. These requirements can be met in any order, but until all three are present there can be no attachment. And attachment is a requirement for perfection. Thus, a creditor who fails to attach is an unsecured general creditor, a *disfavored* position should the debtor default. The three requirements for attachment are:

- the parties have an *agreement* that the security interest will attach;
- the secured party—the creditor—must give *value* to the debtor; and
- the debtor must have *rights* in the collateral.

The requirements for attachment are illustrated in Exhibit 24.2, and are discussed in detail in the sections that follow.

The Security Agreement

The first requirement, the existence of an agreement between the parties, emphasizes the consensual nature of the relationship. This agreement must either be in the form of

Exhibit 24.2

Attachment of a Security Interest

Agreement between the Debtor and the Secured Party	"Authenticated Record" of the agreement with a sufficient description of the collateral *or* Oral agreement between the parties and the Secured Party has or obtains possession *or* control of the collateral
Secured Party gives Value to the Debtor	Consideration sufficient to support a simple contract *or* The Creditor has a preexisting claim against the Debtor *or* The Debtor accepts delivery under a preexisting purchase contract *or* The Secured Party makes a commitment to give future value
The Debtor has rights or acquires rights in the collateral	Debtor owns or possesses the collateral *or* In a sale or lease of goods to the debtor, the goods have been identified to the contract *or* The court determines that the Debtor otherwise has "rights in the collateral"

an *authenticated record* or the secured party must have possession of or control over the collateral. If the secured party has possession or control, the agreement is valid and enforceable even if the agreement is oral. The revision to Article 9 reflects the growing use and acceptance of electronic means of communication. Under prior versions of this article, the security agreement had to be "in writing" and "signed" by the debtor unless the creditor had possession of the collateral.

Section 9-203 (a) provides that a security agreement attaches to collateral when it becomes enforceable against the debtor with respect to the collateral unless the agreement expressly postpones the date of attachment.

Section 9-203 (b) addresses the enforceability of the security interest against both the debtor and any third parties. According to this section, the security interest is enforceable only if:

(1) value has been given;

(2) the debtor has rights in the collateral or the power to transfer rights in the collateral to a secured party; and

(3) one of the following conditions is met:

  (A) the debtor has authenticated a security agreement that provides a description of the collateral and, if the security interest covers timber to be cut, a description of the land concerned;

  (B) the collateral is not a certificated security[12] and is in the possession of the secured party under Section 9-313 pursuant to the debtor's security agreement;

  (C) the collateral is a certificated security in registered form and the security certificate has been delivered to the secured party under Section 8-301 pursuant to the debtor's security agreement; or

  (D) the collateral is deposit accounts, electronic chattel paper, investment property, or letter-of-credit rights, and the secured party has control under Section 9-104, 9-105, 9-106, or 9-107 pursuant to the debtor's security agreement.

The "authenticated security agreement referred to in (b)(3)(A)" is defined rather broadly by the Code, and includes a signed record or the adoption and execution of a symbol or the encryption of a record, in whole or in part, with the present intent to (1) identify the authenticating party, and (2) adopt or accept the record.[13] "Record" is defined as "information that is inscribed on a tangible medium or which is stored in an electronic or other medium and is retrievable in perceivable form."[14] If the security agreement is in "record" form, it must contain a description of the collateral, and this description must be sufficient to reasonably identify the collateral. In perfection, the parties can use a "supergeneric" description, such as "all the debtor's property." In the security agreement (the attachment), the collateral must be described with enough detail that it adequately reflects what collateral the parties intend to designate as the security for the agreement. Thus, a statement that the collateral is "all of the debtor's consumer goods" would be too broad, and would not be effective. However, a statement that the collateral is "all of the debtor's televisions" would be sufficiently detailed and specific, and would satisfy this requirement.

The security agreement may also contain an *after-acquired property clause*, a clause which specifies that the secured party not only has a claim against the collateral described in the agreement, but also has a claim against any property of the type described (for example, equipment) acquired by the debtor after the interest attaches and while the debt is still outstanding, in whole or in part.[15] After-acquired property clauses are relatively common in commercial credit transactions. They are less common in consumer credit transactions. In fact, the Code prohibits the attachment of an after-acquired property clause to consumer goods unless the consumer acquires rights in the goods within 10 days of the time the secured party gave value to the debtor.[16] If the parties intend to include an after-acquired property clause in the agreement, they need to either use the term "after-acquired property" or expressly refer to goods or assets acquired in the future. If they do not, the courts are not likely to recognize any claims on property acquired by the debtor after the agreement has attached.

The Secured Party Gives Value

The purpose of a security interest is to secure payment or performance of an obligation owed to the creditor by the debtor. This payment or performance is in return for something previously done by the creditor—the "giving of value." The UCC defines value in a fairly broad manner in § 1-201 (44). According to this section, a person gives "value" for rights in collateral by acquiring these rights:

a. In return for any consideration sufficient to support a simple contract;

b. As security for a preexisting claim or in partial or total satisfaction thereof;

c. By accepting delivery under a preexisting contract for purchase; or

d. In return for a commitment to give future value. (This commitment must be definite and binding, and not subject to the secured party's subsequent change of mind.)

Once such value is given, the secured party stands to suffer an actual loss if the debtor defaults. This, in turn, justifies allowing the secured party a priority position in the collateral against the debtor, should the debtor default.

The Debtor Acquires Rights in the Collateral

When the parties enter into a security agreement, the creditor agrees to give value to the debtor, and the debtor, in turn, agrees to use his or her *rights* in the collateral as security in the event of non-performance. Thus, the debtor must have "rights in the collateral" before the security interest can attach. Interestingly, the Code does not define "rights in the collateral," leaving courts to determine what this means. It would appear that the debtor must have either some type of ownership or possessory claim to the collateral in order to show that the debtor has "rights" in the collateral.

PERFECTION

Thus far, we have focused primarily on the relationship between the creditor and the debtor. When the debtor and creditor enter into a security agreement, the *attachment* of the creditor's security interest gives the creditor superior rights to those of the debtor in that collateral if the debtor defaults. However, that attachment does not give the creditor superior rights to other competing or conflicting creditors or to a bankruptcy trustee in that collateral. In order to acquire superior rights to other parties claiming an interest in the collateral, the creditor needs to perfect his or her interest, thus giving *notice* to any and all competing creditors of his or her security interest, and thus of his or her priority position.

Perfection is the process by which secured parties establish their position or priority in their claims against the collateral. Perfection is giving notice to "the world" that a particular secured party has a security interest in one or more specific assets of the debtor. Perfection is required in order for a secured party to protect his or her claim in the collateral from the clutches of later creditors who also have given value to the debtor, especially when the debtor has used the same assets as collateral for loans from them. Perfection is extremely important in the determination of rights since it establishes notice and priority. Generally, the Code adopts a "first in time, first in right" approach. The first secured party to file or perfect will normally have the highest priority, although there are some exceptions. The topic of priorities among secured parties is addressed in Chapter 25.

There are four possible ways in which perfection can occur. Care needs to be exercised here to select the most appropriate method since all four methods may not be available in a particular setting or transaction. The possible methods of perfection are:

- Perfection by filing. The secured party files a financing statement, giving notice to the world of his or her interest.
- Perfection by possession of the collateral. The secured party takes possession of the collateral, giving notice to the world of his or her interest.
- Perfection by control of the collateral. The secured party takes control of the collateral, giving notice to the world of his or her interest.
- Automatic perfection. The secured party is automatically perfected *upon attachment* of the security interest, even though there is no notice given to anyone of the existence of the security interest.

Obviously, automatic perfection upon attachment is the easiest method, and the secured party is not required to take any steps beyond attachment. Given the simplicity of this method, every secured party would use this method *every* time if it were always available. Unfortunately for the secured party, this method is not always available. More often than not, especially in commercial credit transactions, automatic perfection is *not* an option and the secured party must use one of the other three methods in order to properly perfect. The methods of perfection, and when each method is available, are illustrated in Exhibit 24.3. Each of the methods is then described in detail in the following sections.

Perfection by Filing

Location. Perhaps the best-known method for perfection is the filing of a financing statement by the secured party. Under the prior law the secured party had to determine *where* to file, and the location for filing could vary from state to state. In addition, even if the secured party initially filed in the correct location, if the debtor moved the collateral it was possible that the secured party would need to refile in a new location in order to retain his or her perfection. The revision to Article 9 made substantial improvements to the filing requirements. Filing is now simpler, the location for filing is much more straightforward, and even the method of filing has changed.

According to § 9-301(1), the proper place to file under Article 9 is in the jurisdiction where the debtor is located. The location of the collateral no longer matters for most purposes (a few exceptions will be addressed later in this chapter). While this rule seems simple, by itself it still does not tell the secured party where to file. The location

Exhibit 24.3

Methods of Perfection

Method of Perfection	Effective with the Following Types of Collateral
Perfection by Filing	Can be used with all types of collateral *except* deposit accounts and letters of credit.
Perfection by Possession of the Collateral	Can be used with goods, money, documents, instruments, certificated securities, and tangible chattel paper.
Perfection by Control of the Collateral	Can be used with investment properties, deposit accounts, letters of credit, and electronic chattel paper.
Automatic Perfection	Can be used with PMSIs in consumer goods, the sale of payment intangibles and promissory notes, and the assignment of beneficial interests in a decedent's estate.
	There are also some *temporary* automatic perfections available: 20 day "grace period" for a PMSI in equipment, although the secured party must "otherwise perfect" before the expiration of the 20 days in order to have a perfected interest;
	20 days from attachment if the secured party gives new value and the collateral is a negotiable document, an instrument, or a certificated security;
	20 days when a secured party makes available to the debtor an instrument, a negotiable document, or goods in possession of a bailee (normally for the debtor to sell the collateral).

depends on the debtor's "location," but what does that mean? If the debtor is an individual, the debtor's "location" is his or her state of residence. And if the debtor has several different residences (for example, a summer home in the Hamptons or a winter home in Florida), the debtor's location is his or her *primary* residence.[17]

If the debtor is a corporation or "registered organization," the debtor is "located" in its state of incorporation.[18] It does not matter where the corporate offices are located, or where any individual store, plant, or operation is located. This means that a creditor extending credit under a security agreement to a store in California *may* need to file in Delaware, if the store is part of a chain and the parent corporation was incorporated in Delaware. If the debtor is an organization *other than* a corporation (trusts, partnerships, societies, etc.), the organization is "located" at its place of business. If the organization has more than one place of business, it is located at its chief executive offices.[19] If the federal government is the debtor, the location for filing is the District of Columbia.[20] Finally, if the debtor is foreign there are two possibilities for the proper location to file the security interest. If the debtor is located in a foreign country that has laws governing perfection that are similar to Article 9, especially in allowing the recording of non-possessory liens, the debtor is located in that foreign country and the creditor needs to file in that foreign country. If the debtor is not located in a country with such laws, the proper place for filing—the "location" of the debtor—is the District of Columbia.[21]

Not only must the secured party know the jurisdiction in which he or she must file in order to properly perfect, the secured party must also perfect in the correct location within that jurisdiction. This requirement caused some confusion prior to the revision of the article because some states required local filing (filing in the county where the collateral was located) while other states required central filing (filing in the state capital of the state in which the collateral was located). In addition, some states required local filing for some types of collateral, but central filing for other types of collateral. Add to this the problems presented if or when the debtor moved the collateral from one state to another, and the potential for confusion and for erroneous filings is obvious. The revised act has virtually eliminated this problem. The secured party is now expected to file *centrally* in the state of the debtor's residence. In addition, the secured party is permitted to file electronically. Thus, in our previous example the California secured creditor will be able to submit a financing statement to the Secretary of State in Delaware in order to perfect his or her security interest against the debtor even though the debtor is a store located in California.

There are still a few potential pitfalls under this new system, but they are significantly fewer than those under the prior law. For example, if the collateral is "related to realty," the secured party must file locally, and not centrally. The filing is in the same office where real estate mortgages would be filed. Such collateral "related to realty" includes minerals, timber to be cut, and fixtures, but it does not include crops.[22] Also, if the debtor is an individual, and he or she moves to another state after the secured party has perfected, the secured party will have a grace period of four months in which to refile in the new state of the debtor's residence in order to retain the security interest. If the secured party does not refile within the four month window, his or her interest will lapse. While the secured party will still be able to file in the new state of residence, the lapse may well permit other creditors who had been junior to this claim to move up the priority list, dropping the secured creditor whose interest had lapsed to a lower priority position. (Remember, the normal rule is "first in time, first in right.")

Effective Date. A filing is considered effective upon the presentation of a financing statement for filing, together with a tender of the filing fees, to the filing officer.[23] The creditor is not responsible for any delays or misfilings of the filing officer. However, the creditor is responsible for making a proper presentation and for proper tender of the filing fees. If the presentation is communicated in a manner or medium that is not authorized by the filing office, it is inappropriate, and thus ineffective. Similarly, if the creditor does not tender an amount equal to or greater than the required filing fee, the attempt to file in invalid.[24]

Once properly filed, the financing statement is effective for a period of five years from the date of filing,[25] and may be continued for additional five-year periods if a continuation statement is properly filed within the last six months before the expiration of the interest.[26]

Sufficiency. In order for a filing to be sufficient, it must contain the name of the debtor and the name of the secured party, and indicate the collateral that is covered by the financing statement.[27] In addition, if the financing statement is for collateral "related to realty," the statement must include a description of the real property, and if the debtor does not have an interest of record in the realty, the name of the record owner must be included.[28]

As stated above, the financing statement must contain the name of the debtor. However, this requirement has a more rigorous meaning under the new provisions. If the debtor is a registered organization, the financing statement must contain the *official* name of the debtor as reflected in the public record of the jurisdiction of the organization. In a similar vein, if the debtor is a decedent's estate, the financing statement must provide the name of the decedent and indicate that the debtor is an estate. If the debtor is a trust, that fact must be reflected. Thus, the secured party must exercise care that the statement contains the *official* name, and not some variation of that name or a different name under which the debtor is doing business. If the financing statement contains only the debtor's trade name, the filing is not sufficient to put other creditors on notice.[29]

At the same time, the drafters did not want to erect too many barriers to the sufficiency of filings. Article 9 has a stated policy that if the financing statement substantially complies with the requirements of § 9-502, that filing is sufficient even if it contains minor errors, so long as those errors are not seriously misleading. In addition, even if there is an error in the name of the debtor in the filing, the filing is sufficient if a search of the records using the debtor's correct name and using the filing office's "standard search logic" (a computer term relating to how a computer program searches for files) would disclose the financing statement, the statement is sufficient despite the technical error in the statement.[30]

Finally, the financing statement can use "supergeneric" terms to describe the collateral, even though such terms are not permitted in the security agreement. Thus, a description of the collateral as "all the debtor's assets" is permissible and serves as adequate notice to any subsequent creditors.

Perfection by Possession

The secured party can perfect his or her interest by taking physical possession of the collateral. In this situation, commonly referred to as a pledge, the perfection is effective as soon as the secured party takes possession and lasts for so long as the secured party retains possession. There is no need to file any statements or worry about any continuations or renewals. However, the secured party must properly store, maintain, and care for the collateral while it is in his or her possession.

Perfection by possession can be used if the collateral is in the form of negotiable documents, goods, instruments, money, or tangible chattel paper. The secured party can also perfect by possession if the collateral is in the form of certificated securities and the secured party takes delivery of the securities under the provisions and guidelines of § 8-301.[31] If the collateral is in the possession of a third person, the secured party is deemed to be "in possession," and therefore to have *perfected*, if the person in possession of the collateral authenticates a record acknowledging that it is holding the collateral for the benefit of the secured party.

eClass 24.2 Finance

PERFECTING A SECURITY INTEREST

eClass recently made a large sale to a large educational customer in the Midwest. The sale was made on credit, and the firm retained a security interest in the goods. A proper security agreement was prepared and signed by the customer, and the firm prepared a financing statement so that it could file and perfect its interest. However, a disagreement has arisen as to where and how to perfect. Yousef thinks that eClass should file the financing statement in the state where the customer is located, since that is where the units were shipped. Ani insists that the statement must be filed where the customer is incorporated, regardless of where any of its schools or the inventory happen to be located. They have asked for your advice. What will you tell them?

BUSINESS CONSIDERATIONS   What policies should a creditor that regularly enters into secured transactions develop to ensure that it will properly perfect its security interests? How would these policies be different under the prior version of Article 9?

ETHICAL CONSIDERATIONS   Is it ethical for a creditor to use "supergeneric" descriptions of collateral in its financing statements when the security agreement requires a more specific description?

Perfection by Control

If a security interest is held in investment property, deposit accounts, letter-of-credit rights, or electronic chattel paper, the secured party is allowed to perfect by taking control of the collateral. The requirements for control of investment property are spelled out in § 8-106, the Investment Securities article. The secured party has perfection by control of a deposit account if the secured party is the bank with which the account is maintained, or the debtor, the bank, and the secured party have agreed in an authenticated record that the bank will follow the instructions of the secured party with respect to the deposit account.[32] The secured party has control of a letter-of-credit right to the extent that the secured party has any right to payment or performance by the issuer of the letter-of-credit, and if the issuer has consented to an assignment of the proceeds of the letter-of-credit to the secured party.[33] Finally, the secured party has control of an electronic chattel paper if (1) there is only one authoritative copy of the record, (2) that copy identifies the secured party as the assignee of the record, and (3) the authoritative copy is communicated to and maintained by the secured party or his or her designated custodian.[34]

Automatic Perfection

Use of automatic perfection upon attachment is limited under the revised act. The reasons for allowing automatic perfection relate to commercial convenience, especially in credit transactions involving consumers, or because there are other protections available to the creditor under other areas of the law.

Purchase Money Security Interest (PMSI) in Consumer Goods. A purchase money security interest (PMSI) in consumer goods is automatically perfected for five years upon attachment. There is no need for the secured party to take any additional steps or to incur any additional expenses in order to be perfected, *provided that* the secured party and the consumer-debtor have entered into a security agreement.[35] A purchase money security interest arises when the secured creditor provides either the money or the credit to allow the consumer to purchase an item, and that purchased item is then used as the collateral to secure the credit. Remember that this applies only to a PMSI for *consumer goods,* goods that are purchased primarily for personal or household use. Also, if the consumer goods purchased are to become fixtures, the secured party cannot rely on automatic perfection. He or she must file a financing statement in order to perfect this interest despite the PMSI nature of the transaction.

Other Automatic Perfections. The Code includes several other types of transactions that perfect automatically and that do not require any additional steps by the secured party. These transactions are listed here.

- ■ The assignment of a beneficial interest in a decedent's estate.

- The assignment of accounts or payment intangibles, so long as the assignment does not constitute a significant portion of the assignor's outstanding accounts or payment intangibles.
- The sale of promissory notes or payment intangibles.

Temporary Automatic Perfections. There are also several areas in which the law grants the secured party an automatic perfection, but the perfection period is temporary. These are also listed here.

- A secured party who has a security interest in negotiable documents, certificated securities, or instruments, and who gives new value to the debtor is automatically perfected for 20 days from the time of attachment even if the debtor retains possession of the collateral.
- If the secured party delivers goods or negotiable documents covering the goods, for the purpose of allowing the debtor to sell or exchange the goods, or for the purpose of loading, shipping, or storing the goods, the secured party is temporarily perfected for 20 days on the goods or the documents.
- Similarly, if the secured party delivers instruments or certificated securities to the debtor for the purpose of sale, exchange, collection, renewal, or registration, the secured party is temporarily perfected on the instruments or the certificated securities.

LEASE INTENDED AS SECURITY

As we have noted, Article 9 broadly defines the term *security interest* as an interest in personal property or fixtures that secures payment or performance of an obligation. One of the strengths of the Code is the flexibility provided by such a sweeping definition. In fact, courts have had few problems in recognizing the existence of a security interest in most circumstances. However, the area of leases *has* presented some difficulty to the courts. If the parties enter into a lease, the lessor retains title to the goods, and there is no need for the lessor to comply with the provisions of Article 9 in order to protect his or her interest in the leased goods. However, some "leases" appear to be disguised sales rather than true leases. In such a transaction the lessor is attempting to circumvent the requirements of Article 9 by *calling* the transaction a lease when it is, in fact, a credit sale with a security interest. These "leases" are recognized by Article 9 as secured transactions, and are subject to all the requirements of any similar Article 9 transactions.

The adoption of Article 2A of the UCC, Leases, did not resolve this problem, nor was it adequately resolved under the provisions of the previous version of Article 9. The revision of Article 9 attempts to address the issue more directly. In § 1-201 (37) the Code states:

Whether a transaction creates a lease or a security interest is determined by the facts of each case; however, a transaction creates a security interest if the

eClass 24.3 Finance

MOVING COLLATERAL

eClass has been selling a significant amount of software in New York, and has, on occasion, had difficulty in providing an adequate supply of the units to meet the requests of its customers. Meg has suggested that the firm should establish a warehouse facility in New York to provide better and quicker service to their customers in the Northeast. She believes that having a ready supply of inventory in the region will actually help to increase sales. Yousef is concerned that the firm's creditors may be opposed to this relocation of inventory, especially the firm's bank, which has a security interest in the inventory to secure a line of credit. He thinks the firm should at least notify the bank of this plan. While Meg does not think that the bank will object, she would like to know what you think they should do. They have asked you for your opinion. What will you tell them?

BUSINESS CONSIDERATIONS   Should a debtor in a secured transaction adhere to a policy of informing the creditor any time removal of the collateral from the jurisdiction occurs? Why or why not? What can the creditor in this situation do to maximize its protection in the event the collateral is removed from the jurisdiction without notice?

ETHICAL CONSIDERATIONS   Is it ethical for a debtor to remove collateral from the jurisdiction without notifying the creditor? Is it ethical for the creditor to demand notice from the debtor in advance before the debtor can move the collateral?

consideration the lessee is to pay the lessor for the right to possession and use of the goods is an obligation for the term of the lease, not subject to termination by the lessee, and

(a) the original term of the lease is equal to or greater than the remaining economic life of the goods,

(b) the lessee is bound to renew the lease for the remaining economic life of the goods or is bound to become the owner of the goods.

(c) The lessee has an option to renew the lease for the remaining economic life of the goods for no additional consideration or nominal additional consideration upon compliance with the lease agreement, or

(d) The lessee has an option to become the owner of the goods for no additional consideration or nominal additional consideration upon compliance with the lease agreement.

While this section expressly provides that the facts of each case will determine whether a given transaction creates a lease or a security interest, it does provide some guidelines to help the courts in making this determination. If the lessee has the right to terminate the lease and to return the goods at any time, the transaction is a "true" lease. If the lessee does not have this right, *and* if the lessee has the option to purchase the goods at the end of the lease for either no or nominal consideration, this is a disguised secured transaction. In addition, if the goods will have no remaining economic value at the conclusion of the lease, this is a secured transaction.

PROCEEDS

The final point we should make about security interests and perfection is that the Code allows a secured party's interest to reach the *proceeds* of the debtor's disposition of the collateral. If the debtor disposes of the collateral, whatever the debtor receives in exchange for that collateral is deemed proceeds. Assuming that the secured party had properly perfected his or her security interest in the original collateral, his or her interest will automatically be perfected in the proceeds under the original perfection. And so long as the proceeds are identifiable, the secured party will retain his or her perfection over those proceeds. However, if the proceeds received by the debtor are in the form of cash, the secured party is perfected in the proceeds only for a period of 20 days.

Suppose the debtor disposes of the collateral for cash, and then uses the cash to purchase some new asset. This newly purchased asset is referred to as "second generation proceeds," and the secured party will need to file a new financing statement that adequately describes these second generation proceeds in order to retain his or her perfection.

Contemporary Case

OHIO GRAPHCO, INC. v. RCA CAPITAL CORP.
2009 U.S. Dist. LEXIS 103791 (W.D. Ky. 2009)

FACTS On November 14, 2008, Graphco sold Unlimited Graphics, Inc. (UGI) a Press Line printing press for $199,247. The contract contained a "Reservation of Title" clause specifying that Graphco retained "exclusive legal title and right of possession" until the full price was paid.

On November 17 UGI made a down payment of $9,247 and the Press Line was delivered to UGI. UGI promptly entered into a lease agreement with RCA Capital Corporation (RCA) for the Press Line, also on November 17. This agreement stated that RCA would buy the Press Line by paying Graphco the $190,000 balance due in order to acquire title, and would then rent the Press Line to UGI.

On November 19, RCA filed a UCC Financing Statement with the Kentucky Secretary of State's

Office claiming a purchase money security interest in the Press Line, with UGI named as the debtor and RCA as the secured creditor. Then on November 20, RCA prepared and issued a "Purchase Order" to Graphco for the Press Line covered by the Graphco—UGI Sales Contract and the proposed UGI—RCA equipment lease agreement. In the Purchase Order, RCA agreed to pay Graphco the balance of the purchase price. Graphco alleges that RCA never acquired the Press Line from Graphco and never paid any part of the $ 190,000.00 balance due. Graphco also alleges that the agreement between UGI and RCA was never consummated because RCA paid the remaining $190,000.00, and that the Purchase Order never became a valid or enforceable agreement between Graphco and RCA because Graphco never signed the Purchase Order; never canceled, waived or otherwise terminated its Sales Contract with UGI; and never delivered possession of the Press Line to RCA.

On January 7, 2009, RCA assigned its rights, title and interest in the UGI lease agreement to APC. Graphco contended that RCA had not purchased the Press Line nor did it have a contract to do so. On January 20, 2009, Graphco filed a UCC Financing Statement with the Kentucky Secretary of State, and on January 30, 2009, an assignment of RCA's security interest in the Press Line to APC was filed with the Kentucky Secretary of State's Office.

When RCA filed for bankruptcy, Graphco filed suit, seeking a determination of rights in the Press Line between Graphco and APC.

ISSUE Which party, Graphco or APC, has the priority security interest in the Press Line?

HOLDING APC has priority. It received an assignment of a properly perfected security interest that predated the perfection by Graphco, and thus has a higher priority.

REASONING Excerpts from the opinion of Chief Judge Thomas B. Russell:

A security interest may become perfected upon several different actions by the secured party; however, the most common, and the one applicable to the collateral at hand, is filing of a UCC Financing Statement with the Secretary of State.... When using filing to perfect a security interest, the security interest is perfected upon filing if all requirements of attachment are met, or immediately upon attachment, if the Financing Statement is filed before attachment has taken place....

In the instance of the Graphco/UGI Sales Contract it appears a valid security interest attached to the Press Line as collateral. First, there is evidence there was value given by the creditor.... Additionally, the debtor acquired rights in the collateral ... the Press Line was delivered to UGI's premises.... Even though the Sales Contract contained a reservation of title, as stated, possession of the collateral alone confers sufficient rights in the collateral on the debtor. Finally, there was an authenticated security agreement. The Sales Contract between UGI and Graphco is a document which created or provided for a security interest because of its "Reservation of Title" language.... Graphco states that it filed its Financing Statement on January 20, 2008.[sic] Since the requirements of attachment had been met prior to that date, the date of perfection for Graphco is January 20, 2009....

RCA filed a Financing Statement on November 19, 2008. The Court finds that the requirements of attachment had been met on that date.... If the Court applies the argument set forth by Graphco that no value could be given until Graphco was paid, the date of perfection for RCA's security interest would be December 9, 2008, when attachment was reached after filing....

On January 20, 2009, RCA or APC filed with the Kentucky Secretary of State an assignment of RCA's UCC Financing Statement. Kentucky's UCC provides means for a secured party to assign its interest to another party.... Filing an assignment is not required to continue the perfected status of a security interest against creditors and transferees of the original debtor.... Therefore, APC, as the assignee, stands in the place of RCA and takes the perfection date of RCA: November 19, 2008.

The general rule for purposes of determining the priority of competing security interest is first in time of filing or perfection, first in priority.... The statute explains, "[p]riority dates from the earlier of the time a filing covering the collateral is first made or the security interest ... is first perfected, if there is no period thereafter when there is neither filing nor perfection." ... A perfected security interest has priority over an unperfected security interest and if both interests are unperfected, the first to attach has priority.... After looking at the security interests competing

in this case, it appears both have been perfected by filing. The date of filing and perfection for the security interest of Graphco was January 20, 2009. The date of filing and perfection for RCA, and thus APC, was November 19, 2008. Applying the priority rules, it appears that APC has priority over Graphco in the Press Line.

Graphco asserts that due to its reservation of title clause in the Sales Contract with UGI it has priority over the Press Line. For support Graphco cites ... the definition of a security interest. While Graphco is correct that reservation of title creates a security interest, that does not mean that the security interest has properly attached or been perfected in order to defeat another perfected security interest. The Court finds that APC has priority in Press Line over Graphco and therefore Graphco's Motion for Summary Judgment is denied.

You Be the Judge

On October 13, 2003, the Debtor, Philip Wayne Dorton, purchased and took possession of a 2000 BMW 328i. The Debtor granted a security interest in the car to the dealer in the purchase contract, which the dealer then assigned to BMW. On December 24, 2003, the District of Columbia Department of Motor Vehicles issued a certificate of title for the car, noting BMW's security interest. BMW did not file a financing statement with the District of Columbia.

On January 30, 2004, less than 90 days after BMW's lien was noted on the certificate of title, the Debtor petitioned for relief under Chapter 7 of the Bankruptcy Code, listing the car as the bankruptcy estate's only asset. The trustee filed a motion for summary judgment in the Bankruptcy Court, arguing that BMW's security interest was never properly perfected since BMW never filed a financing statement, and was thus inferior to the claim of the trustee in bankruptcy.

This case has been brought in *your* court. How will *you* decide? Explain and justify your answer. [See *McCarthy v. BMW Bank of North America*, 346 B.R. 271; 2006 U.S. Dist. LEXIS 54577 (2006).]

Summary

A secured transaction provides added protection to the creditor in the event the debtor defaults on his or her obligation. If the debtor does not pay the creditor as agreed, the creditor's security interest will allow the creditor to repossess the collateral used as security. A secured transaction typically involves a secured party, a debtor, a security agreement, and collateral. The Code categorizes collateral according to its nature or its use. One type of collateral is goods; the different classes of goods are mutually exclusive. Collateral also may consist of documents, instruments, letters of credit, proceeds, accounts, chattel paper, and general intangibles. Article 9 applies to consensual security interests in personal property or fixtures but not to those arising by operation of law. It covers leases meant as security but not "true" leases.

Attachment is the process by which the secured party creates an enforceable security interest in the collateral. A signed security agreement, in conjunction with the occurrence of other events, provides evidence that attachment has occurred. Perfection refers to the method by which a secured party gives notice to the world of his or her security interest. Perfection protects the secured party against claims asserted against the collateral by later creditors of the debtor. Perfection can take place in one of four ways: (1) by the creditor's filing of a valid financing statement, (2) by the creditor's possession of the collateral, (3) by the creditor's control of the collateral, and (4) by automatic perfection. The method of perfection that the secured party should use often depends on the type of collateral involved. If filing is the applicable method, the creditor must use a legally effective financing statement. The revision to Article 9 provides for a simplified filing system. Generally, filing of the financing statement occurs centrally, normally with the office of the secretary of state of the debtor's home state. If the debtor is a corporation, this means the state of incorporation. If the debtor is foreign, the filing may have to be in his or her home nation, or it may be effective if filed in the District of Columbia. Filings may also be made electronically, and the description of the collateral may use "supergeneric" terms such as "all the assets of the debtor."

Discussion Questions

1. What is a secured transaction? Why would a creditor want to enter into a secured transaction rather than a normal credit transaction?

2. Define a security interest. How is a security interest created under the provisions of Article 9?

3. Revised Article 9 recognizes four different methods for perfection of a security interest. What are these methods, and when can each of them be used?

4. If Will does not pay Carla, the mechanic who fixes his car, and she obtains a judgment against him, does Carla have an Article 9 security interest in Will's car? Why or why not?

5. What is the difference between a true lease and a lease intended as security? How does the UCC distinguish between these two types of "leases"?

Case Problems and Writing Assignments

1. John J. and Clara Lockovich purchased a new 22-foot Chapparel Villian III boat from the Greene County Yacht Club for $32,500. The Lockoviches (the debtors) paid $6,000 to the club and executed a security agreement/lien contract that set forth the purchase and finance terms. In the contract, the Lockoviches granted a security interest in the boat to the holder of the contract. When Gallatin National Bank paid the club $26,757.14 on the Lockoviches' behalf, the club assigned the contract to Gallatin. Gallatin then filed financing statements in the appropriate office and with the secretary of the Commonwealth of Pennsylvania. Unfortunately for Gallatin, the Lockoviches resided in New Jersey, so the filing of the financing statements was ineffective to perfect the security interest in the boat. The Lockoviches subsequently defaulted under the terms of the security agreement they had signed with Gallatin. Before Gallatin could take action, the Lockoviches filed for relief under Chapter 11 of the Bankruptcy Code. Gallatin then sought, pursuant to the security agreement, to enforce its rights. The Bankruptcy Court denied Gallatin's motion, holding that because Gallatin had failed to properly perfect its security interest in the boat by filing, it was an unsecured creditor. Pursuant to the bankruptcy laws, as a holder of an unperfected security interest, Gallatin's right to the boat remained inferior to that of the debtor-in-possession, a hypothetical lienholder. What should Gallatin have done in order to perfect its security interest in the boat? Would a different result occur if Gallatin could argue that it held a purchase money security interest in the boat? Explain your answer. [See *In re Lockovich*, 124 B.R. 660 (W.D. Pa. 1991).]

2. Grieb Printing Company, the debtor, executed a lease of equipment with Bayer Financial Services. The lease was for 48 months, had a monthly payment of $4,108.71, and gave the debtor the option to purchase the equipment at the end of the lease for one dollar. The lease, which was executed by the debtor's CEO, granted Bayer a security interest in the equipment and authorized Bayer or its agents to sign and execute on the lessee's behalf any and all necessary documents to effect any filings, including the filing of any such financing or continuation statements without further authorization. Bayer filed a financing statement on the equipment. Pursuant to the lease agreement, Bayer signed the financing statement on behalf of the debtor as the debtor's "attorney-in-fact." Before doing so, Bayer did not request that the debtor sign the lease. Bayer then properly filed the financing statement. Approximately five months after obtaining the equipment, the debtor filed a Chapter 7 bankruptcy petition. When the bankruptcy trustee moved to sell the equipment in which Bayer claimed an interest, the trustee argued that Bayer's interest in the collateral was unperfected. The trustee based its contention on the Kentucky statutory provision that makes invalid any filing of a financing statement not signed by an individual authorized to sign on behalf of the corporate debtor. Was the signature that Bayer, the creditor, had placed on the financing statement for the debtor valid under Kentucky law and thus sufficient to protect the creditor's security interest? [See *In re Grieb Printing Company*, 230 B.R. 539 (Bkrtcy. W.D. Ky. 1999).]

3. Kenneth W. Gibson, an employee of United Airlines, obtained a Visa card from the airlines's credit union. Gibson did not give the credit union any collateral to secure this extension of credit at the time the Visa card was issued. The interest rate for charges always had been 12.96 percent per annum. Some time later, the Gibsons (Kenneth and his wife, Ramona) borrowed approximately $23,000 from the credit union. In connection with this loan, the Gibsons executed a loan and security agreement that provided that the balance due to the credit union would accrue interest at the rate of 8.9 percent per annum. Under the terms of the loan agreement, the Gibsons gave the credit union a security interest in collateral consisting of two cars and Mr. Gibson's shares in the credit union. The back of the loan and security agreement set out a series of pre-printed terms and conditions. One of these pre-printed terms and conditions— the so-called "dragnet clause"—purported to make the collateral security for any debt owed by either of the Gibsons to the credit union in addition to the loan obligation. The Gibsons later contended that no one representing the credit union pointed this language out to them. The loan and security agreement also contained a pre-printed provision (a "choice of law" clause) stating that the agreement "shall be governed by and construed in accordance with the laws of the State of Illinois."

When the Gibsons, who resided in California, ultimately filed a petition for an adjustment of debts under Chapter 13 of the Bankruptcy Code, Mr. Gibson owed the credit union $4,846.06 on the Visa card and the Gibsons owed the credit union $14,759.97 on the 1996 loan obligation. The value of the collateral was sufficient to cover both obligations. The credit union filed two proofs of claim in the Chapter 13 case, one for the Visa card debt and one for the loan obligation. Originally, only the loan claim had been described as secured; the Visa claim had been described as unsecured. However, shortly thereafter, the credit union, in an amended claim, asserted secured status for the Visa claim as well. The Gibsons characterized the dragnet clause as unenforceable and the Visa claim as unsecured. How should a court dispose of this case? [See *In re Gibson*, 234 B.R. 776 (Bkrtcy. N.D. Cal. 1999).]

Notes

1. UCC § 9-102(a)(72).
2. UCC § 9-102(a)(28).
3. UCC § 9-102(a)(73).
4. UCC § 9-102(a)(12).
5. UCC § 9-102(a)(44).
6. UCC § 9-102(a)(23).
7. UCC § 9-102(a)(33).
8. UCC § 9-102(a)(34).
9. UCC § 9-102(a)(48).
10. UCC § 9-102(a)(41).
11. UCC § 9-203(a).
12. UCC § 80102(1)(a). Stated as simply as possible, a certificated security is a share or other interest in an enterprise that is represented by an instrument in bearer or registered form. It is a type of investment security, governed by Article 8.
13. UCC § 9-102(a)(7).
14. UCC § 9-102(a)(69).
15. UCC § 9-204(a).
16. UCC § 9-203(b)(1). See also the federal "Credit Practice Rules," 16 C.F.R. 444; 12 C.F.R. § 227. Under these rules, both the Federal Trade Commission and the Federal Reserve Board prohibit the creation of non-purchase money, non-possessory liens in household goods.
17. UCC § 9-307(b)(1).
18. UCC § 9-307(e).
19. UCC § 9-307(b)(2)–(3).
20. UCC § 9-307(h).
21. UCC § 9-307(c).
22. UCC § 9-501.
23. UCC § 9-516(a).
24. UCC § 9-516(b).
25. UCC § 9-515(a).
26. UCC § 9-515(d).
27. UCC § 9-502(a).
28. UCC § 9-502(b).
29. UCC § 9-503(c).
30. UCC § 9-06(c).
31. UCC § 9-313.
32. UCC § 9-104.
33. UCC § 9-107.
34. UCC § 9-105.
35. UCC § 9-309(1).

25

Secured Transactions: Priorities and Enforcement

Agenda

If eClass is going to grow and prosper, it will need funding. While Ani, Meg, and Yousef expect to generate profits from their operation, they realize that profits alone are not likely to provide sufficient funding. And since they do not want to sell any ownership interests, they know they will need to borrow money occasionally. They also realize that the firm will need collateral for these loans, but the firm does not have many different types of assets that can be used. As a result, they wonder if it is possible to use the *same* assets as collateral for more than one loan, and what effect this might have on any prospective creditors and their ability to obtain loans.

eClass will also be making a number of substantial sales of their inventory to retail purchasers, and many of these sales will be made on credit. The principals understand the need to make credit sales, but they would like to protect themselves and the firm as much as possible by retaining a claim on the merchandise they sell on credit. What type of security interest or other claim on the goods can the firm use in these

783

situations? What will provide the greatest protection to the firm if any of its customers default?

If eClass should default on its obligations, what rights can its creditors assert against the firm and against any collateral used to secure the credit? If a customer defaults, what rights can the firm assert against that customer?

These and other questions are likely to arise during your study of this chapter. Be prepared! You never know when the firm or one of its members will seek your advice.

Classic Case

BORG-WARNER ACCEPTANCE CORPORATION v. TASCOSA NATIONAL BANK

784 S.W.2d 129, 1990 Tex. App. LEXIS 230 (Tex. App. 1990)

FACTS On March 1, 1982, the Tascosa National Bank extended a loan to T&L Ventures, Inc., d.b.a. The Video Collection, in the sum of $30,006.00. A financing statement was obtained and filed with the Secretary of State on March 4, 1982. The Bank's financing statement described the collateral as:

Video software and hardware, computer games hardware and software, all inventory, furniture, fixtures of above located at Amarillo, Potter County, Texas.

From time to time, the indebtedness was renewed and extended and additional funds were provided T&L, with the last note dated April 18, 1986, in the principal amount of $153,613.84. All indebtedness was evidenced by notes and secured by the same collateral.

On March 7, 1982, Borg-Warner and T&L executed and entered into a Security Agreement, granting Borg-Warner a security interest in its inventory purchased with the proceeds of loans made by Borg-Warner. Borg-Warner perfected its security interest as a purchase money security interest (PMSI) under § 9-312(c) by (1) filing a financing statement describing the collateral, with the Office of the Secretary of State of Texas; and (2) notifying the Bank of Borg-Warner's security interest in T&L's inventory.

Following the perfection, Borg-Warner began financing the acquisition of inventory by T&L and continued such financing through May 22, 1986.

Subsequently, T&L defaulted on its indebtedness, and on May 11, 1986, the Bank repossessed the inventory and removed the inventory from T&L's premises and placed it in a warehouse. Borg-Warner made demand on the Bank to deliver the inventory and the Bank refused.

Borg-Warner's then filed suit against the Bank asserting wrongful conversion of the inventory in which Borg-Warner held a PMSI. While the suit was pending, pursuant to an agreement between Borg-Warner and the Bank, T&L's inventory was sold. The net proceeds from the sale totaled approximately $140,771.39.

ISSUE Which creditor, Borg-Warner or the Bank, has a priority?

HOLDING Borg-Warner had a properly perfected PMSI, and its PMSI takes priority over conflicting perfected security interests.

REASONING Excerpt from the opinion of Carlton B. Dodson, Judge:

A security interest is a "purchase money security interest" to the extent that it is (1) taken or retained by the seller of the collateral to secure all or part of its price; or (2) taken by a person who by making advances or incurring an obligation gives value to enable the debtor to acquire rights in or the use of collateral if such value is in fact so used. . . . [T]he general rule of priority among conflicting security interests in the same collateral where both interests are perfected by filing, is that the secured party who first files a financing statement prevails. . . . However, section 9.312(c) states a special rule for a PMSI in inventory. That subsection reads . . . as follows:

> (c) *A perfected purchase money security interest in inventory has priority over a conflicting security interest in the same inventory* and also has priority in identifiable cash proceeds received on or before the delivery of the inventory to a buyer . . .

Under the above provisions, Borg-Warner's security interest is a PMSI. . . .

In determining the priority between Borg-Warner and the Bank, we note that the legislature has provided that a PMSI in inventory such as Borg-Warner's has priority over a conflicting security interest in the same inventory and also has priority in identifiable cash proceeds received on or before the delivery of the inventory to the

debtor. . . . Borg-Warner complied with the statutory code requirements.

The Bank . . . claims that even if Borg-Warner did have a PMSI priority, Borg-Warner lost such priority because its security agreement provided that Borg-Warner had a "future advances" clause and an "after acquired property" clause which contradicted any claim of priority as a PMSI. The Bank argues that the transformation rule applies here because the inventory security agreement by its terms destroyed any priority Borg-Warner might have had as a PMSI holder. . . . Courts applying the transformation rule have done so in cases involving the financing of consumer goods. . . . The underlying policy of the transformation rule applied in consumer goods cases is to prevent overreaching creditors from retaining title to all items covered under a consolidation contract until the last item purchased is paid for. Otherwise, the creditor continues to reserve a PMSI in each item until the entire indebtedness is satisfied. . . .

We have not been directed to, nor has our research revealed circumstances in which the transformation rule has been applied by Texas Courts to cases involving priorities among lienholders. We see no reason to do so now. . . .

The . . . [Texas Code] declares that the code must be liberally construed and applied to promote its underlying purposes and policies. The underlying purposes and policies of the code are to simplify, clarify, and modernize the law governing commercial transactions, to permit the continued expansion of commercial practices through custom, usage and agreement of the parties, and to make uniform the law among the various jurisdictions. We see no need to juxtapose the transformation rule on the clear meaning of the Texas Legislature's mandate. The legislature gave favored treatment to PMSI status. . . . The legislature has made clear that when the inventory financier has complied with the requirements of the Texas Business and Commerce Code, the financier has a PMSI in existing and after acquired inventory, in effect a floating lien over the mass of changing goods available for sale by the debtors to others, with priority over other conflicting security interest[s]. . . .

Borg-Warner has a valid PMSI in the inventory in question which is superior to the Bank's security interest. . . .

INTRODUCTION

In a perfect world, debtors always repay their debts when they are due and creditors do not have to worry about when—or if—they will be repaid. However, the world in which we live is not perfect. Sometimes debtors don't pay their debts when they are due. In fact, sometimes the debtors never repay their obligations. As a result, creditors do worry about when and if they will be repaid. This is one of the main reasons that creditors seek security interests and then take the time and trouble to perfect those interests.

In Chapter 24 we discussed the process of creating a security interest by attachment, and the process of perfecting that security interest, thus giving notice to the world of the secured party's claim against some of the assets of the debtor. If each debtor dealt with only one creditor, we would not need such rules. In that situation, if the debtor defaulted on his or her obligations, everything the debtor owned would be available for the creditor's use in satisfying the creditor's claims. But in reality, debtors are likely to have multiple creditors, and each of those creditors may need to assert claims against assets of the debtor if the debtor defaults on his or her obligations. This is another reason for secured transactions—to allow secured creditors to assert claims against particular assets of the debtor that have been used as collateral on the obligation. Even this is not foolproof, though, since some debtors will use the same collateral as security for several loans or credit transactions. As a result, we need to have rules for establishing priorities among conflicting creditors, both secured and unsecured. We also need rules governing what the creditors can do if the debtor defaults and the creditors have to resort to the collateral in order to satisfy their claims, or at least a portion of their claims. That is the thrust of this chapter.

While many of these rules are found in revised Article 9, there is also an interplay between the provisions of Article 9 and various other state and federal laws in determining priorities. Not all creditor claims are based on a security interest. There may also be claims based on judgments or judgment liens, statutory liens, possessory liens, or the claims asserted by a trustee in bankruptcy. The rules for determining which creditor has priority, and where each of the competing creditors stands in relation to the other creditors and to the collateral is the primary focus of this chapter.

PRIORITIES

A secured party's priority over other creditors can have enormous practical importance. If a debtor defaults on his or her obligation, the parties with the highest priority are the creditors most likely to be able to recover most, if not all, of the money owed to them without having to resort to litigation. Creditors with lower priority, "junior" creditors, may well be prevented from accessing the collateral and may be forced to seek other methods of collecting from the debtor, including filing a lawsuit.

In addition, the debtor may not simply default. He or she may seek relief and protection in bankruptcy. The one catastrophe every creditor probably fears the most is the bankruptcy of the debtor. The reason is simple: In the event of bankruptcy an automatic stay is entered, which prevents the creditors from proceeding against the debtor. If the creditor participates in the bankruptcy proceeding, he or she runs the risk of receiving only a few cents on every dollar loaned to the debtor.

Yet, as we have seen, a creditor who attains the status of a perfected secured party can maximize the chances of recovering the money owed, even in a bankruptcy proceeding. This status gives the creditor first claim on the collateral and thus the best chance (generally by selling the collateral) of realizing most, if not all, of the debt. A creditor with a perfected security interest has priority over general (or unsecured) creditors and lien creditors, including the trustee in bankruptcy. After the secured party has disposed of the collateral, any money in excess of that owed to the secured party may be applied to the claims of these other creditors. In many instances, however, no money remains to satisfy these latter claims. Thus, we cannot overemphasize the importance of becoming a secured party.

In the material to follow, we will first examine priorities among competing security interests. We will then look at the priorities between secured creditors and lien holders. We will finish our coverage of priorities by discussing the conflict between secured creditors and the trustee in bankruptcy. Throughout this discussion, keep in mind that as a general rule first in time is first in right.

CONFLICTING SECURITY INTERESTS

A creditor holding a properly perfected security interest has numerous advantages. As a result, most creditors strive to achieve this status. However, most debtors have either a limited number of assets to use as collateral, or a limited number of *types* of assets (equipment, inventory, etc.) to use as collateral. This fact, in turn, leads to the possibility that several secured parties will claim a security interest in the same collateral. When this happens, how can we determine who among this class of favored parties has priority? Or, in other words, who has "first dibs" on the collateral?

788 Part V: Debtor-Creditor Relations

Article 9 spells out the rules for priority among conflicting security interests in § 9-322, which provides that:

(a) [General Priority Rules] Except as otherwise provided in this section, priority among conflicting security interests and agricultural liens in the same collateral is determined according to the following rules:

(1) Conflicting perfected security interests and agricultural liens rank according to priority in time of filing or perfection. Priority dates from the earlier of the time a filing covering the collateral is first made or the security interest or agricultural lien is first perfected, if there is no period thereafter when there is neither filing nor perfection.

(2) A perfected security interest or agricultural lien has priority over a conflicting unperfected security interest or agricultural lien.

(3) The first security interest or agricultural lien to attach or become effective has priority if conflicting security interests or agricultural liens are unperfected.

This is not as complicated as it sounds. The Code follows a "first in time, first in right" approach in deciding priority. According to this section, the first security interest to *file or perfect* has priority over any conflicting security interests in the same collateral. Thus, if two creditors, each claiming the same collateral as security, both file financing statements seeking to perfect their interests, the first to file would have priority since this creditor won the "race" to record the interest. The second creditor's claim would be subordinate to the first creditor's claim even if the second creditor was the first to attach his or her interest, or the first to give value to the debtor.

Notice that the priority is determined by the first to file *or* perfect. It is quite possible that one creditor may file his or her interest *before* that interest attaches, thus establishing his or her priority position at the time of filing. In this example, since there has not yet been an attachment, this interest, while *filed*, is not perfected. A second, competing creditor might then take possession of the collateral, thus perfecting his or her security interest in the collateral by possession. If the first creditor then has his or her interest attach, probably by giving value to the debtor, the first creditor would have priority in the collateral. Since this creditor filed first, this creditor was first in time and will also be first in right. Note, however, that this creditor must have a perfected interest in order to have priority. If the creditor files first, but his or her interest never attaches, the interest is never perfected. And if it is never perfected, it cannot have priority over a perfected interest.

If for some reason none of the competing parties has perfected its security interest, the first interest to attach enjoys priority. Relying on attachment alone as a vehicle for attaining priority, however, generally makes little sense because an unperfected secured creditor will not enjoy a preferred status in bankruptcy proceedings. In addition, any of the competing creditors can move ahead of the first party to attach simply by perfecting. While the creditor whose interest attached first is celebrating his or her priority position, one or more of the "losing" creditors can file or otherwise perfect, and by so doing gain a priority over the earlier attachment. Remember, to gain priority over other secured parties, other creditors or claimants, and over the trustee in bankruptcy, it is imperative to *perfect* the security interest as soon as possible. Normally this will entail filing a financing statement, if filing is an acceptable mode for perfecting this particular security interest. If filing is not appropriate, the secured creditor needs to perfect his or her interest as soon as possible in the appropriate manner.

EXCEPTIONS

While the Code generally follows the first in time, first in right approach to determining priority among conflicting security interests, there is an exception. A properly perfected security interest will not prevail over a purchase money security interest, a *PMSI*, that is properly perfected even if the PMSI arises later in time. There are also two situations in which a perfected security interest is cut off by the sale of the collateral despite the prior perfection of the security interest covering the collateral prior to the sale. One such situation involves a buyer in the ordinary course of business and the other involves a bona fide purchaser of consumer goods. Each of these three exceptions is discussed below.

Purchase Money Security Interests

According to § 9-324, a perfected purchase-money security interest in goods, other than inventory or livestock, has priority over a conflicting security interest in the same goods.[1] You should recall from Chapter 24 that a purchase-money security interest arises when the secured creditor provides the credit with which the debtor purchases the assets that will be used as collateral to secure the credit. Thus, a debtor who purchases a new computer from a computer company on credit, using the computer as security for the debt, has entered into a PMSI transaction. Similarly, if the debtor goes to the bank to borrow money in order to purchase the computer, and agrees to give the bank a security interest in the computer as collateral, a PMSI transaction is involved. Further, a perfected purchase-money security interest in inventory has priority over conflicting security interests in the same inventory, as well as over any proceeds from the sale of that inventory, provided that the secured creditor has met two criteria: (1) the creditor has perfected the purchase-money security interest by filing before the debtor receives possession of the inventory, and (2) the creditor sends an authenticated notification to any holder of a conflicting security interest stating that the creditor expects to acquire a purchase-money security interest in the inventory, and that notice is received by the conflicting creditor before the debtor acquires the inventory.[2] If the PMSI is in livestock, the creditor also must perfect by filing before the debtor acquires the livestock, and must notify any conflicting creditors by authenticated notification before the debtor acquires the livestock.[3]

Generally speaking, a PMSI has priority over any other type of security interest, regardless of when the other interest attached or was perfected. This may seem unfair at first glance, but it actually makes sense from a business perspective. The debtor who enters into a PMSI transaction has not affected his or her net worth, so prior creditors are no worse off than before the transaction, and they may be better off, depending on the value of the new asset. The debtor's assets will increase by the value of the collateral purchased, and his or her liabilities will increase by the amount of the new debt secured by the new asset. If the debtor finances 100 percent of the transaction, both debits and credits increase by the same amount. If the debtor pays 20 percent down and finances the balance, the debtor's assets increase by the value of the new collateral, but decrease by the 20 percent down payment, a net increase of 80 percent of the asset's value. The liabilities also increase by 80 percent of the asset's value.

You should also recall from Chapter 24 that goods are classified according to their primary use in the hands of the purchaser-debtor. If a debtor acquires goods for personal or household use, those goods are viewed as consumer goods. If the debtor acquires the goods for the purpose of using them in the operation of a business, the goods are viewed as equipment. If the goods are acquired for use in a farming operation, they are deemed to be farm goods. And if the goods are acquired by the debtor with the intention to resell them as part of his or her business, the goods are inventory. The reason for this attention to the classification of the goods is that a purchase-money security interest must be perfected in different ways depending on the classification of the goods.

A PMSI in consumer goods is *automatically* perfected upon attachment, and the perfection is valid for five years. The creditor needs to do nothing beyond attachment in order to enjoy the special priority status of the PMSI. This normally means that the creditor needs only to enter into a security agreement with the debtor. There are numerous reasons for this special treatment, including the fact that consumer goods are not likely to be resold, and that this treatment helps to reduce the cost to consumers who are involved in consumer credit transactions.

A PMSI in equipment must be filed or otherwise perfected in order to protect the creditor. Since the collateral is equipment, and since the debtor is likely to need the equipment in order to operate his or her business, this normally means that the creditor will file in order to perfect. The creditor will enjoy the special priority accorded a PMSI *if* the interest is perfected at the time the interest attaches *or* within 20 days after the debtor receives the equipment. The same rules apply to farm goods other than livestock. Again, the creditor is required to file before, or within the 20 days after, the debtor receives the farm goods.

If the PMSI is in inventory or livestock, the creditor must file *before* the debtor acquires the property, and must *also* provide authenticated notification to any conflicting creditors before the debtor acquires the collateral in order for the creditor to properly perfect the PMSI. Exhibit 25.1 compares the different methods of perfecting a PMSI.

Exhibit 25.1

Perfecting a PMSI

Classification of the Goods	Basis of the Classification	Method(s) of Perfection
Consumer goods	The goods are acquired for personal or household use	The *preferred* method is automatically upon attachment. The creditor can also perfect by filing or by taking possession of the collateral.
Equipment	The goods are acquired for use in operating a business	The creditor has automatic perfection upon attachment, but only for 20 days. The *preferred* method is by filing either before attachment of within 20 days thereafter. The creditor can also perfect by taking possession of the collateral.
Farm goods	The goods are acquired for use in a farming operation	The creditor has automatic perfection upon attachment of farm goods other than livestock, but only for 20 days. The *preferred* method is by filing either before attachment of within 20 days thereafter. The creditor can also perfect by taking possession of the collateral.
		If the collateral is livestock the creditor must file before the debtor acquires the livestock *and* must give authorized notice to any competing/conflicting creditors before the debtor acquires the livestock.
Inventory	The goods are acquired for resale by a business or for consumption within the business	The creditor must file *before* the debtor acquires the property, *and* must give authenticated notification to any conflicting creditors before the debtor acquires the collateral.

If a creditor has an interest in equipment, farm goods, inventory, or livestock that otherwise qualifies as a PMSI, but fails to perfect this interest properly, the creditor will lose his or her "PM" status, but still retains an "SI." This means that an equipment creditor who failed to file within the 20-day grace period, but did file thereafter, would be a secured creditor with a perfected interest, but the interest would *not* be a PMSI and the creditor would not enjoy the special priority rules. Rather, he or she would now be subject to the first in time, first in right provisions of a regular security interest.

We know that a properly perfected PMSI has special priority over other security interests, but which creditor has priority if there are multiple PMSIs in the same collateral? While this situation is likely to be rare, it does occur on occasion. Previous versions of Article 9 did not address this issue, leaving it for the courts to decide on a case-by-case basis. The revision to Article 9 provides a statutory solution to the problem. If a seller and a lender each claim a PMSI in the same collateral, the *seller* of the goods has priority over a lender.[4]

To those who see this "super priority" for purchase money secured parties as unfair to prior secured creditors, the drafters of the Code offer the following policy justifications. The notification procedures required by the Code when the PMSI involves inventory or farm products will tip off the earlier creditor that the debtor is "double financing." At this point, the earlier creditor who believes that he or she is vulnerable may curtail any future advances to the debtor. And, assuming that the earlier security agreement so provides and that this earlier creditor gives notice to the debtor, it may be argued that such double financing constitutes a condition of default, allowing the earlier creditor to demand payment from the debtor. The earlier creditor has means of protecting his or her interest, while the debtor is allowed access to new sources of credit. Remember, the earlier creditors still have priority for the collateral on which they perfected, and they may have a secondary claim on the newly acquired assets covered by the PMSI.

If the security interest covers noninventory collateral (such as equipment, farm products other than livestock, or consumer goods), a purchase money secured party has priority over prior secured parties without the need to give notice to those prior secured parties. Some may wonder why less is required of the PMSI creditors with an interest in equipment or farm goods other than livestock (a 20 day grace period for filing and no need to give notice to conflicting secured creditors) or PMSI creditors with an interest in consumer goods (automatic perfection without filing or giving notice to competing secured creditors) than is required of inventory PMSI creditors. After all, a creditor holding a PMSI in inventory (or farm goods comprised of livestock) must file *and* provide authorized notice to competing creditors, and must do both prior to the debtor acquiring the collateral. Apparently, the drafters of the Code believed that arrangements for periodic advances against incoming property are unusual outside the inventory field; thus, they did not think there was a need to notify noninventory secured parties.

Buyers in the Ordinary Course of Business

Businesses that sell goods from inventory need to make sales in order to be profitable. The creditors who finance the inventory do so knowing that the goods are likely to be sold. If the debtor is successful, the collateral used to secure the credit will leave the possession of the debtor at the time of the sale. But what if the debtor sells the goods and then fails to make payments to the secured creditor? Will the creditor be permitted to proceed against the buyer of the goods, enforcing his or her security interest against the purchaser?

According to § 9-320(a), a buyer in the ordinary course of business takes the goods free from any security interests valid against the seller even if the security interest is perfected and the buyer knows of its existence. (There is an exception to this rule if the buyer is buying farm goods from a person engaged in farming operations.)

The key point to this rule, which effectively "cuts off" the perfected security interest of the creditor, is that the sale is in the *ordinary* course of business. The debtor is simply doing what the debtor was expected to do. He or she is selling inventory to customers. The creditor loses his or her claim against the inventory that has been sold, but the creditor is automatically perfected on the proceeds from that sale, so the creditor is in no worse position than before. In addition, most security interests covering inventory are floating liens that will automatically attach to the replacement inventory the debtor acquires in restocking. And absent this rule, it would be very difficult for the debtor to make sales to customers. If a customer had to worry about whether the debtor would pay his or her creditors, with the customer being subject to the repossession of the goods if the debtor did not pay, the customer would hesitate to make a purchase.

It should also be noted that this rule does not apply if the sale is made *not* in the ordinary course of business. For example, a bulk sale in which the buyer purchases a significant portion of the debtor's inventory and/or equipment does not cut off the rights of the secured creditor in the items sold. In this situation the security interest remains valid and enforceable against the buyer, and if the debtor defaults, the creditor can enforce the interest against the buyer. The buyer, in turn, would then have to sue the seller for any losses suffered due to the seller's default.

Although many people use the terms *bona fide purchaser* and *buyer in the ordinary course of business* interchangeably, they are distinct concepts. A *bona fide* purchaser is normally a consumer who buys goods from another consumer, gives value for the goods, and is unaware of any claims against the goods by any third persons. Buyers in the ordinary course of business, in contrast, are purchasers who are buying from a seller who routinely sells from inventory or otherwise regularly engages in such transactions.

Bona Fide Purchasers of Consumer Goods

Another class of persons who may have "priority" of a sort over a previously perfected security interest is the *bona fide purchaser* of consumer goods. However, before this exception applies several conditions must be met. According to § 9-320 (b), a buyer of goods who purchases the goods from a consumer takes the goods free of any security interests that may exist in those goods, if:

(1) the buyer buys the goods without knowledge of the security interest;

(2) the buyer purchases the goods "for value";

(3) the buyer purchases the goods for his or her own personal or household use; and,

(4) the buyer purchases the goods before a financing statement covering the goods is filed by the creditor.

This means that a consumer who buys goods from a consumer and gives value for the goods will take the goods free of any security interest that the seller granted, provided that the buyer did not know of the security interest, *and* that the secured party had not filed to perfect. Many, if not most, sales of goods from one consumer to another consumer are of a somewhat casual type (think of a yard sale, for example). If the goods being sold by consumer A to consumer B are security for a prior credit transaction by consumer A, the security interest was probably perfected automatically. Unless consumer B knows that there is a security interest in the goods (which is very unlikely), he or she takes the goods "free and clear." If consumer B know of the security interest that was automatically perfected or if the creditor filed to perfect (giving consumer B constructive notice of the perfected security interest), consumer B takes subject to the perfected interest.

Other Exceptions

Two other exceptions need to be mentioned before we complete our discussion of conflicting security interests. The revision to Article 9 permits a secured party holding a security interest in a negotiable instrument or in chattel paper to perfect this interest

eClass 25.1 Finance

SECURITY INTEREST

eClass recently sold some software on credit to a local retail store. The firm retained a security interest in these units and properly perfected its interest by filing in the appropriate office in a timely manner. Unfortunately, Ani, Meg, and Yousef have learned that this retail store is having serious financial problems and may be forced to go out of business. They ask you if they can assert their security interest against the units still in the store's possession if the retailer ultimately should default on the contract. They also want to know what rights, if any, they can assert against any customers who purchased the software from the store if the store eventually defaults on its obligations to the firm. What will you tell them?

BUSINESS CONSIDERATIONS   What should a business creditor that holds a perfected security interest do if or when it hears that one of its debtors is having financial difficulties? How can the business creditor protect its interests without jeopardizing the future of the debtor?

ETHICAL CONSIDERATIONS   Assuming that it would be legal to do so, would it be ethical for a secured creditor to seek enforcement of its security interest against buyers in the ordinary course of business who purchased collateral from a retail seller that also was a debtor of the secured creditor?

by filing. (Under the prior law the creditor had to take possession in order to perfect such an interest in negotiable instruments, with the exception of a 21 day "grace period" if the instrument represented proceeds from the sale of other, covered collateral.) While filing in now a permissible method of perfection, it may not be as effective as the creditor would like. Most people who are purchasing a negotiable instrument or chattel paper are not going to run a record search prior to acquiring the instrument or the paper to determine whether it is subject to a security interest. Such conduct would be unreasonable for the purchaser and would significantly slow down commercial transactions. As a result, the new version of Article 9 addresses these issues in § 9-330.

Under this section, a purchaser of chattel paper has priority over a security interest in the chattel paper, if (1) the chattel paper represents proceeds from the sale of inventory by the debtor, (2) the purchaser gave new value for the paper and took the paper in the ordinary course of his or her business, and (3) the paper itself did not indicate that it had already been assigned to a third party.[5] If the purchaser purchases a negotiable instrument, and qualifies as a holder in due course following this purchase, the purchaser-HDC takes priority over any security interests filed against the negotiable instrument.[6] (The security interest, even if perfected, would be a personal defense, and as discussed in the Negotiable Instruments chapters, an HDC is not subject to personal defenses.)

CONFLICTS BETWEEN SECURITY INTERESTS AND LIENS

As you should already have surmised, there may be a number of conflicting claims in the collateral in which a security interest has been granted to the secured creditor. Among the types of claims that may conflict with the claim of the secured creditor are the various types of liens that may be asserted by other creditors. These liens may take the form of *judicial* liens, *statutory* liens, and *consensual* liens. In the next section we will look at the effect each of these types of liens may have on the priority of a perfected security interest.

Judicial Liens

A judicial lien is a lien acquired by the creditor in a judicial proceeding. The most common method for creating a judicial lien is for the winning party in a lawsuit to have the sheriff, or some other court official, levy on the assets of the debtor. Section 9-102(a)(52) defines a judicial lien creditor as:

> **(a)** a creditor that has acquired a lien on the property involved by attachment, levy, or the like;
> **(b)** an assignee for the benefit of creditors from the time of assignment;

(c) a trustee in bankruptcy from the date of the filing of the petition; or

(d) a receiver in equity from the time of appointment.

In a conflict between a secured creditor and a judicial lien holder, the interests are generally viewed as being equal, and the courts apply the "first in time, first in right" rule to determine the priority among the creditors. Thus, if the security interest is perfected before the judicial lien attaches, the secured party will have priority.[7] Also, if the creditor makes any "future advances" to the debtor, these future advances will also have priority over an intervening judicial lien, if the future advances are made within 45 days after the judicial lien attaches. And if the creditor has no knowledge of the judicial lien or the future advance is made because of a commitment made without knowledge of the judicial lien, the 45-day limit does not apply.[8]

Notice in the definition set out above that each of the judicial liens *except* the one created by attachment or levy also provides for when the lien attaches. For a judicial lien created by attachment or levy, state law controls as to when the interest attaches. Most states hold that the interest attaches at the time of the levy, which means when the sheriff takes physical control of the asset. However, a few states treat the lien as attaching when the court clerk issues a writ of attachment.

Statutory Liens

Statutory liens arise as a result either of a statutory provision establishing the lien, or under common law traditions and customs. Statutory liens are often obtained by landlords against their tenants, artisans or mechanics against the party for whom they have performed work, and attorneys who have not been paid for legal services rendered on behalf of the debtor. Tax liens are also statutory liens. A statutory lien may be possessory or non-possessory. A possessory statutory lien attaches to the debtor's property when the lienholder takes possession of the collateral. For example, if Dan takes his car to Robert, his regular mechanic, for a tune-up, Robert acquires a possessory statutory lien on the car until he is paid for the services. If Dan does not pay, Robert is allowed to retain possession until such time as payment is made. However, if Robert releases the car to Dan, Robert has surrendered the lien and is, at that point, merely an unsecured general creditor. A possessory lien has priority over a properly perfected security interest, regardless of when either arose, unless the statute that creates the lien expressly makes the lien subordinate to a security interest.[9]

Some interesting special rules apply to a tax lien. If a debtor fails to pay his or her federal taxes, a tax lien is created by statute. This lien arises at the moment of "assessment" by the IRS, even though no one except IRS knows of the existence of the assessment or the related lien at that time. This lien is valid against all property owned by the debtor, or anything subsequently acquired by the debtor. However, the Federal Tax Lien Act specifies that a properly perfected security interest that was perfected prior to the attachment of the tax lien will prevail over the tax lien.[10] In addition, the IRS has ruled that a PMSI will also prevail over a tax lien, even if the PMSI arises after the tax lien attaches, provided that the PMSI is properly perfected.[11]

eClass 25.2 Finance

PURCHASE MONEY SECURITY INTEREST

eClass sold an older computer, monitor and printer to Marcy on credit and retained a purchase money security interest in the items, getting her to sign a security agreement at the time of the sale. Since these items were sold to a consumer there was no need for the firm to file, so taking a security interest seemed like a good idea. Marcy is now in default on the debt, and the firm would like to enforce its interest in the units. Yousef learned that the printer is in the possession of a repairperson whom Marcy had hired to work on it. Yousef wants to know what rights the firm has in this situation and also whether the firm can insist that the repairperson turn over the printer to eClass due to its perfected security interest. He also would like to know whether the lack of a filing might reduce the firm's rights in this situation. What will you tell him?

BUSINESS CONSIDERATIONS   Why might a secured creditor want to pay a person who has a possessory lien stemming from repairing the collateral in order to obtain possession of the collateral itself? What can the creditor do if it decides not to redeem the collateral from the possessory lien holder?

ETHICAL CONSIDERATIONS   Is there an ethical reason for allowing a possessory lien holder to gain priority over a properly perfected security interest? What ethical considerations justify such a rule?

Consensual Liens

Consensual liens arise by agreement of the parties. While a secured transaction is a type of consensual lien, that is not the type we are discussing here. The consensual liens that commonly conflict with a secured transaction are likely to involve mortgages on real estate and secured interests in fixtures. A fixture is a good that has become so related to a parcel of real property that any interest in the fixture arises under real property law.[12] Unlike other security interests, an interest in fixtures must be filed locally in the office where a mortgage would be filed. It must also include a legal description of the real property, and it must contain the name of the owner of the property, if the owner is not also the debtor.[13]

If the creditor is financing the construction of a building and has properly perfected a construction mortgage, his or her security interest has priority over any conflicting security interests. This would include a PMSI in fixtures that is perfected before the fixture is attached to the realty or within the 20 days after it is so attached.[14] In any other situation involving a fixture, if the interest in the fixture is a PMSI, and if the secured party perfects by filing before the fixture is attached to the realty or within

20 days after it is attached, the PMSI in the fixture will have priority.[15] If the security interest in the fixture in not a PMSI, or if it is a PMSI that is not timely filed, the interest in the fixture is subordinate to any interests in the realty that were recorded prior to the filing of the interest in the fixture.[16]

CONFLICTS BETWEEN SECURITY INTERESTS AND THE TRUSTEE IN BANKRUPTCY

When a debtor petitions for relief under the provisions of the Bankruptcy Act, or is involuntarily petitioned into bankruptcy, several things happen. (Bankruptcy is discussed in detail in Chapter 27, and the chapter will expand on several of these points.) When a bankruptcy petition is filed, the bankruptcy court enters an order for relief and issues an automatic stay. This automatic stay halts any legal proceedings involving the debtor, including any rights of the secured party to proceed against the debtor for any default on the underlying debt. In addition, in a Chapter 7 Bankruptcy proceeding—the most common type—a trustee is appointed to "manage" the debtor's estate for the benefit of the debtor's unsecured creditors.

The trustee in bankruptcy is treated as a judicial lien holder. As we discussed earlier, a judicial lien is subordinate to a prior perfected security interest. As a result, it would seem as if the secured party is in good position. While there are some obstacles, such as the automatic stay provisions, the secured party retains his or her priority. Given this priority position and the general protections afforded a perfected security interest, what could possibly go wrong? As it turns out, several things could go wrong, depending on the circumstances of the case and the timing of the creation of the security interest.

The trustee is expected to marshal the debtor's assets, prepare an inventory of those assets, and investigate any claims against those assets. This would include the claims of any secured parties and any lien holders. The trustee will determine, under the provisions of the Bankruptcy Code, whether any of these claims were valid against the debtor's estate at the time the bankruptcy petition was filed. If they were, the collateral subject to any such claims is normally released to the secured creditor or the lien holder. (The secured party can also attempt to get a release from the automatic stay in order to be allowed to repossess the collateral.)

The trustee may decide to challenge the validity of the security interest. In this situation, the trustee will attempt to show either that the security interest is fraudulent against any of the unsecured creditors or that the interest is a voidable preference. If either can be shown, the interest is set aside and the secured party becomes an unsecured general creditor for purposes of the bankruptcy proceeding. If the debtor transfers property, or an interest in property, while he or she is insolvent, and the transfer is for less than "fair consideration," the transfer is presumed to be fraudulent and will be declared invalid. If the security interest involves a transfer of property, or an interest in property, and it is made for a preexisting debt, and the debtor is insolvent at the time of the transfer and the transfer is made within 90 days of the petition, the transfer can be challenged as a voidable preference. Thus, the perfected secured creditor retains his or her priority over the trustee as a hypothetical judicial lien holder. Realize, however, this priority position can be lost if the trustee can successfully challenge the creation of the security interest as being fraudulent against any unsecured creditor or involving a voidable preference.

ENFORCEMENT OF THE SECURITY INTEREST

Default

Thus far, we have considered the methods by which a secured party can protect his or her interest in the collateral. Neither the debtor nor the secured party, however, likes to consider the possibility that the debtor will *default*, or fail to meet the obligations set out in the security agreement. Still, this contingency sometimes occurs, and is, in fact, the reason for seeking a security interest in the first place.

The default of the debtor represents a bittersweet moment for the secured party. On the one hand, default distresses the secured party because it reveals that the debtor may be unable or unwilling to pay the debt to the secured party. But, on the other hand, the secured party has worked hard to preserve his or her status. The secured party has a position that is superior to any unsecured lenders, he or she has established a priority position against other secured parties and lien holders, and upon the debtor's default, has certain rights to the collateral. Part 6 of revised Article 9 addresses default and the enforcement of the security interest. It also addresses the rights of the debtor following a default. We will examine these rules in the balance of the chapter.

Interestingly, the Code does not define the term *default*. Basically, the parties decide what events constitute default, and the security agreement may well embody these decisions. Basically *default* means whatever the security agreement says it means. Nonpayment by the debtor perhaps constitutes the easiest definition of default. But default clauses often are broad and lengthy. Security agreements also typically include *acceleration clauses* by which the secured party demands that all obligations be paid immediately under certain specified conditions. In the absence of bad faith and unconscionability, courts routinely uphold these clauses whenever the secured party can show that the debtor has defaulted.

Upon default, the secured party may resort to various alternative remedies. Using non-Code remedies, the secured party may become a judgment creditor, may garnish the debtor's wages, or may replevy (have the collateral returned through judicial action) the goods. Of course, the secured party may also choose to use the remedies provided in Article 9. Code remedies include strict foreclosure (retention of the collateral in satisfaction of the debt after the creditor acquires possession) and resale of the collateral. The secured creditor's rights after default are spelled out in § 9-601:

(a) After default, a secured party has the rights provided in this part and, except as otherwise provided in Section 9-602, those provided by agreement of the parties. A secured party:

(1) may reduce a claim to judgment, foreclose, or otherwise enforce the claim, security, interest, or agricultural lien by any available judicial procedure; and
(2) if the collateral is documents, may proceed either as to the documents or as to the goods they cover.

(b) A secured party in possession of collateral or control of collateral ... has the rights and duties provided in Section 9-207.
(c) The rights under subsections (a) and (b) are cumulative and may be exercised simultaneously.

Exhibit 25.2

A Comparison of Non-Code and Code Remedies

Non-Code Remedies	Code Remedies
Pre-judgment: • Attachment—take possession of debtor's assets pending settlement • Garnishment—judicial order for a third person to retain property of the debtor in the third person's possession pending settlement Post-judgment • Execution—sale of debtor's assets to pay the judgment • Replevy—recover possession of goods from the debtor (goods may then be kept, with value applied to debt or resold with proceeds applied to debt) • Garnishment—third person turns property of the debtor but in possession of third person over to the creditor. [Wages (subject to statutory limitations), bank accounts, and other assets, both liquid and non-liquid may be subject to garnishment]	• Right of Repossession [Creditor may use "self-help" methods so long as the methods do not involve a breach of the peace.] • Sale or Disposal of collateral— — May be by public or by private sale — Sale must be commercially reasonable — Sale must be made in good faith — Notice of the time and place of the sale is normally required • Strict Foreclosure [Creditor retains the collateral in full—and now possible for partial—satisfaction of the debt] — Notice must be given to debtor of intent to use strict foreclosure — Notice must be given to competing secured creditors with a claim in the same goods — Must wait 21 days before effective if there are competing creditors. In any object with the 21 days, strict foreclosure cannot be used. — If the collateral is consumer goods, there are limitations on the availability of strict foreclosure to the creditor.

Obviously, the secured creditor has substantial protections when the debtor defaults. The creditor needs to be aware, however, that there may be problems if he or she attempts to use all available remedies simultaneously. It is possible that the simultaneous exercise of remedies in a particular case may constitute abusive behavior or harassment, thus giving rise to liability despite the apparently permissive language of § 9-601(c).[17]

Assuming that the debtor has defaulted, what can the secured creditor do? Let us examine these rights, first by looking at the non-Code remedies and then by looking at the remedies available under the Code. Exhibit 25.2 provides a comparison of these remedies.

NON-CODE REMEDIES

The Code says that, upon default, secured parties may seek a court judgment, may foreclose, or may otherwise enforce the security agreement by any available judicial procedure. Accordingly, secured parties can use their Code remedies of repossession and resale with the possibility of a deficiency judgment for which the debtor is liable, or they can follow the non-Code remedy of becoming judgment creditors whereby they file suit, obtain a judgment, and have the sheriff use a writ of execution to levy on the goods and then sell the goods at a public sale. The proceeds of this sale are paid to the secured party.

eClass 25.3 Finance

DEFAULT

Third Bank holds a perfected security interest against eClass from a loan the firm took out last year and for which eClass used one of its bank accounts as collateral. Third Bank has perfection of its security interest by control of the collateral (eClass's bank account with Third Bank). Third Bank is asserting that eClass has defaulted on its obligations and that it (Third Bank) intends to seek recovery under the provisions of Article 9. Meg and Yousef ask you what obligations or liabilities Third Bank may owe to eClass under these circumstances, and what obligations or liabilities the firm may owe to Third Bank. What will you tell them?

BUSINESS CONSIDERATIONS   What factors should a secured creditor, like Third Bank, consider before it decides whether to seek a recovery under Article 9 or under common law or other provisions of state law? Why might a business decide to forgo its Article 9 protections and seek a non-code remedy?

ETHICAL CONSIDERATIONS   Is it ethical for a secured creditor to elect *not* to enforce its security interest upon default by the debtor? What impact might such a decision have on the other creditors of the defaulting debtor?

802   Part V: Debtor-Creditor Relations

Another non-Code alternative to levying on the goods involves garnishment. Garnishment can be used on any assets of the debtor that are in the possession of a third party, including bank accounts and wages or salary. If the creditor seeks a garnishment of the debtor's wages, he or she will be limited to receiving only a set percentage of the debtor's wages, as determined by state statute. There may be certain advantages to the creditor from seeking non-Code remedies. This is especially true if the collateral has substantially declined in value. However, most creditors elect the tidier and speedier remedies provided by the Code, most likely the remedies of repossession and disposition by resale or lease.

CODE REMEDIES

Right of Repossession

Article 9 gives the creditor the right to take possession of the collateral if the debtor defaults, unless the parties have agreed to the contrary. This action, generally called a "repossession" even if the creditor never previously possessed the collateral, is the essential first step if the creditor is seeking his or her Code remedies. The act of repossession may be a simple affair with no controversies and no problems, or it may be very complex.

The secured party may decide to use the "self-help" method of repossessing. This involves a repossession by the secured party without the use of any judicial procedures or any court officers. However, while the Code specifically permits "self-help," it also states that the creditor may not *breach the peace* in effecting the repossession.[18] Technically, this means that the creditor is allowed to personally take possession of the collateral from the debtor, but must stop any such efforts if continuation would involve a breach of the peace. Thus, if the debtor or some other person who is present objects to the act of repossession, the creditor must stop. Of course, he or she can try again later. Similarly, the creditor is not allowed to enter the debtor's property in order to make a repossession if doing so involves breaking and entering. However, most courts have upheld a repossession even though the creditor entered onto the debtor's property without permission, thereby committing a trespass. The courts have reasoned that a "mere" trespass, without more, is not enough to constitute a breach of the peace. Courts have also upheld repossessions made through trickery, but not if the trickery involves impersonating a police officer or other court official. The courts have prohibited the use of force or the threat of force in making a repossession, including the fact that the collection agent is armed. If the collection agent is armed, he or she has used an "implied threat" in order to complete the repossession, and this constitutes a breach of the peace.

Needless to say, this aspect of the Code has spawned numerous lawsuits. In general, courts assess such factors as whether the secured party entered the debtor's home or driveway without permission and whether the debtor agreed to the repossession. Although it is difficult to make generalizations in this area, if the creditor repossesses an automobile from a public street and the debtor fails to object to this procedure, most courts will hold no breach of the peace has occurred. Nevertheless, in recent years, some questions have arisen as to the constitutionality of this "self-help" provision of the Code. Specifically, some have argued that repossession without notice to the debtor may deprive the debtor of due process rights.[19] If a creditor is allowed to utilize the "self-help" method of repossession, the debtor may be deprived of something he or she needs in order to earn a living, and he or she has been deprived without having his or her "day in court" to potentially prevent the taking of the property. Wisconsin, for one, has prohibited the use of such tactics by creditors until after there is a court determination that the creditor is entitled to take possession of the collateral.

Self-help is not the only alternative available to the creditor in seeking repossession of the collateral. The agreement may require the debtor to assemble the collateral at some specified place upon default by the debtor.[20] If the debtor refuses to assemble the collateral according to the agreement after being asked to do so by the creditor, the courts are likely to compel the debtor to do so.

If the collateral is equipment, the creditor also has the right to disable the collateral, thus making it unusable, on the debtor's premises. The creditor is also allowed to dispose of the collateral by sale or otherwise without removing it from the debtor's premises.[21]

If the creditor does repossess the collateral, he or she is expected to take reasonable care of the collateral while it is in his or her possession. This includes properly storing the collateral, maintaining it, and so forth.[22]

"Realizing" on the Collateral

Once the secured party is in possession of the collateral, he or she must decide how to proceed. The Code authorizes the creditor to "sell, lease, license, or otherwise dispose" of the collateral.[23] Thus, the creditor must decide whether to keep the collateral in satisfaction, either total or partial, of the debt, or to dispose of the collateral. However, there are some restrictions that may affect what the creditor does or how the creditor does it.

Strict Foreclosure   After default and repossession, the secured party may decide to retain the collateral in complete satisfaction of the debt.[24] This remedy is generally referred to as *strict foreclosure*, although that term is not used in the Code. Strict foreclosure is not always available as an alternative for the creditor, but if it is available it may be an attractive choice. If the collateral is likely to appreciate in value or if the potential costs of any additional action are likely to be prohibitive, strict foreclosure will provide a simple and expedient method for ending the proceedings.

Strict foreclosure can *not* be used *if* the collateral is classified as consumer goods, *and* if the debtor has repaid at least 60 percent of the of the cash price of the goods or the amount of the loan. Instead, the creditor must dispose of the collateral within 90 days of the date of repossession. If the creditor fails to do so, he or she can be held liable for the tort of conversion *or* the consumer debtor can sue for actual damages plus punitive damages, set by the Code as either (1) the finance charges plus 10 percent of the loan amount, or (2) the time-price differential plus 10 percent of the cash price.[25]

If the collateral is not classified as consumer goods, or if it is consumer goods but the debtor has not repaid at least 60 percent of the cash price or the amount of the loan, the creditor may be allowed to use strict foreclosure. However, before strict foreclosure can be used, the creditor must send an authenticated notice to the debtor and to any conflicting creditors, stating his or her intention to retain the collateral in total or partial satisfaction of the debt.[26] If any of these parties object to the creditor's proposed retention within 20 days of the date the notice was sent, the creditor may not use strict foreclosure. Instead, he or she will be required to dispose of the collateral.[27]

An interesting change to Article 9 is the provision allowing strict foreclosure as *partial* settlement of the debt. The law now permits the creditor to notify the debtor and any conflicting creditors that he or she plans to retain the collateral in *partial* satisfaction of the debt, with the balance still due and owing. In order to use strict foreclosure for partial satisfaction, the creditor must give the same type of authenticated notice to the debtor and to the conflicting creditors, and once again, if any of these parties objects within 20 days the creditor may not retain the collateral in partial satisfaction of the debt. But there is an additional requirement here, and a limitation. Before the creditor can retain the collateral as partial satisfaction, the debtor must *consent* in an authenticated record. And if the goods are consumer goods, the creditor may not use strict foreclosure as a partial satisfaction.[28]

Disposition by Sale   As was pointed out above, the secured party is allowed to "sell, lease, license, or otherwise dispose of the collateral." In fact, secured parties use this remedy of *foreclosure by sale* much more frequently than strict foreclosure. The liberality of the Code's provision for resale allows the secured party to realize the highest resale price possible and, at the same time, to reduce the possibility of a *deficiency judgment* (the debtor's liability for the difference between the amount realized at resale and the amount owed to the secured party). In this way, both the secured party and the debtor benefit.

The sale may be either public or private, subject always to the requirement that the method, manner, time, place, and terms of such sale be commercially reasonable.[29] A public sale, or auction, is the more ordinary occurrence; but the Code encourages private sales when, as often is the case, a private sale through commercial channels will increase the chances for a higher resale price. If the debtor or a competing creditor should subsequently challenge the reasonableness of the sale, the burden of proof is on the creditor, who must establish that the sale was made in a commercially reasonable manner.[30]

In order to establish that the sale was made in a commercially reasonable manner, the creditor must first show that he or she gave proper notice of the sale. This notice must be given to the debtor, to any sureties or guarantors of the debtor, and to other creditors that are claiming an interest in the collateral. These "other" creditors include any creditors of record and any creditors who have notified the repossessing creditor of an interest in the collateral. The only exceptions to the notice requirement are (1) if the goods are perishable and are likely to decline in value, or (2) the goods are sold by the creditor in a recognized market.[31] The Code also specifies how the proceeds from the disposition of the collateral are to be applied. According to § 9-615, the proceeds are first applied to the expenses incurred in the sale. This includes the cost of repossession and storage, the cost of the sale itself, and any legal expenses and attorney's fees. If there are still funds available, these funds are applied to the debt owed to the creditor who repossessed and then disposed of the collateral. Again, if there are still funds available, these funds are distributed to junior secured creditors who have sent an authenticated demand for payment. These creditors are paid in order of priority. If any funds remain, the surplus is paid to the debtor. If the funds are inadequate to cover any of the first three categories, the debtor is liable for the deficiency.

DEBTORS' RIGHTS

Because the debtor has the right to redeem the collateral at any time before the secured party has disposed of it, it is possible that no sale will ever occur. *Redemption* consists of the debtor's tendering payment of all obligations due, including the expenses incurred by the secured party in retaking and preparing the collateral for disposition (usually by sale), thereby extinguishing the secured party's security interest in the collateral. Such expenses also may include attorneys' fees and legal expenses. A debtor who can accomplish redemption before sale or strict foreclosure can retain the collateral. The debtor can waive the right to redeem *after* default, but cannot waive this right before default.[32]

SECURED PARTIES' DUTIES

Besides having to observe the previously mentioned duties regarding disposition of the collateral, secured parties also have the duty of taking reasonable care of the collateral while it is in their possession, either before or after default. They are liable for any losses caused by their failure to meet this obligation, but they do not lose their security interests if such a loss occurs. Unless the parties otherwise have agreed, the secured party can charge to the debtor the payment of reasonable expenses, such as insurance and taxes, incurred in the custody, preservation, or use of the collateral. The Code places the risk of accidental loss or damage on the debtor due to any deficiency in insurance coverage. The secured party also may hold as additional security any increase in the value of or any profits (except money) received from the collateral, but the secured party either should turn over any money so received to the debtor or apply it to reduce the secured obligation. There is a duty to keep the collateral identifiable except for fungible collateral that may be commingled. The secured party either may repledge the collateral on terms that do not violate the debtor's right to redeem it or use the collateral (for example, in an ongoing business, the continued operation of equipment that has been given as security) if this will help to preserve it or its value.

Once the secured party defrays the expenses of holding the collateral, as mentioned earlier, the secured party must turn over any remaining proceeds to the debtor. On the other hand, the debtor remains liable for any deficiency—the difference between the available proceeds and the amount of outstanding indebtedness and expenses—unless the parties otherwise have agreed or state law eliminates this obligation.

Debtors sometimes try to argue that the amount received from the sale of the collateral (the usual basis for computing deficiencies or surpluses), if lower than the collateral's market value, makes the sale commercially unreasonable. But courts ordinarily respond unfavorably to such arguments as long as fraud is not present and the secured party has made a good faith effort to attract buyers. Similarly, these arguments generally will not affect the rights of the purchaser at the sale; the purchaser takes the collateral free and clear of such claims if the purchase is made in good faith.

Contemporary Case

BARBER v. GALINDO
2006 U.S. Dist. LEXIS 3356 (E.D. Wisc. 2006)

FACTS The Mercedes-Benz Corporation held title to a Freightliner truck in Tennessee. It sold the truck to Foothill Trucks, Inc. on October 31, 2000, retaining a first security interest. Following this purchase, Foothill applied to register the truck in California, listing Mercedes as the owner of the truck. Foothill through its leasing company leased the truck to Carlos Ayala.

Two weeks after acquiring the truck, Ayala was stopped in Arizona. A search of the truck turned up cocaine hidden with the truck's walls and the truck was seized by Arizona officials. Two days later, the State of California processed the truck's pending registration and registered the truck in the name of Carlos Ayala (though he was not listed as the truck's owner). An Arizona official processing the truck's seizure used the state's criminal justice information system and obtained a report reflecting the truck's California registration to Ayala. The report stated, in part: "THIS RECORD DOES NOT REFLECT OWNERSHIP INFORMATION—USE VIN INQUIRY" This report led the Arizona officer processing the forfeiture to erroneously list Ayala among the owners of the truck. The result of this erroneous report was that forfeiture proceedings went forward with notice being sent only to Ayala and two other individuals rather than to the truck's actual owner or any lienholders.

On December 31, 2000, six weeks after the truck was seized in Arizona, California issued a certificate of title correctly listing Mercedes as the lienholder. Soon after, however, the forfeiture proceedings in Arizona were concluded and, unbeknownst to Mercedes (because it had not received notice), the truck was forfeited to the State of Arizona, which sold the truck in a police auction in 2002. Arlen Sisk purchased the truck at auction and obtained an apparently clear Arizona title and a warranty of the title. Michael Barber then bought the truck and obtained a Wisconsin title free and clear of all liens.

Foothills had stopped making payments to Mercedes after the truck was seized, and Mercedes hired a repossession firm to begin repossession action to recover the truck due to the default in payments.

The repossession firm found the truck parked outside Barber's house, and its agent began attempting to "hotwire" it so that he could start the truck and drive it away. But before doing so, he allowed Barber to remove his personal belongings from the truck. There was no violence or other commotion during the repossession, and the plaintiff himself described the event as peaceful. Officer Bret Galindo of the Crivitz Police Department was present for about six minutes to prevent things from getting out of hand, and at one point while Barber was removing his belongings Officer Galindo instructed him to "calm down." Apart from that there was no direct interaction between Galindo and Barber.

Barber negotiated a settlement with Arizona for the value of the truck due to the breach of warranty, but he then brought suit against Galindo and Mercedes, among others, alleging conversion, trespass, wrongful repossession, and unfair debt collection practices; he also alleged constitutional claims based on the Fourth and Fifth Amendments.

ISSUE Was the repossession of the truck "wrongful"?

HOLDING No. There was no showing of any breach of the peace, nor anything wrongful about the repossession.

REASONING Excerpts from the opinion of William C. Griesbach, U.S. District Judge:

. . . Mercedes had a perfected security interest in the truck and . . . once the truck's owner failed to make its payments, Mercedes was entitled to repossess the truck. It is . . . undisputed that the Arizona forfeiture proceedings were fatally defective and could not have legally deprived Mercedes of its ownership rights to the truck. Finally, it is undisputed that the repossession of the truck occurred in a peaceable manner.

With all of that being uncontested, Barber cannot recover on any of his legal theories because they are all premised . . . on the supposition that Mercedes was not within its rights to effectuate the repossession of the truck. . . . First, it cannot be said that any of the parties "converted" the truck, given that Barber's own interest in the truck was junior to that of Mercedes. By the same token, the complaint's recitation of the trespass count is squarely refuted by the undisputed facts. The amended complaint claims . . . that "None of the defendants had a legal right to immediate possession of the 1997 Freightliner and therefore had no legal justification for entering upon the premises of the Plaintiff's home without Plaintiff's consent or invitation, express or implied." That is now proven false by the undisputed facts. The . . . amended complaint claims that "Once Plaintiff voiced his unequivocal objections to any repossession of the 1997 Freightliner, defendants had no right to remain on the premises regardless of whether or not they had a right to immediate possession of the vehicle." . . . The notion that the plaintiff "voiced his unequivocal objections" to the repossession has also been refuted. . . . The repossession was peaceful and occurred only after Barber removed all of his belongings. . . .

According to the complaint, the acts of Mercedes and the repossession agent were unfair practices because they took "nonjudicial action" to dispossess the truck when there was "no present right to possession of the property as collateral through an enforceable security interest." . . . [H]owever, the undisputed facts show that there *was* a present right to the possession of the property through an enforceable security interest. It is undisputed that Mercedes was a valid lienholder and it is also undisputed that it never received (nor was it sent) notice of the Arizona forfeiture proceedings. Moreover, there was no "debt" at issue here between Barber and Mercedes; Mercedes was simply repossessing its collateral based on the debt owed to it by Foothill Trucks. Accordingly, the Fair Debt Collection Practices Act has no conceivable application to these facts.

The same goes for Barber's claim of wrongful repossession. Because there is no evidence that Barber protested the repossession, self-help was available ... For the same reasons, Barber's constitutional claims fail as well. Given that it is undisputed that all of the parties were within their rights to peacefully repossess the truck, there can be no finding of a taking without due process or an unlawful seizure. Thus, even if the meager actions of Officer Galindo could somehow be construed to turn the private repossession into an action "under color of law" ... there was no underlying violation of any of Barber's privacy or property rights. ...

You Be the Judge

Unlimited Repossessions, LLC, is a commercial firm that specializes in repossessing collateral, especially motor vehicles, from delinquent debtors. It was recently hired by Friendly Finance, Inc. to repossess a car owned by Axel, who financed the car through Friendly Finance. The finance company alleges that Axel is several payments behind and will not return phone calls or otherwise make contact with the finance company, and it hired Unlimited Repossessions to repossess the car for Friendly.

Unfortunately, Axel has made the repossession difficult. He keeps the car either locked in his garage or parked at his place of employment in a fenced and guarded lot, thus preventing Unlimited from gaining access to the vehicle. However, creative repossessions are a specialty of Unlimited, and it devised a clever plan to gain access.

On a Tuesday afternoon when Axel was driving home from work, he saw a car blocking his driveway. The obstructing car was stopped in the street, and the driver was in front of the car with the hood raised as if she was having engine trouble. The debtor stopped his car behind the other vehicle and got out to see if he would help, unfortunately leaving his keys in the ignition. While he was attempting to aid the stranded motorist to get her car running again, an employee of Unlimited came out from hiding, jumped into the debtor's car, started it, and drove away.

Axel has challenged this repossession as an illegal taking that involved a breach of the peace. He alleges that Unlimited used fraud and/or deception, unlawfully blocked his driveway to prevent his gaining access to his home, and failed to identify its agent as a representative of the firm rather than a car thief.

This case has been brought in *your* court. How will *you* decide? Explain and justify your answer. [See UCC § 9-625, Official Comment 3 to § 9-625 and *Problem. Self Help Repossession* at http://law.scu.edu/FacWebPage/Neustadter/article9/main/problems/23.html/.]

Summary

The rules on priorities represent the Code's attempt to decide who, among validly perfected secured parties, has superior rights to the collateral. In general, the Code uses a first-in-time, first-in-right approach. Thus, if competing security interests have been perfected by filing, the first to be filed has priority, whether that security interest attached before or after filing. If neither party has filed, the first party to perfect has priority. And if no one has perfected, the first interest to attach has superior rights to the collateral.

Some exceptions to these priority rules exist. For instance, a properly perfected purchase-money security interest has priority over other security interests, even if the other interest were perfected first. Similarly, in some situations, *bona fide* purchasers of consumer goods and buyers in the ordinary course of business may defeat prior perfected interests. A secured party may also face competing claims against his or her collateral asserted by lien holders. The lien may be classified as a judicial lien, a statutory lien, or a consensual lien. Generally, a conflict between a lien and a security interest is decided by the "first in time, first in right" rule, unless the lien is possessory, in which case the lien is likely to prevail so long as the creditor retains possession. Likewise, certain liens that arise by operation of law have priority over perfected security interests in the collateral.

When a debtor defaults, the secured party may pursue either non-Code or Code remedies. Under the Code, the secured party may take possession of the collateral and either retain it in complete or partial satisfaction of the debt (strict foreclosure) or dispose of it, most often by public or private sale (foreclosure by sale). In either case, if the secured party is to avoid liability, he or she will need to follow the Code's provisions for handling and disposing of the collateral. The secured party's right of strict foreclosure may be limited in certain situations. If a sale is undertaken, the secured party must conduct it in a commercially reasonable manner. Assuming a sale has occurred, the Code also enumerates the order in which the proceeds of a sale should be applied. The debtor's redeeming the collateral prior to foreclosure may cut off the secured party's right to foreclosure by sale or strict foreclosure. When the secured party is in possession of the collateral either before or after default, he or she must take reasonable care of the collateral. Failure to live up to this and other duties subjects the secured party (1) to potential liability for any losses caused thereby, (2) to possible damages under a statutory formula, and (3) to the possible denial of the right to a deficiency judgment. Debtors ordinarily are liable for any deficiency that remains after the sale or other disposition of the collateral.

Discussion Questions

1. Why is the issue of priority important to a secured creditor or to a lien holder?

2. List the rules for becoming a properly perfected purchase money secured party in inventory collateral and in noninventory collateral. Why are

there different rules for proper perfection of a PMSI depending on the type of collateral involved?

3. What is a *bona fide* purchaser? Does such a purchaser always take goods free of any security interest covering the goods? How does this

person differ from a buyer in the ordinary course of business?

4. When does a secured party have priority over the holder of a common law lien? When does a security interest become subordinate to a later lien?

5. Assume that a secured creditor has repossessed collateral from a defaulting debtor. The creditor has decided not to use strict foreclosure. What must the creditor do in order to ensure that he or she preserves all of his or her rights and also that the rights of the debtor are not infringed?

Case Problems and Writing Assignments

1. On April 13, 2005, STR Enterprises, Inc. executed a Promissory Note in the principal amount of $ 250,000 in favor of the Sierra Bank. STR also executed a Commercial Security Agreement giving Sierra Bank a security interest in STR's personal property. The Note was executed by STR representatives. Also on April 13, 2005, John Kallis executed a Small Business Administration (SBA) Unconditional Guarantee in favor of the Bank, which provides that Kallis guaranteed payment to the Bank of all amounts owing under the Note.

The Bank made the loan to STR in the principal amount of $250,000. STR failed to make the required monthly payments to the Bank, so the Bank elected to accelerate the balance on the Note.

On September 14, 2005, Gary Kerr of West Coast Rubber Recycling, Inc., faxed a letter to Janice Castle, a Vice President of the Bank, indicating his desire to purchase STR's collateral for a total of $125,000. Several days later Kerr was informed that the Bank had decided to sell the collateral at a public sale. On September 26, 2005, the attorney for STR sent an e-mail to the Bank indicating Kallis's election to have a private sale conducted in an effort to mitigate his damages. Despite this communication by Kallis, the Bank proceeded to hold a public sale on the steps of the Tulare County City Hall.

Despite the fact that the Bank listed an estimated value of $207,000 for the collateral and that Kerr had offered $125,000, the Bank opened the bidding at $35,000 and sold to the high bidder for $51,000. After application of the sale proceeds, the unpaid balance on the Note totaled $215,905.92, and interest continued to accrue until entry of judgment.

The Bank has demanded payment from Kallis of an amount it contends is due and owing under the Note. Despite his SBA Loan Guarantee, Kallis has not paid any amounts demanded by the Bank. The SBA Loan Guarantee indicates that the guarantor waives defenses based on the lender making a commercially unreasonable disposition of collateral. However, Kallis insists that the method of sale selected by the Bank was so out of the ordinary that it failed to meet reasonable commercial standards, and that he should not be held liable for the alleged deficiency.

How should the court rule in this case? What was the most important fact or factor affecting your decision? Be certain to explain and justify your answer. [See *Bank of the Sierra v. Kallis,* United States District Court for the Eastern District of California, 2006 U.S. Dist. LEXIS 88234.]

2. Between 2002 and 2004, the leaders of several companies collectively known as CyberNET defrauded more than 40 lending institutions of more than $100 million. During these years, Huntington extended a multimillion-dollar line of credit to CyberCo Holdings, Inc., one of the CyberNET companies. As collateral for the line of credit and other liabilities, CyberCo granted Huntington a security interest in nearly all of its assets. One such asset was a bank account CyberCo opened with Huntington, into which CyberCo deposited receipts of the fraud.

In November 2004, the federal government seized ten CyberNET bank accounts at eight different banks, including CyberCo's account at

Huntington. The government eventually sought criminal forfeiture of the Huntington account. After the CyberNET principals agreed to forfeit their interests in the account, the district court entered a preliminary order transferring the account to the United States.

Huntington filed a claim, alleging that a perfected security interest permitted it to retain the account. The district court denied Huntington's claim, reasoning that, because the government's stake in the account predated Huntington's stake in it, Huntington did not have a "superior" interest to the government. Huntington filed a motion for reconsideration, arguing that the timing of its acquisition of the security interest was irrelevant because it was entitled to relief under the second statutory ground: that it was a "*bona fide* purchaser," but the district court denied the motion, concluding that Huntington had forfeited this argument by failing to raise it earlier.

Huntington appealed, and its appeal presented one issue: Did Huntington forfeit its *bona fide* purchaser argument? How should the court resolve this issue? Be certain that you explain and justify your answer. [See *U.S. v. Huntington National Bank*, 574 F.3d 329, 2009 U.S. App. LEXIS 16396, 2009 FED App. 0267P (6th Cir.).]

3. On July 19, 2006, Melendez-Febus and Toyota Credit formed a retail installment sales contract (the "financing agreement") in Caguas, Puerto Rico, for the purchase of a certain 2005 Toyota Echo (the "car"). The financing agreement provided the notice that "the secured creditor shall have the right to possession of the liened [sic] property upon default, without initiating a legal proceeding." Toyota Credit registered the car's title with the Puerto Rico Department of Transportation and Public Works on December 22, 2006.

As of November 19, 2006, Melendez-Febus was in arrears on his payment obligations under the financing agreement. On March 7, 2007, Toyota Credit addressed a letter to Melendez-Febus notifying him that he was in breach of his obligations under the financing agreement. The letter advised Melendez-Febus that if he did not cure his breach by making sufficient payments on or before March 16, 2007, Toyota Credit could either accelerate the balance due under the financing agreement or repossess the car. After Melendez-Febus failed to make the demanded payments, Toyota Credit contacted Isla, a firm specializing in collections and repossessions, on May 25, 2007 to begin repossession of the car. On August 20, 2007, Isla attempted to repossess the car. Juarbe-Torres, who worked for Isla, first located the car parked in front of a police station where Melendez-Febus worked. Melendez-Febus resisted Juarbe-Torres' efforts to repossess the car and drove away.

Later that day, Juarbe-Torres located the car parked in front of Melendez-Febus' attorney's office in Bayamon and proceeded with repossession. After Isla had sealed the car with stickers denoting that the car was subject to self-help repossession, Melendez-Febus appeared and engaged in an angry exchange with Juarbe-Torres. According to Melendez-Febus, he demanded access to the car to retrieve his personal effects, but Juarbe-Torres refused. Melendez-Febus claims that he then "stood his ground" behind the tow truck to compel Juarbe-Torres to grant him access to the car. Melendez-Febus claimed that he had shouted a warning to the tow truck driver to no avail, as the tow truck proceeded to drive in reverse over Melendez-Febus' foot. Melendez-Febus asserts that the tire of the truck momentarily pinned his leg to the ground but that he was able to free himself. Having suffered abrasions from the incident, Melendez-Febus later received treatment at the hospital. Juarbe-Torres claims that he did not see Melendez-Febus being pinned by the tow truck.

Did this repossession involve a breach of the peace, or was it a legitimate use of self-help repossession? Explain and justify your answer. [See *Melendez-Febus v. Toyota Credit de Puerto Rico Corp.*, United States District Court for the District of Puerto Rico, 2009 U.S. Dist. LEXIS 82471.]

Notes

1. UCC § 9-324(a).
2. UCC § 9-324(b), (c).
3. UCC § 9-324(d), (e).
4. UCC § 9-324(g) and Comment 13.
5. UCC § 9-330(a).
6. UCC § 9-330(d).
7. UCC § 9-317(a)(2).
8. UCC § 9-323(b).
9. UCC § 9-333(b).
10. 26 U.S.C. § 6323(a), (h)(1).
11. Rev. Rul. 68-57, 26 C.F.R. 301.6321-1 (1968).
12. UCC § 9-102(41).
13. UCC § 9-502(b).
14. UCC § 9-334(h).
15. UCC § 9-502(b).
16. UCC § 9-334(c).
17. UCC § 9-601, Official Comment 5.
18. UCC § 9-609(b).
19. See, e.g., *Fuentes v. Shevin*, 407 U.S. 67 (1972); *Mitchell v. W.T. Grant Co.*, 416 U.S. 600 (1974).
20. UCC § 9-609(c).
21. UCC § 9-609(a)(2).
22. UCC § 9-207.
23. UCC § 9-610.
24. UCC § 9-620.
25. UCC § 9-620(e).
26. UCC § 9-621.
27. UCC § 9-620.
28. UCC § 9-620(g).
29. UCC § 9-610(b).
30. UCC § 9-626(a)(2).
31. UCC § 9-611(d).
32. UCC § 9-623.

26

Other Credit Transactions

Agenda

eClass recently received an offer from a firm in Canada that seems promising for the firm. The offer included a statement that payment was to be made by a *letter of credit* if the firm decided to accept the offer. The principals are not sure exactly what is involved with the use of a letter of credit, but they want to find out because they are interested in the offer. Ani has heard of a "standby letter of credit," and she would like to know if this is the same thing or a different form of an "ordinary" letter of credit.

While Ani, Meg, and Yousef are primarily concerned with the operation and the success of eClass, they each also have other concerns. As budding young professionals, each has his or her share of the normal wants and needs. Ani would like to buy a new car, Meg would like to travel, and Yousef wants to purchase a house. They realize that they need to wait for these things if they are to pay cash, but they also realize that they can use credit to get them. But they question whether the cost of the credit is worth the reduced waiting period to enjoy these things sooner.

Each of them has several credit cards, and they each regularly receive offers of new credit cards in the mail. Some of these offers carry very attractive interest rates, and they would like to know whether they should just keep their current cards or accept some of the cards they are offered.

One of the firm's employees recently came to Meg asking for an advance on his pay. When asked why he needed the money, he explained that he was past due on a "payday loan" and was worried about getting too far behind and losing everything. Meg had never heard of a "payday loan," and she would like to know what it is and how it compares to a regular loan.

These and similar questions may arise during our discussion. Be prepared! You never know when the firm or one of its members will seek your advice.

Classic Case

PRUTSCHER v. FIDELITY INTERNATIONAL BANK

502 F. Supp. 535, 1980 U.S. Dist. LEXIS 16339 (S.D.N.Y. 1980)

FACTS In March 1974, Prutscher, a limited partnership in Austria, entered into a contract with the Eid Trading Agency (Eid) under which Eid agreed to purchase from Prutscher certain laboratory furniture. On March 13, 1974, Banque Med, located in Beirut, Lebanon, issued to Prutscher a Letter of Credit of 7,097,280 Austrian Shillings. This figure was increased to 10,915,859 Shillings by an amendment dated June 15, 1974, to which Fidelity consented.

The Letter of Credit provided that a full set of bills of lading must be presented to Banque Med as a condition precedent to the availability of funds under the Letter of Credit. It also contained a prohibition against partial shipments and specified July 6, 1974 as the latest date for shipment of the furniture. The Letter became payable 150 days after the date of the shipment.

Fidelity refused to pay the Letter of Credit when it was presented, contending that the furniture was shipped from Trieste in three vessels, violating the prohibition against partial shipments, and that one of the ships didn't sail until July 11, 1974, five days after the final date for shipment. Accordingly, Fidelity argues that the bill of lading presented to Banque Med was false and fraudulent in its certification. Prutscher does not dispute that the furniture was shipped in three vessels, but contends that the bill of lading was true because it was prepared after the entire lot of furniture had been loaded on one ship and before some of it was returned to the warehouse from which it was subsequently loaded onto two other ships.

ISSUE Was Fidelity liable for refusing to honor the Letter of Credit?

HOLDING No, Fidelity was not liable for its refusal to honor the Letter of Credit.

REASONING Excerpts from the opinion of Bonsal, J.:

On June 20, 1979, this Court issued a Letter Rogatory[1] to the Court of Appeals of Trieste, Italy to complete discovery on the alleged forgery of the bill of lading. Evidence developed in Italy establishes that, contrary to Prutscher's assertions, a substantial portion of the furniture was never loaded on the first ship to leave Trieste, the M.S. IRENE STAR. In fact, it establishes that much of the furniture was stored in Warehouse 23 of the ... Port of Trieste on the very day on which the bill of lading states that it was loaded on ship. . . .

The evidence obtained in Italy shows that the M.S. IRENE STAR departed from Trieste on July 4, 1974, carrying 174 pallets of furniture; the M.S. FENKO departed on July 6, carrying 53 pallets; and the M.C. BRIGITTA sailed on July 12, carrying 56 pallets.

A bank which has confirmed a letter of credit is not required to honor a draft presented thereunder if the bank receives information that a bill of lading required by the letter is forged or fraudulent and that the presenter is the original beneficiary or is otherwise chargeable with participation in the alleged fraud. . . .

As noted, evidence developed in Italy does not support the suggestion raised by Prutscher that all laboratory furniture was first loaded on a single vessel. Indeed, the evidence establishes that the furniture was carried by three vessels, one of which sailed after the stipulated date in the Letter of Credit. Accordingly, it seems there was no compliance with two express conditions of the Letter of Credit and the bill of lading submitted to establish such compliance was fraudulent. . . .

[T]he Court finds that Prutscher has presented no evidence raising a triable issue of fact. Fidelity's motion for summary judgment is granted. . . .

INTRODUCTION

The use—and occasional misuse—of credit is an integral part of contemporary American life. Businesses very often will be both a creditor and a debtor during their normal business cycles. A business may need to obtain credit in order to provide its goods and services to its customers, and then may need to grant credit to its customers in order for the customers to purchase the goods or services. Many of these credit transactions take the form of secured transactions, a topic covered in considerable detail in the previous two chapters. However, a significant number of these credit transactions fall outside the coverage of Article 9. The types of credit used by businesses vary widely. Any given business may use letters of credit, covered by Article 5 of the UCC, or promissory notes, covered by Article 3 of the UCC. Similar items are likely to be used by the business when it extends credit to its customers.

Consumers also use credit. Many consumers use credit to purchase major items, such as homes, automobiles, and major appliances. While the major appliance purchases may well be governed by Article 9, other purchases may fall outside the coverage of Article 9 of the UCC. The home loan, while secured by collateral, falls outside the provisions of Secured Transactions coverage. Many consumers also use credit to purchase non-major items, such as clothing, gasoline, and groceries, among other items. For example, a significant number of college students purchase their books and supplies on credit, and students often pay their tuition by means of credit. These transactions also fall beyond the scope of Article 9. In fact, most of these latter transactions do not involve collateral in any sense. These are unsecured credit transactions. Some unsecured credit is procured through the use of promissory notes, while other unsecured credit may be procured through the use of a credit card. Two relatively recent—and controversial—forms of short-term credit that are used by consumers are the "payday loan" and the "title loan." These loans often have an APR (annual percentage rate) in *triple digits*, with interest in some cases exceeding 900% per annum. (These lenders operate within loopholes in the law that exempt them from the provisions of state usury laws, allowing them to legally lend money at exorbitant interest rates.)

LETTERS OF CREDIT

Letters of credit are perhaps the most unique area regulated by the Uniform Commercial Code. Stated as simply as possible, a letter of credit is a device designed to reassure both the buyer and the seller in a transaction, especially a long-distance transaction, that each party will receive the benefit of his or her bargain. The original Article 5 was one of the few areas covered in the UCC that was not based on some prior statute.[2] The laws governing letters of credit prior to the enactment of the UCC were derived primarily from court opinions rather than statutory enactments, and there were not that many cases addressing the issue. As a result, the original article was intended to establish "an independent theoretical frame for the further development of letters of credit."[3] The statutory goal of Article 5 was originally stated to be: "(1) to set a substantive theoretical frame that describes the function and legal nature of letters of credit; and (2) to preserve procedural flexibility in order to accommodate further developments of the efficient use of letters of credit."[4]

The current version of Article 5, which was revised in 1995, reflects the increasing importance of this method of payment. It is estimated that nearly $500 billion in standby letters of credit are now issued annually, with some $250 billion of those originating in the United States.[5] As the use of letters of credit has grown, so has the statutory and code coverage of the area. International letters of credit are regulated by the Uniform Customs and Practices (UCP), which have been revised four times since the 1950s.[6] The current version (UCP 500) became effective in 1994. Article 5 of the UCC regulates domestic letters of credit, although many letters of credit also include language stating that the letter is subject to the Uniform Customs and Practices. In addition the United Nations has proposed a Convention dealing with Independent Guarantees and Standby Letters of Credit through UNCITRAL.

For an example of the use of a letter of credit, suppose that a buyer and a seller enter into a sales contract. The seller may be unwilling to deliver any goods until such time as he or she is paid for the goods. But the buyer is equally unwilling to pay for any goods until he or she has received the goods and can verify that they conform to the contract. This position might well result in a failure to complete the contract, to the detriment of both parties, and possibly to their respective economies. One alternative, discussed under Negotiable Instruments (Chapters 19-23), is to use a *sight draft*.

While the use of such an instrument increases the level of comfort of both the buyer and the seller, it still leaves a bit to be desired. Since the drawee must accept the sight draft before there is any obligation to honor the instrument, the seller is left at the mercy of the drawee to a significant degree.

A letter of credit helps to eliminate this concern, giving the seller a greater degree of control, and thus a greater sense of confidence that he or she will be paid. With a letter of credit the *applicant* (the buyer) obtains a commitment from the *issuer* (the buyer's bank) that the issuer will honor the letter of credit upon the issuing bank's receipt of certain specified documents from the *beneficiary* (the seller). The specified documents that must be presented to the issuing bank will normally include (1) a draft drawn by the seller in the seller's favor against the buyer, (2) a bill of lading covering the goods, (3) an invoice, (4) an inspection certificate, (5) an insurance certificate, and (6) any other documents that might be necessary to show performance by the seller.

When a letter of credit is used the risk to the parties is minimized. The seller knows that he or she will be paid by the issuing bank once the seller ships the goods and provides the required documents to the issuing bank. The buyer knows that he or she will receive a bill of lading that will enable the buyer to obtain the goods from the carrier. The buyer also knows that the goods have been inspected, so that it is reasonable to think the goods are conforming; that the goods are insured, so that the risk of loss during transit is minimized; and that any other necessary documentation has been satisfied.

Revised Article 5 expressly states that the letter of credit is independent of the underlying transaction for which it was issued.[7] In a reflection of modern commercial practices, the revision to Article 5 authorizes the use of electronic technology in the creation, transmission, and presentment of a letter of credit.[8] The letter of credit is deemed to be irrevocable unless the letter itself expressly provides for revocation,[9] which is of great benefit to the beneficiary (the seller). The UCC also requires the issuer to dishonor any letter that does not *strictly* conform, under standard customs and practices, to the terms and conditions contained in the letter of credit.[10] This requirement of "strict compliance" provides protection to the applicant (the buyer), while the limitation as to how "strict" the compliance must be (under standard customs and practices) provides the issuer with some flexibility based on the industry standards of the issuer.

The issuer *is* permitted to dishonor a letter of credit if a required document is forged or materially fraudulent. Under the provisions of § 5-109, if a presentation is made to the issuer that appears on its face to strictly comply with the terms of the letter of credit, but a required document is forged or materially fraudulent, or if honoring the letter would facilitate a material fraud on the applicant or the issuer, the issuer may dishonor the letter. The right to dishonor is limited to some extent. The letter must be honored if the presentation is demanded by a person who has given value in good faith without notice of the forgery or fraud. In addition, an applicant can prevent the honoring of the letter of credit. According to § 5-109(b):

> If an applicant claims that a required document is forged or materially fraudulent or that honor of the presentation would facilitate a material fraud by the beneficiary on the issuer or the applicant, a court of competent jurisdiction may temporarily or permanently enjoin the issuer

from honoring a presentation or grant similar relief against the issuer or other persons only if the court finds that:

(1) the relief is not prohibited under the law applicable to an accepted draft or deferred obligation incurred by the issuer;

(2) a beneficiary, issuer, or nominated person who may be adversely affected is adequately protected against loss that it may suffer because the relief is granted;

(3) all of the conditions which entitle a person to the relief under the law of this State have been met; and

(4) on the basis of the information submitted to the court, the applicant is more likely than not to succeed under its claim of forgery or material fraud and the person demanding honor does not qualify for protection under subsection (a)(1).

Exhibit 26.1 illustrates how a letter of credit works.

Exhibit 26.1

Application and Use of a Letter of Credit

1. Bob's Bedding, the buyer, enters into a contract with Seline's Sheets & Stuff, the seller, for the purchase of $100,000 in sheets, shams, and pillowcases. Before agreeing to the contract, Seline's insisted that Bob's issue a letter of credit to cover the transaction.

2. Bob's, the *applicant*, arranges with its Bank, First National Bank of Des Moines, to issue a letter of credit to Premier Bank of Paris, Seline's bank, the *advising bank*, naming Seline's as the *beneficiary*. (NOTE: First National Bank is agreeing to extend credit to Bob's to cover the amount of the letter of credit.)

3. First National Bank sends a copy of the letter of credit to Premier Bank. (NOTE: at this point First National Bank is liable to Premier Bank on the letter of credit, not Bob's Bedding.)

4. Premier Bank confirms with Seline's that the letter of credit has been received, and what documents must be presented to Premier Bank to receive payment.

5. Seline's delivers the requested goods to a carrier for delivery, receiving a negotiable bill of lading from the carrier.

6. Seline's indorses the negotiable bill of lading and delivers it to Premier Bank, along with any other documents required by the terms of the letter, showing that Seline's has complied with the terms of the contract.

7. Premier Bank indorses the bill of lading and delivers it to First National Bank.

8. First National Bank notifies Bob's Bedding that the bill of lading has been received and that all documents are in proper order.

9. Bob's pays First National Bank the amount called for in the contract, plus any applicable fees, and received the bill of lading.

10. First National Bank issues a check or a draft to Premier Bank, paying the letter of credit.

11. Premier Bank issues a check to Seline's Sheets & Stuff for the amount of the letter of credit.

12. Bob's presents the negotiable bill of lading to the carrier and takes possession of the merchandise.

UNSECURED CREDIT

In an *unsecured credit* arrangement, the creditor agrees to grant credit to the debtor without the use of any collateral. In such an arrangement, the creditor is relying on the debtor to repay the loan or to honor the debt without the benefit of some form of security to use if the debtor defaults on the obligation. Thus, the creditor will *either* restrict the debtors to whom such credit is extended to those debtors who are deemed better credit risks, *or* the creditor will charge a significantly higher interest rate for the credit due to the added risk.

Unsecured credit may take the form of a *signature loan*, in which the lender agrees to make the loan on the basis of the borrower's signature alone. Common examples of unsecured credit include most public utility accounts (telephone, electricity, water, etc), bank credit cards (i.e., Visa and MasterCard), and travel and entertainment cards (i.e., American Express, Diners Club, Carte Blanche). Public utility accounts are regulated by the various state public utility regulatory commissions and by contract law. Credit cards and travel and entertainment cards are discussed in a later section of this chapter. We will discuss other types of unsecured credit transactions next.

eClass 26.1 Finance/Management

LOANS

Yousef recently began looking for a short-term loan to cover the cost of some renovation work he is doing on an old car. After getting terms and conditions from a number of different prospective lenders, he decided that one of the local banks provided him with the best options. The loan officer at the bank gave Yousef two options: a signature loan with a single payment due in six months, and an APR of 10.5 percent; or an installment loan with twelve equal monthly payments and an APR of 9.75 percent. The signature loan would be made without any collateral, while the installment loan would require that Yousef provide some collateral to secure the loan. Yousef has asked you which of these two loans would be better for him. What will you tell him?

BUSINESS CONSIDERATIONS   Although the installment loan has a lower interest rate, Yousef will end up paying more money and more interest to the bank if he chooses the installment loan. Why might a business person prefer a lower rate/longer term loan when such a loan actually increases the amount to be repaid?

ETHICAL CONSIDERATIONS   Is it ethical for a bank to require collateral for a loan in order to grant a lower rate, when the bank was willing to make essentially the same loan to a customer without collateral?

Regulation of unsecured credit transactions is primarily a matter of state law. Federal regulation of these transactions is primarily concerned with ensuring that information is provided to the debtor prior to the creation of the debt, and with acceptable methods of collection in the event the debtor defaults on the agreement. Under Title I of the Federal Consumer Credit Protection Act, better known as the "Truth in Lending Act" (TILA), creditors must provide credit applicants with certain information as to the cost of the credit. This information must be provided in a standard format and in a standard terminology. The most important information that must be given to the applicant is the "APR," the annualized percentage rate to be charged in the transaction. This information must be provided in writing, and the writing must be clear and conspicuous. Failure to provide the necessary information in the appropriate format may make the creditor subject to various penalties and liabilities. (For more detailed coverage of TILA, see Chapter 36, Consumer Protection.)

If a debtor defaults on the credit arrangement, the creditor is allowed to use various methods to enforce his or her claim. For example, the "self-help" provisions discussed in the coverage of secured transactions may be available in certain cases. However, with an unsecured credit transaction, the creditor does not have access to any "self-help" provisions because there is no collateral. The creditor may seek a writ of attachment or a writ of garnishment, or the creditor may elect to file suit for breach of contract. While these methods are often successful, they are time-consuming and relatively expensive. As a result, many creditors choose to hire a collection agent in an attempt to collect the unpaid balance owed. Historically, such debt collection agencies developed a bad reputation. They were known to engage in various types of harassing behavior in their effort to "encourage" the debtor to pay the debt. As a result, the federal Fair Debt Collection Practices Act was passed. This Act only applies to persons who are attempting to collect debts owed to another person, and not to the actual creditor who is acting on his or her own behalf in seeking recovery. However, most creditors also follow the guidelines of the Act in the interests of following sound and fair business practices.[11] (The Fair Debt Collection Practices Act is also covered in detail in Chapter 36.)

The federal regulation in this area is effective in providing debtors with information regarding the cost of the credit, and with protecting defaulting debtors from some unfair or improper collection practices, but it is not very effective as to the terms of the credit agreement. Regulation of the terms and conditions of unsecured credit transactions is left to the states. State regulation in this area includes limits on the interest rates and other finance charges that may be imposed, possible "cooling off" periods for the debtor in some transactions, and other terms and details of the transaction. Each state establishes its own maximum permissible interest rates for various types of loans or credit transactions. If the creditor charges a rate in excess of the state's maximum, the interest is *usurious*. Since usury is defined as charging an illegal rate of interest,[12] the contract is tainted with illegality. In some states, the charging of a usurious rate of interest voids the entire contract. In other states, the interest portion is voided due to the illegality, although the debtor still must repay the principle. Some states void the usurious interest, substituting the state interest maximum into the agreement on the theory that the parties only meant to charge the highest legal rate.

In some states there is a single usury provision for all types of credit. However, most states have different usury rates for different types of credit. A closed-end unsecured loan will have one rate; an installment loan with collateral will have another rate; revolving credit arrangements (credit cards) will have still another rate. It is important for a business that extends credit—and an individual who uses credit to make purchases—to be aware of the state rules in this area.

State regulation also extends to other terms and conditions of the credit arrangement. Among the areas of coverage that may be encountered here are the following:

- The Uniform Consumer Credit Code (adopted by eleven states)[13]
- State consumer loan acts
- State home solicitation sales acts
- Negotiable Instrument law (Articles 3 and 4 of the UCC)
- Contract law.

Again, familiarity with the applicable state statutes will help to ensure that the business person who extends credit is acting in a proper manner and that the individual who is using credit is acting in the most appropriate manner.

INSTALLMENT LOANS

Installment loans are loans for a fixed time period and with fixed periodic payments. Installment loans usually require a monthly payment. While installment loans may be secured or unsecured, most consumer installment loans are secured by some form of collateral. Some of these loans will fall within the coverage of Article 9. For example, if a person purchases a refrigerator on credit and uses the refrigerator as collateral for the loan, the credit arrangement is a purchase money security interest governed by Article 9. However, if a person purchases real estate on credit, using the real estate as collateral for the loan, the transaction falls outside the coverage of Article 9. This transaction will be governed by the state laws governing real property rather than by Article 9.

Installment loans are subject to many of the same regulatory provisions as are unsecured loans. At the federal level the lender is still governed by TILA, and the Fair Debt Collection Practices Act still applies to collection agencies' attempts to collect past due accounts. At the state level, the transaction is still covered by Article 3 of the UCC if a promissory note is involved, as is likely. In addition, the Uniform Consumer Credit Code (UCCC) may apply to the transaction, *if* the transaction takes place in one of the eleven states that have adopted the UCCC, and *if* the debtor is a consumer. Since the parties are involved in a contract, the state laws governing contracts also apply. And if the state has a retail installment sales act, or similar legislation, the provisions of that act will also apply to the transaction.

MORTGAGE LOANS

Mortgage loans involve loans in which real estate is used as collateral by the debtor to secure the credit. Mortgage loans are commonly installment loans with a much longer repayment term. For example, many mortgage loans have a repayment period of thirty years. By contrast, most of the other types of installment loans have a repayment term of five years or less. Since real estate is used as collateral in a mortgage loan, the interest of the state in regulating the transaction is obvious, and state regulations in this area are substantial. However, there are also some important federal regulations that must be met by the parties, particularly the creditor.

The most important federal regulation is, once again, TILA. Debtors must be made aware of the cost of the credit prior to entering the transaction. Given the length of time involved, and the relative size of the credit involved—mortgages are frequently the largest debt a consumer will assume—the need for full and accurate disclosure is obvious. A second area of coverage at the federal level is the Real Estate Settlement Procedures Act (RESPA), which became effective in 1974. RESPA is also a disclosure act. Home mortgage lenders are required to provide loan applicants with a good faith estimate of all settlement and closing costs associated with the loan. The lender must also inform the applicant if any of the settlement business is being referred to a company affiliated with the lender. The applicant must be informed as to the possibility that the loan will be transferred at some point in time. If the loan is transferred, both the lender and the new holder of the note must notify the debtor at that time, as well. Finally, the lender must provide the borrower with a list of the actual settlement and closing costs at the time the loan is formally closed.

Most states have a number of statutes that apply to mortgage loans. Included among these statutes are:

- Mortgage lending acts
- Mortgage banker and broker acts
- Secondary mortgage acts
- Home improvement contract acts

State law will also have provisions regarding the warranties that the seller provides to the buyer, statutes governing recording of the deed, and various other aspects. We should anticipate additional state and federal legislation in this area due to the mortgage debacle of the late 2000's, and the related implosion of the real estate market.[14] (Real property is discussed in more detail in Chapter 39.)

CREDIT CARDS

Credit cards have become ubiquitous in the United States. A significant percentage of the adult population has at least one credit card, and most people are likely to have several different credit cards at any point in time. There are three basic types of credit cards: bank cards such as MasterCard, Visa, and Discover; travel and entertainment cards such as American Express, Carte Blanche, and Diners Club; and store or merchant cards such as Sears, J.C. Penney, Exxon, Texaco, etc. Bank cards and travel and entertainment cards are widely accepted at a variety of locations. By contrast, store or merchant cards are normally only accepted by the stores or merchants who issue the cards. Credit cards involve open-ended credit, and they are often viewed differently from loans for purposes of usury provisions and other state credit coverage. The holder of the card is regarded by the courts as being involved in a "revolving credit" arrangement rather than a loan, and the methods for computing charges and fees are different than the methods used in a "standard" loan. Nonetheless, the number of people who hold credit cards, and the widespread usage of credit cards, has led to a great deal of regulation at both the federal and the state levels.

Federal regulation in this area is based, once again, on the Truth in Lending Act (TILA). The provisions for credit card protection are found in the Truth in Lending Act Regulations (Regulation Z), Subpart B, which deals with "open-ended credit."[15]

eClass 26.2 Finance

CREDIT CARDS

Recently Ani, Meg, and Yousef have been receiving credit card solicitations in the mail and by telephone. Most of these solicitations inform the recipient that she or he has been "pre-approved" for the credit card in question. These solicitations also state that the card has a very attractive interest rate, such as 2.9 percent, and that there will be no fee for any transfers of the balances from any other credit cards to this new one. Ani states that she has heard about "teaser" rates, and also that some of her friends have had problems with changes in the interest rates on cards they accepted. She asks you for your advice regarding these solicitations. What will you tell her?

BUSINESS CONSIDERATIONS   Most college students have minimal income, at best, and yet they regularly receive credit card solicitations from a multitude of credit card issuers. Why would a credit card issuer solicit an application from a person who is probably either unemployed or underemployed, and likely to remain so at least until graduation?

ETHICAL CONSIDERATIONS   Is it ethical for a credit card issuer to use a "teaser" rate to procure applications, and then to change the rate on the cards at some time in the near future, such as after six months? Is it ethical for a credit card company to change the interest rate the first time a customer is late with his or her payments? Is it ethical for colleges to charge credit card companies fees to set up booths on campus to attract student customers?

The credit card issuer must provide a full disclosure of the costs associated with the card, as would be expected under TILA. However, the regulations go much farther.

Section 226.12 (a) prohibits the issuing of unsolicited credit cards. This section states that no credit card may be issued unless it is issued in response to an application from the recipient (the application can be made orally or in writing) or it is a renewal of, or substitution for, a card that has previously been issued and accepted. At this time there is no prohibition against *solicitation* of applications by the card issuer, but the solicitation may not include the card itself. It is not a defense for the card issuer to send a card that requires a telephone call to an "activation center" before the card can be used. The courts have viewed this as an *issuance*, not as a *solicitation* subject to an oral application (the phone call to the activation center).

TILA also limits the liability of card holders in the event that their cards are used without authorization. If a credit card is lost or stolen, the card holder faces a maximum liability of $50 for unauthorized use of the card, and the liability is only for use of the card *before* the issuer is notified of the loss or theft. Once the card issuer is notified, the liability of the card holder ends. However, a different limit applies if the card holder consents to the use of his or her card by another, only to find out that the other person did not use the card as the card holder expected. In this situation, the card holder can be held liable for any charges incurred by the person who is using the card until such time as the card holder notifies the credit card issuer and cancels the "permissive" use of the card by the other person.

Regulation Z also prohibits "offsets" by the card issuer. The card issuer cannot take any action to offset credit card indebtedness by unilaterally asserting a claim on the card holder's funds on deposit with the issuer of the card. However, if the offset is part of a consensual security agreement between the card issuer and the card holder, an offset is permissible. Similarly, the card issuer can proceed against funds on deposit on the basis of a judgment obtained against the card holder, an attachment by the card issuer, or a written plan from the card holder permitting periodic offsets against a credit card balance.

Other federal regulations that apply to credit card use also exist. The Equal Credit Opportunity Act requires businesses that regularly extend credit as a part of their business to make credit available without discrimination. The Fair Credit Billing Act provides a method for card holders to challenge any alleged billing errors without liability until the alleged error is investigated. And the Unsolicited Credit Card Act protects the customer from potential liability for misuse of credit cards issued to that person without an application submitted by that person.

Exhibit 26.2 lists some of the most important federal statutes dealing with credit transactions.

State regulation of credit cards tends to be more enabling than restrictive. However, the state usury provisions regarding credit cards still apply. State contract laws are applicable to the credit card relationship between the issuer and the customer. Further, when store or merchant cards are used, there is the possibility that the store or the merchant will retain a security interest in the purchased item, thus making the transaction subject to the provisions of Article 9 of the UCC.

Exhibit 26.2

Representative Federal Statutes Affecting Credit

Federal Statute	Provisions and/or Protections
Consumer Credit Protection Act (Also known as the Truth in Lending Act, TILA)	Creditors must disclose your exact credit terms to credit applicants in a standard format (APR); There are regulations and restrictions on how creditors advertise consumer credit.
Regulation Z	Provides a "cooling-off" period on some transactions; Provides rules and guidelines in a number of credit card actions, including restrictions on issuing unsolicited card; Prohibits certain acts when the debtor's principal residence secures the credit.
Fair Credit Billing Act	Provides debtor rights when an alleged error in billing occurs; Spells out obligations of creditor for investigating and resolving the controversy; Protects the debtor during the investigation phase; Establishes strict time lines with which the creditor must comply.
Equal Credit Opportunity Act	Prohibits discrimination on the basis of race, color, religion, national origin, age, sex or marital status in extending credit to consumer applicants.
Fair Credit Reporting Act	Designed to assure, to a significant extent, that consumer credit information gathered by credit reporting agencies is accurate and up-to-date; Provides consumers with the right to question the data and to include a statement of explanation if necessary.
Fair Debt Collection Practices Act	Prohibits certain unfair, coercive, or abusive collection practices by third-party debt collectors.
Real Estate Settlement Procedures Act (RESPA)	Addresses closing costs and settlement procedures; Requires lenders to provide a standard Good Faith Estimate that clearly discloses key loan terms and closing costs.

FTC CONSUMER CREDIT RULES

The Federal Trade Commission (FTC) has enacted two special *credit practice* rules designed to provide consumer debtors with protections they might not otherwise enjoy under the various other areas of law. The first of these rules is the Federal Trade Commission Holder in Due Course Rule, in effect since 1976. The second is the Federal Trade Commission Credit Practices Rule, in effect since 1985.

The Federal Trade Commission Holder in Due Course rule requires consumer credit contracts to include a statement that the debtor retains all rights, claims, and defenses that the consumer could have asserted against the seller, even against holders in due course of the consumer credit instrument. This rule does not apply to real estate transactions or to credit card transactions.

eClass 26.3 Finance/Management

CO-SIGNING A LOAN

Amanda, one of Meg's friends has encountered some financial difficulties since she graduated from college, but it appears that she has managed to turn her life around. In fact, she has recently discovered a business opportunity that has tremendous potential and she believes that the risk factor for the opportunity is acceptable. Unfortunately, she lacks the resources to take advantage of the opportunity on her own, and none of the local bankers is willing to lend her the money unless she has more collateral or a co-signer. Since Amanda lacks the collateral to secure the loan on her own, she approached Meg about acting as a co-signer. She also promised Meg a share of the profits from the business, if it is as successful as she thinks it will be. Meg would like to help her friend, but she is concerned about the potential liability if she agrees to act as a co-signer. Meg is not only concerned for herself, but also for the possibility that she might be putting Ani, Yousef, and eClass at risk. She has asked you for advice. What will you tell her?

BUSINESS CONSIDERATIONS   Many businesses have a policy that prohibits the business from co-signing on loans except under extraordinary circumstances. Why might a business have such a policy?

ETHICAL CONSIDERATIONS   From an ethical perspective, how should a business view requests to serve as a co-signer on a loan? Which constituent groups are jeopardized by co-signings if the borrower defaults? Which constituent groups might benefit from co-signing a loan?

The second rule makes it an unfair trade practice for a seller or creditor in a consumer credit transaction to take a contract containing a confession of judgment clause or a waiver of exemptions clause. Nor can the seller or creditor take a contract containing a wage assignment provision or a non-possessory security interest in household goods or furnishing, except in the form of a purchase money security interest.

This second rule also has a special disclosure requirement when a co-signer is involved in a credit arrangement. The required disclosure statement reads as follows:

"You are asked to guarantee this debt. Think carefully before you do. If the borrower doesn't pay the debt you will have to. Be sure you can afford to pay if you have to, and that you want to accept this responsibility.

You may have to pay up to the full amount of the debt if the borrower does not pay. You may also have to pay late fees or collection costs, which increase this amount. The creditor can collect this debt from you without first trying to collect from the borrower. The creditor can use the same collection methods against you that can be used against the borrower such as suing you, garnishing your wages, etc. If this debt is ever in default that fact becomes a part of your credit record.

This notice is not the contract that makes you liable for the debt."

Failure to include this notice is an unfair trade practice under the provisions of the Federal Trade Commission Act.

PAYDAY LOANS AND TITLE LOANS

One of the fastest-growing areas in consumer lending is the "payday loan." These loans are also perhaps the most controversial topic in consumer lending. In a "payday loan" a borrower goes to a lender to borrow funds "until payday." These loans are usually for a short period of time, ranging from a few days to a few weeks. In exchange for the loan, the borrower writes a check payable to the order of the lender and dated for the borrower's next payday. The check written by the borrower is written for the amount of the loan plus any fees and interest to be paid. (A variation of this involves the borrower writing a check for the amount of the loan and then receiving the amount of the loan minus the fees.) When the borrower's check comes due, the borrower can either let the lender present the check to his or her bank, or the borrower can roll the loan over by "buying back" the check, issuing a new check for the amount of the "repurchased" check plus any new fees. Such rollovers may or may not be limited by applicable state laws or by the agreement between the borrower and the lender. The Community Financial Services Association has a code for its members which limits any customer to three rollovers on any one loan.[16] There is now an iphone app that is basically a payday loan on an iphone.

Most payday loans are for relatively small amounts of money, normally from $100 to $500. The most common fee for a $100 loan is $15,[17] which works out to an APR of as much as 390 percent (15% for two weeks is equal to an APR of 390%; had the loan been due in *one* week the APR would be 780%).

Nineteen states prohibit payday loans. However, a loophole in federal banking regulations permits payday lenders to operate even in these states. If a payday lender enters into an arrangement with a national bank, the bank is allowed to "export" its loan rates to any state in which it operates. Thus, a national bank may enter into an arrangement with a payday lender in which the bank "makes" the loan and then sells it to the payday lender. Another option is for the bank to "carry" the loan after paying the payday lender a "finder's fee" for finding the customer.[18]

By one estimate, payday loans numbered more than 77 million loans in 2008, with gross revenues of approximately $27 billion, $20 billion of which came from "churned" loans, renewals of the original loan because the borrower could not pay the loan at the original due date.[19]

A bill has been introduced in Congress that would prohibit any FDIC-insured bank from participating, either directly or indirectly, in payday lending. In addition, a number of recent state laws have addressed the issue, and more states are expected to address it soon. In the interim, it appears that payday loans will be a significant factor in the area of consumer credit.

State and federal attention has increased on payday loans, and regulations are being implemented that will restrict the use and/or the profitability of such loans. In response to this increased scrutiny, a new type of predatory loan has been introduced, the title loan, also called the car title loan. Title loans, like payday loans, are short-term loans with high interest rates. The borrower uses his or her automobile as collateral for the loan, giving the lender the car's title and a key to the vehicle. In exchange, the lender gives money to the borrower at an interest rate that is much higher than those given by banks, often as high as 25 percent per month (a 300% APR), commonly with an expectation that the loan will be repaid at the end of the month. If the loan is not repaid, the borrower must choose to either roll the loan over for another month (for another 25% of the principal amount) or have the lender repossess the car.[20] A number of title loan companies even install a GPS on the vehicle in order to find it more easily if the borrower defaults, and some install a "starter interrupter" that makes it impossible to start the car when activated, making repossession easier.

At the present time there are no federal regulations dealing with title loans, although several states have enacted regulations and restrictions. Some of these regulations and restrictions limit the amount of interest that can be charged, while others limit the number of loan "rollovers" that are allowed. However, the lack of any uniform regulatory scheme makes it difficult to evaluate any given title lender. This area, like the area of payday loans, reaffirms the old adage *caveat emptor*—let the buyer, or in this case the borrower, beware.

Contemporary Case

LANG v. TCF NATIONAL BANK
338 Fed. Appx. 541, 2009 U.S. App. LEXIS 16591
(7th Cir. 2009)

FACTS Steven Lang sued TCF National Bank and Washington Mutual Bank (now JP Morgan Chase Bank) for violating the Fair Credit Reporting Act by failing to correct credit information that he deemed inaccurate. Lang once had personal checking accounts at both banks. In October 2003 Lang opened an account at Washington Mutual Bank. The bank closed that account one year later when Lang had an overdraft balance of $1,224.97. The next day, Washington Mutual reported Lang to ChexSystems, a consumer reporting agency, for "overdrafts," but it did not report any outstanding debt. Washington Mutual then hired a collection agency to recover the outstanding debt, and in September 2005 Lang settled that debt. Lang also had a checking account at TCF, and in 2003 he incurred forty overdraft fees for non-sufficient funds and wrote eight checks that were returned unpaid. In December 2003, TCF closed that account—which was overdrawn by $124—and absorbed the loss. TCF reported the account to ChexSystems for "Non-Sufficient funds (NSF) activity" without mentioning any current debt.

In September 2005, Lang submitted a "Request for Reinvestigation" to ChexSystems. He disputed a report from ChexSystems in which the two banks describe him as having had "overdrafts" and "Non-Sufficient funds." Lang complained to ChexSystems, "The information on your report is inaccurate and should be removed. I owe no monies to any of the institutions listed above. Please correct your information." ChexSystems sent a "Request for Reinvestigation" to both banks. The request from ChexSystems did not include Lang's denial of outstanding debt. Instead, the request stated only

that the banks had reported overdraft or non-sufficient fund activities, and that Lang disputed these reports as "inaccurate." Washington Mutual responded to ChexSystems and confirmed Lang's overdrafts, stating also that "the report is correct." TCF confirmed the information as well, advising that when Lang's account was closed, it was reported for non-sufficient funds activity.

Lang sued TCF, Washington Mutual, and ChexSystems (with whom he later settled). He alleged that because he owed no money to the banks, they provided inaccurate information to ChexSystems and failed to correct their errors, in violation of the Fair Credit Reporting Act. The district judge granted the defendants' motions for summary judgment, and Lang appealed.

ISSUE Did the banks provide inaccurate information and fail to correct their errors in violation of the Fair Credit Reporting Act?

HOLDING No. The information reported was accurate.

REASONING Excerpts from the court's opinion:

... After extensive discovery, the district judge granted the defendants' motions for summary judgment. The judge analyzed two provisions of the FCRA: § 1681s-2(b) (obligating banks to investigate requests from credit reporting agencies) and § 1681s-2(a) (obligating banks to furnish accurate information). The district court found that Washington Mutual and TCF met their obligations under § 1681s-2(b) to conduct an investigation and report to ChexSystems any discovered inaccuracies. The court also concluded that Lang could not sue the banks under § 1681s-2(a) because that provision allows for no private right of action. ...

On appeal Lang argues that the district court erred in concluding that the defendants had met their obligations to investigate the disputed credit information. Lang maintains that had the defendants displayed due diligence, they would have discovered that all debts had been paid. We review the district court's grant of summary judgment *de novo*, construing the evidence in Lang's favor. . . .

As relevant here, under 15 U.S.C. § 1681s-2(b) once the banks received notice of a dispute from ChexSystems, they were required to (a) investigate the disputed information; (b) review the relevant information "provided by" ChexSystems; and (c) report the results to ChexSystems. TCF and Washington Mutual's obligations to investigate were thus limited to the disputed information "provided by" ChexSystems. And, according to that information, Lang disputed only historical information: that he previously had "overdrafts" and account closures for "insufficient funds." The defendants investigated these disputes and confirmed to ChexSystems that these historical reports were accurate. Even Lang acknowledges that he had had overdraft and insufficient fund activities at the banks, and this concession demonstrates that the reports were accurate.

The banks are not liable for the failure to address Lang's other dispute (that he had no *current* debt to the banks) because ChexSystems did not provide that dispute to the banks in its request for investigation. . . . Lang counters that he communicated the true nature of his dispute with the ChexSystems report—that the report misrepresented him as having outstanding debt to the banks—directly to the banks, and they ignored it. But . . . Lang presents no evidence to support this contention. And even if the banks had become aware of Lang's dispute by other means, they were required to investigate only the information reported by ChexSystems. . . .

Lang next argues that the district court erred in concluding that there was no private right of action to enforce the banks' duties under § 1681s-2(a) to furnish accurate information to the reporting agency. Lang argues that the statute is silent on whether there is a private right of action, but he is wrong. Section 1681s-2(c) specifically exempts violations of § 1681s-2(a) from private civil liability; only the Federal Trade Commission can initiate a suit under that section. . . .

AFFIRMED.

You Be the Judge

Guaranteed Credit, Inc. advertised that it would provide its customers with a major credit card, regardless of the applicant's credit history, upon receipt of a one-time up-front payment from the applicant. When the applicant made this payment, Guaranteed Credit Inc. would deposit the funds and then supply the applicant with a list of companies and banks in the customer's geographic area that offer major credit cards. One of the applicants complained about this practice to the Federal Trade Commission. The FTC investigated, decided that this constituted an unfair and deceptive trade practice, and issued a cease and desist order. Guaranteed Credit, Inc. denied thatit was doing anything improper, and filed suit against the FTC. This case has been brought in *your* court. How will *you* decide? [See Bob Garver, "FTC Turns Up Heat on Scam Artists," *The American Banker*, Washington Section, p. 3 (September 6, 2002).]

Summary

While secured transactions form an important part of debtor-creditor relations, they are not the only type of credit transactions involved in this area. This is especially true in the area of consumer credit transactions, where the use of secured transactions under Article 9 tends to be limited to purchase money security interests for furniture and major appliances. There are a number of credit devices that can be used besides secured transactions. Some of these devices are more likely to be used by businesses, while others are more likely to be used by consumers.

Letters of credit are used by businesses as a means of protecting both the seller, who is assured of being paid if he or she complies with the conditions set out in the letter, and the buyer, who is assured that no funds will be released until the conditions established by the buyer have been satisfied by the seller. The buyer, known as the "applicant," establishes the letter of credit with his or her bank, the "issuer." The seller, known as the "beneficiary," provides certain specified documents to the bank to show that the goods called for have been shipped, or arc ready for shipment. If the seller provides all of the required documentation, the funds are released by the bank.

Unsecured credit is commonly used by both businesses and consumers. Many banks grant *signature loans* to their better customers, and most businesses and consumers rely on unsecured credit for the use of public utilities. The regulation of unsecured credit transactions is primarily a matter of state law. Usury is part of the state regulation. Every state has a maximum interest rate that can be charged. Excessive interest is deemed usury, and is illegal. The federal regulation of unsecured credit

is primarily concerned with ensuring that information is provided to the debtor prior to the creation of the debt, and with acceptable methods of collection in the event the debtor defaults on the agreement. Title I of the Federal Consumer Credit Protection Act (TILA) requires creditors to provide credit applicants with certain information as to the cost of the credit. This information must be provided in a standard format and in a standard terminology. The most important information that must be given to the applicant is the "APR," the annualized percentage rate to be charged in the transaction.

Installment loans are closed-end loans, calling for a fixed periodic payment for a predetermined number of periods, normally a monthly payment. Installment loans may be secured or unsecured, although most consumer installment loans are secured by some form of collateral. Some of these loans will fall within the coverage of Article 9. However, if a person purchases a car on credit, using the car as collateral for the loan, the transaction falls outside the coverage of Article 9, and this transaction will be governed by the state certificate of title rules rather than by Article 9. Installment loans are subject to many of the same regulatory provisions as are unsecured loans. Federal regulation is primarily based on the TILA and the Fair Debt Collection Practices Act. State coverage includes Article 3 of the UCC, if a promissory note is involved. The Uniform Consumer Credit Code may apply to the transaction. State laws governing contracts will also apply, as will any state statutes governing retail installment sales or similar legislation.

Mortgage loans involve loans in which real estate is used as collateral by the debtor to secure the credit. Mortgage loans are commonly installment loans, but the repayment term tends to be much longer than other types of installment loans. Mortgage loans often have a repayment period of 15, 20, or 30 years. Both federal and state regulations apply to these transactions.

The most important federal regulation is, once again, TILA. A second important area of federal coverage is the Real Estate Settlement Procedures Act (RESPA), which is also a disclosure act. Home mortgage lenders are required to provide loan applicants with a good faith estimate of all settlement and closing costs associated with the loan. Other information that must be disclosed includes referrals to any company affiliated with the lender, and information about possible transfers of the loan to subsequent parties. State coverage in this area includes mortgage lending acts, mortgage banker and broker acts, secondary mortgage acts, and home improvement loan acts.

Credit card coverage is primarily at the federal level, although some state regulation exists. The main source of federal coverage is Regulation Z, the regulations enacted in support of TILA. Among the prohibitions found under Regulation Z are: credit card issuers are prohibited from issuing unsolicited credit cards; credit card holders are only liable for up to $50 from unauthorized usage of the card; and the issuer is prohibited from using offsets to recover credit card payment deficiencies from deposit accounts of the credit card holder. State law in this area is primarily enabling, although state usury law can have an impact on credit card holders and issuers.

The Federal Trade Commission has issued two credit practice rules designed to provide some protection and some information to consumer debtors. The first, the FTC holder in due course rule, requires the inclusion of language allowing a consumer debtor to retain and use any defenses against subsequent HDCs on a consumer credit note. The second is a disclosure statement warning co-signers of the potential liability faced by co-signing on a loan or credit application.

Payday loans have experienced tremendous growth over the past decade. These loans, normally made for short time periods and for relatively small amounts of money, are readily available virtually anywhere in the nation. Many payday loan companies have reached agreements with national banks, allowing the payday loan company to operate in states that would otherwise prohibit them from doing business in the state. Federal regulation of this area has been proposed, but has not yet been enacted.

Discussion Questions

1. What is a *letter of credit*, and why are letters of credit important in commercial transactions? How does a letter of credit differ from a *sight draft*?

2. What is an unsecured credit transaction? Why would a creditor extend unsecured credit to a debtor? What are some common types of unsecured credit that most consumers are likely to use?

3. What distinguishes a mortgage loan from other types of installment loans? Why is there a different type of coverage for a mortgage loan than for an installment loan taken to purchase an automobile?

4. What are the different types of credit cards? How does a "bank card" differ from a "travel and entertainment card"?

5. What information does TILA require a creditor to provide to a debtor prior to the extension of credit? What format must be used to present this information?

Case Problems and Writing Assignments

1. In 1994, Bank of American sent an unsolicited credit card application to John Cauffiel at his place of business, Galaxie Corporation. Although Cauffiel is the sole shareholder of Galaxie, the application was addressed to Cauffiel individually. Unbeknownst to Galaxie, Cauffiel, or Bank of America, Diadette Mejia, an employee of Galaxie, intercepted and completed the application, putting Cauffiel as the primary cardholder and herself as the secondary cardholder. She also changed the billing address to her private residence. In response to the application, Bank of America issued credit cards in the primary name of Cauffiel with Mejia as the secondary cardholder. From October 1994 to February 1996, Mejia made unauthorized purchases and cash advances amounting to more than $116,000 using the credit card. She paid the monthly credit card statements by forging Cauffiel's signature on stolen checks drawn on the bank account of Galaxie. In February 1996, Cauffiel informed Bank of America of Mejia's criminal conduct and arrest, at which time the bank conducted a fraud investigation and closed the account. Cauffiel and Galaxie Corporation sued Bank of America for damages, alleging that Bank of America was negligent in issuing the credit card to Mejia. The district court granted summary judgment to Bank of America, citing the fact that Galaxie was the only injured party in this case, and determining that Bank of America owed no duty to Galaxie under these facts. Cauffiel and Galaxie Corporation appealed this ruling. Should the court of appeals uphold the district court's determination? [See *Galaxie Corporation v. Bank of America, N.A.*, 165 F.3d 27, 1998 U.S. App. LEXIS 22696 (6th Cir. 1998).]

2. Defendant American Loan is a financial institution licensed by the Illinois Department of Financial Institutions. American Loan is in the business of making "payday loans," that is, small, short-term loans, to individuals whom American Loan characterizes as posing a high risk of default. These payday loans are offered to the public at annual interest rates of 261 percent to 521 percent. Because of the extraordinarily high interest rates, these loans are primarily made to individuals to whom more traditional forms of credit are unavailable. On October 2, 1998, Deborah Jackson obtained a payday loan from American Loan to be repaid on October 15, 1998. On October 12, 1998, Jackson "renewed" her loan in order to gain more time in which to repay the debt. Upon renewal, Jackson was issued a receipt stating that an "extension fee" had been assessed to her in the amount of $35.00. Subsequently Jackson secured at least two additional payday loans from American Loan and on at least two more occasions "renewed" these loans and received receipts listing "extension fees." Similarly, Victoria Davis received multiple payday loans from Defendant and "renewed" these loans. Davis also received receipts listing "extension fees." Jackson sued American Loan for allegedly violating the terms of TILA. According to Jackson, American Loan did not provide adequate disclosure of the finance terms when Jackson "renewed" the "payday loans," and did not properly list the "extension fees" as finance charges, as required by TILA. Is American Loan guilty of violating TILA for either of these alleged offenses? Explain. Was the practice of making "payday loans" or of granting "extensions" at the interest rates charged ethical? [See *Jackson v. American Loan Company, Inc.*, 1999 U.S. Dist. LEXIS 9143 (N.D. Ill. 1999).]

3. On several occasions between 1988 and 1992 Nachson Draiman used his American Express Platinum Card to purchase airline tickets through the Travel Dimensions travel agency. Draiman provided Travel Dimensions with his Platinum Card number, and when he needed tickets he would call and place an order. Travel Dimensions would send the tickets to Draiman and the bill to American Express. American Express would then secure payment from Draiman by including the cost of the tickets plus applicable financing charges in its periodic billing statement. On January 21, 1992 Draiman cancelled his Platinum

Card. Sometime thereafter Draiman deposited an undisclosed sum of money with Travel Dimensions. On July 20, 1992 Draiman purchased four El Al tickets to Israel at $2,077 each, for a total cost of $8,308. Draiman instructed Travel Dimensions to pay for the El Al tickets by drawing upon his deposited funds. Travel Dimensions did not honor that request—instead it charged the amount against the number that it had for Draiman's Platinum Card. American Express knew nothing of Draiman's deposit with, or his instructions to, Travel Dimensions. When American Express received the $8,308 charge from Travel Dimensions, that triggered its reinstatement policy, as set out in these terms in the cardholder agreement:

> If you ask us to cancel your account, but you continue to use the Card, we will consider such use as your request for reinstatement of your account. If we agree to reinstate your account, this Agreement or any amended or new Agreement we send you will govern your reinstated account.

American Express does not communicate with cardholders to confirm that it is in fact their desire to revive their accounts. In accordance with its written policy, American Express reinstated Draiman's Platinum Card on August 26, 1992 and billed him $8,308. Draiman later actually used the El Al tickets (each of which had his Platinum Card number printed on its face) to travel to Israel. On October 15, 1993 Draiman paid American Express $3,399.98 of the $8,308 total and threatened suit if it tried to collect the $4,908.02 balance, citing purported violations of the Fair Credit Billing Act, TILA and other applicable laws. When American Express attempted to collect the debt, Draiman initiated this lawsuit on January 11, 1995 with one twist: Draiman filed not only on his own behalf but also on behalf of a purported class of similarly aggrieved persons.

Did American Express violate the unsolicited credit card provisions of TILA? Was this an unauthorized use of the card, limiting the liability of the cardholder to $50? [See *Draiman v. American Express*, 892 F. Supp. 1096, 1995 U.S. Dist. LEXIS 10195 (N.D. Ill. 1995).]

Notes

1. A "Letter Rogatory" is a letter from a court in one country to a court in another country requesting international judicial assistance. The tribunal of one nation requests a tribunal of another nation to obtain testimony or other evidence from a person located in the latter country.
2. "Prefatory Note to Article 5," *Uniform Commercial Code, 2001 Edition* (West Group 2001), pp. 541-43.
3. *Uniform Commercial Code in a Nutshell*, 5th edition, Bradford Stone (West Group 2002), p. 521.
4. Ibid., p. 522.
5. Note 1, op cit, at 541.
6. UCP 500 is a set of rules established by the International Chamber of Commerce and generally followed by banks that handle letter of credit transactions.
7. UCC § 5-103(d) and § 5-108(f).
8. UCC § 5-102(a)(14) and § 5-104.
9. UCC § 5-106(a).
10. UCC § 5-108.
11. "Summary of Consumer Credit Laws," U.S. Department of Commerce, 1999.
12. *Black's Law Dictionary*, 6th edition (St. Paul: West, 1990), p. 1545.
13. Colorado, Idaho, Indiana, Iowa, Kansas, Maine, Oklahoma, South Carolina, Utah, Wisconsin, Wyoming
14. At the time this text was written there were no new statutes enacted, but there was a "buzz" in Congress, and pressure from the White House, to address these issues through stronger legislation and oversight.
15. 15 USCS 12 CFR § 226.12
16. Ibid.
17. Marcy Gordon, "Payday Loans Targeted in Report," *Financial News* (AP Online, November 13, 2001).
18. John Hackett, "Ethically Tainted," *Consumer Lending*, Vol. III, NO. 11, p. 48 (American Banker-Bond Buyer, November 2001).
19. "Phantom Demand: Short-term due date generates need for repeat payday loans, accounting for 76% of total volume," The Center for Responsible Lending (July 9, 2009).
20. Marietta Jelks, "The Truth About Car Title Loans," *GovGab*, blog.use.gov (August 11, 2009).

27

Bankruptcy

Agenda

Ani, Meg, and Yousef have invested virtually everything they own in eClass. They are aware that any business venture can be risky, but they are making every effort to operate their business as safely and as profitably as possible. Still, they realize that eClass could encounter some difficulties that would force them to terminate the business. They wonder whether they should consider bankruptcy if that should happen.

They also realize that, no matter how carefully they operate eClass, they cannot control the business practices of their customers or their suppliers. It is possible that some of these parties may face financial problems, and could even resort to bankruptcy. They are concerned about what eClass will be able to do if this situation should arise.

Since Ani, Meg, and Yousef have invested so much time and energy into eClass, they would like to know if it would be possible to "salvage" the business if they encounter financial problems. They wonder if liquidating the business is the only option available if they have serious problems. Many large

835

companies have filed for bankruptcy and "survived." Yousef has heard that bankruptcy can be a business strategy in some situations. He doesn't understand how going bankrupt could ever be part of the strategy of a successful business. He would like to learn more about this so that he and the other principals can plan for any contingency that the firm might face.

Each of the principals also has personal debts and obligations, such as student loans. Since eClass is the primary source of income for each of them, they would like to know what their alternatives as individuals would be if the firm should fail. Would they be forced into a liquidation, or is there another avenue they could take under the provisions of the bankruptcy law? What is meant by a "fresh start," and who is entitled to have a "fresh start"?

These or similar questions may arise during our discussion. Be prepared! You never know when the firm or one of its members will seek your advice.

Classic Case

NATIONAL CITY BANK OF NEW YORK v. HOTCHKISS
231 U.S. 50, 34 S. Ct. 20 (1913)

FACTS The case arose upon what is known in New York as a "clearance loan." Brokers need large sums of money to clear or pay for the stocks they receive in the course of the day. The stocks must be paid for before they are received, but they can be pledged as security to raise the necessary funds, which are advanced by the banks. The funds are returned later the same day when the brokers make deposits to their accounts and then draw a check payable to the bank's order to repay the advance received earlier in the day. At the time of the loan the brokers had assets exceeding their liabilities consisting primarily of stock in a coal and iron company. The bank made a clearance loan of $500,000 to the brokers at about 10:00 A.M. Shortly before noon there was a break in the market, the stock went down, and at noon the suspension of trading in the firm's stock was announced. A petition in involuntary bankruptcy was filed against the firm at 3:50 that afternoon.

During the day the bank noticed the drop in the stock and went to the brokerage firm, demanding payment of the clearance loan or securities to cover the obligation owed to the bank. At that time the bank was told of the suspension of trading and that a petition in bankruptcy would be filed against the firm. After negotiating for several hours, the firm delivered the requested securities to the bank between the hours of 2:00 and 3:00. Some of these securities bore no relation to the loan, while others, it may be assumed, had been released by the money obtained in the clearance loan.

The trustee in bankruptcy sought to recover the securities for the bankrupt's estate, challenging the transaction as a voidable preference.

ISSUE Was the transfer of the securities to the bank mere hours before the bankruptcy filing a voidable preference?

836

HOLDING Yes. The loan was unsecured, and receiving security after the loan and just prior to the filing of the petition constituted a preferential transfer.

REASONING Excerpts from the opinion of Justice Holmes:

"In dealing with transactions of this kind we may go far in giving them the form that will carry out the mutually understood intent . . . But if the intent was doubtful or inconsistent with the legal effect of dominant facts, it must fail. For instance, apart from possible exceptions, a man cannot retain a domicil (sic) in one place when he has moved to another and intends to reside there for the rest of his life, by any wish, declaration or intent inconsistent with the dominant fact of where he actually lives and what he actually means to do . . . In the present case it is agreed that it was expected and understood that no portion of the clearance loan was to be used for any purpose other than to clear securities. But, on the other hand, by consent of the bank as it seems, the loan was put into the general deposit account, which was drawn upon for general purposes . . . What happened as between the parties was simply that all monies received in the course of the day from whatever source went into the firm's deposit account with the bank. So that, even if we take it,

as a corollary of what was understood, that the use of the clearance loan was expected to enable the firm to repay the loan, it does not appear to have been expected that the proceeds should be appropriated specifically to that end, but simply that the addition of such proceeds to the general funds of the firm would enable the latter to pay within the time allowed. . . .

[A] lien cannot be asserted upon a fund in a borrower's hands, which at an earlier stage might have been subject to it, if by consent of the claimant it has become a part of the borrower's general estate. But that was the result of the dealings between the parties, and it cannot be done away by a wish or intention, if such there was, that alongside of this permitted freedom of dealing on the part of the bankrupts, the security of the bank should persist. . . .

The suggestions that it does not appear that the bankrupts intended to give a preference or that the bank had reasonable cause to believe that it was obtaining one, hardly need answer. The bank did not confine its demand to proceeds of the loan but asked for and obtained securities without regard to their source. It was notified that it was receiving a preference and that the firm was going into bankruptcy. If this was not sufficient notice it is hard to imagine what would be enough. . . .

HISTORICAL BACKGROUND

Sometimes people have trouble paying their debts. When this problem arises, what should the creditor and/or the debtor do? How should a society address the problem of defaulting debtors? Perhaps the society will decide that the debtor should be punished. Banishment, public humiliation, incarceration, or even the imposition of the death penalty could be used as punishment!

For example, "In medieval Italy, when a businessman did not pay his debts, it was the practice to destroy his trading bench. From the Italian for broken bench, 'banca rotta,' comes the term bankruptcy."[1] This *banca rotta* showed the community that the businessman did not pay his debts, which undoubtedly caused him to be subjected to ridicule and to distrust. In addition, the broken trading bench made it difficult, if not impossible, to continue to ply his trade. How, then, was he to earn enough money to repay his creditors?

The first official law regarding bankruptcy in England was passed in 1542, during the reign of King Henry VIII. Under this law, a bankrupt individual was viewed as a criminal, and when convicted he could be punished for his crime. The punishment for a conviction ranged from incarceration in debtor's prison to execution![2] Over time the seriousness of the "crime" of bankruptcy was reduced, and by the eighteenth century those people in England who were unable or unwilling to pay their debts were very commonly thrown into debtors' prison. A debtor might remain in prison for years waiting for friends or family to raise the funds necessary to repay the debt, or for the creditors to agree to the debtor's release. Less commonly, the debtor might agree to some form of indentured servitude, agreeing to work for a preset number of years at little or no salary to repay the debt.

To prevent such treatment of debtors in this country, the founding fathers made provisions in the Constitution to allow "honest debtors" to make a "fresh start" by providing for relief in the form of bankruptcy. (A problem throughout bankruptcy law has been to determine who is an "honest debtor.") Article I, Section 8 of the U.S. Constitution says: "The Congress shall have the Power ... to establish ... uniform Laws on the subject of Bankruptcies throughout the United States."

It should be noted that the Constitution only *allows* Congress to establish uniform laws on bankruptcy. There is no constitutional *requirement* that Congress create bankruptcy laws or provide relief. In fact, while there were four separate bankruptcy acts passed in the nineteenth century, three of them were very short-lived, and these three did not have wide application or provide much protection for the debtors. The final bankruptcy law of the nineteenth century, and the longest-lived of these laws, was the Bankruptcy Act of 1898. This act made provision for the use of "equity receiverships" as a means of protecting and preserving businesses, and it also provided broader protection for individuals.[3]

The Great Depression led to a number of amendments to the Bankruptcy Act of 1898. These amendments—found in the Bankruptcy Act of 1933, the Bankruptcy Act of 1934, and the Chandler Act of 1938[4]—were especially important to business debtors since they formalized the reorganization provisions used in Chapter XI bankruptcy proceedings.

In 1978, Congress passed the Bankruptcy Reform Act, which took effect October 1, 1979, providing the first major changes in 40 years. The Bankruptcy Reform Act was designed to provide for fair and equitable treatment of the creditors in the distribution of the debtor's property, and, more importantly, it was designed to give an "honest debtor" a "fresh start." The Reform Act attempted to modernize the bankruptcy coverage, providing treatment for both the debtor and the creditors that was consistent with the credit-intensive, consumer-oriented society of the late twentieth century. This new law provided stronger reorganization provisions under the new Chapter 11, and also provided stronger protection for individual debtors in the repayment plan provisions of Chapter 13. The reform act contained a number of defects. Perhaps the most significant defect was its creation of bankruptcy "judges" who were to serve 14-year terms. Such federal "judgeships" violated the lifetime appointment provisions of

Article III of the U.S. Constitution for federal judges. As a result, the Supreme Court declared the Bankruptcy Reform Act unconstitutional in *Northern Pipeline Construction Co. v. Marathon Pipe Line Co.*,[5] but postponed applying this ruling until Congress had an opportunity to restructure the 1978 Act.

In response to the Court's decision Congress passed the Bankruptcy Amendments and Federal Judgeship Act of 1984. This Act clarified the jurisdictional authority of the bankruptcy courts and resolved the constitutional problems discovered in the Bankruptcy Reform Act. Additional changes were made to the Act with the Bankruptcy Reform Act of 1994, again with the aim of balancing protections while ensuring that the basic purpose of bankruptcy was maintained. While far from perfect, the Bankruptcy Reform Act, the accompanying Bankruptcy Amendments and Federal Judgeship Act, and the Bankruptcy Reform Act of 1994 were a vast improvement over the 1898 Act they replaced.

Most recently, Congress passed the Bankruptcy Abuse Prevention and Consumer Protection Act of 2005, which took effect October 17, 2005. This Act was passed because a significant number of people did not believe that the existing bankruptcy laws were appropriate. There was a widely held belief that bankruptcy was too easy to obtain and that the law's provisions did not adequately protect creditors. The resulting Act attempts to ensure that people who are able to pay a significant percentage of their debts cannot avail themselves of Chapter 7, while still leaving Chapter 7 relief available to those people who are truly in need of a liquidation proceeding in order to get a fresh start. (The restrictions imposed by the new Act are discussed later in this chapter.)

Although the Constitution seemingly calls for exclusive federal control of this area, the bankruptcy laws coexist with state law in some areas. In fact, state law often is used to define problems or to provide solutions to bankruptcy problems. For example, each state has its own exemption provisions, a listing of the assets that an honest debtor can retain following a bankruptcy. While there are federal exemptions that might be available to the debtor, state law determines whether the debtor can choose between the state and the federal exemptions or whether the debtor *must* choose the state's exemption provisions.

The current Bankruptcy Act has (from a business law perspective) three major operative sections, called chapters. These chapters are Chapter 7, Liquidation; Chapter 11, Reorganization; and Chapter 13, Adjustments of Debts of an Individual with Regular Income. In a Chapter 7 proceeding, the debtor's nonexempt assets are sold, the proceeds are distributed to the creditors, and a discharge is (normally) granted. Under Chapters 11 and 13, the debtor restructures and rearranges finances and (possibly) organization so that the creditors will be paid, hopefully in full, but at least more than in a liquidation proceeding.

BANKRUPTCY AMENDMENTS AND FEDERAL JUDGESHIP ACT OF 1984

The Bankruptcy Amendments and Federal Judgeship Act of 1984 went into effect on July 10, 1984. As previously mentioned, this act addressed the problems presented by the *Northern Pipeline* opinion by restructuring and redefining the bankruptcy court system and its jurisdiction. In addition, it made a number of substantive changes to the Bankruptcy Reform Act and its coverage.

Since these bankruptcy judges are not Article III judges, the bankruptcy courts have only limited jurisdiction under the law. The 1984 Bankruptcy Amendments grant exclusive and original jurisdiction in all bankruptcy matters to the U.S. district court. The district court may then refer any or all such cases to the bankruptcy court for adjudication. After referral to the bankruptcy court, however, the case may be withdrawn by the district court, either on its own motion or on the motion of any party to the proceedings, "for cause shown."

THE BANKRUPTCY REFORM ACT OF 1994

The Bankruptcy Reform Act of 1994 made several substantial changes in the bankruptcy law. It also created a National Bankruptcy Review Commission charged with studying issues and problems related to bankruptcy. There were numerous substantive changes to the Bankruptcy Code included in the Bankruptcy Reform Act of 1994. Among the more important of these changes are the following:

- The debt limits for Chapter 13 debtors was increased from $450,000 to $1,000,000, and the dollar amounts for involuntary petitions, priorities, and exemptions were doubled.[6]
- Future adjustments for these dollar amounts are included in the act on a three-year cycle, beginning April 1, 1998. These adjustments will be based on the Consumer Price Index for All Urban Consumers published by the Department of Labor, rounded to the nearest $25 amount.
- Purchase money security interests are given a 20-day grace period for perfection to reflect the state law provisions now in effect in a majority of the states, an increase from the ten-day grace period previously allowed.
- Limited liability partnerships are treated in bankruptcy as they would be treated in a non-bankruptcy proceeding reflecting the growing recognition of this relatively new form of business (limited liability partnerships are discussed in Chapters 31 to 33).
- The non-dischargeability of "loading up" debts is triggered at $1,000 rather than $500.
- Bankruptcy fraud is now recognized as a crime. This crime involves filing a petition or a document or making a false representation with the intent to devise a scheme to defraud creditors under Chapter 11.
- A streamlined treatment is provided for small businesses (small businesses are defined as businesses involved in commercial or business activities other than solely real estate and with liquidated debts of $2,000,000 or less) seeking relief under Chapter 11.
- Small business investment companies are not eligible for relief in bankruptcy.

An initial viewing of the Bankruptcy Reform Act of 1994 seemed to provide a balancing of the interests of the debtors and the creditors, providing a more workable structure than did the previous coverage. However, in practice creditors did not seem to be receiving the benefits envisioned when the Act was drafted. This was one of the leading factors behind the push for a *new* reform act.

THE BANKRUPTCY ABUSE PREVENTION AND CONSUMER PROTECTION ACT OF 2005

The Bankruptcy Abuse Prevention and Consumer Protection Act[7] became effective October 17, 2005. The single most important aspect of this new law was the addition of a "means test" as a precondition to the use of a Chapter 7 liquidation proceeding. Debtors seeking relief under Chapter 7 must "pass" this means test before they are allowed to continue under Chapter 7. Those debtors who do not "pass" the means test are given the choice of either converting their cases to Chapter 13 or having their petitions dismissed. The intent of the means test is to ensure that debtors with relatively high incomes are prevented from just eliminating their unsecured debts through the use of a liquidation proceeding. Instead, these debtors would be forced to pay a significant amount of their debts under Chapter 13 or lose the protections afforded by the bankruptcy law, leaving them subject to all the rights and remedies their creditors could assert under other areas of law.

The means test compares the debtor's income and "allocated" living expenses to his or her debts in order to determine whether the debtor is capable of paying a significant amount toward his or her debts. Given that the living expenses of the debtor are "allocated" under IRS guidelines, these expenses are likely to vary a great deal, depending upon the debtor's place of residence and his or her circumstances.

The Act also provided a national limit on homestead exemptions that can be utilized in a bankruptcy proceeding, restricting the ability of debtors who happen to live in some states from investing in lavish homes and then being able to exempt this homestead from the proceeding and from the trustee. The homestead exemption is now capped at $100,000 of equity in the property.

CHAPTER 7: LIQUIDATION, A "STRAIGHT" BANKRUPTCY

To many people, the term bankruptcy means just one thing—a liquidation of the debtor's assets in order for the debtor to obtain a discharge from his or her debts. This form of bankruptcy carries negative connotations to many people. A number of people view a straight bankruptcy, or a Chapter 7 proceeding, as an admission of failure. Rather than viewing this as a "fresh start" for an "honest debtor," they feel that it is a "cop-out" by a "deadbeat." Times are changing, however. More and more people are beginning to realize that a liquidation is a financial and legal option designed to help a person who has been overwhelmed by debt. The stigma of failure is being removed, and the number of Chapter 7 proceedings increases annually.

There are two types of Chapter 7 bankruptcies: voluntary and involuntary. Voluntary bankruptcies are bankruptcies initiated by the debtor. Involuntary bankruptcies are bankruptcies initiated by some combination of the creditors of a debtor. The overwhelming majority of bankruptcy petitions are filed voluntarily by the debtor.[8] Any person, firm, or corporation may file a voluntary bankruptcy petition under Chapter 7, with *five* exceptions:

1. Railroads
2. Government units
3. Banks
4. Savings and loan associations
5. Insurance companies

In addition, any person, firm, or corporation may be subjected to an involuntary petition under Chapter 7, with *seven* exceptions:

1. Railroads
2. Government units
3. Banks
4. Savings and loan associations
5. Insurance companies
6. Farmers (a farmer is defined as an individual who received more than 80 percent of gross income in the prior year from the operation of a farm that he or she owns and operates)
7. Charitable corporations

Filing Fees

The filing fees connected with the various bankruptcy chapters are established by law. For example, effective April 9, 2006 (and still effective as of January 2010), a Chapter 7 proceeding had filing fees of $299; a Chapter 11 proceeding had filing fees of $1,039; the fees for a Chapter 12 proceeding were $239; and a Chapter 13 filing required $274 in fees.[9] The fees are subject to change at any time.

Voluntary Bankruptcy Petition

The debtor who files a voluntary petition does not need to be insolvent. If a debtor desires to eliminate his or her debts, the debtor can file the petition, consent to the court's jurisdiction, go through the proceedings, and hopefully receive a discharge. However, in order to be allowed to use the Chapter 7 procedure the debtor will have to undergo credit counseling within the six months preceding the petition,[10] and then he or she must "pass" the "means test" established in the 2005 Act. (Except for the fact that passing the means test allows the debtor to use Chapter 7, this is a test that most people would not want to "pass.")

The means test is somewhat complicated due to the use of various tables, Internal Revenue-established guidelines, and overly complicated formulae. Here is a *brief* summary of how it is applied:

1. The debtor's average monthly income from the previous six months is determined, and this average is then "annualized" and compared to the median income for his or her state of residence. If the debtor's income falls *below* the state's median income, he or she can use Chapter 7. However, if the debtor's income matches or exceeds the state's median income, he or she must move to the rest of the means test.

2. The test becomes more complicated now. The debtor's monthly income is reduced by his or her monthly living expenses, and the result is multiplied by 60 (60 months represents the five year period that a Chapter 13 proceeding would cover, and the court is finding out how much the debtor can afford to repay over five years).

3. If the result (annualized average monthly income minus allocated monthly living expenses multiplied by 60) is $10,000 ($166.67 of disposable income per month) or more the debtor *cannot* use Chapter 7. If the result is less than $6,000 (no more than $99.99 of disposable income per month), the debtor is allowed to use Chapter 7. If the amount is between $6,000 and $10,000, the debtor goes to the next stage of the test.

4. For debtors with disposable income between $6,000 and $10,000, if the debtor can pay at least 25 percent of his or her debt over the 60-month period, he or she will not be allowed to use Chapter 7. For those debtors who will *not* be able to pay at least 25 percent of their debt, Chapter 7 can be used.

This sounds relatively simple and straightforward, but there is a catch! The "monthly living expenses" deducted from monthly income in step 2 are *not* based on the debtor's actual living expenses. Rather, these expenses are determined by using the IRS Collections Financial Standards guidelines, the method by which the IRS determines the ability of a delinquent taxpayer to pay his or her back taxes. The "living expenses" are (1) food and clothing, (2) housing and utilities, and (3) transportation. The amounts are determined by the *county* in which the debtor lives and the debtor's household. The amount allowed can vary significantly from one community to another within any given state, let alone from state to state.

In addition, the law requires that all debtors be made aware of the alternative provisions of Chapter 13 repayment plans before they are allowed to file a Chapter 7 petition. By so doing, it is hoped that more debtors will elect a repayment plan rather than a liquidation procedure. This will work to the benefit of the creditors and may also help a number of debtors by allowing them to retain more of their assets than they would retain under a Chapter 7 liquidation.

Involuntary Bankruptcy Petition

Often a debtor will get deeply in debt and try to avoid bankruptcy. When this happens, the creditors may decide to petition the debtor into bankruptcy against his or her will. They do so by initiating an involuntary bankruptcy proceeding.

If a debtor does not fall within one of the groups exempted from involuntary petitions, the debtor is potentially subject to an involuntary petition. The vast majority of debtors in this country do not fit into one of these exceptions. That does not mean that most debtors are automatically subject to an involuntary petition, however. The creditors who file the petition must show that three criteria—one related to the *conduct* of the debtor, one to the *number* of creditors of the debtor, and one to the amount of *unsecured debt* of the debtor—are satisfied before they may file an involuntary petition against the debtor.

Debtor Conduct   The petitioning creditors must establish that the debtor is "guilty" of one of two acts: either the debtor is not paying his or her debts as they become due, or the debtor appointed a receiver or made a general assignment for the benefit of the creditors within the 120 days that preceded the filing of the petition. (Under the latter test, the receiver or assignee must have taken possession of the debtor's property.)

Number of Petitioning Creditors   The petition filed with the court must be signed by the "proper number" of creditors. The proper number of creditors for a particular debtor is determined by the total number of creditors that debtor has. If the debtor has a total of 12 creditors or more, at least *three* creditors must sign the petition. If the debtor has fewer than 12 creditors, only *one* creditor must sign the petition, although more may choose to sign the petition.

Debt Requirement   The creditors who file the petition must have an aggregate claim against the debtor of at least $10,000 that is neither secured nor contingent. This means that a debtor with less than $10,000 in general unsecured debts may not be involuntarily petitioned into bankruptcy. It also explains why more than the minimum number of creditors (from the "number of petitioning creditors" requirement) will often need to sign the petition in order to have the proper amount of unsecured debt represented by the petitioning creditors.

The following example shows one problem that petitioning creditors may face.

> *Bob has seven creditors. He has made no payments to any of them for four months. He owes Ralph, one of the creditors, $6,000, of which $2,000 is secured by collateral. Ralph wants to file an involuntary petition against Bob. Since Bob is not paying his debts as they come due, the "conduct" requirement is satisfied. Since Ralph has less than 12 creditors, only one of his creditors must sign the petition to satisfy the*

"number" requirement. However, unless one or more of Bob's other creditors—with a [combined] claim of at least $6,000 in unsecured debt—will join Ralph on a petition, Ralph cannot institute an involuntary petition. Ralph's unsecured claim of $4,000 does not satisfy the "debt" requirement.

In this example, Ralph also needs to exercise care prior to filing the petition. If a debtor is involuntarily petitioned into bankruptcy, the debtor may deny that he is bankrupt and request a trial on this issue. A debtor who wins such a trial can collect damages from the creditors who signed the petition.

THE BANKRUPTCY PROCEEDING

Once a petition is filed, the judge will issue an order for relief (unless the debtor in an involuntary petition files an answer denying bankruptcy and demands a trial). At this point the proceeding is in motion, and it will continue until the final orders are entered. Upon entering the order for relief, the judge promptly appoints a trustee from a panel of private trustees. This trustee takes possession of—and legal title to—the debtor's property and begins the administration of the debtor's estate. (At the first creditors' meeting, a new trustee may be selected. If creditors having collective claims of at least 20 percent of the unsecured claims against the debtor request an election, the creditors can select a "permanent" trustee. If no such request is made, the court-appointed trustee serves throughout the proceedings.)

The Trustee

The trustee is the key figure in the bankruptcy proceeding. The trustee is the representative of the debtor's estate, and the trustee will attempt to preserve this estate to protect the interests of the unsecured creditors. The estate that the trustee preserves is made up of all the property the debtor has when the case is begun and any property the debtor acquires within the 180 days following the petition-filing date, reduced by any collateral removed from the estate and by the exempt assets of the debtor. The trustee must gather all of these assets, liquidate them, and generally handle the creditors' claims. The trustee also raises objections to the granting of a discharge if the debtor gives cause to do so. The trustee may be helped by a creditors' committee, a group of at least three and at most 11 unsecured creditors who consult with the trustee as needed.

The trustee is responsible for representing the interests of the general unsecured creditors in the bankruptcy petition. While the trustee takes legal title to the debtor's estate, the creditors have equitable title—this means that the trustee possesses the estate for the benefit of the creditors. The trustee's job is difficult and demanding. Under the Bankruptcy Act, both individuals and corporations may serve as trustees, although corporations need to be authorized to perform this function in their corporate charter. In order for an individual to serve as trustee, he or she must be "competent to perform the duties of a trustee." The trustee must also satisfy a residency requirement by residing or having an office in the district where the case is pending or in an adjacent district.

Currently in a Chapter 11 proceeding, any interested party may call for a meeting of the creditors in order to elect a trustee, provided the meeting is called within 30 days of the court's appointment of an operating trustee. There is some expectation that similar provisions will be enacted regarding Chapter 7 trustees in the near future.

Automatic Stay Provision

The filing of a petition in bankruptcy operates as an *automatic stay*, placing any legal actions involving the debtor "on hold." The automatic stay operates to stop lawsuits instituted by the debtor, allowing the trustee the opportunity to settle these cases and bringing any amounts recovered through such settlements into the bankruptcy estate. The automatic stay also works against creditors who are involved in any legal actions against the debtor. The creditors must suspend any legal actions already commenced and must delay filing any new actions, pending the outcome of the bankruptcy proceedings. In addition, the creditors may not initiate any repossession actions against the assets of the debtor. This automatic stay provision is designed to ensure that all the creditors are afforded equitable treatment under the bankruptcy proceedings by preventing any one creditor from gaining an advantage through his or her legal actions at the expense of the other creditors.

The Creditors' Meeting

The court will call for a meeting of the creditors within a reasonable time after the order for relief. The debtor, the trustee, and the creditors—but not the judge—will all attend this meeting. The debtor is expected to provide schedules of anticipated income, assets and their locations, and debts and liabilities at that time and to submit to an examination by the creditors concerning the debtor's assets, liabilities, and anything else the creditors feel is important. Although the debtor may not like it, it is best to cooperate fully: A refusal to cooperate may result in a denial of discharge. At this first creditors' meeting, the trustee is required to orally advise the debtor as to the possible repercussion from filing for bankruptcy relief and to explain to the debtor about other bankruptcy chapters that the debtor might want to utilize in lieu of a Chapter 7 liquidation proceeding.

The Debtor

The debtor also has certain duties to perform. The debtor must file a relatively detailed series of schedules that are intended to reveal his or her financial position so that

(1) the bankruptcy court can properly evaluate the need for relief and (2) the interests of the various creditors can be protected. The debtor must provide a list of creditors, both secured and unsecured, the address of each creditor, and the amount of debt owed to each. The debtor also must provide a schedule of his or her financial affairs and a listing of all property owned, even if that property will be claimed as an exempt asset. Finally, the debtor must provide a list of current income and expenses. This list may show that the debtor should be in a Chapter 13 repayment plan rather than a Chapter 7 liquidation proceeding. If it does, the court may, on its own motion, dismiss the Chapter 7 proceeding following a hearing and encourage the debtor to re-file under Chapter 13. However, the law also carries with it a presumption in favor of the debtor. The debtor is presumed to be entitled to receive the order of relief for whatever chapter he or she chooses. The schedules are prepared by the debtor under oath and signed. Knowingly submitting false information on these schedules is a crime under the bankruptcy law.

The debtor also must cooperate fully with the trustee and surrender all property to the trustee. Finally, the debtor must attend any and all hearings and comply with all orders of the court. If this is done, a discharge will normally result.

Secured Creditors

Once the debtor has selected those assets to be exempted for a "fresh start," the trustee must communicate with the secured creditors concerning their status. Each secured creditor must make a selection. Secured creditors may elect to take their collateral in full satisfaction of their claims; dispose of the collateral, applying the proceeds to the debt and surrendering any surplus to the trustee to be included in the bankruptcy estate; dispose of the collateral and participate as unsecured creditors to the extent they are not satisfied by the collateral; or have the trustee dispose of the collateral, paying the secured creditor the proceeds realized (up to the debt amount) and allowing the creditor to participate as an unsecured creditor for any balance owed.

Exemptions

The debtor can exempt some assets from the trustee's liquidation. The exempted assets are intended to provide the foundation for the "fresh start" bankruptcy grants to those honest debtors who successfully complete the bankruptcy proceeding and receive a discharge. This exemption is, surprisingly, governed to a significant extent by state statutes, which determine what the debtor is allowed to exempt. If state law permits, the debtor may elect to take *either* the state exemptions *or* the federal exemptions. If no such choice is allowed by state law, the debtor must take the state exemptions. Under no circumstances may the debtor take both sets of exemptions.

Thirty-six states have elected the override provision, requiring the debtor to take the state exemptions and prohibiting the debtor from using the federal exemptions.

In addition, even if the debtor is in one of the 14 states that allows the choice of either the federal or the state exemptions, another limitation has been imposed by the 1984 Bankruptcy Amendments. In a joint filing, both the husband and the wife must select the same exemptions, either state or federal. They no longer will be allowed to select the exemptions individually, allowing one spouse to take the federal exemptions and the other to select the state exemptions.

The Bankruptcy Reform Act also permits a debtor to convert goods from non-exempt classes to exempt classes before filing the bankruptcy petition. In addition, if there is a lien on, or security interest attached to, otherwise exempt property, the debtor can redeem it—which automatically exempts it—by paying off the lien-holding creditor.

Allowable Claims

Once the permanent trustee has assumed control of the estate and the exempt property has been removed from the estate, the serious business of bankruptcy begins. Those claims of creditors that are "allowable" must be filed. Only allowable debts may participate in the distribution of the estate. Allowable claims may be filed by the debtor, a creditor, or even the trustee, but they must be filed within six months of the first creditors' meeting.

Virtually every debt of the debtor that existed prior to the entry of the order for relief will be treated as an "allowable" claim. The court will *not* allow any claims that would be unenforceable against the debtor outside of the bankruptcy proceeding, such as claims based on fraud or duress by the person asserting the claim. In addition, the court will *not* allow any claims for interest accruing after the petition date. The automatic stay provision of a bankruptcy proceeding stops the accrual of interest on any claims of the creditor.

There are also two classes of claims that are allowable, but for which the amount of the claims may well be restricted. If the debtor has violated a lease agreement, the landlord's claim under the broken lease agreement is allowable, but it may be allowable for only a limited amount. The landlord is entitled to recover any rent already due and payable, and is also allowed to recover for future rent under the lease. However, the claim for future rent is limited to the *greater* of one year's rent or 15 percent of the balance of the lease (with a three-year maximum), plus any unpaid rent already due and payable. Similarly, if the debtor has breached any employment contracts, the employees may assert their claims for damages due to the breach. The employees will be entitled to any wages already due and payable, and they will also be entitled to claim lost future wages, but only for a maximum of one year of unpaid future compensation. The following example illustrates these restrictions.

Milady Formal Wear, Inc. leased office space from River City Realty, signing a 30-year lease in June of 2005. Milady also hired a sales manager, signing her to a five-year employment contract in June of 2005. In August of 2005, Milady hired a designer, signing a three-year employment contract, with an option for another three years. After an auspicious start, Milady encountered financial difficulties, culminating in the filing of a bankruptcy petition in January of 2008. At the time of the petition, Milady was four months behind on its rent to River City Realty, and it had been unable to pay its sales manager or its designer for three months.

River City Realty will have an allowable claim for the four months of rent already due and payable, plus a claim for the breached lease, which still had 27 years and 6 months remaining. However, the claim for the balance of the lease is restricted to the greater of one year or 15 percent of the balance, with an absolute maximum of three years. Thus, River City Realty will be entitled to an allowable claim for 40 months of rent; four months already owed plus 36 months for the future rent.

Each of the employees will also have an allowable claim against Milady. The sales manager will have an allowable claim for three months' wages already due and payable, plus an additional allowable claim for future wages of up to one year. Since the sales manager signed a five-year contract, and the contract still has two years and four months remaining, she has an allowable claim for one year's future compensation. The designer will have a claim for the three months that Milady is in arrears, and will have a claim for future compensation for the remaining six months on the original employment contract. The three-year option will not be considered, nor will any part of it be allowed.

Recovery of Property

While administering a debtor's estate, a trustee may discover that the debtor committed certain improper actions. A trustee who discovers such conduct is obligated to recover the transferred property for the benefit of the unsecured creditor(s). These improper acts fall into two major categories: voidable preferences and fraudulent conveyances.

Voidable Preferences   A voidable preference is a payment made by a debtor to one or a few creditors at the expense of the other creditors in that particular creditor class. This is not as complicated as it may seem at first glance. A transfer is deemed a preference and therefore voidable if *all* the following five conditions are met:

1. The transfer benefits a creditor.
2. The transfer covers a preexisting debt.
3. The debtor is insolvent at the time of the transfer. (A debtor is presumed to be insolvent during the 90 days preceding the date of the petition; this presumption is rebuttable by the debtor.)
4. The transfer is made during the 90 days preceding the petition date.
5. The transfer gives the creditor who receives it a greater percentage of the creditor's claim than fellow creditors will receive as a result of the transfer.

eClass 27.1 Finance

WAS THIS A FRAUDULENT CONVEYANCE?

eClass has purchased a significant amount of its diskettes from the same firm for quite some time. This firm has a reputation for high quality products and competitive prices. Ninety days ago the president of this firm contacted Meg offering to sell eClass some new diskettes. The quantity the firm was offering was larger than any order eClass had placed before, but the price was especially attractive. After a short deliberation, Meg accepted the offer. Now eClass has learned that this supplier has been involuntarily petitioned into bankruptcy, and that the trustee appointed to handle the bankruptcy is investigating all sales made by the company in the past six months. The trustee believes that several of the company's sales were fraudulent conveyances, with the selling price for the goods so far below fair market value that the buyers should have been suspicious. Meg does not believe that she did anything wrong in accepting the offer to buy the diskettes, but she is not sure what evidence the trustee would need in order to establish that a fraudulent conveyance occurred. She has asked you for advice. What will you tell her?

BUSINESS CONSIDERATIONS   Should a business accept an offer that looks "too good to be true" without investigating the reason for the offer, or should the business just be grateful for the opportunity and try to take advantage of it? Why?

ETHICAL CONSIDERATIONS   What ethical issues are raised when a buyer is offered a price that seems unreasonably low? Is it ethical to accept such an offer without investigating the circumstances behind the offer? Is it ethical to refuse such an offer to the detriment of your firm?

A transfer is not deemed a voidable preference if it fits any *one* of the following tests:

1. The transfer is for a new obligation, as opposed to a preexisting debt.
2. The transfer is made in the ordinary course of business.
3. The transfer involves a purchase-money security interest.
4. The transfer is a payment on a fully secured claim.
5. The transfer is for normal payments made to creditors within 90 days prior to the petition, if the payments total less than $600 per creditor.

Fraudulent Conveyance   A fraudulent conveyance is a transfer by a debtor that involves actual or constructive fraud. Actual fraud is involved if the debtor intended to hinder or delay a creditor in recovering a debt. Such a transfer will occur if the debtor transfers assets to a friend or a relative—or hides assets—to prevent any creditors from foreclosing on the assets. Constructive fraud is involved when the debtor sells an asset for inadequate consideration and as a result of the sale becomes insolvent or if the debtor is already insolvent at the time of the sale. It is also deemed constructive fraud to engage in a business that is undercapitalized.

Any fraudulent conveyance made during the year preceding the petition may be set aside by the trustee under federal law. In addition, some state statutes permit the avoidance of such conveyances during the preceding two to five years. The trustee uses the time period that most strongly favors the creditors.

Distribution of Assets

Once the trustee has gathered and liquidated all available assets and admitted all allowable claims, the estate is distributed to the creditors. The Bankruptcy Reform Act contains a mandatory priority list of debts. Each class of creditors takes its turn, and no class may receive any payments until all higher-priority classes are paid in full. All creditors within a given class will be paid on a pro rata basis until either the claims are paid in full or the estate is exhausted. The priority list is set out in Exhibit 27.1. After all priority claims are paid, the balance of the estate is used to pay general unsecured creditors. When all unsecured creditors have been paid in full, any monies left are paid to the debtor. Normally, the funds will not cover the general creditor claims, and

Exhibit 27.1

Distribution of Proceeds in a Chapter 7 Bankruptcy Proceeding

Priority 1:   The expenses of handling the bankruptcy. (All the costs incurred by the trustee in preserving and administering the bankruptcy must be paid first.)

If any funds remain

Priority 2:   Debts that arise in the ordinary course of business between the date the petition is filed and the date the trustee is appointed. (Pro rata if necessary)

If any funds remain

Priority 3:   Wages earned, but not yet paid, by employees of the debtor during the 90 days preceding the petition, up to a maximum of $4,000 per employee. (Pro rata if necessary)

Exhibit 27.1 Continued

If any funds remain

Priority 4:   Unpaid contributions by an employer to employee benefit plans, if they arise during the 180 days before the petition, up to $4,000 per employee. (Pro rata *if necessary*)

NOTE: These claims are reduced by any claims paid in Priority 3, giving a maximum priority for each employee a total of $4,000. Any claims in excess of this amount go to the bottom of the list.

If any funds remain

Priority 5:   Claims of grain farmers against the owner or operator of a grain storage facility and/or to U.S. fishermen who have a claim against individuals who operate a fish storage or fish-processing facility. In either case, the priority is limited to $4,000 per individual creditor. (Pro rata *if necessary*)

If any funds remain

Priority 6:   Claims by consumers for goods or services paid for but not received. The maximum here is $1,800 per person as a priority, with any surplus claim going to the bottom of the list. (Pro rata *if necessary*)

If any funds remain

Priority 7:   Claims against the debtor for alimony, maintenance agreements or obligations, and child support (This category was added as a priority in 1994. To further emphasize this change, the payment of alimony, maintenance, or child support is specifically *not* a voidable preference, nor are such payments subject to the automatic stay provisions of other debts and obligations of the debtor.)

If any funds remain

Priority 8:   Debts owed to government units. This class consists basically of taxes due during the three years preceding the petition.

If any funds remain

General unsecured creditors, together with any creditors who have claims in excess of the amount entitled to priority treatment, then share the remaining funds, pro rata if necessary.

If any funds remain

The debtor receives any funds remaining after these distributions.

a pro rata distribution is necessary. This leaves the creditors with less money than they were owed. The debtor must hope for a discharge to make the balance of the claims uncollectible.

The Discharge Decision

A discharge can be granted only to an individual under Chapter 7 and only if he or she is an honest debtor. A discharge will be denied if the debtor made a fraudulent conveyance or does not have and/or did not keep adequate books and records. In addition, a debtor will be denied a discharge if he or she refuses to cooperate with the court during the proceedings. Furthermore, a discharge will not be granted if a discharge was received during the previous six years. A denial of discharge means that the unpaid portions of any debts continue and are fully enforceable after the proceedings end.

Even if a discharge is granted, some claims are not affected. Under the Bankruptcy Reform Act, certain debts continue to be fully enforceable against the debtor even though the debtor received a discharge. The following 11 major classes of debts are not affected by a discharge:

1. Taxes due to any government unit
2. Loans where the proceeds were used to pay federal taxes
3. Debts that arose because of fraud by the debtor concerning the debtor's financial condition
4. Claims not listed by the creditors or by the debtor in time for inclusion in the proceedings
5. Debts incurred through embezzlement or theft
6. Alimony
7. Child support
8. Liabilities due to malicious torts of the debtor
9. Fines imposed by a government unit
10. Claims that were raised in a previous case in which the debtor did not receive a discharge
11. Student loans, unless the loan is at least five years in arrears.

In addition to these 11 classes of debts, the 1984 Bankruptcy Amendments addressed the problem of debtors who "load up" with debts just prior to filing a petition, expecting to use the bankruptcy proceeding to discharge these recently incurred debts. Under the law, any debtor purchases from one creditor of $1,000 or more in luxury goods or services that are incurred within 90 days of the petition are presumed to be non-dischargeable. Similarly, any cash advances of $1,000 or more that are received from one creditor within the 70 days prior to the petition are presumed to be non-dischargeable. The debtor will have the burden of proof and will have to convince the court that these debts were not fraudulently incurred with the intent of receiving a discharge in order to have these debts discharged. Notice that a discharge is possible but that the debtor has the burden of proof!

Exhibit 27.2 illustrates the steps in a Chapter 7 bankruptcy proceeding.

Exhibit 27.2

A Chapter 7 Bankruptcy Proceeding

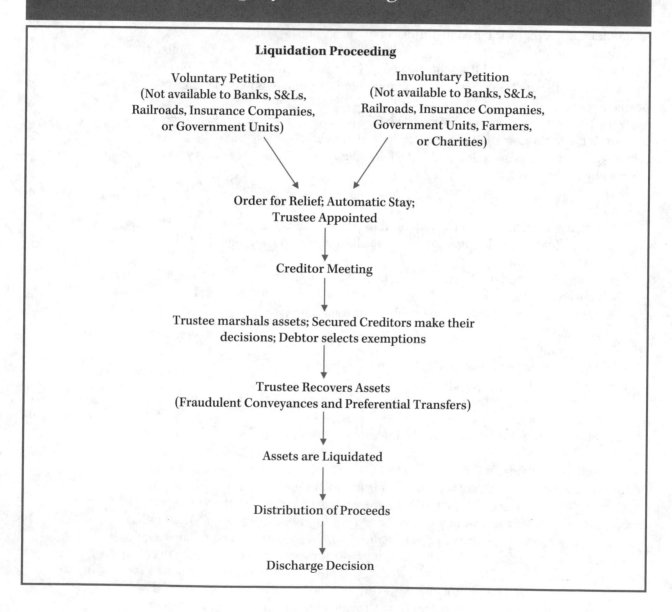

Liquidation Proceeding

Voluntary Petition
(Not available to Banks, S&Ls,
Railroads, Insurance Companies,
or Government Units)

Involuntary Petition
(Not available to Banks, S&Ls,
Railroads, Insurance Companies,
Government Units, Farmers,
or Charities)

Order for Relief; Automatic Stay;
Trustee Appointed

Creditor Meeting

Trustee marshals assets; Secured Creditors make their
decisions; Debtor selects exemptions

Trustee Recovers Assets
(Fraudulent Conveyances and Preferential Transfers)

Assets are Liquidated

Distribution of Proceeds

Discharge Decision

Finally, even if a discharge is granted, it may be revoked. If the trustee or a creditor requests a revocation of the discharge, the request may be granted. The request must be made within one year of the discharge, and the debtor must have committed some wrongful act, such as fraud during the proceedings. The possibility of revocation encourages the debtor to remain honest.

On some occasions, a debtor who has been granted a discharge in bankruptcy may decide that he wants to repay the creditor despite the discharge. If the debtor truly wants to repay the debt, he may voluntarily reaffirm the debt and then repay it. However, the bankruptcy code requires that the reaffirmation must be in writing and the written agreement must be filed with—and approved by—the Bankruptcy Court, and it must be filed with the court prior to the discharge decision. Even if the debtor does so, he or she can rescind the agreement at any time up to 60 days after the discharge decision. (If the debtor has an attorney, the attorney must file a declaration that the debtor was fully informed of his rights, voluntarily agreed to the reaffirmation, and that the agreement will not impose an undue hardship on the debtor or his dependents.) The court will only approve a reaffirmation if it believes that the repayment is in the best interests of the debtor.

CHAPTER 11: REORGANIZATION PLANS

Many people have the mistaken idea that Chapter 7 proceedings are all that the Bankruptcy Code covers. While a Chapter 7 proceeding is the most common type of bankruptcy, several other types of proceedings are also available under the Bankruptcy Code: a reorganization under Chapter 11, which is normally used by businesses; and a wage earner's repayment plan under Chapter 13, which is only available for individual debtors. Neither of these plans calls for a liquidation of the debtor's assets in order to cover the debts; and under these plans, the creditors can reasonably expect to be paid more than they would receive under a liquidation proceeding. In fact, many times the creditors will be paid in full by the debtor. While a Chapter 7 bankruptcy relies on the debtor's assets as of the petition date, plus those assets acquired during the proceedings, each of these chapters involve plans that also rely on the debtor's future earnings.

Chapter 11 bankruptcy proceedings, known as reorganizations, are designed to allow the debtor to adjust his or her financial situation, restructuring the business financially in order to save the enterprise. Chapter 11 is used by debtors to avoid liquidations. Although reorganizations are designed primarily for use by corporate debtors, individuals are also allowed to use the reorganization format.

The major advantage of a reorganization is that it allows a business to continue despite its debts. In fact, if the court approves a reorganization plan, it will force the creditors who object to go along with the plan despite their objections through application of the "cram down" provisions of the Code.[11] Normally the creditors will receive more of the money owed to them in a reorganization than they would receive in a liquidation under Chapter 7.

Any debtor who can use Chapter 7, except stockbrokers and commodity brokers, can also use Chapter 11. Moreover, railroads, which are prohibited from using Chapter 7, can take advantage of the provisions of Chapter 11. Like a liquidation proceeding, a reorganization may be either voluntary or involuntary. The same limitations for an involuntary petition apply under Chapter 11 as apply to a liquidation petition.

The Proceedings

Once the petition has been filed, the court will do three things:

1. It will enter an order for relief.
2. It will appoint a trustee, if requested to do so by any interested party.
3. It will appoint creditor committees to represent the creditors. (Equity security holders will be represented by a separate committee.)

Remember that the *automatic stay* provisions also apply in this chapter. When a petition is filed, any legal actions involving the debtor are subject to an automatic stay, freezing those legal proceedings until the bankruptcy proceedings have been concluded.

The court may appoint a trustee, although the appointment of a trustee is not necessary in Chapter 11. In fact, if no interested party *asks* for the appointment of a trustee, no trustee will be appointed. Instead, the debtor is permitted to retain possession and control of the assets and/or the business (such a debtor is referred to as a debtor-in-possession). This *debtor-in-possession* is deemed to have the same basic duties as a trustee, including the fiduciary duty owed to the creditors. The committees appointed by the court will meet with the trustee, if one is appointed, or with the debtor-in-possession, if no trustee is appointed, to discuss the treatment of the proceedings. The committees also will investigate the debtor's finances and financial potential, and they will help prepare a plan for reorganizing the enterprise that will benefit all the interested parties.

In the event that no one asks for the appointment of a trustee, the court may decide to appoint an *examiner*. The examiner or the trustee will investigate the debtor, the debtor's business activities, and the debtor's business potential. On the basis of this investigation, a recommendation will be made to the court. The recommendation may be a reorganization plan, or it may be a suggestion that the proceedings be transferred from Chapter 11 to Chapter 7 (liquidation) or to Chapter 13 (wage earner plan, if the debtor is an individual). The court normally will follow such a recommendation unless a good reason not to follow it is presented.

eClass 27.2 Finance

CHAPTER 11 BANKRUPTCY

Mail-Mart, a mail-order retail business, is one of eClass's largest customers. Over the past several months it has ordered nearly $12,000 worth of the eClass software, which has been one of Mail-Mart's largest selling computer software items. However, Mail-Mart's business has been in decline for some time, and it recently filed a petition seeking relief under Chapter 11 of the Bankruptcy Act. At the time of the filing Mail-Mart owed eClass nearly $10,000 and had been steadily falling behind on its payments. Mail-Mart has filed a reorganization plan that would have it making payments to its creditors for a longer time period, and would also reduce or eliminate the interest it would normally pay on any of its debts. Ani thinks that Mail-Mart's plan will put eClass in a poor cash-flow position, and she would like the firm to vote against the plan as proposed by Mail-Mart. Meg is also concerned about the cash-flow consequences but thinks that the firm can handle the situation, provided that Mail-Mart pays the entire balance due. She is concerned that if the creditors oppose the plan Mail-Mart will be forced to liquidate, and eClass will only receive a fraction of the money owed. They have asked you what the firm should do in this situation, and they also want to know what rights, if any, eClass can assert. What will you tell them?

BUSINESS CONSIDERATIONS   Any time a business extends credit to a customer that business assumes the risk of default or bankruptcy by the customer, affecting the account. What can a business like eClass do to protect itself, short of refusing to make credit sales? Why would a business not decide to deal strictly on a cash-and-carry basis?

ETHICAL CONSIDERATIONS   Suppose that a customer is encountering financial difficulties and facing the possibility of failure. That customer asks for an extension of the time for making its payments. What considerations would cause a creditor to agree to the extension? When should the creditor take a hard-line stance and refuse to vary the payment terms?

The Plan

The purpose of a reorganization is to develop a plan under which the debtor can avoid liquidation while somehow managing to satisfy the claims of the creditors. Obviously, the right to propose a plan can be very important. If the debtor remains in possession (i.e., no trustee is appointed), only the debtor may propose a plan during the first 120 days after the order for relief is entered.

Note that any interested party (debtor, creditor, stockholder, or trustee) can propose a plan under any of three conditions:

1. If a trustee is appointed, any interested party can propose a plan at any time until a plan is approved by the court.

2. If the debtor fails to propose a plan within the 120-day period, any interested party can propose a plan.

3. If the debtor proposes a plan within 120 days, but it is not accepted by all affected classes of creditors within 180 days of the order for relief, any interested party can propose a plan to the court.

The 1994 Bankruptcy Reform Act includes provisions for a "fast track" reorganization for small-business debtors. This "fast-track" reorganization is covered in § 1121(c). To be eligible for this provision, the business must be a "small business" *and* it must elect to be considered a "small business." Small business is defined in § 101(51C) as a business with less than $2 million in non-contingent liquidated liabilities. If the debtor business has as its primary activity the owning or managing of real estate it is not allowed to use the "fast track" option. The debtor in a "fast track" reorganization must file a plan within 100 days, rather than the 120 days granted under a "regular" Chapter 11. All plans must be filed within 160 days, as opposed to the 180 days granted under a "regular" Chapter 11.

For a plan to be confirmed, it must designate all claims by class as well as specify which classes will be impaired and which will not be impaired. It must also show how the plan can be implemented successfully. Among the factors that the court will examine in reviewing a plan are the following:

1. Plans to sell any assets
2. Plans to merge, consolidate, or divest
3. Plans to satisfy, or modify, any liens or claims
4. Plans to issue new stock to generate funds

If new stock is to be issued, it must have voting rights. No new nonvoting stock may be issued under a reorganization plan. Each class of creditors that is impaired is allowed to vote on the plan.

According to § 1129(a), the court can confirm a plan *only if* a number of requirements are met. Included in this list of requirements are the following:

1. The plan was proposed in good faith and not by any means forbidden by law;
2. Any payments made or to be made under the plan for services, costs, and expenses in connection with the plan have been approved by, or are subject to approval by, the court;
3. With respect to each impaired class of claims or creditors, each class
   a. has accepted the plan, or
   b. will receive or retain property of a value that is not less than the amount that class or claim would receive or retain if the debtor were liquidated under Chapter 7;
4. If a class of claims is impaired, at least one class of claims that is impaired has accepted the plan; and
5. Confirmation of the plan is not likely to be followed by a liquidation.

Exhibit 27.3

A Chapter 11 Bankruptcy Proceeding

Reorganization

Voluntary Petition (Not available to Banks, S&Ls, Insurance Companies, Government Units, Stockbrokers, or Commodities Brokers. Is available to Railroads.)

Involuntary Petition (Not available to Banks, S&Ls, Insurance Companies, Government Units, Farmers, Stockbrokers, or Commodities Brokers. Is available to Railroads.)

Order for Relief; Automatic Stay; Trustee Appointed (if requested) *or* Debtor-in-Possession operates the business Creditor Committees appointed by the Court

Submission of the Plan

If no trustee is appointed: Only the debtor can propose a plan for the first 120 days (100 days in a "Fast Track" proceeding); Any interested party can submit a plan thereafter.

If a trustee is appointed: Any interested party can propose a plan at any time during the proceedings until a plan is accepted.

The Plan must designate claims by creditor class. Must designate how each class will be treated. Must specify which claims will be impaired, if any. Must specify how the business will be restructured/reorganized.

Creditors vote on the plan; the vote is *advisory* for the Court, it is not binding on the Court.

Court approves or rejects the plan.

A class is deemed to have accepted the plan if creditors having at least two-thirds of the dollar amount involved and more than one-half of the total number of creditors vote in favor of the plan. If a creditor class is not impaired by the plan, it does not need to approve the plan. Creditor classes whose claims will be impaired under the plan *must* vote on the plan, and at least one of these impaired classes must approve the plan [§ 1129 (a)(10)]. This requirement sounds very straightforward, but even this has an exception, the so-called "cram down" provisions found in § 1129 (b), which is discussed below.

Despite the vote, no plan can be accepted or rejected by the creditors. The final word is left to the court. The court will hold a hearing on the plan, and the court can confirm or reject it. The court *can* confirm a plan if it is accepted by at least one class of creditors. If all the creditor classes approve the plan, the court normally will confirm it. Similarly, if all the creditor classes reject the plan, the court will reject it. The vote of the creditor classes provides the court with guidance, but the final decision lies with the court, subject to the limitations imposed by the statute.

The court will look at the plan's fairness to each interested group, especially those creditors impaired by the plan. The court also will look at the viability of the plan. If the court feels the plan will not work or is not fair, the court can order the proceedings converted to a Chapter 7 liquidation. This last-ditch power encourages everyone involved to act in good faith, since Chapter 11 usually is better than Chapter 7 for all concerned.

Once the court approves a plan, it becomes binding on all of the interested parties affected by the plan. Suppose that a creditor class objects to the plan, and this class voted against the plan. Despite this objection, if the court approves the plan, the plan will be binding on the disgruntled creditor class. In this situation the court is using the "cram down provision," the plan is being "crammed down" the throats of the dissenting creditors.

Section 1129(b) allows the court to bypass the restrictions imposed by § 1129(a) and to confirm a plan, at the request of the proponent of that plan, if the plan does not discriminate unfairly, and is fair and equitable, with respect to each class of claims that is impaired by the plan and has not accepted the plan.

Exhibit 27.3 illustrates the steps in a Chapter 11 bankruptcy proceeding.

Chapter 11 as a Corporate Strategy

Reorganizations have recently taken on an interesting twist. A number of corporations, some of which are very large and successful, have availed themselves of Chapter 11 to escape or avoid potentially onerous debts or obligations. Johns-Manville was, at one time, a giant in the asbestos industry. When the effect of asbestos on health became known, Johns-Manville was faced with potential liability to its customers and employees that could have literally reached billions of dollars. Despite the size and success of the firm, such liability would have destroyed Johns-Manville. Rather than await the imposition of such a liability, Johns-Manville went to court seeking a reorganization under Chapter 11. The firm proposed the establishment of a trust fund to be used for victims entitled to compensation due to asbestos-related health problems.[12] The court approved the reorganization plan, and the firm endowed the trust with millions of dollars and continued to operate the business. The firm recently paid its first dividends in several years and has once again assumed its position on the Fortune 500 list.

Similar strategies have been used to escape other potentially disastrous liabilities. Several firms have recently used Chapter 11 to avoid burdensome labor contracts. In fact, the use of Chapter 11 to reject a collective bargaining agreement is so prevalent that there is a section of the Bankruptcy Code which addresses this issue. Section 1113, "Rejection of Collective Bargaining Agreements," specifies the conditions under which a collective bargaining agreement can be rejected as a part of the debtor's reorganization plan. The court can only approve such a proposal if:

1. the debtor has made a proposal to the authorized representatives of the employees that provides for any modifications that are necessary to permit the reorganization, and that assures that all affected parties are treated fairly and equitably;
2. the authorized representative of the employees has rejected the proposal without good cause; and
3. the balance of the equities, in the eyes of the court, clearly favors rejection of the collective bargaining agreement despite the action of the authorized representative of the employees.

CHAPTER 13: INDIVIDUAL DEBT ADJUSTMENT

Chapter 13 of the Bankruptcy Reform Act is designed to allow a debtor with a regular source of income to adjust his or her debts in a manner that (hopefully) will repay all creditors. Chapter 13 plans are available only to individual debtors; they cannot be used by corporations. As a further restriction, they are available only to debtors who have less than $1,347,550 of debt, with a maximum of $1,010,650 in secured debts and a maximum of $336,900 in unsecured debts. There is also a cost-of-living adjustment (COLA) provision in the 1994 Bankruptcy Bill. The debt ceiling for Chapter 13 proceedings will be adjusted for inflation every three years, thus (hopefully) allowing this relief to keep up with inflation and negating the need for periodic adjustments by the legislature. The debt ceilings in effect prior to October 6, 1994, made Chapter 13 unavailable to many farmers, which led to the creation of Chapter 12. The increase in consumer debt, coupled with inflation from 1978 through 1994, made the prior debt ceiling an impediment to the public policy objectives of Chapter 13 proceedings, and led to the upward revision on allowable debt and to the inflation adjustment mechanism now in effect.

Debtors who exceed the debt ceiling will have to use Chapter 7, Chapter 11, or some non-bankruptcy alternative. Chapter 13 is only available by means of a voluntary

eClass 27.3 Finance/Management

CHAPTER 13 BANKRUPTCY

When eClass first began operations, it hired Stephanie as an executive secretary. Stephanie has been a wonderful secretary, and the principals have become very fond of her. Stephanie recently encountered some financial difficulties and asked for an advance on her pay. While the firm has no formal policy regarding advances, the principals generally agree that advances on pay should not be given. However, since Stephanie has been with the firm from the beginning and since the firm values her contributions, it was agreed that the firm would advance her $3,000. Several weeks after receiving this advance, Stephanie filed for relief under Chapter 13 of the Bankruptcy Act. Among the creditors she listed was eClass, listing the firm for the amount of the advance. She listed total debts of $22,500, all unsecured except for a car loan from her bank. Her only assets are her car, her computer, her clothing, and her job. She currently takes home $175 per week. In her repayment plan she proposes that she would make weekly payments of $37.50 for the next five years. (eClass would receive $20 per month, or a total of $1,200 under this plan.) Stephanie is single, she shares an apartment with a friend, and her share of the monthly rent is $190. Her car payments to the bank are $211. Yousef is quite upset at this turn of events, and he has asked you if this repayment plan is likely to be approved by the Bankruptcy Court. What would you tell him? Why?

BUSINESS CONSIDERATIONS   Should a business have a formal policy regarding employee salary advances? What can a business do to protect itself from situations such as this if the business does, in fact, allow employees to receive advances on their pay?

ETHICAL CONSIDERATIONS   Suppose that an employee "takes advantage" of his or her employer by getting an advance on his or her pay, and then lists that advance as a creditor's claim in bankruptcy. Should the firm retaliate against the employee through a firing or a reassignment? How should the employee be treated following his or her seeming mistreatment of the employer?

petition. The debtor can seek relief under this option, but the creditors cannot force a debtor to enter a repayment plan. (However, the threat of forcing a debtor into Chapter 7 may persuade the debtor that Chapter 13 is in his or her best interests.)

The Proceedings

In many respects, a repayment plan is the simplest bankruptcy proceeding for an individual debtor. The debtor files a voluntary petition seeking relief. The court will issue an order for relief, an automatic stay takes effect, and a trustee will be appointed. If the debtor operates a business, the trustee will perform the investigation duties normally followed under a reorganization. Otherwise, this step is not required. In addition, the trustee will carry out the plan proposed by the debtor, if the plan is approved by the court.

The Plan

The debtor must file a proposed repayment plan with the court. This plan must be submitted with the petition or within 15 days of the filing unless the court grants an extension. The plan must provide for fixed payments to the trustee on a regular basis, usually monthly or semi-monthly. The trustee will then distribute the money to the creditors according to the terms of the plan. The plan also must make some provisions for clearing up any defaulted debts or defaulted payments on debts. The plan will call for payments for at least three years, and up to five years. The shorter time will apply only if the debtor can pay all of his or her debts in less than 60 months. (For debtors who have average monthly income less than the applicable state median income, the plan will be for three years unless the court approves a longer plan; if the debtor's average monthly income exceeds the applicable state's median income, the plan normally will be for five years.[13])

Creditors are classified as priority, secured, and unsecured. Priority creditors must be paid in full unless any priority creditor agrees to accept less than full payment. Secured creditors must receive at least the value of the collateral if the debtor is allowed to retain the collateral. (In some circumstances, if the collateral was acquired with the loan and the debt was incurred within a specified time frame prior to the filing of the petition, the debt must be paid in full.) Unsecured creditors are not assured of receiving any payment. If the plan calls for the debtor to pay all "projected disposable income" to the trustee, and that "projected disposable income" does not cover the claims of unsecured creditors, they will receive nothing. If it does include some amount for the unsecured creditors, they will share in it pro rata. The debtor must begin making payments within 30 days of the petition date, even if the plan has not yet been approved by the court.

The court will approve the plan if the following conditions are met:

1. The plan appears to be fair to all parties;
2. The plan is in the best interests of the creditors;
3. It appears that the debtor can conform to the plan; and
4. The plan provides for payment to each of the three categories of creditors as outlined above.

Once approved, the plan is binding on all parties, with or without their consent.

If the debtor performs the plan as approved, the court will grant a discharge. The discharge terminates all debts provided for in the plan—if they would be dischargeable in a Chapter 7 liquidation proceeding—that received their full share under the plan. In addition, the court can intercede and grant a discharge during the plan, even though the plan has not been completely carried out. The court will do so only if the following three factors are present:

1. The debtor cannot complete the plan owing to circumstances beyond the debtor's control.
2. The general (lowest-priority) creditors have received at least as much as they would have received in a liquidation.
3. The court does not feel it is practical to alter the plan.

The likelihood of such a court intervention during the plan is not very high, but the option is there. And, once again, the desire to provide a fresh start for an honest debtor is obvious.

In 1993, the Supreme Court handed down its opinion in *Rake* v. *Wade*, 113 S. Ct. 2187 (1993). Wade held a long-term promissory note from Rake, with the note secured by a home mortgage. Wade was classified as an "oversecured" mortgagee since the value of the home was significantly higher than the balance owed on the note. The Court allowed Wade to collect interest, both pre- and post-petition, from Rake even though the note was silent on this matter and state law would not have allowed Wade to recover such interest.

Congress did not like the court's opinion in *Rake v. Wade*. The Bankruptcy Reform Act of 1994 contains a section intended to overrule the court's opinion. The 1994 act provides:

> **Interest on Interest.** This provision is applicable in Chapter 11, 12 and 13 cases, and provides that if a plan cures a default, the liability for interest is to be determined in accordance with the agreement and nonbankruptcy law. The purpose is to overrule *Rake v. Wade* . . . , which required the payment of interest on mortgage arrearages when the chapter 13 debtor attempted to cure the default and reinstate the mortgage even if it is not contained in the agreement and not required by State law.[14]

1984 Bankruptcy Amendments

The Bankruptcy Amendments of 1984 have tightened the requirements for a Chapter 13 repayment plan. The new standards also reduce the burden on the courts, since the good faith of the debtor is not an issue. Rather, a more tangible standard than the apparent good faith of the debtor has been substituted.

The more recent law allows any unsecured creditor to block the debtor's proposed repayment plan, but only if the plan does not meet one of two criteria:

1. The plan calls for the payment of 100 percent of the creditor's claim; if it does not,
2. The plan must call for the debtor to pay 100 percent of all income not necessary to support the debtor's immediate family for at least three years.

Exhibit 27.4

A Chapter 13 Bankruptcy Proceeding

Individual Debt Adjustment Plan

Voluntary Petition (Only) Filed by an
Individual Debtors
(Must have less than $336,900 in unsecured debt
and less than $1,010,650 in secured debt[15])

⬇

Order for Relief; Automatic Stay

⬇

Debtor files plan with the Court
(Plan filed with petition or within 15
days, unless an extension is granted by
the Court)

⬇

Court review plan for:
    Fairness Best interests of the creditors
    Debtor's ability to perform Level and
    amount of scheduled payments Must call
    for payment of all priority debts in full *or*
    call for payment of all projected disposable
    income over the life of the plan.

⬇

Discharge decision is made by the Court
upon successful completion of the plan
unless a petition to review the plan is filed
during the plan

Unless the debtor shows that the plan satisfies one of these two criteria, the Chapter 13 repayment plan will be rejected by the court. The debtor will then have to file a new plan, change over to a Chapter 7 proceeding, or withdraw the petition. Note that these are the *only* criteria available for a creditor to challenge a proposed repayment plan. The creditors do not have a right to "approve" the plan, or even to vote on the plan.

Under the 1978 Bankruptcy Reform Act, debtor payments under a repayment plan did not begin until the plan was confirmed by the court. This gave many debtors a four- to six-month "grace period" in which the debtor retained all of his or her assets but made no payments, to the detriment of the creditors. The 1984 Bankruptcy

Amendments call for payments to begin within 30 days of the filing of the plan, subject to confirmation of the plan by the court. The debtor makes these payments to the trustee, who holds the monies paid until confirmation of the plan by the court and then distributes them to the various creditors. If the debtor fails to make payments to the trustee in a timely manner, the plan can be dismissed by the court.

Finally, the 1984 Bankruptcy Amendments provide for the possible modification of the plan after it is confirmed. The trustee, the debtor, or any creditor can petition the court to increase or decrease the debtor's payments whenever the debtor's circumstances or income warrant such a modification. Prior to the 1984 Amendments, decreases were possible, but increases were not permitted.

Exhibit 27.4 illustrates the steps in a Chapter 13 bankruptcy proceeding.

BANKRUPTCY IN THE INTERNATIONAL ENVIRONMENT

Bankruptcy is not just an American—or even an Anglo-American—phenomenon anymore. There are numerous international statutes and treatments for bankruptcy, and as business becomes more global, it is likely that other statutes and treatments will be enacted. For example, UNCITRAL, the United Nations international trade law body, is developing its "Model Law on Cross-Border Insolvency" with the intention of urging cooperation between the states that are affected, greater legal certainty for trade and investment, and fair and efficient administration in order to protect the interests of all interested parties. The draft of this model law can be found at http://www.uncitral.org/english/texts/insolven/ml+guide.htm. The European Union has developed its own regulations for insolvency proceedings within the Union. The development and recognition of various insolvency statutes and treaties should be an important and an exciting aspect of international business over the next several years.

Contemporary Case

IN RE LISA MARIE CALLICOTT
386 B.R. 232, 2008 Bankr. LEXIS 1301 (E.D. Mo. 2008)

FACTS Lisa Marie Callicott obtained financing from Nuvell Credit Company, LLC on January 20, 2006, to purchase a 2005 Chevrolet Impala. Callicott traded-in a 1999 Chrysler, on which she owed $7,149.65. She received a trade-in allowance of $3,000.00 from Nuvell. After the trade-in allowance, Callicott still owed $4,149.65 on the Chrysler. Nuvell included the balance owed on the Chrysler in the financing package for the Chevrolet.

Callicott also purchased Careguard in the amount of $1,795.00 and GAP protection in the amount of $600.00, which was included in the loan amount.

On July 26, 2007, Callicott filed a Voluntary Bankruptcy Petition under Chapter 13. Nuvell filed a proof of claim in the amount of $26,709.14, secured by the purchase of a vehicle. Callicott filed an Objection to Nuvell's claim, asserting that the purchase money security interest, and therefore the secured claim, amounted to only $20,195.14 under § 506(a)(1) and § 1322(b)(2). She alleged that these sections allowed for a cram down of a secured claim to the retail value of a purchased vehicle if the vehicle owner sought relief under the Bankruptcy Code. She also argued that money advanced by Nuvell to pay off her negative equity went to the lender of the trade-in vehicle and was not part of the price of the Chevrolet. As a result, Collicott asserted that Nuvell should be allowed a secured claim only up to the purchase price of the Chevrolet.

Nuvell argued that the plain language and congressional intent of the "hanging paragraph" immediately following § 1325(a)(9) indicated that a purchase money security interest acquired within the 910-day period preceding a bankruptcy filing was protected from cram down. Nuvell also argued that negative equity is part of a purchase money security interest and should not be crammed down.

ISSUE Does a creditor's purchase money security interest extend to any "negative equity" included in a loan?

HOLDING No. The "negative equity" from the balance owed on a used car trade-in does not give rise to a purchase money security interest. There is no close nexus between the acquisition of the new vehicle and the negative equity financing.

REASONING Excerpts from the opinion of Kathy A. Surratt-States, Judge

... The first issue is whether Debtor may cram down Creditor's claim to the retail value of the purchased vehicle. Pursuant to the unnumbered paragraph immediately following 11 U.S.C. § 1325(a)(9), the cram down provision of § 506, which allows claims to be bifurcated based on whether they are considered secured or unsecured, is inapplicable if:

> ... the creditor has a purchase money security interest securing the debt that is the subject of the claim, the debt is incurred within the 910-day period preceding the date of the filing of the petition, and the collateral for the debt consists of a motor vehicle ... acquired for the personal use of the debtor, or if collateral for the debt consists of any other thing of value, if the debt was incurred during the 1-year period preceding that filing. ...

Debtor states that the Chevrolet was purchased for Debtor's personal use within 910 days of filing bankruptcy. The next issue is whether Creditor held a purchase money security interest in the claim against Debtor. Since no definition for a "purchase money security interest" can be found in the Bankruptcy Code, courts look to state law to define it. Missouri's version of § 9-103 of the Uniform Commercial Code provides ... that a purchase money security interest is a security interest to the extent that the goods are used as collateral to ensure that a party meets its obligation to pay the price or value given to the collateral to acquire rights in or the use of the collateral. ... A purchase money security interest gives the holder priority over other creditors. ...

Debtor purchased the Chevrolet from Creditor. ... Debtor traded-in the Chrysler with a balance due of $7,149.65. Debtor was given a $3,000.00 credit toward the balance due on the Chrysler as a trade-in allowance. Thus, Debtor still owed $4,149.65 on the Chrysler. The excess debt less the vehicle trade-in value is known as negative equity ... Creditor loaned Debtor $4,149.65 to pay off the balance due on the traded-in Chrysler.... Creditor rolled this loan ... into the loan transaction for the purchase of the Chevrolet.

The portion of the loan for the Chevrolet is a purchase money security interest. Since Debtor is in possession of the vehicle, it can be used as collateral if Debtor does not satisfy her obligation to pay the loan.... The issue here is whether Creditor holds a purchase money security interest in the portion of the loan that represents the negative equity from the financing of the balance owed on the traded-in Chrysler ... "The concept of 'purchase money security interest' requires a close nexus between the acquisition of the collateral and the secured obligation" ... The close nexus theory requires that the negative equity be an integral part of the financial transaction. Here, no evidence exists that Creditor financing the payoff of Debtor's traded-in Chrysler was essential to Debtor acquiring the Chevrolet.... [T]he Chrysler was traded-in, and

there is no collateral for that portion of the loan.... [A] close nexus does not exist between the acquisition of the Chevrolet and the loan provided by Creditor ... , because Debtor had the option of paying off the original debt on the Chrysler using other means.

In essence, at the moment the first vehicle was "bought" by the second creditor as a trade-in, the secured debt held by the first creditor is satisfied by the value paid for the car. The deficiency ... is the negative equity. This deficiency is unsecured just as it would be if the first creditor had foreclosed.... [T]he substance of the transaction ... is that the second creditor is paying off the debtor's unsecured deficiency debt on the first vehicle. If the second creditor did not pay that debt off, the debtor would have the option of continuing to make payments to the first creditor, but that debt would be unsecured ... [T]he negative equity does not rise to the status of a purchase money security interest....

You Be the Judge

Congrove was the owner of a McDonald's franchise, under the terms of which he owned and operated two McDonald's restaurants. He initially entered into the franchise arrangement in 1990. Under the terms of the agreement, Congrove had the right to purchase all of the personal property portion of the assets held within the franchise, but McDonald's had the right to unilaterally terminate the franchise upon any default by Congrove. Congrove exercised the option to purchase the personal property of the first restaurant in 1990, paying McDonald's $700,000. He exercised the right to purchase the assets of the second restaurant in 1998, paying an additional $100,095.

By 2001, Congrove's financial condition had become critical, and McDonald's issued a memorandum to Congrove informing him that he was close to default. The memo also stated that the combined value of the two restaurants was down to $850,000. McDonald's and Congrove then proceeded to negotiate a franchise termination agreement. Three options were proposed by McDonald's: (1) the firm would pay Congrove $700,000 for his franchises and would help him to settle with his other creditors; (2) Congrove would file for bankruptcy and let the court decide what should happen to the franchises, or (3) Congrove could voluntarily surrender his franchises and then have McDonald's work with his creditors in an informal manner. Congrove selected option number three in order to minimize his tax liability.

McDonald's then took over the restaurants and paid $768,060.38 to settle some of Congrove's debts, including taxes owed, dishonored paychecks, and utility bills. (Congrove owed a total of more than $1.5 million at the time.) Shortly thereafter, Congrove filed a petition in bankruptcy. He then filed a complaint alleging that his transfer of the franchise and the restaurants to McDonald's had been a fraudulent conveyance in that he had received nothing for the franchise or the restaurants at a time when he was insolvent. He further claimed that any payments McDonald's made to any of his creditors were "voluntary payments," made at McDonald's own risk and without regard to any contract between Congrove and McDonald's. McDonald's countered that the payments it made to Congrove's creditors were consideration for the return of the franchise and the restaurants and constituted "reasonably equivalent value" for the assets. According to McDonald's, these payments were proper and adequate consideration for the return of the franchise and the restaurants and were in no way connected to a fraudulent conveyance.

This case has been brought in *your* court. How will *you* decide the case? In reaching your decision you need to determine whether this was a fraudulent conveyance, allowing Congrove to recover the franchise and the personal property from the restaurants, or a valid purchase of the franchise and the personal property in the restaurants, transferring title to McDonald's.

[Once you have decided this case, see *Congrove v. McDonald's Corporation*, 2007 U.S. App. LEXIS 764, 47 Bankr. Ct. Dec. 166 (2007), and compare your decision and your reasoning with the decision of the court.]

Summary

Federal law governs the topic of bankruptcy, which is designed to give an honest debtor a fresh start. The Bankruptcy Reform Act provided for the establishment of bankruptcy courts as a separate branch of the U.S. district court system. These courts were to be presided over by bankruptcy judges who specialized in handling bankruptcy petitions. Following a constitutional challenge to the bankruptcy courts established by the Bankruptcy Reform Act, Congress modified these bankruptcy courts and severely restricted the authority of the courts and judges through the Bankruptcy Amendments and Federal Judgeship Act of 1984. The Bankruptcy Reform Act of 1994 added a number of additional provisions designed to close loopholes and to further balance the rights of the parties in a bankruptcy proceeding. This Act also includes a built-in adapter in an effort to keep the dollar amounts involved in bankruptcy current without the need to amend the Code every few years.

The Bankruptcy Abuse Prevention and Consumer Protection Act of 2005 substantially changed this area of law. Debtors are now restricted from using Chapter 7 under many circumstances, and are forced to either resort to Chapter 13 and a repayment plan or to use non-bankruptcy alternatives to resolve their financial woes.

Under Chapter 7 (Liquidation), bankruptcy can be initiated voluntarily by the debtor or involuntarily by the creditors. The debtor initiates the proceedings by filing a voluntary petition. The creditors initiate the proceedings by filing an involuntary petition against the debtor. Five types of "public interest" corporations are prohibited from filing a voluntary petition; any other debtor may file such a petition, even if solvent. Creditors may file an involuntary petition against most debtors, although there are seven classes of debtors who are exempt from having an involuntary petition filed against them. Even for those debtors who are legally subject to an involuntary petition, there are safeguards. An involuntary petition can be filed only if the debtor is "guilty" of specified conduct, the proper number of creditors join the petition, and the proper amount of unsecured debts is involved.

Once the petition is filed, a judge appoints a trustee to administer the bankrupt's estate. The trustee is to preserve the estate for the protection of the unsecured creditors. The debtor is allowed some exemptions so that a fresh start is possible. The rest of the estate is available for settling debts. Secured creditors must choose between removing themselves and their collateral from the bankruptcy or surrendering their security interest and participating in the proceedings. Once the exempt property and the collateral securing certain loans are removed, the balance of the estate is liquidated and the proceeds are applied to the allowable claims of the creditors.

The proceeds are applied first to priority classes set up by the Bankruptcy Reform Act. After all priority classes are paid in full, the remaining proceeds are applied to the claims of the unsecured creditors. The debtor will then seek a discharge. If the debtor has been honest and has cooperated, a discharge will probably be granted. If not, the debts will continue.

An embattled debtor need not always go through liquidation in order to make a fresh start. Other bankruptcy and non-bankruptcy remedies may work equally well.

Under bankruptcy, the debtor may seek a reorganization under Chapter 11 or an individual debt adjustment (repayment) plan under Chapter 13. Each of these requires court approval of a plan, and each requires the debtor to propose the plan in good faith. In a reorganization, the debtor adjusts his or her financial position to allow a business to continue. In a repayment plan, the debtor proposes a method of repaying debts over a three-to-five-year period. Courts require good faith and fairness in any plans before they will be approved. Recently, Chapter 11 has been used as a corporate strategy, allowing corporations to escape liabilities or obligations that the firm feels are blatantly unfair or may lead to the demise of the organization.

There is an increasing international development of insolvency laws and regulations. Many of these laws seem to be more concerned with assuring that creditors are paid than with providing a fresh start for an honest debtor. Since more and more businesses are involved in international and multinational activities, the availability of some sort of international remedies is likely to continue to grow.

Discussion Questions

1. What are the five classes of debtors who cannot file a voluntary petition for a Chapter 7 bankruptcy? What are the seven classes of debtors who cannot be involuntarily petitioned into Chapter 7 bankruptcy? What are the public policy considerations for excluding these debtors from a Chapter 7 bankruptcy proceeding?

2. Before a debtor can be involuntarily petitioned into bankruptcy, the petitioning creditors must satisfy three tests. What are the three tests the petitioning creditors must satisfy? Why must these tests be satisfied prior to the imposition of an involuntary bankruptcy proceeding?

3. Why are alimony and child support obligations not discharged in a bankruptcy proceeding? Is such a rule good or bad, from a public policy perspective?

Do the same justifications apply to not permitting the discharge of taxes or student loans?

4. The 1984 Bankruptcy Amendments provide some rather specific guidelines for a repayment plan under Chapter 13. What does the court look at in deciding whether to approve a repayment plan under these guidelines? How does this differ from the requirements for a repayment plan under the original Bankruptcy Reform Act? What can a creditor do to challenge a plan under Chapter 13?

5. What public policy considerations might lead a court to prefer a Chapter 11 reorganization over a Chapter 7 liquidation for a corporation seeking relief in bankruptcy? What considerations will lead the court to order a removal from Chapter 11 to Chapter 7 when a corporation files its petition for reorganization under Chapter 11?

Case Problems and Writing Assignments

1. Egidi filed a petition for relief in bankruptcy. About two months prior to filing her petition, she used some cash advances and some convenience checks from three creditors in order to pay off the $16,065 she owed to MBNA on a credit card account. These payments were made on August 8, 10, and 12. The trustee challenged these payments as preferential transfers and sought to void the transfers and to recover the funds for the bankruptcy estate. MBNA argued that the payments were not preferential transfers, but rather were "bank to bank" transfers and not "property of the debtor." MBNA also argued that there was no diminishing of the estate of the debtor, but rather a substitution of creditors, with the banks that provided the cash advances and the convenience checks replacing MBNA as creditors,

and with the total debt of the debtor being the same after the transactions as it was prior to the transactions. The trustee asserted that the funds transferred by Egidi were "funds under the control of the debtor," and were thus properly classified as "property of the debtor" which were used to pay a preexisting debt, to the detriment of similarly situated creditors, that constituted a preferential transfer.

How should the court rule in this case? What was the most important fact or factor in your decision? [See *Egidi v. Mukamai*, 2009 U.S. App. LEXIS 13198, 21 Fla. L. Weekly Fed. C 1922.] (Bank of America acquired MBNA after these transactions, but prior to this court proceeding. Thus Bank of America shows as a plaintiff-appellant in the court's opinion.)

2. Rivera filed for relief under Chapter 13 of the Bankruptcy Act, and in due course he filed his plan for repayment of his creditors. One of the creditors was DaimlerChrysler Financial Services, which had a perfected security interest in a 2005 Chrysler Town & Country vehicle purchased by Rivera. The first plan submitted by Rivera was objected to by DaimlerChrysler and rejected by the court. Rivera then filed an amended proposed plan that called for the trustees to make disbursements to the creditors from payments submitted by the debtor for the life of the plan. In this amended plan, DailerChrysler was to receive $20,909.80 with 10 percent annual interest as payment for the Chrysler Town & Country vehicle. Once again DaimlerChrysler objected to the plan, alleging that the plan "failed to provide for post-confirmation periodic payments in equal monthly amounts sufficient to provide them with adequate protection, as required by [law]." DaimlerChrysler proposed that the plan be amended to provide for a monthly payment to it of no less than $459. The court held a hearing to consider the amended plan and approved it over the objections of DaimlerChrysler, after which DaimlerChrysler appealed. In its appeal, DaimlerChrysler alleged that the Court had committed a reversible error by approving a plan that did not meet the requirement of equal monthly payments for secured creditors. Rivera answered that, while there was no requirement of an equal monthly payment to the creditor, there also was nothing in the plan to prevent the trustee from making equal monthly payments, and that there was nothing in the record to indicate that DaimlerChrysler would not be adequately protected by the plan, as required by law.

How should the court rule in this case? What was the most important fact or factor in your decision? [See *In re Rivera*, 2008 U.S. Dist. LEXIS 36505, Bankr. L. Rep (CCH) P81 (2008)].

3. Cacioli filed a petition for relief under Chapter 7 of the Bankruptcy Code. His schedule of debts listed 58 creditors holding unsecured non-priority claims totaling $7,313,300. He also attached an affidavit to his schedules asserting that he had no knowledge of the amounts due to 33 creditors whose claims totaled $7,056,000 of the total claims listed on the schedule. Each of these 33 claims arose from "guarantees, co-obligations, or partnership obligations" arising from his involvement in several real estate partnerships and real estate ventures in which he had been involved, but which had been "abandoned" four years earlier. When Cacioli's former partners did not pay the debts, the creditors proceeded to seek recovery from Cacioli. Cacioli then filed for bankruptcy protection.

The creditors object to Cacioli's discharge in bankruptcy, alleging that the debtor failed to keep adequate records as required by law, or to satisfactorily explain any loss of assets. Cacioli explained that he was a high school graduate with no formal training. He was involved in numerous real estate transactions, including the disputed partnerships wherein he located real estate for acquisition, while his partner managed and maintained the partnerships' financial records. The debtor asserted that he failed to maintain records for these particular partnerships because he relied on his partner.

The court faced two related issues: (1) Was Cacioli's reliance on his partner reasonable? (2) Did he fail to keep adequate books and records, so that he should be denied a discharge? How should the court decide this case? What was the most important fact or factor in your decision? [See *In re Cacioli*, 463 F.3d 229 (2d Cir. 2006).

Notes

1. "A Brief History of Bankruptcy in the U.S.," *The 2001 Bankruptcy Yearbook and Almanac*, www.bankruptcydata.com/Ch11History.htm
2. Ibid.
3. Ibid.
4. Ibid.
5. 458 U.S. 50 (1982).
6. Ibid., § 109(e).
7. P.L. 109-8.
8. Ibid. In 1990, 723,886 of 725,484 were voluntary petitions. In 1996, 1,040,915 of 1,042,110 petitions were voluntary.
9. U.S. Courts, Bankruptcy Filing Fees, http://www.uscourts.gov/bankruptcycourts/fees.html, and Total Bankruptcy, found at http://www.totalbankruptcy.com/chapter-7/basics/fees.aspx.
10. As of October 2006, a debtor must undergo credit counseling. A certificate of completion of the counseling must be provided within 15 days after the filing.
11. § 1129.
12. See, e.g., "Reshaping Corporate America," *Management Accountant* 71 (9) (March 1990) p. 21; "Court Reverses Own Ruling: Negotiations Over Revised Manville Payout Plan to Continue," *Business Insurance* 27(21) (May 1993), p. 2; Kevin J. Delaney, *Strategic Bankruptcy* (Berkeley: University of California Press, 1992).
13. U.S. Courts, Bankruptcy Basics, Chapter 13, http://www.uscourts.gov/bankruptcybasic/chapter13.html.
14. H.R. 5116 § 306.
15. The debt limits are revised periodically to reflect changes in the consumer price index.

Part VI

Agency

People *dream* of being in two places at once.

For example, they could be at work and still take in that movie they want to see. Or they could attend that fundraiser *and* play a round of golf. Obviously, this must remain a dream since it is a physical impossibility. However, the law has found a way to do legally what cannot be done physically, and it is a good thing the law has managed to do so. Without this legal flexibility, business as we know it could not be conducted. But through the "magic" of agency law, a person can *legally* be in more than one place at the same time. A person can literally be in one location, and simultaneously, through his or her agent, that same person can *effectively* be in a second place, or a third, or even an unlimited number of places. By using an agent, a person can legally be in more than one place at a time.

If *you* are the principal, an agent is a person empowered to "be you" within the scope of the agency. Whatever the agent hears in the agency, the law treats as if you "heard." Whatever the agent says in the agency, the law treats as if you "said" it. What an agent does at work, the law holds you responsible for, as if you "did" the act.

Agency is essential to business today. Obviously, a businessperson derives benefits from "being" in many places at the same time; however, if the agent does not act properly, many problems may arise. Part 6 explores these areas, discussing the various benefits and problems that may arise in the course and scope of an agency.

28

Agency: Creation and Termination

Agenda

eClass started out as a small firm, and Ani, Meg, and Yousef did most of the work themselves. But as the business grows they will need to hire more workers, and these workers will have varied duties and responsibilities within the firm. As a result, Ani, Meg, and Yousef will need to understand the duties and responsibilities associated with the different jobs being performed. They will also need to understand their responsibilities and obligations owed to employees and to members of the public with whom the employees may interact. What types of relationships might be involved? Is it possible that the firm may be responsible for the actions of its employees?

Initially, eClass will mail eAccounting and the other software directly to customers. Eventually, eClass plans to hire a common carrier to deliver the software. If a common carrier is used, what is the legal relationship between eClass and the carrier? Is it possible that eClass can be held liable for any wrongful conduct by the carrier or by its drivers, such as a traffic accident in which the carrier's driver is at fault?

Ani is also concerned that some of the employees may decide to copy the concepts and products that eClass has developed in order to start their own competing business. She is especially concerned that the sales people, who already have a relationship with the firm's customers, would be in a position to compete effectively almost immediately. Is this a valid concern? What does eClass need to do to protect itself from such competition by former—or current—employees?

These and other questions will arise during our discussion of agency law. Be prepared! You never know when the firm or one of its members will seek your advice.

Classic Case

BAXTER v. MORNINGSIDE, INC.
521 P.2d 946, 1974 Wash. App. LEXIS 1518
(Wash. App. Div. 1974)

FACTS Carl Hoffer terminated his status as a salaried part-time employee with Morningside, Inc., a charitable corporation. However, he expressed a willingness to run errands and perform other tasks as a volunteer. Hoffer's offer was welcomed and accepted by Morningside. On several occasions, Morningside solicited and accepted his gratuitous services. On the date of the incident, Irene Jones, Hoffer's former supervisor at Morningside, called Hoffer and requested his help. She told him that a timber company in Shelton had donated items that could not be left out in the weather, and which needed to be transported to Morningside's warehouse in Olympia. Morningside's truck was disabled so the parties agreed that Hoffer would obtain a trailer to pull behind his own vehicle. As a result of Hoffer's negligence, a collision occurred between Hoffer's vehicle and the vehicle in which the plaintiffs were riding. Hoffer was acting as a volunteer at the time of the accident.

ISSUE Is Morningside vicariously responsible for Hoffer's negligence under the doctrine of *respondeat superior*?

HOLDING Yes, Hoffer was a servant of Morningside at the time of the accident.

REASONING Excerpts from the opinion of Armstrong, J.:

... Plaintiffs may impose vicarious liability against Morningside only if it is established that Morningside engaged defendant Hoffer to perform services in Morningside's affairs and that Morningside controlled, or had the right to control, Hoffer's physical conduct in the performance of the service. ... [I]t is not de facto control nor actual exercise of a right to interfere with or direct the work which constitutes the test, but rather, the *right to control* the negligent actor's physical conduct in the performance of the service. ...

[In precedents], the court held that a man engaged to repair a windmill was a servant even though he was under no obligation to repair, could have quit the job at any time he saw fit, or could have been discharged at any time, and there appeared to be no particular supervision involved. It should also be emphasized that although the appellate courts of this state have not heretofore addressed the question of the effect of volunteer status upon the existence of the master-servant relationship, Mr. Hoffer's status as a volunteer . . . , does not necessarily preclude a finding that a master-servant relationship existed. Other jurisdictions considering this issue have uniformly held that consideration or monetary compensation is not necessary to create the relation. . . . We believe the rule to be that where one volunteers or agrees to assist another, to do something for the other's benefit, or to submit himself to the control of the other, even without an agreement for or expectation of reward, if the one for whom the service is rendered consents to its being performed under his direction and control, then the service may be rendered within the scope of a master-servant relationship. . . .

[W]e are of the opinion . . . that when Morningside engaged Hoffer to transport the donated items to their warehouse, Morningside controlled and had the right to control Hoffer's physical conduct in the performance of the service. A master-servant relationship therefore existed. Mr. Hoffer had performed very similar services for Morningside in the past as part of his duties as a salaried employee. . . . [A]n ongoing volunteer relationship between Hoffer and Morningside continued. . . . [I]t was Hoffer's former . . . supervisor who called Hoffer by telephone and solicited his services, which . . . differed in nature from previous services as a paid employee only in that the service was rendered by one with volunteer rather than staff status. We deem it particularly significant that the result of this telephone call and solicitation was a mutual agreement between Hoffer and Morningside controlling the time, destination, purpose and especially the means of Hoffer's undertaking. The time of performance was implicitly agreed to be as soon as reasonably possible because it was imperative that the materials not be left out in the weather to deteriorate. The parties explicitly agreed upon the destination and purpose of the trip . . . The parties also explicitly agreed that it would be necessary for Hoffer to use his own vehicle and to obtain a trailer as the means to accomplish the desired result. Because of the nature of the service to be performed, any further control, such as direct supervision of the loading or operation of the motor vehicle, would have been uncalled for, impractical, and was not necessary to establish the requisite right of control which vicarious liability contemplates. . . .

Usually the question of control or right of control is one of fact for the jury. . . . However, this is true only where the facts . . . are in dispute, or are susceptible of more than one interpretation. If the facts are undisputed, . . . [and] there can be but one reasonable conclusion drawn from the facts, the nature of the relationship between the parties becomes a question of law. . . . In this case the material facts were undisputed, the negligence of defendant Hoffer had previously been established . . . At that stage of the proceedings, the pleadings, affidavits, and depositions on file clearly indicated that no genuine issue of material fact existed as to the vicarious liability of defendant Morningside for the negligence of defendant Hoffer. The record clearly indicated that as a matter of law Hoffer was acting within the scope of a master-servant relationship. . . .

AGENCY LAW AND AGENCY RELATIONSHIPS

Agency law concerns the relationships between workers and the people who hire workers. It involves their duties and responsibilities both to each other and to the public at large. No one can really avoid agency law; almost everyone at some time works as an employee or hires an employee. Moreover, agency relationships arise not only in business situations, but also in nonbusiness situations. Suppose that Marty has some books that are due back to the university library, but Marty has a review session that he cannot afford to miss. Marty asks Karen, a friend who is planning to go to the library, if she would return the books for him. If Karen agrees to do so, she will be acting as an *agent* for Marty. This is true even though Karen is not being compensated for doing the favor for Marty.

Most agency relationships do not involve litigation because they function smoothly. To resolve the legal problems that do arise, one must look to agency law, contract law, and tort law. In most of these areas, the court will place significant reliance on state law. Much of the law of agency has been studied by the American Law Institute and is discussed in its three *Restatements of Agency.*[1] The *Restatements* are treatises that summarize and make recommendations of what the law should be on a particular subject. Although *Restatements* are not legislature- or court-made law, they become part of the legal precedents when courts rely on them and incorporate them into court decisions. (Legal *precedents* are prior court cases that control future decisions. See Chapter 1 for a more detailed discussion of precedents.) The three agency chapters in this book rely on the provisions found in the second and third *Restatements of Agency* for the formulation of majority rules and for general guidance in the discussion of agency law.[2]

You should note that the position of your state may vary from that in the *Restatement.* You should check for variations followed in your state when issues arise. The *Restatement (Third) of Agency* states:

> Agency is the fiduciary relationship that arises when one person (a "principal") manifests assent to another person (an "agent") that the agent shall act on the principal's behalf and subject to the principal's control, and the agent manifests assent or otherwise consents so to act.[3]

An *agency relationship* is consensual in nature. It is based on the concept that the parties mutually agree that (1) the agent will act on behalf of the principal; and (2) the agent will be subject to the principal's direction and control. The agreement can be expressed or implied. Note that many agency relationships are based on contracts, as discussed in Chapters 9–14, but a contract is not a requirement for an agency relationship. The parties also must be competent to act as principal and agent. A distinguishing characteristic is that an agent represents the principal and derives his or her authority from the principal.

The creation of an agency relationship creates fiduciary duties owed by the agent to the principal.[4] *Fiduciary duties* are the duty to act with the utmost good faith, candor, confidence, and trust. They include the duty to act with the highest degree of honesty and loyalty and the duty to act in the best interests of the person to whom the duty is owed. Ordinary business transactions, such as contracts, do *not* create fiduciary relationships.

Analysis of Agency Relationships

While most agency relationships do not involve litigation, sometimes litigation will occur. When problems arise, you will need to determine which aspect of the agency relationship is involved in order to properly determine what result should occur. To analyze a situation involving an agency relationship, ask these questions:

- Was the dispute between the principal and the agent?
- Was the agency formed voluntarily by the principal and the agent, or is there some other relationship between the parties?
- Did the parties have the capacity to perform their roles as the principal and the agent?
- What authority did the principal vest in the agent?
- Did the agent enter into a contract with a third person or commit a tort or crime harming a third person?

RESTRICTIONS ON CREATING AN AGENCY RELATIONSHIP

Agency law affects a broad range of situations, from a small partnership with two partners and no employees up to and including a corporation with thousands of employees, and from a highly skilled developer of computer peripherals to a 16-year-old babysitter. It even affected Marty and Karen in our first hypothetical. In fact, everything a corporation does, it does through agents. Agency is integral to business as it is conducted in the world today, and business as we know it could not exist without the use of agency law or something very closely related to it.

There are few restrictions on who can form agency relationships and what can be done through agency relationships. In order to form a *lawful* agency relationship, the agreement must specify legal acts for the agent to perform. An agreement to distribute illegal drugs such as "meth," for example, could not be the basis for the creation of a lawful agency relationship. Since the basic agreement specifies an illegal act, no legal agency can be created. You should notice the parallel to the prior discussion of contract law in Chapters 9–14.

Capacity to Be a Principal

Almost any person can appoint an agent. It is generally true that any person having capacity to *contract* has capacity to employ a servant agent or a nonservant agent. (The distinction between these two agents is that a principal has more control over the actions of the former than over those of the latter. The distinction will be discussed in more detail later in this chapter.) Since agency is a consensual relationship, the principal must have the capacity to consent in a legally binding manner.[5]

Some states have determined that a minor lacks capacity to be a principal. In other states, a minor has the capacity to be a principal, but the agency relationship is voidable. The *Restatement (Second) of Agency* § 20 takes the second position. In this second group of states, the agreements entered into by the minor's agent will also be voidable to the same extent that the minor's own contracts will be voidable. The key to understanding this concept is to remember that the contract is really entered into by the principal. The agent is not a party to the contract; he or she is merely a "facilitator" in the formation of the contract. Many states follow similar rules for people who are mentally incompetent.

Capacity to Be an Agent

Generally, anyone can be an agent. Strange as it seems, even persons who do not have the capacity to act for themselves—for example, minors or insane persons—can act as agents for someone else.[6] It is the capacity of the *principal*, not that of the agent, that controls. Obviously, however, principals should exercise care to appoint agents who are able to make sound decisions.

Duties an Agent Can Perform

A principal "appoints" an agent to deal with the public. Generally, an agent can be assigned to do almost any legal task and, depending on the rules we will discuss later, the principal may be liable for the agent's acts. There are, however, some nondelegable duties such as the following:

- an employer's duty to provide safe working conditions[7]
- a person's duty under some contract terms
- a landlord's duty to tenants
- a common carrier's duty to passengers (A *common carrier* is a company in the business of transporting people or goods for a fee and serving the general public.)

- a person's duty under a license issued to that person
- the duty of a person engaged in inherently dangerous work to take adequate precautions to avoid harm

Other nondelegable duties are defined by various state statutes. Each state statute is distinct. If the duty is nondelegable and the principal attempts to delegate the duty to someone else, the principal will be personally liable if the task is not properly completed. Even when a duty is considered nondelegable, the tasks comprising the duty can still be delegated, but the *legal* responsibility for their proper completion cannot be delegated.[8]

TYPES OF AGENCY RELATIONSHIPS

General and Special Agents

The distinction between general and special agents is a matter of degree. A *special agent* is employed to complete one transaction or a simple series of transactions. The relationship covers a relatively limited period and is not continuous. A *general agent* is hired to conduct a series of transactions over time. The amount of discretion the agent has is immaterial in making the distinction between general and special agents. (*Discretion* is the right to use one's own judgment in selecting between alternatives.) The expertise of the agent is also immaterial.

In deciding whether an agent is a general agent or a special agent, courts should examine all of the following factors:

- the number of acts that will need to be completed to achieve the authorized result
- the number of people who will need to be dealt with before achieving the desired result
- the length of time that will be necessary to achieve the desired result[9]

The manager of an electronics store is likely to be viewed as a general agent. He or she can reasonably be expected to have an ongoing, relatively permanent position with broad, general authority. In contrast, a person who collects a payment from a customer of the store on a one-time basis is a special agent. Categorizing an agent who is between these two extremes can be difficult. As Exhibit 28.1 shows, a continuum of relationships exists between the roles of special agents and those of general agents.

Exhibit 28.1

Distinction between Special Agents and General Agents

"Gray Area"

|-------------------[==============]-------------------|

Relevant factors:	Special Agent	General Agent
Frequency of acts	Few acts or simple series of acts	Many acts or long series of acts
Number of people who are expected to be contacted by the agent	Few people	Many people
Length of service	Shorter period of time	Longer period of time

Irrelevant factors:

Discretion granted to agent

Expertise of agent

This line constitutes a continuum and not discrete categories.

The exact number of people contacted and the length of time are subject to interpretation by the court.

In the "gray area," the type of agent is less obvious and is open to the interpretation of the courts. Courts will use different factors to make their determinations.

Gratuitous Agents

Payment is not necessary in a principal-agent relationship. If a person volunteers services without an agreement or an expectation of payment, that person may still be an agent. The requirements for a *gratuitous agency* are that one person volunteered to help another and the second person accepted this "free" assistance. In the terms of the *Restatement*, "[a] gratuitous agent acts without a right to compensation."[10] For example, Susie offers to help Joel with his paper route. Susie goes to a customer's home to collect payment on Joel's behalf, but she fails to give Joel the payment. The courts *can* find that Susie works for Joel as his gratuitous agent, and that her actions bind Joel. Another example is if Beth is not feeling well the morning her legal environment homework is due. Angelica, a sorority sister, is in the same class. Beth asks Angelica to deliver the paper for her. Angelica arrives to class late, and the instructor deducts late points from both Beth's paper and Angelica's paper. Beth will be held responsible for Angelica's acts. Note that, with few exceptions, the rights and duties of a gratuitous agent are the same as those of an agent who is being compensated. The primary differences are that the gratuitous agent can freely terminate his or her duty by giving notice to the principal that he or she will not continue. Since the gratuitous agent is not being compensated there is no contract with the principal and thus no breach of contract by the agent when he or she resigns, with or without advance notice.

SERVANTS AND INDEPENDENT CONTRACTORS

Most workers are *either* servants or independent contractors. The distinction between the terms *servant* and *independent contractor* is confusing, partly because authors and judges apply differing definitions to these terms and partly because common usage differs from legal usage. Using legal definitions, servants and employees are generally synonymous.[11] We generally use the term *servant* to describe someone who is subject to the control of his or her *master*. Either servants or independent contractors can also be agents. Agents have the authority to perform "legal acts." In other words, agents can represent their principals in contractual or other dealings with third parties. Exhibit 28.2 illustrates the legal significance between the two types of workers.

Servants

A master is a special type of principal who has the right to tell his or her worker both what to do and how to do it. The worker then is included in a special class of workers called *servants* or *employees*. (The more modern term is *employee*.) A *servant* is one who works physically for the hiring party. A *master* (employer) has a right to control how the task is accomplished by the servant (employee). The actual exercise of this control is not necessary; it is sufficient that the master has the *right* to control. Thus, interns in hospitals, airline pilots, sales clerks, and officers of corporations are commonly servants.

The distinction between servants and independent contractors is important, because a principal is rarely liable for the unauthorized *physical* acts of an independent contractor. Principals sometimes label a worker as an independent contractor in an attempt to escape liability, but the courts will look behind the designation and make a judgment about the true nature of the relationship. The distinction between servants and independent contractors is also important in determining rights and benefits under unemployment insurance laws, workers' compensation laws, income taxation, the Employee Retirement Income Security Act of 1974 (ERISA), employment discrimination, bankruptcy exemptions, and similar statutes and court precedents. ERISA is a

Exhibit 28.2

What Are the Differences Between Servants and Independent Contractors?

	Servant[1]	Independent Contractor
Hiring party has potential liability under *respondeat superior*	Yes	No
Hiring party generally provides the tools and machines necessary to do the work	Yes	No
Hiring party generally provides the work place	Yes	No
Hiring party must withhold income taxes from pay	Yes	No[2]
Hiring party must pay Social Security and Medicare taxes	Yes	No
Hiring party will provide fringe benefits, such as paid holidays, sick leave, health insurance, retirement plans	Yes	No
Worker entitled to unemployment compensation[3]	Yes	No
Worker entitled to worker's compensation[4]	Yes	Not in most states/not in most situations[5]
Worker entitled to minimum wage and overtime under federal or state statutes	Yes	No

Source: Courtesy of Lynn M. Forsythe, © Lynn M. Forsythe 2010

[1] The IRS calls this a common-law employee. Common law in this context means law that was developed by court decisions as opposed to statutory law.

[2] The hiring party will pay the independent contractor the gross amount. The independent contractor will pay his or her tax liability directly to the state and federal governments. Depending on the situation, the hiring party may still need to file an informational return with the tax agencies. Some workers may be deemed statutory employees under the Internal Revenue Service (IRS) guidelines. The hiring party will have to withhold income taxes for statutory employees. If the hiring party characterizes a worker as an independent contractor and the IRS or a court determines the worker should have been treated as an employee, the hiring party can face a significant bill for past taxes.

[3] The hiring party must pay unemployment tax on the wages paid to the worker during the employment period if the worker is entitled to unemployment compensation.

[4] The hiring party will have to pay for worker's compensation coverage if the worker is covered by the state worker's compensation program.

[5] The independent contractor *may* be able to sue if he or she is injured while working at the hiring party's work site or with the hiring party's equipment.

federal statute that regulates pension plans and employee benefit plans offered by private employers.

The distinction between an independent contractor and a servant is represented in Exhibit 28.3. Remember that this distinction is material when there is a question about whether the hiring party is responsible for the physical acts of the worker. When the worker has entered into a contract for his or her employer, it is irrelevant whether the worker is a servant or an independent contractor.

Independent Contractors

An *independent contractor* is hired to complete a task for someone else. The physical acts of the independent contractor are not controlled or subject to the control of the hiring party. Instead, the independent contractor relies on his or her own expertise to determine the best way to complete the job. Anyone who contracts to do physical work for another does so as either a servant or an independent contractor. It is, however, possible for two people to have multiple working relationships between them and one person can be a servant as to some duties and an independent contractor as to others.

Exhibit 28.3

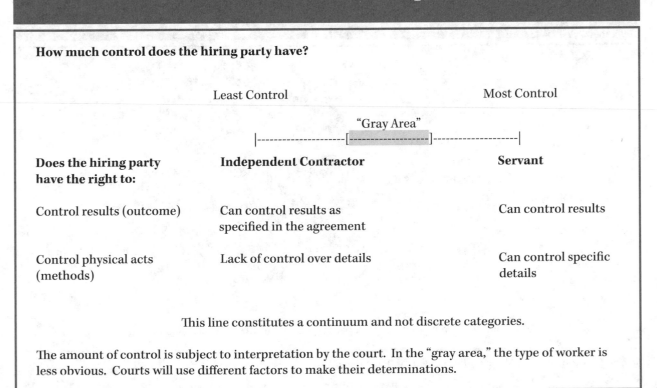

Distinction Between Servants and Independent Contractors

How much control does the hiring party have?

Least Control   Most Control

"Gray Area"

|-------------------[-------------------]-------------------|

Does the hiring party have the right to:	Independent Contractor	Servant
Control results (outcome)	Can control results as specified in the agreement	Can control results
Control physical acts (methods)	Lack of control over details	Can control specific details

This line constitutes a continuum and not discrete categories.

The amount of control is subject to interpretation by the court. In the "gray area," the type of worker is less obvious. Courts will use different factors to make their determinations.

Source: Courtesy of Lynn M. Forsythe, © Lynn M. Forsythe 2010

Courts look at many factors in distinguishing between servants and independent contractors. In addition to considering the *right* to control, courts commonly consider the following factors:

- whether the worker hires assistants
- whether payment is by the number of hours worked or by the job completed
- whether the services will be performed for a short period of time or a longer period of time
- who supplies the tools and equipment to be used
- where the work is being performed
- whether the worker is engaged in a distinct occupation or independent business
- whether the work is a part of the regular business of the principal

Independent contractors may be agents, but that is not a necessary condition for being an independent contractor. This is shown in Exhibit 28.4. If the independent contractor does not represent the hiring party or act for the hiring party in legal or

Exhibit 28.4

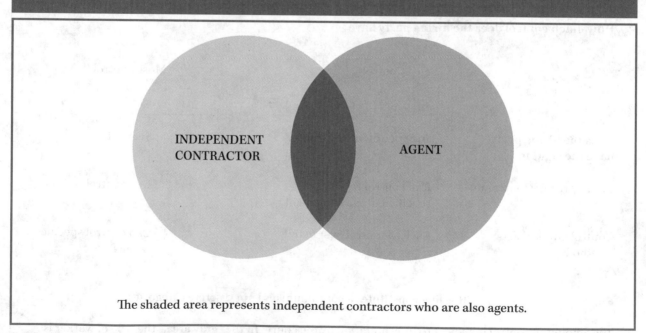

Independent Contractors May also Be Agents

INDEPENDENT CONTRACTOR

AGENT

The shaded area represents independent contractors who are also agents.

Source: Courtesy of Lynn M. Forsythe, © Lynn M. Forsythe 2010

contractual matters with third parties, the independent contractor is not the hiring party's agent. For example, a nonagent independent contractor who is building a house on an owner's lot cannot bind the owner to any additional contracts with third persons. In these situations, the independent contractor does not owe the hiring party any fiduciary duties. (We will not call the hiring party an employer since the independent contractor is not an employee.) Agents do owe fiduciary duties to their principals. Agents represent their principals in legal matters and must act with the utmost loyalty and good faith.

Independent contractors who are also agents (1) have fiduciary duties and (2) can bind their principals to contracts. For example, attorneys owe their clients fiduciary duties when they negotiate settlements and then agree to them on the clients' behalf. On the other hand, attorneys are not the clients' servants. Legal clients have no control over when their attorneys come to work in the morning or when they leave work at the end of the day. These relationships are represented in Exhibit 28.5.

When legal questions concern fiduciary duties or contracts, the worker will simply be identified as an agent, rather than applying the cumbersome term "independent contractor agent."

Exhibit 28.5

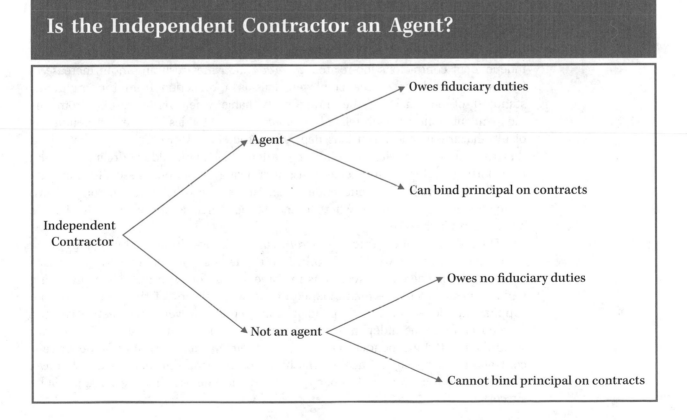

Is the Independent Contractor an Agent?

Independent Contractor

- Agent
  - Owes fiduciary duties
  - Can bind principal on contracts
- Not an agent
  - Owes no fiduciary duties
  - Cannot bind principal on contracts

Responsibility for Independent Contractors

Contract Liability   Principals who engage independent contractors as agents will be liable on the contract *if* the contract was authorized. Authorization is discussed in detail in Chapter 30. This liability complies with the general rule for agents.

Tort Liability   A person who hires an independent contractor is generally not responsible to third parties for the independent contractor's physical wrongdoings. However, there are a number of common exceptions to this general rule, depending on the laws of the specific state. Some of these rules are stated in the *Restatement (Second) of Torts*.[12] These exceptions include:

- The independent contractor is hired to engage in ultrahazardous activities.[13]
- The independent contractor is hired to commit a crime.
- The hiring party reserves the right to supervise or control the work.[14]
- The hiring party actually directs the independent contractor to do something careless or wrong.[15]
- The hiring party sees the independent contractor do something wrong and does not stop it.
- The hiring party fails to adequately supervise the independent contractor.
- The hiring party is negligent in selecting the independent contractor.[16]

In many states, the trend has been to increase the number of situations in which the hiring party can be held liable for the torts of an independent contractor. For example, some courts now will hold the hiring party liable for harm resulting from an independent contractor's job-related *hazardous* activities resulting in an increase in the potential liability of the employer. This is a reduction from the traditional standard of only holding the hiring party liable when harm results from the independent contract's job-related *ultrahazardous* activities. The exact definitions of ultrahazardous and hazardous depend on the state. However, courts have held that the following activites were ultrahazardous: blasting boulders; drilling oil wells; transporting highly volatile chemicals; and using poisonous gases to fumigate buildings. Remember, the independent contractor is also liable for his or her own wrongdoings, regardless of whether the hiring party is liable. Tort liability is depicted in Exhibit 28.6.

The independent contractor *generally* cannot recover from the hiring party if he or she is injured while working. In other words, he or she is not covered by worker's compensation. There are exceptions in some states, for example, when the hiring party is negligent in the maintenance of the work site or of the tools he or she supplies. Employees of the independent contractor, however, have been permitted to recover from the independent contractor. This is because the employees are servants and the independent contractor is their master. Servants of independent contractors have filed suit against the hiring party using the theories listed above. State law and the hiring party's behavior will determine whether the servant will be successful.[17]

Exhibit 28.6

Liability for Tortious Injury to a Third Person

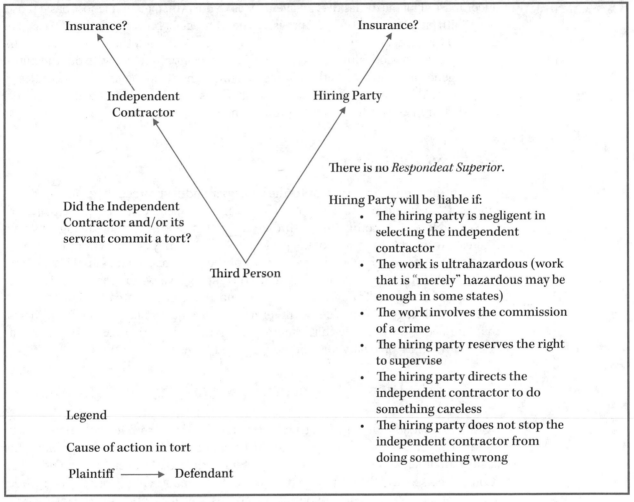

Insurance?   Insurance?

Independent   Hiring Party
Contractor

There is no *Respondeat Superior.*

Did the Independent   Hiring Party will be liable if:
Contractor and/or its   • The hiring party is negligent in
servant commit a tort?   selecting the independent
                                     contractor
                                   • The work is ultrahazardous (work
                                     that is "merely" hazardous may be
Third Person   enough in some states)
                                   • The work involves the commission
                                     of a crime
                                   • The hiring party reserves the right
                                     to supervise
                                   • The hiring party directs the
                                     independent contractor to do
                                     something careless
Legend   • The hiring party does not stop the
                                     independent contractor from
Cause of action in tort   doing something wrong

Plaintiff ——→ Defendant

Source: Courtesy of Lynn M. Forsythe, © Lynn M. Forsythe 2010

DUTIES OF THE AGENT TO THE PRINCIPAL

The agent must protect the interests of the principal, as the duties discussed in the following sections show. Some of the duties overlap. In fact, when an agent breaches one duty, most likely he or she will breach others as well.

Duty of Good Faith

Every agent owes the principal the obligation of faithful service, called the duty of *good faith*. "Good faith is an intangible and abstract quality with no technical meaning,"[18] and it is very difficult to define. This is a very broad duty, and it could theoretically encompass all of the duties that an agent owes to the principal. In its most basic sense, good faith means honesty and fairness. When an agent breaches any of his or her duties to the principal, he or she is also likely to have breached the duty of good faith. In order to act in good faith, the agent must be conscientious in carrying out the duties of the agency and must be faithful in meeting his or her responsibilities and duties to the principal.[19] The most common violations of this duty include concealing essential facts that are relevant to the agency, obtaining secret profits, and self-dealing.

Duty of Loyalty

An agent has a duty to be loyal to the principal and to protect the principal's best interests.[20] This means that an agent must not compete with the principal, work for someone who is competing with the principal, or act to further the agent's own interests without the consent of the principal. An agent may not use his or her agency position for personal benefit at the expense of the principal, such as making a secret profit. Such self-dealings involve a breach of the duty of loyalty. Suppose the principal is searching for a parcel of agricultural land, and the agent locates a suitable parcel. The agent arranges for its sale to the principal without first informing the principal that the agent owns a one-third interest in the parcel. In this case, the agent has violated the duty of loyalty and the duty of good faith.

Duty to Obey All Lawful Instructions

Agents must follow all *lawful* instructions as long as doing so does not subject them to an unreasonable risk of injury *and* the instructions are in the *course and scope* of the agency. In other words, the instructions pertain to the agent's duties for the principal. (Course and scope of the agency involves more than simply being "clocked in" at work.) This duty, also called the duty of obedience, applies even if agents think the instructions are capricious or unwise. Agents must *indemnify* (repay) their principals for damages suffered by the principals because the agents failed to follow lawful instructions that were in the course and scope of their employment.

Duty to Act with Reasonable Care

An agent has a duty to act as a reasonably careful agent would under the same circumstances. This is also called the duty of care. If the agent fails to live up to this obligation and it causes the principal a loss, the agent will be obliged to indemnify the principal. For example, Sita hired Lydia to manage her investments. Lydia was considering various options when Stan suggested that she lend him $45,000 of the investment money secured by a private mortgage on a parcel he owned. Stan and a business associate both told Lydia that the parcel was worth $50,000. Based on their statements, Lydia made the loan of $45,000 secured by the property. She did not view the parcel prior to making the loan. When Stan failed to make the mortgage payments, Lydia began foreclosure proceedings. Then she discovered that the property was worth about $4,000 due to its irregular size and location. Lydia will be liable to Sita for the loss. A reasonable person would look at the property, get an independent appraisal of its value, and consider comparable sales in the area *prior* to making this type of loan.

Duty to Segregate Funds

The agent has a duty to keep personal funds separate from the principal's funds. If the agent wrongfully uses the principal's funds to purchase something, the court can impose a trust for the benefit of the principal. (A *trust* is an arrangement in which the legal title is separated from the equitable or beneficial ownership of the asset.) The court treats the situation as though the purchase was made for the benefit of the principal from the beginning. A trust imposed by a court to prevent unjust enrichment is called a *constructive trust.*

Duty to Account for Funds

An agent has a duty to account for money received. This is really a combined function of recordkeeping and delivery of the funds. The funds usually must be delivered to the principal (or an authorized third party). If the money was received while the agent was *not* in the course and scope of the employment, the agent has a duty to return the proceeds to the third party who gave them to the agent. Compare the agent's duty in each of the following two examples for an illustration of how this duty is applied.

> *Kamal is a sales representative for Fida, Inc. Kamal is authorized to receive payments from the customers with whom he deals. He takes a potential client to dinner to discuss possible orders the client might place with Fida The client, impressed with the presentation Kamal makes during the meal, places an order for $10,000 worth of goods, writing a check as payment in full for the goods ordered. This sale would be considered to have occurred in the course and scope of Kamal's employment, and he would be expected to account to Fida for the proceeds from the client.*

> *Gary is also a sales representative for Fida, Inc., but he is not authorized to accept payments for goods he sells for Fida. He takes his wife to dinner to celebrate their anniversary. While they are eating, a client of Fida recognizes Gary as an employee of Fida. The client approaches Gary's table and hands Gary a check for $10,000 as payment for goods ordered from Fida the previous week. Gary is not authorized to receive payments for his principal. In this situation, Gary would be expected to return the check to the client and to explain to the client that the check should be sent directly to Fida, the principal.*

Duty to Give Notice

The *duty to give notice* requires an agent to inform the principal about material facts that are discovered within the scope of the agent's employment. For example, if a tenant gives an apartment manager notice that the tenant will move out at the end of the month, it is assumed that the manager will inform the owner. In fact, the principal may be bound by this notice even though the agent failed to inform the principal. The law presumes that the principal has notice in such situations under the doctrine of imputed notice.

eClass 28.1 Management

THE RISKS OF HIRING SALESPEOPLE

eClass has decided that it needs to expand its geographic market if it is to be successful in the industry. In order to expand sales geographically, the firm will need sales representatives to work in the new regions. While Yousef does not mind doing some traveling for the business, he does not want to spend too much time "on the road." Neither Ani nor Meg enjoys business travel, and both would prefer to stay in the office, doing their primary jobs. In addition, business travel will interfere with their classes. Ani, Meg, and Yousef recognize that they will need to hire sales representatives for eClass, but they are hesitant to do so. Ani is concerned that any sales agents would be able to cultivate a customer base, copy the eClass products, and then start a competing business using what eClass has taught the agent. Yousef is concerned that the firm will not have adequate control over the agents. Meg does not feel that either of these is a valid concern. She believes there are techniques to protect the firm but is not sure exactly what those techniques are. She has asked for your input about the potential issues. What will you tell her?

BUSINESS CONSIDERATIONS   What policies should a firm establish to maximize its protection in the event an agent violates his or her duty? What are the legal rights of a principal whose agent attempts to utilize technological information obtained in the course of employment for the personal benefit of that agent?

ETHICAL CONSIDERATIONS   What are the ethical implications of acting as a sales agent for a firm that produces a highly technical product? What ethical principles would preclude an agent from attempting to establish a business in competition with his or her former principal based on either the knowledge or the customers he or she developed as an agent?

Duty to Perform the Contract

If the relationship between the agent and principal *is* a contract, the agent must perform the duties specified in the contract. Normally the agent's promise to act is interpreted as being only a promise to make reasonable efforts to achieve the desired result. Consequently, the agent will not be liable for a breach of contract if he or she fails to satisfy the promised act. The agent normally will be held liable only if he or she fails to make reasonable efforts. The agent is expected to try to notify the principal if he or she is unable to perform. For example, an agent who accepts a listing to sell a vacant lot is not guaranteeing that the lot will be sold at the listed price. The agent is committing to make a reasonable effort to try to sell the lot at that price.

DUTIES OF THE PRINCIPAL TO THE AGENT

Many of the duties of the principal may be specified in the contract (if there is one) between the principal and the agent. In general, the principal has the following obligations to the agent:

- to deal with the agent fairly and in good faith[21] (This includes the duty not to interfere with the performance of the agency or thwart the effectiveness of the agency.[22])
- to comply with the express and implied terms of any contract with the agent[23]
- to compensate the agent per the agreement
- to indemnify or reimburse the agent for expenditures and losses incurred in the performance of the duties[24]
- to maintain proper accounts so that compensation and indemnification will be correct
- to provide the agent with the means to do the job
- to continue the employment for the time period specified in the agreement

With the exception of gratuitous agents, agents are entitled to be paid under the terms of their agreements with the principal. Some types of agents are entitled to compensation under special arrangements such as commission sales. These unique situations are usually mentioned in the written contract. For example, in some states real estate agents are entitled to their commissions if they find a buyer who is ready, willing, and able to buy the parcel. This is true even if the transfer does not occur because of destruction of the building, the buyer's inability to obtain a loan, or some other circumstance. Some states follow a different rule, whereby a sale must close and the real estate must be transferred before a commission is earned.

In addition, if the worker is a servant, his or her master has an obligation to provide the servant with a reasonably safe place to work and safe equipment to use. This obligation is based on common law *and* state and federal safety statutes, such as the federal Occupational Safety and Health Act (OSHA). Under OSHA, the secretary of labor *may* pass regulations permitting workers to refuse to work under hazardous conditions.[25] A master also owes a servant an obligation to compensate him or her for injuries occurring on the job under state worker's compensation laws. Worker's compensation laws are discussed in Chapters 30 and 38.

Principals also owe nonservant agents a duty to provide the means to do the job, but the principals' obligations are more limited than when workers are servants. For example, the principal may have the duty to provide the architect's sketches and specifications to the builder.

eClass 28.2 Management

PROTECTING AGAINST WORKPLACE VIOLENCE

Yousef has become very concerned about workplace violence. This topic was discussed in his management class and was cited as one of the fastest-growing problem areas in the 2000s. One example cited in class involved a manager who fired an employee for using drugs at work. The dismissed employee became verbally abusive, and he had to be physically removed from the workplace. At that point the employee went home to get his hunting rifle, returned to the plant with the rifle, and proceeded to shoot the manager and four of his former co-workers.

Although Yousef is unsure as to exactly how to best protect the managers and employees, he believes the firm should at least keep a gun in the office suite for protection if such a situation should arise at eClass. However, he is concerned about potential liability for the firm if something were to happen. He asks for your advice and for any suggestions you have. What will you tell him?

BUSINESS CONSIDERATIONS   Workplace violence is not just a legal problem. It also presents serious business implications. What policies should a business establish to protect its employees and its business operation from workplace violence? Should a business establish policies for some sort of intervention or counseling prior to the dismissal of an employee?

ETHICAL CONSIDERATIONS   What should a firm do, from an ethical perspective, before it fires an employee? Is having a gun in the office area an ethical solution to the potential threat of violence in the workplace?

TERMINATION OF THE AGENCY RELATIONSHIP

Agreement of the Parties

An agency relationship is governed in the first instance by the agreement between the principal and the agent. Commonly the contract will be established for a set period. For example, assume a real estate agent has a listing to sell a house according to certain terms. One of the terms may specify the period for which the contract is going to run, say 90 days; that agreement, therefore, will terminate at the end of 90 days if the house is not sold before the term expires.

The parties can consent to amend the agency agreement to terminate the agency relationship early or to extend it. For example, if the house in the prior example is not sold within 90 days, the owner and agent may specifically extend the agency agreement for an additional 60 days.

If the parties consent to the continuation of the agency relationship beyond the period originally stated, this consent may be implied as a renewal of the original contract for the same period and under the same conditions. This is true only if they have not specifically altered the terms and conditions of the original agreement.

Agency at Will

If the agency agreement does not specify a set date, a set period, or a set occurrence that will terminate it, the relationship is an *agency at will.* This is also called an employment-at-will. In an at-will arrangement, either party can terminate the relationship by giving notice to the other. Neither the principal nor the agent needs cause or justification to terminate the relationship. This is consistent with the theory that agency is a voluntary relationship between the parties. Either party can decide to terminate it. Traditionally, it was perceived that the two parties were relatively equal in their bargaining position and that, consequently, this rule was fair.

The traditional concept of an agency at will is being eroded rapidly. In addition, courts are recognizing various theories for recovery by the discharged agent. Whether a court will utilize these theories for recovery depends on the actual situation and state law. The courts generally use the terms "employer" and "employee" when discussing both agency at will and wrongful discharge, and so will we. Three common examples where the court will find the discharge wrongful include:

1. Courts are recognizing a breach of employment contract where there is an express or implied agreement that the employment will not be terminated *or* will not be terminated without following a specific set of procedures. For example, union–management contracts, called collective bargaining agreements, generally contain express agreements that prevent the dismissal of

union employees without a showing of cause *and* the following of specific procedures. Implied contracts often are based on procedures, policies in personnel manuals, employment interviews, and position announcements.

2. Courts are also recognizing a tort of bad-faith discharge, where the employee has a right of continued employment and has developed a relationship of trust, reliance, and dependency on the employer. It is based on an implicit understanding between the employee and employer that they will deal honestly and fairly with each other. Bad faith is usually evidenced by fraud, malice, or oppression. This is sometimes considered a breach of a covenant of good faith and fair dealing.

3. Some states are holding an employer liable for a tortious discharge if the termination violates public policy. This is based on the theory that employees should not have to forfeit their positions because they act in a manner that supports some *important* public policy. This basis is commonly used to protect whistle-blowers from being discharged, for example, employees who report safety violations to the Occupational Safety and Health Administration (also known as OSHA)[26] or violations of environment protection laws to the Environmental Protection Agency (EPA). Many federal and state statutes now have antiretaliation provisions based on public policy that prevent employers from retaliating against employees who complain to agencies, file reports, or testify in court against them.

Most states recognize implied agreements and public policy exceptions. A few recognize the tort of bad faith discharge. States may not recognize any of these theories, or they may recognize some combination of them.

There are other public policy prohibitions on firing agents at will. If the agent was fired on the basis of gender, race, religion, or national origin, or some other violation of civil rights, the courts may decide that the principal cannot terminate the relationship. In 1991, the National Conference of Commissioners on Uniform State Laws (NCCUSL) approved the Model Employment Termination Act 2 (META), which provides some protection for agents at will. It has not been adopted by many states.[27]

Companies should maintain careful records documenting the reasons a worker is discharged, even if an agency at will is involved. Companies are particularly likely to have difficulty when they terminate a worker after a number of years of successful employment, where the worker has had frequent promotions and commendations.

Notice that wrongful discharge has been used to prevent employers from firing employees, but employees in employment-at-will relationships are still free to quit at any time and for any reason.

The use of an employee handbook or employment manual can be beneficial to an employer in establishing a formal guide for what each party to the employment can expect of the other. However, the handbook can also be somewhat burdensome since it is likely to impose standards for management that must be followed in order to protect the rights of the employees. This is especially true if the handbook or manual becomes part of the employment contract, either expressly or by implication.

eClass 28.3 **Management**

SHOULD AN EMPLOYER HAVE AN EMPLOYEE HANDBOOK?

eClass has grown since its early days and expects to continue to grow in the future. The firm now has 20 regular, full-time employees. The employees have been loyal to eClass, and the firm is appreciative of their contributions to its success. However, the economy has slowed somewhat, and a few of the employees are concerned about their job security with the firm. Ani, Meg, and Yousef would like to reassure the employees, but without making any guarantees they may not be able to honor if the downturn continues. Ani suggests that eClass should write an employee handbook/employment manual to reassure the employees and to establish an employment policy framework for the firm. She thinks the handbook should address a number of issues, including length of employment and procedures for discharge. She has asked for your advice. What will you tell her?

BUSINESS CONSIDERATIONS   Should eClass adopt an employee handbook? If so, what would be the purpose of the handbook? What are the advantages and disadvantages of a handbook? What should it say about the length of the employment or grounds for discharge?

ETHICAL CONSIDERATIONS   Is it ethical for a business to "assure" employees about their status when the business is not willing to make guarantees? What would an act utilitarian do in this situation? What would an *immoral* manager do? What would an *amoral* manager do?

Fulfillment of the Agency Purpose

Logically, an agency relationship terminates when the purpose for which it was created has been fulfilled. It does not make sense to continue the relationship beyond that time.

Revocation

Principals can revoke or terminate the authority of their agents to act on their behalf. They should directly notify their agents of the termination. The notice that the agency relationship is being terminated should be clear and unequivocal. Indirect notice will *sometimes* be sufficient—for example, hiring a second agent to complete all the duties of the first agent.

The principal can terminate the agency at any time even though there was an agreement that the agency relationship would continue for a set time. Even a statement in the agreement that the agency cannot be terminated does not affect the principal's *ability* to terminate it. This is due to the agent's duty to obey his or her principal. Although the principal may have the *ability* to terminate the agency, he or she may not have the legal *right* to do so; in such a case, the agency can be terminated, but the principal may be liable for damages if this termination is a breach of contract.

Renunciation

Renunciation occurs when the agent notifies the principal that he or she will no longer serve as an agent. In other words, the agent resigns. Since an agency relationship is voluntary, an agent can renounce. However, the agent may be liable to the principal if the renunciation is a breach of their contract.

Operation of Law

In the legal system, operation of law means that rights or liabilities are created without the parties' acting in a particular manner or even intending the rights to occur. Sometimes operation of law will automatically terminate an agency relationship without any additional action. These situations include:

- when the agent dies
- when either party becomes insane
- when the principal becomes bankrupt
- when the agent becomes bankrupt, if the bankruptcy affects the agency
- when the agency cannot possibly be performed (for example, when the subject matter of the agency is destroyed)
- when an unusual and unanticipated change in circumstances occurs that destroys the purpose of the agency relationship
- when a change in law makes completion of the agency relationship illegal

The traditional rule is that the death of the principal also terminates the agency relationship immediately. Because this rule can cause hardship, many states modified their laws to implement a more liberal approach. Under this more liberal rule, the death of the principal does not immediately terminate the agency relationship *if* immediate termination will cause a hardship.

When the relationship is terminated by the operation of law, usually it is unnecessary to give notice to the other party or to the public at large. This rule is discretionary, and a court may decide to require notice if lack of notice causes a great hardship.

Importance of Notice

When either an agent or a principal terminates the agency relationship prematurely (as opposed to termination by operation of law), the party terminating the relationship has a duty to notify the other party within a reasonable period of time. This is required to ensure that the other party does not waste effort on a relationship that no longer exists.

If the principal revokes the agency relationship and does not notify the agent, the principal is obligated to indemnify the agent for any expenses and liabilities that the agent incurs in the proper performance of his or her formerly authorized duties.[28]

It may be crucial to notify third parties even if it is not legally required, such as in a termination by operation of law. The agent may find it advantageous to provide notice, but the principal will find that it is even more important to give notice.[29] If the principal fails to notify a third party, the third party may transfer money, such as a rent payment, to the agent with the expectation that the agent will forward the funds to the principal. Remember that the agent ordinarily has a duty to do so. If the agent is unhappy with the termination, there is a risk that the agent may unlawfully abscond with the money. Since the payment to the agent appears to be authorized, the principal will be held responsible and the payment will be credited to the third person's account.

The notice can take various forms. The preferred method is to personally notify the third person by mail, e-mail, electronically transmitted facsimile copy, telephone, or telegram. Personal notice is generally required for all third parties who have had dealings with the agent. The names, addresses, and telephone numbers of these customers are usually in the company data banks or the agent's files. The advantage of using e-mail or electronically transmitted facsimile copy is that it is fast and there is written proof of the notification. Without written proof, the third party may deny receiving the notice. Notice should be distributed promptly, since one of its purposes is to prevent losses caused by a disgruntled agent who feels that the termination is unjust.

In addition, the law accepts notice by publication (also called constructive notice). Usually, such notice is published in the legal notices in the newspaper. This may be the only type of notice that is practical for members of the public who are aware of the agency, but who have not had previous dealings with the agent.

The principal will be protected if the third party actually knows that the agency relationship has been terminated, even if the third party did not receive notice from the principal (that is, the third party may have heard about the termination from the agent or from someone else).

Breach of Agency Agreement

As previously mentioned, generally the principal has the *power* to terminate the agency, even if the principal does not have the *right*. If the principal wrongfully revokes the agent's authority, the agent can sue for breach of express or implied contract. Many principal–agent contracts contain provisions for arbitrating disputes between them. Arbitration is discussed in Chapter 4. If there is an anticipatory breach and the principal notifies the agent in advance of the breach, the agent can sue the principal immediately for the anticipated damages. The agent, at his or her election, may decide to wait until after the contract period and then sue for actual damages. In either case, the agent has an obligation to *mitigate damages* or to keep them as low as possible by searching for another similar position with another principal in the same locality. Mitigating damages is discussed more fully in Chapter 14.

Contemporary Case

VIZCAINO v. MICROSOFT CORP.

120 F.3d 1006, 1997 U.S. App. LEXIS 18869 (9th Cir. 1997)

FACTS Donna Vizcaino and other Workers brought a class action lawsuit against Microsoft and its pension and benefit plans. "Microsoft fully integrated [the Workers] into its workforce: they often worked on teams along with regular employees, sharing the same supervisors, performing identical functions, and working the same core hours. Because Microsoft required that they work on site, they received admittance card keys, office equipment and supplies from the company." Workers submitted invoices to the accounts payable department. Microsoft did not withhold income taxes from their wages. Microsoft did not allow the Workers to participate in the Savings Plus Plan (SPP) or the Employee Stock Purchase Plan (ESPP). The Workers did not complain about being excluded when they were initially hired. Using common law principles, the Internal Revenue Service (IRS) decided that Microsoft should have been withholding income taxes because the Workers were employees and not independent contractors. Microsoft corrected the tax issues and changed the way it handled these Workers. It offered positions to some as acknowledged employees and discontinued others. Those who were let go had the opportunity to work for a temporary employment agency, which supplied workers to Microsoft. The Workers asserted that they were employees and should have had the opportunity to participate in the SPP and the ESPP, which were available to all employees who met certain participation qualifications.

ISSUE Are the Workers common law employees entitled to participate in Microsoft's pensions and benefit plans?

HOLDING Yes, the Workers are common law employees. The SPP plan administrator should determine their rights in the SPP. The district court should determine their rights in the ESPP.

REASONING Excerpts from the opinion of Circuit Judge Ferdinand F. Fernandez:

... [T]here is no longer any question that the Workers were employees of Microsoft, and not independent contractors. The IRS clearly determined that they were.... [T]he IRS made its determination based upon the list of factors which is generally used to decide whether a person is an independent contractor or an employee.... The same essential definition is used for § 401(k) plans ... and for § 423 plans ... [W]hen Congress uses the word "employee," courts "'must infer, unless the statute otherwise dictates, that Congress means to incorporate the established meaning'" of that word.... [O]ne could still question the IRS's application of those factors in a particular case.... [B]oth Microsoft and the SPP have conceded ... that the Workers were common law employees.... [T]hey ... were subject to Microsoft's control as to both "the manner and means" of accomplishing their job, ... they worked for a substantial period, ... they were furnished a workplace and equipment, ... they were subject to discharge, and the like. ...

Each of the Workers and Microsoft signed agreements which stated ... that the worker was "an Independent Contractor for [Microsoft]," and nothing in the agreement should be construed as creating an "employer-employee relationship." As a result, the worker agreed "to be responsible for all of [his] federal and state taxes, withholding, social security, insurance, and other benefits." At the same time, Microsoft had the Workers sign an information form, which explained: "As an Independent Contractor to Microsoft, you are self employed and are responsible to pay all your own insurance and benefits. . . . Microsoft . . . will not subject your payments to any withholding. . . . You are not either an employee of Microsoft, or a temporary employee of Microsoft." . . . [The court is] . . . obligated to construe the agreements. . . . We could decide that Microsoft knew that the Workers were employees, but chose to paste the independent contractor label upon them . . . Or we could decide that Microsoft mistakenly thought that the Workers were independent contractors and that all else simply seemed to flow from that status. . . . [We assume the latter.] As soon as Microsoft realized that the IRS . . . thought that the Workers were employees, it took steps to correct its error. It put some of them on its . . . payroll . . . It also gave the Workers retroactive pay for overtime hours. . . . [I]ts failure to withhold indicates that it did not think that the Workers were a special breed of employee; it simply thought that they were not employees at all. . . .

The . . . terms of the contracts do not add or subtract from their status or . . . impose separate agreements upon them. . . . [T]he other terms merely warn the Workers about what happens to them if they are independent contractors. . . . [T]he Workers were employees, who did not give up or waive their rights to be treated like all other employees under the plans. . . . They did sign agreements, which declared that they were independent contractors, but at best that declaration was due to a mutual mistake . . . Thus, the label became meaningless . . . It could . . . be argued that the statements about benefits . . . stand . . . as a waiver of benefits . . . [W]e think that would be an incorrect interpretation of these agreements . . . Microsoft assured us . . . this is not a waiver case.

Were it one, we would have to consider whether the waivers . . . were knowing and voluntary under ERISA and Washington [state] law. . . .

The SPP is an ERISA plan. . . . [T]he administrative panel of the SPP determined that the Workers are not entitled to benefits. The reasons appear to have been that the Workers were independent contractors and that they waived the benefits. . . . We . . . determine that the reasons given for denying benefits were arbitrary and capricious because they were based upon legal errors which "misconstrued the Plan and applied a wrong standard to a benefits determination." . . . [I]t is the terms of the SPP which control, and the plan is separate from Microsoft itself. Thus, we cannot . . . predict how the plan administrator, who has the primary duty of construction, will construe the terms of the SPP. . . . He has both the right and the duty to decide it, and we must then review his ultimate decision . . . by the usual standard. . . .

The ESPP . . . was an offer to employees . . . [W]e doubt that the corporate officers set out to withdraw the offer from some employees, even if they could have done that. . . . The ESPP was created and offered to all employees . . . and their labor gave them a right to participate in it. Of course, Microsoft's officers would not allow that participation because they were under the misapprehension that the board and the shareholders had not extended the offer to the Workers. That error on the officers' part does not change the fact that there was an offer, which was accepted by the Workers' labor. . . . [Under the ESPP an] employee, who chooses to participate, must pay for any purchase of stock, and the Workers never did that. We . . . leave the determination of an appropriate remedy to the district court. . . .

You Be the Judge

Brendan Bosse and Michael Griffin were part of a group of four teenagers who entered the Chili's Restaurant in Dedham, Massachusetts. They ordered and ate a meal, and their bill totaled $56. The teenagers decided not to pay. They left the restaurant, got into their gold-colored Camry, and headed north up Route 1. A regular customer of the restaurant observed them leave without payment. He followed them in his white sports utility vehicle. They realized that he was following them. They drove into a parking lot at a nearby store, and the pursuing patron followed them. He got out of his SUV and yelled something to the effect that he had seen them skip out on their bill at Chili's and that they would not get away with it. The customer's car had no Chili's insignia. The customer was wearing civilian clothing and not a Chili's uniform. The teenagers drove out of the lot with the patron in pursuit. During the pursuit the customer communicated to a male employee at Chili's by cell phone providing the employee with a description of the teenagers' car and the path of the chase. The male employee gave this information to Frank Conway, the manager. "Conway called 911 and informed the dispatcher (a) that the teenagers had run out on their bill, (b) that some of 'our regulars were leaving and they . . . followed them and they just phoned back saying that they were down by the CVS and the high school.'" Conway described the teenagers' car to the dispatcher. A high-speed chase by the patron ensued through the city streets until the teenagers collided with a cement or brick wall. Bosse and Griffin were injured in the crash. The Chili's customer drove past the crash scene and left the area. He remains unidentified. The teenagers, through their guardians, sued Chili's Restaurant, claiming that the pursuer was acting as a servant of Chili's Restaurant and that his pursuit of them was reckless and negligent. Was the customer acting as a servant of Chili's Restaurant? Should Chili's be liable for his actions? [See *Bosse v. Brinker Restaurant Corporation d.b.a. Chili's Grill and Bar*, 2005 Mass. Super. LEXIS 372 (Super. Ct. Mass., at Suffolk 2005).

Summary

Agency relationships center on the agreement between a principal and an agent that the agent will act for the benefit of the principal. The principal must have the capacity to consent to the relationship. The agent need not have contractual capacity. Most agents are compensated. An agent who does not receive compensation is called a gratuitous agent.

In analyzing the legal rights of the parties, one must determine whether the worker is a servant or an independent contractor. An independent contractor is hired to complete a job. The hiring party does not direct how the independent contractor does the task. In contrast, a master can exert a great deal of control over a servant and how the servant performs the assigned duties. Because the master can control the servant, the master is more likely to be held financially responsible for the servant's physical acts.

An agent has a duty to act in good faith, to act loyally, to obey all lawful instructions, to act with reasonable care, to segregate funds, to account for all funds, and to give notice.

An agency relationship may terminate at a specified time agreed on by the parties, at the will of the parties, or after the purpose of the agency has been fulfilled. It can be revoked by the principal, renounced by the agent, or terminated by operation of law. Even in an agent-at-will situation, the employer can be successfully sued for breach of an expressed or implied employment contract, bad-faith discharge, or tortious discharge in violation of public policy.

A principal generally has the power to terminate an agency relationship even if the termination is wrongful.

Discussion Questions

1. Juan hired Jack to deliver one cord of wood for the fireplace in the house Juan rented. Jack usually just dumps the wood in the driveway—a practice known as a driveway delivery. However, this time he decided to help Juan stack the wood in the garage. Juan was standing in the garage as Jack backed the truck into position. However, Jack backed the truck too far, damaging both the truck and the garage wall. Was Jack a servant or an independent contractor? Who was liable to the injured third party (the landlord), and why? Who would have been liable if the truck had injured Juan? Why?

2. Peter hired Andy to purchase some goods for him on the open market. While Andy was obtaining prices from vendors, Ted offered Andy a $100 rebate if Andy purchased the goods from Ted; Andy did so and kept the $100 for himself. What were the rights of the parties? Why?

3. Rick was hired to serve as a deck hand on Marsha's fishing boat. One day, Marsha ordered him to scrape and repaint a portion of the hull just above the water line. (The boat was not in dry dock.) Rick was directed to perform the task sitting on the rope ladder suspended above the water. Rick complained that he was tired, the job was dirty and dangerous, and the duty was not discussed when he accepted the job as deck hand. What rights did Rick have? What rights did Marsha have?

4. Steve managed a 200-unit apartment complex, which the owners wanted to convert to condominiums. The city council scheduled a hearing on the issue. Instead of sending the notice to the owners, the council sent the notice to Steve. What were the rights and obligations of the parties? Why?

5. Andrea acted as an agent for principals wishing to purchase small businesses. She was trying to assist Rudy in the purchase of a Japanese restaurant for a reasonable price. Rudy called her on her cell phone while she was out of town on other business. She returned the call while she was in the hotel lobby during the evening reception hour. During the discussion with Rudy she revealed most of the details of the business, including an analysis of the business's income statements, projected business, and a reasonable purchase price. Did Andrea violate any duties owed to Rudy? Why?

Case Problems and Writing Assignments

1. José Torres was a self-employed gardener doing business as José Torres Gardening Service from 1980 to 1988. He performed weekly gardening services at a number of homes in Torrance, California, including the home of Michael and Ona Reardon. In 1988, the Reardons began discussing the possibility of having Torres trim a 65- to 70-foot tree in their front yard. An agreement was reached in mid-June that Torres would trim the tree for $350. David Boice, the Reardons' neighbor, was present during the final discussion. Boice indicated that he was concerned about a large branch of the tree that overhung his house. He feared that the branch would fall onto his roof. Torres and one helper arrived at 11:00 A.M. on June 20 to do the job. The Reardons were not at home. Boice was at home working in his garage workshop, and he reminded Torres about the branch. Periodically, Boice came out to watch the progress. He mentioned that Torres was not using safety lines, and Torres responded that he did not need them. Torres used a chain saw to cut the larger branches. When Torres was ready to cut the branch that overhung Boice's house, Boice came out to hold a rope tied to the branch. He was going to pull on it so the branch would not fall on his roof. Torres was wearing a safety belt, but it was not attached to the tree. He did not have enough line to reach a branch that could support his weight. Torres claimed that Boice pulled on "Boice's rope" when Torres did not expect it, causing Torres to lose control of the chain saw and fall. Torres became a paraplegic due to the fall and sued the Reardons. Was Torres a servant of the Reardons and, therefore, entitled to workers' compensation? [See *Torres v. Reardon*, 5 Cal. Rptr. 2d 52 (Cal. App. 2d Dist. 1992).]

2. Joseph Szaller was employed by the Red Cross for three and a half years as a medical team manager. In this capacity, he supervised several other staff members and was responsible for collecting blood from volunteer donors on bloodmobiles in Howard County, Maryland. On February 22, 2001, Szaller placed a telephone call to an anonymous Red Cross hotline. During this call, he reported various blood handling and staff training deficiencies, which he believed violated Food and Drug Administration (FDA) regulations and provisions of a 1993 consent decree between the FDA and the Red Cross regarding training and quality assurance. (A *consent decree* is a court decree agreed to by the parties.) Szaller was suspended from work the day after he called the hotline, and his employment with the Red Cross was terminated on March 7, 2001. Szaller claimed that the American National Red Cross and the American Red Cross Greater Chesapeake and Potomac Blood Services Region wrongfully discharged him in violation of Maryland law. He contended that he was unlawfully terminated for reporting alleged violations of FDA regulations and the consent decree to a Red Cross hotline. Did Szaller's discharge violate a clear mandate of Maryland public policy constituting a wrongful discharge under Maryland law? What about the public policy in most states? [See *Szaller v. American National Red Cross*, 2002 U.S. App. LEXIS 10727 (4th Cir. 2002).]

3. James Matthew Hutchings, a pipe fitter/rigger, was assigned to work on board the vessel M/V CANDY LADY in order to assist with off-loading groceries and equipment from the boat to the Chevron platform. A relief crew of three men was being lowered in a personnel basket from the platform to the vessel by a crane located on Chevron's platform. The personnel basket fell and struck Hutchings, pinning him to the deck. He was unable to grab the personnel basket because there was only one tag line attached to the basket. At the time of the accident, Hutchings was an employee of Danos & Curole Marine Contractors, Inc. (Danos), an independent contractor of Chevron. Danos and Chevron had signed a contract whereby Danos would provide various services for Chevron at the site. The contract was silent about whether Chevron could or could not retain operational control over the work. While Danos assumed contractual responsibility for safety, the contract was ambiguous about whether Chevron relinquished control over the day-to-day operations of the work to Danos. An accident report was completed by Quent B. Gilbert, who listed himself on the report as "Chevron Representative Preparing Report." In addition, Hutchings stated that "Danny" Ragus, Chevron's company man, was the person from whom he generally received instructions, and that a Chevron representative was supervising the Danos employees on the day of the accident. The crane operator responsible for lowering the personnel basket stated that he reported to the Chevron supervisor. Could Chevron legally be held liable for Hutchings's injuries? [See *Hutchings v. Chevron U.S.A. Inc.*, 1999 U.S. Dist. LEXIS 2079 (E.D. La. 1999).]

Notes

1. The American Law Institute published the *Restatement (Third) of Agency* in 2006.
2. Since the third *Restatement of Agency* is relatively new, the provisions in the second *Restatement* are still the precedents in many states. In addition, in many areas the third *Restatement* did not make significant changes from the second.
3. *Restatement (Third) of Agency* (Philadelphia: American Law Institute, 2006), § 1.01.
4. There are other examples of fiduciary duties, such as those owed by a lawyer to his or her client, those owed by a corporate officer to the shareholders, and those owed by a trustee to a trust beneficiary. Principals also owe fiduciary duties to their agents.
5. *Restatement (Second) of Agency* (Philadelphia: American Law Institute, 1958), § 20, Comment b.
6. This is the position of the *Restatement (Third) of Agency* in § 3.05.
7. *Restatement (Second) of Agency*, supra note 5, at § 492, Comment a.
8. *Restatement (Third) of Agency*, § 3.04(c) explains the *Restatement*'s position on duties that cannot be delegated.
9. *Restatement (Second) of Agency*, supra note 5, at § 3, Comment a.
10. *Restatement (Third) of Agency*, supra note 3, at § 1.04.
11. Exceptions occur in areas of unemployment compensation and worker's compensation statutes. These statutes often require that the worker is being paid.
12. *Restatement (Second) of Torts* (Student Edition) (St. Paul, MN: American Law Institute, 1965), Chapter 15.
13. Ibid., Section 423 discusses highly dangerous activities; § 427A discusses abnormally dangerous activities; §§ 413 and 416 address work that creates a peculiar risk.
14. Ibid., § 414.
15. Ibid., § 410.
16. Ibid., § 411.
17. For example, the California Supreme Court decided that an employee of an independent contractor is barred from suing the hiring party for negligently hiring that independent contractor. See *Camargo v. Tjaarda Dairy*, 2001 Cal. LEXIS 3799, 108 Cal. Rptr. 2d 617 (2001), where Carmago was an employee of Golden Cal Trucking when he was killed on the property of Tjaarda Dairy. His widow sued the dairy for negligently hiring Golden Cal Trucking. The Court denied her claim. It felt that this would, in effect, provide a way around the state worker's compensation provisions. Two companion cases also deal with servants of independent contractors—*McKown v. Wal-Mart Stores, Inc.*, 2002 Cal. LEXIS 465, 115 Cal. Rptr. 2d 868 (2002) and *Hooker v. Department of Transportation*, 2002 Cal. LEXIS 464, 115 Cal. Rptr. 2d 853 (2002).
18. *Black's Law Dictionary*, 6th ed. (St. Paul: West 1990), p. 693.
19. "Agency; Agent; Good Faith," LawEasy.com, at http://www.laweasy.com/q/20070606070054/agency—agent—good-faith (accessed 7/11/10).

20. *Restatement (Third) of Agency*, § 8.01 deals with the duty to act loyally. Section 8.08 deals with other duties owed by an agent.

21. *Restatement (Third) of Agency*, § 8.15.

22. Anne E. Melley, "Agency, Rights, Duties, and Liabilities Between Principal and Agent, § 239 Generally; contractual duties, 3 Am. Jur. 2d Agency § 239."

23. *Restatement (Third) of Agency*, § 8.13.

24. There may be a distinction between the duty to indemnify and the duty to reimburse under state law. In many states the duty to repay the agent for necessary expenses, such as hotel bills and meals, may be a duty to reimburse. The duty to repay the agent for damages that result from the execution of the agency, such as damages paid by the agent to a third party for breach of contract by the principal, may be a duty to indemnify. The amount the agent is entitled to receive depends on the agreement and state law. Under the *Restatement (Third) of Agency* § 8.14, a principal has a duty to indemnify an agent in accordance with the contract, and unless otherwise agreed: (1) when the agent make a payment within the scope of the agent's actual authority; (2) when the agent makes a payment that is beneficial to the principal, unless the agent acts officiously in making the payment; or (3) when the agent suffers a loss that should fairly be borne by the principal.

25. *Whirlpool Corp. v. Marshall*, 445 U.S. 1 (1980).

26. OSHA is used to designate both the Occupational Safety and Health Act and the Occupational Safety and Health Administration.

27. On August 8, 1991, the National Conference of Commissioners on Uniform State Laws approved the Model Employment Termination Act 2 (Proposed Official Draft, 1991), commonly called META, which addresses these issues. It provides that employees can only be dismissed for "good cause." Delaware has adopted the Act, and it has been proposed for adoption in the District of Columbia. "A Few Facts About the Model Employment Termination Act," NCCUSL Web site, http://www.nccusl.org/Update/uniformact_factsheets/uniformacts-fs-meta.asp (accessed 2/12/10).

28. Harold Gill Reuschlein & William A. Gregory, *Hornbook on the Law of Agency and Partnership*, 2d ed. (St. Paul, MN: West Publishing Co., 1990), § 89(b), pp. 151–52.

29. The principal should be careful not to defame the agent or invade his or her privacy in the notice. The notice should simply indicate that the agent no longer works for the principal.

29

Agency: Liability for Contracts

Agenda

eClass will use agents in the conduct of its business. Consequently, the firm needs to decide whether eClass should be a disclosed, an undisclosed, or an unidentified principal. The firm also needs to decide what authority eClass should expressly grant to its agents, what additional authority these agents will have, and whether there is some means of limiting the authority of the agents.

Meg is concerned that salespersons will negotiate contracts with buyers and distributors that eClass has not authorized and that eClass will find these contracts unacceptable. What can Meg do to alleviate her concern? In general, what steps should eClass take with its sales force to reduce the risk of this type of problem?

What steps should eClass agents take to minimize their personal liability on contracts they negotiate for eClass?

909

eClass will deal with the agents of suppliers and retailers. In these relationships, eClass will be the third party. What rights will eClass have against these agents and their principals?

These and other questions will arise during our discussion of agency law. Be prepared! You never know when the firm or one of its members will seek your advice.

Classic Case

LIVINGSTON v. FUHRMAN
37 A.2d 747, 1944 D.C. App. LEXIS 175 (D.C. Municipal Ct. of Appeals, 1944)

FACTS Fuhrman (appellee) wished to buy a diamond ring and was given the card of Lassover, which contained Lassover's name and a telephone number and address. The number and address were that of Livingston & Company, a retail jewelry store operated by Livingston (appellant). Fuhrman called Lassover at Livingston's and made an appointment. At the time of the appointment she went to Livingston's store, and Lassover showed her diamond rings. Then, Lassover brought some rings to her home and she purchased one. Later, Fuhrman desired to purchase a waterproof wrist watch for her husband who was in the army. She called Lassover at Livingston's and arranged an appointment. She went to the store, and Lassover showed her some wrist watches. Afterwards, Lassover brought some watches to her home, and she selected and purchased the watch in question for $50. She gave the watch to her husband. Approximately six months later the watch was rusty and would not operate. Fuhrman took the watch to Livingston for repair. Livingston sent the watch to the factory but later informed Fuhrman that the watch could not be repaired. Fuhrman sued Livingston to recover the purchase price of the watch. She testified she thought Lassover was working for Livingston.

Livingston testified that he conducted a wholesale and retail jewelry business; that Lassover was not his employee but was an independent jeweler, who purchased jewelry at wholesale from him and sold it at retail to his own customers; that Livingston permitted Lassover to use the store telephone number for the purpose of receiving customers' calls and in Lassover's absence Livingston would take messages for him; and that Lassover was permitted to use the store for the purpose of meeting customers and showing them merchandise. Livingston provided evidence that Lassover was not his agent; that all merchandise received by Lassover was paid for by Lassover and appellant did not know to whom Lassover sold or for what prices and under what conditions he sold; and that Livingston had nothing to do with Lassover's sales or customers.

ISSUE Did Livingston "clothe" Lassover with apparent authority to act as his agent?

HOLDING Yes, the decision of the trial court is correct. There was apparent authority.

REASONING Excerpts from the opinion of Associate Judge Hood:

. . . The law with respect to apparent authority was well stated in [a prior case] . . . , as follows:

"Apparent authority may result from a manifestation of consent made to a third person or to third persons and inferred from words or conduct which, although ordinarily not indicating such consent, cause the third person because of facts known to both parties reasonably to believe that such consent exists, either where the apparent principal intended to cause such belief on the part of the third person, or where he ought to have anticipated that such belief would be caused."

When appellee went to appellant's retail jewelry store and was there shown jewelry by a salesman, she could reasonably assume that the salesman was the agent of the store and not acting as an independent jeweler; and appellant was bound to anticipate that the situation permitted by him might reasonably lead to such a conclusion. . . .

[The case was reversed for the trial court to hear evidence on the breach of warranty claim.]

A FRAMEWORK FOR CONTRACTUAL LIABILITY

An agent may have many and varied duties. These duties often include negotiating contracts on behalf of the principal. This chapter addresses the obligations of the parties in these contracts, and the potential liability of the agent, the principal, and/or the third party when problems arise during the performance of these contracts. The third party is also called the third person.

While the same broad concepts generally apply, agency law varies from state to state. In addition to applying any given state's rules of agency law, the court will often be influenced by the reasonable expectations of the third party; that is, how the third party reasonably perceives the situation. This perception, coupled with the specific laws of a given jurisdiction, may well influence the results in a particular case.

The distinction between servants and nonservants is *not* significant when the agent has entered into a contract on behalf of the principal. As a result, the courts will treat both types of agents the same in contract cases. Remember, though, that the distinction *is* significant if the agent commits a tort in the course and scope of employment. Because the distinction is irrelevant in contract cases, it is logical to only use the term *agent* in this chapter. These relationships are illustrated in Exhibit 29.1 and will be discussed in detail in this chapter.

In looking at the potential liability that might arise in a contract case, the prime issue for consideration is whether the principal authorized the agent to enter into the contract. This may affect any possible claims the principal might assert against the agent, or that the agent might assert against the principal. Another important factor is whether the principal's identity is revealed to the third party. The principal may be classified as a disclosed, an undisclosed, or an unidentified principal. Each

Exhibit 29.1

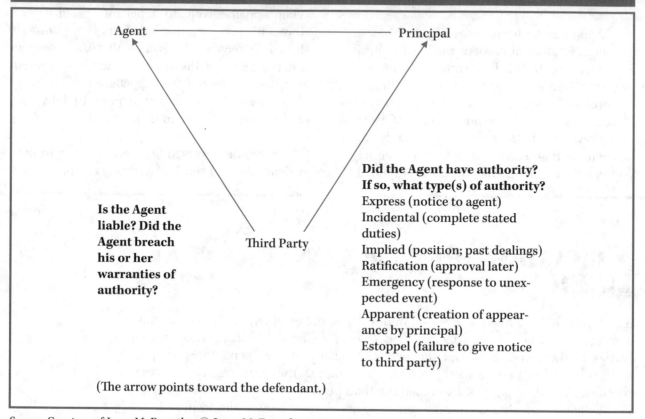

The Agent-Principal Relationship

Agent ———————————————— Principal

Is the Agent liable? Did the Agent breach his or her warranties of authority?

Third Party

Did the Agent have authority? If so, what type(s) of authority?
Express (notice to agent)
Incidental (complete stated duties)
Implied (position; past dealings)
Ratification (approval later)
Emergency (response to unexpected event)
Apparent (creation of appearance by principal)
Estoppel (failure to give notice to third party)

(The arrow points toward the defendant.)

Source: Courtesy of Lynn M. Forsythe, © Lynn M. Forsythe 2010

classification has implications for the potential liability of the agent, the third person, and the principal. The status of the principal in this regard is determined when the agent and the third party enter the contract; the legal relationships are fixed at that time. These issues, among others, will be discussed in detail in the rest of this chapter.

TYPES OF AUTHORITY

Regardless of the principal's classification, the principal will not be liable for every contract entered into by the agent or for every contractual type of act committed by the agent on his or her behalf. To determine whether the principal should be held liable, the court will examine whether the agent was authorized to enter into this type of contract. There are a number of different ways to create authority; they are commonly referred to as *types of authority.* Types of authority can overlap in a given situation, adding confusion for the business student. The types of authority are listed in Exhibit 29.1.

In order for the third person to sue the principal for the conduct of an agent, the third party must show that the agent's actions were authorized and that the contract was breached, to the detriment of the third party. The grounds for a successful suit are set out in Exhibit 9.2, and an explanation of the types of authority that an agent may possess is set out below.

For the third party to enforce the contract agreed to by the agent or to recover a judgment against the principal for breach of contract, all that needs to be shown is that *one* type of authority exists. In fact, if the third person can establish that *apparent* authority exists in the agent, the principal can be held liable to the third person even though the agent's conduct was *not* actually authorized by the principal. Even if the principal had expressly forbidden the conduct, the principal will be held liable if the agent possessed the apparent authority to perform the act. Remember, though, that the authority to act as an agent usually includes authority to act only for the benefit, *not* the detriment, of the principal. This establishes some limitations on the agent's apparent authority.

Actual Authority

Actual authority is the authority that the principal actually grants to the agent and that will establish the limits of what the agent should do in the performance of his or her duties.

Exhibit 29.2

Rights of a Third Party to Sue a Principal

Principal————(Appointment)————▶ Agent   [Agent is the *representative* of the principal. Legally the agent's actions are treated as if done by the principal.]

Agent————(Interacts)————▶ Third Person   [Third person can treat the agent's conduct as equivalent to the principal performing the action, *provided* the agent possess authority.]

Third Person————(Sues)————▶ Principal   [The third person can sue the principal for conduct of the agent, provided that the conduct was authorized.]

Actual authority may be expressed by the principal to the agent or it may be implied by the principal's conduct with the agent. Most courts address the specific type or types of authority that we will discuss next.

Express Authority

Express authority occurs when the principal informs the agent that the agent has authority to engage in a specific act or to perform a particular task. If the agent acts within the limits of his or her express authority, generally the agent will not be liable to the principal even if the results are negative for the principal. Generally, express authority need not be in writing; and, in most cases, it is not. For example, a principal may say to her administrative assistant, "Please order more letterhead stationery." Courts often strictly construe the words the principal uses when giving the authority. If the principal says to the agent, "Locate premises for another card shop," usually the court will interpret this to mean that the agent is authorized only to *find* the premises and not authorized to actually purchase the store. Therefore, an agent should interpret the instructions narrowly or ask for clarification of the scope of his or her authority.

Incidental Authority

In most cases, the principal does not discuss the grant of power in detail, if at all. Generally, the agent is given a brief explanation of his or her authority or he or she is given an objective to accomplish on behalf of the principal. This brief grant of express authority includes the power to do all acts that are incidental to the specific authority that *is* discussed. *Incidental authority* reasonably and necessarily arises in order to enable the agent to complete his or her assigned duties. Suppose an agent is provided with merchandise that is to be sold door to door. The agent will reasonably and necessarily have incidental authority to deliver the merchandise and to collect the purchase price. Incidental authority is also referred to as *incidental powers*.

Implied Authority

Implied authority is based on the agent's position *or* on past dealings between the agent and the third party. One type of implied authority arises when an agent is given a title and a position. It is implied that the agent can enter into the same types of contracts that people with this title normally can enter. A vice president of sales and marketing, for example, will have implied authority to purchase advertising on Google™ and on television and to contract with an advertising agency for a new ad campaign. The agent will have this authority because *most* vice presidents of sales and marketing have such authority. In other words, it is customary for a person with that title to enter that type of contract. When the principal confers the title on the agent, the agent acquires the implied power that accompanies it.

In the alternative, implied authority may exist because of a series of similar dealings in the past between the agent and the third party. If the principal did not object to the past transactions, it is assumed that the principal authorized the earlier contracts and that this type of transaction is within the agent's power. For example, if an administrative assistant customarily orders office supplies for a business on a monthly basis, the administrative assistant has implied authority to continue ordering office supplies in this manner. There is often more than one type of authority present, and in this situation there could also be apparent authority, which will be discussed below.

Ratification Authority

Ratification authority occurs when the agent does something that was unauthorized at the time and the principal approves it later.[1] Ratification requires approval by the principal after the agent forms the contract and after the principal has knowledge of the material facts. When a principal ratifies a contract, the principal must ratify the whole agreement. The principal cannot elect to ratify parts of the contract and disregard other, less advantageous parts.

Furthermore, the principal does not need to communicate the ratification verbally to anyone.[2] Generally, ratification may occur by an express statement or may be implied by the principal's conduct indicating a clear intent to affirm the agent's actions. An example of implied ratification occurs when the principal retains and uses goods delivered under a contract that was originally unauthorized *after* learning of the contract and its terms. Another example of implied ratification occurs when a principal initiates a lawsuit to enforce the terms of such an agreement. The ratification needs to follow the same format required of the original authorization. This means that in a limited number of situations the ratification will have to be in writing. If the agent/third-party contract must be in writing under the Statute of Frauds, then the ratification must be written, too. (You should recall from Chapter 12 that the *Statute of Frauds* is a statute that requires certain contracts to be in writing to be enforceable. Common examples include contracts for marriage, contracts that cannot possibly be completed within one year, contracts for the sale of land, executors' promises to pay the decedents' debts out of the executors' personal funds, guarantee contracts, and contracts for the sale of goods costing over $500.)[3]

Courts have imposed additional limitations on the doctrine of ratification. Both the principal and the agent must have been capable of forming a contract when the original contract occurred *and* when it was ratified. The *relation back doctrine*, as used in this context, states that *if* the contract is properly ratified, it is as if the contract were valid the whole time. Modern courts will not apply the relation back doctrine if it will injure an innocent party who obtains rights in the contract between the time of the original contract formation and the ratification.

Ratification cannot occur if important contract terms are concealed from the principal. Ratification will be effective only if the principal knows all the relevant facts. Also, the agent must have *purported* to act for the principal (indicated that he or she was acting for the principal) when the agent entered into the contract. If the agent did not reveal his or her agency capacity or if the agent was working for an undisclosed principal, there can be no ratification. Undisclosed principals will be discussed later in this chapter.

Emergency Authority

Emergency authority is inherent in all agency relationships. It need not be expressed. It provides the agent with authority to respond to emergencies, even though the principal and agent never discussed the type of emergency or how to respond to it. Suppose Galen, the owner of a jewelry store, leaves Andrea, his manager, in charge and goes out for supper. While Galen is absent, a fire starts in the stock room. In her effort to contain the fire, Andrea rushes to the hardware store next door and "buys" four fire extinguishers on credit. Galen must pay for the fire extinguishers because Andrea had emergency authority to purchase them.

Emergency authority will be found when *all* the following circumstances exist:

■ An emergency or unexpected situation occurs that requires prompt action.
■ The principal cannot be reached in sufficient time for a response or advice.
■ The action taken by the agent is reasonable in the situation and it is expected to benefit the principal.

Apparent Authority

Apparent authority occurs when the principal creates the appearance that an agency exists or that the agent has certain powers. Here, the representation of authority is made by the principal to the third party rather than to the agent.[4] The principal intentionally or carelessly causes the third party to believe that the agent had the authority. Apparent authority is not based on the conduct of the agent. The conduct of the principal must cause a reasonable third party to believe that a particular person has authority to act as the principal's agent. An agent with apparent authority may or may not also have actual authority to perform the same acts on behalf of the principal. For example, the principal hires Saunte to sell his ranch. She has express authority to complete the sale. When Judy asks about purchasing the ranch, the principal tells Judy to speak with Saunte. Saunte has both express authority and, in respect to Judy, Saunte has apparent authority.

Before applying apparent authority, some courts require (1) that the principal's actions give rise to a reasonable belief in the agent's authority and (2) that there be detrimental reliance on the part of the third party.[5] The existence of apparent authority is a factual issue to be determined in each case, and courts faced with very similar fact situations might disagree. In one case, Todd called his insurance company about his automobile insurance. Todd wanted to add a new vehicle to his automobile policy.

The agents on the phone told him to speak to Bridgette and put his call on hold. When Bridgette answered, Todd provided the specific information about his new vehicle, she told him the increase in the premium, and that he had insurance. Unfortunately, he had an accident on the way home with the new car. The court held that Todd's behavior was reasonable and that Bridgette had apparent authority. Notice that in this case the apparent authority was created by the actions of the other agents who spoke to Todd on the phone.

The third party must consider the facts and circumstances surrounding the transaction and the type of action involved. Sometimes, based on the information available, the third party must investigate further before his or her reliance will be deemed reasonable. Obviously, if the third party knows the agent does not have this authority, the reliance cannot be reasonable, and there can be no apparent authority for the conduct of the agent.

Apparent authority can exist even though there is no real agent. The person acting in the agent's role may be considered a *purported agent* (that is, one who claims to be an agent). Sometimes this purported agent is a former agent whose position has been terminated, and sometimes the person never was an agent. For an example of the first situation, suppose a company fires Nathan, a sales representative, but neglects to collect its samples, displays, and order forms from him. Nathan then takes a number of customer orders and disappears with the cash deposits. The company will have to return the deposits or credit the deposits to the customers' orders, because Nathan still has apparent authority to take orders. To help prevent this situation, the company should require Nathan to return the company's sales materials at the time his employment is terminated.

When an agency relationship is terminated, a principal should take certain steps to terminate apparent authority. The principal should inform the agent that the relationship is terminated, call or send notices to people who have dealt with that agent, and sometimes advertise in newspapers and trade journals that the relationship is terminated. The principal should collect all identification tags, samples, displays, order forms, and any other materials that can be used as evidence of the agency relationship. These items are *indicia* of the agency relationship.

Sometimes the principal never employed the purported agent, and yet the principal's conduct may cause the principal to be liable for the "agent's" actions. For example, a department store may not require its clerks to wear identifying jackets, vests, or even name tags. Suppose Rosa, a customer, selects some merchandise and walks toward a cash register. In place of a clerk, JoLynne, another customer steps behind the cash register, "rings up" Rosa's sale, puts the merchandise in the bag, and pockets the payment. In this case, the store cannot charge Rosa again for the merchandise; it is bound by the acts of JoLynne, the purported agent. In a very similar case, the court decided that the customer behaved reasonably and the store was "responsible" for the acts of the purported agent.

Apparent authority may be used to hold a principal liable on contracts entered into by the agent. It *ordinarily* will not be used to make a principal liable for physical harm caused by the agent through negligence, assault, trespass, and similar torts.

Authority by Estoppel

Authority by estoppel prevents a principal from denying the agent's authority. This is also called *ostensible authority*. It occurs when the principal *allows* the purported agent to pass himself or herself off as an agent and does not take steps to prevent the purported agent's representation.

Estoppel authority may occur by itself or in conjunction with other types of authority. When there is only estoppel authority and no other authority, estoppel authority will be used solely for the protection of the third party. It will not constitute the basis of a successful lawsuit by the principal against the third party. It creates rights for the third party and liabilities for the principal; it protects the third party by providing reimbursement for the third party's injuries. As with other doctrines of agency law, the courts are weighing the respective rights of two relatively innocent people—the third party and the principal. The purported agent can be sued for fraud, but generally that person cannot be located or has insufficient funds to cover the resulting losses. (*Fraud* is the intentional misrepresentation of a material fact.)

Authority by estoppel is illustrated in Exhibit 29.3 and in the example that follows on page 920. The types of authority are summarized in Exhibit 29.4.

Exhibit 29.3

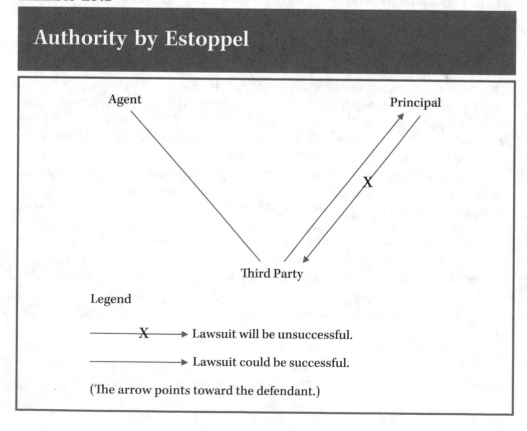

Authority by Estoppel

Agent

Principal

X

Third Party

Legend

⎯⎯⎯X⎯⎯→ Lawsuit will be unsuccessful.

⎯⎯⎯⎯→ Lawsuit could be successful.

(The arrow points toward the defendant.)

Exhibit 29.4

Types of Authority for Agents

Type of Authority	Description	Example
Express	Principal gives the agent the authority by spoken and/or written words. A writing is required in some circumstances because of the Statute of Frauds.[6] This authority is given prior to the agent's actions.	Pablo tells Aaron to purchase a restaurant franchise on Pablo's behalf.
Implied	Agent can acquire implied authority through a series of transactions where the agent enters into agreements with the third party on the principal's behalf. The agent can also acquire implied authority due to his or her position or job title.	Pauline hires Angela to work in her office. Angela was told not to order office supplies for the company. Angela repeatedly orders office supplies, and Pauline pays the bills. If Pauline does not tell Angela to stop, Angela may reasonably believe that she has the authority to continue.
Incidental (also called incidental powers)	Agent will have incidental authority to carry out transactions within his or her actual or apparent authority.	Alissa is given actual authority to obtain a loan for the business. Consequently, Alissa will have incidental authority to sign the loan documents and any other necessary paperwork.
Ratification	Agent did not have authority at the time of his or her acts. The principal approves the action after the fact using words or actions. A writing may be required in some circumstances because of the Statute of Frauds.	Penny tells Ann to research potential restaurant franchises that might be available. Ann is to report back with her findings. Instead Ann purchases a franchise on Penny's behalf. Penny approves the contract in writing.
Emergency	Agent will have emergency authority to enter into a contract as a response to an emergency if (1) an emergency occurs that requires a quick response, (2) the principal cannot be located in a timely manner, and (3) the agent's conduct was reasonable and was reasonably expected to benefit the principal.	Prudence hires Andrea to manage her gift shop. The weather service has announced that a hurricane is headed toward their community. Andrea goes to the hardware store and purchases lumber and nails to board up the store. She has the bill sent to Prudence.

Exhibit 29.4 Continued

Type of Authority	Description	Example
Apparent*	This authority exists when a third party reasonably believes that an agent has authority to act in this manner because of the third party's dealings with the principal and the surrounding facts. The third party's belief that the agent has this authority must be reasonable. Apparent authority will exist even if the principal did not intend to create the authority.	Paul fires Adam, who had worked as his sales agent for three years. After being fired Adam continues to call on his clients and take new orders and collect payments. Note that the court could also use implied authority in this situation.
Agency by estoppel (also called ostensible authority)*	The principal can be held liable for the contracts of a purported agent who is holding himself or herself out as an agent for the principal. The principal will be estopped or prevented from denying the agency relationship if the principal knows that the "purported agent" is representing himself or herself as the principal's agent and the principal does not speak up to prevent the third party's loss.	Able is not an agent for PPP, Inc. However, Able is calling on businesses in town and representing himself as an agent for PPP. PPP becomes aware of Able's activities, but it does not take any action to protect the public from Able.

Source: Courtesy of Lynn M. Forsythe, © Lynn M. Forsythe 2010

* An actual agency relationship is not required for apparent authority or agency by estoppel. The person can be a purported (reputed) agent.

Roy was walking to class one Wednesday when he passed Grace and David, who were standing next to Roy's car. He overheard Grace pointing out all the car's features to David. It was evident that Grace was trying to sell the car to David on Roy's behalf. Roy thought this amusing and did not stop to explain the truth. He went to class instead. He later learned that David made a $200 down payment on the car and that Grace disappeared with the money.

In a lawsuit between David and Roy, David will probably prevail. The court can apply agency by estoppel and decide that Roy is *estopped* (prevented) from denying that Grace was his agent. Roy knew that Grace was pretending to be Roy's agent, and Roy easily could have denied this. Roy's failure to speak helped to cause David's loss. The court will protect David by allowing him to recover.

Note that Grace would also be liable to David if she could be located. She would be liable under fraud and breach of warranty of authority. (*Warranties of authority* are implied warranties that the agent is an agent for the principal and is permitted to act in this manner.)

eClass 29.1 Sales/Management

HONORING SALES AGENT'S CONTRACTS

eClass appointed several sales agents. Each agent was assigned a territory, and each was provided with an "order book" containing standard order forms. These order forms contain the list price for eClass products. Erendida, one of the sales agents, called on a large retail outlet in another state. The retailer expressed an interest in buying a large quantity of eManagement programs, but only if eClass would give the retailer a 10 percent discount on the order. Erendida agreed to these terms and completed the order form, noting the 10 percent discount. Once the form was completed and signed by Erendida and the store's representative, a copy was faxed to eClass. When Yousef received the copy of the order, he was livid. He knows that the discount will remove virtually all the profit from the sale, but he fears that the firm is bound by the signed order. He asks you whether eClass must honor this contract. What will you tell him?

BUSINESS CONSIDERATIONS   What can a firm do to protect itself from overly zealous sales agents? Should a firm have a policy in place for handling situations such as this, or should each case be handled on an individual basis? How should the business communicate with the buyer in this sort of situation in order to (a) avoid the contract and (b) retain the buyer as a future customer?

ETHICAL CONSIDERATIONS   Is it ethical for a firm to refuse to honor a commitment made by one of its agents, even if the agent exceeded his or her authority? Is it ethical for a buyer to utilize its size to force special concessions from a sales agent beyond those normally granted by the firm?

Imputing the Agent's Knowledge to the Principal

In addition to being liable for contracts entered into by an agent, a principal may be legally responsible for information known to the agent but not actually known by the principal. This concept is called *imputing knowledge*. Because an agent has a duty to inform the principal about important facts that relate to the agency, it will be assumed that the agent has performed this duty. (This duty, commonly called the duty to give notice, was discussed in Chapter 28.) If the agent fails to perform this duty and the failure causes a loss, the principal—not the third party—should suffer the loss. Courts justify this result because the principal selected the agent, placed the agent in a position of authority, and had (legal) control over the agent. The principal also has a right of indemnification for any losses caused by the agent's breach of duty, including the duty to give notice. Consequently, the principal has recourse against the agent.

The agent's knowledge is not always imputed to the principal. Before a principal will be bound by knowledge received by the agent, generally the agent must have actual or apparent authority to receive this type of knowledge. In addition, the information received by the agent must relate to the subject matter of the agency. For example, if Valora, the principal, owns a real estate firm, a movie theater, and a hardware store, and Dimas, the agent, works in the hardware store, knowledge that Dimas obtains about the real estate firm will *not* be imputed to Valora. The knowledge must be within the scope of the agency.

DISCLOSED PRINCIPAL

When an agent clearly discloses that he or she is representing a principal and identifies the principal, the principal is *disclosed.* In these situations, the principal may be bound to the contract by any of the types of authority which have been discussed. Exhibit 29.5 illustrates a disclosed principal.

Liability of the Agent

Normally, when an agent indicates that he or she is entering into a contract on behalf of the disclosed principal, the agent will not be liable for the contract. It is clearly understood that the third party should look to the principal alone for performance. As with most legal rules, there are exceptions. For example, if the agent fails to represent

Exhibit 29.5

Disclosed Principal

eClass

Ani Yasuda
Sales Agent for eClass
9876 Appian Way
Maineville, OH 44444
513-555-8375 phone
513-555-8376 fax
Ani@eclass.com

his or her capacity as such, the agent will be personally bound. There have even been cases where the agent was held liable because he or she failed to represent his or her capacity on the written document; even though the agent alleged that he or she orally informed the third party of his or her representative capacity. In addition, the agent will be bound if he or she intends to be bound. For example, the agent may say, "You can rely on me," or "You have my word on it."

Why would an agent want to be liable on the principal's contract? Why would an agent want to undertake additional liability? An agent might do this if it is necessary to make a sale. The prospective buyer may be unsure about the principal and his or her reputation or financial backing. Perhaps the prospect has a long working relationship with the agent, so the agent's guarantee of performance persuades the prospect. The agent does not have valid grounds to complain if the third party takes him or her at his or her word and accepts the guarantee. The third party generally will prefer to sue the principal on the contract instead of the agent, since the principal often has more assets.

The third party, then, has legal rights against both the agent and the disclosed principal in these circumstances. This does not mean that the third party can collect twice. The third party is limited to one reimbursement. The traditional approach also required the third party to make an *election* to sue either the agent *or* the principal. Obviously, an important factor in this decision is who has the funds to pay a judgment. If the third party sues the principal and loses, he or she will be barred from then suing the agent. The reverse is also true. The more modern approach permits the third party to sue both the principal and the agent *together*. However, either defendant can require the third party to make an election prior to judgment.

Warranty of Authority

Whenever an agent of a disclosed principal enters into a contract, the agent makes all of the following implied warranties.[7] The agent does not have to state these warranties; they are implied by the situation.

- The disclosed principal exists and is competent.
- The agent is an agent for the principal.
- The agent is authorized to enter into this type of contract for the principal.

The third party can sue the agent to recover for losses that are caused by the breach of warranty of authority. Suppose the third party has losses because he or she did not receive the goods that are covered by the contract and that the principal is not responsible for the losses because the agent is not authorized to enter into this type of contract. The third party can sue the agent for the breach of warranties.

If the agent fears that he or she does not have the authority to enter into this type of contract, the agent may be concerned about the warranties of authority. He or she would be wise, then, to negate the warranties. This can be accomplished by stating that there is no warranty or by specifically stating to the third party the limitations on the agent's actual authority. The latter situation is illustrated in the following example.

> *Rhoda hires Beth as an agent and tells her to locate a parcel of agricultural real estate. Beth locates a parcel that meets Rhoda's specifications. Edele, the owner of the parcel, wants Beth to sign the purchase contract, but Beth is not sure whether she has authority to sign. If she fully and truthfully discloses the situation surrounding her authority to Edele, Beth will negate the implied warranty of authority. If Edele still wishes to sign the contract with Beth, he will assume the responsibility, and the loss, if the contract is not authorized. Edele would be relying on his own judgment.*

The agent may be liable for fraud if the agent intentionally misrepresents his or her authority. Exhibit 29.6 illustrates the agent's liability.

Liability of the Third Party

Lawsuit by the Principal   When a principal has been disclosed from the beginning, the third party realizes, or should realize, that the principal has an interest in the contract.

Exhibit 29.6

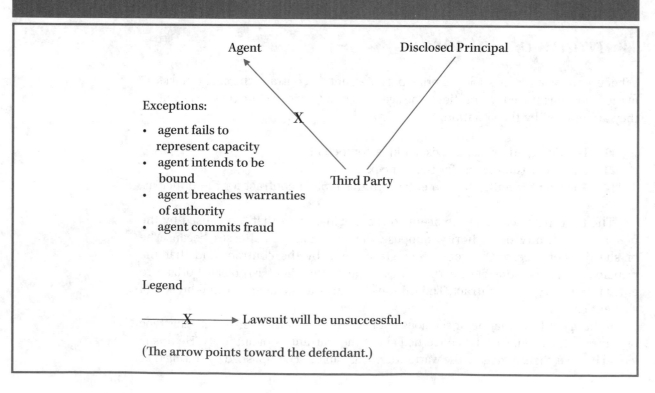

Rights of a Third Party to Sue an Agent of a Disclosed Principal

Agent   Disclosed Principal

Exceptions:

- agent fails to represent capacity
- agent intends to be bound
- agent breaches warranties of authority
- agent commits fraud

X

Third Party

Legend

———— X ————▶ Lawsuit will be unsuccessful.

(The arrow points toward the defendant.)

The principal can successfully sue the third party on the contract, if the agent was authorized to enter into this type of contract for the principal. In other words, the third party will be liable if there is express, implied, incidental, emergency, apparent, or ratification authority. The third party will not be liable if the only type of authority is estoppel authority.

Lawsuit by the Agent   Normally, the agent has no right to sue the third party on a contract. An agent *may* successfully sue the third party, if the agent can show that he or she has an interest in the contract. The most common type of interest is one in which the agent is entitled to a commission on a sale. For example, M.J., a real estate broker (the agent), enters into a contract on behalf of Yolanda, a homeowner (the principal). M.J. is entitled to a 6 percent commission payable from the proceeds of the sale. If the buyer (the third party) breaches the contract, M.J. can sue to recover the lost commission. (In this type of case, Yolanda may decide that it is not worth suing, but M.J. may feel that it is.)[8]

An agent may successfully sue the third party when the agent intends to be bound to the original contract. This rule is based on equitable principles. If the agent is potentially liable to the third party, the third party should be potentially liable to the agent, too. In some cases, a principal may transfer to the agent the right to file the lawsuit. In these cases, also, the agent can sue on the contract. These relationships are illustrated in Exhibit 29.7.

Exhibit 29.7

Rights of an Agent of a Disclosed Principal to Sue a Third Party

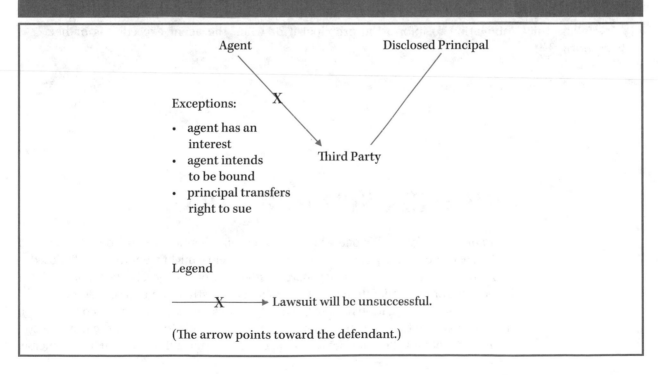

Agent   Disclosed Principal

Exceptions: X

- **agent has an interest**
- **agent intends to be bound**
- **principal transfers right to sue**

Third Party

Legend

——— X ———→ Lawsuit will be unsuccessful.

(The arrow points toward the defendant.)

eClass 29.2 Sales/Management

THE WARRANTY OF AUTHORITY

Alexandra, one of eClass's sales agents, was discussing eManagement with Ellen, a representative of State University system. Ellen was interested in the product, but she was also concerned that the product might malfunction, causing significant damage to the university system's computers. Alexandra told Ellen that, while it was not normal company policy, she was certain that eClass would be willing to guarantee that eClass products would not cause any computer malfunctions, and that the firm would probably be willing to give a two-year guarantee against any losses due to the use of eClass software. Ellen agreed to purchase a site license for eManagement, but only if Alexandra included this two-year guarantee on the order form and gave Ellen a copy of the form. Alexandra did so, and she and Ellen signed the form. When Alexandra sent the order form to eClass, Meg was furious. She would like to cancel the agreement but isn't sure she or the firm has the authority to do so. Meg has asked you about the legal implications of this situation. What will you tell her? (Note that both eClass and State University system are using agents to conduct their business. This is frequently the situation.)

BUSINESS CONSIDERATIONS   How can a firm protect itself from an agent who knowingly exceeds his or her authority in order to make a sale? Is an agent legally liable to the customer if the agent knowingly exceeds the authority granted by the principal?

ETHICAL CONSIDERATIONS   Does an agent have an ethical obligation to disclose to the third person any conduct that might exceed the authority given to the agent? Does the agent have an ethical obligation to inform the principal if or when the agent exceeds his or her authority?

UNDISCLOSED PRINCIPAL

An *undisclosed* principal is one whose existence and identity are unknown to the third party. There are many legitimate reasons why a principal might want to be undisclosed—to be able to negotiate a deal, to negotiate a better deal, or to conceal either an investment in a project or a donation to a charity. Exhibit 29.8 illustrates an undisclosed principal.

There may be situations where the third party would have refused to contract with the principal and the principal and his or her agent decide to mislead the third person in order to obtain the contract. If the agent and principal agree that the principal

Exhibit 29.8

Undisclosed Principal

Educational Systems

Ani Yasuda
9876 Appian Way
Maineville, OH 44444
513-555-8375 phone
513-555-8376 fax
Ani@yahoo.com

should remain undisclosed for the purpose of defrauding the third party, the third party can have the contract set aside by proving this fraud in court. However, the third party cannot have the contract set aside in court merely because the identity of the principal was not disclosed, even if the third party would have preferred not to make any contracts that would benefit the principal, and would not have entered into the contract had he or she known that the principal was the ultimate beneficiary of the contract. The fact that the principal prefers to remain undisclosed to the third person is not sufficient in itself to establish fraud or any other type of wrongdoing.

Liability of the Agent

When the principal is completely undisclosed, the third party believes that the agent is dealing for himself or herself. In other words, the agent is the other party on the contract. Based on the third party's knowledge, that assumption is rational. If there is a default on the contract, the third party can sue the agent. As far as the third party is concerned at the time of contracting, there are only two parties to the contract: the third party and the agent. Thus, the agent is liable to the third person for any breach of the contract.

Liability of the Principal

If the third party later discovers the identity of the principal, the third party can sue the principal. The principal will be held liable if the agent was authorized to enter into this type of contract for the principal. As mentioned before, traditionally the third party must make an *election* to sue either the agent *or* the principal. There is one important exception, however: if the third party sues the agent and loses *before* discovering the principal. In that case, the third party is not considered to have made an election and will be permitted to sue the principal later.

Liability of the Third Party

The third party may not be the one who suffers damages due to the breach of contract but may in fact be the one who committed the breach. Since the third party thought he or she was liable to the agent, it is logical to allow the agent to sue the third party. The law allows this action.

Under some circumstances, the undisclosed principal may, in his or her own name, also be able to sue the third party. There are some limitations, however. Generally, the principal can file a lawsuit by himself or herself only if the contract is assignable. (*Assignable* means that the rights in the contract legally can be transferred from one person to another. See Chapter 13 for a discussion of assignments and of assignable contracts.) If the contract is assignable, the position of the third party will not be jeopardized by either an assignment *or* the suit by the principal. Since the agent can assign the contract to *anyone*, the principal should be able to enforce the contract rights as if those rights had been assigned to the principal. Either way, the third party will be in the same position. Remember that the third party will not have to pay both the agent and the principal: The third party will have to pay damages only once. This relationship is shown in Exhibit 29.9.

Remember that the principal may not be able to sue in his or her own name because the contract is not assignable, or the principal may still wish to keep his or her identity secret. If either of these situations occurs, the principal can still arrange for the agent to file the lawsuit in the agent's name.

Exhibit 29.9

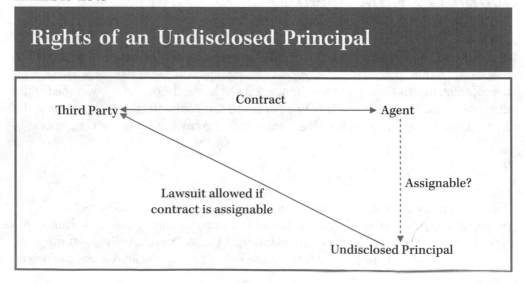

Rights of an Undisclosed Principal

Third Party ← Contract → Agent

Lawsuit allowed if contract is assignable

Assignable?

Undisclosed Principal

UNIDENTIFIED PRINCIPAL

An *unidentified* principal is one whose existence is known to the third party but whose identity is not.[9] In the words of the *Restatement*, "[a] principal is unidentified if, when an agent and a third party interact, the third party has notice that the agent is acting for a principal but does not have notice of the principal's identity."[10] For example, suppose that Hector Dias works as an agent for Smith Manufacturing. Hector approaches Beheshti Tool and Die to have some work done for Smith Manufacturing. Hector then negotiates a contract with Beheshti Tool and Die and signs the contract. However, instead of signing with a full disclosure of his position, Hector signs the contract as "Hector Dias, agent." Obviously, in this situation Beheshti Tool and Die would know that the contract was with the principal, but it would not (yet) know the identity of the principal. If the contract is breached and the work is not paid for as promised, who can Beheshti Tool and Die sue to recover its damages?

The rules that are applied to unidentified principals are similar to those applied to undisclosed principals. The principal may be sued if the contract is breached, and the suit will be successful if the principal authorized the actions of the agent. Once again, the third party can be required to make an election to sue the principal *or* the agent. If the *principal* suffers damages, he or she can sue the third party. The contract need not be assignable, because the third party knew that there was another party with in interest in the contract. Exhibit 29.10 illustrates an unidentified principal.

The general rule is that when an agent is working for an unidentified principal, the agent will be personally liable for the contract. The third party is probably relying on the agent's reputation and credit since the third party knows the identity of the agent but does not know the identity of the principal. It is unlikely that the

Exhibit 29.10

Unidentified Principal

**Ani Yasuda
Sales Agent
9876 Appian Way
Maineville, OH 44444
513-555-8375 phone
513-555-8376 fax
Ani@yahoo.com**

third party is relying on the reputation and credit of the unrevealed principal, a principal who could be anyone. The third party is probably relying on the reputation and credit of the agent, a known party with whom the third party decided to conduct business. An exception arises if the contracting parties agree that the agent will not be held liable. This agreement may occur if the agent indicates that he or she will not be bound and the third party does not object to this limitation.

ANALYSIS OF AGENT'S CONTRACTS WITH THIRD PARTIES

To characterize a contract situation involving any type of principal, you should answer the following questions:

- Was the person acting as an agent for the hiring party?
- Did the agent enter a contract on behalf of the hiring party or make contractual promises?
- Was the agent acting within the scope of his or her contractual authority? What type or types of authority were present?
- Was the hiring party a disclosed, undisclosed, or unidentified principal?
- Did the third party make an election to sue the agent or principal?
- Is the agent liable for the contractual promises?

CONTRACT BETWEEN THE PRINCIPAL AND THE AGENT

The Need for a Writing

The agency relationship is consensual in nature. As previously mentioned, it does not have to be based on a contract. *If* it is a contract, both the principal and agent will give up or promise to give up consideration. As with other contracts, the Statute of Frauds may apply and require written evidence of the contract in order for the contract to be enforceable. The provisions of the Statute of Frauds that are most likely to be applicable are those relating to contracts that cannot possibly be performed within one year and contracts involving the sale of real estate. Even if the Statute of Frauds does not apply, it is wise to write out the contractual provisions.

The *equal dignities rule*, also called the equal dignity rule, requires that some agency agreements be in writing. This rule is an adjunct to the Statute of Frauds and states that the agent/principal contract deserves (requires) the same dignity as

Exhibit 29.11

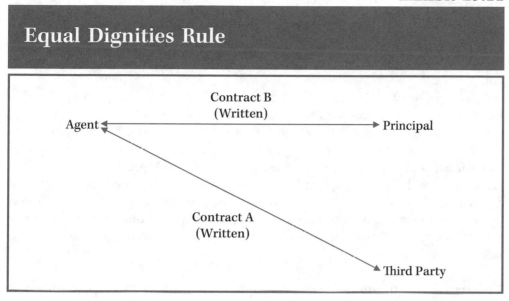

Equal Dignities Rule

the agent/third-party contract. It is illustrated in Exhibit 29.11: If contract A *must* be written, then contract B *must* be written. For example, if the agent is hired to locate and purchase goods costing more than $500, the UCC Statute of Frauds requires that the agent/third-party contract be in writing; consequently, the principal/agent contract must also be in writing.

Covenants Not To Compete

Covenants in Contracts of Employment   Some employment contracts contain *covenants* (promises) that the agent will not work for a competing firm. The contract may provide that (1) the agent will not moonlight with the competition and/or (2) the agent will not compete with the principal after this employment relationship is terminated. The second provision is usually applicable if the agent either quits or is fired. Some contracts contain both prohibitions.

Competing legal considerations arise in disputes about these covenants. On the one hand, the agent agrees not to compete. Perhaps the agent desperately wants the position and feels that he or she will not be hired unless he or she signs the covenant. The agent may not have equal bargaining power with the principal. Generally, parties *are* bound by their contract provisions. On the other hand, it may be a hardship on the agent to unduly restrict his or her ability to locate another position. In addition, it will be detrimental to society if people are not allowed to seek the positions for which they are most highly qualified. For these reasons, courts scrutinize covenants not to compete to determine whether the covenant is legal. As a rule, courts do not favor covenants not to compete in employment contracts. The covenant will be illegal if the court concludes that it is against public policy.

To determine whether the covenant is against public policy, the court will examine its reasonableness. The court will look at the situation surrounding the employment to see whether the principal has a legitimate interest in preventing the competition.

Covenants in Contracts for the Sale of Businesses   Covenants not to compete are also common in contracts in which the owner of a business sells the business to a buyer and the buyer obtains a promise that the seller will not compete with him or her. In such cases, the buyer has an interest in not having competition from the seller. Generally, the buyer pays a larger purchase price so that the seller will sell the goodwill of the business *and* sign a covenant not to compete with the buyer. (*Goodwill* means the good name and reputation of a business and its resulting ability to attract clients.) Courts are more inclined to enforce covenants not to compete in the sale of a business.

Enforceable Restrictions   Additional requirements exist for a valid covenant not to compete. The time and area specifications of the covenant must be reasonable, and what is reasonable depends on the type of employment. Covenants containing time periods of six months to two years are generally acceptable to the courts. The limitation is controlled by the time period during which the agent is able to draw contacts away from the principal or the time period in which these contacts still have value.

The covenant also must be reasonable in the area or distance specified. Another way to consider this is to ask the following question: How far will customers or clients travel to do business with the agent? The answer depends on the field of the agent's expertise. For example, a patient might travel halfway across the country to see a world-famous heart transplant specialist, but many patients will not even go across town to see a general practitioner.

If the principal has a legitimate business interest and the covenant is reasonable, the principal can sue the breaching agent or former agent for an injunction and/or contract damages. However, a principal may structure a covenant not to compete that is too broad. The courts apply one of two approaches in such cases. In one approach, the court declares the covenant void and ignores it. The agent then can do whatever he or she wishes with impunity. A less common approach is for the court to *reform* (modify) the contract to make its restrictions reasonable.

Courts may examine the following criteria in determining whether to enforce a covenant not to compete in an *employment* contract:

- Is the restraint reasonable in the amount of protection it affords the principal, or is it excessive?
- Is the restraint unreasonable because it is unduly harsh on the agent?

eClass 29.3 Manufacturing/Management

CREATING EMPLOYMENT CONTRACTS TO PROTECT TECHNOLOGY

eClass has been more successful than anticipated. Even though eManagement is popular, there have been several suggestions for improvements in the software. eClass would like to hire some programmers to help implement these suggested changes. However, the firm is concerned that some of the new employees might reveal (or "borrow") the technology the firm has developed, to the detriment of eClass. They ask you what protections they have or could add to their employment contracts to help protect them. What advice will you give them?

BUSINESS CONSIDERATIONS   How can a firm prevent employees from revealing or taking confidential business information or technology? What practical protections are available to a firm that is trying to protect its trade secrets?

ETHICAL CONSIDERATIONS   Is it ethical for an employee to utilize information gained in a previous position to benefit a competitor of the former employer? Is it ethical to restrict a former employee from using knowledge or information gained in a job when that knowledge or information makes the former employee a more productive or valuable individual? How can these competing interests be balanced?

- If the agent works for a competitor, will that threaten irreparable injury to the principal?
- Does the principal have a legitimate interest in preventing competition by the agent? Is the agency relationship of a unique and unusual type?

Some state statutes hold that a principal cannot prevent an ordinary employee from engaging in competition once the employment is over.[11]

A principal can prevent an agent from divulging trade secrets or customer lists after the employment is terminated even without a valid covenant not to compete. Under common law, this disclosure is a violation of the agent's duties of loyalty. (The duty of loyalty is discussed in Chapter 28.)

Contemporary Case

LEBLANC v. NEW ENGLAND RACEWAY, LLC

116 Conn. App. 267, 2009 Conn. App. LEXIS 350
(Conn. App. 2009)

FACTS The defendants (New England Raceway, LLC and its principal, Gene Arganese) began to accumulate properties for a proposed National Association for Stock Car Auto Racing, Inc. (NASCAR) raceway. The defendants approached Jeffrey J. LeBlanc and Diane M. LeBlanc regarding the sale of their home. On May 12, 2004, real estate agent Sandra Corn presented the LeBlancs with a purchase and sale agreement. Corn entered a dual agency agreement with the plaintiffs and the defendants. The purchase agreement had been signed by Arganese and had a sale price of $834,750. The LeBlancs increased the price to $894,700. Corn spoke with Arganese on the telephone, and he approved the increase in price. Corn then initialed the change in price on the contract on Arganese's behalf. The contract provided that the property would close within 60 days of all zoning approvals. Prior to the phone call, the LeBlancs made additional changes that indicated the sale would close by December 31, 2005. Corn did not initial these changes, nor did she confer with Arganese on the phone regarding them. The sale did not take place because the defendants were unable to obtain the zoning approvals.

ISSUE Did Corn have authority to agree to the changes in closing dates?

HOLDING No, Corn did not have authority to act for Arganese in this manner.

REASONING Excerpts from the opinion of DiPentima, J:

... [T]he court made the following findings: "Real estate agent Corn did not object to the proposed change in the closing date.... [S]he had a dual agency agreement and was acting for both parties, although her loyalties were clearly with the buyer." ... "Corn had no actual authority to agree to the change in the closing date" ... [T]he plaintiffs "failed to prove that Arganese intended Corn to possess the authority to bind him to the significant change ... in the closing date" and that "Corn, particularly in view of the dual agency agreement, had neither implied nor apparent authority to bind [the defendants]." We conclude that the court's findings are supported by the evidence ...

Agency is defined as "the fiduciary relationship that arises when one person (a 'principal') manifests assent to another person (an 'agent') that the agent shall act on the principal's behalf and subject to the principal's control, and the agent manifests assent or otherwise consents so to act." ... Three elements are required to show the existence of an agency relationship: "(1) a manifestation by the principal that the agent will act for him; (2) acceptance by the agent of the undertaking; and (3) an understanding between the parties that the principal will be in control of the undertaking." ... [O]ur case law provides that authority to perform services on behalf of a principal does not automatically confer either actual or apparent authority to bind a principal in other respects.... "[A] principal is bound to contracts executed by an agent only if it is within the agent's authority to contract on behalf of that principal. ..." ...

An agent acts with actual authority when, "at the time of taking action that has legal consequence for the principal, the agent reasonably believes, in accordance with the principal's manifestations to the agent, that the principal wishes the agent so to act." ... Arganese testified that he would negotiate the terms with the homeowners, giving Corn a parameter for any further negotiations. He explained that he talked to Corn about every contract but that he would have the final say with regard to the terms. He also described Corn's relationship with New England Raceway, LLC, more generally, stating, that as a licensed real estate agent, it was her job to function as a real estate agent in a dual agency capacity. He testified that she was not an employee of New England Raceway, LLC, but a subcontractor ... Arganese testified that at no time did he give Corn the authority to bind New England Raceway, LLC, in a contract. He testified that everyone involved with the company understood that no one, except Arganese himself, had the authority to bind the company. Corn also testified that at no time did Arganese or any other manager ... give her permission to sign contracts on the defendants' behalf. ... Thus, there was evidence that Arganese did not grant Corn authority to enter into contracts on behalf of New England Raceway, LLC, and that Corn understood she did not have the authority to do so. ... [W]e cannot conclude that the court improperly determined that Corn did not have actual authority. ...

Our Supreme Court has defined implied authority as "actual authority circumstantially proved. It is the authority which the principal intended his agent to possess. ... Implied authority is a fact to be proven by deductions or inferences from the manifestations of consent of the principal and from the acts of the principal and [the] agent." ... Arganese ... testified that he and Corn would draw up a contract, which Corn would present to the seller. If the seller made changes to which Arganese agreed, he would initial the changes, and the parties would have a contract. If the seller made changes to the contract to which Arganese did not agree, he would counter with another offer. ... Corn testified that when the seller made

a change to the contract, it was her practice to have the seller initial the change and then bring the contract to Arganese for his approval. She then would mail the approved contract back to the seller. ... Given this factual background, we cannot conclude that the court improperly determined that Corn did not have implied authority to bind the defendants.

"Apparent authority is that semblance of authority which a principal, through his own acts or inadvertences, causes or allows third persons to believe his agent possesses. ... Consequently, apparent authority is to be determined, not by the agent's own acts, but by the acts of the agent's principal. ... The issue of apparent authority is one of fact to be determined based on two criteria. ... First, it must appear from the principal's conduct that the principal held the agent out as possessing sufficient authority to embrace the act in question, or knowingly permitted [the agent] to act as having such authority. ... Second, the party dealing with the agent must have, acting in good faith, reasonably believed, under all the circumstances, that the agent had the necessary authority to bind the principal to the agent's action." ... Whether apparent authority exists is a question of fact, requiring the trier of fact to evaluate the parties' conduct in light of the attenuating circumstances. ... [The trier's decision should only be overturned when it is clearly wrong.]

Jeffrey LeBlanc ... told Corn that she could bring the contract to him but that he intended on further negotiating the purchase price. ... Arganese already had signed the contract. ... LeBlanc testified that after he and Corn negotiated a higher sale price, Corn "told me she [did not] have the authority to change the price, so that's when [Arganese] came into place ..." Jeffrey LeBlanc testified that he remembered hearing Arganese's voice on the other end of the telephone ... and remembered when Arganese agreed on the change in price. . . . He testified that . . . Corn reported that Arganese had agreed to the price change and that Corn was authorized to make that change. He also testified that he did not hear discussion between Corn and Arganese regarding the changes to the closing date, even though the changes were made prior to Corn's telephone call. . . . Jeffrey LeBlanc also testified that on May 12, 2005, he signed Corn's dual agency

agreement. He stated that Corn had explained that he needed to sign the agreement because she was working for both parties to the contract. . . . [H]e understood Corn's authority to be limited and that she was required to obtain Arganese's approval prior to initialing changes to the contract. . . . [T]he court properly determined that Corn did not have apparent authority to approve the change to the closing date. . . .

You Be the Judge

The Croatian Fraternal Union of America (CFU) had an office and museum in Pittsburgh, Pennsylvania. In 1989, CFU contracted with Rollins Protective Service for the purchase and installation of a security detection system, which included a monitoring system, a burglar alarm system, and a fire detection system with a deluge sprinkler system. In 2001, ADT sent CFU a letter indicating that ADT had acquired the prior monitoring service provider. ADT and CFU did not enter into a written contract. After the acquisition, ADT sent CFU the monthly bills for monitoring service. When CFU contacted it, ADT came to the premises to maintain, service, or repair the equipment. ADT would then bill for those services, and it would be paid. When ADT service technicians came to the premises they would prepare an ADT service ticket, service documentation, and/or service authorization. Robert Keber was the primary person at CFU who interacted with the ADT service technicians. Keber was the primary person who dealt with other repair people, too. He was the one who would explain the problem, direct the service people to the equipment, and sign service tickets to confirm that the work had actually been performed. He was also responsible for unlocking the building at 6:00 A.M. in the morning and removing snow from the parking lot.

On November 18, 2004, ADT sent Kevin Ferri to the premises because of a communication error. The control panel could not communicate with the ADT monitoring center because of a problem in a component called the "dialer." Ferri informed Keber that they could remove the panel and send it to California for repair or install a new monitoring system. Keber contacted Ed Pazo, CFU Secretary/Treasurer, to tell him the status of the repair, the repair options, and the fact there would be no service when the panel was removed. Pazo gave Keber express authority to tell ADT to remove the panel and have the panel repaired. Ferri completed an ADT Service Ticket on which he noted that "Customer understands that Security/Fire protection at site will be out of service." Ferri gave the ticket to Keber for review and approval. Ferri told Keber that there was information on the back of the ticket that he should review. Ferri had not done this before, but he testified that it was important this time because the panel was going to be removed. Keber glanced at the back and signed the service ticket. Ferri did not ask Keber if he read and understood the terms and conditions on the back, nor did Ferri ask Keber whether he had authority to enter into contracts for CFU. Keber forwarded this service ticket to Pazo's secretary. Pazo reviewed the ticket for the purpose of approving payment for the services rendered. (This was the procedure followed for earlier tickets, too.) The language on the back of the service ticket claimed to limit ADT's liability for damage to the premises and its contents.

The panel had not been replaced when, on January 23, 2005, a pipe on the sprinkler system broke. The break was not detected for a substantial period of time causing damage to the building and its contents.

Did Keber have authority to bind CFU to the terms and conditions on the back of the ADT service ticket? If *you* were the judge, how would *you* decide this dispute? (Great Northern Insurance Company provided the property insurance coverage on the premises. After Great Northern paid CFU for the damages, it sought reimbursement from ADT.) [See *Great Northern Insurance Co. v. ADT Security Services, Inc.*, 2009 U.S. Dist. LEXIS 91564 (W.D. Pa. 2009).]

Summary

The type of principal affects the rights and obligations of the agent, the principal, and the third party. A disclosed principal is one whose identity and existence are known to the third party. When the principal is disclosed, the principal can sue and be sued on the contract if there is express, incidental, implied, ratification, emergency, or apparent authority. These types of authority often overlap. If the only type of authority present is authority by estoppel, courts will use it to protect a third party but not to protect the principal. Information received by the agent within the course and scope of the job generally will be imputed to the principal. Usually, the agent of a disclosed principal will not be bound on the contract itself, but the agent may be responsible for breach of warranty of authority. The third party will be liable to the principal on the contract and to the agent if the agent has an interest or intends to be bound.

An unidentified principal is one whose existence is known but whose identity is not. In situations with unidentified principals, the agent will be held liable on the contract because the third party is relying on the agent's reputation. When the principal is undisclosed, the third party thinks he or she is dealing only with the agent. In this situation, the agent will be bound on the contract because the third party believes that the agent is a party to the contract.

The agency agreement must be in writing, *if* this is required by either the Statute of Frauds or the equal dignities rule. Covenants not to compete may be valid if the principal has a legitimate interest in preventing the competition, provided that the limitation is reasonable in the length of time and the area specified.

Discussion Questions

1. Sasha, an administrative assistant, often orders office supplies, such as photocopy paper, tablets, and toner cartridges, for her employer. One day, Sasha orders a personal computer and has it delivered to her home. Sasha has the bill sent to her employer. Based on the information provided, does Sasha have authority to do this? Why or why not? What additional information would be helpful? Why?

2. Ani, Meg, and Yousef have recently been issued eClass smart phones. Even though Ani's brother Sam is not part of the business enterprise, he commonly answers "her" phone when she is busy. Assume Sam makes representations about eClass products. Can eClass be held liable for his statements? What if Ani's 14-year-old nephew answers the smart phone and promises delivery within two weeks?

3. What are the business implications of people representing themselves as working for or on behalf of eClass? When is eClass legally obligated for the actions of these people? What are the public relations implications of successfully denying that an alleged agent was working on behalf of the firm?

4. Carmo farms 200 acres planted with grape vines. His neighbor has an additional 100 acres planted with grapes, which are for sale. Since Carmo and his neighbor have been feuding for 12 years, the neighbor will not sell the land to Carmo. Therefore, Carmo hires Rose to act as his agent without revealing his identity. Rose buys the land and starts to transfer it to Carmo. Upon discovering this, the neighbor tries to stop the transfer. What are the legal rights of the parties in this situation?

5. Is it reasonable for a fast-food chain to require all new employees to sign an agreement that they will not work for another fast-food restaurant for six months after leaving the chain? Is this agreement legal in most states? Can an ex-employee legally reveal the recipe for a chain's special blend of 11 herbs and spices? Why or why not?

Case Problems and Writing Assignments

1. Late in 1991, Jo Daviess hired Arlyn Hemmen to serve as its controller. Jo Daviess was a farm service cooperative located in the northwestern Illinois community of Elizabeth, a town of approximately 700 people. Prior to this, Hemmen had worked for a number of banks. As Jo Daviess's controller, Hemmen maintained the company's books and accounts, reviewed and reconciled its bank statements, prepared monthly operating statements and other financial reports, and supervised his coworkers in the absence of the office manager.

Jo Daviess maintained two accounts with Elizabeth State Bank (ESB): (1) an operating account, into which the company deposited all of its revenue and out of which it paid for its day-to-day expenses; and (2) an account reserved for the company's payroll. ESB maintained an account, referred to as the treasury tax and loan (TT&L) account, into which the bank's commercial customers deposited the federal income tax that they withheld from their employees' paychecks. Jo Daviess periodically transferred funds out of its operating account into either its payroll account or the bank's TT&L account. Pursuant to the terms of the operating account, only authorized signers could withdraw or transfer funds from that account. Hemmen was never a signer on the operating account. He did have the authority to sign checks drawn on the payroll account. Hemmen regularly prepared checks drawn on the operating account, both to pay Jo Daviess's suppliers and to transfer funds into one of the other accounts. These checks would be presented to the company's general manager for signature. For purposes of transferring funds into the TT&L account, Hemmen would prepare a check payable to the order of ESB. Jo Daviess did not owe any money to the bank; the only legitimate reason for making a check payable to the bank would be to accomplish a transfer of funds from the operating account to the TT&L account.

Beginning in January 1992, Hemmen began to embezzle money from Jo Daviess. (*Embezzlement* occurs when a person unlawfully takes personal property that has been entrusted to him or her.) Periodically, he would prepare a check on the company's operating account payable to the order of ESB, as if he were making a deposit into the TT&L account. He would then present the check to the general manager, who signed the check assuming that the proceeds were destined for the TT&L account. Hemmen would divert the proceeds of the checks to his own use in one of several ways. Hemmen presented the check to an ESB teller and requested that a portion of the check be deposited into the TT&L account, with the balance to be disbursed to him either in cash or one or more cashier's checks payable to Hemmen's creditors, or he would present the check and have the entirety of the proceeds issued to him. Bank personnel did not realize that Hemmen was diverting the proceeds to his own use; Hemmen would explain that the cash and cashier's checks were necessary in order to pay for supplies, parts, or some other legitimate company

expense. Hemmen would make a false entry in Jo Daviess's internal records indicating that the cash or cashier's check issued to him was used to pay for something.

ESB was aware that Hemmen was not an authorized signer on Jo Daviess's operating account, and Jo Daviess never indicated to the bank that Hemmen had authority to withdraw funds from that account. The bank acceded to Hemmen's requests for cash and cashier's checks without first consulting with Jo Daviess to confirm his authority to receive the proceeds of these checks. The bank did not even ask him to endorse the checks. It was the bank's custom to honor such requests. There was nothing that Jo Daviess did or said that induced the bank to comply with Hemmen's requests. Jo Daviess officials had never discussed with ESB whether Hemmen could legitimately receive the proceeds of any checks payable to the bank. Mutual Service Casualty Company (Mutual), which insured Jo Daviess, compensated the company for its loss. Mutual then filed suit against ESB.

Did Hemmen have either actual or implied authority to receive funds from Jo Daviess's operating account? Is Jo Daviess's system of bank accounts common business practice? What could Jo Daviess do to improve its banking and bookkeeping practices? What should ESB do to improve its procedures? [See *Mutual Service Casualty Insurance Company v. Elizabeth State Bank*, 265 F.3d 601, 2001 U.S. App. LEXIS 20667 (7th Cir. 2001).]

2. Kent Garver owned and operated Paramark Financial Services, a division of Paramark Insurance Corporation. Garver marketed insurance policies and annuities for 40 to 50 companies, including Legacy. Legacy marketed insurance products underwritten by American National Insurance Company (ANICO), as well as other insurance companies. The contract between Legacy and Garver specified that Garver was an independent contractor. Garver was paid on a commission basis, and Legacy retained no rights of control over Garver's actions except that he was forbidden to place client funds for Legacy products into his own company account.

Jimmie Alverson's accountant, William Jordan, referred Alverson to Garver in January 1995. Alverson had retired from his employment and had withdrawn his retirement funds of $275,000. He sought to invest them elsewhere. Alverson was shown a sales illustration for ANICO annuities and researched the company before meeting with Garver. Garver suggested that Alverson purchase ANICO annuities. The annuities were to be purchased in $50,000 increments. Alverson agreed and delivered the proceeds of his retirement accounts to Garver. On April 19, 1995, Alverson signed an ANICO application for a single $50,000 annuity. Garver sent Legacy the application, along with a $50,000 check payable to ANICO. Garver invested only $50,000 in ANICO annuities and transferred the balance of Alverson's money into the "Hallmark High Yield Fund." The Hallmark fund was actually controlled by Garver's own company, Paramark Financial Services. The ANICO annuity turned out to be a legitimate investment, but the money invested in the Hallmark fund was lost when Garver's company went under. Seeking recovery of his lost funds, Alverson filed this action against ANICO, Legacy, and Garver. Was Garver an agent of Legacy and/or ANICO? Did he have apparent or ostensible authority to act on their behalf? Analyze Garver's ethical perspective. Does Alverson bear some ethical responsibility for his loss? [See *Alverson v. American National Insurance Company*, 2002 U.S. App. LEXIS 3132 (6th Cir. 2002) (Not recommended for full-text publication.).]

3. William Powell authorized Debbie Powell, his wife, to obtain a rate quote and an application from Nationwide Mutual Insurance Company for coverage of his two vehicles. Debbie contacted the Nationwide agent from whom she had obtained her own policy, which included Underinsured Motorist (UIM) coverage. (*Underinsured Motorist coverage* pays the insured if another motorist who has insufficient insurance injures her.) South Carolina requires companies to tell applicants about UIM coverage and whether or not it is included in their policy. Debbie informed the agent that her husband desired liability coverage of $100,000 on his two vehicles and that he wanted "full coverage" as he had with his then-current insurer. Debbie met with the agent's assistant, Sherry Volz, and at Volz's direction signed William's name beside several "X" marks on various forms. One of the signatures was in a space indicating that the insurance applicant (William) did not wish to purchase UIM coverage. Another signature was in a space confirming that the applicant had read the explanation of UIM coverage contained in the form. Debbie did not know what UIM coverage was, nor did Volz explain it to her. Additionally, Volz never asked Debbie whether William had authorized her to apply for insurance or reject UIM coverage on his behalf, and Debbie never told Volz that she was so authorized. William was displeased when he learned that Debbie had applied for a policy, but when Debbie assured him that the resulting policy would contain the "full coverage" that he desired, he chose not to rescind the application. Accordingly, when Volz contacted William, he told her that he wanted the policy. Volz did not ask William whether Debbie had been authorized to act on his behalf, nor did she specifically inquire as to whether William desired UIM coverage. Nationwide subsequently issued the policy with William listed as the named insured and Debbie listed as a driver. Although the policy, which Nationwide sent William, indicated that it did not provide UIM coverage, William never read the policy and continued to believe that UIM coverage was included. William never rescinded, modified, or canceled the policy, and he paid the premium. Shortly after he had renewed the policy for an additional six months, Debbie was driving one of William's vehicles when she was involved in an accident caused by another driver. She sustained injuries in excess of the other driver's policy limits. When she subsequently made a claim under William's policy, Nationwide made payments for property damage, towing, and automobile rental but denied that the policy provided UIM coverage. Did Debbie have authority to "reject" the UIM coverage for William? If so, what type of authority existed? If this case were filed in your court, how would you rule? [See *Nationwide Mutual Insurance Company v. Powell*, 2002 U.S. App. LEXIS 10562 (4th Cir. 2002).]

Notes

1. The agency relationship itself can also be formed by ratification. This is often called agency by ratification. It occurs when someone who was not an agent purports to act on behalf of a "principal" and the "principal" affirms the contract.
2. *Restatement (Third) of Agency* (Philadelphia: American Law Institute, 2006), § 4.01.
3. The proposed revision to Article 2 increases the amount to $5,000 or more. We will treat the topic here as if the 2003 revision to Article 2 has not been adopted.
4. Warren A. Seavey, *Handbook of the Law of Agency* (St. Paul, MN: West, 1964), § 8D, p. 19.
5. *General Overseas Films, Ltd. v. Robin International, Inc.*, 542 F. Supp. 684 (S.D.N.Y. 1982), p. 688, n.2.
6. The Statute of Frauds requires some contracts to be evidenced by a writing in order to be enforceable. The Statute of Frauds is discussed in more detail in Chapter 12.
7. *Restatement (Third) of Agency* (Philadelphia: American Law Institute, 2006), § 6.10 deals with warranties of authority.

8. Real estate transactions are governed by state law. In some states, the transaction has to be completed or "close" before the real estate agent is entitled to a commission.
9. The *Restatement (Second) of Agency* and many courts used the label of partially disclosed principals for unidentified principals.
10. *Restatement (Third) of Agency*, supra note 7, at § 1.04(2)(c).
11. California courts do not use the "reasonableness test" for covenants not to compete signed by employees. Former employees can engage in any lawful business, trade, or profession unless it is necessary to enforce the covenant to protect the employer's trade secrets. The statute makes exceptions for covenants in other contexts, such as the termination of partnerships, limited liability companies, and the sale of the goodwill of a business or all of the shares in a corporation. See California Business & Professions Code §§ 16600, 16601, 16602, and 16602.5 and *Edwards v. Arthur Andersen*, LLP, 44 Cal. 4th 937, 2008 Cal. LEXIS 9618 (CA 2008). Other states also restrict the use of covenants not to compete by employers.

30

Agency: Liability for Torts and Crimes

Agenda

As the business grows, eClass will be hiring a number of new employees. Some of these new employees will be making deliveries of eClass's products, while others will be working at one of the firm's facilities. What happens if one of the employees making deliveries for the firm commits a tort, causing injury to a third person? Will eClass be liable for the damages, will the employee be liable, or will the liability be joint and several? If eClass is held liable, will the firm have any recourse against the employee for the damages caused? What should eClass consider in hiring delivery people? What financial risk is involved with hiring employees, and how can eClass best minimize this risk?

Suppose that three eClass employees are involved in some form of "horseplay" during the day, and that one of them is injured as a result. What liability might eClass face in this situation? What protections are available for the firm to either prevent or reduce the potential financial risk the firm might face? What duties does eClass owe its employees?

Ani, Meg, and Yousef designed work shirts with the eClass logo for the "on site" employees and for the delivery personnel. They liked the idea of using the shirts to promote the firm, and decided they would also design t-shirts that could be given away at various functions. They also gave some of these t-shirts to family members and friends to help publicize the firm. Suppose that one of their relatives or friends commits a tort, injuring a third person, while wearing a t-shirt with the firm's logo. Is it possible for the third person to hold eClass liable on the theory that the relative or friend was advertising for the firm and was therefore engaged in a business-related activity for which eClass should be held liable?

These and other questions will arise during our discussion of agency law. Be prepared! You never know when the firm or one of its members will seek your advice.

Classic Case

[Note that this next case involves fraud, so it could have been tried under contract theories instead of tort theories.]

PACIFIC MUTUAL LIFE INSURANCE COMPANY v. HASLIP

499 U.S. 1, 1991 U.S. LEXIS 1306 (1991)

FACTS Lemmie L. Ruffin, Jr. was a licensed agent for two distinct companies, Pacific Mutual Life Insurance Company and Union Fidelity Life Insurance Company. Ruffin, representing himself as an agent of Pacific Mutual, provided Roosevelt City with a single proposal for both health and life insurance for its employees. Union was going to provide the health insurance policies and Pacific Mutual was going to provide the life insurance policies. The packaging of insurance from different companies was not unusual and was approved by Pacific Mutual. The proposal was accepted. Union was to send its bills for health premiums to Ruffin at Pacific Mutual's Birmingham office. The city clerk issued a monthly check for the premiums, which was given to Ruffin. Ruffin misappropriated most of the funds and did not pay Union. Union sent notices of lapsed health coverage to respondents in care of Ruffin and Patrick Lupia, Pacific Mutual's agent-in-charge of its Birmingham office. These notices were not forwarded to the employees. The employees who suffered damages filed this lawsuit against Pacific Mutual and Ruffin claiming fraud and *respondeat superior*.

ISSUE Does it violate Pacific Mutual's constitutional rights to hold it responsible for Ruffin's fraud on the theory of *respondeat superior*?

HOLDING No, it does not violate Pacific Mutual's constitutional rights.

REASONING Excerpts from the opinion of Justice Blackmun:

... Pacific Mutual was held responsible for the acts of Ruffin. The insurer mounts a challenge to this result on substantive due process grounds, arguing that it was not shown that either it or its Birmingham manager was aware that Ruffin was collecting premiums contrary to his contract; that Pacific Mutual had no notice of the actions complained of prior to the filing of the complaint in this litigation; that it did not authorize or ratify Ruffin's conduct; that his contract with the company forbade his collecting any premium other than the initial one submitted with an application; and that Pacific Mutual was held liable and punished for unauthorized actions of its agent for acts performed on behalf of another company. . . . [Consequently,] the burden of the liability comes to rest on Pacific Mutual's other policyholders.

The jury found that Ruffin was acting as an employee of Pacific Mutual when he defrauded respondents. . . . There is no occasion for us to question . . . [this finding], for it is amply supported by the record. Ruffin had actual authority to sell Pacific Mutual life insurance to respondents. The insurer derived economic benefit from those life insurance sales. Ruffin's defalcations related to the life premiums as well as to the health premiums. Thus, Pacific Mutual cannot plausibly claim that Ruffin was acting wholly as an agent of Union when he defrauded respondents. The details of Ruffin's representation admit of no other conclusion. He gave respondents a single proposal—not multiple ones—for both life and health insurance. He used Pacific Mutual letterhead, which he was authorized to use on Pacific Mutual business. There was . . . no indication that Union was a nonaffiliated company. The trial court found that Ruffin "spoke only of Pacific Mutual and indicated that Union Fidelity was a subsidiary of Pacific Mutual." . . . Pacific Mutual encouraged the packaging of life and health insurance. Ruffin worked exclusively out of a Pacific Mutual branch office. Each month he presented to the city clerk a single invoice on Pacific Mutual letterhead for both life and health premiums. Before the frauds in this case were effectuated, Pacific Mutual had received notice that . . . Ruffin was engaged in a pattern of fraud identical to those perpetrated against respondents. There were complaints to the Birmingham office about the absence of coverage purchased through Ruffin. The Birmingham manager was also advised of Ruffin's receipt of noninitial premiums made payable to him, a practice in violation of company policy.

Alabama's common-law rule is that a corporation is liable for both compensatory and punitive damages for the fraud of its employee effected within the scope of his employment. We cannot say that this does not rationally advance the State's interest in minimizing fraud. Alabama long has applied this rule in the insurance context, for it has determined that an insurer is more likely to prevent an agent's fraud if given sufficient financial incentive to do so. . . . Imposing exemplary damages on the corporation when its agent commits intentional fraud creates a strong incentive for vigilance by those in a position "to guard substantially against the evil to be prevented." . . . If an insurer were liable for such damages only upon proof that it was at fault independently, it would have an incentive to minimize oversight of its agents. Imposing liability without independent fault deters fraud more than a less stringent rule. It therefore rationally advances the State's goal. We cannot say this is a violation of Fourteenth Amendment due process. . . . [I]mposing such liability is not fundamentally unfair and does not in itself violate the Due Process Clause. . . .

We . . . conclude that Ruffin was acting as an employee of Pacific Mutual when he defrauded respondents, and that imposing liability upon Pacific Mutual for Ruffin's fraud under the doctrine of *respondeat superior* does not . . . violate Pacific Mutual's due process rights.

A FRAMEWORK FOR TORT LIABILITY

In contract matters there is generally a conscious desire to interact with the public and a conscious decision to enter into business arrangements with the public by means of the agent. In most tort situations, however, neither the master nor the servant desires that the tort occur. But once the tort has occurred, someone has to suffer the financial burden, even if that someone is the innocent victim. Who should pay? The master? The servant? Or the third person?

Vicarious liability is legal responsibility for the wrong committed by another person, in this case the master's liability for the wrongs committed by the servant. Vicarious liability for torts involves different policy considerations from those surrounding an agent's ability to bind the principal in business dealings with third persons. It also involves different legal theories. One important legal theory is *respondeat superior*, where the master has to pay for the torts committed by his or her servant in the course and scope of the servant's job. It is difficult to predict whether the court will conclude that the acts were in the course and scope of the job, making the definition vague and ambiguous. There is significant litigation over whether particular acts were in the course and scope of the job.

The servant will generally be liable for his or her own torts. If *respondeat superior* applies the master can also be held liable for the tort even though the tort was committed by the servant. In most cases, the third party can sue the master and servant together in the same law suit.

SERVANT'S LIABILITY

Servants engage in physical activities or labor on behalf of the master. These activities frequently bring the servant into close contact with members of the general public. When the servant is careless or overly aggressive, there is a good chance that a member of the public will be injured. This chapter discusses the servant's and the master's responsibility to the public for these types of injuries. As we will see, these relationships can occur in business and nonbusiness settings.

The general rule of tort law is that everyone is liable for his or her own torts. This general rule is followed in agency law, but with a twist. Since the servant committed the tort, the servant can normally be held liable for the harm that occurs. The fact that the servant is working for the master at the time of the tort does not alter the general rule. However, this general rule is supplemented under the rules of agency to be discussed in this chapter. Refer to Chapter 6 for a more complete discussion of specific torts.

MASTER'S LIABILITY UNDER *RESPONDEAT SUPERIOR*

When the servant commits a tort that harms a third person, the servant should be responsible for the harm. However, in agency law some circumstances exist in which the master can *also* be held liable for the torts committed by the servant. Notice that in these situations the *master* is being held liable for the conduct of the *servant*. Since the servant is also liable for his or her tortious conduct, the liability is said to be *joint and several.* This means that *either* party may be held liable individually (several liability) or that *both* parties may be held liable (joint liability). If joint liability is found, the plaintiff can seek recovery of any damage award from either party. He or she does not have to seek any set percentage from each.

Respondeat superior is the theory under which masters are held liable for the torts of their servants even though the masters are not personally at fault. Literally, it means "let the master answer." It is also referred to as a "deep-pockets" theory, based on the belief that the master's pockets are likely to be "deeper" (that is, they hold more money) than those of the servant. (This chapter generally uses the traditional terms *master* and *servant* because *respondeat superior* is limited to master–servant relationships.) The *respondeat superior* doctrine is one of the many legal theories that attempt to balance competing interests. In this situation the competing interests are the rights of the injured party to receive compensation for injuries suffered versus the right of the master to avoid liability for acts not actually committed by him or her. Is it better to compensate the victim by holding the master liable, or is it better to "protect" the master, even though the victim may not be able to recover for his or her injuries from the servant?

The *Restatement (Third) of Agency* explains the liability this way:

(1) An employer is subject to vicarious liability for a tort committed by its employee acting within the scope of employment.

(2) An employee acts within the scope of employment when performing work assigned by the employer or engaging in a course of conduct subject to the employer's control. An employee's act is not within the scope of employment when it occurs within an independent course of conduct not intended by the employee to serve any purpose of the employer.

(3) For purposes of this section,
    (a) an employee is an agent whose principal controls or has the right to control the manner and means of the agent's performance of work, and
    (b) the fact that work is performed gratuitously does not relieve a principal of liability.[1]

For example, if Myesha has suffered $175,000 in injuries from an automobile accident caused by the negligence of Sondra, a servant, and Sondra has a total net worth of only $50,000 and no automobile insurance, Sondra cannot fully compensate Myesha. However, if the master is a multimillion-dollar corporation, the master *can* fully compensate Myesha. In these circumstances, the court must evaluate all the facts and determine whether *respondeat superior* should be applied in this particular case. If *respondeat superior* applies, the victim will be allowed to recover from the master; if not, the victim may only seek recovery from the servant.

Respondeat superior has been justified on numerous grounds in court opinions and in legal treatises. The justifications for holding the master liable for wrongful acts of the servant include the following:

- The master will be more careful in choosing servants in order to avoid liability.
- The master will be more careful in supervising servants in order to avoid liability.
- The liability for servants is a cost of conducting business.
- The master is the person benefiting from the servant's actions.
- The master can purchase liability insurance.
- The person with the power to control the conduct should be the person to bear financial responsibility.
- The master can better afford the costs, especially when compared to an innocent third person who is injured by the servant's conduct.

Respondeat superior is not based on the idea that the master did anything wrong. Rather, it involves a special application of the doctrine of strict liability. *Strict liability* is liability for an action simply because it occurred and caused damage, not because it is the fault of the person who must pay. The master hired the servant, and the servant then did something wrong while carrying out his or her obligation to the master, so the master should pay for the wrongdoing. Courts tend to apply a "but for" test in deciding whether to assign liability to the master. "But for" the existence of the master—servant relationship, no harm would have resulted. In other words, someone should pay, and the master is best able to pay and afford the loss; therefore, the master must pay. However, *respondeat superior* does require a *wrongful act* by a servant for which the master can be held liable, and a legally defensible reason for holding the master liable for the wrongful act of the servant. It is not sufficient that the servant committed a wrongful act and that a third person was injured by that act. The wrongful act must be one over which the master can be held legally responsible. It must be an act the master should legally have controlled.

The principal's *right to control* is really what distinguishes servants from nonservants. A principal who has the right to control may be called a *master*, and the worker may be called a *servant*. Remember that *respondeat superior* applies only to servants. It does not apply to nonservants because the principal lacks control over the conduct of the nonservants and, thus, is not a "master" in these situations.

Respondeat superior also does not make the master an insurer for every act of the servant. The master is only liable for those actions that are within the *course* and *scope* of the employment. Therefore, the issue in most cases based on *respondeat superior*, involves a decision as to whether the servant was acting within the course and scope of his or her employment when the tort was committed. To resolve this question, it is important to know the servant's duties, working hours, state of mind, assigned location, and the master's right to control the worker. It is also important to know whether the servant has deviated from his or her route and/or routine, whether the servant has any history of similar sorts of conduct, and any other factors that might show whether the conduct was an extreme deviation from what the master should reasonably have expected. It is immaterial if the master fails to exert actual control over how the worker completes the tasks as long as the master has the *right* to use this control. *Respondeat superior* has been criticized by "masters" on the grounds that it is unconstitutional, but the U.S. Supreme Court has affirmed that *respondeat superior* is not fundamentally unfair or unconstitutional.[2] In most jurisdictions there seems to be a trend toward increasing the master's liability, even for intentional torts or serious wrongs committed by the servant, such as rape. If the courts find that the servant *was* in the course and scope of employment when these intentional torts or serious wrongs occur, they often impose liability on the master.

Factors Listed in the Restatement of Agency

The *Restatement (Second) of Agency* indicates the factors that should be used to determine whether a servant is within the scope of his or her employment.[3] The factors include the following:

General Statement

(1) Conduct of a servant is within the scope of employment if, but only if:
   (a) it is of the kind he is employed to perform;
   (b) it occurs substantially within the authorized time and space limits;
   (c) it is actuated, at least in part, by a purpose to serve the master; and
   (d) if force is intentionally used by the servant against another, the use of force is not unexpectable by the master. . . .[4]
(2) In determining whether or not the conduct, although not authorized, is nevertheless so similar to or incidental to the conduct authorized as to be within the scope of employment, the following matters of fact are to be considered:
   (a) whether or not the act is one commonly done by such servants;
   (b) the time, place, and purpose of the act;
   (c) the previous relations between the master and the servant;
   (d) the extent to which the business of the master is apportioned between different servants;
   (e) whether or not the act is outside the enterprise of the master or, if within the enterprise, has not been entrusted to any servant;
   (f) whether or not the master has reason to expect that such an act will be done;
   (g) the similarity in quality of the act done to the act authorized;
   (h) whether or not the instrumentality by which the harm is done has been furnished by the master to the servant;
   (i) the extent of departure from the normal method of accomplishing an authorized result; and
   (j) whether or not the act is seriously criminal.[5]

In many cases, certain factors may indicate that the servant is within the scope of employment and other factors may indicate the contrary. For example, suppose that

Eric, a servant, is involved in a traffic accident while driving a truck owned by Micheala, the master, and used in Micheala's business. At the time of the accident Eric is driving under the influence according to the state standard and will be cited for the accident. While Micheala in this example furnishes the truck (the instrumentality), she probably has no reason to suspect that Eric will drive under the influence of alcohol (engage in this conduct). Should the court impose liability on Micheala in this situation under the theory of *respondeat superior*? There is no absolute answer to this question. In our example, Eric was driving Micheala's truck or instrumentality which would make *respondeat superior* more likely. However, he was intoxicated while driving, which would make *respondeat superior* less likely.

Each case is different, and no one factor controls this decision; the judge or jury weighs all the factors involved to reach a decision. Since the triers of fact exercise a lot of discretion in these cases, fact situations that seem very similar may result in markedly different decisions by different courts.

Time and Place of Occurrence

Two of the factors that courts analyze in determining the course and scope of employment are the time and place of the act[6]—whether the tort occurred on the work premises and whether it occurred during work hours.

Failure to Follow Instructions

A master can be held liable for a servant's acts even though the master instructed the servant not to perform a specific act or commit torts. The disobedience of the servant does not necessarily exempt the master from liability. If this were not true, a master could avoid all liability by simply instructing all of his or her servants not to commit any torts during the course of employment.

Failure to Act

A master can also be held liable under *respondeat superior* when the servant *fails* to act as directed, as shown in the following example.

> Sammy, a railroad switch operator, is supposed to throw a switch on the track at the same time every day. One day, he carelessly fails to do so, causing a train to derail and passengers on the train to be injured. The master (the railroad) is liable for Sammy's negligence in this situation. Sammy was negligent by failing to act as instructed.

Respondeat superior does not decrease the servant's liability for wrongdoing, but it makes an additional party, the master, also liable. In many legal situations, such as the one just described, multiple parties may be held liable for a single occurrence.

eClass 30.1 Management

LIABILITY FOR DRIVERS MAKING DELIVERIES

As eClass's business has expanded, the firm has begun to hire drivers to make deliveries of its products to customers, especially retail outlets. Yousef recently read an article in the local newspaper about a case in which the driver of a delivery van caused an accident. The local court entered a judgment against the employer of the driver for $1.5 million dollars. Yousef is concerned that a similar case would destroy eClass if the firm employed a driver who caused an accident. Yousef has asked you if there is any way for the firm to avoid liability while still hiring drivers to make deliveries for the firm. What will you tell him?

BUSINESS CONSIDERATIONS   How can a business minimize its potential financial risk when one of its servants is guilty of negligence? What policies should a business initiate to provide the best possible protection when hiring servants who will be driving company-owned vehicles?

ETHICAL CONSIDERATION   Would it be ethical for a firm to state that its delivery personnel are independent contractors, and then to require all of its drivers to drive their personal vehicles and to provide proof of adequate insurance coverage?

Defenses Available to the Master

When an injured third person seeks recovery from the master based on *respondeat superior*, the master has three potential defenses he or she can assert. First, the master may be able to show that the servant's actions were not in the course and scope of employment. If the servant is not within the course and scope of employment the master has no legal right to control the actions of the servant and should not be held liable for the conduct. Assume Shane works for a neighborhood restaurant. Shane is not in the course and scope of employment while he is sitting in his business law class. Similarly, Shane is probably not in the course and scope of employment when he is driving to or from work. In other words, commuting generally is not in the course and scope of the job.[7]

The second possible defense is to show that the servant's action was an extreme deviation from the norm. This will arise when the servant's conduct is so far outside what a servant would normally be expected to do that the master would not expect the conduct: the master could not have done anything to prevent the conduct. For example, if a servant gets into an argument with a customer and viciously assaults that customer with a knife, the master may be able to avoid liability even though the assault occurred at the work place. The conduct is so abnormal that it would not be fair to hold the master liable. Courts have been limiting this defense to a significant extent by expecting a reasonable master to have conducted an appropriate background check on servants and/or being more aware of the servant's personality.

The third possible defense is when the servant goes off on a "frolic of his (her) own," in effect abandoning the employment when he or she was supposed to be working to do something that was purely for his or her self-interest. For example, Sandi, a delivery driver, decides to abandon her route in order to stop by a friend's house for a visit may be "frolicking" when she is supposed to be working. However, if the court disagrees with the master and decides that the servant's deviation is minor, the court will decide that the servant was merely on a detour and will still apply *respondeat superior*. Consequently, the master will be liable for "detours" but not for "frolics." This distinction between detours and frolics can be viewed as an application of the definition of "course and scope" of the job. Courts today expect the master to exert more effective control and supervision over the servant, and the availability of this defense has also declined. You should note that the overall trend is towards increasing liability.

Identifying the Master

Another problem that may arise is deciding *who* the master is. Who controls the manner in which the servant will do the work? The master, or employer, is the one who not only can order the work done, but also can order how it will be done. Identifying the master is especially complex in cases involving borrowed servants. In these cases, who is the master? Is it the lending master, the borrowing master, or both? Again, the important factors are the course and scope of the employment and the master's ability to control the servant. Consider the following example:

> *Jamal works for Computer, Inc., which is having its office remodeled by Redesign Your Space, LLP. (LLP signifies that the business is operating as a Limited Liability Partnership. LLPs are discussed in greater detail in Chapters 31-33.) Since the contractors doing the work are understaffed, Jamal's supervisor tells Jamal to help them. In this situation, Computer, Inc. is referred to as the general master and Redesign Your Space, LLP is referred to as Jamal's special master. (The meanings of general master and special master here are similar to those used to define general and special agents in Chapter 28.) Jamal is classified as a borrowed servant.*

> *Assume that the supervisor for Redesign Your Space, LLP instructs Jamal to paint the walls in the main lobby of the building. After painting the walls in the main lobby, Jamal fails to put up Wet Paint signs. We will assume that Jamal was negligent in failing to post the signs. A customer brushes against the wall and wet paint ruins her clothes. Who is Jamal's master at the time of his negligent act? Who will be held liable under respondeat superior? Recall that Jamal will also liable for his negligence.*

Some courts will decide that both Computer, Inc. and Redesign Your Space, LLP are liable. Jamal was subject to the control of both, and his actions benefited both. Other courts will conclude that Redesign Your Space, LLP is liable because Jamal was working primarily for Redesign Your Space, LLP at the time of the negligence. Still other courts will hold Computer, Inc. liable because ultimately Jamal was subject to its control and it supplied his paycheck. To avoid the uncertainties caused by borrowed servants, prudent employers enter into agreements about which master will be liable when a servant is "loaned" to another master and/or obtain liability insurance for the servant's acts.

A closely related problem occurs when one servant appoints another servant (a subservant) to complete his or her tasks. Under *respondeat superior*, who is responsible for the torts of the subservant? If the servant had authority to appoint the subservant, the master will be held liable for the subservant's acts that are within the course and scope of employment. However, if the servant lacked authority, generally the servant will be liable as the "master" under *respondeat superior*. The primary justification for this rule is that the servant in this situation is the one with the right to control the subservant.

Crimes and Intentional Torts

Courts are more reluctant to hold a master liable under *respondeat superior* for intentional wrongs such as *assault* (a threat to touch someone in an undesired manner) and *battery* (unauthorized touching without legal justification or consent) than they are for negligence on the part of the servant. In fact, a few courts still follow the traditional rule that a master is not responsible for the intentional acts of his or her servant. The modern view, however, is that a master is liable if the servant advanced the master's interests or the servant believed that his or her conduct was advancing the master's interests. Consequently, masters can be held liable under *respondeat superior* for intentional torts such as assault, battery, invasion of privacy, libel, and slander. Many criminal acts are also torts, and the master may be held civilly liable under *respondeat superior* for the financial losses suffered by the victim of the servant's criminal act even if the master is not held liable for the criminal conduct of the servant. For example, in the Classic Case of *Pacific Mutual Life Insurance Company v. Haslip*, Ruffin stole the money for the premiums, and the insurance company was held liable for his acts under *respondeat superior*. *Respondeat superior* is not used to impose criminal liability on the master.

Most courts will hold a master liable for some of a servant's serious wrongdoings but not for others. The question is often one of degree. How serious was the tort or crime? Should the master have expected it? Is there much variance between the assigned tasks and the wrongdoing? There seems to be a trend toward increasing the conduct for which liability will be imposed on masters. In these cases the courts frequently examine the underlying policies for *respondeat superior* that we have already discussed.

eClass 30.2 Management

WHEN IS ANI "OFF THE CLOCK"?

Ani, Meg, and Yousef designed t-shirts with the eClass logo. They gave shirts to family members and friends to help publicize the firm. Ani likes to wear her t-shirt to the gym. One day while wearing her eClass shirt, Ani has a disagreement with Eslanda, another member of the gym, about who is next to use the weight bench. Eslanda claims that Ani hit her. Ani denies the claim. Eslanda is threatening to sue Ani for assault, battery, and intentional infliction of emotional distress, and to sue eClass for *respondeat superior* for Ani's torts. Assuming that Eslanda can prove that Ani hit her, can she successfully sue eClass for damages? Is Ani advertising for eClass, thereby making her conduct "job-related"?

BUSINESS CONSIDERATIONS   Should a business expect to be held liable whenever any person acts negligently or in a tortious manner while wearing a shirt (or other item of apparel) that advertises the firm? Should it matter if the person wearing the logo is, or is related to, a manager of the "advertised" firm?

ETHICAL CONSIDERATIONS   Is it ethical for the plaintiff in a torts case to sue the wealthiest potential defendant, regardless of the degree of fault that may attach to that defendant? Is it ethical for a business to derive the benefits of "free advertising" when people wear its logo on their apparel and yet to deny liability when those same people act in a tortious manner?

DIRECT LIABILITY OF THE MASTER

The worker must be a servant before *respondeat superior* will be applied. However, masters may be held *directly* responsible for some of the wrongs committed by their servants. For example, the master is liable if the master *instructed* the servant to commit the wrong, did not properly supervise the servant, ratified or approved the servant's tort, or was negligent in the selection of the servant. (Negligent hiring is discussed in greater detail in the following section.)

Criminal law may also apply to a master when a servant commits a crime. For example, a master can be criminally liable based on his or her own fault. If a master directs or encourages a servant to engage in criminal activity, the master will probably be held personally liable for such acts as conspiracy, solicitation, or accessory to the crime. (In a *conspiracy*, the participants plan the criminal behavior together. However, in a *solicitation*, one person convinces another to engage in the criminal activity. In an *accessory to the crime*, one person assists the primary actor in the commission of the crime.) In addition, some criminal statutes create liability for the master even though the master does not intend to violate the statute or does not know of the illegal act or condition. For example, state liquor laws often specify that tavern or restaurant owners are liable if minors are served alcohol in their bars. In most states, this is true whether or not the owner approves of such action or even knows that it has occurred. Other examples include statutes that prohibit the sale of impure food or beverages no matter who is at fault. The purpose of these statutes is to assure that the masters take every possible precaution to ensure that such activities do not occur in their establishments; this is accomplished by imposing liability on them if these statutes are violated.

In most states, the hiring party can be held directly liable and/or criminally liable even if the worker is not a servant (that is, the worker was an agent or independent contractor).

NEGLIGENT HIRING

Careful selection of employees is important to an employer. (Courts generally use the employee/employer terminology in this context and so will we.) An employer wants to know if the applicant will do a good job and work well with other members of the staff. In addition, an employer does not want to hire an applicant who will not follow instructions or work within the guidelines established by the employer. Such an employee may be likely to commit torts or harm members of the public while in the course and scope of employment, creating potential liability for the employer.

An employer can be held liable for negligent hiring if he or she is careless in the hiring process. In many states, negligent hiring also applies to the hiring of agents and independent contractors. However, since most of the cases involve employees, we will use the employee/employer terminology. The number of suits based on negligent hiring is on the rise. (Negligent hiring or selection of independent contractors was also discussed briefly in Chapter 28.) *Negligent hiring* assumes that if the company had investigated the applicant's past, it would have learned of the prior anti-social conduct of the applicant, and then the employer would not have hired the person. Instead, the negligent hiring by the employer subsequently placed the employee in a position where he or she could harm someone. Under the theory of negligent hiring, an employer owes a duty to customers and to the public at large. Depending on state law, the employer may also be liable to his or her other employees and agents. Courts in many states also recognize the torts of *negligent promotion* (promoting an employee to a job he or she is not qualified to perform) and *negligent retention* (keeping an employee when he or she should be fired.) In many states, the employee's acts are not required to be in the course and scope of the employment in order to impose liability for negligent hiring. The Florida case of *Tallahassee Furniture Co. v. Harrison* illustrates these principles:

> John Allen Turner, an employee of Tallahassee Furniture Company, delivered a couch to Elizabeth Harrison. (The couch was purchased by her father, a stockholder in the furniture company.) Three months later Turner returned and asked Harrison for a receipt for the broken television she had given him on the delivery date because, he said, they thought he had stolen it. Then he asked to use her bathroom. After gaining access to her home, he brutally beat and stabbed her. Following these events, Harrison filed criminal charges against Turner. In addition to these criminal charges, she sued Tallahassee Furniture Company for her damages, alleging negligent hiring and negligent retention. The employee had a criminal record including several charges of battery. He had been voluntarily committed to a psychiatric hospital two times, where he was diagnosed as a paranoid schizophrenic: he claimed to hear voices telling him to kill himself and telling him to kill other people. He had a known history of drug abuse and he had been fired from his last job. Harrison prevailed in court because the court found that the employer failed to use adequate measures to determine Turner's qualifications for the job or to discover problems with his past conduct. When Turner was hired for the job, the company did not ask him to complete a job application. Company management testified that if they had known of Turner's history, they would not have hired him as a delivery person. The court decided that the company *should* have known of his history, and held the company liable for its failure to act reasonably in hiring Turner.[8]

In negligent hiring cases, the question before the court normally will be whether the employer exercised the level of care that, under all the circumstances, a reasonably prudent employer would exercise in choosing or retaining an employee for the particular duties to be performed. The courts then consider the reasonableness of the employer's efforts to inquire into the applicant's background. The employer's duty depends on the type of position for which it is hiring. This duty is particularly high when the employer is hiring maintenance workers and delivery people who will go into the homes and apartments of customers. In the *Tallahassee Furniture Company* case, the court held that the employer was guilty of negligent hiring.

The liability for negligent hiring poses some difficult practical problems for employers. How does an employer obtain all the necessary information about an applicant, *without* illegally violating his or her right to privacy? What is the employer's responsibility to learn about the applicants' character and background? An employer must consider both federal and state laws. In addition, there are difficult ethical questions involving an applicant's privacy and employer's desire (or need) to know. Exhibit 30.1 contains some practical advice on hiring.

It is common to sue the employer for both negligent hiring and *respondeat superior*. Exhibit 30.2 compares the direct and the vicarious liability of the principal.

Exhibit 30.1

Ten Steps to Reduce Liability for Negligent Hiring

Remember to check the limits of local, state, and federal employment law.

1. Have the applicant complete a job application. The employer should use a job application that is appropriate to the specific job.
2. Obtain a signed release so that the employer can check criminal records, mental health records, and credit histories.

   Most commonly, if the applicant will not sign a release he or she will not be hired.
   This step is particularly important if the applicant may pose a threat to customers.

3. Conduct a careful and detailed interview with the applicant. Ask about periods of unemployment and other items that seem suspicious or confusing.
4. Ask whether the applicant was convicted of any crimes. In many states, it is illegal to inquire about arrests.
5. Talk to the applicant's prior employers.

   Ask whether the employee left on good terms.
   Would the employer rehire the applicant?

6. Check on alcohol use and illegal drug use. This is more critical if the use occurs at work or the use impacts job performance.

   An employer generally cannot prohibit alcohol use by adults during their own time, unless it interferes with work.

7. Ask about driver's licenses, tickets, and driving accidents if the applicant will be driving at work.

   Check with the department of motor vehicles for appropriate states.

8. Check on potential mental or emotional problems.
9. Maintain a written record of the investigation to show the steps taken to screen applicants and the questions asked of applicants and prior employers. This record will be extremely important if there is a lawsuit.
10. Remember to consider the nature of the employment.

    Is the employee going to enter customer's homes?
    Is the employee going to have access to a passkey?

Source: Courtesy of Lynn M. Forsythe, © Lynn M. Forsythe 2010

INDEMNIFICATION

When a master pays a third person under *respondeat superior* for injuries caused by the servant's unauthorized acts, the master is entitled to *indemnification* (the right to be repaid) from the servant. Unlike most other theories, *respondeat superior* is not based on the fault of the master; it only creates legal liability for the master. The master

Exhibit 30.2

Master's Liability

Type of Liability	Proof Necessary	Examples
Direct Liability	The elements of the tort	Negligent Hiring; Negligent Promotion; Negligent Retention; Negligence in Instructing Worker; Negligence in Maintaining the Premises or Equipment
Vicarious Liability	Worker was a servant; worker committed a tort (including the elements of the tort); the tort was in the course and scope of the job	*Respondeat Superior*

should be entitled to recover from the person who caused the loss—the servant—so the law permits reimbursement. As a practical matter, the master generally will have insurance to cover the liability he or she incurred. Remember that the servant normally will not have sufficient funds to cover the liability either to the victim or to the master. If the servant is still employed by the master, the master may be able to withhold part of the reimbursement from each paycheck until the master is completely repaid. Continuing to employ the servant, however, may increase the likelihood that the master will be liable for any similar wrongs by the servant in the future under *respondeat superior* or negligent retention.

Sometimes a servant may be held liable to the third person due to the commission of a tort, but the servant may then be entitled to indemnification from the master.[9] The servant's right to indemnification will depend on the particular facts of the case. Such cases are based either on contract law or on the law of restitution.[10] Courts are influenced by what they believe to be just, considering the business and the nature of the particular relationship between the master and the servant.[11] Under the *Restatement*, a servant is entitled to indemnification *if* the servant, at the direction of the master, commits an act that constitutes a tort but the servant believes that the act is not tortious.[12] In other words, the servant must act in good faith. Obviously, if a servant completes a task that he or she knows to be illegal or tortious, the servant is not entitled to indemnification.[13]

Exhibit 30.3 illustrates the relationships among the primary parties when the servant commits a tort. The servant's right to indemnification is questionable because the courts require that the servant follow the master's instructions in good faith before receiving indemnification. The master's *right* to indemnification is established by law. The master's ability to collect, however, is questionable because, realistically, many servants cannot afford to reimburse the master.

Exhibit 30.3

The Legal Relationships Under *Respondeat Superior*

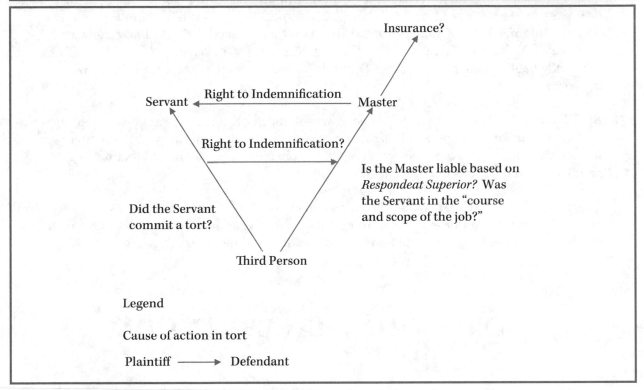

Source: Courtesy of Lynn M. Forsythe, © Lynn M. Forsythe 2010

ANALYSIS OF A SERVANT'S TORTS

To characterize a tort situation, one should answer the following questions:

- Was the person acting as a servant for the hiring party?
- Did the servant commit a tort?
- Was the servant acting within the course and scope of the job?
- Is the servant entitled to indemnification from the master? Is the master entitled to indemnification from the servant?

Remember that the servant is ultimately the one who is liable for the tort, unless he or she is entitled to indemnification from the master. The master may also be liable in his or her own right.

eClass 30.3 Management

COMPANY CD BURNERS AND COMPUTERS

eClass is considering the purchase of a CD burner to produce promotional materials for the company. Ani recently read an article about CD burners being used to copy music or videos from the Internet. In 2001, more blank CDs were sold than prerecorded CDs. Entertainer Sheryl Crow calls CD burning "shoplifting."[14] Ani is concerned that eClass might be held civilly or criminally liable if employees use its CD burner to make unauthorized copies. What will you tell her?

BUSINESS CONSIDERATIONS List some of the inappropriate ways that employees could use computer equipment. What can a business do to minimize its risk that employees will use CD burners and other computer equipment in inappropriate ways? What policies and practices should the business establish?

ETHICAL CONSIDERATIONS What should eClass do if it discovers that its employees are burning music and/or video CDs on its equipment? What is its moral duty? What is the ethical perspective of people who burn CDs of music from the Internet? Why?

INJURY TO THE SERVANT ON THE JOB

Courts generally use the terms *employer* and *employee* when discussing injuries on the job, so we will use the same terminology here. An employer has a duty to provide employees with a reasonably safe place to work and reasonably safe equipment to use at work. Both the place and equipment should be appropriate to the nature of the employment. For example, some places—such as college classrooms—are relatively safe. Other places, like submarines, drilling platforms, and coal mines[15] are likely to be dangerous under the best of circumstances. If the workplace is not safe, the employer should warn employees about unsafe conditions that the employees may not discover even if they are reasonably careful.[16]

Although courts *sometimes* apply similar rules to employees and independent contractors, there are distinct differences in their legal relationships. Nevertheless, courts have, on occasion, allowed independent contractors to recover for injuries sustained on the job.[17]

Under the common law, if an employee is hurt at work, the employer can utilize a number of defenses to avoid an obligation to the employee. Negligence by the employee and the employee's assumption of the known risk are two such defenses. For example, the employee might have been driving a truck too fast for icy road conditions, or the employee might not have been wearing safety goggles provided by the employer. Assumption of the risk, contributory negligence, and its modern counterpart—comparative negligence—are discussed in detail in Chapter 6.

Sometimes the work itself may be inherently dangerous.[18] Some states are reluctant to apply assumption of the risk to bar recovery by injured employees; however, other states are not reluctant to do so.[19] Assumption of the risk can be used as a defense by both the employer and by a third person who may have created the hazardous situation. For example, in one case James Lee Crews, a gas line repairman with over 20 years experience, was injured by an explosion while he was helping repair a gas leak. He sued the worker from another company who hit the gas line causing the leak. The court decided that Crews voluntarily assumed a known risk and barred his recovery.[20] Some states have a "firefighter's rule"[21] that has the same effect as assumption of the risk, it bars suits by firefighters, peace officers, and/or other emergency professionals seeking to recover for on-the-job injuries.[22] The employer also may have a duty to warn the employee if the danger is not commonly known, but the employer knows or should know of the risk inherent in the job.[23]

At common law, the *fellow employee doctrine* also acts to bar recovery by the employee. Traditionally, this concept was called the *fellow servant doctrine*. More recent court cases and treatises call it the fellow employee doctrine. Under this theory, an employee cannot recover damages for work-related injuries if the damages are caused by another employee of the same employer. Like assumption of the risk, this doctrine acts as a complete bar to recovery. This rule is applicable to many worksite accidents. Most of the time when an employee is injured on the job, the injury is caused not by the employer but by another employee at the job site. One justification suggested for this doctrine is that the employer is often remote from the worksite. The employee, on the other hand, is likely to know of hazards at work and to know of careless fellow employees. Another justification used to support this doctrine is that an employee "assumes the risk" of being injured by co-workers.

Assumption of the risk, contributory negligence, and the fellow employee doctrine combined to prevent injured workers from recovering. They were so effective in this regard that they were nicknamed the "three wicked sisters."[24] Their combined effect encouraged the development of state worker's compensation statutes. These theories are summarized in Exhibit 30.4.

Worker's Compensation

Under worker's compensation statutes, payments are made to injured workers for injuries suffered on the job. Generally, these statutes do not apply common law defenses mentioned in the last section. In some states particular types of workers

Exhibit 30.4

Common Law Defenses Available to an Employer When Sued for Work Related Injuries

Legal Defense	Consequence
Contributory negligence of the injured employee*	Bars recovery
Comparative negligence of the injured employee*	Reduces recovery
Assumption of the risk by the injured employee	Bars recovery
Fellow Employee Doctrine (Fellow Servant Doctrine)	Bars recovery

Source: Courtesy of Lynn M. Forsythe, © Lynn M. Forsythe 2010

* The state will use either the contributory negligence or comparative negligence approach.

are not covered under the worker's compensation statutes.[25] For example, in New Mexico agricultural workers are not covered under the state statute.[26]

Worker's compensation statutes may seem to be the opposite extreme of the common law doctrines. They are not based on the fault of the employer, and the employer's negligence need not be shown in court. The worker only needs to show that his or her injury was caused in the course and scope of the job. In many states, the policies underlying these statutes are to "provide prompt and limited compensation benefits for job-related injuries and to facilitate the employee's speedy return to employment without regard to fault."[27] In other words, these statutes are intended to be "economic insurance" for workers. These statutes exist in most states and provide for a fixed schedule of compensation for listed injuries. Moreover, workers can easily determine how much they are entitled to receive. Therefore, this procedure allows for the quick settlement of claims and discourages many lawsuits. When worker's compensation statutes are applied, the statute generally provides the exclusive remedy for the worker. In other words, legal action against the employer based on other theories is prohibited. This is often called the *exclusivity requirement.*

State statutes vary in format. Some states have organized a fund to which the employers contribute; and injured employees collect from the fund. Some states allow employers to purchase insurance or to establish their own funds. In most states, the employee is allowed to recover even if he or she was negligent in causing the injury, assumed the risk, or was injured by a fellow employee. The injured employee generally receives compensation according to a schedule of payments, depending on the type of disability and how long the employee is unable to work. Worker's compensation statutes vary in the following respects:

- Some cover only major industrial occupations.
- Some exclude small shops with few employees.
- Some exclude injuries caused intentionally by the employer or other workers.

Because of the variations, it is important to examine the particular statute at issue.

If the worker's compensation statute does not apply, generally the employee will be permitted to sue based on common law theories. (Worker's compensation is also discussed in Chapter 38.)

Contemporary Case

DRURY v. HARRIS VENTURES, INC.

2010 Ga. App. LEXIS 176 (Ga. App. 3rd Div. 2010)

FACTS Theresa Drury's husband called Harris Ventures, Inc. d/b/a Brunswick Staff Zone (Staff Zone) requesting two workers to help his wife pull weeds in their yard. The husband emphasized that the workers needed to be suitable for working in the yard with his wife at home alone. No one was available. The next day the husband called again, and Staff Zone identified Holmes and his brother for the job, describing them as "trustworthy." That day Staff Zone had the men fill out employment applications in which they denied having any criminal convictions, medical conditions, mental illnesses, or disabilities. They were then sent to work for Drury. Holmes purposely failed to disclose to Staff Zone that he had been diagnosed with and treated for schizophrenia since 1985 and that he had not been taking his prescription medicine. While working for Drury, Holmes

became agitated and annoyed at her. He eventually attacked her from behind, grabbed her throat, pinned her to the ground, and moved up and down on her in a sexual manner as she lay face down. Holmes's brother pulled Holmes off of Drury, who called her husband. The police were also notified, and Holmes pled guilty to the crime of aggravated assault.

ISSUES Is Staff Zone liable to Drury under *respondeat superior*? Is Staff Zone liable for negligently hiring Holmes?

HOLDINGS No, there is no *respondeat superior* because Holmes was not in the scope of employment. No, Staff Zone is not liable for negligent hiring.

REASONING Excerpts from the opinion of Judge Doyle:

Theresa Drury appeals from the grant of summary judgment . . . as to her claims for negligent hiring and *respondeat superior* ... [W]e affirm [the decision of the trial court]. ...

> Two elements must be present to render a master liable for his servant's actions under *respondeat superior*: first, the servant must be in furtherance of the master's business; and, second, he must be acting within the scope of his master's business. If a tort is committed by an employee not by reason of the employment, but because of matters disconnected therewith, the employer is not liable. Furthermore, if a tortious act is committed not in furtherance of the employer's business, but rather for purely personal reasons disconnected from the authorized business of the master, the master is not liable. Summary judgment for the master is appropriate where the evidence shows that the servant was not engaged in furtherance of his master's business but was on a private enterprise of his own. The question of whether the servant ... was acting in the prosecution of his master's business and in the scope of his employment is for determination by the jury, except in plain and indisputable cases. ...

There is evidence in the record that suggests that the attack occurred as Holmes grew more and more aggravated with Drury's critique of his work or work ethic. ... Holmes ... responded to Drury's criticism with violence; we hold that this conduct plainly and indisputably was not in the scope of his employment or in furtherance of Staff Zone's business. ... [T]o the extent that Holmes's attack can be characterized as sexual, "Georgia courts have consistently held that an employer cannot be held liable under *respondeat superior* for an employee's sexual misconduct when the alleged acts were not taken in furtherance of the employer's business and were outside the scope of employment." ... Holmes was a temporary day laborer without management authority and not charged with responding to customer complaints. It is undisputed that Holmes's violence was a result of his schizophrenia, and based on his role as a laborer assigned to pull weeds, the personal attack was in no way a part of his employment or in furtherance of Staff Zone's business. ...

"[A] defendant employer has a duty to exercise ordinary care not to hire or retain an employee the employer knew or should have known posed a risk of harm to others where it is reasonably foreseeable from the employee's tendencies or propensities that the employee could cause the type of harm sustained by the plaintiff." ... "[T]he relevant question is whether [Staff Zone] knew or in the exercise of ordinary care should have known that [Holmes] ... was unsuitable for that position because he posed a reasonably foreseeable risk of personal harm to [people in Drury's position.]" ... Staff Zone inquired in its written application whether Holmes had been convicted of a crime, whether he suffered from mental illness, whether he had been treated by a psychologist, whether he had been treated for any mental condition, and whether there were any disabilities which might affect his performance. ... Holmes ... did not answer the mental illness questions truthfully, and he concealed his schizophrenia diagnosis and treatment to obtain employment. There is no evidence that Holmes had any prior violent outbursts or prior behavioral problems while working. ... [T]he evidence in the record is plain, palpable, and undisputable that Staff Zone did not know, nor reasonably should it have known, of Holmes's mental illness or tendency toward violence while untreated. ... To require an employer to independently verify each area of possible error on the application would render employment decisions in even the most basic settings untenably fraught with potential liability. . . . "Whether or not an employer's investigative efforts were sufficient to fulfill its duty of ordinary care is dependent upon the unique facts of each case," . . . [I]n this case, dealing with temporary day laborers sent to pull weeds at a residence, Staff Zone's reliance on information written in an employment application was not negligent, particularly where there is no evidence that Holmes acted erratically prior to the attack on Drury. . . .

You Be the Judge

Bush Hog manufactured a posthole digger in 1989, which consisted of an auger blade, gear box, and boom. The digger was designed to be attached to and powered by a tractor. Robert Colmore purchased the used posthole digger in Tennessee and brought it to a ranch he rented and operated in Montana. Colmore asked Douglas Forgey to help him by doing some fencing work on the ranch. He gave Forgey the Bush Hog posthole digger and a tractor to use for the work. While using the posthole digger on September 14, 2000, Forgey became entangled in the auger blade. Forgey died as a result of the entanglement. Forgey's widow filed a worker's compensation claim. However, Colmore was not enrolled in the worker's compensation program at the time, so the Montana Uninsured Employers Fund paid her claims. Colmore argued that Forgey was a "casual employee" and that Coleman was not required to have worker's compensation. In *Colmore v. Uninsured Employers' Fund*, 2005 MT 339 (Sup. Ct. 2005), the Supreme Court concluded that he was required to have worker's compensation insurance. Forgey's widow then filed a lawsuit against Colmore and others alleging that they were negligent and negligent per se for providing Forgey with unsafe equipment. Colmore admitted that he was negligent and settled this case with Forgey's widow. Colmore seeks contribution and/or indemnification from Bush Hog, the manufacturer of the digger. Under Montana law, contribution and indemnification both shift the loss. The right to contribution is established by statute and proportions the loss among joint tortfeasors relative to their fault. The right to indemnity is an equitable right. The right to indemnification is an all or nothing proposition because it shifts the total cost to the other party. Is Colmore entitled to sue Bush Hog for contribution or indemnity? If *you* were the judge, how would *you* decide this dispute? [See *State Farm Fire and Casualty Company v. Bush Hog, LLC*, 2009 MT 349, 2009 Mont. LEXIS 500 (Sup. Ct. 2009).]

Summary

A servant is liable for his or her own tortious and criminal acts. The fact that the servant was working at the time is immaterial. The fact that the master may also be liable to the third person is irrelevant as well.

A master may be liable for the acts of his or her servants. Much of this liability is based on the doctrine of *respondeat superior*. A master is liable for the torts committed by a servant if the servant was acting within the course and scope of the employment. The courts have discussed many policy reasons for enforcing *respondeat superior*. These include: masters are encouraged to be careful in selecting servants; masters are encouraged to be careful in supervising servants; liability is a necessary expense of conducting business; the master is benefiting from the servant's acts; the master can purchase liability insurance; the master has control; and the master can better afford these costs.

Numerous factors are used in analyzing what activity is "within the course and scope of the employment." There is no formula, however. Courts look at the factors and determine if *respondeat superior* should be applied. Even when a court

holds a master liable to the third person under *respondeat superior*, this does not mean that the master necessarily will bear the ultimate loss. The master generally will be entitled to indemnification from the servant, although such indemnification may not be practical. The master may also have purchased insurance for this risk.

In rare cases, the master may owe the servant the duty to reimburse the servant for money he or she paid to third persons. A master may also be held directly liable if he or she commits a tort or a crime; this liability is not based on *respondeat superior*. It includes situations in which a master directs a servant to commit a crime or tort or is negligent in selecting or retaining a servant.

The employer owes the employee various duties, some of which were discussed in Chapter 28. The employer has a duty to provide a reasonably safe place to work. At a minimum this includes furnishing appropriate tools and equipment, adherence to safety regulations, and proper supervision. Injuries to employees on the job are normally covered by worker's compensation statutes. State statutes vary as to who is covered, the amount of compensation, and how funds are collected for the payments.

Discussion Questions

1. David hires Annabelle as a housekeeper. Her main duties are to remain in the house and clean, prepare meals, and do the laundry. One afternoon, Annabelle receives a call from One-Day Drycleaners. David's suit is ready to be picked up. Annabelle decides to go and get the suit in her car. On the way back to David's home, she runs a red light and hits Julie's car. The police officer at the scene says that Annabelle's intoxication is the main cause of the accident. Annabelle had a few drinks with her lunch. David knew that Annabelle had a drinking problem when he

hired her and that she is trying to stop drinking. Who is responsible for the damage to Julie's car, and why?

2. Ani Yasuda pays to have the eClass company name, logo, and phone numbers painted on her brother's truck, even though Sam does not work for eClass. One day while driving to his job after class, Sam is involved in a traffic accident with another driver, Erin. Can Erin successfully sue eClass, claiming that Sam is advertising for the firm?

3. Beatrice owns three car dealerships—Toyota, Chevrolet, and Honda—which are located at the major intersection of College Avenue and Main Street. The Chevrolet dealership is located north of College Avenue and faces College Avenue. The Honda and Toyota dealerships are located on the south of College Avenue and face Main Street. Her sales force is authorized to sell vehicles at any of the dealerships. Sales people and clients often jaywalk across College Avenue. Repair people also jaywalk across the street. If potential clients are hit by a car travelling on College Avenue, who would be liable and why? If her servants are injured while jaywalking, who would be liable? Why?

4. Joe's Pizza Parlor advertises that their pizza will arrive at the customer's home hot and tasty within 30 minutes. Their television and radio commercials promise customers that if the pizza does not arrive within 30 minutes of ordering, the pizza will be free. The drivers have the primary responsibility for timely delivery. If a driver delivers more than one late pizza a week, he or she must pay for the additional pizzas from his or her paycheck. The delivery area is limited to a 20-mile radius from Joe's. Drivers are responsible for late delivery, even when the kitchen is busy. During busy periods, like Monday night football games, the pizzas are sometimes boxed 20 minutes after the placement of the order. Drivers compensate by driving fast to abide by the guarantee. Under the work contract, drivers supply their own vehicles and their own automobile insurance. Who is responsible if one of Joe's drivers has an accident? Why? What changes in policy could be implemented to reduce the likelihood of an accident?

5. Some employers ask applicants questions that may violate federal or state law. For example, an employer may mention his or her own children and ask the applicant if he or she has any children. An employer may ask what educational degrees the applicant has and where and when they were earned in order to calculate approximate age. What are the advantages and disadvantages of these inquiries to the employer? What about to the society at large? Assume that the employer is using this information to discriminate against parents or older people. What is the moral perspective of the employer?

Case Problems and Writing Assignments

1. Paul Brierly was a co-op student attending Shelby County Vocational School, and he was working with Alusuisse under the supervision of David Ellison. Alusuisse manufactures materials for packaging and labeling foods and medicines. The printing press components gradually develop a buildup. The workers eliminate the buildup by disassembling the components and running them through a "large-parts washing machine." The washing machine was similar to a dishwasher, but the cleaning solutions used had low flash points and were highly flammable. Three days before the accident, the seal on the main pump of the parts washing machine broke and flammable solvent leaked. An employee shut the washer down. Employees took a number of precautions to minimize the possibility of a fire hazard. Before welding, Alusuisse took additional safety measures including: "(1) water was placed in the pit below the machine so as to prevent sparks from igniting any dried solvent residue left behind from the leaking pump; and (2) welding blankets were placed on and around the filter basket housing and parts washing machine." The lead maintenance man, Reinhold Ritzi, decided that he would do the welding because he had more experience. Wordlow, Ellison, and Ritzi apparently believed that the parts washing room had been monitored with the "LEL" meter, a device which is used to measure the "lowest explosive limit" of solvent vapor in an area before a flammable source, like a welder, is introduced. The meter had not been used. Each of the men involved stated that they had assumed that one of the others had obtained the readings. A "fire watch" crew was assembled. Wordlow and other maintenance crew members, including Brierly, stood by with fire extinguishers watching for stray sparks that could ignite a fire. Brierly, the least experienced member of the crew, was almost 12 feet away from the welding site, further away than any of the other crew members. A spark ignited solvent fumes inside the parts washing machine, causing an explosion. The explosion blew off the steel door of the parts washing machine, and the door struck Brierly, resulting in his death. Wordlow, Ritzi, and one other worker also suffered injuries. Can Brierly's administrator proceed with a tort action against Alusuisse and Ellison? [See *Brierly v. Alusuisse Flexible Packaging, Inc.*, 1999 U.S. App. LEXIS 11927 (6th Cir. 1999).]

2. Owen Hart was a 33-year-old wrestler with the World Wrestling Federation (WWF), wrestling under the name "Blue Blazer." He was fatally injured at a pay-for-view event called "Over the Edge," sponsored by WWF. He was being lowered from the ceiling into the ring by a guy wire when the mishap occurred. He fell about 50 feet hitting his head. The exact cause of the accident is under investigation. Some theories include that he was never properly connected to the harness; the harness malfunctioned; the harness may have caught on the feathers of Hart's costume; or Hart may have released it too soon. Hart was not trained as a stunt man. Thousands of fans in the arena watched the event. Many of them initially thought that it was gag. Robert McCome, a 15-year old spectator, said, "We thought it was a doll at first. We thought they were just playing with us. We were really shocked when we found out that it was no joke."

Vince McMahon, WWF owner, vowed that this particular stunt will not be repeated by any WWF performer, but he has not ruled out other dangerous stunts. "In its quest for higher ratings and its competition with WCW [World Championship Wrestling],[28] the WWF has 'raised the bar' with more dangerous stunts."[29] A memorial to Owen Hart was taped by WWF.

This case poses a multitude of questions and issues, including the following: Was Owen Hart a servant or an independent contractor in this case? Does an accidental death such as this encourage or discourage attendance at future events? Is it ethical to ask servants to perform dangerous stunts for the purpose of notoriety, ratings, and selling tickets? Are these performers being respected as individuals or are they being used merely as a means to greater profit? [See Kia Shant'e Breaux, "Wrestler Hart Dies in Plunge at Arena," *Fresno Bee*, May 24, 1999, p. A8; Nova Pierson, "Wrestler Falls to Death: WWF Star Owen Hart Killed in Ring Accident," *Toronto Sun*, May 24, 1999, Sports p. 5 (Sun Media); M.L. Curly, "Pro Wrestling: McMahon: Stunts Like Hart's Won't Be Repeated," *Detroit News*, May 28, 1999, Sports, p. F2.]

Postscript

In 2010, Owen Hart's widow, Martha Hart filed a lawsuit against Vince and Linda McMahon and the WWE, the successor to WWF. She is alleging that they are continuing to use Owen's name and likeness to promote WWE without permission. Martha claims that she is trying to protect her children from exposure to WWE and the manner in which their father died. [See Brian Fritz, "Martha Hart Files Lawsuit Against McMahons, WWE," 6/22/2010, http://www.fanhouse.com/2010/06/22/martha-hart-files-lawsuit-against-mcmahons-wwe/?icid=main|htmlws-main-n|dl1|link4|http%3A%2F%2Fwww.fanhouse.com%2F2010%2F06%2F22%2Fmartha-hart-files-lawsuit-against-mcmahons-wwe%2F (accessed 6/23/10).]

3. Donna Ivy was a bus driver in the City of Visalia. On September 25, 2000, around noon, Jerry William Knight hijacked the bus she was driving and raped her at knife point. Knight has been sentenced to 89 years in prison for the crime. Ivy has filed suit against the City because the silent alarm on the city-owned bus malfunctioned. The alarm was supposed to activate "Call Police" signs on the front and rear of the bus, sound a loud ringer in the dispatcher's office, and flash the bus number on a small screen in the dispatcher's office. The "Call Police" signs went on, but the ringer in the dispatcher's office did not. Ivy contends that if the alarm system worked properly she would have been rescued. (A cell phone user did eventually call police after seeing the "Call Police" sign from the rear of the bus.) Ivy is suing the City because it owns the bus

system. The City contends that it is not liable since bus drivers are not city employees and the alarm system is the responsibility of Laidlaw Transportation, Inc., the independent contractor that manages and maintains the bus system. The City alleges that Ivy chose to sue the City because Ivy is receiving temporary disability checks from the worker's compensation system and that Ivy cannot sue Laidlaw, her employer. Should Ivy win? Who is responsible for providing Ivy with a safe work place? Is this a nondelegable duty? [See Lewis Griswold, "Raped City Bus Driver Sues Visalia Over Alarm," *The Fresno Bee*, July 13, 2002, p. B4.]

Notes

1. *Restatement (Third) of Agency* (Philadelphia: American Law Institute, 2006), § 7.07.
2. *Pacific Mutual Life Insurance Co. v. Haslip*, 111 S. Ct. 1032 (1991).
3. The *Restatement (Third) of Agency* uses more general terms and does not include a list of factors. However, the factors from the *Restatement (Second)* are precedents in a number of states. Some states are continuing to use them. *Restatement (Third) of Agency*, § 7.07, comment b, as cited in Edward Moomjian & Elizabeth Wolnick, "Raising the Stakes: Corporate Liability for Employees' Private Acts," footnote 29, USLAW Employment Law Section Update (2008), http://www.udalllaw.com/News/raising_the_stakes.pdf (accessed 9/30/2010).
4. *Restatement (Second) of Agency* (Philadelphia: American Law Institute, 1958), § 228(1).
5. Ibid., § 229(2).
6. Ibid., § 229(2)(b).
7. There are exceptions to the general rule about commuting, such as when the servant is running an errand for the master or the servant is a travelling sales person who travels a significant part of the time.
8. See *Tallahassee Furniture Co. v. Harrison*, 583 So. 2d 744, 1991 Fla. App. LEXIS 7598 (Fla. App. 1st Dist. 1991). The Florida Supreme Court denied the petition for review in *Tallahassee Furniture Co. v. Harrison*, 595 So. 2d 558, 1992 Fla. LEXIS 152 (1992).
9. We are continuing to use the *master/servant* terminology in this section; however, the *Restatement (Second) of Agency* uses *agent/principal* terminology in its discussion.
10. Warren A. Seavey, *Handbook of the Law of Agency* (St. Paul, MN: West, 1964), § 168, p. 265.
11. *Restatement (Second) of Agency*, supra note 4, at § 438(2)(b).
12. Ibid., § 439(c) and Comment on Clause (c).
13. Harold Gill Reuschlein & William A. Gregory, *Hornbook on the Law of Agency and Partnership*, 2d ed. (St. Paul, MN: West, 1990), § 89(B), pp. 151-52.
14. In 2001, 1.1 billion blank CDs were sold compared to 968 million prerecorded CDs. See Steve Morse, "CD Burning Protests Still Fall on Deaf Ears," *Fresno Bee*, May 5, 2002, pp. H1 and H2.
15. On July 24, 2002, nine coal miners were trapped in a mine near Somerset, Pennsylvania, when they accidentally broke through the wall of a nearby mine. Fortunately, this time the miners were all rescued. See Judy Lin, "Rescuers Bring Coal Miners to Safety," *Las Vegas Review-Journal*, July 28, 2002, Newsline Second Front Page, pp. 3A and 7A.
16. *Restatement (Second) of Agency*, § 492.
17. *Rodney v. U.S.*, No. 77-4028 (9th Cir. 1980); *Cioll v. Bechtel Corp.*, No. 733794 (San Francisco City Super. Ct., April 23, 1981).
18. Many of the professional and volunteer rescue workers from the 9/11 disaster at the World Trade Center Twin Towers are suffering from some form of respiratory problems. Workers at the site and residents of the area have been exposed to pollutants that are harmful if inhaled, such as asbestos, lead, mercury, and pulverized glass. See Richard Perez-Pena, "Cleaning Set for Exteriors Near 9/11 Site," *New York Times*, April 6, 2002, p. B1, and Margaret Ramirez, "WTC Clinic Opens; Clinton Urges $90 M More for Initiative," *Newsday, Inc.*, August 6, 2002.
19. According to the *Restatement (Second) of Agency*, § 499, absent a statute to the contrary, an employer is *not* legally liable to an employee who is injured by a risk that is inherent in the work.
20. *Crews v. Hollenbach*, 358 Md. 627, 2000 Md. LEXIS 245 (Ct. of App. 2000).

21. It is also called the fireman's rule.

22. The firefighter's rule generally prevents tort recovery for firefighters and police officers who are accidentally injured by accidents within the type normally anticipated by the job. For example, the rule prevents firefighters from suing the individuals who negligently caused the fire requiring the firefighters to arrive on the scene to fight the fire. The South Carolina Supreme Court refused to adopt such a rule. See "S. Carolina High Court Rejects Firefighter's Rule," *National Law Journal*, June 3, 2002, Case, Vol. 24, No. 38, p. B4.

23. *Restatement (Second) of Agency* § 499, Comment c.

24. Bryan A. Garner, *Black's Law Dictionary*, 7th edition (St. Paul: West, 1999), p. 1490.

25. For example, see Cal. Lab Code § 3352 (2001) for a listing of people not considered employees under California Worker's Compensation law.

26. See 52-1-6 Application of Provisions of Act, Part A, of the New Mexico Statutes Annotated 1978/Chapter 51 Worker's Compensation.

27. *Sussman v. Florida East Coast Properties*, 557 So. 2d 74 (Fla. App. 3 Dist. 1990), p. 75.

28. WCW was the main competition to the WWF, until the WWF purchased it in 2001. WWF is now called World Wrestling Entertainment. "Buy Makes McMahon Invincible—WWF Fightin' Talk Edited by Neil Chandler; Lone Star," *Daily Star*, March 26, 2001, WWF, p. 15, Dave Scherer, "WWF, WCW A TV Tag Team," *Daily News* (New York), June 30, 2001, Sports, p. 56.

29. M.L. Curly, "Pro Wrestling: McMahon: Stunts Like Hart's Won't Be Repeated," *Detroit News*, May 28, 1999, Sports, p. F2.

Business Organizations

S hould the entrepreneur (or small business owner) "go it alone" in a sole proprietorship? If so, the entrepreneur will have both absolute authority and total responsibility. Should a partnership be formed? For many businesses, the simplicity of a partnership makes it an ideal form, but the entrepreneur should be aware that a partnership involves the sharing of management powers and duties. Should a corporation be formed? The corporate form offers a number of advantages, including limited personal liability and the ability to franchise, but corporations are subject to heavy federal regulation and taxation. Limited liability companies also provide limited personal liability for the members, but offer different options for tax treatment.

Part 7 compares and contrasts these main forms of business—proprietorship, partnership, corporation, and limited liability company—by showing the legal steps taken in their formation, operation, and termination. In addition, this part discusses variations of these forms, such as limited partnerships and limited liability partnerships. Securities regulation is also addressed.

31

Formation of a Business

Agenda

Ani, Meg, and Yousef realize they have a product—eAccounting—that will have broad appeal. Hence, they need to consider what form of business organization is best for them as owners. They will also want to consider which type of organization will be best for producing, marketing, and distributing this product. Since they are already involved together, should they just form a partnership? What legal implications might arise in such an organization? Should the firm incorporate? If it does, should it "go public," selling stock to investors to help acquire badly needed capital? Would such a sale open the possibility that Ani, Meg, and Yousef may lose control of the business to an outsider? Is there a business form that will allow for outside investment without the fear that investors might take control of management? What benefits are offered by one of the newer forms of organization, an LLP or an LLC? For purposes of Part 7, we will assume that the entrepreneurs are wrestling with these issues.

973

These and other questions will arise as you read this chapter. Be prepared! You never know when the firm or one of its members will seek your advice.

[**NOTE**: Throughout Part 7 the organization form selected by eClass may vary from one eClass problem to the next. This is done to allow you to evaluate the problems presented on the basis of different organizational options. If the facts of a particular case state that eClass has adopted a particular form, answer the questions based on the implications for that particular form. Treat each thread case independently, without reference to the other thread cases or agendas. If no particular form is specified, assume that eClass is operating as a partnership, but the principals are considering the benefits—and the burdens—of changing the structure to another form of business.]

Classic Case

FIRESTONE TIRE & RUBBER COMPANY v. WEBB
207 Ark. 820, 1944 Ark. LEXIS 749 (Ark. 1944)

FACTS D. C. Webb, and his brother, Truett Webb, signed and delivered a financial statement to Firestone Tire & Rubber Company (appellant) which read: "For the purpose of obtaining merchandise from Firestone Tire & Rubber Company, on credit, we make the following statement in writing, intending that your company should rely thereon respecting our financial condition as of February 15, 1940." It was followed by financial details showing a net worth of $ 9,550; and was signed: "Firm name, Truett Webb. Date signed, 2/15, 1940, by Truett Webb, D. C. Webb." The Firestone Tire & Rubber Company immediately commenced shipments as ordered, charging the shipments to "D. C. and Truett Webb." The account continued until January 21, 1942, at which time Firestone claimed a balance due and unpaid of $379.98. Firestone filed suit against Truett Webb and D. C. Webb for this

amount. Truett Webb was in the United States Army, and, as to him, the case was continued under the Soldiers and Sailors Civil Relief Act. D. C. Webb unsuccessfully sought a continuance because of Truett Webb's military service. Then D. C. Webb admitted his signature on the financial statement, but claimed that he signed only to show his financial worth for one note of $500, long since paid to Firestone.

ISSUE Is D.C. Webb liable to Firestone on the theory of partnership by estoppel?

HOLDING Yes, D.C. Webb is liable on the debt.

REASONING Excerpts from the opinion of Justice McFaddin:

. . . It was admitted by D. C. Webb that he and Truett Webb each signed the financial statement. This financial statement read: "Firm name, Truett Webb." The words "firm name" have in this case— in the absence of any corporate status—the same meaning as "partnership name." Ballentine's *Law*

Dictionary . . . says of "firm name," "the name adopted by a partnership under which it transacts its business. Such a name may be the name of one or all the members of the firm, or it may be a fictitious name." . . . Webster's *New International Dictionary* says of "firm": "The name, title or style under which a company transacts business; the firm name; hence, a partnership of two or more persons;" and listed as synonyms are: "company, house, partnership." Bouvier's *Law Dictionary* . . . says: "Firm. The persons composing a partnership, taken collectively. The name or title under which the members of a partnership transact business. The word is used as synonymous with partnership. The words 'house,' 'concern,' and 'company' are also used in the same sense." . . . So we hold that when D. C. Webb signed the statement listing the firm name as "Truett Webb," then D. C. Webb said . . . that D. C. Webb and Truett Webb were partners trading under the firm name of "Truett Webb." . . .

[Parol evidence is not admissible to vary the terms of a written instrument.]

The appellant showed that it relied on the truth of the financial statement and the fact that it was signed by D. C. Webb as a partner, and made shipments on the truth of the statement. No claim was made by D. C. Webb that he had ever notified appellant of any revocation of the statement. In [precedents] . . . , we said: "It is well settled in this state that, when a person holds himself out, by word or deed, to another as a partner, and thereby induces him to extend credit to the partnership on the faith of such representation, he cannot shield himself from liability under the partnership. When a person holds himself out as a member of a partnership, anyone dealing with the firm on the faith of such representation is entitled to act on the presumption that the relation

continues until notice of some kind is given of its discontinuance. . . .

In 40 Am. Jur. 179, in discussing partnership liability by estoppel, it is stated:

"It is a thoroughly well-settled rule that persons who are not as between themselves partners, or as between whom there is in fact no legal partnership, may nevertheless become subject to the liabilities of partners, either by holding themselves out as partners to the public and the world generally or to particular individuals, or by knowingly or negligently permitting another person to do so. All persons who hold themselves out, or knowingly permit others to hold them out, to the public as partners, although they are not in partnership, become bound as partners to all who deal with them in their apparent relation."

And in 40 Am. Jur. 180 it is further stated:

"The liability as a partner of a person who holds himself out as a partner, or permits others to do so, is predicated on the doctrine of estoppel and on the policy of the law seeking to prevent frauds on those who lend their money on the apparent credit of those who are held out as partners. One holding himself out as a partner or knowingly permitting himself to be so held out is estopped from denying liability as a partner to one who has extended credit in reliance thereon, although no partnership has in fact existed."

By signing the statement, D. C. Webb became liable as a partner by estoppel to appellant. . . .

SELECTING A BUSINESS FORM

As we will see, no one form of business organization is perfect. Each has some advantages that the others lack; and each has some drawbacks the others avoid. Deciding on the proper form can be one of the most important decisions a businessperson will make. The decision to choose a type of business organization should never be made lightly or automatically. All the "pros" and "cons" for each potential alternative should be weighed carefully before a decision is made. This decision becomes more complex as new business forms are evolving and tax treatment of the various business forms are changing.

Businesses that purchase franchises can operate in any form allowed by state law unless the contract with the franchisor contains restrictions. (Franchise has multiple meanings in the law. In this context, a *franchise* is the right to engage in business using a particular trademark at a particular location or in a particular territory.) Exhibit 31.1 addresses the complexity of forming any particular type of organization.

SOLE PROPRIETORSHIP

The most simple business form is a sole proprietorship, owned and operated by one person. This one person is the boss and there are no other owners to disagree with him or her. It is easy to form a sole proprietorship. On the other hand, there is no one else to contribute expertise, knowledge, or capital to the business. The sole proprietor can hire agents and servants to assist with the enterprise. The enterprise is highly dependent on the sole proprietor and the business will end when the sole proprietor dies or becomes incapacitated.

Exhibit 31.1

Complexity of Business Forms

Complexity Continuum[a]

Sole Proprietorship	Partnership	Limited Liability[b] Company (LLC)	Limited Partnership[b] & Limited Liability Partnership	Corporation

[a] This continuum illustrates in general the relative complexity associated with forming and operating a business in a particular form.

[b] In given situations, these two categories may be reversed.

PARTNERSHIPS

The Development of Partnerships

The partnership form of business organization can be traced back to ancient Babylon, and perhaps it is even older. It was widely used by the Romans during the height of the Roman Empire. In fact, Roman merchants introduced the partnership throughout Europe as they conducted trade with the peoples conquered by the Romans. England adopted and modified the Roman partnership. The English utilized it in the development of the British Empire, including the colonies in North America that later became the United States. The United States followed the English common law of partnerships for quite some time. Partnership law in the United States, however, has now been codified. Much of the codification has occurred under the leadership of the National Conference of Commissioners on Uniform State Laws (NCCUSL). NCCUSL prepares uniform acts that it encourages state legislatures to adopt. Depending on the state, the controlling law today for general partnerships is found in the Uniform Partnership Act (UPA)[1] or the Revised Uniform Partnership Act (RUPA).[2] In 1997 the NCCUSL amended RUPA to include limited liability for partners in registered limited liability partnerships.

As partnership law continues to evolve, there are a number of significant changes. RUPA has moved away from viewing the partnership as an aggregate of the partners to viewing it as a separate entity. This is called an *entity approach* and is expressly stated in RUPA § 201. Consequently the partnership can sue and be sued in the partnership name.[3] Under RUPA partnership property is owned in the partnership name. A partner has his or her partnership interest, but is not a co-owner of specific partnership property.[4] RUPA has also changed some of the dissolution rules. A dissolution no longer occurs every time a partner leaves. Generally, a partnership can buy the interest of the partner who leaves.[5] RUPA also provides for conversion and merger of partnerships.[6] For example, a partnership can convert from one type of a partnership to another type. "Partnerships based upon aggregate theory are simply more fragile than partnerships based upon entity theory."[7] RUPA also permits, but does not require, the filing of statements when the partnership is formed, dissolved, merged with another partnership, or there are limitations on partnership authority.[8] Other sections of RUPA explicitly state rules that were implicit in the UPA, or build on provisions in the Revised Uniform Limited Partnership Act (RULPA), which is discussed later in this chapter.[9]

Partnerships are formed for a variety of reasons. Many professionals, for example, enter partnerships because they are not allowed to incorporate under some state laws. (In the sense used here, a *professional* is a member of a "learned profession," such as an accountant, a doctor, or a lawyer.) Some people enter partnerships to avoid the technical steps and expense required to form a corporation. (A *corporation* is an artificial person or legal entity created by or under the authority of a state or nation. It is owned by a group of persons known as stockholders or shareholders.) Other people form partnerships because it seems appropriate, sometimes without giving the matter serious consideration.

A partnership has many of the best features of the other major types of business organizations—sole proprietorships, limited partnerships, corporations, and limited liability companies—but also some of the worst features. A partnership is relatively easy to form, and the formation is normally informal. Like a corporation, a partnership may have a wider financial base than a proprietorship. And like a corporation, the partnership has more expertise from which to draw. A partnership can be formed by a simple, oral agreement by two or more people. On the other extreme, it can be very complex with multiple levels of partners with various rights and obligations for the parties at each level.

One disadvantage to a partnership is that it is not "perpetual" as a corporation may be. A partnership will dissolve eventually. Also, the partners face unlimited personal liability for business-related conduct, as does a proprietor. Shareholders in a corporation, in contrast, have limited liability.

Exhibit 31.2 compares the different types of business organizations.

Exhibit 31.2

A Comparison of Different Types of Business Organizations

Attribute	Proprietorship	Partnership	Limited Partnership (L.P.)[a]
Creation	Proprietor opens the business, subject to state and local licensing laws and regulations.	Partners enter into an agreement, either orally or in writing; no formalities are required.	Partners enter into a partnership agreement and file a written form designating the limited partners and the general partners.
Termination	Proprietor closes the business; death, insanity, or bankruptcy of the owner also terminates the business.	Partners agree to dissolve the partnership; death, bankruptcy, or withdrawal of any partner also dissolves the partnership.[b] The terms of the agreement or a court order may dissolve the partnership. If there is a liquidation of the assets after a dissolution, the business will wind up.	Partners follow same procedure as for a partnership, except the assets will be distributed in a different priority in case of a dissolution and liquidation of the business. The death, bankruptcy, or withdrawal of a limited partner does not dissolve the partnership.

Exhibit 31.2 Continued

Attribute	Proprietorship	Partnership	Limited Partnership (L.P.)[a]
Taxation[c]	All business profits are taxed as the regular income of the owner; there are no federal income taxes on the business itself.	The business must file a federal tax return, but it is for information only. The income of the business is taxed as regular income to the partners.	The same tax procedure is followed as for a regular, general partnership.
Liability[d]	Proprietor has unlimited personal liability. First, business assets will be used, and then the personal assets of the owner will be used.	Partners have unlimited personal liability. First, business assets will be used, and then the personal assets of the partners. The partners are jointly and severally liable for the debts.	General partners have unlimited personal liability. First, business assets will be used, and then the personal assets of the general partners. The general partners are jointly and severally liable for the debts. Limited partners are only liable to the extent of their capital contribution. Suit can be brought against any partner to enforce his or her promise to make a contribution.[e]
Advantages	Simplicity of creation; complete ownership and control of the firm.	Informality of creation; greater potential for expertise and capital in management (because there is more than one manager).	Somewhat greater flexibility than a general partnership; increased opportunities to raise capital.
Disadvantages	Limited capital; limited expertise; limited existence (when the owner dies, the business terminates).	Limited existence; lack of flexibility; potential liability.	Some rigidity in ownership and decision making; personal liability for general partners; limited existence.
Capital[f]	Angels and venture capitalists generally will not invest in a sole proprietorship unless the proprietor is willing to incorporate.	Capital can be obtained by selling a partnership interest. Angels and venture capitalists generally will not invest in a partnership.	Capital can be obtained by selling a limited partnership interest. Selling of limited partnership interests may be subject to securities laws. Angels and venture capitalists generally will not invest in a partnership.

Exhibit 31.2 Continued

Attribute	Limited Liability Partnership (LLP)	Corporation (Inc.) (Subchapter C or Subchapter S)	Limited Liability Company (LLC)
Creation	Partners enter into a partnership agreement and the partnership files a copy or some other notice with the state.	Parties prepare and file formal legal documents known as articles of incorporation with the state of incorporation; the entity must comply with any relevant state or federal security statutes or regulations.	LLCs may be formed by one or more members. LLCs must file articles of organization with the state government.
Termination	Partners follow same procedure as for a general partnership.	Parties close the business, liquidate all business assets, surrender the corporate charter, and distribute the assets in accordance with state law; termination may also be due to the state revoking the charter.	Statute and/or agreement may limit the term of the LLC. The trend is to allow an LLC to have a perpetual existence. In many states the LLC will be at will unless it is designated a term LLC and the term is set. The LLC may dissolve when a member dies or withdraws depending on state law and the operating agreement.
Taxation	The same tax procedure is followed as for a regular, general partnership.	A normal corporation (Subchapter C corporation) is treated as a separate taxable entity and pays taxes on its profits. Any dividends are also taxed to the stockholders. This is called "double taxation." A Subchapter S corporation, regulated by the IRS, is taxed as if it were a general partnership despite its corporate status. A Subchapter S corporation is treated differently only for federal tax purposes. States may also tax them as partnerships.	Most LLCs can make an election to be taxed as either a corporation or a partnership. The LLC may have different taxation for state and federal purposes.

Exhibit 31.2 Continued

Attribute	Limited Liability Partnership (LLP)	Corporation (Inc.) (Subchapter C or Subchapter S)	Limited Liability Company (LLC)
Liability	Partner is liable without limit for his or her own wrongs and wrongs of people he or she directly supervises; the partner's liability for the wrongs of others is limited to the partner's contribution to the firm.	Stockholders are *not* personally liable for debts of the corporation, so there is limited liability. Stockholders may lose their investment in the corporation if it fails.	All members are liable for association debts only to the extent of their capital contribution(s). A member can be required to pay any capital contribution contractually promised but not paid.
Advantages	Limited liability except for a partner's own wrongs and the wrongs of people he or she directly supervises.	Longevity, including the potential for perpetual existence; potentially unlimited access to capital and to expertise; freely transferrable ownership (this may intentionally be restricted in some corporations); limited personal liability of the owners.	Limited liability for all the members.
Disadvantages	Unlimited liability for partner's own wrongs; only permitted in some states. State law may restrict LLPs to professional groups, such as accountants, dentists, doctors, and lawyers or require professional LLPs to obtain liability insurance.	Double taxation (except for a Subchapter S corporation); much more federal regulation; considerably more state regulation; formality and rigidity of the organization.	LLC statutes vary from state to state. Professionals may not be permitted to form an LLC in some states. There may be limitations on the transferability of shares.[g] Selling interests in an LLC may be subject to state and federal securities regulations. LLCs may have a limited term of existence.

Exhibit 31.2 Continued

Attribute	Limited Liability Partnership (LLP)	Corporation (Inc.) (Subchapter C or Subchapter S)	Limited Liability Company (LLC)
Capital	Capital can be obtained by selling a partnership interest. Generally partnership interests are sold to junior associates in the profession. Angels and venture capitalists generally will not invest in an LLP.	Capital can be obtained by selling shares as long as the sale conforms to the corporation's rules and securities laws. It is easier to raise capital with corporations. Angels and venture capitalists are more comfortable investing in C corporations than most other forms. C corporations can be used for Initial Public Offerings (IPOs).[h] S corporations would have to change to C corporations for an IPO or if it seeks venture capital.	Capital can be obtained by selling memberships in the LLC as long as the sale conforms to the LLC's rules and securities laws. Angels and venture capitalists are becoming more comfortable with LLCs though some would not invest in an entity with pass-through taxation. Some venture capitalists and angel investor groups are organized as LLCs. The LLC would have to change to a corporation for an IPO.

Source: Courtesy of Lynn M. Forsythe, © Lynn M. Forsythe 2010

[a] This column describes limited partnerships under the Revised Uniform Limited Partnership Act (RULPA) after the 1985 amendments.

[b] This applies to partnerships under the Uniform Partnership Act (UPA).

[c] Any change in the business form may result in tax consequences for the business and its owners.

[d] The business person will be liable on any contract he or she guarantees for the entity regardless of whether the entity would normally protect his or her personal assets.

[e] RULPA § 502 (a).

[f] Banks are willing to loan funds to any of these entities if the entity is financially sound and has good prospects for the future. Banks may require a security interest in the venture's assets and/or a loan guarantee from the venture's participants. Angels and venture capitalists only contribute advice and funds if they believe the venture can be successful.

[g] This may also be an advantage.

[h] IPO offerings are influenced by the economy. For example, there were no IPOs in the United States for the last quarter of 2008 and the first quarter of 2009. These are defined as IPOs with at least one U.S. venture capital investor that trades on a U.S. stock exchange. News Release from Thomson Reuters and the National Venture Capital Association, New York, April 1, 2009, "Venture-Backed Exit Market Remains a Concern in the First Quarter; No IPO Activity for Two Consecutive Quarters; First Time on Record," available at the National Venture Capital Association Web site at http://www.nvca.org/.

Partnerships Defined Under the Uniform Partnership Act

Section 6(1) of the Uniform Partnership Act defines a partnership. According to this section, a partnership has five characteristics. It is:

1. An association
2. Of two or more persons
3. To carry on a business
4. As co-owners
5. For profit.

The 16 words in the definition are deceptively simple. In fact, a tremendous amount of interpretation often is involved in fitting an organization into the definition of a partnership. To illustrate the potential problem, we will discuss the terms in the order listed.

An Association The courts have consistently held that a partnership must be entered into voluntarily; that is, no one can be forced to be a partner against his or her will. Thus, *an association* has been interpreted as being "a voluntarily entered association." Being realistic, the courts also realize that people occasionally disagree. The test for voluntariness is the willingness to associate at the time of *creation* of the relationship. Later disagreements will not automatically destroy the partnership. Thus, *an association* means a mutual and unanimous assent to be partners jointly and severally at the time of the agreement.

Of Two or More Persons *Persons* here is interpreted broadly. It means two or more identifiable entities that elect to associate. Each partner may be a human being, a corporation, a partnership, or even a joint venture. (A *joint venture* is an association of two or more persons to carry out a single business enterprise for profit.)

To Carry on a Business The third element of the definition has two separate segments. First, it must be determined whether there is a business. A *business* is defined as any trade, occupation, or profession; so most associations meet this test. Next, it must be determined whether the business is being "carried on." *Carrying on* implies some *continuity.* A business must be fairly permanent and lasting in order to be carried on. If a business appears to be short term, it is quite possible that the court will rule that no partnership exists. If the other elements of a partnership are present, however, the short-term business may qualify as a joint venture instead.

As Co-Owners The fourth element is probably the most important and the most confusing. Co-ownership does not refer to a sharing of title on the assets used in the business. Instead, it refers to a sharing of ownership of the *business itself.* The business is an intangible asset. A business often uses assets of a tangible nature, but it need not own any tangible assets. For example, several accountants may enter a partnership.

The partnership owns a business that provides services, and services are intangible. The accountants may lease an office; they may rent furniture; they may not own a single tangible asset, and yet they co-own a business. How, then, is one to know if people involved in a business are co-owners? The simplest way is to look at the agreement the people made when the business began. If the agreement states that they are partners, or co-owners, of the business, they *are* co-owners. But all too often the agreement is ambiguous, unclear, or oral. In such a situation, the agreement is of no help in resolving the co-ownership question. Then the courts must look beyond the agreement.

The courts normally will look at how the parties treat profits. If the parties share profits, or net returns, there is *prima facie* evidence that a partnership exists—that is, the partnership is presumed to exist unless disproved by evidence to the contrary. The sharing of profits creates a rebuttable presumption that a partnership was formed. (A *rebuttable presumption* is a legal assumption that will be followed until a stronger proof or presumption is presented. The burden then shifts to the parties to *disprove*, or to rebut, the presumption.) However, note that under the provisions of RUPA, the sharing of profits is recharacterized as an evidentiary presumption, rather than *prima facie* evidence.[10]

The UPA recognizes five rebuttals.[11] If one of the parties can prove that profits were shared for one of the reasons listed below, no partnership exists. If such proof is not made, the sharing of profits establishes that a partnership did exist. The rebuttal is successful if profits are shared for one of the following purposes:

- As payment of a debt, by installments or otherwise (a promissory note or a judgment note should be produced as evidence)
- As payment of wages to an employee or of rent to a landlord
- As payment of an annuity to the representatives of a deceased partner
- As payment of interest on a loan (again, some document probably will be necessary)
- As payment of consideration in the purchase of goodwill or other property, whether by installment payments or otherwise

For Profit   The fifth and final element of the definition of a partnership is probably the easiest to show. A partnership must operate *for profit*. To be specific, all that is needed is a *profit motive*. If the business was created to generate profits and to return these profits to the owners of the business, this test for the existence of a partnership is satisfied. Thus, nonprofit associations cannot, by definition, be partnerships. However, an unprofitable business can be a partnership, provided that profits are the goal of the business. In short, the court is looking at the motive of the organization, not the financial bottom line.

The simplest form of a partnership is a general partnership. In a general partnership, all the partners are "general" partners. General partners may have to pay partnership debts from their personal assets if the partnership does not have sufficient assets. This is called unlimited liability and Chapter 33 includes an explanation of how it operates.

Limited Partnerships

A *limited partnership* is a partnership in which there are two or more "levels," or types, of partners. The liability of each partner is determined by his or her status. The potential liability of some partners is limited to their capital contributions, while other partners face unlimited personal liability. A limited partnership can be created by two or more persons, as long as at least one person is designated a limited partner. A *limited partner* is a partner who furnishes certain funds or assets to the enterprise and whose liability is restricted to the funds provided. There must also be at least one general partner. With the exception of classifying the partners, a limited partnership has the same characteristics as a general partnership set up under the RUPA. A limited partnership is more formal than a general partnership, however. In order to form a limited partnership, the partners must sign and swear to a written certificate that details the important elements of the partnership agreement. This certificate must be filed with the public official specified in the state statutes where the limited partnership is created.

A limited partner is not personally liable for any obligations of the partnership. However, there is a price to pay for this protection: A limited partner is precluded from participating in the management of the business. A limited partner who takes part in management loses the limited status[12] and may be treated as a general partner, subject to unlimited personal liability. This loss of protection only occurs in suits by third persons who actually know of the limited partner's participation in the management of the business. Limited partners who act as agents or employees of a general partner or of the firm or who advise the general partners about business are not considered to be "involved in management." The partnership agreement *may* grant voting rights to limited partners under RULPA (ULPA [1976]), which specifically addresses the type of acts that by themselves will not be considered control.[13] In a significant change, the most recent revision of the Uniform Limited Partnership Act (2001) provides that a limited partner is not liable for partnership debts even if he or she participates in management.[14]

Initially the rules for limited partnerships were codified in either the Uniform Limited Partnership Act (ULPA 1916) or the Revised Uniform Limited Partnership Act (RULPA or ULPA [1976]). ULPA (1916) has little effect today since it is followed only in Vermont. The NCCUSL approved RULPA in 1976,[15] and amended it in 1985.[16] Some form of RULPA was adopted by every state except Louisiana and Vermont.[17] NCCUSL finalized a new version called the Uniform Limited Partnership Act (2001), commonly called ULPA 2001.[18] Louisiana does not follow any of the uniform limited partnership acts.[19]

Under the RULPA the certificate of agreement forming the limited partnership must be filed with the secretary of state for the state in which the limited partnership is formed. RULPA calls for profits and losses to be shared on the basis of capital contributions unless the agreement specifies some other distribution. One of the interesting aspects of the RULPA is § 1105, which specifies that any situations not provided for in the revised act are to be governed by the provisions of the ULPA 1916. Throughout this chapter and Chapters 32 and 33, we will focus on the majority rule contained in RULPA. Any parties who plan to establish a limited partnership, however, need to check the applicable statute for the state of formation.

The Uniform Limited Partnership Act 2001 made some significant changes to RULPA. They include:

- The partnership can exist in perpetuity unless the agreement provides otherwise.
- The exit of a limited partner does not dissolve the partnership.
- Limited partners are protected from obligations of the firm based on their status. (They will not lose this protection by participating in management.)[20]

Some large limited partnerships choose to be master limited partnerships (MLPs). These partnerships are formed under the applicable state law, however, partnership interests are publicly traded either over-the-counter or on organized securities exchanges. The MLP also must comply with the rules of the security exchange on which they are traded. Because they are traded, they provide some liquidity for the interests of the limited partners.

Partnership Property

Although no partnership is *required* to own property, most partnerships do, in fact, own some property. Even if the partnership chooses not to own property, it must have access to possession and use of some physical assets. And this access and use may lead to ownership, at least under the UPA and in the eyes of the court.

UPA § 8 defines partnership property for general partnerships. Under this section, the following kinds of property are deemed to be *partnership property* (property owned by the partnership rather than the partners as individuals):

- All property originally contributed to the partnership as a partner's capital contribution(s)
- All property acquired on account of the partnership
- All property acquired with partnership funds, unless a contrary intention is shown
- Any interest in real property that is acquired in the partnership name
- Any conveyance to a partnership in the partnership name, unless a contrary intention is shown

If an individual partner wants to retain personal ownership but allow the partnership to use property, he or she should be extremely cautious. Unless the intention is made obvious, the partner may discover that the property legally belongs to the partnership. (This is particularly important in dissolution, which is discussed in detail in Chapter 33.)

The Partnership Agreement

A partnership is created by agreement of the partners. The agreement is a contract, and it may be oral unless it falls within the Statute of Frauds. In other words, no formality is required in setting up a general partnership. (Recall that there are formal requirements for creating a limited partnership.) Under RUPA, the partnership agreement is primary, and can include written, oral, or implied agreements. For the most part, the agreement takes priority over RUPA: RUPA covers matters not addressed in the partnership agreement.[21]

A reasonably prudent, cautious person is expected to take great care in negotiating the basic partnership agreement and then reducing the agreement to written form. Yet all too often a partnership is begun with little or no detailed negotiation. Even if the parties are very careful, situations may arise that were never considered and, therefore, are not covered by the agreement. To minimize the harm such situations can create, the UPA *imposes* certain rules, which apply unless the agreement provides otherwise. It also specifies certain areas that the agreement must cover.

Imposed Rules

Some rules are imposed and must be followed by the general partners, no matter what the agreement says. Any attempt to modify these rules in the agreement is contrary to public policy, so any modification will be deemed void. Some of these rules are:

- Each general partner is deemed to be an agent for the partnership and for each partner, as long as the partner is acting in a business-related matter.
- Each general partner is personally liable, without limit, for torts or contracts for which the partnership has insufficient assets to cover the debt or liability.
- Each general partner is expected to devote service to the partnership only and not to any competing business ventures.

Unless the agreement between the parties states otherwise, the following rules are imposed on general partnerships by operation of law:

- Each partner is entitled to an equal voice in the management of the business.
- Each partner is entitled to an equal share of profits, without regard to capital contributions. (The RULPA takes the totally opposite approach for limited partnerships.)
- Each partner is expected to share any losses suffered by the business in the same proportion as profits are to be shared.
- The books of the partnership are to be kept at the central office of the business. (RUPA considers access to the partnership books so important that the partnership agreement cannot waive a partner's right of access.)[22]

Express Terms

In addition to those terms imposed by law, the partnership agreement should cover some other areas. For instance, the agreement should designate the name of the business. This name cannot be deceptively similar to the name of any other company or business, and it cannot mislead the public as to the nature of the business. If a limited partnership is involved, the name should reflect this fact.

The agreement should cover the duration of the business—how long the partnership will last. Such an understanding in the beginning can avoid serious disagreements later. It also should cover the purpose of the business. Understanding the business's functions not only makes it easier to operate the business but also helps to avoid any controversies later.

Finally, the agreement should discuss in detail how, or if, a partner can withdraw from the business. In this area, the rights of a withdrawing partner should be carefully specified so that no one, including a court, will misconstrue the agreement's terms.

Of course, any other items the partners feel should be included can be discussed, agreed on, and added. In fact, the more detailed the original agreement, the better. A carefully drawn, well-thought-out agreement will always benefit honest partners. Where RUPA has been adopted, it will provide terms for the partners only if they failed to specify the terms themselves.

Limited Liability Partnerships

Limited liability partnerships (LLPs) are a relatively new form of business organization. The first statute was enacted in Texas in 1991 partially as a response to suits against partnerships arising out of the saving and loan failures.[23] LLPs are currently permitted in most states. Sometimes the enabling legislation is passed as amendments to the state's partnership act or as part of the state's limited liability company act. The 1997 amendments to RUPA, enacted by a majority of the states, expressly provide for limited liability partnerships.[24]

The advantage of an LLP over a general partnership is, as the name implies, the limit on the liability of all the partners. In an LLP, all the partners are general partners but the partners' personal assets are protected from liability claims against the partnership. There is variation in state laws on the protection afforded partners in an LLP. Generally, under RUPA, the protection is from all liability for partnership obligations.[25] The exception to this is liability created by the partner himself or herself. In other words, a partner has unlimited liability for his or her own wrongdoings and limited liability for the wrongdoings of others. Generally, the statutes broadly interpret the partner's own wrongs to include the wrongs of persons under that partner's direct supervision and control. Under RUPA, the liable partner is still entitled to indemnification from the partnership; however, other partners are not required to make contributions to the partnership when partnership assets are not sufficient.[26]

Many enterprises that were general partnerships have become LLPs. However, as RUPA points out, the decision to become an LLP should not be taken lightly. Like other decisions about business forms, it involves some serious consideration. RUPA suggests that each partner should consider a "personal liability calculus." Each partner gives up the right to receive contributions from other partners in exchange for being relieved of the obligation to contribute towards the personal liability of the other partners. The following factors are relevant in the decision: the size of the business; the type of business; the number of partners; the amount of insurance; and the relative risk of each partner's business practice.[27]

RUPA provides that a decision to change from a regular partnership to an LLP is a major partnership event. The change requires the same percentage vote that is required to amend the partnership agreement.[28] When a partnership votes to become an LLP, the liability "shield" applies, notwithstanding any inconsistent provisions in the partnership agreement. Once there has been an election to become a limited liability partnership, the partnership must register with the state. In addition, it must identify itself as an LLP to those with whom it does business. The registration and identification requirements provide clear notice of the limited liability status. Creditors will evaluate creditworthiness accordingly.[29] Generally under RUPA, the LLP status remains effective until it is revoked by a vote of the partners or is canceled by the secretary of state for failure to file an annual report or pay the required annual fees.[30]

Under RUPA, LLPs are treated as partnerships in all respects.[31] This permits reliance on partnership law to answer many of the questions that might arise. RUPA § 1001 does not restrict the types of businesses that can form LLPs. However, even though most states have adopted RUPA, some of them adopted different LLP statutes causing their LLP statutes not to be "uniform." Some states may not permit professionals to use LLPs. Other states permit professionals to form LLPs, but may require professional LLPs to purchase liability insurance.

Limited Liability Limited Partnerships

Limited liability limited partnerships (LLLPs) are limited partnerships with general partners who serve as managers and limited partners who generally serve as investors. However, *all* the partners have limited liability and creditors are generally limited to collecting from the partnership assets.[32] Depending on the state statutes, the general partners and limited partners might have different exposure to liability. In 1993 Texas was the first state to recognize this business form.[33] This is a relatively new business form, and the statutes and type of liability does vary. LLLPs can be formed in Arizona, Colorado, Delaware, Florida, Georgia, Maryland, and Texas.[34] Under the Uniform Limited Partnership Act 2001, limited partnerships can be limited liability limited partnerships (LLLPs) simply by stating that in the agreement and the certificate that they file.[35]

Many states recognize LLLPs that were formed in other states.[36] These are commonly called foreign LLLPs. In the context of business entities, *foreign* means an entity that was formed under the laws of another state, government, or country. So a Colorado LLLP doing business in California is a foreign LLLP in California.

Taxation of Partnerships

For taxation purposes, the partnership form of business can be either an advantage or a disadvantage. Basically, the partnership is not taxed, but the individual partners are taxed on the receipts of the firm. This is commonly known as pass through taxation. Federal income tax rules and regulations do not recognize the partnership as a taxable entity. The firm must file an IRS Form 1065 annually, but the form is for information purposes only. Each partner is taxed on his or her share of the firm's profits for the year, whether these profits are distributed to the partners or not. Each partner is also taxed on the capital gains and takes the deductions for capital losses that the firm experiences during the tax year. Limited partnerships, LLPs, and LLLPs are also taxed as partnerships.

Many states also treat the partnership as a mere conduit for the transfer of income to the partners. In these states, the partnership is not taxed, but the partners are taxed on the firm's income whether it is distributed or retained by the firm for reinvestment or expansion.

PARTNERSHIPS BY ESTOPPEL

Technically, no partnership can exist without an agreement. A third person who is dealing with someone who *claims* to be a partner when he or she is not, however, may be able to proceed against the partnership and/or the alleged partner. Such a situation may lead to a partnership by estoppel (also called an implied partnership or an ostensible partnership). To use partnership by estoppel, the third party must show:

1. Someone who is not a partner was held out to be a partner by the firm.
2. The third person justifiably or reasonably relied on the holding out.
3. The person will be harmed if liability is not imposed.

RUPA continues most of the prior law of partnerships by estoppel under the new name of "purported partner."[37] Partnership by estoppel is a particular problem for young business enterprises that share space, for example, newly licensed accountants. In order to avoid these problems, people that share office space should make sure that they follow this advice. To reduce potential liability:

- Maintain your own identity. This includes using your own letterhead, business cards, and plaques on office doors.
- Arrange for separate entries on the building directory.
- Maintain your own telephone lines. If you share a receptionist, try to assure that incoming calls are answered with individual names.
- Do not use a group name. If one is used, it should include a disclaimer of joint responsibility *everywhere* it appears, for example, on business cards and telephone listings.

- Be careful to be accurate when talking about the business relationship to business associates and friends. Do not say you are "with" the other individuals or refer to the other individuals as "partners."
- Remind the other individuals to use care, also.
- Be careful if you share work or clients with the others in the office. Clearly identify the working relationship to the client.[38]

JOINT VENTURES

A *joint venture* has all the characteristics of a partnership except one. It is not set up to "carry on a business." A joint venture, by definition, is established to carry out a limited number of transactions, very commonly a single deal. As soon as that deal (or those transactions) is completed, the joint venture terminates. Why is this form important? The agency power in a joint venture is limited; thus, a member of the venture is not as likely to be held responsible for the conduct of the other members of the venture. Also, the death of a joint venturer does not automatically dissolve the joint venture. In all other respects, partnership law is applicable.

CORPORATIONS

The Development of Corporations

It is not known when the first corporation was created, but some evidence suggests that people began to recognize the concept of corporate personality as early as the time of Hammurabi (about 1750 B.C.). By Roman times, corporate personality was created through royal fiat. (A *fiat* is an order issued by legal authority.) From its very origins, the concept of corporateness depended on government authority. The *fiction theory*—that a corporation is an artificial legal person separate from its shareholders—probably developed from the papacy's desire to accommodate priests who had taken vows of poverty forbidding them to hold property. Since controlling the activities and finances of these clergymen was very lucrative, the church devised a way (the corporation) to allow church officers to own property. This separation of the artificial person from the natural person spawned the modern view that the corporation, not the shareholders, owns the corporate property and that the shareholders ordinarily are not liable for debts incurred by the corporation. The development of the law merchant, the forerunner of modern commercial law, mirrored these and similar views of corporateness.

By the 17th century, English monarchs had tightened control over corporations, which were deemed to exist by virtue of concessionary grants of power from the state. Not surprisingly, the concession theory was part of the common law heritage that remained with American colonists after they gained independence from Britain. At first, Americans viewed corporations with suspicion because several well-known, unsavory schemes had been perpetrated through use of the corporate form. However, over time suspicions were reduced and the advantages of corporations became apparent. As the corporate form developed each state jealously guarded its power over these artificial creatures. This careful regulation of corporations, augmented now by federal securities statutes, remains an essential characteristic of the law of corporations in the United States.

Corporate Nature

We define a *corporation* as an artificial person created under the statutes of a state or nation and organized for the purpose set out in the application for corporate existence. A corporation is an invisible, intangible, artificial person. Because it is considered a person, the corporation ordinarily enjoys most of the rights that natural (flesh-and-blood) persons possess. For example, it is a citizen of the state in which it has been incorporated. (As discussed in Chapter 3, for most purposes a corporation is considered a citizen and domiciliary of both the state of incorporation and the state where it has its corporate headquarters.) Thus, under the Fourth Amendment, it cannot be the object of unreasonable searches or seizures. Similarly, under the Fourteenth Amendment, it must be afforded its rights of due process and equal protection.

Advantages of the Corporate Form

Corporations are popular business forms because of their advantages over other types of business organizations. These advantages include:

- *Insulation from liability.* Corporate debts are the responsibility of the corporation. The shareholders' liability ordinarily is limited to the amount of their investment; creditors of the corporation normally cannot reach the shareholders' personal assets to pay for corporate debts.
- *Centralization of management functions.* Centralizing the management functions in a small group of persons possessing management expertise avoids some of the friction that may plague partnerships.
- *Continuity of existence.* The corporation continues to exist in the eyes of the law even after the deaths of the officers, directors, or shareholders, or the withdrawal of their shares. This potential for perpetual existence provides stability. A corporation can exist in perpetuity unless a specific length of time is stated in its articles of incorporation.
- *Free transferability of shares.* This creates opportunities for access to outside capital (as well as allowing investors to sell their interests without the need for unanimous approval or the dissolution of the firm).

These attributes unquestionably convince many large and small businesses to employ the corporate form. In a given situation, however, another form may better suit the business's needs. This is a decision that requires careful thought and the advice of knowledgeable experts, such as a lawyer, accountant, and/or investment adviser. There are also distinct disadvantages that may result from choosing the corporate form.

Formation of a Corporation

The process of forming a corporation involves complicated issues that demand the attention of well-versed professionals. One of these considerations consists of choosing the most desirable type of corporation for the particular circumstances. Another important decision is where to incorporate. Although there are some federal statutes, most corporate activity is controlled by state law.

Types of Corporations

There are a number of special categories of corporations. They include:

- the *publicly held corporation* which has access to capital by selling new shares. There will generally be a large number of shareholders and each shareholder has little say in the management of the firm. Examples include American Telephone & Telegraph (AT&T), General Electric (GE), General Motors (GM), and International Business Machines (IBM).
- the *closely held corporation* which has a few shareholders and restricts the transferability of shares in order to consolidate control. Shares are generally not as liquid or saleable as those of publicly held corporations due to the transfer restrictions.
- the *professional corporation* which is organized for conducting a particular occupation or profession such as accounting, dental work, medical practice, and legal practice. Typically, state statutes limit the ownership of shares to professional persons with the appropriate license. The professional is ordinarily personally liable for his or her own malpractice or similar torts as well as for any such acts performed by others who are under the professional's supervision.
- the *municipal corporation* which is a city, town, or other local political entity. It is formed under the authority of the state.
- the *quasi-public corporation* which is a for-profit corporation that furnishes essential public services such as providing gas, electricity, or water.
- the *nonprofit corporation* which is organized for charitable purposes. These may include educational institutions, charities, private hospitals, fraternal orders, and religious organizations.

eClass 31.1   Finance/Management

OBTAINING NECESSARY CAPITAL

Ani and Yousef believe that the firm needs a large infusion of capital in order to succeed. They have suggested that the firm incorporate and "go public" by offering stock for sale. Ani and Yousef believe that the firm can incorporate, sell 45 percent of the stock, and acquire enough funds to establish the business financially. Meg is opposed to the idea of selling any stock to "outsiders." She feels that these sales create the risk that an "outsider" could later take control of the venture by purchasing its stock. As an alternative, Meg mentions that she has heard about some kind of partnership that might be used to raise money without surrendering any control. Ani and Yousef ask you if you know what type of partnership Meg is talking about. What do you tell them? What alternatives might exist for Ani, Meg, and Yousef that will allow them to raise capital and at the same time retain control of the firm? What will you advise them to do?

BUSINESS CONSIDERATIONS   What factors should a firm consider in evaluating methods to obtain capital? How important is maintaining control of the enterprise?

ETHICAL CONSIDERATIONS   Is it ethical to sell interests in eClass solely to obtain funds and not provide the purchasers with any control over the firm? Is this using investors solely as a means to eClass's ends?

Promoters

Despite the negative connotation of the word, promoters may be vital to the formation of the corporation. Promoters are also labeled *preincorporators*. Although the law does not require the services of promoters to incorporate a business, *promoters* begin the process of forming a corporation by taking affirmative steps toward incorporating, such as hiring a corporate attorney, leasing an office, and procuring subscribers for the stock.[39] Thus, promoters facilitate the creation of the corporation by bringing interested parties together and by encouraging the venture until the corporation is formed.

Promoters' activities raise a host of legal issues. Since the promoter is working on behalf of an entity not yet created, questions arise as to whether the promoter or the corporation is liable on contracts made on the corporation's behalf before its "existence." The general rule is that the promoter will be liable for goods and services rendered to him or her before the corporation's formation. However, the corporation may become liable for the promoter's contracts (and possibly torts) after its formation. In some cases:

- The other party to the contract may agree to release the promoter ending the promoter's liability.
- The other party, the corporation, and the promoter may agree to a novation. (In this context, *novation* means a new contract that replaces the old contract and substitutes the corporation for the promoter.) The novation releases the promoter from his or her liability. The new corporation will be liable instead.
- The corporation may ratify the promoter's contracts. *(Ratification* is accepting an act that was unauthorized when committed and becoming bound to that act upon its "acceptance.") For example, the board of directors might ratify the promoter's contracts at the first meeting of the board of directors.) Ratification will make the corporation liable on the contract. It does not release the promoter from liability.

The *possibility* of double-dealing is inherent in the process of promotion. For this reason, the law treats promoters as owing fiduciary duties to the corporation. Therefore, the promoter must act in good faith, deal fairly, and make full disclosure to the corporation. In a few cases the promoter has had to give back to the corporation secret profits, embezzled funds, and other damages. Therefore, anyone desiring to act as a promoter should seek professional advice in advance.

Articles of Incorporation

The document that signals the official existence of the corporation is the *articles of incorporation.* State statutes prescribe the contents of the articles. Typically the articles include:

- The name of the corporation
- Its purpose
- Its duration
- The location of its principal office or registered agent (A *registered agent,* also called resident agent, is a person designated by a corporation to receive service of process within the state.)
- Its powers
- Its capital structure (that is, the number of shares and minimum *stated capital,* the latter is the amount of consideration received by the corporation for all its shares.)
- The names of the initial directors (these people are usually the incorporators). (An *incorporator* participates in the formation of a corporation by executing the articles of incorporation.)
- The signatures of the incorporators (in most jurisdictions they do not have to be shareholders)

Once the incorporators file the articles with the appropriate state official (ordinarily, the secretary of state) and pay all the required filing fees, the state issues a formal *certificate of incorporation,* or license.

Corporate Charter/Certificate of Incorporation

In most states, corporate existence begins with the issuance of the certificate of incorporation by the secretary of state. After the state issues such a certificate, the state normally will not interfere with its grant of power to the corporation. Unless the corporation by its conduct poses a definite and serious danger to the welfare of the state's citizens, the state will honor the certificate and allow the corporation to conduct its usual business without interference. On the other hand, the state might intervene if the corporation is engaged in wholesale fraud.

Organizational Meeting

In some jurisdictions, official corporate existence does not begin with the issuance of the certificate; it begins after the first organizational meeting of the corporation. The organizational meeting is important because it is during the meeting that (1) bylaws are adopted, (2) the preincorporation agreements are approved, and (3) officers are chosen. It is important to record and maintain accurate minutes of this meeting.

Bylaws

Bylaws are the internal rules and regulations adopted by a corporation for the purpose of self-regulation, especially the regulation of day-to-day matters not covered by other documents. These ordinarily are not filed in a public place as articles of incorporation are. They must, however, be consistent with the jurisdiction's corporation statute and the corporation's articles. Bylaws typically list the location(s) of the corporation's offices and records; describe the meetings of the shareholders and the directors; set out the powers and duties of the board of directors, officers, and executive committee; establish the capitalization of the corporation (that is, what types of shares may be sold and how many shares are authorized to be sold); and establish the methods for conducting the corporation's business, such as execution of contracts, signatures on deeds, and notices of meetings.

De Jure *versus* De Facto *Corporations*

As we have seen, it is relatively easy to obtain corporate status if one *carefully* follows the required statutory procedures. Even so, errors occur so it is necessary to examine the consequences of failure to comply with the statutory requirements. *Defective incorporation*, as this concept is called, may be a matter of degree. If the defect in formation (or noncompliance with the incorporation statute) is slight, the law characterizes the corporation as *de jure* (valid by law). The general rule is that where substantial compliance with all steps necessary for incorporation has occurred, the resultant entity is a *de jure* corporation. If an address is wrong in a provision mandating an address or a relatively insignificant provision has been overlooked, courts will not invalidate corporate status. Such minor flaws ordinarily will not cause the loss of *de jure* status.

Sometimes, however, the defect involved is so serious that the law does not consider the corporation as *de jure*. Corporateness and all its attributes may still be retained, however, if certain conditions are met: (1) A law exists under which the business could have been incorporated; (2) there was a good faith effort to comply with the statute; and (3) there was some use or exercise of corporate powers. Such entities are called *de facto* corporations (corporations in fact, if not in law). Only the state can attack the existence of a *de facto* corporation. Consequently, if the state does not bring an action to dissolve the corporation, the firm will enjoy all the powers and privileges that exist in the corporate form.

This result is probably just, even if the defects in compliance are serious; if both the entity and third parties dealt with each other in the belief that the corporation existed, it would be fair to fulfill their expectations. Yet the law should scrutinize the parties'

eClass 31.2 Management

DE JURE VERSUS *DE FACTO* CORPORATIONS

Ani and Yousef have just about decided that the benefits of incorporating eClass outweigh the disadvantages of the corporate form. They are unsure, however, about the legal steps involved in incorporation and ask your advice as to what they must do to incorporate. What will you advise them to do?

BUSINESS CONSIDERATION What advice and guidelines can you suggest to eClass to ensure that it forms a *de jure* corporation rather than a *de facto* corporation?

ETHICAL CONSIDERATIONS Is it ethical to grant the benefits of limited liability and perpetual existence to a business with only partial compliance with the state statute? Would it be more ethical, due to some minor flaw in the formation of the enterprise, to treat the stockholders as partners? If the creditor or supplier believed it was a *de jure* corporation when it dealt with the business, is it ethical for the creditor or supplier to complain about the status after the fact?

nonfulfillment of statutory requirements in order to avoid frustrating legislative intent. In recent years, statutory provisions have increasingly reflected the view that the issuance of a certificate of incorporation will create a presumption that the corporation has been validly formed (that is, it has attained *de jure* status) except in actions brought by the state. If the state has taken no action and has issued no certificate, the presumption is that corporate status is not yet realized. In this case, third parties can hold individual shareholders personally liable. These developments have greatly eroded the importance of the *de facto* doctrine; but, some courts have continued to make distinctions between *de jure* and *de facto* corporations. It is, therefore, important to understand both the traditional approach and the modern trends in this area of the law.

Corporate Powers

The articles of incorporation may set forth the powers of the corporation. Such provisions actually may be redundant because state statutes normally specify what corporations can permissibly do. These express powers include the ability: (1) to conduct business; (2) to exist perpetually (unless the articles define a shorter period or the state dissolves the corporation); (3) to sue and be sued; (4) to use the corporate name or seal; and (5) to make bylaws. In addition, corporations possess implied powers to do everything reasonably necessary to conduct their business. Typical implied powers consist of holding or transferring property, acquiring stock from other corporations, borrowing money, executing commercial paper, issuing bonds, effecting loans, reacquiring the corporation's own shares, and contributing to charity. Statutes may enumerate these and other implied powers.

Ultra Vires *Acts*

As noted earlier, corporations have more power today than they did years ago. Since the strict application of the concession theory held that corporate status was a privilege (in contrast to a right), corporate acts outside the legal boundaries were considered to be *ultra vires* (beyond the scope or legal power of a corporation) and therefore void. When sued, corporations could use *ultra vires* as a defense to enforcement of a contract. A corporation's use of this doctrine to avoid contractual duties has become largely outmoded due to (1) the advent of implied powers; (2) the relaxation of the concession theory; and (3) an increase in permissible corporate purposes. Thus, the modern trend is to curtail application of the *ultra vires* doctrine as a defense unless the action is a public wrong or forbidden by statute.

State statutes have either abolished the *defense* of *ultra vires* or greatly limited its application. The statutes usually continue to permit suits only in three situations:

1. Shareholder injunctive actions against the corporation (*Injunctive actions* are suits asking a court of equity to order a person to do or to refrain from doing some specified act.)

2. Shareholder derivative suits on behalf of the corporation to recover damages caused by an impermissible act

3. Proceedings by the state to dissolve the corporation because of repeated violations of applicable law

For practical purposes, these situations constitute the only areas where the *ultra vires* doctrine will still be applied.

Taxation of Corporations

The tax treatment of corporations stems from the law's recognition of corporations as separate entities for federal income tax purposes. Often this is a disadvantage of the corporate form. The corporation pays taxes on its income as earned.[40] When this income is distributed to shareholders in the form of dividends, it produces taxable income for them. This structure brings about so-called double taxation. Because corporate losses are not passed on to the shareholders, shareholders do not receive the tax advantages that otherwise accompany such losses.

The creation of what the Internal Revenue Code terms an *S corporation* (regular corporations are labeled *C corporations*) may offset these tax drawbacks and provide tax relief. Subchapter S of the Internal Revenue Code permits certain corporations to avoid corporate income taxes and, at the same time, to pass operating losses on to their shareholders. In this sense, federal tax laws covering S corporations are similar to the laws covering partnerships although there are a few differences. Attaining S corporation status involves an elective procedure and the necessity for strict compliance with statutory requirements.

In order to elect Subchapter S status, the business must:

■ Be a domestic small-business corporation (To be a domestic corporation, it must be incorporated and organized in the United States. Businesses incorporated outside the United States, certain banks, and insurance companies may not become S corporations.) Have only one class of stock issued and outstanding (Generally, there may be different options or voting rights within that one class.)

■ Have 100 or fewer shareholders (Congress has raised the number of shareholders permitted in recent years and may continue to increase the number. In some instances, shareholders may be "aggregated" and treated as one shareholder for this requirement, for example, a husband and wife may be treated as one shareholder.[41])

■ Have no nonresident alien shareholders (If a resident alien moves outside the United States, the Subchapter S status will be terminated.)

■ Have only qualifying shareholders (Individuals, estates, certain tax-exempt organizations,[42] and certain trusts qualify and can be shareholders, but partnerships, corporations, LLCs, LLPs, and nonqualifying trusts are not eligible.)

- Have the consent of all the shareholders
- Not exceed the maximum allowable passive investment income

In order to make a proper election, the consent must be made in writing on IRS Form 2553 and filed in a timely and proper manner. Once the election occurs, renewals are unnecessary; S status remains in effect as long as none of the events that can trigger loss of the election occurs. An S corporation may be subject to state and local income taxes.

Disregarding the Corporate Entity

We have seen that the law sometimes will recognize corporateness when the incorporation has been defective. Now we will examine situations that call for disregarding the corporate entity even when there has been compliance with the incorporation statute. The usual rule is that the shareholders in a corporation enjoy limited liability. Because the corporation is a separate entity from the shareholders, the law normally will not be interested in who owns or runs the corporation. Sometimes, though, it will be necessary to *pierce the corporate veil* in order to serve justice. In other words, the law will ignore the shield that keeps the corporation and its shareholders' identities separate. For example, the corporate veil will be "pierced" to place liability on the shareholder when the corporate form is being used to defraud others or to achieve similar illegitimate purposes. Courts examine the facts closely to see if a particular situation justifies disregarding corporateness. If the corporation is a mere "shell" or "instrumentality," or in reality is the "alter ego" of the shareholder(s), courts can use their powers of equity to impose liability on the controlling shareholder(s). For example, the courts may impose personal liability on shareholder(s) for corporate liabilities when (1) the corporation is so thinly capitalized initially that it cannot reasonably meet its obligations, or (2) the shareholders are draining off the corporation's assets for their personal use.

Courts will uphold corporateness even in one-person corporations as long as the controlling shareholder (1) keeps corporate affairs and transactions separate from personal transactions; (2) adequately capitalizes the business initially and forgoes the draining off of corporate assets; (3) incorporates for legitimate reasons (tax savings, limitation of liability, and so on); and (4) directs the policies of the corporation toward its own interests, not personal ones. Piercing the corporate veil is also an issue in situations involving parent/subsidiary (that is, affiliated) companies. In the parent/subsidiary situation, there are two general theories for holding the parent liable for the acts of the subsidiary: alter ego (piercing the corporate veil) and agency principles (the amount of control the parent exercises over the subsidiary). Most states are using the corporation rules regarding "piercing the veil" for LLCs as well as for corporations. In fact, some courts still call it piercing the *corporate* veil. Exhibit 31.3 illustrates these points.

Exhibit 31.3

Piercing the Corporate Veil

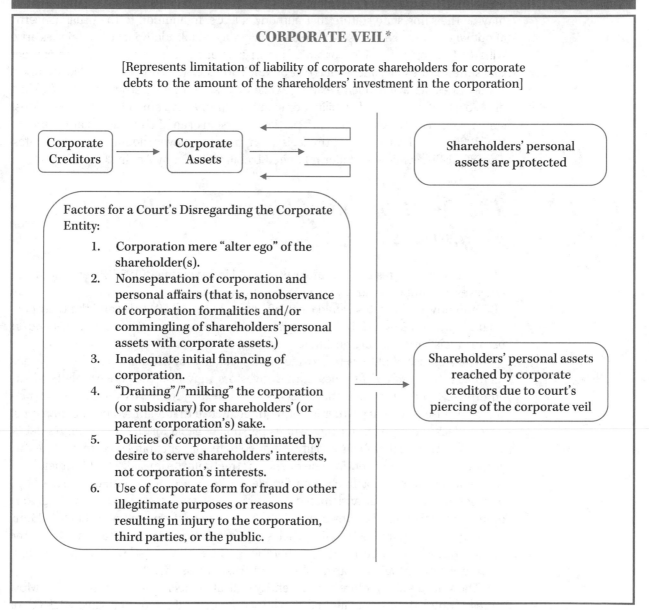

CORPORATE VEIL*

[Represents limitation of liability of corporate shareholders for corporate debts to the amount of the shareholders' investment in the corporation]

Corporate Creditors → Corporate Assets →

Shareholders' personal assets are protected

Factors for a Court's Disregarding the Corporate Entity:

1. Corporation mere "alter ego" of the shareholder(s).
2. Nonseparation of corporation and personal affairs (that is, nonobservance of corporation formalities and/or commingling of shareholders' personal assets with corporate assets.)
3. Inadequate initial financing of corporation.
4. "Draining"/"milking" the corporation (or subsidiary) for shareholders' (or parent corporation's) sake.
5. Policies of corporation dominated by desire to serve shareholders' interests, not corporation's interests.
6. Use of corporate form for fraud or other illegitimate purposes or reasons resulting in injury to the corporation, third parties, or the public.

Shareholders' personal assets reached by corporate creditors due to court's piercing of the corporate veil

* Corporate veils also can be pierced to reach the assets of parent corporations or other related entities.

LIMITED LIABILITY COMPANIES

Limited liability companies (LLCs) are a hybrid form of business organization. Despite some disadvantages, it appears that most small businesses formed today choose to operate as limited liability companies.[43] The state enabling statute that allows LLPs may be the same state statute that authorizes LLCs. In addition to the usual concerns about whether the enterprise will be financially successful, additional uncertainties arise with the LLC form of business organization. In general, businesspeople need to remember that state statutes vary and what is true of New York LLCs may not be true of Florida LLCs. Some states allow for much flexibility while others are more restrictive. The NCCUSL drafted a Uniform Limited Liability Company Act in 1995 and amended it in 1996.[44] Most states had already enacted their own particular version of an LLC enabling statute prior to the 1996 act. However, uniform legislation may be slowly adopted by the states. The NCCUSL revised the Uniform Limited Liability Company Act in 2006.[45]

The Development of Limited Liability Companies

The first United States LLC statute was enacted in Wyoming in 1977. After enactment, however, a number of questions arose about the federal income tax treatment of an LLC and how sister states would treat Wyoming LLCs. All 50 states and the District of Columbia now recognize LLCs. Many states also recognize out-of-state LLCs and/or permit registration of foreign LLCs.

The purpose of LLCs is to provide limited liability for all investors, who are called members. (*Limited liability* means that investors may lose their investments in the enterprise, but not their personal assets.) LLCs have an advantage over limited partnerships because a general partner is not required. Recall that a limited partnership must have at least one general partner who is personally liable for the partnership's debts. With an LLC, each member's liability is limited to his or her capital investment plus any additional capital contributions he or she contractually promised. The LLC members' shares are generally not freely transferable, so LLCs are not suitable where a large number of investors is anticipated. Initially many states required more than one member to form an LLC; however, all states now permit one member LLCs.[46] Many state statutes require LLCs to file articles of organization with the state similar to the articles of incorporation filed by corporations. Generally, state law permits corporations, nonresident aliens, partnerships, and trusts to be members of an LLC.

The statutes also require that the entity indicate in its name that it is an LLC. Most states require the use of "limited liability company," "limited company," "L.L.C." or "L.C." in the title.

Most states require the following information in the LLC's articles of organizationA:[47]

■ Name
■ Duration (The trend is to allow LLCs to exist in perpetuity if the organizers desire.)

- Purpose
- Address of the initial registered office and the name of the initial registere agent at that address
- Statement that the LLC is to be managed by a manager or group of manager or a statement that it will be managed by the members
- Name and address of each initial manager or managers, if applicable, or each initial member
- Name and address of each organizer (Organizers serve the role of promoters in LLCs.)

The articles of organization must be filed with the state. Often the filing fee is less for articles of organization than it is for articles of incorporation. Many states limit what type of business can form an LLC. For example, professional practices and insurance businesses may not be authorized to form LLCs.

Management of Limited Liability Companies

Organizers need to decide whether the LLC should be managed by the members or managed by managers.[48] In a member-managed LLC, the members have the right to manage the enterprise. Generally, each member will have an equal say in the management of the LLC. In a manager-managed LLC, the members appoint one or more managers to manage the business. These managers can be members but they are generally not required to be members. In a manager-managed LLC, the members relinquish their own right to manage. The members generally vote on the selection of managers. They can also retain the right to vote on other matters as specified in the articles of organization and the applicable state law.[49]

Taxation of Limited Liability Companies

The IRS enacted regulations that greatly simplify the federal taxation of LLCs.[50] Unless the entity is actually a corporation or "deemed" to be a corporation under the IRS regulations, it can elect pass-through tax treatment. Consequently, single member LLCs can be taxed as sole proprietorships. Multiple member LLCs can be taxed as partnerships if they are properly structured. (More exactly, they are taxed as limited partnerships with no general partners.) The LLC should follow the rules for filing an Entity Classification Election on IRS Form 8832, commonly called a "check-the-box" (CTB) election.[51] The default for failing to file the form is that most LLCs will be taxed as pass-through entities. There are still uncertainties in the taxation of LLCs due to a lack of IRS rules and court cases, however, the new regulations have greatly simplified questions of tax status for LLCs. The rules pertaining to LLCs in existence prior to January 1, 1997, are a little more complex. In addition, state income tax systems may not honor the federal tax election.

Flexibility and Variance

One of the primary disadvantages of LLCs is that they are a relatively new form of business enterprise. There is not an established body of law interpreting state statutes. Consequently, it is difficult to predict how the law will be applied in specific situations. This problem is amplified when an LLC operates in multiple states due to the variance in state statutes. Which state's laws will be applied? Many statutes authorizing the creation of LLCs include statements that other states *should* honor and enforce the law under which the LLC is formed. However, these provisions have limited effect. One characteristic on which LLC statutes vary is whether professional services associations can form an LLC.[52] Some states will not permit an LLC to continue in perpetuity like a corporation can. Most LLC statutes or the LLC articles greatly restrict the transferability of shares. Another unresolved issue is whether the selling of LLC interests falls under the applicable state and/or federal securities laws. The SEC's position appears to be that LLCs consisting of a large number of members are required to file under the 1933 and 1934 securities statutes. One factor in the determination is whether the members actually manage the enterprise or whether the entity uses centralized managers. It has also been suggested that members in a LLC can distribute profits and losses in different proportions than the membership interests. For example, four members with a 25 percent interest each could agree to give one member 50 percent of the profits and losses.[53]

eClass 31.3 Finance

LIMITED LIABILITY WITHOUT DOUBLE TAXATION

Ani and Yousef have decided to incorporate eClass in order to take advantage of the corporate form, including the protection of limited liability. Meg, however, is concerned that the firm will face "double taxation" if it incorporates. She knows that other methods of organization exist whereby eClass can gain limited liability but not be subject to double taxation. She is unsure what those methods are, however, or how eClass could organize under one of them. Meg asks you what methods are available for organizing the business with limited liability for members of the firm but without double taxation. What will you tell her?

BUSINESS CONSIDERATIONS   What factors should be considered by a group of people *before* they decide on the appropriate form of organization? Is there a single best form for businesses?

ETHICAL CONSIDERATIONS   What is the ethical duty of a business in regard to the tax code? Is it ethical to select a particular form of organization to avoid or reduce taxation?

Contemporary Case

DOUBLE CONSTRUCTION COMPANY, LLC v. ADVANCED HOME BUILDERS, LLC

2008 Conn. Super. LEXIS 1998 (Superior Ct. of Conn, Hartford Dist., 2008)

[NOTICE: This Decision Is Unreported and May Be Subject To Further Appellate Review. Decision as Corrected September 19, 2008.]

FACTS Plaintiff (Double C), owned by Chris Chiulli, sued Advanced Home Builders, LLC (Advanced), Robert A. Chiulli, Sr., and Laura Chiulli, his daughter, claiming money damages for breach of contract for work performed at the request of the defendants on a subdivision development. Laura had little experience in developing a subdivision. Robert and Laura were the sole members and had complete control of Advanced, which owns no equipment and has never had employees.

Laura and Robert claimed that the plaintiff had not done much of the work under the agreement. Chris submitted daily work sheets to show that the work was done. There was no indication that the work was performed negligently or was inferior. The Town of Rocky Hill, through its engineers, approved the work. Defendants did not submit evidence to show that the work had to be redone or that it had to be corrected. Other witnesses testified that they believed the work to be satisfactory.

Advanced set up an escrow account with its attorney, James Ripper, to pay some of the contractors who worked on the subdivision. Ripper assured Chris that plaintiff would be paid promptly when the work was completed and approved by the town engineer. However, when the work was completed Robert directed the attorney to withhold payment which Ripper did.

The Court finds Chris more credible than the defendants. The Court finds that the defendants have breached their contract with the plaintiff and that they have been unjustly enriched. The plaintiff performed the work required of it and fulfilled its obligations under the various contracts between the parties and has not been fully compensated for the work by the defendants.

ISSUE Are Robert Chiulli, Sr. and Laura Chiulli personally liable under the principle of piercing the corporate veil?

HOLDING Yes, the veil of the LLC should be pierced.

REASONING Excerpts from the opinion of Judge Trial Referee Richard M. Rittenband:

In [a prior Connecticut case] . . . , the Court stated that "the corporate veil will be pierced when 'the corporate entity has been so controlled and dominated that justice requires liability to be imposed on the real actor.'" . . . The Court stated that the corporate veil may be pierced under the "instrumentality rule" upon proof of three elements:

(1) Control, not mere majority or complete stock control, but complete domination, not only of finances but of policy and business practice in respect to the transaction . . . so that the corporate entity as to this transaction had at the time no separate mind, will or existence of its own;

(2) that such control must have been used by the defendant to commit fraud or wrong,

to perpetuate the violation of a statutory or other positive legal duty, or a dishonest or unjust act in contravention of plaintiff's legal rights; and

(3) that the ... control and breach of duty must proximately cause the injury or unjust loss complained of.

[The same piercing of the corporate veil and alter ego principles apply to an LLC.] ...

The Court finds that, under the totality of the evidence, all three elements have been proven by clear, unequivocal, precise and convincing evidence:

(1) Robert and Laura Chiulli conspired to and did exercise complete domination of the defendant LLC with respect to finances, policy and business practice with respect to the defendant LLC's relationship and transactions with the plaintiff so that the defendant corporations ... had at the time no separate mind[,] will or existence of its own.

(2) Robert and Laura Chiulli conspired to and did use such control to commit a wrong (i.e. not pay the monies due to the plaintiff), to perpetrate a violation of a positive legal duty (breaching the contract with the plaintiff) which was in contravention of plaintiff's legal rights; and

(3) The control and breach of contract and the aforesaid duties proximately caused, actually solely caused, the unjust loss or injury complained of; i.e. non-payment of a fair and reasonable value of the plaintiff's services and breach of the contract and agreements with the plaintiff.

Additionally, Robert and Laura Chiulli were the alter egos of the defendant corporations and are ... personally liable. "When the corporation is the mere alter ego, or business conduit of a person, it may be disregarded." ... Accordingly, the Court finds that the corporate veil (LLC veil) is pierced, Robert and Laura Chiulli were alter egos of the defendant LLC and that Robert and Laura Chiulli are individually liable as well as the defendant LLC for all of the plaintiff's claims. ...

You Be the Judge

Douglas Bishop was an Iowa farmer and president of the local co-op. He began meetings with representatives of the Department of Agriculture to explore the feasibility of building an ethanol plant in the Manchester area to increase the amount that the farmers would get from their crops. Consequently, the Northeast Iowa Ethanol, LLC was formed and shares were sold to raise financing for the plant. Northeast had difficulty raising sufficient funds for the project so it turned to alternative financing. Since none of the Northeast directors had experience with this type of alternative financing, Northeast decided to use Dorchester Enterprises, which requested that Northeast place its $3,865,000 in an escrow account as security for the alternative financing. Dorchester designated Martin Ubani as the administrator for the escrow account, and he was formally appointed as the administrator by a Northeast corporate resolution. However, Northeast restricted Ubani's ability to invest the escrow funds, permitting investments only with the prior written approval of Northeast. In 2001 the escrow funds were deposited with the Wells Fargo Bank in Des Moines, Iowa. Dorchester then convinced them to transfer the funds to a bank in Florida. Dorchester promised that Northeast would receive a letter of credit but it did not.

In early 2001 Jerry Drizin and Peter Topol set up Global Syndicate International, Inc. (GSI) in Las Vegas, Nevada, capitalizing it with $250. GSI was established for the purpose of buying and selling commercial paper and assisting others in obtaining financing. Drizin had worked as an insurance and real estate broker, but he had no experience in buying and selling commercial paper, had never been licensed to sell investments, and was not a stockbroker. Ubani became a consultant to GSI and started to use GSI stationery. GSI did not object to his use of the stationery. Ubani proposed that GSI assist in the investment of Northeast's funds. GSI was given a copy of the Northeast corporate resolution indicating that the funds were only to be invested with prior written approval from Northeast and Ubani's agreement to the condition.

Most of the escrow funds were transferred to GSI's bank account on November 13, 2001. Only Drizin was authorized to sign on the bank account. On November 19th, $2 million was sent to a trust account of the Greenspoon law firm for the benefit of Gravity Entertainment and its principal, Michelle Arsenault. This was done pursuant to Ubani's instructions and a $2 Million "guarantee" that Ubani had given Arsenault on GSI letterhead. Drizin did not receive any information about what was being guaranteed and why GSI would wire $2 million to Arsenault. No one ever claimed that Arsenault had done or would do anything for Northeast. "Drizin now claims to have no explanation for what he did other than to say that Mr. Ubani was his client and that Mr. Ubani assured GSI that the money would be replaced shortly." GSI did not receive written permission from Northeast and there is no evidence that Ubani had received permission. Drizin claims that he thought about contacting Northeast, but he did not do so because Ubani forbade him from having any such contact. (By December 31, 2001, GSI had suspended Ubani's position as GSI's consultant.)

Shortly after receiving Northeast's funds, GSI transferred $2 million to Arsenault; $512,741.06 to GSI's travel and expense account; and $500,000 to Barry Marvel, an attorney for GSI. Later Drizin sent another $500,000 to Barry Marvel because he said that he was having trouble with Ubani and he needed to diversify Northeast's portfolio. "Drizin frittered away the remaining $1.8 million over the next four months." Drizin wrote checks to his other enterprises, various attorneys, and a gold prospector. He also purchased a gold mine and a judgment with Northeast's funds.

Should the court pierce GSI's corporate veil and hold Drizin liable? If *you* were the judge, how would *you* decide this dispute? [See *Northeast Iowa Ethanol, L.L.C. v. Drizin*, 2006 U.S. Dist. LEXIS 4828 (N. Dist. Iowa, E. Div. 2006), and affirmed by *Northeast Iowa Ethanol, L.L.C. v. Global Syndicate International, Inc.*, 2007 U.S. App. LEXIS 21689 (8th Cir. 2007)(unpublished opinion).]

Summary

Every business enterprise must have an organizational form, generally choosing among a proprietorship, a partnership, a limited partnership, a limited liability partnership (LLP), a limited liability company (LLC), and a corporation. A partnership has the advantages of being easily formed and of having multiple contributors, whose different opinions and expertise are always available. A partnership also has the disadvantages of somewhat limited existence and unlimited personal liability for each general partner. A partnership is defined in the UPA as an association of two or more persons carrying on a business as co-owners for profit. This definition requires that the partners voluntarily agree to enter the business and that the business be somewhat permanent in nature. Co-ownership is the key element of the definition. This element is so important that a sharing of profits by the people involved creates a presumption of co-ownership, which, in turn, creates a presumption that a partnership exists.

A limited partnership is similar to a regular, or general, partnership with a few exceptions: There must be at least one general partner and at least one limited partner who generally may not participate in the management of the business. Somewhat formal documents must be prepared and correctly filed in order to establish the limited partnership. A limited liability limited partnership is a special type of limited partnership where the general partner also has some protection from liability.

In a limited liability partnership, there are no general partners. Each partner is personally liable for his or her own wrongs and for the wrongs of people he or she supervises. A partner will not be personally liable for the wrongs of other partners.

A partnership by estoppel is very similar to a partnership but there is no partnership agreement, however, the parties act as if there was a partnership to the detriment of some third party. A joint venture is not set up to "carry on a business." It is established to carry out a limited number of transactions, often a single deal.

A corporation is an artificial entity created and endowed with certain powers by the state. The incorporators begin the process by filing the articles of incorporation with the state. The corporation comes into existence when the state issues the certificate of incorporation. Some jurisdictions require an organizational meeting before the corporation officially exists. In general, corporate status will not be lost if there is substantial compliance with the incorporation statute; courts will view the entity as a *de jure* (legal) corporation. Courts will even grant corporate status to *de facto* (in fact, but not in law) corporations on the fulfillment of certain requirements. The modern trend is to presume *de jure* status, except in actions brought by the state.

As a business form, corporations have the advantages of limited liability, centralization of management functions, continuity of existence, free transferability of shares, and sometimes favorable tax treatment. Corporations enjoy certain express and implied powers.

At times, courts will disregard corporate status even when there has been complete compliance with the state statute. Courts consider a number of factors in deciding whether to "pierce the corporate veil" and impose personal liability on a shareholder or parent corporation. This doctrine is also used to pierce the veil of limited liability companies.

LLCs have a number of advantages over other forms of business. The LLC can be a hybrid of the favorable features of partnerships and corporations. Generally the formation of the LLC is an attempt to provide for pass-through tax treatment, including both income and active losses and to insulate personal assets from the LLC's debts. However, many state statutes restrict the transferability of

LLC shares and limit the life of the organization. Care must be used in establishing an LLC. Members must conform to the applicable state statute.

In order to be entitled to partnership tax treatment on the federal level, the LLC should comply with the IRS rules on making an election.

Discussion Questions

1. Porsche, Tim, and Dennis have a business concept they are sure will succeed if they can establish it properly. Unfortunately, they are short of capital and cannot afford to begin the business without financial support. Marge is willing to put up the necessary capital, but she is unwilling to face the liability of a general partner. Therefore, Marge agrees to be a limited partner in the business. What must the parties do to establish a limited partnership under the RULPA?

2. Larry and Vincente form a partnership. Vincente contributes $10,000. Larry, on the other hand, permits the partnership use an office building he owns, rent free. Three years later, the business dissolves. Vincente claims the building is partnership property. Larry claims he still owns the building personally. Who is correct, and why?

3. Mohamed and Eliza are partners. In order to get a loan, they tell the bank that Denise is also a partner. Relying on Denise's credit, the bank makes the loan. Mohamed and Eliza default, and the bank sues Denise. What must the bank prove in order to hold Denise liable for the loan?

4. Assume that Ani, Meg, and Yousef have decided to incorporate eClass to protect their personal assets. What must they do to avoid having the corporate veil pierced? What advice and guidelines can you provide them?

5. Jesse, José, and Esmeralda want to form an LLC that will be taxed as a partnership. What type of taxation do they desire? What should they do to help assure taxation as a partnership?

Case Problems and Writing Assignments

1. William Gosselin sued his former attorney, James O'Dea, for mishandling an employment claim. He also sued attorneys Marshall Field, William Hurley, Raymond Webb, and Arthur Sullivan. These lawyers practiced law in Lowell, Massachusetts, using the name of Field, Hurley, Webb & Sullivan. (Field, Hurley, Webb, and Sullivan were not partners, but they shared office space and some expenses.) O'Dea had an office with them. In the lobby of the building, the directory listed "Field, Hurley, Webb, Sullivan, Attorneys at Law" followed by the names of Field, Hurley, Sullivan, and O'Dea. O'Dea told Gosselin that he was "with" Field, Hurley, Webb & Sullivan. Prior to hiring O'Dea, Gosselin checked on the reputation of Field, Hurley, Webb & Sullivan, because Gosselin

wanted to hire an attorney with an established firm behind him. Gosselin had meetings with O'Dea at the Field, Hurley, Webb & Sullivan office. He met with Sullivan when O'Dea was not available. Gosselin's wife also met with Sullivan. Was there a partnership by estoppel? [See *Gosselin v. Webb*, 242 F.3d 412, 2001 U.S. App. LEXIS 3979 (1st Cir. 2001).]

2. Abrahim & Sons Enterprises and 42 other independent dealers operated Shell or Texaco gasoline stations in southern California. All appellants leased their stations from, and had dealer agreements with, Shell or Texaco. In 1998, Shell and Texaco addressed growing concerns about declining oil prices, declining profits, and increased competition by combining their refining and retail marketing activities into one LLC, called Equilon Enterprises. They contributed all of their western refining and marketing assets to Equilon and assigned the gas station leases and dealer agreements to Equilon. Shell transferred title of its real property to Equilon by deed. Shell and Texaco, as the sole members of Equilon, received 100 percent of the ownership interests in the LLC. Texaco's SEC form stated that Texaco and Shell jointly control Equilon. The individual gas stations continued to sell Shell and Texaco products under their same leases and agreements. The California Business & Professions Code § 20999.25(a) reads in relevant part:

> In the case of leased marketing premises as to which the franchisor owns a fee interest, the franchisor shall not sell, transfer, or assign to another person the franchisor's interest in the premises unless the franchisor has first ... made a bona fide offer to sell, transfer, or assign to the franchisee the franchisor's interest in the premises. ...

Under California law did the contribution of assets by Shell and Texaco to Equilon require Shell and Texaco to first offer to sell the stations to the independent dealers? [See *Abrahim & Sons Enterprises v. Equilon Enterprises, LLC*, 2002 U.S. App. LEXIS 15847 (9th Cir. 2002).]

3. Patricia Holmes and Sandra Kruger Lerner[54] became friends. At Lerner's mansion outside of London, Holmes developed her own nail color. On July 31, 1995, the two women returned from England and stayed at Lerner's West Hollywood condominium. Lerner and Holmes worked with the colors in a nail kit to try to recreate the purple color Holmes had made in England. Holmes said that she wanted to call the purple color she had made "Plague." The two women decided that "Urban Decay" was a good name for their concept. Lerner said to Holmes: "This seems like a good [thing], it's something that we both like, and isn't

out there. Do you think we should start a company?" Holmes responded: "Yes, I think it's a great idea." Lerner told Holmes that they would have to do market research, determine how to have the polishes produced, and that there would be many things they would have to do. They did not separate out which tasks each of them would do, but planned to do it all together. Lerner went to the telephone and called David Soward, the general partner of & Capital, and her business consultant. Holmes heard her say "Please check Urban, for the name, Urban Decay, to see if it's available and if it is, get it for us." Holmes knew that Lerner did not joke about business, and was certain that Lerner was serious about the new business. The telephone call to secure the trademark for Urban Decay confirmed in Holmes' mind that they were forming a business based on the concepts they had originated in England and at the kitchen table that day. Holmes knew that she would be taking the risk of sharing in losses as well as potential success, but the two friends did not discuss the details at that time. Although neither of the two women had any experience in the cosmetics business, they began work on their idea immediately. Holmes and Lerner discussed their plans for the company and agreed that they would attempt to build it up and then sell it.

The participants in the business attended meetings that they called board meetings. They discussed financing, and Soward reluctantly agreed to commit $ 500,000 towards the project. Urban Decay was financed entirely by & Capital, the venture capital partnership composed of Soward as general partner, and Lerner and her husband as the only limited partners. Holmes was spending four to five days a week at the warehouse. Holmes was reimbursed for mileage, but received no pay for her work. Holmes inquired about her role in Urban Decay a number of times. When it became obvious that they were excluding her, she initiated this lawsuit. Did Holmes and Lerner form a partnership? Was Lerner's behavior ethical? Why or why not? [See *Holmes v. Lerner*, 1999 Cal. App. LEXIS 774, 88 Cal. Rptr. 2d 130 (Cal. Ct. App. 1st Dist. Div. 1, 1999).]

Notes

1. Officially, this is the UPA (1914). The following states have adopted UPA (1914): Georgia, Indiana, Massachusetts, Michigan, Missouri, New Hampshire, New York, North Carolina, Pennsylvania, Rhode Island, South Carolina, Utah, and Wisconsin. Email from Katie Robinson, Communications Officer, National Conference of Commissioners on Uniform State Laws (NCCUSL), February 22, 2010.
2. The NCCUSL made the Revised Uniform Partnership Act available in 1992. Officially, it is the Uniform Partnership Act or UPA (1992). Unofficially, it is called RUPA, even by the NCCUSL. We will use the standard nomenclature and call it RUPA. The commissioners further amended RUPA in 1993 and 1994; in 1994, they released UPA (1994), which is basically the 1992 version with the 1993 and 1994 amendments. The following states have adopted the 1994 version of RUPA (without the 1997 amendments): Connecticut, West Virginia, and Wyoming. The 1997 amendments provided for limited liability partnerships. The following states have adopted the RUPA with the 1997 amendments: Alabama, Alaska, Arizona, Arkansas, California, Colorado, Delaware, District of Columbia, Florida, Hawaii, Idaho, Illinois, Iowa, Kansas, Kentucky, Maine, Maryland, Minnesota, Mississippi, Montana, Nebraska, Nevada, New Jersey, New Mexico, North Dakota, Ohio, Oklahoma, Oregon, Puerto Rico, South Dakota, Tennessee, Texas, U.S. Virgin Islands, Vermont, Virginia, and Washington. (The versions in South Dakota and Texas are substantially similar.) "A Few Facts about the Uniform Partnership Act (1994)(1997)," NCCUSL Web site, http://www.nccusl.org/Update/uniformact_factsheets/uniformacts-fs-upa9497.asp (accessed 2/21/10).
3. "Revised Uniform Partnership Act Reflects Modern Business Practices, 28 Jurisdictions Have Now Updated Venerable 80-year-old Partnership Law," NCCUSL Web site, http://www.nccusl.org/pressrel/upa799.htm.
4. "Summary Uniform Partnership Act (1994)," NCCUSL Web site, http://www.nccusl.org/Update/uniformact_summaries/uniformacts-s-upa1994.asp (accessed 2/21/10).
5. "Revised Uniform Partnership Act Reflects Modern Business Practices, 28 Jurisdictions Have Now Updated Venerable 80-year-old Partnership Law," supra note 3.
6. "Summary Uniform Partnership Act (1994)," supra note 4.
7. Ibid.
8. Ibid.
9. Revised Uniform Partnership Act § 602 Comment 1 and § 601 Comments 1 and 5.
10. Revised Uniform Partnership Act § 16202 (c)(3).
11. Uniform Partnership Act § 7(4).
12. Uniform Partnership Act § 303.
13. "Revised Uniform Limited Partnership Act, A Summary," NCCUSL Web site, http://www.nccusl.org/summary/ulpa.html/ (accessed 10/11/99).
14. "Summary Uniform Limited Partnership Act (2001)," NCCUSL Web site, http://www.nccusl.org/Update/uniformact_summaries/uniformacts-s-ulpa.asp (accessed 2/21/10).
15. The following states have adopted ULPA (1976) (RULPA) without the 1985 amendments: Connecticut, Maryland, Michigan, Montana, Missouri, Nebraska, New Jersey, South Carolina, and Wyoming. Email from Katie Robinson, Communications Officer, National Conference of Commissioners on Uniform State Laws (NCCUSL), February 22, 2010.
16. The following states have adopted ULPA (1976) or RULPA with the 1985 amendments: Alaska, Arizona, Colorado, Delaware, District of Columbia, Georgia, Indiana, Kansas, Massachusetts, Mississippi, New Hampshire, New York, North Carolina, Ohio, Oklahoma, Oregon, Pennsylvania, Rhode Island, South Dakota, Tennessee, Texas, U.S. Virgin Islands, Utah, Vermont, West Virginia, and Wisconsin. Email from Katie Robinson, Communications Officer, National Conference of Commissioners on Uniform State Laws (NCCUSL), February 22, 2010. The NCCUSL has enacted the 2001 Revision of the Uniform Limited Partnership Act (ULPA 2001). It has been adopted by Alabama, Arkansas, California, Florida, Hawaii, Idaho, Illinois, Iowa, Kentucky, Maine, Minnesota, Nevada, New Mexico, North Dakota, Virginia, and Washington. In 2010 it was introduced in the District of Columbia, Missouri, and Oklahoma. See "A Few Facts about the Uniform Limited Partnership Act (2001)," NCCUSL Web site, http://www.nccusl.org/Update/uniformact_factsheets/uniformacts-fs-ulpa.asp (accessed 2/21/10).
17. Officially, NCCUSL refers to them as ULPA (1916), ULPA (1976), and ULPA (1976) with 1985 amendments. Unofficially, NCCUSL and most writers refer to the 1976 revision as RULPA. We will call it RULPA.
18. The 2001 draft of the Uniform Limited Partnership Act (ULPA 2001) is available at http://www.law.upenn.edu/bll/archives/ulc/ulc_final.html#final.
19. Email from Katie Robinson, Communications Officer, National Conference of Commissioners on Uniform State Laws (NCCUSL), November 4, 2002.
20. "Why States Should Adopt the Uniform Limited Partnership Act (2001)," NCCUSL Web site, http://www.nccusl.org/Update/uniformact_why/uniformacts-why-ulpa.asp (accessed 2/21/10).

21. See "Revised Uniform Partnership Act Reflects Modern Business Practices, 28 Jurisdictions Have Now Updated Venerable 80-year-old Partnership Law," supra note 3.

22. See "Uniform Partnership Act (1994)," NCCUSL Web site, http://www.nccusl.org/nccusl/uniformact_summaries/uniformacts-s-upa1994.asp (accessed 9/4/02).

23. Excerpt entitled Limited Liability Partnership from West's Encyclopedia of American Law published at http://www.wld.com/conbus/weal/wlimlpar.htm (accessed 12/27/02).

24. Note 2 lists the states that have adopted RUPA with the 1997 amendments.

25. Revised Uniform Partnership Act, Addendum.

26. Ibid.

27. Ibid.

28. Revised Uniform Partnership Act § 1001(b).

29. "A Few Facts about the Uniform Partnership Act (1994)(1997)," NCCUSL Web site, http://www.nccusl.org/factsheet/upa-fs.html (accessed 10/11/99).

30. Revised Uniform Partnership Act, Addendum.

31. "A Few Facts about the Uniform Partnership Act (1994)(1997)," supra note 29.

32. See Uniform Limited Partnership Act (2001) § 404 (c) which states "An obligation of a limited partnership incurred while the limited partnership is a limited liability limited partnership, whether arising in contract, tort, or otherwise, is solely the obligation of the limited partnership. A general partner is not personally liable, directly or indirectly, by way of contribution or otherwise, for such an obligation solely by reason of being or acting as a general partner. This subsection applies despite anything inconsistent in the partnership agreement that existed immediately before the consent required to become a limited liability limited partnership under Section 406(b)(2)."

33. Carter G. Bishop, "Unincorporated Limited Liability Business Organizations: Limited Liability Companies and Partnerships," 29 SUFFOLK U. L. REV. 985 (Winter, 1995), at p. 1003.

34. Information about the states that permit the formation of LLLPs is a composite of information from Business Owners Toolkit, "The Limited Liability Limited Partnership (LLLP)," http://www.toolkit.com/small_business_guide/sbg.aspx?nid=P12_4275 (accessed 7/21/10); J. William Callison, "Limited Liability Partnerships & Limited Liability Limited Partnerships," The 'Lectric Law Library, http://www.lectlaw.com/files/buo04.htm (accessed 7/20/10); and Daniel S. Kleinberger, "Two Decades of 'Alternative Entities': From Tax Rationalization Through Alphabet Soup To Contract As Deity," 14 FORDHAM J. CORP. & FIN. L. 445 (2009), p. 457. As this area matures, updated information will be added to the Web site for this text.

35. "Why States Should Adopt the Uniform Limited Partnership Act (2001)," supra note 20. ULPA 2001 implicitly authorizes LLLPs. However, not all states which enact ULPA 2001 authorize the formation of LLLPs in their state.

36. California does not permit the formation of LLLPs, but recognizes LLLPs formed in other states. California Franchise Tax Board, Limited Liability Limited Partnership (LLLP), http://www.ftb.ca.gov/businesses/bus_structures/LLLpartner.shtml (accessed 7/20/10).

37. Revised Uniform Partnership Act § 308.

38. John W. Marshall, "Partnership by Estoppel—Liability by Surprise" in the Boston Bar Journal, May/June 2002, http://www.bostonbar.org/members/bbj/bbj0506_02/casefocus_estoppel.htm (accessed 12/27/02).

39. Subscribers enter into agreements to purchase stock from the company. Subscribers often agree to purchase stock before the actual formation of the company. There are a number of special rules that govern stock subscriptions, especially those prior to incorporation.

40. Corporate income tax is a complex subject. However, corporations are allowed deductions and credits.

41. For additional information about treating family members as one shareholder, see Internal Revenue Code § 1361(c)(1) and Notice 2005-91, 2005-51 I.R.B. 1164.

42. For example, I.R.C. § 501(c) (3) corporations are permitted to be shareholders of S corporations.

43. "[T]he number of new LLCs formed in America in 2007 now outpaces the number of new corporations formed by a margin of nearly two to one." Rodney D. Chrisman, "LLCS Are the New King of the Hill: An Empirical Study of the Number of New LLCS, Corporations, and LPS Formed in the United States Between 2004-2007 and How LLCS Were Taxed For Tax Years 2002-2006," 15 FORDHAM J. CORP. & FIN. L. 459 (2010), p. 460.

44. The states that have adopted the Uniform Limited Liability Company Act are Alabama, Hawaii, Idaho, Illinois, Iowa, Montana, South Carolina, South Dakota, U.S. Virgin Islands, Vermont, and West Virginia. "A Few Facts about the Uniform Limited Liability Company Act," NCCUSL Web site, http://www.nccusl.org/Update/uniformact_factsheets/uniformacts-fs-ullca.asp (accessed 2/21/10). The states that have adopted the Uniform Limited Liability Company Act (2006) are Idaho and Iowa. In 2010 it was introduced in the District of Columbia. "A Few Facts about the Uniform Limited Liability Company Act (2006)," supra note 29.

45. Idaho and Iowa have adopted the 2006 version. In 2010 the 2006 version was introduced to the state legislatures in the District of Columbia and Nebraska. Some of the primary features of the 2006 revision include providing for perpetual existence, clarifying the duties of loyalty and care owed by members and managers, allowing the parties to specify the rights of departing members in their contract, and providing that a member may not transfer his or her membership unless the operating agreement provides that power.

"A Few Facts about the Uniform Limited Liability Company Act (2006)," supra note 29.

46. For example, the Uniform Limited Liability Company Act permits one person to form an LLC. "Summary Revised Uniform Limited Liability Company Act (2006)," NCCUSL Web site, http://www.nccusl.org/Update/uniformact_factsheets/uniformacts-fs-ullca.asp (accessed 2/21/10). Carter G. Bishop, "Reverse Piercing: A Single Member LLC Paradox," 54 S.D. L. REV 199, 209 (2009), citing Carter G. Bishop & Daniel S. Kleinberger, *Limited Liability Companies: Tax and Business Law*, p. 1.07[7], (1994, 2008-2 Supplement).

47. Depending on the state, articles of organization can be called certificates of formation or certificates of organization.

48. Under the Uniform Limited Liability Company Act (2006) § 407(a), the LLC will be presumed to be managed by the members unless stated otherwise.

49. For states that have adopted it, the Uniform Limited Liability Company Act (2006) § 407 sets out the types of matters that must be put to a vote of the members and whether or not that vote must be unanimous for both management structures.

50. Treas.Reg. §§ 301.7701-1 to 7701-3 (as amended by T.D. 8697, 1997-2 I.R.B. 11).

51. Form 8832 is available at the IRS web site at http://www.irs.gov/pub/irs-pdf/f8832.pdf/. One reason for the check-the-box election was that by 1996 all states had LLC statutes and the number of requests for determinations of tax status by the IRS was crushing. Carter G. Bishop, "Reverse Piercing: A Single Member LLC Paradox," p. 201.

52. California specifically forbids LLCs from providing professional services, Cal. Corp. Code § 17000 (1996). Section § 101(3) of the Uniform Limited Liability Company Act, drafted by the NCCUSL, expressly permits professional LLCs.

53. Fred S. Steingold, *The Legal Guide for Starting & Running A Small Business* (Berkeley, CA: Nolo Press 1992), 1/20.

54. Sandra Lerner is a successful entrepreneur and an experienced businessperson. She and her husband were the original founders of Cisco Systems. She received a substantial amount of money when she sold her interest in Cisco, which she invested in a venture capital limited partnership called "& Capital Partners."

32

Operation of a Business Organization

Agenda

When eClass was being established, Ani, Meg, and Yousef were unsure as to what form of business they should select for eClass. If they choose to form a partnership, how would they delegate authority and responsibility for the decisions that need to be made? How would they share profits and responsibility? If they decide to incorporate, how should the corporation be structured? Obviously, it will be a for-profit enterprise, but should it be publicly owned or closely held? If they decide to incorporate the business, what legal steps must they follow in managing and operating the firm? How do these steps compare to those followed in a partnership, a limited partnership, or a limited liability company? Can they be compelled to distribute profits, or can they retain the firm's earnings to help it grow?

These and other questions will arise during our discussion of business organizations. Be prepared! You never know when the firm or one of its members will seek your advice.

[**NOTE:** Throughout Part 7 the organization form selected by eClass may vary from one eClass problem to the next. This is done to allow you to evaluate the problems presented on the basis of different organizational options. If the facts of a particular case state that eClass has adopted a particular form, answer the questions based on the implications for that particular form. Treat each thread case independently, without reference to the other thread cases or agendas. If no particular form is specified, assume that eClass is operating as a partnership, but the principals are considering the benefits—and the burdens—of changing the structure to another form of business.]

Classic Case

MEINHARD v. SALMON

249 N.Y. 458, 1928 N.Y. LEXIS 830
(N.Y. Ct. of Appeals, 1928)

FACTS Louisa M. Gerry leased the premises known as the Hotel Bristol to the defendant Walter J. Salmon for a twenty-year period. Under the lease Salmon promised to modify the building at a cost of $200,000. Salmon and Morton H. Meinhard, the plaintiff, agreed that Meinhard would pay half of the moneys necessary to reconstruct, alter, manage and operate the property. In return, Salmon was to pay to Meinhard 40 percent of the net profits for the first five years of the lease and 50 per cent for the years thereafter. The parties would share losses equally. Salmon was to have sole power to "manage, lease, underlet and operate" the building.

Near the end of the 20 years, Elbridge T. Gerry became the owner of the reversionary interest in the Hotel Bristol. He owned a substantial amount of property in the neighborhood. Elbridge negotiated with Salmon and they agreed to a 20-year lease for the whole tract including the Hotel Bristol to the Midpoint Realty Company, which is owned and controlled by Salmon. The lease could

be renewed and could possibly extend to a maximum of 80 years. Under the lease the existing buildings could remain unchanged for seven years and then they are to be torn down, and replaced by a new building costing $3,000,000. Salmon personally guaranteed the performance by Midpoint Realty Company.

Salmon did not tell Meinhard anything about the negotiations or the new lease. When Meinhard found out about the lease, he demanded that the lease be held in trust as an asset of the venture.

ISSUE Did Salmon breach a fiduciary duty to Meinhard?

HOLDING Yes, Salmon breached a fiduciary duty. Meinhard is entitled to an interest in the new lease.

REASONING Excerpts from the opinion by Chief Judge Cardozo:

... The two were coadventurers, subject to fiduciary duties akin to those of partners.... The heavier weight of duty rested, however, upon Salmon. He was a coadventurer with Meinhard, but he was manager as well. During the early years of the enterprise, the building, reconstructed, was operated at a loss. . . . For each [of them], the venture had its phases of fair weather and of foul. The two were in it jointly, for better or for worse. . . . Joint adventurers, like copartners, owe to one another, while the enterprise continues, the duty of the finest loyalty. Many forms of conduct permissible in a workaday world for those acting at arm's length, are forbidden to those bound by fiduciary ties. A trustee is held to something stricter than the morals of the market place. Not honesty alone, but the punctilio of an honor the most sensitive, is then the standard of behavior. As to this there has developed a tradition that is unbending and inveterate. Uncompromising rigidity has been the attitude of courts of equity when petitioned to undermine the rule of undivided loyalty by the "disintegrating erosion" of particular exceptions. . . . Only thus has the level of conduct for fiduciaries been kept at a level higher than that trodden by the crowd. It will not consciously be lowered by any judgment of this court. . . .

[Mr. Gerry] figured to himself beyond a doubt that the man in possession would prove a likely customer. To the eye of an observer, Salmon held the lease as owner in his own right, for himself and no one else. In fact he held it as a fiduciary, for himself and another, sharers in a common venture. If this fact had been proclaimed, if the lease by its terms had run in favor of a partnership, Mr. Gerry, we may fairly assume, would have laid before the partners, and not merely before one of them, his plan of reconstruction. The pre-emptive privilege, or, better, the pre-emptive opportunity, that was thus an incident of the enterprise, Salmon appropriated to himself in secrecy and silence. . . . The trouble about his conduct is that he excluded his coadventurer from any chance to compete, from any chance to enjoy the opportunity for benefit that had come to him alone by virtue of his agency. This chance, if nothing more, he was under a duty to concede. The price of its denial is an extension of the trust at the option and for the benefit of the one whom he excluded.

Little profit will come from a dissection of the precedents. None precisely similar is cited in the briefs of counsel. . . . Authority is, of course, abundant that one partner may not appropriate to his own use a renewal of a lease, though its term is to begin at the expiration of the partnership. . . . Certain it is . . . that there may be no abuse of special opportunities growing out of a special trust as manager or agent. . . . If conflicting inferences are possible as to abuse or opportunity, the trier of the facts must make the choice between them. There can be no revision in this court unless the choice is clearly wrong. . . . A constructive trust is then the remedial device through which preference of self is made subordinate to loyalty to others. . . .

We have no thought to hold that Salmon was guilty of a conscious purpose to defraud. Very likely he assumed in all good faith that with the approaching end of the venture he might ignore his coadventurer and take the extension for himself. He had given to the enterprise time and labor as well as money. He had made it a success. . . . Salmon had put himself in a position in which thought of self was to be renounced. . . . He was much more than a coadventurer. He was a managing coadventurer. . . . For him . . . , the rule of undivided loyalty is relentless and supreme. . . . A different question would be here if there were lacking any nexus of relation between the business conducted by the manager and the opportunity brought to him as an incident of management. . . . [However, here] the subject-matter of the new lease was an extension and enlargement of the subject-matter of the old one. . . .

OPERATION OF A PARTNERSHIP

A partner has certain rights by virtue of his or her status as a partner. These rights *may* be limited or defined by the partnership agreement, the type of partnership formed, and any statutory restrictions. If there is no agreement to limit the rights, each partner is a manager for the enterprise, an agent for the partnership and every other partner, and a principal of every other partner. As a result, all the regular rules of agency apply. This means, among other things that each partner is a fiduciary of the other partners, and that when a partner deals with some third party, the firm is bound by the conduct of that partner if the conduct was apparently or actually authorized. Remember that if the partnership is a limited partnership or a limited liability partnership, some of these rules will be modified. This discussion focuses on general partnerships.

Rights of the Partners

A person who enters a partnership acquires certain rights. Some of these rights are gained through the agreement, and some are gained through the terms of the Uniform Partnership Act (UPA)[1] or the Revised Uniform Partnership Act (RUPA).[2] This book cannot cover all the rights that might be included in the agreement, but it can examine some of those rights imposed by the uniform acts.

Management   By virtue of his or her status as a partner, each partner is entitled to an equal voice in management. In conducting the ordinary business of the partnership, a majority vote controls. In order to conduct any extraordinary business, a unanimous vote is required.[3] A matter is considered extraordinary if it changes the basic nature or the basic risk of the business.

While the UPA requires that each partner be given an equal voice in managing the business, the partners are allowed to agree on the definition of "equal." Such an agreement can be beneficial to a dynamic business. If the partnership is forced to conduct its business by majority vote, opportunities may be lost because a vote cannot occur quickly enough to take advantage of them as they arise.

To avoid this problem, many partnership agreements *define* the management voice of each partner. Remember that the agreement must include such a definition to be valid. For instance, a partnership composed of Ali, Ben, Chris, and Dee might provide the following management divisions:

- Ali is in charge of inventory.
- Ben is in charge of marketing.
- Chris is in charge of personnel.
- Dee is in charge of technology.
- Any other areas are governed by a vote.

Under such an agreement, Ben can make marketing decisions immediately, without needing to meet with the partners to vote on the issue. Likewise, Ali can decide matters concerning inventory; Chris can make personnel decisions; and Dee can upgrade the operating system on their computers without first consulting the other partners. Absent such an agreement, each partner has a truly equal voice in management: decisions will be made by majority vote.

RUPA permits but does not require the filing of a statement of partnership authority with the appropriate state office.[4] The partnership's existence is not dependent upon the filing of *any* statement. If the statement is filed, it has an impact upon a third party dealing with the partnership. It can grant extraordinary authority to partner(s) and/or limit the ordinary authority of partner(s). If the third party deals with a partner with authority provided in the statement, the third party is assured that the partnership will be bound. Any limitation upon a partner's authority, however, generally does not affect any third party who does not know about the statement.[5] The statement concerns the authority of the partners to bind the partnership to third persons. The relationship among the partners is governed by the partnership agreement or RUPA, and not by the statement of partnership authority.

Reimbursement   Each partner is entitled to repayment by the partnership for any money spent to further the interests of the partnership. In addition, each partner is entitled to interest on the advances or payments made, unless the agreement says otherwise. Each partner is also entitled to a return of his or her capital contribution at the close of the partnership, provided enough money is present after all the other liabilities have been satisfied.[6] (*Capital contribution* is money or assets invested by the business owners to commence or promote an enterprise.)

Profits and Losses   Unless the agreement states otherwise, each partner is entitled to an equal share of the profits of the business.[7] The profits are not automatically divided in the same percentage as the partners contributed capital, nor are they automatically divided in any other unequal manner. Profits are the only remuneration to which any partner is always entitled.[8] No partner is automatically permitted to draw a salary from the enterprise even if that partner devotes extra time to running the business. However, the agreement can be worded in such a manner that a partner receives a salary from the business, with the remaining profits then divided in some predetermined manner. Any salary provision for partners must be expressly set out in the agreement. Losses are divided among the partners in the same ratio as profits are shared, unless the agreement expressly provides for a different allocation of losses.

Books and Records   Each partner is entitled to free access to the books and records of the business. This includes the right to inspect the records and to copy them as the partner sees fit. Similarly, each partner is expected to give, and entitled to receive, detailed information on any matter that affects the partnership.[9]

Partnership Property   Under the UPA, each partner is a co-owner of partnership property with the other partners. This ownership is called a tenancy in partnership.[10] This tenancy entitles the partner to possess the property for partnership purposes, but not to possess it for nonpartnership purposes. However, a majority of the states have now adopted RUPA. RUPA has moved away from viewing the partnership as an aggregate of the partners to viewing it as a separate entity.[11] RUPA states simply that since a partnership is a separate entity, its property belongs to it and not to the partners.[12] A partner has his or her partnership interest, but is not a co-owner of specific partnership property.[13] This is a significant departure from the UPA.

Right to an Account Any general partner is entitled to a formal *account*—that is, a statement or record of business transactions or dealings—if he or she feels mistreated in the partnership.[14] Specifically, any partner who is excluded from the business or from use of business properties is entitled to an account. And the UPA provides for an account in any other circumstances that render it just and reasonable. In effect, any time an internal argument or disagreement arises about the business operation, the courts will say an account is just and reasonable.

Each partner is a fiduciary for every other partner and is expected to account to the other partners and to the partnership for any benefits received or any profits derived without the knowledge and consent of the other partners.[15]

Duties of the Partners

Agency Duties Each general partner is an *agent* of the partnership and of every other partner. Thus, any conduct by a partner that is *apparently* authorized is binding on the partnership. Because each partner is *personally* liable for partnership debts, such an act makes each partner at least *potentially* personally liable. This obviously creates a possible financial hazard to the partners. To reduce the danger that a reckless partner can present, the UPA restricts some agency power. Under UPA § 9(3), there is no apparent authority to do any of five specific acts unless *unanimously approved.* These five acts are as follows:

1. Making an assignment for the benefit of creditors by transferring partnership property to a trust for the creditors of the business (*Assignment for the benefit of creditors* is an assignment in trust made by debtors for the payment of their debts.)
2. Selling or otherwise disposing of the goodwill of the business (*Goodwill* is the favorable reputation of an established and well-conducted business.)
3. Performing any act that makes it impossible to carry on the business
4. Confessing a judgment against the partnership (In this context, *confessing a judgment* is an acknowledgment in court that the partnership is legally to blame. Standard form contracts may provide that the party contracting with the partnership has authority to confess judgment against it.)
5. Submitting a partnership claim or liability to an arbitrator (An *arbitrator* is an independent person chosen by the parties or appointed by statute. The issues are submitted to the arbitrator for settlement outside of court.)

Notice the scope of these acts. The first three frustrate business, and the last two remove the partners' rights to their "day in court." Except for these five exceptions, any other act of a partner within the scope of apparent authority is binding.

Since each partner is an agent, *notice* given to any partner on a partnership matter is as valid as notice given to each of the partners.[16] This is simply the application of basic agency law to a partnership/agency situation. Similarly, knowledge gained, or *remembered*, while one is a partner is imputed to each partner. Generally knowledge acquired before becoming a partner is not imputed to the partnership. However, there are exceptions. Assume Josie learned important information prior to becoming a partner. After she became a partner she is shown to have the facts in mind when she acted on behalf of the partnership, the knowledge will be imputed to the partnership.

If a partner acts, or fails to act, within the course and scope of the business, and the act or omission causes harm to a third person, the partnership is liable to the third person, as is the partner who committed the tort.[17] The other partners face joint and several liability for torts. Under RUPA, the liability of the partnership and the partners is joint and several for *all* debts of the partnership. However, RUPA defines joint and several liability in a different sense than is commonly used in law. Generally, RUPA requires the creditor to exhaust the partnership's assets before going against the individual partners.[18]

Likewise, if a partner *misapplies* money or property of a third person that is in the possession of the partnership, the partnership is liable. All the partners, or each of them, may need to answer for the breach of trust by one partner.[19] Again, the liability is joint and several.

Obviously, being a partner *may* be hazardous to your financial health. Even if you are a careful, cautious person, you face potential financial liability, maybe even disaster, from the conduct of your partners. What rights do you have that protect you? What rights are available for the protection of any partner from the excesses of another partner?

One such right protects the other partners and the partnership from a creditor of a partner. For example, assume that Arturo, Bill, and Cindi are partners. The business is very profitable, and Bill and Cindi are solvent. However, Arturo is in deep financial trouble. Several of Arturo's creditors sue Arturo to collect their claims. They win the suit, only to discover that Arturo cannot pay the judgment from his personal assets. Can these creditors foreclose on Arturo's share of the partnership assets? No. All the creditors can do is to get a charging order from a court.[20] A *charging order* is a court order permitting a creditor to receive a portion of the profits from the operation of a business; it is especially common in partnership situations. Under a charging order, the debtor/partner's *profits* are paid to the creditors until the claims are completely paid. Thus, the partnership can continue, and Bill and Cindi are protected. Only Arturo, the debtor, suffers.

On the other hand, suppose that the partnership is in financial difficulty but that some of the partners are solvent. Can the partnership's creditors proceed directly against the individual partners, bypassing or ignoring the assets of the firm? No. Generally, the creditors of the firm must first proceed against the assets of the firm.[21]

Fiduciary Duties   Another protection given to the partners is the legal status assigned to each partner. Each member of a partnership is a *fiduciary* of the other partners and of the business itself.[22] The fiduciary position carries with it certain responsibilities and certain duties. Each partner is required to account for, and to surrender to the firm, any profits derived from the business or from the use of business assets. No partner is allowed to have a conflict of interest with the partnership. And each partner is entitled to indemnification from a partner who causes a loss or liability from misconduct in the course and scope of employment. RUPA explicitly addresses the fiduciary duties of partners to each other, including the obligations of loyalty, due care, and good faith.[23]

Rights of Third Persons Who Deal with Partnerships

When partners are dealing internally, each is aware of the rights and duties of the other partner(s). Each general partner should know the terms of the basic agreement and the

eClass 32.1 Finance/Management

LIABILITY IN A GENERAL PARTNERSHIP

Assume that eClass is continuing to operate as a general partnership. Meg, a partner, signed a contract with a marketing consulting firm to develop a new marketing plan at a cost of $20,000. She entered this contract without consulting with the other partners in the firm, believing that the new consultants would improve eClass's opportunity to establish its niche in the industry. Unfortunately, when the plan is implemented, it is a disaster. Ani thinks that Meg should have consulted with the partners before signing the contract and asks you whether eClass and/or the other partners are liable for this contractual agreement. What will you tell her? In this situation what is Meg's personal liability, if any, to the consulting firm and/or eClass?

BUSINESS CONSIDERATIONS   Assume that a partnership does not want an individual partner to unilaterally enter into specialized service contracts for the firm. What should the partnership do to prevent such conduct? How could a statement of authority under RUPA affect the result?

ETHICAL CONSIDERATIONS   Suppose that an individual partner *does* enter into a contract without consulting with his or her partners. Is it ethical for the firm to refuse to honor the contract because the partners did not discuss it? Why or why not?

limits of his or her authority. A third person who deals with the partnership, however, has no such advantage. Any nonpartner who deals with the firm must rely on *appearances*. As a result, a third person who deals with the partnership may be given certain rights by the court that are contrary to the basic partnership agreement.

Contracts   As noted earlier, each partner is an agent of the partnership. Thus, if a partner negotiates a contract on behalf of the partnership, that partner is negotiating as an agent. From agency law, we know that if the agent has the *apparent authority* to perform an act, the principal is bound by the act. The same rule applies here. If the partner has the apparent authority to enter the contract, the partnership is bound to honor the contract. Under the prior law, partners were jointly liable on partnership contracts. Under RUPA, the liability of the partnership and the partners is joint and several for all obligations of the partnership. (Remember that RUPA defines joint and several liability in a different sense.[24])

In many instances, the partner has the actual authority to enter the contract. If so, the partnership is obviously bound, and the partner who negotiated the contract is no more liable than the other partners.

In some cases, the partner has the apparent authority to enter the contract but lacks the actual authority. (Recall, for example, the division of duties discussion earlier in this chapter.) Under these circumstances, the partnership must still honor the contract with the third person. But the partner who negotiated the contract will be liable to the partnership for any losses that arise because the partner exceeded his or her authority.

In still other cases, the partner does not have even apparent authority. If the partner exceeds his or her authority and negotiates a contract, the negotiating partner is personally obligated to perform, but the firm is *not* liable on the agreement.

When the court examines these agreements, the apparent authority of the partner is of overriding importance. When deciding the scope of authority, courts often look at the type of business the firm is conducting. If the partnership buys and sells as its primary business purpose, the court views the partnership (unofficially) as a *trading* partnership. If the primary business purpose is to provide services, the court views it (unofficially) as a *nontrading* partnership. In a trading partnership, the partners are presumed to have broad powers. In a nontrading partnership, partners are deemed to have much narrower powers. A partner in a trading partnership is presumably authorized to perform *any* management-related duties. In contrast, a partner in a nontrading business is apparently authorized to do only those things reasonably necessary to further the main business purpose of the partnership.

A third person who is dealing with a partnership for the first time needs to exercise care. The partner with whom the third person is dealing may exceed his or her authority, and the resulting contract will not be binding on the partnership.

Borrowing in the Partnership Name   Perhaps the most important area in which the court applies the trading-versus-nontrading distinction is in the borrowing of money. In a trading partnership, the firm deals from inventory. Inventory must be purchased. Purchases require money. Thus, a partner in a trading partnership has the apparent authority to borrow money in the firm's name.

In a nontrading partnership, the need for money is less obvious. As a result, the courts are less apt to impose liability on the firm for a loan that was made to a single partner even though that partner borrowed the money in the partnership name.

Torts and Crimes   Again, remember that each partner is an agent (and servant) for the partnership and every other partner. Consequently, when a partner commits a *tort*, the partner is liable as the tortfeasor. (A *tortfeasor* is a wrongdoer; the one who commits a tort.) The partnership may also be liable jointly and severally with the partner who committed the tort, under the theory of *respondeat superior* if the injured person can establish that the partner was performing in "the course and scope of employment" when the tort was committed. Their liability is joint and several in the traditional sense. Under prior law, the partnership and each of the partners individually were jointly and severally liable in the traditional sense. Under RUPA, the liability of the partnership and the other partners is joint and several for all debts of the partnership. No distinction is made for liability for contracts or torts. For an example, assume Mary, Ned, and Oscar are partners. Ned is driving to a business meeting to represent the business in some negotiations. On the way to the meeting, Ned runs a stop sign and hits Sam. Since Ned was on a job-related trip, Ned and the partnership are liable to Sam. Under RUPA, the other individual partners will be liable only when the partnership assets are exhausted.

If the tort is willful and malicious, however, the firm is normally not liable. Assume Oscar, another of the partners, is driving to a business meeting to represent the firm and sees Tom crossing the street. Oscar is still angry with Tom for an insult from long ago. Oscar accelerates the car and *intentionally* runs over Tom. Since the tort was willful and malicious, neither Mary nor Ned nor the firm is liable to Tom. However, if the willful and malicious tort is one that furthers any business interests of the firm, the partnership *may* be held liable despite the intentional nature of the tort. And even if the intentional tort is not related to the business purpose, the partnership can still be held liable, provided that it assents to or ratifies the tortious conduct.

If a partner commits a crime, what liability do the noncriminal partners face? For most crimes, the other partners are not liable. Most crimes require a specific criminal intent. To be convicted of such a crime, a person must commit the crime or aid and abet in its commission. (To *aid and abet* means to help, assist, or facilitate the commission of a crime.) Unless evidence of involvement is shown, only the partner who committed the crime will be liable. However, some crimes can be committed *without* a specific criminal intent. Such crimes are normally *regulatory* in nature; in other words, these crimes involve violations of administrative areas rather than violations in traditional criminal areas. If one of these crimes is committed, all the partners are criminally liable. A common example is a liquor control law that provides criminal fines for bars or restaurants that serve alcohol to a person who is underage, and that also fine their owners. Generally the owners are liable whether or not they are aware that a customer is underage (or even if the bartender was not aware that the customer was underage.)

OPERATION OF A LIMITED PARTNERSHIP

Although a limited partnership is an actual partnership, the limited partners are more like investors than regular partners. They have contributed cash, property, or services, and in exchange they receive an interest or "share." Courts often treat the limited partners like investors in limited liability companies or corporations. As you would expect, the inspection rights of a limited partner are more restricted than those of general partners. Under the traditional approach, a limited partner may lose his or her protected status by managing the firm. This is not true under the Uniform Limited Partnership Act (2001).

OPERATION OF A CORPORATION

The corporation's actions are governed by three documents—the corporation code for the state of incorporation, the articles of incorporation, and the bylaws, as illustrated in Exhibit 32.1. The officers and the board of directors bear the responsibilities for the day-to-day operations and the overall policies of a corporation, respectively. They also act as agents for the corporation. The board of directors usually acts as an agent collectively. The management of the entity is centralized. Directors, officers, and controlling shareholders are often called "managers" for the sake of simplicity. The managers are ultimately answerable to the shareholders, the owners. Shareholders exert only indirect control, generally through the election of directors. Exhibit 32.2 shows the legal relationship between the three primary groups. Some writers contend that the legal model is inaccurate and that often the board of directors actually controls the stockholders instead. When individual shareholders are displeased with the management or

Exhibit 32.1

Governance Documents

State Corporation Code	+	Articles of Incorporation	+	Bylaws

Source: Courtesy of Lynn M. Forsythe, © Lynn M. Forsythe 2010

Exhibit 32.2

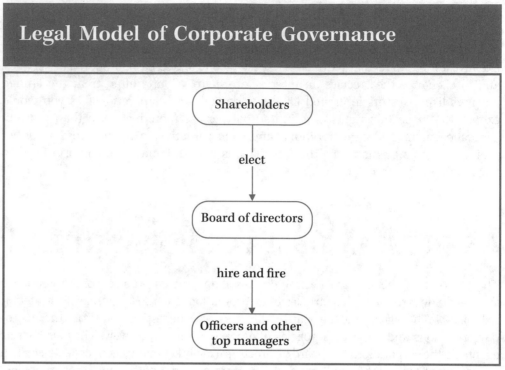

Legal Model of Corporate Governance

Source: Courtesy of Lynn M. Forsythe, © Lynn M. Forsythe 2010

performance of a firm, the shareholders are likely to do the "Wall Street walk" by selling their shares and walking away.

Increasingly, shareholders are walking away when they do not trust the accuracy of the corporate financial records. In 2002, the National Conference of Commissioners on Uniform State Laws (NCCUSL) approved a new Uniform Securities Act (USA).[25] Like other uniform acts, the USA is a *state* act. If adopted, it would replace or supplement existing state securities laws. It prohibits fraud in the sale of securities and imposes registration requirements for brokers and investment advisors.[26] The federal government also has enacted a number of securities laws. (Securities laws are discussed in more detail in Chapter 34.)

Rights of the Shareholders

Stock Certificates   Shareholders exert indirect control over the corporation by virtue of their ownership of shares; the more they own, the more power they wield. Ownership is generally evidenced by a stock certificate. Stock certificates became prevalent in the United States by the late 1800s. They were often elaborately designed and played a role as financial document, advertising pitch, and public relations ploy.

The stock certificate is becoming obsolete, especially in large publicly traded companies. Ownership is increasingly evidenced by an "electronic book entry."[27]

Types of Stock Owned   A shareholder may own *common stock*, which allows the shareholder to receive dividends, to vote on corporate issues, and to receive property upon the corporation's liquidation. Some shareholders may own *preferred stock*, which, as its name suggests, confers priority with regard to dividends, voting, or liquidation rights. Not all corporations issue preferred stock. If the corporation does issue preferred stock, there may be several classes, or series, that set out different gradations of priority for each class. Under most state statutes, the articles of incorporation must spell out the preferences; such preferences generally will not be implied.

The most common preference involves priority with regard to *dividends* (cash, property, or other shares that the board of directors declares as payment to shareholders). For example, preferred stockholders may receive dividends paid at a specified rate (for example, 7 percent) before any other classes of stock receive any dividends. If any funds for dividends remain after payment to the various classes of preferred stockholders, some preferred shareholders may have *participation* rights; that is, they take part in this additional distribution of dividends with the common shareholders.

In addition to dividend and participation rights, preferred shareholders may receive corporate assets before any other stockholder if the corporation is liquidated. After the debts of the corporation are paid, preferred shareholders are the first to receive the par value of their stocks plus any outstanding dividends. (*Par value* is the face value assigned to a stock and printed on the stock certificate.)

Common stockholders receive corporate assets only if sufficient assets remain to pay their stocks' par values. If there are any additional assets after payment to the common stockholders, the preferred and common shareholders normally share this balance in proportion to their shares. Preferred shareholders also may enjoy *conversion* rights (the shareholder's option to change preferred stock into common stock or corporate bonds) and/or *redemption* rights (the corporation's right to buy the shares in certain authorized circumstances). These features are summarized in Exhibit 32.3.

Shareholders' Meetings

As is the case with other corporate business, the shareholders' meetings should be conducted in accordance with the articles of incorporation, the bylaws, and the state corporation code. These "rules" may require an annual meeting of the shareholders. Sometimes, an annual meeting is not required for small closely held corporations. However, it is important for the corporation to observe the normal formalities. Failure to observe formalities is one of the considerations when a court is considering piercing the corporate veil, which was discussed in Chapter 31. The board of directors can also call special meetings of the shareholders, for example, the directors may call a special meeting to discuss an offer to purchase the corporation.

Exhibit 32.3

Stock Characteristics from the Stockholder's Perspective

Type of Stock	Characteristics
Common	Basic shares issued by a corporation; they generally have a lower priority for dividends and distribution of assets upon dissolution. Includes voting rights.
Preferred	Shares that include special rights to dividends and/or distribution of assets upon dissolution; often the rights to dividends is at a specified rate.
Participating Preferred	Shares that include special rights to dividends and/or distributions; in a successful year after the owners of these shares receive their "preferred" rights they receive an extra dividend; usually so that the total dividend is at least equal to that of the common stockholders.
Cumulative Preferred	Shares that include the right to a specified dividend; any unpaid dividends owed to these shareholders must be paid before dividends can be paid on the common stock.
Convertible Preferred	Shares that include the shareholder's right to convert them into another type of stock; generally they are convertible into common stock or corporate bonds.
Redeemable Preferred	Shares that the corporation can repurchase according to the terms of the redemption agreement.

Source: Courtesy of Lynn M. Forsythe, © Lynn M. Forsythe 2010

Notice   In general, the corporation must send written notice of the meeting to all shareholders of record. Statutory and bylaw provisions often spell out the procedures for giving notice. Such notice ordinarily contains the time, date, and place of the meeting, as well as a statement of the purpose of the meeting. Most statutes require at least ten days' notice before a meeting can legitimately be conducted. States are beginning to provide for the use of electronic media in shareholder meetings, including notice of meetings.[28] Shareholders can expressly waive the notice requirement in writing before or after the meeting, or they can impliedly waive it by not protesting the lack of notice.

The corporation will specify a record date for the meeting. The record date may be specified in the bylaws. A shareholder must be registered in the corporate books on the record date in order to be entitled to vote at the shareholder's meeting. There is also a record date for dividends and the shareholder on that record date is entitled to the dividend even if he or she sells the stock after that date. The owner of the stock on the record date is called the owner of record or stockholder of record.

Quorum   Shareholder meetings cannot take place in the absence of a quorum. State statutes and corporate bylaws or articles usually state the percentage of *outstanding shares* or shares entitled to vote, that constitutes a quorum. A majority of such votes is usually necessary; yet some states authorize articles of incorporation that set the quorum requirement at one-third of all outstanding shares. Delaware *permits* a corporation to conduct shareholder meetings by "remote communication" under some conditions. The board of directors can choose whether to use "remote communication" and how the meeting will be conducted.[29] As technology advances, the shareholders at remote sites may be able to be counted as part of the quorum and to vote. For example, ballots submitted by "electronic transmission" will satisfy the written ballot requirement of the Delaware statute.[30]

Dissident shareholders (those who disagree with the actions of management) may prevent a quorum by not attending meetings; but the law remains unsettled as to whether a subsequent walkout of dissident shareholders, once a quorum is present, invalidates the meeting.

Election and Removal of Directors   One of the foremost powers held by shareholders is their capacity to elect and remove directors. Although the articles of incorporation usually designate the people who are to serve as the initial directors, these directors may serve only until the first annual meeting. At that time, the shareholders *may* elect some (or all) of them to the board of directors. If vacancies occur on the board because of deaths or resignations, the shareholders normally vote to fill these vacancies. The articles of incorporation or bylaws, however, may permit the directors to fill these posts. Directors usually serve staggered terms. This means that only a certain proportion of directors (for example, one-third) will be up for reelection at any given meeting. Such staggered terms ensure continuity of leadership on the board. In recent years, there has been a trend toward adding outside directors to the board. *Outside directors* are directors who are not employees and who have little or no direct interest in the corporation.[31]

Shareholders have *inherent* power (that is, power regardless of the articles or bylaws) to remove a director for cause. Previous cases have upheld the exercise of such rights when directors have engaged in embezzlement or other misconduct; have failed to live up to their duties to the corporation; or have undertaken unauthorized acts. The director, of course, may appeal his or her removal to a court of law. Statutes, articles of incorporation, and bylaws may also allow removal without cause.

Amendment of the Bylaws   Bylaws are provisions intended to regulate the corporation and its management. To be valid, bylaws must comply with state incorporation statutes and the articles of incorporation. Shareholders retain inherent power to amend (or repeal) bylaws. State law generally mandates the proportion of outstanding shares needed to approve an amendment.

Voting   The voting rights exercised by shareholders at meetings allow them *indirect control* of the corporation and the board of directors. Shareholders of record ordinarily appear on the voting list and can vote on matters that are lawfully on the agenda.

Owners of nonparticipating preferred stock generally do not have the right to vote on most matters. Shareholders can either be present at the meeting and vote in person, or they can assign their voting rights to others, who then vote their shares for them by proxy. (A *proxy* is a person appointed and designated to act for another, especially at a public meeting. The term proxy can be used to designate both the person and the document used to appoint the person.) If a shareholder in a public-issue corporation does not want to participate personally in the meeting, he or she can sign a proxy, giving the proxy holder authority to act as his or her agent.[32] Exhibit 32.4 shows a proxy. Delaware permits stockholders to appoint proxies by transmitting telegrams, cablegrams, or other electronic transmissions.[33] The controlling "rules" may permit shareholders to vote on specific proposals by mail, telephone, or Internet.

Whoever controls large blocs of proxies in a public-issue corporation may, in effect, dictate the outcome of the election. For this reason, management (and sometimes dissident stockholders) in such corporations may solicit proxies in order to consolidate voting power. Not surprisingly, then, vicious proxy fights have occurred at various times in U.S. corporations. Because of the high stakes and the possibilities for abuse, federal law now ensures that proxy solicitations are carried out fairly. Within the corporation, impartial parties called inspectors, judges, or tellers oversee the election to ensure fairness.

Exhibit 32.4

Proxy

_____, a California Corporation.

The undersigned, as record holder of the shares of stock of _____, described above, revokes any previous proxies and appoints _____ as the undersigned's proxy to attend the special shareholder's meeting on _____, and any adjournment of that meeting.

The proxy holder is entitled to cast a total number of votes equal to, but not exceeding _____ which the undersigned would be entitled to cast if the undersigned were personally present.

The undersigned authorizes the undersigned's proxy holder to vote and otherwise represent the undersigned with regards to any business that may come before this meeting in the same manner and with the same effect as if the undersigned were personally present.

THIS PROXY MAY BE REVOKED AT ANY TIME IN WRITING.

Dated: _____, 20_____

Source: Courtesy of Robyn Esraelian, Richardson, Jones and Esraelian, Attorneys-at-Law, Fresno, California

In most corporate matters, a shareholder can cast one vote for each share held. This is called *straight voting*. Unless the voting involves an extraordinary corporate matter (such as dissolution, merger, amendment of the articles of incorporation, or sale of substantially all the assets), the decision made by a majority generally controls. Thus, votes of more than 50 percent for any ordinary corporate matter usually bind the corporation. In extraordinary matters, statutes may require a higher proportion (for example, two-thirds) of votes for the proposal to be approved.

To offset shareholders who own large blocs of votes and who may therefore be able to wield significant control, most state statutes today either permit or require *cumulative voting*. Cumulative voting applies only to the election of directors and is a method to assist minority shareholders in obtaining representation on the board.

The following simple example illustrates the difference between straight and cumulative voting. Assume that at the annual shareholders' meeting, three directors will be elected from a field of six candidates—Umberto, Victoria, Wally, Xavier, Yvette, and Zack. Under straight voting, shareholder Amir, who owns 100 shares, can cast 100 votes for each of three directors, say Umberto, Victoria, and Wally. If, instead, cumulative voting is used, Amir can cast 300 votes (the number of votes equals the number of shares times the number of directors being elected). Amir can cast 300 votes for Umberto or can divide 300 votes among the candidates in any proportion he wishes (that is, 150 for Umberto, 100 for Victoria, and 50 for Yvette). In this fashion, Amir's votes accumulate—hence, the term cumulative voting. A minority shareholder can have a larger impact on the election of directors under cumulative voting than under straight voting.

To dilute any advantage that the minority might gain through cumulative voting, management may stagger the terms of directors, reduce or enlarge the size of the board, or remove directors elected by the minority. To counter such steps, lawmakers in many jurisdictions have passed statutory provisions that protect cumulative voting rights by making such steps illegal or by mandating statutory formulas that safeguard the beneficial effects of cumulative voting.

Voting trusts, like proxies and cumulative voting, represent devices used to consolidate votes for control. A shareholder can create a voting trust by transferring to trustees the shares he or she owns. (In this context, *trustees* are persons in whom a power to vote is vested under an express or implied agreement.) Once the shareholder has entered into such a trust, the shareholder has no right to vote the shares until the trust terminates. The trustees issue a *voting trust certificate* to the shareholder to indicate that the shareholder retains all rights incidental to share ownership except voting. In contrast to proxies, which are generally revocable, voting trusts are normally irrevocable. State statutes, however, usually limit the duration of voting trusts to a specified time period, such as 10 years (with possible extensions).

Pooling agreements are similar to voting trusts. In such agreements, each shareholder agrees to vote the shares he or she owns in a specified way. Both voting trusts and pooling agreements remain valid and enforceable as long as they do not, in effect, preempt the directors' managerial functions. This could happen if the shareholders who enter into these arrangements are also directors. For example, it is legal for the shareholders to agree through voting trusts or pooling agreements to vote for director

Ali at the annual election of directors (even if director Ali is also one of the shareholders who enters into the arrangement). However, voting trusts or pooling arrangements to bring about the dismissal of the chief executive officer (CEO) normally will be unenforceable. Why? Selection of officers is ordinarily a function of the directors.

Shareholders of close corporations probably utilize voting trusts and pooling arrangements more than their counterparts in publicly held corporations. Modern statutes recognize that close corporations are more similar to partnerships than most other corporate entities. Consequently, some states will enforce agreements that treat shareholders as if they were directors, when all the shareholders are parties to the agreement. Such statutory developments illustrate the law's ability to change whenever modifications become necessary.

Dividends   Most shareholders buy shares of for-profit, public-issue corporations primarily to receive dividends. Such shareholders normally care more about dividends than about control. We have spoken of a *right* to receive dividends, but that constitutes a very loose use of the term "right." Actually, there is no absolute right to receive dividends. The power to declare dividends resides with the board of directors. Shareholders cannot compel the directors to declare dividends without proving bad faith. The directors alone decide, first, *if* dividends will be distributed. If so, they also determine the timing, type, and amount of the dividend.

Of course, shareholders hope to receive the financial profits represented by dividends. *Cash dividends* are the most common type. However, dividends may also take the form of *property* or *stocks*. Property dividends are also called asset dividends. They are usually paid in the company's product. For example, a large distillery once paid its dividend in barrels of whiskey.[34] When the dividend is paid in stock, it is usually expressed as a percentage of the number of shares already held by the shareholder.[35] The dividend may be in additional shares of the issuing company or in shares of another company, usually a subsidiary company.[36] The directors must make certain that the dividends will be paid from a *lawful source*. This is particularly true of cash dividends. In general, statutes limit the sources of dividends to *current net profits* (those earned in the preceding accounting period) or *earned surplus* (the sum of the net profits retained by the corporation during all previous years of existence). Any declaration of dividends that will impair the corporation's *original capital structure* (the number of shares originally issued times their stated value) is illegal and may subject the directors and shareholders to personal liability. Similarly, payment of dividends during the corporation's insolvency or any payment that will bring about insolvency or financial difficulties is illegal. Exhibit 32.5 illustrates the decision-making process in declaring dividends.

As noted earlier, preferred stockholders enjoy priority with regard to the distribution of dividends. Preferred shareholders are also protected from improper dividend declarations. Directors normally cannot declare dividends if the declaration will jeopardize the liquidation preferences of the preferred shareholders. (*Liquidation preferences* are priorities given to creditors and shareholders when the enterprise is terminated and the assets are distributed.) Once a dividend is lawfully declared, preferred stockholders receive their dividends first. Common stockholders receive

Exhibit 32.5

The Decision to Issue Dividends: A Flowchart

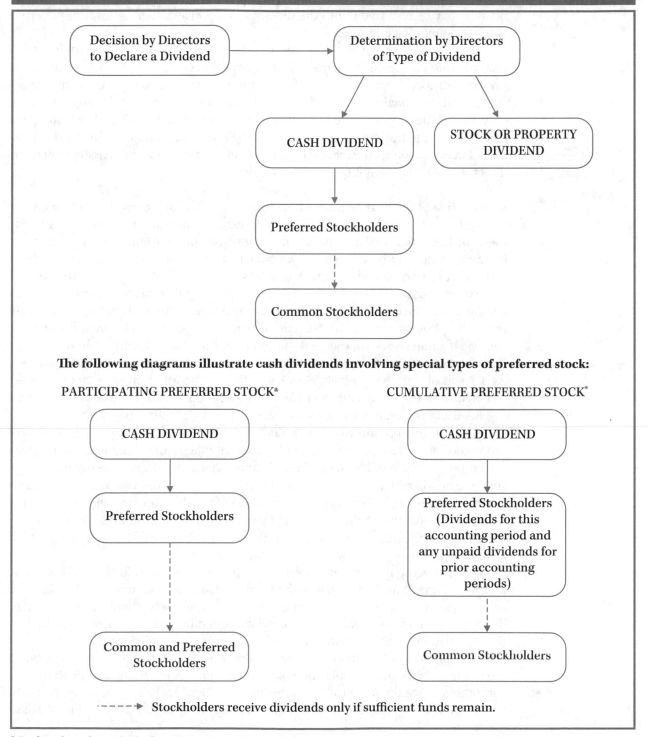

The following diagrams illustrate cash dividends involving special types of preferred stock:

PARTICIPATING PREFERRED STOCK[a]   CUMULATIVE PREFERRED STOCK[*]

- - - - ▶ Stockholders receive dividends only if sufficient funds remain.

* Preferred stock can be both participating and cumulative.

dividends only if adequate funds remain after the preferred stockholders have been paid. Sometimes preferred stockholders have *participating* preferred stock. This means they not only receive their original dividend but also share (or participate) with the common stockholders in any dividends that are paid after the preferred stockholders have received their initial dividends. In other words, participating preferred stockholders may be able to dip into the dividend fund twice. Usually, however, preferred stock is nonparticipating.

There is another complexity in declaring preferred dividends. Preferred dividends may be *cumulative,* which means that the sum (or accumulation) of all unpaid prior preferred dividends must be paid before common shareholders receive any dividends. In contrast, in *noncumulative* preferred dividends, the preferred stockholder receives only the dividend preferences for the *current accounting period;* and the common stockholders then receive their dividends should any funds remain. Under this type of preference, the preferred shareholders lose all dividends for any years in which the directors have chosen not to declare a dividend.

Preemptive Stock Rights   Sometimes it is necessary for a corporation to increase its capital by issuing new shares. This is an extraordinary matter involving amendment of the articles of incorporation because the original number of shares and their par value will be changed. Shareholders must vote on the issuance of these new shares. A shareholder's interest in this matter extends beyond voting rights. For example, assume Bonnie owns 10 shares of Samp Corporation. Samp's original capitalization involved 100 shares sold at $100 each ($10,000 stated capital). At that time, Bonnie owned 10 percent of Samp Corporation (10 shares/100 total shares). If Samp issues another 100 shares as a result of the amending of the articles, Bonnie then will own 5 percent of the corporation (10 shares/200 total shares). As a result of this new capitalization, her voting power will decrease proportionately. Her right to receive dividends and corporate assets on liquidation will also decrease.

Realizing the unfairness of this sequence of events, courts began to protect the Bonnies of the corporate world by a doctrine called *preemptive rights.* These courts promoted the notion that the right of first refusal inheres in stock ownership. Before the corporation can sell to anyone else, it must offer to sell to Bonnie the number of shares that will restore her proportionate share of ownership. This allows Bonnie to preempt the rights of other would-be purchasers of the stock because she can purchase before they have the chance to do so. Once the corporation notifies Bonnie of her preemptive rights, she has a limited time to exercise them. If she does not take advantage of the offer, she waives her rights of preemption.

Preemptive rights normally apply only to new shares issued for cash and will not apply to shares issued in exchange for property (such as a commercial building) or services (such as shares issued to lure a CEO to Samp), or to shares issued as share dividends, or to *treasury stock* (stock originally issued but subsequently reacquired by the corporation). In this last situation, there is no new issue and, hence, no reduction in Bonnie's proportionate interest in Samp Corporation. In the first two situations, preemptive rights may cripple the corporation's financing efforts and obstruct the corporation's legitimate, profit-maximizing activities, such as acquiring property and recruiting top-flight executives. Because of the possible frustration of these worthwhile aims, courts and statutes alike deny Bonnie's preemptive rights, however, her ownership interest is still diluted. In addition, judicial and statutory treatment of Bonnie's preemptive rights might be different in a publicly held (as opposed to a close) corporation.

Inspection of Corporate Books and Records   The rights of shareholders to inspect corporate records arise from both common law doctrines and express statutory provisions. In light of the recent situations, such as Enron and MCI Worldcom, shareholders may increase the amount and frequency of their inspection of corporate records. In general, shareholders have access to such corporate materials as stockholder lists; minutes of shareholders' meetings; minutes of board or officers' meetings; financial records, such as books of account or other periodic summaries; and business documents, including tax returns, contracts, and office correspondence or memoranda.

At common law, inspection rights were qualified (rather than absolute) because shareholders needed to demonstrate that the reason for inspection involved a "proper purpose." Shareholders had to show that the motivation for the inspection related to their status as a shareholder. Requests for shareholder lists to communicate with shareholders about corporate matters, or corporate financial records to determine the value of shares, the propriety of dividends, or possible mismanagement ordinarily qualify as proper purposes. On the other hand, shareholder requests that ask for information to learn trade secrets for the benefit of the corporation's competitors or to bring *strike suits* (those without any real merit) in order to impede management normally will constitute improper purposes. Assuming the inspection is for a proper purpose, the shareholder generally can employ attorneys, accountants, and other personnel to aid in examining records, making copies or summaries, and the like. Note the similarity between a shareholder's inspection rights and those of a limited partner.

Most statutes require a showing of proper purpose; but once the shareholder has made an initial showing of a proper purpose, the burden of proof shifts to the corporation to rebut the presumption by showing an improper purpose on the part of the shareholder. Sometimes statutes change the burden of proof or the party who has the burden, depending on the type of record being requested. Statutes may also restrict inspection rights only to certain shareholders (for example, those who have held their shares for at least six months or who own at least 5 percent of the outstanding shares). These statutory restrictions, however, do not eliminate the shareholder's common law inspection rights. But, as mentioned, the shareholder, not the corporation, has the burden of proving proper purpose under these common law doctrines.

Federal securities law and state statutes that mandate annual disclosure of profits and losses, officer compensation, and so on have made inspection rights somewhat less important. The information made available to the shareholder under these statutes encompasses the type of information that shareholders previously could obtain only by exercising their rights of inspection.

Transfer of Shares   As discussed earlier, ownership of share (stock) certificates signifies ownership of a portion of the corporation. Thus, these shares are the shareholder's property. Shareholders, like other owners of property, generally can transfer their shares to someone else (by gift or sale). A transfer of shares generally occurs through endorsement and delivery of the stock certificate in conjunction with a surrender of the certificate for subsequent reissue to the new owner by the corporation's secretary or, in a large corporation, by its transfer agent. Exhibit 32.6 shows various types of stock from the corporation's perspective. Stock exchange rules regulate the conduct of *transfer agents*, who are professionals who help the corporate secretary with the myriad details attendant on large-scale transfers of stocks. Transfers of stock in these situations, including the actual physical transfers of stock certificates, cause numerous administrative headaches. Recent developments, such as when a brokerage firm holds title to stock through bookkeeping entries rather than possession of actual certificates, will likely lead to the abolition of stock certificates and their replacement by computer printouts.

Generally, the right to transfer stock remains unfettered. Restrictions placed on the stock itself, however, may limit this right of transferability. It is easy to understand why these restrictions may be advisable. Such restrictions commonly occur in close corporations. We have already discussed the fact that close corporations are like partnerships in that the controlling shareholders actively take part in the day-to-day management of the corporation. Consequently, shareholders in close corporations often attempt to preserve their control over the corporation through voting trusts and pooling arrangements. Such attempts at consolidation of power will be meaningless without restrictions on the stock's transferability.

Exhibit 32.6

Stock Characteristics from the Corporation's Perspective

Type of Stock	Characteristics
Authorized (also called capital stock)	Shares that a corporation may issue under its charter or articles of incorporation.
Issued	Shares that are authorized and sold by the corporation to shareholders. Shareholders may vote these shares.
Outstanding	Shares that have been issued by the corporation but have not been reacquired by it.
Treasury	Shares that were issued and then reacquired by the corporation. The corporation can either hold the shares or cancel them.

Courts try to balance the legitimate interests of the shareholders in limiting ownership to a few congenial shareholders with the competing right of a shareholder to transfer his or her property. In our legal system, this right of alienation is considered to be inherent in the ownership of property. (*Right of alienation* is the right to transfer ownership to another.) A *right of first refusal,* where the shareholder who wishes to sell must first offer his or her shares to the corporation or to the other shareholders, is enforceable as a valid restriction on transfer. A common valid restriction is "No shareholder may encumber or dispose of his or her shares except (1) by sale only if such shareholder first offers his or her shares to the corporation, or to the other shareholders, on the same terms as such shareholder can sell to a bona fide prospective purchaser and (2) by gift, bequest, or intestate descent to, or in trust for, certain described members of such shareholder's family." The agreement will generally specify which family members, for example, spouse, children, and grandchildren. In contrast, a restriction that states that "these shares are nontransferable" will probably be unreasonable and, therefore, unenforceable.

Buy-sell agreements are also prevalent in small closely held corporations. The agreement states the events that will trigger it, such as the death of a shareholder. In these events the shareholder (or his or her estate) agrees to sell the company shares. The agreement will specify who must buy the shares. It will be either the corporation itself or one or more of the other shareholders. It will also specify the price or the method for determining the price. The parties should strive for a fair and equitable agreement because they do not know who will be selling or purchasing the shares. In addition, a buy-sell agreement can be invalidated by a court if the court decides that it is an unreasonable restraint on alienation.

Any of these restrictions must be conspicuously placed on the stock certificate to be valid. A conspicuous notice is meant to protect any subsequent purchaser of the shares by informing him or her of the restriction. If this notice is missing, the purchaser will not be bound by the restriction unless he or she otherwise has notice of it. If the restriction is reasonable and appears on the face of the stock certificate, however, the corporation can refuse to transfer the shares to the purchaser. The purchaser's remedy involves forcing the seller to return the money paid to the seller for the shares.

If the transfer satisfies all legal requirements, including the applicable provisions of Article 8 of the Uniform Commercial Code (UCC) and state securities laws, the purchaser (transferee) pays the price asked and the shareholder (transferor) then endorses and delivers the stock to the purchaser. The corporation, when notified, must register the transfer and change corporate records to denote the new ownership. This is necessary to guarantee the new owner the rights incidental to stock ownership in the corporation.

Liabilities of Shareholders

As we learned in Chapter 31, one of the most significant advantages of the corporate form is the limited liability afforded to shareholders. In other words, the shareholders risk only their investment. Except for situations in which courts can disregard the corporate entity, shareholders normally do not become personally liable for corporate debts. In this section, we will look at some other circumstances that may cause a shareholder to be personally liable for obligations of the corporation.

Watered Stock   At the time of the formation of the corporation, the articles of incorporation spell out its *capital structure*. The money to operate the corporation initially results from the issuance of securities to investors. The authorization for such securities ordinarily occurs early in the formation process, commonly by board action at the organizational meeting.

The consideration the corporation receives for these shares constitutes the stated capital of the corporation. The board of directors establishes a fixed value for each share of such capital stock (for example, $10 per share). This is called *par value stock*. The corporation may also issue no-par value stock, which has no fixed value but may be sold at whatever price the directors deem reasonable (called *stated value*). No-par value shares permit a corporation to issue stock in return for corporate assets that currently are worth little but have the possibility of high, though speculative, returns (such as technological developments).

If no statutory provisions exist to the contrary, the corporation may issue shares in exchange for any lawful consideration, including cash received, property received, or services actually rendered. Just as the board of directors generally sets the price of the shares, it also normally fixes the value of the property received or services rendered. As long as the board makes these decisions in good faith and in the absence of fraud, courts will not impose legal liability on the directors for these decisions.

However, the shareholder who receives shares of a corporation that are issued as fully paid, when, in fact, the full par or stated value has not been paid by the purchaser, owns *watered stock*. The shareholder is personally liable for the deficiency, that is, "the water." For example, if a shareholder pays $8 per share and the par value or stated value is $10 per share, the shareholder is liable to the corporation for the $2 per share deficiency.

The purpose of state laws which make the shareholder liable for the "water" is to protect innocent shareholders from dilution of their interests and to protect corporate creditors who may have relied on the fact that the stock was supposedly issued at or above par. The most common examples of watered stock occur when stock is transferred in exchange for property or services.

For example, eClass incorporates and issues $4,000 worth of its shares to Eduardo in exchange for his efforts in developing a Web site. If Eduardo's efforts are later found to be worth only $2,000, Eduardo will be liable for $2,000. In effect, this is the amount that remains unpaid for the value of his stock. Depending on the state Eduardo may be liable to the corporation. Some states will allow corporate creditors to impose liability on Eduardo if eClass becomes insolvent and unable to meet its obligations as they come due. A later purchaser from Eduardo normally will not be liable for watered stock unless he or she knew the stock was watered stock or participated in the transaction that created the "water."[37]

The use of no-par value stock and the impact of federal and state securities regulation have greatly reduced the incidence of suits alleging liability for watered stock. Still, shareholders should be aware of this legal doctrine.

Stock Subscriptions *Stock subscriptions* are agreements by investors ("subscribers") to purchase shares in a corporation. The law views a subscription as an offer. However, most state statutes make subscriptions irrevocable for a certain period unless the subscription itself provides otherwise. A subscriber may enter into such agreements either before or after the corporation's formation. If the stock subscription occurs before the corporation's formation (usually as a result of promoters' activities), some states treat the subscription as an offer that is automatically accepted by the corporation upon its formation, creating a valid contract. Other states, however, require formal acceptance of the subscription (offer) before a valid contract exists between the subscriber and the corporation.

Because an accepted stock subscription constitutes a contract, various types of liabilities arise if it is breached. Thus, the corporation can sue the subscriber for the subscription price if the subscriber refuses to pay as agreed. In some cases, creditors of a corporation that has become insolvent may force the subscriber to pay the amount owed on the subscription. By the same token, the subscriber can sue the corporation if the corporation refuses to issue the shares that are the object of the subscription. As in the case of watered stock, securities laws have reduced the incidence of shareholder liability for stock subscriptions.

Illegal Dividends We noted earlier that cash dividends must be paid from a lawful source. Any declaration of dividends that will impair the original capital structure of the corporation is illegal and may subject both the directors and the shareholders to personal liability. Shareholders who receive an illegal dividend are liable for its return if the corporation is insolvent at the time the dividend is paid. In such cases, the corporation's creditors can sue the shareholders directly for the amount of the illegal dividend. If the corporation is solvent when an illegal distribution takes place and remains solvent even after it, however, only shareholders who knew the dividend was illegal (that is, from an improper source) must repay the dividend to the corporation. Innocent shareholders can retain the dividends. Directors who have been held financially liable for distributing illegal dividends can force shareholders who knew of the illegal dividends to pay the amounts received back to the directors. The shareholders and directors thus share liability in such circumstances.

Dissolution Dissolution signals the legal termination of the corporation's existence. It may occur *voluntarily* (by actions of the incorporators or shareholders), or *involuntarily* (by court actions initiated by the state or a shareholder). It is important to note that majority (or controlling) shareholders may incur liability if the purpose of the dissolution is to freeze out minority stockholders and to strip them of rights or profits they would otherwise enjoy. The basis of this liability is that controlling shareholders owe fiduciary duties to minority shareholders. Generally speaking, controlling shareholders must exert control for the benefit of all shareholders, not just for themselves. Majority shareholders may be personally liable for dissolutions that prejudice the interests of minority shareholders while substantially enhancing the interests of majority shareholders.

Rights and Duties of the Board of Directors

The right to manage the affairs of the corporation falls squarely on the board of directors. The board is legally responsible for the management of the corporation although it delegates day-to-day authority to the officers. Although shareholders, the ultimate owners of the corporation, retain the power to elect and remove directors, this prerogative does not give shareholders a direct voice in management. Nor can shareholders compel the board to take any action. The directors are not agents of the shareholders; they owe loyalty primarily to the corporation. As we discussed, however, different rules may apply if the corporation is a close corporation.

Boards of directors and executives have been criticized for their roles in recent corporate failures, including those at Adelphia, Enron, Global Crossing, Tyco, Xerox, and WorldCom. The Sarbanes-Oxley Act of 2002 (SOX) was enacted to prevent similar failures in the future.[38] In addition, the Securities and Exchange Commission (SEC) and the stock exchanges have strengthened their rules concerning boards of directors and other corporate managers. SOX will be addressed in Chapter 34.

Number and Qualifications The articles of incorporation usually name the initial directors. Older statutes required at least three directors, but the modern trend—due, no doubt, in part to the increased numbers of close corporations—is to permit as few as one or two directors. To avoid deadlocks, the articles or bylaws usually authorize an uneven number of directors.

Unless otherwise provided in the relevant statutes, articles, or bylaws, directors need not be either shareholders in the corporation or residents of the state where the corporation has its principal place of business. Where there are qualifications, the election of unqualified persons is voidable, not void. In other words, until the corporation employs proper proceedings to displace the unqualified directors, the law considers them *de facto directors* (that is, directors in fact if not in law). Consequently, most of their acts as directors are effective; and *de facto* directors must live up to the same corporate duties and standards as qualified directors do. Directors generally have the right to appoint interim replacements on the board when vacancies arise owing to the death, resignation, or incapacity of a director.

Term of Office Directors serve for the time specified in state statutes, unless the articles or bylaws limit the term to a shorter period. Directors usually serve for one year unless the corporation has set up a *classified board* (a board divided into classes of directors with staggered election dates). Directors continue to hold office until the shareholders elect their successors and the latter take office. Thus, sitting directors do not automatically leave the board at the end of their terms.

Sometimes shareholders remove directors before their terms on the board end. Shareholders may remove directors for cause. For cause was the only basis for removal at common law. Modern statutes relax this standard by permitting a majority of shareholders to remove directors at any time during their terms without cause. In those jurisdictions that require cumulative voting, however, directors cannot be removed if the number of votes cast for retention would have been sufficient to elect those directors to the board. In most jurisdictions, directors who have been removed can seek court review of such dismissals to determine if the proper procedures were followed.

Meetings   Traditionally, the board could validly exercise its powers only when acting collectively, not individually. The law emphasized the value of decision making arrived at through collective debate, deliberation, and judgment. For this reason, statutes set out rules permitting the board to act only when it was formally convened. Directors traditionally had to be present to vote, they could not vote by proxy or send substitutes to deliberate for them. Directors could vote only at a properly announced formal meeting.

Today, most modern statutes dispense with the formalities previously required of directors' meetings. Thus, even though the bylaws usually fix the times for regular or special board meetings, statutes today allow meetings to occur even without prior notice. To make a meeting valid, however, either before or after the meeting, each absent director must—in writing—waive the right to prior notice, consent to the meeting, or approve the minutes of the meeting.

Similarly, some states even allow the board to act without a meeting, assuming the articles or bylaws permit informal action, as long as all directors consent and file their consents in the corporate minute book. In fact, telephone conference calls suffice in several states. In Delaware the directors can use all forms of teleconferencing, videoconferencing, and other communication means as long as the participants can "hear" each other.[39] In California, the directors can also meet by "chat room" meetings or committee meetings over the Internet.[40] Given this trend toward informality, the board can hold its meetings anywhere unless the articles or bylaws declare otherwise. Meetings outside the corporation's state of incorporation or principal place of business are, in general, perfectly legal.

A quorum is required under state law. Unless the articles or bylaws set a higher or lower percentage, a simple majority of the directors ordinarily constitutes a quorum. Actions taken by a quorum of directors are binding on the corporation. Two important questions still arise in any discussion about quorums. First, can directors who intentionally miss a meeting to prevent a quorum later question the validity of the action taken at the meeting? Since different cases have produced different results, you should check the law on this matter in your particular jurisdiction. Second, can directors count toward the quorum (or vote) if the board will be voting on matters in which they are personally interested? Modern statutes generally allow directors to participate as long as there has been compliance with statutory provisions meant to ensure fairness to the corporation (such as disclosure of the interest). If there is no statutory provision, the case results vary from jurisdiction to jurisdiction. Some cases have allowed interested directors to be counted; other cases have not.

Directors usually cannot agree in advance about how they will vote on corporate matters. Such a formal agreement is not binding because it is against public policy; directors owe fiduciary duties to the corporation and must be free to exercise their judgment in a totally unrestricted fashion. Such agreements may be valid, however, among directors in a close corporation if all the shareholders-directors agree to the plan.

Delegation of Duties   Most statutes authorize the board of directors to delegate managerial authority to officers and executive (or other) committees. Common examples of specialized committees are the compensation committee and the investment committee. Such delegations of duties ensure the smooth running of the day-to-day affairs of the corporation and promote efficiency by utilizing the expertise of the various committee members.

If no statutory provisions specifically allow the delegation of duties, courts will interpret any attempts at delegation very strictly. Moreover, if the delegation becomes too broad and pervasive, such actions will probably be void because it is too great a relinquishment of the board's management functions. Similarly, attempts to place control of the corporation in fewer persons than the entire board of directors will be illegal (even in close corporations), because the corporation deserves the best efforts of all its directors, who, in turn, owe fiduciary duties to the corporation. Delegation of authority to arbitrators, management consultants, or others who are not directors or officers, is difficult to justify legally.

Compensation   In the past, the corporation had no duty to compensate directors for their services. Older cases ruled that directors were not to be paid for their services unless the articles or bylaws authorized the compensation before the directors had rendered the services. Even under these circumstances, however, directors could receive payment for extraordinary services taken at the board's request (such as recruitment of executive officers), despite the lack of a prearranged, specific agreement. This payment is based on quasi-contractual grounds. Today, although many corporations still pay their directors little or no compensation, an increasing number of corporations do pay rather hefty sums. Since directors are subject to ever-expanding duties and potential liability, compensation seems more justifiable. Directors often are not substantial shareholders, and consequently they do not profit as owners of the firm.

The directors normally determine the salaries of the officers of the corporation. Possible conflict of interest concerns may arise when directors also serve as officers because, in effect, the directors will be participating in setting their own salaries. As noted earlier in the discussion of quorum requirements, statutes may empower interested directors to vote on these issues as long as disclosure of the interest has been made and the transaction is otherwise fair to the corporation. The board can hire officers to serve for periods longer than the board's tenure as long as the period involved is reasonable in length. The amount of compensation paid to officers also must be reasonable. The compensation package commonly consists of salary, bonuses, share options, profit sharing, annuities, and deferred-compensation plans. Large compensation packages may be attacked as a "waste" of corporate assets by the directors.

Corporate salaries in the millions of dollars have become common today. It has also become a relatively common strategy for the board to give "golden parachute" packages to their chief executive officers when the board's corporation is the target of a hostile takeover attempt. (*Golden parachutes* pay the officers a hefty salary after their severance from the corporation for doing no additional work.) Since the acquirer will be obligated to pay these inflated salaries after the acquisition, golden parachutes become a strategy for fending off a takeover attempt. Golden parachutes raise controversial questions about possible conflicts of interest and waste of corporate assets.

Liabilities   State corporation statutes, common law doctrines, and federal securities and antitrust laws may impose liability on a director for noncompliance with the duties or requirements set out in those doctrines and statutes. Directors, by the very nature of their positions, make numerous decisions, collectively and individually. Increasingly, the performance of these duties exposes directors to potential personal liability, either individually or with the other members of the board who have approved or engaged in the forbidden conduct. Directors must use great caution in order to avoid liability in the form of civil damages or criminal fines. Scrutiny of directors' decisions is likely to increase in the light of recent problems, such as those at Adelphia and Enron.

Although not always the case, today it is legal and common for corporations to *indemnify* (pay back) their directors for liabilities accruing from their corporate positions. Through indemnification, directors are repaid by the corporation for the losses and expenses incurred from litigation brought against them personally for actions undertaken on behalf of the corporation in their corporate capacities. Statutes may limit the right of indemnification in certain circumstances. For instance, indemnification for criminal fines may be prohibited when directors have knowingly engaged in unlawful activities. Statutes often empower corporations to purchase liability insurance for their directors, officers, and other employees to cover nonindemnifiable liabilities. These policies are commonly called *D and O liability insurance*. At the corporate level, the purchase of D and O policies may be authorized in the bylaws or by a resolution of the board of directors. Exhibit 32.7 on the following page summarizes the management responsibilities in a corporation.

Other Rights   Because directors alone have the right to declare dividends, they may be personally liable for improper dividends. (We have already discussed the shareholders' potential liability for improper dividends.)

Directors may enter into agreements about how they will vote as directors. But if such agreements unduly hamper the board's managerial functions, the agreements will be void on public policy grounds. These agreements ordinarily will be valid in close corporations in which *all* the shareholders-directors have assented to the terms.

The rights of directors to inspect corporate records are even more compelling than shareholders' rights. This is rather obvious since access to corporate records is essential if directors are to discharge their fiduciary duties and decision-making functions. Unlike shareholders' rights, many states characterize the directors' right of inspection as absolute. Yet this right will probably be lost if directors abuse the right by using it for an improper purpose that damages the corporation, such as misappropriation of trade secrets or confidential trade information.

Constituency Statutes   Thirty-one states have enacted constituency statutes (also called "other constituency" statutes) that either require or permit the board of directors to consider the interests of other constituents of the corporation in their decision making. The statutes are varied in their approaches. Depending on the statute other

Exhibit 32.7

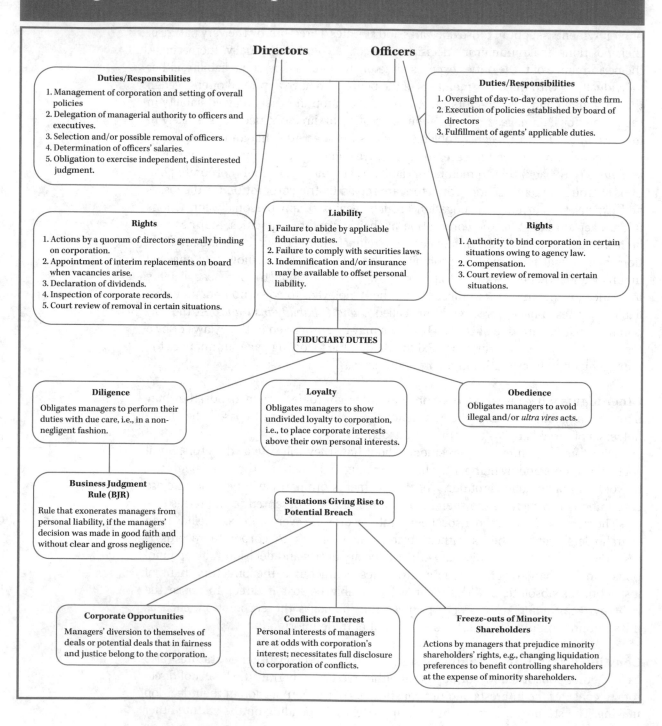

Management of the Corporation

Directors   **Officers**

Duties/Responsibilities
1. Management of corporation and setting of overall policies
2. Delegation of managerial authority to officers and executives.
3. Selection and/or possible removal of officers.
4. Determination of officers' salaries.
5. Obligation to exercise independent, disinterested judgment.

Duties/Responsibilities
1. Oversight of day-to-day operations of the firm.
2. Execution of policies established by board of directors
3. Fulfillment of agents' applicable duties.

Rights
1. Actions by a quorum of directors generally binding on corporation.
2. Appointment of interim replacements on board when vacancies arise.
3. Declaration of dividends.
4. Inspection of corporate records.
5. Court review of removal in certain situations.

Liability
1. Failure to abide by applicable fiduciary duties.
2. Failure to comply with securities laws.
3. Indemnification and/or insurance may be available to offset personal liability.

Rights
1. Authority to bind corporation in certain situations owing to agency law.
2. Compensation.
3. Court review of removal in certain situations.

FIDUCIARY DUTIES

Diligence
Obligates managers to perform their duties with due care, i.e., in a non-negligent fashion.

Loyalty
Obligates managers to show undivided loyalty to corporation, i.e., to place corporate interests above their own personal interests.

Obedience
Obligates managers to avoid illegal and/or *ultra vires* acts.

Business Judgment Rule (BJR)
Rule that exonerates managers from personal liability, if the managers' decision was made in good faith and without clear and gross negligence.

Situations Giving Rise to Potential Breach

Corporate Opportunities
Managers' diversion to themselves of deals or potential deals that in fairness and justice belong to the corporation.

Conflicts of Interest
Personal interests of managers are at odds with corporation's interest; necessitates full disclosure to corporation of conflicts.

Freeze-outs of Minority Shareholders
Actions by managers that prejudice minority shareholders' rights, e.g., changing liquidation preferences to benefit controlling shareholders at the expense of minority shareholders.

possible constituents include the corporation's employees, customers, suppliers, and creditors. Some statutes even permit the directors to consider the economy of the state and the country.[41] Most of the state statutes are permissive and do not require the directors to consider the interests of these other constituents. Courts have not yet provided a detailed analysis of the legal effect of these statutes, although it appears that directors can use the statutes as a defense when they make a decision to benefit long-term non-shareholder interests at the expense of short-term shareholder interests.

Rights and Duties of the Officers

The selection or removal of officers represents an important managerial function of the board of directors. While directors are responsible for the overall policies of the corporation, officers conduct the day-to-day operations of the firm and execute the policies established by the board. These lines of authority are well established in American law. The directors should manage, and the officers should carry out the management goals delegated to them by the directors.

Qualifications   Officers are agents of the corporation and, therefore, must live up to the fiduciary duties placed on agents. Statutes often name the officers that a corporation must have, and usually either these statutes or the corporate bylaws spell out each respective officer's authority. Typical officers include president, vice president, secretary, and treasurer (or comptroller). The top executive may also be called the chief executive officer (CEO). The same person ordinarily can serve in more than one office, but some statutes prohibit the same person from serving as both president and secretary. In closely held corporations, the CEO may often also serve as chairman of the board.

Term of Office   The board ordinarily appoints the officers, who serve at the will of the directors. Some modern statutes, on the other hand, allow the shareholders to elect the officers. Either the board or the president can appoint junior or senior officers.

Officers usually serve at the pleasure of the board because the board in most jurisdictions can remove an officer with or without cause, even when the officer has a valid employment contract. But after removal *without cause,* the corporation may be liable in damages to the former officer for breach of the employment contract. As we shall see later in this chapter, the directors normally escape personal liability if they have removed the officer in accordance with the *business judgment rule;* that is, they have exercised due care while making corporate decisions. In rare instances, the state, the courts, or the shareholders can remove officers. These instances nearly always involve a removal with cause.

Compensation   Traditionally, officers, like directors, served without pay because they usually were shareholders who expected their investment in the corporation to multiply by virtue of their work on the corporation's behalf. Thus, there was no need to supplement these corporate profits with a salary. Today, since neither directors nor officers are required to be shareholders, the corporation usually pays a prearranged, fixed salary. In addition, the corporation commonly adds to this salary such benefits as profit-sharing plans, bonuses, share options, deferred-compensation plans, pensions, annuities, and other fringe benefits like health care and expense accounts. Golden parachutes may also be included. Such compensation packages often turn out to be substantial.

Compensation, to be lawful, should be reasonable and not represent waste of corporate assets. If waste is present, both directors and officers may be liable to the corporation for this waste. Courts have even ordered officers to return amounts deemed excessive compensation to the corporation. The amount of officers' compensation has been an issue recently, particularly in corporations that are doing poorly. Some of these corporations requested government bailout funds or protection under bankruptcy laws while they provided substantial compensation packages to their officers.

Agency Law Because officers are agents of the corporation, they have authority to bind the corporation to contracts. (To help with this section, you should review the material on agency in Chapters 28 through 30.) Briefly, an officer's authority may be actual (either express or implied) or apparent.

Express authority derives from state statutes, the articles, or the bylaws. Any of these three sources may spell out the duties, responsibilities, and authority of the respective officers. The bylaws are the most common source of express authority. Under express authority, the corporation has determined the boundaries within which the officer shall act on behalf of the corporation.

Implied authority, on the other hand, can be derived by virtue of the office or title of the person. Presidents have implied authority to direct corporate meetings and to act on behalf of the corporation with regard to transactions occurring in the ordinary and regular course of business. For example, a president normally has authority to hire real estate brokers for the purpose of selling corporate property. Yet the president normally cannot validly sell or mortgage corporate assets without the approval of the board (and sometimes that of the shareholders). The president can have authority, however, to bind the corporation to sale or services contracts arising in the usual course of business; for instance, the president of a grain elevator can authorize purchases of wheat from local farmers.

Vice-presidents normally possess no authority by virtue of their office. Similarly, neither the treasurer nor the secretary can normally bind the corporation. The law ordinarily limits them to fairly ministerial intracorporate functions. Some jurisdictions, however, do give the treasurer authority to write, accept, endorse, and negotiate corporate checks and promissory notes.

Corporate officers may have *apparent authority* to bind the corporation. Apparent authority arises when the corporation, by its actions, indicates to a third party that an officer or agent is empowered to engage in certain transactions on behalf of the corporation. The corporation's actions can be intentional or careless. To constitute apparent authority, the third party's reliance must be reasonable. When apparent authority exists, the contract will be binding on the corporation and the third party.

Subsequent *ratification* or approval of previously unauthorized acts will also bind the corporation. Even if the president had no prior authority to buy real estate, a later board resolution that approves the purchase constitutes ratification and binds the corporation to the completion of the transaction.

Liabilities   Officers who attempt to contract on behalf of the corporation without authority may be personally liable to the other contracting party. Similarly, nondisclosure of the fact that the officer is acting on behalf of the corporation, even when the officer's actions are authorized, will lead to the personal liability of the officer. This is really an application of general agency law. Officers who commit torts may be personally liable to the injured party; however, the corporation may also be liable for torts committed by the officer during the scope of his or her employment under the doctrine of *respondeat superior. Respondeat superior* will be applied by the court only if the tort is in "the course and scope" of the employment.

Fiduciary Duties Owed to the Corporation

Directors, officers, and controlling shareholders owe fiduciary duties to the corporation and sometimes to shareholders and creditors. The source of these duties is the fact that directors, officers, and controlling shareholders occupy a position of trust and faith with regard to the corporation and other constituencies. Generally speaking, these obligations fall into three broad categories: the duty of obedience, the duty of diligence (or due care), and the duty of loyalty. These duties may arise from statute but, more often, they issue from case law.

Obedience   Directors, officers, controlling shareholders, and other corporate managers must restrict their actions and those of the corporation to lawful pursuits. Any action taken beyond the scope of the corporation's power is an illegal, *ultra vires* act. By definition, violation of a positive rule of law or statute constitutes an illegal act. Any such actions by managers violate the duty of obedience and may subject them to personal liability.

Diligence   Because corporate managers act on behalf of the corporation, they are obligated to perform their duties with the amount of diligence or due care that a reasonably prudent person would exercise in the conduct of his or her own personal affairs in the same or similar circumstances. You probably notice the familiar ring of this language. We discussed this kind of standard when we addressed negligence (see Chapter 6). Basically, the duty of due care obliges a corporate manager to perform his or her duties in a nonnegligent fashion. Note that the law does not expect a director, officer, or controlling shareholder to be perfect or all-knowing. Honest errors of judgment will not lead to liability for breach of the duty of diligence. If liability were imposed in such situations, who would ever consent to be a director or officer?

Instead, the law excuses the conduct if the manager has made the error in good faith and without clear and gross negligence. This is the *business judgment rule*.

The legislatures or courts in some states have modified the tradition business judgment rule. A jury must decide whether the manager's decision satisfies the business judgment rule or is grossly negligent and, hence, unacceptable. A manager who is ill prepared because he or she fails to attend corporate meetings or pays no attention to corporate affairs may incur liability for breach of the duty of diligence. Similarly, failure to fire an obviously unworthy employee, failure to obtain casualty insurance, failure to heed warning signs suggesting illegal conduct (such as embezzlement), or reliance on unreasonable statements by attorneys or accountants may lead to liability.

Nonetheless, the manager will incur liability only for such losses caused by his or her own negligent conduct. Consequently, if a director formally dissents about a matter that is later held to be negligent, that director will avoid liability.[42] If the director does not dissent, it is usually no defense that the director was only a figurehead or served without pay. However, a manager's reasonable reliance on expert reports, such as those by accountants or attorneys, usually exonerates the manager from liability unless violations of securities statutes are involved.

Loyalty   Because directors, officers, and controlling shareholders enjoy positions of trust with the corporation, they must act in good faith and with loyalty toward the corporation and its shareholders. The undivided loyalty expected of fiduciaries means that managers must place the interests of the corporation above their own personal interests. Sometimes these corporate interests and personal interests "collide," and it

eClass 32.2 Management/Finance

AVOIDING LIABILITY

Meg contracted for a unique marketing plan that she expected to dramatically increase sales. Unfortunately, the plan was a disaster, and the firm lost a significant amount of money on the plan. While the firm will weather this financial storm, the setback made Meg consider what might have happened if the firm was publicly owned. She is afraid that if this situation occurred in a publicly held firm, she might have been dismissed and/or held personally liable for the losses. Meg has asked you what liabilities she would have faced if eClass had been publicly owned at the time she made the decision to purchase the marketing plan. What will you tell her?

BUSINESS CONSIDERATIONS   What must a manager be able to show in order to avoid liability for a decision gone bad? Is this a difficult defense to prove? Why or why not?

ETHICAL CONSIDERATIONS   What ethical duties do managers owe to the firm and/or the shareholders? To whom do managers owe the greatest duty?

becomes necessary to resort to applicable statutes and case law. Usually such issues involve (1) corporate opportunities or (2) conflicts of interest.

The *business opportunity doctrine*, also called the corporate opportunity doctrine, forbids directors, officers, and controlling shareholders from diverting to themselves business deals or potential deals that in fairness or in justice belong to the corporation. Personal gains at the expense of the corporation represent a breach of the managers' fiduciary duties. A corporate opportunity is commonly found (1) if the manager discovers the opportunity in his or her capacity as director, and (2) it is reasonably foreseeable that the corporation will be interested in the opportunity because it relates closely to the corporation's line of business. Consider this example:

> *Juanita is a director in a real estate development corporation (Coast-to-Coast Properties, Inc.) and Joel offers to sell property to Juanita because he knows she is a director of Coast-to-Coast Properties, Inc. Juanita should not buy the property for herself. To do so will violate her duty of loyalty. If the corporation might reasonably be interested in the land for its corporate development program, Juanita must disclose this opportunity to the corporation. Once she has given the corporation this right of first refusal, Juanita ordinarily can purchase the property in her own right, but only after the corporation refuses the opportunity or is financially unable to implement the purchase.*

If Juanita breaches the duty of loyalty and purchases the land for herself, corporate remedies will include damages (the profits Juanita makes as a result of the sale) or the imposition of a constructive trust. (A *constructive trust* is a trust imposed by law to prevent the unjust enrichment of the person in possession of the property). A court will treat Juanita as a trustee who is holding the property for the benefit of the corporation. A court then can force Juanita to convey the property to Coast-to-Coast Properties, Inc. and to pay Coast-to-Coast any profits she has already realized on the transaction.

When a director, officer, or controlling shareholder is interested in an opportunity that might be subject to this rule, he or she should make a full and fair disclosure of all the facts and wait for a definitive statement that the corporation is not going to proceed with the opportunity. Generally the disclosure should be to the board of directors and the decision to decline it should be made by the disinterested board members. In some cases it should be made to the shareholders.

Another common example of a possible conflict of interest occurs when a director, officer, or controlling shareholder personally contracts with the corporation. To continue with the previous example:

> *Juanita, a director of Coast-to-Coast Properties, Inc., is willing to sell a piece of her own property to the corporation. Because of her personal interests, Juanita will undoubtedly hope to make as much money as possible on the transaction. Yet her position as a director of Coast-to-Coast Properties, Inc. obligates her to accept as low a price as possible in order to benefit the company. Juanita obviously faces a difficult dilemma. Most states will allow the*

transaction (1) if Juanita makes a full disclosure of her interest to the board of directors of Coast-to-Coast before the board begins its deliberations on the proposed contract, and (2) if the resultant contract is fair and reasonable to the corporation. If Juanita does not fully disclose her interest or if the terms of the contract are unfair or unreasonable, the contract will be voidable by the corporation.

An additional concern in these situations stems from whether Juanita (who is called an interested director) should be allowed to vote on the contract. At common law, Juanita could not vote—or even be counted toward the quorum—at the meeting where the matter was to be discussed. Although modern statutes (and articles or bylaws) vary, in general, Juanita can vote and be counted toward the quorum if, as noted earlier, she discloses her interest and the resultant contract is fair to the corporation.

A recent development in the conflict of interest area occurs when directors and officers trade in corporate stock. Although generally they are selling the stock on the open market, they may be tempted to postpone announcements or to "camouflage" transactions on the balance sheets in order to dispose of their shares first. These issues will be discussed in greater detail in Chapter 34.

eClass 32.3 Finance

SUBCHAPTER S CORPORATIONS

Ani, Meg, and Yousef have decided either to incorporate eClass as a Subchapter S corporation or to remain a general partnership. They are concerned, however, about the need to satisfy several of the more burdensome and/or time-consuming aspects of corporate existence. They need to know what requirements they will face as a Subchapter S corporation in such matters as annual meetings, distribution of authority, tax returns, and rights of shareholders. They also need to know how these requirements might vary if they were just to remain a partnership. What advice will you give them?

BUSINESS CONSIDERATIONS   What business criteria are important in making the decision to adopt any particular business form? What personal factors should a businessperson consider?

ETHICAL CONSIDERATIONS   Will the businesspersons have different ethical duties if they operate the business as a partnership as compared to a corporation? Why or why not?

As previously discussed, the duty of loyalty also prohibits directors, officers, or controlling shareholders from prejudicing minority shareholders' rights. This includes freezing out minority shareholders through such actions as forcing dissolution of the corporation or modifying the distribution of assets on liquidation.

In the context of corporate takeovers, allegations of breach of fiduciary duties commonly arise. As the sophistication of both the "raider" and the target corporation has increased, directors of the target have responded creatively to initiate a host of defensive moves meant to blunt the would-be acquiring firm's desire for the target corporation. This has led to the development of thrusts and countermeasures such as greenmail and poison pills. (*Greenmail* is the process by which a firm threatens a corporate takeover by buying a significant portion of a corporation's stock and then selling it back to the corporation at a premium when the corporation's directors and executives, fearing for their positions, agree to buy the firm out. A *poison pill* is any strategy adopted by the directors of a target firm in order to decrease their firm's attractiveness to an acquiring firm during an attempted hostile takeover.) The critical issue remains whether the law will approve of these deterrent efforts.

OPERATION OF A LIMITED LIABILITY COMPANY

Nine states have adopted the Uniform Limited Liability Company Act of 1995 with the 1996 amendments.[43] Two have adopted the Uniform Limited Liability Company Act of 2006.[44] The other states have enacted their own versions of Limited Liability Company (LLCs) statutes. The state statutes have diverse provisions. As the number of LLCs increase, legislatures and courts create additional laws concerning their operation. Generally, it is easier to operate an LLC than a corporation. However, many rules of corporation law are also being applied to LLCs.

Many of the practical aspects of other business forms are also being applied to LLCs. Some LLCs have a complicated structure for members. There may be the Managing Members, Voting Members, and "regular members" who have control over all matters that are not reserved to the Managing Members and Voting Members. LLCs may have buy-sell agreements that permit or require members to sell their membership interests to the LLC or other members under set circumstances. There may be restrictions on a member's ability to transfer ownership interests. For example, an LLC operating agreement may include:

> "No member shall sell, assign, transfer, pledge or encumber any interest in the Company without the prior written consent of the Manager and the other Members. Any person acquiring rights with respect to any interest in the Company in a transaction which is an Adverse Act shall not be deemed a substituted Member and shall be restricted to the right to receive any distributions made with respect to such interest."[45]

Statutes may specify the manager's legal liability. For example, under the Arkansas statute a manager of an LLC is not liable to the company or other members unless he or she engages in "gross negligence or willful misconduct."[46] In Maryland, a majority interest holder owes a fiduciary duty to the minority interest holders.[47]

Contemporary Case

IN RE: CUMBERLAND FARMS, INC.

284 F.3d 216, 2002 U.S. App. LEXIS 4998 (1st Cir. 2002)

FACTS Cumberland Farms, Inc. (Cumberland) is a close corporation started by Haseotes's parents. The six siblings of the Haseotes family now own all the shares. Demetrios B. Haseotes is one of Cumberland's directors. Independent of Cumberland Haseotes purchased an oil refinery. Haseotes also organized Cumberland Crude Processing, Inc. (CCP) to purchase crude oil, transfer it to the refinery, and sell the refined product to Cumberland and others. Based on a sense of common purpose, the family and Cumberland promptly loaned large sums of money to the refinery and to CCP.

Cumberland's largest lender, Industrial Bank of Japan Trust Company (IBJ) was not pleased to learn that Cumberland had loaned roughly $70 million to the refinery and CCP. IBJ arranged for CCP and Cumberland to enter into a subordination agreement under which CCP was to give a priority to the debt it owed to Cumberland, and subordinate the debts to Haseotes and the other family members. CCP became unable to repay its loan to Cumberland, causing devastating consequences for Cumberland. When Cumberland filed for bankruptcy in 1992, it had not received any

payment on its loan to CCP since 1988. However during this period, Haseotes caused CCP to repay approximately $4 million it owed to Haseotes and his own companies. During the course of Cumberland's bankruptcy reorganization, CCP paid another $1.75 million to Haseotes's enterprises.

ISSUE Did Haseotes breach his fiduciary duty to Cumberland by usurping a corporate opportunity?

HOLDING Yes. Haseotes usurped a corporate opportunity.

REASONING Excerpts from the opinion of Circuit Judge Lipez:

... Corporate directors must "act with absolute fidelity [to the corporation] and must place their duties to the corporation above every other financial or business obligation." ... The fiduciary duty is "especially exacting where the corporation is closely held." ... In an attempt to give substance to the general duty of loyalty, courts have recognized several more specific obligations. We focus here on a particular variant known as the corporate opportunity doctrine, which prohibits a director "from taking, for personal benefit, an opportunity or advantage that belongs to the corporation." ... The corporate opportunity doctrine is best understood as a "rule of disclosure." ... When a corporate director learns of an opportunity that could benefit the corporation, she must inform the disinterested shareholders of all the material details of the opportunity so that they may decide whether the corporation can and should take advantage of it. . . . It is inherently unfair for the director to deny the corporation that choice and instead take the opportunity for herself. Thus, Massachusetts courts hold that "the nondisclosure of a corporate opportunity is, *in itself,* unfair to a corporation and a breach of fiduciary duty." . . . Accordingly, it makes no difference whether . . . his decision to cause CCP to repay the shipping operation before Cumberland was "a business judgment that seemed fair at the time." . . . [T]he decision as to how to use that money was not his to make if the availability of the $5.75 million was an "opportunity" that rightfully belonged to Cumberland. We must determine . . . whether the availability of money in CCP constituted an "opportunity" within the meaning of the corporate opportunity doctrine. . . .

Normally, a corporate opportunity is thought of as a business or investment opportunity within the sphere of, or somehow related to, the corporation's own activities. . . . Although the facts here diverge somewhat from the prototypical corporate opportunity case, we agree with the bankruptcy court that the disputed repayments fall well within the contours of the doctrine. . . . [T]he Supreme Judicial Court of Massachusetts . . . noted that recent formulations of the corporate opportunity doctrine have "given a . . . broad definition to the scope of potential corporate interests, and have focused on the responsibility of the fiduciary to present these possibilities to the corporation for its consideration." . . . [A]ny funds that became available in CCP provided an opportunity to pay down CCP's $50 million debt to Cumberland. That opportunity was more than "conceivably advantageous" to Cumberland; it was desperately

needed. . . . [T]here is no question that the money was within Cumberland's sphere of interests—not only was it owed to Cumberland under the promissory note, but the subordination agreement explicitly required Haseotes to apply any available money toward Cumberland's loan before paying down CCP's debt to himself or other family members. . . . Yet, instead . . . Haseotes had CCP pay more than $5 million on the loan from his own shipping operation. . . . In so doing, Haseotes took for himself an opportunity that properly belonged to Cumberland, in violation of his duty of loyalty. . . . The key point is that he "placed himself in a position in which . . . his own pecuniary interests *could have* prevented him from acting in [Cumberland's] best interest." . . . In such circumstances, Haseotes was obligated to seek approval from Cumberland's board before acting. The requirement of disclosure "takes from the fiduciary the power to decide whether the opportunity or self-dealing transaction is in the corporation's interest and removes the temptation posed by a 'conflict between self-interest and integrity.' " . . .

As a matter of law, any disclosure must be "full." . . . A director plainly violates his duty of loyalty if his disclosure of the corporate opportunity is "misleading, inaccurate, and materially incomplete." . . . Haseotes does not attempt to show that he made the kind of full and explicit disclosure required by Massachusetts law. Instead, he argues that disclosure was unnecessary because the other members of Cumberland's board knew that money was available in CCP, and that Haseotes was using it to repay the loan from his shipping operation. . . . [T]he bankruptcy court found that Cumberland's directors were *not* aware of the opportunity for repayment. . . . [W]e conclude that the bankruptcy court did not err in finding that Haseotes breached his duty of loyalty to Cumberland. . . .

You Be the Judge

Michael D. Eisner was the chief executive officer (CEO) and chairman of the board of the Walt Disney Company (Disney). Eisner recruited Michael S. Ovitz to serve as the new president of Disney and possibly succeed Eisner as CEO. At the time Ovitz was the head of a talent agency and was regarded as one of the most powerful figures in Hollywood. He earned over $20 million per year at the talent agency. In its effort to recruit Ovitz, the Disney board unanimously approved a five-year contract for him. It also provided that Disney could terminate Ovitz for "good cause" without liability. "Good cause" was defined as gross negligence or malfeasance in the performance of his duties. If Disney terminated Ovitz without good cause or if Ovitz resigned with the consent of the board, Ovitz would get his remaining salary payments, $7.5 million per year for unaccrued bonuses, an immediate vesting of his first group of stock options, and a $10 million payment for the second group of stock options. Irwin Russell, the Chairman of the Compensation committee, participated in the negotiations. He noted that the compensation package represented an extraordinary level of compensation, but he acknowledged that Ovitz was an "exceptional corporate executive."

Ovitz was appointed president under the contract and was elected to the board of directors. There was a lot of publicity about Ovitz joining Disney and the stock market responded favorably to his appointment. However, within a year it became obvious that the relationship was not working well. Ovitz was encouraged to begin looking for other employment. After only 14 months Ovitz's term as president was ended. Eisner and other Disney officials decided to treat the termination as a no-fault termination. Consequently, Ovitz's severance pay package was worth approximately $130 million. Several Disney shareholders claim that the board of directors breached their duty to the shareholders in the hiring of Ovitz, the firing of Ovitz, and agreeing to pay him the severance package. They contend that Ovitz should have been terminated for "good cause." Assume that this case was brought in your court. If *you* were the judge, how would *you* decide this dispute? [See *Brenn v. Eisner (In re the Walt Disney Company Derivative Litigation)*, 906 A.2d 27, 2006 Del. LEXIS 307 (Del. Sup. Ct. 2006).]

Summary

Each partner has certain rights in a partnership by virtue of his or her status as a general partner. These rights may be limited or defined by the agreement. If no agreement exists, each partner has an equal voice in management, a right to an equal share of profits or losses, equal access to books and records of the enterprise, and an equal right to use partnership property for partnership purposes.

Each general partner is an agent for every other partner and is a principal of every other partner. As a result, all the rules of agency apply. Each partner is a fiduciary of the other partners. When a partner deals with some third party, the firm is bound by the conduct if it was apparently or actually authorized. Partners are jointly and severally liable for the contracts of the partnership under RUPA. However, RUPA generally requires the firm creditor to exhaust the partnership assets before going after the partners' individual assets. Agency principles also apply to the torts of a partner. If the tort is in the course and scope of employment, the partners are jointly and severally liable.

Limited partners are more like investors. They are not automatically entitled to access all the books and records and generally they cannot manage the firm.

Ownership of corporate shares carries with it certain rights. The types of rights shareholders enjoy may vary depending on the type of stock involved. Ownership of common stock permits the shareholder to receive dividends (without priority) and to vote on corporate issues. In contrast, ownership of preferred stock confers priority as to dividends, voting, and/or liquidation rights. In addition, preferred stock may have participation rights, conversion rights, and/or redemption rights.

Shareholders' meetings are the vehicle for common and preferred stockholders to exercise their most significant control over the corporation. Corporate bylaws usually require an annual meeting (primarily for election of directors) and may authorize special meetings in appropriate circumstances. Such meetings ordinarily cannot occur without prior notice and a quorum. One of the shareholders'

foremost powers involves the election and removal of directors. Shareholders have inherent power to remove a director for cause and also may have power to remove a director without cause. They may also amend or repeal the bylaws.

Shareholders can cast their votes either in person or by proxy. For most corporate matters, straight voting is used. However, for the election of directors, many state statutes either permit or require cumulative voting. Cumulative voting protects the interests of minority shareholders but may be countered by such strategies as staggered terms for directors. Other devices used to consolidate voting power include voting trusts and pooling arrangements. These devices are especially useful in close corporations.

Shareholders' rights to inspect corporate records arise from both common law doctrines and express statutory provisions. Ordinarily, if a shareholder can demonstrate a proper purpose for requesting access to the records, the shareholder will be able to examine certain corporate documents.

Shareholders may be liable to the corporation or creditors for watered stock, and a subscriber may be liable to the corporation or to creditors if the subscriber breaches a stock subscription. Declaration and distribution of illegal dividends may subject both directors and shareholders to personal liability. Controlling shareholders also may incur liability if the purpose of the corporation's dissolution is to freeze out minority stockholders and to strip these stockholders of rights or profits they would otherwise enjoy.

The right to manage the corporation falls squarely on the board of directors. Shareholders cannot compel directors to take any action, because the directors are not the agents of the shareholders but, rather, owe loyalty *primarily* to the corporation. The modern trend is to lower the number of directors and to lessen the traditionally stringent rules concerning directors' qualifications.

Most statutes authorize the board of directors to delegate managerial authority to officers and executive committees. Broad delegations of authority to persons outside the directorial ranks are usually invalid.

Directors may or may not receive compensation from the corporation. The directors normally determine officers' compensation. Such compensation packages are usually legal if reasonable in amount. Otherwise, a shareholder can attack the compensation as a waste of corporate assets.

Performance of directorial duties may lead to personal liability for directors. Occasionally, the corporation will indemnify the directors for liabilities accruing from their corporate positions. Directors have the right to declare dividends, enter into agreements, and inspect corporate records.

The board of directors ordinarily appoints the officers, who serve at the will of the directors. Officers are agents of the corporation and, thus, must live up to the fiduciary duties placed on agents.

Directors, officers, and controlling shareholders owe fiduciary duties to the corporation. Broadly speaking, these duties fall into three categories: the duty of obedience, the duty of diligence (or due care), and the duty of loyalty. The duty of obedience forbids *ultra vires* acts. The business judgment rule constitutes a defense to liability for violation of the duty of diligence. Under this rule, the manager will not be liable if he or she makes an erroneous decision in good faith and without clear and gross negligence. The duty of loyalty, among other things, precludes directors, officers, and controlling shareholders from usurping corporate opportunities or prejudicing the corporation because of undisclosed conflicts of interest.

Limited Liability Companies (LLCs) are now authorized in all states. Courts and legislatures are wrestling with the various issues that arise with LLCs. Many concepts in corporate law are also being applied to LLCs.

Discussion Questions

1. Tim and Ed are partners. Tim, however, is tired of the business and sells it to Eugenia. Ed objects to the sale and sues to have it declared void. Eugenia claims Tim has the apparent authority to sell. How should the court rule, and why?

2. April, Jim, and Dan are partners in a retail business. Dan borrows $10,000 from the bank to "buy more goods." The loan is made in the partnership name. Dan, however, takes the money to Las Vegas and loses it all at the roulette table. If the bank sues April and Jim on the loan, what should be the result? Explain. Would the results be the same under the UPA and the RUPA? Why?

3. How can liability arise for watered stock, stock subscriptions, illegal dividends, and dissolution?

4. What are the limitations on directors' delegations of authority to officers and corporate committees?

5. In what ways can corporate managers prevent charges of conflicts of interest from being levied against them?

Case Problems and Writing Assignments

1. The Red Hawk partnership, consisting of 20 (1 deceased) limited partners and one corporate general partner, G&A, was formed in 1986. Pursuant to their partnership agreement, the Partners contributed capital which ultimately they allocated to two distinct partnership projects, Timber Knolls and Chestnut Woods. In 1987, Red Hawk and Cedar Ridge entered into a joint venture agreement forming the Chestnut Woods Partnership, with both Red Hawk and Cedar Ridge as general partners.

Under the joint venture agreement, Red Hawk would provide the capital funds for the project and Cedar Ridge would provide the general management. Cedar Ridge agreed to act as both the managing partner and the general contractor of the project. Cedar Ridge had the right to incur liabilities on behalf of the partnership, borrow money in the name of the partnership, and incur reasonable and legitimate expenses related to Chestnut Woods. Red Hawk and Cedar Ridge entered into a second and distinct joint venture agreement to form the Timber Knolls partnership. Red Hawk contributed $2.3 million and Cedar Ridge again agreed to act as both the managing partner and the general contractor. The Timber Knolls project never commenced operations. The Red Hawk Partners entered into an agreement with Cedar Ridge requiring the latter to return Red Hawk's capital contribution. This money was returned to the limited partners.

Cedar Ridge, as general contractor for Chestnut Woods, entered into a written subcontract with Henkels & McCoy, Inc. (Henkels), to have Henkels furnish the labor, materials, and equipment for the installation of the storm and sanitary sewer systems for the project. Cedar Ridge agreed to pay Henkels a fixed-price of $300,270 under the contract. Henkels completed the installation of the storm and sewer systems but Chestnut Woods defaulted in making the payments due under the contract. Henkels filed a lawsuit against Cedar Ridge and Red Hawk followed by a lawsuit against G&A. In both suits, Henkels obtained a judgment which was not paid. Henkels brought suit against the limited partners of Red Hawk. Are the limited partners obligated to return capital contributions distributed to them in violation of their partnership agreement? [See *Henkels & McCoy, Inc. v. Adochio*, 138 F.3d 491, 1998 U.S. App. LEXIS 4101 (3d Cir. 1998).]

2. William Granewich was a shareholder and director in a closely held corporation called Founders Funding Group, Inc. (FFG). Granewich, Ben Harding, and Jeannie Alexander-Hergert each owned one-third of the stock. They were all directors, officers, and employees of FFG. They agreed to accept inadequate compensation from the corporation, with the expectation that they would be well compensated in the future. They were each going to receive the same amount of compensation. They also agreed that they would be "employed continually and perpetually by the corporation." The business became quite successful. On May 5, 1993, Harding and Alexander-Hergert met with Granewich and told him that he was removed as a director, officer, and employee effective immediately. Harding and Alexander-Hergert, acting on behalf of the corporation, hired attorney Michael Farrell to provide legal services to the corporation. Granewich claims that Farrell assisted the other shareholders in amending the corporate bylaws, removing Granewich as director, and taking action to dilute the value of Granewich's interest in the corporation. Granewich sued Farrell. Was Farrell liable to Granewhich? What ethical issues are raised? [See *Granewich v. Harding*, 985 P.2d 788, 1999 Ore. LEXIS 383 (Sup. Ct. Ore. 1999).]

3. Adelphia Communications Corporation was the cable television company founded by John Rigas. Five former executives—John Rigas (chief executive officer), his sons, Timothy Rigas (chief financial officer) and Michael Rigas (vice-president for operations), Michael Mulchey (former director of internal reporting), and James Brown (vice-president for finance)—were indicted on September 23, 2002.

U.S. authorities accused the Rigases of hiding debt and looting the company. The criminal indictment charged 24 counts of conspiracy and fraud, including that the Rigases: (1) used company money to cover $250 million in personal stock purchases and build a golf course, and (2) failed to disclose $2.3 billion in loans to the family. Authorities alleged that the Rigases made phony bookkeeping entries to make it appear that the company's debt was declining and its operating performance was improving. Shareholders, Adelphia, and the U.S. Securities and Exchange Commission (SEC) have filed more than 40 lawsuits against the Rigases. Federal prosecutors wanted the Rigases to forfeit $2.5 billion. The independent directors removed

Rigas from control of Adelphia in May 2002 and the company filed for Chapter 11 bankruptcy in June. In July 2002, the SEC filed a civil fraud suit accusing the Rigases of "rampant self-dealing."

Originally Brown entered a plea of innocent. However, as part of a plea bargain, on November 14, 2002, Brown pleaded guilty to conspiracy to commit fraud, securities fraud, and bank fraud. He faced a maximum of 45 years in prison under the plea. Brown admitted to the court that he conspired with John, Timothy, and Michael Rigas and Michael Mulchey to cheat investors. He said he overstated earnings, lied to Moody's Investor Service and several banks, and issued misleading statistics about the number of subscribers the cable company had. Presumably, Brown will aid the investigators by telling them how the financial statements were manipulated. Brown's testimony could be particularly damaging to Timothy Rigas, who was the chief financial officer and Brown's supervisor.

There is also a legal battle over the family's money. In August 2002, John Rigas was about to sell two properties, when the bankruptcy court blocked the sales of the parcels. The court can implement a freeze on the family assets. Complete and partial freezes of assets are common in cases like this. The court will have to decide "How to balance the family's right to pay for their defense with creditors' desire to safeguard money that they contend was stolen."

The family would like to have the case moved to U.S. district court. The stated reason is that the bankruptcy court lacks the necessary expertise to handle the legal issues under the Racketeer Influenced and Corrupt Organizations Act (RICO) and the federal securities laws. However, bankruptcy courts also may be more protective of unpaid creditors than the district court. There is also a question of whether the bankruptcy filing under Chapter 11 will prevent the five defendants from receiving payments under the director and officer liability insurance policies. The bankruptcy judge hearing the case said that the former Adelphia executives can request $300,000 each from Adelphia D and O liability insurance policies to cover legal bills and defend fraud suits by investors. According to the ruling by Judge Robert E. Gerber, the men could ask the 3 insurers to advance legal fees and other costs of their defense. The judge also stated that if the insurance companies deny coverage, the men may not sue to demand payments until after the criminal cases are over. Assume that the judge's ruling has been appealed to your court. How will you decide? [*See* "Adelphia Ex-Officials Plead Not Guilty," *New York Times*, October 3, 2002, http://www.nytimes.com/2002/10/03/business/adelphia-ex-officials-plead-not-guilty.html (accessed 7/29/10), "Former Adelphia VP Pleads Guilty to Fraud Charges," CNN, November 14, 2002, http://archives.cnn.com/2002/LAW/11/14/adelphia.plea/index.html (accessed 7/29/10), and David Voreacos, "Adelphia's Rigases Deserve 215 Years, Prosecutors Say," June 13, 2005, Bloomberg, http://www.bloomberg.com/apps/news?pid=newsarchive&sid=aUIWI39CYdRE&refer=us (accessed 7/29/10).]

Notes

1. Uniform Partnership Act (UPA) refers to the 1914 act drafted by the National Conference of Commissioners on Uniform State Laws (NCCUSL). The following states have adopted UPA (1914) but none of the later uniform acts: Georgia, Indiana, Massachusetts, Michigan, Missouri, New Hampshire, New York, North Carolina, Pennsylvania, Rhode Island, South Carolina, Utah, and Wisconsin. Email from Katie Robinson, Communications Officer, National Conference of Commissioners on Uniform State Laws (NCCUSL), February 22, 2010.

2. The following states have adopted the 1994 version of RUPA, without the 1997 amendments: Connecticut, West Virginia, and Wyoming. The 1997 amendments provided for limited liability partnerships. The following states have adopted RUPA with the 1997 amendments: Alabama, Alaska, Arizona, Arkansas, California, Colorado, Delaware,

District of Columbia, Florida, Hawaii, Idaho, Illinois, Iowa, Kansas, Kentucky, Maine, Maryland, Minnesota, Mississippi, Montana, Nebraska, Nevada, New Jersey, New Mexico, North Dakota, Ohio, Oklahoma, Oregon, Puerto Rico, South Dakota, Tennessee, Texas, U.S. Virgin Islands, Vermont, Virginia, and Washington. (Although technically Puerto Rico and the U.S. Virgin Islands are not states, the NCCUSL treats them as states and for purposes of uniform laws we will also.) The versions in South Dakota and Texas are substantially similar. "A Few Facts About The Uniform Partnership Act (1994)(1997)," NCCUSL Web site, http://www.nccusl.org/ Update/uniformact_factsheets/uniformacts-fs-upa9497.asp (accessed 2/21/10).

3. Uniform Partnership Act § 18(h).

4. Revised Uniform Partnership Act § 303.

5. "Summary Uniform Partnership Act (1994)," NCCUSL Web site, http://www.nccusl.org/nccusl/uniformact_summaries/ uniformacts-s-upa1994.asp (accessed 2/21/2010).

6. Uniform Partnership Act § 18(a), (b), and (c).

7. Revised Uniform Partnership Act § 401 (b).

8. Uniform Partnership Act § 18(f).

9. Ibid., §§ 19 and 20.

10. Ibid., § 25.

11. Revised Uniform Partnership Act § 201.

12. Revised Uniform Partnership Act § 203.

13. "Summary Uniform Partnership Act (1994)," supra note 5.

14. Uniform Partnership Act § 22.

15. Ibid., § 21.

16. Ibid., § 12.

17. Ibid., § 13.

18. Revised Uniform Partnership Act §§ 306 and 307.

19. Uniform Partnership Act § 14.

20. Ibid., § 28.

21. Revised Uniform Partnership Act § 307(d).

22. Uniform Partnership Act § 21.

23. "A Few Facts About The Uniform Partnership Act (1994)(1997)", NCCUSL Web site, http://www.nccusl.org/ nccusl/uniformact_factsheets/uniformacts-fs-upa9497.asp (accessed 2/21/10).

24. Revised Uniform Partnership Act §§ 306 and 307.

25. "New Uniform Securities Act Approved, Law Governing Regulation of Securities by States Modernized," NCCUSL Web site, Press Release, Section: Newsroom, August 5, 2002, http://www.nccusl.org/nccusl/pressreleases/pr080502_ SEC.asp (accessed 2/28/10). It has been adopted by Georgia, Hawaii, Idaho, Indiana, Iowa, Kansas, Maine, Michigan, Minnesota, Mississippi, Missouri, New Mexico, Oklahoma, South Carolina, South Dakota, U.S. Virgin Islands, Vermont, and Wisconsin. "A Few Facts About the Uniform Securities Act (2002), NCCUSL Web site, http://www.nccusl.org/Update/ uniformact_factsheets/uniformacts-fs-usa.asp (accessed 3/ 2/10).

26. "New Uniform Securities Act Approved, Law Governing Regulation of Securities by States Modernized," supra note 25.

27. "The Art of the Market" (book excerpt), *Fortune,* September 27, 1999, pp. 230-39. Book excerpt from Bob Tamarkin and Les Krantz, with commentary by George LeBarre, *The Art of the Market,* (New York: Stewart Tabori & Chang, 1999).

28. Del. Code Ann. § 232 (2000) provides that stockholders *may* consent to notice by "electronic transmission." New York Bus. Corp. Law § 605 (1988) and Conn. Gen. Stat. Ann. § 33-603(c)(2)(2000) authorize electronic notice of shareholders' meetings. Delaware enacted a revision to its corporate code effective July 1, 2000. It permits Delaware corporations to use electronic transmissions in additional aspects of corporate affairs. It includes a definition of "electronic transmission." The purpose of the amendments are to (1) enable corporations to use them but not require their use; (2) operate fairly and maintain the balance of powers and responsibilities among corporate constituencies, (3) anticipate technological advances; (4) be flexible; and (5) permit economic efficiency and cost savings. Prior to passage of the statute, only electronic proxies by shareholders were permitted. Delaware permits stockholders to consent to notice by "electronic transmission" under § 232 of the corporate code. The Securities and Exchange Commission (SEC) has also issued two releases providing for the use of electronic media in a limited number of situations. James L. Holzman & Thomas A. Mullen, "A New Technololgy Frontier for Delaware Corporations," 4 DEL. L. REV. 55 (2001).

29. Del. Code Ann. § 211. Holzman & Mullen, supra note 28.

30. Holzman & Mullen, supra note 28.

31. Bryan A. Garner, *Black's Law Dictionary,* 7th edition (St. Paul: West, 1999), p. 473.

32. A common reason for not participating is because the meeting is far from the shareholder's home.

33. Del. Code Ann. § 212 (c)(2). Electronic proxies were permitted prior to the 2000 revisions. Holzman & Mullen, supra note 28.

34. Christine Ammer & Dean S. Ammer, *Dictionary of Business and Economics* (New York: Free Press, 1984), p. 136.

35. Garner, supra note 31, p. 492.

36. Ammer & Ammer, supra note 34, at p. 442.

37. Laura Hunter Dietz et al., "Liability of Transferee of Stock," 18A Am. Jur. 2d *Corporations,* (West Group 2010), § 760.

38. Pub. L. No. 107-204, 116 Stat. 747 (2002).

39. Del. Code Ann. § 141(i). Holzman & Mullen, supra note 28.

40. Cal. Corp. Code § 307. This provision in the California Code was enacted on a trial basis until January 2003. Holzman & Mullen, supra note 28.

41. Ohio Rev. Code Ann. 1701.59(E) (2009), Minn. Stat. § 302A.251(5) (2008).

42. State law will specify the steps necessary to formally dissent. Often the director must have his or her dissent entered into the minutes of the directors' meeting when the vote was taken.

43. The states that have adopted the Uniform Limited Liability Company Act (1995 with 1996 amendments) and have not adopted the 2006 version are: Alabama, Hawaii, Illinois, Montana, South Carolina, South Dakota, US Virgin Islands, Vermont, and West Virginia. "A Few Facts About the Uniform Limited Liability Company Act, NCCUSL Web site, http://www.nccusl.org/nccusl/uniformact_factsheets/uniformacts-fs-ullca.asp (accessed 2/21/10).

44. Idaho and Iowa have adopted the Uniform Limited Liability Company Act (2006). It was introduced in the District of Columbia in 2010. "A Few Facts About the Uniform Limited Liability Company Act (2006), NCCUSL Web site, http://www.nccusl.org/Update/uniformact_factsheets/uniformacts-fs-ullca06.asp (accessed 2/21/10).

45. *Ault v. Brady,* 2002 U.S. App. LEXIS 11684 (8th Cir. 2002), Unpublished Opinion, footnote 6.

46. Ark. Code Ann. § 4-32-402(1) (Repl. 2001).

47. *Robinson v. Geo Licensing Company, L.L.C.,* 173 F. Supp. 2d 419, 427, 2001 U.S. Dist. LEXIS 18867 (Md. 2001).

33

Business Terminations and Other Extraordinary Events

Agenda

eClass may be a big success in developing and marketing eAccounting and eManagement. On the other hand, the enterprise may fail miserably. If the firm is a success, it is likely that a large corporation may wish to acquire eClass. Ani, Meg, and Yousef do not wish to give up ownership of the company at this time, and they would resist any takeover efforts. If the other firm persists in its efforts to acquire eClass, how can our entrepreneurs prevent a takeover? What legal or ethical restrictions may limit eClass's actions? If the enterprise is a failure, Ani, Meg, and Yousef are afraid that they will lose everything they have acquired over the years. How can they protect their personal assets while providing adequate support to the firm to give it an opportunity to succeed?

These and other questions will arise as you read this chapter. Be prepared! You never know when the firm or one of its members will seek your advice.

[**NOTE**: Throughout Part 7 the organization form selected by eClass may vary from one eClass problem to the next. This is done to allow you to evaluate the problems presented on the basis of different organizational options. If the facts of a particular case state that eClass has adopted a particular form, answer the questions based on the implications for that particular form. Treat each thread case independently, without reference to the other thread cases or agendas. If no particular form is specified, assume that eClass is operating as a partnership, but the principals are considering the benefits—and the burdens—of changing the structure to another form of business.]

Classic Case

PAGE v. PAGE
55 Cal. 2d 192, 1961 Cal. LEXIS 201 (Cal. 1961)

FACTS Plaintiff and defendant are brothers and partners in a linen supply business in Santa Maria, California. Plaintiff appeals from a judgment declaring the partnership to be for a term rather than at will. The partners entered into an oral partnership agreement in 1949. Within the first two years each partner contributed approximately $43,000 for the purchase of land, machinery, and linen needed to begin the business. From 1949 to 1957 the enterprise was unprofitable. The partnership's major creditor is a corporation, wholly owned by plaintiff, which supplies the linen and machinery necessary for the day-to-day operation of the business. This corporation holds a $47,000 demand note of the partnership. The partnership operations began to improve in 1958. Despite this improvement plaintiff wishes to terminate the partnership.

ISSUE Did the partners establish a partnership at will?

HOLDING Yes, the business was a partnership at will.

REASONING Excerpts from the opinion of Justice Traynor:

... The Uniform Partnership Act provides that a partnership may be dissolved "By the express will of any partner when no definite term or particular undertaking is specified." ... Viewing this evidence [in a light] most favorable for defendant, it proves only that the partners expected to meet current expenses from current income and to recoup their investment if the business were successful.

Defendant contends that such an expectation is sufficient to create a partnership for a term under ... [precedents]. In that case we held that when a partner advances a sum of money to a partnership with the understanding that the amount contributed was to be a loan to the partnership and was to be repaid as soon as feasible from the prospective profits of the business, the partnership is for the term reasonably required to repay the loan. ... [O]ther cases hold that partners may impliedly agree to continue in business until a certain sum of money is earned ..., or one or more partners recoup their investments ..., or until certain debts are paid ..., or until certain property could be disposed of on favorable terms. . . . In each of these cases, however, the implied agreement found support in the evidence. . . . In each of these cases the court properly held that the partners impliedly promised to continue the partnership for a term reasonably required to allow the partnership to earn sufficient money to accomplish the understood objective. . . .

[Here] defendant failed to prove any facts from which an agreement to continue the partnership for a term may be implied. The understanding to which defendant testified was no more than a common hope that the partnership earnings would pay for all the necessary expenses. Such a hope does not establish even by implication a "definite term or particular undertaking" as required by . . . [statute]. All partnerships are ordinarily entered into with the hope that they will be profitable, but that alone does not make them all partnerships for a term and obligate the partners to continue in the partnerships until all of the losses over a period of many years have been recovered.

Defendant contends that plaintiff is acting in bad faith and is attempting to use his superior financial position to appropriate the now profitable business of the partnership. . . . Defendant fears that upon dissolution he will receive very little and that plaintiff, who is the managing partner and knows how to conduct the operations of the partnership, will receive a business that has become very profitable because of the establishment of Vandenberg Air Force Base in its vicinity. . . .

There is no showing in the record of bad faith or that the improved profit situation is more than temporary. In any event these contentions are irrelevant to the issue whether the partnership is for a term or at will. Since . . . this action . . . will be the basis for future action by the parties, it is appropriate to point out that defendant is amply protected by the fiduciary duties of copartners. Even though the Uniform Partnership Act provides that a partnership at will may be dissolved by the express will of any partner . . . , this power, like any other power held by a fiduciary, must be exercised in good faith. We have often stated that "Partners are trustees for each other, and in all proceedings connected with the conduct of the partnership every partner is bound to act in the highest good faith to his copartner and may not obtain any advantage over him in the partnership affairs by the slightest misrepresentation, concealment, threat or adverse pressure of any kind." . . .

A partner at will is not bound to remain in a partnership, regardless of whether the business is profitable or unprofitable. A partner may not . . . by use of adverse pressure "freeze out" a copartner and appropriate the business to his own use. A partner may not dissolve a partnership to gain the benefits of the business for himself, unless he fully compensates his copartner for his share of the prospective business opportunity. . . .

Likewise in the instant case, plaintiff has the power to dissolve the partnership by express notice to defendant. If, however, it is proved that plaintiff acted in bad faith and violated his fiduciary duties by attempting to appropriate to his own use the new prosperity of the partnership without adequate compensation to his copartner, the dissolution would be wrongful and the plaintiff would be liable . . . for violation of the implied agreement not to exclude defendant wrongfully from the partnership business opportunity.

TERMINATION OF A SOLE PROPRIETORSHIP

The termination of a sole proprietorship is a relatively simple matter. The owner simply pays the business debts and then the remaining assets belong to him or her. As an alternative, the owner might sell the business to someone else. Care must be used to assure that business liabilities are handled correctly, however. Often, but not always, this is an obligation undertaken by the buyer. It is critical that the parties discuss existing liabilities and reach an agreement about who will pay them.

TERMINATION OF A PARTNERSHIP

The ending of a partnership is different from what most people expect. The *partnership* may end while the business *enterprise* continues; if so, a dissolution occurs. Or the partnership and the business enterprise may both end. If so, a dissolution and a winding up occur. (A *winding up* consists of paying the accounts and liquidating the assets of a business for the purpose of making distributions and dissolving the concern.) A dissolution is diagrammed in Exhibit 33.1. Note that a dissolution does not necessarily result in a termination of the business.

Dissolution of a Partnership

Technically, a *dissolution* is "the change in the relation of the partners caused by any partner ceasing to be associated in the carrying on as distinguished from the winding up of the business."[1] This means that any time a partner leaves the business, the partnership is dissolved. The change in the relations of the partners changes the basic structure and nature of the partnership, "dissolving" the former partnership.

The fact that a partner leaves the business does not mean that the *business* must cease to exist. The remaining partners may be able to continue the business, or they may need to terminate the business. Their options depend on the method and manner of dissolution.

The Uniform Partnership Act (UPA) lists several different causes of dissolution.[2] Exhibit 33.1 illustrates partnership dissolution under UPA. Any of these events will cause a dissolution of the partnership, but they may not require a winding up of the business. We shall examine these causes of dissolution next. Note that references in this chapter to the Uniform Partnership Act (UPA) are to the UPA (1914), which 13 states still follow.[3]

Dissolution Without Violation of the Agreement   A dissolution may be caused by the terms of the partnership agreement. For example, the time period established in the agreement may expire, or the original purpose of the partnership may be fulfilled.

Exhibit 33.1

Partnership Dissolution under the Uniform Partnership Act (UPA)

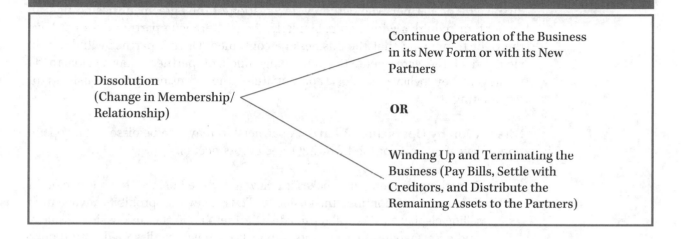

Dissolution
(Change in Membership/
Relationship)

Continue Operation of the Business
in its New Form or with its New
Partners

OR

Winding Up and Terminating the
Business (Pay Bills, Settle with
Creditors, and Distribute the
Remaining Assets to the Partners)

If a partnership was established to operate for two years, and two years have elapsed, the partnership is dissolved. If a partnership was established to sell 100 parcels of land, and all the land has been sold, the partnership is dissolved. Of course, a new agreement may be made to extend the time or to modify the purpose, if the partners so desire.

If the agreement does not specify a particular time period or a particular, limited purpose, a partner may simply decide to quit unless the agreement states otherwise. Such a decision operates as a dissolution without violation of the agreement.

All the partners may decide to terminate the partnership. If so, the partnership is dissolved without violating the agreement. This is true *even if* a definite time period was specified and that time has not yet expired. And it is true *even if* a particular purpose was declared and the purpose has not yet been achieved.

Finally, a partnership is dissolved if any partner is expelled from the partnership by the others; this dissolution does not violate the agreement *provided* that the agreement permits the expulsion. Thus, if Xavier, Yvette, and Zara vote to remove Patricio from the firm, and the agreement permits such a vote, the partnership is dissolved without violation of the agreement.

Normally, a dissolution in accord with the agreement will lead to a winding up *unless* the agreement itself provides for a continuation of the business. If the agreement does not specify that a continuation is permitted, the partner who causes the dissolution may demand that a winding up take place. Such a demand must be obeyed, even though it normally will harm the remaining partners who may wish to continue the business. Thus, every partnership agreement should contain some provisions for continuing the business. (Of course, an *expelled* partner cannot demand a winding up of the business if the expulsion was done in good faith by the other partners.)

Dissolution in Violation of the Agreement   No one can be forced to be a partner against his or her will. Thus, any partner has the *power* to withdraw from any partnership at any time—but a partner does not have the *right* to withdraw at any time. A withdrawing partner may violate the terms of the partnership agreement by withdrawing. If so, the remaining partners may continue the business if they desire: This is true even though the partnership technically has been dissolved. The partner who withdrew in violation of the agreement has no right to demand or require a winding up. Similarly, the withdrawing partner does not have the right to demand that the business be continued. Once a partner withdraws in violation of the agreement, the remaining innocent partners may decide to do whatever they believe is most appropriate—either continuing the business or terminating it.

Dissolution by Operation of Law   A partnership may also be dissolved by operation of law, if any one of the following three events occurs:

1. Something happens that makes it unlawful for the business to continue or for the partners to continue the business. (Thus, a law that prohibits anyone from selling elephant tusks will terminate a partnership in the tusk-selling business. And a partnership that loses its import license will be dissolved even though importing itself is still legal.)
2. A partner dies.
3. A partner or the partnership becomes bankrupt.

Dissolution by Court Order   The final method for dissolving a partnership is by court order. As explained in § 32 of the UPA, a court will order a dissolution only if *asked* to do so. The person who wants to dissolve the partnership must petition the court; the court will not go searching for partnerships that should be dissolved. Most commonly, one of the partners or a representative of one of the partners files the petition. Even if a petition is filed, dissolution is not automatic. The court must have *grounds* to grant the request. The following grounds will justify a court ordered dissolution:

- Insanity of any partner
- Incapacity, other than insanity, of a partner that prevents that partner from performing the contractual duties called for in the agreement
- Misconduct by any partner that makes continued operation of the business difficult
- Intentional or repeated breach of the agreement by a partner, or any behavior that makes the continuation of the business impossible or impractical
- Evidence that the business can be continued only at a loss without a prospect that it will become profitable in the near future
- Any other circumstances that, in the court's opinion, justify dissolution as the equitable response

Note that insanity does *not* automatically dissolve the partnership; a petition must be filed seeking dissolution. If the remaining partners wish to continue the business with an insane partner, they have the right to do so.

It is also possible that some person may purchase the interest of a partner and then decide to seek a court-ordered dissolution.[4] A court may grant this request only if one these situations can be proven:

- The agreement had a specific term or a particular purpose that has been fulfilled or satisfied.

  OR

- The partnership was a partnership at will at the time of the purchase. (*At will* means it has no specific date or circumstance to bring about a dissolution.)

Termination Under RUPA

Where it has been adopted, the Revised Uniform Partnership Act (RUPA) has modified the partnership termination rules due to its clear adoption of the entity theory.[5] Partnerships under the entity theory are more durable than partnerships based on the aggregate theory.[6] The entity theory provides a conceptual basis for continuing the firm despite a partner's withdrawal or expulsion. An example of this shift in perspective is the addition of sections in RUPA on partnership "mergers" and "conversions." For example, two or more partnerships may merge and form a new partnership. A general partnership can convert to a limited partnership and vice versa.

RUPA adopted the term "dissociation," and § 601 discusses the events that cause a partner's dissociation.[7] These events will sound familiar. As summarized and paraphrased below, a partner is dissociated if:

- The partnership has notice that the partner wants to withdraw now or at a later date specified by the partner.[8] (RUPA calls this "notice of the partner's express will.")
- An event occurs that is specified in the agreement as causing the partner's dissociation.
- A partner is expelled pursuant to the partnership agreement.
- There is a unanimous vote of the other partners to expel a partner under certain circumstances listed in RUPA.
- Any partner or the partnership can apply to the court to have a partner expelled if:
  - The partner engaged in wrongful conduct that adversely and materially affected the partnership business.
  - The partner willfully or persistently committed a material breach of the agreement or of a duty owed to the partnership or other partners under § 404 of RUPA.
  - The partner engaged in conduct that makes it not reasonably practical to carry on the business in partnership with him or her.

■ The partner becomes a debtor in bankruptcy;[9] executes an assignment for the benefit of creditors; seeks, consents, or agrees to the appointment of a trustee, receiver, or liquidator of that partner or substantially all that partner's property; or fails to have the appointment of a trustee, receiver, or liquidator canceled or postponed within 90 days after appointment.

■ If the partner is an individual, the partner's death;[10] the appointment of a guardian or general conservator for the partner; or a judicial determination that the partner has become unable to perform his or her partnership duties under the agreement.[11]

Under RUPA, a partner has the power to withdraw at any time even though he or she may not have the right to do so.[12] A partner who wrongfully withdraws is liable to the partnership and to the other partners for any damages caused by the withdrawal.[13] A partner, who dissociates wrongfully, is not entitled to participate in the winding up of the firm.[14] A dissociated partner remains a partner for some limited purposes and retains some residual rights and duties. He or she is a partner for some purposes but a former partner for other purposes. Section 701 provides that in most situations there is a buy out of the dissociating partner's interest, rather than a winding up of the business. Section 801 specifies the situations in which the dissociation of a partner causes a winding up of the business.

RUPA also provides for conversion and merger of partnerships.[15] A dissociation under RUPA is diagrammed in Exhibit 33.2. Note that a dissociation does not necessarily result in a termination of the business.

Exhibit 33.2

Partnership Dissociation Under the Revised Uniform Partnership Act (RUPA)

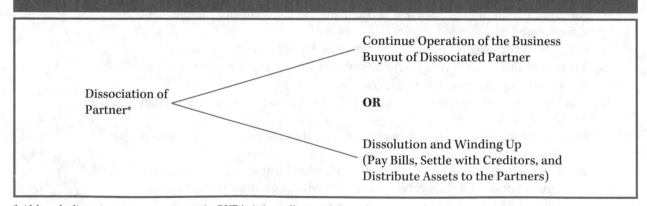

Dissociation of Partner*

Continue Operation of the Business
Buyout of Dissociated Partner

OR

Dissolution and Winding Up
(Pay Bills, Settle with Creditors, and
Distribute Assets to the Partners)

* Although dissociation is a new term in RUPA, it is really a withdrawal or removal of a partner.

Continuation of the Partnership Business

Once a dissociation occurs under RUPA or a dissolution occurs under UPA, an important decision must be made. Will the business terminate through a winding up, or will the business continue? In most cases, an ongoing business is more valuable than the assets that make up the business; in other words, the sum is greater than its parts. Thus, the remaining partners normally want to continue operating the business if they can possibly do so. This may not be satisfactory to a withdrawing partner, however. For this reason, the partners should consider the problem of a continuation when they draw up the original agreement, and they should make provisions for the "solution" at that time.

The remaining partners have the *right* to elect to continue the business under any one of the following circumstances:

- The withdrawing partner withdraws in violation of the agreement.
- The withdrawing partner consents to the continuation when he or she could have demanded a termination and winding up.
- The agreement permits a continuation following a dissociation or a dissolution.

Unless one of these circumstances occurs, a dissociation or a dissolution will be followed by a winding up.

Withdrawing Partners   Any time the business is continued following a withdrawal, the continuing partners have a duty to the withdrawing partner. The withdrawing partner must be both *indemnified* (that is, secured against partnership debts) and bought out. The purpose of the indemnification is to protect the withdrawing partner from any claims of creditors of the partnership. The withdrawing partner is still liable for any debts owed that arose during his or her membership in the partnership. Without an indemnification agreement, a withdrawing partner might be tempted to force a winding up in order to minimize his or her potential liability. But the indemnification agreement is assurance that the continuing partners will repay any losses the withdrawing partner may suffer on account of partnership obligations. The indemnification agreement provides the withdrawing partner with legal rights. All the parties should be aware that, as a practical matter, the partners and the remaining partners may not have the funds and assets to indemnify.

Withdrawing partners are also entitled to payment for their interest in the business at the time of withdrawal, including any undistributed profits. However, if a withdrawal is in violation of the partnership agreement, the continuing partners may first deduct *damages,* based on breach of contract theories. The amount of these damages should adequately cover the harm caused by the breach.

The continuing partners may pay former partners in a lump sum and settle the matter. If they do not, or cannot, make a lump-sum payment, the withdrawing partners are allowed to elect how payment will be made. They can either: (1) receive interest on the unpaid portion until they receive payment in full; or (2) elect to receive a portion of profits that corresponds to the unpaid portion of their share until they are paid in full. This election must be made at the time of withdrawal, and once the election is made, it cannot be modified unless the continuing partners agree to the change.

Entering Partners   Occasionally, a new partner is brought into the business. When this happens, a continuation obviously occurs. No one wants to enter a business in order to see it go through a winding up. The continuation is treated slightly differently when a new partner enters the firm. As a partner, the new entrant is liable for the debts of the partnership. But existing creditors did not rely on the new partner's credit rating when they decided to extend credit to the (previous) partnership. As a result, it seems unfair to impose unlimited liability on the new partner. UPA § 41(7) resolves this problem by specifying that the new partner is liable to preexisting creditors only up to the amount of his or her capital contribution. In other words, an entering partner has limited liability to preexisting creditors but faces unlimited personal liability with respect to future creditors. This rule is continued under RUPA.[16]

Winding Up the Partnership

Winding up is the termination of the business enterprise. In winding up, one must marshal and liquidate the assets of the business and then distribute the proceeds of this process to the proper parties. (To *marshal* means to collect assets or claims against others so that the firm's debts can be paid. To *liquidate* means to settle with creditors and debtors and apportion any remaining assets to the partners.)[17]

General Partnerships   The priority for distributing the proceeds is set out in the UPA § 40. The first priority is the claims owed to creditors who are not partners. If the proceeds are sufficient to pay this class entirely, they will be so paid. Any surplus carries over to the next priority class. Any deficit will cause two things to happen: (1) a pro rata distribution of the proceeds within the class; and (2) a collection of the balance from the personal assets of the partners, jointly and severally.

The second priority in receiving the proceeds is claims owed to the partners as *creditors* of the business. Again, any surplus will be applied to the next priority class, and any deficit will be made up from the personal assets of the partners. Note that a partner who wishes to be treated as a creditor of the firm will need to present clear and convincing evidence of the debt. It is normally presumed that any monies advanced to the firm were advanced as a capital contribution, not as a loan. The court probably will demand some written proof, such as a promissory note, that the funds were meant as a loan. Without such proof, the court will probably determine that it was a capital contribution.

The third priority is the return of the capital contributions of the partners. Any surplus will be carried over to the fourth and final priority. Any deficit will be allocated among the partners pro rata.

The fourth and final priority category is profits. Any monies left over after all the other classes have been satisfied will be distributed as profits, according to the terms of the partnership agreement. There can be no deficit here.

Creditors of the partnership have first claim on any partnership assets. If the partnership is actually in bankruptcy, the Bankruptcy Reform Act of 1978 § 723 provides that partnership creditors can recover from the individual partners at the same time as the individual creditors of the partners.

If an individual partner cannot pay his or her creditors, the creditors of the individual partner can claim against that partner's partnership interest. However, these creditor claims are limited by the UPA § 28. Usually, if the partnership is solvent, the creditors of the individual partner will be given a charging order by the court. (A *charging order* is a court order permitting a creditor to receive profits from the operation of a business; it is especially common in partnership situations.) This charging order allows the business to continue to operate and minimizes the amount of disruption to the partnership, while providing some recovery for the creditor.

The three examples that follow illustrate how the various interested parties may be treated in a dissolution of a partnership and a winding up of the business. In each example, there are three partners—Carmen, Eric, and Jerrod—whose net worths are shown in the first example. In addition, each partner has made the capital contributions specified, and Jerrod has made a loan to the firm. Notice the effect the different asset positions of the partners have on the partners individually.

Partners	Personal Assets	Personal Liabilities	Net Worth
Carmen	$ 80,000	$ 40,000	$ 40,000
Eric	40,000	100,000	(60,000)
Jerrod	100,000	20,000	80,000

Each partner has already contributed $50,000 to the partnership; profits and losses are to be shared equally. Jerrod has already loaned the firm $30,000 (there is a signed promissory note for this loan).

Example 1   Further assume that the partnership has $200,000 in proceeds and $290,000 in liabilities to regular creditors, plus the $30,000 owed to Jerrod.

Step 1.   Partnership proceeds are distributed to regular creditors (priority 1), leaving a deficit of $90,000.

Step 2.   Each partner owes an additional $30,000 to priority 1 creditors. However, Eric has no money, and so Jerrod and Carmen must pay the full $90,000 between them (Jerrod will pay $50,000 and Carmen will pay $40,000) and hold claims against Eric (Jerrod for $20,000, and Carmen for $10,000). Both Carmen and Eric are now insolvent.

Step 3.   Under priority 3, Jerrod, Carmen, and Eric each owe Jerrod $10,000. Jerrod "pays" himself, and Carmen and Eric each owe Jerrod $10,000.

Consequently, Jerrod had a net worth of $80,000, which has decreased to $30,000 plus $40,000 in debts owed by Carmen and Eric. Carmen had a net worth of $40,000, which has decreased to ($10,000), including the amount that Carmen owes Jerrod.

Carmen also has a claim of $10,000 against Eric. Eric had a net worth of ($60,000), which has technically decreased to ($100,000).

Example 2 Assume instead that the partnership has $309,000 in proceeds and $300,000 in liabilities to regular creditors, plus the $30,000 owed to Jerrod.

Step 1. The priority 1 debts are paid in full, and the $9,000 surplus is carried over.

Step 2. Priority 2 debts are paid until the money runs out. Thus, Jerrod receives the $9,000 carried over from priority 1 and is still owed $21,000. Jerrod "pays" himself $7,000; Carmen pays Jerrod $7,000; Eric owes $7,000. Eric is insolvent, and Jerrod probably will not collect from Eric.

Consequently, Jerrod, who had a net worth of $80,000, now has increased it to $96,000 plus a $7,000 debt owed by Eric. Carmen had a net worth of $40,000, which has decreased to $33,000. Eric had a net worth of ($60,000), which has technically decreased to ($67,000).

Example 3 Assume instead that the partnership has $500,000 in proceeds, $200,000 in liabilities to regular creditors, and the $30,000 owed to Jerrod.

Step 1. Priority 1 debts are paid in full, leaving a surplus of $300,000.

Step 2. Priority 2 debts are paid in full (Jerrod gets his $30,000), leaving a $270,000 surplus.

Step 3. Priority 3 is taken care of next. Each partner receives a full return of his or her capital contribution, leaving a surplus of $120,000.

Step 4. The final priority is satisfied; the $120,000 is distributed as profits, with $40,000 going to each of the partners.

Consequently, the partners will also be paid in full in this case. Jerrod now has:

```
$ 30,000 loan payment
$ 50,000 return of capital
$ 40,000 profits
  80,000 prior net worth
$200,000 new net worth
```

Carmen and Eric each receive:

```
$ 50,000 return of capital
  40,000 profits
$ 90,000 distribution
```

Carmen had a net worth of $40,000, which has increased to $130,000. Eric had a net worth of ($60,000), which has increased to $30,000.

Limited Partnerships A change in the limited partners does not dissolve the partnership. Under most statutes and agreements, new general or limited partners can be added only with the written consent of all the limited partners.

The distribution of assets in a limited partnership is substantially different from that in a normal, general partnership. Also, the Uniform Limited Partnership Act (ULPA) and the Revised Uniform Limited Partnership Act (RULPA) differ from each other in their treatment of distributions. We will discuss RULPA since the majority of states follow it.[18] RULPA calls for distribution in the following order:

- Claims of nonpartner creditors and claims of partners as creditors
- Any amounts owed to former partners prior to their withdrawal from the firm
- Return of capital contributions of all partners
- The remainder distributed as profits to all of the partners

The two examples that follow illustrate how various interested parties may be treated in a dissolution of a limited partnership and a winding up of the business under the RULPA. In each example, there are two general partners—Alice and Bob—and two limited partners—Chuck and Diane. The financial positions and contributions of each of the four are set out as follows.

Partners	Personal Assets	Personal Liabilities	Net Worth
Alice	$150,000	$ 75,000	$ 75,000
Bob	375,000	135,000	240,000
Chuck	100,000	150,000	(50,000)
Diane	200,000	185,000	15,000

Each partner has already contributed $75,000 to the firm. The general partners are to receive 30 percent of the profits each, and the limited partners are to receive 20 percent of the profits each. Chuck has already loaned the firm an additional $50,000 and has a signed promissory note.

Example 1   Further assume the partnership has $400,000 in proceeds and $500,000 in liabilities to nonpartner creditors. Under the RULPA, the distribution is as follows:

Step 1.   Claims of creditors, both partner and nonpartner, are first priority. Here, the $400,000 in proceeds are allocated to the $550,000 in debt owed to nonpartners and to Chuck. These debtors are paid at the rate of approximately 73 percent each, which is calculated by dividing $400,000 by $550,000. The balance of $150,000 in debt is owed by the general partners individually. Since Alice and Bob have the funds, they share this liability equally.

Step 2.   Amounts owed to former partners are paid next; however, there are no former partners in this example.

Step 3.   Capital contributions of all partners are returned. Since the firm has no money left, the general partners are personally liable for this $300,000 ($75,000 times 4) claim. Bob "pays" himself, and he pays Chuck and Diane $75,000 each. Alice already owes Bob; she does not collect $75,000 from him. Alice "pays" herself and owes Bob $75,000 for her share of the payments to Chuck and Diane.

Step 4.   Remaining funds are distributed as profits; however, no funds remain in this example.

Example 2   Assume instead that the partnership has $500,000 in proceeds and $100,000 in liabilities to nonpartner creditors. Under the RULPA, the distribution is as follows:

Step 1.   Claims of creditors, both partner and nonpartner, are satisfied first. The entire $150,000 owed is paid, leaving $350,000.

Step 2.   Any amounts owed to former partners are paid; however, there are none in this example.

Step 3.   Capital contributions of all partners are returned. The entire $300,000 is paid, leaving a balance of $50,000.

Step 4.   The balance is distributed as profits. Each general partner gets $15,000 (30 percent each), and each limited partner gets $10,000 (20 percent each).

The Uniform Limited Partnership Act (2001) made some significant changes to RULPA.[19] These changes for limited partnerships include:

- The limited partnership can exist in perpetuity unless the agreement provides otherwise.[20]
- The exit of a limited partner does not dissolve the partnership.[21]
- A limited partner generally cannot disassociate until the termination of the limited partnership except for those events mentioned in § 601 (b) or if the power is provided in the partnership agreement.[22]

CHANGES IN CORPORATE STRUCTURE

In Chapter 32, we briefly touched on the subject of corporate dissolution when we discussed shareholders' rights in the event of corporate liquidation. So far, though, we have paid little attention to fundamental changes in the corporate structure that might endanger the rights of shareholders and creditors. We will now focus on actions bringing about some of these fundamental changes—dissolution, merger and consolidation, sale of substantially all the corporate assets, and stock acquisition.

Exhibit 33.3 illustrates these four major changes in corporate structure.

Liquidation of the Corporation

The process of *liquidation* consists of winding up the affairs of a business in order to terminate the business. It includes marshaling assets and converting those assets to cash in order to pay the claims of creditors. During this winding up, the corporation pays all debts and creditors from the corporate assets and then distributes any

Exhibit 33.3

Fundamental Changes in Corporate Structure

Merger or Consolidation	Sale of Substantially All the Assets
Rationales:	**Formalities:**
– Economies of scale	– Simpler than merger procedures
– Knowledge (i.e., acquisition of "know-how")	– Approval only by seller's shareholders (i.e., approval of buyer's shareholders unnecessary)
– Diversification	– Provision of appraisal rights to seller's dissenting shareholders and compliance with applicable statutory procedures
– Securing of competitive advantages	
– Tax savings	
– Utilization of assets	– Compliance with statutory provisions protecting creditors' rights
– Preservation of management prerogatives	
	– These formalities not applicable to sale, in the regular course of business, of substantially all the assets created by the corporation
Formalities:	
– Both boards' adoption of merger plan Both corporations' shareholder approval (usually 2/3 of outstanding shares or more needed) unless short-form merger involved	**Effect:**
	– Liabilities of seller ordinarily not assumed by purchaser by operation of law
– Filing of plan with state	
– Issuance of certificate of merger	
– Provision of appraisal rights to dissenting shareholders and compliance with statutory procedures covering such rights, including:	
• Dissenting shareholders' written notice of objection to merger	
• Dissenting shareholders' written demand on corporation for fair market value (fair value)/ market value of shares	
• On failure to agree, either corporation or dissenting shareholders petition court for an appraisal proceeding	
Effect:	
– Assets, rights, and liabilities of acquired firm assumed by surviving firm by operation of law	
– Dissolution of acquired firm	

Exhibit 33.3 Continued

	Dissolution	
Stock Acquisition	**Voluntary (Initiated by shareholders)**	**Involuntary (Initiated by shareholders or other entitites)**

Formalities:
– Simpler than procedures for merger or sale of substantially all the assets
– Compliance with all applicable state statutes and federal securities laws
– Neither board action nor shareholder approval by either corporation needed: necessary only for shareholders of target firm to decide to sell to would-be acquirer or refrain from selling
– Transactions may be deemed *de facto* mergers and set aside by courts
	Formalities:
	– Board recommendation
	– Shareholder approval (usually 2/3 of outstanding shares or more needed)
	– Filing of notice to creditors
	– Filing of certificate of dissolution
	– Liquidation of corporation either before or after dissolution
		Types:
		– At request of state, owing to
		  • Securities fraud; or
		  • Noncompliance with state statutory procedures (e.g., failure to pay taxes or file annual reports)
		– At request of shareholders, owing to
		  • Mismanagement; or
		  • Deadlock among directors or controlling shareholders so serious as to warrant dissolution
		– At request of creditors, owing to the need to preserve creditor's rights

remaining assets to the shareholders. The process of *dissolution*, which denotes the end of the corporation's legal existence, may immediately precede or follow liquidation. Although the terms "dissolution" and "liquidation" are often used together, they are not synonymous.

Throughout the liquidation period, the corporation has all the rights and powers reasonably necessary to effect liquidation. The corporation can even sue and be sued during this period. Under most statutes, the board of directors continues the management of the corporation unless there is a court ordered dissolution and liquidation. In the latter case, the court may appoint a receiver to oversee the liquidation. (A *receiver* is an unbiased person appointed by a court to receive, preserve, and manage the funds and property of a party.) If the directors unlawfully continue the business after dissolution and beyond the time reasonably necessary to wind up the corporation's affairs, they may become personally liable for the corporation's debts. Therefore, the directors (and controlling shareholders) must be cautious during the liquidation process.

State statutes normally protect creditors during liquidation because the creditors have rights superior to those of the stockholders. The statutes require the corporation to notify creditors of dissolution and liquidation so that these creditors can file their claims against the corporation in a timely manner. A creditor who receives notice but does not file a claim may lose the right to sue later on this claim. Retention of this right, on the other hand, allows the creditor to recoup from shareholders any distributions of corporate assets that have occurred before payment of creditors' claims. To protect creditors, the law characterizes the illegal distributions as held "in trust" for the benefit of the creditors. The directors also may incur liability for distributions illegally declared up to the amount of the unpaid claims.

After the corporation has satisfied its debts to its creditors, the shareholders ordinarily receive their proportionate share of the remaining net assets. As discussed earlier, however, the articles of incorporation may set out one or more classes of shares as meriting liquidation preferences over another class or classes of shares. For instance, preferred stockholders usually receive their shares of the net assets before holders of common stock do. (Note, however, that preferred shareholders *never* receive payment before creditors do.) But if the preferred shareholders do not enjoy liquidation preferences, they will participate with the common shareholders on a share-for-share basis. Sometimes the articles give the preferred shareholders both liquidation preferences and participation rights with the common shareholders. Because cash is the usual method for satisfying liquidation preferences, the corporation may need to sell its assets to raise the amount required to pay these preferences. Under most statutes, the corporation can distribute property instead of cash in satisfying liquidation preferences; but it will be illegal to favor some shareholders through grants of property (as when a corporation gives controlling shareholders valuable patents or trademarks) while doling out cash to minority shareholders.

Dissolution of the Corporation

Dissolution involves termination of the corporation as a *legal entity*. The term *dissolution* is not synonymous with *liquidation*, which refers to the winding up or termination of the corporation's business or affairs. Corporate existence remains impervious to most events, including such unusual occurrences as bankruptcy or the cessation of business activities. Dissolution represents an extraordinary circumstance, or an organic change in corporate structure, that must occur formally in order to have legal effect. Dissolutions are of two types: voluntary and involuntary.

Voluntary Dissolution   As we learned in Chapter 31, corporations theoretically can exist perpetually. On the other hand, a corporation's articles may limit the period of corporate life to, say, 10 years. Alternatively, the incorporators may decide at some point to end the corporation's existence, even though the articles specify the perpetual duration of the corporation. In both cases, such voluntary dissolutions must be carried out through formal procedures.

Statutes ordinarily set out the requirements for these nonjudicial, voluntary dissolutions. Typically, these statutes mandate (1) board action recommending dissolution, (2) shareholder voting to approve the dissolution (usually by the holders of two-thirds of the outstanding shares), and/or (3) filing of a notice to creditors prior to dissolution.

On compliance with these and any other necessary procedures, a certificate of dissolution is filed with the secretary of state or other designated state officer. At this time, the dissolution is legally effective. Remember, though, that liquidation may follow or precede dissolution; so it is possible that some limited corporate activity may occur after dissolution. In voluntary liquidation, the shareholders share proportionately—subject, of course, to any liquidation preferences—in the net assets of the corporation that remain after satisfaction of creditors' claims. As discussed in earlier chapters, some courts prohibit dissolutions that freeze out minority shareholders, especially if a controlling shareholder initiated the dissolution. Also, be aware that the rules regarding dissolutions may vary when a close corporation, instead of a publicly held corporation, is involved.

Involuntary Dissolution   Occasionally, the state, the shareholders, or the corporation's creditors may request the dissolution of the corporation because of wrongdoing or prejudice to shareholders or creditors. Such judicial proceedings are involuntary because the corporation itself is not asking for dissolution. Involuntary dissolutions occur less frequently than voluntary ones.

Dissolution at the Request of the State   Because the corporation is a creation of the state, the state retains the power to rescind the corporation's certificate when the corporation's actions present a clear danger to the public. For instance, the state may ask for involuntary dissolution of a corporation that has engaged in systematic securities fraud. More often, however, grounds for involuntary dissolution involve noncompliance with state requirements, such as failure to pay taxes or to file annual reports.

Rather than seek dissolution, the state may seek suspension of the corporation. *Suspension* works as a deprivation of the corporation's right to conduct its business and certain other powers, but is not as drastic or as permanent a remedy as dissolution. When the firm is once again in compliance with the corporate statutes, the corporation can be reinstated.

Dissolution at the Request of Shareholders   Shareholders can petition the courts for dissolution of the corporation. Statutes generally authorize shareholder actions based on freeze-outs (or oppression) of minority shareholders' interests, allegations of corporate waste of assets, and other examples of corporate mismanagement. Courts sometimes order dissolutions in similar circumstances even in the absence of express statutory provisions. Deadlock among directors or shareholders constitutes an additional ground for involuntary dissolution. For example, courts intervene when a shareholder shows that the deadlock among directors or controlling shareholders has so paralyzed the corporation that it can no longer conduct its business advantageously.

As a less severe alternative, some state statutes permit the appointment of a provisional (or temporary) director who breaks the deadlock and thus allows the corporation to continue functioning. Statutes also may allow holders of a majority of the corporation's outstanding shares to purchase the shares owned by the shareholders who are requesting dissolution. Statutes may contain provisions setting out a minimum number of shareholders (for example, one-third of the corporate shareholders) who must join in the petition for involuntary dissolution before it can be presented to a court.

In contrast to these potential actions, shareholders in close corporations frequently agree in advance that upon the occurrence of a certain event, such as deadlock, each shareholder will be able to request dissolution. Courts ordinarily enforce such agreements.

Dissolution at the Request of Creditors   The theory of corporate personality normally prevents creditors from compelling the involuntary dissolution of the corporation. But in order to protect creditors' rights during dissolution and liquidation, statutes require prior notice to creditors. Statutes also allow the appointment of a receiver who takes over the corporation's business and conducts it for the benefit of the creditors. In some circumstances, creditors can petition for the involuntary bankruptcy of the corporation to preserve their rights. Neither the appointment of a receiver nor the institution of involuntary bankruptcy proceedings results in the dissolution of the corporation, however. As we have seen, formal statutory procedures spell out the necessary steps for implementing this fundamental change in corporate structure. Courts are reluctant to force dissolution and generally do so only if they have no other alternative.

Corporate Merger and Consolidation

Like dissolutions, mergers and consolidations bring about fundamental, or organic, changes in the corporation's structure. Dissolution is also related to these two concepts because dissolution of a corporation (or corporations) occurs automatically when either a merger or a consolidation occurs. The procedures for carrying out a merger or consolidation are similar to dissolution procedures. The National Conference of Commissioners on Uniform State Laws (NCCUSL) wrote the Model Entity Transactions Act (2007), which deals with mergers and conversions.[23] A *conversion* occurs when a business changes its form, for example a corporation becomes a limited liability company or a limited partnership.[24] A change in business form may cause changes in the owners' liability and taxation.

Technically, a merger differs from a consolidation. In a *merger,* one corporation (called the *acquirer* or *acquiring firm*) purchases another firm (called the *acquired* or *disappearing firm*) and absorbs it into itself. This new entity is called the *survivor corporation;* the acquired firm no longer exists.

A *consolidation* is similar, except that in a consolidation two or more existing corporations combine to form a wholly new corporate entity. Since most statutes treat the procedures for mergers and consolidations as if the two were identical transactions, this part of our discussion focuses only on mergers. But, as noted, they are analytically different ways of bringing about major changes in corporate structure.

Rationales For Merger   During certain periods of the economy, we experience a phenomenal number of mergers.[25] We will review some of the common motivations for mergers.

Economy of Scale   *Economy of scale* refers to a decrease in the unit cost of a product or service due to production on a larger scale.[26] A number of things may result in an economy of scale such as lower prices for volume purchases of raw materials or parts, more efficient use of machinery, sizable creation of by-products that can be sold to create new profits, or greater bargaining power. A merger may permit a firm to achieve economies of scale and thus to compete much more efficiently. Accumulation of resources resulting from merged firms also facilitates access to financing. Large firms may engage in more research and development. A merged firm, for example, ordinarily is able to allocate more funds to these activities. Mergers can cut costs by allowing the new firm to reduce the number of workers, the number of managers, and the number of facilities. *Horizontal mergers* are mergers between competitors who provide similar products in the same region. Mergers between manufacturers and customers (called *vertical mergers*) may lessen transaction costs, also bringing about economies of scale. A firm can use economies of scale to drive out smaller, less efficient firms through its dominance due to size and wealth ("deep pockets"). Antitrust laws attempt to protect the competitive environment from any retaliatory, abusive conduct by large firms. Antitrust laws are discussed in Chapter 35. In the absence of antitrust concerns, mergers to effect economies of scale are legal and customary.

Knowledge   Often a larger company will merge with a smaller company because the latter possesses valuable technological information or know-how. An established computer firm, for example, may find a merger with a software firm valuable if the software firm has made important technological breakthroughs. The merged firm may be able to retain the staff of the smaller firm and thereby realize future gains from these persons' expertise and inventive capacities.

Diversification   The 1970s marked a large increase in the number of mergers undertaken for the purpose of diversification. Many firms jumped into areas previously unrelated to their principal lines of business through conglomerate mergers. (*Conglomerate mergers* are mergers between noncompeting firms in different industries.) Diversification minimizes the risks that are inherent in being restricted to one industry and the risks caused by economic cycles. It permits a company to gain access to new technologies, markets, skills, and workers. For instance, a traditional retailer may acquire an e-commerce firm. At this time, governmental regulators are not enforcing a strict policy against conglomerate mergers. (Antitrust enforcement policies often change with the political and economic climate of the country.) Even without regulatory concerns, a company should limit its mergers to firms which are similar in culture and related to its core competencies.

Competition   Inherent in much of what we have discussed so far is an underlying desire to control, if not curtail, competition. One firm clearly does not want to be at the mercy of another firm in times of scarcity. Therefore, a merger between a supplier of aluminum and a fabricator of aluminum, for instance, seems a viable strategy for cutting down on some of the supply-side uncertainties. Naturally, though, antitrust concerns may also lurk in mergers designed to control the competitive process, so caution is warranted.

Other Rationales   Other rationales for mergers include tax savings, utilization of cash-rich entities to infuse businesses that need assets for expansion and growth, and preservation of rights of management. The controversies over hostile takeovers, "golden parachutes," "poison pills," and defensive mergers (for example, a merger in which Abbott Corporation merges with Precision Graphics Corporation to avoid Abbott's being taken over by Belmont Corporation) often arise in the context of mergers.

Procedure

Board of Directors   Whatever the rationale for the merger, once the firms have decided to merge, state statutes set out the steps that must be followed in bringing about the merger. Such statutes generally require that each corporation's board of directors adopt a merger plan that includes (1) the names of each corporation and the

eClass 33.1 Finance/Management

SHOULD eCLASS DIVERSIFY?

Yousef read about the opportunities in operating franchises in an entrepreneurship magazine. Yousef has suggested that eClass might want to purchase a tutoring franchise to provide a steady source of cash until eClass establishes its reputation and builds a regular market. He feels that the tutoring business will be steady and that the funds generated from tutoring should carry the firm for the first year or two. Ani and Meg, however, are unsure about this suggestion and ask for your opinion. What legal complications might arise if eClass tries to expand into tutoring?

BUSINESS CONSIDERATIONS   What are the advantages and disadvantages of diversification by a newly formed business? What information should a firm obtain in order to make an informed decision in this instance?

ETHICAL CONSIDERATIONS   Does a business have any duties to expand or not expand when an opportunity presents itself? Do these duties vary depending on the business form of the enterprise—corporation, limited liability company, limited partnership, partnership, or sole proprietorship?

surviving corporation, (2) the appropriate terms and conditions of the merger, (3) the method for converting the acquired firm's securities into the securities of the acquiring firm (stock for cash, stock for stock, and the like), and (4) any amendments to the articles of the acquiring corporation that have resulted from the merger. Difficult issues may arise as the board follows these procedures.

Shareholders   After each of the boards of directors has adopted a merger plan, the shareholders of both corporations ordinarily must approve the merger. Depending on the timing of the merger, this may require a special meeting of the shareholders. As with dissolutions, normally the holders of two-thirds of the outstanding shares must approve this fundamental change, although in a few states approval by a simple majority of the holders of the outstanding stock suffices.

In some states, statutes dispense with the necessity for shareholder approval in *short-form mergers* (those involving a merger between a subsidiary and a parent company that owns 90 to 100 percent of the subsidiary's stock). Because the parent's ownership interest is so high, a vote of approval is a mere formality; therefore requiring such a vote makes little practical sense.

Once all the required steps have been followed, the directors file the plan with the appropriate state office. After the state approves this plan, the surviving corporation receives a certificate of merger and can begin conducting business.

eClass 33.2 Finance/Management

HOW TO DISCOURAGE A TAKEOVER

eClass has had success in developing and marketing eAccounting. This product has been featured in articles in education journals and in the news. As a result of this success and publicity, Online University, Inc. wishes to acquire eClass. Online University specializes in online courses and educational software. Ani, Meg, and Yousef have a meeting (which you attend) and decide they are not ready to sell the firm. They ask for your advice about resisting this takeover attempt. Assume that eClass is a regular (Subchapter C) corporation. What can Ani, Meg, and Yousef legally do to discourage or prevent a takeover? What legal limitations may restrict their options? Why is this problem less likely with a Subchapter S corporation?

BUSINESS CONSIDERATIONS   From a practical perspective, what can a business do to discourage or prevent a takeover? Which techniques are most effective? Why?

ETHICAL CONSIDERATIONS   From an ethical perspective, what can a business do to discourage or prevent a takeover? What ethical limitations may restrict its options?

Effect of Merger   Once the state issues the certificate of merger, the acquired corporation is formally dissolved and ceases to exist; only one corporation survives. The survivor takes on all the assets, rights, and liabilities of the disappearing (acquired) corporation by operation of law. This means, among other things, that creditors of the acquired corporation are now the creditors of the survivor corporation. Lawsuits, like products liability cases, pending against the acquired corporation, if successful, will be paid by the survivor corporation.

Appraisal Rights   Thus far, we have focused on the positive qualities of a merger from the point of view of those who want it. In any given merger, however, some shareholders will object to, or dissent from, the merger. Many people believe it is unfair to require someone to become a shareholder in a new corporation that may be totally different from the one in which he or she originally invested. Therefore, statutes in most states give dissenting shareholders appraisal rights. *Appraisal rights* allow dissenters to sell their shares back to the corporation for cash. State statutes vary in the amount that the dissenters receive for their shares. Some statutes specify fair value, market value, or fair market value of the shares. Notice how the court defines fair value in *Pueblo Bancorporation v. Lindoe, Inc.*, the Contemporary Case in this chapter. *Market value* is generally defined as the current price the stock will sell for on a stock exchange. Not all stock has a market value. *Fair market value* is the current price for selling an asset between an informed willing buyer and an informed willing seller. With appraisal rights, a dissenting shareholder can avoid becoming a shareholder in the survivor corporation and still protect his or her original investment.

To be eligible for appraisal rights, a shareholder ordinarily must follow a set statutory procedure. Although the state statutes vary, in general, such statutes require the following steps:

1. The dissenter must send a written notice of his or her objection to the merger before the meeting at which the merger will be considered.
2. The shareholder must make a written demand on the corporation for the fair value of the shares after the merger has been approved.
3. The corporation must then make a written offer to purchase at a price it believes represents the fair value (or the fair market value) of the shares.
4. If the corporation and the dissenting shareholder disagree about the fair value of the shares, either party may petition a court to determine the fair value in an appraisal proceeding.

Valuation of shares is quite complicated and requires a sophisticated understanding of valuation issues. This task becomes somewhat easier if the stock is traded on the New York, American, Tokyo, or other stock exchanges; in such cases, a court will place great importance on the market price of the stock when assigning a fair value to it. Otherwise, a court usually will arrive at its valuation determination by weighing a number of factors, including market price, investment value, net asset value, and dividends.

Some jurisdictions deny appraisal rights for certain types of mergers (for example, shareholders of the parent company in a short-form merger may have no appraisal rights) and certain types of corporations (those with stock listed on a national securities exchange or those with more than 2,000 shareholders). Since appraisal rights generally represent the exclusive remedy for a dissenting shareholder who opposes a merger, the shareholder must use vigilance in complying with the strict statutory provisions and short time periods involved.

The Delaware Supreme Court, in *Weinberger v. UOP, Inc.*[27] expanded the scope of the appraisal process, thereby making it more appropriate in minority freeze-out cases. The court approved the use of cash-out mergers to eliminate minority interests in a firm. The court held that appraisal should be a minority shareholder's exclusive remedy in most cases. Still the court provided for judicial review of majority action where "fraud, misrepresentation, self-dealing, deliberate waste of corporate assets, or gross and palpable overreaching are involved."[28] Since then, Delaware courts have permitted minority shareholders to challenge the "entire fairness" even when the alleged harm could have been remedied in an appraisal. Where directors are on both sides of a transaction, they have the burden of demonstrating the "entire fairness" of the transaction, which has two aspects: fair dealing (or procedural fairness) and fair price. The fair dealing prong "embraces questions of when the transaction was timed, how it was initiated, structured, negotiated, disclosed to the directors, and how the approvals of the directors and stockholders were obtained."[29] Fair price "relates to the economic and financial considerations of the proposed merger, including all relevant factors: assets, market value, earnings, future prospects, and any other elements that affect the intrinsic or inherent value of a company's stock."[30] In many states other than Delaware, the trend is still to view appraisal as the sole check on conflicts of interest by majority shareholders. It will be interesting to see which states decide to follow the Delaware approach.

Sale of Substantially All the Assets

Rather than acquire another firm through a merger, a corporation can instead buy all, or substantially all, of another firm's assets. For example, a shipping company may buy the ships of a rival company as an alternative to merging with it. This method of acquisition enjoys favor over a merger because it has less procedural complexity. Approval by the shareholders of the acquired firm ordinarily is necessary, but approval by the acquiring firm's shareholders is not. Even then, a sale of substantially all the assets made in the regular course of the corporation's business (as when a corporation is formed to build a tanker, and the tanker is then sold to an oil company) would not normally require shareholder approval. Shareholder approval thus becomes necessary only in the event of a fundamental change in the corporate structure (that is, the disposal of operating assets in order to terminate the corporation's business activities.). Most states provide appraisal rights for dissenting shareholders in these circumstances as well. In addition, various methods of protecting creditors are included in the statutes governing sales of substantially all the assets. In a merger, the acquiring firm takes on all the liabilities of the acquired firm by operation of law; but this is not ordinarily the case when all or substantially all the assets are sold. Court precedents, state corporate codes, and Article 6 of the UCC dealing with bulk transfers have provisions to protect creditors if such sales prejudice their rights.

Stock Acquisition

An alternative method for acquiring the business of another corporation involves stock acquisitions. Instead of buying substantially all the assets of a corporation, the acquiring corporation's directors may decide to buy the stock of the "acquired" corporation. Because the acquisition implicates only the acquired corporation's individual shareholders, who can decide for themselves whether to sell at the price offered for the stock, the directors of the acquired corporation have no right to approve or disapprove the stock acquisition. Similarly, no requirements usually exist for shareholder approval or appraisal rights. However, federal securities laws may apply to such corporate takeovers.

eClass 33.3 Finance/Management

MERGERS AND ACQUISITIONS

A business that manufactures the plastic cases for eClass software is experiencing financial difficulties. If this firm fails, eClass will need to find another manufacturer, probably at a substantially higher cost per unit. The owner of the business has proposed either selling his firm to eClass or merging with eClass. If eClass buys the firm, it will expend a substantial amount of cash. If eClass agrees to merge, the manufacturer wants 20 percent of the common stock in eClass. Ani, Meg, and Yousef have asked your advice as to their best course of conduct. What do you recommend?

BUSINESS CONSIDERATION   Should a business have a policy regarding potential mergers, or should it analyze and decide on each opportunity separately as it arises?

ETHICAL CONSIDERATIONS   What duties does a business owe to its manufacturer in a situation like the one confronting eClass? What duties does it owe its owners and other constituents?

Because sales of substantially all the assets and stock acquisitions may have the ultimate effect of mergers, some companies have characterized their acquisitions in one of these fashions in order to avoid the strict statutory procedures required for mergers. Transactions that take the *form* of sales of assets or stocks but nevertheless have the *effect* of mergers are called *de facto mergers.* Because shareholders and creditors can be injured through *de facto* mergers, in some jurisdictions courts can set aside the transactions and require compliance with the relevant merger statutes (shareholder approval, appraisal rights, and so on).

TERMINATION OF A LIMITED LIABILITY COMPANY

As we mentioned in the prior chapter, the law of Limited Liability Companies (LLCs) is often based on laws of other business organizations. The 1995 Uniform Limited Liability Company Act has not been adopted widely.[31] LLCs are governed by the operating agreement. Organizers will choose to create either an at-will LLC or a term LLC. An *at-will LLC* will continue as long as the members want to continue. A *term LLC* will terminate at the end of the specified term. Either one may fail financially prior to this time. Unless the operating agreement provides otherwise, a member has the *power* to withdraw from either one.[32] The member's disassociation from an at-will LLC will not be wrongful unless the operating agreement makes it wrongful.[33] A member's disassociation from a term LLC before the expiration of the term is wrongful and the disassociating member will be liable for damages.[34] In the latter case, the LLC only has to purchase the disassociating member's distributional interest on the expiration of the term of the LLC.[35] Any damages caused by the wrongful disassociation can be offset from the purchase price.[36]

In a term LLC, some of the members may wish to continue the LLC. Prior to the expiration date, the members can vote to continue the LLC for an additional term. This requires the unanimous vote of all the members and filing an amendment to the articles of organization with the secretary of state. If there is not the requisite unanimous vote, the LLC may be continued as an at-will LLC by a majority vote of the members.[37]

If the LLC is not continued, it follows a winding up procedure similar to other types of organizations. The assets will first be used to pay off the creditors. Then the remaining amount will be paid equally to the members unless the operating agreement provides for an unequal payment.[38]

Under the Revised Uniform Limited Liability Company Act of 2006, the parties may contractually provide for the rights of exiting members.[39] The revised act specifies that LLCs can merge into other types of business entities and other types of entities can merge into LLCs.[40] Following the developing case law, it permits a member to seek a court order to dissolve the LLC on the grounds that managers or controlling members are acting in a manner that is oppressive or a manner that will be directly harmful to the member.[41] This act clarifies the rights of a member's creditor to use charging orders to obtain the member's rights to distributions from the LLC. It provides the rules governing charging orders and foreclosing on them and makes clear that a purchaser of a foreclosed interest only obtains financial rights, and does not become a member of the LLC.[42]

Contemporary Case

PUEBLO BANCORPORATION v. LINDOE, INC.

63 P.3d 353, 2003 Colo. LEXIS 53 (Colo. 2003)

Rehearing Denied Feb. 24, 2003.

FACTS Pueblo Bancorporation (Holding Company), a Colorado corporation, is a bank holding company. Lindoe, Inc. owned 6,525 (5.71%) of Holding Company's outstanding shares. Holding Company was taxed as a corporation under subchapter C of the Internal Revenue Code (IRC). Holding Company could not qualify under subchapter S. Because of certain changes to the rules, Holding Company became eligible to elect S corporation status in 1997. Holding Company's board of directors sought to convert the company into an S corporation. However, an S corporation cannot have a corporation as a shareholder. Lindoe and several other shareholders could not hold stock in an S corporation.

An election to become an S corporation requires the unanimous approval of its shareholders; a single dissenting vote can block the conversion. Consequently, Holding Company created a second corporation, Pueblo Bancorp Merger Corporation (Merger Corp.), which was organized as an S corporation. Holding Company and Merger Corp. entered into a merger agreement which was approved by the shareholders of both companies. The resulting entity was an S corporation. Only those shareholders who could legally own shares in an S corporation were eligible to remain shareholders of the surviving corporation. Shareholders that were ineligible received a cash payout in exchange for their Holding Company stock. Lindoe chose to dissent. Holding Company's expert argued for a fair value of $344 per share. Lindoe's experts argued the fair value of the shares was between $725 and $775 per share.

ISSUE Should the court apply a discount to reflect the lack of marketability in determining the "fair value" of Lindoe's shares?

HOLDING No, under Colorado law a discount should not be applied for lack of marketability.

REASONING Excerpts from the opinion of Justice Rice:

. . . We granted certiorari to resolve a conflict in the court of appeals regarding the question of whether a marketability discount may be applied in determining "fair value" under the Colorado dissenters' rights statute. . . . This case requires us to determine what the General Assembly meant by "fair value." . . . If the language of the statute is ambiguous, we may pursue alternate modes of construction, including consideration of the legislative purpose, the circumstances under which it was adopted, and the consequences of a particular construction. . . . We conclude that the meaning of "fair value" is ambiguous. It is a term that does not have a commonly accepted meaning in ordinary usage, much less in the business community. . . . [T]he phrase "fair value" has been subject to inconsistent judicial interpretations [by the Colorado court of appeals]. . . .

We conclude that the meaning of "fair value" is a question of law, not a question of fact to be opined on by appraisers and decided by the trial court. . . . A case-by-case interpretation of "fair value" results in a definition that is too imprecise to be useful to the business community. Under a case-by-case approach, the parties proceed to trial without knowing what interest the trial court is valuing. In some cases, the trial court may determine that it is "fair" to award the shareholder his pro rata ownership interest in the corporation; in other cases, the court may conclude that it is "fair" to award only the fair market value of the shareholder's specific allotment of shares. Although the difference between the two measures is the single largest variable in the appraisal process, the court's choice of which interpretation to adopt is largely determined by whichever expert the court finds more persuasive. . . . Both the corporation and the dissenting shareholder are disadvantaged because of the subjective and unpredictable nature of the case-by-case approach. A case-by-case interpretation encourages unnecessary litigation; it is a costly and inefficient means to settle disputes between a corporation and a dissenting shareholder. A definition of "fair value" that varies from one courtroom to another is no definition at all; this could not be the scheme the legislature intended. . . . "Fair value" must have a definitive meaning. . . .

In the sixty year history of Colorado's dissenters' rights statute, the measure of compensation has changed from "value" to "fair value," but the legislature has never required that dissenters be paid "fair market value" for their shares. . . . Fair market value is typically defined as the price at which property would change hands between a willing buyer and a willing seller when neither party is under an obligation to act. . . . If the General Assembly intended to create a fair market value measure . . . , it knew how to provide it; the phrase has been used many times in a wide variety of other statutes. . . .

We hold that the proper interpretation of fair value is the shareholder's proportionate ownership interest in the value of the corporation, without discounting for lack of marketability. This view is consistent with the underlying purpose of the dissenters' rights statute and the strong national trend against applying discounts. Historically, the dissenters' rights statutes were intended to compensate minority shareholders for the loss of their veto power and to provide liquidity for dissenting shareholders who found themselves trapped in an involuntarily altered investment. . . . The consensus that has developed among courts and commentators is that the modern dissenters' rights statute exists to protect minority shareholders from oppressive conduct by the majority. . . . In this case, the sole purpose of the merger between Holding Company and Merger Corp. was to cash out minority shareholders, such as Lindoe, who did not qualify to hold stock in an S corporation. . . . The time and price at which Lindoe was cashed out was determined entirely by Holding Company. The purpose of the dissenters' rights statute would best be fulfilled through an interpretation of "fair value" which ensures minority shareholders are compensated for what they have lost, that is, their proportionate ownership interest in a going concern. . . . An interpretation of "fair value" that gives minority shareholders "less than their proportionate share of the whole firm's fair value would produce a transfer of wealth from the minority shareholders to the shareholders in control. Such a rule would inevitably encourage corporate squeeze-outs." . . . The interpretation of fair value which we adopt today is the clear majority view. . . .

We hold that the term "fair value," for the purpose of Colorado's dissenters' rights statute, means the dissenting shareholder's proportionate interest in the corporation valued as a going concern [without discount]. . . .

You Be the Judge

On January 15, 2009, the Bank of America board of directors had a conference call. Kenneth D. Lewis, the chairman, wanted to explain the bank's problems to the board. The bank was about to receive its second taxpayer bailout, but on more severe financial terms than originally expected. In addition, the bank had recently acquired Merrill Lynch, and Merrill's losses were far more than earlier estimates. During the conference call, Charles K. Gifford, one of the directors, emailed to Thomas May, another director, "Unfortunately it's screw the shareholders!!" Thomas May replied, "No trail." Gifford said his comments were made in "the context of a horrible economy!!! Will effect everyone." To which May replied, "Good comeback." It is uncertain exactly what was being discussed during the conference call at the time of the e-mails. "E-mails are often the best trails to what a person is really thinking. . . . That kind of spur-of-the-moment reaction provides grist for the mill of plaintiffs' lawyers where issues of honesty and integrity are at issue," said Mark C. Zauderer, a corporate litigator. Shareholders are unhappy, claiming that they might not have approved the merger if they knew how poorly Merrill was really doing and the hefty bonuses Merrill paid its traders and bankers. Evidence shows that Lewis had concerns about the extent of Merrill's losses and that he had told the government that he was thinking of backing out of the deal prior to its implementation. The government urged him to stay with the deal because of its concerns over the financial markets. One anonymous source said that Gifford was the only board member to argue against the merger before the deal. (Congress, Attorney General Andrew M. Cuomo of New York, and the Securities and Exchange Commission are all investigating the Merrill merger.) Assume that the shareholders brought suit in your court alleging that the officers and directors failed to properly investigate the Merrill merger. In other words, that they failed to do "due diligence." If *you* were the judge, how would *you* decide this dispute? [*See* Louise Story & Eric Dash, "E-Mail Shows Concerns Over Merrill Deal," *New York Times*, October 14, 2009, pp. B1 and B4.]

Summary

Under the UPA, when a partnership undergoes a change in the relationship among the partners, a dissolution occurs. Thus, a withdrawal by any partner is a dissolution, whether the agreement allows such conduct or not. Likewise, a dissolution will occur when the purpose of the agreement has been carried out or when its time has expired. A dissolution will happen by operation of law: (1) if a partner dies; (2) if any partner goes bankrupt; or (3) if the purpose becomes illegal, or the partners cannot legally continue in the business. A dissolution can also happen by court order. When a dissolution occurs because a partner withdraws, the remaining partners may be allowed to continue the business. If they do, then the withdrawing partner must be bought out and indemnified. The RUPA discusses dissociation instead of dissolution.

Often the partnership must be wound up if a dissolution occurs. In a winding up, the assets of the firm are marshaled and liquidated, and the proceeds are distributed according to law. In a general partnership under the UPA, the proceeds must be used first to pay debts that the partnership owes to nonpartner creditors. Next, the creditors who are also partners must be paid. After that, the partners recover their capital contributions. Anything left is distributed as profits.

The process of liquidation (or winding up) of a corporation occurs when it pays all debts and creditors from the corporate assets and then distributes any remaining assets to the shareholders. Directors may incur personal liability if they continue the business of the corporation beyond the time reasonably necessary to wind up the corporation's affairs. Creditors who have preserved their claims against the corporation can recoup from shareholders any distributions of assets that happened prior to payment of creditors. Directors may also incur liability for the remaining unpaid claims. After creditors' claims have been satisfied, the shareholders normally receive the proportion of the remaining net assets represented by their proportionate ownership, subject to any liquidation preferences that the corporation has authorized.

Dissolution of a corporation involves the termination of the corporation as a legal person. It is not synonymous with the term *liquidation,* which refers to the winding up of the corporation's business. Dissolutions may be either voluntary or involuntary. Statutes set out the formal requirements for a voluntary dissolution. Typically, voluntary dissolution involves board action, shareholder approval, and notice to creditors. Upon voluntary dissolution, the shareholders share proportionately in the net assets that remain after satisfaction of creditors' claims. Involuntary dissolutions—those effected by judicial proceedings—occur less frequently than voluntary dissolutions.

The state can rescind or suspend the corporation's certificate when the corporation's actions present a clear danger to the public. When the corporation complies again with the statutes, the state often orders the corporation's reinstatement. Shareholders also can petition the courts for dissolution of the corporation. Statutes sometimes limit the conditions under which shareholders can petition for involuntary dissolution. Creditors normally cannot compel involuntary dissolution of the corporation.

Mergers and consolidations can bring about fundamental changes in the corporation's structure. Technically, mergers and consolidations differ, because in a merger one firm absorbs another, whereas in a consolidation both firms combine to produce a wholly new entity. The increase in mergers stems from a desire to effect economies of scale, to gain technical knowledge, to diversify, to control competition, and to avoid taxes. The negative aspects of mergers include the possible sacrifice of shareholders' interests, personnel displacement, and the uprooting of firms from the local community. State statutes set out the procedures necessary for bringing about a merger. The directors ordinarily adopt a merger plan, which the shareholders of both firms must approve. Shareholder approval is not necessary in short-form mergers. After the state approves the filed merger plan, the surviving corporation receives a certificate of merger and can begin conducting business. At this time, the acquired corporation ceases to exist. The surviving corporation takes on all the assets, rights, and liabilities of the acquired corporation by operation of law.

Most state statutes permit appraisal rights for stockholders who object to the merger. Appraisal rights allow dissenters to sell their shares back to the corporation for cash equal to the shares' value.

To be eligible for appraisal rights, shareholders usually must follow a set statutory procedure.

Rather than merge, a corporation instead can buy all or substantially all the assets of another firm. This method of acquisition entails far fewer procedures than a merger. Care must be taken to avoid *de facto* mergers, which are transactions that take the form of either a sale of substantially all the assets or a stock acquisition but have the effect of a merger.

Limited liability companies continue to be hybrid entities borrowing some rules from corporation law and others from partnership law.

Discussion Questions

1. Julio is an equal partner is an accountancy partnership with Justin and Alex. However, Julio is engaged to Christy. Julio and Christy wish to establish their own accountancy partnership after their marriage. Julio is unsure of his obligations to his current partners and their obligations to him. He also wants to continue to provide accounting advice and tax return preparation for some of his present clients even after he has established an office with Christy. What legal rights and obligations does Julio have? What decision do you recommend Julio make and why?

2. Demetrio is in a partnership, but is also heavily in debt. One of his creditors has gone to court and obtained a charging order against Demetrio's share of the business. Under what circumstances can this creditor seek a court-ordered dissolution of the business?

3. Given the following figures, work out the final financial position of each of the partners (net worth, cash, amounts owed, amounts receivable) following a winding up of their general partnership business:

	Bill	Charles	Larry	BCL Partnership
Assets	$70,000	$50,000	$50,000	$200,000
Liabilities	20,000	45,000	85,000	190,000
Capital contribution	50,000	25,000	25,000	
Profits	50%	25%	25%	

4. In 1999, Mattel Inc. acquired the Learning Company for $3.8 billion. Five months after the merger Mattel announced that due to problems at the Learning Company, it would have a $50 million to $100 million third quarter after-tax loss. "A Mattel spokesman said that the company had done due diligence on the Learning Company and that its problems came as a big surprise." However, analysts say that the problems at the Learning Company were well known for years prior to the merger. What constitutes due diligence for the managers at the acquiring company? What can an investor do to protect him or herself?[43]

5. Explain the meaning and importance of appraisal rights. Why would a stockholder want—or need—to seek an appraisal?

Case Problems and Writing Assignments

1. A limited partnership was created in 1982 to provide cellular telephone service in the Los Angeles area. The limited partnership, known as the Los Angeles SMSA Limited Partnership (Los Angeles Partnership) has three partners: U.S. Cellular, AirTouch Cellular, and GTE Wireless Incorporated (GTE). The Los Angeles Partnership Agreement includes Section 13.1 which provides that the general partner may "transfer or assign" its general partner's interest only with the consent of all the other partners. AirTouch Cellular owns a 40 percent general partner interest. Vodafone AirTouch (Vodafone) is the ultimate parent of AirTouch Cellular. AirTouch Communications, Inc. owned all of the stock of AirTouch Cellular when AirTouch Cellular first acquired its partnership interest. AirTouch Communications is a wholly owned subsidiary of Vodafone. Cellco is a joint venture (or alliance) created in 1999 between Bell Atlantic Corporation and Vodafone. Under the Alliance Agreement, Vodafone would transfer all its United States wireless interests to Cellco. In April 2000, AirTouch Communications transferred all of its AirTouch Cellular stock to Cellco. Thus, AirTouch Cellular remains the 40 percent general partner of the Los Angeles Partnership and it also retains its limited partnership interest, but Cellco now owns all of AirTouch Cellular's stock. AirTouch Cellular remains a bona fide operating company, with thousands of employees, substantial assets, interests in wireless systems throughout California, and general partnership interests in other communities in addition to Los Angeles. When AirTouch Communications transferred the AirTouch Cellular stock to Cellco, did it withdraw as the general partner under the agreement and give up control to Cellco? [See *United States Cellular Investment Company of Los Angeles, Inc. v. GTE Mobilnet, Inc.*, 281 F.3d 929, 2002 U.S. App. LEXIS 2618 (9th Cir. 2002).]

2. Horizon/CMS Healthcare appealed the final judgment in favor of Southern Oaks Health Care, Inc. Horizon is a large, publicly traded provider of both nursing home facilities and management for nursing home facilities. It wanted to expand into Osceola County. Southern Oaks was already operating there. Horizon and Southern Oaks decided to form a partnership to own the proposed facility. They agreed that Horizon would manage both the Southern Oaks facility and the new Royal Oaks facility. Southern Oaks and Horizon entered into several partnership and management contracts in 1993. In 1996, Southern Oaks filed suit alleging numerous defaults and breaches of the twenty-year agreements. The court ordered that the partnerships be dissolved, finding that "the parties to the various agreements . . . are now incapable of continuing to operate in business together" and that because it was dissolving the partnerships, "there is no entitlement to future damages. . . ."

The pertinent contracts provided in section 7.3, "Causes of Dissolution":

> . . . [T]he Partnership shall be dissolved in the event that: (a) the Partners mutually agree to terminate the Partnership; (b) the Partnership ceases to maintain any interest (which term shall include, but not be limited to, a security interest) in the Facility; (c) the Partnership, by its terms as set forth in this Agreement, is terminated; (d) upon thirty (30) days prior written notice to the other Partner, either Partner elects to dissolve the Partnership on account of an Irreconcilable Difference which arises and cannot, after good faith efforts, be resolved; . . . (g) pursuant to a court decree; or (h) on the date specified in Section 2.4.

The term "irreconcilable difference" used in the above quote is defined in the contracts as:

[A] reasonable and good faith difference of opinion between the Partners where either (i) the existence of the difference of opinion has a material and adverse impact on the conduct of the Partnerships' Business, or (ii) such difference is as to (x) the quality of services which is or should be provided at the long-term care facilities owned by the Partnership, (y) the adoption of a budget for a future fiscal year, or (z) any matter requiring unanimous approval of the Partners under the terms of this Agreement. . . .

Did Horizon wrongfully cause the dissolution of the partnership? [See *Horizon/CMS Healthcare Corporation v. Southern Oaks Health Care, Inc.*, 732 So. 2d 1156, 1999 Fla. App. LEXIS 4902 (Florida App. 5th Dist. 1999).]

3. Frank Sorenson replaced worn-out brake assemblies and clutch disks containing asbestos for Fowler Oliver Sales, Inc. from 1964 to 1971 and 1977 to 1993. The parts were used in Oliver brand and White Farm brand tractors and combines. The Oliver brand name was discontinued sometime after Oliver was purchased by White Farm. Fowler was a White Farm dealership of new equipment, but continued to provide service and maintenance on the discontinued Oliver product line as well as the White Farm product line. In 1985, White Farm was placed in involuntary bankruptcy by its creditors. On October 9, 1985, Allied entered into an Asset Purchase Agreement with White Farm where Allied would purchase White Farm assets related to the manufacturing of tractors, planters, and tillage equipment. Allied agreed to issue and deliver to White Farm 340,000 shares of a new series of preferred stock. The Agreement specifically provided that:

Allied shall not assume or in any way become liable for, any claims, liabilities or obligations or [sic] any kind or nature, whether accrued, absolute, contingent or otherwise, or whether due or to become due or otherwise arising out of the events or transactions of facts which shall have occurred prior to the final closing date except as expressly assumed by Allied. . . .

The bankruptcy court ruled that White Farm was authorized to immediately consummate the acquisition agreement with Allied and that the reorganization assets shall immediately be transferred to Allied free and clear of all liens, claims, and encumbrances. On November 11, 1987, the bankruptcy court confirmed a plan of reorganization. In 1986, Allied entered into new dealer contracts with a number of White Farm dealers, including Fowler. Allied also began selling replacement brakes and clutches to dealers of old Oliver and White Farm brand tractors and combines.

Sorenson became sick in late 1993 and died on April 24, 1994 of mesothelioma from asbestos exposure. The doctor that diagnosed Sorenson with mesothelioma stated that the latency period for the effects of asbestos exposure is thirty to fifty years. He concluded that Sorenson must have been exposed to asbestos prior to 1986, when Allied bought White Farm's assets. Sandra Sorenson, his wife, brought a claim against Allied alleging that Allied supplied the brakes and clutches that Sorenson inspected, serviced, and repaired. Is Allied liable as a successor of White Farm? [See *Sorenson v. Allied Products Corporation*, 706 N.E.2d 1097, 1999 Ind. App. LEXIS 361 (Ind. Ct. App. 3rd Dist. 1999).]

Notes

1. Uniform Partnership Act § 29.
2. Uniform Partnership Act § 31.
3. The following states have adopted UPA (1914): Georgia, Indiana, Massachusetts, Michigan, Missouri, New Hampshire, New York, North Carolina, Pennsylvania, Rhode Island, South Carolina, Utah, and Wisconsin. Email from Katie Robinson, Communications Officer, National Conference of Commissioners on Uniform State Laws (NCCUSL), February 22, 2010.
4. Uniform Partnership Act §§ 27 and 28.
5. The following states have adopted the 1994 version of RUPA (without the 1997 amendments): Connecticut, West Virginia, and Wyoming. The following states have adopted the RUPA with the 1997 amendments: Alabama, Alaska, Arizona, Arkansas, California, Colorado, Delaware, District of Columbia, Florida, Hawaii, Idaho, Illinois, Iowa, Kansas, Kentucky, Maine, Maryland, Minnesota, Mississippi, Montana, Nebraska, Nevada, New Jersey, New Mexico, North Dakota, Ohio, Oklahoma, Oregon, Puerto Rico, South Dakota, Tennessee, Texas, U.S. Virgin Islands, Vermont, Virginia, and Washington. (The versions in South Dakota and Texas are substantially similar.) (Although technically Puerto Rico and the U.S. Virgin Islands are not states, the NCCUSL treats them as states and for purposes of uniform laws we will also.) "A Few Facts about the Uniform Partnership Act (1994)(1997)," NCCUSL Web site, http://www.nccusl.org/Update/uniformact_factsheets/uniformacts-fs-upa9497.asp (accessed 2/21/10).
6. "Summary Uniform Partnership Act (1994)", NCCUSL Web site, http://www.nccusl.org/nccusl/uniformact_summaries/uniformacts-s-upa1994.asp (accessed 2/21/10).
7. The special rules for dissociating partners that are partnerships, corporations, trusts, estates, or other types of business entities have been omitted from this discussion.
8. If the partner specifies a future date, other partners can still dissociate before the date specified.
9. Under RUPA, this includes a person who files a voluntary petition or against whom an involuntary petition is ordered under any chapter of the Bankruptcy Code.
10. Usually, the deceased partner's transferable interest in the partnership will pass to his or her estate, and then the partnership will buy the estate's interest under Article 7 of RUPA.
11. The drafters intended for this to include physical incapacity. Revised Uniform Partnership Act § 601, Comment 8.
12. Revised Uniform Partnership Act § 602 addresses a partner's power to dissociate and wrongful dissociation.
13. Section 603 of the Revised Uniform Partnership Act addresses the effect of a partner's dissociation.
14. Revised Uniform Partnership Act § 804.
15. "Summary Uniform Partnership Act (1994)," supra note 6.
16. Revised Uniform Partnership Act § 306(a) and (b).
17. Liquidation is described in the Uniform Partnership Act § 40 and the Revised Uniform Partnership Act § 807.
18. The following states have adopted ULPA (1976) (RULPA) without the 1985 amendments: Connecticut, Maryland, Michigan, Montana, Missouri, Nebraska, New Jersey, South Carolina, and Wyoming. The following states have adopted ULPA (1976) or RULPA with the 1985 amendments: Alaska, Arizona, Colorado, Delaware, District of Columbia, Georgia, Indiana, Kansas, Massachusetts, Mississippi, New Hampshire, New York, North Carolina, Ohio, Oklahoma, Oregon, Pennsylvania, Rhode Island, South Dakota, Tennessee, Texas, U.S. Virgin Islands, Utah, Vermont, West Virginia, and Wisconsin. Email from Katie Robinson, Communications Officer, National Conference of Commissioners on Uniform State Laws (NCCUSL), February 22, 2010.
19. The Uniform Limited Partnership Act (2001) has been adopted by Alabama, Arkansas, California, Florida, Hawaii, Idaho, Illinois, Iowa, Kentucky, Maine, Minnesota, Nevada, New Mexico, North Dakota, Virginia, and Washington. In 2010 it was introduced in the District of Columbia, Missouri, and Oklahoma. See "A Few Facts about the Uniform Limited Partnership Act (2001)," supra note 5.
20. "Why States Should Adopt the Uniform Limited Partnership Act (2001)," NCCUSL Web site, http://www.nccusl.org/Update/uniformact_why/uniformacts-why-ulpa.asp (accessed 2/21/10).
21. Ibid.
22. "Summary Uniform Limited Partnership Act (2001)," NCCUSL Web site, http://www.nccusl.org/Update/uniformact_summaries/uniformacts-s-ulpa.asp (accessed 2/21/10).
23. The Model Entity Transactions Act has been adopted in Idaho and Kansas. Email from Katie Robinson, Communications Officer, National Conference of Commissioners on Uniform State Laws (NCCUSL), March 15, 2010. The Model Entity Transactions Act was a unique collaborative effort between the NCCUSL and the American Bar Association.
24. Conversions are addressed in Article 4 of the Model Entity Transaction Act (2007).
25. In 2000, there were substantial changes in the Fortune 500 companies due to mergers. The rate and size of mergers may have slowed somewhat since then due to the economy, falling share prices, and government scrutiny of proposed

mergers. See Peter Thal Larsen, "The Year the Giants Chose to Merge: M&A," *Financial Times* (London), May 11, 2001, Survey—FT 500, p.10.

26. More production does not always result in economies of scale: it can result in diseconomies of scale.

27. 457 A.2d 701 (Del. 1983).

28. Ibid., p. 714, quoted in *Krieger v. Gast*, 179 F. Supp. 2d 762, 2001 U.S. Dist. LEXIS 18678 (W. Dist. Mich., S. D. 2001), at 775.

29. Ibid., p. 711, quoted in *Krieger v. Gast*, note 25, at 775.

30. Ibid., p. 714, quoted in *Krieger v. Gast*, note 25, at 775.

31. The states that have adopted the Uniform Limited Liability Company Act are Alabama, Hawaii, Idaho, Illinois, Iowa, Montana, South Carolina, South Dakota, U.S. Virgin Islands, Vermont, and West Virginia. "A Few Facts about the Uniform Limited Liability Company Act," NCCUSL Web site, http://www.nccusl.org/Update/uniformact_factsheets/uniformacts-fs-ullca.asp (accessed 2/21/10). Idaho and Iowa then adopted the 2006 act. "A Few Facts about the Uniform Limited Liability Company Act (2006)," NCCUSL Web site, http://www.nccusl.org/Update/uniformact_fact-sheets/uniformacts-fs-ullca06.asp (accessed 3/11/10).

32. Uniform Limited Liability Company Act § 602(a).

33. Uniform Limited Liability Company Act § 602(b).

34. Uniform Limited Liability Company Act § 602(c).

35. Uniform Limited Liability Company Act § 701(a)(2).

36. Uniform Limited Liability Company Act § 701(f).

37. Uniform Limited Liability Company Act § 411(b).

38. Uniform Limited Liability Company Act § 806.

39. "A Few Facts about the Uniform Limited Liability Company Act (2006)," supra note 5.

40. "Why States Should Adopt the Revised Uniform Limited Liability Company Act (2006)," NCCUSL Web site, http://www.nccusl.org/Update/uniformact_why/uniformacts-why-ullca.asp (accessed 3/11/10).

41. Ibid.

42. Ibid.

43. Gretchen Morgenson, "Market Watch: On the Acquisitions Road, Stay Alert to the Hazards," *New York Times*, Late Edition-Final, October 10, 1999, Sec. 3, p. 1.

34

Securities Regulation

Agenda

The firm members have incorporated eClass, and they must now raise money for needed expansion and growth. They will consider issuing stocks and/or bonds, as well as incurring debt. They will need to know which of these will involve "securities," and therefore potentially be subject to federal and/or state regulations. An "offering" by a company of securities is heavily regulated in the United States, and undertaking such an offering may increase their liability, even if the offering is just to friends and family of the founders. If eClass is successful enough, the founders may consider offering shares to the public in an IPO—and they must be aware of the additional responsibilities that come with having publicly traded stock. In addition, the firm is considering an expansion into the international marketplace. If the expansion occurs, Ani, Meg, and Yousef are likely to have questions about the Foreign Corrupt Practices Act and its impact on their dealings. These and other questions may arise as you study this chapter.

Be prepared! You never know when the firm or one of its members will seek your help or advice.

Classic Case

SECURITIES & EXCHANGE COMMISSION v. W. J. HOWEY CO.
328 U.S. 293, 66 S. Ct. 1100, 1946 U.S. LEXIS 3159
(S. Ct. 1946)

FACTS W. J. Howey Company and Howey-in-the-Hills Service, Inc. are Florida corporations under direct common control and management. The Howey Company owns large tracts of citrus acreage in Florida. During the past several years it has planted about 500 acres annually, keeping half of the groves itself and offering the other half to the public. Howey-in-the-Hills Service, Inc. is a service company engaged in managing citrus groves. The companies offer customers the opportunity to purchase land in the groves and to obtain a service contract under which the land so purchased can be effectively managed.

Basically, a person purchases land from the Howey Company and obtains a warranty deed to a parcel of land. The parcel is not fenced or overtly marked; the sole indication of individual ownership is found in small land marks intelligible only through a plat book record.

The purchaser is also encouraged to make arrangements with a service company that will manage the parcel. While any service company can be used, 85 percent of the acreage sold during the three-year period ending May 31, 1943, was covered by service contracts with Howey-in-the-Hills Service, Inc. These service contracts are generally for ten years, there is no cancellation option, and Howey-in-the-Hills retains a leasehold interest giving it full and complete possession of the land.

The purchasers for the most part are non-residents of Florida. They are predominantly business and professional people who lack the knowledge, skill, and equipment necessary for the care and cultivation of citrus trees. They are attracted by the expectation of substantial profits. It was represented, for example, that profits during the 1943-1944 season amounted to 20 percent and that even greater profits might be expected during the 1944-1945 season, although only a 10 percent annual return was to be expected over a ten-year period.

The companies admitted that they used the mails and instrumentalities of interstate commerce in the sale of the land and service contracts and that no registration statement or letter of notification has ever been filed with the SEC in accordance with the Securities Act of 1933 and its rules and regulations.

The SEC filed suit, seeking to restrain the respondents from using the mails and instrumentalities of interstate commerce in the offer and sale of unregistered and non-exempt securities in violation of § 5 (a) of the Act.

ISSUE Did these transactions (the land sales contract, the warranty deed, and the service contract) constitute an "investment contract" within the meaning of § 2(1) of the Securities Act of 1933?

HOLDING Yes. The test for what constitutes an "investment contract" is whether the scheme involves an investment of money in a common enterprise with profits to come solely from the efforts of others.

REASONING Excerpts from the opinion of Justice Murphy:

The term "investment contract" is undefined by the Securities Act or by relevant legislative reports.

But the term was common in many state "blue sky" laws in existence prior to the adoption of the federal statute and, although the term was also undefined by the state laws, it had been broadly construed by state courts so as to afford the investing public a full measure of protection. Form was disregarded for substance and emphasis was placed upon economic reality. An investment contract thus came to mean a contract or scheme for "the placing of capital or laying out of money in a way intended to secure income or profit from its employment." ... This definition was uniformly applied by state courts to ... situations where individuals were led to invest money in a common enterprise with the expectation that they would earn a profit solely through the efforts of the promoter or of some one other than themselves.

By including an investment contract within the scope of § 2 (1) of the Securities Act, Congress was using a term the meaning of which had been crystallized by this prior judicial interpretation. It is therefore reasonable to attach that meaning to the term as used by Congress, especially since such a definition is consistent with the statutory aims. In other words, an investment contract for purposes of the Securities Act means a contract, transaction or scheme whereby a person invests his money in a common enterprise and is led to expect profits solely from the efforts of the promoter or a third party, it being immaterial whether the shares in the enterprise are evidenced by formal certificates or by nominal interests in the physical assets employed in the enterprise. ...

The transactions in this case clearly involve investment contracts as so defined. The respondent companies are offering something more than fee simple interests in land, something different from a farm or orchard coupled with management services. They are offering an opportunity to contribute money and to share in the profits of a large citrus fruit enterprise managed and partly owned by respondents. ...

Thus all the elements of a profit-seeking business venture are present here. The investors provide the capital and share in the earnings and profits; the promoters manage, control and operate the enterprise. It follows that the arrangements whereby the investors' interests are made manifest involve investment contracts, regardless of the legal terminology in which such contracts are clothed ... And respondents' failure to abide by the statutory and administrative rules in making such offerings, even though the failure result from a bona fide mistake as to the law, cannot be sanctioned under the Act. ...

This conclusion is unaffected by the fact that some purchasers choose not to accept the full offer of an investment contract by declining to enter into a service contract with the respondents. The Securities Act prohibits the offer as well as the sale of unregistered, non-exempt securities. Hence it is enough that the respondents merely offer the essential ingredients of an investment contract. ...

The test is whether the scheme involves an investment of money in a common enterprise with profits to come solely from the efforts of others. If that test be satisfied, it is immaterial whether the enterprise is speculative or non-speculative or whether there is a sale of property with or without intrinsic value. ... The statutory policy of affording broad protection to investors is not to be thwarted by unrealistic and irrelevant formulae.

Reversed.

WHAT ARE "SECURITIES" AND WHY REGULATE THEIR SALE?

Because the offer and sale of securities is heavily regulated in the United States, it is important to understand what constitutes a "security." The definition of a "security" has been expanded through case law over the years, and essentially covers anything that involves:

(1) an investment of money
(2) in a common enterprise
(3) whereby the investor has no managerial functions but instead expects to profit solely from the entrepreneurial or managerial efforts of others.

In our classis case, the U.S. Supreme Court decided that an orange grove, together with a management contract for the grove, constituted a "security."[1] Mortgage-backed securities, which are bundles of mortgages that are packaged up by banks and sold, are also "securities." Common and preferred stock (discussed in detail in Chapter 32) are examples of securities, as are bonds or other evidence of debt that is packaged up and sold (also known as debentures). Whether something is a "security" is an important consideration, because if something qualifies as a "security" then the extensive body of laws governing securities issuances applies to the company issuing the security.

The federal regulation of securities in the United States began as a consequence of the stock market crash of 1929. In the boom years leading up to the crash, companies and brokers tried to convince investors to purchase securities with inflated and sometimes absolutely untrue or fraudulent claims. After congressional hearings exposed the scope of the fraud, Congress enacted the Securities Act of 1933 and the Securities Exchange Act of 1934 (known as the "'33 Act" or the "Securities Act" and the "'34 Act" or the "Exchange Act," respectively). Both the '33 and '34 Acts have been subsequently amended, and the Securities and Exchange Commission (SEC), the federal agency charged with primary responsibility for the enforcement and administration of the federal laws covering securities, has issued extensive rules and regulations relating to the '33 and '34 Acts.

Essentially, the '33 and '34 Act are *disclosure statutes*: they require companies to disclose information to investors about the company that is issuing the securities—including financial information, results of operations, management, and prospects—and the Acts provide consequences for non-compliance, including failure to disclose or fraudulent disclosure of the required information.

FEDERAL LAW: GENERAL REQUIREMENTS OF THE '33 AND '34 ACTS

Registration and Disclosure   The '33 Act provides that any security that is not exempt must be *registered* with the SEC before it is sold, and that investors must be provided with information about the company issuing the security prior to the sale. Smaller sales (in both number of securities and dollar amount raised) are generally, but not always, exempt from these requirements. Note, however, that there are no exemptions from the antifraud provisions of the '33 Act, which we examine later in this chapter. The rules governing the exemptions from the '33 Act are complex, and you should always watch your step if you are considering selling a security.[2] When firms "go public," this means that a company is issuing a large number of securities (to more than 500 holders) and the company's stock will then be traded on a securities exchange such as the New York Stock Exchange (NYSE) or the NASDAQ stock market. Companies that have publicly traded stock (commonly referred to as "public companies") are subject to the registration and disclosure requirements of the '33 Act before they issue any new stock, and must also comply with ongoing information requirements mandated by the '34 Act. The ongoing information requirements under the '34 Act include quarterly and annual updates about a company's business (known as 10-Q and 10-K reports, respectively), reports filed within four days after significant transactions or occurrences in the business (a form 8-K report), and reports with information about a company's shareholder meetings (proxy statements or "DEF 14A" reports).

The initial disclosure requirements and the ongoing requirements outlined above mean that publicly traded companies must file a lot of information about themselves—and this information is required to be filed electronically with the SEC and posted on the company's Web site. It is possible to find out almost anything you want to know about a publicly traded company with just a few clicks on your computer, including the salaries of a company's executives, the results of their most recent quarter or fiscal year, their future plans, detailed financial statements, and risk factors that could cause the company's business to suffer. For example, in 2009 the salary for Jeffery R. Immelt, Chairman of the Board and CEO of General Electric, was $9,885,240, 308 times the average worker's pay for that same year.[3] It should be noted that Mr. Immelt declined an $11.7 million bonus in 2008 when GE's stock was declining.[4] The information required to be included in these disclosures is intended to make an investment in a company's securities more transparent so an informed investment decision can be made, and to give shareholders recourse if proper information is not available.

Because of the stringent and significant disclosure requirements, "going public" is not a decision to be taken lightly. Companies must plan for significant management time to be devoted to securities law compliance, must retain an independent public accountant to comply with the financial statement and audit requirements, and must hire a law firm or assemble an internal legal team to assist in navigating the disclosure requirements. In addition, the securities exchanges, such as the NYSE and NASDAQ, impose additional requirements on companies with securities listed on those exchanges—including requirements for shareholder approval of certain corporate transactions and corporate governance requirements such as independent committees of the board of directors.

Registration Exemptions Under the '33 Act   Not all securities a business offers must be registered with the SEC before they can be sold under the '33 Act. There are several provisions for exemptions from the registration requirement, the most common of which are:

- Private offerings to a limited number of persons or institutions;
- Offerings of limited size;
- Intrastate offerings; and
- Securities of municipal, state, and federal governments.[5]

A private offering is one in which a limited number of "sophisticated investors" who would have access to the sort of information that is normally included in a prospectus and who agree not to resell or distribute the securities to the general public are given the opportunity to purchase the securities. The firm may not use any general advertising or public solicitations to use this exemption.

An offering of limited size (a "small offering") exemption exists for a firm that offers no more than $5 million in securities in any 12-month period. However, the business must submit an offering statement containing certain specified information to the SEC for review before it can take advantage of this exemption.

An intrastate offering exemption is given to firms that are incorporated in the state in which the security is offered for sale, will carry out a significant amount of its business within that state, and only offers the securities to people residing within the state.

Antifraud Provisions   In addition to registration requirements, the '33 and '34 Acts contain antifraud provisions prohibiting misstatements or omissions of material facts in connection with the offer or sale of any security or in any disclosure document filed with the SEC.[6]

Any purchaser of securities who relied on untrue statements (or statements that contained an omission) when purchasing a company's securities is entitled to damages not exceeding the purchase price of those securities. The liability for misstatements or omissions extends to the company itself, every person who signed the registration statement (usually the CEO and CFO and each director of a company), every accountant, engineer, appraiser, or any other professional expert whose statement or report appears in a document filed with the SEC; and on every underwriter (a firm who promotes or sells the company's securities).

THE SARBANES-OXLEY ACT OF 2002

In 2001, it was revealed that the Enron Corporation, through its CEO and CFO, had repeatedly misled investors, hidden corporate losses, and inflated financial statements in order to prop up the company's stock price. The ultimate bankruptcy of Enron was at the time the largest corporate bankruptcy in U.S. history and resulted in millions of dollars of losses to the company's shareholders and creditors. Not to be outdone, in early 2002 internal auditors at WorldCom unearthed similar fraudulent activity—the

CEO and upper management had inflated the company's financial statements for years, again in order to maintain or increase the company's stock price.

In light of these and other scandals involving misstatement of earnings, inflation of financial statements, and hiding of assets and similar fraudulent activity, in 2002 Congress passed the Sarbanes-Oxley Act (known as "SOX" or "Sarbox"[7]). Among other things, SOX requires that:

(1) companies establish a whistleblower hotline or other reporting procedure where anonymous "tips" relating to a company's accounting practices can be safely reported;

(2) the CEO and CFO of every publicly traded company must certify as to the accuracy of the financial statements contained in public filings with the SEC; and

(3) companies satisfy increased requirements relating to corporate governance and the independence of audit firms.

In addition, SOX called for the formation of a new quasi-public agency, the Public Company Accounting Oversight Board, or PCAOB; and resulted in the issuance of new rules relating to internal controls disclosure and evaluation and requiring lawyers to report to a company's board of directors if unusual activities are noticed.

SOX also requires that publicly traded companies establish a code of ethics for senior management, and that any waivers or violations of the code of ethics be reported to the public.

In most companies, especially large, publicly traded companies, the financial statements are not prepared by the CEO and they are probably not prepared by the CFO personally, and yet the CEO and the CFO must certify as to their accuracy. Each of these executives faces potential liability under SOX if the statements are, in fact, not accurate. This places a significant burden on them to be as careful as possible in ensuring that the financial statement are accurate, and requires the CEO and the CFO, at a minimum, to be certain that the firm's internal and external accountants and auditors are highly qualified and have solid credentials and reputations. (One consequence has been for CEOs and CFOs to require the employees involved in the preparation to certify the documents' accuracy.) Because of this potential liability, some people question whether it is fair or ethical to require the CEO to certify the accuracy of the statements. The answer would seem to be that anything less increases the likelihood of another Enron or WorldCom scandal.

INSIDER TRADING

Insider Trading   "Insider trading," the act of an "insider" trading securities of a publicly traded company while in possession of material nonpublic information about that company, is prohibited. Interestingly, insider trading is not prohibited directly by the language of the '34 Act—rather, the prohibition has evolved over

eClass 34.1 Finance/Management

ISSUING STOCK IN eCLASS

Ani, Meg, and Yousef want to issue stock in eClass to generate funds for the expansion of the firm. They believe that, if successful, this issuance of stock will result in a huge inflow of cash for the firm. However, they also know that the firm's issuance of stock may be subject to regulation under the '33 Act, and that subsequent to the offering the firm may be subject to the disclosure requirements of the '34 Act and of SOX. They ask you if they could structure their offering in order to qualify for an exemption from registration under the '33 Act, or in the alternative, what they will need to do to comply with the registration requirements. What advice will you give them?

BUSINESS CONSIDERATIONS   Why might a business prefer a potentially smaller inflow of funds if this meant that the company qualified for an exemption from registering under the '33 Act? What factors should a company consider in deciding whether a larger public offering is justified?

ETHICAL CONSIDERATIONS   Is it ethical for a company to tailor its securities offerings so as to avoid registration of the securities under the '33 Act?

time through SEC and judicial interpretations of the '34 Act's antifraud provisions and rules prohibiting the use of deceptive or manipulative practices.[8]

In order to establish a case against someone alleged to have engaged in insider trading, the following must have occurred:

1. The person must be an "*insider*"—in other words, must owe a duty of confidentiality to the company whose securities are traded (more on this later).
2. The person must be in possession of *material* information about the company, which information has not yet been disclosed to the public.
3. The person must trade in the securities of the company in order to achieve personal gain.

The standard for whether information is "material" is, for the most part, well settled and involves whether the relevant fact would have been viewed as significant by a reasonable investor.[9] Similarly, whether an individual traded in the securities of a company in order to achieve personal gain is not usually a matter of argument. Consequently, most insider trading cases delve into whether the person trading was an "insider"—and whether he or she owed a duty of confidentiality to the company in question. The fact is, not everyone who has material nonpublic information is prohibited from making trades. The examples that follow with provide some guidelines regarding who can or can't trade.

The *Chiarella v. United States* case[10] explored whether remote "tippees"—individuals who hear about the information from someone who clearly is an insider—should be liable for insider trading. Chiarella was a printer who worked for a firm that printed takeover bids. Although the identities of the firms had been left blank, Chiarella—using the information contained in the documents he was preparing for printing—was able to deduce the names of the target companies. Without disclosing his knowledge, Chiarella purchased stock in the target companies and sold the stock when the takeover attempts became public knowledge. Chiarella thereby gained $30,000 in 14 months. The SEC indicted him on 17 counts of insider trading violations under the '34 Act. The Supreme Court held that because Chiarella was a complete stranger who had dealt with the sellers only through impersonal market transactions, he did not owe a fiduciary duty of confidentiality to the company and therefore was not liable for insider trading. According to *Chiarella*, "outsiders"—those who are not in positions of trust or confidence within the companies involved—do not have a duty to abstain from trading on nonpublic material information.

In *United States v. O'Hagan*, 521 U.S. 642 (1997), the U.S. Supreme Court established the "misappropriation" theory of insider trading, which holds that a person commits fraud in connection with a securities transaction when that person misappropriates confidential information for securities trading purposes, in breach of a duty owed to the source of the information.[11]

On the heels of the *Chiarella* and *O'Hagan* cases, in 2000 the SEC promulgated Rule 10b5-2, which sets forth a non-exclusive list of instances that will give rise to a "duty of trust or confidence" for purposes of the misappropriation theory. These instances include whenever a person has agreed to maintain information confidentially; whenever the individuals sharing the communication have a history or practice of keeping information confidential such that each should know and/or expect the other to maintain confidentiality; and whenever a person receives confidential information from an immediate family member.[12]

The SEC has the ability (under the Insider Trading Sanctions Act of 1984[13]) to penalize insider traders up to three times the amount of the profit gained or the loss avoided as a result of the unlawful purchase or sale. Such penalties are payable to the U.S. Treasury; private parties cannot seek relief based on this Act. This Act also increases the criminal penalties that can be levied against individual violators from $10,000 to $100,000. In addition, the Insider Trading and Securities Fraud Enforcement Act of 1988[14] creates an express private right of action in favor of market participants who traded at the same time as those who violated the '34 Act or SEC rules by trading while in possession of material nonpublic information, and also allows private individuals who provide information that leads to the imposition of penalties to receive a bounty of up to 10 percent of any penalty.

The situations in which a person might acquire inside information are diverse, and not all such situations involve illegal or improper conduct by the person in possession of the information. Suppose Lucinda, a senior officer of a company, accidentally leaves a memorandum describing a proposed corporate transaction in the seat pocket of an airplane. Alvin later boards the plane, occupies the seat that Lucinda had occupied on an earlier portion of the flight, and discovers the memo. Alvin reads the memo, appreciates the potential value of the information contained therein, and trades in the firm's securities (to great profit) based on the information contained in the memo. Based on the misappropriation theory of insider trading, would Alvin be liable for insider trading? Probably not, since he does not appear to fall within the SEC's definition of an "insider." It also would appear that Lucinda has not violated any SEC rules or regulations, although she was careless with this sensitive document. However, situations like this can, and occasionally do, happen. Ask yourself the following questions:

1. What steps can and should a company take to ensure its employees do not inadvertently disclose material nonpublic information?
2. Is it *ethical* for Alvin to trade on the information he has discovered?

Short-Swing Profits   The '34 Act contains a provision (known as Section 16) that requires a publicly traded company's senior management to disclose any purchase, sale, or other transaction made in the securities of the company they manage. This provision includes all directors of the company, the CEO and CFO, and senior officers, and the disclosure must be made online at the SEC's Web site. For most transactions, the public report must be filed within two days of the transaction and must indicate the price at which the security was purchased or sold and any other relevant details about the trade.

In addition to the reporting and disclosure requirement, Section 16 also forces those who report their trades to disgorge (that is, give up and return to the corporation) any profits they realize from the purchase or sale of any security that takes place in any time period of less than six months—that is, *short-swing profits*. Section 16 covers transactions resulting in profits *even when the transactions were not actually based on inside information*. In essence, this is the application of strict liability (discussed in the context of tort cases in Chapter 7) to trades by insiders. Thus, if director Wallis sells stock in Continuing Corp. for $5,000 and five months later buys an equal number of shares for $3,000, Wallis will have to pay back to the corporation the $2,000 in profits so realized—regardless of whether Wallis had any inside information during the time of purchase or sale. Section 16 is designed to *prevent* any "short-swing" profit-making by senior officers and directors of a corporation.

The short-swing profit rule allows the company or any holder of the company's securities to enforce the rule. Remember that under Section 16, any profits are disgorged *to the company*, not to any individual. In order to spur enforcement, Section 16 provides that the company must reimburse the legal fees of any lawyers who successfully "catch" a short-swing profits violation. Reporting a transaction within two days can be difficult, but a firm needs to establish processes and procedures to ensure that all trades by senior officers and directors are accurately and quickly reported. The company also needs to realize that § 16 allows for the reimbursement of legal fees. On the one hand this promotes enforcement of the law, but on the other

eClass 34.2 Finance/Management

INSIDER TRADING RULES UNDER THE '34 ACT

eClass stock is being traded on a national exchange and these sales subject the firm to regulation under the '34 Act. The initial public reaction to the firm and its prospects has been good, and the stock has had steady increases in its market price. eClass is currently negotiating with a small firm that has "know-how" that will speed up the response time for both eClass products. This new technology holds great promise for increased sales. No one outside the immediate family is aware of these negotiations or the potential impact on eClass of this development. Ani, Meg, and Yousef want to purchase a significant number of eClass shares before the news "leaks out" about the negotiations. However, they are concerned that if they do so, they will be guilty of insider trading. They ask you what they should do to avoid liability in this situation. What will you tell them?

BUSINESS CONSIDERATIONS   What should the officers, directors, and controlling shareholders of a firm whose stock is publicly traded be concerned about when they trade in their firm's securities? What can the firm do to minimize its potential liability if/when an insider trading scandal erupts?

ETHICAL CONSIDERATIONS   Is it ethical for an insider to trade in securities when he or she has information that is not yet available to the general public? Is it ethical to prevent people from using the knowledge or information they have acquired through their jobs from making a profit based on that knowledge or information?

it may provoke overzealous enforcement by attorneys seeking profit in the form of legal fees.

Exhibit 34.1 compares the three major federal securities regulation statutes.

STATE REGULATION OF SECURITIES

Because the assorted federal statutes preserve the states' power to regulate securities activities, any transactions involving securities may be subject to state law as well as federal law. Such state laws, often called "blue sky" laws, normally include three types of provisions: (1) antifraud stipulations, (2) registration requirements for brokers and dealers, and (3) registration requirements for the sale and purchase of securities. The National Securities Markets Improvement Act of 1996, or NSMIA, exempted securities that are publicly traded from regulation by state securities laws—but

Exhibit 34.1

A Comparison of the Three Major Securities Statutes

The Securities Act of 1933 ("truth in securities" law)	The Securities and Exchange Act of 1934	Sarbanes-Oxley (2002) (SOX)
• Requires that investors receive significant information about securities being offered for sale to the public prior to the sale • Prohibits deceits, misrepresentation, or fraud in the sale of securities • Requires that securities be registered to obtain its objectives	• Provides broad power to the SEC to oversee all aspects of the securities industry • Identifies and prohibits certain conduct in the market • Provides disciplinary power to the Commission • Allows the SEC to require the filing of periodic reports by companies issuing publicly traded securities • Provides rules governing the information required in proxy solicitations • Prohibits fraudulent activities of any kind in securities dealings, including "insider trading"	• Reforms financial disclosures and corporate responsibility • Provides regulations dealing with corporate and/or accounting fraud • Creates the Public Company Accounting Oversight Board, to oversee the auditing industry

states still maintain rights of action for fraud with respect to these securities. State blue sky laws vary widely, and consequently, any securities offering not exempted by NSMIA requires a local expert to assist in navigating the local laws.

THE FOREIGN CORRUPT PRACTICES ACT

In December 1977, then-President Jimmy Carter signed into law the Foreign Corrupt Practices Act (FCPA). The FCPA resulted from post-Watergate congressional hearings about questionable payments made to foreign officials by hundreds of U.S. firms, including Exxon, Northrop Corporation, Lockheed Aircraft Company, Gulf Oil, and GTE Corp. Testimony revealed that, in order to land sizable contracts for themselves, companies had given foreign officials large payments, or bribes. In their own defense, these U.S. firms argued that foreign officials often demanded such payments as a condition of doing business and that without such "grease" payments, or sums paid to facilitate transactions by minor governmental functionaries, bureaucratic red tape would have brought business dealings to a complete halt.

Congressional investigators found that such questionable payments often took the form of secret slush funds, dubious transfers of funds or assets between subsidiaries and parent companies, improper invoicing methods (e.g., false payments for goods or services that never were received), and bookkeeping practices designed to camouflage improper payments or procedures. Indeed, these corrupt practices by U.S. corporations even included payments to engineer the overthrow of foreign governments hostile to U.S. business interests and bribes to foreign officials to keep competitors out of certain countries. To compound the improprieties, these same firms often deducted such so-called business expenses from their tax returns.

Because accounting irregularities, including secret funds and falsified or inadequate books, formed the vehicle by which firms most often had effected these questionable payments and bribes, Congress attempted to put an end to these practices by enacting the FCPA. The FCPA's antibribery sections provide criminal penalties for actions taken by issuers (that is, firms subject to the '34 Act) or any domestic concern (even those not subject to the '34 Act) when an officer, director, employee, agent, or stockholder acting on behalf of such businesses corruptly pays money (or anything of value) to foreign officials for the purpose of influencing the foreign officials to assist the firm "in obtaining or retaining business for or with, or directing business to, any person."[15]

Gifts or payments that are lawful under the written laws and regulations of the foreign country involved or that constitute *bona fide* reasonable expenditures (such as travel or lodging) incurred by such persons during the performance of a contract with the foreign government do not fall within the FCPA's proscriptions. These antibribery provisions do not extend to payments made to these classes of persons when the payments' purpose is to expedite or facilitate the performance of "routine governmental action." Hence, "grease" payments to obtain permits or licenses to do business in the foreign country, visas, work orders, phone service, police protection, or inspections are legal as long as the employee receiving them is not a person known as someone who is acting as a conduit for governmental officials to whom the FCPA forbids corrupt payments or gifts.

Critics of the FCPA argue that its provisions and resultant regulations have greatly increased both U.S. businesses' costs of doing business and the enforcement agencies' costs, all of which negatively affect the public. On the other hand, such laws and supplementary regulations carry the attendant advantages of heightened investor information and fewer scandals involving U.S. bribery of foreign officials. Regardless of criticism, the U.S. Department of Justice (DOJ) continues to aggressively enforce the FCPA.

■ In December 2008, Siemens Aktiengesellschaft ("Siemens") agreed to pay $800 million in combined fines and penalties to settle FCPA charges for a pattern of bribery the DOJ termed "unprecedented in scale and geographic scope." The combined fines and penalties against Siemens (a global corporation organized under the laws of Germany with shares listed on the New York

Stock Exchange since March 2001) are easily the largest ever levied against an FCPA violator. Enforcement actions were brought by both the SEC and the DOJ.[16]

■ In January 2010, the DOJ announced the indictments of 22 executives and employees of companies in the military and law-enforcement products industry. The indictments stemmed from an FBI undercover operation in which the employees and executives thought they were agreeing to pay bribes to foreign officials in exchange for lucrative military supply contracts—when in fact the "foreign official" was an undercover FBI officer.[17]

■ The FCPA also applies to individuals who use bribes to further their business aims as well as corporations. In late 2009, two Los Angeles film executives were convicted of FCPA violations in connection with paying kickbacks to the former governor of the Thailand Tourist Authority. In exchange for the payments, the executives were awarded contracts to host the Bangkok International Film Festival, among other lucrative contracts.[18]

WALL STREET REFORM AND CONSUMER PROTECTION ACT OF 2010[19]

On July 21, 2010, President Obama signed the Wall Street Reform and Consumer Protection Act into law. This Act, the culmination of more than two years of debate, is intended to protect the United States economy against another financial meltdown. It also provides a broad range of consumer protections, as well as various provisions dealing with executive compensation, corporate governance, and securities disclosure requirements. While a number of provisions in the statute will not take effect immediately, others will have an impact on corporate reports and reporting in the 2011 reporting cycle. Many of the provisions will not take effect until later due to the need for rulemaking by the SEC, the Federal Reserve Board, and/or the Federal Trade Commission.[20]

Among the most important areas of reform in this statute are:

1. The SEC is given oversight over hedge funds and credit reporting agencies;
2. The creation of the Consumer Financial Protection Bureau, an independent agency charged with protecting consumers from deceptive financial practices and with enforcing rules on banks and mortgage companies;
3. Large companies are required to provide "funeral plans," plans to ensure a safe method of shutting the company down should it fail;
4. A requirement that any consumer who is turned down for a loan due to his or her credit score (FICO score) or who is charged a higher-than-expected interest rate on the loan has the right to see the score without charge. (Getting a copy of one's credit score currently costs about $15.);

5. Various state mortgage regulations will be subject to federal guidelines, including the elimination of pre-payment penalties included in many adjustable rate mortgages (ARMs); and

6. The creation of an Office of Credit Ratings, charged with supervising rating agencies like Moody's and Standard & Poor's.[21]

Obviously, it is too soon to gauge the impact of this legislation at this point in time, but the increased size and scope of the statutory coverage promises to provide some interesting changes in corporate conduct, especially in the financial sector. It also promises a number of lawsuits as the courts work to provide interpretations of the various provisions of the law.

eClass 34.3 Marketing/International

HOW SHOULD eCLASS BEHAVE IN A FOREIGN MARKET?

eClass is investigating the possibility of selling the firm's products internationally. Yousef thinks he recalls learning in one of his management classes that bribery of governmental officials as a way of procuring business is a common occurrence in many countries. Yousef therefore advocates following that old adage, "When in Rome, do as the Romans do." He consequently supports giving eClass's sales personnel a "slush fund" the staff can use for making "facilitation payments" to assist the appropriate officials in whichever country they target for obtaining sales. Ani and Meg suggest that Yousef immediately undertake a close reading of the FCPA. What will the FCPA teach Yousef about the advisability of embracing bribery as a corporate strategy?

BUSINESS CONSIDERATIONS The International Chamber of Commerce in recent years has added antibribery provisions to its organizational rules. The Organization for Economic Cooperation and Development similarly has advocated that its member states criminalize the bribery of foreign officials. What policies should a business institute so as to ensure compliance with the provisions of the FCPA and these other organizations' rules? Do you believe that the FCPA hampers the ability of U.S. firms to compete in a global market? Why or why not?

ETHICAL CONSIDERATIONS Does the FCPA improve the ethical conduct of U.S. firms? Does the FCPA represent a type of "cultural imperialism" in which the United States expects the rest of the world to accede to its view of what is—or is not—ethical?

Contemporary Case

U.S. v. BHAGAT

436 F.3d 1140, 2006 U.S. App. LEXIS 3008 (9th Cir. 2006)

FACTS Bhagat was an employer of Nvidia Corporation when it successfully acquired the contract to develop the X-Box, a video game console, for Microsoft. Upon acquiring the contract, on Sunday night the CEO of Nvidia sent a company-wide e-mail announcing the contract award, and the following day several follow-up e-mails were sent. The first of these follow-up e-mails advised Nvidia employees that the X-Box information should be kept confidential. The other e-mails imposed a trading blackout on the purchase of Nvidia stock for several days, and required Nvidia's employees to cancel any open or outstanding orders for Nvidia stock. All of these emails were on Bhagat's computer when he arrived at work Monday morning.

Roughly 20 minutes after the final company-wide e-mail was sent, Bhagat purchased a large quantity of Nvidia stock—his largest purchase in nearly three years. There were rumors about Nvidia and the X-Box contract leaking in the industry the day after Bhagat purchased his stock, and the price of the stock rose sharply. Three days later, the news was made public and the price of Nvidia stock skyrocketed. Another four days later, Bhagat sold his stock, reaping a substantial profit.

Less than one-half hour after Bhagat made his purchase, two of his friends, Puneet Mehrotra (Mehrotra) and Mamat Gill (Gill), purchased Nvidia stock. There was no direct evidence that Bhagat contacted Mehrotra or Gill prior to their purchases. However, Bhagat did send Gill an e-mail during the blackout period, the day after Gill purchased the Nvidia stock, containing a link to an internet article discussing Nvidia and the X-Box. Evidence was also introduced that Bhagat provided his real estate agent with the X-Box information before it was made public. Finally, Gill's purchase was his largest purchase of the year.

ISSUE Was Bhagat guilty of insider trading and securities tipping in violation of federal securities laws?

HOLDING Yes. There was ample evidence that Bhagat took advantage of an insider's knowledge to personally benefit, and also that he tipped others to the information.

REASONING Excerpts from the opinion of Rawlinson, Circuit Judge:

The principal theory of the prosecution during the trial was that Bhagat knew about the contract from reading his own e-mail. . . . [H]owever, the prosecutor also questioned Bhagat about conversations among his co-workers that he had heard that morning concerning the X-Box contract. This line of questioning set the stage for what the parties refer to as the "office 'abuzz' theory." . . .

Evidence is sufficient to support a conviction if, considering the evidence in the light most favorable to the prosecution, any reasonable juror could have found the essential elements of the offense beyond a reasonable doubt. . . . For the following reasons, we hold that sufficient evidence supported Bhagat's convictions on all grounds.

To convict Bhagat of insider trading, the government was required to prove that he "traded stock on the basis of material, nonpublic information." . . . The government offered significant evidence to support the jury's conclusion that Bhagat was aware of the confidential X-Box information before he executed his trades. The X-Box e-mails were sent prior to his purchase. The e-mails were found on his computer. Bhagat was at his office for several hours prior to executing his trade, which provided him the opportunity to read the e-mails. Finally, Bhagat took virtually no action to divest himself of the stock, or to inform his company that he had violated the company's trading blackout. The fact that this evidence was all circumstantial does not lessen its sufficiency to support a guilty verdict. . . .

To convict Bhagat of tipping Gill, the government was required to prove that the tipper, Bhagat, provided the tippee, Gill, with material, inside information, prior to the tippee's purchase of stock. . . .

Viewing the evidence in the light most favorable to the prosecution, we cannot say that no reasonable trier of fact could have found Bhagat guilty. Bhagat and Gill were friends; Bhagat had provided inside information to his real estate broker, with whom he shared a more distant relationship; Gill purchased stock shortly after Bhagat; and Gill's purchase was his largest purchase of the year. . . . The government's use of the "office abuzz" theory did not constructively amend the indictment or create a material variance between the facts alleged in the indictment and the evidence presented at trial.

Sufficient evidence supported Bhagat's convictions on all counts.

A limited remand of Bhagat's sentence . . . is appropriate.

You Be the Judge

From 1990 to 2003, Chiquita Banana made payments to two Colombian organizations known as the FARC (Fuerzas Armadas Revolucionarias de Colombia) and AUC (Autodefensas Unidas de Colombia). The payments were essentially bribes made to the AUC and FARC in order to ensure the safety of the employees of Chiquita in areas of Colombia that were not adequately governed by public authorities. When the organizations were formally listed as "terrorist" organizations in 2001 by the U.S. Department of State, the payments took on not only an ethical dilemma but a legal complication. Ultimately, Chiquita voluntarily disclosed the payments to the U.S. Department of Justice. Should Chiquita be found guilty of violating the FCPA even though the payments were necessary to ensure the safety of its employees? [See J. Holcomb, D. Mayer & K. O'Brien, "Chiquita Brands and Terrorism: Legal Challenges and Ethical Dilemmas," Center for International Business Ethics Research, 2008.]

Summary

The Securities Act of 1933 and the Securities Exchange Act of 1934 extensively regulate securities. In essence, a "security" involves an investment in an enterprise whereby the investor has no managerial functions but instead expects to profit solely from the efforts of others. The United States securities laws require significant disclosure and registration in connection with the offer and sale of securities, with certain exemptions, and contain antifraud provisions.

Disclosure requirements for publicly traded companies include quarterly and annual reports, proxy statements, and reports about current material events. The Sarbanes-Oxley Act of 2002 and the rules and regulations of the securities exchanges impose additional requirements on publicly traded companies.

The antifraud provisions of the '34 Act have been interpreted by the courts to prohibit insider trading. However, not everyone who knows nonpublic information about a company is prohibited from trading. The "misappropriation" theory of insider trading requires that the person in possession of material nonpublic information must owe a duty of trust or confidence to the person or company disclosing the information.

Under the '34 Act's section on short-swing profits, directors and officers of publicly traded corporations must refrain from buying or selling securities within a six-month period, or they will be required to disgorge any such short-swing profits.

The Foreign Corrupt Practices Act forbids U.S. businesses from making payments to foreign officials for the purpose of obtaining foreign business. Noncompliance with the FCPA's antibribery provisions and recordkeeping standards may subject individuals or corporations to civil and/or criminal penalties.

The Wall Street Reform and Consumer Protection Act of 2010 is a broad statute that was passed with the objective of preventing another financial meltdown like the one that devastated the U.S. economy beginning in 2007, and now dubbed the "Great Recession." It imposes new regulations and restrictions on big banks and financial firms. It also creates a Consumer Financial Protection Bureau and an Office of Credit Ratings, establishes new national rules for regulating mortgages, and a host of other areas are affected. The impact of this Act will not be known for several years even though some of the new rules are already in place.

Discussion Questions

1. What is a *security*?

2. Explain the primary purposes of the Securities Act of 1933 and the Securities Exchange Act of 1934.

3. List the types of information a publicly traded company must disclose.

4. What is the "misappropriation" theory of insider trading?

5. Discuss the laws regarding short-swing profits and why the '34 Act prohibits these profits.

Case Problems and Writing Assignments

1. The Securities and Exchange Commission charged Dallas entrepreneur Mark Cuban with insider trading for selling 600,000 shares of the stock of an Internet search engine company, Mamma.com, on the basis of material nonpublic information concerning an impending stock offering. The SEC's complaint alleged that in June 2004, Mamma.com Inc. invited Cuban to participate in the stock offering after he agreed to keep the information confidential; that Cuban knew that the offering would be conducted at a discount to the prevailing market price and that it would be dilutive to existing shareholders; and that he used the information for personal gain. Cuban avoided losses in excess of $750,000 by selling his stock prior to the public announcement of the offering. Under the misappropriation theory of insider trading, should Cuban be held liable? Because the transaction was executed between a willing seller and a willing buyer, who was harmed by Cuban's actions to sell his stock ahead of the public announcement? [See *Securities and Exchange Commission v. Cuban*, Civil Action No. 3-08CV-2050-D, Northern District of Texas; Order Filed July 17, 2009.]

2. On October 14, 2003, the SEC filed an action against John Montana and others for their alleged involvement in the fraudulent sale of approximately $30 million in investment securities to approximately 29 investors located in several different states. Montana and his colleagues were said to have sold interests in a bank-trading program that purportedly invested money in the trading of a variety of instruments, including medium term notes. The investors were assured that, in exchange for a minimum investment of $1 million, they would earn significant returns risk-free in the program. They were also assured that their investments were fully insured and that the transactions would be monitored and controlled by the Federal Reserve Bank. They were assured that all they had to do was invest the funds, keep quiet about the opportunity, and await their returns on their investments. Unfortunately, none of these claims were true except that the minimum investment was $1 million. Montana personally raised about $23 million from 22 investors over four months in 1999.

Montana and his colleagues invested some of the funds in high-risk ventures and spent significant amounts of money on personal expenses and purchases. Eventually, most of the fund had been depleted and the investors suffered major losses. The SEC then became involved, filing suit against Montana and his cohorts for violations of § 10-6 of the Securities Act of 1934 and SEC Rule 10b-5.

How should this case be decided? What must the SEC show in order to prevail in this case? Should any of the blame be placed on the investors, none of whom investigated the claims put forward by Montana and the others nor, seemingly, questioned the validity of such a "risk-free, guaranteed high return" investment opportunity? [See *SEC v. Montana*, 464 F. Supp. 2d 772 (S.D. Ind. 2006).

3. Steven G. Cooperman and five other purchasers of the common stock of Individual, Inc. (Individual) sued Individual, its board of directors, and the underwriters who had participated in Individual's March 1996 IPO. The plaintiffs claimed that the defendants had made materially false and misleading statements and had omitted material facts in connection with the registration statement and prospectus for the IPO. Specifically, the plaintiffs alleged that the defendants had failed to disclose that, at the time the IPO became effective, a conflict exited between Yosi Amram—the director, founder, chief executive officer, and president of Individual—and a majority of the board of directors about the strategic direction the company should take. In 1989, Yosi Amram had founded the company, a provider of electronic customized information services, and was largely responsible for the firm's rapid growth. According to the plaintiffs, Amram believed that the company should grow and expand through rapid, often costly, acquisitions of new businesses. The majority of the board, however, believed that Individual should grow through building its core business by, among other things, expanding the subscriber base, extending its information base and providers, and enhancing its knowledge processing systems. The prospectus did not disclose the existence of any disagreement between Amram and the majority of the board. Instead, the prospectus stated that the company's

future objective was to maintain growth through the development of Individual's existing core business. The plaintiffs further maintained that, owing to this conflict, Amram ultimately had left Individual and thereby had caused a sharp decline in the company's stock. Hence, the plaintiffs alleged that the defendants' failure to disclose the conflict between Amram and the majority of the board at the time of the IPO constituted an omission of a material fact in violation of Section 11 of the '33 Act. Should the court rule in favor of Cooperman and the other plaintiffs? [See *Cooperman v. Individual, Inc.*, 171 F.3d 43 (1st Cir. 1999).]

Notes

1. See *Securities and Exchange Commission v. W. J. Howey Co.*, 328 U.S. 293 (1946).
2. The full text of the '33 Act, '34 Act, and all associated rules and regulations is consolidated and regularly updated by the University of Cincinnati College of Law and available online at http://www.law.uc.edu/CCL/xyz/sldtoc.html.
3. AFL-CIO Executive Paywatch Database, found at http://www.aflcio.org/corporatewatch/paywatch/ceou/database.cfm?tkr=GE&pg=1.
4. "GE CEO Declines More Than $12M in Bonus, Incentives," *USA Today*, (February 2, 2009), at http://www.usatoday.com/money/companies/management/2009-02-18-ge-bonuses_N.htm.
5. "Registration Under the Securities Act of 1933," U.S. Securities and Exchange Commission Web site, at http://www.sec.gov/answers/regis33.htm.
6. Section 10(b) of the '34 Act makes it "unlawful for any person . . . [t]o use or employ, in connection with the purchase or sale of any security . . . any manipulative or deceptive device or contrivance in contravention of such rules and regulations as the Commission may prescribe as necessary or appropriate in the public interest or for the protection of investors." 15 U.S.C. § 78j(b). Rule 10b-5, promulgated pursuant to the SEC's § 10(b) rulemaking authority, provides: "It shall be unlawful for any person . . . (a) To employ any device, scheme, or artifice to defraud, (b) To make any untrue statement of a material fact or to omit to state a material fact necessary in order to make the statements made, in the light of the circumstances under which they were made, not misleading, or (c) To engage in any act, practice, or course of business which operates or would operate as a fraud or deceit

upon any person, in connection with the purchase or sale of any security." 17 C.F.R. § 240.10b-5 (2009).
7. 116 Stat. 745.
8. See 17 C.F.R. § 240.10b-5 (2009) and 15 U.S.C. § 78j(b).
9. See *Basic Incorporated v. Levinson*, 485 U.S. 224 (1988) and *TSC Industries v. Northway, Inc.*, 426 U.S. 438 (1976).
10. 445 U.S. 222 (1980).
11. See *O'Hagan*, 521 U.S. at 652.
12. See 17 C.F.R. § 240.10b5-2 (2009).
13. 98 Stat. 1264, 15 U.S.C. 78a.
14. 102 Stat. 4677.
15. See 15 U.S.C. § 78(dd-1), (dd-2).
16. See "Siemens Settles Largest Ever FCPA Enforcement Action and Agrees to Pay $800 Million in Combined Fines and Penalties, Worldwide Resolution Tops $1.6 Billion," December 22, 2008, at www.fcpaenforcement.com.
17. See Department of Justice News Release, January 19, 2010, "Twenty-Two Executives and Employees of Military and Law Enforcement Products Companies Charged in Foreign Bribery Scheme" at www. justice.gov.
18. See Department of Justice News Release, September 14, 2009, "Film Executive and Spouse Found Guilty of Paying Bribes to aSenior Thai Tourism Official to Obtain Lucrative Contracts," at www.justice.gov.
19. Pub. L. 111-203.
20. "The Financial Reform Act: New Corporate Governance and Executive Compensation Provisions," JD Supra, http://www.jdsupra.com/post/documentViewer.aspx?fid=e57bd3df-abed-47ad-a550-f5b068b13e53.
21. Dalia Fahmy, "Top 6 Changes That Financial Reform Brings To Consumers," ABC News (June 25, 2010), http://abcnews.go.com/print?id=11012343.

Part VIII

Government Regulation of Business

Government regulation of business is a controversial area. There are people who believe that such regulation is an inappropriate exercise of the government's power and that the nation would be better served by a return to a *laissez-faire* economy. Other people believe that the government does not go far enough in regulating business and that the nation would be better served by a government that was more actively involved in the regulation and operation of business.

However, for better or for worse, government regulation of business is a fact. The government regulates competition through the Sherman, Clayton, Robinson-Patman, Cellar-Kefauver, and Federal Trade Commission Acts. It also provides consumer protection through various consumer credit and consumer product safety acts and regulations. The government also imposes regulations on business to provide environmental protections and to establish guidelines for labor relations, fair employment practices, and workplace safety.

Government regulation of business is closely related to the Social Contract Theory discussed in Chapter 2. It is also an area that creates controversy concerning whether business should be proactive or reactive in meeting its social and legal obligations. Throughout the rest of this section of the text, consider the topics in light of the Social Contract Theory and the benefits and burdens of being either proactive or reactive to a changing environment.

35
Antitrust Law

Agenda

eClass has entered the market for its product on the "ground floor," providing a good that virtually no one else is providing. This has placed the firm in a position to take control of a significant part of the market. This potential market position has benefits, but it also carries risks. The firm may be able to generate large profits and to gain "name" recognition, allowing it to remain profitable for quite some time. However, it may also lead to charges that eClass is improperly maintaining its position or otherwise violating the antitrust laws. The firm needs to be aware of the scope of the various antitrust laws, and it needs to take steps to insure that it does not violate any of these laws. It will also need to be aware of what constitutes an "unfair trade practice." This is all new territory for the firm and its principals, and may lead to a significant number of questions.

Be prepared! You never know when the firm or one of its members will seek your advice.

Classic Case

WARNER-LAMBERT COMPANY v. FEDERAL TRADE COMMISSION

562 F.2d 749, 183 U.S. App. D.C. 230, 1977 U.S. App. LEXIS 11599 (D.C. Cir. 1977)

FACTS Warner-Lambert, the producer of Listerine mouthwash, had advertised for more than 50 years that using Listerine would help to prevent colds or sore throats, and that a person who had a cold or a sore throat could lessen its severity by using Listerine. These advertisements were found to be false, and the Federal Trade Commission (FTC) issued a cease-and-desist order, requiring Warner-Lambert to stop running ads containing such claims.

However, the FTC also found that the prior advertising had created a belief in the mind of the public about the alleged benefits to be obtained from using Listerine, and determined that this belief had to be "dislodged" from the public's mind. In order to achieve this objective, the FTC ordered Warner-Lambert to run "corrective advertising," which disclaimed the prior statements about the remedial and/or medicinal benefits of using Listerine in treating colds and sore throats. Warner-Lambert objected, asserting that such a requirement was an infringement of its First Amendment right to free speech.

ISSUE Did the FTC's order that Warner-Lambert run corrective advertising infringe the First Amendment rights of the company?

HOLDING No. Since the claims had been made for more than 50 years, such corrective advertising was required to "dissipate the effects of respondent's deceptive representations."

REASONING Excerpts from the opinion of Wright, Circuit Judge:

In *Virginia State Board of Pharmacy v. Virginia Citizens Consumer Council* ... the Supreme Court rejected prior precedents holding that commercial speech is "wholly outside the protection of the First Amendment." ... In reaching this conclusion the Court emphasized the interest of consumers in the free flow of truthful information necessary for formulation of intelligent opinions and proper resource allocation. ... Consistent with this concern, the Court was careful to distinguish truthful commercial speech from that which is false, misleading, or deceptive ... [T]he Court went on to suggest that, because of the "commonsense differences" between commercial speech and other varieties, even commercial speech subject to First Amendment protections may nonetheless enjoy a "different degree of protection" than that normally accorded under the First Amendment. ...

Applying these principles to the case at bar, there can be no question of the legitimacy of the FTC's role in regulating and preventing false and deceptive advertising. In this case it has been found that Warner-Lambert has, over a long period of time, worked a substantial deception upon the public; it has advertised Listerine as a cure for colds, and consumers have purchased its product with that in mind. That the Commission has authority to prohibit Warner-Lambert from continuing to make such false and deceptive claims in its advertisements is not disputed, for it is only truthful claims which are protected under the First Amendment. Here, however, the FTC has determined on substantial evidence that the deception of the public occasioned by Warner-Lambert's past advertisements will not be halted by merely requiring Warner-Lambert to cease making such claims in the future. To be sure, current and future advertising of Listerine, when viewed in isolation, may not contain any statements which are themselves false or deceptive.

But reality counsels that such advertisements cannot be viewed in isolation; they must be seen against the background of over 50 years in which Listerine has been proclaimed—and purchased—as a remedy for colds. When viewed from this perspective, advertising which fails to rebut the prior claims as to Listerine's efficacy inevitably builds upon those claims; continued advertising continues the deception . . . It will induce people to continue to buy Listerine thinking it will cure colds. Thus the Commission found on substantial evidence that the corrective order was necessary to "dissipate the effects of respondent's deceptive representations." . . .

Under this reasoning the First Amendment presents no direct obstacle. The Commission is not regulating truthful speech protected by the First Amendment, but is merely requiring certain statements which, if not present in current and future advertisements, would render those advertisements themselves part of a continuing deception of the public. As the Supreme Court recognized in *Virginia State Board*, in some cases it may be "appropriate to require that a commercial message appear in such a form, or include such additional information, warnings,

and disclaimers, as are necessary to prevent its being deceptive." . . . We must conclude . . . that this is such a case. . . .

On the facts of this case, no burden is imposed upon truthful, protected advertising since, as the Commission makes clear, Listerine's current advertising, if not accompanied by a corrective message, would itself continue to mislead the public. Even if . . . the current and future advertising of Listerine is considered constitutionally protected speech, however, we think the corrective advertising order in this case remains appropriate. . . .

And the facts of this case make it eminently clear that this interest will not be substantially served by . . . a cease and desist order. Whatever one may conclude as to the effect of Warner-Lambert's long history of deception on the protected status of its current advertising, we see no basis . . . for questioning the Commission's conclusion that, absent a corrective remedy, consumers will continue to purchase Listerine as a cure for colds. . . .

Taking all these factors into account, we think it beyond doubt that the FTC order is a valid one.

THE BASIS OF REGULATORY REFORM

For the first 114 years of U.S. history, business had a fairly free field in which to work. There was little federal regulation and little effective state regulation. The courts and the federal government took a "hands-off" attitude toward business. In such an environment, Cornelius Vanderbilt, buccaneering railroad tycoon of the 1800s, was able to crow, "What do I care about the law? Hain't I got the power?"

The tide began to turn in the late 1800s as the public tired of the irresponsible behavior of some of the so-called *robber barons*. The press began to call for reforms and for protection from "big business." Finally, in 1890, Congress enacted the Sherman Antitrust Act. While the Sherman Antitrust Act began the era of government regulation, it proved to be inadequate in curbing business excesses. One of the problems with the Sherman Act is that the act is *remedial*, only applying to situations *after* the conduct has occurred and the harm has been inflicted. In an effort to provide *preventative* protections, Congress subsequently bolstered the antitrust area with the passage of:

- the Clayton Act (1914)
- the Federal Trade Commission Act (1914)
- the Robinson-Patman Act, an amendment to § 2 of the Clayton Act (1936)
- the Cellar-Kefauver Act, which amended § 7 of the Clayton Act (1950)

The growth in both the size and importance of international trade and its impact on the domestic market led to further amendment of the Sherman Act with the passage of the Foreign Trade Antitrust Improvement Act in 1982. We examine the effectiveness of this comprehensive statutory package over the balance of this chapter.

THE SHERMAN ANTITRUST ACT

Congress passed the Sherman Antitrust Act in 1890. The intended purpose of the act was to preserve the economic ideal of a pure-competition economy. To reach this ideal, the Sherman Act prohibits combinations that restrain trade, and it prohibits attempts to monopolize any area of commerce. Violations of the act can result in fines, imprisonment, injunctive relief, and civil damages.

Section 1: Contracts, Combinations, or Conspiracies in Restraint of Trade

The Sherman Antitrust Act is a fairly short statute, but its few words cover a great number of actions. Section 1 states:

> "Every contract, combination in the form of trust or otherwise, or conspiracy, in restraint of trade or commerce among the several States, or with foreign nations, is hereby declared to be illegal. Every person who shall make any contract or engage in any combination or conspiracy hereby declared to be illegal shall be deemed guilty of a felony, and, on conviction thereof, shall be punished by fine not exceeding $10,000,000 if a corporation, or, if any other person, $350,000, or by imprisonment not exceeding three years, or by both said punishments, in the discretion of the court."[1]

[The original statute provided that the crime was a misdemeanor, and called for a maximum fine of $5,000, with a maximum imprisonment of one year for anyone convicted of violating the Act.] Violations of § 1 require a contract, a combination, or a conspiracy. Each of these three requires two or more persons acting in concert in some manner that restrains trade or commerce among the states or with a foreign nation. Thus, § 1 requires two or more persons acting together before a violation can be found. One person cannot be guilty of a § 1 violation, since one person is acting alone, by definition.

As originally enacted, § 1 presented problems to the courts. Because nearly every contract can, at least in theory, be viewed as a restraint of trade, the prohibition against contracts "in restraint of trade" seemed too broad. In fact, if this section were to be interpreted literally, virtually all business dealings that affect interstate commerce (including foreign trade) could, theoretically, be prohibited by § 1 of the Sherman Act. As a result, the courts initially interpreted the Sherman Act very narrowly. The courts were willing to rule against combinations or conspiracies "in restraint of trade," but had a more difficult time ruling that any contracts were "in restraint of trade." However, the courts *did* rule that some union activities were combinations or conspiracies in restraint of trade in violation of § 1 of the Sherman Act. Unfortunately, these rulings tended to promote—rather than hinder—the "big business" of the era. These interpretations virtually negated the Act.

The Rule of Reason   Eventually, the Supreme Court found a method for evaluating conduct, particularly contracts, that allegedly restrains trade among the several states in violation of § 1 of the Sherman Act. In the case of *Standard Oil Co. of New Jersey v. United States,*[2] the "rule of reason" concept was introduced by the Supreme Court. According to this "rule," the Sherman Act does *not* prohibit *every* contract, combination, or conspiracy in restraint of trade among the several states. Rather, the Act only prohibits those contracts, combinations, or conspiracies that *unreasonably* restrain trade among the several states. If the contract, combination, or conspiracy is *reasonable* under the circumstances, the conduct is not in violation of the law. By applying this "rule" the Court can determine whether a defendant accused of violating the Act conducted his or her business in a reasonable manner and adhered to the law, or acted in an unreasonable manner in violation of the law. Although the Court determined in this particular case that the conduct by Standard Oil of New Jersey was unreasonable, the Court did accept, in theory, this defense. Thus was born the "rule of reason" defense to charges of violations of § 1 of the Sherman Act.

Once it was established, the "rule-of-reason" defense provided business with an opportunity that it lost no time in pursuing to its best advantage. Given a sufficient amount of time to prepare a defense, almost any business can develop a strong argument that its conduct was "reasonable" under the circumstances. Because of the results produced by the rule, the courts had to reevaluate their approach. The amended approach retained the rule of reason but added a new category: The courts declared some conduct to be so lacking in social value as to be an automatic violation of § 1. These actions, called *per se* violations, tend to contradict directly the economic model of pure competition.

***Per se* Violations**   As noted in the preceding section, the courts restricted the availability of the rule-of-reason defense for alleged Sherman Act violations by finding that the conduct in question was a *per se* violation. (A *per se* violation is inherently a violation; the act alone proves the violation.) The acts that are deemed to be *per se* violations are acts that are inherently contradictory to the economic theory of pure competition. If a firm is found guilty of a *per se* violation, it is not permitted to defend its conduct; it will be found guilty of the alleged violation of the Sherman Act by definition.

Historically, the *per se* violations under § 1 of the Sherman Act were:

1. Horizontal price fixing (agreements on price among competitors)
2. Vertical price fixing (agreements on price among suppliers and customers)
3. Horizontal market divisions (agreements among competitors as to who can sell in which region)
4. Group boycotts (agreements among competitors not to sell to a particular buyer or not to buy from a particular seller)

Clearly, few businesses would be careless (or stupid) enough to actually and overtly agree to such conduct. As a result, the courts have had to infer such agreements from the conduct of the parties. For example, in the area of price fixing, if the courts find that the parties have acted in a manner that amounts to conscious parallelism, a violation is likely to be found. Conscious parallelism, by itself, is not conclusive proof of a violation of § 1. However, it is to be weighed—and weighed heavily—by the courts in determining whether a § 1 violation is present. Generally, conscious parallelism coupled with some other fact, however slight, is sufficient to support a jury verdict of price fixing in violation of § 1. But if the conduct of the firms amounts only to price leadership, no violation is present. How can anyone distinguish conscious parallelism from price leadership? There is no answer to this problem; it poses a dilemma for the court every time it is raised.

Both the rule of reason and the economic theory of competition seemed to be invoked by the Court in a recent case.[3] Sears, Roebuck and Company (Sears) applied for membership with Visa, USA, the association of credit card issuers who offer the Visa card in the United States. The association denied the application by Sears, and Sears filed suit against Visa, USA, alleging that the credit card association was combining or conspiring illegally in an effort to prevent Sears from issuing Visa cards. The Court found that the harm to competition would be greater if the association admitted Sears than it would be if Sears was prevented from joining the association. According to the Court, the credit card industry was better served by having Visa, MasterCard, American Express, Diners/Carte Blanche, and Discover (issued by and through Sears). Competition was keen, and the market was highly competitive. Admitting Sears to the association would reduce the number of competitors in the credit card industry, and would seriously harm banks that issue Visa in head-to-head competition with Sears for the potential Visa customers in the market. According to the Court, the association acted in a reasonable manner under the circumstances. Under the rule of reason, the conduct of Visa, USA was reasonable, and therefore appropriate. It did not violate § 1 of the Sherman Act.

"Quick Look" Analysis   The courts have recently added a third method for evaluating allegations that certain conduct violates § 1 of the Sherman Act. This method, the *"quick look"* analysis, provides a "middle ground" between the rule of reason and the *per se* violations. Under the quick look analysis, a defendant firm that is charged with what has historically been treated as a *per se* violation is given an opportunity to rebut the presumption that the conduct is automatically anticompetitive, and thus to avoid conviction under the *per se* standards. If the court agrees with the rebuttal evidence of the defendant firm, the court removes the conduct from the *per se* category and applies a "rule of reason" analysis to the case.

Under the traditional approach, the *per se* rule absolutely prohibits certain conduct. This effectively denies the firms accused of violating the Act the opportunity to show that there is a business justification for the conduct. By contrast, the rule of reason allows the accused firms an opportunity to present a *reasonable* business justification, and thus to avoid being held in violation of the statute. When a "quick look" analysis is applied, the courts allow the firms charged with a traditional *per se* violation an opportunity to argue that the conduct should not be treated as an automatic violation, but rather should be judged under the more lenient rule of reason standards. If the court accepts this initial argument, this "quick look," it gives these firms the opportunity to show that there *is* a business justification for their conduct, and that they should not be found in violation of the law. Exhibit 35.1 compares the three approaches to allegations of violations of § 1 of the Sherman Act.

In 1967, the Court ruled that non-price vertical restrictions imposed by a supplier on its customers was a *per se* illegal market division.[4] The following year, the court ruled that a maximum resale price-fixing arrangement was also illegal *per se*.[5] However, by 1979 the Court had begun to restrict the application of the *per se* doctrine, beginning to apply the "quick look" analysis to certain types of cases. In *Broadcast Music, Inc. v. CBS, Inc.*,[6] the Court upheld the right of an association of music copyright holders to establish a common price for the "blanket license" of their compositions. In rejecting the challenge by CBS, the Court stated that, in determining whether to apply the rule of reason or the *per se* rules, the court should decide "whether the practice facially appears to be one that would always or almost always tend to restrict competition and decrease output," or is "one designed to increase economic efficiency and render markets more, rather than less, competitive." This formulation provides the framework for the "quick look" analysis.

To date the "quick look" has been limited in its application to some vertical restraints and some cooperative pricing agreements. Thus, while horizontal price fixing, horizontal market divisions, and group boycotts still are viewed as *per se* violations, some vertical market division cases and some maximum price arrangement cases have been evaluated under the "quick look" provisions. In addition, some tying arrangements are now being evaluated under a "quick look" analysis. The businesses charged with violations of § 1 of the Sherman Act are allowed the opportunity to rebut the presumption of anticompetitive effect in these cases. If they are successful, the case is decided under the rule of reason. If they are not, the conduct is found to be a *per se* violation of § 1 of the Sherman Act.

Exhibit 35.1

Sherman Act § 1 Analyses

Type of Analysis	Violations Alleged	Treatment
Rule of Reason	Contract, combination, or conspiracy in restraint of trade (excluding price fixing, market divisions, or group boycotts)	A "totality of the circumstances" test. The firm must show a reason for the conduct undertaken and the effect on competition in the industry. If the conduct is found to unreasonably restrain trade, it is illegal.
Per se violation	Price fixing Market division Group boycotts	Conduct that has a "pernicious effect" on competition or lacks any redeeming value. Practices that "always or almost always tend to restrict competition and decrease output." Evidence of a *per se* violation is, by definition, unreasonable and the firm is guilty of a violation of § 1.
Quick Look Analysis	To date: Some Price fixing Some vertical Market division	The defendant must present some evidence that the conduct is "designed to increase economic efficiency and render markets more, rather than less, competitive." If the court finds that the evidence is persuasive the case is decided under the rule of reason.

Foreign Trade Antitrust Improvement Act

Another change to the Sherman Act occurred in 1982 when Congress passed the Foreign Trade Antitrust Improvement Act (FTAIA),[7] an amendment to the Sherman Act that addressed antitrust issues involving foreign trade. The FTAIA was intended to facilitate the *exporting* of domestic goods by providing an exemption to the Sherman Act for export transactions that did not injure the U.S economy, thus relieving exporters from competitive disadvantage in foreign trade.[8] The act precludes subject matter jurisdiction over claims by foreign plaintiffs against defendants when the *situs* of the injury is overseas and the injury arises from effects in the non-domestic market.[9]

Section 2: Monopolizing and Attempts to Monopolize

Section 2 of the Sherman Act is nearly as brief as § 1 and is equally as broad. Section 2 makes the following provision:

"Every person who shall monopolize, or attempt to monopolize, or combine or conspire with any other person or persons, to monopolize any part of the trade or commerce among the several States, or with foreign nations, shall be deemed guilty of a felony, and, on conviction thereof, shall be punished by a fine not exceeding $10,000,000 if a corporation, or, if any other person, $350,000, or by imprisonment not exceeding three years, or by both said punishments, in the discretion of the court."

[The original statute provided that the crime was a misdemeanor, and called for a maximum fine of $5,000, with a maximum imprisonment of one year for anyone convicted of violating the Act.]

Section 2 can be violated *either* by one person acting alone *or* by multiple parties acting in concert. In contrast, § 1 can be violated only by multiple parties acting together. (To avoid confusion, remember that it takes two people to violate § 1, while it takes only one person to violate § 2.)

Many people mistakenly believe that monopolies are prohibited by § 2. In fact, no law prohibits having monopoly power. It is not illegal to gain a monopoly position through making a superior product or providing superior service, and a firm that does so would not be found in violation of § 2 of the Sherman Act. The objective of § 2 of the Sherman Act is to prohibit *monopolizing*, which involves either *seeking* to acquire monopoly power or attempting to exclude or limit competition in order to keep monopoly power once such power is attained. A business that is shown to have committed either of these prohibited acts is guilty of monopolizing and would be found to be in violation of § 2.

Obviously, very few "pure" monopolies exist in the U.S. market, and those that do exist often exist for a valid reason, such as the so-called "natural monopolies." Some areas, for example, may only be served by one railroad or may only have one source of electric power. However, the provisions of § 2 do not require that a "pure" monopoly exists. Monopoly *power* may be present even if an area of commerce has several businesses in existence and seemingly competing with one another. If a firm is found to dominate an industry it may also be found to possess monopoly power. As a rule of thumb, control of 70 percent or more of the *relevant market* is deemed to be sufficient to establish that the firm has monopoly power. However, defining the relevant market may be difficult. In determining the relevant market, the courts must determine the relevant *geographic* market—where the product is sold—and the relevant *product* market—what is being sold or provided by the seller. In so doing, the courts examine the *product* produced by the challenged firm, *substitute* goods produced by other firms, and the elasticity of demand between the challenged product and

eClass 35.1 Sales/Management

DOES eCLASS HAVE A MONOPOLY IN THE RELEVANT MARKET?

While eClass has enjoyed success in its initial entry into the market, the firm has hardly become dominant in its industry. Nevertheless, eClass's major competitor in the Indiana-Illinois region recently filed for protection under the bankruptcy law and closed its operations in this two-state region. As a result, eClass now controls more than 70 percent of the Indiana-Illinois market. Yousef jokingly stated that, with the withdrawal of this competitor, eClass now is in position to monopolize the Indiana-Illinois market. Meg replied that the firm does not have a large enough share of the national market to be accused of monopolizing. However, Ani remembers some discussion about relevant product markets from one of her classes, and she is concerned that the firm *could* be accused of violating § 2 of the Sherman Act if it acts improperly in the region. She has asked for your opinion. What will you tell her?

BUSINESS CONSIDERATIONS   Is there any problem with a business gaining a dominant position in its market? Should a business aim for a lesser degree of control to avoid potential problems under the Sherman Act, or should it maximize its potential and deal with Sherman Act problems if or when they arise?

ETHICAL CONSIDERATIONS   Section 2 of the Sherman Act prohibits monopolizing, and a "virtual-monopoly" position is defined by the courts as controlling 70 percent or more of the relevant product market. Economic theory states that a monopoly exists when an industry only contains one firm. Is it ethical for the courts to define a virtual-monopoly position differently than economic theory defines monopoly position, when the purpose of the Sherman Act is to provide for industrial conduct that is more in line with economic theories and economic competition?

the substitutes. If the courts find that the firm controls 70 percent or more of this relevant market with its product, the firm will be found to possess monopoly power under the courts' interpretation of § 2 of the Sherman Act. If the firm possesses less than 70 percent of the relevant market, it lacks monopoly power under § 2 of the Sherman Act.

United States v. E.I. DuPont de Nemours and Co.[10] is a landmark in U.S. antitrust law involving relevant product market. Dupont acquired the exclusive U.S. right to produce cellophane from the French patent holder of the process. By 1947, Dupont had acquired 75 percent of the cellophane market in the United States, which led the Justice Department to file charges against Dupont for violating § 2 of the Sherman Act. At trial, Dupont admitted that it controlled the market for *cellophane*, but denied that it controlled the relevant product market. According to Dupont, the relevant product market was for *flexible wrapping materials*, including aluminum foil, wax paper, saran wrap, and various other materials. In this broader market, Dupont only had a 20 percent market share. The court agreed with Dupont's argument, establishing a precedent for the determination of relevant product market.

When a dominant position in the relevant product market is present, there is a presumption that § 2 was, or is, violated. However, a number of defenses exist to rebut this presumption. The dominant firm may argue that it is not attempting to retain its power, or that it acquired its position legally, or that its position was "thrust upon" it.

This hypothetical case shows how the "thrust upon" defense can be applied:

> *Ralph developed a new product, Kleenzall, which does what other soaps or cleansers do, except that it does it better and is cheaper. Kleenzall is good for washing dishes, clothes, floors, walls, and even hair. Kleenzall is so good a product that Ralph has 95 percent of every cleanser and soap market. The major soap producers sue Ralph for monopolizing the industry in violation of § 2 of the Sherman Act. The court, however, finds that Ralph is not guilty. He did nothing wrong in acquiring his market share. Rather, this monopoly was "thrust upon" him by sheer efficiency. However, if Ralph subsequently takes steps to prevent other firms from entering the cleanser market or acts in any manner that seems to be precluding or preventing competition, he may be found guilty of monopolizing. Possessing his monopoly power is legal, but attempting to retain it is illegal!*

The government, in a number of monopolization cases over the years, has used the Sherman Act quite successfully, beginning with *Standard Oil Co. v. United States*,[11] decided in 1911. The Standard Oil Company was found guilty of monopolizing, using regional price-cutting to drive competition out of the market, and then asserting domination over that market segment. The court ordered Standard Oil divided into a number of smaller companies, effectively ending its ability to dominate the domestic oil market. The Justice Department was also successful in attacking American Tobacco, Alcoa, and AT&T. The most recent § 2 case occurred in 2000 when the government obtained a conviction against Microsoft.

In the Microsoft case, the judge found that Microsoft was guilty of monopolizing and was also guilty of illegal tying arrangements. He ordered that the company be divided into two separate companies, one handling the Windows operating system and the other handling Internet Explorer, Microsoft Office, and all other Microsoft holdings. These two companies were to remain separate and independent for at least ten years.

The judge also (1) prohibited Microsoft from taking any actions against computer makers who support competing technologies, (2) required that the Windows system had to be sold at the same price to all computer makers, and (3) required that Microsoft disclose certain parts of the Windows source code to software developers in order to ensure that newly developed software would be compatible with the Windows system.

Microsoft subsequently reached a settlement with the Justice Department and nine of the states that participated in the initial case.[12] This settlement avoided the break-up of the firm previously ordered by the court, although numerous other remedies were imposed. While some of the states that initially joined in the complaint did not participate in the settlement, Microsoft survived this action without being broken into two or more companies and has continued to thrive.

The settlement prohibited Microsoft from reaching exclusive deals with vendors that could harm Microsoft's rivals, and it ordered Microsoft to allow PC vendors and purchasers to designate software or programs from other computer companies as the preferred option on new computers. Interestingly, the settlement did not address Microsoft's activities in the area of delivering services over the Web, nor did it address the development of computer "servers" that power Web sites, or hand-held computers and software. These areas are expected to be the next major area in the development of computers and software. Despite these seeming weaknesses in the settlement, the success of the government in gaining a conviction shows the continued potential for using the Sherman Act.

Remedies

When a Sherman Act violation is shown, both criminal and civil remedies are available. As originally enacted, the Sherman Act did not provide for individual civil remedies. Instead, the law only provided for governmental prosecution of the prohibited conduct. However, § 4 of the Clayton Act[13] provides for civil remedies for violations of *any* antitrust statutes, including the Sherman Act. Under this section, "any person who shall be injured in his business or property by reason of anything forbidden in the antitrust laws may sue therefore . . . and shall recover threefold the damages by him sustained, and the cost of suit, including a reasonable attorney's fee."[14] In addition, as was previously mentioned, an individual who is convicted of a violation of the Sherman Act can be fined up to $350,000 and can receive up to three years in prison; a corporation that is convicted can be fined up to $10,000,000. Also, § 4 of the Sherman Act provides that an injunction can be issued against the prohibited conduct.

THE CLAYTON ACT

By 1914, Congress realized that the Sherman Act alone was not sufficient to solve the major anticompetitive problems of the country. The Sherman Act was remedial in nature: If a problem existed, the Sherman Act could be used to help correct the problem. Unfortunately, it is possible (if not probable) that by the time the "remedy" is sought the injured party has suffered irreparable harm or has ceased to exist as a business entity. Unfortunately, there were no federal statutes or regulations available to prevent a problem from developing. In an effort to correct this regulatory deficiency, Congress decided to enact some preventative legislation. The result was the Clayton Act, which was designed to nip problems "in their incipiency." The Clayton Act has four major provisions addressing different antitrust conduct. And, as previously discussed, the Clayton Act has a number of other provisions dealing with implementation of the antitrust laws, including the provision for treble damages for violations of *any* of the antitrust laws.

Section 2: Price Discrimination

The Clayton Act, § 2, prohibits price discrimination. The original § 2 made it illegal for a *seller* to discriminate in price between different purchasers unless the price difference could be justified by a difference in costs. This provision soon placed a number of sellers in a terrible bind. Major purchasers often demanded special prices from their sellers, many of whom were not as powerful or influential as the major purchaser. If the sellers refused to give these special prices they lost the business; if they agreed, they violated the law. This placed some sellers in an untenable position, while shielding the buyers—who often initiated the price discrimination—from liability, since the law only applied to the seller. As a result, § 2 was amended in 1936 when the Robinson–Patman Act became law. Under the Robinson–Patman Act, *buyers* were prohibited from knowingly accepting a discriminatory price. In addition, the act prohibited buyers from knowingly accepting indirect benefits such as dummy brokerage fees and promotional kickbacks. And, of course, sellers were still prohibited from granting discriminatory prices to their customers absent a cost differential justifying the price.

In interpreting and applying the provisions of the Robinson–Patman Act, the courts have developed a "checklist" of elements that are required in order to find that a firm is guilty of violating the law. It appears that all of these elements must be present before a violation will be found. The elements are:

1. There must be discrimination in price; a different price must be charged to two or more different buyers.
2. There must be at least two consummated sales. Mere offers will not suffice; there must be at least two contracts involved.
3. There must be a difference in price quoted by the "same seller."
4. At least one of the sales must cross state lines. Since this is a federal statute, interstate commerce must be involved before the statute applies.
5. The sales must either be contemporaneous or they must occur within a relevant time period.
6. The sale must relate to "commodities."
7. The goods sold must be of "like grade and quality."
8. The law only applies to goods that will be used, consumed, or resold within the United States.
9. There must be a showing of an adverse affect on competition.[15]

The mere fact that a different price is granted to different buyers is not enough to assure a conviction for price discrimination. In fact, a number of potential defenses exist. These include:

1. The person accused of price discrimination can defend against the charge by showing that he or she is *meeting*, but *not* beating, the price being offered by a competitor.
2. The accused can also defend by showing that the lower price is being offered because of obsolescence, seasonal variations, or damage to the goods being sold.

3. The accused can also show that the price differential is based on legitimate cost savings based on quantity discounts, *and* that such discounts are generally available to any other customers who place orders of sufficient size.

4. The accused can avoid being found liable if it charges two different prices—a normal price and a reduced price—if it can show that the reduced price is realistically available to any individual customer, but that the particular customer chose not to take advantage of this reduced price for whatever reason.[16]

Standard Oil Co. (of Indiana) v. FTC,[17] a landmark opinion, involved an allegation of price discrimination and a defense of meeting—but not beating—the competition. Standard Oil was selling gasoline to four large "jobbers" in the Detroit area at a lower price than it was selling gasoline to numerous smaller competitors in the same market. Standard Oil showed that its lower price for the "jobbers" was only to meet—and not to beat—the price of a competitor, thus allowing Standard Oil to retain its customers. The court accepted this defense, finding that Standard Oil was not guilty of price discrimination.

The Robinson–Patman Act also changed the standards needed to show a violation. Under the original § 2, it was necessary to show that general competition had been harmed. Under the Robinson–Patman Act, a case can be prosecuted on a showing that one single competitor was injured. There are two types of injuries that the courts look for when hearing a Robinson–Patman case: a *primary-line injury* and a *secondary-line injury*. A primary-line injury involves competition at the seller's level. The seller is providing discriminatory prices in order to gain a competitive advantage over one of the seller's competitors. A secondary-line injury involves competition at the buyer's level. One or more of the buyers who receive the discriminatory price are given an advantage over one or more of the buyer's competitors who did not receive the same price.

An interesting Robinson–Patman issue was raised in a recent Puerto Rico case.[18] Caribe BMW purchased new automobiles directly from the manufacturer. Caribe's competitors in the market purchased their new BMWs from a wholly owned subsidiary of the manufacturer, and were able to purchase at a lower price than that offered to Caribe. The court ruled that a manufacturer and its wholly owned subsidiary are a single entity for purposes of applying the Robinson–Patman Act so that there was a discriminatory pricing practice in effect, entitling Caribe to remedies for violation of the Act. [This ruling involves the "single seller" test, the third item listed in the "checklist" set out above.]

Section 3: Exclusive Dealings and Tying Arrangements

The second major prohibition under the Clayton Act is found in § 3. This section bans exclusive-dealing contracts and tying arrangements when their "effect may be to substantially lessen competition or tend to create a monopoly in any line of trade or commerce." Notice again the preventative intent of the Act: Actual harm need not be shown, merely the *likelihood* that harm will eventually occur.

In an exclusive-dealing contract, one party requires the other party to deal with him, and him alone. For example, the seller tells the buyer that unless the buyer buys only from the seller, and not from the seller's competitors, the seller will not deal with the buyer. For such a demand to be effective, the seller must be in a very powerful market position.

In a tying arrangement, one party—usually the seller—refuses to sell one product unless the buyer also takes a second product or service from the seller. For example, a manufacturer of cosmetics might refuse to sell a facial moisturizer unless the buyer agrees to also purchase the manufacturer's soap. Usually for this sort of arrangement to work, the seller needs a highly valued, unique product to which he or she can "tie" a commonly available product. As a defense to a charge that such an arrangement tends to lessen competition or create a monopoly, the seller may attempt to show that the tied product is tied for quality-control reasons. To do so, the seller must prove that no competitors produce a competing product that works adequately with the controlled product.

Franchising is one area in which tying arrangements still present an ongoing problem. Franchisors insist that they must be allowed to tie the products and the

eClass 35.2 Management/Manufacturing

TYING ARRANGEMENTS

A rapidly growing publishing company has significantly expanded it eBook division, especially for college text books. This company has approached eClass with what it considers a "can't miss" deal. The publisher wants to enter a contract with eClass that links the firm's eBooks with the eClass software, using this packaged offer to allow each firm to gain a larger market share in their respective industries. However, the publisher wants eClass to make the publisher the exclusive dealer for any such package arrangement. Although the idea is intriguing, the firm is afraid there may be some legal implication they have overlooked. They ask you what you think of the idea. What advice will you give them?

BUSINESS CONSIDERATIONS   What potential problems could arise under the various antitrust laws from tying eClass's products to the products of another firm? Could this be considered an attempt by each firm to monopolize its respective industry? Is this more or less of a problem than would be faced if a firm tied one of its products to another of its products?

ETHICAL CONSIDERATIONS   What ethical issues are raised when one firm ties its products to the products of another firm? Is it ethical to put the stakeholders of one firm in a position where those stakeholders are relying on the performance of another firm for success?

materials that franchisees use to the franchise contract in order to assure consistent quality and to preserve the reputation of the franchise. However, many franchisees insist that these tying arrangements lead to substantially higher prices for their materials without assuring consistent quality. Instead, the franchisees argue that the tying arrangements are merely a method allowing the franchisor to gain additional profits from the franchise arrangement at the expense of the franchisees. This area has not yet been resolved, and there will doubtless be continuing litigation over this issue.[19]

The Supreme Court has ruled that a "not insubstantial" amount of commerce must be affected in order to have an illegal tying arrangement.[20] The Ninth Circuit went even further, ruling that there is no requirement for multiple purchasers in order to have an illegal tying arrangement,[21] so long as the effect on commerce is not insubstantial. The amount involved was approximately $100,000 per year for an indeterminate number of years, and the Court ruled that such an amount was sufficiently substantial to allow the trial to proceed even though only one firm was precluded from the market due to the tying arrangement.

Section 7: Antimerger Provisions

The third major section of the Clayton Act, § 7, concerns mergers. As originally written, the only prohibited type of merger was one in which the stock of another firm was acquired with the effect "substantially to lessen competition, or [to] tend to create a monopoly in any line of trade or commerce." This prohibition was so narrow that it was easily evaded by merging firms.

To broaden the scope of the law, Congress amended § 7 in 1950 by passing the Cellar–Kefauver Act. The amended § 7 prohibits the acquisition of stock or assets of another firm that may tend to have a negative effect on any line of commerce. As a result, firms are now subject to § 7 in almost any type of merger—horizontal, vertical, or conglomerate. A horizontal merger is one between competing firms; a vertical merger is one between a firm and one of its major suppliers or customers; a conglomerate merger is one between firms in two noncompetitive industries.

Not all mergers are prohibited by § 7. The government must establish that if the merger is allowed, the result "may be to substantially lessen competition" in an industry. For example, as a challenge to a merger, the government might argue that a "concentration trend" has been established, or that one of the firms was a "potential entrant" into one of the industries affected by the merger. The government would thus argue that the industry *after* the proposed merger was less competitive than the industry *prior* to the proposed merger. The burden then shifts to the defendants to justify the proposed merger by showing that a substantial lessening of competition is not the probable effect. For example, the merging firms might raise the "failing-company" doctrine, showing that without the merger one of the firms would have gone out of business. If one of the firms would have gone out of business anyway, the same number of firms remain in the industry following the merger as would have existed without the merger, and jobs were saved in the firm that would otherwise have ceased to exist. The following example illustrates the failing-company doctrine.

> *Fred's Stereo is in severe financial difficulty. Irv's Interstate Sound Store, the largest stereo dealer in the region, buys Fred's (a merger under revised § 7). Under the failing-company doctrine, if Fred's would have gone bankrupt, the merger with Irv's is probably permissible. [Of course, such a merger would be less likely to be challenged if the firm taking over Fred's had not been the largest competitor in the region. In such a case, the merged firms would be better able to compete with Irv's, the largest firm, and might be able to show that competition would be enhanced with the merger even if Fred's was not about to go out of business.]*

Section 8: Interlocking Directorates

The final substantive section of the Clayton Act is § 8, which prohibits interlocking directorates. In other words, no one may sit on the boards of directors of two or more competing corporations if either of the firms has capital and surplus in excess of $1 million *and* if a merger between them violates any antitrust law.

THE FEDERAL TRADE COMMISSION ACT

The year 1914 was a very busy year for antitrust regulation. Congress passed not only the Clayton Act but also the Federal Trade Commission Act. The Federal Trade Commission Act did two important things:

1. It created the Federal Trade Commission (FTC) to enforce antitrust laws, especially the Clayton Act.
2. In § 5 it provided a broad area of prohibitions to close loopholes left by other statutes.

Section 5 of the act prohibits "unfair methods of competition" and "unfair and deceptive trade practices." This broad language permits the FTC to regulate conduct that technically might be beyond the reach of the other, more specific antitrust statutes. The area of unfair and deceptive trade practices was intentionally made broad and somewhat vague to grant the FTC leeway to proceed against any commercial practices that seem to be unfair or deceptive under the circumstances. If the statute was more specific, businesspeople would more easily find methods to circumvent it, methods that may be unfair or deceptive but are within the technical limits of a more specific law. The strength of the law has been its breadth, as well as the willingness of the FTC to attack practices that had, in some cases, been followed for many years.

To further strengthen the FTC position, a violation can be found without proof of any actual deception. A mere showing that there is a "fair possibility" that the public will be deceived is sufficient to establish that the conduct is unfair and deceptive. In addition, if a representation made by a company is ambiguous, with one honest meaning and one deceptive meaning, the FTC will treat it as deceptive and as a material aspect of the transaction so that remedies are available.

If the FTC opposes a business practice as unfair or deceptive, it issues a cease-and-desist order. The business must stop the challenged conduct or face a fine for disobeying the order. The fine is $10,000 per violation. This may sound small, but realize that each day the order is ignored constitutes a separate violation. Thus, ignoring the order for one week costs $70,000 in fines; for a month, $300,000 in fines; and so on.

In recent years, the FTC has become particularly concerned about two business practices: deceptive advertising and "bait-and-switch" advertising. In an effort to force

eClass 35.3 Management/Marketing

WHAT IS AN "UNFAIR TRADE PRACTICE"?

Text World, one of eClass's largest customers, recently placed an order for a large quantity of the firm's software. The order was so much larger than normal that Ani called the purchasing manager to verify the number of units being ordered. The purchasing manager told Ani that Text World plans to launch a "you can't fail with eClass" advertising campaign. The idea is that customers will be told that *if* they buy the eClass software from Text World, *and* they buy the required textbooks and study guides from Text World, and *if* they use the product properly, they "can't fail" to pass the class for which the text, study guide, and software was purchased. The company's marketing department thinks this is a wonderful ad campaign that will benefit both Text World and eClass. However, Ani is afraid that this might be viewed as an unfair trade practice. Before she agrees to fill the order, she would like your opinion as to whether there is anything wrong with the campaign, and whether any problems might reflect badly on eClass. What advice will you give her?

BUSINESS CONSIDERATIONS   Is a manufacturer responsible for the conduct of its customers when that conduct involves potential violations of antitrust law? What responsibility should a manufacture have for the conduct of its customers after the sale is completed?

ETHICAL CONSIDERATIONS   Is it ethical for a manufacturer to deal with a customer if the manufacturer believes that customer is violating the law or public policy, and using the products of the manufacturer in this illegal conduct? Does the manufacturer have an ethical duty to report the suspected improper conduct to a government agency?

truth in advertising, the FTC has been carefully studying the commercials run by corporations and ordering corrective advertising when the advertising was deemed especially misleading.

Bait-and-switch advertising involves advertising a product at an especially enticing price to get the customer into the store (the "bait") and then talking the customer into buying a more expensive model (the "switch") because the advertised model is "sold out" or has some alleged defect. An advertiser who refuses to show the advertised item to the customer or who has insufficient quantities on hand to satisfy reasonable customer demand is engaging in an unfair trade practice in violation of § 5 of the FTC Act.

UNFAIR TRADE PRACTICES

We should also mention some common law unfair trade practices, such as palming off goods and violating trade secrets. Palming off involves advertising, designing, or selling goods as if they were the goods of another. The person who is palming off goods is fraudulently taking advantage of the goodwill and brand loyalty of the imitated producer. This practice also frequently involves copyright, patent, or trademark infringements.

Trade secrets are special processes, formulas, and the like that are guarded and treated confidentially by the holder of the trade secret. Employees of a firm that has trade secrets must not betray their loyalty to the firm by revealing the trade secrets to others. Revealing the trade secret is a tort, and the employee can be held liable for any damages suffered by the employer. In addition, the firm or person who receives the information is guilty of appropriating the trade secret, and use of the secret can be stopped by injunction; the recipient of the information will also be liable for damages suffered by the trade secret holder. As we just mentioned, palming off frequently involves the infringement of a copyright, a patent, or a trademark. These three areas, along with a few others, such as service marks and trade names, are protected by federal statutes, as well as under various state laws. A copyright, filed with the Copyright Office of the Library of Congress, is the protection given to artists, composers, and writers. The creator of a book, song, work of art, or similar item has the exclusive right to the profits from the creation for the life of the creator plus 70 years. Any infringement can result in an infringement action in federal court, with injunctive relief and damages being awarded to the holder of the copyright.

A patent is a federally created and protected monopoly power given to inventors. If a person invents something that is new, useful, and not obvious to a person of ordinary skill in the industry, the inventor is entitled to a patent. In exchange for making the method of production public, the patent grants the inventor an exclusive right to use, make, or sell the product for 20 years (14 years for a design patent). If anyone violates this exclusive right, the patent holder can file an infringement suit. If the court upholds the patent, the infringer will be enjoined from further production and will be liable for damages to the holder of the patent.

A trademark is a mark or symbol used to identify a particular brand name or product. Copying the trademark of a competitor or using a symbol deceptively similar to that of a competitor is a violation of the Lanham Act of 1946, and the violator is subject to an injunction and the imposition of damages.

EXEMPTIONS

Labor unions are exempt from the provisions of the Sherman Act by the Norris–LaGuardia Act, passed in 1932. They are also exempt from the Clayton Act by § 6 of the Act. The exemption applies only to "labor disputes" and normal union activities.

Farm cooperatives are also exempt from antitrust coverage so long as they are engaged in the sale of farm produce. (A number of other exemptions exist, but they have little impact on business law.)

Contemporary Case

[This case is ongoing, but the challenged conduct potentially falls within the scope of § 1 of the Sherman Act.]

AMERICAN NEEDLE, INC v. NATIONAL FOOTBALL LEAGUE
2010 U.S. LEXIS 4166 (S. Ct. 2010)

FACTS The National Football League (NFL) is an unincorporated association of 32 separately owned professional football teams (also parties in this case). The teams, each of which owns its own name, colors, logo, trademarks, and related intellectual property, formed the National Football League Properties (NFLP) to develop, license, and market that property. Initially, NFLP granted nonexclusive licenses to American Needle and other vendors to manufacture and sell team-labeled apparel. In December 2000, however, the teams authorized NFLP to grant exclusive licenses. NFLP granted an exclusive license to Reebok International Ltd. to produce and sell trademarked headwear for all 32 teams. When American Needle's license was not renewed, it filed this suit alleging that the agreements between the NFLP and Reebok violated § 1 of the Sherman Act, which makes "[e]very contract, combination . . . or, conspiracy, in restraint of trade" illegal. Respondents answered that they were incapable of conspiring within § 1's meaning because the NFL and its teams are, in antitrust law jargon, a single entity with respect to the conduct challenged. The District Court granted NFLP's summary judgment, and the Seventh Circuit affirmed.

ISSUE Did the NFLP and Reebok violate § 1 of the Sherman Act when they entered into the exclusive licensing agreement?

HOLDING Perhaps. NFLP and Reebok's conduct may be covered by § 1. Accordingly, the judgment of the Court of Appeals is reversed, and the case is remanded for further proceedings consistent with this opinion.

REASONING Excerpts from the opinion of Justice Stevens:

Every contract, combination in the form of a trust or otherwise, or, conspiracy, in restraint of trade" is made illegal by § 1 of the Sherman Act . . . The question whether an arrangement is a contract, combination, or conspiracy is different from and antecedent to the question whether it unreasonably restrains trade. This case raises that antecedent question about the business of the 32 teams in the National Football League (NFL) and a corporate entity that they formed to manage their intellectual property. We conclude that the NFL's licensing activities constitute concerted action that is not categorically beyond the coverage of § 1. The legality of that concerted action must be judged under the Rule of Reason. . . .

Taken literally, the applicability of § 1 to "every contract, combination . . . or conspiracy" could be understood to cover every conceivable agreement, whether it be a group of competing firms fixing prices or a single firm's chief executive telling her subordinate how to price their company's product. But even though, "read literally," § 1 would address "the entire body of private contract," that is not what the statute means . . . Not every instance of cooperation between two people is a potential "contract, combination . . . , or conspiracy, in restraint of trade." . . .

The meaning of the term "contract, combination . . . or conspiracy" is informed by the "'basic distinction'" in the Sherman Act "'between concerted and independent action'" that distinguishes § 1 of the Sherman Act from § 2. . . . Section 1 applies only to concerted action that restrains trade. . . .

We have long held that concerted action under § 1 does not turn simply on whether the parties involved are legally distinct entities. Instead, we have eschewed such formalistic distinctions in favor of a functional consideration of how the parties involved in the alleged anticompetitive conduct actually operate.

As a result, we have repeatedly found instances in which members of a legally single entity violated § 1 when the entity was controlled by a group of competitors and served, in essence, as a vehicle for ongoing concerted activity. . . . We have similarly looked past the form of a legally "single entity" when competitors were part of professional organizations or trade groups. Conversely, there is not necessarily concerted action simply because more than one legally distinct entity is involved. Although . . . we once treated cooperation between legally separate entities as necessarily covered by § 1, we now embark on a more functional analysis. . . .

"[S]ubstance, not form, should determine whether a[n] . . . entity is capable of conspiring under § 1." . . . This inquiry is sometimes described as asking whether the alleged conspirators are a single entity. That is perhaps a misdescription, . . . because the question is not whether the defendant is a legally single entity or has a single name; nor is the question whether the parties involved "seem" like one firm or multiple firms in any metaphysical sense. The key is whether the alleged "contract, combination . . . , or conspiracy" is concerted action—that is, whether it joins together separate decisionmakers. The relevant inquiry . . . is whether there is a "contract, combination . . . or conspiracy" amongst "separate economic actors pursuing separate economic interests," . . . such that the agreement "deprives the marketplace of independent centers of decisionmaking," . . . and therefore of "diversity of entrepreneurial interests," . . . and thus of actual or potential competition. . . .

Football teams that need to cooperate are not trapped by antitrust law. "[T]he special characteristics of this industry may provide a justification" for many kinds of agreements. . . . The fact that NFL teams share an interest in making the entire league successful and profitable, and that they must cooperate in the production and scheduling of games, provides a perfectly sensible justification for making a host of collective decisions. But the conduct at issue in this case is still concerted activity under the Sherman Act that is subject to § 1 analysis.

When "restraints on competition are essential if the product is to be available at all," *per se* rules of illegality are inapplicable, and instead the restraint must be judged according to the flexible Rule of Reason. . . . And depending upon the concerted activity in question, the Rule of Reason may not require a detailed analysis; it "can sometimes be applied in the twinkling of an eye." . . .

Other features of the NFL may also save agreements amongst the teams. We have recognized, for example, "that the interest in maintaining a competitive balance" among "athletic teams is legitimate and important". . . . While that same interest applies to the teams in the NFL, it does not justify treating them as a single entity for § 1 purposes when it comes to the marketing of the teams' individually owned intellectual property. It is, however, unquestionably an interest that may well justify a variety of collective decisions made by the teams. What role it properly plays in applying the Rule of Reason to the allegations in this case is a matter to be considered on remand.

You Be the Judge

Pretty Playthings, a toy company, has a very successful line of toys, but the line is aging and the company is looking for something fresh and new to reinvigorate its product line. One of Pretty Playthings' toy designers proposes a new product that is "hipper" and "edgier" than the old line of toys, although it is within the same genre and will appeal to the same base market as the older line. However, before the company begins to produce this new line, the designer resigns, goes to work for MegaToys, a competitor, and soon thereafter MegaToys introduces the new line of toys that Pretty Playthings had been planning. This new line is an immediate hit, generating sales of over $1 billion in its first year.

Pretty Playthings has filed suit against MegaToys and the designer for various unfair trade practices. The case has been brought in your court. How will you rule? Be certain that *you* explain and justify *your* decision. [See Greg Risling, "In Federal Copyright Trial, Mattel Says Rival Stole Bratz Doll Concept," *Washington Post* (May 28, 2008).]

Summary

Since 1890, the federal government has regulated business in an attempt to ensure competition in the marketplace. This legislative effort is referred to as antitrust law. The cornerstone of antitrust law is the Sherman Act, which prohibits joint conduct that unreasonably restricts competition (§ 1), and also prohibits monopolizing or attempting to monopolize any area of trade or commerce (§ 2). Some conduct is considered so lacking in social value that it constitutes a *per se* violation. Other questionable conduct is measured under the "rule of reason." Recently a third test, the "quick look" analysis, has been developed. This allows a defendant firm to rebut the presumption of harm to competition in some of the traditional *per se* areas by showing that there is a *bona fide* reason for the conduct. If the rebuttal is found persuasive by the court, the case is decided under the rule of reason. In any case, if a violation is found, the injured parties are entitled to recover treble damages from the violators. The Sherman Act has also been amended by the Foreign Trade Antitrust Improvement Act, which attempts to restrict Sherman Act enforcement to conduct that affects domestic trade. The FTAIA exempts export trade from coverage of the Sherman Act unless the conduct has a direct and substantial impact on the domestic markets involved.

While the Sherman Act was effective in attacking conduct that reduced or eliminated competition in a number of industries, it did not suffice in *preventing* violations. The Sherman Act is remedial in

nature, only applying to a situation *after* harm has occurred. Often this harm is irreparable. As a result, Congress enacted some preventative legislation, laws designed to *prevent* economic or competitive harm before it caused irreparable injury. One of these statutes is the Clayton Act, which prohibits price discrimination, exclusive-dealing contracts and tying arrangements, some types of mergers, and interlocking directorates. The price discrimination provisions were expanded and strengthened by the enactment of the Robinson–Patman Act, and the anti-merger provisions were expanded and strengthened by the enactment of the Cellar–Kefauver Act. The purpose of the Clayton Act is to stop anticompetitive conduct "in its incipiency." In order to do this, the government can attack conduct within the regulated areas if the effect of such conduct may be to substantially lessen competition in any line of trade or commerce. Notice that the government does not have to prove that competition will be harmed; it merely must show that competition is likely to be harmed. This provides a powerful tool to the government in its antitrust campaigns.

As a means of protecting competition, Congress passed the Federal Trade Commission Act. This act has two major aspects: It created the Federal Trade Commission to act as a watchdog in the antitrust area, and it prohibits unfair and deceptive trade practices. There are numerous other unfair trade practice areas as well, but most of these are regulated under state law.

Discussion Questions

1. Section 1 of the Sherman Act is intended to protect competition by prohibiting restraints on trade. In order to apply this section, the court frequently uses the so-called "rule of reason." What is the rule of reason, and how does it affect § 1 of the Sherman Act?

2. The courts have decided that a number of actions are likely to be so anticompetitive that the conduct cannot be defended under the rule of reason analysis. These actions have been deemed *per se* violations of § 1 of the Sherman Act. What are the traditional *per se* violations? What public policy

or economic theory considerations justify treating these actions as violations *per se*?

3. Can a firm totally dominate an industry and not be guilty of monopolizing in violation of § 2 of the Sherman Act? Can a firm be found guilty of monopolizing an industry if it only controls three-quarters of the relevant market?

4. Section 2 of the Clayton Act prohibits price discrimination; however, it has been found to be less effective than originally expected. As a result, the Robinson–Patman Act was passed to supplement the provisions of § 2 of the Clayton Act. What are the major prohibitions that the Robinson–Patman Act added to § 2 of the Clayton Act?

5. What is the major difference in philosophy between the coverage of the Sherman Act and the coverage of the Clayton Act and the Federal Trade Commission Act? Which philosophy is more effective in protecting competition?

Case Problems and Writing Assignments

1. Discon, Inc. sold "removal services"—the removal of obsolete telephone equipment—through Materiel Enterprises Company, a subsidiary of NYNEX Corporation, for the use of New York Telephone Company, another subsidiary of NYNEX. Materiel Enterprises began to purchase "removal services" from AT&T Technologies rather than Discon, and Discon filed suit, alleging that the arrangement between AT&T, Materiel Enterprises, and NYNEX violated the Sherman Act. According to Discon, Materiel Enterprises paid AT&T more than Discon had charged for the same services. Materiel Enterprises then passed these higher costs on to New York Telephone, which, in turn, passed the higher costs on to consumers. (This was approved by the New York regulatory agency, which characterized the costs as approved service charges.) Discon also alleged that Materiel Enterprises received a year-end "rebate" from AT&T Technologies, and then shared this "rebate" with NYNEX. According to its complaint, Discon alleged that this conduct amounted to a prohibited group boycott, which had, in effect, driven Discon out of business. Does this conduct amount to a prohibited group boycott? Would the argument put forward by Discon be stronger if the firms were not interrelated? [See *NYNEX Corp. et al. v. Discon, Inc.*, 119 S. Ct. 493, 1998 U.S. LEXIS 8080 (1998).]

2. This case involves the market for digital subscriber line (DSL) service, which is a method of connecting to the Internet at high speeds over telephone lines. AT&T owns much of the infrastructure and facilities needed to provide DSL service in California. In particular, AT&T controls most of what is known as the "last mile"—the lines that connect homes and businesses to the telephone network. Competing DSL providers must generally obtain access to AT&T's facilities in order to serve their customers. Until recently, the Federal Communications Commission (FCC) required incumbent phone companies such as AT&T to sell transmission service to independent DSL providers, under the theory that this would spur competition. In 2005, the Commission largely abandoned this forced-sharing requirement in light of the emergence of a competitive market beyond DSL for high-speed Internet service; DSL now faces robust competition from cable companies and wireless and satellite services. As a condition for a recent merger, however, AT&T remains bound by the mandatory interconnection requirements, and is obligated to provide wholesale "DSL transport" service to independent firms at a price no greater than the retail price of AT&T's DSL service.

Linkline is an independent Internet service provider (ISP) that competes with AT&T in the retail

DSL market. It does not own all the facilities needed to supply its customers with this service, instead leasing DSL transport service from AT&T. AT&T thus participates in the DSL market at both the wholesale and retail levels; it provides plaintiff and other independent ISPs with wholesale DSL transport service, and it also sells DSL service directly to consumers at retail.

In July 2003, Linkline brought suit in District Court, alleging that AT&T violated § 2 of the Sherman Act, by monopolizing the DSL market in California. The complaint alleges that AT&T refused to deal with the plaintiffs, denied the plaintiffs access to essential facilities, and engaged in a "price squeeze." Specifically, Linkline contends that AT&T squeezed its profit margins by setting a high wholesale price for DSL transport and a low retail price for DSL Internet service. This maneuver allegedly "exclude[d] and unreasonably impede[d] competition," thus allowing AT&T to "preserve and maintain its monopoly control of DSL access to the Internet." According to Linkline, such a claim can arise when a vertically integrated firm sells inputs at wholesale and also sells finished goods or services at retail. If that firm has power in the wholesale market, it can simultaneously raise the wholesale price of inputs and cut the retail price of the finished good. This will have the effect of "squeezing" the profit margins of any competitors in the retail market. Those firms will have to pay more for the inputs they need; at the same time, they will have to cut their retail prices to match the other firm's prices. The question before us is whether such price-squeeze claim may be brought under § 2 of the Sherman Act when the defendant is under no antitrust obligation to sell the inputs to the plaintiff in the first place. How should the Court rule in this case? Is ATT&T guilty of monopolizing in violation of § 2 of the Sherman Act? [See *Pac. Bell Tel. Co. v. Linkline Communications, Inc.*, 129 S. Ct. 1109, 172 L. Ed. 2d 836, 2009 U.S. LEXIS 1635 (S. Ct. 2009)]

3. Sun Microsystems, Inc. (Sun) has filed suit against Microsoft Corp. (Microsoft), alleging

numerous claims for illegal tying, monopolization, and exclusive dealing. Sun's suit alleges that Microsoft's actions undermined the ability of Sun's Java technology to offer an alternative to the Windows operating system. Sun bases its suit, at least in part, on the finding by the U.S. Court of Appeals for the District of Columbia Circuit that Microsoft engaged in a series of illegal acts to choke off the distribution channels for the Navigator browser and Java platform.

The complaint alleges Microsoft violated the Sherman Act, §§ 1 and 2, by:

- illegally maintaining a monopoly in the Intel-compatible PC operating system market;
- illegally monopolizing the Web browser market;
- unlawfully tying the Internet Explorer browser to the Windows operating system;
- attempting to monopolize the workgroup server operating system market (workgroup servers connect to and interoperate with PCs to perform a variety of functions, including file management, printing and communications);
- illegally tying the Windows workgroup server operating system to the PC operating system; unlawfully tying its IIS Web server to the workgroup operating system (a Web server sends Web pages to client computers over the Internet or other computer network);
- unlawfully tying its .NET "middleware" platform to its PC and workgroup server operating systems;
- engaging in exclusive-dealing and other exclusionary agreements with Internet service providers, computer manufacturers, and other companies; and
- illegally monopolizing the market for office productivity suites.

The complaint seeks injunctive relief, compensatory damages, treble damages under the Sherman Act, and costs and attorneys' fees.

This case has been brought in *your* court. What must Sun show in order to establish that Microsoft is guilty of monopolizing in violation of § 2 of the Sherman Act? How will you decide this case?

[See "Sun Microsystems Files Antitrust Suit Against Microsoft," *E-Business Law Bulletin*, Antitrust, Vol. 3, No. 8, May 2002 (Andrews Publications, Inc., 2002) p. 12.

Notes

1. 15. U.S.C. § 1.
2. 221 U.S. 1 (1911)
3. *SCFC ILC, Inc. v. Visa, USA, Inc.*, 36 F.3d 958 (10th Cir. 1994).
4. *United States v. Arnold, Schwinn & Co.*, 388 U.S. 365 (1967).
5. *Albrecht v. Herald Co.*, 390 U.S. 145 (1968).
6. 441 U.S, 1 (1979).
7. 15 U.S.C. § 6(a).
8. *Carpet Group Int'l v. Oriental Rug Importers Ass'n*, 227 F.3d 62 (2000).
9. *Den Norske Stats Oljeselskap As v. Heereman VOF*, 241 F.3d 420 (2001).
10. 351 U.S. 377 (1956).
11. 221 U.S. 1 (1911).
12. "Judge Oks Microsoft's Antitrust Settlement," *Los Angeles Times*, November 2, 2002, p. 1.
13. 15 U.S.C. § 15.
14. 15 U.S.C. § 15(a).
15. List compiled from "Executive Legal Summary," a publication of *Business Laws, Inc.* (1997).
16. Ibid.
17. 340 U.S. 231 (1951).
18. *Caribe BMW, Inc. v. Bayerische Werke Aktiengesellschaft*, 19 F.3d 745 (1st Cir. 1994).
19. See, e.g., *Siegel v. Chicken Delight, Inc.*, 448 F.2d 43 (9th Cir. 1971) and *Collins v. International Dairy Queen, Inc.*, 939 F. Supp. 875 (M.D. Ga. 1996).
20. *Jefferson Parish Hospital District #2 v. Hyde*, 466 U.S. 2, 104 S. Ct. 1551 (1984).
21. *Datagate, Inc. v. Hewlett-Packard Co.*, 60 F.3d (9th Cir. 1995).

36

Consumer
Protection

Agenda

eClass plans to sell its products to customers both directly and indirectly. For direct sales, the firm is considering extending credit to some customers. The firm members would like to know what consumer protection statutes eClass needs to follow, if any, if it does extend credit to these customers. Ani, Meg, and Yousef also want to know what information they can expect to receive if they seek a credit report on prospective employees.

These and other questions are likely to arise as you study this chapter. Be prepared! You never know when the firm or one of its members will need your help or advice.

MOURNING v. FAMILY PUBLICATIONS SERVICE, INC.

411 U.S. 356, 93 S. Ct. 1652, 36 L. Ed. 2d 318, 1973 U.S. LEXIS 129 (S. Ct.)

FACTS Leila Mourning, a 73-year-old widow, entered into a five-year subscription contract to purchase four magazines from Family Publications Service, Inc. By the terms of the contract, Mourning was to pay $3.95 at the time of the contract and then make 30 monthly payments of $3.95 each. The contract form she signed contained a clause stating that the subscriptions could not be canceled and also included an acceleration clause similar to that found in many installment undertakings, providing that any default in installment payments would render the entire balance due. The contract did not recite the total purchase price of the subscriptions or the amount which remained unpaid after the initial remittance, and made no reference to service or finance charges. The total debt assumed by Ms. Mourning was $122.45; the balance due after the initial payment was $118.50.

Mourning made the initial payment, began to receive the magazines for which she had contracted, and then defaulted. Upon this default, Family Publications declared the entire balance of $118.50 due and threatened legal action. In reply, Mourning brought this suit in United States District Court, alleging that Family Publications had failed to comply with the disclosure provisions of the Truth in Lending Act, as implemented by the Federal Reserve Board in Regulation Z. She sought recovery of the statutory penalty and reimbursement for the costs of the litigation, including reasonable attorney's fees. The District Court granted summary judgment for Mourning, and Family Publications appealed.

The Fifth Circuit reversed, and the Supreme Court granted certiorari.

ISSUES Is the imposition of a mandatory disclosure requirement on all installment contracts to discourage evasions by some a violation of the Fifth Amendment? Is the imposition of a minimum penalty for nondisclosures when there are no finance charges an impermissible sanction?

HOLDINGS No to both.

REASONING Excerpts from the opinion of Chief Justice Burger:

... Section 121 of the Truth in Lending Act requires merchants who regularly extend credit, with attendant finance charges, to disclose certain contract information "to each person to whom consumer credit is extended and upon whom a finance charge is or may be imposed. ..." Failure to disclose renders the seller liable to the consumer for a penalty of twice the amount of the finance charge, but in no event less than $100 or more than $1,000. The creditor may also be assessed for the costs of the litigation, including reasonable attorney's fees ...

Passage of the Truth in Lending Act ... culminated several years of congressional study and debate ... By the time of passage, it had become abundantly clear that the use of consumer credit was expanding at an extremely rapid rate. ... Yet ... consumers remained remarkably ignorant of the nature of their credit obligations and of the costs of deferring payment. Because of the divergent, and at times fraudulent, practices by which consumers were informed of the terms of the credit extended to them, many consumers were prevented from shopping for the best terms available and, at times, were prompted to assume liabilities they could not meet. ... The Truth in

Lending Act was designed to remedy the problems which had developed. . . .

It was against this legislative background that the Federal Reserve Board promulgated regulations governing enforcement of the Truth in Lending Act. . . . The Four Installment Rule was included in the original published draft of the regulations. . . . [E]ven as to sales in which it was impossible to determine what, if any, portion of the price recompensed the creditor for deferring payment, the regulation at least required that the consumer be provided with some information which would enable him to make an informed economic choice. . . .

We see no reason to doubt the Board's conclusion that the rule will deter creditors from engaging in the conduct which the Board sought to eliminate. The burdens imposed on creditors are not severe, when measured against the evils which are avoided. . . . That some other remedial provision might be preferable is irrelevant. . . . Since the deterrent effect of the challenged rule clearly implements the objectives of the Act, respondent's contention is reduced to a claim that the rule is void because it requires disclosure by some creditors who do not charge for credit and thus need not be deterred. The fact that the regulation may affect such individuals does not impair its otherwise valid purpose. . . .

We are also unable to accept [the] argument that § 130 does not allow imposition of a civil penalty in cases where no finance charge is involved but where a regulation requiring disclosure has been violated. Section 130 provides that the penalty assessed shall be twice the amount of the finance charge imposed, but not less than $100. Since the civil penalty prescribed is modest and the prohibited conduct clearly set out in the regulation, we need not construe this section as narrowly as a criminal statute providing graver penalties, such as prison terms. . . . Finally, the Four Installment Rule does not conflict with the Fifth Amendment. . . . The rule was intended as a prophylactic measure; it does not presume that all creditors who are within its ambit assess finance charges, but, rather, imposes a disclosure requirement on all members of a defined class in order to discourage evasion by a substantial portion of that class.

The Truth in Lending Act reflects a transition in congressional policy from a philosophy of "Let the buyer beware" to one of "Let the seller disclose." By erecting a barrier between the seller and the prospective purchaser in the form of hard facts, Congress expressly sought "to . . . avoid the uninformed use of credit." . . . That the approach taken may reflect what respondent views as an undue paternalistic concern for the consumer is beside the point. The statutory scheme is within the power granted to Congress under the Commerce Clause. It is not a function of the courts to speculate as to whether the statute is unwise or whether the evils sought to be remedied could better have been regulated in some other manner.

Reversed and remanded.

INTRODUCTION

For many years, state laws regulated consumer credit activities. But the lack of uniformity among such laws, coupled with the increasing need to protect consumers from fraudulent practices, erroneous information found in credit reports, discrimination in the extension of credit, and harassing debt-collection practices has led to the enactment of numerous federal laws. Product safety also remains a significant issue for the vast majority of the American public. In this chapter, we consider the most noteworthy of these consumer protection laws.[1]

Consumer credit has become a gargantuan business in the United States and increasingly draws the attention of federal lawmakers and regulators. On a given day, we in the United States purchase 500,000 appliances, 40,000 motor vehicles, and 15,000 homes on credit.[2] The ubiquity of such credit transactions in turn has led to a giant industry involving the sale of credit reports by credit bureaus. To generate the 2 million such reports that are sold every working day, credit bureaus retain information on 90 percent of the adults in our country—some 170 million people.[3]

THE CONSUMER CREDIT PROTECTION ACT

Title I of the Consumer Credit Protection Act of 1968, more commonly known as the Truth in Lending Act (TILA), represents the landmark modern consumer protection law. After its enactment, other federal legislation followed.

TILA, in essence, is a disclosure statute designed to force creditors to inform consumers, via a standardized form and terminology, of the actual costs of credit. This information enables consumers to make more informed decisions about credit. Indeed, to comply with TILA, creditors, prior to the consummation of a credit transaction, must provide every consumer with a separate disclosure statement that satisfies the dictates of both TILA and the Federal Reserve Board (FRB), which enforces TILA. Failure to comply with TILA's disclosure provisions subjects the creditor to various civil, criminal, and statutory liabilities.

Although primarily a disclosure statute, TILA also regulates transactions in which a consumer uses his or her home as collateral for a loan (that is, for home equity or home improvement loans), with the exception of transactions involving the purchase or initial construction of a home. For situations covered by the statute, TILA allows a three-day cooling-off period, during which the consumer may decide to rescind (that is, cancel) the loan. Congress apparently wanted to allow the consumer the opportunity to reconsider any transaction that may encumber the consumer's title to his or her home. The power of rescission potentially lasts for three years from the consummation of the transaction or the sale of the property, whichever occurs first.[4]

Upon its initial enactment, TILA resulted in a great deal of litigation that benefited consumers, much to the chagrin of the lending industry. Largely in response to lobbying efforts by lenders, in 1980 Congress enacted the Truth in Lending Simplification and Reform Act, which the FRB subsequently labeled the "new" truth-in-lending act. Designed to simplify the disclosures mandated by the 1968 Act (which, according to the FRB, resulted in consumer confusion owing to the detail required), the 1980 Act makes creditor compliance easier. However, some people wonder whether providing consumers with *less* information actually furthers the law's overriding purpose of enhancing his or her ability to shop meaningfully for credit. Litigation under the new act nonetheless has decreased dramatically.

Regulation Z, prepared by the FRB, summarizes the scope of TILA, so it is important to read the statute in conjunction with this regulation. In general, Regulation Z covers persons who regularly offer or extend credit to consumers, if the credit will be used for personal, family, or household purposes and the transaction is subject to a finance charge or, by written agreement, is payable in four or more installments (the Four Installments Rule referenced in our classic case). In the initial disclosure statement, the creditor must provide detailed information in a clear and conspicuous manner and in a meaningful sequence. This information must address finance charges (including interest, time differential charges, service charges, points, loan fees, appraisal fees, and certain insurance premiums), any other charges, whether the creditor is retaining a security interest, and a statement of billing rights that, when taken together, outlines the consumer's rights and the creditor's responsibilities.

Creditors must also furnish the consumer with periodic statements that disclose various items: the previous balance, credits since the last statement, the amount of the finance charge, the annual percentage rate charged, the closing date of the billing cycle, the new balance, the address to be used for notice of billing errors, and so on. The creditor also must promptly credit consumer payments and refund credit balances.

Occasionally, a consumer may believe that his or her bill contains an error. This is also covered under Regulation Z, and should be covered in the "billing rights" section of the bill the consumer receives. In order to maximize his or her protection, the consumer must notify the creditor in writing of an alleged billing error within 60 days. (TILA and Regulation Z tell the consumer exactly how to satisfy these notification procedures.) The creditor must then notify the consumer *in writing* that it received the disputed billing information. The creditor then has up to 90 days after receiving the notice to (a) investigate the transaction giving rise to the alleged error, and then either (b) correct the disputed bill or, (c) explain *in writing* why the creditor believes the account is correct and supply copies of documented evidence of the consumer's indebtedness.

A creditor who complies with these provisions has no further obligations to the consumer, even if the consumer continues to make substantially the same allegations regarding the alleged error. Until the creditor has either corrected the dispute bill or notified the consumer that it (the creditor) believes the bill is correct, the creditor may *not*:

- try to collect the cost of the disputed item;
- close or restrict the consumer's account during the controversy, although the creditor can apply the disputed amount to the consumer's credit limit; or
- make or threaten to make an adverse report that the consumer is in arrears or that his or her bill is delinquent because of nonpayment of the disputed amount.

Any creditor who fails to comply with these provisions forfeits the amount in dispute, plus any finance charges, provided the amount does not exceed $50.

These requirements cover "open-ended" credit transactions, such as those involving credit cards (Visa, MasterCard, American Express, and so forth) or department store revolving charge accounts. [Note that if you check a credit card bill, you will notice that it sets out the information required under Regulation Z, normally on the back of the bill. Most creditors also include a toll-free number to call with billing inquiries. Remember that calling the number does *not* satisfy the requirements of TILA and Regulation Z and does *not* provide the maximum protection available.]

Regulation Z (as well as TILA) also applies to "closed-end" credit transactions, such as consumer loans from finance companies; credit purchases of cars, major appliances, and furniture; and real estate purchases. Different disclosure rules exist for closed-end transactions.

Other provisions of TILA prohibit the issuance of a credit card except in response to an oral or written request or application and limit the liability of the cardholder to $50 in cases of unauthorized use of the card if the cardholder notifies the creditor of an unauthorized use because of the loss or theft of the card. In some circumstances, a person who knowingly and fraudulently uses or traffics in counterfeit access devices (that is, credit cards, plates, codes, account numbers, or any means of account access) and during a one-year period obtains $1,000 in value as a result of this conduct, is subject to a maximum fine of not more than the greater of $100,000 or twice the value obtained by the offense or imprisonment of not more than ten years (or both).

Remedies sought by individuals for creditors' violations of TILA include actual damages and statutory damages of twice the finance charges (but not less than $100 or more than $1,000). Class actions for actual damages as well as statutory damages of an amount equal to the lesser of $500,000 or 1 percent of the creditors' net worth also are possible. Awards of attorneys' fees to successful litigants are available under the statute as well. Criminal penalties for each willful and knowing failure to make the proper disclosures required by the act include fines of not more than $5,000 and one year's imprisonment. Several agencies—the FRB and the Federal Trade Commission (FTC), for example—have responsibility for the administrative enforcement of TILA. Defenses to liability include the expiration of the one-year statute of limitations (for disclosure violations), creditor *bona fide* clerical errors, and the creditor's timely correction of an error.

THE FAIR CREDIT REPORTING ACT

Banks and other lenders, would-be secured creditors (about whom we learned in Chapters 24 and 25), landlords, insurance companies, department stores, and employers often seek information about consumers. Credit transactions are pervasive in our society, affecting most people in their domestic (and in some cases, international) lives. Virtually everyone in our country has a credit history, which seems to come as a surprise to many college students. Any person who has a credit card, a loan, a utility account in his or her name, a lease in his or her name, or any number of other transactions and/or obligations has begun to establish a credit history, and every subsequent transaction or obligation adds to that credit history. Therefore, each credit card use, phone bill payment (or non-payment), rent payment, and so forth becomes part of the credit history of the user. This credit history, in turn, is used to determine how much of a credit risk a person is when that person applies for a loan, a lease, a credit card, or any other type of credit. However, that credit history may also be used to determine whether a company should hire an applicant for a position with the firm. [A person's credit history may be a key factor in the hiring decision of some businesses, especially if the applicant is seeking a managerial job or a job that entails being bonded or handling significant amounts of money!]

Credit histories are gathered, and credit ratings are determined, by credit-reporting agencies (also called credit bureaus). Experian, TransUnion, and Equifax are the three major national credit-reporting agencies in the United States. These credit-reporting agencies summarize the information of any given person into credit (or consumer) reports and sell these reports to lenders, landlords, insurers, retailers, and employers. There are also local or regional credit bureaus that may provide information on a person's credit history, especially to local or regional businesses.

Given the statistics cited earlier, it is easy to see the importance of credit bureaus to the U.S. economy. Credit bureaus continually update the information they hold regarding consumers—by some estimates, a total of 2 billion pieces of information concerning private consumer transactions and 2 million pieces of public record information (that is, bankruptcies, tax liens, foreclosures, court judgments, and so forth) are reported each month.[5] Credit-reporting services facilitate a given consumer's access to various avenues of credit and speed up credit transactions. However, the centralization of these vast stores of information covering virtually the entire adult population has raised concerns about the accuracy of the information and the adequacy of the safeguards employed by these agencies to protect the privacy of individual consumers. At least one study reported that as many as 80 percent of the credit reports generated contained errors, although most were minor. Unfortunately, 25 percent of the reports contained major errors, errors significant enough to either prevent the applicant from getting credit or causing the applicant to receive the credit on less favorable terms than he or she should have received.[6]

Given these abuses, in 1970 Congress passed the Fair Credit Reporting Act (FCRA) as a part of the Consumer Credit Protection Act. Congress enacted the FCRA to require consumer-reporting agencies to adopt reasonable procedures for meeting the needs of commerce for consumer credit, personnel, insurance, and other information in a manner that is fair and equitable to the consumer and ensures the confidentiality, accuracy, relevancy, and proper use of such information. It applies to all persons or entities that collect information concerning a consumer's creditworthiness, credit standing, credit capacity, character, general reputation, personal characteristics, or mode of living when third parties use this information either to deny or to increase the amount charged for credit or insurance used primarily for personal, family, or household purposes.

In addition, the FCRA applies whenever such information is used for the purposes of employment, governmental benefits or licenses, insurance underwriting, or other legitimate business transactions. Credit reports and licenses issued for any other reasons require a court order or the permission of the consumer.

Interestingly, the FCRA does not apply to all such credit reports but only to those compiled by any entity that *regularly* engages in the practice of disseminating or evaluating consumer credit or other information concerning consumers for the purpose of furnishing consumer reports to third parties. Thus, the Act covers credit reports generated by credit bureaus, whose reports ordinarily set out only financial information about the consumer in question—bank accounts, charge accounts and other indebtedness, creditworthiness, marital status, occupation, income, and perhaps some nonfinancial information. The act also covers credit-reporting bureaus whose reports focus not so much on credit information of the type compiled by credit bureaus but rather involve more personal information typically gathered through interviews with neighbors, colleagues, and the like. Whether the report centers on financial matters or investigatory matters relating to a prospective employment or landlord/tenant relationship, both types of credit reports raise significant privacy issues.

In placing obligations on third-party users of credit information and those credit agencies or bureaus that report information about consumers, the FCRA attempts to protect such consumers from invasion of privacy and breach of confidentiality. It expressly obligates every consumer-reporting agency to maintain reasonable procedures designed to avoid violations of the Act. Among other things, this obligation means that such agencies must report only accurate and up-to-date information and report these data only to those persons or entities eligible to receive the information.

Unfortunately, Congress set out no test for ensuring the relevancy of the information when it enacted this legislation. Thus, while agencies must report information that is accurate and up to date, consumers have little recourse against credit bureaus and credit-reporting bureaus that report irrelevant information (for example, political beliefs or lifestyle issues) that arguably encroaches on the subject's privacy.

Besides setting out limitations on consumer-reporting agencies, the FCRA places on both reporting agencies and users certain obligations regarding the proper disclosure of the information gathered or reported. The limitations on the uses of such information discussed earlier (employment, governmental benefits or licenses, insurance underwriting, or any other legitimate business purpose) fulfill this goal, and the act requires that every consumer-reporting agency undertake reasonable procedures to verify that the users of the information use the report for only these purposes. Reasonable procedures include requiring prospective users to identify themselves and to certify the purpose for which they are seeking the information. Prospective users also must certify that they will use the information only for this—and no other—purpose.

Users of consumer reports also must satisfy certain statutory obligations. Unless the report is an investigative one concerning employment for which the consumer has not yet specifically applied, users of investigative consumer reports must notify the consumer in advance that he or she may be the subject of an investigation concerning his or her character, general reputation, personal characteristics, and mode of living. Whenever a user of a consumer report denies credit, insurance, or employment or charges a higher rate for credit or insurance and bases the denial or increase wholly or in part on the information contained in a credit report, the user must advise the consumer of the adverse action and supply the name and address of the reporting agency that compiled the report. Adverse actions involving only denial of credit or an increased charge for the extension of credit based on information obtained from persons other than a consumer-reporting agency obligate the user, upon request, to disclose to the consumer the nature (but not the source) of the information. In this latter situation, the user also must inform the consumer of his or her statutory right to learn of the information that caused the adverse decision.

Consumers' rights, in addition to the FCRA's prohibition on the use of inaccurate and outdated information, include notification of an agency's reliance on adverse information contained in consumer reports. The consumer also is entitled to limited access to any files concerning him or her, as well as the right in certain circumstances to correct erroneous information. The information that the consumer can receive from a consumer credit-reporting agency includes the nature and substance of all information (except medical information) in its files concerning the consumer, the sources of information (except for the sources of information compiled pursuant to investigative reports), and the recipients of any consumer reports that the agency has furnished concerning the consumer for employment purposes within the last two years or for *any* purpose within the six-month period preceding the request.

Note that under the FCRA the consumer cannot actually see his or her file. But once the consumer receives the information, he or she can dispute the completeness or accuracy of any information contained in the file. When the consumer directly conveys to the reporting agency such questions, the agency must investigate the information disputed by the consumer within a reasonable time, unless the agency has reasonable grounds to believe the consumer's claim is frivolous or irrelevant. If the agency's reinvestigation fails to resolve the dispute, the consumer can file a statement that sets forth the nature of the dispute. Unless it has reasonable grounds to believe the statement is frivolous or irrelevant, the agency must clearly note in any subsequent consumer report containing the disputed information that the consumer disputes the information and provide either the consumer's statement or a clear and accurate codification or summary thereof. At the request of the consumer, the agency must send a similar notice to any users that the consumer can identify as receiving a report concerning employment within the past two years, or receiving a report for any purpose within the previous six months. The statute expressly mandates that the agency clearly and conspicuously disclose to the consumer his or her right to make such a request.

The FCRA sets out civil remedies for violations of the Act. For willful failure to comply with the Act, suits for compensatory or punitive damages are possible; for violations stemming from negligent noncompliance, an injured consumer can recover only compensatory damages. In addition, for either type of violation, the injured party who successfully sues can recover court costs and attorneys' fees.

The FCRA prohibits court actions brought for defamation, invasion of privacy, or negligence with respect to the reporting of information, unless the suit involves false information furnished with malice or with a willful intent to injure the consumer. Any person who knowingly and willfully obtains information concerning a consumer under false pretenses faces a fine of $5,000 and/or one year's imprisonment.

eClass 36.1 Management

CREDIT-REPORTING AGENCIES

eClass recently fired one of its employees. Following this firing, a credit-reporting agency contacted the firm and asked questions about the former employee. Fearing possible liability for the firm under the Fair Credit Reporting Act if the information reported by the firm turns out to be inaccurate or if the agency misuses the information, Ani believes that eClass should not answer the questions. Meg does not see these reservations as legitimate concerns. Rather, Meg thinks that eClass should provide the information, especially since eClass uses this credit-reporting agency when eClass seeks information concerning prospective employees. Meg and Ani ask your opinion on this matter. What will you advise them?

BUSINESS CONSIDERATIONS　Should a business establish a policy for providing information concerning employees—or former employees—to credit-reporting agencies? What factors would affect the formation of such a policy?

ETHICAL CONSIDERATIONS　Is it ethical for a former employer to provide information about a former employee to a credit-reporting agency? How can the employer, from an ethical perspective, relate the employment performance of a person to the latter's creditworthiness?

The Federal Trade Commission (FTC) functions as the principal enforcement agency for violations of the FCRA, because the law views violations of the Act as unfair or deceptive trade practices. As such, the FTC can order various administrative remedies (such as cease-and-desist orders) against consumer-reporting agencies, users, or other persons not regulated by other federal agencies (such as the Federal Reserve Board) that themselves have enforcement authority when credit-reporting agencies and users' activities fall within these agencies' regulatory purview.

The Fair and Accurate Credit Transactions Act (FACTA)

As a further protection for consumers, in 2003 Congress passed the Fair and Accurate Credit Transactions Act (FACTA). This Act provides new rights to consumers including allowing each consumer (1) the right to a free credit report every 12 months from each of the three credit-reporting agencies; (2) the right to receive his or her credit score; and (3) the key factors used in computing that score. The three major credit reporting agencies are also required to provide a single point of contact so that a consumer can order all credit reports from all three companies with one communication—either a phone call to the toll-free number, a letter, or by use of the Internet Web site. (The Privacy Rights Clearinghouse recommends using the mail or telephone rather than the Internet.[7])

FACTA also requires the truncation of account numbers for credit cards and debit cards on a customer's receipt, using only the last five digits of the account number, preceded by a series of Xs. It also prohibits the inclusion of the expiration date for the card. These measures were included as a protection against identity theft.[8]

THE EQUAL CREDIT OPPORTUNITY ACT

When Congress first passed the Equal Credit Opportunity Act (ECOA) in 1974, it prohibited only discrimination based on sex or marital status whenever creditors extend credit. Congress at that time was responding to evidence showing that creditors denied credit to single women more often than to single men and that married, divorced, and widowed women often could not get credit in their own names. Instead, these women had to obtain credit in their husbands' names.

To broaden the protections available to low-income consumers to enable them to have access to credit comparable to the credit opportunities enjoyed by more affluent consumers, in 1976 Congress amended the statute to also prohibit discrimination based on race, religion, national origin, age (provided the applicant has the capacity to contract), receipt of public assistance benefits, and the good faith exercise of rights under the Consumer Credit Protection Act (TILA). Although part of TILA, the ECOA covers more than consumer credit transactions, it covers any creditor who deals with any applicant in any aspect of a credit transaction.

Federal Reserve Board (FRB) Regulation B (extensively revised in 1985), the implementing regulation for ECOA, broadly defines a credit transaction as involving every aspect of an applicant's dealings with a creditor regarding an application for credit or an existing extension of credit, including but not limited to:

- information requirements;
- investigation procedures;
- standards of creditworthiness;
- terms of credit;
- the furnishing of credit information, revocation, alteration, or termination of credit; and
- collection procedures.

ECOA and Regulation B exempt certain transactions, such as those made pursuant to special-purpose credit programs designed to benefit an economically disadvantaged

eClass 36.2 Finance/Management

EXTENDING CREDIT

eClass has been discussing credit sales to consumers, especially if the firm adds some hardware or other items to its product line. While Yousef and Ani realize that direct sales to consumers—often on credit terms established by the firm—probably will increase sales substantially, they also agree that some of these customers inevitably will default. To minimize the risk of default, Meg proposes that the firm should extend credit only to consumers who have a minimum family income and a minimum credit bureau rating. All other applicants would be rejected. While the three members agree that this policy sounds like a good idea, they wonder whether this proposed strategy will violate the law. If they ask for your advice, what will you tell them?

BUSINESS CONSIDERATIONS   The extension of consumer credit is likely to increase the sales of a business, but it also will increase losses because of bad debts and defaults. When eClass decides whether to provide credit to its consumer customers, what factors should the firm consider? Should a firm that decides to extend credit to consumer debtors revisit the decision periodically and reevaluate it?

ETHICAL CONSIDERATIONS   Is it ethical for a firm to decide not to extend credit to its consumer debtors, thereby possibly precluding lower-income customers from acquiring the product? Is it more ethical to provide such consumer credit, even though the firm may lose some of its profits because of defaults?

class of persons, from coverage. Partial exemptions also exist for public utility services credit transactions (for example, public utilities can ask questions about an applicant's marital status) and incidental consumer credit transactions, such as those involving physicians, hospitals, and so on.

Since creditors generally evaluate applicants' creditworthiness as a precondition of extending credit, Regulation B sets out rules that creditors must follow in making such evaluations and specifies the forms that creditors can use to ensure that they do not discriminate on any of the prohibited bases while they undertake these evaluations. In addition, ECOA requires creditors to give notice to applicants of any actions taken by the creditors concerning the applicants' requests for credit.

Creditor actions typically take three forms: approval of the application; extension of credit under different terms than those requested; or an adverse action (for example, denial of the application). Regulation B then prescribes a notification regime specifically tailored to the type of action taken. Exhibit 36.1 represents a communication that generally will satisfy these notification requirements. Creditors typically must send such a notification within 30 days of receiving a completed application.

Exhibit 36.1

Form C-2, Sample Notice of Action Taken

FORM C-2—SAMPLE NOTICE OF ACTION TAKEN AND STATEMENT OF REASONS[9]

Date Dear Applicant: Thank you for your recent application. Your request for [a loan/a credit card/an increase in your credit limit] was carefully considered, and we regret that we are unable to approve your application at this time, for the following reason(s):

Your Income: _____ is below our minimum requirement. _____ is insufficient to sustain payments on the amount of credit requested.

_____ could not be verified.

Your Employment: _____ is not of sufficient length to qualify. _____ could not be verified. *Your Credit History*: _____ of making payments on time was not satisfactory. _____ could not be verified.

Your Application: _____ lacks a sufficient number of credit references. _____ lacks acceptable types of credit references. _____ reveals that current obligations are excessive in relation to income.

Other: _____

The consumer-reporting agency contacted that provided information that influenced our decision in whole or in part was [name, address and [toll-free] telephone number of the reporting agency]. The reporting agency played no part in our decision and is unable to supply specific reasons why we have denied credit to you. You have a right under the Fair Credit Reporting Act to know the information contained in your credit file at the consumer-reporting agency. You also have a right to a free copy of your report from the reporting agency, if you request it no later than 60 days after you receive this notice. In addition, if you find that any information contained in the report you receive is inaccurate or incomplete, you have the right to dispute the matter with the reporting agency. Any questions regarding such information should be directed to [consumer-reporting agency]. If you have any questions regarding this letter, you should contact us at [creditor's name, address and telephone number].

NOTICE: The federal Equal Credit Opportunity Act prohibits creditors from discriminating against credit applicants on the basis of race, color, religion, national origin, sex, marital status, age (provided the applicant has the capacity to enter into a binding contract); because all or part of the applicant's income derives from any public assistance program; or because the applicant has in good faith exercised any right under the Consumer Credit Protection Act. The federal agency that administers compliance with this law concerning this creditor is (name and address as specified by the appropriate agency listed in Appendix A).

    Remedies under ECOA include actual damages and/or punitive damages, to a maximum of $10,000 for individual actions or a maximum of $500,000 (or 1 percent of the creditor's net worth—whichever is greater) for class actions. Equitable relief, attorneys' fees, and costs also may be granted. A two-year statute of limitations generally applies. The usual administrative remedies are available as well. The enforcement agencies can also ask the U.S. attorney general to institute civil actions against any creditor who has engaged in a pattern or practice of denying or discouraging credit applicants in violation of the Act.

THE FAIR DEBT COLLECTION PRACTICES ACT

In 1977, Congress passed the Fair Debt Collection Practices Act (FDCPA) as Title V of the Consumer Credit Protection Act (TILA). This part of TILA regulates the activities of those who collect bills owed to others (including attorneys who regularly engage in consumer debt-collection activity, even when the activity consists of litigation).[10] The Act specifically exempts from its coverage the activities of secured parties, process servers, and federal or state employees who are attempting to collect debts pursuant to the performance of their official duties. This Act only covers the conduct of debt-collection agents and agencies and does not apply to the original creditors who extended the credit.

The law was intended to eliminate abusive, deceptive, and unfair debt-collection practices and thereby to protect consumers. The Act limits the manner in which a debt collector can communicate with the debtor. For example, the statute expressly prohibits any communications made at an unusual or inconvenient time (generally before 8:00 A.M. and after 9:00 P.M. local time) at the debtor's location without the consumer debtor's consent. The debt collector cannot communicate with the debtor at the debtor's place of employment if the debt collector knows or has reason to know that the debtor's employer prohibits the consumer from receiving such communications. In addition, in most circumstances, if the debt collector knows an attorney represents the consumer with respect to the debt, the debt collector can contact only the attorney, not the debtor. A debt collector typically cannot communicate with third parties (for example, the debtor's neighbors, co-workers, or friends) concerning the collection of the debt, either.

The statute also requires the termination of further communication with the debtor if he or she notifies the debt collector in writing that he or she refuses to pay the debt and wishes all communications to stop. At that point, the debt collector can advise the consumer only of the termination of further efforts to collect the debt or of the debt collector's intention to invoke any available remedies.

Similarly, debt collectors must refrain from unfair or unconscionable means of debt collection. For example, the debt collector is prohibited from accepting post-dated checks, making collect phone calls to debtors, or adding amounts—interest, fees, or expenses—not expressly allowed by the underlying debt agreement or by state law.

So that the debtor can dispute the debt if he or she has grounds to do so, the Act requires the bill collector to send the debtor a written verification of the debt. The debtor then has 30 days in which he or she must dispute the debt in writing; otherwise, the debt collector can assume the validity of the debt.

The FTC has primary enforcement responsibilities under the FDCPA. Civil remedies of actual damages plus additional damages, not to exceed $1,000, are possible in individual suits. In class actions, $1,000 per person may be awarded; but the total damages so awarded cannot exceed the lesser of $500,000 or 1 percent of the debt collector's net worth.

Under a separate statute, a criminal penalty of $1,000 or a sentence of one year's imprisonment, or both, may be imposed on anyone who, during the course of debt-collection efforts, uses the words *federal*, *national*, or *the United States* to convey the false impression that the communication originates from, or in any way represents, the United States or any of its agencies or instrumentalities. Successful litigants may recover costs and attorneys' fees as well.

THE UNIFORM CONSUMER CREDIT CODE

The Uniform Consumer Credit Code (UCCC) was designed to replace state laws governing consumer credit. It resulted from the drafting efforts of the National Conference of Commissioners on Uniform State Laws and was meant to make the widely varying state laws concerning installment sales and loans, revolving charge accounts, home solicitation sales, home improvement loans, and truth-in-lending consistent from state to state. The drafters wished to do for consumer law what the Uniform Commercial Code had done for commercial law.

eClass 36.3 Finance/Management

CREDIT COLLECTION

Several of eClass's credit customers have fallen behind in making their credit payments; a few have even defaulted. All efforts by the firm to collect these amounts have failed, and Ani and Meg think that the firm should hire a collection agency to recover the firm's money. Yousef, preferring a low-key approach to collection, wants the firm to write to these customers and remind them of their obligation to repay the debts. The firm members all agree that they would like to recover the funds, but they remain unsure of the legal implications of various collection efforts. They ask you what they should do. What will you advise them?

BUSINESS CONSIDERATIONS   Why would a business be willing to hire a debt-collection agency to recover past due accounts? What factors should a business consider before it takes such a step?

ETHICAL CONSIDERATIONS   Is it ethical for a business to turn its debt collections over to an independent third party who was not involved in the extension of credit? Is it ethical for a firm to accept collections that the debt-collection agency may have acquired in an unethical manner?

First promulgated in 1969 and later revised in 1974, the UCCC has failed to gain wide acceptance. To date, only nine states have enacted it; and many of them have chosen to replace the UCCC's provisions with their own. Still, it represents an additional statutory attempt to benefit consumers.

THE CONSUMER PRODUCT SAFETY ACT

The Consumer Product Safety Act of 1972 established the Consumer Product Safety Commission (CPSC). An independent federal regulatory agency, the CPSC consists of five members appointed by the President with the advice and consent of the Senate. The CPSC has authority over a great number of consumer products; but products expressly excluded from the Commission's jurisdiction include tobacco and tobacco products, motor vehicles, pesticides covered under FIFRA (a statute discussed in Chapter 37), firearms and ammunition, food, and cosmetics.

To help protect the public from injuries from consumer products, the Commission can do the following:

- set and enforce safety standards;
- ban hazardous products;
- collect information on consumer-related injuries;
- administratively order firms to report publicly defects that could create substantial hazards;
- force firms to take corrective action (repair, replacement, or refund) with regard to substantially hazardous consumer products in commerce;
- seek court orders for recalls of imminently hazardous products;
- conduct research on consumer products; and
- engage in outreach educational programs for consumers, industry, and local government.

Products banned by the CPSC include certain all-terrain vehicles, unstable refuse bins, lawn darts, tris (a chemical flame-retardant found in children's apparel), products containing asbestos, and paint containing lead. Products subject to CPSC standards include matchbooks, automatic garage door openers, bicycles, cribs, rattles, disposable lighters, toys with small parts, and the like.

Contemporary Case

JERMAN v. CARLISLE, McNELLIE, RINI, KRAMER & ULRICH LPA

130 S. Ct. 1605, 176 L. Ed. 2d 519, 2010 U.S. LEXIS 3480, 22 Fla. L. Weekly Fed. S 247 (S. Ct. 2010)

FACTS Carlisle, McNellie, Rini, Kramer & Ulrich, a law firm, and one of its attorneys (hereafter Carlisle), filed a lawsuit in Ohio state court on behalf of its client, Countrywide Home Loans, Inc., a mortgage company, to foreclose a mortgage on real property owned by Karen L. Jerman. The complaint included a notice that the mortgage debt would be assumed to be valid unless Jerman disputed it in writing. Jerman's lawyer sent a letter disputing the debt, and, when the mortgage company acknowledged that the debt had in fact been paid, Carlisle withdrew the suit. Jerman then filed this action, contending that by sending the notice requiring her to dispute the debt in writing, Carlisle had violated provisions of the Fair Debt Collection Practices Act (FDSPA), specifically § 1962g(a), which governs the contents of notices to debtors. The District Court held that Carlisle had, in fact, violated the § 1692g(a) by requiring her to dispute the debt in writing, but granted Carlisle a summary judgment under the "bona fide error" defense found in § 1692(k). The Sixth Circuit affirmed the District Court's ruling, holding that the "bona fide error" defense is not limited to clerical or factual errors, but also extends to mistakes of law.

Given that there was a division of authority on this issue, the U.S. Supreme Court issued a writ of certiorari to hear the case.

ISSUE Does the "bona fide error" defense apply to errors of law?

HOLDING No. the bona fide error defense found in § 1692k(c) does not apply to a debt collector's mistaken interpretation of the law.

REASONING Excerpts from the opinion of Justice Sotomayor:

The Fair Debt Collection Practices Act (FDCPA or Act) imposes civil liability on "debt collector[s]" for certain prohibited debt collection practices. Section 813(c) of the Act . . . provides that a debt collector is not liable in an action brought under the Act if she can show "the violation was not intentional and resulted from a bona fide error notwithstanding the maintenance of procedures reasonably adapted to avoid any such error." This case presents the question whether the "bona fide error" defense . . . applies to a violation resulting from a debt collector's mistaken interpretation of the legal requirements of the FDCPA. We conclude it does not. . . .

The parties disagree about whether a "violation" resulting from a debt collector's misinterpretation of the legal requirements of the FDCPA can ever be "not intentional" . . . Jerman contends that when a debt collector intentionally commits the act giving rise to the violation (here, sending a notice that included the "in writing" language), a misunderstanding about what the Act requires cannot render the violation "not intentional," given the general rule that mistake or ignorance of law is no defense. Carlisle and the dissent, in contrast, argue that nothing in the statutory text excludes legal errors from the category of "bona fide error[s]" . . . and note that the Act refers not to an unintentional "act" but rather an unintentional "violation." The latter term, they contend, evinces Congress' intent to impose liability only when a party knows its conduct is unlawful. Carlisle urges

1161

us . . . to read § 1692k(c) to encompass "all types of error," including mistakes of law. . . .

We decline to adopt the expansive reading . . . that Carlisle proposes. We have long recognized the "common maxim, familiar to all minds, that ignorance of the law will not excuse any person, either civilly or criminally." . . . Our law is therefore no stranger to the possibility that an act may be "intentional" for purposes of civil liability, even if the actor lacked actual knowledge that her conduct violated the law. . . . Likely for this reason, when Congress has intended to provide a mistake-of-law defense to civil liability, it has often done so more explicitly than here. In particular, the FTC Act's administrative-penalty provisions . . . apply only when a debt collector acts with "actual knowledge or knowledge fairly implied on the basis of objective circumstances" that its action was "prohibited by [the FDCPA]." . . . Given the absence of similar language in § 16922(c), it is a fair inference that Congress chose to permit injured consumers to recover actual damages, costs, fees, and modest statutory damages for "intentional" conduct, including violations resulting from mistaken interpretation of the FDCPA, while reserving the more onerous penalties of the FTC Act for debt collectors whose intentional actions also reflected "knowledge fairly implied on the basis of objective circumstances" that the conduct was prohibited. . . .

Congress also did not confine liability under the FDCPA to "willful" violations, a term more often understood in the civil context to excuse mistakes of law. . . .

We draw additional support for the conclusion that bona fide errors . . . do not include mistaken interpretations of the FDCPA, from the requirement that a debt collector maintain "procedures reasonably adapted to avoid any such error." The dictionary defines "procedure" as "a series of steps followed in a regular orderly definite way." . . . In that light, the statutory phrase is more naturally read to apply to processes that have mechanical or other such "regular orderly" steps to avoid mistakes—for instance, the kind of internal controls a debt collector might adopt to ensure its employees do not communicate with consumers at the wrong time of day . . . or make false representations as to the amount of a debt. . . . We do not dispute that some entities may maintain procedures to avoid legal errors. But legal reasoning is not a mechanical or strictly linear process. For this reason, we find force in the suggestion . . . that the broad statutory requirement of procedures reasonably designed to avoid "any" bona fide error indicates that the relevant procedures are ones that help to avoid errors like clerical or factual mistakes. Such procedures are more likely to avoid error than those applicable to legal reasoning, particularly in the context of a comprehensive and complex federal statute such as the FDCPA that imposes open-ended prohibitions on, inter alia, "false, deceptive" . . . or "unfair" practices. . . .

To the extent the FDCPA imposes some constraints on a lawyer's advocacy on behalf of a client, it is hardly unique in our law. "[A]n attorney's ethical duty to advance the interests of his client is limited by an equally solemn duty to comply with the law and standards of professional conduct." . . . In sum, we do not foresee that our decision today will place unmanageable burdens on lawyers practicing in the debt collection industry. . . . Absent such a showing, arguments that the Act strikes an undesirable balance in assigning the risks of legal misinterpretation are properly addressed to Congress. . . . This Court may not . . . read more into § 1692k(c) than the statutory language naturally supports. We therefore hold that the bona fide error defense ... does not apply to a violation of the FDCPA resulting from a debt collector's incorrect interpretation of the requirements of that statute.

... [T]he judgment of the United States Court of Appeals for the Sixth Circuit is reversed, and the case is remanded for further proceedings consistent with this opinion.

It is so ordered.

You Be the Judge

A Marin County, California, woman who lost $70,000 while gambling online with 12 credit cards sued MasterCard, Visa, and the banks that had issued the credit cards. She argued that because gambling is illegal in California, the credit card companies never should have authorized her charges. She claimed that the credit card companies in effect are aiding and abetting illegal Internet gambling and making a lot of money from these activities. In a related vein, a Minneapolis attorney recently filed a class action lawsuit alleging that credit card firms' fomenting such illegal online gambling amounts to racketeering and precludes the companies from collecting on the debts (state laws oftentimes make the collection of gambling debts unenforceable). The operators of online gambling Web sites argued that the absence of laws specifically outlawing Internet gambling—only three states explicitly ban Internet gambling, although many prosecutors construe a federal law banning interstate sports betting over the telephone and state laws banning gambling in general as providing a basis for prohibiting online gambling—makes such betting legal. For the more than 800 Web sites that offer such gambling, business is booming, with revenues likely in excess of $20 billion per year. Assume you are the judge who must decide these cases. In whose favor will you hold? Why? Should a business that provides products or services that involve potentially addictive and harmful behavior take steps to protect its customers from the potentially harmful consequences if the customers' conduct becomes addictive? What responsibility does the business have to the customer or to society for the harm resulting from addictive behavior "aided and abetted" by the goods or services provided by the company to the addict? Is it ethical for a consumer credit-granting business, especially credit card companies, to provide a means for its customers to participate in addictive behavior on credit, even if such activities are legal?[11] [See Tom Lowery, "Debtors Take Credit Cards to Task for Allowing Bets," *USA Today*, August 17, 1999, p. B1; *Datamonitor*, "Bright Future for Online Gambling," July 14, 2001, http://nua.com.]

Summary

Various federal and state statutes protect consumers' rights. The Consumer Credit Protection Act of 1968, better known as the Truth in Lending Act (TILA), mandates the disclosure (via a standardized form and terminology) of the actual costs of credit to enable consumers to make more informed decisions about credit. Failure to comply with TILA's disclosure provisions (or with its implementing regulation, Regulation Z) subjects the creditor to various civil, criminal, and statutory liabilities. The Fair Credit Reporting Act of 1970 (FCRA) requires consumer-reporting agencies to adopt reasonable procedures for guaranteeing the accuracy of information disseminated in credit reports. The FCRA also limits the uses that one can make of such information. Consumers enjoy a variety of rights under the statute, including notification of an agency's reliance on adverse information and mechanisms for disputing the accuracy of information contained in files. Civil, criminal, and administrative remedies are available under the Act. The Equal Credit Opportunity Act of 1974 (ECOA) prohibits discrimination based on sex, marital status, race, religion, national origin, age (provided the applicant has the capacity to contract), receipt of public assistance benefits, and the good faith exercise of rights under TILA. Regulation B extensively implements ECOA by, among other things, setting out the rules that creditors must follow when they evaluate the credit-worthiness of any applicant and when they provide notification to the consumer of the action taken. The remedies available for violations of ECOA resemble those granted under TILA. The Fair Debt Collection Practices Act of 1974 (FDCPA) regulates the activities of debt collectors. Congress intended the law to eliminate abusive, deceptive, and unfair debt-collection practices and thereby to protect consumers. The FDCPA limits the manner in which the debt collector can communicate with the debtor and limits the third parties the debt collector can contact about the debt. Remedial awards are similar to those granted under other statutes, but the Federal Trade Commission has primary enforcement responsibilities under the FDCPA. The Uniform Consumer Credit Code represents yet another statute—this time at the state level—that protects consumers. The Consumer Product Safety Act established the Consumer Product Safety Commission (CPSC). The CSPC regulates hazardous products and can even ban those that pose imminent hazards to the public.

Discussion Questions

1. Explain the disclosures a creditor typically must make to the consumer under the Truth in Lending Act (TILA).

2. Describe the remedies available for creditors' violation of TILA.

3. Explain what Regulation B of the Equal Credit Opportunity Act (ECOA) requires of creditors for compliance.

4. Outline the general requirements of the Fair Debt Collection Practices Act (FDCPA).

5. Set out the civil and criminal penalties that can result from violations of the FDCPA.

Case Problems and Writing Assignments

1. In 1994, Gregory Hawthorne opened a checking account at a Washington, D.C., branch of Citicorp Data Systems, Inc. (Citibank). Three years later, Hawthorne withdrew all the funds from his Citibank account before moving from Washington, D.C., to New York City. In December 1997, Citibank sent him an invoice alleging an overdraft balance of $2,600 on his Washington, D.C., account. After comparing his records with the Citibank charges, Hawthorne discovered that he owed less than claimed by Citibank. He wrote to Citibank on May 8, 1998, detailed the discrepancies, and enclosed a check for the amount that his records indicated was owed. Citibank did not respond to Hawthorne's claim of a discrepancy. Instead, Citibank sent him numerous computer-generated letters demanding payment and, at various times, threatened either "collection action," legal action, or referral of the matter to a credit-reporting bureau. Hawthorne tried numerous times, by phone and by letter, to explain to Citibank the nature of his dispute. Citibank neither cleared up the matter over the phone nor indicated in any letter to Hawthorne that it acknowledged that a discrepancy might exist. On January 17, 2001, Hawthorne purchased his credit report from Experian, a leading credit-reporting bureau. That report included an entry from Citibank indicating that Hawthorne was more than 60 days in arrears. On February 14, 2001, Hawthorne wrote to three of the largest credit reporting agencies (Experian, TransUnion, and Equifax) and disputed Citibank's report against his account. On February 26, 2001, Hawthorne received from a director of executive communications at Citibank a letter (the first non-form one) indicating that Citibank could not find any discrepancies in his account, that he currently owed a balance of $2,167.97, and that Citibank might be unable to resolve disputes involving statements that are three or four years old. In April 2001, when Hawthorne sought a home mortgage loan, only one lender offered Hawthorne a loan; and four days before the closing, that lender demanded an additional .875 percent on the interest rate. Hawthorne alleged that the lack of lending options and the lender's last-minute interest rate hike had resulted from Citibank's report to the credit-reporting agencies that Hawthorne was a "bad debt." Further, Hawthorne claimed that the difficulty he had experienced in obtaining a mortgage served as evidence that the Citibank discrepancy continued to have a negative, ongoing effect on his credit. Section 1681i(a)(2) of the FCRA provides in relevant part that when "a consumer reporting agency receives notice of a dispute from any consumer . . . the agency shall provide notification of the dispute to any person who provided any item of information in dispute. . . ." Section 1681i(a)(2) further states that "the consumer reporting agency shall promptly provide to the person who provided the information in dispute all relevant information regarding the dispute that is received by the agency from the consumer. . . ." Among other things, the FCRA creates a private right of action by which consumers may bring suit for damages against "any person" who violates or fails to comply with "any requirement imposed" under Section 1681. As defined in § 1681a, the term "person" means "any individual, partnership, corporation, . . . association, government or governmental subdivision or agency, or other entity." Would the FCRA allow a consumer like Hawthorne to sue a furnisher of information such as Citibank for damages? [See *Hawthorne v. Citicorp Data Systems, Inc.*, 216 F. Supp. 2d 45 (2002).]

2. Johnson paid for merchandise at a 7-Eleven with a check for $2.64. The check bounced and was referred to the defendant lawyer, whose firm specializes in collecting dishonored checks. Utah law permits a service charge on dishonored checks as long as the charge does not exceed $15. The state's shoplifting statute, on the other hand, imposes civil liability on an "adult who wrongfully takes merchandise by any means" in the amount of the retail price of the item plus "an additional penalty" of up to $500, with costs and attorneys' fees. The defendant demanded payment for the value of the check plus a statutory penalty of $250. The plaintiff paid the defendant $17.64 (the value of the check plus the $15 service charge), which he accepted. The plaintiff then sued under the FDCPA on the grounds that the statute prohibits a debt collector from using "unfair or unconscionable means to collect or attempt to collect any debt," which is defined in Section 1692f(1) as the collection of any amount "unless such amount is expressly authorized by the agreement creating the debt or permitted by law." Had the attorney violated the FDCPA? [See *Johnson v. Riddle*, 305 F.3d 1107 (10th Cir. 2002).]

3. In 1999, Congress enacted the Gramm-Leach-Bliley Act (GBLA) so as to enhance competition in the financial services industry, by eliminating many federal and state law barriers to affiliations among banks and securities firms, insurance companies, and other financial providers. Title V of the GLBA contains a number of provisions designed to protect the privacy of "nonpublic personal information" (NPI) that consumers provide to financial institutions, thereby reflecting the congressional policy that each financial institution has an affirmative and continuing obligation to respect the privacy of its customers and to protect the security and confidentiality of those customers' nonpublic personal information. Accordingly, by requiring that the financial institution provide the consumer with notice of the institution's disclosure policies and the opportunity for the consumer to "opt out" of disclosure, the GLBA restricts the ability of a "financial institution" to disclose NPI to a nonaffiliated third party. The GLBA further mandates that an unaffiliated third party recipient of NPI "shall not, directly or through an affiliate of such receiving third party, disclose such information to any other person that is a nonaffiliated third party of both the financial institution and such receiving third party, unless such disclosure would be lawful if made directly to such other person by the financial institution." To implement its disclosure restrictions, the GLBA gives the FTC and other agencies broad rulemaking authority to promulgate such regulations as may be necessary to carry out the purposes of the Act with respect to the financial institutions subject to their jurisdiction. TransUnion, LLC, a "credit-reporting agency" (CRA) under the FCRA, challenged the regulations promulgated by the FTC and other federal agencies to implement the privacy provisions of the GLBA. TransUnion contended that the regulations unlawfully restrict a CRA's ability to disclose and reuse certain consumer information because (1) a CRA is not a "financial institution" subject to the FTC's rulemaking authority under the GLBA; (2) the regulations' definition of the statutory term "personally identifiable financial information" (PIFI) is overbroad; (3) the regulations' restrictions on the reuse of information are inconsistent with the GLBA; and (4) the challenged regulations infringe TransUnion's right of free speech under the First Amendment. If this case were in your court, how would you rule? [See *TransUnion, LLC v. FTC*, 295 F.3d 42 (2002).]

Notes

1. See, e.g., Jonathan Sheldon ed., *Fair Credit Reporting Act*, 3d ed. (Boston: National Consumer Law Center, 1994). This and other National Consumer Law Center publications, such as Ernest L. Sarason ed., *Truth in Lending* (1986); Gerry Azzata ed., *Equal Credit Opportunity Act* (1988); and the annual cumulative supplements to these works provide more detailed information on consumer law, as does Gene A. Marsh, *Consumer Protection Law in a Nutshell* (St. Paul, MN: West Group, 1999) and Howard J. Alperin & Ronald F. Chase, *Consumer Law: Sales Practices and Credit Regulation* (Minneapolis, MN: West Publishing Co., 1986).

2. Jonathan Sheldon ed., *Fair Credit Reporting Act*, 3d ed. (Boston: National Consumer Law Center, 1994), p. 31.
3. Ibid.
4. *Beach v. Ocwen Federal Bank*, 523 U.S. 410 (1998).
5. Jonathan Sheldon, supra note 2, p. 32.
6. Candace Heckman, "Study assails accuracy of credit reports," *Seattle Post-Intelligencer* (June 21, 2004).
7. "Fact Sheet 6a: Facts on FACTA, The Fair and Accurate Credit Transactions Act," at http://www.privacyrights. org/fs/fs6a-facta.htm.
8. Ibid.
9. FDIC Sample form, at http://www.fdic.gov/regulations/laws/ rules/6500-2900.html7#fdic6500appendixctopart202.
10. *Heintz v. Jenkins*, 514 U.S. 291, 299 (1995).
11. Some of the facts and figures in this question are now out of date. Congress passed a law attempting to regulate internet gambling in 2006, the Unlawful Internet Gambling Enforcement Act, but in 2010 Congress is considering a bill to legalize and tax Internet gambling.

37

Environmental Protection

Agenda

Initially eClass will be a regional firm, but as it grows eClass plans to sell its software nationally, with the hope that someday it can be sold internationally. As the firm grows it will likely need distribution centers at various locations throughout the country. While some buyers will want to download the software, others will want to purchase a CD-ROM containing the program, which will require packaging and shipping, although some direct deliveries may also be used. The firm wants to make certain that any packing materials used are stored and disposed of properly and that any vehicles it uses for deliveries or other business-related purposes are environmentally friendly. The entrepreneurs are concerned about the differing state environmental protection standards and whether these differing standards will force the company to adapt location-specific responses to such laws for any or all of their distribution centers. The firm members want each community to view eClass as a "good neighbor," and they want to know what they must do to meet this objective in each community in which the firm operates a facility. They have decided to develop a company policy to ensure that the firm will make every effort to "go green" at all of its locations. Ani, Meg and Yousef also want to ensure that the firm meets or exceeds all federal and state environmental standards and expectations in every location. They also want to avoid dealing with any suppliers or carriers that are not recognized as environmentally friendly businesses. In pursuing these objectives they will need to decide what constitutes "green," or environmentally friendly, business practices.

These and other questions are likely to arise as you study this chapter. Be prepared! You never know when the firm or one of its members will need your help or advice.

Classic Case

COOK v. CITY of DU QUOIN
256 Ill. App. 452, 1930 Ill. App. LEXIS 50
(Ill. App. 4th Dist. 1930)

FACTS Cook (appellee) is the owner of a farm with improvements thereon used as a residence by Cook and his family; Du Quoin (appellant), a city of 10,000 inhabitants, constructed a sewer system, the main outlet of which is into Reese Creek on the outskirts of the city. Reese Creek is a natural watercourse, flowing through Cook's premises. When he acquired his farm, Reese Creek was suitable for watering stock. As a result of the emptying of sewage into Reese Creek, the creek has become contaminated and polluted so that it can be no longer used by Cook. Noxious odors are continually emitted from the stream which flows within a few yards of his dwelling and as a result he has been deprived of the comforts and enjoyment of his home and his health and that of his family are greatly endangered. This condition has existed for more than five years prior to the filing of the suit and he has suffered damages.

Du Quoin denied the material allegations and alleged that if the water in the creek had become polluted it was caused by other towns and villages discharging sewage into the creek.

ISSUE Did the City of Du Quoin create and maintain a continuing nuisance to the detriment of Cook?

HOLDING Yes. The evidence established that the city was responsible for the nuisance.

REASONING Excerpts from the opinion of Justice Newhall:

. . . The evidence shows that [Cook] moved upon the premises in question about the year 1920 and occupied the same with his family as a home; that the creek is about 40 yards from his house and three miles upstream was located the packing plant of the Du Quoin Packing Company; that the City of Du Quoin has about 10,000 inhabitants and some time prior to 1920 had constructed a sewer system, with a septic tank located above the packing plant and discharged the sewage through a tile sewer into a ditch leading to Reese Creek.

For some years after appellee moved onto his premises he used the water in the creek for watering stock, but for five years prior to the filing of the bill he had been unable to use it for that purpose; that by reason of the stream being used for a sewage outlet, the stream had become contaminated and noxious odors arose therefrom, particularly in the summertime. At times the family had to leave the home, being unable to sleep, and the odors were such as to render the members of the family sick; that the water in the stream was filled with sediment, sewage, and other deleterious elements which killed the fish in the stream and rendered the water unfit for farm uses. . . .

It is the right of every owner of land over which a stream of water flows, to have it flow in its natural state and with its quality unaffected. It is a part of the freehold, of which the owner cannot be disseized except by due process of law, and the pollution of a stream constitutes the taking of property, which may not be done without compensation. . . .

Appellant did not attempt to offer any evidence which would refute that of appellee, but the only offered proof . . . that other sources . . . may have been responsible for contributing to the pollution of Reese Creek. . . . Though other wrongful acts than that of the . . . city may have been responsible for the collection of this objectionable sewage, such fact furnishes no defense to the . . . city, if it in fact contributed to the nuisance complained of and participated in the pollution of the water that caused injury to appellee. . . .

Where the acts of several persons, although separate and distinct as to time and place, culminate in producing a public nuisance, which injures the person or property of another, they are jointly and severally liable. . . .

No claim was made in the bill, or proofs, as to permanent damage to appellee's real estate and the jury were instructed that the measure of damages was compensation for physical discomfort and deprivation of the comfortable enjoyment of a home, and it is clearly evident that the chancellor allowed compensation to appellee based upon this theory.

Where the injury is physical discomfort and results in deprivation of the comfortable enjoyment of a home, the measure of damages is not the depreciation in the rental value of the premises but compensation for such physical discomfort and deprivation of the use and comforts of home and is to be determined by the sound judgment, experience and discretion of the court or jury that may be called to determine such question in view of the facts in each particular case. . . .

After careful review of the record we are of the opinion that the decree of the court below is supported by the evidence and that the court did not err in its rulings, and that said decree should be affirmed.

INTRODUCTION

We all would like to have clean air, clean and safe water, and land that is neither polluted nor covered with litter or waste. Most of us would also like to avoid exposure to an unduly noisy environment and would like to see efforts to sustain a clean, safe, and healthy environment. There is widespread agreement that our "carbon footprint" needs to be reduced in order to sustain—and even to improve—the environment, so there is a great deal of emphasis on going "green" as a necessary step in doing so. At the same time, most people want continued access to—and availability of—a multitude of goods and services. Few people today, if given the choice, would want to be totally self-sufficient or to try to adapt to life without the goods, the services, or the technological devices and advances of modern life. Unfortunately, these "benefits" of modern life have a cost, and that cost is often "paid" by the environment. As a result environmental protection has become a very important topic in the recent past, and its importance can be expected to grow for the foreseeable future.

Environmental protection and its related laws constitute an extremely complex and controversial area of the law. The statutes and regulations are highly technical and laden with acronyms. Given the technical nature of the area, the somewhat unique terminology that is used, and the plethora of statutes and regulations covering the various areas, understanding environmental law poses a genuine challenge to students and legal practitioners alike. A thorough coverage of the material is well beyond the scope of this text. However, we are able to provide a broad overview of the topic and we will discuss some of the major principles and goals of this area.[1]

The environment has taken a great deal of abuse, both inside and outside of the United States. However, it is possible that the tide is beginning to turn. Environmental issues are viewed as increasingly important, and there is a growing national and international effort to reverse some of the harm that has been done to the environment.

In the United States environmental protection is predominantly accomplished by statute, with most of the statutory provisions being federal laws. State laws can be used to complement the federal laws, but not to override them. Thus, for example, we have "California emissions controls" on cars that are to be sold in California and various state laws regulating fuels, as well as "bottle laws" in at least ten states.

Many of the early environmental protection statutes were based to a significant extent on common law nuisance principles, primarily by prohibiting uses or conduct that interfered with the rights of others. While nuisance principles did provide a framework for some of the initial provisions, the sheer size and complexity of the environmental issues we face today require more than protection from "nuisances" or similar problems. As a result, the statutory and regulatory coverage today tends to be very technical and scientific.

COMMON LAW ACTIONS

The common law recognized that certain conduct unreasonably interfered with the occupancy, use and enjoyment of property, and allowed the persons whose rights were thus interfered with to seek remedies. One such action was a suit alleging *nuisance*. For example, if a new factory was constructed in an area, and that factory produced smoke or soot or a stench that interfered with the rights of homeowners in the area, those homeowners could file a suit against the factory on the basis of nuisance. The court would then have to weigh the benefits the community might derive from the factory's continued operation against the loss of use and enjoyment of the homeowners, deciding whether to shut down the factory (or at least order it to reduce or eliminate the nuisance-causing factor, if possible), or to award damages to the homeowners for the decrease in their property value due to the presence of the factory. While the benefits from the factory might well be sufficient to outweigh the cost to the homeowners, other nuisances would not. Thus, a neighbor who does not maintain adequate sanitation on his or her property might be ordered to clean up the property; a neighbor who decided to begin raising goats, pigs, or chickens—each of which brings an "exotic ambience" to the neighborhood—might be forced to stop such activities due to the negative impact the activities would have on the neighbors. [NOTE: if a "nuisance activity" comes to a neighborhood, the neighbors may be able to seek remedies; if a person moves to a neighborhood that already has such "nuisance activity" he or she cannot successfully seek remedies due to the presence of the activity.] The availability of remedies for a nuisance work well locally, but they do not address the bigger problem of environmental protection for the region, the state, or the nation.

Another common law cause of action could be brought for *negligence* where a person or a business breached a duty of care to others in the community. A factory that did not provide adequate ventilation in its building, causing harm to its employees, could be sued for negligence. A private party who recklessly sprayed an herbicide in his or her yard, with the herbicide being blown into a neighbor's yard and destroying a garden might also be sued for negligence. Again, the available remedies for the negligence might work well locally or for a relative few, but they do not address the bigger problem of environmental protection.

In some instances, a business or an individual might even be held liable under strict liability theories for harm caused while engaged in ultrahazardous activities or imminently dangerous activities, such as blasting. The common law provides remedies for the individuals harmed by such activities even if the actor exercised due care and there is no showing of negligence on his or her part. And once again, such remedies may work well locally, but they will not address the larger issues. A more broad-based approach is needed if the environment is to be protected on a larger scale.

THE NATIONAL ENVIRONMENTAL POLICY ACT

The National Environmental Policy Act of 1969 (NEPA) was intended "To declare a national policy which will encourage productive and enjoyable harmony between man and his environment; to promote efforts which will prevent or eliminate damage to the environment and biosphere and stimulate the health and welfare of man; to enrich the understanding of the ecological systems and natural resources important to the Nation. . . ."[2]

Section 101 of NEPA declares that it is the federal government's continuing responsibility, in cooperation with state and local governments and other concerned private and public organizations, to use all practicable means, consistent with other essential national policy considerations, to attain the broadest range of beneficial uses of the environment (including the preservation of healthy and aesthetically and culturally pleasing surroundings) while at the same time avoiding the degradation of the environment, risks to health and safety, and other undesirable or unintended consequences. In fulfilling this purpose, NEPA directs that, to the fullest extent possible, all agencies of the federal government shall live up to these environmental responsibilities.

THE ENVIRONMENTAL PROTECTION AGENCY

The primary responsibility for enforcing the various environmental protection statutes, and for enacting regulations to help in such enforcement, lies with the Environmental Protection Agency (EPA) an administrative agency. The EPA was established by executive order in 1970, and was given the power to enforce environmental laws, adopt regulations, conduct research on pollution, and assist other governmental entities concerned with the environment. To enforce federal environmental laws, the EPA can subject suspected violators to administrative orders and civil penalties and can refer criminal matters to the Department of Justice.

The laws Congress passes and the EPA enforces consider the economic aspects of environmental law; take a technological approach to environmental concerns; mandate risk assessment in the implementation of these laws; and use the imposition of liability, sometimes even strict liability, as a "hammer" to ensure compliance. Early legislation required compliance primarily by business and industry, especially the chemical industry. In the last thirty-plus years, however, small businesses and state and local governments increasingly have borne the burden of environmental compliance costs.

ENVIRONMENTAL IMPACT STATEMENT

All of these responsibilities listed in § 101 of NEPA sound overwhelming. How can the provisions of the statute possibly be carried out? These goals and responsibilities under NEPA are satisfied, or at least addressed, primarily by requiring virtually all federal agencies to prepare a detailed environmental impact statement (EIS) whenever the agency proposes legislation, recommends any actions, or undertakes any activities that *may* affect the environment. Among other things, an EIS must:

- Describe the anticipated impact that the proposed action will have on the environment

- Describe any unavoidable adverse consequences of the action or activity
- Examine the possible alternative methods of achieving the desired goals
- Distinguish between long-term and short-term environmental effects
- Describe the irreversible and irretrievable commitments of resources that will occur if the proposed action is implemented

The statute requires wide dissemination of EISs in draft form to other federal, state, and local agencies, as well as the President.

Once an EIS is prepared, the public has 30 days to review the statement and to submit any comments or observations to the EPA. The EPA will then consider any comments it receives and issue an order as to whether the project should proceed. The order issued by the EPA can be challenged by an appeal to the U.S. Court of Appeals. (If a positive recommendation of the EPA is challenged, the EIS can be used as evidence to support the EPA's decision.)

A number of states[3] have also enacted their own state-oriented environmental policy legislation (SEPA), often called "mini-NEPAs," in order to allow the state to address issues that are seen as problems in the particular state. These "mini-NEPA" statutes operate in conjunction with the NEPA standards and often impose higher standards for the given state than the standards imposed nationally by NEPA.

AIR POLLUTION

Concerns with air pollution, and the desire for clean air have been at the forefront of our environmental protection efforts since the enactment of the Air Pollution Control Act of 1955.[4] This was followed by the Clean Air Act of 1963,[5] which has been expanded by amendments numerous times The original aim of the law was to control air pollution at its source, which was generally viewed as stationary and local. Thus, these first statutes were designed to provide federal assistance to the states in their own efforts to combat air pollution. It quickly became apparent that this initial effort was inadequate, and subsequent acts and amendments broadened the regulatory scope, setting new standards for mobile pollution sources (i.e., motor vehicles) and, in subsequent amendments, addressing the issues of air quality and hazardous pollutants.

(A listing of the various acts addressing clean air can be found on the web site resources for this chapter.)

Stationary Sources

Stationary sources of air pollution, so-called "smokestack pollution," have long been recognized as detrimental to air quality, especially in those areas near to the stationary source. Factories, oil refineries, and public utilities are all major sources of air pollution. So, too, are homes, schools, and non-manufacturing commercial sites. The Clean Air

Act recognizes that state and local governments should take the initiative in regulating this area, subject to the air quality standards established by the EPA.

The EPA was directed to establish two kinds of air quality standards: (1) primary standards that, in the judgment of the administrator and allowing for an adequate margin of safety, are necessary in order to protect the public health; and (2) secondary standards that, in the judgment of the administrator, are necessary to protect the public welfare—crops, livestock, buildings, and the like—from any known or anticipated adverse effects associated with the presence of such air pollutants. After these standards are established, each state must submit an implementation plan detailing how the state proposes to implement and maintain the standards. Before the EPA administrator can approve a state implementation plan, the plan must provide for establishing procedures necessary to monitor and control ambient air quality and include a program providing for the enforcement of emissions regulations. The plan must provide for the attainment of primary standards "as expeditiously as practicable" but in no case later than three years from the date the administrator approves the plan. The state must also attain secondary standards within a "reasonable time."

Mobile Sources

Air pollution does not arise solely from "smokestack sources." Motor vehicles of all types also produce pollutants that affect air quality, more so in some areas than in others. Automobiles, buses, airplanes, motorcycles, and even lawn mowers and tractors are mobile sources of air pollution. Beginning with the move to unleaded gasoline in 1975, and inclusion of catalytic converters on automobiles beginning in 1975 and becoming standard by the early 1980's, the EPA has sought methods for reducing harmful exhaust emissions in motor vehicles. Today ethanol is a standard gasoline additive, and gasoline with a higher blend of ethanol[6] (giving a higher oxygen content) must be sold in forty-one U.S. cities that have serious smog problems. In the nation's most polluting cities service stations must sell even cleaner-burning gasoline.

Congress also established fuel mileage requirements for motor vehicles in 1975 with its introduction of Corporate Average Fuel Economy, or CAFÉ, standards. Each automobile manufacturer is required to meet the CAFÉ standards for its *fleet* of vehicles, with the vehicles categorized by size and style, with the standard based on average miles per gallon based on the performance of randomly selected cars and trucks on a standardized driving model. (For 2010 cars are required to achieve an average of 27.5 mpg and the combination of cars and light trucks must achieve an average of 23.5 mpg.[7]) In May 2009, President Barack Obama announced plans for a new fuel economy and greenhouse gas standard that would significantly change this area of the law. His plan calls for average of 39 mpg for cars and 30 mpg for trucks by 2016 and would set a national standard on greenhouse gas emissions by motor vehicles for the first time.[8] (California passed a landmark law restricting the greenhouse gas emissions from motor vehicle tailpipes in 2002, but the EPA denied California's request to implement the law.)

Hazardous Pollutants

The 1990 amendment to the Clean Air Act addressed, among other things, the issue of *hazardous pollutants*. It identified 188 specific pollutants (the original list has been modified several times) that are either known to cause, or can reasonably be expected to cause, adverse effects on human health or on the environment. These "adverse effects" are generally irreversible, and include cancer, neurological injuries, and reproductive harm. The federal government establishes National Emissions Standards for hazardous air pollutants that are issued to limit the release of specified hazardous air pollutants, but these standards are not based on health risk considerations. Instead, these standards are "technology-based," meaning that they represent the best available control technology an industrial sector could afford. While the level of emissions allowed under the law has not been determined to be safe for the public, such emissions are limited to the greatest extent possible through the application of a standard known as MACT—The Maximum Achievable Control Technology.

Penalties for Violations

Violators of the Clean Act face a number of possible penalties. The EPA can assess "administrative penalties" of up to $25,000 per day for violations of the emission standards, with fines of up to $5,000 per day possible for violations of other aspects of the law, such as failure to keep adequate records. In addition, criminal actions can be brought by the U.S. Attorney General, with potential fines of up to $1,000,000 for each violation and/or imprisonment of up to 15 years in cases where one knowingly releases hazardous air pollutants into the ambient air. In setting civil penalties, the administrator or the courts may take into account the size of the business, the economic impact of the penalty on the business, the violator's full compliance history and good faith efforts to comply, the duration and seriousness of the violation, and so forth. In addition to any actions taken by the EPA or the U.S. Attorney General, private citizens can file suit against firms suspected of violating the Clean Air Act. Those citizens who mount successful suits may receive attorneys' fees and recoup their court costs, as well as having the courts enforce the provisions of the statutes.

WATER POLLUTION

Water, like air, is essential to human life. In addition, water provides a means of transportation, especially commercial transportation, that is of significant national interest, both commercially and in the area of national defense. As a result the interstate or international navigable waters of the United States are subject to exclusive federal jurisdiction.

eClass 37.1 Manufacturing/Management

WHAT SORT OF VEHICLES SHOULD THE FIRM PURCHASE?

The firm has just opened a distribution and delivery center in Massachusetts and plans to buy at least two vehicles for use by the staff in making deliveries. Yousef has recommended that they buy high-mileage diesel automobiles, but Meg thinks that Massachusetts is one of the states that prohibits the use of diesels. She would prefer to have them purchase hybrids, or even electric cars. The firm does not want to violate Massachusetts state law, nor does it want to buy any vehicles that are not environmentally friendly. The firm also wants to take steps to minimize any pollution that might be attached to the firm, however tangentially. The principals ask you what they should do in this situation. What advice will you give them?

BUSINESS CONSIDERATIONS   Can a business be too concerned about environmental issues, at the expense of efficiency? How can a firm get "ahead of the game" on environmental issues, being a leader rather than a follower, while also remaining competitive and profitable? What factors would influence such a decision?

ETHICAL CONSIDERATIONS   Is it ethical for a business to do less than the law requires in the area of environmental protection if the business in so doing is meeting the existing legal requirements and industry standards? Is it ethical for a business to decide to exceed legal requirements and industry standards in order to be more environmentally protective, if doing so will reduce net income and therefore cost the shareholders?

The federal government began regulating water use in 1889 when it passed the Rivers and Harbors Act[9], the oldest federal environmental law in U.S. history. The Act makes it a misdemeanor to discharge any refuse into any navigable waters or tributaries of the United States without a permit. It also made it a misdemeanor to excavate, fill, or alter the course or condition of any port, harbor, or channel covered under the act without a permit. (The Act is still valid today, although some of the regulations now fall under the Clean Water Act.) Today the Clean Water Act covers navigable waters, drinking water, wetlands, and ocean dumping, in addition to the coverage of Rivers and Harbors under the original statute.

Navigable Waters

Building from the Rivers and Harbors Act, Congress passed the Federal Water Pollution Control Act[10] in 1948 in an effort to regulate and control water pollution.

Various amendments to this act comprise what we now refer to as the Clean Water Act. The Clean Water Act has three main goals:

1. To make the nation's waters safe for swimming and recreational use;
2. To protect all varieties of wildlife that rely on the waters; and
3. To eliminate the dumping or discharge of pollutants into the waters.

Municipal and industrial parties who wish to discharge any pollutants into any navigable waterways must seek a permit from the government before doing so, and they must use the "best available technology" to control the pollutants and their effects on the waterways.

The EPA has broad regulatory powers under the Clean Water Act. It is authorized to establish water pollution standards for *point sources* of water pollution, and to require any such point sources to maintain records and monitoring equipment, to keep samples of those pollutants discharged into the waterways, and to otherwise adhere to the standards established. (Point sources of water solution are stationary sources such as factories and plants, municipal waste treatment facilities, and public utilities.)

While the Clean Water Act allows for the discharge of some pollutants into the navigable waterways, it specifically prohibits thermal pollution, the discharge of heated waters into those same waterways. Thermal pollution decreases the oxygen level in the water, causing harm to fish and wildlife. This type of discharge is strictly regulated and monitored by the EPA.

Drinking Water

The Safe Drinking Water Act[11] of 1974 authorized the EPA to establish a set of national drinking water standards that set the minimum acceptable quality of water to be used for human consumption. Public water systems must use the best available technology that is feasible, both economically and technologically, in satisfying the EPA's standards. Suppliers of public drinking water must also provide an annual statement to each of its household consumers that lists the source of the water, the level of contaminants found in the water, and possible health hazards presented by the contaminants found in the water.

The statute specifically prohibits the dumping of waste into wells used for drinking water. Such waste will obviously affect the water from that particular well, and may reach the water tables and from there enter into one of more sources of public drinking water. The EPA is also concerned about other underground pollutants that can leak or seep into the water tables and eventually could contaminate public drinking waters. Leakage from landfills, runoffs from agricultural lands that contain pesticides, seepage from underground storage tanks and facilities, and other potential pollution sources can affect drinking water. To date no solution has been found for this problem.

Wetlands

Wetlands are defined by the EPA as "those areas that are inundated or saturated by surface or ground water at a frequency and duration sufficient to support, and that under normal circumstances do support, a prevalence of vegetation typically adapted for life in saturated soil conditions. Wetlands generally include swamps, marshes, bogs and similar areas."[12] The Clean Water Act forbids the filling or dredging of wetlands without a permit issued by the U.S. Army Corps of Engineers, which is authorized to adopt regulations to protect the wetlands.

Ocean Dumping

Congress passed the Marine Protection, Research, and Sanctuaries Act,[13] more commonly known as the Ocean Dumping Act, in 1972. This act regulates the dumping of *any* materials into ocean waters, and it specifically prohibits the dumping of radioactive wastes and radiological, chemical, or biological warfare agents.

In 1990 Congress passed the Oil Pollution Act,[14] a rather prompt reaction to the Exxon Valdez oil spill in Alaska in 1989, at the time the worst oil spill/disaster in U.S. history. More than 10 million gallons of crude oil were spilled into the Prince William Sound, the damage to the wildlife in the region was incalculable, and the cost of the clean-up exceeded $1.3 billion! In an effort to avoid such oil spills or leaks in the future, the act established new design standards for ships operating in U.S. waters. These new standards mandate that new ocean-going tankers must be of a double-hulled construction unless or until the U.S. Coast Guard approves a superior design to protect against oil spills.[15] Single-hulled tankers must be phased out by 2010. (It was estimated in 1992 that these new standards might increase the cost of shipping oil to the U.S. by as much as $2 billion per year.[16]) It also imposes liability on ship owners whose ships discharge oil in any manner in U.S. waters.

The 2010 Deepwater Horizon oil spill, also known as the BP oil spill, is the largest oil spill in history. Its impact is not yet known, and it may be years before the final tally is complete. However, its impact is already being felt from a regulatory perspective. A moratorium on off-shore drilling was imposed almost immediately, new inspection standards for off-shore oil rigs were imposed, and Congressional actions are expected after further investigation of the cause of the disaster and its impact are assessed.

Penalties for Violations

Violations of the Clean Water Act can result in civil and/or criminal penalties. The civil penalties run from $10,000 to $25,000 per day, depending on the type of violation. Criminal penalties, which can only be imposed for intentional violations of the Act, range from a fine of $2500 per day and possible imprisonment for up to one year to fines of up to $1 million dollars and imprisonment for up to fifteen years.

Violations of the Ocean Dumping Act can result in a civil penalty of up to $50,000, while knowingly violating the act is a criminal penalty carrying a fine of up to $50,000 and possible incarceration for up to one year.

Violations of the Oil Pollution Act potentially carry the most significant penalties: civil liability of $1000 per barrel of oil spilled or $25,000 per day and the party responsible for the oil spill is responsible for all the costs of the clean-up, to a maximum of $1 billion.[17] [In June 2010 British Petroleum agreed to create a $20 billion "spill response fund" to cover at least some of the costs of the 2010 spill in the Gulf of Mexico.[18]]

NOISE POLLUTION

Probably owing to the fact that noise seems less noxious to us than filthy water or foul-smelling air, Congress did not address the issue of noise until 1965 when it passed the federal Noise Control Act. Prior to that time, litigants seeking remedies to limit the increasingly higher decibel levels caused by post-World War II urbanization and mechanization relied on common law nuisance theories. The Noise Control Act established a national policy to promote an environment for all Americans free from noise that jeopardizes their health and welfare.

In 1972 Congress amended the law by passing the Noise Control Act of 1972,[19] hoping to "promote an environment for all Americans free from noise that jeopardizes health or welfare."[20] The 1972 amendments also created the Office of Noise Abatement and Control (ONAC) within the EPA and charged it with overseeing noise-abatement activities and coordinating its programs with those of other federal agencies. (The ONAC was terminated in 1981.)

In 1978 Congress passed the Quiet Communities Act, an amendment to the Noise Pollution Act, to reinforce the significant role that state and local governments play in noise control. The amendments provide federal financial and technical assistance aimed at facilitating state and local research related to noise control and developing noise abatement plans. Similar to the remedies we have seen in other statutes, civil and criminal penalties are possible for violations of the Noise Control Act, as are citizens' suits.

LAND CONSERVATION AND POLLUTION

The protection and preservation of land constitute the most obvious areas of federal environmental regulation. As early as the presidency of Theodore Roosevelt, concern for protecting the environment and preserving America's natural resources surfaced in the United States. The *public domain*, defined as land owned and/or controlled by the federal government, includes nearly 677 million acres. To put that in perspective, federally controlled land, national parks, and wildlife refuges in the United States occupy about as much land as the subcontinent of India does. Each state also owns and/or controls land within its borders, adding significantly to the total acreage that is government-owned. In an effort to protect and preserve the land, whether in the public domain, owned by one of the states, or owned privately, the federal government has enacted a number of statutes. Several of the more important ones are discussed below.

Toxic Substances

The Toxic Substances Control Act (TSCA), passed by Congress in 1976, represents the first statutory enactment that comprehensively addresses toxic chemicals and their impact on health and the environment. The Act authorizes the EPA to study chemicals, and to either ban the chemicals or limit their use, if such conduct is required to protect public health and/or the environment.

Under the terms of the Act, chemicals are classified as either "existing" or "new," and the emphasis of the law is to ensure that "new" chemicals are properly tested and approved by the EPA prior to their release. The manufacturer of a new chemical must provide the EPA with specific test data 90 days prior to the planned introduction of the chemical. The EPA then determines what regulations are needed in regard to the chemical. The EPA may request additional information and can ban production or distribution until such data is supplied.

The Act permits the EPA to require special labeling, to limit the use, to establish production quotas, or even to ban chemicals. Manufacturers of regulated chemicals are required to keep careful and detailed records of their production and distribution of the chemicals.

The EPA is expected to balance health and environmental issues on the one hand with economic considerations on the other. In effect, the agency is only to issue regulations covering any particular chemical or chemical compound when there is an *unreasonable* risk to health and/or the environment—and there is not an accepted definition of what constitutes a *reasonable* risk. This restriction, combined with the cost of testing and the regular introduction of new chemical compounds, makes the Toxic Substances Control Act very difficult to apply. Making matters worse for the agency, private citizens have the right to sue the EPA for any alleged failures to follow the TSCA or to properly apply its standards.

Sprays, chemicals, and other devices used for eradicating insects, fungi, or rodents have a valid and valuable purpose. They are also quite often toxic substances, with potentially serious consequences to unintended targets. By 1947 the use of pesticides and insecticides had become prevalent, and such use was recognized as posing a potential threat to the environment. In response to this concern, Congress passed the Federal Insecticide, Fungicide, and Rodenticide Act (FIFRA). This early version of FIFRA mandated the registration of "economic poisons [pesticides] involved in interstate commerce and the inclusion of labels, warnings, and instructions on such pesticides."

In 1970 the EPA, which had just been established, took over the enforcement of FIFRA (it had been administered by the Department of Agriculture prior to 1970). In 1972 Congress amended FIFRA when it passed the Federal Environmental Pesticide Control Act, changing the focus of regulation in this area from the accuracy of labeling to recognizing and addressing concerns for the environment. Under the amended Act all persons who distribute or sell pesticides must register them with the EPA. Before the EPA will approve the registration, however, it must determine that the pesticide will not generally cause unreasonable adverse effects on the environment when it is used properly. The EPA registration of an approved pesticide can designate that the pesticide is for general use or for a restricted use, such as a use only by exterminators. The EPA can also cancel or suspend the registration of any pesticide whenever such action is necessary to prevent an imminent hazard.

Although FIFRA is at heart a risk-assessment statute, the amendments to the Act make it clear that in determining "unreasonable adverse effects on the environment" the EPA must take into account the benefits, as well as the costs, associated with the use of the pesticide. It is possible, then, for the EPA to register an economically beneficial pesticide even though it might pose harm to health or the environment.

Hazardous Waste Disposal

Waste disposal has the potential to cause significant harm to health and to the environment. Some of the waste contains toxic chemicals, but the disposal of such chemicals is not covered by the Toxic Substances Control Act. Even the waste that does not contain any toxic chemicals can cause environmental harms, ranging from merely being eyesores to serving as a breeding ground for various types of vermin.

The Resource Conservation and Recovery Act was passed by Congress in 1976 to address the growing concern over waste disposal in general, and toxic waste disposal in particular. The EPA was charged with monitoring this area, which includes the handling of toxic waste and solid waste. (So-called "solid waste" includes, in reality, liquids, gases, sludges, and semisolids as well as solid waste. The disposal of solid waste involves landfill use and regulation.) The objectives of the Act include:

- ■ Protecting human health and the environment from the potential hazards of waste disposal
- ■ Conserving energy and natural resources
- ■ Reducing the amount of waste generated
- ■ Ensuring that wastes are managed in an environmentally sound manner

In carrying out its charge, the EPA is to determine which types of waste are hazardous and then to develop regulations to monitor and control the disposal of these hazardous wastes. Treatment of hazardous waste is covered by Subtitle C of the Act, commonly referred to as the "Cradle to Grave" system. Subtitle C imposes stringent bookkeeping and reporting requirements on generators, transporters, and operators of treatment, storage and disposal facilities handling hazardous waste. In other words, the wastes are monitored from creation (cradle) to final disposal (grave) under the (hopefully) watchful eye of the EPA.

The landfill of today has replaced the "town dump" of yesteryear. Under the provisions of the law, landfills generally are well-engineered facilities that are located, operated, and designed to protect the environment from contaminants which may be present in the solid waste stream. In addition, many new landfills are now collecting potentially harmful landfill gas emissions and converting the gas into energy.

Congress passed the *Comprehensive Environmental Response, Compensation, and Liability Act* (CERCLA), better known as the "Superfund," in 1980. Congress intended to fill in the gaps in the treatment of hazardous waste with this statute by regulating hazardous waste disposal sites. CERCLA authorizes the EPA to regulate "hazardous substances," which, when released into the environment, may present substantial danger to the public health or welfare, or the environment. (NOTE: The act specifically excludes petroleum and natural gas from its definition of hazardous substances.) The purpose of this "Superfund" is to finance the clean-up of hazardous waste disposal sites when the responsible party or parties cannot be found. However, if the responsible party (referred to in the statute as a potentially responsible party, or PRP) can be found, he or she faces *strict liability* If there are multiple PRPs, they face *joint and several liability* for the clean-up expenses. PRPs include any and all of the following:

1. The person who generated the waste disposed of at the site;
2. The person who transported the waste to the site;
3. The person who owned or operated the property at the time of disposal; and
4. The current owner or operator of the property.

Any PRP who is held liable can bring a "contribution action" against any other persons who are, or potentially might be, liable for his or her percentage contribution of the costs incurred.

Penalties for Violations

The Toxic Substances Control Act is essentially a monitoring and licensing statute. Violations of the Act, however, carry the potential for fines of up to $27,500 per day. It should also be kept in mind that private citizens can file suit against the EPA for its failure to carry out its duties under this Act.

It is a violation of FIRFA to sell any pesticide or herbicide that is unregistered, or to sell either if the registration has been suspended or revoked. It is also a violation to sell a pesticide or herbicide that is mislabeled or one on which the label has been destroyed. Any commercial dealer found in violation faces a fine of up to $25,000 and incarceration for up to one year. Private users who violate these regulations face a fine of up to $1,000 and up to 30 days in jail for each offense.

Any company found in violation of the Resource Conservation and Recovery Act is subject to a civil fine of up to $25,000 per violation. Criminal penalties call for fines of up to $50,000 per day, imprisonment for up to two years, or both.

eClass 37.2 **Management/Ethics**

PURCHASING A POSSIBLE WASTE SITE

Given the robustness of the sales of the firm's products, eClass is considering the purchase of a site for the firm's headquarters. Yousef has learned of a site that seems advantageous, a former convenience store location that is within reasonable commuting distance from each of the principals' homes. However, when Yousef mentions this location to the others, Ani reminds him that the convenience store that once operated there also sold gas to its customers, and the underground gas storage tanks may still be on the property. Hence, she expresses some apprehensions about buying the property without investigating the potential liability these storage tanks may create. Despite Ani's concerns, Yousef wants to move forward quickly before another potential buyer shows an interest in the property. Out of deference for Ani's judgment, however, Yousef calls you for advice. How will you respond to him after he explains the circumstances to you?

BUSINESS CONSIDERATIONS   When a firm decides to purchase property, why should it concern itself with the possibility of earlier pollution on the site? Explain whether such environmental issues should rank high or low on the firm's priorities as it contemplates the acquisition of a given parcel.

ETHICAL CONSIDERATIONS   Is it ethical for a firm to ignore the possibility that a parcel of land is polluted and thus take a "wait-and-see" attitude regarding this possibility? Or will a firm that tries to emulate admirable ethics be more proactive in such circumstances?

Liability for violations of CERCLA is, basically, the cost of cleaning up the site. Remember, though, that the statute imposes strict liability and that the liability is joint and several for any and all potential responsible parties, up to a maximum of $50 million. If the action leading the situation is deemed to be willful conduct or willful negligence, the $50 million cap does not apply.

Brownfields Legislation

Given the potential liability that can be imposed under CERCLA, many urban areas have been left virtually abandoned. Many developers preferred to expand outward from the city's center, developing new areas while leaving "derelict land" behind and increasing urban sprawl. In response to this problem, in 2001 Congress passed the Small Business Liability Relief and Brownfields Revitalization Act, which President Bush signed into law on January 11, 2002. This Act, an amendment to CERCLA, encourages the redevelopment of "brownfields" by reducing the potential liability under CERCLA and by providing funding for the assessment and clean-up of these "brownfields."

Brownfields are defined as "real property, the expansion, redevelopment, or reuse of which may be complicated by the presence or potential presence of a hazardous substance, pollutant, or contaminant."[21] However, cleaning these properties and reinvesting in them is good for the economy and for the environment. Such use can reduce blight while also reducing pressure on greenspaces and working land.[22] The Act "promotes the cleanup and redevelopment of brownfields sites through policies, laws, and initiatives that explore sector-based solutions, enhance environmental quality, spur economic development, and revitalize communities."[23] The Act exempts certain contributors from potential CERCLA liability, and supports state and tribal response programs in clean-up efforts, expands the activities that qualify for funding of State programs, and provides Superfund liability relief for certain properties cleaned up under State programs.[24]

Under the Act the EPA awards grants to communities, non-profit organizations, workforce investment boards, and academic institutions for job training programs intended to lead to cleaning up these contaminated sites and turning them into productive assets within the community.

WILDLIFE CONSERVATION

Section 7 of the Endangered Species Act of 1973 requires every federal agency, in consultation with the secretary of the interior, to ensure that no agency action is likely to jeopardize the continued existence of an endangered or threatened species or result in the destruction or adverse modification of any critical habitat of such species. Congress enacted this legislation, the world's first attempt to protect wildlife in a comprehensive manner, so as to prevent the extinction of various animals and plants. (According to scientific estimates, the world loses approximately 100 species per day.[25])

Since 1973, the ESA has helped bring about the stabilization or the improvement of the conditions of about 300 threatened or endangered species, including the national symbol of the U.S., the bald eagle.[26] But the impact of the statute reaches beyond the borders of the United States because its prohibitions concerning the international trading of wildlife and its protection of the American habitats of migrating birds affect transnational interests.

The national commitment to protecting species and their habitats invokes more than mere sentimentality or altruism—fully 40 percent of all ingredients in prescription medicines (including digitalis and penicillin) derive from plants, animals, and micro-organisms.[27] This means that the loss of any given species may involve the loss of the medicinal capacity to save thousands of lives.

There are different degrees of violations provided in the Endangered Species Act. The most punishable offenses are for trafficking (smuggling of an endangered species) or any act of knowingly "taking," including the harming, wounding, or killing of an endangered species. The criminal penalties for such violations call for a maximum fine of up to $50,000, imprisonment for one year, or both. Civil penalties of up to $25,000 per violation, may be assessed. No penalty can be imposed, however, if the accused can establish that the act was done in self-defense. No criminal penalties can be imposed for the accidental killing of an endangered species while performing farming or ranching duties.

SUSTAINABILITY

Sustainability embodies "stewardship" and "design with nature," well established goals of the design professions and "carrying capacity," a highly developed modeling technique used by scientists and planners.[28]

The most popular definition of sustainability can be traced to a 1987 UN conference. It defined sustainable developments as those that "meet present needs without compromising the ability of future generations to meet their needs." Robert Gillman, editor of the *In Context* magazine, extends this goal oriented definition by stating "sustainability refers to a very old and simple concept (The Golden Rule)... do onto future generations as you would have them do onto you." [29]

Sustainability has become a "hot topic" on college campuses and across industrial lines as the fears of global warming and the renewed interest in environmental protection take root across society.

GOING "GREEN"

Time magazine now runs a weekly news column addressing environmental issues. Exxon recently announced a $600 million partnership with the biotech company Synthetic Genomics Inc. to develop fuel from algae.[30] The public is being asked to change from the traditional incandescent light bulb to compact fluorescent bulbs to save energy and money. There appears to be a movement in the U.S. for people and business to "go green." What does this movement imply for the future?

INTERNATIONAL CONSIDERATIONS

Environmental regulation is not only on the rise in the United States, but around the world as well. While some European countries—Germany and the Netherlands, for example—have traditionally undertaken regulatory efforts that rival those of the United States, in many other countries environmental laws are nonexistent or, at best, embryonic. The environmental contamination and degradation found in post-Communist Eastern European countries, besides providing telling examples of what

eClass 37.3 Marketing/Management

ENVIRONMENTAL CONCERNS vs. CUSTOMER PREFERENCES

The firm received a sales report recently stating that slightly less than 80 percent of the eClass customers are downloading the program, with slightly more than 20 percent opting to order the CD-ROM version. This caused Meg to raise an interesting argument about their sales. Meg would prefer to see the business no longer offer the program on CD-ROM for environmental protection reasons. She points out that each diskette is produced from polycarbon plastic and is coated on one side with a thin aluminum layer. By buying these diskettes, the firm is using a polycarbon plastic, which leaves a "carbon footprint" and harms the environment. In addition, the diskette must be packaged and mailed, requiring the use of packing materials and motor vehicles to make each delivery. She would like to see eClass make every viable effort to be as "green" as possible, and she believes that only providing the program via download would be less expensive, more environmentally aware, and better for the firm's image. Ani points out that they use recycled packaging materials, they purchase the diskettes from a reputable company, and deliveries are made by the U.S. Postal Service, so the firm is not adding to the use of motor vehicles in its deliveries. In an effort to avoid a disagreement that might escalate into something more serious, they have asked you for your opinion. What will you tell them? In formulating your answer, consider how far a business should go in trying to be environmentally active.

BUSINESS CONSIDERATIONS   Should an environmentally active firm try to force its customers to "go green"? When does "environmentally active" become "environmentally obsessed"?

ETHICAL CONSIDERTIONS   Is concern for the environment more of a legal question, a business questions, or an ethics question? How much should the environmental attitude of the principals of a business affect the environmental posture of the business?

results from lax environmental standards, have discouraged much-needed privatization and foreign investments.

Realizing the need for environmental oversight and modeling its efforts on U.S. legislation, the European Union (EU) has adopted the Eco-audit Management and Audit Scheme Regulation that mandates environmental registers at each plant to catalog pollution emissions, land contamination, and the like; public disclosure of such environmental statements; and external verification of the company's environmental management system. Recently enacted environmental laws covering products now regulate product features (such as shape and recyclability), labeling, packaging, hazardous chemicals, and waste (its generation, trans-boundary shipment, etc.).[31] These laws also ban certain products such as asbestos, heavy metals, and vinyl chloride.

Closer to home, the passage of the North American Free Trade Agreement (NAFTA) also shows sensitivity to environmental concerns. A subsequent environmental side agreement between the United States and Mexico attempts to address the degradation of the environment along the U.S.-Mexican border.

The EPA is working to implement the Montreal Protocol on Substances that Deplete the Ozone Layer, a treaty to which the U.S. is a signatory nation. As part of its efforts, the EPA will establish and enforce rules aimed at controlling the production and emission of ozone-depleting compounds and at identifying safer alternatives that reduce depletion. The Uruguay Round of the General Agreement on Tariffs and Trade (GATT) included a discussion of environmental issues.

The Kyoto Protocol, an international agreement linked to the United Nations Framework Convention on Climate Change, is designed to reduce greenhouse gas emissions. The protocol sets binding targets for the reduction of these emissions for thirty-seven industrialized nations and the European Community. The initial goal of the protocol is for industrialized countries to reduce their combined greenhouse gas emissions by at least 5.2 percent compared to 1990 levels by 2008-2012. It went into effect in 2005 when Russia ratified the protocol, giving the necessary ratification by at least 55 nations, with those nations producing at least 55 percent of the global production of greenhouse gases. To date 184 nations have now ratified the Kyoto Protocol. The United States, the world's largest producer of greenhouse gas emissions, is *not* one of the ratifying nations.

Contemporary Case

[This case, decided by a 5-4 vote of the Justices, points to the concern and the uncertainty surrounding issues of global warming / climate change and the problems the EPA will undoubtedly confront in the future.]

MASSACHUSETTS v. ENVIRONMENTAL PROTECTION AGENCY

549 U.S. 497, 2007 U.S. LEXIS 3785 (S. Ct. 2007)

FACTS A number of private organizations petitioned the Environmental Protection Agency (EPA) to begin regulating the emission of four "greenhouse gases," including carbon dioxide, under § 202(a)(1) of the Clean Air Act in response to the problem of global warming. The EPA denied the petition, alleging that it did not have the authority to issue mandatory regulations in order to address global climate change. It further alleged that it would be unwise to issue such regulations at this time because no causal link between greenhouse gases and global warning has been conclusively established.

The private organizations, joined by groups of states and local governments, sought review of the EPA's order. The Court of Appeals determined that the petitioning parties lacked standing to bring their suit, and also determined that the EPA had properly exercised its discretion in concluding that regulation of greenhouse gas emissions from motor vehicles was not warranted.

ISSUES Did the petitioners have standing to bring suit? Had the EPA properly exercised its discretion in this case?

HOLDINGS Yes, the petitioners had standing. They alleged that they had already suffered harm, and would continue to do so if action was not taken. No. The EPA's action was arbitrary, capricious, or otherwise not in accordance with law because it offered no reasoned explanation for its refusal to decide whether greenhouse gases caused or contributed to climate change.

REASONING Excerpts from the opinion of Justice Stevens:

Article III of the Constitution limits federal-court jurisdiction to "Cases" and "Controversies." Those two words confine "the business of federal courts to questions presented in an adversary context and in a form historically viewed as capable of resolution through the judicial process." ... It is therefore familiar learning that no justiciable "controversy" exists when parties seek adjudication of a political question ... or when the question sought to be adjudicated has been mooted by subsequent developments. ... This case suffers from none of these defects.

The parties' dispute turns on the proper construction of a congressional statute, a question eminently suitable to resolution in federal court. Congress has moreover authorized this type of challenge to EPA action. ... EPA maintains that because greenhouse gas emissions inflict widespread harm, the doctrine of standing presents an insuperable jurisdictional obstacle. We do not agree. At bottom, "the gist of the question of standing" is whether petitioners have "such a personal stake in the outcome of the controversy as to assure that concrete adverseness which

sharpens the presentation of issues upon which the court so largely depends for illumination." ... Only one of the petitioners needs to have standing to permit us to consider the petition for review. ... We stress here ... the special position and interest of Massachusetts. It is of considerable relevance that the party seeking review here is a sovereign State and not ... a private individual. ...

The scope of our review of the merits of the statutory issues is narrow. As we have repeated time and again, an agency has broad discretion to choose how best to marshal its limited resources and personnel to carry out its delegated responsibilities. ... That discretion is at its height when the agency decides not to bring an enforcement action. ... Some debate remains, however, as to the rigor with which we review an agency's denial of a petition for rulemaking.

There are key differences between a denial of a petition for rulemaking and an agency's decision not to initiate an enforcement action. ... In contrast to nonenforcement decisions, agency refusals to initiate rulemaking "are less frequent, more apt to involve legal as opposed to factual analysis, and subject to special formalities, including a public explanation." ... They ... arise out of denials of petitions for rulemaking which (at least in the circumstances here) the affected party had an undoubted procedural right to file. ... Refusals to promulgate rules are ... susceptible to judicial review, though such review is "extremely limited" and "highly deferential." ...

EPA concluded in its denial of the petition for rulemaking that it lacked authority ... to regulate new vehicle emissions because carbon dioxide is not an "air pollutant" as that term is defined. ... In the alternative, it concluded that even if it possessed authority, it would decline to do so because regulation would conflict with other administration priorities. ... The statutory text forecloses EPA's reading. The Clean Air Act's sweeping definition of "air pollutant" includes "*any* air pollution agent or combination of such agents, including *any* physical, chemical . . . substance or matter which is emitted into or otherwise enters the ambient air. . . ." On its face, the definition embraces all airborne compounds of whatever stripe, and underscores that intent through the repeated use of the word "any." . . . The statute is unambiguous. . . .

The alternative basis for EPA's decision—that even if it does have statutory authority to regulate greenhouse gases, it would be unwise to do so at this time—rests on reasoning divorced from the statutory text. While the statute does condition the exercise of EPA's authority on its formation of a "judgment," . . . that judgment must relate to whether an air pollutant "cause[s],

or contribute[s] to, air pollution which may reasonably be anticipated to endanger public health or welfare," . . . [T]he use of the word "judgment" is not a roving license to ignore the statutory text. It is . . . a direction to exercise discretion within defined statutory limits. . . .

EPA has refused to comply with this clear statutory command. Instead, it has offered a laundry list of reasons not to regulate. . . . EPA has offered no reasoned explanation for its refusal to decide whether greenhouse gases cause or contribute to climate change. Its action was therefore "arbitrary, capricious, . . . or otherwise not in accordance with law." . . . The judgment of the Court of Appeals is reversed, and the case is remanded for further proceedings consistent with this opinion.

You Be the Judge

The American Bird Conservancy claimed that the Federal Communication Commission failed to comply with the requirements of the National Environmental Policy Act (NEPA), the Endangered Species Act (ESA), and the Migratory Bird Treaty Act (MBTA) when it erected communication towers in the Gulf Coast region without preparing an environmental impact statement. According to the various environmental groups, including the American Bird Conservancy, communications towers killed between 4 and 50 million birds per year, a significant number of them "migratory birds." The number of bird deaths allegedly caused by communication towers constituted a "sufficient environmental effect to warrant" action by the FCC. Industry members and the FCC asserted that the number of bird deaths caused by colliding with the towers was significantly overstated and did not constitute a hazard to avian life. The FCC also contended that the erection of communication towers fell within a "categorically excluded" class of federal actions that did not require the preparation of an environmental impact statement, and that it had therefore done nothing in violation of NEPA, the ESA, or the MBTA. However, a provision of NEPA requires agencies falling within the "categorical exclusion" to provide for "extraordinary circumstances in which a normally excluded action may have a significant environmental effect."

The issue to be resolved is whether there is sufficient evidence to establish that the erection of these towers "may have a significant environmental impact, requiring the completion of an environmental assessment, or even an environmental impact statement, prior to the erection of any additional towers.

This case has been brought in *your* court. How will *you* decide? What is the most important factor affecting your decision?

[See *American Bird Conservancy, Inc. v. Federal Communication Commission*, 516 F.3d 1027, 380 U.S. App. D.C. 102 (D.C. Cir. 2008).

Summary

The National Environmental Policy Act of 1969 mandates that virtually all federal agencies prepare detailed Environmental Impact Statements whenever any agency undertakes any activities that may affect the environment.

The Clean Air Act, enacted in 1963 and amended subsequently, takes a technology-forcing approach to air pollution. It directs the EPA to establish national ambient air quality standards and state implementation plans that set out how each state proposes to implement and maintain those standards. The 1990 amendments attack urban air pollution brought on by motor vehicle emissions, toxic pollutants, and acid rain. Among other things, beyond controlling emissions from mobile sources, these amendments set up a permit process aimed at minimizing emissions from major point sources. Civil, criminal, and administrative actions (including citizens' suits) are possible for violations of the act.

The Clean Water Act sets out an extensive program for preventing, reducing, and eliminating water pollution. States must comply with EPA-mandated standards designed to ensure the maintenance of desirable water quality standards. The Act takes an especially stringent approach to toxic pollutants such as asbestos, mercury, lead, PCBs, and so forth. The penalties imposed for violations of this Act resemble those set out in the Clean Air Act.

The Safe Drinking Water Act of 1974 regulates the water supplied by public water systems to home taps. This act uses EPA-issued national primary drinking water regulations that have as their goal the reduction of contaminant levels in drinking water.

The Noise Control Act of 1972 leaves to the federal government control over noise sources that require national uniformity of treatment or protection of the public health and welfare with an adequate margin of safety. Otherwise, the primary responsibility for controlling noise lies with state and local governments.

The Toxic Substances Control Act of 1976, by giving authority to the EPA to regulate chemicals before they come onto the market, screens pollutants before humans and the environment are exposed to the effects of these substances. The congressional mandate requiring the testing and regulation only of chemicals that pose an "unreasonable risk" of injury to health or the environment has undercut the statute's worthy goals.

The Federal Insecticide, Fungicide, and Rodenticide Act of 1947 mandates the registration of all insecticides and pesticides with the EPA. The EPA will register only those products that, when used in accordance with widespread and common practice, will not generally cause adverse effects on the environment. The EPA also can cancel the registration of any pesticide that fails to live up to this standard and can suspend a registration whenever it is necessary to prevent an imminent hazard. Civil and criminal penalties, as well as EPA "stop sale" or seizure orders, are available under the FIFRA.

The Resource Conservation and Recovery Act of 1976 requires the EPA to regulate nonhazardous solid waste, typically through approved state management plans. The EPA's "cradle-to-grave" regulation of hazardous waste involves a permit/manifest system that covers those who own or operate treatment, storage, or disposal facilities. Under this Act the EPA enjoys broad enforcement powers. Anyone involved in the handling, transport, storage, or disposal of solid or hazardous waste that presents an immediate and substantial endangerment to health or the environment faces the imposition of strict liability.

The Comprehensive Environmental Response, Compensation, and Liability Act (or "Superfund") regulates hazardous waste disposal sites. CERCLA authorizes cleanups of hazardous waste sites and makes generators, owners, operators, and transporters of hazardous wastes strictly liable for cleanup costs. CERCLA also establishes a "Superfund" to finance cleanups whenever the government cannot identify the parties responsible for the damage.

The Endangered Species Act of 1973 attempts to conserve endangered or threatened species of plants and animals by protecting the critical habitats of wildlife, International efforts to improve the environment in this and other nations are on the rise and therefore bear watching.

Discussion Questions

1. When does an agency need to prepare an environmental impact statement (EIS), and what must this statement contain? Be certain to address both issues fully.

2. Explain how the Clean Air Act has addressed the problem of air pollution from its initial enactment in 1963 through its amendments in the 1990s. What caused the change in emphasis over time?

3. How does the Safe Drinking Water Act differ from the Clean Water Act? Why did Congress decide to treat these as separate topics?

4. Describe some of the international aspects of environmental law. Does international environmental law tend to parallel U.S. environmental law, or is international law more rigorous?

5. April 20, 2010 saw the collapse of the of a BP offshore oil rig in the Gulf of Mexico, leading to the largest oil spill in U.S. history. The site released millions of gallons of oil into the Gulf, threatening the coastlines of at least five states and causing untold—and possible unmeasurable—environmental harm. The clean-up is likely to take years. In the interim, the environmental and economic impact will be immense. BP was initially allowed to take action to try to stop the leak, with Coast Guard supervision. Should the government have allowed a private company to control the initial attempts to stop the leak, or should the government have taken control immediately? What safeguards for off-shore oil exploration and drilling are likely to be implemented as a result of this ecological disaster?

Case Problems and Writing Assignments

1. Dow Chemical Company (Dow), while under the control of and at the direction of the federal government, operated a plant that produced synthetic rubber during World War II. The need for rubber during the war effort was critical. Hence, the government, even though it did not manufacture the product, owned the site and all the equipment and materials, knew what the manufacturer was doing, had unfettered control over all the manufacturing activities and approved of them, had an agency relationship that would ordinarily require it to indemnify the manufacturer for its actions, and had made an express written promise to hold the manufacturer harmless for what it did during the war effort. When Cadillac Fairview/California, a land developer, sued Dow and the government for damages to cover the expenses of investigating the soil pollution that had resulted from the wartime production of rubber, Dow counterclaimed for indemnity and contribution under the CERCLA. In deciding the case, the district court found for the plaintiff and allocated 100 percent of the remediation expenses to the government. Did the district court abuse its discretion in placing all the response costs on the government? [See *Cadillac Fairview/ California v. Dow Chemical Company*, 299 F. 3d 1019 (9th Cir. 2002).]

2. Power Engineering Company (PEC) has operated a metal refinishing and chrome electroplating business in Denver, Colorado, since 1968. Each month PEC produces over 1000 kilograms of waste, including arsenic, lead, mercury, and chromium. This waste is covered by the Resource Conservation and Recovery Act and is defined as a "hazardous waste." After the Colorado Department of Public Health and Environment learned of a discharge of hexavalent chromium into the Platte River, it conducted inspections of PEC and discovered that chromium emanating from PEC was the source of this groundwater contamination. The agency also found that PEC had treated, stored, and disposed of hazardous wastes without a permit. The Colorado Department issued a notice of violation in June 1993 and again in July 1994. The Colorado Department issued a final administrative compliance order on June 13, 1996, requiring PEC to comply with hazardous waste laws, to implement a cleanup plan for the chromium-contaminated soil, to conduct frequent

inspections, and to submit periodic reports. When PEC failed to comply with this order, the Colorado Department, on December 23, 1996, assessed civil penalties of $1.13 million. When PEC refused to pay these penalties, the Colorado Department brought suit in state court to force PEC's compliance with both orders. On March 23, 1999, the Colorado state court found that the final administrative compliance order and the administrative penalty order were enforceable as a matter of law. Before the Colorado Department issued its final administrative compliance order, the EPA had filed a lawsuit seeking financial reassurances from PEC based on the ongoing Resource Conservation and Recovery Act violations. Once the state order was issued, PEC argued that *res judicata* would bar the enforcement of the EPA's suit. How should the court decide this case? [See *U.S. v. Power Engineering Company*, 303 F. 3d 1232 (10th Cir. 2002).]

3. The reality of an ever-increasing backlog of spent nuclear fuel (SNF) in temporary storage has created a national problem. Temporary on-site storage of SNF holds approximately 38,500 metric tons of SNF. But licensed nuclear reactors are expected to generate at least an additional 70,000 metric tons of SNF over their commercial lifetimes. In 1982, Congress passed the Nuclear Waste Policy Act (NWPA). The NWPA requires the Department of Energy to construct a permanent repository for the disposal of SNF. Pursuant to the terms of NWPA, the Department of Energy entered into a contractual agreement with all utilities that control one or more nuclear reactors to accept the SNF generated by these reactors no later than January 31, 1998. However, the Department of Energy estimates that, at the earliest, it will not have a permanent repository to receive SNF until 2010. Hence, a consortium of utility companies formed Private Fuel Storage, L.L.C. (PFS) as a temporary solution to the storage problem. PFS proposed to build an off-site, private SNF storage facility on a portion of the reservation of the plaintiffs, the Skull Valley Band of Goshute Indians (Skull Valley Band) in Utah. On May 20, 1997, PFS entered into a lease of tribal reservation lands with the Skull Valley Band to allow the construction of a SNF storage facility. After the Bureau of Indian Affairs (BIA) conditionally approved the lease, PFS submitted a license application to the Nuclear Regulatory Commission (NRC) in which PFS sought to construct and operate the proposed SNF storage facility. The NRC has yet to rule on PFS's application. The State of Utah objected strenuously to PFS's plan, and the Utah Legislature passed five pieces of legislation directed at blocking the proposed facility. The plaintiffs, the Skull Valley Band and PFS, sued for declaratory and injunctive relief from the application of these Utah laws. The defendants—several high-ranking officials in the Utah state government—then filed a counterclaim alleging that: (1) the NRC has no authority to license a private, for profit, off-site storage facility; (2) an NRC license will necessarily violate the National Environmental Policy Act (NEPA) and therefore will be invalid; (3) the Skull Valley Band has not lawfully approved the lease; (4) the conditional approval of the lease by the BIA occurred in violation of governing laws and rules; and (5) any BIA approval of the lease will be invalid as a breach of the Government's trust obligations. The plaintiffs asserted: (1) that the passage of state licensing schemes for the storage and transportation of SNF duplicates the NRC's licensing procedures and therefore is pre-empted by federal law under

the Supremacy clause and (2) that the Utah statutes violate the Commerce Clause. In moving for judgment on the pleadings, the defendants first argued that the plaintiffs lacked standing, claiming that, because federal law prohibited the plaintiffs from operating an off-site, private SNF facility, the plaintiffs had not alleged a violation of a legally cognizable interest. Consequently, the defendants submitted, the plaintiffs had not shown the standing required for a court to exercise jurisdiction over the matter. The defendants next argued that that the plaintiffs' claims are not ripe because the NRC has yet to grant PFS a license for the facility. The plaintiffs countered that Utah's enactment of various laws aimed at thwarting the construction and operation of a SNF facility, by creating uncertainty about whether it is futile for the plaintiffs to attempt to obtain a license from the NRC and whether the costs imposed by the laws make the construction of the facility prohibitively expensive, render the issue ripe for adjudication.

In whose favor should the court rule? In reaching your decision be certain to address the issue of standing and whether the Utah legislature's attempt to prevent the construction of this site was preempted by federal law. [See *Skull Valley Band of Gashute Indians v. Leavitt*, 215 F. Supp. 2d 1232 (D. Utah 2002).]

Notes

1. John Henry Davidson & Orlando E. Delogu, *Federal Environmental Regulation*, 2 vols. (Salem, NH: Butterworth Legal Publishers, 1994); Roger W. Findley & Daniel A. Farber, *Environmental Law in a Nutshell*, 4th ed. (Minneapolis: West Publishing Co., 1996); and William H. Rodgers, Jr., *Handbook on Environmental Law*, 2nd ed. (Minneapolis: West Publishing Co., 1994) provide more detailed and comprehensive information concerning environmental law.
2. 42 U.S.C. § 4321, Sec. 2, Purpose.
3. At least 15 states, Puerto Rico, and the District of Columbia have enacted SEPA—or "mini NEPA"—legislation.
4. Public Law 84-159.
5. Public Law 88-206.
6. Whitten, Gary Z., *AIR QUALITY AND ETHANOL IN GASOLINE*, "Ethanol in gasoline can favorably impact mobile source emissions in five main air quality areas."
7. The Energy Independence and Security Act signed into law on December 19, 2007 mandates a 40 percent increase in fuel economy by 2020.
8. Mike Allen & Eamon Javer, "Obama Announces New Fuel Standards," *Politico* (May 18, 2009).
9. 33 U.S.C. §§ 401 *et seq.*
10. 33 U.S.C. §§ 1251-1387.
11. 42 U.S.C. §§ 300(f)-300(j)(5).
12. EPA Regulations, 40 CFR 230.3(t).
13. 16 U.S.C. §§ 1401-1445.

14. 33 U.S.C. §§ 2701-2761.

15. Thomas D. Hopkins, "Oil Spill Reduction and Costs of Ship Design Regulation," Contemporary Policy Issues, Vol. 10, p. 59 (1992).

16. Ibid.

17. "Oil Pollution Act," *The Environment, A Global Challenge*, http://library.thinkquest.org/26026/Politics/oil_pollution_act.html.

18. Noah Brenner, "Hayward Says Spill 'Never Should Have Happened.'" *Upstream Online* (June 17, 2010, NHST Media Group).

19. 49 U.S.C. §§ 4901-4918.

20. *Noise Control Act of 1972*, at http://www.pollutionissues.com/Na-Ph/Noise-Control-Act-of-1972.html.

21. www.smarte.org/smarte/resource/sn-glossary.xml.

22. "Brownfields and Land Revitalization," EPA Web site, found at http://epa.gov/brownfields/index.html.

23. Ibid.

24. "Benefits of Brownfields Legislation—Summary of Public Law 107-118," EPA Web Site, at http://www.epa.gov/swerosps/bf/laws/2869ben.htm.

25. Tim Eichenberg & Robert Irvin, "Congress Takes Aim at Endangered Species Act," *The National Law Journal* (February 13, 1995), p. A21.

26. Ibid.

27. Ibid., pp. A21 and A22.

28. *Defining Sustainability*, at http://www.arch.wsu.edu/09%20publications/sustain/defnsust.htm.

29. Ibid.

30. "Exxon Makes First Big Biofuel Investment," MSNBC.com (July 14, 2009).

31. Turner Y. Smith, Jr., "Environmental Regulation on the Rise Worldwide," *National Law Journal* (September 19, 1994), pp. C15 and C16.

38

Labor and Fair Employment Practices

Agenda

As eClass grows and prospers, it will hire more employees. This means the firm will need to ensure that it complies with all applicable federal and state laws regulating labor and employment. eClass also may have to deal with one or more unions. The firm must make certain that it uses fair employment practices and avoids any prohibited discrimination in its hiring and promotion practices. The firm must take steps to protect against sexual harassment. eClass must provide a reasonably safe work environment as well. The firm will have concerns about Social Security, worker's compensation, and unemployment compensation. These legal areas require careful attention to detail and strict compliance with the applicable laws and regulations.

These and other issues are likely to arise during your study of this chapter. Be prepared! You never know when the firm or one of its members will seek your advice.

GRIGGS v. DUKE POWER CO.
401 U.S. 424 (1971)

FACTS This suit was filed by 13 Negro employees who worked at Duke Power Company's Dan River Steam Station. (The court uses the term Negroes, which was the socially correct term at the time.) Prior to the Civil Rights Act of 1964, Duke Power openly discriminated on the basis of race. The plant was organized into five operating departments. Negroes were employed only in the Labor Department. In 1965 when the Company abandoned its policy of restricting Negroes to the Labor Department, it made high school graduation a prerequisite to transfer from the Labor Department to any other department. White employees hired before the education requirement continued to perform satisfactorily and achieve promotions. The Company added a requirement for new employees hired on or after July 2, 1965, the date on which the Civil Rights Act became effective. To qualify for positions in all department except the Labor Department, applicants had to have a high school education and to achieve satisfactory scores on two professionally prepared aptitude tests, the Wonderlic Personnel Test, which purports to measure general intelligence, and the Bennett Mechanical Comprehension Test. Neither test was created or intended to measure the ability to learn to perform a particular job or category of jobs. The test standards were more stringent than the high school requirement, since they would screen out approximately half of all high school graduates. The 1960 North Carolina census data shows that 34 percent of white males had completed high school, and only 12 percent of Negro males had done so. In one case the EEOC found that use of a battery of standardized tests, including the Wonderlic and Bennett tests, resulted in 58 percent of whites passing the tests, as compared with only 6 percent of the blacks. There was no showing of a racial purpose or invidious intent in the adoption of the high school diploma requirement or general intelligence tests. These standards have been applied fairly to whites and Negroes alike.

ISSUE Does the Civil Rights Act of 1964 prohibit an employer from requiring a high school education or the passing of standardized general intelligence tests as a condition of employment in or transfer to jobs when (1) neither standard is shown to be significantly related to successful job performance, (2) both requirements operate to disqualify Negroes at a substantially higher rate than white applicants, and (3) the jobs in question formerly had been filled only by white employees as part of a longstanding practice of giving preference to whites?

HOLDING Yes, the Civil Rights Act prohibits the use of these requirements.

REASONING Excerpts from the opinion by Chief Justice Burger writing for a unanimous court:[1]

... The objective of Congress in the enactment of Title VII is plain from the language of the statute. It was to achieve equality of employment opportunities and remove barriers that have operated ... to favor an identifiable group of white employees over other employees. Under the Act, practices, procedures, or tests neutral on their face, and even neutral in terms of intent, cannot be maintained if they operate to "freeze" the status quo of prior discriminatory employment practices. ... Congress did not intend by Title VII ... to guarantee a job to every person regardless of qualifications. ... What is required by Congress is the removal of artificial, arbitrary, and unnecessary barriers to employment when the barriers operate invidiously to discriminate on the basis of racial or other impermissible classification.

... The Act proscribes not only overt discrimination but also practices that are fair in form, but discriminatory in operation. ... If an employment practice which operates to exclude Negroes cannot be shown to be related to job performance, [it] is prohibited. ... [N]either the high school completion requirement nor the general intelligence test is shown to bear a demonstrable relationship to successful perfor-mance of the jobs for which it was used. Both were adopted ... without meaningful study of their relationship to job-performance ability. ... [T]he requirements were instituted on the Company's judgment that they ... would improve the overall quality of the work force. The evidence ... shows that employees who have not completed high school or taken the tests have continued to perform satisfactorily and make progress ... Congress directed the thrust of the Act to the *consequences* of employment practices, not simply the motivation. ... Congress has placed on the employer the burden of showing that any given requirement must have a manifest relationship to the employment in question.

... The Equal Employment Opportunity Commission [EEOC] ... has issued guidelines interpreting § 703 (h) [of the Civil Rights Act] to permit only the use of job-related tests. The administrative interpretation of the Act by the enforcing agency is entitled to great deference. ... Since the Act and its legislative history support the Commission's construction, this affords good reason to treat the guidelines as expressing the will of Congress. ... Nothing in the Act precludes the use of testing or measuring procedures ... What Congress has forbidden is giving these devices and mechanisms controlling force unless they are demonstrably a reasonable measure of job performance. Congress has not commanded that the less qualified be preferred over the better qualified simply because of minority origins. Far from disparaging job qualifications as such, Congress has made such qualifications the controlling factor, so that race, religion, nationality, and sex become irrelevant. ...

INTRODUCTION

Labor law and fair employment law provide the framework under which workers are regulated and protected. Labor law deals with the relationship between management and the workers. It tends to view the workers as a group and provides for group protection. It defines unfair labor practices and unfair management practices. Fair employment practices law deals with employer rights and responsibilities that help to guarantee the equitable treatment of all the employees. Fair employment practices view the workers as individuals and provides for the protection of each worker within the employment setting. Most of these protections consist of federal regulations. Important state laws also exist, so employers and employees should check the applicable state laws. You will find that both of these areas are in a state of flux which requires the student and business person to check the laws for important changes. Many federal and state laws require that written notice be given to employees. Employers often comply with this requirement by posting appropriate signs in the workplace.

FEDERAL LABOR STATUTES

Unions are a fact of life in the United States today. But this was not always so. Violence and bloody battles between employers and pro-union workers marked the rise of unionism in this country. The courts were also hostile to unions. In fact, in the 1800s and early 1900s, both state and federal courts viewed workers' concerted activities (such as strikes and picketing) as common law criminal conspiracies, tortious interference with contract, or antitrust violations. The Sherman Act was initially used against unions since union activities were viewed as "combinations in restraint of trade." Although Congress passed the Clayton Act in 1914 in part to shield unions from liability under the antitrust laws, subsequent Supreme Court decisions narrowed this statutory protection. Exhibit 38.1 provides an overview of the most significant federal labor laws.

Exhibit 38.1

Significant Labor Statutes

Name of Statute	Behavior Allowed or Prohibited
Norris-LaGuardia Act (Labor Disputes Act) [1932]	Protects certain activities from federal court action; protected activities include peaceful refusals to work, boycotts, and picketing. It also promotes collective bargaining.
Wagner Act (National Labor Relations Act) [1935]	Allows employees to organize and to engage in collective bargaining; specifies employer unfair labor practices; establishes the National Labor Relations Board (NLRB).
Taft-Hartley Act (Labor Management Relations Act) [1947]	Prohibits unfair labor practices by unions; separates the NLRB's functions; empowers courts to grant various civil and criminal remedies; creates the Federal Mediation and Conciliation Service.
Landrum-Griffin Act (Labor Management Reporting and Disclosure Act) [1959]	Requires extensive reporting of unions' financial affairs; allows civil and criminal sanctions for union officers' financial wrongdoings; mandates democratic procedures in the conduct of union elections and meetings.

The Norris-LaGuardia Act (1932)

Congress passed the Norris-LaGuardia Act, also called the Labor Disputes Act, in 1932. This act immunized certain activities from federal court actions, for example peaceful *strikes* (organized refusals to work), *boycotts* (concerted refusals to deal with firms so as to disrupt their business), and *picketing* (demonstrations near a business to publicize a labor dispute and to encourage the public to refuse to do business with the employer). The act barred the issuance of federal injunctions in the context of labor disputes and the institution of *yellow dog contracts* (promises to refrain from union membership as a condition of employment). In doing so it allowed employees to organize and to engage in collective bargaining free from court or employer intervention, as long as the concerted activity did not involve *wildcat strikes* (unauthorized withholdings of services or labor during the term of a contract), violence, sabotage, trespass, and similar activities.

The Norris-LaGuardia Act signaled a policy aimed at keeping the courts out of labor disputes. Free from court involvement, employees and employers could advance their respective goals using the economic weapons available to them. The unions resorted to strikes, picketing, and boycotts; and the employers discharged employees.

The Wagner Act (1935)

In 1935, Congress passed the Wagner Act, also called the National Labor Relations Act. This legislation heralded the beginning of a positive—as opposed to a neutral—approach to labor organizations. In §7 of the Wagner Act Congress approved the right of employees to organize themselves and "to form, join, or assist labor organizations, to bargain collectively through representatives of their own choosing, and to engage in concerted activities for the purpose of collective bargaining or other mutual aid or protection." The right to refrain from engaging in concerted activities is protected as well. Section 8 enumerates employer *unfair labor practices* (that is, activities that are prohibited by law as injurious to labor policies), such as (1) coercion of or retaliation against employees who exercise their §7 rights, (2) domination of unions by employers, (3) discrimination in employment (hiring and firing, for instance) designed to discourage union activities, and (4) refusals by employers to bargain collectively and in good faith with employee unions. Section 9 sets out the process for conducting secret elections for employees to choose their representative in the collective bargaining process.[2] The Wagner Act also established a new administrative agency, the National Labor Relations Board (NLRB), to oversee such elections and also to investigate and remedy unfair labor practices. Section 10 permits the appropriate federal circuit court of appeals to review any NLRB order. The Wagner act was declared to be constitutional in *NLRB v. Jones & Laughlin Steel Corp.*[3]

The Taft-Hartley Act (1947)

After the passage of the Wagner Act, unions grew in size and influence. As a result, the power balance between employees and employers became so pro-union that in 1947 Congress passed legislation to counter the perceived excesses of the NLRB and the pervasive court deference to its orders.

The Taft-Hartley Act, also called the Labor Management Relations Act (LMRA), attempted to curb union excesses. It amended § 8 of the Wagner Act to prohibit certain unfair labor practices by unions, including (1) engaging in *secondary boycotts* (boycotts at an employer's customers or suppliers in an attempt to influence the employer), (2) forcing an employer to discriminate against employees on the basis of their union affiliation or lack of union affiliation, (3) refusing to bargain in good faith, (4) requiring an employer to pay for services not actually performed by an employee (*featherbedding*), and (5) *recognitional picketing* (picketing in which a union attempts to force recognition of a union different from the certified bargaining representative). Congress also amended § 7 to allow employees to refrain from joining a union and participating in its collective activities.

In addition, the Taft-Hartley Act cut back the NLRB's authority by separating the NLRB's functions. The Office of General Counsel became responsible for the board's unfair labor practices cases, leaving to the five-person board the decision-making (or *adjudicatory*) function. This reconfiguration significantly changed the nature of the NLRB, which previously had served as both prosecutor and decision maker.

The Taft-Hartley Act also (1) empowered courts of appeals to set aside NLRB findings concerning unfair labor practices cases where and when appropriate, (2) authorized district courts to issue labor injunctions requested by the NLRB to stop unfair labor practices, (3) created the possibilities of fines and imprisonment for anyone resisting NLRB orders, and (4) provided for civil remedies for private parties damaged by secondary boycotts or various union activities.

Other sections (1) protect the employer's right of free speech (by refusing to characterize as unfair labor practices an employer's expressions of its opinions about unionism when the expressions contain no threats of reprisal), (2) preserve the employees' rights to engage in peaceful *informational picketing* (picketing for the purpose of truthfully advising the public that an employer does not employ members of, or have a contract with, a labor organization), and (3) prohibit *closed shop agreements* (contracts that obligate the employer to hire and retain only union members). While closed shop agreements are prohibited, *union shop clauses* (provisions that require an employee, after being hired, to join a union in order to retain his or her job) are legal. The Taft-Hartley Act also created a Federal Mediation and Conciliation Service for settling disputes between labor and management. To further foster conciliation efforts, the act established a cooling-off period that is required in certain circumstances before strikes can occur. It also preserved the power of states, under their right-to-work laws, to invalidate other union devices designed to consolidate the unions' hold on workers. Right-to-work laws are discussed later in this chapter.

The Landrum-Griffin Act (1959)

By the 1950s, Congress had discovered substantial corruption among union leadership. Union members had been harmed by officers' plundering of union treasuries and by officers' often tyrannical treatment of the rank-and-file members. Congress responded with the Landrum-Griffin Act, also called the Labor Management Reporting and Disclosure Act (LMRDA). As this latter title suggests, the act (1) requires extensive reporting of financial affairs; (2) allows civil and criminal sanctions for financial wrongdoings by union officers; and (3) mandates democratic procedures in the conduct of union affairs by providing a "bill of rights" for union members. In addition, the Landrum-Griffin Act amended portions of the Taft-Hartley Act to outlaw *hot cargo clauses* (provisions in contracts requiring the employer to cease doing business with nonunion companies).

In combination these acts apply to almost all employers and employees, excluding federal, state, and local government employers and employees; employers covered under the Railway Labor Act; agricultural workers; domestic workers; independent contractors; and most supervisors.[4] Even though government workers are not covered, federal workers can organize themselves under the authority of Executive Order 11491, entitled Labor-Management Relations in the Federal Service, issued in 1969. In addition, about two-thirds of the states have enacted laws permitting collective bargaining in the public sector for state and municipal employees. Such executive orders and statutes ordinarily forbid strikes by public employees (such as police officers and firefighters), but nevertheless such strikes have occurred. Collective bargaining in the public sector is relatively new, but it will have significant implications for the future as our economy becomes more service oriented and the number of government employees increases.

Further Issues

Although we cannot describe fully the pervasive federal regulation of labor, we will highlight a few of the more important issues. Questions invariably arise when employees select their bargaining representative. The Wagner Act sets forth the procedures that must be followed during this process. Upon a showing of employee interest, the union will petition for an election that it hopes will lead to its recognition as the exclusive bargaining representative of the employees. The NLRB decides whether the election has been conducted appropriately and, if so, certifies the union as the exclusive bargaining agent.

Once the bargaining representative has been chosen, the Wagner Act requires *good-faith bargaining* by both the employer and the union. This is a nebulous term; in essence, it mandates that both sides meet and discuss certain issues with as much objectivity as possible. Under this duty, an employer cannot bypass the union to deal directly with the employees. Even with good faith bargaining, the parties may not reach an agreement.

The Wagner Act requires good-faith bargaining over "wages, hours, and other terms and conditions of employment." The duty to bargain covers only those topics that have a direct impact on the employees' job security. Decisions that are not essentially related to conditions of employment but rather are managerial decisions "which lie at the core of entrepreneurial control"[5] are not mandatory bargaining subjects. Pay differentials for different shifts, piecework and incentive plans, transfers, fringe benefits, and severance pay are mandatory subjects. Courts have had more trouble classifying bonuses and meals provided by the employer. Managerial decisions to terminate the company's business or to shut down a plant are ordinarily *permissive*, or nonmandatory, subjects. An employer might be forced to bargain about the *effects* of such decisions that impinge on the conditions of employment, for example, *severance pay* (wages paid upon the termination of one's job).

The NLRB can require either side to begin bargaining and to cease and desist from engaging in any unfair labor practice associated with bad-faith bargaining. The NLRB also can use its powers to end employer or union unfair labor practices that have occurred outside the bargaining context.

NLRB orders are not self-enforcing. They become law only when imposed by a federal circuit court of appeals. These limitations on the NLRB's enforcement powers make policing the actions of maverick employers or unions more difficult. If the court affirms the NLRB order, the court issues an injunction. In the meantime, the allegedly unfair labor practices may have continued and may have successfully stifled the opponent's interests.

The application of federal labor laws to the intersection of employer-instituted rules concerning technology and employees' rights to engage in concerted activities under § 7 of the Wagner Act has put many of these issues in a new light. For example, the NLRB recently faced such questions as (1) the degree of statutory protection the federal labor laws grant to employees' use of email, (2) the appropriate bargaining unit when employers have no fixed work location but rather conduct all their business electronically, and (3) union access to employees in a virtual workplace. Many of the precedents the NLRB follows are based on theories of real property (which is characterized by discrete physical boundaries), rules concerning what constitutes work areas (also characterized by discrete physical boundaries), and distinct separations between working hours and nonworking hours. The realities of a digitized environment may force the employer's "business only" computer usage policies to give way to unions' right of access. The customary methods of organizing traditional workplaces—face-to-face communications, handbilling, and home visits—provide unions with several options for encouraging workers to join the bargaining unit. While the union may view such personalized contacts as the preferred choice during solicitation drives, they are not the union's only alternative.

Face-to-face interactions are normally absent in the digitized workplace. Consequently, the employer's denial of access to email may foreclose all communications to employees. Employers should exercise caution when they tie no-solicitation rules to their email policies. Broad prohibitions on the use of an email system may constitute an unfair labor practice, since denial of access to email systems will arguably result in a greater interference with employees' rights to engage in concerted activities than would be the case in traditional, physical, workplace settings. The potential use of electronic ballots in representation elections may change the future contours of labor law as well. Given the numerous issues and the unsettled nature of the law, you should pay attention to such developments.

STATE LABOR LAW

The supremacy clause of the Constitution empowers Congress to pass laws, such as the federal labor laws, that will preempt the states' regulation of labor. Supreme Court decisions have held that federal preemption powers are broad in the area of labor law. Given the NLRB's expertise and the desire for uniformity of results, federal laws usually supersede state efforts to govern labor-related activities.

Matters that only peripherally affect the federal statutory scheme or matters that are of deep local concern may constitute legitimate state interests that state legislatures and courts may control. The law in this area is unsettled; generally, however, state courts can adjudicate lawsuits involving damages from violence or other criminal or tortious activity, retaliatory discharges, and those causes of action covering all employers and employees exempted from the federal statutes.

States may enforce any right-to-work statutes that they have enacted.[6] A right to work law is a statute that prohibits requiring union membership as a condition for employment. In other words a state can prohibit "agency shop" union security agreements between unions and management if it deems that to be an appropriate policy. In addition, state courts will have jurisdiction to enforce the state right-to-work statute.

eClass 38.1 Management

UNIONS

eClass has been wildly successful, and the firm has increased its workforce significantly. Beth, a newly hired worker, is a strong union advocate. She has started discussing the possibility of forming a union at eClass. Several of the employees, believing that a strong bargaining representative will help them, seem to favor forming a union. Others, including a number of the original employees, oppose the formation of a union. They believe that Ani, Meg, and Yousef have treated the workers fairly and that a union will set up an "us versus them" mentality that will not be in the best long-term interests of the firm or the employees. Yousef is concerned that such discussions will divide the loyalty of the workers and harm the firm. He asks you what the firm can legally do to prevent the formation of a union and what it must legally do if the employees decide to proceed. What will you tell him?

BUSINESS CONSIDERATIONS   What should a business do if it learns that its employees are considering petitioning the NLRB for a union-certification election? Should the business take steps to discourage the formation of a union, or should the business wait and then choose a course of conduct after the vote?

ETHICAL CONSIDERATION   Is it ethical for a business to take affirmative steps to thwart union-organizing activities if the management of the firm honestly believes that the union will have harmful long-term effects on the business?

FAIR EMPLOYMENT PRACTICES LAWS

Besides the extensive regulation of labor just discussed, several federal and state statutes have been enacted designed to ensure equal employment opportunity for persons historically foreclosed from the workplace. Exhibit 38.2 provides an overview of the most significant of these employment laws.

Exhibit 38.2

Representative Employment Statutes

Name of Statute	Workers Protected	Who is Covered*
Age Discrimination in Employment Act [1967]	Protects certain workers (in general those aged 40-70) from discrimination in employment based on age.	All private employers with 20 or more full- or part-time employees for each working day in each of 20 or more weeks in the current calendar year or the prior calendar year; includes state and local governments, employment agencies, and labor organizations.[7]
Title I of the Americans with Disabilities Act [1990]	Protects disabled workers from employment discrimination. Disabilities are defined as physical or mental impairments that substantially limit one or more major life activities.	Employers with 15 or more full- or part-time employees for each working day in each of 20 or more weeks in the current calendar year or the prior calendar year; also applies to labor organizations and employment agencies.
Title VII of the Civil Rights Act [1964]	Prohibits discrimination in the terms, conditions, and privileges of employment on the basis of color, race, religion, sex, or national origin.	Employers in interstate commerce with 15 or more full- or part-time employees for each working day in each of 20 or more weeks in the current calendar year or the prior calendar year; includes federal, state, and local governments; also applies to national or international labor organizations and employment agencies.
Civil Rights Act [1991]	Amends earlier civil rights statutes to broaden the scope of protections afforded under antidiscrimination law; prohibits "race norming" of employment tests; in some circumstances, allows compensatory and punitive damage awards and jury trials.	Employers in interstate commerce with 15 or more full- or part-time employees for each working day in each of 20 or more weeks in the current calendar year or the prior calendar year; includes federal, state, and local governments; also applies to national or international labor organizations and employment agencies.

Exhibit 38.2 Continued

Name of Statute	Workers Protected	Who is Covered*
Consolidated Omnibus Budget Reconciliation Act (COBRA) [1985]	Allows employees or qualified beneficiaries to extend their coverage under the employer's group health insurance for a period of time; the employee or beneficiary has to pay the entire premium for the coverage.	Employers with 20 or more employees on a typical business day during the last quarter; does not apply to churches or government entities.
Equal Pay Act [1963]	Prohibits discrimination in wages on the basis of sex.	Executive, administrative, and professional employees; outside sales people; and all employees who are covered by the federal minimum wage laws.
Family and Medical Leave Act [1993]	Mandates that eligible employees receive up to 12 weeks of leave during any 12-month period for certain family- or medically-related events.	Public employers of any size and private employers with 50 or more employees for each working day in each of 20 or more weeks in the current calendar year or the prior calendar year.
Immigration Reform and Control Act [1986]	Prohibits immigration-related discrimination based on national origin or citizenship status.	Employers with 4 or more employees.
Lilly Ledbetter Fair Pay Act [2009]	Specifies the statute of limitations to file a suit based on pay discrimination begins to run with each discriminatory pay check. Amends Title VII, the Age Discrimination in Employment Act, and the Americans with Disabilities Act.	Victims of pay discrimination who do not learn of the discrimination until some time after it bgan.
Occupational Safety and Health Act [1970]	Mandates safe and healthful workplace conditions.	Most employers that are involved in interstate commerce and employ at least one employee. Atomic energy workers are not covered.
Pregnancy Discrimination Act [1978]	Protects workers from pregnancy-related discrimination based on pregnancy or pregnancy-related symptoms. Amends Title VII.	Employers in interstate commerce with 15 or more full- or part-time employees for each working day in each of 20 or more weeks in the current calendar year or the prior calendar year; includes federal, state, and local governments; also applies to national or international labor organizations and employment agencies.

Exhibit 38.2 Continued

Name of Statute	Workers Protected	Who is Covered*
Rehabilitation Act [1973]	Directs federal contractors to take affirmative action with regard to "otherwise qualified" handicapped individuals.	Employers doing business with the federal government.
Social Security Act [1935]	Provides federal benefits to retired workers, disabled workers, and the workers' spouses and minor children.	Most employers and people who are self-employed. Some state and local governments do not use Social Security and have created their own retirement system. Some churches and religious organizations are exempt.[†]
Federal Unemployment Tax Act [1954]	Provides (through a coordinated federal and state effort) economic security for temporarily unemployed workers.	Employers who paid wages of $1,500 or more to employees in any calendar quarter during the current or prior calendar year; also employers who had one or more full or part-time employee for at least some part of a day in any 20 or more different weeks in the current or prior calendar year.[8]
State Worker's Compensation Statutes	Provide financial benefits to reimburse workers for workplace-related injury or death.	Wide variation across the states as to which employers/employees are covered. Some states even cover independent contractors.

Source: Courtesy of Lynn M. Forsythe, © Lynn M. Forsythe 2010

* The Federal government's control of employment is generally based on the Commerce Clause and is limited to enterprises involved in Interstate Commerce.

[†] This box only describes new employment. For example, in the past self-employed workers, federal government workers, members of the military, and workers for nonprofit organizations were not covered. Past employees of this type may or may not be covered due to complicated rules.

The Civil Rights Act of 1964

Foremost among these laws is the Civil Rights Act of 1964. Title VII of that statute prohibits discrimination in employment on the basis of color, race, religion, sex, or national origin. Under Title VII, an employer cannot lawfully make decisions to hire, discharge, compensate, or establish the terms, conditions, or privileges of employment for any employee based on the categories just enumerated. In addition, an employer cannot segregate, limit, or classify employees or applicants for employment in discriminatory ways. Title VII's coverage, in general, extends to employers in interstate commerce that have on their weekly payrolls at least 15 full- or part-time employees[9] for at least 20 weeks per year, to any national or international labor organizations that consist of at least 15 members or that operate a hiring hall, and to employment agencies that regularly procure employees for employers or work opportunities for potential employees.

None of the three groups (employers, unions, or employment agencies) can discriminate against any individual because the individual has opposed unlawful employment practices. An employer that relegates blacks to manual labor jobs or an employment agency or labor organization that refers only white males for executive jobs or only women for nursing or administrative assistant jobs is in violation of Title VII. Advertisements that indicate a discriminatory preference also violate Title VII.

Title VII authorized the creation of the Equal Employment Opportunity Commission (EEOC), a bipartisan, five-member group appointed by the president. The EEOC presently serves as the enforcement agency for (1) Title VII, (2) the Pregnancy Discrimination Act of 1978, (3) the Equal Pay Act of 1963, (4) the Age Discrimination in Employment Act of 1967, (5) the Rehabilitation Act of 1973, (6) the Americans with Disabilities Act of 1990, (7) the Civil Rights Act of 1991, and other statutes. The EEOC also can bring lawsuits relating to broad patterns and practices of discrimination. Complaints by individual grievants or charges filed by the EEOC or state fair employment or human rights commissions may trigger the EEOC's jurisdiction. The jurisdictional requirements including the time period for filing a suit are complex and outside the scope of our discussion.

Employers should be aware that many employment practices that seem neutral actually lead to discrimination. Several cases have been filed that involved testing procedures and mandatory high school diplomas. These cases show that selection criteria that seem outwardly neutral may foreclose blacks and other protected persons from jobs merely because statistically fewer blacks than whites graduated from high school. Selection criteria that require a certain score on an aptitude test or a high school diploma may, as our Classic Case notes, "operate as 'built-in' headwinds for minority groups and [may be] unrelated to measuring job capability.... [Title VII] proscribes not only overt discrimination but also practices that are fair in form, but discriminatory in operation. The touchstone is business necessity. If an employment practice which operates to exclude [minorities] cannot be shown to be related to job performance, the practice is prohibited."[10]

Disparate Impact   Any job requirement that prevents a disproportionate number of blacks or other minorities from securing employment or promotion has a *disparate impact* (that is, an unequal effect) on minorities and *may* be illegal. The victim of the alleged discrimination begins by establishing his or her *prima facie* case by presenting statistical evidence that the employment practice has an adverse impact on a protected group.[11] The Supreme Court has said that in determining the type of statistical evidence necessary to establish a prima facie case, great deference should be given to the guidelines issued by the EEOC.[12] The EEOC, in its Uniform Guidelines of Employee Selection Procedures,[13] sets out a 4/5 rule. Under the 4/5 rule, if the selection rate for a protected class is less than 4/5 (or 80%) of the selection rate for the group with the highest selection rate this constitutes statistical evidence that there is a disparate impact. For a simple example, if 90 percent of the white applicants are accepted (and they are the group with the highest selection rate) and only 30 percent of the black applicants are accepted then the 4/5 rule is violated. Black applicants would have to be accepted at a rate of 72 percent or more under the rule. This 4/5 rule, then, should be given "great deference;" however, it is not a part of the statutory law. The Supreme Court has also recognized that a statistical disparity of more than two standard deviations from the mean create an inference of discrimination.[14] Once the plaintiff has made a prima facie case, the employer has the burden of proving either that (1) the employment practice does not cause a disparate impact or (2) that the requirement is legitimately job-related for the position in question (a *bona fide* occupational qualification, or BFOQ). As you might expect, there is a significant amount of litigation over whether a requirement is a BFOQ. The plaintiff may respond to a claim that a requirement is a BFOQ by showing that the requirement is a pretext for unlawful discrimination. (A *pretext* is a false or weak motive used to hide the real or strong motive.)

Disparate Treatment   Besides facing liability stemming from disparate impact, employers also may be liable for the *disparate treatment* of their employees. Such cases may involve an employer who only considers women for clerical positions; only considers men for positions on an assembly line; or only considers white males for managerial positions. An employer that allows whites or males to break rules without punishment but institutes penalties if blacks or women break the same rules is also likely to be found guilty of disparate treatment. The reverse is also true.[15] The term reverse discrimination refers to claims by whites that they have been subjected to adverse employment decisions because of their race and the application of employment discrimination statutes designed to protect minorities.

Affirmation Action Plans   The allegations of reverse discrimination that spring from another source—affirmative action plans—pose some of the most controversial issues in the area of fair employment practices involving race. Title VII requires the employer to maintain a racially balanced workforce. Yet if the employer takes affirmative steps—setting aside certain opportunities or positions for blacks, for example—to bring about such racial balance, these actions may adversely affect the white applicants who wish to take part in these opportunities or positions. Two diametrically opposed policies clash here: the interests of the minority candidate who in the past has been disadvantaged because of race and of the white candidate who has taken no part in this discrimination but who now, must lose employment opportunities because the employer is seeking to bring about equal opportunity for black workers. Whites have sued alleging reverse discrimination.

Religious Discrimination   Besides racial discrimination, Title VII also prohibits religious discrimination. Sincere religious beliefs (or the lack thereof) are protected under Title VII. Typically, cases arise when an employee is scheduled to work on his or her Sabbath. If a person's religion forbids work on Fridays after sundown, for instance, Title

VII mandates that the employer make a "reasonable accommodation" to the employee's beliefs unless doing so would pose an "undue hardship" on the conduct of the business.

Bona Fide Occupational Qualifications (BFOQs)   Religion, sex, or national origin *can* be a BFOQ. Race, however, cannot. Educational institutions may make religion a BFOQ. Consequently, a Jesuit university could hire only Jesuit professors to teach philosophy if it wishes.

BFOQs can constitute a limited defense to charges of sex discrimination. For example, it is not a violation of Title VII for a movie director to cast only women in women's roles. However, it is a violation to hire based on stereotypical beliefs that equate gender with the ability to perform certain jobs, such as believing that only men can be heavy equipment operators or that only women can be childcare providers. The use of height/weight requirements that are not job-related may also result in violations since women are usually smaller than men. Sex-plus cases can also be violations. In sex-plus cases, the employer adds a selection criterion for women that is not added for men (such as when women with pre-school-aged children are not hired but men who have such children are).

Sexual Harrassment   Recent Title VII cases have protected women from sexual harassment in the workplace by imposing liability on employers for sexual advances or requests for sexual favors made by the employer's agents and supervisory employees (so-called *quid pro quo* sexual harassment) and for sexual misconduct that creates an intimidating, hostile, or offensive working environment for women (so-called *hostile environment* harassment). Courts have relied on the decision in *Meritor Savings Bank v. Vinson*,[16] the landmark Supreme Court case that held that an employer could face liability for harassment that created a hostile or offensive working environment, even though the plaintiff had suffered no "tangible" losses of an "economic character." Since the *Meritor* decision, the courts of appeals and employers have continued to struggle with the issue of when an employer is liable for the conduct of its supervisors for sexual harassment.

Although most cases have involved harassment of women by men, men who face harassment from women supervisors have standing to sue under Title VII. In addition, workplace sexual harassment is actionable under Title VII when the offender and the victim are the same sex.[17]

Employers can face large recoveries if they fail to take corrective actions to end sexual harassment once they know, or should have known, that it had occurred. Prudent employers should establish, publicize, and vigorously enforce anti-sexual harassment policies.[18]

National Origin Discrimination   National origin claims are not as common as those made under many other Title VII categories.[19] They are likely to become increasingly important since immigration is hot political topic. Title VII's ban on national origin discrimination similarly prevents harassment in the form of ethnic slurs based on the country in which one was born or the country from which one's ancestors came. Repeated ethnic jokes and other derogatory statements directed at one's ethnic origins may constitute national origin discrimination.

National origin discrimination often takes the form of "covert discrimination." To illustrate, height/weight requirements may foreclose Spanish-surnamed Americans from employment opportunities. Language difficulties or accents also may pose problems for perspective employees from certain countries. If an employer fails to hire a worker on the basis of such criteria, the employer must prove that the criteria are job related. Some employers have established English-only rules, requiring that employees speak English at the work place. These work rules have been challenged as a form of national origin discrimination. The courts have been very inconsistent in their treatment of these rules.

Narrow BFOQs may exist in national origin cases. It *may* be legal to refuse to hire non-American citizens because the prohibition in Title VII does not include citizenship[20] unless the discrimination in favor of citizens has the purpose or effect of discrimination on the basis of national origin. The protected categories under Title VII do not specifically include being an alien.[21] Other anti-discrimination laws may protect legal residents however. It is not a violation of Title VII for an employer to refuse to hire persons who are unable to obtain security clearances because they are not U.S. citizens or have relatives in countries that have hostile relationships with the United States.

The Pregnancy Discrimination Act of 1978

The Pregnancy Discrimination Act of 1978 (PDA), passed by Congress as an amendment to Title VII, dictates that an employer treat pregnancy in the same fashion as any other disability. Failure to do so constitutes actionable sex discrimination. *International Union UAW v. Johnson Controls, Inc.*[22] illustrates an interesting interpretation of the PDA. Johnson Controls's battery-manufacturing process used lead. Occupational exposure to lead entails health risks, including the risk of harm to a fetus carried by a female employee. Eight of its employees became pregnant while maintaining blood lead levels exceeding those the Occupational Safety and Health Administration (OSHA) thought were safe for a worker planning to have a family. Johnson Controls then announced a policy barring all women, except those whose infertility could be medically documented, from jobs involving actual or potential lead exposure exceeding the OSHA standard. The International Union UAW filed a suit on behalf of the employees claiming that the policy constituted sex discrimination in violation of Title VII. The question before the Supreme Court focused on whether Johnson Controls's sex-specific fetal-protection policy of excluding fertile female employees from certain jobs violated Title VII's ban on sex discrimination. According to the Court, by excluding women with childbearing capacity from lead-exposed jobs, Johnson Controls's policy created a facial classification based on gender and explicitly discriminated against women on the basis of their sex under Title VII. When Johnson Controls used the words "capable of bearing children" as the criterion for exclusion, it explicitly classified on the basis of potential for pregnancy, which constitutes explicit sex discrimination under the

eClass 38.2 Management

HIRING REQUIREMENTS

From its inception, eClass has had a policy of refusing to hire any full-time, nonfamily applicants who are not high school graduates. The firm's members have included this requirement in the firm's hiring manual because they believe that any high-tech firm—and eClass is high-tech—needs a well-educated workforce if it is to succeed. Ani is concerned that this requirement makes eClass vulnerable to lawsuits claiming that the firm is guilty of racial discrimination in its hiring practices. She asks you what eClass should do in this situation. What advice will you give her? Why?

BUSINESS CONSIDERATIONS   Should a business have a policy for evaluating and changing job requirements? What factors should any such policy include? Could a firm's changing its job descriptions or hiring qualifications make it vulnerable to legal challenges?

ETHICAL CONSIDERATIONS   Would it be ethical for a business to establish higher job requirements for a given position than are absolutely necessary to perform the described job? What ethical concerns would such a job description raise? What should a company do to act ethically, as well as legally, in this situation?

Pregnancy Discrimination Act. Johnson Controls professed moral and ethical concerns about the welfare of the next generation would not suffice to establish a BFOQ of female sterility. The Court concluded that decisions about the welfare of future children must be left to the parents who conceive, bear, support, and raise them rather than to the employers who hire those parents.

The Immigration Reform and Control Act of 1986

The Immigration Reform and Control Act of 1986 (IRCA) is principally aimed at stemming the flow of illegal aliens into the United States. However, it also bans discrimination based on national origin or citizenship. This act prohibits an employer's turning away job applicants because they appear to be aliens or noncitizens. IRCA is narrower in scope than Title VII because it only covers hiring, recruitment of workers for a fee, and discharges. Title VII preempts this act whenever Title VII covers the conduct in question. IRCA's legislative history makes it clear that Congress did not intend this act to expand the rights granted under Title VII.

eClass 38.3 Management

HARASSMENT POLICY

eClass employs several drivers, who operate company trucks delivering the firm's products to customers. Each driver is assigned a particular truck. Sam, one of the drivers, took a personal leave day. Toni, another driver, was assigned the truck that Sam normally drives. At the end of the day, Toni informed Yousef that Sam had taped several "girlie" pictures to the dashboard of the delivery truck and that Toni found the pictures sexist and insulting. Yousef apologized to Toni and promised to look into the situation. Yousef later seeks your advice as to what eClass should do and also what liability eClass could face based on these circumstances. What would you tell him?

BUSINESS CONSIDERATIONS   Should a business establish a strong policy addressing discrimination and harassment before any complaints arise, or should the business wait until there is a problem and then address that particular problem? If the business decides to become proactive, what sorts of conduct should its policy cover?

ETHICAL CONSIDERATIONS   Is it ethical for a business to prohibit the free speech or expression of some employees if other employees find such speech offensive? How can an employer protect the freedoms and rights of each employee and simultaneously protect all employees from discrimination and harassment?

The Equal Pay Act of 1963

The Equal Pay Act of 1963 prohibits discrimination in wages on the basis of sex. This means that men and women performing work in the same establishment under similar working conditions must receive the same rate of pay *if* the work requires equal skill, equal effort, and equal responsibility. Note that the law does not *just* require equal pay for doing equal work. It is based on the skills required, the effort required, and the responsibilities included in the job rather than the job title. Different wages may be paid if the employer bases the pay differential on seniority, merit, piecework, or any factor other than sex (for example, participation in training programs).

The Age Discrimination in Employment Act of 1967

The Age Discrimination in Employment Act of 1967 (ADEA), in general, protects workers aged 40 or older from adverse employment decisions based on age. BFOQs based on safety or human and economic risks, such as requiring police officers or airplane pilots to retire at age 60, may be upheld. An employer claiming an age related BFOQ based on public safety must convince the court that the challenged practice is effective in protecting the public and that there is no acceptable alternative. Courts have reached various results in interpreting the public safety standard. For example, in one case the court held that the employer could not be successful in court until it established and enforced minimum fitness standards for all its employees.[23] The Supreme Court recently held that a plaintiff who alleges discrimination under the ADEA does not have to show, as part of his or her *prima facie* case, that the employer replaced the plaintiff with a worker under age 40. According to the Court, the fact that one person in the protected class has lost out to another person in the protected class is irrelevant, so long as the plaintiff can show that he or she has lost out because of his or her age.[24]

The Lilly Ledbetter Fair Pay Act of 2009

The Lilly Ledbetter Fair Pay Act was the first major piece of legislation signed by President Obama.[25] The act was a response to the Supreme Court's decision in *Ledbetter v. Goodyear Tire & Rubber Co.*[26] The Supreme Court ruled against Ledbetter because she failed to file her complaint within 180 days of the *first* act of discrimination when Goodyear started paying her less than male employees performing the same jobs.[27] Unfortunately for the claimant, he or she may not be aware of the discrimination at that time. In many cases the claimant may not be aware that he or she is being paid less. Even when the claimant is aware that his or her pay is less, the claimant may believe that the disparity is based on other grounds and not illegal discrimination. The act amends Title VII of the Civil Rights Act of 1964, the Age Discrimination in Employment Act of 1967, and the Americans with Disabilities Act by specifying that the individual "may file a charge within 180 (or 300) days of any of the following:

- when a discriminatory compensation decision or other discriminatory practice affecting compensation is adopted;
- when the individual becomes subject to a discriminatory compensation decision or other discriminatory practice affecting compensation; or
- when the individual's compensation is affected by the application of a discriminatory compensation decision or other discriminatory practice, including each time the individual receives compensation that is based in whole or part on such compensation decision or other practice."[28]

The Civil Rights Act of 1991

Congress enacted the Civil Rights Act of 1991 in part to overturn a series of Supreme Court cases that had significantly eroded the rights of plaintiffs alleging employment discrimination. The 1991 act's amendments to § 1981 of the Civil Rights Act of 1866 specify that this statute covers all forms of racial discrimination in employment (including racial harassment). The 1991 act's amendments to Title VII reaffirm the holdings of such cases as *Griggs v. Duke Power Co.,*[29] where the Supreme Court established the basic framework for disparate impact cases.[30] However, the act has been criticized as providing vague standards for disparate impact.[31]

The act mandates the impartial use of tests and in so doing it prohibits "race norming" of employment tests. In other words, employers must record and report actual scores and will be unable to modify scores, use different cutoff scores, or otherwise adjust the results of employment-related tests on the basis of color, race, religion, sex, or national origin even if employers have taken these actions to assure the inclusion of minorities in the applicant pool.

In a similar vein, the act effects no changes in the law regarding what constitutes lawful affirmative action and/or illegal reverse discrimination. It does restrict challenges to court-ordered consent decrees by individuals who had a reasonable opportunity to object to such decrees or whose interests were adequately represented by another party.

The act broadens the scope of federal antidiscrimination law. It makes clear that Americans employed abroad by U.S.-owned or U.S.-controlled firms can use the protection of Title VII, the Americans with Disabilities Act (ADA), and the ADEA, unless compliance with these laws will constitute a violation of the host country's laws. The act extends coverage of the antidiscrimination laws to congressional employees and executive-branch political appointees and sets up separate internal mechanisms for addressing such claims. Nevertheless, in 2001 the Supreme Court held that state employees cannot sue their employers for damages under the ADA because Congress had exceeded its power under the 14th Amendment to enforce the equal protection clause when it applied the ADA to state workers.[32] In barring such suits, the Court added the ADA to the growing list of federal statutes that cannot be enforced against states that refuse to consent to such suits.[33]

The act broadens the categories of victims who can seek compensatory and punitive damages based on intentional discrimination. Any complainant eligible for compensatory or punitive damages may request a jury trial. The act also allows successful complainants to recover expert witness fees and attorneys' fees. Other amendments deal with (1) the availability of interest payments for delayed awards, (2) extensions of filing deadlines for lawsuits brought against the government, (3) notification by the EEOC to the complainant when the EEOC dismisses charges under the ADEA, and (4) a longer statute of limitations period for a claimant who brings an action under the ADEA.

Court decisions will continue to answer the various questions spawned by the act. For example, courts may award punitive damages in Title VII cases without a showing of "egregious" misconduct.[34] The 1991 act limits compensatory and punitive damages awards to cases of intentional discrimination (in other words, disparate treatment). The availability of punitive damages is conditioned on a showing that the defendant engaged in a discriminatory practice "with malice or with reckless indifference to the federally protected rights of an aggrieved individual."[35] An award of punitive damages is predicated on the defendant's state of mind and does not require a showing of egregious or outrageous discrimination independent of the employer's state of mind. In the punitive damages context, an employer may not be held vicariously liable for the discriminatory employment decisions of managerial agents where these decisions are contrary to the employer's good faith efforts to comply with Title VII.[36]

The Rehabilitation Act of 1973

The Rehabilitation Act of 1973 directs federal contractors to take affirmative action with respect to "otherwise qualified" handicapped individuals. A handicapped individual includes any person who "has a physical or mental impairment which substantially limits one or more of such person's major life functions, has a record of such impairment, or is regarded as having such an impairment." Federal contractors must make "reasonable accommodation" to such a person's impairments unless to do so would pose an "undue hardship" on the operation of their programs.

Other Protections

The Vietnam Era Veterans' Readjustment Assistance Act of 1974, various executive orders, and the Civil Rights Acts of 1866 and 1871 also guarantee equal access to the workplace. State law often augments this extensive federal scheme.

THE AMERICANS WITH DISABILITIES ACT OF 1990

The Americans with Disabilities Act of 1990 (ADA) seeks to rectify employment discrimination against individuals with disabilities and to guarantee such individuals equal access to public services (including public accommodations and transportation), public services operated by private entities, and telecommunications relay services, to name a few. Title I, which prohibits employment discrimination, adopted the Rehabilitation Act of 1973's definition of handicap but used the more up-to-date label of "disability." It was amended by the ADA Amendments Act in 2008.[37] The changes to the act are significant. The amendments:

■ codified a rule of interpretation requiring that the disability definition be construed in favor of broad coverage of individuals under the ADA.

- stated "the question of whether an individual's impairment is a disability under the ADA should not demand extensive analysis."
- broadened the definition of disability by stating that "[a]n impairment that substantially limits one major life activity need not limit other major life activities in order to be construed as a disability."
- stated that an impairment that is episodic or in remission qualifies as a disability if it would substantially limit a major life activity in active state. (If an employee has a condition in remission, courts must consider whether the disease would substantially limit a major life activity in its active phase.)
- directed the EEOC to redefine the term "substantially limits" as used in the ADA
- codified and expanded the EEOC definitions of "major life activity" in the ADA. The nonexclusive list of "major life activities" now includes all the activities identified in the EEOC regulations and also eating, sleeping, standing, lifting, bending, reading, concentrating, thinking, and communicating. The definition adds the operation of "major bodily functions" including "functions of the immune system, normal cell growth, digestive, bowel, bladder, neurological, brain, respiratory, circulatory, endocrine, and reproductive functions."
- broadened the definition of disability by making clear that the courts should not take into consideration mitigating measures in determining whether an individual is impaired.[38]

The EEOC was directed to revise its regulations to reflect the new standard. Exhibit 38.3 contrasts the ADA employment provisions with the public access provisions, which will be addressed in Chapter 39.

The ADA requires an employer to provide "reasonable accommodation to the known physical or mental limitations" of a person with a disability unless such accommodation "would impose an undue hardship on the operation of the business." Reasonable accommodation under the ADA includes such actions as making existing facilities accessible to and usable by persons with disabilities, restructuring jobs, and providing part-time or modified work schedules. However, the act does not require the employer to implement any job accommodation if the employer can demonstrate that the accommodation would impose an "undue hardship" on the operation of the business. The ADA defines *undue hardship* as an action requiring "significant difficulty or expense" with reference to the following factors: (1) the nature and cost of the accommodation; (2) the size, type, and financial resources of the specific facility where the accommodation would have to be made; (3) the size, type, and financial resources of the covered employer; and (4) the covered employer's type of operation, including the composition, structure, and functions of its workforce and the geographic separateness and administrative or fiscal relationship between the specific facility and the covered employer.

The legislative history indicates that the "significant difficulty or expense" standard encompasses any "action that is unduly costly, extensive, substantial, disruptive, or

Exhibit 38.3

Comparison of the American with Disabilities Act Provisions

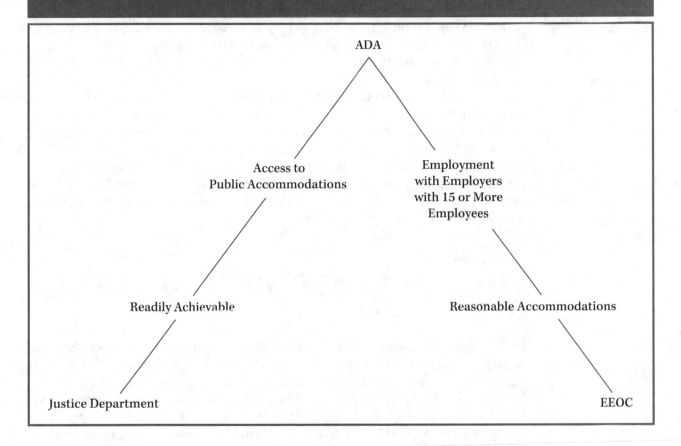

that will fundamentally alter the nature of the program." Congress rejected attempts to put a cap on the level of difficulty or expense that would constitute an "undue hardship."

The employment discrimination provisions under Title I cover employers that have on their weekly payrolls 15 or more full- or part-time employees for each working day in each of 20 or more calendar weeks in the current or preceding calendar year. Like the Civil Rights Act of 1964, the ADA covers employers, employment agencies, labor organizations, and joint labor/management committees, but exempts religious entities. Thus, the ADA's coverage goes beyond that of the Rehabilitation Act of 1973, which applies only to employers doing business with the federal government. The ADA also expressly protects employees or applicants who have completed (or who are participating in) drug rehabilitation programs and no longer are engaging in the use of illegal drugs. Without fear of violating the ADA, employers can impose sanctions against employees who currently are using illegal drugs and may hold such employees (and/or employees who are alcoholics) to the same performance and conduct standards to which it holds other employees, even if the unsatisfactory performance or behavior *is* related to the employees' drug use or alcoholism. The ADA also protects from discrimination persons who have AIDS or who are HIV-positive.

At the congressional hearings for the ADA, experts testified that the ADA potentially would cover about 43 million Americans and that its enactment might cause a flood of litigation. Indeed, the EEOC itself predicted that the EEOC would file between 12,000 and 15,000 charges during the first year the statute took effect—a prediction borne out by the number of actual filings.[39] From 1992 to the fall of 2008, the agency resolved over 284,000 ADA-related charges.[40] The overall impact of the ADA remains unclear. Many employers, particularly small firms, are concerned about the costs including the costs associated with the hiring process, the costs related to the increases in litigation, and the expenses of converting existing facilities to make them accessible to individuals with disabilities.[41]

THE FAMILY AND MEDICAL LEAVE ACT OF 1993

The Family and Medical Leave Act of 1993 (FMLA) covers public employers of any size and private employers that have on their weekly payrolls 50 or more employees during each of 20 or more calendar workweeks in the current or preceding calendar year. Employees eligible to take leave under the act must have worked for the employer for at least 12 months and for at least 1,250 hours in the 12 months immediately preceding any leave taken under the act. Employees who work at job facilities that employ fewer than 50 persons are ineligible for FMLA leave unless the employer has 50 or more employees working within a 75-mile radius of any work site. Part-time employees count, but laid-off employees do not.

The FMLA provides generally that "an eligible employee shall be entitled to a total of 12 work weeks of leave during any 12 month period" for the following family-related events: (1) the birth of a child; (2) the placement of a child with the employee for adoption or foster care; (3) the care of a seriously ill spouse, child, or parent; and (4) a serious health condition of the employee that makes him or her unable to perform any of the essential functions of his or her job.[42] The FMLA does not require the employer to pay for any leave taken under the act. However, eligible employees can use any accrued vacation or personal leave for FMLA purposes. Similarly, an eligible employee may elect to use any paid leave, sick, family, or disability leave" in accordance with the terms of the employer's leave policies. In fact, the employer can require employees to exhaust all "banked" personal, sick, and vacation leave as part of the 12 weeks' leave. In such cases, though, employers are prohibited from imposing more stringent conditions on leave taken under the act than the employers would require under their own leave plans. The act obligates employers to reinstate an employee who has used FMLA leave to the employee's former position or to one that involves "substantially equivalent skill, effort, responsibility, and authority."

Interestingly, the FMLA exempts the highest-paid 10 percent of salaried employees within the 75-mile radius from the right to reinstatement after they have taken a leave. In short, the FMLA allows an employer to refuse restoration of employment to these "key employees" if an employer can show that "substantial and grievous" economic injury would occur if the key employees were restored to their original positions. The regulations do not establish a precise test for calculating the level of hardship that an employer must sustain before it can deny restoration to key employees. Once the employer has determined that a given worker is a key employee, the employer must notify the employee in writing of its determination when the employee requests FMLA leave. The employer's failure to comply with the specific notification requirements will cause the forfeiture of its rights to deny restoration. Furthermore, the employer cannot require an employee to "requalify" for such benefits as life or disability insurance or profit-sharing plans once the worker completes his or her FMLA leave.

Although the act itself does not specifically define the term *family*, the regulations do and they contemplate coverage of a wide spectrum of persons beyond the traditional family unit. The regulations define spouse as a husband or wife recognized as such for purposes of marriage under state law (including common law marriages in jurisdictions that recognize these relationships). Partners in homosexual "marriages" presumably do not qualify for benefits and protection under the FMLA. The parental relationship described in the act can be either biological or one that is *in loco parentis*; but parents "in law" are not included. *Son* or *daughter* means a biological, adopted, or foster child, a stepchild, a legal ward, or a child of a person standing *in loco parentis* and who either is under 18 or 18 and older and incapable of self-care due to a mental or physical disability. The regulations define a person who is *in loco parentis* as including anyone with day-to-day responsibilities to care for and financially support a child. A biological or legal relationship specifically is not required under the regulations.

The act defines a *serious health condition* as "an illness, injury, impairment, or physical or mental condition that involves ... inpatient care in a hospital, hospice, or residential medical care facility; or ... continuing treatment by a health care provider."[43] The regulations further explain that a *serious health condition* is (1) one that requires either an overnight stay in a hospital; (2) a period of incapacity requiring an absence from work of more than three days and that involves continuing treatment by a health care provider; or (3) continuing treatment for a chronic or long-term health condition that, if left untreated, likely will result in a period of incapacity for more than three days. Prenatal care and care administered for a long-term or chronic condition that is incurable (such as Alzheimer's disease) and for which condition the person is not receiving active treatment by a health care provider are included.

FMLA also allows employees to take *intermittent leave*, that is, "leave taken in separate blocks of time due to a single qualifying reason."[44] Intermittent leave can consist of leave taken for medical appointments, chemotherapy, and the like. The regulations require the employee to give notice to the employer of the need for intermittent leave.[45] Employees instead may opt for a *reduced leave* schedule, which the regulations define as a reduction in an employee's usual number of working hours per week or in the working hours per day.

The act allows an employer to require an employee who has requested intermittent or reduced leave to transfer to another position. The transfer must be temporary, and the new position must reflect equivalent pay and benefits (if not equivalent duties). Employers also have the right, consistent with the leave being taken, to transfer an employee to a part-time position. These transfer provisions give the employer some leeway to place the affected employee in a position that more easily accommodates recurrent and unpredictable absences.

Like other federal fair employment practices laws, the FMLA contains antidiscrimination/antiretaliation provisions. Violations of these provisions may result in civil lawsuits, liquidated damages, or administrative remedies.

THE OCCUPATIONAL SAFETY AND HEALTH ACT OF 1970

The Occupational Safety and Health Act (OSHA) attempts to assure safe and healthful workplace conditions for employees. The act does so by (1) authorizing enforcement of the standards developed under the act (through the Occupational Safety and Health Administration); (2) by assisting and encouraging the states' efforts to assure safe and healthful working conditions; and (3) by providing for research, information, education, and training in the field of occupational safety and health, through the National Institute for Occupational Safety and Health (NIOSH). OSHA requires each employer to furnish to its employees a safe and healthful workplace, one that is free from "recognized hazards" that may cause or are likely to cause death or serious physical harm to employees. An example of a recognized hazard might include excessive toxic substances in the air. The act covers most employers and employees, including agricultural employees, nonprofit organizations, and professionals (such as accountants, brokers, doctors, and lawyers). In fact, the act reaches almost any employer that employs at least one employee and whose business in any way affects interstate commerce. Atomic energy workers, however, are exempted.

Illnesses and injuries arising from the workplace produce significant burdens in terms of lost production, lost wages, medical expenses, and disability payments, so Congress designed an act meant to highlight these factors and to provide standards for preventing future illnesses, injuries, and losses. To this end, OSHA sets out methods by which employers can reduce workplace hazards and encourage attention to safety. The act authorizes the secretary of labor to set mandatory occupational safety and health standards for businesses and to create an Occupational Safety and Health

Review Commission for hearing appeals from OSHA citations and penalties. The Supreme Court held that when this "split enforcement" structure (that is, the secretary's powers of enforcement and rulemaking versus the commission's adjudicatory powers) leads to reasonable but conflicting interpretations of an ambiguous OSHA regulation promulgated by the secretary of labor, courts should defer to the secretary's interpretations.[46]

OSHA allows inspectors to enter the workplace to inspect for compliance with regulations. Inspections are generally unannounced. OSHA regulations now require the inspector to obtain a warrant if the employer refuses to admit the inspector. The employer's refusal by itself does not constitute probable cause for the issuance of the warrant. The standards for demonstrating the need for the warrant are relatively easy to meet and ordinarily do not impede OSHA's functions very much. Employees may request an inspection by writing to the secretary of labor if they believe a violation exists. When an employee has initiated the complaint, OSHA will withhold the employee's name if it is requested to do so.

Inspections typically involve a tour through the business and an examination of each work area for compliance with OSHA standards. After the inspector has informed the employer of the reason for the inspection, the inspector will give the employer a copy of the complaint if there is one or the reason for the inspection if it results from an agency general administrative plan. An employer representative and an employee-selected representative generally accompany the inspector on this walk-around tour. The inspector may order the immediate correction of some violations, such as blocked aisles, locked fire exits, or unsanitary conditions. The inspector also reviews OSHA mandated records, including records of deaths, injuries, illnesses, and employee exposure to toxic substances. After the inspection, the inspector and employer hold a closing conference, during which they discuss probable violations and methods for eliminating these violations. The inspector then files his or her report with the commission.

Citations and proposed penalties may be issued to the employer, and a copy of these will be sent to the complaining party, if there is one. OSHA requires the prominent posting of citations in the workplace. Normally, citations are limited to violations where there is an immediate or direct relationship to safety or health. However, a notice of a minimal violation (without a proposed penalty) *may* be sent to the employer.

Penalties, when imposed, are severe: fines of up to $70,000 for each violation may be levied for willful or repeated violations. An employer also will be fined up to $7,000 for each serious violation—one in which there is a "substantial probability" that the consequences of an accident resulting from the violation will be death or serious harm. Employers can defend by showing they did not, and could not with the exercise of "reasonable diligence," know about the condition or hazard. For even nonserious violations (such as a failure to paint steps and banisters or to post citations), fines of up to $7,000 are possible. Prison terms are possible in the event of willful violations that cause an employee's death. The OSHA Commission assesses these penalties in light of the size of the employer's business, the seriousness of the violation, the presence or absence of employer good faith, and the past history of violations.

An employer that wishes to contest any penalties can utilize the procedures established by the commission. In general, these require an investigation and a decision by an administrative law judge (ALJ). The commission, in turn, can review this decision. An employer or the secretary of labor can appeal to the appropriate federal circuit court of appeals for review if either one disagrees with the commission's decision.

Employers may request temporary exemptions from OSHA standards by proving that they cannot comply within the required time because of the unavailability of materials, equipment, or personnel. Permanent exemptions may be granted when the employer's method of protecting employees is as effective as that required by the standard. These exemptions are not granted retroactively.

Other provisions of OSHA protect employees from discrimination or discharge based on filing a complaint, testifying about violations, or exercising any rights guaranteed by the act. The act prohibits employees from stopping work or walking off the job because of "potential unsafe conditions at the workplace" unless the employee would subject "himself [or herself] to serious injury or death arising from a hazardous condition at the workplace"[47] The Supreme Court held that the secretary of labor had the authority to promulgate a regulation allowing workers to refuse to perform in hazardous situations. According to the Court, the promulgation of the regulation was a valid exercise of the authority granted the secretary of labor under OSHA, especially given the act's fundamental purpose of preventing occupational deaths and serious injuries.[48]

GROUP HEALTH INSURANCE

One common and popular employee benefit is the availability of group health insurance. The premiums are generally significantly less than the cost of purchasing health insurance as an individual. When employees lose their jobs, have their hours reduced, or voluntarily sever their employment they generally lose their health insurance. The Consolidated Omnibus Budget Reconciliation Act of 1985 (COBRA) allows employees or qualified beneficiaries to continue their health insurance with the group, so long as the employee or qualified beneficiary pays for the insurance. If an employee has health insurance that is partly paid for by the employee and partly paid for by the employer, the ex-employee will have to pay the full amount during the extension. COBRA does not apply to health plans of small employers, churches, or government entities. Small employers are defined as employers with fewer than 20 employees on a typical business day during the last quarter. A number of "qualifying" events will trigger COBRA, including death, termination (other than for misconduct), reduction of hours, retirement, Medicare entitlement, or employer's bankruptcy.[49] Reduction of hours is important because at many companies employees are only eligible for health insurance if they work a specified number of hours per week. For a qualified beneficiary, a divorce or legal separation from the employee spouse or the cessation of a child's dependency is a qualifying event. COBRA requires that the employee benefit plan administrator provide notice of the right to extend health insurance coverage. It does not specify the form for this notice, but courts have held that the notice should provide sufficient information for the employee or qualified beneficiary to make an informed decision. The employee or qualified beneficiary must be given a specified period in which to decide whether to accept the COBRA coverage. This period must be at least 60 days long. COBRA specifies various lengths for extension of the coverage depending on the situation: it generally ranges from 18 to 36 months.[50]

SOCIAL SECURITY

The Social Security Act, first enacted in 1935, created retirement benefits for workers. Since then, Social Security benefits have been extended to the worker's spouse and minor children (1939) and severely disabled workers (1956). The 1939 amendments added coverage for families of retired workers and workers who had died.[51] The states also can supplement this federal scheme if they so choose. The current debate about Social Security centers on fears that the system will become bankrupt and on proposed plans to prevent its bankruptcy.

In general, federal Social Security benefits are computed on the worker's earning records. This is true for all four basic types of payments—retirement, disability, dependents, and survivors. A *fully insured* worker is one who has worked at least 40 quarters (10 years). To use 2007 as an example, such workers will earn one-quarter of coverage for each $1,000 in covered earnings, including wages, farm wages, or income from self-employment, up to a maximum of four quarters per year.[52] A worker or his family may be eligible for benefits other than retirement benefits with less than 40 quarters.

Computing the actual benefits amount involves complicated arithmetical formulas based on the worker's age; date of retirement, disability, or death; and yearly earnings history (including the amount of salary). The amount of the benefit is dependent on the type of payment—retirement, disability, dependent, or survivor—and who is receiving it. Cost-of-living escalators tied to the *consumer price index* (the measurement of how the price of a group of consumer goods changes between two time periods) may raise benefits.

Disability benefits are available for covered workers who have been disabled at least five months. For eligibility, generally the worker must prove that he or she no longer can engage in substantial gainful employment. The disability must be expected to last at least 12 months or to result in death within 1 year.[53] Receipt of benefits paid under worker's compensation or other federal, state, or local disability plans may lessen the amount of benefits received from Social Security.

Monthly payments made to a retired or disabled worker's family or to the survivors of an insured worker are equal to a certain percentage (usually 50 or 75 percent) of the worker's benefits. For example, if a worker were entitled to $379 per month in benefits, the worker's wife or divorced wife who was married to the worker for at least 10 years and is not now married will receive $189.50 or $284.25 in monthly benefits. The act limits the amount one family can receive in total benefits. Similarly, benefits for a nondisabled child who no longer is attending high school normally end at age 18. Lump-sum death benefits to eligible persons cannot exceed $255. In 2000, earnings realized by retired persons between 65 and 69 could not exceed $17,000 without loss of benefits. The loss of benefits will be one dollar for every three dollars earned over the limit.

Those who have been denied Social Security benefits may appeal the Social Security Administration (SSA) decision. Usually, such persons file a request for reconsideration within 60 days of the date of the initial determination. The agency then conducts a thorough and independent review of the evidence. After this reconsideration, a person who is still adversely affected can file for a hearing or review by an ALJ. After the hearing, the ALJ issues a written decision setting out his or her findings of fact. All parties receive copies of this decision. The decision is binding unless appealed to the Appeals Council of the SSA or to a federal district court.

The Federal Insurance Contribution Act (FICA) taxes are paid by both employees and employers on wages earned by workers. FICA taxes fund Social Security and Medicare. In 2009, the combined tax rate paid was 7.65 percent (6.2 percent Social Security tax and 1.45 percent Medicare tax). Social Security tax is not assessed on that portion of the annual wages that exceed $106,800.[54] The Medicare tax is assessed on all wages.

Medicare (Part A) is often called hospital insurance and covers part of the expenses of reasonable and necessary care associated with a stay in a hospital or nursing facility.[55] In addition to receiving Medicare Part A, qualified persons can pay for a government-subsidized plan called Medicare Part B that will cover medical services beyond hospitalization, such as doctors' services and related medical expenses involving outpatient and rehabilitation costs, ambulance services, lab tests, and the like. It generally pays 80 percent of Medicare's approved charge for a covered treatment. In order to fill in the gaps in health care protection left by the Medicare program, some persons also purchase Medicare supplemental insurance, called Medigap insurance, from insurance companies. Another program, Medicaid, provides broad medical assistance to "categorically needy" individuals.

UNEMPLOYMENT COMPENSATION

Unemployment compensation represents a coordinated federal and state effort to provide economic security for temporarily unemployed workers. Generally, unemployment compensation only covers employees as defined in Chapter 28. The funds used for payments come from taxes, or "contributions," paid predominantly by employers. In a few states, employees also pay these taxes. Under the Federal Unemployment Tax Act (FUTA) employers must report and pay the tax on their employees' wages.[56] "Wages" include anything paid as compensation for employment and may consist of salaries, fees, bonuses, and commissions. In 2009, the maximum amount of wages subject to FUTA was $7,000 per employee and the FUTA rate was 6.2 percent on each employee's wages up to $7,000. The federal government allows a credit for participating in a state unemployment program. After the credit for state participation, most employers pay 0.8 percent or less in FUTA.[57]

State rates generally utilize "experience rating" or "merit rating" systems whereby the rate employers pay reflects each individual employer's experience with unemployment. Under such systems, employers whose workers suffer the most involuntary unemployment pay higher rates than employers whose workers suffer less unemployment. Since the aim of unemployment compensation involves the achievement of regular employment and the prevention of unemployment, such systems provide incentives to employers to keep their workforces intact.

State provisions regarding the criteria for eligibility and the amount of benefits vary greatly. However, generally a worker will not be eligible if he or she

- is discharged for good cause
- quits voluntarily without cause
- is unemployed due to a strike in which he or she is actively participating
- refuses to remain available to work and/or refuses to accept a similar substitute position

WORKER'S COMPENSATION

In contrast, the worker's compensation laws in the various states attempt to reimburse workers for injuries or death arising in the employment context. Generally, only employees are covered by worker's compensation. "Compensation" in this area does not refer to wages or salaries but rather to the money paid to indemnify the worker for employment-related injury or death. The employer usually self-insures; buys insurance; or, pays money into a state fund at a "merit" or "experience" rate reflective of the employer's actual incidence of employee injuries. Injured workers receive compensation for their injuries in the form of medical care and disability benefits, the latter often based on a specific statutory scale.

Worker's compensation acts impose *strict liability* on the employer for injuries to employees during the scope of their employment. In many states the employee can elect to sue under the common law or to collect under worker's compensation. However, under common law three defenses tend to prevent recovery by the employee: they are contributory negligence, assumption of the risk, and the fellow servant rule.[58] See Exhibit 30.4 for a summary of these doctrines. They were so effective at preventing recovery that they were labeled the three wicked sisters.[59] Worker's compensation statutes arose in part as a response to these "wicked sisters." Worker's compensation statutes were intended to be the exclusive remedy for work related injuries, although some states listed specific exceptions where employees could sue under other laws. Under worker's compensation statutes employees can receive compensation without engaging in costly litigation; and the employer, by passing these costs on to consumers, can recoup the costs of worker's compensation benefitting both sides.

The classes of employees covered by such acts depend on the particular statute involved. Agricultural, domestic, or casual laborers often are not covered because the right to compensation ordinarily depends on the nature of the work performed, the regularity of such work, and/or the status of the worker. To be covered, an employee ordinarily must be a worker—that is, a person who performs manual labor or similar duties. For this reason, worker's compensation statutes presumably do not cover directors, officers, or stockholders. Yet under the dual capacity doctrine, such persons can receive compensation if, when they suffer injury, they are performing the ordinary duties of the business. For example, a general manager of a tree-pruning service who is injured while pruning trees will be able to recover.

Typically the covered employee is eligible for workers' compensation for just about any employment-related injury or disease. Even a negligent employee usually can recover for injuries suffered while he or she was acting as an employee. Recent decisions allow recoveries for occupational diseases such as asbestosis, for work-related stress, and even for injuries suffered before or after work hours. Although worker's compensation generally takes the place of an employee's suing the employer, employees may be able to maintain product liability suits against manufacturers or suppliers and suits against fellow employees who cause their injuries.

ISSUES IN EMPLOYMENT LAW CREATED BY TECHNOLOGY

The digital age has had a profound impact on the workplace. Computers have replaced typewriters as the common medium for producing documents and telephones as the primary mode of communication. The Internet has made conducting research and finding information much easier—one can access data while at one's computer terminal instead of having to go to a library. Email and cell phone technologies have substantially accelerated both inter- and intra-firm exchanges. Consequently, employees' usage of computers has enlarged employees' control over their working hours (through telecommuting, job-sharing, and flex-time), increased productivity, lowered costs, and raised employee morale. The proliferation of technology also has multiplied the challenges in the employment context.

The alternative working arrangements made possible in an Internet-based world, though novel variations, implicate many traditional workplace issues—for instance, whether the workers in question are employees or independent contractors. As discussed in Chapter 28, such distinctions become legally important for a number of issues including the possible application of the federal antidiscrimination laws, worker's compensation, Social Security, and overtime pay. However, distinguishing between employees and independent contractors in the Internet environment can be especially problematic, given the fact that start-up companies often demand long hours from their workers. A misclassification can subject the employer to costly penalties, including the payment of retroactive overtime and overdue employee taxes.

The on-line recruiting revolution has brought about similar transformations. Employers who wish to attract younger staff must take into account these workers' tendency to use the Internet as their job-search tool of choice. The proliferation of company Web sites that list job openings and solicit résumés has led to the issue of when a person becomes an "applicant" under federal law.[60] This is a significant legal issue because the federal enforcement agencies, notably the EEOC and the Office of Federal Contract Compliance Programs (OFCCP), mandate that employers collect EEO data on all applicants. The compilation of these data, which focus on race, gender, and ethnicity, enable federal contractors to discharge their obligation to undertake affirmation action with regard to certain protected groups. "Applicants" used to consist of the people who walked into a personnel or recruiting office, filled out an application, and provided the requested EEO data. It was relatively simple for employers to manage their documentation and data collection responsibilities. Now, anyone seeking employment can, with a keyboard stroke, send generic résumés to the Web sites of innumerable firms. Employers fear that anyone who submits a résumé to the company's Web site may be an applicant, triggering the requirement to collect EEO data from that individual. This would be true regardless of whether a given employer has any openings, is recruiting, or is even accepting applications. Employers believe this interpretation would impose costly, time-consuming, and unjustified burdens on them without providing the benefits desired by the enforcement agencies (for example, guaranteeing an applicant pool that is as large as possible and ensuring recruiting practices that are fair, inclusive, and nondiscriminatory). Employers also fear that such an interpretation could lead to frivolous lawsuits by unqualified persons.[61]

Job applicants are also exposed to some new risks. Increasingly employers are using the "power of the Internet" to investigate applicants. For example, the employer can locate and view information that the applicant has posted on social networking sites, such as Facebook™ and YouTube™. Even the applicant's choice of username may cause the employer some concern.

The very nature of the technology heightens the potential for legal liability in a variety of contexts. For example, email can be the basis for hostile-working-environment sex discrimination under Title VII. Typical cases involve employees' uploading, downloading, or displaying inappropriate content (for example, pornographic materials on a firm's electronic bulletin board) or employees' using email to make unwelcome sexual overtures to other people. Companies will want to monitor any shared systems (such as bulletin boards) to identify and remove any inappropriate content. Employers also will want to adopt an anti-harassment policy that makes it clear that this policy also applies to the firm's email system.

Besides technology-related claims of discrimination, liability can arise from defamatory statements, copyright violations, and the disclosure of trade secrets or other proprietary information. Consequently, preventing such claims is a powerful rationale for monitoring employees' usage of the Internet and email. One common misconception is that deleting files destroys email; however, retrieval specialists are quite adept at locating these messages and these retrieved messages are often admissible in court.

Before implementing any monitoring regime, employers should inform employees (ideally through a written policy and/or employee handbook) that employee Internet and email usage are intended only for company business and may be monitored. A well-crafted policy will inform employees of the types of conduct that constitute illegal or improper use and the bases for discipline and discharge under the policy. Still, employers should confine monitoring activities to work-related email and target specific problems (for example, reduced productivity stemming from employees' "surfing" the Internet during work hours) rather than totally banning all personal email and Internet usage.[62]

Any policy that is adopted should state that because the firm owns and maintains the equipment, employees have no expectations of privacy regarding computer and Internet usage and consent both to monitoring and to the disclosure of the results of any monitoring. Employees who wish to challenge such work rules have limited options because the federal Constitution does not protect private sector employees in the same way it protects *public sector* (governmental) employees. Even as to public sector employees, prior notice of the surveillance generally will defeat these employees' expectations of privacy. Similarly, the rights of freedom of speech and the prohibition on unreasonable searches and seizures generally do not curtail the employer's right to monitor. A few states have enacted laws pertaining specifically to the monitoring of email, so you should check the coverage of these statutes. You should make a conscious effort to keep up-to-date as these areas of law evolve.

Contemporary Case

PENNSYLVANIA STATE POLICE v. SUDERS
542 U.S. 129, 2004 U.S. LEXIS 4176 (2004)

FACTS[63] The Pennsylvania State Police (PSP) hired Nancy Drew Suders as a police communications operator for the McConnellsburg barracks, where she was supervised by three officers. These three supervisors subjected Suders to a continuous barrage of sexual harassment. Suders took a required computer-skills exam several times. Each time, her supervisors told her that she had failed. Suders found her exams in a set of drawers. She concluded that her tests had not been graded and the reports that she had failed were false. Suders removed the tests. When her supervisors discovered that the exams had been removed, they devised a plan to arrest her for theft. They dusted the drawer with a theft-detection powder that turns hands blue. When Suders attempted to return the tests to the drawer, her hands turned blue. The supervisors apprehended and handcuffed her, photographed her blue hands, and commenced to question her. Suders had already prepared a written resignation, which she gave the supervisors soon after they detained her. They still brought her to an interrogation room and continued to question her. Suders reiterated that she wanted to resign, and then they let her leave. Suders spoke to the Equal Employment Opportunity Officer twice before she resigned, but did not file a formal complaint.

ISSUE When a plaintiff sues for constructive discharge based on actions of her supervisors, can the employer use its reporting procedures as a defense?

HOLDING Yes. An employer can use as an affirmative defense that it has effective procedures for reporting and dealing with sexual harassment and that the plaintiff failed to use them.

REASONING Excerpts from the opinion of Justice Ginsburg:

... This Court granted certiorari ... to resolve the disagreement among the Circuits. ...

Under the constructive discharge doctrine, an employee's reasonable decision to resign because of unendurable working conditions is assimilated to a formal discharge for remedial purposes. ... The inquiry is objective: Did working conditions become so intolerable that a reasonable person in the employee's position would have felt compelled to resign? ... Our starting point is the framework *Ellerth* and *Faragher* established to govern employer liability for sexual harassment by supervisors. ... [T]hose decisions delineate two categories of hostile work environment claims: (1) harassment that "culminates in a tangible employment action," for which employers are strictly liable, ... and (2) harassment that takes place in the absence of a tangible employment action, to which employers may assert an affirmative defense. ... [The question is into which category do hostile-environment constructive discharge claims fall.] A tangible employment action ... "constitutes a significant change in employment status, such as hiring, firing, failing to promote, reassignment with significantly different responsibilities, or a decision causing a significant change in benefits." ... Ordinarily, the tangible employment decision "is documented in official company records, and may be subject to review by higher level supervisors." ... We acknowledged that a supervisor's "power and authority invests his or her harassing conduct with a particular threatening character ...".

The Court reasoned that tying the liability standard to an employer's effort to install effective grievance procedures would advance Congress' purpose "to promote conciliation rather than litigation" of Title VII controversies. ... [W]e held that when no tangible employment action is taken, the employer may defeat vicarious liability for supervisor harassment by establishing ... both that "the employer exercised reasonable care to prevent and correct promptly any sexually harassing behavior," and that "the plaintiff employee unreasonably failed to take advantage of any preventive or corrective opportunities provided by the employer ...".

For an atmosphere of sexual harassment or hostility to be actionable, ... the offending behavior "must be sufficiently severe or pervasive to alter the conditions of the victim's employment and create an abusive working environment." ... A hostile-environment constructive discharge claim entails something more: A plaintiff who advances such a ... claim must show working conditions so intolerable that a reasonable person would have felt compelled to resign. ... [H]arassment so intolerable as to cause a resignation may be effected through co-worker conduct, unofficial supervisory conduct, or official company acts. ... But when an official act does not underlie the constructive discharge, the *Ellerth* and *Faragher* analysis ... calls for extension of the affirmative defense to the employer. ... [A]n official act reflected in company records—a demotion or a reduction in compensation, for example—shows "beyond question" that the supervisor has used his managerial or controlling position to the employee's disadvantage.

... Absent such an official act, the extent to which the supervisor's misconduct has been aided by the agency relation ... is less certain. That uncertainty ... justifies affording the employer the chance to establish . . . that it should not be held vicariously liable. . . .

[T]he plaintiff who alleges no tangible employment action has the duty to mitigate harm, but the defendant bears the burden to allege and prove that the plaintiff failed in that regard. . . . [This] case . . . presents genuine issues of material fact concerning Suders' hostile work environment and constructive discharge claims. . . . [We] remand the case for further proceedings consistent with this opinion.

You Be the Judge

The "Rooney Rule"[64] was implemented in 2003 and requires National Football League (NFL) teams to interview at least one minority candidate for head coaching positions. In 2009 the rule was broadened to include openings for the team's senior operations position. The actual name of the position varies by team. (There are exceptions, such as when the senior operations position is held by the owner, a member of the owner's family, or there is a pre-existing contract promising to promote someone to the position.) There are currently seven minority head coaches in the 32-team NFL or 22 percent. There are only nine minority head coaches in the 120 major colleges. About 47 percent of the college players are African American but six percent of the coaches are.

In January 2009, the New Jersey Legislature introduced a bill urging the National Collegiate Athletic Association (NCAA) to adopt the Rooney Rule. The Oregon Legislature went further passing legislation (2009 Ore. ALS 780) that requires Oregon universities to interview at least one minority candidate before hiring a head football coach. The statute applies to the six state universities with football teams. Does college football need a version of the "Rooney Rule?" If *you* were on the governing board of the NCAA, would *you* support a "Rooney Rule?" [See Mark Anderson, "BYU's Mendenhall Prefers Ending Las Vegas Bowl Streak," *Las Vegas Review-Journal*, July 22, 2009, 11C; Associated Press, "NFL Broadens 'Rooney Rule' to Include Senior Posts," *Sports News*, June 15, 2009; Rachel Bachman, "'Rooney Rule' Bill in Rotation," *The Oregonian* (Portland, Oregon), Sports, March 3, 2009.]

Summary

The Wagner, Taft-Hartley, and Landrum-Griffin acts set out a pervasive federal scheme for the regulation of labor. This blueprint of federal labor law broadly regulates employees' rights to organize and to engage in concerted activities in furtherance of their objectives. Both employees and employers are protected from unfair labor practices. The National Labor Relations Board (NLRB) retains jurisdiction over labor disputes, oversees elections, and arbitrates disputes about the duty to bargain.

A host of federal statutes extensively regulates fair employment practices. Title VII of the Civil Rights Act of 1964 prohibits employers, labor organizations, or employment agencies from engaging in employment discrimination based on color, race, religion, sex, or national origin. The Equal Employment Opportunity Commission (EEOC) enforces many of these federal laws and sets out the procedures. Employment criteria that have a disparate impact on minorities are illegal unless the employer can show that the criteria are job-related. Employers also may be liable for the disparate treatment of their employees. The issue of reverse discrimination remains controversial in the Title VII context. Limited defenses based on bona fide occupational qualifications (BFOQs) are available for the protected categories of religion, sex, and national origin; a BFOQ never can be based on race. The Immigration Reform and Control Act of 1986, the Equal Pay Act of 1963, the Age Discrimination in Employment Act of 1967, the Rehabilitation Act of 1973, the Americans with Disabilities Act of 1990, the Civil Rights Act of 1991, the Family and Medical Leave Act of 1993, and other federal statutes protect qualified individuals against employment discrimination. State law often supplements this comprehensive federal scheme.

The Occupational Safety and Health Act (OSHA) attempts to ensure safe and healthful working conditions for American workers. Federal and state benefit programs aid workers, the disabled, the blind, and the aged. Unemployment compensation is designed to provide economic security for temporarily unemployed workers. The funds generally come from taxes paid by the employer and/or employee.

State worker's compensation statutes attempt to reimburse workers for injuries or death resulting from the employment relationship. The classes of employees covered in such acts depend on the particular statute involved; but eligible employees may recover for occupational diseases and injuries resulting from the employee's own negligence.

Discussion Questions

1. List a few of the rights guaranteed and the practices prohibited by the Wagner, Taft-Hartley, and Landrum-Griffin acts.

2. Explain the boundaries of state regulation of labor.

3. What are the protected classes of employees under Title VII? How do these protections relate to bona fide occupational qualifications?

4. Why is the issue of reverse discrimination such a difficult problem?

5. Name other statutes that guarantee fair employment, and explain how these more recent statutes build on earlier fair employment statutes.

Case Problems and Writing Assignments

1. On February 27, 1995, Abner J. Morgan, Jr., a black male, filed a charge of discrimination and retaliation against the National Railroad Passenger Corporation (Amtrak) with the EEOC and cross-filed with the California Department of Fair Employment and Housing. Morgan alleged that during his employment with Amtrak, he was "consistently harassed and disciplined more harshly than other employees on account of his race." The EEOC issued a notice of right to sue on July 3, 1996, and Morgan filed this lawsuit on October 2, 1996. Some of the allegedly discriminatory acts about which Morgan complained occurred within 300 days of the time in which he had filed his complaint with the EEOC. However, many took place prior to that time period. Amtrak filed a motion, arguing that it was entitled to summary judgment on all incidents that had occurred more than 300 days before the filing of Morgan's EEOC charge. The district court, holding that the company could not be liable for conduct that fell outside the 300-day filing period, granted partial summary judgment to Amtrak. Morgan appealed. The United States Court of Appeals for the Ninth Circuit reversed, relying on its previous statement of the continuing violation doctrine, which allows courts to consider conduct that would ordinarily be time barred as long as the untimely incidents represent an ongoing unlawful employment practice. When determining liability in hostile work environment suits under Title VII, may courts consider acts that have occurred outside the applicable statute of limitations time period? [See *National Railroad Passenger Corporation v. Morgan*, 536 U.S. 101 (2002).]

2. In his application for employment with Waffle House, Inc., Eric Baker agreed that "any dispute or claim" concerning his employment would be "settled by binding arbitration." All prospective Waffle House employees were required, as a condition of employment, to sign an application form containing a similar mandatory arbitration agreement. Baker began working as a grill operator at a Waffle House restaurant on August 10, 1994. Sixteen days later, he suffered a seizure at work and soon thereafter was discharged. Baker did not initiate arbitration proceedings in 1994; but, in 2001, he filed charges with the EEOC. Specifically, Baker claimed that his discharge violated the ADA. The EEOC charged Waffle House with disability discrimination and requested injunctive relief, as well as backpay, reinstatement, and compensatory and punitive damages in order to make Baker whole. Waffle House filed a petition under the Federal Arbitration Act (FAA) to compel arbitration or to dismiss the EEOC's action. The circuit court of appeals concluded that, because the EEOC was not a party to the otherwise valid and enforceable arbitration agreement between Waffle House and Baker and because the EEOC had independent statutory authority to bring suit, the arbitration agreement would not foreclose EEOC's enforcement action. It limited the EEOC's remedies to injunctive relief and precluded the agency from seeking victim-specific relief because in its view the FAA policy favoring the enforcement of private arbitration agreements outweighed the EEOC's right to proceed in federal court when it seeks primarily to vindicate private, rather than public, interests. Does a private arbitration agreement prevent the EEOC from pursuing victim-specific relief in suits brought on behalf of employees who had agreed to arbitrate employment-related disputes? [See *EEOC v. Waffle House, Inc.*, 534 U.S. 279 (2002).]

3. Eastern Associated Coal Corporation and the United Mine Workers of America (UMA) were parties to a collective-bargaining agreement. The agreement specified that in order to discharge an employee, Eastern must prove it had "just cause."

Otherwise, the arbitrator would order the employee reinstated. The arbitrator's decision was final. James Smith worked for Eastern as a member of a road crew, a job that required him to drive heavy, trucklike vehicles on public highways. As a truck driver, Smith was subject to Department of Transportation (DOT) regulations requiring random drug testing of workers engaged in "safety-sensitive" tasks. In March 1996, Smith tested positive for marijuana. So, Eastern sought to discharge Smith. When the union took Smith's case to arbitration, the arbitrator concluded that Smith's positive drug test did not amount to "just cause" for discharge. The arbitrator ordered Smith's reinstatement, provided that Smith (1) accept a suspension of 30 days without pay, (2) participate in a substance-abuse program, and (3) undergo drug tests at the discretion of Eastern (or an approved substance-abuse professional) for the next five years.

Between April 1996 and January 1997, Smith passed four random drug tests. But in July 1997, he again tested positive for marijuana; and Eastern once more sought to discharge Smith. The arbitrator again concluded that Smith's use of marijuana did not amount to "just cause" for discharge, because of two mitigating circumstances: First, Smith had been a good employee for 17 years. And, second, Smith had sworn that a personal/family problem had caused this one-time lapse in drug usage. The arbitrator ordered Smith's reinstatement subject to five more rigorous conditions. Eastern, seeking to have the arbitrator's award set aside, argued that the award contravened a public policy aimed at prohibiting the operation of dangerous machinery by workers who test positive for drugs. How should this issue be resolved? [See *Eastern Associated Coal Corporation v. United Mine Workers of America*, 531 U.S. 57 (2000).]

Notes

1. Justice Brennan did not participate in the case.
2. The proposed Employee Free Choice Act will make secret ballots unnecessary if a majority of the employees sign authorization cards. Fred S. Steingold, *The Employer's Legal Handbook* (Nolo, Berkeley, CA: 2009), p. 256.
3. See 301 U.S. 1 (1937).
4. Courts and the NLRB have wrestled with the question of who is a supervisor.
5. *Fibreboard Paper Products Corp. v. NLRB*, 379 U.S. 203, 223 (1964).
6. 29 U.S.C.A. § 164(b), cited in James Buchwalter et al., § 528 State Right-to-Work Statutes, 48 Am. Jur. 2d Labor and Labor Relations.
7. Federal Laws Prohibiting Job Discrimination, Questions and Answers, http://www.eeoc.gov/facts/qanda.html (accessed 12/31/09).
8. IRS 2009 Instructions for Form 940, http://www.irs.gov/pub/irs-pdf/i940.pdf (accessed 1/4/10).
9. *Walters v. Metropolitan Educational Enterprises, Inc.*, 519 U.S. 202 (1997).
10. *Griggs v. Duke Power Co.*, 401 U.S. 424, 431-32 (1971).
11. In *McDonnell Douglas Corp. v. Green*, 411 U.S. 792, 802 (1973), the Supreme Court said that to establish a prima facie case of discrimination, plaintiffs must demonstrate that the tests being used select applicants in a racial pattern significantly different from the pool of applicants. Michael J. Songer,

"Going Back to Class? The Reemergence of Class in Critical Race Theory Symposium: Note: Decline of Title VII Disparate Impact: The Role of the 1991 Civil Rights Act and the Ideologies of Federal Judges," 11 Mich. J. Race & L. 247, 251 (2005).
12. *Griggs*, 401 U.S. 424, 433-34, as cited in Songer, p. 251.
13. 29 C.F.R. 1607.4(D) (1979).
14. *Hazelwood School District v. United States*, 433 U.S. 299, 311 (1977).
15. A 1976 case, *McDonald v. Santa Fe Trail Transportation Co.*, 427 U.S. 273 (1976) held that whites can sue for racial discrimination when they receive disparate treatment. In this case, the employer had accused two whites and one black of misappropriating a shipment of antifreeze. The company fired both white employees but retained the black worker. The Supreme Court concluded that Title VII prohibits all forms of racial discrimination, including *reverse discrimination* of this type.
16. 477 U.S. 57 (1986).
17. *Oncale v. Sundowner Offshore Services, Inc.*, 523 U.S. 75 (1998).
18. To illustrate the need for an effective policy, in 1994, a female secretary in one of the largest law firms in the country won a $3.5 million judgment against the firm and the partner who allegedly had harassed numerous women over a 14-year period. More recently, in 1999, Ford Motor

Company agreed to pay $7.5 million in damages and millions more in training costs as part of its settlement of an EEOC-initiated sexual discrimination complaint brought on behalf of female workers in two Chicago area plants. This settlement followed the 1998 one involving Mitsubishi Motor Manufacturing Company's record-breaking $34 million agreement to settle a similar case at its Normal, Illinois, plant. Courts will frequently ask employees whether they were aware of the sexual harassment policy and the extent to which they used it to resolve their claims.

19. Andrew J. Robinson, "Comment: Language, National Origin, and Employment Discrimination: The Importance of the EEOC Guidelines," 157 U. Pa. L. Rev. 1513 (2009) citing EEOC data in endnote 8.

20. *Espinoza v. Farah Mfg. Co., Inc.*, 414 U.S. 86 (1973).

21. Legal aliens generally have the right to work under the Fourteenth Amendment's Equal Protection Clause. They may be excluded from certain jobs if it is necessary to the public welfare. Laura Hunter Dietz et al., § 1874 Basic Rule of Right to Work, 3B Am. Jur. 2d Aliens and Citizens.

22. 499 U.S. 187 (1991).

23. *E.E.O.C. v. Com. of Pa*, 829 F.2d 392 (3d Cir. 1987), cited in Kenneth W. Biedzynski et al., § 264 Safety-Related BFOQs, 45A Am. Jur. 2d Job Discrimination.

24. *O'Connor v. Consolidated Coin Caterers Corporation*, 519 U.S. 1040 (1996).

25. After John McCain spoke against corrective legislation, Lilly Ledbetter became a figure in the 2008 presidential campaign making an ad for Barrack Obama and speaking at the Democratic National Convention. Lani Guinier, "Symposium The Most Disparaged Branch: The Role of Congress in the Twenty-First Century: Panel IV: Beyond Legislatures: Social Movements, Social Change, and the Possibilities of Demoprudence: Courting the People: Demoprudence and the Law/Politics Divide," 89 B.U. L. Rev. 539 (2009).

26. 127 S. Ct. 2162 (2007).

27. A five-justice opinion spoke for the majority. Justice Ruth Bader Ginsburg wrote and spoke for the four dissenting justices. She read her dissent aloud from the bench to express "more than ordinary disagreement." Justice Ruth Bader Ginsburg, The 20th Annual Leo and Berry Eizenstat Memorial Lecture: The Role of Dissenting Opinions (October 21, 2007), http://www.supremecourtus.gov/publicinfo/speeches/sp_10-21-07.html cited in Guinier, Symposium.

28. EEOC Notice Concerning the Lilly Ledbetter Fair Pay Act of 2009, http://archive.eeoc.gov/epa/ledbetter.html (accessed 1/3/10).

29. 401 U.S. 424 (1971).

30. Songer, supra note 11, p. 250.

31. Songer, supra note 11, where the author compares disparate impact decisions prior to and following the 1991 act.

32. Board of Trustees of the *University of Alabama v. Garrett*, 531 U.S. 356 (2001).

33. *Kimel v. Florida Board of Regents*, 528 U.S. 62, 92, (2000). States that refuse to consent are entitled to immunity from private damage suits under the ADEA, also.

34. *Kolstad v. American Dental Association*, 527 U.S. 526 (1999).

35. Ibid., 534.

36. Ibid., 542.

37. The amendments redefined disability and created new rules for interpreting the term because Congress thought that the standard set out by the Supreme Court in *Toyota Motor Manufacturing, Kentucky, Inc. v. Williams* was too high. Kathy E. Hinck et al., § 2 ADA and Implementing Regulatory Provisions, Am. Jur. 2d Americans with Disabilities Act Analysis and Implications § 2.

38. See Philip A. Kilgore & John T. Merrell, "Redefining 'Disabled': The ADA Amendments Act of 2008," 21 S. Carolina Lawyer 24 (July 2009) and its summary of the 2008 Amendments.

39. See http://www.eeoc.gov/eeoc/statistics/enforcement/ada-charges.cfm (accessed 12/31/09).

40. Ibid.

41. However, data from a pre-ADA survey of federal contractors showed that the compliance costs/workplace changes incurred under the Rehabilitation Act of 1973 for half of the companies amounted to zero dollars and for 30 percent of the companies it was less than $500. In only 8 percent of the cases did the changes cost more than $2,000.

42. FMLA § 102.

43. *Stimpson v. United Parcel Service*, 2009 U.S. App. LEXIS 24245,18 (6th Cir. 2009), Not recommended for full-text publication, citing 29 USC § 2611(11).

44. *Brown v. Eastern Maine Medical Center*, 514 F. Supp. 2d 104, 110 (Dist. of Me. 2007), citing the text of 29 CFR § 825.203(a).

45. It is not necessary for the employee to obtain the employer's permission in advance for intermittent or reduced leave taken for the purpose of caring for a family member or for a serious health condition of the employee. The employer and employee must agree to any intermittent or reduced leave that the employee takes for the birth or adoption of a child, however.

46. *Martin v. Occupational Safety and Health Review Commission*, 499 U.S. 144 (1991).

47. *Whirlpool Corp. v. Marshall*, 445 U.S. 1, 3 (1980), footnote 3 citing the text of 29 CFR § 1977.12 (1979).

48. Ibid.

49. Mary Babb Morris et al., § 160 Employer's Notice Requirements, 27 Am. Jur. 2d Employment Relationship.

50. Ibid. Laura Hunter Dietz, P 7615 Group-Health Plan Continuation Coverage (COBRA), 33A Am. Jur. 2d Federal Taxation. During difficult economic times, employees may be eligible for a subsidy on their premiums.

51. Social Security Online, In-Depth Research, Legislative History, 1939 Amendments, http://www.socialsecurity.gov/history/1939amends.html (accessed 1/4/10).

52. Ibid., p. 23.

53. In *Barnhart v. Walton*, 535 U.S. 212 (2002), the Supreme Court upheld the Social Security Administration's interpretation of this statutory provision.

54. The rates and the cut-off point change annually.

55. There have been large-scale changes to the Medicare program under the Medicare Modernization Act of 2003. In addition, in 2004 the EEOC issued proposed regulations permitting employers to reduce or eliminate health coverage for their retirees aged 65 or older. The EEOC was sued over this rule, and the court of appeals upheld the EEOC's position. *American Association of Retired Persons v. Equal Employment Opportunity Commission*, 489 F.3d 558 (3rd Cir. 2007).

56. The Federal Unemployment Tax Act was amended in 2008.

57. Fred S. Steingold, *The Employer's Legal Handbook*, 9th edition, (Berkeley, CA: Nolo, 2009), p. 109.

58. The fellow servant rule (also known as the fellow employee rule) bars recovery from the employer when the employee was injured by the acts of a fellow employee.

59. Bryan A. Garner, *Black's Law Dictionary*, 7th edition, (St. Paul: West, 1999), p. 1490.

60. Federal guidance as of 2002 defined an applicant as "a person who has indicated an interest in being considered for hiring, promotion, or other employment opportunities."

61. In 2002 the pertinent agencies assembled a taskforce to come up with a reasonable clarification of the range of possible definitions.

62. In this regard, some employers dedicate a computer terminal that employees can use for a limited duration for personal emails—during their breaks, for example—as long as the usage is lawful and nondisruptive of ordinary business operations.

63. The facts are contested, but they are considered in the light most favorable to Suders because of the District Court's summary judgment.

64. The rule is named for Pittsburgh Steelers owner Dan Rooney, who chaired the NFL's diversity committee that drafted the rule.

Part IX

Property Protection

I n the United States, the right to own property is one of our most fundamental rights. Preserving the right to pursue and maintain property was a primary concern of our founders; this is evident in the Constitution, especially in the search and seizure limits of the Fourth Amendment and the taking and due process clauses of the Fifth Amendment.

The Constitution balances the right to own property with the need for government to maintain order and promote the good of society. Consequently, Congress has the right of eminent domain, or the right to take private lands if they are necessary for a "public use." Balancing the rights of businesses and individuals with the needs of government continues to be a pressing issue.

Part IX examines how local, state, and federal laws treat property and property rights, as well as the manner in which property is created and transferred. This part addresses real property and personal property in Chapter 39 and intellectual property in Chapter 40.

39

Property and Joint Ownership

Agenda

A number of property issues will arise as eClass conducts business.
For example, eClass owns the right to produce eAccounting. How can Ani,
Meg, and Yousef protect this asset? What type of property is it? What are the
rights and obligations that accompany ownership? How can eClass best
protect its property?

Ani, Meg, and Yousef will need to purchase or rent real property for
manufacturing plants and warehouse space. What information do they need
as they engage in these undertakings? If eClass purchases real estate, what
type of deed would it prefer? Why? Ani's parents have a barn on their
property. eClass would like to purchase the property and renovate the barn
into a warehouse. If the land is not zoned for commercial use, can eClass
lawfully do this? What problems may arise from such activity?

Yousef read an article about a firm purchasing an office building for its
own office and renting out the remaining space to other companies. He
believes that this may provide eClass with a method of financing an office

building from the rents generated by renting out the excess space. Yousef suggested that the firm consider this as an effective method to acquire an office building. What should eClass consider before implementing such a plan?

eClass leases equipment from an electronics firm. Meg is concerned that eClass may be liable for any damages to the equipment and she feels this equipment should be insured by eClass during the period of the lease. Yousef disagrees. He argues that in leases of industrial equipment, the party leasing the equipment assumes the risk relating to damages. Who is correct? Why? When eClass rents extra delivery trucks, what are the legal rights of the lessor and eClass?

Assume an eClass debtor is a joint owner in an apartment complex. If this debtor defaults on his obligations to the firm, can eClass attach the debtor's interest in the apartment complex and force a sale of the property to satisfy its claim? What issues would affect eClass's rights?

Be prepared! You never know when the firm or one of its members will seek your advice.

Classic Case

LUCAS v. SOUTH CAROLINA COASTAL COUNCIL

505 U.S. 1003, 1992 U.S. LEXIS 4537 (1992)

FACTS In the late 1970s, David H. Lucas and others were involved in extensive residential development on the Isle of Palms, a barrier island east of Charleston, South Carolina. In 1986, Lucas paid $975,000 for two residential lots for his personal investment, intending to build single-family homes on the lots. At the time, the lots were zoned for single-family residential use and there were no other restrictions on them. In 1988, the state legislature passed the Beachfront Management Act, based on an official report that the beaches named in the act were seriously eroding. The act directed the South Carolina Coastal Council to establish a baseline and permanently prohibited the building of *any* inhabitable structures between the baseline and the ocean. The legislature concluded that the area was not stabilized and setback lines were required to protect people and property from storms, high tides, and beach erosion. No exceptions were allowed under the act.[1] When the baseline was established, Lucas's lots were between the baseline and the ocean, thereby preventing Lucas from building any inhabitable structures on either of his parcels.

ISSUES Did the state take Lucas's property in violation of the Fifth Amendment of the Constitution, which prohibits the taking of property without due process of law? Must the state pay Lucas for the lots because the act deprived him of all economically viable use of the property?

HOLDINGS Yes, there appears to be a taking in violation of the Constitution. The issue of payment is to be decided on remand.

REASONING Excerpts from the opinion of Justice Scalia:

... [T]he Fifth Amendment is violated when land-use regulation "does not substantially advance legitimate state interests *or denies an owner economically viable use of his land.*" ... [I]n the extraordinary circumstance when *no* productive or economically beneficial use of land is permitted, it is less realistic to indulge our usual assumption that the legislature is simply "adjusting the benefits and burdens of economic life". . . . [S]upporting a compensation requirement is the fact that regulations that leave the owner of land without economically beneficial or productive options for its use—typically . . . by requiring land to be left substantially in its natural state—carry with them a heightened risk that private property is being pressed into some form of public service under the guise of mitigating serious public harm. . . . The many statutes on the books, both state and federal, that provide for the use of eminent domain to impose servitudes on private scenic lands preventing developmental uses, or to acquire such lands altogether, suggest the practical equivalence in this setting of negative regulation and appropriation. . . . [W]hen the owner of real property has been called upon to sacrifice *all* economically beneficial uses in the name of the common good, that is, to leave his property economically idle, he has suffered a taking. . . . [O]ur "takings" jurisprudence . . . has traditionally been guided by the understandings of our citizens regarding the content of, and the State's power over, the "bundle of rights" that they acquire when they obtain title to property. . . . [T]he property owner necessarily expects the uses of his property to be restricted . . . by various measures newly enacted by the State in legitimate exercise of its police powers. . . . When . . . a regulation . . . goes beyond what the relevant background principles would dictate, compensation must be paid to sustain it. . . . The "total taking" inquiry . . . will ordinarily entail . . . analysis of . . . the degree of harm to public lands and resources, or adjacent private property, posed by the claimant's proposed activities . . . , the social value of the claimant's activities and their suitability to the locality in question, . . . and the relative ease with which the alleged harm can be avoided through measures taken by the claimant and the government (or adjacent private landowners) alike . . . The fact that a particular use has long been engaged in by similarly situated owners ordinarily imports a lack of any common-law prohibition (though changed circumstances or new knowledge may make what was previously permissible no longer so . . .) So also does the fact that other landowners, similarly situated, are permitted to continue the use denied to the claimant. It seems unlikely that common-law principles would have prevented the erection of any habitable or productive improvements on petitioner's land; . . . [common-law principles] rarely support prohibition of the "essential use" of land. . . . The question, however, is one of state law to be dealt with on remand. . . . [T]o win its case South Carolina must do more than proffer the legislature's declaration that the uses Lucas desires are inconsistent with the public interest. . . . Instead, . . . South Carolina must identify background principles of nuisance and property law that prohibit the uses he now intends in the circumstances in which the property is presently found. Only on this showing can the State fairly claim that . . . the Beachfront Management Act is taking nothing. . . .

PROPERTY RIGHTS

There are two distinctly different meanings for *property*. First, the term means an object that is subject to ownership, a valuable asset. Second, property means a group of rights and interests that are protected by the law. These rights and interests are commonly called "a bundle of rights" and are illustrated in Exhibit 39.1. A multitude

Exhibit 39.1

The Bundle of Rights

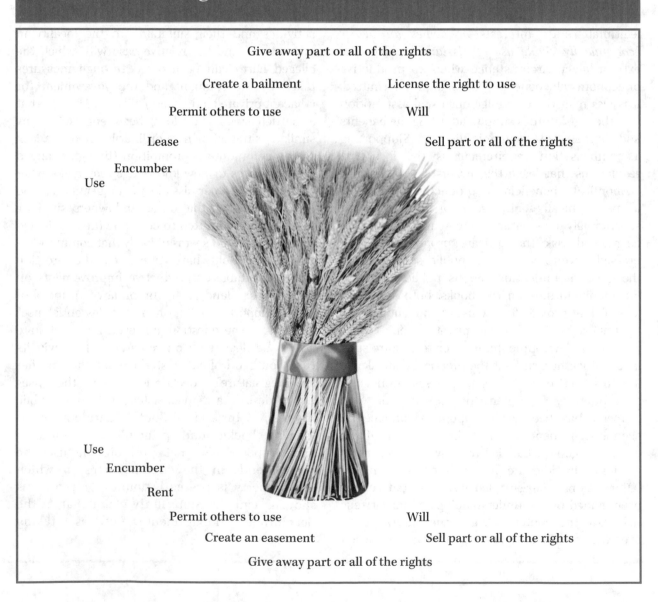

Give away part or all of the rights

Create a bailment   License the right to use

Permit others to use   Will

Lease   Sell part or all of the rights

Encumber

Use

Use

Encumber

Rent

Permit others to use   Will

Create an easement   Sell part or all of the rights

Give away part or all of the rights

of rights are associated with property ownership. Ownership entitles a person (1) to use the property personally; (2) to make improvements to the property; (3) to give someone else the use of the property; (4) to rent the use of the property to someone else; (5) to sell the property; (6) to use the property to secure a loan; or (7) to abandon the property. The rights include the rights to enjoy and use the property; to economically exploit the property based on present and potential uses; and to exclude others from occupancy or use of the property. Even though the owner has a bundle of rights, there are limits on his or her rights.

When one owner has rights, it may limit the rights of other owners. Ownership of real property normally entitles the owner to continued use and enjoyment of the property in its present condition. For example, suppose you owned a house with a beautiful view of the mountains. If someone purchased an adjacent lot and started constructing a three-story house that would block your view, you can sue for an injunction to prohibit that person from interfering with the view. Such a lawsuit will succeed in some states.[2] Your rights will limit their rights. Many states also recognize that property owners have the right of support from adjoining lands; the right to use bodies of water adjacent to the property; limited rights to the airspace above it; the right to things growing on it; the right to things attached to it; and the right to things, like minerals, below its surface. However, owners or prior owners may have transferred some of these rights. Many communities now recognize and protect the right to have sun fall on existing solar collectors.

There are three *main* components of property ownership—ownership, possession, and title. Ownership includes all the rights related to the ownership of property. Possession includes the right to control the property by having it in one's custody or by directing who shall have custody of it. The concept of title includes both the current legal ownership of the property and the methods of its acquisition. Title also refers to the written evidence of ownership that appears on a certificate of title for the property, such as a real estate deed or a certificate of title for an automobile.

CLASSIFICATION OF PROPERTY

Property is divided on two dimensions. Real property is land and things that are growing on the land, attached to the land, or constructed on the land. Everything else is considered personal property. Property is also divided into tangible and intangible property. Tangible property is property that has a physical, material existence—it can be seen and touched. Tangible real property includes soil, crops, and buildings. Laptop computers and desks are examples of tangible personal property. On the other hand, intangible property has a conceptual existence, but no physical existence—it cannot be touched. Intangible real property includes *easements* (the right to use the real estate of another), real estate leases, and mortgages. Copyrights and patents, discussed in detail in Chapter 40, are examples of intangible personal property. Money, negotiable instruments, and stock certificates, among others, are also classified as intangible personal property. While each has physical existence, the value of each is intangible and that value is the "property,"

Exhibit 39.2

Types of Property

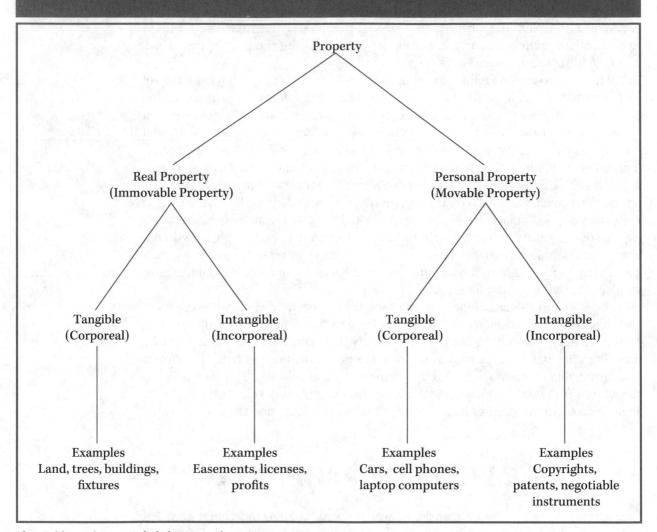

The civil law titles are included in parentheses.

the paper on which they are printed does not have value in and of itself. Exhibit 39.2 illustrates the Types of Property. It shows both the common law and the civil law terms. We will use the common law terms used by most states. It is important to remember that most property law is state law and the rules vary by state.

Real Property Defined

Our discussion will begin with *real property* or, as it is commonly called, *real estate*. Significant differences exist between real and personal property. Ownership of land and things growing on the land is a society-based concept. The idea that individuals can own land, trees, and plants is prevalent in European countries and the United States; however, it is not universal. A notable exception is found in Native American cultures. Real property is land and things that are permanently attached to the land, including buildings, roadways, and storage structures. Property that is permanently attached to buildings is also considered real property and is called a *fixture*.

A *fixture* is property that at one time was movable and independent of real estate but became attached to it. Examples are water heaters, central air-conditioning units, furnaces, built-in ovens, installed dishwashers, bathroom sinks, and copper pipes for plumbing. A builder who is constructing a house will buy a water heater (personal property at the time of the purchase), take it to the construction site, and permanently attach it to the plumbing lines and the gas or electric lines. After the personal property has been attached, it becomes a fixture.

In determining whether an item is a fixture as opposed to personal property, courts will look at the reasonable expectations and understandings of most people. For instance, most people would be shocked if they purchased a house and then discovered that the sellers had removed the handles on the kitchen cabinets and the plates over the light switches when the sellers moved out. The same buyers, however, expect the sellers to remove the tables, chairs, and other furniture. Ceiling lights are fixtures, while table lamps are household goods. Plants in a flower bed are real property; plants in pots are personal property. Wall-to-wall carpeting is real property; area rugs are personal property. Refrigerators, mirrors, and paintings are generally personal property but may be treated as real property if they are an integral part of the building.

In making this distinction between fixtures and personal property, courts also consider how much damage would occur to the overall property if the item in question were removed.

The Nature of Plants

Another issue concerns plants: Are they real property or personal property? Real estate includes plants that are growing on the land, such as fruit and shade trees, tomatoes, strawberries, artichokes, and trees that are being grown for timber. If a farmer sells land with crops still growing on it, the farmer is clearly selling real estate.

Sometimes a farmer or another landowner may sell the plants but keep the land. In this case, did the landowner sell real or personal property? The common law rule is that if the plants were still growing when the title passed to the buyer, the contract was for the sale of real estate. (In this context, *common law* is the body of law that has developed from prior case decisions, customs, and usage. *Title* is the legal ownership of property or the evidence of that ownership.) If the title passed after the plants were severed from the land, the sale was of personal property. This rule is difficult to apply because in many instances the buyer and seller never discuss when title should pass.

Since the common law rule was difficult to apply, the Uniform Commercial Code (UCC) now uses a different test when the owner is selling the plants but retaining the land. Under the UCC, the determining factor is *who* is going to remove the plants or trees. If the *buyer* is going to remove them, the buyer has purchased real property. If the seller is going to remove them, the sale is of personal property. The UCC test is generally easier to apply because the parties probably discussed who was going to provide the labor. Often they do not address when title is going to pass. After defining the difference between real and personal property, the UCC generally is not concerned with real estate, although some sections of the UCC discuss crops and fixtures. A few states still follow the common law rule, and some states use different rules.

ACQUISITION AND TRANSFER OF PROPERTY

Original Occupancy of Real Property

Original occupancy (original entry) occurs when the government allows the private ownership of land that was previously owned by the government. In the United States, title may have been acquired by grant from either the U.S. government or other countries that colonized here. Original occupancy may be accomplished under an outright grant to specific people or families, or it may have occurred under homestead entry laws. *Homestead entry laws* are laws that allowed settlers to claim public lands by entering the land, filing an application with the government, and paying any required fees. Homesteading was a popular way to settle large amounts of land during pioneer days, but it is not generally available today.

Original Possession of Personal Property

Original possession occurs when the owner is the first person to possess the property. In other words, the owner created the property rather than receiving it by transfer from another person. One way to obtain ownership by original possession is to create the property through physical or mental labor. For example, Sanjay, an artist, acquires ownership through original possession by creating a painting or a sculpture.

Another way to obtain ownership by original possession is to take something that was not owned before and reduce it to possession, as when someone pans for gold in a wilderness area and takes possession of any nuggets found. When a person creates property, there is usually no dispute about who actually owns it. Disputes do arise, however, when people are hunting or trapping wild animals. For example, suppose that a group of hunters is about to trap a fox when Spiro, a farmer, spots the fox near his chicken coops and shoots it. A dispute may ensue about who owns the fox. A court would probably decide that Spiro owned the fox and its pelt because the hunters had not yet taken possession of the fox; they had not reduced the fox to their possession.

Spiro took control over it first.[3] Today, state statutes may declare that the state is the owner of wild animals, unless the animal was hunted or trapped in accordance with state hunting statutes.

Voluntary Transfers of Possession

Individuals can also acquire real and personal property by having it transferred to them voluntarily by the previous owner. The transfer can occur by purchase, gift, gift *causa mortis*, inheritance, or intestate succession. In the case of real estate, the transfer should be evidenced by a deed as previously mentioned. Exhibit 39.3 on page 1252 illustrates the options.

Purchases   The most common way to acquire property owned by another is to *purchase* it. When property is sold by the previous owner, there is an exchange of consideration: The buyer gives up one form of property, often money, and the seller gives up another form of property. Sometimes the parties *barter,* or exchange goods or services for the property. Bartering for goods is increasing in popularity; organizations even exist to assist businesses in locating other businesses with which to barter.

Gifts   A person can also obtain ownership of property through a *gift.* The person who transfers the property is called the *donor,* and the person who receives the property is called the *donee.* Three requirements must be satisfied for a valid transfer by gift.

First, the donor (the previous owner) must *intend* to make a present gift—that is, to transfer the property without receiving full and fair consideration. This includes the intent to pass title to the donee now, and not in the future. For example, if the donor says, "I want you to have this," the donor is showing a *present intent* to make the transfer. By contrast, if the owner says, "I want you to have this next Sunday," the donor is showing a *future* intent to make a transfer. It is not a valid gift because it is not a present transfer. In most gift situations, the donor is freely giving up the property without receiving any consideration at all. Sometimes it is difficult to determine whether the intent of the donor was to make a gift or, alternatively, to sell or to lend the property. This is particularly true if the donor has died or if the donor and the donee have had a disagreement. However, if the transfer is to be treated as a valid gift, it must be shown that the donor's intent was to make a gift.

The second requirement for a valid gift is that the donor *deliver* the gift property to the donee. When the donor hands the gift to the recipient, *actual delivery* occurs. Sometimes actual delivery is not practical because of the situation of the parties or the type of property being transferred. Consequently, courts permit *constructive delivery.* For example, assume Roberto is hospitalized. He has some antique coins in his safe deposit box and wants to give them to his son, Fernando. Roberto can give Fernando the keys to the safe deposit box and a note that will allow him access to the box, thereby effecting *constructive* delivery of the gift property.

The third requirement for a valid gift is *acceptance* by the donee. The donee must be willing to take the property from the donor. In most cases, this is not an issue.

However, a donee may refuse to accept a gift if the donee feels it will "obligate" him or her to the donor, as when a sales agent making a bid for a contract offers the purchasing agent a two-week vacation in Hawaii. Sometimes a donee may refuse a gift because the gift property has little use or value to the donee or creates legal liabilities for the donee. For instance, Firhana, a donee, might refuse a gift of real estate if it is substandard tenement housing that has many building code violations.

A transfer by gift may be subject to a *transfer tax* (tax on the ability to transfer assets), such as a gift tax. If so, usually the donor must pay the tax. Most state and federal gift taxes also apply when the transfer is for less than full and adequate consideration. An example would be when the donor receives something back in exchange for the "gift," such as nominal consideration. *Nominal consideration* occurs when the consideration is very small in proportion to the value of the property. For example, if Markus, a donor, transfers a diamond ring worth $700,000 to Andrea, a donee, for $5, the value of the gift will be treated as the fair market value of the ring ($700,000) less the $5 that was paid for it. Any gift tax is figured on this amount ($699,995) and Markus is obligated to pay the tax. The gift is *not* subject to income tax when Andrea receives it.

If the donor intends to make a gift, delivers the property, and the donee accepts it, the transfer is a valid gift. Once transfer of a gift has been completed, it generally cannot be revoked. The ability to revoke the gift and reacquire the property is considered inconsistent with surrendering control of the property. The donor cannot legally take the property back from the donee, no matter how much the donor wants or needs to have it returned. In most cases a completed gift, also called an *executed gift*, is final. However, the gift can be set aside or revoked if the donee engaged in fraud, duress, or undue influence that resulted in the making of the gift. *Fraud* is the use of a false statement of material fact in order to obtain a gift. *Duress* is the wrongful use of force and u*ndue influence* is the wrongful use of a position or relationship of trust and confidence to obtain a gift. Remember that fraud, duress, and undue influence can also be grounds to set aside a contract.

There are other situations where a gift may be revocable. Conditions that make a gift revocable *may* be stated by words or inferred from the circumstances. Justice may require the creation of a condition even though the donor had no condition in mind. A number of states consider engagement rings to be conditional gifts. Courts reason that an engagement ring is given as a pledge or symbol of the promise to marry. It is given subject to the implied condition that if the marriage does not take place either because of death, a disability recognized by the law, breach of the promise by the donee, or mutual agreement, the gift shall be returned. It only becomes the absolute property of the donee if the marriage takes place. When the marriage does not occur due to the fault of the donor, courts take one of two primary approaches to engagement rings, the fault rule or the no-fault rule. An increasing number of jurisdictions are adopting the no-fault rule. Under the no-fault rule devised by many states, absent an agreement to the contrary, the ring must be returned to the donor regardless of why the engagement is terminated. Under the fault rule, the donee may keep the engagement ring if the donor breaks the engagement.

A promise to make a gift at some time in the future is not binding on the promisor. The promisor can change his or her mind with impunity. However, an executory promise to make a gift may be enforceable in the case of *promissory estoppel*. This equitable doctrine is applied by the courts to avoid injustice. When the promisor makes a definite promise that he or she expects, or should reasonably expect, will induce the donee to act or refrain from acting, the donor can be held to his or her promise to prevent injustice.

Gifts fall into three categories: *inter vivos* gifts, testamentary gifts, or gifts *causa mortis*. *Inter vivos* gifts are made while the transferor is still alive; they are lifetime gifts. *Testamentary gifts* are completed when the owner dies; they are the types of gifts that a person puts in a will and are commonly called *testamentary transfers*. These transfers do not actually take place until death. Gifts *causa mortis* must meet special requirements about the donor's intention.

Gifts *Causa Mortis*   Gifts *causa mortis* occur while the property owner is still alive. The donor is making the gift because he or she expects to die soon. Generally, the donor is contemplating death from a specific cause. The requirements for a gift *causa mortis* are that (1) the donor must intend to make the gift, (2) the gift must be made in contemplation of death, (3) the gift property must be actually or constructively delivered, and (4) the donor must die from the contemplated cause. If the donor does not die from the contemplated cause, the gift will be revoked. In this case, the donor or the donor's estate can reclaim the gift property. Since the donor was motivated, at least in part, by the expectation of death, it is logical that if the donor does not die, he or she should be able to get the property back. A gift *causa mortis* is a legal concept and is distinct from various tax concepts that require some lifetime gifts to be included in the estate for tax purposes.

Transfers by Will or Intestate Succession   A person can arrange to transfer real or personal property by provisions in a valid will. If a person does not have a valid will covering the property, the property will pass under an intestate succession statute. (An *intestate succession statute* is a statute which determines who will inherit assets if a *decedent* does not have a valid will disposing of them.) For real estate the land will generally pass under the intestate succession statute of the state where the property is located. Personal property will generally pass under the intestate succession statute of the state where the person was domiciled. Like gifts, inheritances may be subject to state and/or federal transfer taxes.

Title Evidence for Real Property

The owner of real property may sell, trade, or give title to another by *executing* (signing) and delivering a deed. The recipient can be a private individual, business entity, or government body. In these cases, the transfer of title occurs by the execution and delivery of a written deed. A *deed* is the type of title evidence that is used for real estate and indicates who owns the land. Recall that the Statute of Frauds requires a written contract to convey any interest in land in order for the contract to be enforceable. A deed must adequately describe the property and the interest that is being transferred.

Exhibit 39.3

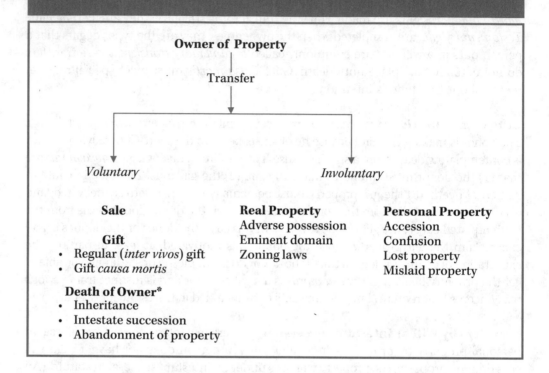

Transfer of Ownership from the Owner to "Recipient"

Owner of Property

Transfer

Voluntary   *Involuntary*

Sale	**Real Property**	**Personal Property**
	Adverse possession	Accession
Gift	Eminent domain	Confusion
• Regular (*inter vivos*) gift	Zoning laws	Lost property
• Gift *causa mortis*		Mislaid property

Death of Owner*
• Inheritance
• Intestate succession
• Abandonment of property

It will generally include the following items:

- ◼ The names of the *grantor(s)* (transferor) and the *grantee(s)* (transferee)
- ◼ The amount of consideration, if any, that was paid by the grantee
- ◼ A statement that the grantor intended to make the transfer (commonly called *words of conveyance*)
- ◼ An adequate description of the property (the street address by itself may not be sufficient; usually this description contains information provided by a private or government survey)
- ◼ A list and description of any ownership rights that are not included in the conveyance (such as mineral rights, oil rights, or easements) (*Easements* are the rights to the access and use of the real estate by someone other than the owner.)
- ◼ The quantity of the estate conveyed
- ◼ Any covenants or warranties from the grantor or grantee (Some covenants or warranties may be implied under state law; others may be expressed in the deed, such as the grantee can never permit alcohol to be sold on the premises.

Usually the deed specifies that these covenants are binding on the grantee and his or her heirs and legal transferees.)
■ The signature of the grantor or grantors

There are three major types of deeds. While each type conveys rights to the grantee, the rights conveyed and the warranties that are included vary significantly among the three types.

A Warranty Deed   A *warranty deed* contains a number of implied covenants (or promises) made by the grantor to the effect that a good and marketable title is being conveyed. All the following covenants are included:

■ Covenant of title (The grantor owns the estate or interest that he or she is purporting to convey.)
■ Covenant of right to convey (The grantor has the power, authority, and right to transfer this interest in the property.)
■ Covenant against encumbrances (There are no encumbrances on the property except for those listed on the deed; encumbrances include easements, mortgages, and similar restrictions on ownership.)
■ Covenant of quiet enjoyment (The grantor promises that the grantee's possession or enjoyment of the property will not be disturbed by another person with a conflicting lawful claim of title.)
■ Covenant to defend (The grantor promises to defend the grantee against any lawful or reasonable claims of a third party against the title of the grantee. This usually includes providing a legal defense in court, if it is necessary.)

A Grant Deed   A *grant deed* contains fewer promises than a warranty deed. Basically, it includes only a covenant that the grantor has not conveyed this property interest to anyone else. The grantor also promises that all the encumbrances are listed on the deed.

A Quitclaim Deed   With a *quitclaim deed,* the grantor makes no promises about his or her interest in the property. The grantor simply releases to the grantee any interest in the property that he or she *may* possess.

Delivery of the Deed   To complete a transfer of real property, the grantor *must* deliver the deed to the grantee or have it delivered to the grantee by a third person. The delivery establishes the grantor's intention to transfer the property.

Instead of handing the deed directly to the grantee, the grantor may use a third person to make the transfer. Sometimes it is important to use an impartial third party to assist in the transfer to protect both the buyer and seller. This third party has the obligation of supervising the transfer, including such activities as (1) collecting the deed, (2) collecting the funds, (3) checking that past utility bills, liens, and tax bills have been paid, (4) prorating real estate taxes, (5) prorating interest payments if a mortgage is being assumed, and (6) assuring that the parties have fulfilled any conditions, such as repairs and inspections of the premises. This procedure is called an *escrow* and is a common method of transferring property in some states. The person who supervises this type of delivery may be an attorney, an *escrow officer* (an employee of a bank or escrow company who oversees the escrow transaction), or another agent.

Recording of the Deed   Recording is accomplished by filing the deed with the proper authority, usually the county clerk or county recorder. The recorder files the deed or a copy of it in a deed book. Deed books usually are arranged in chronological order. The recorder also enters information about the transfer in an index, which is organized by the names of the grantors and grantees or by the location of the property. The index simplifies the task of locating information about a particular parcel. The recording gives the whole world "notice" of the transfer to this grantee. Recording is not a legal prerequisite to the transfer, but it does establish the grantee's interest in the property, and in many states recorded deeds have precedence over unrecorded deeds.

Title Evidence for Personal Property

Certain types of personal property require special formalities before the owner can transfer them. To transfer a *chose in action* (a right to bring legal action), the transferor must make an assignment of the right. An *assignment* is a formal transfer of a contract right. (Assignments are discussed in detail in Chapter 13.) To transfer negotiable instruments, the transferor must make either an assignment or a negotiation. (*Negotiable instruments* are formal written documents used as credit instruments or as substitutes for money. Examples include checks, drafts, promissory notes, and certificates of deposit.) Automobile owners register their title with the state department of motor vehicles.

Abandonment

When property is abandoned, it can be considered a voluntary act of the owner. If the owner throws the property out without intending to reclaim it, the property is abandoned. Abandonment is more likely with personal property than with real property. Real property tends to be more valuable. However, homeowners whose homes have declined in value and who owe more on the mortgage than the current value often abandon the homes. A number of people decided to just "walk away" from their mortgaged homes during the recent economic downturn, effectively abandoning their homes rather than attempting to honor the mortgage or to sell the home in a weak seller's market. The mortgage company then forecloses on the property.

Escheat and Unclaimed Property

When the rightful owner of property cannot be located, the property can *escheat*, or revert, to the state government. The effect of escheat is that the property is given to the government. Usually the property is in a third person's custody, and possession is transferred to the state. The policy behind this doctrine is that the state is more deserving of the property than anyone else if the true owner cannot be found. Escheat tends to occur when a person dies and the heirs or relatives cannot be located. (*Heirs* are the people who actually inherit property from the decedent.) In effect, the state becomes the person's heir. It also can occur when a person does not keep careful financial records and so forgets about small bank accounts, stocks and bonds, or other assets. Often there is an assumption that the owner has died if the owner does not contact the property holder after a period of time. Escheat is governed by the appropriate state statute, and the rules vary from state to state. Often, escheated property becomes part of the state's general fund. For a specified period after the escheat, the rightful owner can reclaim the property from the state.

Many states have enacted unclaimed property acts. Unclaimed property statutes differ from escheat statutes. Under escheat laws, title passes to the government; In unclaimed property acts title does not transfer to the government. Unclaimed property acts provide rules about when the property is considered "unclaimed." For purposes of these statutes, the term *unclaimed property* replaces the term *abandoned property*. The acts generally proscribe the following steps:

- the holder is required to report to the state that it has unclaimed property;
- the holder attempts to formally notify the owner;
- the property is transferred to the state;
- and the state once again tries to notify the owner.

The state then holds the property for the owner in perpetuity.[4] The advantage of giving custody to the state is to conserve and maintain the property for the owner. Otherwise, the holder with custody of the property may assess fees and deplete the asset.[5] These fees are called *dormancy charges*. Unclaimed property acts generally place restrictions on dormancy charges.[6]

PROTECTION OF PROPERTY

Property may be lost by operation of law or due to actions of the government, of another person, or of nature. These losses are generally involuntary on the part of the owner. To prevent them, the owner should be alert to these potential causes of loss. Some types of losses can occur only with real property, while others can occur only with personal property. Other types can occur with both types of property.

Involuntary Transfers by Operation of Law

An owner who defaults on a mortgage or loan may lose the property due to the default. The lender may institute foreclosure proceedings and take possession of the real estate or security. The lender must follow the appropriate state laws. Usually, the property will be sold at a foreclosure sale.

In most states, if the owner has not paid a court judgment, the judgment creditor may ask the court for a writ of execution. Following the applicable state procedures, the sheriff will attach the property and sell it at a judgment sale. Under state law, some real and/or personal property may be exempt from attachment to pay a court judgment.

If the owner has not paid people who supplied labor or materials for his or her real estate, these suppliers may also be able to force a sale under state law. These workers may have mechanic's liens for the value of the supplies or services rendered to improve the property. Even if they do not force a sale of the real property, generally they can prevent a voluntary sale by the owner unless they are paid from the proceeds. Automobile mechanics are entitled to mechanic's liens in most states.

The government may also take property if the owner has not been paying the taxes on it. If the state or local government imposes real estate or personal property tax on the property, the government may attach and sell the property if the owner is behind in paying the taxes.

Involuntary Transfers by Government Action

Real Property   Government bodies have the right to take private lands if they are necessary for a public purpose.[7] This is called the right of *eminent domain*. Under this doctrine, the government must have a legitimate "public use" that requires taking the land and must pay the owner a reasonable amount for it. Generally the "reasonable amount" is the fair market value.

A different type of taking occurs when the government enacts land use laws. Zoning and planning laws restrict how property may be used. They may prevent certain types of structures from being built on the property; for example, some areas may be limited to single-family residences. Or certain industries may not be permitted to operate plants in particular areas because of the air pollution these plants would cause. Sometimes these ordinances restrict the number and placement of establishments that sell alcohol. Commonly, bars are not allowed within one-quarter mile of public schools. In order to be valid, zoning and planning laws must be based on a compelling government interest, and the restrictions must be reasonable. The constitutionality of zoning laws was addressed in the Classic Case for this chapter, *Lucas v. South Carolina Coastal Council*,[8] and the cases that have followed it. Two of the federal statutes that restrict land use are the National Historic Preservation Act (1966)[9] and the National Environmental Policy Act (1969).[10]

Personal Property   Governments may have the right to take personal property. For example, state or local governments may take and destroy livestock or crops that are diseased to prevent the spread of the disease. Governments also confiscate contraband.

eClass 39.1 Management

ZONING RESTRICTIONS

Ani's parents have a large barn on their rural, residential property. This barn has been vacant for quite some time. Ani thinks that, with minor renovations, it will make an excellent warehouse from which to ship eClass's products. Ani recommends that eClass purchase the barn from her parents. Meg points out that the property is zoned for residential and agricultural use, not for commercial activities and such a use might be a crime. Yousef thinks that, since eClass is a closely held business, such restrictions do not apply. Before approaching Ani's parents, Ani, Meg, and Yousef seek your advice. What will you tell them?

BUSINESS CONSIDERATIONS   What are the advantages and disadvantages of renovating the barn into an eClass warehouse? What factors should the closely held business consider in making this sort of decision? Would different factors enter into the decision for a partnership or a publicly owned corporation?

ETHICAL CONSIDERATIONS   Among the factors that might affect any decisions on this issue are: Will there be an increase in traffic and/or noise in the neighborhood? How will such a use affect the neighbors? What ethical obligations exist for eClass under these circumstances?

Nongovernmental Transfers and Restrictions

Personal Property   Depending on the state law and the situation the owner of personal property *may* lose custody of or title to the personal property if

- a person takes personal property that he or she does not own and adds to it. The owner of the "original" property may lose it. This is called *accession.*
- the personal, fungible property of two or more people is mixed together and cannot be separated. This is called *confusion.*
- the owner drops or loses personal property. The property is then called *lost property.*
- the owner puts down his or her property and forgets to reclaim it when he or she walks away. The property is then called *mislaid property.*

Property is occasionally lost at sea. The rights of the owners of the ship, the owners of the property on board, and the salvors is governed by admiralty law.

Private Restrictions on Land Use   Subject to the government regulations, an owner can use real property as he or she wishes. (*Land use regulations* are laws that regulate the possession, ownership, and use of real property.) *Restrictive covenants* also limit how land may be used. These are private agreements between landowners on the use of the property and may take the form of building restrictions or *covenants, conditions, and restrictions (CC&Rs)*. These are the techniques used by condominiums and planned developments to control the building on and use of the lots. Restrictive covenants may be enforced by private lawsuits *if* they are lawful. Formerly, restrictive covenants were used to enforce racial segregation. The covenant would state that no owner could sell his or her property to a nonwhite person. The U.S. Supreme Court declared that restrictive covenants based on race are illegal in the landmark decision of *Shelley v. Kraemer.*[11]

Adverse Possession of Real Estate   *Adverse possession* occurs when an individual takes title and possession of real estate from the owner. A person who has physical possession of real property has better legal rights to that property than anyone else, except for the true owner and people who claim possession through the true owner. If the possession is of an adverse nature and it continues for a sufficient length of time, the adverse possessor may actually take ownership from the true owner. This doctrine applies only to privately owned real property. Government land may not be taken by adverse possession.

For possession to be adverse, it must be actual, open, and notorious. *Actual* possession means that the adverse possessor is actually on the land and is using the real estate in a reasonable manner for that type of land—as a residence, a farm, a ranch, or a business office. It is not sufficient that the adverse possessor state that he or she is using the land; actual use is required.

For possession to be *open*, it must be obvious that the adverse possessor is on the property. It will not be sufficient if the person stays out of sight during the day and walks around the property only at night. Openness is required to reasonably put the owner and the rest of the world on notice that the adverse possessor is using the property.

Finally, for possession to be *notorious*, it must be adverse or hostile to the true owner. Generally, people who occupy or use the property with the owner's permission, such as co-owners and renters, cannot be adverse possessors.

The required holding period varies from state to state and is specified by state statute. The period may range from 5 to 30 years. Entry under color of title may affect the holding period. Entering under *color of title* means that the holder thought that he or she had a legal right to take possession of the real property and had title to it. For example, a person with a defective deed would enter under color of title. Some states specify a shorter holding period if the holder entered under color of title and/or if the holder paid real estate taxes. In some states, the payment of real estate taxes is a necessary requirement for adverse possession; in some others, color of title is required. The possession must be continuous for the specified time period. However, the adverse possessor may leave the property for short periods to go to work, to classes, or on a brief vacation. He or she may not leave the property for an extended period of time.

The policy behind the doctrine of adverse possession is to encourage the use of land, a very valuable resource. The doctrine tends to encourage the use of land by someone else, if the owner is not using it. As the old adage says, possession may be nine-tenths of the law. If the owner is not using or renting the property, he or she should periodically check to make sure that no one else is using it. If it is being used without permission, the owner should take prompt legal steps to remove the occupant or the owner may learn a very expensive lesson about the effect of adverse possession on his or her title.

Easements   In some situations, a person may be entitled to use the land of another in a particular manner. This right is called an *easement*. An easement is not a right to *own* the property. Rather, it is the right to *use* the property in a particular manner. An easement may belong to a particular person, or it may run with the land. The latter means that the easement belongs to the owner of a particular parcel of land, called the *dominant parcel*. The parcel that is subject to the easement is the *servient parcel*.

An easement may be an *express* easement; in other words the person who created the easement used written or oral words. Or it can be created by *prescription*, which is much like adverse possession: A person starts to use the servient parcel openly and, after the state's statutory period, he or she will be entitled to continue the use. Easements also are created by *contract*, when an owner of property sells someone a right to use it. For example, an owner may sell an easement to an oil company to come onto the property to drill exploratory oil wells. An easement can also be created by *necessity*. The most common example of necessity occurs when an owner divides a parcel and deeds a landlocked portion to someone else: The only method of access is across the servient estate. (*Landlocked* means that the land is surrounded by land owned by others.) A requirement for an easement by necessity is that both parcels were originally one larger parcel.

Easements can also be created by *implication*. This can occur when a parcel is divided, and the owner of the dominant parcel "needs" to use the servient parcel. However, the need is not required to be as great as it is for an easement by necessity. For example, suppose an owner of a parcel of land decides to sell the northeast corner of the parcel. The owner had previously run a sewer system from this northeast corner to the main sewer line under the rest of the parcel. The buyer can reasonably expect to use the same sewer line when he or she owns the northeast corner. It would be *possible* to run a new sewer line to the northeast corner, but it was implied that the new owner could use the existing one.

The manner and type of use are restricted by the easement. A person who exceeds the amount of use that is permitted under the easement will lose the easement, and his or her rights will be extinguished.

RENTAL OF REAL PROPERTY

The owner of real property may decide to allow another person or persons to use the property. If the owner is willing to exchange temporary possession of the property for money or other consideration, there is a rental agreement. In other words, there is a contract between the landlord and the tenant. (We use landlord in the generic sense to include both men and women.) Most students are tenants because they live in a university dormitory, an apartment near campus, or rent a house with others. The National Conference of Commissioners on Uniform State Laws (NCCUSL) has enacted the Uniform Residential Landlord and Tenant Act which has been adopted by 21 states.[12] According to the NCCUSL the purpose was "[t]o remove the landlord and tenant relationship from the constraints of property law and establish it on the basis of contract law."[13] However, in many states tenancies are governed by both the rules of contract law and real estate law. Some states are very protective of tenants' rights and other states are more protective of landlords.

Types of Tenancies

Several basic types of tenancies exist, which are based on the length of the rental period. These include tenancies for a fixed term, periodic tenancies, tenancies at will, and tenancies at sufferance.

A *tenancy for a fixed term* is a tenancy for a set period of time; the beginning and ending dates are established. Generally, the Statute of Frauds requires a written lease if the tenancy is for one year or longer. Such tenancies automatically end at the set time. (Some states have set a maximum allowable term for a tenancy for a fixed term.) If the tenant has not vacated the premises by the end of the lease period, the landlord can explicitly execute a new lease with the tenant or can elect to treat the tenant's actions as an implicit renewal of the lease for another term of the same length. However, an implicit renewal cannot exceed one year due to the Statute of Frauds.

A *periodic tenancy* starts at a specific time and continues for successive periods until terminated. It may be established to run from year to year, month to month, week to week, or for some similar period. Either party may terminate it after proper notice. The lease normally specifies how much notice is necessary and to whom the notice should be addressed. In a periodic tenancy the beginning date of the tenancy is specified, but the ending date is not.

A *tenancy at will* can be terminated any time at the desire of *either* the landlord or the tenant.

A *tenancy at sufferance* is one in which the tenant entered into possession properly and with the landlord's permission, but wrongfully remained in possession after the period of the tenancy.

Rights and Duties of Tenants

The tenant rents the right to exclusive possession and control of the premises, which means that the tenant is the only one entitled to be in possession. Generally, the lease specifies that the property can be used only for a particular, stated purpose. Some leases specify that the property can be used only for lawful purposes.

At common law, the landlord is not entitled to enter the premises. The landlord often obtains permission from the tenant to enter the premises either on an *ad hoc* basis or because such a right is reserved in the lease. Even at common law, the landlord has the right to enter the premises in case of an emergency.

If the tenant is a business, it may need to install trade fixtures, such as neon signs, commercial refrigeration units, and industrial ovens. If a tenant attaches trade fixtures to the property, the tenant is allowed to remove them before the end of the lease. But if the removal causes any damage, the tenant must repair the damage. Even though the common law provides for trade fixtures, it is advisable for the parties to specifically address them in the written lease. For clarity, the trade fixtures can be listed in the lease. The parties' memories about ownership may not be accurate after a long-term lease, for example, 20 or 30 years.

Under a normal lease, the landlord is required to make sure the property is in good condition for the purposes specified in the agreement and must maintain the property in good condition. Tenants do not have an obligation to make major improvements or repairs. However, a tenant may contractually agree to make certain modifications or improvements. For example, in exchange for an exceptionally low rent, a tenant might agree to remodel a property at his or her own expense. In such a case, it is wise to specify who will pay for these improvements and who will get the benefit of them at the end of the lease.

Warranty of Habitability   Some states have held that an implied warranty of habitability exists in residential housing leases. That is, the landlord impliedly promises that the premises will be fit for living—for example, that the heating system will work, that there will be running water, and that there will be indoor plumbing. When the courts recognize this warranty, the tenant can use a breach of warranty as a basis for terminating a lease, as a means of reducing the rent, or as a defense for nonpayment of the rent.

Constructive Eviction   Most states recognize an implied covenant that the owner will protect the tenant's right to quiet enjoyment (use) of the premises. Constructive eviction occurs when the owner does not protect this interest of the tenant and allows a material interference with the tenant's enjoyment of the premises. Suppose, for example, that you rent an apartment and that Ronnie lives in the next apartment. Ronnie has a habit of playing drums in the middle of the night which interferes with your sleep. Although Ronnie's behavior is in violation of the lease, the landlord refuses to enforce the lease provisions. The landlord's behavior may constitute constructive eviction, which will allow you to "escape" the lease and to move out without any further liability to pay rent. However, if you do not take some action promptly, the court may decide that you waived your right to complain about the noise. Even if you plan to act promptly, you would be well advised to consult with an attorney before claiming that you have been constructively evicted. Otherwise, you may improperly break your lease and may be liable for the balance of the rent.

Assignments and Subleases   The transfer of the tenant's entire interest in the lease is an *assignment*. If the tenant transfers only part of his or her interest and retains the balance, the transfer is a *sublease*. (Note that this terminology is slightly different from that in Chapter 13.) Ordinarily, assignments and subleases are allowed unless the lease specifically provides that they are not. Most leases do prohibit assignments and subleases without the prior written approval of the landlord.

Retaliatory Eviction   *Retaliatory eviction* occurs when a landlord evicts a tenant who has filed complaints about violations of law, including building- or health-code violations. To recover for retaliatory eviction, generally, the tenant must prove *all* of the following elements:

- The tenant's complaint was *bona fide,* reasonable, and serious in nature.
- The tenant did not create the problem himself or herself.
- The complaint was filed before the landlord began the eviction proceedings.
- The primary reason the landlord began the eviction proceedings was to retaliate against the tenant for filing the complaint.

Retaliatory eviction may be prohibited based on court precedents and/or legislative statutes.

Rent Control   Some states and/or cities have rent control statutes that prohibit landlords from raising the rent.[14] Although rent control is intended to protect tenants, many economists argue that it is ineffective. They argue that instead it creates a shortage of rental housing, because investors choose other investments that provide a higher rate of return. Also, landlords may not provide necessary repairs. After unsatisfactory results, rent controls were abolished in some areas. Massachusetts's voters abolished rent controls in 1994. The California legislature enacted a statute allowing landlords to raise the rents on vacant apartments even where there are local rent controls.[15]

Rights and Duties of Landlords

Landlords have the right to retake possession of their property at the end of the lease. In most rental situations, the landlord expressly reserves the right to terminate the lease if the tenant breaches any promises contained in it, including the promise to adequately care for the property.

Rent   Rent is the compensation that the landlord receives in exchange for granting the tenant the right to use the landlord's property. Most leases require the tenant to pay the rent in advance. Many landlords require tenants to pay the first and last month's rent in advance, which provides added protection for the landlord. If the tenant is behind in paying the rent, it usually takes a number of weeks to force the tenant to leave the premises. If the tenant has not paid the rent, the landlord has a number of available options. The landlord can sue for the rent that has not been paid or can start procedures to have the tenant *evicted* (removed) from the premises. In some states, the landlord has a lien on the tenant's personal belongings that are on the premises. This allows a form of self-help called a *lockout*: the landlord locks the tenant out of the premises while the tenant's personal property is inside. For example, North Carolina law allows a landlord to gain possession of the property by peaceable means, including lockouts.[16]

States generally select one of the following approaches to determine the amount of self-help allowed to a landlord who is entitled to possession of the premises:

1. A landlord can use necessary and reasonable self-help.
2. A landlord must rely only on the remedies provided by the courts.
   Or
3. A landlord can gain possession by *peaceable* means.

Damage by the Tenant   When a tenant moves into an apartment or home, the tenant and the landlord or the landlord's agent should walk through the home and check for any damage. The tenant and landlord should also walk through the property when the tenant moves out. The landlord has the right to reimbursement from the tenant for any damage caused by the tenant. For example, assume Rudy, a tenant, negligently fills his waterbed, and it leaks and causes substantial damage to the premises. Rudy is liable for the damage. Tenants are also responsible for any damage caused to the premises by their guests. This right to collect for damages exists at common law and is usually stated in the lease. The tenant is responsible for damage caused negligently or intentionally but not for *ordinary wear and tear* (ordinary wear and tear is the deterioration that occurs through ordinary usage).

Security Deposits   For protection, the landlord will usually collect a security deposit. This money is to be used after the tenant has vacated the premises to repair any damage negligently or intentionally caused by the tenant. It is not to be used to clean the premises or to repair normal wear and tear. Consequently, a security deposit generally cannot be used to repaint walls that have become dirty through normal use. However, it can be used to replace doors in which holes have been punched. Any money that remains should be returned to the tenant within a reasonable period after the tenancy terminates. Some states have statutes that establish deadlines for the return of the security deposit.[17] Some states require the payment of interest on security deposits.

Duty to Protect a Tenant and His or Her Guests   Landlords generally have the same responsibility to their tenants' guests as they do to the tenants themselves. The landlord does not warrant that the premises are safe, but the landlord does have the duty to warn the tenant of *latent defects*—defects that are not immediately obvious and of which the tenant may not be aware. This duty of the landlord extends only to latent defects that the landlord knew or should have known existed.

Rights after Abandonment by a Tenant   If the tenant wrongfully abandons the premises during the term of the lease, the landlord has various options. The landlord can make a good faith effort to find a suitable tenant, but if one cannot be found, the landlord can leave the premises vacant and collect the rent from the tenant who abandoned the premises. The tenant is legally obligated to pay the rent, and the landlord can obtain a court judgment for the payment. Practically the landlord will only be able to collect *if* the tenant can be located and is solvent. If the landlord is able to rerent the premises, he or she is technically renting the premises on the tenant's behalf. If a lower rent is obtained, the original tenant is liable for the difference.

As an alternative, the landlord can repossess the premises and rerent them on his or her own behalf. The original tenant who abandoned the premises is relieved of any liability for additional rent. If the landlord is able to re-rent the premises for more money, the landlord will benefit. There may be a factual issue whether the re-renting is for the landlord's or the tenant's behalf.

Discrimination in Housing

Two federal statutes address discrimination in housing—the Civil Rights Act of 1866 and the Civil Rights Act of 1968. The 1968 Fair Housing Act, which is contained in the latter act, is the more comprehensive of the two acts and is the basis for most of the

eClass 39.2 Management/Manufacturing

LONG- OR SHORT-TERM LEASE?

eClass wants to rent a new plant in order to start its production and shipping. The firm has located a parcel that is ideal for its needs: it has good access, adequate space, and a reasonable rent. eClass prefers a relatively long-term lease, due in part to the renovations eClass will need to make to the leased property. Howie, the landlord, is only willing to sign a five-year lease. He is willing to insert a clause stating that the lease will be renewable for additional periods of five years each, subject to certain conditions. Because Howie is not willing to meet the terms proposed by eClass, Ani, Meg, and Yousef ask you whether the firm should sign the lease. What advice will you give them? What additional information would be helpful?

BUSINESS CONSIDERATIONS   What terms should be included in the lease in order to protect eClass's rights? What concerns should Ani, Meg, and Yousef have with regard to the renovations? How should they protect themselves and their interests?

ETHICAL CONSIDERATIONS   Suppose a prospective tenant explains planned renovations for a rental property during the negotiations. The landlord recognizes that the building will be worth a great deal more after the renovations and decides to negotiate a shorter lease term than was originally anticipated. Does such conduct raise any ethical concerns? Why? How should such a situation be treated from an ethical perspective?

recent litigation. As originally passed, it prohibits discrimination based on race, color, religion, or national origin. Age, disability, sex, and familial status were added later. Familial status includes having children under18 years of age. Some examples of illegal discrimination include:

- Advertising or making any statement that indicates a preference for people of a particular group
- Falsely stating that no rental unit is available
- Setting more restrictive standards for certain tenants, such as higher income levels
- Refusing to rent to members of certain groups
- Terminating a tenancy for a discriminatory reason
- Setting different terms for some tenants than others, for example having an inconsistent policy for late rent payments
- Refusing to make reasonable accommodations for disabled tenants, such as refusing to allow a guide dog or other service dog

The 1988 amendment increased the amount of protection by providing three methods for enforcement: (1) the Department of Housing and Urban Development can initiate a lawsuit in federal court or before an administrative law judge, *if* all the parties agree; (2) the person claiming that he or she was subjected to discrimination can file a suit in either state or federal court, and the court may award actual damages, punitive damages, or equitable relief; or (3) the U.S. attorney general can file a suit if the attorney general believes a pattern or practice of discrimination exists. As with most statutes, there are exceptions. For example, single-family units owned by a private investor with less than four houses *may* be exempt from the act as a whole, and housing solely for the elderly (over 62 years of age) is exempt from the age discrimination provisions.

The Civil Rights Act also prohibits discrimination in the sale of homes. States also have statutes governing discrimination in the rental and/or sale of homes.

AMERICANS WITH DISABILITY ACT PROVISIONS

Title III of the Americans with Disabilities Act (ADA) regulates property that is open to the public. These properties are commonly called *public accommodations* and include motels, hotels, restaurants, movie theaters, and retail stores. Under the act, newly constructed public accommodations must be designed to accommodate handicapped individuals. Architects and builders must comply with regulations established by the Department of Justice (DOJ). Generally, new structures must be designed and built to be readily accessible to and usable by individuals with disabilities unless it is structurally impossible to do so. When existing structures are being renovated, the areas being renovated must be made accessible too. The act itself does not specify the types of accommodation necessary. Court decisions and the DOJ regulations provide guidance in interpreting the statute. Critics of the statute claim that the act is ambiguous as to what handicaps must be accommodated and what accommodations are required. Under the statute, disabled Americans can initiate private litigation or the DOJ can bring litigation. In addition to actual damages, violators may be subject to civil penalties of up to $50,000 for the first violation and penalties of up to $100,000 for subsequent violations. Note that the ADA also includes employment provisions that are administered by the EEOC.[18] The employment provisions of the ADA are discussed in Chapter 38.

BAILMENTS OF PERSONAL PROPERTY

A *bailment* arises when a person delivers custody of personal property to someone else. The *bailor* is the owner of the property or is the person or entity in rightful possession of it. The *bailee* is the one who has possession of (but not title to) the property. Whenever an owner allows another person to have custody of the owner's personal property, a bailment exists. It is understood that the bailee is to use the property in a specific way. For example, the attendants of a parking garage are expected to drive a customer's car to park it or safeguard it. The attendants breach their duty as bailees if they drive it for other purposes. It is also understood that the bailee is to return the property at the end of the bailment.

If the bailee is giving up consideration, a contract also exists. When an individual or company rents personal property, he or she is creating a bailment. For example, if Emma rents a car from Silva's Car Rental Company, a bailment relationship exists. Emma is the bailee and Silva's Car Rental Company is the bailor. Their relationship will be governed by *both* the rules of bailments and the rules of contracts. However, a contract is not a requirement for a bailment. A bailment can occur gratuitously. All the following elements are necessary for a bailment:

1. The bailor must retain the right to reclaim/recover the goods.
2. The possession of the property must be delivered to the bailee.
3. The bailee must accept possession.
4. The bailee must have possession of the property for a specific purpose and must have temporary control of the property.
5. The parties must intend that the property will be returned to the bailor unless the bailor directs that the property be delivered to another person.

A bailment is not a sale of personal property. A sale involves a transfer of title and requires an exchange of consideration. A permanent change of possession occurs with the sale.

It is not always easy to recognize whether a situation is a bailment. A particularly controversial question is whether parking in a garage constitutes a bailment or the rental of a space to park a car. Generally, the question is resolved by examining whether the driver has relinquished control over the car. If the driver retains control of the vehicle by driving into a self-service parking garage, parking the car, locking it, and removing the keys, courts will decide that there was a license of space. At the other extreme, if a person drives to a hotel where an attendant parks the car, keeps the keys, and gives the driver a claim check, there is a bailment. Transfer of possession of the car is essential. However, courts have held that the *keys* do not necessarily have to be surrendered.

Bailee's Duty of Care

Disputes often arise when the property is damaged while in the hands of the bailee. In a lawsuit, the issue concerns whether or not the bailee took proper care of the property while it was in his or her custody. Liability will depend on provisions in local statutes, the language of any bailment contract, and the type of bailment.

Classifications of Bailments

Bailments are divided into types based on who benefits from the bailment relationship. The classification affects the bailee's obligation and his or her liability if any damage occurs to the property. This relationship is summarized in Exhibit 39.4.

Bailor Benefit Bailments   When the bailment is established solely to benefit the bailor, it is a *bailor benefit bailment.* The bailee will be responsible only for gross negligence in caring for the property. An example of a bailor benefit bailment is when Sergio, the owner, leaves his laptop computer with Melvin, his friend, until Sergio returns from his lunch. When Sergio returns from lunch he discovers that his laptop computer was knocked off a table and damaged. He alleges that Melvin should be liable for the damages since they occurred while Melvin was in possession of the laptop. Melvin denies liability, claiming that the bailment was for Sergio's benefit so that Melvin can only be held liable for gross negligence. Melvin alleges that there is no evidence of gross negligence. The degree of negligence that can be attributed to Melvin is a question of fact that will need to be determined by the court if this case goes to trial. What is considered to be gross negligence in court will depend on the circumstances and the evidence presented.

Mutual Benefit Bailments   When a bailment is established for the benefit of both the bailor and the bailee, a *mutual benefit bailment* exists. Both parties expect to gain from the bailment relationship. In such bailments, the bailee is responsible for ordinary negligence. A mutual benefit bailment occurs, for example, when the owner of a suit takes it to a dry-cleaning establishment. The owner will benefit by having the suit

Exhibit 39.4

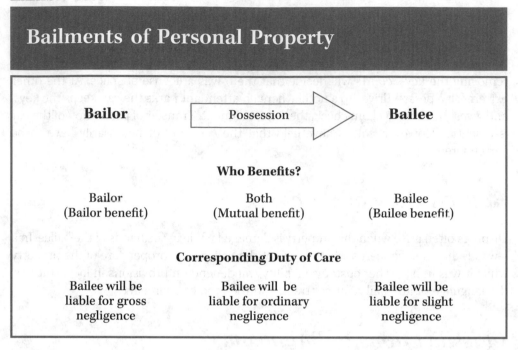

Bailments of Personal Property

cleaned and pressed. The dry cleaner will benefit because it is going to be paid. The dry cleaner will be responsible if it carelessly cleans the suit in cleaning fluid that is too hot and causes the suit to shrink.

Bailee Benefit Bailments   When a bailment is established solely for the benefit of the bailee, a *bailee benefit bailment* exists. The bailee will be responsible for slight negligence in caring for the property. When Alberto loans his car to Jaime, his fraternity brother, to drive to a job interview, a bailee benefit bailment occurs. Since Alberto is receiving no benefit from this arrangement, Jaime will be held responsible for any damages occurring to the car if Jaime was negligent in even a slight manner. Again, the question of negligence is a question of fact to be determined by the court, if the case is taken to trial.

Constructive Bailments

Many states also recognize constructive bailments. *Constructive bailments* occur even though there is no formal agreement between the owner and the possessor who lawfully comes into possession of the property. The court may determine that the possessor should be treated as a constructive bailee in order to serve justice. A constructive bailee may also be called a *bailee by operation of law*. An example would be if a grain silo were sold to Filzah. The transfer documents did not mention the grain inside the silo at the time of the transfer. The prior owner of the silo was a bailee of the grain, and Filzah would become the constructive bailee of the grain.[19]

Limitations on a Bailee's Liability

Some states and localities have statutes or ordinances that provide maximum limits on the liability of the bailee in certain types of bailments. If the bailment is based on a contract, the terms of the contract may increase or decrease the liability of the bailee.

A *quasi-public bailee* offers services to the public. For example, he or she may operate a common carrier, a garage, a hotel, or a public parking lot. A quasi-public bailee generally will not be permitted to limit his or her liability contractually unless specifically permitted to do so by statute. Even when a statute permits a bailee to restrict liability, any limitation on liability must be reasonable.

A private bailee can restrict his or her liability under the terms of the agreement *if* this restriction does not conflict with the real purpose of the contract between the bailee and the bailor. The bailee must inform the bailor of any limitation on the bailee's liability. Most courts hold that a printed ticket stub or a posted notice on the premises does not adequately inform the bailor of the limitations *unless* the bailor's attention is directed to the sign or the ticket stub.

Termination of a Bailment

A bailment terminates at the end of the period that the parties specify or when a specified condition occurs. A bailment terminates when the purpose or performance of the bailment has been completed. If the bailment was for an indefinite time, it may be terminated at the will of either the bailor or the bailee. If either party causes a material breach of the bailment relationship, the victim can terminate the bailment and the wrongdoer will be liable for any damages he or she caused. The bailment terminates if the bailed property is destroyed or becomes unfit or unsuitable for the purpose of the bailment. Generally, a bailment also terminates by operation of law if the death, insanity, or bankruptcy of either party makes performance by the bailee impossible.

Bailee's Duty to Return the Property

A bailee has a general duty to return the bailor's property to the bailor; however, there are exceptions to this rule. The bailee is not liable to the bailor if the property is lost, destroyed, or stolen through no fault of the bailee. The bailee is not liable if the property is taken away by legal process such as an attachment for a sheriff's sale. The bailee is not liable if the property is claimed by someone who has a better legal right to possession than the bailor has.

Sometimes a bailee has a duty to return the property to someone other than the bailor. For example, there may be a duty to "return" the property to a transferee who purchased the property from the bailor. A common business practice involves transferring property to a warehouse or common carrier that has an obligation to hold this property and then transfer it to a purchaser who presents a receipt or bill of lading.

eClass 39.3 Manufacturing/Management

SHOULD eCLASS PURCHASE INSURANCE ON LEASED PRODUCTION EQUIPMENT?

eClass leases some of its production equipment from a large electronics firm. This equipment is extremely expensive and relatively fragile. Meg is concerned that eClass will be responsible for any damage to the equipment. She feels that eClass should purchase insurance to protect the firm from liability in the event the equipment is damaged. Yousef insists that the electronics firm is responsible for maintenance and bears the risk of loss for any damage done to the equipment. He contends that, since the equipment was leased for industrial use, the electronics firm alone is responsible. They ask you which of their positions is correct. What will you tell them?

BUSINESS CONSIDERATIONS   The leasing of equipment creates a bailment, but it also entails a contract for the lease of goods, governed by Article 2A of the UCC. Does Article 2A change the common law treatment of bailments in this sort of situation? Does the lessor or the lessee bear the risk of loss if leased equipment is damaged during the lease, presuming that the equipment is being used by the parties in the manner expected?

ETHICAL CONSIDERATIONS   From an ethical perspective, and without regard to who is legally responsible for risk of loss, how should eClass behave in this situation? Is it ethical to underinsure a piece of equipment if the insuring party knows that the other party legally bears the risk of loss? Is it ethical for an owner or lessee to overinsure a piece of equipment in the hope that the insurer will not notice the over-insurance in the event of a loss?

The bailee does not have to return the property if the bailee has a lien on it. Many states have statutes that permit the bailee to keep the property in his or her possession until the bailor pays for the bailment; this is called a *possessory lien*. If the bailor fails to make payment, most statutes permit the bailee to sell the property. A common type of bailee's lien is a mechanic's lien, which arises when services have been performed on personal property. For example, if Lupe hires a garage to repair her automobile and she does not have the money to pay for the repairs, the garage can keep the automobile until Lupe pays. In most cases, the bailee loses the lien if the bailee willingly releases the goods to the bailor. For example, if the bailor comes to reclaim the property and the bailee releases it without receiving payment. Generally, there is no bailee's lien if the bailor and bailee agree at the beginning that the bailor is going to pay on credit.

JOINT OWNERSHIP OF PROPERTY

Joint ownership exists when two or more people have concurrent title to property; that is, they own the property at the same time. There are five forms of joint ownership: tenancy in common, joint tenancy with rights of survivorship, tenancy by the entireties, community property, and partnership property. (Chapter 31 discusses partnership property; it is not covered in this chapter.) Some states have created special hybrid forms of joint ownership.[20] Generally, these forms of joint ownership can exist with personal property as well as with real property. Most of these forms can be created voluntarily by the tenants, or they can be created by someone else for the tenants. In this context, the tenants are the co-owners.

A legal characteristic of most forms of joint ownership is that each of the co-owners has an undivided right to use the whole property. Thus, the parcel is not divided equally among the tenants; instead, each of them has the right to use all the property. If a dispute arises about the use of the property that the tenants are unable to resolve among themselves, they can file their complaint with the court. The primary remedies available to resolve such a dispute are (1) to sell the property and divide the proceeds or (2) to divide the property equitably and give each tenant a separate parcel. Both of these are considered actions for partition. Because the usable value of adjoining portions may differ, the separate parts may differ in size and shape. Exhibit 39.5 summarizes joint ownership of property. Since state law governs property rights, there may be some variation from state to state.

Tenancy in Common

A *tenancy in common* can occur when two or more people own the same property. Each tenant has an undivided right to use the whole property. Usually, a tenancy in common is indicated by words like "Peluso and Paulovich, as tenants in common" on the deed or other evidence of title. If the deed simply says "Peluso and Paulovich," most courts will presume that they are tenants in common.

There is no legal limit on the number of tenants in a tenancy in common. Practically speaking if there are too many tenants, conflicts will probably arise among them regarding the use of the property. Each tenant may sell, assign, or give away his or her interest. A tenant may also will away the interest in a valid will. If the tenant has no valid will, then the interest in the tenancy will pass to his or her heirs under the state intestate succession statute. A creditor of an individual tenant can attach his or her interest in the tenancy in common.

Tenants in common do not have to have equal interests in the property. For example, if there are four tenants in common, one may have a one-half interest, one may have a one-quarter interest, and the other two may have a one-eighth interest each.

Exhibit 39.5

Comparison of Forms of Joint Ownership[a]

	Tenancy in Common	Joint Tenancy with Rights of Survivorship	Tenancy by the Entireties	Community Property
Requirements for Creation				
Requires equal ownership interests		●	*	*
Restricted to married couples			*	*
Limited to two people			*	*
Restricted to human beings		√	*	*
Applicable to both real and personal property	*	√	√	*
Rights of One Tenant Acting Alone to Transfer or Encumber His or Her Share Without the Consent of the Others				
May use the whole property (undivided right to the whole)	*	*	*	*
May be transferred by will	*			*
May not be transferred by will		*	*	
Will pass to surviving tenants at death, if there is no valid will[b]		*	*	√[c]
Will pass to intestate heirs at death, if there is no valid will	*			√[c]
May be sold during life	*[d]	√		√●

Exhibit 39.5 Continued

	Tenancy in Common	Joint Tenancy with Rights of Survivorship	Tenancy by the Entireties	Community Property
May be mortgaged or assigned during life	*d	√		√
May be transferred by gift during life	*d	√		
May be attached by a creditor of a tenant[e]	*	*		■

[a] Remember that because property rights are governed by state law, a wide variation may exist from state to state.

[b] In some types of tenancies, courts would say the interest "remains" with the surviving cotenants instead of "passing" to them.

[c] Most community property states have different intestate succession provisions for the passage of separate property and community property. The community property commonly passes to the surviving spouse if there is no valid will provision covering the property.

[d] Generally, a tenant in common will have this power. However, in many states, if the tenancy in common is between spouses and consists of real estate, the signature of the second spouse will be required.

[e] Creditors of the unit (husband and wife together) may attach Tenancies by the Entireties and Community Property.

Legend
* The trait applies to the specific form of joint ownership.
√ This is true in most states.
● This is true in many situations.
■ This depends on state law and the situation, including when and how the debt was incurred.

Joint Tenancy with Rights of Survivorship

A *joint tenancy with rights of survivorship* can occur when two or more people own property together. Again, there is no legal maximum number of tenants. However, the practical question remains: How many cotenants can get along with one another? As in a tenancy in common, each tenant has an undivided right to use the whole property. Generally, each tenant has an equal interest in the property. Joint tenancies differ from tenancies in common in that when one tenant dies, his or her interest passes to the remaining cotenants. The survivors continue to hold an undivided interest in the whole property. Generally, a will does not have any effect on a joint tenancy with rights of survivorship. (There is a movement in the U.S. legal community that advocates changing state laws regarding the ability to will joint tenancies and insurance policies. A few courts are devising theories to this effect.) The interest in the cotenancy property will pass from one tenant to another immediately on death by operation of law. Eventually, the tenant who outlives the others will own the complete interest. In most states, corporations are not allowed to be joint tenants because corporations do not die.

Because of the survivorship feature, joint tenancies often are used as substitutes for wills. Given the potential for disputes during life, however, this practice may be unwise. In most states if a joint tenant wrongfully causes the death of another joint tenant, he or she will not be allowed to benefit and will be prevented from taking the decedent's interest.

Joint tenancies may be divided during a court action for partition. In most states, a joint tenant can sell, make a gift of, or assign his or her interest during his or her life. A creditor of the joint tenant can attach the interest. A transferee of the joint tenant will take the interest as a tenant in common. A transferee includes a purchaser, a donee, an assignee, or a creditor who obtained rights through an attachment procedure. The transferee does not receive the survivorship rights of a joint tenant because the other joint tenants never agreed to share the risk of survivorship with the transferee.

Tenancy by the Entireties

In a *tenancy by the entireties,* two tenants, who must be husband and wife, share the property. Each tenant is a joint owner in the whole property. This type of ownership has a survivorship feature. If one spouse dies, the survivor receives the whole property. Unlike joint tenants with rights of survivorship, many states allow a tenant who wrongfully caused the death of his or her spouse (cotenant) to benefit and to take title to the whole. Generally, only creditors of the family unit can attach entireties property. One spouse normally cannot unilaterally dispose of his or her interest, unless the parties obtain a legal separation or a divorce. However, the tenants can agree to sever the tenancy. A valid will does not affect distribution of entireties property. Tenancies by the entireties are not recognized in all states; for example, community property states do not have tenancies by the entireties.

Community Property

Community property is recognized in eight states—Arizona, California, Idaho, Louisiana, Nevada, New Mexico, Texas, and Washington—as well as the Commonwealth of Puerto Rico. This discussion emphasizes the general features of community property laws, which vary from state to state. Louisiana community property law is most dissimilar, because it is based on Louisiana's French heritage. The community property laws in the other states are based predominantly on Spanish civil law.[21] Community property laws are also evolving.

Community property is a form of co-ownership that can occur only between husband and wife. It is based on the concept that financially the marriage is a partnership. One-half of most of the property that is acquired or accumulated during marriage belongs to each spouse. Technically, this assumes that one-half of each asset belongs to the husband and one-half belongs to the wife. Consequently, most states require that both the husband and the wife sign any deeds to transfer real property. In most states, this requirement does not extend to personal property. In fact, the names of both spouses do not have to appear on the community property or on any title evidence to the property. For example, although a paycheck may bear the name of only one spouse, it is nonetheless community property and belongs to both spouses. The primary source of community property for most couples is wages and earnings.

A couple begins to form community property once they are married. In most situations, they stop forming community property once they establish separate residences. In a divorce proceeding, the community property usually is divided.

This is not meant to imply that a married couple will have only community property. Each may own property separately, just as in separate property states. (*Separate property states* are states in which married couples cannot create community property.) In community property states, separate property normally includes the following:

- Property owned by either spouse before their marriage
- Property given to *one* spouse alone by gift, by will, or by intestate succession
- Property that is acquired with separate property funds

In addition, in some states—California, for example—income, rents, or profits earned from separate property are also separate property; in other states—Idaho, Texas, and Louisiana—this income is community property if it is received during the marriage. In Louisiana, a husband or wife can file a declaration that this income should be separate property instead of community property. All property other than that previously mentioned is usually community property.

For most purposes, a husband and wife can contractually agree to split their community property into two shares of separate property. However, if they are careless and mix their respective separate properties and/or community properties, it may all become community property. If the property becomes so mixed together that it cannot be separated into community and separate property, the courts decide that it is hopelessly commingled and treat all of it as community property.

Community property does not have a survivorship feature. A spouse can will his or her share of the community property to someone else. If the decedent does not have a valid will, most intestate succession statutes provide that the community property will pass to the surviving spouse.

The NCCUSL adopted the Uniform Marital Property Act.[22] When a state legislature enacts the act, it modifies the property rights of married couples and makes the state more like a community property state. Wisconsin adopted the Act in 1983.[23] Initially, a number of other states introduced the bill; however, Wisconsin is the only state that adopted it.[24]

Distinguishing among the Forms of Joint Ownership

The words used on the deed or other title evidence are controlling as to whether the tenants are tenants in common, joint tenants with rights of survivorship, or tenants by the entireties. If the language on the deed is not clear, under state law there will be a presumption as to the form of joint ownership. If the tenants are husband and wife, most states will presume that the property is community property or entireties property. If the state recognizes neither form of ownership, it will presume a joint tenancy with the right of survivorship. If the tenants are not husband and wife, most states will presume that they are tenants in common.

Transfer on Death Ownership

Transfer on death or pay on death ownership should be distinguished from forms of joint ownership. When an owner opens a bank account, purchases securities, or acquires other assets, he or she may designate the form of ownership as transfer or pay on death. Transfer on death (TOD) is used for investment securities. Pay on death (POD) is generally used for bank accounts. The NCCUSL has drafted a Uniform Transfer on Death Securities Registration Act that has been adopted in 46 states and the District of Columbia.[25] With this type of ownership, the recipient does not have an interest in the asset during the owner's life. The recipient cannot withdraw the assets or mortgage them. The recipient only is entitled to the assets at the owner's death, if the owner has not changed the name to indicate a new recipient. In 2009, the NCCUSL promulgated the Uniform Real Property Transfer on Death Act.[26] TOD and POD forms of ownership are relatively new. However, they are becoming popular as substitutes for wills.

Contemporary Case

IN THE MATTER OF EMINE BAYRAM AGAINST CITY OF BINGHAMTON

**2010 NY Slip Op 20116, 2010 N.Y. Misc. LEXIS 660
(Sup. Ct. of New York,[27] Cortland County 2010)**

FACTS Emine Bayram owns a single-family residence located in an R-1 Residential Single-Unit Dwelling District. Bayram entered into a written agreement to lease the property to seven Binghamton University students, for a term of approximately two years. The City of Binghamton Department of Building and Construction received a complaint that the property was being "rented to a frat house." After conducting an investigation, the Department sent Bayram a Notice that the seven individuals residing at the property did not constitute a functional and factual family equivalent and that their continued occupancy was a violation. Bayram sought review of the Notice by the Zoning Board of Appeals (ZBA). Following a public hearing, the ZBA upheld the Department's determination.

ISSUE Did leasing to seven college students violate the zoning law?

HOLDING Yes, the lease violated the zoning law.

REASONING Excerpts from the opinion of Justice Phillip R. Rumsey:

... The interpretation by a zoning board of appeals of terms defined in its ... zoning ordinance is entitled to great deference, and must be upheld if it is neither irrational nor unreasonable; judicial review is limited to an examination of whether there is a rational basis for the determination.... Any dwelling unit located in a residential zoning district may be occupied only by a family or the equivalent of a family.... [A] functional and factual family equivalent is ... [a] group of unrelated individuals living together and functioning together as a traditional family.... [I]t cannot be said that the ZBA's decision is irrational. The record of its deliberations ... and its written decision ... reflect that the ZBA considered each of the enumerated factors in reaching a determination that is supported by the evidence that was before it.... [T]he ZBA first concluded that the occupants do not share the entire dwelling unit, instead acting as separate roomers, based on evidence—including photographs—showing that each has a separate room with his own refrigerator, computer, and television, and that each resident has his own car.... The ZBA found that the tenants' living arrangement is temporary, limited at most to the two-year lease term, based on evidence that the tenants are in the area only for the purpose of attending Binghamton University.... This determination is also supported by the acknowledgment of petitioner's counsel that the tenants could not be present at the ZBA hearing because they were then "on break"..., and ... that there is no expression of intent by the tenants to continue living together after leaving Binghamton University. There are no minor, dependent children residing at the property. The ZBA noted ... that this fact was not dispositive.... While recognizing that the lease designates Kim as "head of the family," the ZBA found little evidence that he functions in the role of a traditional head of household. It ... determined that petitioner attempted to depict the tenants as a functional and factual family equivalent—in part by naming Kim as head of household—to circumvent the occupancy limitations imposed by the Zoning Ordinance.... The ZBA concluded that there was not substantial evidence of shared expenses. While acknowledging that there was some proof that the tenants shared payment of utility expenses, the ZBA noted that there was no evidence with regard to pooling of money or resources toward payment for food or other expenses.... [T]he Zoning Officer initially determined that each tenant separately paid his share of the rent directly to petitioner ... With respect to common ownership of furniture ... the ZBA decided that the evidence ... showed that most significant items, such as computers and televisions, were individually owned and not shared. In reaching its conclusion that the household is a temporary living arrangement ..., the ZBA noted that ... none of the residents' automobiles was registered to the property address, none of their driver's licenses listed the property as a residence address, and none of the tenants was registered to vote in local elections.... [T]he

ZBA considered an additional factor, namely that the monthly rent of $2,800—which it believed is three to four times the monthly rent typically paid for a single-family residence in Binghamton—is indicative of a lease to seven individuals, rather than to a single family unit. . . .

[T]he ZBA's decision was rational in light of the evidence before it. . . . [It] is also supported by caselaw, which has sustained the view that a group of college students temporarily residing together and commuting to a nearby school, lacks the permanency or community required in order to constitute a functional and factual family equivalent. . . . [I]t has long been settled that . . . police power may be legitimately used to further the goal of providing for a stable, uncongested single family environment, and that uses associated with occupancy by numbers of transient persons, such as fraternities or housing for college students, may be restricted to further that goal. . . . Thus, the decision of the ZBA must be upheld.

You Be the Judge

Parking is difficult during the home football games of the Fresno State Bulldogs. For the first home game of the season, a number of fans parked their cars at a shopping center approximately 4 blocks from the stadium. The owner of the shopping center arranged with a towing service to have the cars towed during the game. The fans returned to the shopping center after the game to find that their cars had been towed away. Suppose a group of fans who had their cars towed challenge the towing in *your* court. If you were the judge, how would *you* decide this dispute? Do you think the Bulldog fans behaved in a reasonable manner? Do you think the owner of the shopping center behaved in a reasonable manner? Did the fans behave ethically? Did the owner of the shopping center? [See "Bulldog Fans' Cars Aren't Deterring Business," letter to the editor by Michael Boone, *Fresno Bee,* September 20, 2009, p. B4.]

Summary

Property ownership includes title to the property and the right to control possession of the property. Real property consists of land and objects that are constructed on the land, growing on the land, and/or permanently attached to the land. A fixture is property that was personal in nature before it was permanently attached to a building. An owner may trade, sell, give, or will his or her property. If the owner dies without a valid will, the property will pass by intestate succession.

For some types of property, ownership may be designated by title evidence. Title evidence for real property is a deed. Government entities may place restrictions on the use of a person's land through zoning laws. Governments may take property for a "public use" through eminent domain. An owner may lose his or her interest by the adverse possession of another person. Easements can restrict the owner's use of the property.

Ownership of personal property may escheat to the state, when a custodian of property cannot locate the owner. A more modern approach is unclaimed property statutes.

An owner can enter into a rental agreement called a lease. The real estate lease is the contract that will govern many terms of the landlord-tenant relationship. The landlord can require a security deposit in order to assure that there are funds for making repairs. The tenant is justified in leaving the premises when there is constructive eviction. A landlord can evict a tenant if the tenant fails to pay the rent.

A bailment occurs when the bailor transfers the possession of personal property to someone else, the bailee. The owner keeps title. After the purpose of the bailment has been completed, generally possession is returned to the owner. The bailee's duty of care is affected by whether it is a bailor benefit bailment, a mutual benefit bailment, or a bailee benefit bailment relationship.

Two or more people, called cotenants, can own an interest in the same piece of property at the same time. They may be tenants in common, in which case each tenant owns an undivided right in the whole parcel and there are no survivorship rights. Or they may be joint tenants with rights of survivorship. Such tenants can dispose of their interests during life; at death, their interest will pass to the remaining cotenants by operation of law. Tenants in a tenancy by the entireties must be husband and wife. In community property states, a husband and wife can create community property.

Discussion Questions

1. After Al's mother and father died, Al, who is responsible for their estate, decides to sell their home. After locating buyers for the property and entering into a sales contract with them, Al removes the petunias, his father's prize-winning roses, and a load of topsoil that is on the flower beds. The buyers are unhappy about this. Who has the right to these items? Why?

2. Domingo and Rosie are neighbors. In 1990, Rosie built a fence around her property. However, she did not have the boundary surveyed, and the fence was built four feet into Domingo's property. Who owns this four-foot strip of land now? Why?

3. Suppose that a business wishes to rent premises to use as a sports bar in a shopping mall. What provisions might the business want to include in the lease? Why?

4. cClass is considering purchasing an office building and renting the excess office space to others.

Yousef thinks that this would be a good idea. It would provide some diversification. In the future, when eClass expands it can refuse to renew the leases and expand into the tenant-occupied areas. What are the advantages and disadvantages of this idea? Why?

5. eClass is considering purchasing a fleet of cars for key employees. eClass would purchase four vehicles and assign them to employees who could operate the cars for both business and personal use. What are the advantages and disadvantages of such a plan? Why?

Case Problems and Writing Assignments

1. Del Monte Dunes tried to develop a parcel of land within the city of Monterey. Although the zoning requirements permitted the development of more than 1,000 units for the entire parcel, the landowners' proposal was limited to 344 units. The city's planning commission denied the application but stated that a proposal for 264 units would receive favorable consideration. The landowners submitted a revised proposal for 264 units. The planning commission again denied the application saying a plan for 224 units would be received with favor. The landowners prepared a proposal for 224 units, which the planning commission denied. The landowners appealed to the city council, which referred the project back to the commission, with instructions to consider a proposal for 190 units. The landowners again reduced the scope of their proposal. The planning commission rejected the landowners' proposal. The council overruled the commission. The council found the proposal satisfactory and in conformance with previous decisions. The landowners' final plan was designed, in accordance with the city's demands, to provide the public with a beach, a buffer zone between the development and the adjoining state park, and view corridors so the buildings would not be visible to motorists on the nearby highway. The proposal also called for restoring and preserving as much of the sand dune structure and buckwheat habitat as possible. The planning commission denied the development plan. The city council also denied the final plan, declining to specify measures the landowners could take to satisfy its concerns. The council did not base its decision on the landowners's failure to meet any of the specific conditions earlier established by the city. After five years, five formal decisions, and 19 different site plans, Del Monte Dunes concluded that the city would not permit development of the property under any circumstances. Del Monte Dunes commenced a lawsuit against the city. The District Court submitted some of the claims to a jury. The jury delivered a general verdict for Del Monte Dunes on the takings claim, and awarded $1.45 million in damages. Was this matter properly submitted to the jury? [See *City of Monterey v. Del Monte Dunes at Monterey, Ltd.*, 119 S. Ct. 1624, 1999 U.S. LEXIS 3631 (1999).]

2. Alex Popov claims that he caught Barry Bonds's 73rd home-run baseball on October 7, 2001 at Pacific Bell Park. It was the last day of the 2001 season. Popov, who at least touched the ball with his glove, says that the ball was wrestled away from him. In the end, Patrick Hayashi ended up with the ball. Popov claims he was mugged by Hayashi. The parties were not able to resolve their dispute in three mediation sessions. Experts say that ball could be sold for more than $1 million. It is locked in a safety deposit box under the judge's order. Assume that Popov files suit in your court to reclaim the baseball. How will you decide this case? Why? What additional information would be helpful in making your decision? [See "Claims on Bonds; 73rd Go to Trial," *Newsday* (New York), Nassau and Suffolk Edition, October 16, 2002, p. A60; Dean E. Murphy, "A Ball in the Hand Is Worth a Lot—to the Lawyers," *New York Times,* October 16, 2002, p. A16.]

3. William Seebold, president of Eagle Boats, was contacted by *Trailer Boats*, a boating magazine, about doing a feature article on a motorboat manufactured by Eagle. The article was to include pictures taken on Grand Lake in Oklahoma. At the time of the inquiry, a boat owned by Hoppies Village Marina (Hoppies) was in the Eagle Boat repair facility undergoing minor paint repairs. This boat was a 1991 Seebold Eagle 265 Limited Edition motorboat with a 1990 Buccaneer Deluxe Tri-Axle trailer. This boat is considered "to be the 'cadillac' of motorboats in its class." Seebold contacted Paul Hopkins, the owner of Hoppies and Michael Atkinson, the sales manager there. Hopkins agreed to loan this boat and trailer to Eagle Boats, Ltd. and William Seebold. It was also agreed that the magazine article would include information about the boat, Eagle Boats, Ltd., and Hoppies Village Marina. Seebold would transport the boat to Oklahoma and then return it to Hoppies using Hoppies's trailer.

The night before the magazine demonstration, Seebold parked the boat, trailer, and Eagle's truck in the parking lot of a motel. They were parked near the roadway parallel to the fence across the parking lot from the one dusk-to-dawn light. The trailer did not have a locking device that would lock it onto the truck. No one was left to guard the boat and it was not locked in any manner. Although other boats and trailers were in the parking lot, this was the most expensive boat there. It was also the closest to the road. Both the boat and trailer were stolen between 11:00 P.M. and about 5:00 A.M. Seebold offered evidence that failure to use locks is common in the industry. He testified that at his facility, he simply chains the boats together and locks the chain. He also produced sworn statements by Hopkins and Atkinson that it is common not to use locking devices. Seebold admitted that he could have put a chain around the boat and trailer and locked it to the truck; he did not have a chain with him. Suit was filed by a group of insurance underwriters that had issued a policy on this boat and had paid Hoppies for its losses. Legally, the group substituted for Hoppies in its claim against the defendants. Did the bailee fail to exercise proper care over the bailed property? [See *Institute of London Underwriters v. Eagle Boats, Ltd.*, 918 F. Supp. 297 (E.D. Mo. 1996).]

Notes

1. In 1990, after this lawsuit was begun, the state legislature amended the act to authorize the council to issue special permits for building or rebuilding of single-family residences.
2. This is not always the case. In the classic case of *Fontainebleau Hotel Corp. v. Forty-Five Twenty-Five, Inc.*, 114 So. 2d 367 (Fla. 1959), the court held that there was no rights to sunlight or view.
3. The classic case on this subject is *Pierson v. Post*, 3 Cai.R. 175 (N.Y. 1805).
4. "Summary Uniform Unclaimed Property Act (1995)," National Conference of Commissioners on Uniform State Laws (NCCUSL) Web site, at http://www.nccusl.org/Update/uniformact_summaries/uniformacts-s-uupa1995.asp (accessed 4/29/10). The following states have adopted the Uniform Unclaimed Property Act (1995): Alabama, Arizona, Arkansas, Hawaii, Indiana, Kansas, Louisiana, Maine, Montana, Nevada, New Mexico, North Carolina, U.S. Virgin Islands, Vermont, and West Virginia. (Although technically the U.S. Virgin Islands is not a state, the NCCUSL treats is as a state and for purposes of uniform laws we will also.) "A Few Facts About the Uniform Unclaimed Property Act (1995)," NCCUSL Web site, at http://www.nccusl.org/Update/uniformact_factsheets/uniformacts-fs-uupa.asp (accessed 4/29/10).
5. "Why States Should Adopt the Uniform Unclaimed Property Act (1995)," NCCUSL Web site, at http://www.nccusl.org/Update/uniformact_why/uniformacts-why-uupa.asp (accessed 4/29/10).
6. Ibid.
7. In *Kelo v. City of New London*, 545 U.S. 469 (2005), the Supreme Court accepted the argument that economic development could constitute a "public use" under the Fifth Amendment to the Constitution.
8. 112 S. Ct. 2886 (1992).
9. 16 U.S.C. §§ 461 *et seq.*
10. 42 U.S.C. §§ 4321 *et seq.*
11. 334 U.S. 1 (1948).

12. The Uniform Residential Landlord and Tenant Act has been adopted by Alabama, Alaska, Arizona, Connecticut, Florida, Hawaii, Iowa, Kansas, Kentucky, Michigan, Mississippi, Montana, Nebraska, New Mexico, Oklahoma, Oregon, Rhode Island, South Carolina, Tennessee, Virginia, and Washington. NCCUSL Web site, "A Few Facts About The Uniform Residential Landlord and Tenant Act," at http://www.nccusl.org/Update/uniformact_factsheets/uniformacts-fs-urlta.asp (accessed 4/29/10).

13. Ibid.

14. Currently, communities in only five states have rent control. Those states are California, District of Columbia, Maryland, New Jersey, and New York. Shae Irving, Kathleen Michon & Beth McKenna, *Nolo's Encyclopedia of Everyday Law* (Berkeley, CA: Nolo, 2002); and National Multi Housing Council Web site, Rent Control Laws by State, February 10, 2006, at http://www.nmhc.org/Content/ServeContent.cfm?isPrinterFriendly=1&IssueID=66&ContentItemID=1162 (accessed 4/29/10).

15. "Slow Death for Rent Control," *Fortune*, August 5, 1996, pp. 24, 26.

16. See *Spinks v. Taylor*, 278 S.E.2d 501 (N.C. 1981).

17. Rentlaw.com has a Web site on landlord tenant law, http://www.rentlaw.com/. It includes information on security deposits, at http://www.rentlaw.com/securitydeposit.htm (accessed 09/07/09).

18. Laura M. Litvan, "The Disabilities Law: Avoid the Pitfalls," *Nation's Business*, January 1994, pp. 25-27.

19. *German National Bank v. Meadowcroft*, 95 Ill. 124, 1880 WL 10015 (Ill.), and *Christensen v. Hoover*, 643 P.2d 525 (Colo. 1982).

20. California now recognizes a community property joint tenancy with rights of survivorship.

21. For an excellent discussion of the historical basis for community property law in each state, see W. S. McClanahan, *Community Property Law in the United States* (Lawyers Cooperative and Bancroft-Whitney, 1982), ch. 1-3. For an interesting discussion of the origins of community property in Europe and its adoption in other countries, see William Q. DeFuniak & Michael J. Vaughn, *Principles of Community Property* (Tucson, AZ: University of Arizona Press, 1971), ch. II.

22. For a copy of the act as adopted by the NCCUSL, see 9A Uniform Laws Annotated (U.L.A.) 97 (1987) and pocket parts. The NCCUSL has changed the Uniform Marital Property Act to the Model Marital Property Act. Email from Katie Robinson, Public Affairs Coordinator, NCCUSL, 11/26/02.

23. See Wisconsin 1983, Act 186, Effective 1-1-86, W.S.A. 766.001 to 766.97.

24. "A Few Facts about the Uniform Marital Property Act," NCCUSL Web site, at http://www.nccusl.org/Update/uniformact_factsheets/uniformacts-fs-umpa.asp (accessed 4/29/10).

25. The Uniform TOD Security Registration Act has been adopted by Alabama, Alaska, Arizona, Arkansas, California, Colorado, Connecticut, Delaware, District of Columbia, Florida, Georgia, Hawaii, Idaho, Illinois, Indiana, Iowa, Kansas, Kentucky, Maine, Maryland, Massachusetts, Michigan, Minnesota, Mississippi, Missouri, Montana, Nebraska, Nevada, New Hampshire, New Jersey, New Mexico, New York, North Carolina, North Dakota, Ohio, Oklahoma, Oregon, Pennsylvania, Rhode Island, South Carolina, South Dakota, Tennessee, Utah, Vermont, Virginia, Washington, West Virginia, Wisconsin, and Wyoming. NCCUSL Web site, "A Few Facts about the TOD Security Registration Act," at http://www.nccusl.org/Update/uniformact_factsheets/uniformacts-fs-tsra.asp (accessed 4/29/10).

26. "New Act Provides Procedures for Transferring Real Property without Probate," NCCUSL Web site, NCCUSL Press Release, July 15, 2009, at http://www.nccusl.org/nccusl/DesktopModules/NewsDisplay.aspx?ItemID=216 (accessed 09/07/09).

27. In New York State, the Supreme Court is the name for the trial court with general jurisdiction.

40

Intellectual Property, Computers, and the Law

Agenda

eClass is a software firm, and its success is ultimately tied to the popularity and uniqueness of its software. The principals are concerned about their ability to obtain a copyright on the software and also how to enforce their rights if they are able to obtain a copyright. They would also like to get trademark protection on the name of the product but are unsure about how to do so. Ani has expressed interest in acquiring a service mark by seeking an endorsement of the product from the American Education Association (AEA) or the American Association of University Professors (AAUP) as a marketing tool. Yousef recognizes the necessity of computers for the firm's customers, and he is concerned about any changes in the laws regarding computers and computer usage. These and other issues are likely to arise as you study this chapter. Be prepared! You never know when the firm or one of its members will seek your advice.

Classic Case

THE COCA-COLA COMPANY v. THE KOKE COMPANY OF AMERICA

254 U.S. 143, 41 S. Ct. 113, 1920 U.S. LEXIS 1177 (1920)

FACTS Coca-Cola filed suit, seeking an injunction to restrain The Koke Company of America, the alleged infringer, from using the words "Koke" and "Dope" to describe its product, alleging that the words infringed Coca-Cola's trademark and constituted unfair competition. Coca-Cola also asserted that Koke was a trademark infringement, clearly intended to capitalize on Coca-Cola's goodwill.

The Koke Company argued that Coca-Cola's trademark should be declared void because it fraudulently represented the contents and/or effects of the product.

ISSUES Did Koke infringe on the trademark of Coca-Cola? Was Koke's action an unfair competition? Was the Coca-Cola trademark a fraudulent representation of the product?

HOLDINGS Yes, Koke infringed the Coca-Cola trademark and was guilty of unfair competition. No, the Coca-Cola trademark was not a fraudulent representation of the product.

REASONING Excerpts from the opinion of Justice Holmes:

"This is a bill in equity brought by the Coca-Cola Company to prevent the infringement of its trade-mark Coca-Cola and unfair competition with it in its business of making and selling the beverage for which the trade-mark is used. . . .

Both the Courts below agree that subject to the one question to be considered the plaintiff has a right to equitable relief. Whatever may have been its original weakness, the mark for years has acquired a secondary significance and has indicated the plaintiff's product alone. It is found that defendant's mixture is made and sold in imitation of the plaintiff's and that the word Koke was chosen for the purpose of reaping the benefit of the advertising done by the plaintiff and of selling the imitation as and for the plaintiff's goods. The only obstacle found by the Circuit Court of Appeals in the way of continuing the injunction granted below was its opinion that the trade-mark in itself and the advertisements accompanying it made such fraudulent representations to the public that the plaintiff had lost its claim to any help from the Court. That is the question upon which the writ of certiorari was granted and the main one that we shall discuss.

Of course a man is not to be protected in the use of a device the very purpose and effect of which is to swindle the public. But the defects of a plaintiff do not offer a very broad ground for allowing another to swindle him. The defense relied on here should be scrutinized with a critical eye. The main point is this: Before 1900 the beginning of the good will was more or less helped by the presence of cocaine, a drug that, like alcohol or caffeine or opium, may be described as a deadly poison or as a valuable item of the pharmacopoeia according to the rhetorical purposes in view. The amount seems to have been very small, but it may have been enough to begin a bad habit and after the Food and Drug Act of June 30, 1906 . . . if not earlier, long before this suit was brought, it was eliminated from the plaintiff's compound. . . . It is argued that the continued use of the name imports a representation that has ceased to be true and that the representation is reinforced by a picture of coca leaves and cola nuts upon the label and by advertisements, which however were many years before this suit was brought, that the drink is an "ideal nerve tonic and stimulant," . . . and that thus the very thing sought to be protected is used as a fraud.

The argument does not satisfy us. We are dealing here with a popular drink not with a medicine, and although what has been said might suggest that its attraction lay in producing the expectation of a toxic effect the facts point to a different conclusion. . . . The name now characterizes a beverage to be had at almost any soda fountain. It means a single thing coming from a single source, and well known to the community. It hardly would be too much to say that the drink characterizes the name as much as the name the drink. . . . [W]e see no reason to doubt that, as we have said, it has acquired a secondary meaning in which perhaps the product is more emphasized than the producer

but to which the producer is entitled. The coca leaves and whatever of cola nut is employed may be used to justify the continuance of the name or they may affect the flavor as the plaintiff contends, but before this suit was brought the plaintiff had advertised to the public that it must not expect and would not find cocaine, and had eliminated everything tending to suggest cocaine effects except the name and the picture of the leaves and nuts, which probably conveyed little or nothing to most who saw it. It appears to us that it would be going too far to deny the plaintiff relief against a palpable fraud because possibly here and there an ignorant person might call for the drink with the hope for incipient cocaine intoxication. The plaintiff's position must be judged by the facts as they were when the suit was begun, not by the facts of a different condition and an earlier time . . .".

INTRODUCTION

In this chapter, we will examine the law's treatment of intellectual property, or the property that comes from the human capacity to create. The body of law that addresses intellectual property derives from a variety of common law, state, and federal statutory and nonstatutory sources. Intellectual property law encompasses several substantive legal areas: patents, copyrights, trademarks, service marks, trade dress, trade secrets, and unfair competition. Computer usage can have a significant impact on intellectual property, especially given the ease with which a computer can be used to infringe on someone's intellectual property rights, so we will also address some of the more important areas of the law that deal with the regulation of computers and computer usage.

Article I, Section 8 of the U.S. Constitution authorizes Congress "to promote the Progress of Science and the useful Arts, by securing for limited Times to Authors and Inventors the exclusive Right to their respective Writings and Discoveries." This Constitutional grant of authority to Congress is the cornerstone on which intellectual property law in the United States is built. The "exclusive right" to authors is the basis of copyright law, and the "exclusive right" to inventors is the basis of patent law. These "exclusive rights" provide the holders of copyrights and/or patents with a government-issued monopoly on their covered works, thus encouraging creativity. The "limited times" mentioned in this section ensures that the monopoly will not last forever, but rather will expire after a reasonable time (to be set out by Congress in its statutes), allowing others to compete with the owners of either or both of these rights.

Although not specifically addressed in the Constitution, other types of intellectual property have been recognized, as well. The symbol, mark or device that identifies a business or an organization (trademark, service mark, certification mark, trade dress) is entitled to protection under the law today. Trade secrets are somewhat protected, although to a lesser degree, provided the person who has the secret treats it with an appropriate level of confidentiality. These issues will be addressed in more detail in the rest of this chapter.

Exhibit 40.1 sets out the broad categories of intellectual property.

Exhibit 40.1

An Overview of Intellectual Property Law

Patent	A government-issued monopoly to the inventor of a new, useful, and non-obvious device for a period of 20 years (utility patent) or 14 years (design patent).
Copyright	A government-issued protection for original works of art, once captured in a tangible medium, for the life of the author plus 70 years (for a work owned by a business, the copyright lasts the shorter period of time of 95 years from the date of first publication or 120 years from creation).
Trade Mark	An exclusive right to use a word, term, mark, or symbol to identify one's goods. A registered trademark is valid for 10 years, but can be renewed every ten years for an indefinite period.
Service Mark	A service mark is like a trademark only it covers services provided by the owner rather than goods produced and sold.
Certification Mark	A word, mark, term, or symbol that certifies the membership in a group, approval by a group or trade association, or geographic origin of the good being sold. A certification mark is not used by the owner of the mark, but rather by a producer of goods who has secured permission from the owner as evidence of compliance with the group's certification process.
Trade Dress	Also covered by trademark law, trade dress is a unique design, shape, color, or other decorative aspect of a product that identifies its producer.
Trade Secret	A method of doing business that gives its owner a competitive advantage, and which the owner treats in a confidential manner to prevent is dissemination to competitors and the public.

PATENTS

As mentioned, Article I, Section 8 of the Constitution grants "for limited times ... to inventors ... exclusive rights ... to their ... discoveries." These "exclusive rights" are in the form of *patents*. A patent is a federally authorized and issued monopoly granted to the "inventor"—the "exclusive right"—for twenty years (for a utility patent) or fourteen years (for a design patent)—the "limited time." In exchange for this legal monopoly, the inventor must file for the patent with the U.S. Patent and Trademark Office (PTO), and the filing requires a full description of the item or design. Assuming that the patent is granted, the patent holder has the exclusive right to use and/or sell the item or the design for the patent's life. Once the patent protection ends, anyone can copy the item or the design, and these people can then make, use, or sell the invention with impunity.

The Standards of Patentability

To be eligible for patent protection, the invention must be (1) new, (2) useful, and (3) not obvious to persons of ordinary skill in the trade or area. All three requirements must be satisfied before a patent will be issued.

It is fairly obvious that a person seeking a patent, and the exclusive rights that go with the patent, must invent something new. The patent application will be denied if:

- There is already something substantially similar to the invention in existence or available
- There has been public use by others in this country prior to the application, *or*
- The inventor has either sold or publicly used the invention more than one year prior to his or her application.

Before the PTO will issue a patent, the invention must be shown to be useful. In order to acquire exclusive rights to an invention for twenty years, the person gaining those exclusive rights needs to demonstrate that there is the potential for society to obtain significant current benefits from the invention.

Finally, the invention must involve a development that is not obvious to others in the field. If the invention would be obvious to a person of ordinary skill in the field, the public will not benefit by permitting the inventor to have a 20-year monopoly. There is an assumption here that if the invention is truly useful and it is obvious, someone would come forward with the idea in due time, and the protections afforded by a patent would therefore not be beneficial to society.

Since the first patent statute in 1790, the statutory categories of patentable subject matter have consisted of:

(1) any process (the earlier term was "art," but the term "process" now includes a process, art, or method);

(2) machine;

(3) manufacture;

(4) composition of matter, including certain nonnaturally occurring plants, such as hybrids;[1] and

(5) any new and useful improvement thereof.

The Supreme Court has held that such utility patents may cover genetically engineered living matter as well. As in copyright law, ideas *per se* are not patentable. Neither are laws of nature (for example, "for every action there is an equal and opposite reaction"), mathematical formulas, scientific truths or principles, and mental processes. Business methods were historically excluded from being patentable, but the technological developments of the late twentieth century led the PTO to "rethink" this area. Today business methods can be patented, provided that the business method is shown to produce a useful, concrete and tangible result.[2]

By making an application to the U.S. Patent and Trademark Office (PTO), inventors who believe they have met these requirements begin the process of receiving a patent. This application includes a declaration that the applicant first discovered the invention for which he or she solicits the patent; any drawings necessary to explain the patent; detailed descriptions, specifications, and disclosures (including all prior art) of the subject matter the applicant claims as his or her invention; and the required filing fees. The substantive information provided in the specifications should (1) enable any person skilled in the art to make or use the invention after the expiration of the term of the patent and (2) inform the public of the limits of the monopoly asserted by the inventor for the life of the patent.

The Commissioner of Patents and Trademarks will issue a patent if the PTO examiner to whom the Commissioner has given the application approves the application. Common grounds for rejection include the finding of prior art or the existence of "double-patenting" (two patents for the same invention). Applicants who receive rejection notices can appeal to the PTO Board of Patent Appeals and Interferences and then either to the U.S. Court of Appeals for the Federal Circuit or the U.S. District Court for the District of Columbia.

The PTO reports that in 2006, it granted 183,187 patents, from the 443,652 applications it received.[3]

Protection and Infringement

A patent can be extremely valuable. Possession of a patent gives the patent holder exclusive rights to the invention and a 20 year head start over his or her competitors—if the patent is upheld. Patent litigation normally arises when a patent holder sues another party, alleging that the other party has infringed on his or her patent.

A person can infringe a patent intentionally or accidentally. A patent gives the patent holder exclusive rights, and the issuance of a patent serves as constructive notice to the world of the patent's existence. Since there is no need to intend to infringe a patent in order to be held liable for infringement, the person being sued for patent infringement will try to prove that the patent is invalid owing to some omitted condition of patentability (for example, novelty); if the patent is found to be invalid, there is no infringement since there is no longer any valid patent that could be infringed.

A defendant may also try to argue that the patent holder has abused the patent rights by, for example, using the patent as a means of engaging in anticompetitive behavior or to extend its monopoly beyond the scope of the patent rights. If the defendant can establish that the patent holder violated antitrust laws in the use of the patent, the defendant will be found not guilty of infringement. Remember, however, that it is not a misuse of the patent if the patent holder refused to sell or license the patent to others, or even to use the patent he or she has acquired.

In 1996, the U.S. Supreme Court held that when an infringement action involves the interpretation of a patent claim (that is, the portion of the patent document that defines the scope of the patent holder's rights), such an interpretation is a question of *law* exclusively within the province of the court; juries are not empowered to engage in such interpretive activities. However, juries can decide questions of fact, such as whether infringement has occurred.[4]

Remedies

Remedies for actionable patent infringement include damages and equitable relief in the form of injunctions. The statute directs courts to award damages in an amount adequate to compensate the holder of the patent for the infringement (such amounts will include lost profits attributable to the infringement) but in no event less than a reasonable royalty representative of the infringer's use of the invention.

The act also allows courts to impose costs and to award reasonable attorneys' fees to the prevailing party in exceptional cases, such as circumstances involving clear fraud and wrongdoing or in circumstances in which the court believes the award of attorneys' fees will prevent gross injustice. But given the enormity of the attorneys' fees in typical patent cases, courts rarely award such fees.

In either jury or nonjury trials, courts have authority to treble the damages assessed. A court's award of damages denies the infringer its ill-gotten gains and also restores to the patent holder the benefits he or she would have derived from the legal monopoly had the infringement not occurred. The Patent Act expressly allows courts to use expert testimony for determining the damages or royalties that would be reasonable under the circumstances.

International Dimensions

With the growing globalization of business, coupled with the relative ease and speed of communication and transportation, many patents have significant value beyond the patent holder's national borders. As a result a number of nations have signed treaties that recognize and protect the rights of the patent holder within the borders of all the signatory nations. Prior to the adoption of these international treaties an inventor had to patent the invention in each foreign jurisdiction in which he or she sought protection, and the filing had to conform to the requirements of the patent law of that particular nation.

The Paris Convention for the Protection of Industrial Property, administered by the World Intellectual Property Organization (WIPO), came into existence in 1883. It has been amended a number of times, most recently in Brussels in 1990. About 140 nations, including the United States, are members of the Paris Convention. The Paris Convention emphasizes the concept of national treatment of patents. This allows each member nation to determine the nature and extent of the substantive protections afforded to patents, which means that patented inventions may not be fully protected in each member nation. As a result, the Paris Convention has done little to alleviate the need for separate filings in each signatory nation's jurisdiction, and it has no enforcement mechanisms for policing violations of the convention.

Owing to these shortcomings, the Patent Cooperation Treaty[5] (PCT) became effective in 1978. It has been modified several times, most recently in 2001. The PCT's procedures—especially the filing system—allow inventors in the 133 or so nations, including the United States, that have signed the treaty to use one filing for securing patent rights in the jurisdictions represented by the signatory nations. The present GATT round and NAFTA, international efforts discussed in Chapter 8, also provide transnational patent protection to inventors. In particular, the recent GATT changes appear to involve practical steps that will result in further harmonization of the international treatment of patents.[6]

Computers

Neither the prior patent law nor the recent amendments contemplated the inclusion of computers or program-related inventions. As a result, by the 1960s, the PTO and the Court of Customs and Patent Appeals (CCPA) had drawn strict battle lines regarding the patentability of computer programs and other software. The CCPA was for it; the PTO against it.

After several cases in the 1970s holding computer-related inventions unpatentable, the Supreme Court in *Diamond* v. *Diehr*[7] held that a process for curing synthetic rubber, which includes in several of its steps the use of a mathematical formula and a programmed digital computer, was patentable subject matter. A subsequent CCPA decision, *In re Pardo*,[8] ruled that a compiler program, one designed to convert a high-level programming language into binary or machine code so as to translate source code to object code, alone may constitute patentable subject matter. It now appears that computer programs are patentable in the United States, provided that they satisfy the three requirements of novelty, uniqueness, and non-obviousness. The European Union reached a similar position in 2005, although the language of the policy as adopted is extremely difficult to read or to decipher.

COPYRIGHTS

Similar protections are also given to creators of artistic works. While inventors have the potential protection of patents, artists (writers, composers, and other types of artists) have the protection of copyrights. The U.S. Copyright Act[9] was enacted in 1976 and went into effect in 1978. (Works copyrighted prior to January 1, 1978 are still governed by the Copyright Act of 1909, as amended.) The Copyright Act has been amended several times since 1978, including the Berne Convention Implementation Act[10] of 1988 and four amendments passed in 2008 and 2009.[11]

The Copyright Act protects an original work of authorship fixed in any tangible medium of expression now known or later developed, from which they can be perceived, reproduced, or otherwise communicated, either directly or with the aid of a machine or a device. Works of authorship include, but are not limited to, (1) literary works; (2) musical works, including any accompanying music; (3) pantomimes and choreographic works; (4) pictorial, graphic, and sculptural works; (5) motion pictures and other audiovisual works; (6) sound recordings; and (7) architectural works. Note that copyright laws protect only *expressions of ideas*, not the ideas themselves. In order to acquire protection, the artist must express his or her original artistic idea in some tangible medium, thus providing proof of his or her creation of the artistic work.

Copyright protection extends much longer than patent protection. Generally, for works created after January 1, 1978, a copyright runs for the life of the author plus 70 years. If the author is anonymous, the work was created under a pseudonym, or it was a "work for hire" the copyright runs for the lesser of 95 years from it first publication or 120 years from its creation. These copyrights cannot be renewed. For works first published prior to January 1, 1978, several different rules may apply.

Under current law, since March 1, 1989 an artistic work is automatically entitled to copyright protection as soon as it is fixed into tangible form. This means that a person does not need to register with the Copyright Office, affix the copyright symbol (©) or take any other steps in order to enjoy the protection afforded by the law to the exclusive rights to his or her creative work. Prior to that date the artist had to register the work or provide some other notice that he or she was claiming a copyright on the work in order to have protection against infringement of the work by others. In order for an artist to acquire copyright protection today, his or her work must simply be original, it must be at least somewhat creative or artistic, *and* it must be fixed in a tangible medium of expression. However, in order for the copyright holder to file suit for damages against an infringer the copyright must be registered with the Copyright Office. If the copyright is not registered, the holder can seek other remedies (e.g., an injunction) but cannot sue for damages.[12] A copyright cannot be obtained in a mere recitation of facts (the listings in a telephone directory, for example) or in an idea (although the method of expressing the idea may well be copyrighted).[13]

The Copyright Office of the Library of Congress administers copyrights in the United States. Among other things, the Copyright Office registers copyrights; issues certificates of registration; keeps records of copyright registrations, licenses, and assignments; and oversees deposits of copyrighted materials. Unlike the Patent and Trademark Office's stringent and detailed oversight of patents and trademark, the Copyright Office merely determines whether applications involve copyrightable subject matter and have fulfilled all the registration requirements. Consequently, the registration process is relatively simple and inexpensive. The author or artist can register the copyright online for a nominal fee. In 2008 the Copyright Office registered 232,100 works, down from 524,700 in 2007.[14]

Protection and Infringement

While a copyright lasts much longer than a patent, the rights granted to the copyright holder are not as great as those given to the holder of a patent. A copyright provides a bundle of rights that enables the copyright owner—usually the author or one to whom the author has transferred rights—to exploit a work for commercial purposes. These exclusive rights include: (1) reproducing the copyrighted work; (2) preparing derivative works (or adaptations) based on the copyrighted work; (3) distributing copies or phono records of the copyrighted work; (4) performing publicly literary, musical, dramatic, and choreographic works, pantomimes, and motion pictures or audiovisual works; and (5) displaying the works themselves or individual images of the works mentioned in (4) as well as pictorial, graphic, or sculptural works.

However, the law also provides for certain uses of the copyright-protected work without requiring the permission of the copyright holder, in some situations without even acquiring his or her permission. Under the fair use provisions of the Copyright Act[15] certain reproductions are permitted without obtaining permission from the copyright holder. In order to qualify as a "fair use," the use must be for purposes such as criticism, comment, news reporting, teaching, scholarship, and research. Section 107 set out four factors that should be considered in deciding whether a challenged use qualifies as a fair use, and thus is exempt from the "exclusive use" of the copyright holder:

1. the purpose and character of the use, including whether the use is for a commercial purpose or is for nonprofit educational purposes;
2. the nature of the copyrighted work;
3. the amount and substantiality of the portion used to the copyrighted work as a whole;
4. the effect of the use upon the potential market for, or value of, the copyrighted work.[16]

Because the distinction between fair use and infringement is not clear, it is best to always seek permission, and to avoid using the copyrighted material if such permission is not obtained. However, if a person believes that the use is necessary, and he or she is unable to obtain permission, he or she should carefully review the standards generally followed for determining whether the use will qualify as fair use, such as

Reproduction of Copyrighted Works by Educators and Librarians,[17] provided by the U.S. Copyright Office. The user should also document his or her analysis of why the use was "fair."

The fair use doctrine also includes parody to some extent. A work done by one person in which he or she imitates another person's work as a parody or a satire of a copyrighted work is likely to be viewed as a fair use. While the owner of the copyrighted work may not appreciate the parody or satire, the courts tend to allow such use, even without permission from the copyright holder. The Supreme Court reached such a conclusion in a 1994 opinion, upholding the use by the rap group 2 Live Crew in which the group performed a parody of *Oh, Pretty Women*, a song written by Roy Orbison and William Dees in 1964. (Orbison and Dees had assigned their rights in the song to Acuff-Rose Music, Inc.) When 2 Live Crew asked for permission to use the song, they were denied by Acuff-Rose.[18] Rather than being deterred, they used the song anyway in their recording of *Pretty Woman*. Acuff-Rose sued for infringement, but the Court found for 2 Live Crew, noting that parody was within the scope of fair use and thus not an infringement.

Many copyright holders of recorded music assign their rights to control public performance of their music to either the American Society of Composers, Authors, and Publishers (ASCAP) or to Broadcast Music, Inc. (BMI) to ensure that they receive royalties when their songs are publicly played. Both ASCAP and BMI collect royalties from various entities that play songs and then distribute these royalties to their signed artists on a predetermined schedule of payments. By assigning their rights to either of these organizations, the artist loses some control over the use of the covered recordings. During the 2008 Presidential election campaign, John McCain used songs by John Mellencamp, Jackson Brown, and Gretchen Peters, all without the direct permission of the copyright holders. However, when the holders of the copyrights objected to the usage, they were informed that permission had been granted and all appropriate royalties had been paid, so that there was no copyright infringement. Further, since they had been paid they had no control over how the songs were used, nor did they have a right to limit or restrict the usage. (There are also *compulsory* licensing sections in the act that apply to cable television systems' secondary transmissions of primary broadcasts, satellite retransmissions, operators of electronic video game arcades, and operation of jukeboxes.)

Copyright infringement does not require intent on the part of the infringing party. A totally innocent reproduction of another's copyrighted work is still an infringement of that person's copyright, absent permission or the fair use exception.[19] Typically, the owner of the copyrighted work will show that the defendant had access to the copyrighted work and that the defendant's work shows a striking similarity to the copyrighted work. If the court finds that the similarities are more likely than not to have been the result of copying the protected work, it will find that an unlawful appropriation of that work has occurred. At that point the owner of the copyright is entitled to remedies to end the infringement. These remedies may include damages, if the copyright was registered with the U.S. Copyright Office.

Remedies

Civil remedies for infringements include injunctions, the impoundment and destruction of infringing items, and damages. Plaintiffs can choose between actual damages, including the infringer's profits attributable to the infringement if the court, in computing the damages, did not take these into account, or statutory damages ranging from a minimum of $750 to $30,000 for all infringements involved in the action with respect to one work and which the court thinks is just under the circumstances. A court may increase the damages to $150,000 for willful infringements. Similarly, the court may lower the damages to $200 if the infringer can prove it was unaware that its actions constituted an infringement. The court in its discretion can award court costs to either party and may award attorneys' fees to either prevailing plaintiffs or prevailing defendants.[20]

Criminal penalties range from a maximum of $10,000 and one year's imprisonment (or both) to a maximum $25,000 and one year's imprisonment (or both) for the first offense involving willful infringement and a maximum of $50,000 and two years' imprisonment (or both) for subsequent offenses.

The No Electronic Theft Act of 1997 provides for both civil and criminal penalties for copyright infringement involving the Internet. Infringement is a crime only where it is done "willfully and for purposes of commercial advantage or private financial gain."[21] According to this Act:

> The penalties for criminal infringement, set forth in Title 18 of the U.S. Code, are determined by the extent of the infringement: if the infringer has made, in any 180-day period, ten or more copies of one or more copyrighted works with a total retail value of $2,500, the crime is a felony entailing up to five years imprisonment and/or a fine of up to $250,000 for individuals and $500,000 for organizations.[22] For cases not meeting this threshold, the crime is a misdemeanor, with the maximum penalty of imprisonment for up to one year and/or a fine of up to $25,000 for individuals and $100,000 for organizations.[23] There is also an increased penalty for repeat offenders, authorizing a sentence of up to 10 years.[24]

International Dimensions

As noted earlier, U.S. copyright laws have undergone some changes since the United States became a member of the Berne Convention (the International Union for the Protection of Literary and Artistic Works) in March 1989. The Berne Convention makes national treatment of copyrights the linchpin of the treaty. In other words, each member nation must automatically extend the protection of its laws to the other signatory nations' nationals and to works originally published in a member nation's jurisdiction. The Berne Convention is not self-executing; each member nation therefore must enact implementing legislation.

The United States has taken a minimalist approach to compliance with the Berne Convention, not accepting every provision of the treaty. But since the United States has enacted into law many of the treaty's provisions, it is important to U.S. intellectual property law. The World Intellectual Property Organization's (or just WIPO's) December 1996 treaties have updated the Berne Convention to reflect the changes in information technology and to set intellectual property standards for the digital age. These new treaties, among other things, have closed some loopholes that had left the U.S. recording industry without copyright protection in the international arena.

The Universal Copyright Convention (UCC), administered by the United Nations, represents another international treaty that covers copyrights. Although it imposes fewer substantive requirements on copyrights than does the Berne Convention, some Berne Convention members also have joined the UCC as a means of establishing relationships concerning copyrights with UCC members who have not signed the Berne Convention. (The U.S. signed the Berne Convention in 1989).

Recent amendments to the General Agreement on Tariffs and Trade (GATT) expand the protections afforded to copyrighted works, including computer programs.

eClass 40.1 Management

COPYRIGHT INFRINGEMENT

Ani has come up with what she believes is a creative idea for a commercial for the eClass software. She has described it to Meg and Yousef, and they also think it could be a very successful ad. In the ad Ani envisions a point-counterpoint type of discussion between a professor who advocates using eClass and a professor who prefers a traditional "talk and chalk" approach to teaching. Her ad is very similar to a series of Windows—Mac commercials with actors representing each computer: this ad campaign has been quite popular and effective. While Meg and Yousef agree that the idea for the ad is good, they are concerned that the similarity to the Mac commercials might infringe a copyright. The firm members ask you if this ad might infringe a copyright. What will you tell them?

BUSINESS CONSIDERATIONS   Why do businesses use the voices, names, and likenesses of famous people to sell their products? Are these types of ads less effective if the advertiser uses unknown people to show the use of the product?

ETHICAL CONSIDERATIONS   Is it ethical for a business to use computer imaging to place famous people who have died into commercials with contemporary stars or contemporary settings? What ethical concerns do the use of the likenesses of deceased celebrities in raise?

The European Union's (EU's) "Directive on the Legal Protection of Computer Software," slated to cover EU members as of January 1, 1993, represents another promising initiative in the international arena.

Computers

When computer usage first became widespread, it was unclear whether computer programs could be copyrighted. By 1964 the Copyright Office began to allow computer programs to be registered as "books," and therefore copyright-eligible. Even the passage of the Copyright Act of 1976 did not resolve this issue. The issue was finally resolved with the 1980 amendments to the Copyright Act. Under the 1980 amendments, "[a] 'computer program' is a set of statements or instructions to be used directly or indirectly in a computer in order to bring about a certain result." According to the 1980 amendments, computer databases also are copyrightable as "compilations" or "derivative works."

There are some important limitations and differences in the copyright protections for computer software as compared to protections for a book, movie or song. While it would probably be viewed as an infringement for a person to buy a book and then make a copy of it for his or her "archives," such an act with software is not an infringement. It is also not considered an infringement if a person makes a copy or an adaptation of a computer program when such a copy or adaptation is essential for proper utilization of that program on the buyer's computer.

The fair use doctrine also applies to software. Software that is protected by copyright can be used in the classroom for instructional or demonstration purposes without acquiring permission from the copyright owner and without the need to pay royalties for the use. In addition, libraries can reproduce and distribute software in some circumstances without infringing the copyright.

It must be remembered that while the computer program can be copyrighted, the idea behind the program cannot be so protected. Original works can receive a copyright, but ideas—even original ideas—cannot receive a copyright for their protection. Thus, a program that provides a word processing function can be copyrighted, but the idea of word processing cannot be copyrighted, nor can the copyright prevent other software developers from devising competing word processing programs. The software program for the video game DOOM® can be copyrighted, but the idea behind the game is "fair game" for others to "borrow" by creating a similar game with a different program to run the game.

Similarly, the audiovisual display aspects of a video game may be copyrightable whereas the idea—a crazy character that "munches" everything, for instance—behind the game, or the game *per se*, ordinarily will be ineligible for copyright protection. The same may be true in general of flowcharts, components of machines, and printed circuit boards that do not have computer programs embedded in them: These normally are not copyrightable. The unsettled state of the law in this area merely complicates the problems of software developers.

TRADEMARKS, SERVICE MARKS, AND TRADE DRESS

Trademarks, service marks, and trade dress each involve a distinctive mark or design that identifies the provider of goods or services. As a business develops a reputation and establishes goodwill, customers who see the mark recognize the provider and rely on that provider's reputation as evidence of the quality customers expect from the business. As a result, these distinctive marks can be quite valuable to business.

From their inception, trademarks have served as a means by which tradespeople and craftspersons identify goods as their own. Archaeologists have found centuries-old artifacts bearing such symbols. In recognition of the social and economic dimensions of such marks, the medieval guilds used trademarks as a means of controlling quality and fostering customer goodwill. Statutes as early as the thirteenth century codified these ideas. These early statutory developments were intended to prohibit "palming off," an act where one producer passes off its goods as if they are the goods of a competitor by copying the trademark.

Present-day trademark law continues this tradition, protecting against consumer confusion as to the origin of goods by providing protection for registered trademarks. There is no Constitutional provision for protecting trademarks, but the Commerce Clause grants the federal government exclusive authority to regulate interstate commerce providing the basis for federal regulation of trademarks. In addition, state laws protect trademarks.

Over the years, an extensive body of state trademark law had developed in the common law, principally through the application of state laws governing unfair competition. At the federal level, the 1946 Lanham Act[25] provides the most important federal protection of trademarks. The Lanham Act provides for the registration of trademarks with the Patent and Trademark Office (PTO). The PTO oversees the federal registration of trademarks. In 2008 there were 233,900 applications for trademarks, with 233,900 being issued.[26] Just as the Lanham Act allows the registration of various marks, so too, some states have statutory registration provisions.

Protection and Infringement

The Lanham Act defines a trademark as "a word, symbol, or phrase, used to identify a particular manufacturer or seller's products and distinguish them from the products of another."[27] Trademarks are used to distinguish one manufacturer's goods from those of its competitors. Trademark protection can also extend to the *shape* of a product (e.g., the iconic Coca-Cola bottle), the *color* of the product (e.g., the pink of Owens-Corning fiberglass insulation), or other items of *trade dress*. However, a product's shape cannot be protected by trademark if that shape would provide a competitive advantage, such as making the product easier to stack.

Service marks, trade dress, and certification marks are given similar treatment and protection. Each of these can also be registered with the PTO and can acquire trademark protection. A service mark is the use of a "word, symbol, or phrase used to identify" the provider of that service. Trade dress, as previously mentioned, is the use of a specific design, including shape or color, to identify a business, its goods, or its services. Trade dress has even been extended by the courts to include floor plans, color schemes, and even menu designs for some restaurants. Certification marks are used to identify the specific geographic region from which a product comes (e.g., Sunshine Tree for citrus from Florida), to certify that the goods or services meet certain standards in relation to quality, materials, or mode of manufacture (e.g., Good House-keeping Seal of Approval or the Underwriters' Laboratories seal), or to certify that the work or labor on the products or services was performed by a member of a union or other organization, or that the performer meets certain standards (e.g., ISO 9000 certified,). [Note that a certification mark is not used by the owner of the mark, nor does it identify the provider of the goods or services. It merely certifies that the goods or services possess certain traits or characteristics often identified with quality.]

To deserve protection, the trademark—whatever its form—must be distinctive. In determining whether any given "word, symbol, or phrase" is distinctive, and thus deserving or protection, the courts have established four classifications:

1. arbitrary and fanciful
2. suggestive
3. descriptive
4. generic

Arbitrary and fanciful terms are distinctive by definition. For example, "Exxon" and "Xerox" are trademarked words, each of which is an arbitrary and fanciful word that had no meaning until it was related to the respective companies and their products. Suggestive terms are terms that conjure an image or an idea of what the product is intended to do rather than what the product is. As a result such terms are also distinctive. For example, "Coppertone," a sun tanning product, suggests what the product does rather that what it is. Note that all these marks embody some degree of imaginativeness. Without distinctiveness, identifying the source of the goods and avoiding consumer confusion become decidedly more difficult. Such marks in themselves also serve narrow marketing functions.

Descriptive marks are marks that basically describe the business that the mark intends to portray. "Holiday Inn" is a descriptive mark, "describing" what the mark represents—an INN for people on HOLIDAY, or a hotel / motel. (Sometimes the description is less obvious, as in "Vision Center," a mark for a business that sells glasses and contact lens. While not selling vision per se, the business is selling products that enhance one's vision.) Purely descriptive marks—adjectives such as "sweet" or "chicken"; geographic designations like "California" or "New York" in reference to wines; and people's surnames like L.L. Bean used as marks—do not qualify as distinctive until they have acquired "secondary meaning." In other words, when the consuming public no longer views the marks as purely descriptive terms but rather as indicative of the source of the goods or products, the marks have become distinctive. In a similar vein, common geometric shapes, flowers, or slogans generally lack the required distinctiveness and will not merit trademark status unless the owner can demonstrate an acquired secondary meaning.

Generic marks are not entitled to trademark protection. Generic marks describe the classification or category of the product rather than the product itself. If a computer company decided to incorporate as Computers, Inc., and to sell its product as "Computer," it would not be able to acquire a trademark on "Computer" and thus prevent other companies from advertising that they were selling computers. While generic terms never can qualify for trademark protection, some terms that were once trademarked have lost that protection because the term became generic! Trademark law shows numerous examples of words that have passed into generic usage and thereby have lost their trademark status. Aspirin, calico, cellophane, escalator, linoleum, shredded wheat, thermos, yo-yo, and zipper represent a few such former trademarks.

The Lanham Act also prohibits the issuance of a trademark for a deceptive mark or for marks that are immoral, scandalous, or offensive. Similarly, the Lanham Act specifically excludes trademark protection for marks that disparage any person (living or dead), institution, belief, or national symbol; that use the name, portrait, or signature of a living person without that person's consent; that use the name, portrait, or signature of a deceased U.S. President during the lifetime of his or her spouse without the spouse's consent; and/or that so resemble an already registered mark as to be likely to cause confusion, mistake, or deception.

The person or entity that first uses, and then continues to use, a mark in trade or commerce is recognized as the owner of that mark. Under the provisions of the Lanham Act, in order to register the mark with the PTO, the owner must demonstrate either prior use or a *bona fide* intent to use the mark in the future. An applicant submits his or her application, which includes the "word, symbol, or phrase" to be covered to the PTO, which then examines the application for compliance with the statute and also to ensure that the mark is not confusingly or deceptively similar to previously registered marks. Once the mark is approved, the PTO publishes the mark in its *Official Gazette*. Once granted, registration ordinarily lasts for ten years and is renewable for ten-year periods so long as the mark remains in commercial use.

The law protects the trademark owner from infringement when the infringer's use will likely cause an appreciable number of consumers to be confused about the source of the goods or services. The factors courts have used to determine the "likelihood of confusion" include, but are not limited to, the following: (1) similarities in the two marks' appearance, sound, connotation, meaning, and impression; (2) similarities in the customer base, sales outlets (that is, "trade channels"), or the character of the sale ("impulse" versus "nonimpulse" sales); (3) the strength of the mark; (4) evidence of actual confusion; and (5) the number and nature of similar marks on similar or related products and services.

Defenses to infringement include "fair use." As we have noted earlier, one can use one's surname—even if it is the same as another famous, trademarked name like McDonald's, Campbell's, or Hilton—as long as one's use does not create the likelihood of consumer confusion. Abandonment of the mark, whether actual (that is, discontinuation of the use of the mark with the intent not to resume usage) or constructive (acts or omissions by the owner that bring about the loss of distinctiveness), constitutes a defense to infringement as well. The Lanham Act expressly provides that nonuse of the mark for two consecutive years constitutes *prima facie* evidence of an intent to abandon the mark.

The plaintiff's registration of the mark on the Principal Register gives him or her certain advantages in an infringement action, since registration serves as *prima facie* evidence of the mark's validity and the registrant's exclusive right to use the mark in connection with the goods or services described in the registration. Ordinarily, then, at least until the mark becomes incontestable (indisputable), defendants challenging the validity of the mark must prove the registrant's noncompliance with the prerequisites of the Lanham Act (or the common law). Incontestability status derives from the registrant's continuous use of the mark in interstate commerce for five consecutive years, the absence of any decision adverse to the registrant's claim of ownership or any pending proceeding, and the registrant's filing an affidavit to this effect with the Commissioner of the PTO.

Attainment of incontestability status gives the registrant of the mark a decided edge. For example, loss of an incontestable mark can occur only through cancellation of the mark, in certain limited statutorily enumerated circumstances, or through the challenger's showing one of the statutorily enumerated defenses to incontestability. Such defenses, among others, include proof that the mark is generic; registration or incontestability has been obtained fraudulently; the registrant has abandoned the mark; the mark falls within the aforementioned categories prohibited as deceptive marks; or the use of the mark constitutes a violation of the antitrust laws. In the context of descriptive products or services, incontestability substitutes for proof of secondary meaning. Hence, even though the registrant of a generic mark can never use incontestability to protect the mark, owing to this presumption of secondary meaning, the registrant of a merely descriptive mark can avail himself or herself of the protection represented by the incontestability doctrine. On the other hand, one can assert fair use and certain equitable defenses against even an incontestable mark.

Remedies

The Lanham Act sets out certain statutory remedies for trademark infringement, including the equitable remedies of an injunction or an accounting to recover the profits the defendant unfairly has garnered from the infringing use. In addition, the plaintiff may recover actual damages; and the court in its discretion can treble these damages if the circumstances (for example, willfulness or bad faith on the infringer's part) so dictate. The court also can adjust the amount recovered for lost profits to a figure the court considers "just." The court can award court costs and in exceptional cases may award reasonable attorneys' fees to the prevailing party. Special rules apply to counterfeit marks. Treble damages, attorneys' fees, and prejudgment interest awards usually result from the use of counterfeit marks.

eClass 40.2 Management

TRADEMARK INFRINGEMENT

A new business in the MP3 market recently unveiled its new logo, which is very similar to the trademark eClass has been using since its inception. Ani wants eClass to file a trademark infringement suit against this firm. Meg and Yousef, expressing concern, point out that while eClass does have a relatively distinctive name, its symbol has not yet acquired widespread recognition. Also, while the new business has a very similar symbol for its logo, there is little likelihood that any customers of either that firm or eClass will be confused about the provider of the goods being sold. All three of the principles fear that if they do not take steps to prevent this other business from using the logo, eClass will lose its right to the trademark protection it has acquired since it will no longer be unique. The firm members ask for your advice. What will you tell them?

BUSINESS CONSIDERATIONS   How can a business protect its trademark so that the trademark does not become a generic term for the product it is intended to promote? Should a business consider changing its logo periodically so as to make the logo appear "fresh" and "new" to the public?

ETHICAL CONSIDERATIONS   What ethical concerns derive from a firm's apparent copying of the logo of a more successful rival? Is a firm that attempts to prevent any competitors from using a trademarked logo even remotely similar to its own behaving in an ethically admirable fashion?

International Dimensions

The Paris Convention mentioned earlier in our discussion of patent law applies to trademarks. The "national treatment" rationale of the Paris Convention provides the same protection to trademark holders from member nations that the nation grants to its own nationals—no more and no less. Under this rationale, one can register a trademark in another member nation either by complying specifically with that nation's requirements or by registering the mark in one's home country. Member nations then cannot refuse to register any such marks unless the mark is confusingly similar to a preexisting mark, or the mark is nondistinctive, immoral, deceptive, or uses the insignia of a member nation without that nation's consent.

The requirements of U.S. trademark law (for example, use in trade and commerce as a prerequisite to registration and the cancellation provisions of U.S. law) decidedly limit the usefulness of the Paris Convention to many international applicants for trademark protection in the U.S. The same shortcomings discussed earlier—the lack of substantive guarantees, enforcement mechanisms, and a centralized filing system—have led to the creation of the Madrid Protocol and the Trademark Registration Treaty, although neither of these initiatives has attracted very many members. The United States, for example, has refused to sign either treaty. The recent changes under GATT seem promising, since they provide heightened protections against international infringement and piracy of trademarked products.

TRADE SECRETS

Protection

Patents and copyrights each offer significant protection to a person who successfully applies for either of them. However, not all applications are approved, and even if an application is approved, the information concerning the covered material becomes available to the public and increases the likelihood that a competitor may use that information to copy the protected item and engage in competition with the holder of the right. Some people would prefer to treat their intellectual property as a secret, avoiding the need to reveal how something is done in order to seek protection. When a business does this, the business is treating its method as a trade secret, and relying on its ability to keep the information confidential. The business is also relying to a much greater extent on state law to provide legal protection, although some federal protections now also exist.

We already have seen some of the limitations on the protection of software under copyright law, in that only the written expression of the software and not the ideas embodied in it are protectable. Patent law also has limitations, in that strict compliance with statutory requirements is necessary for a valid patent. However, various state and common law doctrines, such as trade secrets, unfair competition, and misappropriation, may apply to certain aspects of software—including know-how, information, and ideas—and thus encompass concepts too nebulous for copyright or patent protection. These doctrines may cover computer hardware as well. According to the *Restatement (First) of Torts*, § 757(b), a trade secret may include:

> [a]ny formula, pattern, device or compilation of information which is used in one's business, and which gives [one] an opportunity to obtain an advantage over competitors who do not know or use it. The subject matter of a trade secret must be secret . . . so that, except by the use of improper means, there would be difficulty in acquiring the information.

In determining whether given information is a trade secret, courts generally consider:

1. The extent to which the information is known outside the owner's business
2. The extent to which it is known by employees and others involved in the business
3. The extent of measures taken by the owner to guard the secrecy of the information
4. The value of the information to the owner and to its competitors
5. The amount of effort or money expended by the owner in developing the information
6. The ease or difficulty with which others could properly acquire or duplicate the information

To qualify as a trade secret, the know-how, manufacturing processes, customer lists, or other proprietary information must be used continuously in the business. In addition, the owner must show that it has taken steps to protect and to ensure the confidential manner in which the information is handled. This is likely to require a showing that steps were taken to ensure the physical security of the information, disclosure of the information was limited to only those who actually need the information in order to complete their jobs, and putting those who have access to the information on notice that the firm expects them to retain it in confidence. For example, the business may (1) require employees to sign confidentiality agreements and restrictive covenants, (2) review papers that employees will present publicly, (3) conduct exit interviews with departing employees, and so on. One need only take reasonable precautions to guard and/or prevent access to the proprietary information.

Common knowledge is not protectable under trade secrecy law because such knowledge presumably is of little value to the owner of the information. Similarly, if through reverse engineering one can easily acquire or duplicate the information, it may not qualify as a trade secret.

Liability

Courts base liability for misappropriation of a trade secret on two principal theories: (1) breach of contractual or confidential relations (note the way in which courts often blur the distinction between contract and tort law) and (2) acquisition of the information through improper means. Under the first line of reasoning, courts will prohibit persons in an agency relationship (including employment) and/or a fiduciary relationship from disclosing or using information acquired in the course of employment. Sometimes an employee expressly promises not to compete with the employer for a given period of time in a given geographical area if the employee leaves this particular job.[28] In the absence of such an express contract, courts generally will not imply such a restrictive covenant. But in some circumstances—for example, where a third party learns of confidential information from the employee—the law *will* imply a confidential relationship between the third party and the owner of the trade secret. In such circumstances, the third party's disclosure or use of the information will represent actionable misappropriation.

The law also imposes liability for impropriety in the methods used to acquire the trade secret. The law will not tolerate conduct that falls below generally accepted standards of commercial morality. If a competitor of a firm induces that firm's key engineer to disclose proprietary information, the competitor will have acquired the information through improper means. Liability will also result from the acquisition of information through bribery; commercial espionage; or other illegal conduct such as fraud, theft, and trespass. However, as we discussed earlier, information obtained through reverse engineering, independent discovery, or the owner's failure to take reasonable precautions is probably a lawful acquisition of information.

Remedies

Remedies for misappropriation of a trade secret include injunctions and actions for damages. Such damages may include the plaintiff's lost profits, the profits made by the defendant, or the royalty amount a reasonable person would have agreed to pay. State criminal laws may apply to misappropriations of trade secrets as well.

On the federal level, the Economic Espionage Act of 1996 (EEA) seeks to punish a broad spectrum of activity that interferes with an owner's proprietary rights in commercial trade secrets. In establishing a comprehensive and systemic approach to trade secret theft and economic espionage, the EEA facilitates investigations and prosecutions by federal authorities. In enacting the EEA, Congress apparently was responding to the losses—estimated at $1.5 billion in 1995[22] alone—resulting from competitors' activities (the "raiding" of employees, for example) and misappropriations by foreign enterprises. Hence, the substantive provisions of the EEA address "economic espionage," including activities on behalf of foreign instrumentalities, and "theft of trade secrets" resulting from certain domestic commercial endeavors. Prohibited activities include misappropriating, concealing, procuring by fraud or deception, possessing, altering or destroying, copying, downloading-uploading, or conveying trade secrets without permission.

The EEA covers both "traditional" acts of misappropriation, that is, when conversion removes protectable information from the owner's control, as well as "nontraditional" methods—when "the original property never leaves the control of the rightful owner, but the unauthorized duplication or misappropriation effectively destroys the value of what is left with the rightful owners."[23] The sanctions that can be levied against those who engage in such prohibited activities include fines, imprisonment, and criminal forfeiture. Organizations acting in concert with or on behalf of foreign instrumentalities may be fined no more than $10 million. Other organizations may be fined no more than $5 million. Individuals acting in concert with or on behalf of foreign instrumentalities may be fined no more than $500,000 or imprisoned no more than 15 years, or both.[24] Other individuals also may be fined and/or imprisoned up to 10 years. The criminal forfeiture provision permits the seizure and forfeiture of the property used to facilitate the misappropriation or impermissible possession of a trade secret. The EEA in such provisions thus mirrors the broad seizure powers enjoyed by the government under antidrug enforcement criminal statutes.[25] Try to keep abreast of the developments that stem from this relatively new statute.

Exhibit 40.2 compares the different types of intellectual property.

Exhibit 40.2

Comparison of Different Types of Intellectual Property

Intellectual Property	Who Is Protected	Length of Protection
Patent	The person who files for and receives the patent from the U.S. Patent and Trademark Office; licensees of the patent holder	20 years for a utility patent, 14 years for a design patent. Non-renewable
Trademark or service mark	The person registering the mark; licensees of the holder of the registered mark	10 years for the initial registration and 10 years for each renewal period. Unlimited renewals are possible
Trade secret	The person who develops the trade secret	Undefined. So long as the secret remains a secret no one else can use it
Copyright	The author of an original work unless the author produced the original work as a "work for hire" The person who hired the author in a "work for hire"	If the author created the original work for himself or herself, the life of the author plus 70 year; if the work was produced as a "work for hire," the employer for whom the work was prepared owns the protection for the *lesser* of 95 years from its first publication or 120 years from its creation
Internet domain name	The person who registers the name or the person to whom he or she assigns it	Registration of a domain name is from 1 to 10 years, at the option of the registrant; registration is renewable at the expiration of the registration period; there is no limit in the number of renewals

Source: Courtesy of Daniel V. Davidson, © Daniel V. Davidson, 2009

eClass 40.3 Management

COPYRIGHT OR TRADE SECRET?

eClass has invested a great deal of time, energy, and money in the development of its software, and eClass wants to derive as much protection for its software as the law allows. Meg believes the firm will receive the greatest protection by applying for a copyright on the basic software and then applying for additional copyrights on each new version as it is developed. Yousef prefers to treat the software as a trade secret, treating the information as confidential and restricting access to the information available to the smallest number of people possible. All three ask for your advice. What will you tell them?

BUSINESS CONSIDERATIONS   What factors should an inventor consider before deciding to seek a patent? What drawbacks might need to be considered before one seeks a patent? What should eClass do if it decides to treat the software as a trade secret?

ETHICAL CONSIDERATIONS   Is it ethical for a firm to copy a patented item and then hope that it can prevail in any litigation that results from the patent litigation? Is it ethical for a firm to attempt to enforce questionable patents and to use the expense of litigation as a means of preventing competitors from making the product?

Computers

Actions that employers can take to protect trade secrets about software (or hardware) include the creation of nondisclosure, noncompetition, and confidentiality agreements with employees. Employers also should limit physical access to areas where the development of privately and exclusively owned—or proprietary—software is taking place as well as to storage areas. All software and documents containing trade secrets should bear proprietary labels; and, to ensure the security of the information, the software should use encrypted code so that only those who have the key for unscrambling it can make the program intelligible. Last, employers should provide constant reminders to employees about secrecy obligations and conduct exit interviews with departing employees regarding the information the company considers proprietary.

If the owner of the trade secret will be licensing the software, it will need to take special care. Besides restricting disclosures by the licensee, the licensor/owner should limit the rights the licensee obtains in the software by virtue of the license. The licensor should specifically prohibit copying except for use or archival purposes, and also should (1) formulate special coding techniques to identify misappropriated software, (2) distribute the software in object code as opposed to source code, and (3) stipulate that the breach of any confidentiality provision will result in the immediate termination of the licensing agreement. As we learned earlier, the loss of a protectable trade secret may occur through another party's independent discovery of the secret or any other legitimate means, such as reverse engineering or the public dissemination of the knowledge underlying the trade secret through either a failure to keep the information secret or flaws in the methods the owner has employed to ensure secrecy. Mass distribution of software copies to those with whom the software owner has a confidential relationship generally does not eliminate trade secret protection as long as the owner otherwise has taken precautions to preserve secrecy.

UNFAIR COMPETITION

Our system of law allows rather freewheeling and wide-ranging activities in the name of "competition." However, courts will give remedies to those injured by activities such as the solicitation of a former employer's customers or employees, the competition between an employee and his or her employer while the employee still works for the employer, and the "palming off" of one's goods as those of another.

Protection and Remedies

The common law and statutory restrictions on "unfair competition" often form the legal bases on which aggrieved persons file suit. Misappropriation, another basis for relief, derives from the common law principles of unfair competition and often becomes a "catch-all" theory used in situations in which patent, copyright, and trade secret law do not cover the aspect of the business in dispute. One note of caution is in order, however. The Supreme Court in several decisions has held that federal law will preempt such state causes of action if they interfere with federal policies.[29]

Palming off probably represents the oldest theory of unfair competition. When a firm is accused of palming off, it is accused of conduct in which it tries to divert another firm's patronage or business to itself by deceptively "passing off" his or her goods or services as originating from the other firm. The common law recognized the unfairness of one firm's "free-riding" on the effort, investment, and goodwill of another and thus granted injunctions and/or damages to those injured by such conduct.

Since such activities often involved the wrongdoer's misrepresenting or copying the plaintiff's trademark or trade dress, the Lanham Act, in outlawing trademark infringement, basically "federalizes" these common law theories, although it changes them in certain significant ways. Indeed, § 43(a) of the Lanham Act also provides protection to business people even in the absence of federal trademark registration. As a result, it has carved out broad civil remedies for commercial activities that affect interstate commerce.

Section 43(a) recognizes three different types of "unfair competition" claims: (1) "palming off" claims (the act prohibits any person's falsely designating the origin of particular goods or services if these false designations are likely to cause confusion, mistake, or deception with regard to this person's affiliation or connection to another person's goods, services, or commercial activities); (2) false advertising claims; and (3) product disparagement-type claims (that is, derogatory, false, injurious statements about a competitor's product, service, or title). To recover under § 43(a), the plaintiff must show that the defendant's activities affected interstate commerce; the defendant made material, false, misleading, or deceptive statements or designations that led to a likelihood of confusion among consumers; and actual harm or the likelihood of injury to the plaintiff.

While consumers ordinarily have no standing to sue (only injured competitors do), by allowing injunctive relief upon the plaintiff's showing a likelihood of damage, § 43(a) indirectly protects consumers' interests; the plaintiff need not show the defendant's actual diversion of patronage or trade. A showing of such a loss of business will be necessary if the plaintiff seeks money damages, however. Otherwise, the remedies ordinarily available for infringement of trademarks apply to § 43(a) claims.

The Federal Trade Commission (FTC) has jurisdiction over "unfair or deceptive acts or practices in or affecting commerce." The FTC's enforcement mechanisms, particularly the wide latitude the FTC has in fashioning cease and desist orders, represents yet another avenue for protecting the owners of intellectual property from unfair trade practices. In the international arena, the Paris Convention protects businesses in its signatory nations against unfair trade practices.

Antidilution Statutes   In recent years, the legal system has begun to recognize that competitive injury can result even if the parties are not competitors and even if there is an absence of confusion as to the source of the goods. In other words, the law in some circumstances will protect one who owns strong, distinctive, well-known marks from another's use of an identical or similar mark if such use is likely to tarnish, degrade, or dilute the distinctive power of the mark. The states that have enacted these so-called "antidilution" statutes recognize that even nonconfusing uses of identical or similar marks may, over time, gradually erode the distinctive value of the mark, as well as advertising and other public promotional efforts the mark owner has undertaken to promote product goodwill and to capture, as well as retain, market share.

In granting relief, state courts have utilized the dilution doctrine. The law protects truthful, nondeceptive commercial speech. Hence, like the *2 Live Crew* case we discussed under copyright law, some cases brought under the dilution theory implicate aspects of the First Amendment, particularly if the defendant's use involves parody.

The recently enacted Federal Trademark Dilution Act of 1995 adds to rather than replaces state antidilution statutes. This act codifies as federal law the principle that no one can undertake a diluting use of a famous mark even in circumstances in which there is an absence of the likelihood of customer confusion as to the source of the goods. This statute apparently ushers in a new era of federal trademark protection, an era that potentially will greatly expand the protection afforded to famous, strong, distinctive marks. Be alert for the legal developments that will result from this congressional enactment.

Contemporary Case

IN RE CASINO DE MONACO TRADEMARK LITIGATION

2010 U.S. Dist. LEXIS 33950 (S.D.N.Y. March 31, 2010)

FACTS Societe des Bains de Mer et du Cercle des Estrangers a Monaco's (SMB) is the operator of all casino properties and other attractions in the Principality of Monaco. SBM has registered the mark "Casino de Monaco" with the U.S. Patent and Trademark Office for use in providing casino services in a hotel environment, and has applied for another mark for use in connections with casino services alone.

Playshare PLC is an operator of online casino websites. Playshare used the domain names "Grand Monaco" and "Grand Monaco Casino" for its website casino games. SBM claims that these names infringe its copyright, and it has sued Playshare, alleging trademark violations and unfair competition under both federal and state laws as to SBM's mark "Casino de Monaco." Playshare has countersued SBM in a separate action seeking a declaratory judgment that Playshare is not infringing SBM's trademark, and also seeking to overturn a decision by the World Intellectual Properties Organization (WIPO) awarding various domain names held by Playshare to SMB.

These actions were consolidated in this case.

ISSUES Do Playshare's domain names, Grand Monaco and Grand Monaco Casino, infringe on SBM's registered trademark? Is SBM's registered trademark a valid and enforceable trademark?

HOLDINGS SBM's registered trademark is invalid, and is cancelled. Since the trademark has been cancelled, Playshare did not infringe.

REASONING Excerpts from the opinion of Deborah A. Batts, U.S. District Judge:

"SBM owns the mark CASINO DE MONACO . . . in connection with 'providing casino services within a hotel environment.' SBM's trademark is based on a bona fide intent to use the mark. . . .

Playshare argues that . . . SBM has no protectable rights in its mark. Playshare's rationale is that SBM does not provide goods or services in the U.S., so that it has no trademark rights in the mark. . . . Mere advertising and promotion of a mark in this country are not enough to constitute 'use' of the mark 'in commerce,' to bring the activity with the scope of the Lanham Act. . . . In relation to SBM's mark CASINO DE MONACO, SBM's activities in the United States do not constitute 'services' within the meaning of the Lanham Act. . . . SBM has not used the mark in any meaningful way anywhere. And SBM has not shown that it has used the mark in the United States at all. . . . First, there does not exist in Monaco, or anywhere else, a casino identified by the name Casino de Monaco. . . . There is no real evidence that the claimed . . . term that signifies CASINO DE MONACO has ever existed in the United States. . . . SBM's utter lack of use of the mark CASINO DE MONACO anywhere, let alone in the United States, requires this Court to refuse to enforce SMB's right in the mark CASINO DE MONACO. . . .

In this opinion, the Court cancelled SBM's mark . . . as it does not constitute a protectable service mark under the Lanham Act. . . . Since the mark is no longer owned by SBM, as a matter of law, Playshare cannot be in violation of the Anticybersquatting Consumer Protection Act . . . in relation to its use of the Monaco Domain Names and any infringement of SBM's (former) mark. . . . The Court vacates the WIPO decision and the Monaco Domain Names shall remain with [Playshare]. . . .

You Be the Judge

DirecTV, Inc. sued NDS Group, a Rupert Murdoch-controlled company that manufactures "smart" cards that prevent the piracy of digital television signals. Although it at one point had a contract with NDS with regard to such "smart" card technology, DirecTV ultimately moved its encryption technology in-house. In September 2002, DirecTV sued NDS on several theories, including misappropriation of trade secrets. DirecTV retained the Los Angeles office of Jones, Day, Reavis and Pogue as its outside legal counsel for this lawsuit. Documents filed in court indicated that DirecTV delivered to the law firm about 27 boxes of confidential materials related to the case. To facilitate the management of these documents, the law firm in turn hired Uniscribe Professional Services, a Norwalk, Connecticut, document-copying service that does imaging work for not only law firms but accounting firms, investment banks, universities, and museums. Owing to the sensitivity of the documents, Uniscribe set up an imaging center at the law firm's offices and greatly restricted the number of persons who had access to these materials. Michael Peker, a Uniscribe employee who did have access to the materials, enlisted the assistance of his nephew, a 19-year-old, University of Chicago student named Igor Serebryany, after the firm indicated its desire that the copying work proceed more quickly. The law firm had not approved the hiring of Serebryany. During the course of his work, Serebryany allegedly came across information concerning the design and architecture of DirecTV's latest "P4 access card" technology, a device that prevents free access to digital television signals by the company's 11 million subscribers. Serebryany allegedly distributed this information—which cost DirecTV about $25 million to develop—to several Internet sites that cater to hackers. Court documents indicated that Serebryany removed copies of the documents from the law firm's offices, took them to his own home, and used his father's computer to send electronic copies of the information to at least three Web site operators. Serebryany apparently was motivated by a desire to facilitate the hacking community's activities rather than by personal monetary gain. DirectTV has decided to file suit against the law firm, the document-copying firm, and Serebryany for misappropriation of a trade secret. This case has been brought in *your* court. How will *you* decide this controversy? Be certain that you explain and justify your decision. [See Debora Vrana, "U. of C. Student Arrested for Document Piracy," *Chicago Tribune*, January 3, 2003, section 1, p. 15.]

Summary

Intellectual property encompasses several substantive areas of the law: patents, copyrights, trademarks, trade secrets, and unfair competition. Intellectual property law strives to serve two oftentimes competing goals: ensuring incentives to create a wider array of products and services in the marketplace while at the same time promoting competition by providing public access to intellectual creations. The law serves the first goal when it grants property rights (sometimes even monopolies) to creators and the second when it limits the duration of such exclusive rights and/or circumscribes the rights thus granted so as to maximize the amount of information found in the public domain. This area of the law also seeks to protect creators and businesspeople from injurious trade practices.

The Patent Act of 1952 grants to inventors the exclusive right to their respective discoveries that consist of patentable subject matter. The Supreme Court has held that such utility patents may cover genetically engineered living matter as well. Utility patents last for 20 years from the filing date, while design patents last for only 14 years from the date of the grant of the patent, after which time the monopoly granted by the patent ends. At that point others can make, use, or sell the invention with impunity. Ideas *per se* are not patentable. To be patentable, an invention must be new, useful, and non-obvious. Obtaining a patent involves detailed disclosures to the Patent and Trademark Office. Infringements may be either direct or contributory and may consist of inducements to infringe. Persons sued for patent infringement may claim lack of patentability or patent misuse as a defense. Remedies for infringement include injunctive relief as well as damages.

The copyright laws protect any original works of authorship. To be copyrightable, works of authorship must show originality and the works must be fixed in a tangible medium of expression. Ideas are not copyrightable. A copyright consists of a bundle of exclusive rights that enables the copyright owner—usually the author or one to whom the author has transferred the rights—to exploit a work for commercial purposes. Violations of any of the copyright owner's exclusive rights constitute infringement. The courts have imposed liability for both direct and contributory infringement. The most common defense against charges of infringement is the "fair use" doctrine. Civil remedies for infringement include injunctions, the impoundment and destruction of infringing items, and damages. Criminal penalties also are available.

Over the years, an extensive body of state trademark law has developed, principally through the state common law relating to unfair competition. By providing a structure by which the enforcement of these common law principles can occur through federal oversight, the 1946 Lanham Act—the most important federal protection of trademarks—builds on these common law roots. The Lanham Act defines a trademark as any word, name, symbol, device, or any combination thereof used to identify and distinguish the services of one person from the goods or services of others and to indicate the source of the goods, even if the source is unknown. This definition underscores the fact that a trademark only exists in a commercial activity or use and may cover an extensive array of things, including the distinctive features of the product such as the product's shape, the product's packaging, the logo or artwork on the product, and so on. To obtain protection, the trademark—whatever its form—must be distinctive; generic terms never can qualify for trademark protection. Purely descriptive marks do not qualify as distinctive until they have acquired "secondary meaning."

The law protects the trademark owner from infringements that will result in a likelihood of confusion concerning the source of the goods. Defenses to a cause of action based on infringement include "fair use" and abandonment of the mark. Registration of the mark on the Principal Register gives the owner certain advantages in an infringement action, as does the mark's becoming incontestable. Under the Lanham Act, an owner may resort to certain equitable and legal remedies.

Trade secret law protects proprietary information that gives the owner a differential advantage over his or her competitors. To qualify as a trade secret the information must be treated in a confidential manner and it must be used continuously in the business. The law does not protect as trade secrets either common knowledge or information easily acquired from reverse engineering. Misappropriation can occur through breach of contractual or confidential relations or the use of improper means to acquire the secret. Remedies include injunctions and damages. State and federal criminal laws may apply to such misappropriations as well.

The Lanham Act allows recovery on three bases: (1) "palming off," (2) false advertising, and (3) product disparagement. State and federal "antidilution" laws also protect one who owns a strong, distinctive, well-known mark from another's use of an identical or similar mark if such use is likely to tarnish, degrade, or dilute the distinctive power of the mark. As we have seen in other contexts, parody may constitute a defense to actions brought under this theory.

The Federal Trade Commission also has authority to protect the owners of intellectual property from unfair trade practices. Several international treaties regulate intellectual property as well.

Discussion Questions

1. What does the law require before it will grant copyright protection?

2. What factors constitute "fair use" under the Copyright Act?

3. What does the law mandate before it will grant patent protection?

4. What is a trademark, and what does the law require before it will grant trademark protection?

5. What must one do to protect information as a trade secret? In determining whether information constitutes a trade secret, what factors might a court consider?

Case Problems and Writing Assignments

1. Tiffany sells jewelry under the registered federal trademarks TIFFANY and TIFFANY & CO. It takes significant care to protect its brand name and its trademarks against counterfeit products, a problem faced by many "brand name" products. The internet marketing and auction site eBay offered Tiffany products for sale, advertising that it carried Tiffany-brand jewelry on its home page and providing a link to the Tiffany mark. When this link was clicked, the prospective customer was taken to listing offering Tiffany jewelry for sale through the eBay site. Unfortunately, some of the jewelry so listed was counterfeit, infringing on the Tiffany

trademark. When Tiffany discovered that counterfeits of its jewelry were being sold on eBay, it decided to file suit against eBay for facilitating the sale of the counterfeit jewelry and/or for failing to stop such sales once it had notice that such sales were occurring.

Tiffany alleges that hundreds of thousands of counterfeit silver jewelry items were offered for sale on eBay's Web site over the past few years. Tiffany seeks to hold eBay liable for direct and contributory trademark infringement, unfair competition, false advertising, and direct and contributory trademark dilution, on the grounds that eBay facilitated and allowed these counterfeit items to be sold on its website. Tiffany acknowledges that individual sellers, rather than eBay, are responsible for listing and selling counterfeit Tiffany items. Nevertheless, Tiffany argues that eBay was on notice that a problem existed and accordingly, that eBay had the obligation to investigate and control the illegal activities of these sellers—specifically, by pre-emptively refusing to post any listing offering five or more Tiffany items and by immediately suspending sellers upon learning of Tiffany's belief that the seller had engaged in potentially infringing activity.

In response, eBay contends that it is Tiffany's burden, not eBay's, to monitor the eBay website for counterfeits and to bring counterfeits to eBay's attention. eBay claims that in practice, when potentially infringing listings were reported to eBay, eBay immediately removed the offending listings. It is clear that Tiffany and eBay alike have an interest in eliminating counterfeit Tiffany merchandise from eBay—Tiffany to protect its famous brand name, and eBay to preserve the reputation of its website as a safe place to do business. Both Tiffany and eBay are interested in ensuring that counterfeit Tiffany items are not sold on eBay, so the issue is which of the two parties should bear the burden of policing Tiffany's valuable trademarks in Internet commerce. How should this case be decided? Explain and justify your ruling. [See *Tiffany, Inc. v. ebay, Inc.*, 576 F. Supp. 2d 463 (S.D.N.Y. 2008).]

2. The litigation between the parties brought out the following information: Barbie was born in Germany in the 1950s as an adult collector's item. Over the years, Mattel, Inc. (Mattel) transformed her from a doll that resembled a "German street walker," as she originally had appeared, into a glamorous, long-legged blonde. Barbie has been labeled both the ideal American woman and a bimbo. She has survived attacks both psychic (from feminists critical of her fictitious figure) and physical (more than 500 professional makeovers). She remains a symbol of American girlhood, a public figure who graces the aisles of toy stores throughout the country and beyond. With Barbie, Mattel created

not just a toy but a cultural icon. In 1997, Aqua, a Danish band, produced the song, "Barbie Girl," on the album *Aquarium*. The female singer (a band member who sings in a high-pitched, doll-like voice) and who calls herself Barbie, is "a Barbie girl, in [her] Barbie world." She tells her male counterpart (named Ken), "Life is plastic, it's fantastic. You can brush my hair, undress me everywhere/Imagination, life is your creation." And off they go to "party." The female singer further explains, "I'm a blond bimbo girl, in a fantasy world/Dress me up, make it tight, I'm your dolly." "Barbie Girl" singles sold well; and, to Mattel's dismay, the song made it onto the Top 40 music charts. Mattel sued the music companies who had produced, marketed and sold "Barbie Girl:" MCA Records, Inc., Universal Music International Ltd., Universal Music A/S, Universal Music & Video Distribution, Inc., and MCA Music Scandinavia AB (collectively, MCA). Mattel's theories included trademark infringement, dilution of its mark (under the Federal Trademark Dilution Act [FTDA]), and unfair competition. MCA in turn challenged the district court's jurisdiction under the Lanham Act and its personal jurisdiction over the foreign defendants, Universal Music International Ltd., Universal Music A/S, and MCA Music Scandinavia AB. MCA also argued that its conduct fell within the FTDA's exemption that permits uses that, though potentially dilutive, involve noncommercial, or fully constitutionally protected speech. Evaluate the strength of the arguments each party will make in its own behalf and then decide who should win. [See *Mattel, Inc. v. MCA Records, Inc.*, 296 F.3d 894 (9th Cir. 2002). Also, visit the Web site for more information in the creation of Barbie and some of the other controversies that have accompanied her over the years.]

3. Random House, Inc. seeks to enjoin Rosetta Books LLC and its Chief Executive Officer from selling in digital format eight specific works on the grounds that the authors of the works had previously granted Random House—not Rosetta Books—the right to "print, publish and sell the work[s] in book form." Rosetta Books, on the other hand, claims it is not infringing upon the rights those authors gave Random House because the licensing agreements between the publisher and the author do not include a grant of digital or electronic rights. Relying on the language of the contracts and basic principles of contract interpretation, this Court finds that the right to "print, publish and sell the work[s] in book form" in the contracts at issue does not include the right to publish the works in the format that has come to be known as the "ebook." Accordingly, Random House's motion for a preliminary injunction is denied.

Do you agree with the court's decision? Should ebooks be treated differently than "traditional" books under copyright law? Explain why. [See *Random House, Inc. v. Rosetta Books, LLC.*, 283 F.3d 490 (2d Cir. 2002).]

Notes

1. *J.E.M. Ag Supply, Inc., v. Pioneer High-Bred International, Inc.*, 534 U.S. 124 (2001).
2. Michael Cohen, "Patentability of Business Methods," *Ezine articles*, found at http://ezinearticles.com/?Patentability-of-Business-Methods&id=129647.
3. InventionStatistics.com, found at http://www.invention statistics.com/Number_of_New_Patents_Issued.html.
4. *Markman v. Westview Instruments, Inc.*, 517 U.S. 370, 371 (1996).
5. Information about the Patent Cooperation Treaty can be found at the following Web sites, among others: http://www.wipo.int/pct/en/treaty/about.htm *and* http://www.uspto.gov/web/offices/pac/dapp/pctstate.html
6. David V. Radack, "GATT Brings Major Changes to U.S. Patent Law," 47 (5) JOM p. 79 (1995), http://www.tms.org/pubs/journals/JOM/matters/matters-9505.html/.
7. 450 U.S. 175 (1981).
8. 684 F.2d 912 (CCPA 1982).
9. 17 U.S.C. §§ 101–810
10. 17 U.S.C. 101note.
11. Prioritizing Resources and Organization for Intellectual Property Act of 2008 P.L. 110-403), signed Oct. 13, 2008, Webcaster Settlement Act of 2008 (P.L. 110-435), signed Oct. 16, 2008, Vessel Hull Design Protection Amendments of 2008 (P.L. 110-434), signed Oct. 16, 2008, and Webcaster Settlement Act of 2009, P. L. 111-36, signed June 30, 2009.
12. Note 5, op cit.
13. *Feist Publications, Inc. v. Rural Telephone Service Co., Inc.*, 499 U.S. 340 (1991).
14. Statistical Abstract of the United States, U.S. Department of Commerce, Bureau of the Census (128th ed.) (Washington, DC, 2010), Table 756, found at http://www.census.gov/compendia/statab/cats/business_enterprise/patents_trademarks_copyrights.html.
15. I7 U.S.C. §§ 107-18.
16. U.S. Copyright Office, Fair Use, at http://www.copyright.gov/fls/fl102.html.
17. http://www.copyright.gov/circs/circ21.pdf.
18. Note that the copyright holder is unlikely to grant permission for a parody based on his or her work.
19. George Harrison was found to have innocently and inadvertently infringed the copyright held by Bright Tunes Music for the song *He's So Fine*, recorded by The Chiffons in his recording of *My Sweet Lord*. See *Bright Tunes Music v. Harrisongs Music*, 420 F. Supp. 177 (S.D.N.Y. 1976).
20. 17 U.S.C. § 504.
21. 17 U.S.C. § 506(a).
22. 18 U.S.C. §§ 2319(a), 3571(b).
23. 18 U.S.C. §§ 2319(c), 3571(b).
24. 18 U.S.C. § 2319(b).
25. 15 U.S.C.A. §§ 1051 *et seq.*
26. Statistical Abstract of the United States, U.S. Department of Commerce, Bureau of the Census (128th ed.) (Washington, DC, 2010), Table 754, found at http://www.census.gov/compendia/statab/cats/business_enterprise/patents_trademarks_copyrights.html.
27. 15 U.S.C. § 1127.
28. States vary in their willingness to enforce these covenants not to compete.
29. See, e.g., *Sears, Roebuck & Co. v. Stiffel Co.*, 376 U.S. 225 (1964); *Compco Corporation v. Day-Brite Lighting, Inc.*, 376 U.S. 234 (1964); *Bonito Boats, Inc. v. Thunder Craft Boats, Inc.*, 489 U.S. 141 (1989).

Table of Cases

Classic and Contemporary cases indicated by italics.

Index